Writings of Charles S. Peirce

Volume 6

This volume
is dedicated to

JOHN GALLMAN

Amicus librorum

Conjectural south elevation of Peirce's Milford, Pennsylvania, home in 1888—the year that Charles and Juliette bought the house. The simple farmhouse would be buried within a series of major expansions during the final twenty-six years of Peirce's life; today it serves as a Park Service facility within the Delaware Water Gap National Recreation Area. Adapted from "Charles S. Peirce House," a 1983 National Park Service Historic Structure Report by Penelope Hartshorne Batcheler.

Writings of
CHARLES S. PEIRCE

A CHRONOLOGICAL EDITION

Volume 6
1886–1890

EDITED BY THE PEIRCE EDITION PROJECT

NATHAN HOUSER, *General Editor*
ANDRÉ DE TIENNE, *Associate Editor*
CORNELIS DE WAAL, *Assistant Editor*
CATHY L. CLARK, *Editorial Associate*
LUISE H. MORTON, *Research Associate*
JONATHAN R. ELLER, *Textual Editor*
ALBERT LEWIS, *Associate Editor*
D. BRONT DAVIS, *Technical Editor*
LEAH CUMMINS, *Editorial Associate*
DIANA D. REYNOLDS, *Editorial Assistant*

Indiana University Press
Bloomington and Indianapolis

Preparation of this volume has been supported in part by grants from the Program for Editions of the National Endowment for the Humanities, an independent federal agency.

The paper used in this publication meets the minimum requirements of American National Standard for Information Sciences—Permanence of Paper for Printed Library materials, ANSI Z39.48–1984.

∞™

Manufactured in the United States of America

Library of Congress Cataloging-in-Publication Data
(Revised for volume 6)

Peirce, Charles S. (Charles Sanders), 1839–1914.
Writings of Charles S. Peirce

Vol. 6– : Peirce Edition Project
Includes bibliographies and indexes.
Contents: v. 1. 1857–1866.—v. 2. 1867–1871.—[etc.]—v. 6. 1886–1890
1. Philosophy. I. Peirce Edition Project
II. Title
B945.P4 1982 191 79–1993
ISBN 0-253-37201-1 (v. 1)
ISBN 0-253-37206-2 (v. 6)

1 2 3 4 5 04 03 02 01 00

The Peirce Edition Project

Indiana University–Purdue University Indianapolis

Contents

Preface

This is the sixth volume of the chronological edition of the writings of Charles S. Peirce, started in 1975 under the leadership of Max H. Fisch and Edward C. Moore and expected to run to thirty volumes. The edition is selective but comprehensive and includes all writings, on any subject, believed to shed significant light on the development of Peirce's thought. The selections are edited according to the guidelines of the Modern Language Association's Committee on Scholarly Editions, and Volume 6 has been awarded the Committee's seal as an approved edition.

During the six years since Volume 5 appeared, the Peirce Edition Project has been reorganized and its production methods revamped to more fully integrate computing technology at all stages of operation and to put a system in place that can better support parallel volume editing. The integrity and continuity of the edition has remained a principal concern, but there have been a few changes in policy and practice that should be noted. These changes concern (1) the manuscript base that supports the edition, (2) the expected publication order of forthcoming volumes, and (3) the internal organization and style of the volumes.

1. The Peirce Edition Project will no longer attempt to definitively reorganize all of Peirce's manuscripts and to assign new chronologically-determined manuscript numbers. That effort, which involved only a virtual reorganization as the manuscript originals are not physically located in Indianapolis, was found to be unnecessarily time-consuming because it required the thorough study and reorganization of all Peirce's manuscripts, including many that were not candidates for publication. For the purposes of the chronological edition, a less definitive rearrangement of manuscripts is satisfactory, one that integrates every manuscript within a unified chronology of all of Peirce's writings, but which accepts in many cases the manuscript arrangements of the holding archives. The chronological catalogs beginning with this volume will number Peirce's writings in their order of composition year by year, after the style of the Burks catalog in Volume 8 of the *Collected Papers,* and manuscripts will be identified by their Robin numbers (for Harvard's Houghton Library collection) or by standard archive identifiers (for other collections). Future volumes will continue to be chronological, with their published texts generally identified by selection number and title

rather than by a newly assigned manuscript number. (See the introduction to the Chronological Catalog, pp. 512–14, for further discussion.)

2. Plans for forthcoming volumes are now being reconsidered and some revisions have already been made. For example, some advance work has been assigned on the manuscripts for Peirce's 1901–02 "Minute Logic" and 1903 "Lowell Lectures" and it is possible that the volumes containing those writings will be published out of sequence. Other volumes that will contain single works or unified series of lectures are candidates for out-of-sequence publication, as are Peirce's definitions for the *Century Dictionary* and Baldwin's *Dictionary of Philosophy and Psychology.* Although some of Peirce's early work on definitions for the *Century Dictionary* was published in Volume 5, the editors have decided against further piecemeal publication of that work. Volume 7 will be devoted exclusively to a selection from Peirce's thousands of contributions to the *Century,* and will include some of his contributions to the two-volume *Century Supplement* of 1909. Although this will require a slight departure from the strict chronological arrangement of texts that has characterized the Indiana edition, the editors believe it will prove to be the most useful and effective presentation of Peirce's definitions. This special volume fits best into the general chronology following Volume 6 which runs to the middle of 1890, about half-way through the three-year period during which the *Century* first appeared in print and Peirce devoted more time to his dictionary work than to anything else. Volume 7 will appear out of sequence, the next volume scheduled for publication being Volume 8 which will include writings for the years 1890–92.

3. A few changes to layout and format will be obvious on comparison of Volume 6 with earlier volumes. The selection headers have been redesigned and list the date of composition or publication and the location of copy-text manuscript or place of publication. Further information about text sources is recorded in the Textual Apparatus. The Chronology at the front of the volume has been slightly expanded for the period covered by Volume 6 (a practice that will be continued for future volumes). The Annotations have been slightly expanded from the corresponding Notes of earlier volumes, and include more quotations from unpublished manuscript material of the period. Some supplementary annotations will be published in the Electronic Companion for Volume 6 (www.iupui.edu/~peirce), which will be updated and expanded in the coming years. The Chronological Catalog (pp. 512–30), mentioned above, has been reconceived and includes more information about writings not selected for publication than was included in the Chronological Lists of earlier volumes. Discussions of editorial methods and practices, symbol use, and textual theory that were included in Prefaces to earlier volumes, have been moved to appropriate sections in the back matter, in particular to the Editorial Symbols section and the Essay on Editorial Theory and Method. In making these and other changes, the editors have been attentive to the need for continuity with the earlier volumes of the

edition and hope that readers will find the transition to be smooth and the changes helpful.

We wish to acknowledge our indebtedness to our host institution, Indiana University, for stewarding the Peirce Edition Project's core staff resources through a time of fiscal austerity at both the university and the national level, and for providing increasing support through the late 1990s as the Project won new federal and private-sector grant commitments. We are grateful to the National Endowment for the Humanities for funding from pre-1993 grants that was used during the earliest stages of volume preparation, and for a renewed commitment beginning in 1997 that in part supported final volume preparation. Significant private-sector support came from the Gladys Krieble Delmas Foundation and from the Prince Charitable Trusts. We are most grateful to these organizations and to the late Helen Peirce Prince, Peirce's grandniece, who was an enthusiastic supporter of the edition. We are grateful to the Charles S. Peirce Society and the Philosophy Documentation Center for financial support and for encouragement. We are especially grateful to the many individuals who have demonstrated their support by making private contributions.

Acknowledgment is due as well to the Harvard University Department of Philosophy for permission to use the original manuscripts, and to the officers of the Houghton Library, especially Manuscripts Curator Leslie Morris, for their cooperation regarding the Charles S. Peirce Papers. Access to Peirce's government papers and correspondence was provided by the National Archives and by the National Ocean Survey, the National Oceanic and Atmospheric Agency's successor to the old Coast Survey of Peirce's time. Special thanks go to individual staff members of these institutions and to the many scholars and archivists who have provided important research support, including Melanie Wisner of the Harvard Houghton Library; to Webb Dordick for his research assistance in the Harvard Libraries; to Marjorie Ciarlante of the National Archives, and Grace Sollers and Sharon Tomlinson of NOAA's Geodesy Library; to graduate assistants Jeffrey DiLeo, Adam Kovach, and Jack Musselman, of the Department of Philosophy, Indiana University (Bloomington), all now pursuing postdoctoral careers; to on-site graduate research assistants Ginger Johnson, Brian C. McDonald, and David Beck, of the Department of English at Indiana University–Purdue University Indianapolis; to Joshua Garrison, editorial assistant; to on-site undergraduate intern Brandy Yaeger; to Gerald McCollam of New York University for his work at Milford and at the New York Public Library; to Richard Tursman (York University, Ontario) for his indispensable assistance in editing Peirce's scientific papers; to Vania Goodwin, University Library, IUPUI; to Pier Bierbach (Martin-Luther-Universität Halle-Wittenberg), Janice Deledalle-Rhodes (Montbazin, France), Alan Gauld (University of Nottingham, UK), Don Hebert (East Texas Baptist University), Ron

Knott (most recently a Visiting Fellow, University of Surrey, UK), Eric Luijten (Thomas Instituut Utrecht), Kelly Parker (Grand Valley State University), Volker Peckhaus (Universität Erlangen–Nürnberg), David Pfeifer (Principia College), Stephen Pollard (Truman State University), Bruce Thompson (Erie County Library System, Erie, PA), and José Vericat (University of Madrid), for their expert assistance at several points.

We are also indebted to Stephen Schmidt and the Interlibrary Loan department of IUPUI and to the Texas Tech University Institute for Studies in Pragmaticism for permission to use duplicates of its annotated photocopy of the Harvard Peirce Papers. Members of the Charles S. Peirce Society, as well as the editors of the Society's *Transactions,* have been a constant source of support and scholarly information. Our thanks also go to Darryl Rehr, journalist and editor of *ETCetera,* the journal of the Early Typewriter Collectors Association, for his detailed information on the typewriter models used by Peirce during the 1880s. Professor Peter Weil of the University of Delaware kindly provided rare original documentation for the Hammond type shuttles which Peirce used on his Hammond typewriters throughout the period covered by this volume. Robert Hirst, General Editor of the Mark Twain Project (University of California, Berkeley), has provided expert advice both as a fellow editor and as a member of the Peirce Project's Advisory Board. We are grateful to him for coordinating the Modern Language Association's Committee on Scholarly Editions during the CSE inspection process, and to Larry Hickman, General Editor of the Dewey Edition (Southern Illinois University), for conducting the MLA inspection on behalf of the CSE.

We are also grateful to the contributing editors listed on the series page of this volume for the specialized scholarship they brought to bear on many of the selections. Special thanks go to our copy editor and production manager Aleta Houser, who saw a number of selections through the first stage of review by contributing editors, and to former staff members Kyle Barnett and Beth Eccles, who provided administrative and development support for the edition. The executive support of Tracie Peterson has been essential at every stage of production. Throughout the period of volume preparation, we were fortunate to have the expert counsel of Arthur Burks of the University of Michigan and Don Cook of Indiana University, Bloomington, who continue to serve as advisory editors for the Peirce Project, and Don Roberts of the University of Waterloo (Ontario), who has provided outstanding support as Advisory Board Chair for the last five years. We are grateful as well for the memory of Max H. Fisch, who devoted a half century to Peirce research and, after his retirement, fifteen years to the Peirce Project. His work and inspiration will live on through the donation of his books and papers to Indiana University.

Special acknowledgment is due to Christian J. W. Kloesel, former Director and Editor of the Peirce Edition Project. Work on Volume 6 began under his direction and the present Project organization and methods evolved from the structures he left in place when he completed his tenure in 1993.

A final note of thanks goes to four administrative officials of Indiana University: President Myles Brand, Chancellor and Vice President Gerald L. Bepko, Executive Vice Chancellor and Dean of the Faculties William M. Plater, and Dean Herman Saatkamp of the School of Liberal Arts. Dean Emeritus John D. Barlow, who led the School of Liberal Arts through eleven crucial years in the development of the Peirce Project, provided institutional and personal support throughout his tenure. We are fortunate to have the same high level of commitment from Dean Saatkamp, a scholarly editor in his own right and long-time General Editor of the Works of George Santayana. As both an administrator and a colleague, he has already helped the Peirce Project plan for the challenges of the twenty-first century.

Chronology

(Years of W6 period in **boldface** type)

1839 Born in Cambridge, Mass., to Benjamin and Sarah Hunt (Mills) Peirce, 10 Sept.

1847–50 Worked his way through Liebig's method of chemical analysis

1858 First publication: "Think Again!" *Harvard Magazine,* Apr.

1859 Graduated (A.B.) from Harvard
Temporary aide in U.S. Coast Survey, fall to spring '60

1860 Studied classification with Agassiz at Harvard, summer–fall

1861 Entered Lawrence Scientific School at Harvard
Appointed regular aide in Coast Survey, 1 July

1862 Received graduate degree (A.M.) from Harvard
Married Harriet Melusina Fay, 16 Oct.

1863 Graduated summa cum laude (Sc.B.) in Chemistry from Lawrence Scientific School

1865 Delivered Harvard lectures on "The Logic of Science," spring
Began Logic Notebook, 12 Nov.; last entry in Nov. '09

1866 Delivered Lowell Institute lectures on "The Logic of Science; or Induction and Hypothesis," 24 Oct.–1 Dec.

1867 Elected to American Academy of Arts and Sciences, 30 Jan.

1869 Wrote first of about 300 *Nation* reviews; last in Dec. '08
Assistant at Harvard Observatory, Oct. '69–Dec. '72
Delivered Harvard lectures on "British Logicians," Dec.–Jan.

1870 First Coast Survey assignment in Europe, 18 Jun. '70–7 Mar. '71

1871–72 Founded Cambridge Metaphysical Club in spring, or in Jan. '72
In charge of Survey office, spring–summer
Put in charge of pendulum experiments, beginning in Nov.
Promoted to rank of Assistant in the Survey, 1 Dec.

1875 Second Coast Survey assignment in Europe, Apr. '75–Aug. '76
First official American delegate to the International Geodetic Association, Paris, 20–29 Sept.

1876 Separated from Melusina, Oct.

1877 Elected to National Academy of Sciences, 20 Apr.
Third Coast Survey assignment in Europe, 13 Sept.–18 Nov.
Represented U.S. at International Geodetic Association conference in Stuttgart, 27 Sept.–2 Oct.

1878 *Photometric Researches* published in Aug.

1879–84 Lecturer in logic at Johns Hopkins University

1879 First meeting of Johns Hopkins Metaphysical Club, 28 Oct.

1880 Elected to London Mathematical Society, 11 Mar.
Fourth Coast Survey assignment in Europe, Apr.–Aug.
Addressed French Academy on value of gravity, 14 June
Designed and supervised construction of the first of four gravity pendulums bearing his name
Death of Peirce's father, Benjamin, 6 Oct.

1881 Elected to American Association for the Advancement of Science in Aug.

1883 *Studies in Logic* published in spring
Divorced Melusina, 24 Apr.
Married Juliette Froissy (Pourtalais), 30 Apr.
Fifth and final Coast Survey assignment in Europe, May–Sept.

1883–91 Prepared about 15,000 definitions for *Century Dictionary* (published 1889–91)

1884 Forced to resign from Johns Hopkins; moved to Washington, D.C. in Sept.
In charge of U.S. Office of Weights and Measures, Oct. '84–22 Feb. '85

1884–86 Directed pendulum operations to determine relative gravity at Washington, D.C. and various field sites, Jul. '84–Feb '86

1886 Moved from Washington, D.C. to New York City, Mar.
Operations at Stevens Institute, Hoboken, summer
Relieved of field operations for the Coast Survey, 15 Aug.

1887 Received first inquiries about his correspondence course in logic, Jan.
Submitted, under pressure, his report on General Greely's pendulum work at Fort Conger, 11 Apr.
Moved with Juliette to Milford, Penn. 28 Apr.; by May 11 rented a house (in town) for the summer
Finished first paper after moving to Milford, "Criticism on

Phantasms of the Living," 14 May. Published in Dec.
Death of Peirce's mother, Sarah Mills, 10 Oct.

1887–88 Turned "One, Two, Three" (1885–86) into "A Guess at the Riddle"

1888 Appointed by President Cleveland to U.S. Assay Commission, 1 Jan.
Death of Charlotte Elizabeth Peirce, his aunt, 4 Feb.
Rented Scheinmee Homestead on Broad Street, Milford, 28 Apr.
Assigned a clerk, Allan Risteen, for Coast Survey work
Risteen and wife stay with Peirces in Milford, Apr.–Jul.
Purchased with Juliette the Quick farm about two miles northeast of Milford, 10 May; renamed Arisbe in 1891

1889 First edition of *Century Dictionary* published; continues till 1891
Started renovations on Quick farmhouse, Jan.
O. H. Mitchell, 37, died of pneumonia at Marietta, 29 Mar.
Juliette diagnosed with tuberculosis in May
Thomas Corwin Mendenhall succeeded Thorn as superintendent of the Coast Survey, 9 Jul.
After many delays, submitted report on gravity at Smithsonian, Ann Arbor, Madison, and Cornell, 20 Nov. Never published
Juliette travelled to Mediterranean for her health, Nov. 27–spring '90

1890 Ernst Schröder resumed correspondence with Peirce, 1 Feb.
Helped organize the *New York Times* debate on Spencer; contributed under the name "Outsider," 23 Mar.–27 Apr.
Invited by Paul Carus to write article for inaugural issue of the *Monist,* 2 Jul.; submitted "The Architecture of Theories," 3 Aug. (too late for the first issue), launching one of his most important publishing relationships

1891 Forced to resign from Coast and Geodetic Survey, 31 Dec.

1892 Delivered Lowell lectures on "The History of Science," 28 Nov. '92–5 Jan. '93

1893 *Petrus Peregrinus* announced; prospectus published, Oct.
"Search for a Method" announced by Open Court (not completed)
"The Principles of Philosophy" (in 12 vols.) announced by Henry Holt Co., Dec. (not completed)

1894 "How to Reason" rejected by both Macmillan and Ginn & Co.

1895 "New Elements of Mathematics" rejected by Ginn & Co.

1896 Consulting chemical engineer (till '02), St. Lawrence Power Co.

1896–97 Reviewed Ernst Schröder's works on logic of relatives

1898 Delivered Cambridge lectures on "Reasoning and the Logic of Things," 10 Feb.–7 Mar.

"The History of Science" announced by Putnam's (not completed)

William James introduced "Pragmatism" to Berkeley Philosophical Union, naming Peirce its father, 26 Aug.

1901 Contributed to Baldwin's *Dictionary of Philosophy and Psychology*

Presented "On the Logic of Research into Ancient History" to National Academy of Sciences, 12–14 Nov.

1901–02 Completed the first four chapters of "Minute Logic"

1902 Applied to Carnegie Institution for grant to fund "Proposed Memoirs on Minute Logic" (rejected)

1903 Delivered Harvard lectures on "Pragmatism," 26 Mar.–17 May

Delivered Lowell lectures on "Some Topics of Logic," 23 Nov.–17 Dec.

Began correspondence with Victoria Lady Welby

1905–06 Published three *Monist* papers on pragmatism (series incomplete)

1906 Presented paper on existential graphs to National Academy of Sciences, Apr.

Presented paper on phaneroscopy to National Academy of Sciences, Nov.

1907 Delivered three Harvard Philosophy Club lectures on "Logical Methodeutic," 8–13 Apr.

Wrote lengthy letter to the *Nation* and *Atlantic Monthly* on pragmatism (especially R 318)

1908 Published "A Neglected Argument for the Reality of God," *Hibbert Journal,* Oct.

1908–09 Published *Monist* series on "Amazing Mazes"

1909 Originated a matrix method for three-valued logic; recorded in his Logic Notebook (R 339), 23 Feb.

1911 Wrote "A Sketch of Logical Critics" for volume to honor Lady Welby (not completed)

Last public presentation: "The Reasons of Reasoning, or Grounds of Inferring" at meeting of National Academy of Sciences, 21–22 Nov.

1914 Died of cancer at Arisbe, 19 Apr.

Bibliographical Abbreviations in Editorial Matter

CD [page #] *The Century Dictionary and Cyclopedia,* 10 volumes, ed. William D. Whitney (New York: The Century Company, 1889–). The pagination is that of Peirce's personal interleaved copy, which was the dictionary's first printing. Unless specified otherwise all quotations are considered Peirce's and were marked by him in his own copy.

CN [page #] Contributions to The Nation, 4 parts, ed. Kenneth L. Ketner and James E. Cook (Lubbock: Texas Tech Press, 1975–88). A searchable CD-ROM edition is published by InteLex Corporation (1999) as part of Charles Sanders Peirce: Published Philosophy (I).

CP [volume #.para #] *Collected Papers of Charles Sanders Peirce,* volumes 1–6 eds. Charles Hartshorne and Paul Weiss; volumes 7–8 ed. Arthur Burks (Cambridge: Harvard University Press, 1931–35, 1958).

EP [volume #] *The Essential Peirce,* volume 1 eds. Nathan Houser and Christian Kloesel; volume 2 ed. Peirce Edition Project (Bloomington, IN: Indiana University Press, 1992, 1998).

ISP [page #] Numbers Bates-stamped in 1974 on each sheet of an electro-print copy made from *The Charles S. Peirce Papers* (Cambridge: Harvard University Library, 1966, microfilm, 33 reels including supplement) and kept at the Institute for Studies in Pragmaticism, at Texas Tech University, Lubbock. With some exceptions the numbering follows closely the order of the pages on the microfilm. Harvard documents that were not microfilmed, including those in R 1600 and RL 100, do not have ISP numbers.

NARG [accession #] National Archives Record Group.

NEM [volume #] *New Elements of Mathematics,* 4 volumes in 5, ed. Carolyn Eisele (The Hague: Mouton, 1976).

O [catalog #] A publication by someone other than Peirce listed in *A Comprehensive Bibliography of the Published Works of Charles Sanders*

Peirce, 2nd edition rev., ed. Kenneth L. Ketner (Bowling Green: Philosophy Documentation Center, 1986).

P [catalog #] A Peirce publication listed in *A Comprehensive Bibliography.*

R [catalog #; ISP #] A Harvard manuscript listed in Richard Robin's *Annotated Catalogue of the Papers of Charles S. Peirce* (Amherst: University of Massachusetts Press, 1967). Manuscript numbers preceded by an S are listed in Robin's "The Peirce Papers: A Supplementary Catalogue" (*Transactions of the Charles S. Peirce Society* 7 [1971]: 37–57).

RL [catalog #; ISP #] Correspondence listed in Richard Robin's *Annotated Catalogue.*

RLT [page #] *Reasoning and the Logic of Things,* ed. K. L. Ketner (Cambridge: Harvard University Press, 1992).

W [volume #] *Writings of Charles S. Peirce* (Bloomington, IN: Indiana University Press, 1982–).

WMS [list #] A Peirce manuscript listed in the Chronological List published in W1–W5.

Introduction

The period from 1887 through the spring of 1890, though not without hope and accomplishment, was a time of disillusionment and defeat for Peirce.[1] Only a few years earlier, Peirce's father, Benjamin, the great mathematician and astronomer, had proudly proclaimed to the Boston Radical Club that his son Charles would carry on his life's work and would develop and fertilize vistas he had only glimpsed. No one doubted it. Charles's star was rising. During the first half of the 1880s, he was one of America's elite scientists and the only American logician known the world over. Peirce had just begun teaching at Johns Hopkins and had every reason to expect that he would spend his life there as Professor of Logic. But in April 1883, Peirce divorced his first wife, Melusina Fay, and married his reputed mistress, Juliette Froissy Pourtalais, a woman of unknown, or at least of unspoken, origin.[2] Nothing for Peirce would ever be the same again. Within a year he had been forced out of Johns Hopkins and by 1886 his scientific career with the Coast and Geodetic Survey was falling apart. By 1887 Peirce had come to be spurned by the society that had nurtured him—he was no longer welcome even in his family home. A sense of defeat grew in Peirce as he struggled with the realization that all the paths he had chosen were blocked and that he could neither have the life he wanted nor provide for Juliette the life her extravagant tastes demanded. In April 1887, Peirce and Juliette packed up and moved to Milford, Pennsylvania, a mountain village with a small but thriving French community, where they hoped to make a new start and where they imagined they could afford to live well. At first Peirce expected his exile to be temporary but he soon

1. In writing this introduction, I have depended on the results of Max H. Fisch's many years of research, contained in his files and data collections at the Peirce Edition Project. To reduce the number of footnotes, I do not give references for items that can be easily located by keeping the following in mind: all references to manuscripts and Peirce family letters, unless otherwise indicated, are to the Peirce Papers in the Houghton Library at Harvard University; correspondence with employees of the Coast Survey is in Record Group 23 in the National Archives.

2. The Fisch Collection at IUPUI contains records of extensive research into Juliette's origin, primarily conducted by Maurice Auger, Victor Lenzen, and Max H. Fisch, but no final conclusions were drawn. Elisabeth Walther's *Charles Sanders Peirce: Leben und Werk* (Agis-Verlag, 1989), Joseph Brent's *Charles Sanders Peirce: A Life* (Indiana University Press, 1993; revised ed. 1998), and Kenneth Laine Ketner's *His Glassy Essence* (Vanderbilt University Press, 1998), each contain helpful discussions of Juliette's origin but do not settle the question.

came to understand that he would be a man apart. When in the spring of 1890, mainly for the income, he helped organize a journalistic attack on Herbert Spencer, Peirce signed his contributions "Outsider." That is what he had become.

In 1884, after his dismissal from Johns Hopkins, Peirce moved to Washington D.C. to refocus his career on his scientific work for the Coast and Geodetic Survey. In July he had begun an intensive program of field operations which he expected to continue until a vast expanse of the continental United States was linked through gravity determinations and added to the international geodetic network that would serve to calculate the figure of the Earth. This was a principal concern of mathematical geodesy and Peirce had already contributed to its solution (W4: sel. 76). At some point he knew he would have to turn a growing mass of data into a publishable report on gravity, but he kept putting it off in favor of continued field work. He assumed that when the time came to prepare reports he would have whatever computing help he needed, as he always had before. Then in March 1885, Grover Cleveland was inaugurated as the twenty-second President of the United States and Peirce's plans were dashed. Cleveland came to power intent on reforming government service and by July had targeted the Coast Survey as the agency he would make an example of.[3] Superintendent Julius Hilgard was fired and all administrators and field officers, including Peirce, were subjected to intense scrutiny. Frank Manly Thorn, a lawyer and friend of Cleveland, was installed as acting superintendent to carry out the President's reform agenda. Greatly discouraged by what was happening, Peirce left Washington in March 1886 and moved with Juliette to New York City. He supposed that New York would be a better place to start a new life in case his Survey job should be lost. He carried out pendulum field operations at the Stevens Institute station in Hoboken until August when Thorn relieved him of further field duty and ordered him to prepare for publication the backlog of results already obtained. Funding for field operations had been slashed and Peirce's gravity work, among the most costly, could no longer be supported. If pendulum operations were to continue they would have to be scaled back to meet only the demands of practical science, not those of pure science that guided Peirce. On 20 August Peirce wrote to University of Wisconsin astronomer, Edward S. Holden: "The president seems to have decided to keep Thorn in as Superintendent as long as he can, and under the influence of these men of Red Tape all the life and energy has gone from the Survey. . . . I am utterly discouraged and disgusted, and want

3. See Thomas G. Manning's *U.S. Coast Survey vs. Naval Hydrographic Office: A 19th-Century Rivalry in Science and Politics* (University of Alabama Press, 1988), especially ch. 4, and his "Peirce, the Coast Survey, and the Politics of Cleveland Democracy," *Transactions of the Charles S. Peirce Society* 11 (1975): 187–94. Also see Brent, ch. 3, and the introduction to W5.

to get out. . . ." In October, trying to cheer him up, Peirce's mother wrote: "Cleveland is a Dolt."

Somehow Peirce managed to hang on to his Survey job for another five years, although it seems certain that he would have given it up many times over had he not needed the income so desperately. Peirce was clearly disaffected and frequently spoke of resigning, but then always reconsidered. His relations with Survey headquarters became increasingly strained, sometimes quite bitter, and except for brief periods of respite, the remainder of his tenure was marked by a suspicion in Washington that Peirce was not doing enough work and by a concern on Peirce's part that there was a cabal conspiring to get him dismissed. One period of promise came just after July 1889 when Thomas Corwin Mendenhall, a trained scientist, succeeded Thorn as Superintendent. But it soon became evident that Mendenhall's plans for gravity determinations left no room for pendulum operations of the sort Peirce practiced. By the close of the period covered in the present volume, Peirce's second major gravity report, representing years of labor, was at risk of being rejected for publication, and Mendenhall's patience with Peirce was rapidly reaching its limit.

Amidst the turmoil of a life in constant transition and a career that was falling apart, Peirce managed to carry on at least a thread of philosophical inquiry, inspired in part by his late work at Johns Hopkins and his reading of the 1885 books by Royce and Abbot, and fueled by his continuing lexicographic research for the *Century Dictionary*.[4] In the August 1886 letter to Holden quoted above, Peirce added: "You remember that I told you something of a sort of evolutionist speculation of mine. This has grown much. . . ." When he wrote to Holden, he had already begun to write a book entitled *One, Two, Three* in which he would make a guess about the constitution of the universe and use his categories as the key to an all-encompassing system of philosophy (W5: sels. 47–50). After his move to Milford in 1887 this work would grow into his "A Guess at the Riddle" (sels. 22–28) and, although never finished, it would set the course for much of his subsequent thought. But as 1886 drew to a close, it was logic that was uppermost on Peirce's mind. For a while he resumed work on a book on general logic (W5: sel. 54) which would evolve into his "How to Reason" of 1894. But as his insecurity with his career increased, his interest turned from the advancement of the science of logic to how he could use his specialty to make a living adequate to the demands of the lifestyle he and Juliette had set for themselves in Baltimore in the first months of their marriage. Peirce's income had taken a serious hit with the loss of his lectureship at Johns Hopkins, and now that his

4. See Francis Ellingwood Abbot's *Organic Scientific Philosophy: Scientific Theism* (Boston: Little, Brown, & Co., 1885) and Josiah Royce's *The Religious Aspect of Philosophy, A Critique of the Bases of Conduct and of Faith* (Boston: Houghton Mifflin Co., 1885). For Peirce's reviews of these works, see W5: sels. 33, 46. For a brief account of Peirce's work for the *Century Dictionary*, leading up to 1887, see the Introduction to W5, pp. xliii–xliv. See also W5: sel. 57.

Coast Survey salary was in danger, he had to find a substantial new source of income. He began writing elementary accounts of his logic of relatives (W5: sels. 55–56) and Boolean algebra (sel. 1), perhaps initially for a course of lectures he hoped to deliver at the University of Wisconsin, but at least in the latter case it is likely he had paying students in mind.

Peirce entered 1887 with some confidence that he had found a way to survive his anticipated separation from the Survey. Were there not hundreds, nay, thousands of citizens abroad in the land in the greatest need of improving their reasoning skills? Would not a good course in reasoning, customized for individual capabilities and taught by a master logician, increase opportunities and, in general, better the lives of students—and thereby serve well the country as a whole? Could not one expect to attract large numbers of occasional students to sign up for a course of study that virtually guaranteed a high degree of self-improvement? Peirce was convinced that he had found a niche and that with clever marketing and efficient operations he could make good money with a correspondence course on the art of reasoning. He wrote to Cyrus W. Field, financier for the first transatlantic cable, that for years he had carried in his pocketbook a clipping quoting Field on the value of right reason: "My fortune was made by working a gold-mine, and that gold-mine is the power of right reason." Peirce might not make a fortune, but surely he would make a good living.

To set this promising plan into motion, Peirce needed capital. Brochures would have to be printed, lessons duplicated, typewriters purchased, assistants hired, and field-agents engaged. Peirce wanted fifteen hundred students and imagined that once things got rolling he would send out around five hundred letters a day. He would begin by advertising in popular magazines and would send out a hundred thousand circulars. He wrote to his cousin, Henry Cabot Lodge, and asked for a loan to get his scheme off the ground. Lodge declined and apparently with no other prospects Peirce decided to start up piecemeal. In May an advertisement for his course circular (reproduced on p. 14) ran in the *Century Magazine* and he sent circulars (sel. 2) to seven hundred people. He wrote to his brother James Mills (Jem) that he doubted he would attract "a single pupil from so small a number," but letters of interest began to come in. Records for the course are very incomplete, so it is difficult to tell how many responded or exactly what the content of the course was, but it is clear that by the end of March Peirce had received more than fifteen inquiries and at least eight students had begun lessons. While far from what Peirce needed to make a living, and certainly not enough to let him resign from the Survey, the response was promising and indicated that a major promotional effort could succeed. Peirce imagined an army of agents dispersed throughout the country, all soliciting students to sign up for his course. He drew up directions for agents (sel. 5) which bring to mind the hucksterism of turn-of-the-century medicine peddlers or of modern telephone solicitors: "The levers upon which you have to rely are first, cupidity, second, shame, and third, fatigue." Still, there is no doubt that Peirce believed he could deliver good value for the price of his course, and from what can be reconstructed from the fragments that remain (see sels. 3–13), that belief seems justified.

Peirce's plan for the correspondence course was set out in his circular (sel. 2) and his follow-up letter (sel. 3). The course would be divided into three parts—traditional logic, mathematical reasoning, and scientific reasoning—and the full course would require a minimum of one hundred and eighty letters. From the exercise sets that have survived—only a small part of the series Peirce had prepared—and from surviving student letters, it is possible to get a sense of what Peirce taught and how he interacted with his students. He seems to have gone to some lengths to address his students' individual interests and capabilities, but it is likely that he was aiming too high. Certainly the reasoning exercises (sel. 9) and the three lessons in Boolean algebra with additional exercises (sels. 10 and 13) involved rather high-level logical content; there is a one-page fragment (in RL 100) that indicates that Peirce even hoped to convey some of his favorite philosophical ideas through his reasoning exercises. For example, the second exercise from the fragment gives a brief lesson in Peirce's theory of signs:

> Let us use the word "sign" to mean anything which on being perceived carries to a mind some cognition or thought which is applicable to some object. Thus, I would call a portrait a sign. I would call a pointing finger a sign. I would call a spoken sentence a sign. I now ask you to make a list of a good many different kinds of signs, and to attempt to classify them according to their different modes of standing for their objects. To do this will require a good deal of thought.

Such questions might well serve the purpose of evaluating student preparedness but they seem aimed at minds more elastic and capable than might be expected to turn out in the large numbers Peirce expected. Still, a letter he wrote at the end of March to J. M. Hantz of Northwestern University indicates continuing enthusiasm for his course and reveals no dissatisfaction with his initial students:

> It is my fate to be supposed an extreme partisan of formal logic, and so I began. But the study of the logic of relations has converted me from that error. Formal logic centers its whole attention on the least important part of reasoning, a part so mechanical that it may be performed by a machine, and fancies that that is all there is in the mental process. For my part, I hold that reasoning is the observation of relations, mainly by means of diagrams and the like. It is a living process. This is the point of view from which I am conducting my instruction in the art of reasoning. I find out and correct all the pupil's bad habits in thinking; I teach him that reasoning is not done by the unaided brain, but needs the cooperation of the eyes and hands. Reasoning, as I make him see, is a kind of experimentation, in which, instead of relying on the intelligible laws of outward nature to bring out the result, we depend on the equally hidden laws of inward association. I initiate him into the art of this experimentation. I familiarize him

with the use of all kinds of diagrams and devices for aiding the imagination. I show him just what part abstract thought has in the process—a quite subsidiary one.

Peirce added that he assigns his students "a large number and great variety of exercises in dealing with real facts" and that "the invention of these exercises is the thing for which I hope to be remembered, for I believe they are destined to exert no little influence in the future." In the years that followed, as Peirce used his exercise sets for other purposes, the package of exercises was broken up and dispersed. The small set that has been reassembled (sels. 9, 10, 13) is at best an indication of what Peirce was so proud of, as many of the exercises derive from other authors. Had Peirce's students successfully worked their way through all of his lessons, they would likely have become the proficient reasoners he promised, but in the end no one ever finished the course. Peirce did carry on with a few students for a year or two, and later even tried to revive the course, but his lack of capital from the outset and his move to Milford in April thwarted any real chance for success.

Still, in the spring of 1887, prospects seemed good, though Peirce's circumstances were becoming more and more difficult. New York was an expensive place to live and Peirce's salary from the Survey was barely enough to maintain a satisfactory lifestyle. With enough paying students he would have welcomed separation from the Survey, but with only a handful he could not afford to resign. Unfortunately, his Survey work, now confined to the reduction of observation data—which in better times would have been handled by computing assistants—was extremely time-consuming, and severely limited the time he could spend answering letters and promoting his logic course. More disturbing, starting in September of 1886 a crisis had been brewing over the report on pendulum operations from the ill-fated Greely Expedition to Lady Franklin Bay in the Arctic, and Peirce was caught in the middle of it.[5] In 1881, then Lieutenant Adolphus Greely led an Army expedition of twenty-five men to the northeastern part of Ellesmere Island to establish a scientific station above the 81st parallel at Fort Conger off Lady Franklin Bay. Greely's party had been organized to participate in the first International Polar Year, an eleven-nation effort to advance earth science in the Arctic and Antarctic during 1882–83. The astronomer for Greely's party, Sergeant Edward Israel, had been specially trained by Peirce in the use of pendulums for gravity determinations, and for sixteen days in January 1882 he diligently swung Peirce Pendulum No. 1 in a specially constructed ice shelter. Greely's party met with disaster when supply ships failed to reach Fort Conger in 1882 and 1883, and when a navy vessel finally reached the retreating expedition about two hundred miles south of Lady Franklin Bay at Cape Sabine in June 1884, only seven men had survived and

5. For some background remarks on Peirce's involvement with the scientific assignment of the Greely expedition, see the introduction to W4, p. xxxi.

only six would make it home. Throughout the agonizing final winter, with starvation threatening his men, Greely took great pains to preserve the scientific data obtained at such a high price. Knowing that the heavy pendulum was a dangerous burden as his party retreated from Fort Conger to Cape Sabine, Greely had given his men the option of abandoning it, but they had declined. Fearing that his party's camp might be missed by the much hoped-for relief expedition, he sent a party on 23 October 1883 to a prominent point on an island a few miles south of Cape Sabine in Payer Harbor to cache the records. Peirce's pendulum, sealed in its case, was erected as a towering marker over the cache (see woodcut on p. 219).

The rescue of the expedition made international headlines, and Greely became an instant celebrity. There was some initial concern that the tragedy might have resulted from poor judgment on his part, and it was rumored that the survivors had resorted to cannibalism, but Greely was quickly exonerated. However, discord over the cost of the expedition and rescue troubled President Arthur and Secretary of War Lincoln, and they remained cool to Greely and even used his disaster as an opportunity to argue against future federal support for dangerous scientific missions. Not until Cleveland was elected President would Greely be duly recognized for his achievement and promoted first to Captain in 1886 and then to Brigadier General in 1887. The initial controversy over his leadership and the attempt to use his misfortune as an argument against federal support for science made Greely very sensitive to any criticism of his party's achievements.

In his first dispatch following the rescue, Greely had stated with much satisfaction that his party had saved and brought back the records of the meteorological, tidal, astronomical, magnetic, and pendulum observations, and he mentioned proudly that he had brought back the pendulum. In the 19 September 1884 issue of *Science,* the President of the British Association for the Advancement of Science proclaimed that "nothing in the annals of scientific heroism exceeded the devotion of those hungry men in sticking to that ponderous piece of metal." In consequence of the criticism of his expedition, and the considerable attention given to the pendulum, Greely was determined to include Peirce's account of the Ft. Conger pendulum observations in his official report. Yet by September 1886, over two years after Peirce had been given the pendulum records, and with everything else in hand, Greely was still waiting for the gravity results. Knowing that Superintendent Thorn feared bad publicity, Greely threatened to go to press without Peirce's report: "It is needless for me to point out the comments which will be called forth in America and Europe, if these observations are wanting when the final report appears."[6] Responding as Greely hoped, Thorn put tremendous pressure on Peirce to turn in his report at once.

6. Greely to Thorn, 29 March 87. NARG 23.

Thorn knew that Peirce had delayed his report because of some remaining uncertainties over the expansion coefficient for Pendulum No. 1 which he believed could not be resolved without taking No. 1 to a northern station, preferably St. Paul or Minneapolis, where it could be swung in the summer and again in the winter under extreme conditions as similar as possible to those at Ft. Conger. Peirce felt it his duty to turn Greely's hard-won data into the most significant results possible and he knew what that required. As early as April 1886, he had informed the Assistant in Charge of the Survey's Washington office, Benjamin A. Colonna, of his concerns and of his plan to swing the pendulum at a suitable northern location, and by September he had informed Superintendent Thorn directly. As the Coast Survey authority on pendulum operations, and given the importance of the Greely observations, Peirce probably expected his recommendation to be accepted without opposition, but he did not count on, nor perhaps even fully comprehend, the political pressures on Thorn. Peirce's stubbornness, however justified from the standpoint of pure science, rankled Thorn, who threatened to take the matter entirely out of Peirce's hands. Finally seeing the urgency of issuing the report, even if not fully adequate, Peirce reluctantly conceded: "You are aware that my judgment is averse to the publication of the Greely matter; but as you were plainly determined upon it, I thought it my duty to do all I possibly could to try to render that publication useful . . ." When Peirce wrote this on 22 March 1887 he added: "I have wasted more time upon this than I should have thought it worth while to do, except for my desire to make the best of this Greely publication. . . . I perceive you are becoming very impatient, and I will give up trying to perform the impossible, and send on the work as soon as I can."

Three weeks later Peirce submitted his report, but instead of settling things down it made matters worse. Although in muted terms, Peirce had included all of his criticisms and concerns. In accordance with Peirce's instructions, after the pendulum at Ft. Conger had been swung for eight days, the knives had been removed and interchanged. But after that interchange, the periods of oscillation were noticeably different, too different to be accounted for, Peirce believed, by the contraction of the pendulum due to colder temperatures or by slippage of a knife, as suggested by one of Peirce's past assistants, Henry Farquhar (see annotation 220.4), who, in the past, had frequently been assigned to assist Peirce. There was a remote possibility, Peirce suggested, that the change was the result of frost accumulation on the knives during the interchange, but he thought it really could not be satisfactorily explained and would detract from the usefulness of the results until further experiments could be made at a northern station. To make matters worse, he pointed out that the pendulum appeared to have lost between 10 and 15 grams of mass,[7] probably as a result of an accident

7. In his published report (sel. 30), Peirce gave 10 to 15 grams as the probable weight loss, but in a 28 February 1887 letter to Thorn (NARG 23), he estimated that 15 to 20 grams had been lost.

during the difficult retreat from Ft. Conger to Cape Sabine. Such a loss of mass would explain a variation in the pendulum's period of oscillation after its return. In raising these concerns, it is clear that Peirce's purpose was to present the Ft. Conger results in a way that made sense, and being fully aware of how often damage occurs to scientific equipment, especially in rough conditions, he had no idea his report would give offense. But Greely's high sensitivity to criticism blinded him to Peirce's good intentions and he became furious. Thorn set the Survey office to work to diffuse the tension. Farquhar was asked to write a supplementary report to mitigate Peirce's account and Greely added a memorandum (pp. 243–44) in which he fervently denied that any accident had happened to the pendulum. He went so far as to accuse Peirce of having given Sergeant Israel inadequate training and of failure to supply any written instructions, even though he had earlier praised Peirce for the care with which he had instructed Israel—care documented by Peirce's detailed written instructions, which have survived and can be found with the papers that Greely brought back from Ft. Conger (see annotation 216.19).

When he saw Greely's memorandum, Peirce was dismayed that such offense had been taken, and he immediately submitted a conciliatory note to be printed with Greely's memorandum (pp. 244–45). In this note, Peirce stressed that he had no intention whatsoever of imputing any blame for what he considered to be normal occurrences under the circumstances, and he emphasized that Greely and Israel deserved nothing less than the highest honor for their "signally successful" gravity determination. He did refer, though, to "the only doubt which affects the result, namely, that which relates to the temperature-correction," but added that this doubt was destined to be resolved when further experiments could be made in the North. Greely's two-volume report, including Peirce's Ft. Conger "Pendulum Observations" (sel. 30), finally appeared in the fall of 1888, and Peirce's "Explanatory Note" was inserted to appear with Greely's "Memorandum." Greely was satisfied and wrote to Peirce on 30 November 1888 that he understood that no blame had been intended. He added: "I beg to assure you that I have always been impressed with your earnestness and zeal in connection with these observations, and I know that you were very decided in insisting upon the conditions under which the work should be done. I cannot well believe that any one should consider you as desirous of pulling down a house which has been substantially built with your hands; for to your assiduity, skill, and knowledge must be credited, as I have always understood, the latest and most important advances in the methods of application of pendulum observations." That brought to an end an unfortunate episode largely fueled by misunderstanding; but while Peirce's relations with Greely seemed to have been mended, his relations with the Survey had suffered further damage.

As he grappled with the Ft. Conger pendulum results, Peirce continued working on his definitions for the *Century Dictionary*—before long his main concern. And, typically, from time to time other topics would catch his attention. In 1886, three members of the English Psychical Research Society, Edmund Gurney, Frederic Myers, and Frank Podmore, published a book which recounted hundreds of cases of the hallucination of the appearance of a person who would die or had died within twelve hours of their "appearance" and a scientific case was made for the authenticity of telepathic and apparitional phenomena. William James, a close friend of Gurney and a member of the English Psychical Research Society as well as of its American counterpart, gave the book, *Phantasms of the Living,* a very positive review in the January 1887 issue of *Science.* Peirce, who would have known of the book in any case because of his many acquaintances in the American branch of the Society (to which he never belonged), including his own brother Jem, must have been struck by James's praise for the book. Only two years earlier, Peirce had speculated (W5: sel. 24) that presumed telepathic phenomena were the result of faint sensations, and he had endorsed the field as worthy of further scientific study. So in early 1887, Peirce was working his way through the main argument of this huge book with his own review in mind—it would appear later in the year in the *Proceedings of the American Society for Psychical Research* (sel. 16) and trigger a controversy with Gurney that would continue for two years.

Probably in March, Peirce and a few other prominent American scientists were asked to contribute short articles to *The Christian Register* for a series on how science viewed belief in a future life. Peirce agreed to participate and drew material from his ongoing examination of *Phantasms* for his contribution (sel. 14). He wrote to his mother on 3 April 1887 that his work for his correspondence course was improving his writing style and that he hoped in a year or two to be "as good a writer as these men who write the editorials in the New York papers, who turn out so much good English and good sense." The little piece for the *Register,* published on 7 April, gave Peirce an opportunity not only to try out his developing style, but also to "announce" a few ideas that were growing more and more important for him and that would become signature doctrines. Among these were his ideas that the variety in the universe could not have come about by strict adherence to mechanical law and that there are no definite limits to human knowledge. According to Max Fisch, it is here that Peirce first made his case in print against the doctrine of necessity.[8] Peirce thought that although the evidence in favor of afterlife was not strong, it might be expected to become stronger. As to the "shades" who supposedly survive physical death, existing evidence could only bring Peirce to conclude that they were mere ghosts of their former selves—and so painfully solemn. Perhaps revealing more of his own

8. Fisch, p. 229.

circumstances than he intended, he wrote that were he suddenly to find himself "liberated from all the trials and responsibilities of this life, my probation over, and my destiny put beyond marring or making, I should . . . regard the situation as a stupendous frolic, should be at the summit of gayety, and should only be too glad to leave the vale of tears behind." He certainly would not "come mooning back . . . to cry over spilled milk."

Probably while he was working on his contribution for the "Science and Immortality" series, possibly slightly later, Peirce wrote a paper entitled "Logical Machines" (sel. 15) for the November inaugural issue of G. Stanley Hall's *American Journal of Psychology*. Peirce argued for the superiority of Allan Marquand's logic machine over that of Jevons, but he offered some improvements and suggested that it should be possible to construct a machine "which should work the logic of relations with a large number of terms." Peirce believed that the study of such machines was a good way to improve logic. In this paper Peirce did not mention his recent recommendation to Marquand to use electrical switching circuits for logical operations (W5:421–22),[9] but he did, in passing, make some interesting remarks about "the secret of all reasoning machines" and the appropriateness of calling such machines "reasoning machines," and then suggested that to some extent every machine is a reasoning machine—to the extent that they depend on "the objective reason embodied in the laws of nature." Peirce claimed that "reasoning machines" are destitute of originality and initiative: "it cannot find its own problems; . . . it cannot direct itself between different possible procedures." The absence of originality, however, is no defect for a machine: "we no more want an original machine, than a house-builder would want an original journeyman, or an American board of college trustees would hire an original professor"—a clear reference to himself.

It is not surprising that what we see of Peirce's life mirrored in his writings from this period appears as troubled and somewhat embittered. He had been forced to leave Johns Hopkins and, though not without hope, saw no good prospect of an appointment at another university. The Coast Survey was in disarray and he knew that it was just a matter of time until his career there would come to an end. His one hope was his correspondence course.

9. Around 1950, Alonzo Church discovered in Marquand's papers at Princeton a fairly elaborate circuit diagram for a logic machine, thus establishing that Peirce's recommendation had been acted on. It is not known whether an electrical logic machine was built. Ken Ketner has argued that Peirce himself drew the wiring diagram, probably in 1887. See Ketner's article, with Arthur F. Stewart: "The Early History of Computer Design: Charles Sanders Peirce and Marquand's Logical Machines," *The Princeton University Library Chronicle,* Vol. 45, 1984, pp. 187–211. Alice and Arthur Burks discuss the Marquand diagram in Appendix A of *The First Electronic Computer: The Atanasoff Story* (University of Michigan Press, 1989), pp. 339–48, and conclude that it marks a significant advance in computing engineering theory—or would have had it become known. Although they do not believe that Peirce drew the elaborate circuit diagram, they do argue that it is plausible to credit Peirce with being the first to have conceived of an electrical general-purpose programmable computer, but they find no clear evidence that Peirce's or Marquand's ideas had any influence in the development of electronic computing.

He felt sure it could succeed—but without the capital to begin his scheme at full strength it would have to grow to a critical mass before he could devote himself to it fully, and reaching that point would take time. Could he and Juliette survive in New York while they waited? On 3 April, Peirce wrote to his mother:

> It seems to be pretty certain that there is going to be enough to live on from my lessons any way, even in New York. But I shall go into the country the first of May and economize a little; and can stay there next winter if necessary. The expenses have so far eaten largely into the profits, but I have made arrangements to reduce the cost of my advertising, and at the same time make it more effective. My clerks will get trained and will make the letters less costly, and the purchases of type-writers, etc. will cease, or nearly so, as I reach my maximum. For the next few months, this will be a heavy expense, but then I expect to retain the Coast Survey two, and perhaps three, months more. That gives me more than enough to pay for type-writers. I think I shall eventually make a handsome thing of this. At any rate, I shall make a living, and earn the everlasting gratitude of the country, when the effects of the training come to be seen. I have had an enormous quantity of extremely interesting letters from teachers, professors, lawyers, business men, etc. I am also getting numerous suggestions to invest money. But I have not yet been obliged to purchase a steam coupon-cutting machine.

Peirce's spirits sound high but he must have been putting his best face on for his mother—in fact, during most of this period he was in emotional turmoil. He was under constant, often extreme, pressure from Thorn to submit reports, yet congressional budget cuts made it virtually impossible for him to receive sustained computing assistance, especially since he had moved out of Washington. There were some exceptions, but Peirce was left to his own devices most of the time. He thus confronted a mountain of data at the very time he found his powers as a mathematical computer to be weakening. A few years later, in December 1891, as he was about to resign, Peirce wrote to then Superintendent T. C. Mendenhall what amounted to a confession about his hidden struggle with his loss of computing proficiency.

> My mind, as it seems to me, is generally sound and decidedly strong. But of late years, in a certain direction a singular weakness has been growing upon me; though I cannot but believe that with a good rest I should recover. When Thorn had been in about a year I think it was that I found I got all mixed up about my computations, and at first complained of it openly. Then, I began to see that it would injure me and kept quiet about it. We were constantly expecting that Mr. Thorn would go, and I was determined that when he did I would ask to be sent into the field. Then I came into the country and found myself better at first. Besides, I got upon hydrodynamics which did not affect me the same way. I worked very hard, and could find nobody who could give me much help. But my tendency to become confused about complicated computations increased, and was aggravated by having no aid. I became almost incapable of reading certain kinds of mathematics, though other kinds, much more difficult to most minds, afford me little difficulty. The more trouble I had, the less I liked to acknowledge it. So I temporized and got along as well as I could . . . (18 December 91)

It is easy to imagine Peirce's frustration when Thorn pushed him beyond limits he was prepared to acknowledge. Peirce's relations with Thorn grew acrimonious and they became impatient and sarcastic with each other. To make matters worse, Peirce imagined that there was some kind of conspiracy to get him out of the Survey. While this may have been a paranoid response, there is evidence that B. A. Colonna (who during Thorn's tenure[10] was officially in charge of the Survey's Washington office but unofficially acted as the de facto superintendent) was working behind the scenes to turn Thorn against Peirce. It was Colonna who had created a stir in the scientific community during the 1885 investigation of the Survey by describing Peirce's gravity work as of "meager value" (see W5:xxix) and Peirce's letters to Thorn frequently contain marginal notes added by Colonna, seemingly intended to dispose Thorn against him. For example, in the margin of a 30 September 1886 letter to Thorn in which Peirce outlined some of his concerns with the Greely data and asked for help with the computations, Colonna wrote: "It is plainly evident that if we depend on Peirce we get nothing. I would suggest a letter to him directing that he turn over to the office all the Greely records and any others that he may already have made bearing on them & that he do so at once." And when on 9 July 1887 Peirce sent in a few unpaid vouchers from his pendulum operations at Hoboken the previous year, Colonna sent this exasperated note to Thorn: "Mr. Peirce extended time and time again his allotment and still left these bills unpaid. Open with him again and where will you stop?" The simple fact is, there was bad blood between Peirce and Colonna,[11] and whatever his motives, Colonna did want Peirce out of the Survey: "Charles Peirce about crazes me. He has no system, no idea of order or business & with all his talent is a dead-weight. I wish he could get a larger salary somewhere else and leave us. We could spare his talent for the sake of a better order."[12]

More stressful than his career instability were his increasingly bad relations with his family and friends over his marriage to Juliette. Established society wanted no part of Juliette and even old friends, including Samuel P. Langley, withdrew from Peirce. Peirce's Aunt Elisabeth (Lizzie), who owned the house his mother and brother Jem lived in, despised Juliette, and made it plain that she was not welcome in her home. Aunt Lizzie wrote to Peirce's sister Helen after the death of Herbert's (Berts's) baby girl: "I had a little talk with Berts about Juliette & he feels about her just as I do. . . . It seems she is studying for the theater to learn how to act; it will be an easy lesson for her—though I don't see that there is much left for her to learn" (22 April 1886). She wrote later (4 July 1886): "I have many sad hours thinking of Charles. He did wrong to marry Zina—& he suffered for it—but he was young then. Now there is no excuse for him in tying himself to that

10. Manning (1988), p. 90.
11. Brent, pp. 171–2.
12. B. A. Colonna to George Davidson, 17 December 86. National Archives RG 23.

miserable Juliette—whom we ought not & cannot receive. There is no question about it. She is, I feel sure, a very dangerous person—& our only course is to keep her at a distance." In January 1887, Peirce had a flare-up with Jem over Juliette. Peirce had written to Jem pleading with him to warm up to her:

> If you had any discernment of human nature you would see that the worst thing you could do for me and the worst thing all round is to treat Juliette with any want of love & confidence. We have bad things to face in the near future, all of us; and you may be sure we had best stick together. That we can't do if you are going to be distrustful of Juliette. She burns under a sense of your injustice to her. Half our misery comes from that. (c. 20 January 1887)

Jem's reply was not conciliatory. He wrote that he had "no wish to enter on a disagreeable discussion," but he went on to say that he could not permit himself "to be called to account for sentiments & conduct to which I am driven by the hard stress of facts" (21 January 1887). He insinuated pointedly that Juliette had acted disloyally to Peirce during that very week. Peirce responded sharply: "As you insist on putting me into the position of choosing between you and my wife,—quite unnecessarily—of course I choose my wife. You thus get rid of a troublesome relative very neatly, & at a time when he is more troublesome than ever" (c. 22 January 1887). The fact was, however, that Peirce's own feelings for Juliette were mixed. Though he had become completely committed to her, he was aware that she had already caused him much harm and he did not fully trust her. When he had written to Jem earlier in January about the plans for his correspondence course, he said plainly that he was afraid Juliette would somehow interfere: "She may intercept letters from pupils & break up correspondence. . . ." He added that Juliette would not permit him to have a clerk at their flat, nor have any woman work for him at all, and he revealed that he even suspected that Juliette was somehow to blame for his troubles with the Coast Survey. "Uncle Sam and Juliet [sic] are enough to drive me out of my wits." But his feelings for Juliette fluctuated wildly. He ended by asking Jem to burn the letter, "which is imprudent, because I love her devotedly."

As Peirce's old social and family ties unraveled, he and Juliette began to associate with a more bohemian crowd—people like New York playwright and director Steele MacKaye and his wife Mary, writer and editor Titus Munson Coan, poet and stockbroker—and editor of the works of Edgar Allan Poe—Edmund Clarence Stedman, geologist and chemist Persifor Frazer, known for his atheism, and artists Albert Bierstadt, Alfred L. Brennen, and George B. Butler.[13] One of Juliette's New York friends, Mary Eno Pinchot, had a country estate in the Pocono Mountains just outside of Milford, Pennsylvania. Peirce and Juliette had visited Milford and were much attracted to the beauty of the surrounding countryside and, in partic-

13. See Brent, p. 185.

ular, to the French community that had gathered there. The Peirces found that they were most easily accepted by people of French heritage. The need to economize, together with the attraction of an accepting community, convinced them to pull up stakes and move to Milford. It did not detract from this decision, as Joseph Brent has pointed out,[14] that the Pinchot family had great wealth and that they regularly entertained the likes of the Vanderbilts, Stuyvesants, Harrimans, and Belmonts. Here seemed to be an opportunity for Peirce and Juliette to enter a rich society even if not the society of Peirce's heritage. In later years, Peirce remembered the time differently. In a draft of his 1908 paper, "A Neglected Argument for the Reality of God," (R 842), Peirce reminisced: "In 1887, when I had attained a standing among American scientific men sufficiently to satisfy a man of very little ambition, I retired to the wildest country of the Northern States, south of the Adirondacks and east of the Alleghanies, where I might have the least distraction from the study of logic." But though this may be what he came to value most highly about his retreat from city life, it is far from certain that this motive had anything to do with his decision to move to Pennsylvania.

The Peirces arrived in Milford on Thursday, 28 April 1887, and checked into the Hotel Fauchère. Within two weeks the Peirces had leased a house in Milford, characterized by Peirce's mother as "luxurious quarters" (3 June 87), and proceeded to enter into the village life. Peirce joined the Episcopalian church and became friendly with the local clergy.[15] He and Juliette became frequent guests of the Pinchots at their Norman-style mansion they called "Grey Towers." Brent has described how they spent many afternoons and evenings at Grey Towers playing charades, capped with Peirce reading and reciting, and in September the Peirces "wrote, produced, directed, and acted" in a play given in the Pinchot's private theatre.[16]

Although the move disrupted Peirce's correspondence course and the preparation of his reports for the Coast Survey, it did not take him long to resume those efforts. The correspondence course would never achieve a critical mass and would gradually expire, but his Survey work would continue for another four and a half years. His official assignment at that time was to reduce the data from his post-1881 pendulum observations and produce publishable results, but his main interest would soon become the theory of the hydrodynamical effect of air on pendulum movement. Peirce also went back to work on his definitions for the *Century Dictionary*, and would spend the following three years working more intensively on his definitions than on anything else.

Peirce's relations with his family deteriorated further after the move to Milford. Aunt Lizzie became even more vitriolic about Juliette. She wrote to

14. See Brent, p. 186.

15. From Henry Leonard's notes of conversation with Mrs. Robert G. Barkley, Milford resident. Fisch Collection.

16. Brent, p. 187.

Peirce's sister: "I think that your mother blames me for the stand I take about Charles & Juliette. . . . We can not have them here at all. In fact I know Juliette enough from my own observation, that she would be a dreadful creature to have in the house. She is a liar & very artful, & she cares for nobody but herself, & she wd be worse than a rattle-snake in the house" (8 August 1887). She wrote of Juliette's alleged genius for acting that "she always has been on the stage & ought to be an adept by this time" but that "if she is a genius I fear it is a cracked one," and that "I utterly distrust her & hope I never see her again" (5 May and 9 June 1887). Even Peirce's mother, who had alone seemed always to maintain a genuine concern in Juliette, seemed to turn against her. In August, Mrs. Peirce traveled to Newport with Jem after vaguely inviting Charles and Juliette to meet them, but Jem waited until it was too late—nine days into their visit—to write that they could come. When Charles learned of this, he was furious and wrote a scathing letter draft that he never sent:

> It is best I should say once for all a few plain words which I shall not repeat concerning an expression in your last. You say you hope Juliette will let me come on to Cambridge. I wish Juliette would not urge me to go but would resent as I think she ought your insufferable and vulgar insolence. You insult me deeply in supposing or pretending to suppose I ever would go into that house. Whatever your object may have been in driving me to this decision, you have succeeded in that.
>
> Your inviting us to meet you and mother in Newport and then not letting us know till you had been there 9 days when mother writes that I can put any construction I like on her silence, confirms me in [the] decision self-respect ought to have brought me to long ago.
>
> I was deeply attached to you all, but you have all behaved ignobly & contemptibly, & I will pay up what I owe & be done with you. (22 Aug. 1887)

He did send a telegram that he immediately regretted sending and wrote to Jem to express his "sorrow and shame at having used an insulting expression." He promised that "As long as mother lives, at least, I want to have the best relations possible with those she loves" (21 Sept. 1887).

Peirce's mother would not live for much longer. On 4 October, Peirce was called to her bedside and she died six days later. Unfortunately, the tensions toward Juliette, who accompanied Peirce to the funeral and stayed on with him as he helped settle affairs, did not let up during the period of mourning. On the 15th, Aunt Lizzie wrote to Helen: "I hope I shall hear today when Charles & Dulcinea are going. I hope today but this I cannot expect. I wish she was at the South Pole, the North being too much in the neighborhood. . . ." She wrote again on the 21st: "I do not hear any thing yet of Charles' going—I hope & trust they will go this week & never return." A few days later she could finally write: "Charles is going tomorrow & then I shall breathe freely. I am always afraid she will make an invasion. I feel quite sure that she has got Charles into her power—& she would like to get us all if she could. . . . However we need not be afraid of her if we can only keep her at a distance." When Peirce's mother's estate was eventually settled about a year later, his share came to about $2000, including $1000 he had borrowed in 1885. He also got back some books he had given his mother, in particular a *Leopold Shakespeare* which had been dear to her.[17]

The move from New York and his family troubles did not prevent Peirce from making some progress on the intellectual front. By mid-May 1887, he had finished his review of *Phantasms of the Living*, his first paper after arriving in Milford. Although Peirce did not believe that the postulation of telepathy and apparitions, Gurney's "ghosts," formed a good hypothesis for explaining the unusual phenomena recounted in *Phantasms*, that conviction was not why he devoted so much attention to that gigantic book. Gurney, Myers, and Podmore had put forward their results as a serious scientific study and had presumed to build their argument on the basis of probabilities, hoping to show that in an earlier investigation by Charles Richet the probability in favor of telepathic phenomena had been found to be too low.[18] The critical use of probability theory in the design of scientific experiments and the analysis of results was relatively new, although not for Peirce, who was an expert in two sciences that were exceptions, astronomy and geodesy. In the preceding decade Peirce had devoted much thought to extending the use of statistical reasoning to new sciences, and in the 1883–84 experiments with Jastrow, he had introduced the first modern randomized experimental design for psychology.[19] Peirce saw at once that the method of Gurney and his associates was inadequate to their task and that they had seriously misapplied the logic of probability. However well-intentioned, their work amounted to an attack on the logic of science, and Peirce could not let it go unanswered. It only made matters worse that William James had been impressed by the absurd claim made in *Phantasms* that the odds in favor of "ghosts" was about "a thousand billion trillion trillion trillions to one."[20] In the first paragraph of his "Criticism" (sel. 16), Peirce alluded to this claim—"I shall not cite these numbers, which captivate the ignorant. . . ."—and pointed out that "no human certitude reaches such figures as trillions, or even billions to one." Gurney, Myers, and Podmore had presented thirty-one cases[21] which they claimed established their hypothesis to this remark-

17. *The Leopold Shakespeare. The Poet's Works in Chronological Order, from the Text of Professor Delius* (London: Casser, Petter, & Galpin, 1877).

18. Charles Richet, "La suggestion mentale et le calcul des probabilités," *Revue Philosophique de la France et de l'Étranger* 18 (1884): 609–74. See Ian Hacking's "Telepathy: Origins of Randomization in Experimental Design," *ISIS* 79 (1988): 427–51, for an account of the circumstances giving rise to *Phantasms,* and the Peirce-Gurney dispute. Many of the details of this paragraph are taken from Hacking's article. Also see Stephen E. Braude's "Peirce on the Paranormal," *Transactions of the Charles S. Peirce Society* 34 (1998): 203–24.

19. See Hacking op. cit. and W5:xxv–xxvi.

20. Gurney, Myers, and Podmore were using the British system where a billion equals a U.S. trillion and a trillion equals, in U.S. terms, a billion billions.

21. Abstracts for these thirty-one cases, and others mentioned in selections 16–19, are available on the Electronic Companion for W6 (http://www.iupui.edu/~peirce).

able degree of certitude and Peirce's aim was to show how their results were vitiated by inadequate sampling and control procedures; specifically, that in each of the thirty-one cases they had failed to meet one or more of sixteen conditions of an adequately designed experiment.

Peirce's review was forwarded to Gurney for a reply to be published along with it. These papers, together with a rejoinder by Peirce probably written in the late summer or fall, appeared in the December 1887 issue of the *Proceedings of the American Society for Psychical Research.* In his review (sel. 16) Peirce's criticism of the thirty-one cases was somewhat casual and perhaps slightly derisive, containing a number of inaccuracies and exaggerations that Gurney, in his lengthy "Remarks" (sel. 17), pounced on. He answered Peirce point for point, often with an impatience that matched Peirce's swagger. He did admit that perhaps he and his colleagues fell "far short of Mr. Peirce's standard in respect of caution, shrewdness of observation, and severity of logic," but he supposed that his deficiencies were not so great as to override the weight of the evidence. Peirce, stung a bit by some of Gurney's rebuttals, wrote a "Rejoinder" (sel. 18) almost as long as Gurney's "Remarks" and more technical and precise than his original criticism. He reiterated why he had felt the need to take a stand against Gurney, namely, that "to admit the existence of a principle, of which we certainly only meet with manifestations in very exceptional observations, is to rashly set the prosperity of scientific progress at hazard." He then answered all of Gurney's rebuttals and attempted to show that once the suspicious or problematic cases were weeded out there really was no "weight of evidence" at all. Peirce praised Gurney for adopting a statistical method "with a view of putting this question to rest," but his badly designed study "leaves the question where he found it." In response to Gurney's claim that any bias he might have in favor of the supernatural was no greater than Peirce's bias against it, Peirce agreed, but he added that "a bias against a new and confounding theory is no more than conservative caution; while a bias in favor of such a theory is destructive of sound judgment." Gurney set about answering Peirce's "Rejoinder," but had not finished his remarks when, in 1888, he apparently took his own life. It is thought that the impetus for his apparent suicide was the revelation that his assistant, George Albert Smith, had manufactured evidence (annotation 61.23). Gurney's final but unfinished answer to Peirce appeared posthumously in 1889 as "Remarks on Mr. Peirce's Rejoinder," with a concluding "Postscript" by Myers (sel. 19). In his final "Remarks" Gurney wanted to make it clear that he was really not an *advocate* for the supernatural and that, in fact, he agreed with Peirce "in professing 'a legitimate and well-founded prejudice against the supernatural.'" The entire controversy had been acrimonious, with both parties sometimes verging on the scornful. Ian Hacking says "It is Peirce at his crankiest (but none the less sound for that)," and he suspects "that many of the Boston skeptics were egging him on."[22] On his side, Gurney had the

22. Hacking, p. 445.

resources and encouragement of the *Psychical Research Society* behind him, along with his co-editors and assistants. But, all in all, one senses that the disputants did not lose respect for each other and even understood that they were in a curious way working together in an effort to advance human knowledge. About a dozen years later, when Peirce revisited this subject for a paper he was writing on "Telepathy and Perception," he reminisced: "I had a somewhat prolonged controversy with Edmund Gurney which was only interrupted by his death; and this brought me into fine touch with the spirit of the man. I was most strongly impressed with the purity of his devotion to truth" (CP 7.612).

After returning to Milford in October, following his mother's funeral, Peirce finished the year working on the theory of hydrodynamics, concerned with the effects on pendulums of the viscosity of air, and he worked on other matters related to his Coast Survey investigations, including his postponed report on the construction of a practical standard of length calibrated against a specified wave length of sodium light (W4:269–98). Peirce was probably stimulated to resume that work by three papers on wavelengths that appeared in 1887, one of them a study by Michelson and Morley precisely on the point of Peirce's own research. Michelson and Morley's paper, and the others by Louis Bell and Henry Rowland, made reference to Peirce's work.[23] Peirce also resumed work on his "Guess" and continued to write his definitions for the *Century Dictionary*. Possibly in connection with his dictionary work or his study of hydrodynamics, or his interest in mathematical pedagogy, and stimulated by an 1887 article in the *Journal für die reine und angewandte Mathematik*,[24] Peirce began a systematic study of curves that he would carry on for at least two more years (see sel. 42; also see c.1888.4 and 1889.3, 20–22 in the Chronological Catalog). Apparently in response to an invitation from Peirce to join in this study, Survey computer and occasional aid to Peirce, Allan Risteen, replied on 4 August: "It has often occurred to me that a collection ought to be made of these properties that are common to all curves of given kinds—say, closed curves—and that perhaps the close examination of such a set of general propositions might lead to others equally general, so that after a time we should have a *general geometry* in the truest sense." Sometime during the year Peirce also returned to his work on the theory of number and applied quantification theory to his

23. All three papers appeared in *The London, Edinburgh, and Dublin Philosophical Magazine and Journal of Science:* Henry A. Rowland, "On the Relative Wavelengths of the Lines of the Solar Spectrum," vol. 23: 257–65; Louis Bell, "On the Absolute Wave-length of Light," vol. 23: 265–82; Albert A. Michelson and Edward W. Morley, "On a Method of making the Wave-length of Sodium Light the actual and practical Standard of Length," vol. 24: 463–66.

24. The article in *Journal für die reine und angewandte Mathematik*—referred to by Peirce as Crelle's Journal—has not been identified. It is clear, from Risteen's 4 Aug. 1887 letter, that Peirce had recommended a "demonstration," probably in an 1887 issue, in connection with the study of curves.

1881 axiomatization (sels. 20 and 21).[25] It is noteworthy that in "Logic of Number" (sel. 21), Peirce gives a technical definition of the "hereditary character" for number that brings to mind Frege's "hereditary property" (see annotation 156.11), but Peirce's regrettable inattention to Frege, probably because of Schröder's dismissal of him,[26] argues that Peirce's innovations arose from an independent course of thought. It is not definite when or how Peirce's interest in number theory was rekindled; perhaps it was in connection with his study of number for his *Century* definition. A few years later, in 1896, he would present a lecture on number to the mathematics department at Bryn Mawr College (probably R 25), and number theory would periodically occupy him for the rest of his days.

In the latter months of 1887, Peirce began a correspondence with Francis C. Russell, a Chicago attorney who had taken a sudden interest in Peirce's logic. Russell soon became something of a disciple of Peirce and, after he became associated with the Open Court Press, was instrumental in paving the way for Peirce to publish in *The Monist*. Peirce also resumed correspondence with William James, writing to him in October about his "admirable work on Space."[27] This was Peirce's first letter to James after moving to Milford, and it may have been the first in two years—since his letter of October 1885 in which he had mentioned to James that he was working on "something very vast . . . an attempt to explain the laws of nature . . . to trace them to their origin & to predict new laws by the laws of the laws of nature." Then Peirce had been at the seminal stage of what would become the systematic metaphysics of his "A Guess at the Riddle," and not much later, his *Monist* metaphysical series. By October 1887, Peirce had penetrated much deeper into his "vast" undertaking, and he had been working through some of the same issues addressed by James in his article on space. After telling James how much he had learned, Peirce expressed some reservations: "I fancy that all which is present to consciousness is sensation & nothing assignable is a first sensation." He was not ready to admit "that size is so nearly a primary sensation as red or blue." Peirce suggested that "objective space" might be "built up" by a synthesis of fragmentary spaces and speculated that in the same way "objective time" might be built up by a synthesis of fragmentary times. Peirce concluded his letter by remarking that James had apparently not seen "Mayer's argument against Helmholtz's theory of audition."

25. Peirce's landmark 1881 paper, "On the Logic of Number" (W4:299–311) is discussed in the introduction and annotations to W4 (see especially pp. 575–76, annotation 222.24).

26. See Ernst Schröder's review of Frege's *Begriffsschrift* in *Zeitschrift für Mathematik und Physik* 25 (1880): 81–87, 90–94.

27. Peirce must have been referring to James's "The Perception of Space," which appeared in *Mind*, vol. 12, in four parts: I (Jan. 1887, pp. 1–30), II (Apr. 1887, pp. 183–211), III (Jul. 1887, pp. 321–53), and IV (Oct. 1887, pp. 516–48).

Perhaps Peirce's most intellectually stimulating correspondent of the time was Alfred Bray Kempe who, in November 1886, had sent him an inscribed copy of his recently published "Memoir on the Theory of Mathematical Form."[28] Peirce may have first learned of Kempe in July 1879, when it had been reported in *Nature* that he had proved the four-color conjecture that for any map only four colors are required to avoid having a boundary separating areas of the same color. Peirce seems to have had pre-publication access to Kempe's paper, which had been submitted to J. J. Sylvester for publication in the Johns Hopkins *American Journal of Mathematics*, and in 1880, before Kempe's paper appeared, Peirce offered some improvements on Kempe's method.[29] But it was Kempe's 1886 "Memoir" that would have a profound impact on Peirce, whose expertise in the logic of relations and interest in spatial logics enabled him immediately to see the genius of Kempe's graphical approach to relations. In order to exhibit essential forms, Kempe had introduced a graphical notation of spots and lines modeled on chemical diagrams, and this notation would play an important role in Peirce's innovation of his Existential Graphs (EG).[30] On 17 January 1887, after carefully reading Kempe's memoir and making a list of new terms that he thought might be included in the *Century Dictionary*, Peirce wrote to Kempe with some suggestions that led Kempe to make revisions which he credited to Peirce.[31] In January of 1889 Peirce would return to Kempe's "Memoir" and still find it "so difficult that I was at work on it all day every day for about three weeks" (RL 80:105). Kempe's influence can be found in Peirce's correspondence course exercises (sel. 9), especially those on relational graphs, and in the 1889 paper, "Mathematical Monads" (sel. 34), and in many other writings. In R 714 (1889.4), his fragmentary "Notes on Kempe's Paper on Mathematical Forms," Peirce even introduced lines to stand for individuals, an important move in the direction of EG.

The year 1888 began on a positive note for Peirce. On 1 January, President Cleveland appointed him to the Assay Commission, charged with testing coins from different U.S. mints for fineness and weight. Peirce served on two committees for the Commission, the Committee on Counting and the Committee on Weighing, and was a signatory for the final reports, signed on 10 February in Philadelphia. On 13 January Peirce and Juliette went to New York to see Steele MacKaye's new play, "Paul Kauvar," which had opened to acclaim on Christmas Eve. Mary MacKaye had sent them tickets. The Peirces continued to be frequent guests of the Pinchots,

28. *Philosophical Transactions of the Royal Society of London* 177 (1886): 1–70.

29. Peirce's "improvements" were presented to the Johns Hopkins Scientific Association and reported in *Johns Hopkins University Circulars* 1 (1880): 16. Kempe's paper, "On the Geographical Problem of the Four Colours," appeared in *American Journal of Mathematics* 2 (1879): 193–200.

30. For a treatment of Kempe's influence see Roberts (1973), pp. 20–25.

31. "Note to a Memoir on the Theory of Mathematical Form," *Proceedings of the Royal Society* 42 (1887), 193–96.

mingling with their well-heeled friends, and they had successfully entered into village life in Milford.

On 4 February, Peirce's Aunt Lizzie died in the family home in Cambridge. Jem wrote in her obituary that she had been "a woman of remarkable character & intelligence" but that she had been "very singular, almost eccentric" and that her "greatest real fault was a certain streak of jealousy which she could not always conquer." He said that she had been devoted to reading, "especially to German literature & above all to Goethe, whom she esteemed the paragon of geniuses and of men." In fact she had held virtually the same opinion of her brother, Benjamin, to whom, as Jem put it, she had been "devotedly attached." Aunt Lizzie's funeral was held on 8 February and Peirce attended, but it is not likely that Juliette was with him. Aunt Lizzie's estate was divided among Benjamin's children and Peirce's share came to about $5000.

Peirce's inheritance, from Aunt Lizzie and from his mother, created the possibility for a life in Milford that would otherwise have been impossible. Even though Peirce still held out hope that he could make a success of his correspondence course, it was hardly lucrative nor likely to be so any time soon, and his combined income from the Survey and from the Century Company was quite inadequate to the life he and Juliette had assumed in Milford—with its socializing in the Pinchot circle and with frequent trips back to New York. And, of course, Peirce's income from the Coast Survey was tenuous at best. To make matters more difficult, there were few suitable homes available for rent in Milford. When at the end of their first year the lease expired on their first house, it seemed that there was no place to go and that they would have to leave Milford. On 26 April a note appeared in the Port Jervis *Evening Gazette* (taken from *Milford News*): "We fear that we are about to lose Prof. Charles A. Pierce [sic] and his excellent lady because of their inability to secure a suitable residence for the coming year." At the last minute Peirce did find a house to rent, the Scheinmee Homestead on Broad Street, but his inheritance made it possible to consider something more permanent. On 10 May, the Peirces bought a farm about two miles northeast of Milford in the direction of Port Jervis. They paid $1000 for the 130 acres on the Delaware River, which included a parcel called "Wanda Farm" that had been the homestead property of John T. Quick, one of the colorful early settlers in the area, and another parcel known as the "Quick Saw Mill Property." The property as a whole was called "Quicktown." Altogether, there were two houses, two barns, a large ice-house, a sawmill, and some other outbuildings. The farmhouse on Wanda Farm, built in 1854, was the main house and the one the Peirces would begin renovating in January 1889 with the aim of turning it into a magnificent resort that could accommodate summer guests and perhaps even a residential school of philosophy. But on 10 May, when the Peirces bought Quicktown, there was an understanding that they would not move in immediately and that some members of the

Quick family could continue living in the main house for a period of time. That understanding would lead to complications later in the year, and descendants of the Quicks would come to believe that they had lost their property to the Peirces by some trick.[32]

It is hard to tell how Peirce divided his time in 1888, but as the year got underway it seems certain that his intellectual work was mainly devoted to three efforts: to his Coast Survey reports, to his definitions for the *Century Dictionary*, and to the articulation of a system of thought founded on his categories and his evolutionary metaphysics. After Peirce submitted his report on the pendulum work at Fort Conger, he turned his attention to working up results from the considerable unreduced records of the gravity work he had carried out during the preceding five years, and some from even earlier. It was becoming more and more difficult for Peirce to sustain the mental focus and intensity required for the complex calculations that typified these reductions and he persistently tried to convince Superintendent Thorn that he needed assistance with the computations. Early in April Thorn finally agreed to assign Allan Risteen to work with Peirce on a temporary basis. Risteen and his wife moved to Milford and probably stayed with the Peirces until sometime in July. During those months it is likely that the reduction of data from gravity determinations was a constant in Peirce's daily routine. But the fact that Risteen was there to help with the reductions probably allowed Peirce to work more on the related hydrodynamical theory, and it also freed him to spend more time on the *Century Dictionary*. Although Peirce had been working on definitions for at least five years, he was just beginning his most sustained and concentrated effort. Definitions were now being set in galleys and there was no choice but to turn considerable attention to that work. When the local newspaper had printed the notice that Milford might lose Peirce, it noted that he was engaged "in compiling a dictionary to be issued by the Century Company of N.Y." Clearly, Peirce's lexicographic work was a prominent part of his life at that time.

The third undertaking that must have occupied Peirce a great deal as 1888 got underway was his philosophical system building. Sometime after moving to Milford, probably after his mother died, Peirce resumed work on his book, "One, Two, Three" (W5: sels. 47–50, but see also 35 and 36), rechristened as "A Guess at the Riddle" (sels. 22–28). It had been over three years since he had begun articulating his "evolutionary speculation" which by 20 August 1886, as he wrote Holden, had become "a great working hypothesis of science" (W5:xxxix). Peirce's "speculation," his "guess," was that because of an "original, elemental, tendency of things to acquire determinate properties, to take habits" the universe itself has evolved from a state of "all but pure chance" to "the present almost exact conformity to law."

32. Lenzen to Fisch, 11 July 1961. Fisch Collection.

Peirce had come to conceive of the grand cosmic history of the universe as of a kind with the evolutionary growth of biological systems.

What led Peirce to these cosmological speculations at that time can only be surmised. Although it is clear that many of the roots of Peirce's grand idea ran deep into the earliest layers of his thought, it does seem that after his marriage to Juliette in 1883, and after he found out that his career at Johns Hopkins had been lost, he became decidedly focused on the riddle of the universe.[33] In his outline of how the argument of his book had developed (sel. 23, pp.175–176), he noted that after he had turned his illuminating categories to "the domain of natural selection," he had been "irresistibly carried on to speculations concerning physics": "One bold saltus landed me in a garden of fruitful and beautiful suggestions. . . ." That "bold saltus" may have been the "guess" itself, perhaps as expressed in his January 1884 "Design and Chance" lecture to the Johns Hopkins Metaphysical Club: "Now I will suppose that all known laws are due to chance and repose upon others far less rigid themselves due to chance and so on in an infinite regress . . . and in this way we see the possibility of an indefinite approximation toward a complete explanation of nature. . . . May not the laws of physics be habits gradually acquired by systems." For three or four years following his Metaphysical Club lecture, Peirce roamed in his Epicurean "garden of fruitful and beautiful suggestions":—his "One, Two, Three" writings of 1885–86 were part of that exploration. By the fall of 1887, as he began writing "A Guess at the Riddle," Peirce's initial exploration had worked itself out and he had started looking for further implications or illuminations of his guess for sociology and theology.[34] The final two chapters, projected but probably never written, were to be expositions of the triad in those two subjects.

Another possibility is that the "bold saltus" was the "leap" he took, probably in the summer of 1885, from his growing understanding of the usefulness of his categories for logic to the speculation that they provided the key to a rich and unified system of science. By fall 1885 at the latest, he could show how "the whole organism of logic may be mentally evolved from the three conceptions of first, second, and third." He would conclude that "if these three conceptions enter as we find they do as elements of all conceptions connected with reasoning, they must be virtually in the mind when reasoning first commences" and he would add that "in that sense, they must be innate ideas" and "there must be in consciousness three faculties corresponding to these three categories" (W5:245) which, in turn, "must be capable of a physiological explanation from three fundamental properties of the nervous system" (W5:247). It was Peirce's conjecture that his categories, firstness, secondness, and thirdness, or perhaps even the underlying concep-

33. See the introduction to W5, pp. xxxix–xlii for a discussion of the influences on Peirce.
34. Fisch, p. 229.

tions "one," "two," and "three," were the building blocks for a vast, integrated system of knowledge, that led him by mid-1886 to turn the evolutionary speculation of his "Design and Chance" lecture into his guess at the riddle of the universe, namely, that the universe may be understood as a process in which chance brings forth *first,* or original, events, which, because of an inherent tendency "to acquire determinate properties, to take habits," become more and more systematic and law governed. The evolving law produces *seconds* and the tendency to take habits, which generates law, is the *third* "or mediating element" between firsts and seconds (W5:293). By early 1888, when he sketched chapter seven for "A Guess at the Riddle" (sel. 28), he had refined his guess to this succinct statement: "three elements are active in the world, first, chance; second, law; and third, habit-taking."

The main thrust of "A Guess at the Riddle" was an exploration of the fecundity of Peirce's categories for different sciences and the construction of a unifying structure of fundamental conceptions. In each of the extant chapter sketches Peirce used his categories as a device for rethinking and refining old ideas. For example, in chapter 1, "Trichotomy" (sel. 23), he showed how ubiquitous firstness, secondness, and thirdness are by connecting them with common conceptions such as spontaneity, result, and bridge, or beginning, end, and process. But why stop with one, two, three, he asked. Because, he said, "any number, however large, can be built out of triads; and consequently no idea can be involved in such a number radically different from the idea of three." He used a model of a road with three-way forkings to demonstrate his point. Peirce's analysis of degenerate categories revealed that there are two distinct varieties of secondness, one internal and one external. It may have been Hegel's failure to understand this, Peirce suggested, that led him to commit "the trifling oversight of forgetting that there is a real world with real actions and reactions."

Chapter 2, "The Triad in Reasoning," was probably never written, unless Peirce intended "One, Two, Three: Fundamental Categories of Thought and of Nature" (W5: sel. 35) to be a preliminary draft, or at least a precursor of it. However, it is very suggestively outlined in the "Contents" (sel. 22) with particular reference to Peirce's 1885 paper in the *American Journal of Mathematics* (W5: sel. 30) where it was stressed that for "a perfect system of logical notation" it is necessary to employ three kinds of signs: icons, indices, and tokens (what would later be called "symbols"). Immediately following "A Guess at the Riddle" is a short selection on Steele MacKaye's theory of dramatic expression entitled "Trichotomic" (sel. 29). This paper, probably written for oral presentation during the early part of 1888 while "Guess" was in progress, effectively though very briefly summarizes four of its chapters (1, 2, 4, and 5). The discussion of signs complements the outline given in the "Contents" (sel. 22), and, together, they give a good idea of what Peirce had in mind for Chapter 2.

Chapter 3, "The Triad in Metaphysics," (sel. 24) is only a fragment of a sketch of what Peirce planned to write, but it strongly indicates that Peirce viewed his cosmology in relation to Greek thought, particularly pre-Socratic philosophy. His plan was to "run over all the conceptions that played an important part in the pre-Socratic philosophy and see how far they can be expressed in terms of one, two, three." He did not get far, but he pointed out that the Greek *arche,* the "primal matter out of which the world [was] made," was quintessentially his *first.* A fragmentary list of pre-Socratic doctrines (annotation 181.4–5), probably to be used as a source-list for Chapter 3, indicates further some of what Peirce might have included had he completed that chapter. For example, the thirtieth item on this list is a quotation of Parmenides taken from Plato's *Symposium* (178b): "He devised Love the very first of all the gods." Peirce then remarked: "But this doctrine was of course infinitely more ancient. Hesiod, quoted by Plato in the same place in the *Symposium,* puts Chaos first, earth second, and love third."

In Chapter 4, "The Triad in Psychology" (sel. 25), the application of his categories revealed to Peirce that there are "three radically different elements of consciousness": immediate feeling (consciousness of the first), polar sense (consciousness of the second), and synthetical consciousness (consciousness of a third or medium). In Chapter 5, "The Triad in Physiology" (sel. 26), Peirce used his categories to find a threefold division in the physiology of the nervous system that would account for the three kinds of consciousness. As though anticipating that he might be accused of reductionism, Peirce wrote: "No materialism is implied in this, further than that intimate dependence of the action of the mind upon the body, which every student of the subject must and does now acknowledge" (p. 188). Peirce concluded that three fundamental functions of the nervous system were, "1st, the excitation of cells, 2nd, the transfer of excitation over fibers, 3rd, the fixing of definite tendencies under the influence of habit," and he considered further whether these functions were "due to three properties of the protoplasm or life-slime itself" (p. 193).

In Chapter 6, "The Triad in Biological Development" (sel. 27), Peirce's examination led him to three principle factors in the process of natural selection: "1st, the principle of individual variation or sporting; 2nd, the principle of hereditary transmission, which wars with the first principle; and 3rd, the principle of the elimination of unfavorable characters." Peirce concluded that the principle of sporting is a principle of chance corresponding to his category of first, the principle of heredity is a principle of compulsion corresponding to his category of second, and the principle of the elimination of unfavorable characters is a principle of generalization corresponding to some extent to his category of third. But he acknowledged that the correspondence of the main principles of natural selection with his categories was not perfect and he speculated that "its imperfection may be the imperfection of the theory of development" (p. 202).

In Chapter 7, "The Triad in Physics" (sel. 28), the last extant chapter sketch for the book, Peirce delivered his guess that there are three active elements in the universe: "first, chance; second, law; and third, habit-taking." Finally, we know from the "Contents" that Peirce intended to finish with chapters on sociology and theology, but there is not much indication of what fundamental triads he expected to find. He does note under "The triad in sociology" that "consciousness is a sort of public spirit among the nerve-cells" and under "The triad in theology," that "faith requires us to be materialists without flinching," but this only gives a little of the flavor of what Peirce might have written. It is true, though, that in his first chapter, "Trichotomy," when he was discussing "absolutes" in cosmology, he alluded to the theological triad: "The starting-point of the universe, God the Creator, is the Absolute First; the terminus of the universe, God completely revealed, is the Absolute Second; every state of the universe at a measurable point of time is the Third" (sel. 23, pp. 173–174). Although Peirce tended to identify the third with representation, here we find, that in leading from first to last (second), third is process. Insofar as Christian theology holds that the universe is developing from "God the Creator" toward "God completely revealed," Peirce regarded it as an evolutionary doctrine. Perhaps this is the approach he wanted to develop in Chapter 9.

Peirce had a remarkable confidence in the importance of "A Guess at the Riddle." He was convinced that not only was it "destined to play a great part in the future," as he wrote to Holden (W4:xxxix), but that he was inaugurating a new philosophy which, like the earlier system of Aristotle, was so comprehensive that "for a long time to come, the entire work of human reason . . . shall appear as the filling up of its details" (sel. 23, pp. 168–169). He envisioned his new system as a "philosophical edifice," constructed on a deep and massive foundation, which unlike the Schelling-Hegel mansion—found to be uninhabitable almost immediately upon opening its doors—would be the principal habitat of philosophers long into the future. But Peirce's book was never published, nor even completed, and even though he managed to get some of his architectonic ideas into print in his 1891–93 *Monist* series, he remained virtually the only inhabitant of the "Peirce mansion" during his own lifetime. After May 1888, when Peirce and Juliette purchased the house that would become Arisbe, Peirce would become preoccupied with architectural renovations. Chapter 1 of Peirce's "Guess" (sel. 23), which was written out of order, may have been composed about the time Peirce began planning the renovation of his country house—when sound architectural structures became a matter of immediate practical importance for him. It is lamentable that Peirce would never finish either of his mansions and that, in their different ways, they would trammel him.

The evidence for when the Peirces moved to Wanda Farm and into their new house is inconclusive as it stands. By early June Peirce was using "Westfall Township," where his new estate was located, as his return address, and by July he was using the name "Quicktown." In an 8 June letter to Thorn, Peirce remarked that "on leaving Milford" he had lost his local clerk and on 2 July he said that his "movings" had taken five days. Yet as late as November he and Juliette stayed for a few weeks in a hotel in Milford while they dealt with legal issues pertaining to the eviction of the Quicks, which finally took place on 18 December. Probably the Peirces had moved to Quicktown shortly after they purchased it and occupied the secondary house, or some portion of the Quick house until the difficulties with the Quick's continuing occupancy became acute, but so far nothing conclusive has come to light. In any case, it was not until January 1889 that the Peirces finally moved fully into the main house and began rebuilding it to suit their purposes.

Wherever Peirce was residing during the second half of 1888, it is certain that his new estate was much on his mind. Except for the legal difficulties that arose concerning the Quick family, Quicktown was a place of promise for Peirce, a chance to make a good life for Juliette and himself. Together they must have spent many hours making plans and thinking about the hopeful future that now seemed within their grasp. Peirce tried to keep his Coast Survey work on track but without much success. He did manage on 10 August to send in a new paper on the mean figure of the earth, expanding on his previous paper of 1881 (W4:529–34), but Thorn, suspecting that it was somehow a ploy to ease the pressure he had been exerting on Peirce to complete his major gravity report, had it evaluated by Schott who returned an indecisive verdict. Schott made a vague insinuation that Peirce may have made some unattributed use of similar results of F. R. Helmert—"whose work came under the author's notice while writing his report"—and recommended that work on the earth's shape should be kept separate from "regular pendulum matter" in any case. Of course, for Peirce, determining the shape of the earth was the principal goal of his geodetic labors, and it was hardly beside the point to keep his gravity researches integrated with their ultimate purpose. But Peirce's paper (which has not been located) was not published, although it was probably the source for the results that Peirce used in his definition of "Earth" for the *Century Dictionary*. Peirce's work on the earth's figure and on its compression would continue to be mentioned in his monthly reports.

The texture of Peirce's life can only be painted in pale outline in an introduction such as this one in which the aim is to provide a context for and a sketch of the intellectual development that gave birth to the writings in this volume. A more complete account of 1888 would describe more fully Peirce's family relations, especially concerning the settlement of his mother's and aunt's estates, and would say more about his and Juliette's social and domestic lives. It would also say more about some of the correspondents who have been passed over in silence, and about some unmentioned incidents and flare-ups with the Survey's Washington office and scientific activities that have been left out—and, of course, there would be more about

Peirce's friends and colleagues and external matters that affected his life and thought. Chapter three of Joseph Brent's *Charles Sanders Peirce: A Life* should be consulted for a more complete account of these matters. Perhaps the main thing still to be said about the last half of 1888 is that Juliette's health took a turn for the worse and she would sometimes stay in New York, perhaps to be near New York physicians or because of the unsettled living conditions in Quicktown. Her health had always been worrisome for Peirce, but beginning in the spring of 1889 it would become a major concern.

On Thanksgiving Day, 29 November, Peirce wrote a newsy letter to his brother Jem. He thanked Jem for a remittance toward his inheritance and for the explanation of "fleflexnode" which "went straight into the dictionary." He said he had been "much occupied with small but pressing matters," and mentioned in particular the lawsuit concerning the eviction of the Quicks. He told Jem he was taking Juliette to New York on the following day and would return to the farm by himself. He reported that "Mrs. Pinchot wants us to change the name *Quicktown,* but I dont know that I agree with her. It is the name we found & 'Tom Quick' is rather a romantic figure in the history of the valley"—the following year a monument to Tom Quick was erected in Milford to mark the one hundred and fifty-sixth anniversary of its settlement. Peirce told Jem that if he was reading novels he should get *Le Capitaine Fracasse* by Gautier. "For my part I read little literature & I find serious novels dull. I am loitering through Pepys again, & have been reading Sidney's *Arcadia,* Dr. Dee's preface to Euclid, Thirion's *History of Arithmetic,* Browning, Shelley, Keats, Wordsworth, Montaigne (of which I have an old French copy), *Mémoires de Casanova, Our Mutual Friend,* some old Arithmetic & other old books." He finished by remarking that the dictionary was coming along quickly. This letter gives a nice sense of the tone of Peirce's life as the year was winding down. The final weeks of 1888 were dominated by the prospect of finally having full occupancy of the Quick house and plans for its renovation.

Peirce woke up at about 7:30 a.m. on New Year's Day, 1889, at Quinn's Halfway House, near Quicktown, from which he and Juliette would direct preparations for their move into their new house. He divided his day in a way that modeled how he would spend his time during the coming year. He devoted the morning to philosophy, in particular, to starting a new book, "Reflections on the Logic of Science" (sel. 31). After lunch he and Juliette drove to Port Jervis in their carriage to see a carpenter about an addition to the house. In later years, when Henry S. Leonard traveled from Harvard to interview elderly Milford residents about Peirces life, Mrs. Robert G. Barkley recalled that Peirce "drove a Phaeton with a white horse and gently waved a whip as he drove along."[35] Upon leaving Port Jervis, the Peirces crossed back into Pennsylvania to the village of Metamoras where they saw a

35. A record of this interview is in the Fisch Collection.

second carpenter. After dinner that evening, Peirce and Juliette worked on accounts—Peirce noted in his diary that "there was some disagreement." Later he turned to galley proofs for the *Century Dictionary,* which he noted had reached "game," and to his overdue Coast Survey reports—at least he recorded these tasks in his diary for 1 January.

A few days later the reconstruction of the Quick house was underway and, although more or less completed stages would be reached, remodeling would continue with varying degrees of intensity and disruption for the rest of Peirce's life, and even afterwards under Juliette's direction. Their home would become their prison in the way that Peirce's philosophical mansion would imprison him, catching him up in a vision he could not resist but causing him much suffering as he steadfastly struggled against insurmountable odds to achieve it. But as 1889 lay before him, there was good reason to suppose that his hopes for his estate, as well as for his philosophy, would be realized. He could not then know what a great struggle he would endure trying to build these parallel edifices. Leonard recorded some anecdotes that give an idea of how this process appeared from the outside. Miss May Westbrook remembered: "When the Peirces built their house they built around an original house on the property. Mr. and Mrs. Peirce sometimes quarreled. Once when I was at their house for dinner the quarrel was violent. I don't know what it was about because they talked in French. Mrs. Peirce was an unreasonable person." Miss Westbrook noted that whenever she visited, Peirce was always in his study except for meals, but she added that when Juliette was in Europe, Peirce "took one meal a day here with mother. He was very pleasant. Mrs. Peirce sometimes spoke well of him and sometimes not." Gifford Pinchot also talked with Leonard about the Peirces' reconstruction project: "The alterations were of an absurd character. The attempt was to make the house irresistible as an Inn or a Gentleman's Estate. Mrs. Peirce had two passions: devotion to Peirce and interest in land. In the latter respect she showed a characteristic common among French peasants. Peirce was extremely impractical. He submitted to her plans for alterations in the house loyally and cheerfully, living in one room while all the others were in a turmoil with carpenters." Pinchot remembered how in 1887 and 1888 he had discussed forestry with Peirce and that those discussions had been instrumental in his decision to study forestry in Germany. Pinchot went on to become Theodore Roosevelt's Chief Forester and would play a large role in establishing the National Park System in the United States. He also recalled that it was Peirce who had calculated the settings for a sundial built into the stone front of Grey Towers, "so that it gave exact normal time for the longitude and latitude" and that he "calculated the true North and South that were marked in the sidewalk in front of the house." These markings are still visible today.

The book Peirce started writing on 1 January (sel. 31), might have been an outgrowth of Chapter VII of Peirce's "A Guess at the Riddle," where he had made a number of the same observations he now planned to examine in detail—for example, that in order to have any hope of making progress in physics, we cannot simply work through one hypothesis after another without some hint to guide our initial choices. Peirce wanted to set out in detail the logic of science that supported his guess and that would recommend it as the hypothesis to guide physics. It may be that Peirce intended "Reflections" to be his "Illustrations of the Logic of Science" (W3:242–74) brought up to date. It is interesting that on the following day, 2 January, Francis Russell wrote to Peirce that "when your 'Illustrations of the Logic of Science' came out the papers initiated in me a new era in my mental history and I am one of a necessary many who recognize in you a master to be followed." Russell then asked Peirce if he had changed his views since the "Illustrations." Peirce replied on the 8th, "Suffice it to say that I have not given up any of the more fundamental of my younger opinions so far as I recollect them, but am perhaps more sceptical & materialistic."

Peirce did not get very far with "Reflections." He began the second chapter with a discussion of the doctrine of chances but soon decided that a prior discussion of mathematics was needed. On 9 January he wrote a few paragraphs of a new draft of Chapter 2 and continued it on the 17th, but that was the end of it. On that day he began working on a mathematical paper, "Note on the Analytical Representation of Space as a Section of Higher Dimensional Space" (sel. 32), elaborating on a proof he had just sent to Simon Newcomb with the hope, soon dashed by Newcomb, that it would be published in the *American Journal of Mathematics.* It may have been Peirce's interest in the mathematical foundations of the logic of science that caught him up in new mathematical investigations, or it may have been his work on hydrodynamics, but he continued working on mathematical topics throughout January and there are a number of other 1889 selections that may have been composed around that time. These include "Ordinal Geometry" (sel. 33), "Mathematical Monads" (sel. 34), "On a Geometrical Notation" (sel. 38), "On the Number of Forms of Sets" (sel. 39), "The Formal Classification of Relations" (sel. 40), "Dual Relatives" (sel. 41), and "Notes on Geometry of Plane Curves without Imaginaries" (sel. 42). Some of these papers, perhaps especially selection 34, and also the mathematical chapter of selection 31, may have been inspired by Peirce's January study of Kempe's paper on mathematical forms, and others may have been outgrowths of his work on mathematical definitions for the *Century* or his correspondence with mathematicians such as Alfred Mayer and his own brother Jem.

Peirce's enthusiasm for what was coming to pass in Quicktown was dampened by a continuing decline in Juliette's health. His diary reveals his growing concern. On 3 January he noted that "Juliette weighs 104 with thick clothes & heavy shawl" and on the 6th he wrote: "Much alarmed about Juliette's health. She spits so much blood. Juliette getting quite ill. If I should lose her, I would not survive her. Therefore, I must turn my *whole* energy to saving her." Peirce suspected tuberculosis and knew that living in a house under construction in the winter time was putting Juliette at serious risk, so he arranged for her to travel to the South. She left sometime in February, staying for a time in Brunswick, a resort town on the Atlantic coast of Southern Georgia, and then offshore at the very exclusive and expensive Jeckyl Island Club, where, at the request of Mr. Henry E. Howland, she had been extended privileges for two weeks. From Jeckyl Island, Juliette traveled to the new Hotel Ponce de Leon in St. Augustine where, Peirce wrote to Jem, "she found the greatest benefit" (30 March 89). She telegraphed Peirce from Jacksonville, Florida, on 30 March to say that she was much improved and would like to return, but Peirce tried to discourage her: "You must not think of coming back here so soon. This house is very unwholesome. I have not had a single well day since you left. The spring air would also be the death of you. You cannot come back till after the carpenter work is done. . . . We are rushing the work all we can, but I don't expect it will be ready for you to move into the front part before May 1 & not into the new part for another month at the very least. To move into a new house with the plaster not thoroughly dry would be madness." It must have added to his worry about Juliette to learn that on 29 March his friend and former student, O. H. Mitchell, had died of pneumonia at thirty-seven years of age.

As the days grew warmer Peirce's own health improved and he became excited at the prospect of farming Quicktown. He purchased two farm horses for harvesting hay, decided to raise a calf that had been born to his Guernsey cow, had five hundred Palmetto asparagus plants set out, and was probably as content as he had been for many years. He missed his young wife and considered renaming Quicktown "Sunbeams" in her honor. When Juliette returned she had not improved and in May Peirce asked for a two-week leave from his Coast Survey duties to take her to New York for medical tests. The diagnosis was tuberculosis, as Peirce had feared. They returned to Milford for the summer and fall knowing that Juliette could not spend the next winter in Milford. That realization was perhaps less worrisome than it would have been had Peirce not recently received fairly substantial payments from the estates of his mother and aunt—$1450 in April alone.

Certainly given the demands of the farm and the renovations to the house, and his preoccupation with Juliette's health, along with the pressure from his continuing responsibilities to the Century Company and the Coast Survey, Peirce had little time for anything else. But occasionally something would happen to turn his thought from its main course. Perhaps this happened most frequently as a result of the great variety of subjects he had to look into for his definitions, but there were other sources of intellectual stimulation and diversion. At the beginning of the year, Kempe's paper on mathematical form had played that role. In March, Wolcott Gibbs had written to Peirce to ask if he had published any results from his color experiments that had been funded fourteen years earlier by the National Academy of Sciences with a grant from its Bache Fund. Gibbs's request seemed to reawaken Peirce's interest in color studies and for several days beginning 4 April, he recorded results of a new series of color experiments in a notebook labeled "Hue" (1889.12). Peirce traveled to Washington D.C. during the third week of April to present a paper "On Sensations of Color" (1889.14) to the National Academy. He presented a second paper, "On Determinations of Gravity" (1889.15), in which he discussed his work with the invariable reversible pendulums he had designed. The spring issue of the *Proceedings of the American Society for Psychical Research* carried Gurney's final reply to Peirce (sel. 19) which must have caught his attention, but with Gurney by then deceased, Peirce probably had no thought of any further response. Within a few months, however, he would take up the subject again for *The Forum.* And in June at Harvard's commencement, Percival Lowell delivered the annual Phi Beta Kappa poem and took the occasion to commemorate Peirce's father, Benjamin, and Oliver Wendell Holmes. Lowell's Peirce stanza ended: "Though but an echo find itself in verse, The Cosmos answers to the name of Peirce."[36] Charles would surely have heard of this and it could not but have reminded him that he was expected to wear his father's mantle. No doubt he felt the irony that while such grand things were being said about his father, he was, largely by his own doing, living in exile from his father's social world. The promise of a new life may have made things easier for Peirce, but that would not last long.

During the years covered in this volume, the one continuous focus of Peirce's intellectual energy was his lexicographic work for the *Century Dictionary,* which in its first edition ran to 7046 quarto pages. He had begun writing definitions as early as 1883 and he continued with varying degrees of concentration from then on, but his most sustained and intensive effort came between 1888 and 1891. Peirce's contribution to the *Century Dictionary* was massive. He was responsible for six major subject areas—logic, metaphysics, mathematics, mechanics, astronomy, and weights and measures—but he contributed to many other areas including color terms, general philosophy, geodesy, psychology, and education (in particular, the words related to universities). Altogether he probably contributed or approved over 15,000 definitions, with many of them taking many hours of thought and research.[37]

From the beginning, Peirce's lexicographic work had a decided impact on his intellectual development. At Johns Hopkins, where Peirce began working for the Century Company, he developed a course in philosophical terminology structured around his dictionary work. His desire to express

36. Ferris Greenslet. *The Lowells and Their Seven Worlds.* Boston: Houghton Mifflin Co., 1946, p. 356.

37. Peirce estimated that he had been responsible for about 16,100 words (RMS 1163:2). For a more complete account see "Peirce's work for the *Century Dictionary*" by Jeffrey R. Di Leo and André DeTienne, *Peirce Project Newsletter* 3 (1999): 1–2.

usefully but as fully and accurately as possible the meanings of words such as "classification," "color," "continuity," "formal," "law," "logic," "nominalism," "predicate," "probability," "real," "relation," "science," "sign," "theorem," "truth," and "university," among many others, often led to significant developments in his ideas or in the direction of his thought. Max Fisch believed it was Peirce's return to the Greek philosophers for his dictionary work that led him to his evolutionary metaphysics, and it is likely that some of the mathematical selections in the present volume were stimulated by his lexicographic work (e.g. sel. 40). Certainly Peirce's increasing interest in classification, in the history of language, in the ethics of terminology, and in such matters as spelling reform, grew directly out of his work for the *Century Dictionary.*

It is unclear in what order Peirce took up his dictionary work, but he appears to have begun in 1883 by working his way through the *Imperial Dictionary* (the basis for the *Century*) letter by letter, pronouncing judgment on the *Imperial*'s treatment of his words, emending what could be saved and supplying what more was needed—often a great deal. By 1886 he had reached "Words in E" (W5: sel. 57). But Peirce also worked on his definitions by subject areas, beginning in 1883 with definitions for selected mathematical terms, followed in the intervening years by similar efforts for color terms, metrological terms, university terms, and so on. The *Century* was an etymological dictionary and included carefully chosen quotations to illustrate the history of the use of its words, so during these years Peirce's intellectual purview was profoundly expansive, covering the wide range of subject areas he was responsible for and the full history of the words from those areas, from their baptisms, if that could be found out, to their most current uses. He was always on the look-out for illustrative quotations to send in to the Century Company's New York office.

Sometime near the beginning of 1888, but perhaps not until the spring, Peirce started to receive galley proofs for his definitions. The *Century* began appearing in print the following year in bound fascicles of about three hundred pages. This process of working over the galleys incrementally, while publication was proceeding with earlier fascicles, would continue until the final fascicle, the twenty-fourth, was published early in 1891. By the end of November 1888, Peirce was through the first galley proofs for the F's and on 7 January he wrote Jem that he had received a second galley for "function." By the spring of 1890, the end of the period covered in this volume, about half of the *Century* was in print. Because of this piecemeal production process, from 1888 to 1891 Peirce had to revisit all of the definitions he had written during the previous five years and compose for each fascicle, as a continuing matter of priority, any definitions he had put off along the way. There is nothing that occupied Peirce more completely during these years than his dictionary work, neither his work for the Coast Survey nor his philosophical system building. It was likely this concentration that led him to set aside his "A Guess at the Riddle" manuscript, just as he seemed to have the book well in hand.

It did not take long after the first of the twenty-four slim volumes of the *Century Dictionary* appeared in print for reviews to follow. One lone voice of dissent was heard—the voice of Simon Newcomb. In a letter to the editor of the *Nation,* published on 13 June 1889, Newcomb complained of certain *Century* definitions that were "insufficient, inaccurate, and confused to a degree which is really remarkable." The examples he gave were for "Almagest," "albedo," "eccentric anomaly," "absorption lines," "law of action and reaction," "apochromatic," "alidade," and "achromatic lens," five of which, it turned out, were Peirce's. Peirce replied in the 27 June issue of the *Nation,* admitting that his definition of "anomaly," "perhaps the first I wrote in astronomy," was flawed, but defending the rest. Newcomb confessed to great surprise when he found out it was Peirce he had taken to task, but privately, in a letter to William D. Whitney, Editor in Chief for the *Century,* he wrote: "I may say to you confidentially that several years ago I should have regarded Peirce as the ablest man in the country for such work but I fear he has since deteriorated to an extent which is truly lamentable."[38] A few days earlier, Whitney had written to his brother that he did not understand why Newcomb felt "called upon to strain the truth and misjudge things in order to find fault" with the dictionary. "It seems," he went on, "as if he must have some private grudge to satisfy."[39] But Newcomb's criticism quickly faded out against the countervailing tide of acclaim. Overall Peirce was quite satisfied with the results of his work, even though he would often remark, as he did to Paul Carus on 25 September 1890, "God forbid I should *approve* of above 1/10 of what I insert."

The second major preoccupation of Peirce in 1889 was the preparation of scientific reports for the Coast Survey. For years he had accumulated gravity data with painstaking effort and at great expense, and beginning about 1887 had been trying to prepare results for publication. He had not published a major report since 1884, and that was a report on gravity determinations made in Pennsylvania in 1879 and 1880 (W5: sel. 1). Since then he had published some smaller reports, mainly on theory (e.g. W5: sels. 42, 43, 51–53) and, of course, his report on pendulum operations at Ft. Conger, but his principal gravity findings since 1880 remained unpublished. Most importantly, with the exception of the Greely report, these included all of the gravity work carried out with the Peirce invariable reversible pendulums. These unpublished results involved ten stations, six running along a north-south line between Montreal and Key West (including Albany, Hoboken, Ft. Monroe, and St. Augustine), three along an east-west line between Ithaca and Madison (including Ann Arbor), and the base station at the Smithsonian

38. Simon Newcomb to William D. Whitney, 9 July 1889, Yale (Beineke).
39. William D. Whitney to Henry Whitney, 26 June 1889, Yale (Beineke).

in Washington D.C., which provided the constants for all the Peirce pendulum operations.

In addition to reports on gravity work involving the Peirce pendulums, results still had to be worked up for earlier operations with Repsold or Kater pendulums at Hoboken, Cambridge, and Baltimore and for some of Peirce's early gravity work with less refined pendulums in Massachusetts (at the Hoosac Tunnel, Northampton, and Cambridge). Also, there were at least three volumes of unreduced data from observations made at Paris, Geneva, and Kew during Peirce's final trip to Europe in 1883. All of these records together, in their raw data form, filled more than one hundred volumes of pendulum transit records and scores of chronograph sheets recording time observations.

Finally, in conjunction with his principal work of determining gravity, Peirce had applied his results to the problem of determining the shape of the earth and had made many studies and investigations of such issues as the flexure of the pendulum staff and the effect of air resistance (involving hydrodynamical theory). For that, too, he needed to prepare reports.

Peirce had begun in earnest reducing data and writing a report on operations with the Peirce pendulums in the fall of 1886, after being relieved of field duty, but his attention had soon turned to the Greely report. Upon settling in Milford, Peirce turned again to the preparation of the report he believed would carry forward the U.S. contribution to geodesy he had initiated with his 1876 "Report on Gravity at Initial Stations" (W4: sel. 13) and his "Determinations of Gravity at Allegheny, Ebensburgh, and York, Pa., in 1879 and 1880" (W5: sel. 1). His plan in June 1887 was to write first a report on what he thought was the best work done with the Peirce pendulums, the results from Ithaca, Madison, Ann Arbor, Key West, and perhaps Fort Monroe, and to give "a full account" of the pendulums, including a discussion of their theory and of the work that had been done at the Smithsonian, the base station, to determine their constants. Then, for a separate report, he planned to prepare the results from Hoboken, Albany, Montreal, and St. Augustine, also done with Peirce pendulums, but not "in the last approved way" (9 June 1887).[40] But by the end of the year, Peirce had decided to organize the work into two series of stations grouped by their approximate location on either the same east-west or north-south meridian. After he finished his reports on work with the Peirce pendulums, he planned to clean up the remaining backlog.

Peirce went to work on the report for the east-west series of stations and wrote to Thorn on 28 June 1887 that it was "shaping up" and that he would soon have a draft ready, but he added: "it is a larger job than I fully realized." Two months later Peirce still had not finished his draft and he was forced to admit that he had run into a serious difficulty: he had found an error in the

40. Peirce did not mention Ann Arbor in this letter, but that was probably an oversight.

mathematical theory used to calculate the effects of the viscosity of air on the period of the pendulum. "This is one of the most difficult mathematical problems conceivable," Peirce wrote to Thorn (29 Aug. 1887), but he expected that his work would lead to an improvement in Stokes' hydrodynamical theory which would justify the delay; by the end of September Peirce decided that he should put off further treatment of hydrodynamics for a separate memoir. The final illness and death of Peirce's mother kept him in Cambridge for most of the month of October 1887, but by the end of November he wrote Thorn that his "long report" was almost ready, "requiring only final touches." Two months later, on 30 January 1888, Peirce sent in what he had ready "for the sake of suggestions of which I may avail myself in making the copy of it." He acknowledged that a lot of work, mostly clerical, remained unfinished and asked if he could have some assistance. Thorn declined and returned the draft unreviewed to be finished and copied.

Weeks passed by and Thorn's displeasure increased. On 30 March Peirce felt the need to explain the continuing delay. Pendulum work, he pointed out, is much more complicated than other geodetic work such as triangulation, longitude work, and leveling, because there are so many more sources of error that have to be studied and corrected for. "If these difficulties are only slightly increased, there results an enormous increase, first in the precautions which have to be taken in the field, and second in the puzzle of interpreting the observations." Defects in the construction of the Peirce pendulums, which Peirce attributed to poor American craftsmanship, made it all the more difficult to reach useful results, and the problem of hydrodynamics, now to be treated separately, had taken considerable time. "Now anybody who has ever done such a Work in such a way,—ask such men as Langley or Newcomb,—will tell you that it is impossible to make any reliable estimate of how much time it will take." Peirce's emotions were at a high pitch and he could not resist an allusion to Colonna's obstructionism: "In addition to this, I was subjected to false accusations of the most disgraceful kind, and the newspapers were filled with unbounded lies about me readily traceable to important personages. All of these things, and others which I omit to mention, distracted the equanimity of my mind considerably." In the margin of Peirce's letter, Colonna added the sarcastic remark: "What about other people's distractions of mind[?] Also what distracted his mind at all except the last 3 stations?" This was a clear reference to Peirce's relations with Juliette, and the fact that she had accompanied Peirce on many of his field assignments. Even though Peirce would not have seen Colonna's remark, Thorn and others in the Washington office would have; it indicates that rumors of scandal had infected Peirce's Coast Survey relations with the poison that had driven him from Johns Hopkins and had virtually sent him into exile. Peirce felt compelled to respond to the irritation and displeasure Thorn had been exhibiting:

The tone of your letters would seem to betray the opinion that I am myself completely insensible to the disparity between the time I estimated for the work and the time it has occupied. But can you suppose that I do not look upon the labor of my life seriously? Or that anything that you or the Hon. Secretary could say or do about it could possibly be as grievous to me as the want of my own self-commendation? When I agreed to do this work by myself my intention was to hire a computer; for I do not believe that anybody in the world could do such work advantageously without aid. The papers amount to at least a hundredweight and the mere picking out of such as are wanted in one day will all together often occupy hours.

Peirce took time in July to work on the method for calculating the figure of the earth from gravity determinations and on 10 August submitted his results for publication. For the rest of the year, again without an assistant, Peirce continued to work on reductions of data and on flexure and time calculations. On 31 December 1888, following a recommendation from C. A. Schott, he wrote to Thorn suggesting that both series of stations be included in one comprehensive report: "The amount of additional computation required is considerable, although not so great by any means as if the constants & behaviour of the instruments had not been studied." Peirce added, with some obvious bitterness: "The labour of writing the report,—of composing it, writing it, copying, verifying copies,—which is in part mechanical and in part requires all the ability I can bring to the task,—but in every part the utmost care and consideration, has mostly to be done over."

You will remember that about a year ago, I sent you my report in a substantially complete state (though then only embracing 4 stations) with the request that it be submitted to such critical examination as might be practicable and the result communicated to me for my aid in revision. The request was refused; and your letter embodying the refusal, conveyed to me the conviction that any flaws however trifling which might be detected would be husbanded to form material for an attack after the report was printed. Under these circumstances, my caution about parting my MS. out of my hands is naturally increased. . . . I am unable to say more definitely at what time my report will be ready, than that it will be during next spring.

On 11 January 1889, Peirce reassured Thorn that "the full report on the meridional line from Montreal to Key West inclusive & from Albany to Madison inclusive will be completed during the Spring," but Thorn, at Colonna's instigation, had lost faith in Peirce and decided that it was time to see exactly where things stood. He ordered Peirce to package up all of his work on the report and ship it to Washington for examination. Peirce complied, and two days later had packed and shipped twenty large books of reduced data and 2037 carefully inventoried and numbered manuscript pages and draft materials (see p. 636). Peirce could not let pass unaddressed the distrust that Thorn's order so clearly revealed. He told Thorn that he was glad to send all of his working documents because, for one thing, it would rebut the insinuation that the draft report he had sent the previous year had represented little effort on his part. But Thorn would also see that a great deal had been accomplished since then "and that the principal cause of the delay in completing the work has been the great amount of time spent upon the general method of pendulum observations and reductions,—which lay directly in my way." Peirce estimated that he needed at least three more months to complete the report and he asked again if he could submit it in draft to be looked at by specialists before making his official submission. Taking Thorn to task for a previous refusal, he added presciently:

> You say your object was to prevent my shifting the *blame* for the report to other shoulders. Now, for my part, I really do not think the report will sink below the zero of merit; but anyway, you overlook the fact that I never asked for binding directions but only for suggestions which I might be free to adopt or not. My main, not to say my only, motive was that I had reversed the usual order of presentation in a scientific memoir by stating the conclusions before the premises; and I wished to know how this would strike another mind competent to judge of it. (30 January 1889)

Peirce's relations with Thorn were at a very low point, yet, having unburdened himself, Peirce put his rancor aside and tried to resume normal relations. He wrote to Thorn on 4 February to say that, while the Peirce pendulum records were in Washington, he had gone to work on the Kater pendulum records from his Hoboken observations. He asked if he might go into the field again in the South—without mentioning that he was about to send Juliette to Southern Georgia for her health. Thorn declined. A few days later, Thorn returned all of Peirce's records "precisely as received from you—with the exception of Ms. report of pendulum work, which is in your handwriting and is retained for safe keeping in the archives here . . ." (13 Feb. 1889).[41] Peirce resumed his work on the long report and by the end of April had finished the reductions for the Montreal and Albany stations.

Whether Peirce knew on 30 January, when he wrote his spirited letter, that Thorn was about to resign is uncertain, but by mid-February it was common knowledge that Thorn would tender his resignation in March to be effective when a new superintendent was appointed. Peirce had hoped for this for a long time; he thought that a new superintendent, if a scientist were chosen and not another lawyer, would want him back playing a more active role in Survey operations. This may have had something to do with Peirce's request to go back into the field and was surely on his mind in May when he wrote to Thorn about a plan he had conceived "by which pendulum stations may be occupied perhaps at the rate of one a day, with good result, and not at an extravagant expense" (28 May 1889). He asked Thorn again to send him back into the field to institute his new plan as soon as he finished his pendulum report, which he said would be forwarded soon. Thorn replied on 14 June with a reminder of Peirce's "repeated promises during the past

41. The National Archives "Register of Records" indicates that this report was received and stored as GO–401, 902 HG in Box 395. It is now missing.

winter" that he would soon forward the report, "and now the Spring has passed." He advised Peirce "that no other enterprise or scheme be permitted to interfere with the prompt completion of that long delayed report, upon receipt of which your plan of daily pendulum stations will be in order for submission and consideration."

On 10 July 1889, Thorn was succeeded by Thomas Corwin Mendenhall as Superintendent of the Coast Survey. Mendenhall, who had been a student of Simon Newcomb,[42] was a physicist who had taught at universities in Ohio and Tokyo before joining the U.S. signal-service in 1884. In 1886 he had assumed the presidency of Rose Polytechnic Institute in Indiana, and it was from there that he had been called to the superintendency of the Coast Survey. Mendenhall seemed well suited to lead the Survey and Peirce was delighted with his appointment. Peirce's telegram of congratulations, sent to Indiana, was the first that Mendenhall received and he replied that it had given him great satisfaction. Peirce sent his first monthly report to Mendenhall on 31 July and took the opportunity to give a very detailed account of his pendulum work for the many years he had been in charge of gravity research. He also described at length his relations with Thorn and his general unhappiness with the direction the Survey had taken over the last half-decade.

> When Mr. Thorn came in, certain charges were made against me. Later, all these were retracted with the exception of one, which was a very vague one to the effect that I had not been under proper control and discipline. Now, if I were to be informed what the questions about gravitation were, and what the facts of the case on which the solution of those questions must depend, all the discipline in the world could hardly prevent my having my way, for the simple reason that "my way" is simply what I deem reasonable, and as my ideas on this subject are clearer than other persons', they must prevail with those very persons themselves. Accordingly, to prevent my having "my way," I have of late years been kept as far as possible ignorant of pendulum matters. I trust you will reverse this policy, and restore me to the charge of investigations into gravitation.

As to the report Thorn had been waiting for so impatiently, Peirce wrote that it was in a typist's hands. He had been working on a new arrangement for the report and now intended to submit it in two parts with the first one covering the work done at the Smithsonian, Ann Arbor, Madison, Cornell, and Key West. There were yet further delays, but finally on 20 November Peirce was able to write the agreeable letter that would accompany his long-delayed report (sel. 36). Although it did not include the Key West results, his submission included all of the theory, history, and discussion of constants needed for the complete report on the Peirce pendulum operations. As it was, the report ran to one hundred and forty oversize typescript pages. Peirce promised that a report on Montreal, Albany, Hoboken, Fort Monroe, St. Augus-

42. Brent, p. 195.

tine, and Key West would soon follow, and could be published later as the concluding part of the comprehensive report.

Although Peirce's report included all of the basic component sections present in his 1879 report (W4: sel. 13), it strikingly reversed their arrangement. Peirce also used radically different methods, the most obvious one being the introduction of "logarithmic seconds" as a unit of measurement. He also made a different application of the "resistential formula" which occurs in both reports as the basis for calculating the effect of air resistance. It is in this determination of corrections for the "second atmospheric effect" that Peirce hoped to improve on the classical theory of G. G. Stokes. As the annotations in this volume help to make out, though all of the necessary components are present, they do not all fit together entirely smoothly, and the report is marred by computational errors. This is not surprising, given the massive quantity of calculations that Peirce had to make in order to achieve his results; it is clear, however, that the report needed a thorough overhaul before it could be published.

Perhaps had Thorn still been superintendent, Peirce's report would have followed a standard course of technical examination, proofreading, and publication, but Mendenhall was new, and he had been encouraged not to fully trust Peirce's work, so he chose to have Peirce's report examined by specialists for "form, matter, meaning and suitability for publication." One of the three people he asked to examine the report was his own mentor, Simon Newcomb. On 28 April 1890, only four days after Peirce's long memoir had been mailed to him, Newcomb wrote to Mendenhall that it appeared to be "a careful and conscientious piece of work," but that its form was wrong:

> A remarkable feature of the presentation is the inversion of the logical order throughout the whole paper. The system of the author seems to be to give first concluded results, then the method by which these results were obtained, then the formulae and principles on which these methods rest, then the derivation of these formulae, then the data on which the derivation rests, and so on until the original observations are reached. The human mind cannot follow a course of reasoning in this way, and the first thing to be done with the paper is to reconstruct it in logical order.

Newcomb also objected to Peirce's reliance on logarithmic seconds, which he believed accomplished nothing except to confuse the reader. "On the whole the paper does not seem to me one which would prove useful scientifically or would redound to the credit of the Survey if published in its present form." Ultimately, Mendenhall would decline to publish Peirce's laboriously ground-out report and would justify his decision with words that echoed Newcomb. On 21 September the following year, having decided that Peirce's report as submitted was not publishable, and still waiting for the report for the north-south stations, Mendenhall would inform Peirce that his services would be discontinued at the end of 1891. That would bring to an end Peirce's thirty-one years of federal service and, without a pension,

Peirce would have no regular income. As for Peirce's 1889 report, it would be bundled up in brown wrapping and sent to the archives where it would disappear, mislaid, for more than seventy-five years.

At the end of the period covered by the writings in this volume, Peirce's report was still under review, and nearly a year and a half would pass before Mendenhall would write the letter informing Peirce that his services were no longer desired. But given how much time Peirce spent preparing the 1889 report, and how crucial a role it played in determining his fate, it seems appropriate to consider a little further some of the circumstances pertaining to the report's composition and quality. A number of delaying factors have already been noted, including Peirce's commitment to other writings and projects, his attending to family matters, and also his discouragement, perhaps even depression, over his treatment by the Washington office. But Victor Lenzen, in the best study to date of this report,[43] emphasized two additional factors that must be taken into account.

Since 1883, Peirce had waited in vain for new pendulums from Paris, with which he hoped to improve upon the results obtained with the set of Peirce pendulums. The latter had been manufactured in the U.S. in 1881, and data obtained from their use required many corrections that could be avoided with better constructed pendulums. While in Paris in 1883, Peirce had arranged with P. F. Gautier, instrument maker for the French Bureau of Longitude, for new pendulums to be constructed according to his own improved design, and it was a constant source of frustration that he had not been allowed to stay in France until the pendulums were finished. He kept hoping until his final days with the Survey that they would be sent for.

A related but more general reason for Peirce's slow progress was his insistence, for his own reputation and that of the Survey, that his pendulum work met the highest standards of scientific performance. He could not accept the view that had become entrenched in all levels of U.S. Government that only fast *practical* results were wanted. Peirce was working to advance science, and it was thanks to the precision of his research that he had earned the respect of his peers. He could not surrender to what he believed to be anti-science.

Another important factor in that contributed to the demise of Peirce's report was Mendenhall's disagreement on how gravity results should be represented. Peirce was adamant in his view that gravity is best understood as an acceleration, not a force,[44] and that relative determinations of gravity—where gravity at a location is measured relative to gravity at

43. Victor F. Lenzen, "An Unpublished Scientific Monograph by C. S. Peirce," *Transactions of the Charles S. Peirce Society* 5 (1969): 5–24.

44. In his definition of "gravity" for the *Century Dictionary,* Peirce wrote: "The words *gravity* and *gravitation* have been more or less confounded; but the most careful writers use *gravitation* for the attracting force, and *gravity* for the terrestrial phenomenon of weight or downward acceleration which has for its two components the gravitation and the centrifugal force."

another location—provide greater accuracy than absolute determinations and are all that is needed for determining the figure of the earth. In his report on gravity at Fort Conger (sel. 30), Peirce had introduced a new relative measure that he called "logarithmic seconds." These new units, reintroduced in the 1889 report (sel. 36, pp. 289–90), were meant to facilitate the calculation and use of gravity results. Lenzen explains that when gravity is expressed in logarithmic seconds, "a difference of values of gravity at two stations in log. secs. is numerically equal to the difference in the corresponding numbers of oscillations per day at the stations of a pendulum that beats seconds at the mean equatorial station."[45] Mendenhall, for his part, was equally adamant that gravity should always be expressed in units of force called "dynes" and, besides, he thought that Peirce's logarithmic seconds were obscure and confusing. He was not moved by Peirce's defense that they were not obscure to mathematical geodesists, "men who have to deal with the most intricate parts of the calculus," and that they had the very useful effect of "making all the operations of reduction and comparison additions & subtractions in place of multiplications and divisions" (22 July 1890). Mendenhall told Peirce that of course it was his own business how he wanted to restrict the meaning of "g" for his personal use, but that "when acting for the public . . . one must be guided by the general consensus of opinion of those generally admitted to be the highest authorities; personal preferences and especially any weakness towards 'eccentricity' must often give way" (24 July 1890). Mendenhall was unwilling to recognize that at that time there was no one in the United States who was a higher authority in these matters than Peirce.

A more important disagreement between Peirce and Mendenhall concerned the method for conducting gravity operations and the precision to be aimed for. Mendenhall had become persuaded that it was acceptable to give up absolute determinations altogether and, in general, to sacrifice precision for economy as long as results were satisfactory for ordinary practical purposes. Accordingly, Mendenhall, following the lead of Robert von Sterneck of Austria-Hungary, had adopted a new style short "half-seconds" invariable pendulum that could be carried from station to station and put into operation at a fraction of the cost associated with Peirce's use of the yard and meter pendulums, especially their use in the complex operations required to determine absolute values.[46] In his first gravity report, published in 1892, Mendenhall explained that the Coast Survey would no longer follow the traditional European-style gravity studies that Peirce had instituted in the U.S. because they were too expensive, cumbersome, slow, and inefficient. The half-second pendulum, by contrast, solved all of these

45. Lenzen (1969), p. 13.

46. Victor F. Lenzen and Robert P. Multhauf, "Development of Gravity Pendulums in the 19th Century," *Contributions from the Museum of History and Technology* (Smithsonian Institution, Bulletin 240, 1966), pp. 301–47.

difficulties: "One of the principal advantages of this apparatus is the ease with which it may be used, and the few and inexpensive preparations necessary for its installation."[47]

In June 1894, two and a half years after Peirce's forced resignation, Mendenhall testified before the Congressional Committee on Naval Affairs where he was questioned about Peirce.[48] He told the Committee that much of Peirce's work "was of the highest character, and it has received praise from the European geodesists and others, physicists, etc., but it lacked the practical quality which I believed to be essential." He explained that after the successful introduction of his half-second pendulums, he "became convinced that Professor Peirce's services to the Survey were no longer necessary." Mendenhall added that the results Peirce had been working on in his final years had not been published because Newcomb and other experts had judged that they were "not valuable."

Was that a fair assessment of the results Peirce worked so hard to obtain during his last years at the Survey? It is difficult to evaluate scientific work that never became part of the public record, but Lenzen concluded that Peirce's unpublished monograph was much more important than Mendenhall supposed. Some of Peirce's accomplishments, according to Lenzen, are the following:[49] 1. Peirce's calculation of "provisional maximum values of the departure of the geoid from the mean spheroid" (pp. 289ff.) is one of the earliest applications, if not the first, of Stokes's theory of the form of the geoid. 2. Several of the corrections used in the report were original with Peirce. These include the correction for flexure of the pendulum support (pp. 295–99), which Peirce had introduced in his 1876 "Report on Gravity at Initial Stations" (W4:131–33); the correction for the unequal expansion of the upper and lower parts of the pendulum, introduced by Peirce in 1885 (W5: sel. 53) but first applied in the 1889 report (p. 341); the correction for the inclination of the knife-edge (pp. 340–41); and the correction for the second atmospheric effect. 3. Peirce's calculation of the absolute value of gravity for the Smithsonian station, appropriately converted, appears to match a result obtained seventeen years later by the Geodetic Institute at Potsdam, which became the reference value throughout the world.[50]

47. *Report of the Superintendent of the U. S. Coast and Geodetic Survey for the Fiscal Year Ending June 30, 1891*, part II, Appendix no. 15, pp. 503–64.

48. See Lenzen (1969), pp. 6–7.

49. See Lenzen (1969), passim.

50. Peirce's best value for gravity at the Smithsonian was 980.1037 cm/sec^2, but that was not the value given in the 1889 report; it comes from a letter of 3 July 1890 from Peirce to Herbert Nichols, Professor of Physics at Cornell University. The value from the report is 99.095 cm (as the length of the mean equatorial seconds' pendulum), which converts to an acceleration slightly less than Peirce's "best value." Lenzen points out, however, that the value given in the 1889 report had not been corrected for flexure, which may account for the difference (see Lenzen 1969: 17–20).

In considering the importance of the 1889 paper, Lenzen emphasized the significance of Peirce's "second atmospheric effect," the effect of the viscosity of air on the motion of a pendulum. Peirce had introduced this correction in his report for 1876 (W4:104–106) but only as an a posteriori correction. In the 1889 paper he applied and compared both a priori and a posteriori corrections, for he had designed the Peirce pendulums to facilitate just such a comparison for the viscosity correction. The theory Peirce applied was that of G. G. Stokes, but the formula Peirce used for his calculations took account of more factors than did Stokes's formula. Lenzen concluded that it was unfortunate that Peirce's "highly original discussion of the second atmospheric effect" had not been published, for it would certainly have been of interest to "Professor Stokes, Lucasian Professor of Mathematics, and in charge of the British Gravity Survey." Lenzen closed his study with the following assessment: "In the light of a review that I have made of the development of pendulums for the determination of gravity, it is my firm judgment that the experimental and theoretical work represented in *Peirce's Report on Gravity at the Smithsonian, Ann Arbor, Madison, and Cornell* was the best work of its kind in the nineteenth century."[51] However, as was pointed out above, Peirce's report was far from finished, and had it been published without improvements, his innovations might well have gone unheeded.

Life for the Peirces in their new house, during its renovation in the summer of 1889 could not have been idyllic. Overseeing construction and running the estate would have been pressure enough, but Peirce was expected to give full days of attention to his work for the Coast Survey, and somehow find time to write his definitions. Besides, many other lines of thought were constantly working themselves out under his pen. In August, Peirce published in the *Nation* a review of St. George Stock's *Deductive Logic* (sel. 35). It was Peirce's first review for the *Nation* since reviewing Abbot's *Scientific Theism* (W5: sel. 46) in 1886. Peirce's review of Stock was the kind of review an author dreads; the best Peirce could say was that "it would be impossible for a man who has been studying and teaching logic at Oxford for seventeen years to write a thoroughly bad book on the subject," but he added immediately that any teacher who decided to use Stock instead of Bain "would be doing his pupils an injury." Peirce was not one to mince words. He declared that "the best expositions of the subject" force students step by step to see the close connection between "formal rules and the trains of thought which actually go on in their own mind" and that every logic text should have at least a brief treatment of symbolic logic. Stock's book failed on both counts. Peirce announced that "there is no subject in which there is more urgent need of a new book," probably knowing he would soon resume his own effort to fill that need (see W5, sels. 54–56). By the end of 1890, he

51. Lenzen (1969), p. 20.

was working to transform his correspondence course lessons into a text book entitled "Light of Logic." The fragment that the present editors have entitled "Reasoning" (sel. 37) probably dates from early 1890 and may have been written with such a book in mind.

By the end of September the first phase of construction at Quicktown was complete. Peirce wrote to Jem with some satisfaction that "our house" is "very comfortable, very pretty" and "not in the least in the Queen Anne nor any other style. It is our own original style" (30 September 1889). He continued with a description of his estate and plans for its development and added: "I am confident that we shall eventually make money from this place." But this was to remain the elusive silver lining. Peirce's enthusiasm for Quicktown, his dream of a comfortable, even elegant, country life with Juliette, had already begun to fade. In part this was due to the combined demands of managing the renovations, running the farm, and his professional work, but that was not all. He continued his letter to Jem: "But now I must turn to quite another side of the canvass." The other side was "dear Juliette's health." Peirce told Jem that her diseased lungs were even worse than they had been the previous year when she had been warned not to spend her winters in the North. Clearly, she would have to winter elsewhere again this year. To make matters worse, Juliette had become very depressed, a condition Peirce might have been prone to as well.[52] On 11 July in an outburst of anger and frustration, Peirce struck a domestic helper, Marie Blanc, and a few days later was charged with assault. Joseph Brent speculates that Peirce may have lost his temper while attempting to upbraid Miss Blanc for not following Juliette's orders.[53] Such domestic tension could only have added weight to the pall that was descending over Quicktown. The case was not resolved until October when Peirce pled guilty to one count of assault and was fined twenty-five dollars plus court costs. Everything taken into account, life for the Peirces in the summer and fall of 1889 had taken a decided turn for the worse and tensions were mounting. But Charles and Juliette were resilient and still usually hopeful. In November they added significantly to their land holdings by purchasing an additional 1200 acres of woodland. Apparently Peirce was growing used to his new life. He continued his 30 September letter to Jem: "This living in the country is highly conducive to reading long works in many volumes. I have not a rage for reading; indeed I think an impulse to study and an impulse to read are rather antagonistic; but I get through a good many books here. I find nothing wears better than Sainte Beuve."

Had Peirce and Juliette been content with modest country living, with an excellent library to fill their idle hours and with only infrequent trips back to New York for a fashionable dinner or an evening at the theater, they might

52. See Brent, pp. 14–15, especially in revised edition.
53. This opinion was expressed in a private communication.

have managed to avoid the terrible poverty that lay ahead. But they seemed determined to amass a great estate—adding yet another five hundred acres the following year—and modest living seemed to be out of the question. When it became necessary to deal with Juliette's winter convalescence, much of Peirce's inheritance had been used up—the greater part that he had already received. Yet cost does not appear to have been a factor. Peirce explained to Jem that because of Juliette's depression, he thought it "absolutely indispensable that she should be where she finds amusement" (30 September 89), and he thought that Sicily might be the place for her. As it happened, Jem had been in Europe for nearly three months and would be there for several more. Relations with Jem had improved since Aunt Lizzie's death, and Peirce was relieved to have him there to watch out for Juliette.

On 21 November 1889, one day after Peirce had finally submitted his long overdue gravity report, a notice appeared in the *Milford Dispatch* announcing that Juliette would soon make a journey abroad for the winter in quest of health. Six days later Peirce watched Juliette and their dog, Bliss, board the SS Entella in the New York harbor, bound for Naples. Two days later Peirce wrote to Juliette: "What a terrible afternoon & night it was after you sailed! How did you get through? I was terribly anxious." He told her he had seen the Pinchots, who lived in New York City except for the summers, and they had invited him to dinner, but he had declined because he did not have dress clothes with him. He had taken his Thanksgiving dinner at the Century Club with John La Farge and Clarence King. "I expect to get away this afternoon, but may not. They haven't been very polite to me at the Lenox, & are evidently trying to get rid of me. I could not stay there with the least self-respect. I don't pay enough. . . . Dear little girl! I do nothing but think of you, & can't help talking too much about you. Good bye! Write from Gibraltar."

Indeed, Peirce could not stop thinking about Juliette or his money woes. He wrote to his friend Annibale Ferrero, an Italian mathematician and geodesist who lived in Florence, to ask if there was not some position for him in Europe. He indicated that he would be prepared to leave the U.S. at once—perhaps hoping secretly to find a way to join Juliette while she convalesced. He had inquired of G. S. Hall a few weeks earlier about the possibility of a position at Clark University, so apparently he had begun shedding his illusions about Quicktown. Ferrero wrote back on 25 November urging Peirce to be patient. He was sure there could be something for Peirce with the International Geodetic Association, something appropriate to a scientist of his international reputation, but that sort of arrangement could not be hurried. With Juliette away, Peirce decided to spend as much time as he could in New York to see if he could find a way to turn his writing into cash. By now he must have understood that the correspondence course would never bring him much income and that if the farm were ever to make a profit, it would not be soon. He may have been feeling a little more secure about his Coast Survey salary, having just turned in the long report, but he had promised, quite unrealistically, that the second part would be finished promptly and he knew that before long he would be asked to turn it in. But even if he could keep his income from the Survey, that would not be enough—at least not until the farm could generate a substantial annual income. The immediate problem was to keep Quicktown operating and to provide for Juliette in Europe. Peirce had used up all of his reserves, and he was not sure how he would earn the money for the monthly disbursements he had promised Juliette.

Peirce wrote to Juliette again on the 6th of December. At the top of his stationary in place of "Quicktown" he inscribed "Sunbeams," a name he sometimes called Juliette as an endearment. He was feeling lonely and greatly missed her. Beside the word "Sunbeams" Peirce made the impression of a kiss. André De Tienne has speculated that it may be from an anagram play on "baiser," the French word for kiss, that Peirce first got the idea to rename his estate "Arisbe" as he soon would do.[54] He wrote to Juliette about finances. He told her that he had returned to the farm and had been working twelve and thirteen hour days. In New York, Pinchot had encouraged him about the prospects for an arithmetic book he had started, but Peirce thought it doubtful that such a book could bring in more than $1000 a year, and other books he thought he could produce would not bring in more than half that. "Thus, you see if I write 4 with my own hand, the most I can expect is $3000 a year from them; and from all I can write myself or ever get written $5000 a year will be the most. We are spending that now." On a more positive note, he told Juliette that he had learned that tuberculosis was not incurable, even though some lung damage might be permanent. Finding this out had been such a relief to him.

Peirce was running out of options. He tried to borrow from his friend George Butler. On 8 December, Butler wrote that he was "awfully sorry" but that he simply had nothing to loan: "I am probably harder up than you are." Peirce did manage to raise a little money to ease the tension of the moment, but nothing would be more destructive of his relationship with Juliette or of his life overall than his constant and never diminishing, sometimes extreme, need of money. The problem would become almost intolerable in another year, after the loss of his income from the Coast Survey, but the expenses of Juliette's trip abroad made the first half of 1890 almost as difficult. The day before Christmas, Peirce sent Juliette a check for six hundred and fifteen francs, apologizing for the delay and warning her that he might have some difficulty with "the next remittance." Peirce knew that Juliette's steamer had reached Gibraltar on the 16th, but did not know that she had reached Naples when he wrote to her on the 24th: "I have had no letter from you yet. . . . I shall pass Christmas with the old bachelors of the club."

54. See De Tienne's "The Mystery of Arisbe," *Peirce Project Newsletter* 3 (1999): 11–12.

Peirce spent New Year's eve with George Butler and his wife at their country home in the Hudson Valley north of New York City. He had by then received a letter from Juliette, from Gibraltar, and was greatly distressed at how ill Juliette told him she was. He wrote back on New Year's day expressing his concern: "I never would live without the sunbeam of my soul!" But Jem's letters to Peirce suggest that Juliette's stay in Europe came much closer to being the pleasant amusing time Peirce had wanted for her than she was ever willing to admit. On 23 January 1890 Jem wrote from Rome: "Your cablegram did not reach me till the 16th. . . . I telegraphed & wrote to the hotelkeeper at Palermo, & learned that Juliette had already left for Cairo. She is sure not to have been seriously ill, & to have been well lodged & cared for." Jem's opinion is confirmed by an extant medical report from a Cairo physician who examined Juliette on the 24th and found nothing seriously wrong with her. Juliette stayed in Cairo until the end of March. Jem wrote on 5 April that he had seen Juliette several times recently and that he wanted to send his impressions about her state of health. "I cannot help thinking that her winter has been of substantial benefit to her. She speaks of the serious attacks which she still has, & seems to regard herself as doomed. But whenever I saw her, she looked & appeared strong & vigorous, & has evidently enjoyed much in her Cairene life and is familiar with Cairo through frequent visits to its streets & bazaars. . . . I have a strong faith that you will find that she has gained ground since she came abroad." Later Jem would write that he did not believe Juliette was as ill as she imagined but that "She is easily excited & depressed" (13 June 1890). After Cairo, Juliette stayed in Alexandria for two or three weeks and then traveled back to Naples where, according to Jem, she stayed "at the Grand Hotel, a delightful house," waiting for a steamer to New York. There is some obscurity about Juliette's final days in Italy and when she finally sailed for New York, but it seems unlikely that she arrived back before early June.

Juliette had been away for half a year. During that time, Peirce periodically returned to Quicktown to tend to the estate and probably to spend long hours on his definitions, but he spent the greater part of these months in New York where he had friends and where there was more opportunity to make money. On the first of February, Ernst Schröder wrote to Peirce, resuming a correspondence that had lapsed for five years. Schröder told Peirce that the first volume of his *Vorlesungen über die Algebra der Logik (exakte Logik)* would soon be published and that he had asked his publisher to forward a copy to Peirce. He was concerned that Peirce might have broken off their correspondence out of anger for "some unknown reason." Their ensuing exchange of letters, until Schröder's death in 1902, was a great stimulus to Peirce, especially concerning the logic of relations. On 5 March, Peirce received a letter of self-introduction from Ventura Reyes y Prósper, who also corresponded with Schröder.

Such communications, and meetings with scholarly friends for dinners or at the Century Club, were important intellectual anchors for Peirce during a difficult time. Juliette's absence caused Peirce much distress. At first he just missed her and was worried about her health, but the hardship he endured trying to provide the money she needed led to anxiety and a growing sense of failure. Gradually, with so few letters from her and with those he did receive expressing disaffection and disapproval, his frustration turned to disillusion and sometimes bitterness. Peirce wrote on 23 January, after she had been away for two months: "I have only had two letters. . . . I hear *nothing*, nothing. Good God, I shall go crazy if I don't hear soon. This is terrible." Three months later, feeling that he had done his best for her but having received not the slightest indication of any appreciation from her, Peirce wrote: "Your letters to me are so full of hate and rage, that I know not how to write to you. What my difficulties have been you do not know."[55] Using the third person, Peirce went on to describe the changes in Juliette's character that he had observed, starting with when they had met.

> She was a very true and noble heart, that nothing ever could corrupt. And then I knew her in Washington when she showed capacities which surprized me. Then there was a dreadful period when everything in life was terribly terribly embittered. I wish now I had been drowned before I had to pass through such things. Very gradually, the curse seemed to pass away, & there was a time in Milford when there seemed to be much happiness, shaded by some doubts only. All this time, I was getting to know and to adore this dear lady more and more and to love her more deeply. In the future I don't know how it will be. The present is dreadful.

The letter from Juliette that had agitated Peirce so much is no longer extant, but it is evident that Juliette had made an urgent and probably indignant plea for more money, perhaps claiming that she could not return without it. She must have threatened to sell a watch Peirce had given her for he pleaded with her not to do it and promised to send more money "no matter what happens, very soon." He tried to borrow from friends and acquaintances but apparently without success. He urged Pinchot to hire him to tutor his children at fifteen dollars a week, and probably asked for an advance, but on 5 May Pinchot replied that he could not immediately make up his mind. On 14 May, Peirce wrote to C. R. Miller of the *New York Times*, with whom he had just concluded a successful newspaper debate on Spencer, proposing a series of fifty articles on evolution, but Miller did not think it could sustain the interest of his readers. As late as the first week in June, Peirce sought a consulting assignment with the Astor Library. By this time, however, Juliette must have already been on a steamer for New York, if she had not already arrived. The record does not indicate how she managed to settle her final accounts in Europe.

55. The first two lines of this letter of 22 April 1890 have been heavily crossed out. This reading is based on Max H. Fisch's study of the document.

It is difficult to know whether Juliette ever understood or even cared about how Peirce had managed to support her European convalescence, or whether Peirce became a changed man as a result. The scant evidence suggests that her anger over what he had not provided outweighed any appreciation for what he had managed to send. The fact is, Peirce *had* managed to raise money from his writing, and his urgent need for cash had disposed him to try writing as a tool to make money rather than for the straightforward exchange of ideas. Of course Peirce's stock in trade *was* his ideas, but he had been more willing than ever to turn them, if he could, to commercial ends. How successful he was still remains to be discovered. Extensive searches of New York newspapers and of contemporary magazines remain to be made with the purpose of digging up anonymous reports or hack writings that might have come from his pen (or typewriter). More may be discovered, but we will probably never know how much he managed to sell during that difficult time.

Sometime early in 1890, Peirce and Wendell Phillips Garrison, editor of the *Nation,* reached an understanding that significantly increased the number of books sent to Peirce for review. Peirce had occasionally reviewed books for the *Nation* since 1869, but he had never reviewed more than three in a single year, and his August 1889 review of Stock's *Logic* had been his first *Nation* review in three and a half years. Peirce published ten reviews during 1890, and would publish even more in each of the next five years. Only two of Peirce's 1890 *Nation* reviews appeared during the period covered in this volume. The first was the review of Noel's *Science of Metrology* (sel. 43). Noel was an Englishman who was opposed to the metric system of measurement but who believed that the English system should be reformed. Noel proposed changing the ratios of inches to feet, pounds to gallons, and so forth. Although Peirce saw some merit in Noel's proposal, he suggested that to challenge the metric system was "like challenging the rising tide" and that the only thing more futile would be to try to change the length of the inch." The second *Nation* review was a review of F. Howard Collins's *Epitome of the Synthetic Philosophy* (sel. 46). This was a very brief notice praising Collins' "second-hand synopsis" for reducing Spencer's "heart-breakingly tedious" five thousand pages to a mere five hundred, but lamenting that Collins had gone over fifty.

If Peirce's increasing number of reviews for the *Nation,* many of them also appearing in the *New York Post,* was in fact an outcome of his overwrought effort to raise money during Juliette's European convalescence, then it should be regarded as his most striking success. For he would produce nearly three hundred more reviews for the *Nation* and the income supplement from those reviews would be crucial for his and Juliette's survival—and the loss of that income in 1906, after Garrison's retirement, would be a serious blow.[56]

56. See Brent, pp. 303–08.

But Peirce's most notable achievement in raising funds while Juliette was away was his success, working with *New York Times'* editor C. R. Miller, in organizing a debate about the soundness of Herbert Spencer's philosophy that ran for six consecutive Sundays, from 23 March to 27 April. Altogether, the debate consisted of twenty-nine articles and notes. At Miller's urging, Peirce made a great effort to recruit respondents for this debate. One of his prospects, William James, replied on 16 March that nothing would please him more "than to help stone Uncle Spencer, for of all extant quacks he's the worst—yet not exactly a quack either for he *feels* honest, and never would know that a critic had the better of him." But James begged off because he was so pressed to finish *Principles of Psychology*. Peirce had sent James copies of his opening article for the *Times* and probably also his *Nation* review of Collins, and James wrote that the columns were clever but "possibly a bit too interrogative and transcendentally suggestive to captivate the vulgar." Not having what it takes to "captivate the vulgar" was James's usual criticism of Peirce's writing. He closed by asking when Peirce's own "radical evolutionary speculations" would see the light.

A 17 March letter from Miller to Peirce serves to illustrate the nature of their collaboration and how the Spencer series was organized.

> I wanted to hold the Spencer article until I could be assured of something in reply to or in support of it for the following Sunday. Prof. Marsh and Prof. Dana . . . are both too busy to take a hand, but Prof. Sumner is coming in, probably for a week from next Sunday, that is a week after we print the article. Won't you stir up Powell and Cope or any of the other combatants you may have in mind and get them to send in their contributions promptly? It is a good thing to have King's article appear on the same day with Sumner's by way of ballast, can you get him? For Sunday, the 30th. None of them need sign the articles unless they wish, though we should prefer signatures.

William Graham Sumner, a Yale sociologist, was probably the leading exponent of Social Darwinism in the U.S., and could be counted on to give strong support to the mechanistic principles that Spencer preached—but apparently Sumner never came through with a contribution. The Powell that Miller wanted was Peirce's friend John W. Powell, Director of the U.S. Geological Survey, but he did not enter the debate either. He wrote to Peirce that he would like to join in but did not have the time. King must have been Clarence King, the geologist who advanced the theory that catastrophes and cataclysms are important factors in evolution, particularly with respect to rapid evolutionary developments. King may have contributed as "Kappa."

The debate opened on 23 March with an introductory editorial and a piece by Peirce, "Herbert Spencer's Philosophy. Is it Unscientific and Unsound?" (sel. 45), and was framed as a set of questions, but the tone was such as to raise the temperature of Spencer supporters. For example, Peirce took Spencer's recommendation that a good way to make intellectual progress was to compare competing opinions and settle on those that survive mutual cancellation, as an occasion to ask: "Are thinkers ever really obliged to give all opinions equal votes . . . ?" He pointed out that there are some things—matter, space, time, law—which Spencer's "somewhat clumsy conception of evolution has left him no room to explain in any evolutionary sense." Spencer claimed that these "inexplicables spring directly from the Unknowable" but, Peirce asked, is this resort to the Unknowable really "thoroughgoing evolutionism"? Finally Peirce explained that since Spencer's intention was to produce "a great scientific theory, a philosophy worthy to form the crown of modern science"—Spencer's own "guess at the riddle"—it should be evaluated by "the recognized touchstone of a scientific theory": successful prediction. What scientific discoveries, Peirce wanted to know, can be attributed to Spencer's synthetic philosophy? Almost at once, after his opening article appeared, Peirce wrote to Miller asking to be paid. Miller replied that "checks for contributions to *The Times* are made out on Fridays" and he added: "I hope you will stir up as many combatants as possible and promptly."

Peirce stayed on the sidelines for the following two Sundays while the first seven respondents weighed in, but he contributed a second article on 13 April: "'Outsider' Wants More Light" (sel. 47). Claiming once again that he was only seeking light—"an attack would be very different"—he replied to all seven respondents, but principally to three who had tried to answer from the standpoint of science. Henry Osborn, a well-known paleontologist, received Peirce's most serious and polite reply. Peirce drew support from Osborn for his "doubt" that Spencer's work would have permanent value. He treated Hiram Messenger and Edgar Dawson much less respectfully, essentially ridiculing them; his intent throughout was to stir up interest and emotions to keep the series going. Peirce did raise two or three interesting points that he would develop more fully in later years. In response to Messenger's claim that he could find no mathematical errors in Spencer's extensive writings, Peirce gave a single example. Spencer claimed that all phenomena are "necessary results of the persistence of force." Peirce pointed out that it would be perfectly consistent with the principle of the persistence of force if at any given moment all the molecules in the universe were assumed to be in their actual positions but with reversed velocities. From that moment on, history would run in reverse. But "eggs grow into birds, not birds back to eggs," so clearly not all the phenomena of evolution can be mathematical consequences of the persistence of force. In response to "Kappa," Peirce outlined the seven tasks that have to be performed by a good critic of philosophy. That was a subject that would interest Peirce for the rest of his days. In response to "R.G.E." he made the interesting observation that his dissatisfaction with Spencer "is not that he is evolutionist, but that he is not evolutionist enough."

Peirce's use of the pseudonym "Outsider" for his contributions to this debate may have been partly a ploy to add an air of mystery to the proceedings but it was also intended to situate Peirce outside the prevailing ethos of Social Darwinism. When Miller introduced the debate he indicated that the pseudonym allowed "Outsider" to "stand apart from the adepts whom he calls upon to speak their minds." He added, however, that the name, "Outsider," was really too modest for "he is himself eminent for his attainments in science and might speak with some authority upon the questions he raises." But it may be that Peirce's use of a pseudonym was not so much to set himself apart from his respondents as it was a prudent decision based on his understanding that he could no longer pretend not to be standing apart and that his own name might keep some interested parties from participating. That he chose the pseudonym "Outsider" may have been Peirce's wry way of stating an unpleasant truth.

Around the same time Peirce took up the cause against Spencer, perhaps a few weeks before, he arranged with Lorettus Sutton Metcalf to contribute to a series of articles on spiritualism Metcalf was organizing for his journal, *The Forum.* Peirce was known to be a skeptic concerning such matters, especially because of his recent dispute with Gurney, and Metcalf had engaged him to present a case against spiritualism. It is not known whether Peirce sought out Metcalf to offer his services, or whether Metcalf had become aware that Peirce was looking for magazine work, but it is likely that it was not until after the first article in the series had appeared that Peirce struck his deal with Metcalf. The first in the series was a piece by Mary J. Savage entitled "Experiences with Spiritualism," which appeared in the December 1889 issue. The second, "Truth and Fraud in Spiritualism," by Richard Hodgson, appeared in April 1890. Peirce's article was to follow. It was never given a title by Peirce, but for the present volume the editors have entitled it "Logic and Spiritualism" (sel. 44). It could also have been called "The Case against Spiritualism."

Initially Peirce must have thought he would make an easy go of this assignment, for he had worked through the arguments quite thoroughly during the Gurney controversy. But by the end of March he had run into a snag. His first draft ran to 6700 words and Metcalf had set a limit of 5000. Metcalf would not budge and Peirce was equally determined to say everything he wanted to say, so there ensued a curious battle of wills. Peirce finally conceded to Metcalf's word limit, probably because he was in such great need of the remuneration, but Metcalf had to agree to Peirce's peculiar way of cutting his article down to size. Peirce simply struck out hundreds of articles and pronouns transforming his paper into something not quite a poem but not really prose either. Peirce's paper was set in galleys on 7 April, but he continued making revisions. He could not make it work and asked if he could start over. Metcalf agreed but asked Peirce to hurry it up and "please remember not to exceed 5000 words" (21 June 1890). Peirce never rewrote the paper.[57] Back in Quicktown, after Juliette's return from Europe, other priorities had taken center stage.

Peirce began his essay by admitting that he was a man of science—a scientific specialist—and made it plain that he believed that "no mind with which man can communicate can act or feel otherwise than through its residential nerve-matter." But he did not doubt that "unrecognized avenues of sense may exist" and he believed that telepathy was not an impossibility. Nevertheless, he thought that science had to reject spiritualism and telepathy as viable hypotheses to explain unusual and unexpected phenomena. His argument against spiritualism is complex and cryptically stated because of the many revisions and cuts his manuscript had suffered. Important for his argument are three assumptions which he believed psychology had sufficiently established: 1. The obscure part of the mind is the principal part. 2. It acts with far more unerring accuracy than the rest. 3. It is almost infinitely more delicate in its sensibilities. It is this vast "unconscious or semi-conscious" part of the mind, which evolves through generations of interaction with external forces into instinct and common sense, which must be trusted to guide us in situations where reason does not know which way to turn. This is our "mother-wit" which, for all we know, may have access to the "unrecognized avenues of sense." The secret of mother-wit is that over the course of her education, her evolution, she has "learned" to follow nature's laws—nature's reason. Now the general conclusions of mother-wit, our common sense, should not be dismissed in the face of some "special experience." It is barely possible, of course, that any given strange occurrence might be an exception to law, a rebuff to common sense. But, generally, where there is a strange occurrence, the probability of a trick is greater than the likelihood that it is an exception to law.

After further development of his argument, Peirce looked back to Gurney's attempt to prove telepathy by amassing favorable cases and proclaimed that "the myriad strange stories prove nothing." Such supposed evidence for telepathy or spiritualism loses its force when we consider four simple facts: 1. "the fact that all men are liars"; 2. "the fact of deranged imagination, hypnotism, hysteria"; 3. "the fact that we may receive and act upon indications of which we are quite unconscious"; and 4. "the fact that a certain number of coincidences will occur by chance." Taken together, these facts serve as a basis for explaining unusual and surprising perceptions without resort to ghosts or spirits. In an earlier draft Peirce wrote: "why should we draw upon such an extreme rarity as telepathy, so long as we have such ordinary elements of human experience as superstition, lying and self-lying (from vanity, mischief, hysteria, mental derangement, and perverse love of untruth), exaggeration, inaccuracy, tricks of memory and imagination, intoxication (alcohol, opiate, and other), deception, and mistake, out of which to shape our hypotheses?"

57. See the textual editor's headnote to selection 44 (pp. 658–663) for further discussion of Peirce's relations with Metcalf and the import on Peirce's composition.

In his final paragraph, Peirce made it clear that he was not dismissing the importance of psychical research; on the contrary, it "should receive every encouragement." But properly conducted, it would become a branch of experimental psychology—the branch of science "destined to be the most important experimental research of the twentieth century." Even though this paper remained unpublished, some of the ideas would make their way into the fourth article of Peirce's *Monist* metaphysical series, "Man's Glassy Essence"; that series would, in fact, reverberate with ideas from this period, especially ideas from "A Guess at the Riddle" and the Outsider pieces.

Working out definitively how the writings in this volume contributed to the overall development of Peirce's thought is a task for the community of scholars who will study them for that purpose, but a few additional thoughts might be helpful. Following again the method used in the introduction to W5, it may be revealing to consider how the W6 writings fit into Peirce's general intellectual development as traced by Murphey and Fisch.[58] According to Murphey, the most telling demarcations in Peirce's intellectual development are revisions to his system of categories necessitated by discoveries in logic. For Fisch, the single most important gauge of the growth of Peirce's thought was its movement toward the robust three-category realism of his later years.

Murphey divides Peirce's intellectual life into four phases dominated in turn by Kant's system of philosophy, by syllogistic logic, by the logic of relations, and by the logic of quantification. According to Murphey, the fourth and final phase began about 1885 after Peirce, with his student O. H. Mitchell, discovered the quantifier. Only then could Peirce add pure indexical signs to his logic, signs that refer to individuals per se and not to conceptions. The individual, the non-general, quickly took on a special importance for Peirce as he came to realize that a non-conceptual acquaintance with individuals can provide a direct and immediate link to reality. According to Murphey, this allowed Peirce to retreat from the conceptualism of his "end of inquiry" theory of reality without having to resort to "first impressions of sense."[59] Although Murphey makes the long final period of Peirce's intellectual development range over the last three decades of Peirce's life, he does notice that around 1896 Peirce formed a new conception of the continuum after discovering that continua must involve unactualized possibilities: "Whatever is continuous therefore involves real possibility and is accordingly of a general nature."[60] Murphey notes that Peirce announced this discovery to William James in March of 1897 and that it led to a strengthening of Peirce's realism. It is surprising that Murphey did not count the period

58. Max H. Fisch, *Peirce, Semeiotic and Pragmatism,* eds. K. L. Ketner and C. J. W. Kloesel, (Indiana University Press, 1986) and Murray G. Murphey, *The Development of Peirce's Philosophy,* (Harvard University Press, 1961; Indianapolis: Hackett Publishing Co., 1993).

59. See Murphey, pp. 301–03.

60. Murphey, p. 396.

following this important logical insight, the period of Peirce's synechism—"the new Scholastic realism"[61]—as a new and final phase of Peirce's development, one dominated by modal logic (and by Peirce's Existential Graphs).

In Fisch's account, Peirce's thought is shown to have developed gradually from an early nominalism that attributed generality only to cognitions and that held all realities to be "nominal, significative, cognitive" (W2:181), to a robust form of realism that gave ontological place to each of the three categories. Fisch marks the major stages of Peirce's intellectual journey by three principal revisions to his ontology: his acceptance, beginning around 1868, of "the long run" as providing an independence condition for reality; his admission, around 1890, that reality extends to the non-cognitive realm of actuality; and his admission in 1897 that even possibility is real. In line with Murphey's understanding of the importance of Peirce's logical discoveries of the mid-1880s, Fisch notes that Peirce had taken large strides toward acknowledging the reality of secondness with his 1884–85 acceptance of the necessity of indexes for logic and his 1885 reaction to Royce's idealism (W5: sels. 30, 33), but he believes it was not until about 1890, when he accepted Scotus's haecceities, that he saw that ultimate reality should be ascribed to seconds.[62] It seems likely, however, that Fisch's principal reason for locating this important intellectual event in about 1890 was his belief, following Hartshorne and Weiss, that Peirce's "A Guess at the Riddle" had been composed then. It was there, in the chapter on physics, that Peirce stated clearly for the first time that what "Scotus calls the hæcceities of things, the hereness and nowness of them, are indeed ultimate" (p. 205). But it now seems much more likely that Peirce composed that important chapter as early as 1887 or 1888, and that he had started his "Guess," as "One, Two, Three," by 1886. These considerations, as well as the many references to the necessity of indices for logic, beginning as early as 1881 (W4:251), and his work, beginning as early as 1886, on definitions for "haecceity" and "scotism" for the *Century Dictionary* (see W5:389), all suggest that Peirce's acceptance of the reality of secondness is better dated "around 1887" than "around 1890." Accordingly, the step to Murphey's fourth phase and Fisch's second stage occurred near the beginning of the years covered by the present volume so that the writings in W6 may be viewed as inaugurating what Fisch calls Peirce's period of two-category realism.

Fisch's account of Peirce's journey from nominalism to a robust realism has been challenged by a number of scholars, including Don D. Roberts, Fred Michael, and, most recently, T. L. Short. Roberts argued in 1970, soon after Fisch's account first appeared, that there is no compelling reason for concluding that Peirce ever was an out and out nominalist and that it would be safer to conclude that he was always a realist. Roberts accepted, however,

61. Ibid.
62. Fisch, p. 190.

that there were nominalistic elements in Peirce's thought.[63] Michael agrees with Fisch that Peirce was at first a nominalist, but argues that his nominalism continued until the mid-1880s, when he became a realist by taking the crucial step of accepting that there are singulars outside of cognition—what Fisch identifies as accepting the reality of secondness. Earlier declarations of realism were, at most, nominal.[64] Short, the most recent dissenter to Fisch's account, argues that in at least one important sense, Peirce remained a nominalist all his life, namely, in his "continuing inclination toward a 'nominalism' that identifies reality with a world external to cognition." Peirce's "nominalism," rather than something to be overcome, was an important component of Peirce's realism, actually contributing to its depth.[65] These are valuable studies, each contributing important insights concerning Peirce's development as a philosopher, and the disagreements, though going much deeper, serve to highlight the difficulty in reaching consensus on the meaning of "nominalism" and "realism" and on what constitutes a significant change with respect to these two positions. But whatever labels they use, these scholars all agree that there was a significant development within Peirce's thought and that the repercussions that followed his introduction of logical quantifiers in the mid-1880s clearly constitute one of his major periods of change. Another would come around 1897 when he accepted that there are generals external to thought, a change that would breathe new life into his slumbering pragmatism.

Thus the present volume, most notably with "A Guess at the Riddle" (sels. 22–28), inaugurates a new period of philosophy for Peirce, one distinguished by a commitment to a thoroughgoing architectonic approach based on his categories. The difficult task of reforming his entire system of thought, always with an eye for improving it, would occupy Peirce for the remainder of his life. Having accepted the reality of seconds, Peirce could begin to build an account of perception that would make sense of direct acquaintance with reality and that would provide reason to hope that inquiry could be guided toward the truth by the obstinacy of reality rather than by a conception of it. In his definition of "real" for the *Century Dictionary*, Peirce distinguished between "real objects . . . external to the mind," which are "independent altogether of our thought," and internal objects which "depend upon thought," though "not upon thought about them." By 1903, this distinction became a basic feature of his semeiotic (EP2:276) and by 1906 it had turned into the now familiar dynamical object/immediate object duo (EP2:477).

63. Don D. Roberts, "On Peirce's Realism," *Transactions of the Charles S. Peirce Society* 6 (1970): 67–83.

64. Fred Michael, "Two Forms of Scholastic Realism in Peirce's Philosophy," *Transactions of the Charles S. Peirce Society* 24 (1988): 317–48.

65. T. L. Short, "Review Essay," *Synthese* 106 (1996): 409–30.

Among the other noteworthy ideas that seem to have originated or come much more clearly into focus during this period, we find in Peirce a growing conviction that instinct and evolutionary attunement to the laws of nature—to the "objective reason embodied in the laws of nature"—give humans a predisposition for guessing nature's laws (sels. 8, 15) and explain the importance of common sense (sel. 44). Peirce's intensive work on reduction of observational data and modeling of hydrodynamic effects for his gravity reports, and perhaps even his critique of the design of Gurney's "experiment" to prove telepathic phenomena (sels. 16, 18), strengthened his conviction that probable reasoning is "the logic of the physical sciences," as he proclaimed in his definition of "probability" in the *Century Dictionary*. We find Peirce placing more stress on regulative principles, perhaps a step toward his later recognition of the normativity of logic, and on intellectual hopes (see sel. 28 and W5:221–34). There is an indication in some of the W6 writings that Peirce has begun moving toward his later accommodation with religion and his innovative theological ideas (sels. 14, 22, 23, 44). In science, including even his work for the Coast Survey, Peirce's interest shows a definite turn toward dynamic and process-oriented concerns and, also, toward foundational and cosmological questions (sels. 25–28, 31, 36). Peirce reveals a timely grasp of the crisis that was developing in physics at the end of the 19th century[66] and perceptively recommended that progress would depend on a better understanding of physical matter at the molecular level and on fruitful new theories (sels. 28, 31). Peirce offered his "guess" as a candidate for a new paradigm in physics and began a book intended to promote and justify its embrace (sel. 31).

Peirce's 1887 polemic against Herbert Spencer's "mechanical notion of the universe" (sel. 14) provided his first occasion for stating his case against the doctrine of necessity,[67] and turned him into a public critic of necessitarianism, even a prophet of its doom. Peirce's aggressive rejection of mechanical causation as adequate for the explanation of growth and development, forced him to defend a teleological form of evolution and moved him in the direction of a theory of sign action, or semiosis. Peirce's "guess at the riddle," as expressed about 1888, was that "three elements are active in the world: first, chance; second, law; and third, habit-taking"; there was not yet any explicit inclusion of signs among the basic components of the universe. But he was already committed to a close analogy between the growth of mind and the growth of physical law and he would make that connection explicit in 1892 when he proclaimed his tychistic thesis that matter is specialized or "effete" mind (R 972; see also, EP1:312). At least by 1907, Peirce would recognize that the end of semiosis of the highest kind is an intellectual habit, which realization may lead us to wonder whether the third basic element

66. See Murphey, pp. 327–48.
67. Fisch, p. 229.

that is active in the universe, habit-taking, is a form of semiosis, and if that is what imparts the teleological current that Peirce finds in evolution.

In 1887, in a sketch of his "A Guess at the Riddle," Peirce noted that he wanted a "vignette of the Sphynx" placed below the title.[68] Then after stating his guess in Chapter VII, he added, "Such is our guess of the secret of the sphynx." On 5 April 1890, almost two years after he had put his manuscript aside, Jem wrote to him from Egypt: "I am now passing a few days on the edge of the desert & directly at the base of the Great Pyramid. It is by far the most stupendous structure I have ever seen, and the Sphinx is more imposing than I ever thought possible. . . . no calm that living man can experience approaches the sublime sweet god-like serenity of the sphinx under the full moon." Although Peirce's Sphinx was no doubt the one of Greek mythology, Jem's letter would have moved him, and it must have been difficult not to take up his manuscript again; but he was working on "Logic and Spiritualism" for *The Forum,* and was still hard at work as the Outsider trying to raise money to send to Juliette in Europe. In July, Carus would invite him to contribute to his new journal, *The Monist,* and Peirce would take that opportunity to turn his "Guess" into the six articles known as the "*Monist* Metaphysical Series." That would appease his sphinx.

Nathan Houser

68. It is commonly believed that Peirce's allusion to "the riddle" and his reference to the Sphinx were beholden to Emerson's poem, "The Riddle of the Sphinx." But the story is more complicated: see the introduction to W5, pp. xli-xlii and annotation 165.title in this volume on pp. 438–39.

Writings of Charles S. Peirce

1

Boolian Algebra— Elementary Explanations

Fall 1886 ***Houghton Library***

There is a very convenient system of signs by which very intricate problems of reasoning can be solved. I shall now introduce you to one part of this system only, and after you are well exercised in that, we will study some additional signs which give the method increased range and power. We use letters in this system to signify statements or facts, real or fictitious. We change their signification to suit the different problems. Two statements a and b are said to be equivalent when equal, provided that in every conceivable state of things in which either is true, the other is true, so that they are true and false together, and we then use a sign of equality between them, and write $a = b$. We use the words addition, sum, etc., and the symbol + in such a sense that, if a is one fact, say that the moon is made of green cheese, and b is another fact, say that some nursery tales are false, that is $a + b$, or a added to b, or the sum of a and b, signifies that one or the other (perhaps both) of the facts added are true, so that $a + b$ is a statement; true if one or both of the statements a and b are true and false if both are false. Giving to a and b the above significations, it would mean that the moon is made of green cheese, or some nursery tales are false, or both. In translating it into ordinary language, you generally omit the words "or both" as unnecessary.

We use the words multiplication, product, factor, etc., and the signs of multiplication, or we write the two factors one after the other with no sign between them to mean that both of the two statements multiplied are true, so that ab is a statement which is true only if both the statements a and b are true, and false if either a or b is false. With the above significations it would mean that the moon is made of green cheese, and that some nursery tales are false. When we wish to signify the multiplication of a whole sum by any factor, we write that sum in parenthesis. Thus, $(a+b)c$ would mean the product of $a+b$ into c while $a+bc$ would mean the sum of a and of the product of b and c; giving the above significations to a and b, and letting c mean some proverbs were false, $(a+b)c$, there we signify the combined statements of, some proverbs are false, and that either the moon is made of green cheese, or some nursery tales are false, while $a+bc$ would mean that either the moon is made of green cheese, or else some proverbs and some nursery tales are false. There are certain rules which facilitate the application of these symbols to reasoning. Thus, $a+a$ will mean neither more nor less than a written alone, so that we may write $a+a = a$, for $a+a$, according to what has been said, is that statement which is true if a is true, and is false only if a is false.

The statement aa is also the same as a standing alone, for it merely asserts the fact a twice over so that we may write $aa = a$. We also say that $a+b$ is the same as $b+a$ and that ab is the same as ba. This is usually expressed by saying that addition and multiplication are commutative operations. Also that $(a+b)+c$ is the same as $a+(b+c)$, and $(ab)c$ is the same as $a(bc)$. This is usually expressed by saying that addition and multiplication are associative operations. We also have $(a+b)c = (ac+bc)$, for if we say that c is true and also that either a or b is true, we state neither more nor less than if we say that either both a and c are true, or both b and c are true. In like manner we have $a+bc = (a+b)(a+c)$, for if we say that either a is true, or else both b and c are true, we state neither more nor less than if we say that either a or b is true, and also that either a or c is true. As this is perhaps not quite evident, I will give a proof of it. We have seen already that $(a+b)c = ac+bc$. Now this has nothing to do with the particular letters used, but will be as true for any other three letters. We will therefore write $(a+b)x = ax+bx$. Now x may be any statement whatever. Let it then be the statement $a+c$ and substitute this in the place of x in the conclusion; then we get $(a+b)(a+c) = a(a+c)+b(a+c)$. Now, on the same principle the first term of the second member of this conclusion $a(a+c)$ is equal to $aa+ac$, and aa we have just seen to be equal to a, so that the first term is $a + ac$; the second term $b(a + c)$ is equal to $ba + bc$, so that the whole expression $(a + b)(a + c)$ equals $a + ac + ab + bc$. Now it is plain that $a + ac$ equals a, for $a + ac$ is only false if both a and either a or c are false. Now if a is false, plainly, either a or c is false, that is, one of those two, a and c, is false, so that $a + ac$ is false whenever a is false and only then.

And on the same principle $a + ab$ is equal to a, and thus the second member of the last conclusion reduces to $a + bc$, and the whole conclusion is $(a + b)(a + c)$ equals $a + bc$, which is the very conclusion we had to prove. The two principles that $(a + b)c = ac + bc$, and $a + bc$ equals $(a + b)(a + c)$ are commonly referred to by saying that multiplication is distributive with reference to addition, and that addition is distributive with reference to multiplication. I shall now introduce two statements which have special symbols in this system; the first is $, and means any fact necessarily true. All facts that are necessarily true are equal, because we agreed that we should say that two statements are equal provided they are true and false together in all conceivable states of things. The other special symbol for a statement is 0. This signifies any statement that is false. All false statements are equal for the same reason that all true statements are equal. There are a number of rules facilitating the use of these symbols $ and 0. The first is $a + 0 = a$. This means that to say that either a is true, or else a false statement is true, is the same as to say at once that a is true. In like manner $\$a = a$; for this means that to say a is true and also that any undesignated true statement is true, is no more than to say that a is true. Second, $\$ + a = \$$, for this means that to say that either a is true or something true is true, is no more than to say that something true is true, which is not saying anything at all. And in like manner $0a = 0$; for this means that to say that a is true and that something false is true, is to say something false. Third, since every statement is either true or false, if we replace any letter, say a, by $ throughout any formula and find the formula is then necessarily true, and if, on afterwards replacing the same letter by 0, we find that the formula so resulting is true also, then the original formula must be true any way. This affords quite a valuable means of proving any doubtful formula. For instance, let us apply it to proving the formula demonstrated above, $a + bc = (a + b)(a + c)$. First, replace a by \$ and the formula becomes, $\$ + bc = (\$ + b)(\$ + c)$. Now, \$ added to anything gives \$; so that $\$ + bc = \$$, $\$ + b = \$$, and $\$ + c = \$$. The whole formula thus reduces to $\$ = \$\$$ which is true. Now replace a by 0 and the formula becomes, $0 + bc = (0 + b)(0 + c)$. Now 0 added to anything does not alter it, so that we may drop these added 0s, and the formula reduces to $bc = bc$, which is true. Thus, it has been shown that the formula is true when a equals \$ or a equals 0; and as a must equal one or the other, it is true any way. We must now introduce a new sign. $a = \$$ is the same as a written alone; it means that the statement a is true. But we have as yet no simple expression for $a = 0$, meaning that the statement a is false. Let us denote this by making a line over the *a;* thus, $\bar{a}$; this we call the negative or denial of *a.* There are several rules facilitating the use of denials. First, $a\bar{a}$ equals 0, or nothing can be true and false at the same time; this is called the principle of contradiction. Second, $a + \bar{a}$ equals \$, or everything is either true or false; this is called the principle of excluded middle.

We will now proceed to show this system of signs is to be used for the purpose of drawing conclusions from premises. The simplest possible kind of reasoning is the immediate application of a rule. Thus, a little girl says that whatever mamma forbids is wrong, but mamma forbids this, therefore, this is wrong. Let a mean that anything is forbidden by mamma, b that it is wrong. Then, to say that anything is forbidden by mamma is wrong is the same as to say that either it is not forbidden by mamma, or else it is wrong. This proposition is therefore written $\bar{a} + b$. The other proposition is *a.* These propositions are asserted to be both true and therefore, they must be multiplied together, and we have, $a(\bar{a} + b)$. On performing this multiplication, that is, on applying the distributive principle, we get $a\bar{a} + ab$, but $a\bar{a}$ is 0 by the principle of contradiction, and may therefore be dropped. We therefore have ab. ab is therefore asserted of both the propositions a and *b.* It therefore asserts *b,* and therefore the act in question is wrong. Now it would of course be perfectly ridiculous to use this cumbrous system of signs for the purpose of bringing out the conclusion of such a simple mode of argument as this, but it will be found that the system is well adapted to complicated cases but this very feature makes it cumbrous for simple ones.

It will be observed in the above example that after we get the conclusion ab, we drop the factor a, leaving only b. We obviously have the right to do this at any time. We are always entitled to drop a factor from any additive term, and we are also at liberty to add a term to any factor. In consequence of this, whenever we have given an expression in the form $a(b+c)$ we are at liberty to drop the parenthesis and write $ab+c$. For the distributive principle gives us $ab+ac$, and on dropping the factor a from the last term, we get $ab+c$.

In my different publications I have used a sign like Y turned over on its side, $\prec$, to signify the relation between the antecedent and consequent of an hypothetical proposition. It is a very convenient sign, but as I have no such sign on this typewriter, I shall use a colon for the same purpose, according to the practice of Mr. Hugh McColl. Then, we may write $a{:}b = \bar{a}+b$. But although the use of this sign does simplify some cases, and I have been one of its principal advocates, and it certainly is useful for a learner, yet it makes a good deal of difficulty in complicated problems. The best way for a beginner to do is to use this sign first, to write down the relations of antecedent and consequent, and afterwards to replace it by +, at the same time negativing the antecedent.

Let us now take a slightly more complicated kind of reasoning, the direct syllogism. If you tell one lie you will tell a hundred, and if you tell a hundred lies you will corrupt your integrity. Let a mean that you tell a lie, b that you tell a hundred, c that you corrupt your integrity. Then, the premises are $a{:}b$ and $b{:}c$. Multiplying them together we have $(a{:}b)(b{:}c)$. This is equivalent to $(\bar{a}+b)(\bar{b}+c)$. Breaking down the first parenthesis, according to the rule just given, we have $\bar{a}+b(\bar{b}+c)$. Now breaking down the second parenthesis, according to the same rule, we have $\bar{a}+b\bar{b}+c$. But $b\bar{b}$ is 0 and may be dropped. Thus, we reach the conclusion $\bar{a}+c$ or $a{:}c$, if you tell a lie you will corrupt your integrity.

I will now show how to treat a little more complicated arguments called indirect syllogisms. Take these premises: if Enoch and Elijah are mortal the Bible errs; but all men are mortal. Let a mean that any given person is Enoch or Elijah, b that he is a man, c that he is mortal, and d that the Bible errs. Then $a{:}c$ means that if any person is Enoch or Elijah he is mortal, or what is the same thing, that Enoch and Elijah are mortal. Then, $(a{:}c){:}d$ means that if Enoch and Elijah are mortal the Bible errs, which is the first premise. The second premise is $b{:}c$, or if any person is a man he is mortal. Multiplying the two premises together, we have $[(a{:}c){:}d](b{:}c)$. Now $a{:}c = \bar{a} + c$ and $(\bar{a} + c){:}d$ is to be converted into the regular form by negativing the antecedent and putting a + instead of the colon. We have, therefore, to find the negative of $\bar{a} + c$. The rule for finding the negative of any expression is this: put a line over every letter that has no line over it, and take a line off every letter that has a line over it, and everywhere substitute multiplication for addition and addition for multiplication. Applying this rule, the negative of $\bar{a} + c$ is $a\bar{c}$. That is to say, to deny that anything is either not Enoch or Elijah, or else is mortal, is equivalent to asserting that something is Enoch or Elijah and at the same time is not mortal. To prove that this is so it will be sufficient to show that these two expressions satisfy the formulae of contradiction and excluded middle. By the principle of contradiction their product ought to vanish. Now their product is $(\bar{a} + c)a\bar{c}$. By the distributive principle this is the same as $\bar{a}a\bar{c} + ca\bar{c}$, but $a\bar{a} = 0$ and $c\bar{c} = 0$, so that the whole is $0\bar{c} + 0a$. Now $0\bar{c} = 0$ and $0a = 0$, so that it comes to $0 + 0$ which is 0.

Thus, the principle of contradiction is satisfied. According to the principle of excluded middle, the sum of any expression and its negative gives $\$$. Adding the two expressions we have $\bar{a} + c + a\bar{c}$. By the distributive principle of addition with respect to multiplication this is the same as $(\bar{a} + c + a)(\bar{a} + c + \bar{c})$. Now $\bar{a} + a = \$$ and $c + \bar{c} = \$$, so that the whole becomes $(\$ + c)(\bar{a} + \$)$.

But $\$ + c = \$$ and $\$ + \bar{a} = \$$, so that it reduces to $\$ + \$$ which is $\$$; and thus, the principle of excluded middle is also satisfied. Our first premise, then, is $a\bar{c} + d$, and the product of the two premises is $(a\bar{c} + d)(\bar{b} + c)$. We may arrange this by the associative principle in the following order, $(\bar{b} + c)\bar{c}a + d$. We now put in a new parenthesis, which we are entitled to do by the associative principle, so as to write $[(\bar{b} + c)\bar{c}]a + d$. We now break down the inner parenthesis and thus have $[\bar{b} + c\bar{c}]a + d$, and since $c\bar{c} = 0$ this is $\bar{b}a + d$, or $(a{:}b){:}d$, which means that if Enoch or Elijah is a man the Bible errs.

I will now give an example of another variety of indirect syllogism. Take the premises, Translated persons are not mortal and All men are mortal. Let *a* mean that any person is translated, *b* that he is a man, *c* that he is mortal. The first premise, no translated persons are mortal, might be written $ac = 0$. But if we take the negative of both members of this conclusion we have $\bar{a} + \bar{c} = \$$, or simply $\bar{a} + \bar{c}$. The other premise is $\bar{b} + c$. The product of the two premises is this, $(\bar{a} + \bar{c})(\bar{b} + c)$. Treating this precisely as in the case of a direct syllogism we get the conclusion $\bar{a} + \bar{b}$, or no translated persons are men.

We now go on to a slightly more complicated kind of reasoning, the dilemma. The dilemma is a reasoning in which you show that there are two (or more) possible alternatives, and then show that in either case a consequence follows. This kind of reasoning, although treated in books on Rhetoric, was first introduced into the treatises on logic about the year 1500 by Laurentius Valla. In point of fact the dilemma was very little used during the middle ages and it forms the most elementary example of the falsity of the traditional and Aristotelian notion that all reasoning is syllogistic. In the present system of signs, however, we fail to see anything peculiar about the dilemma, for the reason that we have in this system arbitrarily twisted every syllogism into a dilemmatic form, by writing all *a* is *b* in the form of either non-*a* or *b*. The truth is that this system of signs is altogether framed to meet the case of the dilemma. Syllogistic reasoning is so easy that it is got rid of by a little artifice. The old stock example of a dilemma is as follows: "It is not good to marry a wife, for if she be fair she will be common, if foul then loathesome" (Blundeville, *Art of Logic,* 1599). Let *a* mean that any object is a wife, *b* that she is fair, *c* that she is foul, *d* that she is eligible. Then, the first premise is $\bar{a} + b + c$, or any object is either a wife, or is fair, or is foul. The other two premises are $ab{:}d$ and $ac{:}d$, that is, if any object is a fair wife it is not eligible, and if any object is a foul wife it is not eligible. These two propositions may be otherwise written, $\bar{a} + \bar{b} + \bar{d}$ and $\bar{a} + \bar{c} + d$. Now, multiplying the three premises we have $(\bar{a} + b + c)(\bar{a} + \bar{b} + \bar{d})(\bar{a} + \bar{c} + \bar{d})$. By the application of the distributive principle of addition with respect to multiplication, this is the same as $\bar{a} + (b + c)(\bar{b} + \bar{d})(\bar{c} + \bar{d})$ and by the application of the distributive principle of multiplication with respect to addition, this is the same as $\bar{a} + b(\bar{b} + \bar{d})(\bar{c} + \bar{d}) + c(\bar{b} + \bar{d})(\bar{c} + \bar{d})$. Again, applying the same principle, and striking out $b\bar{b}$ and $c\bar{c}$, we have $\bar{a} + b\bar{d}(\bar{c} + \bar{d}) + c\bar{d}(\bar{b} + \bar{d})$, and by the striking out of factors this reduces to $\bar{a} + d + d$, or $\bar{a} + d$, or if any object be a wife she is not eligible, or no wife is eligible.

Without the introduction of any further signs, the above kind of reasoning is all that this system can comprehend, but it is useful in two ways. First, the practice of the method gives us great facility in imagining facts in other logical relations, so that we reason much more easily than we did before, even without the use of the method. Secondly, the algebra is itself very useful whenever we meet with a very complicated state of things, provided it is not so excessively complicated as to be unmanageable even with this aid. I shall now add a number of examples sufficient to thoroughly exercise the student and give him a mastery of this really very simple system.

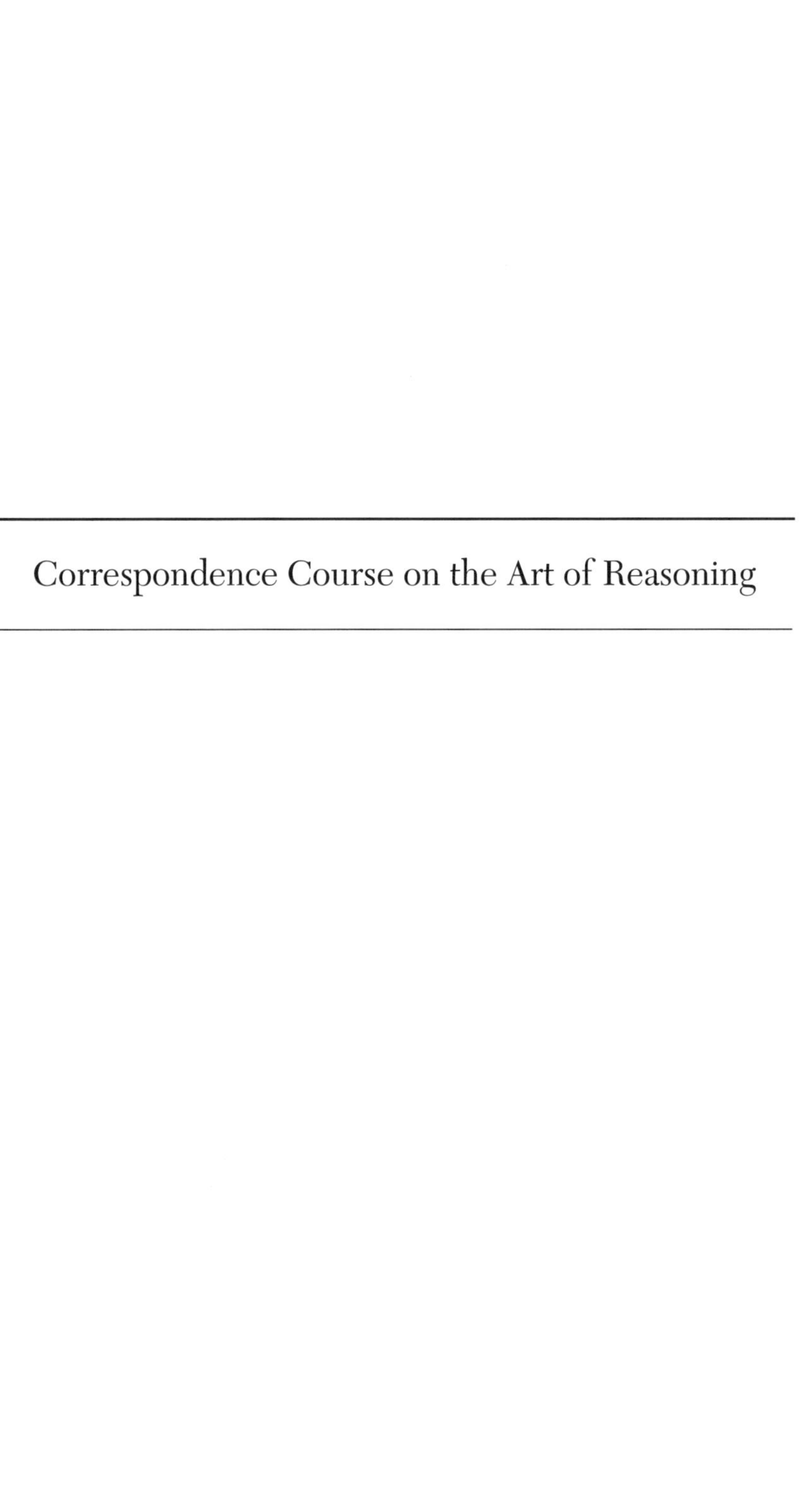

Correspondence Course on the Art of Reasoning

2

[Circular for Course on the Art of Reasoning]

January 1887 *Houghton Library*

MR. C. S. PEIRCE

Member of the National Academy of Sciences of the United States, etc., formerly Lecturer upon the Logic of Science in Harvard and the Johns Hopkins Universities, and author of many scientific memoirs, gives instruction *BY CORRESPONDENCE* in

THE ART OF REASONING.

The education best entitled to be called liberal is that which is calculated to put the student in full possession of his powers and to enable him to direct them as he will. But if this be true, the art of thinking must be acknowledged to be the soul of liberal training, and to constitute, indeed, an education by itself. It is true that no single branch of learning can replace a rounded culture; but if circumstances compel the choice of a single branch, that one should be the science of thought itself. If, on the other hand, many studies are pursued, the only rule by which the student can keep his knowledge in order and render it efficient is never to lose sight of the doctrine of method as the goal of every other discipline. "Dialectic," says the old text book which was everywhere used throughout the middle ages, "dialectic is the art *of* arts; it is the science *of* science; and it holds the road to the principles of all methods."

The instruction of Mr. PEIRCE is conducted entirely by means of practical exercises to be performed by the pupil, each being accompanied by the necessary explanations of how it is to be executed, and followed by reflections upon the nature of the proceeding and why it has been successful, with criticism of faults, and with answers to questions and resolutions of perplexities. The theory of reasoning is not neglected; but it is never divorced from its practical applications nor touched upon before living examples make the necessity and significance of it apparent. All education, broad or narrow, is intended to teach the student to *do* something (unless mere information be reckoned as education); and there is but one way of learning to do anything, namely, by graduated exercises leading up to the final performance of it, with close attention to the modes of executing each of those exercises. Even when the old technical logic was taught with success in the universities, it was by practical exercises, namely, by continual disputes, of which the lectures were only exemplifications. The student disputed every day. He disputed before breakfast, during breakfast, after breakfast, all day, and often half the night. Now modern science has shown us that it is not by disputations that truth is to be attained; and mere debating cannot for an instant be recommended as suitable to train a man in genuine, solid, and remunerative reasoning. But other exercises, every whit as strenuous and invigorating, can be, and have been devised to replace disputations and to do for the reasoning of the nineteenth century what those did for that of the fourteenth. Mr. PEIRCE has prepared such a series of exercises, as the fruit of long experience and intense study, and no intending student need doubt that the full course will make him an acuter, a broader, and a higher mind. The ordinary course is designed to meet the wants of those young men and women who have been debarred from the privileges of a college education, and even from the training preparatory to it. Although it is not claimed that this course is a full substitute for a liberal education, yet the student who follows it out to the end will surely find that doing this work will, in some important respects, more than compensate him for the college instruction he may have missed. Abridged and modified courses have been arranged for law-students, for divinity-students, and for college graduates generally.

The following list shows the subjects of the exercises.

PART I.—TRADITIONAL LOGIC. Exercises in common-sense syllogistic reasoning, to be rapidly passed over. Logical analyses. Arranging ideas. Divisions and classifications. Definitions.

This part is given in thirty to sixty letters.

PART II.—MATHEMATICAL REASONING. Solution of logical problems by algebra. Problems in higher arithmetic. Problems in geometry. Stating ordinary questions of life in mathematical terms. Problems in probabilities. Errors of observations.

This part requires sixty to ninety letters.

PART III.—SCIENTIFIC REASONING. Exercises in sampling. Inductions. Extrapolations. Framing hypotheses. Analogies. The generalization of problems and methods. The art of asking questions. Precautions in considering moral and spiritual questions: the world not governed by blind law.

This part is treated in sixty letters.

The plan of Correspondence is as follows: Each letter from Mr. PEIRCE contains answers to the student's difficulties, general criticisms, corrections of the last exercise and two new ones with explanations, the whole being sufficient to occupy the pupil for four hours. As soon as possible after the receipt of the letter, the student should carefully read it, go through the corrected task, and then perform the first of the new ones with the aid of the explanations sent, spending about two hours upon all this. He then forwards in duplicate all that he has done since his last letter, states how long he has worked on each part, and puts any questions he desires to ask. There remains in his hand material for two hours more work before the reply to his letter is received.

Under this system, the student will not be treated as if he were in a class. His peculiar difficulties will receive special attention, and the teaching will be moulded to his individual needs. Hence, nobody who feels impelled to seek the instruction need hesitate on account of any apprehended unfitness. He may confidently leave the resolution of such doubts with Mr. PEIRCE, who is under no temptation to accept any pupil for whom he cannot do good service.

A complete course usually requires one hundred and eighty letters extended over a period of from a year and a half to three years. The terms are $30.00, in advance, for each quarter of thirty letters. Any person desiring instruction should write to Mr. PEIRCE making application for the same, enclosing $5.00 (by postal note or otherwise) as a guarantee of good faith, giving his name and address, age, and full particulars in regard to previous education. Should the application not be entertained, the fee is returned. Otherwise, the name of the person is at once added to the end of the list of Accepted Applicants, from which pupils are taken in regular order as fast as vacancies in Mr. PEIRCE'S time permit. Any person whose name has remained upon the list of Accepted Applicants for more than three months can withdraw it, and will then receive back the fee, less postage. As soon as a person is made a pupil, he is notified, and must immediately remit the balance of the $30.00 for the first quarter. Old pupils are requested to state at about the twentieth lesson whether they desire to go on with another quarter, and if so, whether to continue without intermission.

Address by letter only, C. S. PEIRCE,
36 West 15th Street, New York.

SCHOOLS 10

The Art of Reasoning

TAUGHT BY CORRESPONDENCE.

BY C. S. PEIRCE, A. M., S. B. (in Chemistry, *summâ cum laude*), MEMBER OF THE U. S. NATIONAL ACADEMY OF SCIENCES, OF THE LONDON MATHEMATICAL SOCIETY, etc., DELEGATE TO THE EUROPEAN GEODESICAL ASSOCIATION, FORMERLY LECTURER ON THE LOGIC OF SCIENCE IN HARVARD AND THE JOHNS HOPKINS UNIVERSITIES.

Mr. Peirce has for a quarter of a century been a devoted student of methods of reasoning, and his proficiency in the subject is widely acknowledged. He has elaborated with great care, and as the fruit of much experience, a system of mental gymnastics and reflections, calculated to develop genuine practical skill in reasoning.

The exercises are molded to the individual needs of each pupil. His bad habits in thinking are corrected, and he is made familiar with valuable methods of attacking problems. The general course embraces three parts. Part First teaches all that is useful in the old logic, the art of arranging ideas, and how to make the thoughts clear and distinct. Part Second teaches mathematical precision in reasoning, with instruction in the doctrine of chances. Part Third teaches the art of investigation, how to ask questions, how to consult a library, how to select fair and instructive instances of any phenomenon, with all the precautions to be used in making induction and hypotheses.

The instruction is conducted by correspondence. Thirty letters are called a "quarter," calculated to occupy about three months. The entire course usually requires six quarters. Each lesson gives the pupil work for four hours.

The improvement is at the end of each quarter brought to a positive and indisputable test, consisting, not in an examination of the memory, but in the performance of a task of real reasoning in comparison with the performance of a like task at the beginning of the quarter.

Diplomas on the completion of the course.

Circulars sent on application. Letters of inquiry cannot be answered.

TERMS $30.00 PER QUARTER, IN ADVANCE.

Address MR. C. S. PEIRCE, 36 WEST 15TH STREET, NEW-YORK.

The President of a University, one of the ablest and most celebrated men in the country, writes: "I am not sure that I sha'n't ask you myself to teach me how to think. I have found it an extremely difficult and painful task." Many applications are received from highly educated people; but the instruction is particularly useful to those who have not had a college training. Instructors by old methods are earnestly invited to acquaint themselves with this system.

"The Art of Reasoning" advertisement from the May 1887 issue of the Century Magazine. *Until this ad appeared, enrollments depended primarily on mass mailings of the course circular (selection 2) which Peirce had printed in January 1887. Bibliographical annotations in the top margin have been removed from this image of Peirce's personal copy. Each issue's advertising supplement was separately paginated, and was not usually included in bound volumes. (Photo courtesy of the Houghton Library, Harvard University.)*

3

[Follow-up Letter to Circular]

13 March 1887 ***Houghton Library***

Dear Sir:— No full account of my method of teaching "The Art of Reasoning" has yet been printed, but I will give you some information additional to what you will find in my circular.

First:— The machinery of the instruction is this. The correspondence is treated as strictly confidential, and no person will learn anything about it from me, except my clerks, who will see only what it is necessary and fitting they should. The pupil exercises his own discretion as to what he will say on the subject. The instruction is divided into quarters of thirty lessons each, each lesson giving the student four hours of intense mental exercise, or say about an hour each day. I begin by sending work enough to last at least four hours, and after the pupil has done two hours' work he reports the result. After that he reports at the end of every four hours' work; and I continue to send him work fast enough to keep him occupied. His thirty-first letter, like the first, reports upon only two hours' work, thus making up the total of 120 hours. My letters of aid, criticism, and explanation, are similar in form to this I am writing to you. They average from 1000 to 2000 words in length. Besides these letters, he writes me two others, one at the beginning and the other at the end of the quarter. The first letter gives me all the particulars about himself, his age, history, education, purposes, plans, prospects, turn of mind, etc., that he may see fit to communicate; it also encloses a piece of his writing of say about a half a dozen pages as a favorable exhibit of the product of his brain at the outset. The letter at the end of the quarter gives some specimen of his powers at that time, so that he and I may be sure that satisfactory progress has been made. There is a similar positive test at the end of every quarter. At the end of the course I give a diploma on parchment.

Second:— I do not call the subject of my instruction Logic, but "The Art of Reasoning"; for the ordinary text books of logic are occupied mainly with teaching simple syllogisms and dilemmas, matters forming an insignificant part of the business of thinking. Prof. Allan Marquand (there is no impropriety in my saying he is one of my pupils) has invented a machine into which premises being fed, conclusions are turned out, and that of reasonings far more complicated than are usually treated in the text books (I have remarks on this machine in the forthcoming number of the *American Journal of Psychology*). The fact that this work can be done by a machine sufficiently shows that it is the smallest part of the mind's function in thinking. I teach formal logic, as well as the rest of reasoning, but I do not dwell unduly upon it. I treat rather the living process; I observe all the scholar's bad habits of thought, and see that he corrects them. I teach him methods and artifices by which he may make difficult problems easier; and I exercise his mind in such a way that it gains strength and skill at the same time. The first point, for instance, which I bring to the test, in nearly every case, is the brightness, inventiveness, liveliness of the mind; and some exercises are devoted to waking up this faculty should it be in a dormant state, as it often is. There is much in my exercises throughout the course calculated to stimulate and strengthen this faculty, so that I only devote one or two exercises to it exclusively, at the beginning. The next thing necessary is to see that the man makes a vigorous distinction between fact and fancy. Commonly this is sufficiently developed before my pupils come to me; but young people who have had little experience of the realities of life, and a few dreamy natures, need sometimes to be led into a line of thought which will emphasize this. Some fancy that reasoning has to be performed within the private chambers of their own brains, and do not appreciate, at first, how intimately it is connected with the real world. At this point, I am in the habit of giving my pupils some lessons in the art of learning, without always explaining what it is that I am then teaching. I find it quite important, in most cases, to see that they receive some advice and training as to just how they are to go to work, and what the attitude of their mind is to be in learning. We then come to the last of the preliminary studies, namely, learning some things about the English language. Everybody knows that accuracy of speech is an important condition of accurate thinking. Consequently, I take up seriatim a considerable number of words and forms of expression, and substitute definite ideas of their meaning for the loose ones which are current with untrained minds. In the course of these lessons, the pupil picks up something of the philosophy of speech. By this time he already begins to show some signs of greater strength of thought. I now explain how to unravel complicated inferences which involve no considerations of quantity, nor any but very simple relations. Here, for example is one of these exercises.

—A young king, on coming to the throne, found himself attacked by a powerful neighbor, and thereupon made the following reflections. I shall either prove myself a great man and conquer in the first campaign, or a prudent man and trust implicitly in my chancellor, or a fool and ruin the dynasty by headstrong rashness. If I am a great man, and popular with the army, my soldiers will not mutiny. If I am a prudent man, or have good counsellors, I shall obtain the assistance of some of the neighboring princes. If I am a fool, or behave like a coward, I shall alienate my people. If my soldiers do not mutiny and I conquer in the first campaign, I shall reduce my enemy to vassalage, unless I ruin the dynasty by headstrong rashness in spite of good counsellors. If I gain the assistance of a neighboring prince, and trust implicitly to my chancellor, I shall be compelled to behave like a coward, but I shall not ruin the dynasty by headstrong rashness. If I am positively popular with the army, I shall conquer in the first campaign. Of all these things I am profoundly convinced; and they afford me a legitimate ground of confidence; for I have only to resolve that I will do nothing to alienate my people unless it assures my popularity with the army, and that if I have good counsellors I will trust implicitly to my chancellor, and thus I shall be assured of reducing my enemy to vassalage. Was this conclusion well drawn?

Thence I proceed to inferences about relations presenting considerable more difficulty than the example above. Then I set the pupil to analyzing some piece of real argumentation, such as Mr. George's

Progress and Poverty, or Butler's *Analogy*. Some exercises upon definitions, the analysis of ideas, and how to form clear conceptions, complete the first part. The course, in this part as in the others, is modified to suit the individual needs and purposes of each pupil. It occupies either one or two quarters. The second part of the course exercises the pupil in reasonings in which quantity is involved. It shows him how to take a mathematical view of many subjects not usually so regarded, as "Political Economy," etc. It initiates him into the methods of thinking about mathematical questions. It also includes a course in the doctrine of chances with practical examples ranging from the easiest to really difficult ones. It gives the main principles of insurance, in all its forms; and the method used by scientific men in estimating errors of observations.

Part 3 teaches how to deal with real facts. It does not enter into methods of scientific observation, but does show by practical problems what observations are needed to be made. It exercises the pupil in the art of making good inductions and hypotheses by means of a series of problems, in the invention of which I have spent a great deal of time and thought. These are of the most various description. The reading of cipher dispatches is one kind. I then teach the pupil how to use a library. That is to say, required a certain piece of information, and given a library, the problem is to obtain that information in the shortest possible time. There are also exercises in asking questions so as to elicit a given piece of information as quickly as possible. Two quarters are devoted to this third part.

The above will give you some idea of the nature of my course, and will enable you to form some opinion as to its usefulness. No pupil fails to profit by it more or less; and I would not keep on with any pupil who should not have profited greatly by his last quarter. The better the man's previous training, the more he will profit under me, as a general rule. At the same time, I find persons whose minds are quite undeveloped usually reap more good from my course, than they would be likely to do from any other teaching which is within their reach.

Yours truly,

4

A Few Specimens of Exercises in the Art of Reasoning

April–May 1887 ***Houghton Library***

CONFIDENTIALLY COMMUNICATED. N.B. IT MUST NOT BE SUPPOSED THAT THESE REPRESENT MORE THAN A FEW OUT OF A LARGE NUMBER OF VARIETIES OF EXERCISES.

—— If your making your men work in your powder-mill at night would lose you much money, you would get your property insured. If fire is dropped into a barrel of gunpowder, there will be a terrific explosion. If the certainty that a terrific explosion would lose you much money would lead you to insure your property, you would be sure to find that no company would take the risk. Hence, if your making your men work in your powder-mill at night would make danger of fire being dropped into a barrel of gunpowder, you cannot get any company to insure your property. Show whether or not this follows.

—— A young king, on coming to the throne, found himself attacked by a powerful neighbor, and thereupon made the following reflections. I shall either prove myself to be a great man and conquer in the first campaign, or a prudent man and trust implicitly in my chancellor, or a fool and ruin the dynasty by headstrong rashness. If I am a great man, or popular with the army, my soldiers will stand by me. If I am a prudent man, or have good counsellors, I shall obtain the assistance of some of the neighboring princes. If I am a fool, or behave like a coward, I shall alienate my people. If my soldiers stand by me and I conquer in the first campaign, I shall reduce my enemy to vassalage, unless I ruin the dynasty by headstrong rashness in spite of good counsellors. If I gain the assistance of a neighboring prince, and trust implicitly to my chancellor, I shall certainly be compelled to behave like a coward, but I shall not ruin the dynasty by headstrong rashness. If I do not conquer in the first campaign, I shall not be positively popular with the army. Of all these things I am profoundly convinced; and they afford me a legitimate ground of confidence; for I have only to resolve that I will do nothing to alienate my people unless it assures my popularity with the army, and that if I have good counsellors I will trust implicitly to my chancellor, and thus I shall be assured of reducing my enemy to vassalage. Was this conclusion well-drawn?

—— In a certain college, there is at least one student having an examiner and never studying unless during the recitation of some one or other of his examiners. (But it is not herein implied that there are any recitations.) Moreover, every examiner lectures at some time during the studying of all those whom he examines. Draw two conclusions, one without saying anything about examining, the other without saying anything about studying.

—— Required the conclusion from the following premises: 1st. There is somebody who accuses everybody to everybody, unless perhaps not to some persons who have servants who love the parties who would otherwise be accused. 2nd. There are two persons one of whom accuses every servant of the other to everybody whom that other does not benefit.

—— Explain how the conclusion of the following argument might be false, though the premises were true, and give the additional premise required to make it irrefragable.

> Every Corsican kills a Corsican;
> But nobody is killed by more than one person;
> Hence, every Corsican is killed by a Corsican.

—— Truth being the conformity of a statement with fact, what are the facts conformity with which constitutes the truth of a hypothetical proposition, such as, "If A is true, then B is true"?

—— It has been held that a man is responsible for the proximate, but not for the remote, effects of his actions and negligences. Define these two kinds of effects.

—— Criticise the ordinary definition of a pronoun, showing that it yields no positive idea; and propose a better definition.

—— Show that the ordinary definition of a circle contains something superfluous.

5

Directions to Agents

Winter–Spring 1887 ***Houghton Library***

CLASSES TO BE ADDRESSED. The mayor. Clergymen, lawyers, doctors. Superintendent of schools, principal of the high-school (having interested him, you get permission to address the pupils, most easily on a Saturday. The same applies to all other classes of teachers). Teachers of private schools, young ladies' academies, business colleges, law schools, divinity schools, etc. Leave circulars in the bookstores and apothecaries, after making friends with the booksellers and the apothecaries. Get hold of the young men directly wherever you can. In the country, you can interest one young man, and take him about in a buggy to pick up others whom he knows on promise of $1 to him for everyone you get.

GENERAL METHOD OF TALKING. You must never lose yourself in your talk. Keep wide awake to the situation. Know exactly what effect you are aiming to produce, and watch to see when it is produced. Hammer away until you produce it, and then at once go on to the next point. Though you will have great need of arguments, you must not, of course, suppose that these are to produce their effect by their action on the understanding alone. The levers upon which you have to rely are first, cupidity, second, shame, and third, fatigue. You can offer a clergyman or a teacher a commission. You will put it in this way: that Mr. Peirce insists upon paying it in every case, whether it is asked for or not, but with the distinct understanding that no portion is to be refunded to the pupil, and to that end nothing is paid on the first pupil an agent (resident) obtains. You will understand that if you offer such commissions, you will have to pay them yourself out of your own. Whenever you are talking to a young man, who may become himself a pupil, you will represent the certainty of success in life which this instruction brings with it. Say it is unfortunate that pupils almost always insist on their names being kept secret; otherwise your interlocutor would be surprised to learn how many successful Wall Street men there are among the number, and the sons of Bankers form a large proportion of those who are now taking the course. In Wall Street, the value of sound reasoning is understood, etc. 2nd, whenever you see an opportunity to do so, you should manoeuvre to put the person to whom you are talking into a position in which he is ashamed to send you away empty-handed. Americans are particularly subject to the passion of shame. As soon as you see that a man begins to be strongly interested, pretend that you are going, say you have much more interesting things to tell him, but you will not allow yourself to trespass on his indulgence longer. When he says you need not mind, say that to tell the truth you have an appointment to see a gentleman who has agreed to take one ticket, but is doubtful about another for another member of his family, and owing to his high position you dare not offend him, but you will stay a few minutes, and then stay a good long while, so as to be able to hint that you have fooled away a lot of valuable time, satisfying your present man's curiosity, and so make him ashamed not to take one ticket at least. Remember this: that if the person whom you address is very rude at the outset, it gives you an immense advantage. Such men are generally unskillful in talk, and are more easily handled than others. You will behave with perfect good temper, dignity, and politeness. Make him feel that he has a gentleman to deal with, for whose good opinion he cannot but have some regard. You say: I have not come to sell you anything. I do not expect you to enter as a pupil. I have simply come because I have understood that you were one of the most prominent and respected citizens of the town, who would be likely to take an interest in anything tending to ameliorate the condition of the people and calculated to conduce to the well-being of the community. Without a pause, you then proceed to explain what you mean by "ameliorating the condition of the people and conducing to the well-being of the community" and draw him into conversation. Afterward, when he begins to be interested and to entertain a respect for you, you can say that your reception was not, you must confess, quite that which his reputation about the town had led you to expect it would be. If he says something apologetic, do not make light of the incident, but say that never having been an agent for any other enterprise than this, it had never happened to you to be subjected to such treatment before in your life; and in short, convey the idea that while you are ready to accept any apology, you had been considerably wounded. Some men will hear you attentively through to the end, and then give you a firm, emphatic, but polite negative. In such a case, you would probably waste your time in trying to effect anything. Still, the man is sure to be a valuable friend if you can get him, and your one chance is to make him fear he may have gone off the handle too soon. Answer him briefly and forcibly, showing that there is some material circumstance which he has left out of consideration. Do not wait for a rejoinder, but wind up by saying that you do not want to detain him with a long argumentation, and take your leave with sufficient deliberation to give him time to call you back should he see fit to do so. 3rd, you should never fail to take the measure of your man's nervous energy and endurance. Nobody is ever convinced, in any practical sense, until he is tired of objecting. You must take care not to vex a man (unless you see how you are going to make the vexation pass away) nor bore him, you must make your conversation pleasant; but if you can at the same time tire him quite out, by keeping his attention long on the stretch, and making him exert his mind in an unusual way, you will find it highly advantageous.

Of course, you will use these suggestions according to your judgment. I suppose that you are a man of sense. You will fully understand that I should not counsel to tell the slightest untruth, and far less to treat your fellow-citizens as if they were so many fish to be angled for. The object of life is not to make money, you know, but to prepare you for another better and far different world than this; and you will behave accordingly.

ORDER OF YOUR TALK. You will find it best to stick closely to a certain scheme of persuasion, never varying from it unless for some definite reason, or because you instinctively feel that with a given man some slight variation will be useful. There are many reasons for this plan. You get a greater mastery of the method, you are able to make modifications on a better basis of experience, etc. You begin with talk calculated to incline your man to put confidence in you. You cannot generally give a man confidence in you in a few minutes, but you must incline him to have confidence. For this purpose, you must have a remarkably straightforward and artless way in the beginning. You announce your business, without delay or circumlocution, say "I wish to call your attention to an educational undertaking for which I am soliciting pupils," and immediately hand out a circular and ask if he will kindly cast his eye over that. Throw in any naive remark you find takes, as "I don't suppose you will care for it. Nobody does in this town. I cannot understand how they can be so indifferent to such a matter." The next effect you want to produce is that you are deeply convinced of the value of this instruction yourself. Do not protest; but let your conviction crop out unconsciously as it were. The next thing you have to do is to fascinate your man, to interest him, to amuse him, or in short to cause him for no matter what reason to take pleasure in talking with you. The next thing you have to do is to give him a favorable impression of Mr. Peirce. You should produce these four effects, coolly and watchfully, in the order here set down; but you may so far run them together as to begin on each before you have quite done with the one that goes before.

Here is the point where you will generally thank your man for his kind attention, and say you only wanted to sow a little seed on good ground, so that you may go on at his request.

You will now go into cool argumentation to show the benefits of the plan. Be grave. To begin with, you state clearly what the system of instruction is and what its purpose is. It is a system of mental gymnastics, intended to develope 1st, the power of making a stupendous mental effort, 2nd, the power of keeping up a moderate exertion for a long time without undue fatigue, and 3rd, skill in reasoning or practical familiarity with the best methods of attacking every kind of practical problem. All the teaching is conducted by practical exercises; by giving the pupil some real thinking to do, and then making him observe not only where he has not done well, and what his failure has been due to, but also, what is even more useful, showing him where he has done well, and making him note exactly what the exertions were that he had to make to succeed, and then making him repeat the same process in the case of another problem. Having learned to perform the process of thinking, the theory of it can be made perfectly clear in comparatively short metre. The matters taught are divided into three parts. The first part consists of the recognition of the logical relations of thoughts, the analysis of them, and the logical arrangement of them. This makes of the pupil what would be called a good clear-headed thinker. The second part consists of the mathematical precision of thought, of mathematical views of things in general, and of the doctrine of chances. These exercises give a piercing distinctness to thought, which penetrate every wrapping, and at the same time impart great moderation and caution, by habituating the pupil to put a definite measure and value upon everything. The exercises in the doctrine of chances are carried sufficiently far to prevent his being taken in by any sophistry of gambling, speculation, or injudicious insurance. The third part consists of judgments about matters of fact. This part has cost Mr. Peirce far more trouble to get it up than anything else. He has been studying it for years, and has at last succeeded in inventing a course of exercises, by which a man can get a lifetime of experience in the exercise of good judgment in the course of a few months. The precise nature of these exercises is for the present a secret between Mr. Peirce and his pupils, until the whole method can be properly set forth in a book upon which Mr. Peirce is now engaged. He does not wish it to be judged by experiments made with it by people who do not thoroughly understand it. The instruction is carried on by correspondence. Each letter from Mr. Peirce gives a criticism of the exercise last received, in a good deal of detail, and sets two more exercises, each to occupy the pupil two hours, accompanied with explanations as to how they are to be done. As soon as the first one of these is done, the pupil sends it on to Mr. Peirce, retaining the other one to occupy him until he gets Mr. Peirce's reply. Thirty lessons are called a quarter, and the pupil pays $30 in advance for each quarter. At the end of each quarter, there is a positive practical test of the improvement made by the pupil, and should it not be very marked Mr. Peirce reserves the right to bring the lessons to a close, but this never happens with serious pupils. Having thus stated the case, you will go on to give the general advantages of the scheme as hereinafter stated. You will then argue that the man that reasons the best is the most successful man, other things being equal. You will then show that people can be taught to think. You will then show that the only way to teach anything is by practical exercises. You will then show that this kind of instruction can be conducted by correspondence as well as in any other way. You will then make a careful résumé of the argument.

Having thus fully argued the question, you next aim to suggest to the mind of your man that it would be an excellent thing, either for himself or for somebody in whom he takes an interest. You do not directly say this, you only instance some other cases in which great advantage has been got from it. Speak of its advantages over any college training. Do not make this part too long. Excite your man about as much as you can do quickly. Beyond that you will not be able to go.

Finally explain that if the step is to be taken at all, it must be taken at once. Ask him to hand you anything, or do any little service for you. That will put him into the attitude of compliance, and make it easier for him to say "Yes" when you ask him to take a ticket.

THE SUBSTANCE OF YOUR TALK. 1st, Who is Mr. Peirce? Charles Sanders Peirce was born in 1839, and is therefore 47 years old. He successively took three degrees in Harvard, the last, Doctor of Science, was conferred *summa cum laude*, being one of the very few Harvard degrees to which that distinction has been appended. He has been during the greater part of his life attached to the Coast Survey, where he has charge of the most scientific branches of the work, relating to the figure of the earth, etc., and to the determination of the force of gravity, weighing the earth, etc. He has resigned his regular position in the Survey, though still exercising a supervision over the work, in order to devote his energies to the education of his fellow countrymen in right thinking, which he thinks is the way in which he can make himself most useful. He has carried on his branch of the Survey in a manner to win the encomiums of the greatest European authorities. In 1875, he happened to be invited to attend the meetings of the delegates of the different governmental Surveys of Europe which was held in the Ministry of Foreign Affairs in Paris, and Mr. Peirce was asked to say what he thought of the method used at that time throughout Europe for determining the force of gravity. He condemned it, and said it gave results enormously in error. Pendulums were used, and these pendulums swung from brass tripods, and Mr. Peirce stated that he had found by actual measurement that these tripods swayed under the pendulums, by an amount so minute that no ordinary microscope would detect it, but yet that owing to a complicated mechanical effect, the time of oscillation was lengthened in consequence quite considerably. The European delegates were so surprised at this statement, that they had very little to say, but adjourned to meet in Brussels the following year. At this Brussels meeting (at which Mr. Peirce was not present) reports were received from two or three of the Surveys, those of Austria and Switzerland among the number, where the matters in question had been most studied. These different Surveys reported that they had undertaken special investigations of the facts alleged by Mr. Peirce, and that they found that "our American colleague" was quite mistaken. These reports did not reach Mr. Peirce until the following year, barely in time for him to reach a third meeting of the European Surveys, which was called to meet in Stuttgart in order to reach a final decision in regard to this important question. He at once applied for orders to attend that meeting, but owing to the influence of Mr. Randall the Washington authorities declared they did not care what the European Surveys said or did, and refused to issue the orders. Several of the most influential New York newspapers, however, protested against this view, and the result was that the orders were finally issued. Mr. Peirce hurried over with all speed, and entered the meeting in the midst of a heated discussion of the question. The venerable president General Baeyer of Berlin, who had been endeavoring to defend Mr. Peirce's views, fell upon his neck and kissed him. Mr. Peirce addressed the meeting and showed that the experiments instituted by the Surveys of Austria, Switzerland, etc., were not well-calculated to bring out the phenomenon in question. He then exhibited his own experiments, and then showed by an elaborate mathematical discussion that they led demonstratively to the conclusion that he had announced. At the end of his address, those who had opposed his views one after another arose and declared themselves convinced, and his proposition was adopted by a unanimous vote. Since then the methods used in Europe for the determination of gravity have been reversed. The king next day invited Mr. Peirce to dinner. Mr. Peirce's main study, however, for the last quarter of a century, has been the methods of reasoning in science. He has lectured upon the subject before the Lowell Institute in Boston, for two years in Harvard University, for five years in the Johns Hopkins University, etc. As long as the Coast Survey continued as a scientific institution, Mr. Peirce was unwilling to accept any permanent engagement which would cut off his connection with that. Now that it has been apparently broken up, he prefers to set up a school of reasoning rather than connect himself with any college, because he disapproves the methods of instruction in the colleges and has a small opinion of their results. Mr. Peirce's writings have mostly been confined to scientific memoirs, which have appeared in the scientific and philosophical journals of this country, of England, of France, and of Germany, as well as in the memoirs of learned societies in all those countries. Professor Schroeder, the highest authority on logic in Germany, today, in the advertisement to his last work, says: "It has been necessary to bring out an entirely new work, instead of a mere new edition of my former one, on account of the very remarkable *(hoechst bedeutende)* progress which the science has made in the interval, mainly through the works of the American Charles S. Peirce and those of his pupils." You can also supply yourself with anecdotes respecting Mr. Peirce, to show his skill in reasoning.

FACTS ABOUT THE INSTRUCTION. The letters are generally about the length of a page of *Harper's Magazine.* This is the shortest. There are 750 words on a page of *Harper's.* There are 1100 on a page like this. The shortest letter is nearly a page like this. The letters not infrequently run up to three pages. Mr. Peirce uses the fewest words consistent with perfect clearness, and with fully saying all that is essential, and he trains his pupils to the same habit. One class of exercises consists in exercises in endurance. These are exceptional in their nature; they require the pupil to give up his whole time to them, or else to do them by himself, in the course of his business, with only general instructions and help from Mr. Peirce. The following gives information in some detail concerning the nature of the exercises. PART I. The first thing is to exercise the pupil in not being deceived by the jingle of words, but always imagining the facts set forth, by a simple method which will guard him against ever being taken in by such juggles as are usually served up as examples in the books on Logic. The next examples that are taken up are in drawing up formal definitions. The method of going to work in framing such definitions, which are rather useful for various purposes, is fully explained, and the pupil exercised on it. After this, the pupil is taken through a series of exercises calculated to show, that while formal definitions do something toward rendering thought clear and distinct, they nevertheless leave the main part of the business incomplete, and the method of attaining scientific clearness of thought is exhibited, and the pupil is thoroughly practised in it. The pupil is next introduced to exercises in the arrangement of ideas. He is given, for example, a list of a thousand words, of somewhat kindred nature, and is required to arrange them according to their meanings, so clearly that any one can be found with the least possible effort of mind by another person. He is required to make a table of contents for a book, with an analysis of all it contains. PART II. The pupil is in this part first taught how to apply diagrams and algebra to the solutions of puzzling questions of logic formed by Mr. Peirce on the basis of Boole's algebra of logic. This includes the logic of relations. The method of aiding the mind by drawing or imagining curves is next taught. Then the art of making numerical scales to aid the judgment about all sorts of observations which seem not to have anything to do with quantity. Also, the art of giving precision to our thoughts by the introduction of the conception of quantity, where at first sight it does not seem to be at all applicable. Next the use that can be made of various conceptions which have hitherto only been employed in mathematics is fully illustrated and the pupil familiarized with them. The doctrine of chances is next taken up and taught mainly by examples, which are made as practical as possible. The theory of errors of observations is explained and its use taught. The principles of insurance are illustrated. PART III. This part teaches how to deal with matters of fact. The pupil has now to make his own observations, because in this kind of reasoning observation and reasoning are inextricably entwined. The first lessons are in judging of a lot of things by a sample, which the pupil selects for himself. Considerable study is paid to the art of picking out a characteristic sample. Next come exercises in the method of detecting regularities in phenomena, and coincidences of all sorts. Quasi-periodic phenomena. Then, exercises in interpolation and extrapolation, and the precautions necessary in this dangerous kind of reasoning. Exercises in explaining facts by making hypotheses, and the whole art of this kind of reasoning. Reading cipher dispatches; solving various kinds of puzzles. The art of guessing. Exercises in asking questions. Exercises in the art of using a library. Exercises in reasoning by analogy, and the precautions necessary.

GENERAL ADVANTAGES OF THE INSTRUCTION. The art of reasoning is the very essence of education. It is the main thing a man goes to college to learn. But the Colleges fail to teach it, as they fail in most of their teaching. There is nothing they fail in so miserably as in this. Mr. Peirce does teach it. He has never had a failure, after the first quarter had shown the pupil was in earnest. Even when he was under the trammels of the university system, he had great success. The entire course, which will occupy two or three years, costs $180. But the pupil is not obliged to interrupt his business in order to take it. On the contrary, Mr. Peirce considers that it is most advantageous for the pupil to have a business, which shall keep his mind bent to practical things, so as to take a serious and practical view of this instruction. Logic as it has been taught is trifling. The very word trivial owes its origin to this circumstance, because logic was the principal study of the trivium or threefold road (grammar, logic, rhetoric) which formed the staple of instruction in the Roman and medieval schools. But the new logic taught by Mr. Peirce is eminently practical; and the great thing is not to allow the pupil to fall into trifling subtleties,—and to teach him to unite scientific profundity and even a philosophical insight with thoroughly practical aims. The practical must never be lost sight of, or the reasoning becomes dry and worthless. Practical exercises form the only instrument by which anything can be taught. If you want to teach a man to box, you must set him to boxing. But you must carefully analyze each motion for him. In other words, the exercises must be analytic. The analytical gymnastics of the mind is what this instruction consists in.

This witnesses that______________________
has paid me $2 and will be received____________
as a pupil in

THE ART OF REASONING

for 10 lessons, on remittance by mail to me at 36 West 15th St., New York City, of this ticket and $8.

C. S. PEIRCE.

No.________ ______________________Agent.

The Agent is not authorized to modify these terms.

This witnesses that______________________
has paid me $2 and will be received____________
as a pupil in

THE ART OF REASONING

for 30 lessons, on remittance by mail to me at 36 West 15th St., New York City, of this ticket and $28.

C. S. PEIRCE.

No.________ ______________________Agent.

The Agent is not authorized to modify these terms.

"The entire course, which will occupy two or three years, costs $180." Peirce divided his correspondence course in "The Art of Reasoning" into quarterly terms of thirty lessons each. The admission tickets allowed students to enroll through Peirce's field agents for $2, then pay either $8 for ten lessons (top) or $28 for an entire quarter of instruction (bottom). Peirce also provided other installment options when students wrote directly to him. (By permission of the Houghton Library, Harvard University.)

SUCCESS IN LIFE DEPENDS LARGELY ON REASONING WELL. It is a fact that the average American can see well enough, that to succeed better than your neighbors, you must be a little smarter than they are. This is felt keenly in Wall Street, where the elements which make the successful man are brought out into vivid distinctness by the contrast in the fate of the successful and the unsuccessful man. Tell the story of Cornelius Vanderbilt and his grandfather.

It is true we see plenty of men who can tell so well exactly how anything should be done; and yet when it comes to doing it they are not there. We also see men who can reason soundly enough, and yet want tact, grace, and subtlety of perception in dealing with men. But it is one of the points of Mr. Peirce's method that it dwells upon the regions where reasoning shades off into vigor of action, and into observation.

It may be thought that success depends more upon good morals than upon right reason. But the truth is that the best way to teach people morals is to teach them to think.

PEOPLE CAN BE TAUGHT TO THINK. Ignorant and uncultivated people have a strange idea that men cannot be taught to think. The foundation of this is no doubt in part that they observe that educated men often reason no better or not so well as they do themselves. This is because education generally is so ill designed to fulfill its chief purpose. Every function of the body is strengthened by exercise, and if every tissue of the body can learn, how can it be thought that the mind should want the faculty of learning? The truth is, that exercise is immensely more telling on the mind than on the body. Any ordinary man not too old can in three months learn to lift twice the weight he could at the outset. This is an understatement. But in three months mental gymnastics, he can triple or even quintuple his mental energy. Mr. Peirce *[ ]*

6

[Letter to New Students]

January 1887 ***Houghton Library***

36 W 15th St, New York City

My dear Pupil:

The first thing that you and I have to do is to form one another's acquaintance. You have hitherto probably been taught in a class, but my instruction is to be fitted to your individual mind. It is a custom-made and not a ready-made education. Very likely you are of opinion that ready-made things pay the best for the purchaser. But you will agree, I think, that if every day-laborer knew how to work with wood, the carpenter trade would be worse than it is; if every man could conduct a law suit as well as a lawyer, the lawyers would not get large fees; if all the world had foreseen the success of the Atlantic cable as clearly as Cyrus Field did, he would not be today many times a millionaire. Thus, every man's success in life depends upon his being a little smarter than his neighbor. Very well; now that you have become my pupil, I will declare to you what I do not proclaim to the general public, because I do not wish to make boasts that I may not have the opportunity to make good; but I declare to you privately that I intend to make you smarter than your neighbors. No, no; what am I saying? It is beyond human power for one man to add to the mental vigor of another. That I cannot do; but I will guide you in the way of making yourself smarter than your neighbors. Plainly, a wholesale education which is extended to all the children in the country can raise nobody above the general level.

Few men can excel in all their powers of mind. My experience has shown me that men's minds are as various as their faces. Having minutely studied multitudes, I find that each is naturally strong in one kind of thinking and naturally feeble in another. I have then a two-fold task. I must train the pupil up to respectable strength where he is weak and up to remarkable strength where he is strong. I have to arrange his exercises so that the work done is more serviceable than the same amount otherwise distributed could be. I am a sort of physician for the mind; and to know what to prescribe I must study my patient's symptoms. Then I may be able to make him a better man than I myself am. That is why the first thing I have to do is to make your acquaintance.

I want you to begin by writing me a letter. This will not count as one of your 30 exercises, and yet it will be more important than most of them, and will give more work both to you and to me. I wish you to select some subject upon which you have thought a good deal, and write me an account of what you think. No matter what subject you select. Perhaps it had better not be so purely personal, local, or technical, that I could not possibly know anything about it, although even such matters are not positively ruled out. The main point is not to think out something for the occasion, for that would, I know, not do you justice, but to take a subject upon which you have already thought. I ask you to set forth your reflections in an orderly manner, plainly, fully, and yet as briefly as may be. I will give you no further directions. Do the thing in your own way; and let the letter be a favorable exhibit of what your mental factory can turn out now. It will thus serve two purposes. It will show me to what my first efforts must be directed. I shall not, if I can avoid it, recur to the subject of this letter during the whole period of our correspondence; but at the end of each quarter, I wish you to write me a new letter on the same subject, and these successive letters will be evidence, both to you and to me, of the increment of your mental strength.

Yours truly,

C. S. Peirce

7

[Orientation Letter to Marie Noble]

11 May 1887 ***Houghton Library***

Milford, Pa., 1887 May 11.

MISS MARIE B. D. NOBLE,

Care Messrs. Gorham, Turner, & Co., Mills Building, New York City.

My dear pupil:

I am glad that you have applied to me; for I am entirely confident of being able to be of service to you. Your letter is a very clear one, and shows good intellectual powers. You have had a long period of ill-health, which has impaired the vigor of your will-power. Your difficulty of seeing two sides of every practical question is a familiar fact to me, though I have never experienced it myself. It is no symptom of intellectual weakness, but rather the contrary. Almost every question has two sides, and it is only the thoughtless and the passionate who can fail to see it. But what we have to do, after we have considered the question as long as it is convenient to do, is somewhat arbitrarily to make a choice between the two sides, and having once made our choice to stick to it. Your difficulty lies, no doubt, in making a vigorous choice, in the absence of the *vis a tergo* of demonstrative reasons. Will is also needed for the act of concentrating the mind, although this is a less willful kind of will. We often see people whose external will is weak, but whose control over themselves is strong. I suspect this is the case with you. How is it? Have you good power of concentration? Next, I want to know how your observing powers are. "A little botany" is the only study of observation that you mention. You also say nothing about any studies, except school-studies. What else have you applied your mind to, and with what success? Have you any taste or turn for mathematics? Do you learn readily? I do not mean lessons merely. But are you pliant? Do you readily adapt yourself to a new situation? I would like to have you answer all these questions. Then, I want to know whether you are prepared to give an hour a day of good, solid and intense work to my exercises. One of the things that is the quickest improved by exercise is the power of making an exertion. And if my diagnosis is correct, one of the things you want is the power of making suddenly a violent effort. For that reason, I will not allow you to spend a long time over the exercises, you must do them as well as you can in a short space of time, and learn to throw yourself into them with sudden energy. During this time you must be absolutely alone, without fear of interruption. If an hour a day is too much, name a shorter time; but the time once fixed, let it be as the Law of the Medes and Persians. I will thank you to enclose in your letter about 5 or 6 pages of your writing on any subject you please, written for the occasion, to serve as a favorable exhibit of your intellectual powers at the outset. This will not only furnish me with needful information, but it will serve as a term of comparison with something similar that I shall ask you to write at the end of the Quarter, so that there may be no difference of opinion as to the amount of benefit that you have received from the exercises.

Yours very truly,

C. S. Peirce.

P.S. I have taken a house here for the summer, and my address until further notice will consequently be Milford, Pa.

8

[Letter to Noble on the Nature of Reasoning]

28 May 1887 ***Houghton Library***

Milford, Pa., 1887 May 28th.

MISS MARIE B. D. NOBLE,

Care Messrs. Gorham, Turner, & Co., New York City.

My dear pupil:

I wish to begin by giving you some general idea of the nature of reasoning. All reasoning involves observation. A chemist sets up an apparatus of flasks and tubes, he puts certain substances in the former, he applies heat, and then he watches closely to see what the result will be. The procedure of the mathematician is closely analogous to this. He draws a diagram, for example, conforming to certain general conditions, and then he observes certain relations among the parts of this diagram, over and above those which were used to determine the construction of it. The result that the chemist observes is brought about by Nature, the result that the mathematician observes is brought about by the associations of the mind. But this does not constitute so radical a distinction as it seems at first sight to do; for were the laws of nature not intelligible, that is, were they not such as naturally occur to the human mind, the chemist's observation could never teach him anything, while on the other hand the power that connects the conditions of the mathematician's diagram with the relations he observes in it is just as occult and mysterious to us as the power of Nature that brings about the result of the chemical experiment. You do not quite see the truth of this? No, why should you: I have stated it in abstract terms, which give you nothing to observe this fact in, and the mind can see no truth except by observation. To enable you to see it, I will give two instances of simple mathematical reasoning; you will please first see that they are proofs, and then remark the fact that even after you know the proofs you have no direct consciousness of the necessity that binds the conclusion to the conditions supposed. First take this simple proposition in geometry, an interesting one in itself, and probably unknown to you. On a plane, take any point, O, and through it draw 3 straight lines. Take 3 new points, A, B, C, lying severally on these 3 straight lines. Take also 3 other points, A′, B′, C′, lying, A′ in the line through O and A, B′ in the line through O and B, C′ in the line between O and C. Now if we draw the straight lines AB and A′B′, and continue them till they intersect at a point which we may designate as X, if we draw the straight lines BC and B′C′, and continue them until they intersect in a point which we may designate as Y, and if we draw the straight lines CA and C′A′, and continue them till they meet in a point which we may designate as Z, then we shall find that the points X, Y, Z *lie on one straight line.* More briefly stated, if two triangles are so situated that the lines joining corresponding vertices meet in one point, then the points of intersection of corresponding sides (produced if necessary) lie in one straight line. To prove this, through the point O imagine a line not lying in the plane of the triangles, and on this line we imagine any two points, which we may distinguish as S and S′. Now any 3 points whatever lie in some one plane. Consider, then, the plane OSA. S′ lies on this plane, because it is in the line between S and O, both of which are on the plane. A′ too lies on the plane, because it is in the line through A and O. Then, since the point S′ and A′ lie on the plane the whole line through these points lies on the plane. Thus, the lines SA and S′A′ lie on one plane. But any two lines in one plane cross, if sufficiently produced (unless, indeed, they happen to be parallel, a case not necessary to consider, because easily evaded by shifting S or S′). Consequently, the lines SA and S′A′ (produced, if necessary) intersect in a point which we may designate as A″. Similar reasoning would show that the lines SB and S′B′ intersect in a point which we may designate as B″, and that the lines SC and S′C′ intersect in a point which we may designate as C″ Now the points S, A, and A″ lie in a straight line, for A″ designates the intersection of the line SA with another line. And in like manner, the points S, B, and B″ lie in a straight line. These two lines have the point S in common; they therefore lie in one plane. Consequently, the lines AB and A″B″ lie on this same plane, which we may designate as plane No. 1. Likewise, the points S′, A′, and A″ lie in a straight line, and the points S′, B′, and B″ lie in a straight line, and these two lines intersect at the point S′, so that they lie in one plane, which we may designate as the plane No. 2. Consequently, the lines A′B′ and A″B″ lie in plane No. 2. Now the lines AB and A′B′ lie on the original plane of the two triangles first spoken of, which we may call plane No. 3. These three planes, like any three planes, must meet in some one point, and this point lies in the line common to planes 1 and 3, and also in the line common to planes 2 and 3. It also lies in the line common to planes 1 and 2. But the line common to planes 1 and 3 is AB, and the line common to planes 2 and 3 is A′B′, and the point of intersection of AB and A′B′ is the point we called X. Thus, X lies in the line through A″ and B″. It therefore lies in any plane on which this line lies, and thus in the plane of A″B″C″. In like manner, it could be shown that the points Y and Z are on the plane A″B″C″. But these three points are also on the original plane. They are therefore on the intersection of the original plane with the plane A″B″C″ and thus are on a straight line, which is what we had to prove.

As another illustration of mathematical reasoning I will prove a proposition in arithmetic, namely, that no power of a whole number whose exponent is one less than a prime number can, on division by that prime, leave a remainder greater than 1. Thus, 5 being a prime number, the series of 4th powers is 1, 16, 81, 256, 625, 1296, 2401, 4096, 6561, 10000, etc., and as these all end with a 1, a 6, a 5, or a 0, it follows that the remainders, after division by 5 will all be either 0 or 1. The general proof is as follows. If the base, or root of the power, is divisible by the prime, then the power itself is so too, and there is no remainder. But if the base is not so divisible, then its product by any number less than the prime will, on division by the prime, leave a remainder different from any other product of the base by a number less than the prime. For if two such products were to leave the same remainder, the difference between them would leave no remainder at all, and would thus be divisible by the prime. But this difference would be equal to the base multiplied by some number less than the prime number. Now if a prime number does not divide either of two numbers, neither can it divide their product. Thus the difference of the products cannot be divisible by the prime, and consequently all products of the base by numbers less than the prime must, on division by the prime, give different remainders. But the remainder after division by a number is of course less than that number. Hence the products of the base by the different numbers less than the prime will after division by the prime give those same numbers as remainders, in some different order. Thus, suppose the prime is 5, and the base 6. Then the products of 6 by the numbers, 1, 2, 3, 4, less than 5, are

$$6 = 5 \cdot 1 + 1, \quad 12 = 5 \cdot 2 + 2, \quad 18 = 5 \cdot 3 + 3, \quad 24 = 5 \cdot 4 + 4.$$

But if 7 had been the base, the products would have been 7, 14, 21, 28, which leave as remainders after division by 5, 2, 4, 1, 3, the same numbers in a different order. Consequently, the product of all the products of the base by the different numbers less than the prime (which for the sake of brevity may be called the product of products) *[. . .]*

9

[Reasoning Exercises]

Winter 1887 ***Houghton Library***

[Number Series]

The following rows of numbers are called Fermat's series:

0 1 3 7 15 31 63 127 255 511 1023 2047 etc.
2 3 5 9 17 33 65 129 257 513 1025 2049 etc.

Find out the rules of the succession of numbers in these two series.

The numbers in the following row are called the phyllotactic numbers. The series is also called Fibonacci's series, because first studied in the XIIIth century by the mathematician Leonardo of Pisa, called Fibonacci.

0 1 1 2 3 5 8 13 21 34 55 89 144 etc.

Find out the rule of succession of these numbers.

Do the same for the series

2 1 3 4 7 11 18 29 47 76 123 199 322 etc.

The following series are called Pell's series:

0 1 2 5 12 29 70 169 408 985 2378 etc.
2 2 6 14 34 82 198 478 1154 2786 6726 etc.

Find the rule of succession for these.

0 1 1 0 –1 –1 0 1 1 0 –1 –1 etc.

Find the rule of succession here.

What is the product of two corresponding numbers in Fermat's series?

Compare the square of any number in any series with the products of those which precede and follow it. What rules can you find?

If two numbers one over another in any pair of series are both prime, what is true of the number of their place in the series? (N.B. The places are to be numbered beginning with 0.)

What relation can you find between the phyllotactic number whose place in the series is expressed by the sum of any two numbers, say m and n, and the numbers in the mth and n^{th} places in that series and in the series underneath it?

Every third number in the series of Fibonacci is even, every 4th number is divisible by 3. What about every 5th number, every 6th etc.? Is there anything analogous in any of the other series?

Compare the greatest common divisor of two phyllotactic numbers with the greatest common divisor of their places in the series.

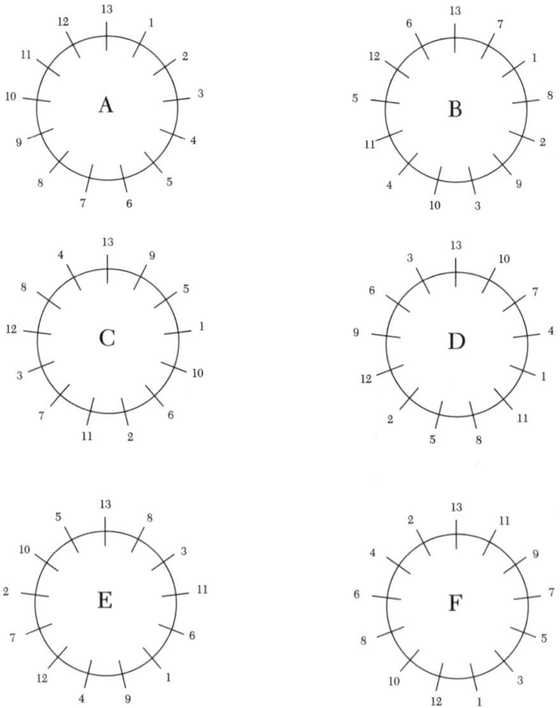

Give the rule or plan of each arrangement.

What is the relation between arrangements B and F? What between C and D? What is so related to E?

Show that as B is to A, so is D to B, E backwards to D, C to E backwards, F to C, and A backwards to F.

*[*Relational Graphs*]*

Represent by graphs that one person is the second cousin of another.

" " " that a man marries his grandmother.

" " " that a man has children by two sisters.

" " " that a man has a child by his father's mother-in-law.

" " " that A injures B, B injures C, C injures D, D injures E, E injures A, while the brother of E injures the brother of D, who injures the brother of C, who injures the brother of B, who injures the brother of A, who injures the brother of E just mentioned.

Required to make some graphs in which every spot is just like every other and has connections exactly like those of every other spot. See how many different forms of graphs you can make under these conditions, with 3, with 4, and so on up to 12.

Make some graphs in which the spots are of two colors and in each color of two shapes and the lines are of two kinds and every line runs from a spot of one color to a spot of another color and the lines are not barbed. See how many different kinds of graphs you can draw under these conditions beginning with the simplest.

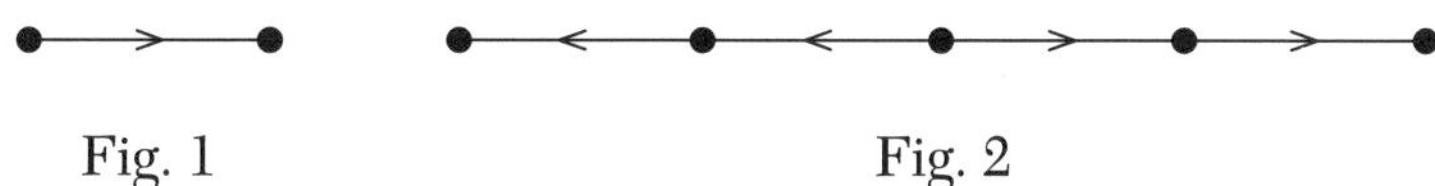

Fig. 1 Fig. 2

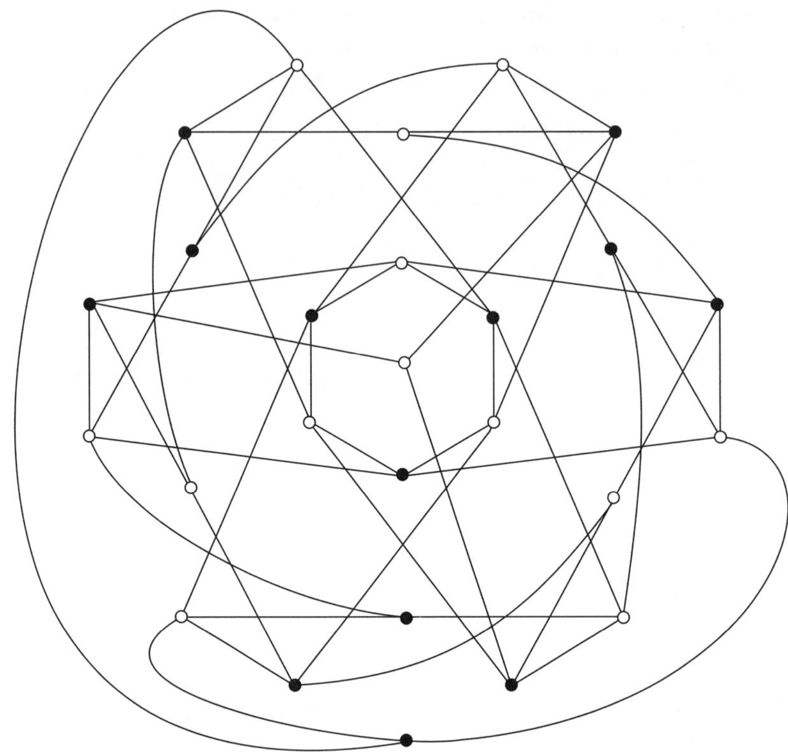

Fig. 3

Let the black spots ● denote points and the circles ○ lines, and let the connections signify that points lie on lines. Thus ●——○ (A B) means the point A lies on the line B.

Problem: to draw *straight* lines so that the state of things represented in Fig. 3 shall be carried out.

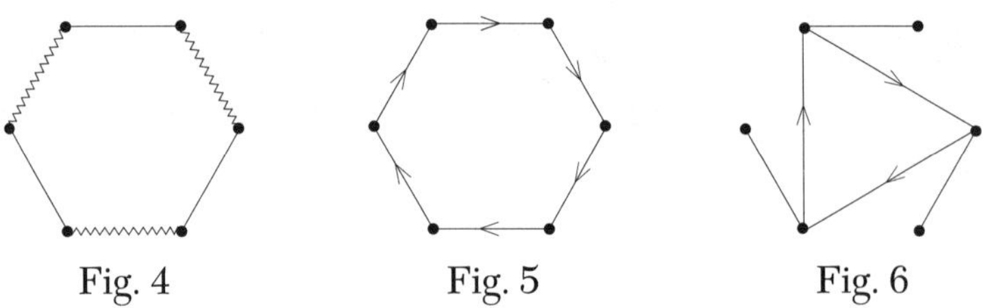

Fig. 4 Fig. 5 Fig. 6

Figs. 4 and 6 are substantially the same, but Fig. 5 is different.

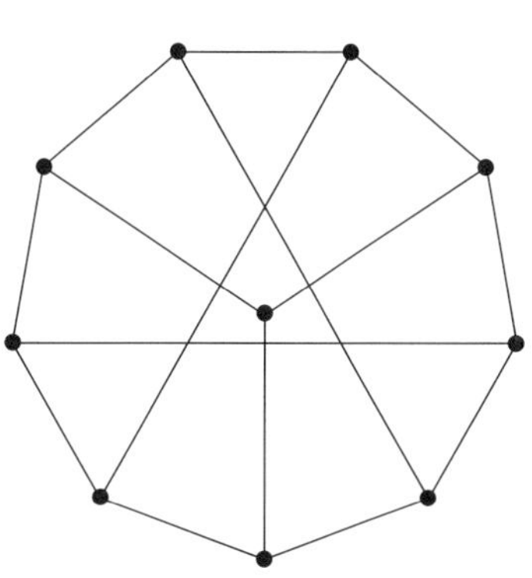

Fig. 7. Draw two triangles, having their vertices on three lines that meet in one point. Then the corresponding sides, produced if necessary, meet in 3 points lying on a 10th line. Show how this graph represents the relations either of the points or lines.

Fig. 8. The dots stand for the edges of a cube. Show that the junctions may signify either that two edges meet or that they do not lie in one plane.

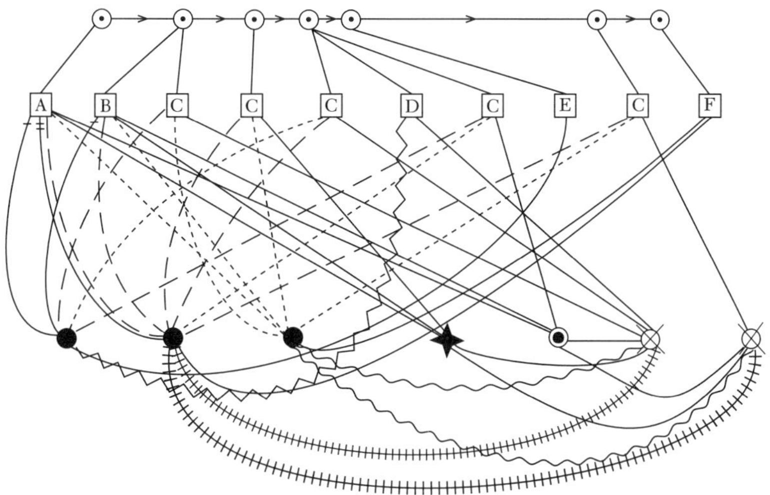

Fig. 9

⊙ An instant of time. Joined by barbed line →— to a later instant. The length of the interval is roughly represented by that of the barbed line. Instants are joined by plain lines to the events that take place about that time.

● A person or firm. ✦ Goods. ◉ A sum of money.

⊗ A bill. Amount due and goods joined by plain lines. Party making out bill joined by wavy line ~~~~~. Party to whom made out joined by line ++++++++++.

[A] A verbal contract. Negotiators joined by lines +——— ++———. The contract is for the sale of goods joined by plain line, for each payment of sum joined by plain line. Goods to be delivered by party joined by dotted line ---------- to party joined by broken line — — — —.

[B] Order for goods joined by plain line. Order delivered by party joined by line +———. Goods to be sent by party joined by dotted line ---------- to party joined by broken line — — — —. Price to be sum joined by plain line, to be paid as usual at end of month.

[C] Act of delivery by party joined by dotted line --------- of object joined by plain line, to party joined by broken line — — — —.

[D] Receipt by party joined by scraggly line, ⋀⋀⋀⋀⋀⋀⋀, of bill joined by plain line.

[E] Disappearance of party joined by plain line.

[F] Quarrel between parties joined by plain lines.

[Card Games]

Take a pack of cards, select from it the spades and the hearts, rejecting only the kings. Arrange each of these suits in sequence,—ace, 2, 3, . . . 9, 10, Knave, Queen,— the ace being at the back, the queen at the front. Put the hearts on the table in a pile, backs up. Deal off the spades one by one into two piles, turning each card over and laying it down, face up. The cards in this dealing are, of course, alternately placed on the left hand and the right hand piles. But when you come to the last card, which will be the queen, instead of putting it down on the pile where it would regularly go, you put it down on the table, face up, to form the first card of a new pile. In the place where the queen would have gone had you proceeded regularly, now put instead the top card of the pile of hearts, which is the ace, turning it face up. Now cover the pile upon which you have just laid this card, with the other pile of six spades, and take up the combined pile into your hand, faces down. Repeat this operation: that is, deal out the cards you hold in your hands into two piles, until you come to the last card which will be the knave, which you place on the queen, as the second card of that pile, and in place of the knave you put on the second pile, the top card of the pile of hearts, which will be the two. You then cover this pile with the other pile of six, and take up the combined pile, as before. Do this over and over until you have done it twelve times in all, when you will hold all the hearts in your hand, and all the spades will lie in a pile on the table. Now I say that there is a singular relation between the arrangement of the spades and that of the hearts, so that when you have once remarked the secret of it, by examining the spades which you hold in your hand, you can readily tell off the hearts in the order in which they lie on the table. What I ask you to do is, preserving their order, to spread out the spades and the hearts on the table, and try if you can see what this relation between the two orders is.

Take a pack of cards, and arrange them in sequence, proceeding from back to face, as follows:—Spades: ace, 2, 3, . . . 10, Knave, Queen, King. Diamonds: ace, 2, 3, . . . 10, Knave, Queen, King. Clubs: ace, 2, . . . Queen, King. Hearts: ace, 2, . . . Knave, Queen, King. Thus, the ace of spades will be at the back, and the king of hearts at the face of the pack. Take the pack in your hand, face down, and deal the cards out singly, into five piles, in regular rotation, turning each card face up as you lay it down. Take up the third pile and lay it face up on the first, so as to make one pile of the two. Place this combined pile on the last pile but one, so as to make one pile of them. Take up this still larger pile and lay it on the first pile, so as to combine these. Take up this pile and lay it on the last of the original piles, so as to unite the whole pack. Take up the pack into your hand, faces down, and deal the cards out one by one into six piles in regular rotation, turning them up as you lay them down. Place the fifth pile on the fourth, this united pile on the third, this pile on the second, this on the first, and this again on the last, so as to reunite the whole pack, spread the cards out in four rows, of thirteen in a row, as follows, where the numbers show the places of the cards in the pack before they are spread out.

1	2	3	4	5	6	7	8	9	10	11	12	13
14	15	16	17	18	19	20	21	22	23	24	25	26
27	28	29	30	31	32	33	34	35	36	37	38	39
40	41	42	43	44	45	46	47	48	49	50	51	52

You will now find a singular relation between a card and a certain other, in respect to their suits and numbers in the suits, their rows and places in the rows. Try to discover that relation.

Take a pack of 52 cards, and select all the plain cards of three suits. Arrange them in order from 1 to 10, one suit after another, in a pack, beginning at the back with the ace, and a ten at the face of the pack. Then you have thirty cards, and the second suit you can conceive as numbered from 11 to 20, and the third suit from 21 to 30. Now hold the pack in your hand with backs up, and deal them out into a number of piles which may be either 2, 3, 5, 6, 10, or 15. The cards are to be dealt out singly, and each card is to be turned up as it is laid down on the table and you are to deal them out to the different piles in regular rotation. When the cards are all dealt out, you place the first pile on the second, and you place that combined pile on the third, you place that combined pile on the fourth, and so on until you have united the whole pack. Now, I wish to know whether you can find a rule or general statement by which, when you know how many piles the cards have been dealt out into, you can tell what their order will be beginning at the back of the pack, and proceeding to the face. Also, what will be the effect of dealing them out twice or three times.

When you have ascertained the rule asked for in the last problem, take the cards in their original order and deal them out into eight piles; as eight does not divide thirty, it will follow that the last two piles will have each one card fewer than the others. Put the seventh pile on the sixth, put this combined pile on the fifth, put this combined pile on the fourth, put this combined pile on the third, put this combined pile on the second, put this combined pile on the first, and this combined pile on the remaining pile. Now, you will find that the rule which you have already discovered in regard to the order of the cards, holds good in this case. This is because you pick up the piles in this particular order. Now I want to know if you can tell me in what order the piles must be taken up, in order to make this same rule hold good when the cards are dealt out into other numbers of piles than eight.

10

Boolian Algebra [Three Lessons]

Spring 1887 ***Houghton Library***

In this system of signs, each letter of the alphabet is the abbreviated statement of a fact, simple or complex. Thus, x might be taken to signify that twice two is four, and that either all men are mortal or else Napoleon Bonaparte was born in Salem, Mass. Every letter is an abbreviated statement. It may be of all that is stated in a book, it may be of something very simple.

The sign = is used in ordinary algebra to signify equality. Thus, $x = y$, read "x equals y," can be written when the quantity named x is known to be equal to the quantity named y. In the Boolian Algebra the same sign is used, and is read in the same words, but a different meaning is attached to the sign and to the words "equal," etc. with which it is associated. Two facts are considered to be equal when every possible state of things in which either is true is or would be a state of things in which the other is or would be true, and *vice versa.* Thus, "this polygon has three sides," and "this polygon has three angles" are equal or equivalent facts, although the statements refer the one to sides, the other to angles. If you ask what is meant by a "possible" state of things, I reply that the possible is that which is not known to be non-existent,—and that either in the state of knowledge in which we find ourselves, or else in some feigned condition of ignorance. The "possible" of this Algebra may be any variety of the possible,—as the logically possible, the physically possible, etc. Only the same meaning must be attached to the possible throughout any one discussion. Or if different varieties are used, these must be carefully distinguished. It must be understood that when $x = y$ is written the facts x and y are not stated; it is only stated that they are either both actual or neither.

The sign + is used in ordinary algebra to denote addition. Thus, $x + y$, read "*x plus y*," denotes the sum of the quantities named x and y. This sign, with the words "plus," "sum," "add," etc. associated with it, are also used in the Boolian Algebra, but by most writers (myself included) in a sense not strictly analogous to the arithmetical sense. The expression $x + y$ is a *statement,* and it states that either x or y (perhaps both) is a fact, without saying which. The expression $x + y$ is that statement which is true if either of the statements x and y is true, and is false if both x and y are false. It follows that $x + x = x$, contrary to the analogy of arithmetic.

The signs $\times$ and $\cdot$, and the writing one after another of two expressions, are used in ordinary algebra to denote multiplication. Thus, $x \times y$, or $x \cdot y$, or xy, read "xy," or "x into y," or "x multiplied by y," denote the product of x and y. The same signs and words are used in the Boolian Algebra in a different sense. The expression xy is a *statement,* and it is the statement of both facts x and y. More precisely, it is that statement which is true if both the statements x and y are true, and is false if either of them is false. It follows that $xx = x$, which in ordinary algebra would be an equation satisfied by $x = 0$, $x = 1$, and $x = \infty$.

Exercise. Ascertain whether the following formulae necessarily hold good, whatever statements x, y, and z may be.

$$x + y = y + x \qquad xy = yx \qquad x(yz) = (xy)z$$

[N.B. Parentheses are used to signify that the statement in parenthesis is to be combined as one statement by addition or multiplication with the one outside of the parenthesis.]

$$x + (y + z) = (x + y) + z$$
$$x(y + z) = xy + xz$$
$$x + yz = (x + y)(x + z)$$
$$(x + y)(y + z)(z + x) = xy + yz + zx$$

N.B. The exercises should be done, and the formulae verified by the definitions of logical addition and multiplication in the way shown in the following example: $x + yz$ is true if either x or yz is true; otherwise it is false. But yz is only true if both y and z are true. Hence

$x+yz$ is true 1st if x is true and 2nd if both y and z are true. The statement $(x+y)(x+z)$ is true only if $(x+y)$ and $(x+z)$ are true. $x+y$ is true 1st if x is true, and 2nd if y is true. $x+z$ is true, 1st if x is true, and 2nd if z is true. Hence both $(x+y)$ and $(x+z)$ are true, 1st if x is true, and 2nd if both y and z are true. But these are the same circumstances under which $x+yz$ is true. Hence, the two statements $x+yz$ and $(x+y)(x+z)$ are equivalent, and we can write $x+yz = (x+y)(x+z)$. Do all these exercises before going further.

Boolian Algebra—Second Lesson

The equations $x+(y+z) = (x+y)+z$ and $x(yz) = (xy)z$ are called respectively the Associative Principle of Addition and the Associative Principle of Multiplication. The formulae $x+y = y+x$ and $xy = yx$ are called the Commutative Principle of Addition and Multiplication. The formula $x(y+z) = xy+xz$ is called the Distributive Principle of Multiplication with respect to addition. The formula $x+yz = (x+y)(x+z)$ is called the Distributive Principle of Addition with respect to multiplication.

From those formulae with $x+x = x$ and $xx = x$ all others can be deduced, without recourse to the meanings of the operations. Thus, to prove $(a+b)(c+d) = ac+ad+bc+bd$ we proceed as follows. By the distributive principle $(a+b)(c+d) = (a+b)c + (a+b)d$. By the commutative principle this equals $c(a+b) + d(a+b)$ and, again applying the distributive principle, this equals $ca+cb+da+db$ or by the commutative principle $ac+bc+ad +bd$. The associative principle is assumed in leaving off the parentheses.

Exercises. Prove in this way the following.

$ab+cd = (a+c)(a+d)(b+c)(b+d)$

$a+ab = a$

$a(a+b) = a$

$(a+b)(b+c)(c+a) = ab+bc+ca$

$(a+b)(b+c)(c+d)(d+a) = ac+bd$

$$(a+b+c)(a+b+d)(a+c+d)(b+c+d) \\ = ab+ac+ad+bc+bd+cd$$

$$(a+b+c)(a+b+d)(b+c+e)(c+a+f)(a+d+f)(b+d+e) \\ (c+e+f)(d+e+f) = ae+bf+cd$$

$$(a+e)(b+f)(c+d) = abc + abd + bce + caf + adf + bde + cef + def$$

$$(a+b)(a+c)(a+d)(b+c)(b+d)(c+d) = (abc + abd + acd + bcd)$$

$$(b+f)(c+g)(d+h)(a+e)(b+d)(b+g)(d+g)(c+f)(c+h)(f+h) = (abcd + abgh + adfg + bche + cdef + efgh)$$

Third Lesson

We now introduce a new sign. A line drawn over a statement denies it. Thus, $\bar{x}$ is the statement that x is not true. Then, show that $x = \bar{\bar{x}}$. Also that $\overline{x+y} = \bar{x}\bar{y}$. Also that $\overline{xy} = \bar{x}+\bar{y}$. Also that $\overline{\bar{x}\bar{y}} = x+y$. Also, that $\overline{\bar{x}+\bar{y}} = xy$. Also, that $\overline{x+\bar{y}} = \bar{x}y$. Also that $\overline{x\bar{y}} = \bar{x}+y$.

Let the sign of dollars \$ be used to signify a statement that is true in every possible case, that is, which is known to be true. Then, to write $x = \$$ is the same as to write x simply; or $x = (x = \$)$. Let naught, 0, be used to signify a statement known to be false. Then, to write $x = 0$ is the same as to write $\bar{x}$ simply; or $\bar{x} = (x = 0)$.

Exercises. Show that

$x + 0 = x$

$x\$ = x$

$0x = 0$

$\$ + x = \$$

$x\bar{x} = 0$ [This is the principle of contradiction.]

$x + \bar{x} = \$$ [This is the so-called principle of excluded middle.]

11

[Two Letters from J. B. Loring on Algebra Lessons]

22 and 27 December 1887 ***Houghton Library***

New York Dec 22/87

Mr C. S. Peirce

Dear Sir:

I enclose my solutions of the questions relating to 1st lesson. Please excuse pencil. I am a poor penman and can write plainer and more quickly with pencil than with pen.

Am somewhat doubtful as to the last solution but it is the best I can do with it. I do not see how there can be any other. It is required to demonstrate that

$$(x+y)(y+z)(z+x) \ = \ xy+yz+zx.$$

The statement at the left of the sign of equality relates to multiplication and its truth depends upon the truth of each of the 3 statements in parenthesis. Each of these 3 statements is a plus statement whose truth depends upon the truth of either one of its members. In the 1st statement is x, in the 2nd z and in the 3d are both z and x. Hence it seems to me that if both z and x are true then each of the 3 statements in parenthesis is true, and if each of the 3 statements in parenthesis is true then the whole statement at the left of the sign of equality is true. The statement at the right of the sign of equality is a plus statement whose truth depends upon the truth of either one of its 3 members. As each of these 3 members relates to multiplication, the truth of each depends upon the truth of both of its parts. One of these members is zx. Hence if both z and x are true then this one member is true, and if this one member is true, the whole statement at the right of the sign of equality is true. And these conditions, the truth of both z and x, are the same as are those under which the statement at the left of the sign of equality is true.

The last two lines of page 2 of the sheet that you sent me are somewhat blurred. May I trouble you to send me a copy of these two lines and oblige

Yours Truly
J. B. Loring
Box 555
New York

Dec 27 1887

Mr C. S. Peirce

Dear Sir:

In demonstrating that

$$(a+b)(c+d) = ac+ad+bc+bd$$

you begin by saying "by the distributive principle

$$(a+b)(c+d) = (a+b)c+(a+b)d \text{ .''}$$

May I trouble you to explain to me how by the distributive principle you arrive at this result.

And in connection with this demonstration you also say "the associative principle is assumed in leaving off the parentheses." I do not understand that.

In your first lesson you say "the expression $x + y$ is that statement which is true if either of the statements x and y is true and is false if both are false". Then am I to understand that the above expression in the 3[d] line from top of this page—$(a+b)c+(a+b)d$ — is true if either of the statements, $(a+b)c$ and $(a+b)d$, is true and is false if both are false

Yours Truly
J. B. Loring
Box 555 New York

12

[Reply to Loring]

30 December 1887 ***Houghton Library***

Milford, Pa., 1887 Dec. 30.

Mr. J. B. Loring, Box 555 New York.

My dear pupil:

I congratulate you on the way you are taking hold of the subject. I have received yours of Dec. 22 and 27. You will please make it a rule to report to me at the end of each four hours' work, so that we shall know when the quarter ends; for its length is determined by the amount of work that you have done, measured in time.

I will first consider the equation

$$(x + y)(y + z)(z + x) = xy + yz + zx.$$

Your reasoning in your letter is pretty well. It does not fully meet the case. You show that the two statements are both true provided that both x and z are true. But that is not enough. You must also show that neither can be true without the other being true. Besides, as a matter of practice in this system of signs, I want you to prove it symbolically. First, multiply together the first two factors of the first member. That will give by the distributive principle of addition with respect to multiplication $(x + y)(y + z) = y + xz$. Now multiply in the third factor. That will give

$$\begin{aligned}(y + xz)(z + x) &= y(z + x) + xz(z + x)\\ &= yz + yx + xzz + xzx\\ &= yz + yx + xz + xz\\ &= yz + yx + xz.\end{aligned}$$

In your second letter, you ask how the distributive principle proves that $(a + b)(c + d) = (a + b)c + (a + b)d$. The formula of the distributive principle of multiplication with respect to addition is $x(y+z) = xy+xz$. Put $x = a+b$, $y = c$, and $z = d$, and you have the result. Of course, in the general formula, x, y, z, may be any statements; hence, it is legitimate to adopt the equivalents just given.

The next question is what I mean by saying that the associative principle is assumed in leaving off the parentheses. By the associative principle $x + (y+z) = (x+y)+z$; so that we may as well write simply $x+y+z$, for whether this means that x and y are first to be added and then z added on to them, or that to x is to be added the sum of y and z makes no difference according to the preceding formula. In like manner, in the particular case in which I make the remark and to which your inquiry relates, without the associative principle, I should only reach the statement $(ac+bc)+(ad+bd)$. But by the associative principle, this would be the same as $ac+[bc+(ad+bd)]$ and as $ac+[(bc+ad)+bd]$, and in short, without giving all the equivalents, it obviously makes no difference how the parentheses are put in, so long as the factors of no one term are separated, so that they may as well be dropped altogether. All students have to ask such questions at first.

The blurred lines are $x+0 = x$ $x\$ = x$ $0x = 0$ $\$+x = \$$ $x\bar{x} = 0$ [This is called the principle of contradiction.] $x+\bar{x} = \$$ [This is the so-called principle of excluded middle.] In the last two formulae please observe the second x is in each case negatived.

I will not send you any further exercise today, as I think you have enough for 8 hours, at least. These things are puzzling, at first.

Yours very truly,

13

[Additional Exercises in Boolian Algebra]

Summer 1887 ***Houghton Library***

I saw a man in the street who had a way of looking up and squinnying his eyes which showed me that he was either excessively near-sighted or somewhat foolish. He went up to a post-box at the corner and tried to put some object through the top, until he finally found the slit in the side of the box. He was not foolish enough to account for this conduct, and was certainly not intoxicated; so that he was plainly either excessively near-sighted or else absent-minded. Having put something small into the box he next sat down on the curbstone. Nearsightedness would not account for this, which showed him to be either absent-minded or rather foolish. But absentmindedness would not account for his squinnying his eyes; so that I was puzzled. He might be both absent-minded and somewhat foolish, and if so undoubtedly was under the impression he was in a bob-tailed horse-car, and had deposited a nickel in the box. If he was somewhat foolish and excessively near-sighted, the same conclusion would result. If he was absent-minded and excessively near-sighted, the inference will be the same.

Let a mean he was absent-minded; f, that he was foolish; n, that he was excessively near-sighted; c, that he thought himself in a horse-car. Then the premises are

$(a+f)$, he was absent-minded or rather foolish;

$(f+n)$, he was rather foolish or excessively near-sighted;

$(n+a)$, he was very near-sighted or else absent-minded;

$(\bar{a}+\bar{f}+c)$, if he was both absent-minded and foolish, he thought himself in a bob-tailed horse-car;

$(\bar{f}+\bar{n}+c)$, if he was both foolish and near-sighted, he thought himself in a bob-tailed horse-car;

$(\bar{n}+\bar{a}+c)$, if he was both near-sighted and absent-minded, he thought himself in a bob-tailed horse-car.

The product of the premises is

$$(a+f)(f+n)(n+a)(\bar{a}+\bar{f}+c)(\bar{f}+\bar{n}+c)(\bar{n}+\bar{a}+c)$$
$$(a+f)(f+n)(n+a)[(\bar{a}+\bar{f})(\bar{f}+\bar{n})(\bar{n}+\bar{a})+c]$$
$$(a+f)(f+n)(n+a)(\bar{a}\bar{f}+\bar{f}\bar{n}+\bar{n}\bar{a}+c)$$
$$[(a+f)\bar{a}\bar{f}+(f+n)\bar{f}\bar{n}+(n+a)\bar{n}\bar{a}+c](a+f)(f+n)(n+a)$$
$$= c(af+fn+na)$$

He must have thought himself in a bob-tailed horse-car.

1. Wherever there is smoke, there is fire or light. Wherever there is light and smoke there is fire. There is no fire without either smoke or light. What if there is smoke? What if there is not smoke? What if there is no light?

2. The members of a board were all either bondholders or shareholders, but no member was both bondholder and shareholder; and the bondholders were all on the board. State the relation between bondholders and shareholders.

3. Three persons are set to sort a heap of books. The first is to collect all English political works and bound foreign novels; the second, the bound political works and English novels not political; the third, the bound English works and unbound political novels. What books will be claimed by two and by all of them?

4. The members of a scientific society are divided into three sections, which are denoted by A, B, C. Every member must join one, at least,

of these sections, subject to the following conditions: 1st, whoever is a member of A but not of B, of B but not of C, or of C but not of A, may read a paper if he has paid his subscription, but otherwise not; 2nd, whoever is a member of A but not of C, of C but not of A, or of B but not of A, may exhibit an experiment if he has paid his subscription but otherwise not; 3rd, every member must either read a paper or exhibit an experiment annually. Find the least addition to the rules necessary to compelling every member to pay his yearly subscription.

5. In a certain lot of calicos, every piece with lilac spots and green spots has also black spots and yellow spots, and *vice versa;* and every piece with red spots and orange spots has also blue spots and yellow spots, and *vice versa.* Eliminate yellow and express the conclusion in terms of green.

6. In the Kingdom of Mbugwam, all freemen together with all cannibal cooks and slaves neither cannibals nor cooks are attached either to the army or the court. The army cooks not attached to the court as well as all men in the army attached to the court except cooks are, so many as are cannibals, slaves. The cooks and slaves belonging to the army are in attendance at court if they are not cannibals but not if they are; while all other men are in attendance at court if they are cannibals, but not if they are not. Without distinguishing slaves from freemen, 1st state the composition of the army, 2nd state of what classes the cooks consist. 3rd, without distinguishing either slaves from freemen or men in the army from men out of it, describe the cooks. 4th state the composition of the nation neglecting the same distinctions and also that between cooks and non-cooks.

14

[Science and Immortality]

7 April 1887 ***The Christian Register***

What is the bearing of positively ascertained facts upon the doctrine of a future life?

By the doctrine of a future life, I understand the proposition that after death we shall retain or recover our individual consciousness, feeling, volition, memory, and, in short (barring an unhappy contingency), all our mental powers unimpaired. The question is, laying aside all higher aspects of this doctrine, its sacredness and sentiment,—concerning which a scientific man is not, as such, entitled to an opinion,—and judging it in the same cold way in which a proposition in physics would have to be judged, what facts are there leading us to believe or to disbelieve it?

Under the head of direct positive evidence to the affirmative would be placed that of religious miracles, of spiritualistic marvels, and of ghosts, etc. I have little to say to all this. I take the modern Catholic miracles to be the best attested. Three members of the English Psychical Research Society have lately published a vast book of fourteen hundred pages, large octavo, under the title of *Phantasms of the Living*. This work gives some seven hundred cases of apparitions, etc., of a dying person to another person at a distance. The phenomenon of telepathy, or perception under conditions which forbid ordinary perception, though not fully established, is supported by some remarkable observations. But the authors of the book I am speaking of—Messrs. Gurney, Myers, and Podmore—think they have proved a kind of telepathy by which dying persons appear to others at great distances. Their most imposing arguments are based upon the doctrine of probabilities, and these I have examined with care. I am fully satisfied that these arguments are worthless, partly because of the uncertainty and error of the numerical data, and partly because the authors have been astonishingly careless in the admission of cases ruled out by the conditions of the argumentation.

But, granting all the ghost stories that ever were told, and the reality of all spiritual manifestations, what would it prove? These ghosts and spirits exhibit but a remnant of mind. Their stupidity is remarkable. They seem like the lower animals. If I believed in them, I should conclude that, while the soul was not always at once extinguished on the death of the body, yet it was reduced to a pitiable shade, a mere ghost, as we say, of its former self. Then these spirits and apparitions are so painfully solemn. I fancy that, were I suddenly to find myself liberated from all the trials and responsibilities of this life, my probation over, and my destiny put beyond marring or making, I should feel as I do when I find myself on an ocean steamer, and know that for ten days no business can turn up, and nothing can happen. I should regard the situation as a stupendous frolic, should be at the summit of gayety, and should only be too glad to leave the vale of tears behind. Instead of that, these starveling souls come mooning back to their former haunts, to cry over spilled milk.

Under the head of positive evidence apparently unfavorable to the doctrine, we may reckon ordinary observations of the dependence of healthy mind-action upon the state of the body. There are, also, those rare cases of double consciousness where personal identity is utterly destroyed or changed, even in this life. If a man or woman, who is one day one person, another day another, is to live hereafter, pray tell me which of the two persons that inhabit the one body is destined to survive?

There is certainly a large and formidable mass of facts, which, though not bearing directly upon the question of a future life, yet inclines us to a general conception of the universe which does not harmonize with that belief. We judge of the possibility of the unseen by its analogy with the seen. We smile at Aladdin's lamp or the elixir of life, because they are extremely unlike all that has come under our observation. Those of us who have never met with spirits or any fact at all analogous to immortality among the things that we indubitably know must be excused if we smile at that doctrine. As far as we see, forms of beauty, of sentiment, and of intelligence are the most evanescent of phenomena.

"The flower that once has bloomed forever dies."

Besides, scientific studies have taught us that human testimony, when not hedged about with elaborate checks, is a weak kind of evidence. In short, the utter unlikeness of an immortal soul to anything we cannot doubt, and the slightness of all the old arguments of its existence, appear to me to have tremendous weight.

On the other hand, the theory of another life is very likely to be strengthened, along with spiritualistic views generally, when the palpable falsity of that mechanical philosophy of the universe which dominates the modern world shall be recognized. It is sufficient to go out into the air and open one's eyes to see that the world is not governed altogether by mechanism, as Spencer, in accord with greater minds, would have us believe. The endless variety in the world has not been created by law. It is not of the nature of uniformity to originate variation, nor of law to beget circumstance. When we gaze upon the multifariousness of nature, we are looking straight into the face of a living spontaneity. A day's ramble in the country ought to bring that home to us.

Then there is the great fact of growth, of evolution. I know that Herbert Spencer endeavors to show that evolution is a consequence of the mechanical principle of the conservation of energy. But his chapter on the subject is mathematically absurd, and convicts him of being a man who will talk pretentiously of what he knows nothing about. The principle of the conservation of energy may, as is well known, be stated in this form: whatever changes can be brought about by forces can equally happen in the reverse order (all the movements taking place with the same velocities, but in the reverse directions), under the government of the same forces. Now, the essential of growth is that it takes place in one determinate direction, which is *not* reversed. Boys grow into men, but not men into boys. It is thus an immediate corollary from the doctrine of the conservation of energy that growth is not the effect of force alone.

The world, then, is evidently not governed by blind law. Its leading characteristics are absolutely irreconcilable with that view. When scientific men first began to understand dynamics, and had applied it with great success to the explanation of some phenomena, they jumped to the anticipation that the universe could be explained in that way; and thus what was called the Mechanical Philosophy was set up. But a further study of the nature of force has shown that it has this conservative character, which absolutely refutes that mechanical notion of the universe. As well as I can read the signs of the times, the doom of necessitarian metaphysics is sealed. The world has done with it. It must now give place to more spiritualistic views, and it is very natural now to anticipate that a further study of nature may establish the reality of a future life.

For my part, I cannot admit the proposition of Kant,—that there are certain impassable bounds to human knowledge; and, even if there are such bounds in regard to the infinite and absolute, the question of a future life, as distinct from the question of immortality, does not transcend them. The history of science affords illustrations enough of the folly of saying that this, that, or the other can never be found out. Auguste Comte said that it was clearly impossible for man ever to learn anything of the chemical constitution of the fixed stars, but before his book had reached its readers the discovery which he announced as impossible had been made. Legendre said of a certain proposition in the theory of numbers that, while it appeared to be true, it was most likely beyond the powers of the human mind to prove it; yet the next writer on the subject gave six independent demonstrations of the theorem. I really cannot see why the dwellers upon earth should not, in some future day, find out for certain whether there is a future life or not. But at present I apprehend that there are not facts enough in our possession to warrant our building any practical conclusion upon them. If any one likes to believe in a future life, either out of affection for the venerable creed of Christendom or for his private consolation, he does well. But I do not think it would be wise to draw from that religious or sentimental proposition any practical deduction whatever,—as, for instance, that human happiness and human rights are of little account, that all our thoughts ought to be turned away from the things of this world, etc.,—unless such deduction has the independent sanction of good sense.

15

Logical Machines

November 1887 ***The American Journal of Psychology***

In the "Voyage to Laputa" there is a description of a machine for evolving science automatically. "By this contrivance, the most ignorant person, at a reasonable charge, and with little bodily labor, might write books in philosophy, poetry, politics, laws, mathematics, and theology, without the least assistance from genius or study." The intention is to ridicule the *Organon* of Aristotle and the *Organon* of Bacon, by showing the absurdity of supposing that any "instrument" can do the work of the mind. Yet the logical machines of Jevons and Marquand are mills into which the premises are fed and which turn out the conclusions by the revolution of a crank. The numerous mathematical engines that have been found practically useful, from Webb's adder up to Babbage's analytical engine (which was designed though never constructed), are also machines that perform reasoning of no simple kind. Precisely how much of the business of thinking a machine could possibly be made to perform, and what part of it must be left for the living mind, is a question not without conceivable practical importance; the study of it can at any rate not fail to throw needed light on the nature of the reasoning process. Though the instruments of Jevons and of Marquand were designed chiefly to illustrate more elementary points, their utility lies mainly, as it seems to me, in the evidence they afford concerning this problem.

The machine of Jevons receives the premises in the form of logical equations, or identities. Only a limited number of different letters can enter into these equations—indeed, any attempt to extend the machine beyond four letters would complicate it intolerably. The machine has a keyboard, with two keys for the affirmative and the negative form of each letter to be used for the first side of the equation, and two others for the second side of the equation, making four times as many keys as letters. There is also a key for the sign of logical addition or aggregation for each side of the equation, a key for the sign of equality, and two full stop keys, the function of which need not here be explained.[1] The keys are touched successively, in the order in which the letters and signs occur in the equation. It is a curious anomaly, by the way, that an equation such as A = B, which in the system of the transitive copula would appear as two propositions, as All A is B and All B is A, must not be entered as a single equation. But although the premises outwardly appear to be put into the machine in equations, the conclusion presents no such appearance, but is given in the form adopted by Mr. Mitchell in his remarkable paper on the algebra of logic. That is to say, the conclusion appears as a description of the universe of possible objects. In fact, all that is exhibited at the end is a list of all the possible products of the four letters. For example, if we enter the two premises All D is C, or D = CD, and All C is B, or C = BC, we get the conclusion in the following shape, where letters in the same vertical column are supposed to be logically multiplied, while the different columns are added or aggregated:

A	A	A	A	a	a	a	a
B	B	B	b	B	B	B	b
C	C	c	c	C	C	c	c
D	d	d	d	D	d	d	d.

The capital letters are affirmatives, the small letters negatives. It will be found that every column containing D contains B, so that we have the conclusion that All D is B, but to make this out by the study of the columns exhibited seems to be much more difficult than to draw the syllogistic conclusion without the aid of the machine.

Mr. Marquand's machine is a vastly more clear-headed contrivance than that of Jevons. The nature of the problem has been grasped in a more masterly manner, and the directest possible means are chosen for the solution of it. In the machines actually constructed only four letters have been used, though there would have been no inconvenience in embracing six. Instead of using the cumbrous equations of Jevons, Mr. Marquand uses Professor Mitchell's method

1. *Philosophical Transactions* for 1870.

throughout.[2] There are virtually no keys except the eight for the letters and their negatives, for two keys used in the process of erasing, etc., should not count. Any number of keys may be put down together, in which case the corresponding letters are added, or they may be put down successively, in which case the corresponding combinations are multiplied. There is a sort of diagram face, showing the combinations or logical products as in Jevons's machine, but with the very important difference that the two dimensions of the plane are taken advantage of to arrange the combinations in such a way that the substance of the result is instantly seen. To work a simple syllogism, two pressures of the keys only are necessary, two keys being pressed each time. A cord has also to be pulled each time so as to actualize the statement which the pressure of the keys only formulates. This is good logic: philosophers are too apt to forget this cord to be pulled,

2. It would be equally true to say that the machine is based upon Mrs. Franklin's system. The face of the machine always shows every possible combination; putting down the keys and pulling the cord only alters the appearance of some of them. For example, the following figure represents, diagrammatically, the face of such a machine with certain combinations modified:

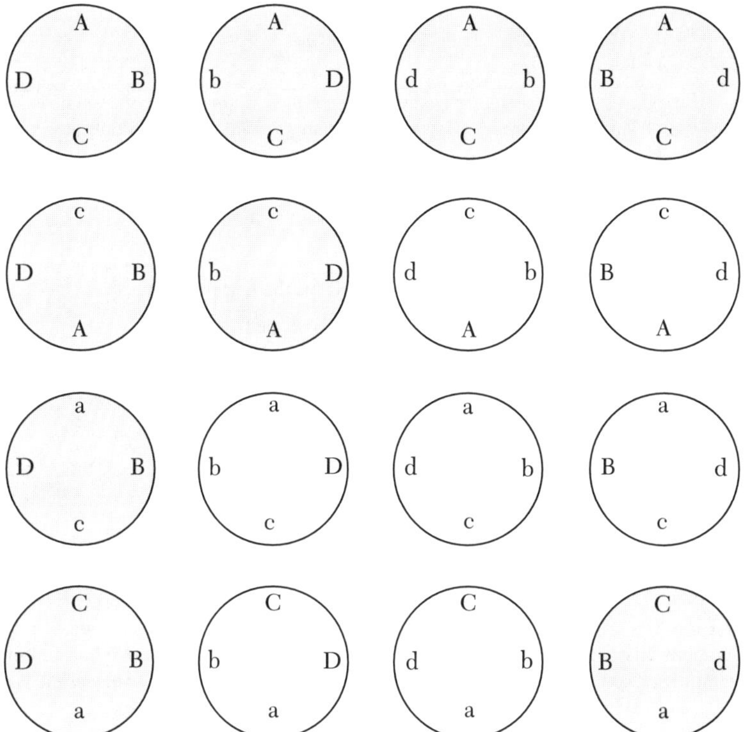

this element of brute force in existence, and thus to regard the *solvet ambulando* as illogical. To work the syllogism with Mr. Jevons's machine requires ten successive movements, owing to the relatively clumsy manner in which the problem has been conceived.

One peculiarity of both these machines is that while they perform the inference from (A + B)C to AC + BC, they will not perform the converse inference from AC + BC to (A + B)C. This is curious, because the inference they refuse to perform seems to be merely syllogistic, while the one they do perform, and in fact continually insist on performing, whether it is wanted or not, is dilemmatic, and therefore essentially more complicated. But in point of fact neither of the machines really gives the conclusion of a pair of syllogistic premises; it merely presents a list of all the possible species in the universe, and

---

This face may be interpreted in several different ways. First, as showing in the shaded portions—

$$(A+B+C+D)(A+b+C+D)(A+b+C+d)(A+B+C+d)$$
$$(A+B+c+D)\ (A+b+c+D)$$
$$(a+B+c+D)$$
$$(a+B+C+D) \qquad\qquad (a+B+C+d),$$

which is the same as what is seen on the unshaded portions if we regard the small letters as affirmative and the capitals as negative, and interchange addition and multiplication, that is, as—

$$aBCD + abCD$$
$$+ABCd + ABCD + AbCD$$
$$+ABcd + ABcD.$$

Or, looking at the unshaded portion, we may regard it as the negative of the above, or—

$$(A+b+c+d)\ (A+B+c+d)$$
$$(a+b+c+D)\ (a+b+c+d)\ (a+B+c+d)$$
$$(a+b+C+D)(a+b+C+d),$$

or, what is the same thing, as—

$$abcd + aBcd + aBcD + abcD$$
$$+abCd + aBCd$$
$$+AbCd$$
$$+Abcd \qquad\qquad + AbcD.$$

There are two other obvious interpretations. We see, then, that the machine always shows two states of the universe, one the negative of the other, and each in two conjugate forms of development. In one interpretation simultaneously impressed terms are multiplied and successively impressed combinations added, and in the other interpretation the reverse is the case.

leaves us to pick out the syllogistic conclusions for ourselves. Thus, with Marquand's machine, we enter the premise All A is B in the form a + B, and the premise All B is C in the form b + C; but instead of finding the conclusion in the form a + C, it appears as—

$$\begin{aligned} &ABCD + ABCd \\ &+ aBCD + aBCd + abCd + abCD \\ &\qquad + abcd + abcD. \end{aligned}$$

As we only want a description of A, we multiply by that letter, and so reduce the conclusion to ABCD + ABCd, but there is no elimination of the B nor of the D. We do not even get the full conclusion in the form ab + BC, although it is one of the advantages of Marquand's machine that it does give the conclusion, not only in the form just cited, but also, simultaneously, as

$$\begin{aligned} &(a + B + c + d)\ (a + B + c + D) \\ &(a + B + C + d)(a + B + C + D)(a + b + C + D)\ (a + b + C + d) \\ &\qquad (A + b + C + D)(A + b + C + d). \end{aligned}$$

The secret of all reasoning machines is after all very simple. It is that whatever relation among the objects reasoned about is destined to be the hinge of a ratiocination, that same general relation must be capable of being introduced between certain parts of the machine. For example, if we want to make a machine which shall be capable of reasoning in the syllogism

If A then B,
If B then C,
Therefore, if A then C,

we have only to have a connection which can be introduced at will, such that when one event A occurs in the machine, another event B must also occur. This connection being introduced between A and B, and also between B and C, it is necessarily virtually introduced between A and C. This is the same principle which lies at the foundation of every logical algebra; only in the algebra, instead of depending directly on the laws of nature, we establish conventional rules for the relations used. When we perform a reasoning in our unaided minds we do substantially the same thing, that is to say, we construct an image in our fancy under certain general conditions, and observe the result. In this point of view, too, every machine is a reasoning machine, in so much as there are certain relations between its parts, which relations involve other relations that were not expressly intended. A piece of apparatus for performing a physical or chemical experiment is also a reasoning machine, with this difference, that it does not depend on the laws of the human mind, but on the objective reason embodied in the laws of nature. Accordingly, it is no figure of speech to say that the alembics and cucurbits of the chemist are instruments of thought, or logical machines.

Every reasoning machine, that is to say, every machine, has two inherent impotencies. In the first place, it is destitute of all originality, of all initiative. It cannot find its own problems; it cannot feed itself. It cannot direct itself between different possible procedures. For example, the simplest proposition of projective geometry, about the ten straight lines in a plane, is proved by von Staudt from a few premises and by reasoning of extreme simplicity, but so complicated is the mode of compounding these premises and forms of inference, that there are no less than 70 or 80 steps in the demonstration. How could we make a machine which would automatically thread its way through such a labyrinth as that? And even if we did succeed in doing so, it would still remain true that the machine would be utterly devoid of original initiative, and would only do the special kind of thing it had been calculated to do. This, however, is no defect in a machine; we do not want it to do its own business, but ours. The difficulty with the balloon, for instance, is that it has too much initiative, that it is not mechanical enough. We no more want an original machine, than a house-builder would want an original journeyman, or an American board of college trustees would hire an original professor. If, however, we will not surrender to the machine, the whole business of initiative is still thrown upon the mind; and this is the principal labor.

In the second place, the capacity of a machine has absolute limitations; it has been contrived to do a certain thing, and it can do nothing else. For instance, the logical machines that have thus far been devised can deal with but a limited number of different letters. The unaided mind is also limited in this as in other respects; but the mind working with a pencil and plenty of paper has no such limitation. It presses on and on, and whatever limits can be assigned to its capacity today, may be over-stepped tomorrow. This is what makes algebra the best of all instruments of thought; nothing is too complicated for it. And this great power it owes, above all, to one kind of symbol, the importance of which is frequently entirely overlooked—I mean the parenthesis. We can, of course, dispense with parentheses as such. Instead of $(a+b)c = d$, we can write $a+b = t$ and $tc = d$. The letter t is here a transmogrified parenthesis. We see that the power of adding proposition to proposition is in some sort equivalent to the use of a parenthesis.

Mr. Marquand's machines, even with only four letters, facilitate the treatment of problems in more letters, while still leaving considerable for the mind to do unaided. It is very desirable a machine on the same principle should be constructed with six letters. It would be a little more elegant, perhaps, instead of two keys to each letter, to have a handle which should stand up when the letter was not used, and be turned to the right or left, according as the letter was to be used, positively or negatively. An obvious extension of the principle of the machine would also render it possible to perform elimination. Thus, if six letters, A, B, C, D, E, F, were used, there could be an additional face which should simply take no notice of F, a third which should take no notice of F or E, a fourth which should take no notice of F, E or D; and these would suffice. With such a machine to represent AB + CD, we should proceed as follows: Put down handle E to the left. (The left hand would naturally signify the negative.) Leaving it down, put down handle A to the right and then bring it back after pulling the cord. Put down handle B to the right and pull the cord, and then restore handles B and E to the vertical. Next, put down handle F to the left and successively put down the handles C and D to the right, as before. After restoring these to the vertical, put down handles E and F to the right, and pull the cord. Then we should see on the third face

(A + B + C + D)(A + b + C + D)(A + b + C + d)(A + B + C + d)
(A + B + c + D) (A + b + c + D)
(a + B + c + D)
(a + B + C + D) (a + B + C + d)

or, what comes to the same thing,

$$\begin{array}{c} aBCD + abCD \\ ABCd + ABCD + AbCD \\ ABcd + ABcD \end{array}$$

I do not think there would be any great difficulty in constructing a machine which should work the logic of relations with a large number of terms. But owing to the great variety of ways in which the same premises can be combined to produce different conclusions in that branch of logic, the machine, in its first state of development, would be no more mechanical than a hand-loom for weaving in many colors with many shuttles. The study of how to pass from such a machine as that to one corresponding to a Jacquard loom, would be likely to do very much for the improvement of logic.

The Peirce–Gurney Dispute
over
Phantasms of the Living

16

Criticism on *Phantasms of the Living*: An Examination of an Argument of Messrs. Gurney, Myers, and Podmore

December 1887 ***Proceedings of the American Society for Psychical Research***

The most imposing of the arguments of Messrs. Gurney, Myers, and Podmore, in favor of spontaneous telepathy, popularly called ghosts, as presented in their *Phantasms of the Living* is this. Only one person in three thousand each year has a visual hallucination. Hence it is easy to calculate from the annual death-rate that in a population of fifty millions there would be each only one visual hallucination fortuitously coinciding within twelve hours, before or after, with the death of the person represented. But these gentlemen, having addressed, as they estimate, a public of only 300,000 persons, claim to have found thirty-one indubitable cases of this kind of coincidence within twelve years. From this, they cipher out some very enormous odds in favor of the hypothesis of ghosts. I shall not cite these numbers, which captivate the ignorant, but which repel thinking men, who know well that no human certitude reaches such figures as trillions, or even billions to one.

But every one of their thirty-one coincidences sins against one or more of eighteen different conditions to which such an argument must conform to be valid. This I proceed to show.

1st. Every case should have occurred between January 1st, 1874, and December 31st, 1885, for the calculation of the probabilities depends upon this supposition. Now Case 199 occurred in 1873 and Case 355 occurred in 1854.

2nd. The percipient should in each case have been drawn from their public, which they estimate at 300,000 persons who are supposed to have seen the advertisement. But no person could have seen the advertisement who was dead at the time of its publication; and this was the state of the percipients in Cases 170, 214, 238, and 695.

3rd. According to their calculations, there ought not to have been among their 300,000 persons any having had two hallucinations fortuitously. Such cases must, if their calculations are correct, be in some way abnormal, and ought to be thrown out. Now the percipient of Case 184 seems to have hallucinations nearly every day. The percipient of Case 175 has had them frequently without any coincidence. In Cases 173 and 298 the percipients had had other hallucinations without significance.

4th. The general frequency of hallucinations, upon which the whole argument depends, was ascertained by asking of certain persons whether or not they had had any visual hallucinations, within the last twelve years, *"while in good health, free from anxiety, and wide awake."* It is, therefore, an indispensible requisite to the validity of the argument from probabilities, that no account should be taken of coincidences where the percipient was not in good health. This happened in Cases 28, 174, 201, 202, 236, and 702.

5th. For the same reason, cases should be excluded where the percipient was not clearly free from anxiety. But they certainly were anxious in Cases 27, 28, 172, 174, 184, 231, and 240; and were probably so in Cases 182, 195, and 695.

6th. For the same reason, all cases should be excluded where the percipient would not certainly have been confident of having been *wide* awake, even if no coincidence had occurred. Now the percipient of Case 175 says, "I cannot yet answer to my satisfaction whether I was awake or asleep." One of the witnesses to Case 195 calls it a "vivid dream." In Case 702, the percipient is doubtful whether it was anything more than a dream. It is difficult to admit any case where the percipient was in bed, which happened in Nos. 26, 170, 172, 173, 174, 182, 184, 199, and 697. This objection applies with increased force to cases where the percipient was taking an afternoon nap, which happened in Nos. 28 and 201.

7th. All cases should be excluded in which the person who died was not clearly recognized in the apparition. This applies with great force to No. 170, where the apparition was distinctly recognized as the percipient's own mother, who did not die, though a person who resembled her did. It also applies to Case 201, where the percipient says she "could not say who it was." Also, to Case 236, where the percipient's original statement was that she saw "a dark figure"; although after having been shown the testimony of a second witness, who testifies that it "resembled her [the percipient's] brother," she assents to this statement. In Case 249 the supposed ghost only showed his hat and the top of his head. In Case 697, the percipient does not seem to have recognized the apparition until after the news of the death had reached her.

8th. It is absolutely essential to the force of the argument, that the death should have occurred within twelve hours before or after the time of the apparition; and it is not sufficient that the evidence should satisfy a mind that already admits the existence of ghosts, but the proof must be strong enough to establish the fact, even if we assume that it is due only to hazard. This is a point which the authors totally fail to appreciate. They have admitted among their thirty-one cases no less than thirteen which might well enough be set down as falling probably within the twelve-hour limit, *once we have admitted any special antecedent likelihood of such an occurrence;* but which beg the question entirely, when, the evidence of the coincidence being but slight, they are used to prove the existence of such a likelihood. In Case 26, for example, on the morning after the apparition, the percipient says he searched the newspapers,—and that day was Saturday. His words are, "The next day, I mentioned to some of my friends how strange it was. So thoroughly convinced was I, that I searched the local papers that day, Saturday." The authors interpret this as meaning that he told his friends one day, and searched the papers the day after that, which is directly contrary to his statement, and unlikely in itself. Their only warrant for this is, that he says the vision occurred on Friday at 2 A.M. But it is certainly more natural to suppose that he inadvertently used this expression meaning the night of Friday at 2 A.M. This is the *more* likely of the two suppositions; but the case ought not to be included, unless it can be shown beyond all reasonable doubt, and irrespective of considerations drawn from the time of the death, that the vision occurred on the night of Thursday. In Case 170, the death was not heard of for months. "Time passed, and all was forgotten." Under these circumstances, as no written note was taken of the time of the apparition, the coincidence is plainly doubtful. I shall discuss Cases 182 and 197, which violate this rule, under another head. In Cases 195, 201, 202, 214, 231, 237, and 355, the date is wholly uncertain. In Case 199, the vision occurred, if at all, on Saturday; the death on Wednesday. In Case 702, the date given for the apparition differs from that of the death by one day; but this is only a blunder, for it is admitted that the date was changed, after ascertaining the day of death, by four days.

9th. Cases ought to be excluded in which it is possible that a real person was seen. In Case 202, the percipient, who "had been ordered by the doctor to take absolute rest, and not read at all, and do no work whatever," and who is excessively near-sighted, when she was out driving, in the neighborhood of London, met a carriage, containing, as she thought, the person who died (although this person's head was turned away) together with another who did not die. It surely seems a little unnecessary to suppose that this was anything more than a case of mistaken identity. In Case 249, a man, looking out of his window on Christmas day, saw, on the other side of a brick wall, the hat and the top of the head of what he took to be one of his neighbors coming to see him. He turned round to remark upon it to the persons in the room; and his first surprise came when there was no knock at the door (we may assume after the lapse of more than a minute). Then, looking out of the window, he did not see anything at all. It appears quite unnecessary to suppose any hallucination here, unless possibly some slight aberration of the senses connected with the festivities of the season. I should suggest, as possible, that some boy had stolen the old man's hat, and was perpetrating some Christmas joke, which he was ashamed to confess when it turned out that the person impersonated was at that moment dying. When so simple a hypothesis is admissible, it cannot be said that the appearance of something that was not there has been positively established. There are several other cases which might easily be explained by supposing that a real person was seen.

10th. Every case should be excluded which can be explained on the supposition of trickery. In Case 350, one evening three maidservants in the kitchen saw a face outside the window. They could see all around it, so that there was no body attached to it; and while they were looking at it, it turned slowly through a considerable angle, about a vertical axis. Now, the lady of the house is so exceedingly superstitious that she gravely testifies that her dog howls whenever there is a death in the village; and it is more than likely that the maids take after the mistress in this respect. The dog was howling at the moment that the face appeared,—so that this circumstance may have helped them to identify the face with that of a woman who was at that moment expiring under the surgeon's knife, in an operation for cancer. Although the mistress thinks that they were unaware of the operation, yet, as the cook shortly afterward married the widower, it is not impossible that the servants were better informed than the mistress thought, and that they were, in fact, talking about the woman and her danger (and perhaps even dared to hint at another wedding) when they were confounded by this dreadful sight. One of the three servants testifies that it looked like the "face of a skeleton"; while the other two identify it with that of the woman who died. Meantime, it appears that there were certain young men who had a way of tapping at that window in the evening, and looking in and smiling at the girls, and who had not been treated with quite the politeness to which they probably thought themselves entitled. What, then, can possibly be more natural, than to suppose that these young men had contrived, in some way, to let down a skull by a string from above, perhaps from the roof, to frighten the girls and punish them for their rudeness? Clearly, this cannot be admitted as a proved case of seeing something that was not there.

11th. No case should be admitted upon the unsupported and unverified statement of a superstitious, ignorant, and credulous person. And a common sailor or skipper may be assumed to be such a person. This throws out Cases 300 and 355.

12th. Cases should be excluded in which there is any room to suspect that the percipient was intoxicated. This applies to Nos. 29 and 249; and no doubt to others.

13th. Cases should be excluded which can possibly be explained by the delirium of fever. In Case 214, the percipient first told of the apparition after four months of severe illness, with constant delirium or unconsciousness. It is not at all unlikely that the whole story is the product of a delirious imagination.

14th. No case should be admitted which can be attributed to the effect of imagination. In Case 195, the percipient herself is inclined so to explain her vision.

15th. All cases ought to be excluded in which the percipient did not tell of having seen the vision until after the news of the death had been received. Otherwise, all sorts of exaggerations would creep in. There might even be cases of downright lying, besides cases in which the well-known sensation of having undergone a present experience on some previous occasion might have given rise to the idea of an apparition which was really not experienced. This would be a rare case, but we are dealing with rare cases. This objection applies to Cases 172, 173, 174, 184, and 214.

16th. No case can be admitted which rests largely on the testimony of a loose or inaccurate witness. Inaccuracies of more or less importance can be detected in Cases 27, 170, 182, 197, and 199. For example, in Case 182, a young lady on shipboard, going from London to the Cape of Good Hope, saw one night, a good while after the lights were out, an apparition of a young girl, a friend or acquaintance of hers who, as she knew, was out of health, and who had the consumption. She is positive that this vision took place at half past ten; and, as no bell is rung at that time, this positive precision is already suspicious. She also testifies positively that she mentioned the occurrence the next morning to four persons, who all severally took written notes of it; but the only two of these persons who can be reached now profess to know nothing whatever of the matter. She gives May 4th as the date of the vision, but the death occurred on May 2nd. She says, however, that she is sure she wrote to her father from the Cape, giving the date of the vision, before she heard of the death. Her father, on the other hand, is certain he wrote to his daughter the news of the death by the very next mail after it occurred. Now, since taking this testimony, the letter which she wrote to her father has been found by him. The whole passage about the apparition is not given, as it should be; but it is stated that the letter gives the date of May 4th. Now the date of the letter is June 5th; and it only takes three weeks or less for news to go from London to the Cape of Good Hope, so that she must have already heard of the death, if her father's statement is accurate. But why is the passage of this letter withheld?

In Case 197, the percipient is a lady. She was at Interlaken at the time of the vision, and the death took place in Colorado. She testifies positively that written notes were taken at the time of the occurrence, both by herself and another; but she is unable now to give the date, and the other witness has not been called upon. Now Messrs. Gurney, Myers, and Podmore request us to accept this as a positively proved case of coincidence, because this one witness avers, with all the solemnity the matter calls for, that, when the news of the death did arrive, it was found to be absolutely simultaneous with the vision, after making the necessary allowance for difference of longitude. But the lady remembers the time of day at which the vision occurred, namely, it was before breakfast when she was lying on her bed. The time of day of the death is also known; and the best supposition that can be made with regard to the date of the vision will make it eight hours from the time of death. We are asked, in the face of this demonstrated inaccuracy, to accept a coincidence of date as beyond question, because this witness testifies that it was a coincidence exact to the minute.

17th. No case can be admitted where there is only a meagre story told in outline, and we are not furnished with any means of judging of the reliability of the witnesses, or where questions might have been asked which would have brought the matter to a test, and have not been asked. Thus, in Case 231 the date is quite doubtful; but it could have been verified by means of the letter which the percipient wrote that day to a newspaper. In Case 236, whatever the story possesses is due to the statements of a second witness, who does not seem to have been cross-examined at all. In Cases 237, 240, 298, 300, 355, 695, and an unnumbered case, the story is so excessively meagre as to be worthless.

18th. After all, the reader, who cannot cross-examine the witnesses, and search out new testimony, must necessarily rely upon Messrs. Gurney, Myers, and Podmore having on the whole performed this task well; and we cannot accept any case at all at their hands, unless, as far as we can see, they have proved themselves cautious men, shrewd observers, and severe logicians.

Although there is not a single one of the thirty-one cases considered which can be accepted for the purpose of the argument, yet some of them may be genuine for all that. It can only be guess-work to say how many; but in my opinion not more than two or three.

Let us now glance at the other numerical data used in the argument. The ratio of frequency of hallucinations without coincidences has been ascertained by inquiries addressed to a large number of persons, going back for twelve years. The authors have thus assumed that a hallucination with coincidence of the death of the person represented is no more likely to be remembered for a period of twelve years than one which is unaccompanied by such a coincidence. Yet there are numerous cases in their book in which, the death not having been heard of, the vision had been totally forgotten after the lapse of a few months, and was only brought to mind again by the news of the death. I think it would be fair to assume that, in considering so long a period as twelve years, a coincidental apparition would be four times as likely to be remembered as one without coincidence. I also strongly dissent from the authors' estimate that their coincidences have been drawn from a population of only 300,000. I should reckon the matter, for my part, in this way: every case of an apparition simultaneous with the death of the person represented, or nearly so, becomes known to a circle of 200 to 300 persons, on the average. If any one of this circle of persons, some of whom have had an interest in apparitions excited by the story, learn and are interested in the advertisement of Messrs. Gurney, Myers, and Podmore, these gentlemen would learn of the case. Now, I suppose that the advertisement, being of a very peculiar and sensational character, interests one person for every hundred copies of the newspaper printed. On this assumption, since a million and a half is given as the circulation of the newspapers, the instances obtained would really have been drawn from a population of three to four millions. Adopting these figures, they ought to have heard, on the doctrine of chances, of three or four purely fortuitous cases of visual hallucination with coincidence of death. In view of the utter uncertainty of all the data, it would be very rash to draw any conclusion at all. But the evidence so far as it goes, seems to be rather unfavorable to the telepathic character of the phenomena. The argument might, certainly, have been constructed more skillfully; but I do not think that there is much prospect of establishing any scientific fact on the basis of such a collection as that of the *Phantasms of the Living*.

17

Remarks on Professor Peirce's Paper

December 1887 ***Proceedings of the American Society for Psychical Research***

BY EDMUND GURNEY

The foregoing review has been to me a source of genuine pleasure and profit; not so much in respect of the special points which the writer raises,—though my pleasure is not diminished by the sense that on most of these his objections can be fairly met,—as on account of the business-like and thorough spirit in which he has gone to work. Criticism, as my colleagues and I should allow, and even insist, is what the exponents of every new doctrine must expect; and in the case of a doctrine so new to science as telepathy, the criticism cannot be too searching. But, on this subject, searching criticism is as rare as loose and hasty comment is the reverse. The world is roughly divided into two parties,—those who will not so much as look seriously at any of the alleged facts, and those who swallow them all wholesale. Thus the evidence is either wholly neglected, or is admitted without due warrant, and discredited by being mixed up with all sorts of baseless rumors and uncritical fancies. One person recognizes no difference between the strongest case that can be adduced and some anonymous "ghost-story," and would accept telepathy or any other marvel on the score of a few third-hand reports or vague personal experiences. Another turns away from the facts in whatever strength accumulated, on the ground that they are *à priori* impossible or unprovable. Both are equally remote from the rational scepticism which alone is the proper attitude for approaching psychical investigation. Apart from such an attitude of mind, no treatment of the subject, whether constructive or critical, can be of any value; and here Mr. Peirce and I are wholly at one. But, in an inquiry so novel and difficult, it is likely that two persons, even though they both begin as rational sceptics, will develop differences of opinion; and it is at least equally likely that they will both make mistakes. Thus, some of Mr. Peirce's strictures depend (as I shall hope to show) on distinct errors and misconceptions, while others appear to me to be unreasonable and overstrained. On the other hand, he has pointed out some errors on my part; and in so doing, and generally in enabling me to make the present *apologia,* he has done me a valuable service.

Mr. Peirce prefaces his detailed criticisms with a more general remark which cannot be quite passed over. Referring to *Phantasms of the Living,* Chap. XIII, he objects to the "enormous odds ciphered out in favor of the hypothesis of ghosts,"—more correctly, to the enormous improbability that a certain series of coincidences were due to chance alone—as calculated to "captivate the ignorant," but to "repel thinking men, who know that no human certitude reaches such figures as trillions or even billions to one." It is as well to be accurate, even at the risk of repelling "thinking men." But most thinking men, whose thoughts have been directed to the subject of probabilities, will, I imagine, support me in dissenting from Mr. Peirce's view. There are many cases of practically absolute certitude, where the actual degree of certitude can be measured. For instance, if dice turned up sixes a hundred times running, which could any day be made to happen, the mathematical probability that the dice were not both evenly weighted and honestly thrown would reach a figure higher than those which have offended Mr. Peirce.

To proceed now at once to his numbered list of objections.

1st. Case 199. The discovery that this incident occurred as long ago as April, 1873, was only made after the work was printed off. (That it was made so late was partly due to a very rare accident—a misspelling of a name in the Register of Deaths at Somerset House. Much time was wasted in the search there, before it occurred to me to apply to the Coroner.) The date has been rectified in the "Additions and Corrections"; and it was careless of me not to remember, when this was done, that the case had been included in the list in Chap. XIII, so as to have added a warning in reference to that list. But, of course, the limitation of the list to cases occurring in a period of twelve years, starting from Jan. 1, 1874, was purely arbitrary. Had a period of thirteen years, starting from Jan. 1, 1873, been selected instead, the numerical argument would not have suffered appreciably, if at all.

Case 355. The inclusion of this case was a bad blunder, for which I take the fullest blame. My eye was misled by the date in the first line of the account; but that, of course, is no excuse.

2nd. This objection seems to me fallacious. We can scarcely doubt that our number of cases would have been increased had we prosecuted our search during the whole period (1874–85), instead of during the last quarter of it only. Had we done so, I should still have been perfectly justified in representing the size of the group of persons to whom we had had access by the number of them all alive at any one time—say half a million—though the half-million would not have throughout consisted of the same individuals. The reason why this would have been legitimate is that in the calculation the *whole population* is similarly treated. Of course a much larger number of persons are alive during some portion of a period of twelve years than are simultaneously alive on the day of it when the census is taken. And if the group of half a million were increased so as to allow for persons becoming adults during the period, and thus joining the group (so to speak) at one end while others died off it at the other, the size of the whole population would have to be reckoned in a similar way; and the two increases would balance each other in the calculation, which would only be made more complex without being made more correct. Thus any case of percipience within the given period (where the evidence which reaches us is on a par with first-hand (see Vol. I, p. 148)) may be legitimately included, even though the percipient be dead, if it is practically certain that we should equally have obtained it direct from the percipient, had he or she survived. This applies to three of the four cases which Mr. Peirce cites (his number 237, is, I suppose, a mistake for 238). Cases 170 and 695 were obtained through private channels, and Case 238, though our first knowledge of it was due to a published account, would have been at once procured at first-hand from the percipient had we been at work in 1876. The receipt of Case 214, however, was due to a newspaper-appeal of our own, which it is not certain that the deceased percipient would have independently seen and acted on, had it been published during her lifetime; and as, moreover, it is only by straining a definition (as I have pointed out) that this case can be regarded as on a par with first-hand, it would be best to drop it from the list.

3rd. Case 184. Mr. Peirce says that the percipient "seems to have hallucinations nearly every day." He has had only one other hallucination in his life. This occurred many years ago, in his boyhood, and represented a vague, unrecognized figure. But the list is confined to cases where the appearance was recognized; and the only subjective hallucinations which have to be considered *per contra* are those presenting the same characteristic. The other experiences from the same informant, Nos. 21, 38, 56, have, in the first place, been coincidental, and have a fair claim to be considered telepathic; and, in the second place, have not been hallucinations at all. They have conveyed no impression of external reality, but are distinctly described as impressions and "mind's-eye" visions, parallel to those which a good visualizer can summon up at will. Thus Mr. Peirce's objection is doubly out of place.

Case 175. The percipient draws a distinct line between the experience which he here describes and those which he has had without any coincidence. In the latter he "quite believes he was asleep,"—*i.e.*, there is no ground for regarding them as hallucinations at all, in the sense in which I throughout employ the word.

As regards Cases 173 and 298, Mr. Peirce's use of the plural "other hallucinations" is misleading. Each of the two percipients has had *one* other hallucination, and neither of these was of a nature to affect the legitimacy of including their cases in the list. The narrator of Case 173 had once seen an *unrecognized* figure, which seems curiously to have corresponded in aspect with a person who, unknown to her, had recently died in the room in which it appeared; but it has been impossible to obtain corroboratory evidence of this incident. The other hallucination of the narrator of Case 298 was *not visual*.

4th. The percipient in Case 29 was in perfect health. (Query—Is it Case 28 that Mr. Peirce means, where the percipient "had a headache"? If so, does he really consider that such a condition at the end of a day's work amounts to not being "in good health"?)

Case 201. The percipient says, "I had been in ill-health for some years, but at that time was stronger than I ever was in my life, the warm climate suiting me—so well that I felt a strength and enjoyment of life for its own sake, which was a delight to me." Many of us would be glad enough to be "not in good health" on these terms.

Case 202. The percipient had been ordered to rest and do no work. But hers was not a condition which would have prevented me from counting her hallucination *against* my argument, as a purely subjective specimen, had she happened to be included in the census, and had no coincidental event occurred.

Case 214. The percipient's illness *succeeded* the vision.

In Case 174, the percipient, Miss P., was still "far from well," having recently had a distinct attack of illness; and in Case 702, the percipient, Mr. G., was weak but convalescent after fever. My information on the subject of hallucinations does not lead me to suppose that there was anything in Mr. G.'s state especially favorable to an experience of the sort; as to Miss P., I cannot tell. Unless their state *was* so favorable,—indeed, unless visual hallucinations, representing recognized figures, are markedly common in such states—which is certainly, I think, not the fact—the cases remain very striking ones. There would, of course, be some force in Mr. Peirce's objection, if my census-list of *non-coincidental* hallucinations would have been considerably larger than it is but for the condition as to health (or as to anxiety—see his 5th objection). But I have explained (p. 7) that the interrogatories were put in separate parts—questions as to the person's bodily or mental state at the time of the experience being kept separate from the question as to the fact of the experience; and the number of *yeses* struck off the list used in the computation, on the ground of an exceptional bodily or mental state at all comparable to that which existed in a few of the coincidental cases, amounted at most to two or three.

5th. I cannot admit the objection in more than one of the cases referred to, and only partially in that one.

The percipient in Case 702 says, "I had no idea of the lady's being ill, and had neither been anxious about her nor thinking about her."

The percipient in Case 174 was not personally intimate with the gentleman who died; and, though she was "aware that he was in a critical condition," she says, "At the time of his death he had been quite out of my thoughts and mind."

The percipient in Case 182 "had not been thinking about her [the girl who died] at all; she was an acquaintance and neighbor, but not an intimate friend."

The percipient in Case 184, having absolutely no ground for anxiety, was naturally not anxious. This boy was perfectly well when he parted from him, and he had since received excellent accounts of him, including an "assurance of the child's perfect health," within three days of the experience described.

The percipient in Case 28 knew that his friend had had an attack of indigestion, and had been given some medicine for it by a chemist. A medical man "thought he wanted a day or two of rest, but expressed no opinion that anything was serious"; and even this not very appalling professional diagnosis did not come to the percipient's knowledge till afterwards.

The percipient in Case 195 was not expecting the death of a relative who "had been ailing for years," and whose "death occurred rather suddenly." The attitude of mind of young persons towards chronic invalids whom they are not personally tending, and whose death is not held to be imminent, is too habitual and continuous, and not sufficiently exciting or abnormal, to be fairly described as *anxiety,* for the purpose of the present argument.

A similar remark applies in Case 27. The percipient had heard two months before that his friend had a complaint which was likely sooner or later to be fatal, but was "in no immediate apprehension of his death." No more had been heard of him, and the fact that "his name had not been mentioned for weeks" between Mr. R. and his wife is a tolerably conclusive sign that he was not occupying a foremost position in their thoughts. I can scarcely think Mr. Peirce seriously believes that the hallucination here was due to anxiety.[1]

In Case 172, the percipient says that her friend "had been for some time seriously ill, and I was anxious about her, though I did not know that death was near." Here again, though the word "anxious" is used, the anxiety, such as it was, was chronic, not acute; and I certainly should not have felt justified in making such a condition of mind the ground for not reckoning the hallucination, had it happened to fall on the other side of the account, as a non-coincidental instance.

As regards Case 231, I can only quote my own remark,—that it would be pedantic to apply the hypothesis that anxiety may produce purely subjective hallucinations "to cases which occur in the thick of a war, where the idea of death is constant and familiar. In such circumstances, the mental attitude caused by the knowledge that a comrade is in peril seems scarcely parallel to that which similar knowledge might produce among those who are sitting brooding at home. At any rate, if anxiety for the fate of absent comrades be a natural and known source of hallucinations during campaigns, it is odd that, among several hundreds of cases of subjective hallucination, I find no second instance of the phenomenon."

In Case 240, the percipient, Mrs. E., knew the person whose face she saw to be ill, but "did not know he was so near death." They were not on friendly terms at the time, and there was probably no anxiety; but the sick man lived only five miles off, and it is possible that Mrs. E.'s mind reverted to him more frequently than to other absent acquaintances. It might be safer, therefore, to drop this case from the list.

Anxiety is clearly a condition which admits of all degrees, while at the same time it cannot be accurately measured; but all that logic demands is that coincidental cases should be excluded when the anxiety was acute enough to be regarded with any probability as the sufficient cause of the hallucination. A person who has been for some time ill, but whose condition has not been seriously dwelt on, is in fact not a bit more likely to be represented in a friend's hallucination than the friend's most robust acquaintance. Such, at any rate, is the conclusion to which a wide study of subjective hallucinations has led me. And, to be on the safe side, I have included in the purely

1. An objection might possibly be taken to this case which Mr. Peirce has not taken,—the vision was not absolutely externalized in space; the percipient says that it arose "in my mind's eye, I suppose." At the same time, as I have pointed out, "it took on a sort of vividness and objectivity which he believes to have been unexampled" in his life. And this, combined with the fact that the experience (which occurred while he was dressing in the morning) began with a certain conviction that some one was in the room,—a conviction which made him look round,—seems to justify the treatment of it as a hallucination rather than as a mere vivid idea.

subjective group (any increase of which, of course, tells against my argument) "several cases where there was such an amount of anxiety or expectancy on the part of the hallucinated person as would prevent us, if it were present in a *coincidental* case, from including such a case in our telepathic evidence."

6th. Case 175. Mr. Peirce ought to have quoted a few additional words: "I only am sure that as the figure disappeared [N.B., not *after* it disappeared] I was as wide awake as I am now."

Case 195. Surely a second-hand informant's use of the word "dream" cannot weigh against the "while yet fully awake" of the percipient, and her statement that she "sat up to see what it was," and looked round the room to discover if the appearance could be due to some reflection.

Case 702. I cannot understand Mr. Peirce's remark, which contradicts the percipient's emphatic statement. He most expressly distinguishes the dream from the waking experience.

Case 28. The "nap" is an inference of Mr. Peirce's from the fact that the percipient had just leaned back on the couch. The inference is incorrect, and surely ought not to have been put forward as though it was a fact which appeared in the evidence.

Still more inexcusable is the assertion that the percipient in Case 201 was napping. She was reading Kingsley's *Miscellanies*, and she says: "I then [*i.e.*, after the apparition] tested myself as to whether I had been sleeping, seeing that it was 10 minutes since I lay down. I said to myself what I thought I had read, began my chapter again, and in 10 minutes had reached the same point."

In saying that "it is difficult to admit any case where the percipient was in bed," Mr. Peirce has apparently not observed that similar non-coincidental cases, where the hallucinated person was in bed, but awake, have been reckoned on the other side of the account. (See Vol. II, p. 12, second note.) It is not less legitimate, and decidedly more instructive, to admit such cases on both sides than to reject them on both sides. It is worth adding—what Mr. Peirce has not perceived—that for purposes of comparison with the census-cases, the question is not whether people were awake, but whether they *believed* they were awake.

7th. Case 170. I have myself drawn attention to the peculiarity of this experience, as regards recognition. The case, however, is one which I am inclined to drop from the list, for a reason which will appear later.

Case 201. Mr. Peirce has misquoted the account. He makes the percipient say, "I could not say who it was." Her words are, "I knew the face quite well, but could not say whose it was, but the suit of clothes impressed me strongly as being exactly like one which my husband had given to a servant named Ramsay the previous year." She suggests what seems a very reasonable explanation of the fact that the face, though familiar, did not at once suggest its owner.

Case 236. I cannot think on what Mr. Peirce founds his assertion—which is contrary to the fact—that the percipient had been shown the testimony of a second witness. She states clearly that the apparition reminded her of her brother; and this is independently confirmed by another person to whom she described her experience immediately after it occurred.

Case 249. The important point is surely not how much of a figure is seen, but whether it is unmistakably recognized.

Case 697. Mr. Peirce's remark is again contrary to the facts. The percipient had *not* heard of Z.'s death when she announced that it was his face that she had seen. Most readers would, I think, infer this from the printed account, which I had not perceived to be ambiguous.

8th. Case 26. I am obliged to differ from Mr. Peirce in respect both of what he thinks unlikely, and of what he thinks likely. He thinks it unlikely that the percipient should have told his friends of his experience on one day, Friday, and have searched the local paper on the next day, Saturday. But he did both things on the earliest opportunity, the local paper not being published till Saturday. Mr. Peirce thinks it likely, on the other hand, that when he said "About 2 o'clock on the morning of October 21," which was a Friday, he meant "the night of Friday at 2 A.M.," *i.e.*, 2 o'clock on the morning of Saturday. Now, had he made the statement which Mr. Peirce incorrectly attributes to him, "The vision occurred on Friday, at 2 A.M.," there might be some ground for this view; for "Friday at 2 A.M." is a phrase which one could imagine to be laxly used for 2 A.M. on the night of Friday-Saturday. But the use of the precise phrase "on the morning of," which Mr. Peirce suppresses, and the giving of the day of the *month*, not of the *week*, surely makes a very distinct difference. On what ground can it be held that a person is likely to say "2 o'clock on the morning of October 21," when he means "2 o'clock on the morning of October 22"?

Case 170. I agree that the degree of exactitude in the coincidence is here doubtful, and I would drop the case from the list in consequence.

Case 182. I do not think that there is much doubt here, as the date of the percipient's experience was particularly remarked at the time, and might well be remembered for a month.

Case 197. I have myself pointed out that it is possible that the limit was exceeded by some hours. But two or three such cases may, I think, fairly be included in the estimate, considering what the object and upshot of the estimate is. The reader may of course be trusted to perceive that had the arbitrary limit been fixed at twenty-four hours instead of twelve, the overwhelming character of the odds against chance would remain. The precise figures would differ, according as a limit of six, twelve, eighteen, or twenty-four hours was selected; but considering that any selection, with the calculation based on it, would lead us to the same conclusion, I see nothing misleading in the inclusion of a case where the interval may have exceeded the actually selected lower limit, provided that it is equally likely *not* to have done so, and provided due warning is given. These remarks apply equally to Cases 201 and 231.

Case 195. It ought to have been stated that the percipient returned home almost immediately after—she and her mother think the very day after—the death, thereby missing a letter which was sent to her, and finding her grandmother dead. She would thus only have to carry her memory back a day or two to identify the date of her vision with that of the death.

Case 202. The percipient distinctly states that she saw the announcement of the death "two or three days" after her experience; to which, therefore, there is again a very high probability that she assigned the right date.

A similar remark applies to Case 237, where the percipient heard of the death "a day or so after" her experience. The interval certainly cannot have been much longer, as she saw her dead friend before the funeral.

In Case 214 we are told that the percipient "noted the day and the hour"; but the testimony to this effect is second-hand, and there was no written note, so that here there is reasonable ground for doubt as to the closeness of the coincidence. The case has been already dropped from the list for another reason; as also has Case 355, where, however, the coincidence, on the evidence, was extremely close.

Case 199. Mr. Peirce says that "the vision occurred, if at all, on a Saturday; the death on a Wednesday." This seems unwarranted. The narrator thought that *both* the vision and the death had been on a Saturday, but he recollects and says nothing which independently marks the day of the week of the vision. Why is it to be assumed that his memory is right as to the quite uninteresting and little noticeable point of the day of the week, and wrong as to the extremely interesting and noticeable point that the day of the two events was the same? The fact remains, however, that he has made one definite mistake; and the probability that the closeness of the coincidence has been exaggerated in memory seems here sufficiently appreciable to condemn the case for the purpose of this particular list—even had not its retention been made impossible by its having occurred before 1874, as already stated.

Case 702. Mr. Peirce says, "The date given for the apparition differs from that of the death by one day." This is contrary to the fact. The apparition is stated to have taken place on June 11, the day of the death; and as the death occurred in England at 5:20 A.M., and the apparition in Jamaica at a few minutes past 12 A.M., the coincidence of hour would be extraordinarily close if the coincidence of day is correctly remembered. Mr. Peirce's next sentence conveys a totally false impression. In conversation with me, Mr. G. said that he fancied the date of the two events had been June 15, but that he could not be sure of this till he referred to the letter. What he was sure of was the *identity* of the two dates, which, according to his account, was noted both by his friend and himself with special care. Mr. Peirce's way of putting it would imply that there was some independent reason—apart from Mr. G.'s idea that the 15th was the date of the *coincidence*—for believing that the 15th was the day of the *apparition*. But this is not the case; and surely it is obvious that correctness of memory as to a very striking coincidence does not necessarily involve infallibility as to the perfectly insignificant point on what particular day of the month the coincidence fell.

9th. Case 202. "The percipient, who is excessively near-sighted,"—this is Mr. Peirce's version of the sentence, "She is short-sighted, but wears suitable glasses, and was wearing them on this occasion." "This person's head was turned away,"—this is his version of "I saw only the three-quarter face." He has omitted to notice the improbability, specially pointed out in the account, that a lady of flesh and blood should be wearing a seal-skin jacket in August, and also the fact that the bonnet was recognized; nor does he seem to have remarked the importance of the recognition of the child, which tells strongly against the hypothesis of mistaken identity.

Case 249 (I presume that this is the case meant, though the number given is 201). Most readers of the whole case will, I think, agree with me that, if the facts are correctly stated, mistaken identity is a highly improbable explanation. And I cannot think that it is much helped by the hypothesis of the facetious and then conscience-stricken boy. If that hypothesis be adopted, however, I would venture to suggest the further feature of *stilts,* both as adding to the humor of the "Christmas joke," and as probably necessary in order to enable the boy's head (which he would naturally have practised before a mirror in the method of Mr. X's "peculiar droop") to be visible above the wall.

10th. Case 350. One of Mr. Peirce's suppositions contradicts what is plainly stated in the account—that it was not known that the woman was dying, or in any way near death. She was a chronic invalid. I cannot guess how Mr. Peirce knows that she had cancer, which is nowhere mentioned. The hypothesis of the skull is quite inconsistent with M. J. F.'s and Mrs. R.'s evidence. I may add that "looking in and smiling at the girls" is rather a free version of "trying to look in," which is the expression used in the account.

11th. Case 355 has been already excluded on the ground of the date; but Captain A. impressed our friend and helper, the Rev. J. A. Macdonald, as a reliable witness; and personal knowledge, though not an infallible guide in such matters, is, at any rate, a safer one than such a sweeping presumption as Mr. Peirce enunciates. As to Case 300, I can well imagine a difference of opinion. But, again, the witness appeared to be honest and truthful to a clear-headed cross-examiner, who had begun by disbelieving the story.

12th. By "any room to suspect" I suppose that Mr. Peirce means any appreciable grounds for suspecting. I should be interested to know what his own grounds are. As regards Case 29, would he supplement his assumption that all sea-captains are ignorant and superstitious by the still more robust hypothesis that all gardeners get drunk? The hypothesis, however, whether general or particular, would not at all affect the case, if the percipient's wife is correct in saying that he mentioned the dying lady, as the person whom he had seen, immediately on his return home; *i.e.,* before the news of her death had arrived. But then, perhaps, all gardeners' wives are liars,—a particular hereditary taint, derived from our first parents, may cling to this walk in life. I had better, therefore, quote the words of the Rev. C. F. Forster, vicar of the parish, in a letter written to me on August 18, 1887: "I think the hypothesis that B. was intoxicated is quite untenable. Mine is only a small parish, and I should be certain to know of it if a man was inclined that way. I never heard the slightest suspicion of it. On the contrary, I should have said that, whatever faults he had, he was a thoroughly sober man. Added to this you ought to know that he had come three miles on his bicycle before entering the churchyard; and I should have thought this almost impossible if a man was so intoxicated as this account would make out. Again, we have to account for the coincidence that this appearance to him (drunk or sober) occurred at the time of Mrs. de F.'s decease."

As regards Case 201, though quite in the dark as to Mr. Peirce's principle of selection, I cannot quite believe that he would pitch on this particular informant in connection with this particular suspicion. If he has really done so, I shall not insult a lady who is my esteemed friend by making a syllable of reply. But I am fain to hope that by No. 201 he again means No. 249, in speaking of which in another place he has mentioned " the festivities of the season" as a possible element in the case. Not that the idea would be any less absurd in connection with this percipient. Even on Christmas-day, men of business in England are not usually intoxicated at 4 o'clock in the afternoon; and the suspicion seems specially extravagant in the case of an elderly and respected member of the Society of Friends—"a typical Quaker," as Mr. Podmore describes him in a letter which lies before me. Is it likely, moreover, that a man in his position, if he had really been the worse for liquor, would have cared to revive the recollection of the fact in his friends' minds, by calling them to bear witness to the occurrence of a hallucination which took place while he was in that state?

Mr. Peirce seems to have taken a rather unfair advantage of the fact that, though much time has been spent in forming a judgment as to witnesses' characters by personal interviews, and often by prolonged correspondence, I have expressly avoided giving the results in the shape of definite testimonials.

13th. Case 214. There is not a word in the account about "constant delirium," or about any delirium at all. Like the cancer in a former case, it is a contribution of Mr. Peirce's. And what authority has he for regarding illness, caused by shock, as likely to produce a single perfectly distinct and isolated "retrospective hallucination"?

14th. This objection seems to me quite fallacious. The fact of experiencing a hallucination of the senses does not make a person an expert in regard to such phenomena, any more than having an illness would make him an expert in disease. If, in the course of long study of the subject, including the formation of a large collection of cases of purely subjective hallucination, I have found no evidence that affectionate thoughts directed to a person, even though that person has been "ailing for years," as in Case 195, have the power of evoking a distinct visual impression representing *that person and another*, I am justified in not inventing the hypothesis for this particular case. Nor even if I did invent it, could the *coincidence* do otherwise than enormously detract from its plausibility.

15th. Mr. Peirce's axiom seems to me decidedly too sweeping. As to the hypothesis of lying, I must hold that our mode of conducting the investigation reduces the scope of its possible application to an extremely small proportion—I do not myself believe it to be applicable to a single one—of our cases. Each case must be judged on its merits, with the aid of all the knowledge attainable of the witness's character.

The central fact in Case 173 is an extremely simple one, and there is no attempt at adornment. The account of Case 174 may, to the best of our judgment, be relied on. The absence of any personal relation between the person who died and the percipient makes the narrative a particularly unlikely one to have been consciously invented. In Case 184—also, I believe, quite reliable—we have a second person's testimony to the percipient's depression, and his anxiety about the child, though he did not mention the cause before the news of the death arrived. In Case 214 we are told that the percipient was clear-headed and truthful, and never varied in her statement.

I do not quite understand Mr. Peirce's suggestion that some of the cases may be explained by "the well-known sensation of having undergone a present experience on some previous occasion." Does he mean that the witness had a sensory hallucination representing the deceased person on some occasion subsequent to the death, accompanied by the delusion of having had it before? But this would involve a double improbability. The supposed delusion is not of the vague sort, unlocalized in time, and often in space, which is the common form of the "well-known sensation" referred to, but a very distinct picture of an experience belonging to a particular hour and a particular place. And, stranger still, the supposed *real* sensory hallucination, which actually does belong to a particular place and time, is clean forgotten—vanishes from the mind—its place being wholly usurped by the retrospective delusion to which it is supposed to give birth.

16th. Case 27. As Mr. Peirce gives no clue to the "inaccuracy of more or less importance" which he detects in this case, and as careful scrutiny fails to reveal any, I can make no reply with regard to it. Is it, perchance, that while the percipient says "Every feature of the face and form of my old friend X," his wife, to whom he immediately mentioned his experience, merely says "X's face"?

Case 180. This case is not included in my list, and I presume that Mr. Peirce has included it in his through rough inadvertence. As he has mentioned it, however, I may quote my comment on it. "It seems practically beyond doubt," as will be admitted, I think, on a perusal of the account, "that at the time that the news arrived, Mr. C., as well as his wife, fixed the date of the dream [more correctly 'Borderland' hallucination] as Monday, the 19th; and the fact that in his letter to us, written more than three years afterwards without reference to documents, he says 'about the 25th,' is therefore unimportant."

Case 182. Mr. Peirce says that the percipient "is positive that her vision took place at half-past ten; and, as no bell is rung at that time, this positive precision is already suspicious." The reader will be surprised to learn that Mr. Peirce is the sole authority for the suspicious circumstance. There is not a word as to the hour of the vision in the percipient's account; and in the passage quoted from her letter to her father, the only indication of time is in the words, "in the night, or rather morning."

The percipient says that she mentioned her experience to "two or three passengers on board, who made a note of it." Afterwards she gives the names of four persons whom she told "next day," but adds nothing there about a note. Mr. Peirce's version of these statements is: "She testifies positively that she mentioned the occurrence the next morning to four persons, who all severally took written notes of it." (I am forced to notice these frequent inaccuracies in his versions of the facts, as they would, of course, be extremely misleading to any one who did not take the pains to study the original cases.) "Two of these persons," Mr. Peirce adds, "now profess to know nothing whatever about the matter." Even this is not quite accurate, as "the matter" was not mentioned by me to one of these two persons; he was merely asked generally if he remembered any singular announcement made by Miss J. during the voyage. I have, however, now received the independent recollections of one of the persons told, to whom I was unable to apply last year, as he was travelling and his address could not be ascertained. He writes as follows:—

June 1, 1887.

> It was some years [four] ago that the voyage referred to in your note took place; but I distinctly remember that one morning during that voyage, Miss K. J. told me that during the previous night she had dreamed that a lady friend of hers was dead, or (for I cannot now remember which) that this friend had appeared to her on that night and announced her death.[2]
>
> A short time after arriving at the Cape (about the time that would be required for the transmission of a letter), Miss J. informed me that she had heard that her friend had died on the identical night of the dream or supposed appearance.

In answer to the question whether he made a written note, he says: "It is possible I may have at the time noted the date and the supposed apparition in an ordinary pocket-book; but if I did so, this pocket-book is now lost. I have some recollection of having seen the letter announcing the death of the lady, but none of comparing the date with that in a pocket-book; it is possible, however, that I have forgotten this circumstance."

I regard it as not improbable that Miss J. is wrong in thinking that any of the persons to whom she mentioned her experience made a written note of it. This is just the sort of feature that is likely enough to creep into an account without warrant, owing to the tendency of the mind to round off and complete an interesting story. One might expect *à priori* that this would be so; and the fact is illustrated by the far greater commonness of written notes in second-hand than in first-hand accounts. But in Miss J.'s case, though she is only a second-hand witness as regards the note, I think it probable that the idea of it had some real origin at the time of the event. Very likely one or more of the persons to whom she mentioned her experience said that it was worth making a note of, or that they were going to make a note of it—which has left in her mind the impression that the note was actually made.

2. The second of these alternatives is the right one, but it is not quite correct. The visual experience was certainly a waking impression, not a dream; but there was no impression of an announcement or of any words. This is a good instance of the way in which lapse of time affects memory as to details, without the evidence becoming in the least untrustworthy as to essentials.

Mr. Peirce's sentence, "She gives May 4th as the date of the vision, but the death occurred on May 2nd," is extremely misleading. When she wrote her account (as I explain), she had nothing independent by which to mark the day of the vision, and fancied that the vision and the death had both occurred on May 4th. But afterwards (without the real date of the death being recalled to her mind) she stated that she was not sure of the exact date, but that she knew it had been mentioned in a letter from the Cape to her father. It is contrary to what is stated to say that the letter (*i.e.*, the first letter) written to her father has been found by him. He expressly states that he cannot find it. And why does Mr. Peirce make the assumption, for which there is not the slightest ground, that the whole passage about the apparition, in the letter which is quoted, is not given? Why, again, does he assert that "it is stated that the letter gives the date of May 4th," when it is nowhere so stated, and when the very first words of the extract quoted are, "On the 2nd of May"?

The evidence would, of course, be more complete if it could be proved that the percipient gave a written account of her experience (as well as the verbal account which we now have corroborative testimony that she did give) before hearing of the death. In spite of both her own and her father's belief that she did so, I think it more probable that she did not, and that the letter of June 5th was really the first letter; as the way in which the fact of the vision is there mentioned does not suggest that it has been mentioned before. The idea that letters have *crossed*, in a case of this kind, is a likely first dereliction from perfect accuracy. The direction in which imagination and failure of memory gradually tend is just this, of neatening the facts, and supplementing the essential point by details which enhance its interest. Of course it is to be regretted that human memory is not infallible, and that time acts in any way as a distorting medium. But it is very important to avoid confounding the natural growths on the margin (so to speak) of a telepathic record with the vital point at its centre, or concluding that the latter is as likely to be unconsciously invented as the former. Supposing the mistake which I here think probable to have been really made, the substance of the case is not affected. Having specially observed the date, the percipient was likely to retain it correctly for the short period before hearing of the death; and her ability at that time to identify it could not be seriously impugned on the ground of a subsequent mistake as to the date of her first writing home. We should note, too, that in its essentials the case is a specially unlikely one (even apart from the corroborative testimony) to have been the work of imagination; as the percipient was not personally attached to the lady who died, nor had she been thinking about her.

Case 197. Mr. Peirce's phrase, "A coincidence exact to the minute," is not used in the account. What the narrator says is that the date of the death, "allowing for the difference of longitude, coincided" with that of the vision. Mr. Peirce is wrong also in saying that I ask him to accept the coincidence of date in this case as "beyond question," or as "positively proved." I have again and again urged that exaggeration of the closeness of a coincidence is a common and natural form for exaggeration to take;

and I have pointed out that there certainly had been some exaggeration[3] in this particular case. I have quite recently learnt that the error was greater than at first sight appeared. The vision took place on the morning of Sept. 6, that is *the day before* the death. The date is fixed by the entry in the diary of the narrator's friend, Miss K.;[4] under the head of September 5 is written, "On this night Isabella saw Jim vividly appear to her as if dead." The vision was actually in the early morning—that is, at the close of the night Sept. 5–6. The case, therefore, if telepathic, is one in which the telepathic impulse coincided not with death, but with a time of exceptional danger and probably excitement on the side of the agent. Another document which has lately been recovered further strengthens the evidence. This is a letter, sent at the time by the narrator to her sister, which, though it contains no date, leaves no doubt as to the record of the hallucination having been written and sent away before the news of the death arrived. This is really a better and rarer form of documentary evidence than an entry in a diary, which sometimes allows of the hypothesis that it was written later than the day under which it figures. The following is the account in the letter:—

> Hotel Interlaken,
> Wednesday.
>
> A few days ago, about seven in the morning, I had lain down again after drawing up my blind to let in the beautiful view of the rose-flushed morning, when I saw an appearance of Mountain Jim, looking just as he did when I last saw him. There was an impression on my mind as though he said: "I have come as I promised. Farewell." It was curious, and if I had not heard that he was getting well and going about, I should have thought he was dead.

This record, which closely corresponds with the printed account, written more than eleven years afterwards, makes it almost certain that the narrator's memory was at fault as to one unimportant detail, when she said in that account that she was lying on her bed and *writing to her sister* at the moment when the apparition occurred; for had she been so employed she could hardly have failed to mention the experience in that letter, instead of waiting some days.

17th. Case 231. The date could not be verified in the way that Mr. Peirce suggests, since, as I have stated, we have been unable to obtain the address of the witness. The original letter containing the account was not preserved by the editor of the paper in which it was published.

3. I take this opportunity of noting another instance of exaggeration which I have discovered since the book was published. In Case 29 it is stated that Mrs. de F. was found dead at 7:30 P.M. I learn from a near relative of hers that the time was certainly some hours earlier, about 2 P.M.

4. Before this diary was recovered, Miss K. wrote to me, "I distinctly remember that on my going into her room in the morning she told me immediately what she has related to you."

Case 236. Mr. Peirce's remark seems to me utterly without foundation. The percipient's account is quite as precise as that of her friend, who, however, completely corroborates her.

As to Case 237, I can only wish that Providence would bless us with more such "meagre" accounts, with essentials stated in a perfectly clear and straightforward manner, and with not a word suggestive of adornment or exaggeration. If Mr. Peirce really considers such a narrative, if true, as "worthless" for the purpose for which it is used, I am afraid that nothing I can say is likely to influence him.

The same remarks apply with almost equal force to the other cases to which Mr. Peirce refers—to Nos. 298 and 695 with quite equal force. As to Case 300, it would be improved for evidential purposes by being a little *more* meagre, there being, as I have pointed out, some suggestion of exaggeration in respect of details.

18th. It is possible that my colleagues and I fall far short of Mr. Peirce's standard in respect of caution, shrewdness of observation, and severity of logic. I think, however, that some readers of the book may feel the connection between our deficiencies and the evidence which we present less vital than he does—that they may find themselves able to judge the cases on their merits, and to "accept" any case so far as it seems trustworthy (not, of course, as a proof of telepathy, but as an item in the proof), without receiving from us anything beyond the assurance that in our opinion it was certainly given in good faith.

To sum up my view as to the cases in the list. Nos. 199 and 355 must certainly be omitted, as having occurred before Jan. 1, 1874; and Nos. 214 and 240 had better also be omitted, though on grounds different from those which Mr. Peirce adduces. Mr. Peirce seems to be logically right in demanding the exclusion of Nos. 174 and 702, on the ground that *non-coincidental* hallucinations, falling at a time when the percipient was so decidedly below par in point of health as in those cases, would probably not have been reckoned on the other side. If the census of hallucinations had not included so explicit a condition as to health, these two cases might have been reckoned, without any considerable alteration in the estimate from an increase of the number of subjective hallucinations representing recognized figures to be reckoned on the other side. No. 702 remains, anyhow, a strong case, and may become stronger still if the diary-entry can be recovered when the writer returns to England. As regards closeness of coincidence, the recent information as to case 197, though improving the quality of the evidence, removes it from this particular death-list; and there is enough room for doubt as regards Nos. 170, 201 (a very valuable case), and 231, to make it wiser to exclude them also; though I must point out that I never represented the coincidence as actually proved in every instance to have been close to within twelve hours; that the doubt has been clearly expressed in connection with the particular cases (except in respect of Case 170, an omission which I regret); and that the list and the calculation would necessarily be taken subject to that doubt in respect of a few of the items.

It will be observed that in dropping these cases I am merely conceding their omission from a particular calculation. The omission will not at all detract from their worth, and scarcely at all from the worth of the argument which the calculation exemplifies; since, for this to be appreciably affected, it would be necessary that a large majority of the records in the list should be substantially false, *i.e.*, that the professing percipient should have had no such experience as is described at all in close proximity to the death. The collective force, even of the excluded cases, say of the group 174, 197, 199 (and a case which happened a few months earlier, No. 500), 201, 231, 702, as evidence of a causal link between the death and the percipient's experience, is alone quite enough to give us pause; and as for the list as it stands without them, most candid students will, I think, find in it good evidence for a sufficient number of highly abnormal experiences, in correspondence with unexpected deaths at a distance, to supply material for a legitimate and exceedingly strong numerical argument. Of the retained cases, there are only seven in which we have not a second person's testimony to the percipient's mention of his or her experience at the time, before the fact of the death was known; or six, if we do not count No. 184, where, though the actual experience was not so mentioned, the special anxiety to which it gave rise was. As for the evidential point in respect of which the substantial accuracy of a certain proportion of the cases may with most reason be questioned—the degree of closeness in the coincidence—it is not of cardinal importance; if the arbitrary limit had been three days, or even a week, instead of twelve hours, the objectionable odds of billions to one against the proximity in time being due to chance would still be attained. Points of this sort were so obvious that I did not think it necessary to encumber the exposition with them; a very little good-will would enable any reader to see that the particular calculation, based on the particular data assumed, was a mere sample, serving to show what an immense margin there was to the argument, and how little any reasonable abatement would affect its force.

It may be well to point out in a more general way what has already been shown in respect of the particular point of degree of coincidence, that the admission of possible inaccuracies in the cases used is not in any way an afterthought, or in any degree a condemnation of my treatment of them. In the very first page of the chapter which Mr. Peirce has criticised, I say: "It is very necessary to distinguish these two questions—whether the evidence may be trusted; and if trusted, what it proves. It is the latter question that is now before us. The character of the evidence was discussed at some length in the fourth chapter, and is to be judged of by the narratives quoted throughout the book. In the present chapter it is assumed that these narratives are in the main trustworthy; that in a large proportion of them the essential features of the case—*i.e.*, two marked experiences and a time-relation between them—are correctly recorded." These words naturally refer the reader to the actual cases, and the comments which accompany them, for the means of judging as to their evidential value. He will find that incompleteness and doubtful points are abundantly recognized; but I believe he will also find that the probable or possible mistakes do not generally touch the real core of the case,[5] and that enough reliable ground remains to support *a* numerical estimate—if not my particular one, another conducted on the lines which that illustrates—of a sort that science cannot afford to disregard.

Mr. Peirce's concluding remarks on "the other numerical data used in the argument" require but brief comment. He says that I "have assumed that a hallucination with a coincidence of the death of the person represented is no more likely to be remembered for a period of twelve years than one which is unaccompanied by such a coincidence." All that I have assumed is that a hallucination of the waking senses, so distinct as those which have occurred in the coincidental cases, is likely to survive in the mind on its own account, or at any rate to be recalled when the person who has experienced it is put into the right attitude for recalling it by being asked a definite question on the subject. (See Vol. II, pp. 10, 11.)

Mr. Peirce adds, "There are numerous cases in which, the death not having been heard of, the vision has been totally forgotten after the lapse of a few months, and was only brought to mind again by the news of the death." I doubt if there are as many as three such cases in the book; and there is not one in respect of which the expression "totally forgotten" would not be thoroughly misleading. A thing may be totally forgotten in the sense that it is not likely to recur spontaneously to the mind; but this is a very different thing from total forgetfulness in the sense that a question with respect to that very thing will wake no memory of it. There is no coincidental case in the book in which it seems at all likely that such forgetfulness as this followed the hallucination; so that Mr. Peirce's *à priori* argument as to the forgetableness of the non-coincidental experiences of the same kind comes to nothing.

Mr. Peirce's final objection seems to rest on the assumption that, having supposed a quarter of a million of newspaper-readers, I forgot that each of these had a circle of persons sufficiently closely connected with him to make it likely that he would hear of a remarkable experience befalling any one of them, of which he might then let us know, so that the number of persons tapped by newspaper appeals should have been reckoned not as a quarter of a million only, but as a quarter of a million multiplied by the average number of each person's acquaintances. I have been guilty of no such stupendous blunder. Had the cases of the type which is used in the calculation been mainly obtained by means of public appeals,[6] it would, of course, have been very necessary, in estimating the area from which they were drawn, to distinguish the direct from the indirect results of the appeals—that is, to distinguish the cases which were from percipients who had encountered the appeal from those where the percipients had not themselves encountered it, but had been applied to for their accounts on the strength of it. Only five cases, however, out of the whole list, were obtained in this

5. I am, of course, not assuming that a case is necessarily a strong item of evidence if it is free from substantial error. There are many weaknesses which are in no sense mistakes; but I do not think that this specially applies to the cases in the list in question. Granted their substantial correctness, those cases form a very strong group.

6. A sentence in Chap. XIII (Vol. II, p. 14) is certainly not calculated to mislead. I say, "our chief means of obtaining information has been by occasional requests in newspapers." I ought to have added, "apart from information derived from our own circle of friends."

way through public channels; and of these, only one, Case 300, was an indirect result, in the sense just explained. That case was certainly not known to a wide circle; and as I was making a rough, but as I believed a very liberal, estimate of the area, I felt justified in including it.

In this connection I may repeat the substance of some remarks which Mr. Peirce has perhaps not observed, and which seem to me of great importance. Of the 64 coincidental experiences of three sorts—vivid dreams of death, and visual and auditory hallucinations—used in the calculations of Chapters VIII and XIII, five, or about one-thirteenth, were obtained by canvassing a body of about 5,535 persons, taken at random. It is not unreasonable, therefore, to suppose that the body from which the whole 64 were drawn amounts to 13 times 5,535 or 71,955. No doubt the number of coincidental (or, as we should now say, probably telepathic) experiences yielded by a random group of 5,535 persons is too small for us to be confident that it represents the average proportion in other groups of the same size. But the estimate is probably not so inexact but that it may safely be taken as showing my assumption of 300,000 to be decidedly unfair to the telepathic argument. I have further supposed this area of 300,000 persons to have been drained dry—an extravagant concession; for, though it is easily assumed that any one who has ever had a "psychical experience" is desirous to publish it abroad, as a matter of fact people do not usually take the trouble to write a letter to perfect strangers, about the family and personal matters of themselves or their friends, on the ground of a newspaper-appeal. Would that Mr. Peirce's view of the general eagerness to communicate with us were anywhere near the truth. We know of much evidence which the reluctance or indifference of the parties concerned has made unavailable for our collection; we can scarcely doubt, therefore, that much more remains unelicited, even among those whom our appeal has reached. A further strong argument for the existence of these unelicited facts is the very large proportion of our actual cases (specially large in the group with which Mr. Peirce and I have here been concerned) that has been drawn from a circle of our own, for the most part quite unconnected with "psychical" inquiry—from the friends, or the friends' friends, of a group of some half-dozen persons who have had no such experiences themselves, and who have no reason to suppose their friends or their friends' friends better supplied with them than anybody else's. In view of this latter fact, Mr. Peirce's guess that the cases in the list (or, at any rate, a sufficient number of them amply to support the argument) are "drawn from a population of three to four millions" clearly becomes grotesque.

As to the concluding paragraph, in which Mr. Peirce sums up his view, I may be allowed to point out, that if "the evidence, so far as it goes, seems to be rather unfavorable to the telepathic character of the phenomena," that is a most important result, and one which would amply repay the time and pains bestowed on collecting and examining the cases. The prime reason why it seems a scientific duty to collect and examine such evidence is not to support a foregone conclusion, not to prove this or that, but to see what is really involved in it; how far, when rationally criticised, it reveals facts which our previous knowledge fails to explain. No rational opinion could be formed on the subject, no rational guess even could be hazarded, till a wide effort had been made, and a large body of material got together and arranged. Mr. Peirce's provisional conclusion is, therefore, a quite sufficient justification for the book; for I do not imagine that he would deny that, if this collection actually goes some distance towards *disproving* telepathy, telepathy is not very likely to be proved. At the same time, his is not a conclusion which I can pretend that I expect many to share who devote an equal amount of study to the matter. He regards me, no doubt, as an advocate rather than a judge; and he is so far justified, in that the mistakes which I have made are all mistakes which tell in favor of my conclusion. He will pardon me if I say that he is in the same position; he has made (I think) a larger number of mistakes in seven pages than I in as many hundreds; and they all tell in favor of *his* conclusion. Thus the impartial reader who may be led to the book by this controversy will start fair; and that some may be so led is, I trust, one probable and useful result of a controversy which, I gratefully acknowledge, has not been without other uses.

Finally, let me urge on American readers that good as criticism is, cases to criticise are even better. I have expressly stated in *Phantasms of the Living*, that, though the book may reasonably be accepted as supplying a proof of Telepathy, the proof is not one which all candid minds are likely to accept. More cases, and contemporary cases, are needed; and for this we must largely depend on the wide assistance of educated persons in many countries. We trust that it is from the United States that the next considerable batch of evidence will come.

18

Mr. Peirce's Rejoinder

December 1887 — *Proceedings of the American Society for Psychical Research*

[*Note.*—In the copy of the above criticism, which was sent to Mr. Gurney, and on which he has based his reply, the following errata occurred:—

Objection	Line	True reading	Reading sent Mr. G.
2	5	238	237
4	8	28	29
4	8	236	214
5	4	695	702
9	9	249	201
12	3	249	201
13	4	or	and
16	3	170	180

C. S. P.]

When *Phantasms of the Living* appeared, I desired for my own satisfaction to examine the arguments for spontaneous telepathy. But, as I lacked the leisure to study the whole, I was forced to confine my attention to a single argument,—the most important one. Having reached a definite opinion in regard to the validity of this, I found myself in the possession of a good many notes which I thought might be useful in economizing the time of another student of the book. I, therefore, abridged these notes as much as possible, and so constructed an article afterwards communicated to the American Psychical Research Society and now printed above. In the abridgment of my notes a number of errors have crept in; but none of these are such as to alter my conclusion; only one or two are important; most of them consist in misstating my points; several are absolutely without significance, and some are errors favorable to the telepathic hypothesis. The reader may well ask whether I have not corrected in the proof-sheets as many of these errors as I have been able to discover; for to bring before the public a paper containing acknowledged faults certainly seems like an act of presumption. In truth, none of the errors have been corrected, except those in the list above, which are of a purely clerical nature. My excuse for pursuing this course will, I hope, be admitted. One of the chief points of Mr. Gurney's reply is that I have committed as many mistakes as he has. Accordingly, instead of simply dropping the cases against which he is forced to admit fatal objections for the purpose of the argument under examination, he labors to show that I have fallen into some small errors in my account of them. This line of argumentation seems more appropriate to a school disputation than to a scientific inquiry; for it would not help the theory of spontaneous telepathy in the least to prove me never such a blunderer. With Mr. Gurney's own intellectual character it is different. He stands to a certain extent as endorser of the witnesses to his ghost-stories. The public, which comes into contact with these witnesses only through him, is obliged to confide in his sagacity; and it thus becomes very important to ascertain whether he is an accurate and stern logician, or not. Now, the manner in which he conducts his reply might be judged quite significant in this regard; and hence I was unwilling to make corrections which might interfere with the development of Mr. Gurney's thought. I must beg pardon of the reader for the extent to which this course has lengthened the discussion. As long as I allow my errors to stand, since the reply is of the nature of an attack upon my scientific morals, involving accusations of garbling, suppression, and invention of testimony, it is incumbent upon me to notice the strictures in detail; and I have preferred to review the whole argument, repeating as little as possible what I have already said, but rearranging the matter in such a form as to render the force of my various objections more clear. My first paper was intended only for the use of close students of the book, and the several objections were indicated as briefly as possible. The present rejoinder is sufficiently expanded to permit any one who has read the work attentively, and who will actually turn to the pages I cite, to form a judgment of the correctness of what I allege.

Every attempt to explain ghost-stories without admitting anything supernatural (by which I mean anything counter to the great body of human experience) has dealt largely with supposed fortuitous coincidences; and students of the theory of probabilities must have entertained no little doubt whether a larger number of such coincidences were not supposed than was morally possible. Mr. Gurney has, for the first time, undertaken a statistical inquiry with a view of putting this question to rest; and he thinks he has reached an irrefragable conclusion. But I maintain he leaves the question just where he found it. (In the last paragraph but one of his reply, he does not observe the significance of my phrase "as far as the evidence goes." My judgment, I repeat, is that, "in view of the uncertainty of all the data, it would be very rash to draw any conclusion at all." I abstain, after reading the book as I did before, on account of the doubt just mentioned, from any positive denial, though I decidedly incline to disbelieve in any supernatural theory of ghost-stories.)

Mr. Gurney does not demur to my *résumé* of his argument. He says, "It may be calculated that the odds against the occurrence, by accident, of as many coincidences" within twelve hours, of visual hallucinations with the deaths of the persons presented, as a natural explanation would require, are, from the thirty-one cases he takes as established, "about a thousand billion trillion trillion trillions to one." To my remark that no human knowledge can reach such a probability as this he dissents, and gives an illustration from the throws of a die. I will grant, at once, that problems of that sort can be imagined which yield probabilities indefinitely nearer certainty than the above. For instance, if a die be thrown but once, the odds that one or another of the six faces will turn up is, upon the usual assumptions, absolute certainty, or infinity to one. But this only refers to an imaginary state of things. In any actual case there is a possibility—ordinarily very rightly neglected, but far greater than one out of trillions of trillions—that the die may rest on its vertex, or fly up to heaven, or vanish altogether, or that before it reaches the table earth and heaven shall be annihilated. The continuance of the order of nature, the reality of the external world, my own existence, are not as probable as the telepathic theory of ghosts would be if Mr. Gurney's figures had any real significance. And for that it would be requisite, too, that each one of his thirty-one cases should be established with a degree of certainty far transcending the odds he gives. He might reply that the enormous number given does not profess to be anything but the calculated probability of the thirty-one coincidences happening by chance; but this would be admitting at once what I allege, that the number has no real significance; and it is because the thinking man will see this, while the vulgar may not, that I say such figures may be calculated to overawe the latter, but can only repel the former. Mr. Gurney, in his reply, continues to insist upon the number, for the sake, as he says, of accuracy. To my mind, it is precisely against strict accuracy of thought that such insistence offends.

I will first consider the census of 5,705 persons, taken at random, of whom only 21 could recall having had within twelve years a visual hallucination of a living person while they were in good health, free from anxiety, and wide awake, two of these having had two such experiences. If it would answer the purpose to accept these answers in the rough, as Mr. Gurney has done, the census would be large enough; but this is not so. It is essential to ascertain the proportion of hallucinations that have been forgotten. I have pointed out that Mr. Gurney assumes that hallucinations with coincidence of death within twelve hours of the person presented are no more likely to be remembered for twelve years than similar hallucinations without coincidence! Mr. Gurney, in his reply, has the air of denying that he has made this assumption; but I submit that a careful reading of the passage will show that, on the contrary, he fully admits it. Mr. Gurney sharply censures me for saying that there are numerous cases in the book of an apparition being totally forgotten after the lapse of a few months. The remark is certainly somewhat exaggerated; I should have said, so far forgotten that in the absence of coincidence they would not have been called to mind in answering the census-question. But I think it is unjust to say that the expression "totally forgotten" is "thoroughly misleading," since it is a very common exaggeration, and I add the qualifying clause, "and was only brought to mind again by the news of the death." Mr. Gurney doubts if there are as many as three cases of forgetting an apparition in the book. I cannot say how many there are;

I have noticed the following, and I suppose there are others. In Case 170, "all seemed forgotten." In Case 177, it was not until long after hearing of the death that it occurred to the percipient to "put two and two together" and to associate the apparition with the death, although the recognition was perfect. In Case 235, the percipient says, "but for the fact of his death I should never probably have recalled the circumstance." In Case 258, the percipient only "happened to remember" the apparition. In Case 306, the percipient's mind "recurred to it from time to time," and no doubt would soon have forgotten the apparition in the absence of any coincidence. In Case 552, the percipient testifies that she heard of the death after six weeks, but did not mention the apparition for many months. Mr. Gurney, however, on the ground of subsequent conversation, says that this appears to be an error. In Case 579, the percipient thought no more about the vision, and therefore probably would have forgotten it. In Case 588, "the thing was in great measure forgotten." In Case 607, "no more was thought of it;" but that may not mean by the percipient, who was a child. Perhaps a pedantic accuracy might object to calling these cases "numerous," though there are doubtless others. There are not a great many cases in the book in which an apparition has been recalled at all where the death constituting the coincidence has been heard of only after the lapse of long time, unless the experience had created the fear of the death of a relative or friend, or was brought to mind by some record, or was kept in remembrance by being a collective or reciprocal experience. I am confident that Mr. Gurney is wrong in supposing that hallucinations are experiences particularly well remembered. They are so with the few persons who take a special interest in them; but whatever has no apparent bearing upon facts we consider important or interesting is quickly lost from mind. I should have said unhesitatingly that I personally had never had a visual hallucination, until almost as I write these words I recollect such an occurrence about thirty years ago. At any rate, the question cannot be settled by discovering microscopic errors in my criticism; the average index of forgetfulness, in these cases, ought to be positively ascertained; and the census proves nothing until it is made so large that the affirmative replies can be classified according to their dates, without too much diminishing the numbers in the several classes. It would also be needful, in order to arrive at satisfactory results, to separate the different kinds of hallucinations. First, the genuine hallucination, the product of an overwrought brain, which is preceded by great depression, accompanied by faintness (manifesting itself in damp weather as an icy chill as soon as the skin has had time to cool), and followed by an access of terror; second, the dream continued through the process of waking up and even for a second into the wide-awake state; and third, the mere illusion, or imaginative misinterpretation of something really seen, without any disorder of the brain, should be distinguished in this inquiry. There was no good reason for limiting the census-question to a period of twelve years; on the contrary, it would have been better to use all the available data. It was a mistake, too, to limit the question by the clause relative to being in good health, free from anxiety, and wide awake. The entire answers should rather have been printed, and the subtractions on account of illness, anxiety, and drowsiness have been made within the view of the public. Finally, a fallacy seems to be involved in limiting the question to hallucinations presenting persons really (and not merely supposed to be) alive; for there may be a decided tendency for hallucinations to represent those who are approaching their end. A new census should be undertaken upon a larger scale and with the sufficient means to carry it out in a thoroughly scientific manner.

In the estimate which I made of the size of the circle from which the coincidental cases were drawn, I relied on the statements in the *Phantasms of the Living*. We there read[1] in the discussions of these cases, "Our chief means of obtaining information has been by occasional requests in newspapers." But Mr. Gurney now says, "Had the cases used been mainly obtained by means of public appeals," this calculation of the population from which the coincidences were drawn, made as it was, would have involved "a stupendous blunder." In point of fact, however, as he says, "Only five cases . . . out of the whole list were obtained in this way." But on the same page of the book last cited he allows 250,000 as the number of persons who have become acquainted with the inquiry through the newspapers, and only 50,000 as the number of those who have derived the same information through private channels. If the former class have furnished

1. Vol. II, p. 14

only 5 cases, or 1 for every 50,000, while the latter class have furnished 26 cases, or 1 for every 2,000, it would seem that the bulk of Mr. Gurney's cases have been drawn from a class which is twenty-five times as fertile in ghost-stories as the general population. This furnishes food for reflection. An attempt is made to check the estimate by a piece of imaginative statistics. "Would any one," he asks, "suppose that if he canvassed the first one thousand adults whom he met in the streets of any large town, he would find that twelve or thirteen of them had within the last three years been aware of what we wanted, and of the address to which information might be sent?" Perhaps not; but here again the author forgets that people not only send their *own* experiences, but also cause those of others to be sent, of which they have heard. I have estimated that the advertisements in the newspapers ought to have drawn the really remarkable ghost-stories from a population of three millions; and though I admit the extreme uncertainty of this estimate, I still see no reason to modify it. Mr. Gurney puts forth two objections to it. One is that 5 of his 64 coincidental cases have been obtained by canvassing a body of 5,535 persons taken at random. The other is that a very large proportion of the 31 cases on which the argument under examination has been based, have been the experiences of the friends and friends' friends of half-a-dozen persons. These objections seem at first glance crushing; but they both involve one and the same *petitio principii.* For the whole question is whether the advocate of naturalistic explanations of ghost-stories is forced to assume a greater number of purely fortuitous coincidences than the doctrine of chances will permit. Now this devil's advocate, whose office I endeavor to fill, is not by any means forced to attribute the whole of the 31 visual and 33 auditory cases to the operation of chance alone. I have only examined the former class, but of these I find only one which I am obliged to call a purely fortuitous coincidence. It is the case of Mrs. Duck, number 238. This case did not come from the 5,535 persons, nor from the friends' friends, but was taken from the *Englishman* newspaper of May 13, 1876. If we are to suppose that every very striking ghost-story published in any prominent newspaper back to 1876 and susceptible of investigation has come to Mr. Gurney's ears, surely three or four million is not a very large number to assign to the population from which they were drawn. In my view of the matter, then, what Mr. Gurney calls his well-attested coincidental cases are of two classes: one derived from closely questioning a relatively small number of persons, not one of these stories being capable of sustaining a severe criticism; the other confined mainly to the more remarkable of the experiences of a far larger population, among which one visual case seems to involve a purely fortuitous coincidence. That something like this is the truth of the matter will, I am confident, be the final judgment of students.

Mr. Gurney takes as the chance that a given hallucination will fall accidentally within twelve hours of the death of a person whom it represents, the ratio of deaths in a day to the number of the population. This would be correct if the death-rate for persons represented in hallucinations were the same as that of the whole population. But the examples given in the book are sufficient to show that this is not the case. Persons who, from the percipient's stand-point, appear particularly likely to die are, we find, particularly apt to appear in hallucinations. This is not surprising, for genuine hallucinations are accompanied by a peculiar terror, as one of their physiological symptoms; so that it is quite natural that they should tend to take the forms of those whose death the percipient has most reason to expect, rather than of those in whom he may be more interested. This is, at least, a natural supposition; the burden of proof is not upon me to show it actually is the rule; for I am not trying to prove anything, but only to show that nothing has been proved. Until we obtain some positive statistics, we can only assume that the thirty-one cases under consideration are fairly representative of hallucinations in general in regard to the lengths of time that the percipients might expect the apparitor to live. Suppose, now, that a given person is to have a hallucination on a given occasion. The apparition might take the form of a person belonging to one of several classes having different death-rates. Let d, d', d'', etc., be the antecedent probabilities to the percipient in the given case that individuals belonging to these several classes will die on a given day. Let h, h', h'', etc., be the antecedent probabilities that the apparition in the same case will take the form of individuals of those several classes. Then, $hd + h'd' + h''d'' +$, etc., will be the antecedent probability that the hallucination in the given case will be accompanied within twelve hours by the death of the apparitor (but it will usually be unnecessary to take account of more than one term of the algebraical expression); and the reciprocal of this quantity will be the number of hallucinations like this among which, in the long run, there would be one accompanied by such a coincidence. We do not, it is true, in our existing ignorance of the subject, know whether more or fewer ordinary hallucinations than of hallucinations *like this* would be requisite to yield such a coincidence. But we can only assume that if we sum these numbers for the whole thirty-one cases (or as many of them as are admitted into the argument), we shall obtain about that number of hallucinations among which there would be thirty-one coincidences of this sort. If there are two different natural explanations of a ghost-story, one giving P and the other Q as the number of hallucinations per coincidence, and if the respective probabilities of these theories are p and q, where $p + q = 1$, then the number to be adopted is $p\mathrm{P} + q\mathrm{Q}$. If one of the explanations is complete, we need only take account of one of the terms of this last formula, since the other will be very small. If there is a probability, r, that the case ought to be excluded from the calculation, then P is to be multiplied by $(1 - r)$. I have estimated the numbers given below to the best of my judgment, but it will be seen that for the most part considerable changes might be made in them without essentially affecting the conclusion. But logic will forbid the making of any changes in favor of the telepathic hypothesis, except where the number given by me may be unquestionably wrong.

It will be seen that, in treating the stories upon these principles, I have somewhat refined upon the method of my first criticism. This I have done in response to Mr. Gurney's protest that I have pinned him down to too hard and fast an interpretation of his argument. I thought it fair to meet a roughly stated argument by a roughly stated reply. But since he seems to desire to leave his demonstration of his theory hazy, while insisting on great precision in my objections, I so far comply with his wish as to attempt to estimate numerically the effect of the latter, instead of ruling the case out altogether, when the objections are not absolute in their nature.

In the discussion of each story, I shall endeavor either to show that it has no bearing on the argument under examination, or else to explain it in a way that is more probable than the telepathic theory. This explanation is either *complete*, if it leaves nothing to be accounted for by a chance coincidence, or *partial* if it serves to increase very greatly the probability of the coincidence. It is necessary and sufficient that the explanation which I propose for each story should be more probable than the telepathic explanation. This opens the question how antecedently probable that theory is. Now there is a considerable body of respectable evidence in favor of telepathy, in general. Yet I am clear that we cannot probably infer that there is any influence of mind upon mind otherwise than through the recognized avenues of sense. It must be regarded as exceedingly unlikely that such a proposition should ever be established by means of evidence of the kind hitherto chiefly relied upon. For this proposition, being counter to some of the fundamental elements of the general conception of nature which we have formed under the influence of our aggregated experience, has against it antecedently odds of hundreds of thousands, perhaps, to one. In order to refute it, then, for the time being, it is only necessary to bring some other explanation of the facts less improbable than that. Telepathy might conceivably, by another method, be put out of all doubt. You might, for example, begin by establishing a proposition, A, not in itself very improbable, which in turn might lend so much probability to a second proposition, B, that it might be possible to establish this by evidence; and this again might render a third proposition, C, sufficiently probable to be capable of being established by observations; and by proceeding thus, you might bridge over the profound chasm which separates telepathy from the solidarity of our ordinary experience. This is the way in which all the marvels of science have been made credible. But to mix with the well-compacted body of scientific truth sporadic propositions contrary to the main principles of science, simply because we find ourselves without any other ready explanation at hand for certain outlying facts, would be a proceeding calculated to throw our whole knowledge into confusion, even if but a small minority of the propositions so accepted should be false. To admit the existence of a principle, of which we certainly only meet with manifestations in very exceptional observations, is to rashly set the prosperity of scientific progress at hazard. Moreover, though nature gives us examples enough of rare substances, a rarely operative fundamental principle is yet to be discovered. On the contrary, every force or other cause we know works almost everywhere and at all times. But telepathy, as the evidence stands at present, if it acts at all, does so only with the extremest infrequency.

The degree of my disbelief in telepathy in general is such that I might say that I think the odds against it are thousands to one. But even were I convinced of the general phenomenon, I should find the telepathic explanation of ghost-stories but little more acceptable than I do at present. Even if telepathy exists, we know next to nothing of the conditions of its action. I have heard ignorant persons attribute table-tipping to electricity, an agent which they only knew from sporadic manifestations. I thought such persons not only ignorant, but foolish; and it appears to me that we should be imitating them if we were to try to explain anything by an agency that we know so little about as we do about thought-transference. The phenomena, so far as we know them, seem to depend for one condition upon a vigorous effort on the part of the telepathic agent; and it is fair to presume that this would be impaired with other powers in sickness, and would cease with death. Then again, why should we draw upon such an extreme rarity as telepathy, so long as we have such ordinary elements of human experience as superstition, lying and self-lying (from vanity, mischief, hysteria, mental derangement, and perverse love of untruth), exaggeration, inaccuracy, tricks of memory and imagination, intoxication (alcohol, opiate, and other), deception, and mistake, out of which to shape our hypotheses? For these reasons, I hold the telepathic theory of ghost-stories to be an unwarrantable and wild surmise. I would prefer to this an explanation which I deemed antecedently very improbable, provided it was not utterly preposterous. I do not therefore think it incumbent upon me in opposing the telepathic theory to suggest only positively probable explanations. No explanation within the bounds of common sense can well be so unlikely as that one. Mr. Gurney, in his reply, admits that he has the bias of an advocate; but thinks that I, on my side, have so too. Perhaps: I certainly profess a legitimate and well-founded prejudice against the supernatural. But observe that a bias against a new and confounding theory is no more than conservative caution; while a bias in favor of such a theory is destructive of sound judgment.

Before I take up the stories in detail, there are a few of my objections concerning which a few additional words seem necessary. In referring to these objections, I preserve the original numbering.

2nd. Certain percipients were dead before the advertisements of Messrs. Gurney, Myers, and Podmore were inserted in the newspapers. I propose to surrender this objection altogether. It is logically sound; but the estimate of the population from which the cases have been drawn is so exceedingly uncertain, that is hardly worth while to insist on this point. Accordingly, I now admit one case of purely fortuitous coincidence, No. 238.

3rd. I have not clearly expressed this objection. What I say is that every case must be thrown out in which the percipient has "had two hallucinations fortuitously." But I intended to say, what the logic of the case required, that every case must be thrown out in which the percipient remembers having had any other insignificant hallucination;—for Mr. Gurney has shown that only 1 person in 59 remembers having had the illusion of a voice in twelve years, and only 1 in 248 remembers having seen an apparition of a person in the same period. Hence, as not over half-a-dozen cases of pure coincidence from his list can be admitted by any careful critic, if any of the percipients in these cases remembers a hallucination of any kind at any time of his life, the probability is large that he is abnormally subject to hallucinations. It is to be observed that the census question very rightly says nothing about the recognition of the apparition.

6th. Mr. Gurney says that I have not perceived that the question is not whether the percipients were awake, but whether they believed they were awake. *First,* I think it would be absurd to include dreams in this inquiry. *Second,* waiving this, the question is, not whether the percipients do believe themselves to have been awake, but whether they would have continued to do so had there been no coincidence. For a like reason, the including of cases in the census where the percipient was in bed cannot balance the objection to this circumstance in the coincidental cases.

12th. The percipient may have been intoxicated. I should have added that he may have taken opium, chloral, or other exciting drug. This throws a certain suspicion upon every case in which the percipient was even slightly unwell. Of course, such cases may be thrown out on the ground of ill-health. But that is not an explanatory objection,—it only going to show that the cases have no relevancy to the argument. In the present view of the matter, it appears that there may have been circumstances rendering hallucinations specially probable (relatively to ordinary circumstances), thus partially explaining the coincidences.

15th. If the percipient has not told of the vision until after having received news of the death, several modes of explanation are suggested.

A. He may be lying. This is a disagreeable hypothesis, especially when it is more probable that he is telling the truth. Still, an almost inappreciable possibility of lying may outweigh the probability of the telepathic explanation.

B. In ordinary indistinct vision, if the person is led to think that he ought to recognize what is seen as a certain person or thing, he will often feel sure he has already so recognized it, although the perception may be quite incompatible with the identification made. The same is true with dreams. So far as my own are concerned, I have long convinced myself that they are largely fabricated after I wake up, in trying to recover and go over in my mind what I had been dreaming. I am confident, therefore, that, in some cases, the memory of the hallucination could be greatly modified by subsequent suggestion.

C. Just as a person often has considerable difficulty in persuading himself that he has not previously been in the same situation in which he finds himself, so if, on hearing sudden news of another person, an image of that person is presented before his eyes, he might think he had seen that vision before.

16th. If the principal witness is shown to be inaccurate even in a small matter, we, who have no opportunity to cross-examine him, must make up for that disadvantage by throwing out the case; for an essential perversion of the truth,—an unintentional one,—by such a witness is more likely than the telepathic hypothesis. It is not necessary in such a case to make a definite hypothesis of what the truth may be.

17th. A story so meagre that we cannot judge of the thoroughness of the cross-examination nor of the real character of the witnesses, and which does not fully detail the circumstances, must go for nothing. Anyone in a large city by frequenting the right company,—that of highly cultivated people, too,—may, with a little encouragement, hear such stories in an endless flood.

I will now consider, one by one, Mr. Gurney's thirty-one cases of visual hallucinations with coincidence of the death of the person represented within twelve hours, and show the force of my objections.

Case 26 (Vol. I, p. 207). An old farmer sees the apparition of a cousin. See objections 6 and 8.

The percipient was in bed, but says he was "perfectly wide awake."

There is a doubt about the date; for he says he searched the papers on the same day he told his friends. Namely, his words are, "The next day I mentioned to some of my friends how strange it was. So thoroughly convinced was I, that I searched the local papers that day [Saturday]." The local papers appeared, as Mr. Gurney now tells us, on Saturday. On Saturday, then, the percipient first told his friends. But three of his friends sign a statement that he told them he had the vision "during the previous night." This does not quite agree with his testimony that it occurred "about two o'clock in the morning of October 21st;" for the 21st was Friday. I think the odds, then, two to one that he meant it occurred about two o'clock in the morning of the night of October 21–22, which would harmonize the whole, but spoil the twelve-hour coincidence. Mr. Gurney, on the other hand, thinks that by the statement first quoted he means to say: That same day I mentioned it to my friends, and the next day (Saturday) I searched the local papers. He still insists on using the case as a premise from which to draw a conclusion to which (since "it is as well to be accurate") he assigns a probability of a thousand billion trillion trillion trillions to one.

The percipient's age is seventy-two. He would seem to have no immediate relations; so that I shall assume that those who might be represented in his hallucinations would be as old as he. The probability of dying on a given day at that age is 1:5000. But the probability that there was a twelve-hour coincidence is only 1/3. Then, the probability of such a coincidence, *if this was one,* is 3:5000.

Case 27 (Vol. I, p. 209). A gentleman, while dressing in the morning, sees in his mind's eye the face and form of an old friend. See objections 5 and 16. I have reckoned this case among those in which inaccuracies, small or great, might be detected in the testimony. In this case, the inaccuracy I meant, if it be one, is very small. It was supposed to consist in the lady's saying that her husband "had always been particularly unbelieving as to anything supernatural." Everybody who has patiently listened to many such stories knows that phrases like this are so perpetually in the mouths of cultivated people inclined to superstitious credulity, that they are just a little suspicious in themselves. Now, in this case the percipient did not have a regular hallucination at all; so that there was probably no physiological fear; and yet he was more agitated and impressed by the occurrence than a person uninclined to credulity would have been by the most substantial apparition. It therefore clearly conveys an erroneous impression to say that he is "particularly unbelieving." The lady's account contains no sentence attributable to a desire to bring to light any circumstance telling against the supernatural character of the vision; but both matter and phraseology ("strange to say") are directed to heightening the effect. The story is very well told.

I have also reckoned this case among those in which the percipient was anxious. My reasons are as follows: The decedent was an old friend of the percipient, so intimate that the latter was informed of the death by a letter received the next morning; and the peculiar illusion seems (on any hypothesis) to reveal a close bond of sympathy between the two men. Now the percipient knew that the decedent had a mortal disease. Hence, I think a certain degree of anxiety must have existed. This may not have been so great that a really vivid non-coincidental hallucination affected by it would have been on this account unnoticed in replying to the census-question; but the vision in question was only seen "in the mind's eye," and was so little removed from an imagination that the percipient's wife thinks it necessary to say, "My husband is the last person in the world to imagine anything." I think, therefore, that, had there been no coincidence, husband and wife would have concluded that the apparition, if it can be called one, was a product of an imagination worried by anxiety. Mr. Gurney says, "I can scarcely think Mr. Peirce seriously believes that the hallucination was due to anxiety." But it is not the question whether the hallucination was really due to anxiety or not, but whether it is certain that there was not sufficient anxiety to prevent such a case from being reported in the census, provided it had proved to have no significance. In my opinion the chance is that the case ought to be excluded for this reason.

At the same time if it were a pure coincidence it would be nothing remarkable. Though the percipient was not very anxious, he was probably more anxious about the decedent than about any other friend; so that it may be assumed that the probability that this decedent would be represented in any hallucination that the percipient might have at this time was four-fifths. The decedent was known to have a cancer; and that cancer was a mortal one, because it was an "incurable" one, and the phrase that "we were in no immediate apprehension of his death" shows that he was expected to die of it at some time. The average duration of such a cancer may be five hundred days. But the percipient does not seem to have been very well informed in regard to the particulars; and we may therefore presume he did not know how long the malady had been going on. If so, it was an even chance that the decedent might die in two hundred and fifty days. That is, there was one chance in two hundred and fifty that he would die that day. The antecedent probability of the coincidence is 4/5 of this, or 1 in 312. The case is thus insignificant, even if it be admitted. In view of the anxiety, I will reckon its antecedent probability as 1 in 156.

Case 28 (Vol. I, p. 210). An employé in an office while on a sofa in the evening sees an apparition of a fellow-employé. See objections 4, 5, and 6. There was a certain inaccuracy in my putting this case among those in which the percipients were taking afternoon naps. But my notes were only the briefest references for students. By the word "nap" I meant that the percipient was not in bed, but either snoozing or liable to do so.

This is a very impressive case, owing both to the unexceptionable character of the testimony and to the numerous details which the fine observation of the percipient brings out. Nevertheless, I do not think it proves anything; and I am gratified to find my judgment borne out by the witness A. C. L. (p. 212, at the end of his letter), who was in so much better a position to judge it than the public can be. The present discussion of the case must of course be limited to its bearing on the single argument under examination.

The percipient was apparently reclining upon a couch at nine o'clock in the evening; but he had only leaned back the minute before. He was, however, not well. He not only had a headache, but he said to his wife that he was, what he had not been for months, rather too warm. He was, therefore, probably feverish. It is possible that he may have taken some exciting medicine. This degree of illness would not have been sufficient of itself, I suppose, to prevent such a case, if not coincidental, from being reported in the census; but it is significant on another account. For I believe that the derangement of the percipient's health was brought on by sub-conscious anxiety concerning his friend the decedent. Mr. Gurney, in his answer to my criticisms, represents that the only knowledge the percipient had of the illness of his friend was that he knew he had an attack of indigestion. But there was nothing to be called an "attack" of indigestion. On Monday, the decedent "complained of having suffered from indigestion;" that is to say, he had, no doubt, had a pain which he referred to his stomach, and which had been so severe that he mentioned it after it was over; and he still felt that something was the matter, for he consulted an apothecary. This apothecary "told him that his liver was a little out of order, and gave him some medicine," doubtless a blue pill. On Thursday "he did not seem much better," so that it was apparent that there was something more than mere biliousness the matter. Nor was this all; for on Saturday he was absent from the office. All these symptoms were known to the percipient; and, besides these, there must have been indescribable indications of illness. For a man can hardly have an aneurism of the aorta and be so little ill that the derangement of his health wholly escapes the notice of a sympathetic and observant friend who sees him every day. Such a wonderful sympathy existed between these two men, that when A. L., the brother of the decedent (the same whose opinion of the case has been cited above), came to announce the death to N. J. S., the percipient, the following extraordinary conversation took place: "A. L. said, 'I suppose you know what I have come to tell you?' N. J. S. replied, 'Yes, your brother is dead.' A. L. said, 'I thought you would know it.' N. J. S. replied, 'Why?' A. L. said, 'Because you were in such sympathy with one another.'" Here was a man in a better situation to judge the case than any one can now be, and who is so little given to marvels that after this occurrence he continues to disbelieve in telepathic visions, and who says he gives his testimony "to strengthen a cause I am not a disciple of;" and yet this excellent judge thought the percipient would know of the death. The same good judge must, then, have thought the percipient would have been anxious. The reason he gave for his surmise shows that, like a good observer of human nature, he knew that deep sympathy, as the word implies, may produce a wonderful exaltation of sensibility. In such a condition perceptions of the truth may be reached which are founded on differences of sensation so slight that even an attentive scrutiny of the field of consciousness may not be able to detect them, and which may be almost magical in their effects.

I would propose, then, the following hypothesis to account for this story. The exalted sensibility of sympathy had unconsciously detected alarming symptoms in the decedent, and given rise to very great anxiety. But anxiety is a vague sensation, which frequently escapes recognition, even though it be enough to make the person sick. So I suppose it was in the present case. Fever resulted, with headache due to over-excitation and exhaustion of the brain (owing both directly to the heat of fever), and faintness due to an irritation of the sympathetic nerves. When the percipient leaned back on the couch I suppose he felt the weakness of approaching faintness; then, a moment later, an icy chill passed through him,—a sure sign that the blood had been withdrawn from the periphery long enough for the skin to cool. The brain must have been already left bloodless; and this withdrawal of the blood, in the condition in which the brain was, sufficed to bring on a hallucination. I submit that this hypothesis keeps nearer to the facts, and is less far-fetched, than that of spontaneous telepathy, and is also far more antecedently probable.

I assume it to be practically certain antecedently that any hallucination that the percipient might have on that day would refer to the decedent, and further that his unconscious, anxious clairvoyance showed that the decedent was a very sick man. It is, therefore, fair to say that the latter's antecedent chance of dying was ten times that of the average man, or say 1 in 2,000, which is, therefore, the antecedent probability of the coincidence.

Case 29 (Vol. I, p. 212). See objections 4 and 12, with Mr. Gurney's replies, especially under the former head, where he communicates the important additional fact that the percipient was in perfect health.[2] I am sorry he does not say on whose testimony he states this, for such supplementary testimony must be received with special caution.

This gardener stumbling about the churchyard in the evening suggests an Ingoldsby legend. When he got home he half thought what he had seen must have been his fancy. Such uncertainty is odd, and seems to show something was the matter with the man. I suspect drunkenness; but perhaps this is too gratuitous, for the man has an excellent character. Yet I do not think that the drunkenness of a man to whose character the vicar of the parish certifies is quite so improbable as the telepathic hypothesis. Let us, however, assign to the former only one-third the probability of the latter.

But, further, as the percipient on his return half thought what he had seen must have been his fancy, he perhaps would have settled down to that belief had there been no coincidence, and consequently would not have reported the case, had the census-question been put to him. Observe that I am not supposing there was such a case among the persons to whom the census-question was put; but probability deals wholly with what would happen in an indefinitely long run, and in the long run there would have been such a case; besides, though there may not have been any case in the census exactly analogous to this, yet to balance this defect there were probably cases of suppression of hallucinations which find no precise analogues among the coincidental cases. Still, as the case might have been reported under the circumstances supposed, I will not cut it off altogether on account of this objection, but only reduce its weight by one-third.

Finally, it appears to me that this case has not been sufficiently inquired into. I cannot help thinking, for example, that if we knew as much about it as we do about No. 28, that if we had a better acquaintance with the witness than is conveyed by the vicar's banal certificate to the man's character, and that if we were fully informed concerning the events of that day, some explanation might offer itself which does

2. I only refer the reader to Mr. Gurney's replies in cases where they include new testimony.

not now occur to us. I will estimate the probability of this at one-third that of the telepathic hypothesis, to which I think I have thus been unduly liberal. These probabilities sum up to the equivalent of the telepathic hypothesis.

As the news of the death reached the town the next morning, it is fair to assume that the gardener was aware of the illness of the decedent. We may, then, reasonably estimate the antecedent probability that the hallucination would relate to the invalid whose tomb was before his eyes as four-fifths. I further assume that the widow in a coal-scuttle bonnet was sixty-five years of age, and that, being poorly, her chance of dying was five times the normal. According to the table of the English Institute of Actuaries, out of 49,297 assured persons living at the age of sixty-five, 2,141 die in the year, or say 1 in 23. Then the chance that such a person will die on a given day is 1 in 365 times 23, or 1 in 8,400. But this woman's chance was five times that, or 1 in 1,700. However, there was only a probability of four-fifths that she would be the object of the hallucination; so that the probability of the coincidence was only $4/5$ of $1/1700$, or $1/2100$. In other words, there would have in the long run to be 2,100 hallucinations before a coincidence equivalent to this would occur. But there is an even chance that one of the above objections is valid, when we are not obliged to fall back on fortuitous coincidence, so that in the long run only 1,050 hallucinations would be necessary.

Case 170 (Vol. I, p. 428). A woman saw an apparition of her mother, and her aunt died. See objections 2, 6, 7, 8, and 16. Owing apparently to an error of a copyist, Mr. Gurney understands me, under the 16th head, to object to Case 180, instead of to this; and hence his smooth remarks on my "rough inadvertency."

The percipient was in a delicate condition, and consequently, perhaps, not in good health.

It was in the morning, and she had not risen, though she had been awake, and probably still was so.

She did not recognize the apparition as the person who died, but as another person.

The date is altogether doubtful.

Owing to the lapse of time the testimony is not good.

The case has not been very thoroughly investigated.

Mr. Gurney gracefully surrenders this case, which must go for nothing.

Case 172 (Vol. I, p. 430). See objections 5, 6, and 15. A housekeeper, alone in the house, as she is going to sleep at night, sees the apparition of a dear friend.

The honesty of the witness cannot be doubted. She did not tell the experience, apparently, until long after she had heard of the death; but in this case that could hardly make any difference, unless we suppose outrageous lying without any known motive.

It is quite possible that a real person may have been seen; yet there is no positive indication whatever of the presence of such a person.

The percipient was in bed, and at the beginning of the hallucination, at least, not wide awake, as required by the census-question. Such a case, if non-coincidental, would probably not be reported in the census, and therefore should not be counted in the argument under examination.

Moreover, the percipient expressly says, "I was anxious about her." Mr. Gurney replies that she was not anxious in the sense in which he uses the word. But she would have understood the word "anxiety," in the census-question, as she herself uses it. For this reason, I must positively exclude the case.

Yet, even if all the above objections fail, it has no value. For it was antecedently practically certain that the dream would relate to the decedent, an "intimate friend" about whom the percipient was anxious; and since the decedent "had been for some time seriously ill," and anxiety existed, the antecedent probability of death, and, therefore, of the coincidence, may be put at 1 in 200.

Case 173 (Vol. I, p. 431). See objections 3, 6, and 15. The captain of a steamer was killed by the fall of a spar at six o'clock in the morning. The percipient was the stewardess, and was then asleep in her berth. I suppose there was loud talk about the event, and that this talk, being heard by the stewardess in her sleep, produced a vivid dream. This dream was continued for an instant after she woke or half woke up, "probably between six and seven." She rose at once and went to the pantry and there heard what had happened, being very likely not yet wide awake. This explanation is complete and satisfactory.

Were it necessary to suppose any fortuitous coincidence, we should have to take into the account that the percipient has had another hallucination.

Case 174 (Vol. I, p. 431). A young lady in bed saw a vivid apparition of an acquaintance, Major G., walking in the room. See objections 4, 5, 6, and 15.

The percipient did not mention the vision to the family for fear of ridicule until after the news of the death. Hence, upon general principles, we should entertain a doubt whether her recognition of the person she seemed to see was quite as absolute as she afterwards thought it had been. Yet, in view of the details, "neither his features nor his figure any whit altered,"—I do not think we can attribute any importance to her having kept her experience to herself.

The percipient was not in good health. Mr. Gurney says that unless the percipient's health was favorable to subjective hallucination, her illness is of no consequence.[3] But he himself sufficiently refutes this notion in his summing up. It is not so; for as she was far from being in good health, if the hallucination had been non-coincidental, it would not have been reported in answer to the census-question; and a case which would not have been reported if non-coincidental must not be counted as coincidental. Mr. Gurney is obliged to admit that this is logical. He says he cannot tell whether the percipient's particular malady would be favorable to subjective hallucination or not. But the young lady says, "An attack of rheumatism and nervous prostration left me far from well for some weeks last spring, and one night," etc. This seems to mean that she had not recovered from her nervous prostration. On that night she "had gone to bed early," showing she felt more tired than usual, so that her brain must have been unusually taxed. I should think it plain that such a condition was favorable to the production of hallucinations.

I have reckoned this as a case in which the percipient was certainly anxious. I do not, however, think that she was so to such a degree as to exclude the case on that ground. But she knew that the person seen in her vision was fatally ill, and his case had been "a topic of conversa-

3. I note in the second proof sheet, that Mr. Gurney has modified this statement. The passage, as it will go to the reader, furnishes a curious illustration of how the census was constructed.

tion" in the family. "We had also received bad accounts a few days before, and were aware that he was in a critical condition." This, I think, implies such a degree of inquietude about the decedent as to give an antecedent probability of nine-tenths that he would be the object of any hallucination which she might have at that time.

After no hopes of his recovery were any longer entertained, further bad accounts were received, and he was "known to be in a critical condition." His chance of dying on any given day may therefore be put at one in ten. Hence, nine-tenths of one-tenth, or one-eleventh, was the antecedent probability of the coincidence.

But, for the reason given above, the case cannot be counted at all.

Case 175 (Vol. I, p. 433). A gentleman dreamt he saw his neighbor lying on the bed between him and his wife, and, waking, still thought he saw him. See objections 3 and 6.

The percipient has had other hallucinations many years before. He describes them as "day-mares." "That is, . . . I quite believe I was *asleep* while experiencing them." The present case was of the same general character, but more vivid, and continued into, or at least up to, a fully waking condition. Probably the old experiences were more vivid than he now remembers them as being; and even if they were not so, I cannot think they were of a radically different nature. He admits that "it is difficult to define the difference in these cases." Mr. Gurney says, "There is no ground for regarding them (the former experiences) as hallucinations at all, in the sense in which I throughout employ the word." But they were so according to the definition of the census-question; that is, they were "vivid impressions of seeing" human beings. The percipient says, "In the earlier cases many years ago I concluded that *waking* had caused what looked real to disappear." The phrase implies that he was some time in coming to this conclusion, and there can be little doubt to an unprejudiced mind that, in the absence of coincidence, he would have come to the same conclusion regarding the present case.

The percipient falls into confusion in trying to make out whether his state during this vision was that of waking or sleeping. He says, "I reflected, 'Am I awake, or is this a dream?' I cannot yet answer this question to my own satisfaction; I cannot tell when my dream merged in my waking thoughts. I only am sure that as the figure disappeared I was as wide awake as I am now." That is, he fully woke just as the figure disappeared, and he knows not whether to call his previous state sleeping or waking. "I had not a peculiar sense of breaking out of sleep at once, and with a snap, as it were. . . . I believe I might be awake, I even *think* I was awake, with the image of a dream still strongly on my mind. . . . Briefly, I cannot be sure . . . that I was asleep, although all experience would go to say that I was." All this shows it was a dream continued through a slow process of waking up and just into the fully waking state. Cases of this sort are so common, and so little attention is paid to them, that they could not possibly get fully reported in the census, and should be altogether excluded from the class of hallucinations for the purpose of this argument. I am willing, however, to give it one-fourth weight.

There seems to be nothing surprising in the percipient's dreaming of the decedent, who seems to have been an intimate acquaintance, and who was a sufferer from bronchial asthma. There probably was no other acquaintance about whom he was more anxious. I will put the antecedent probability of the hallucination relating to the decedent at two-thirds. A man could not die of asthma without it being generally known to his friends that his attacks were frightful. Hence, I think we may assume that the antecedent probability of his dying on a given day was 1 in 2,500. This would make the probability of the coincidence 1 in 3,800. In other words, 1 hallucination in 3,800 would present a coincidence as remarkable as this. But, owing to the percipient being exceptionally subject to hallucinations of this nature, say more so than 1 man out of 20, we must divide the 3,800 hallucinations by 20, making 190. Finally, as the case is to have only one-fourth weight, we divide again by 4, and so reach the number 48.

Case 182 (Vol. I, p. 441). The case of the young lady on the voyage to the Cape of Good Hope. See objections 3, 5, 6, 8, and 16, and Mr. Gurney's replies, especially under 16. I regret that a number of material errors have crept into my account of the case. Mr. Gurney also now furnishes new testimony, he does not say whose, affording important corroboration of that of the principal witness.

The percipient experienced another apparition shortly afterwards of a dressmaker who died about that time, the dates not being ascertainable. This shows that the percipient was at that time very unusually liable to hallucinations. But it seems to me that the rough coincidence of the second apparition with death almost forbids the hypothesis that either coincidence was purely fortuitous. I can see but two alternatives. The first is, that there has been some important suppression or falsification of the testimony, the nature of which I cannot divine. This possibility should be gravely considered, though in my numerical estimate I will not take account of it. The second is, that this young lady had a wonderful hypnotoid sensitiveness, by which she was sometimes able to make unconscious estimates, or rather unconscious mental modifications analogous to estimates, of how long consumptives approaching their end would live, with a probable error of perhaps a few months, at the end of which time she would have apparitions of them. It would then be a chance result that in the hallucination on shipboard the error was, say, only three or four hundredths of the probable error. The telepathic hypothesis would leave it very strange that the young lady should have visions of two persons in whom she had no special interest, and whom she had not seen nor probably thought of for a long time.

I assume that the antecedent probability that the hallucination would relate to the decedent was one-half, and that the antecedent probability of death was 1:200, so that the probability of the coincidence was 1:400.

Case 184 (Vol. I, pp. 444, 546, lxxx, 196, 235, 255). Mr. Keulemans, in Paris, has two visions of his little boy in London. See objections 3, 5, 6, and 15.

I have said that the percipient seems to have hallucinations nearly every day. Mr. Gurney replies: "He has had only one other hallucination in his life. This occurred many years ago in his boyhood, and represented a vague, unrecognized figure." The census-question asks whether the person addressed has "had a vivid impression of seeing . . . a human being." This defines what we have to understand by a hallucination for the purposes of the argument under examination. Now we find (Vol. I, p. 256, note) that on New Year's eve, 1881, this percipient, Mr. Keulemans, had "a vivid picture of his family circle in Holland." Nor was there any coincidence of the death which this vision had led him to expect. What I meant by saying that Mr. Keulemans seems to have hallucinations nearly every day (for I made no positive statement) was that he has constant vivid impressions of seeing objects, not always human beings. Mrs. Keulemans says (p. 256), "My husband looked at some eggs, and made the remark that he had seen them before." This shows that Mr. Keulemans speaks of these experiences as acts of seeing. Mr. Gurney tells us (p. 196), "He has experienced so many of these coincidences that, even before our inquiries quickened his interest in the matter, he has been accustomed to keep a record of his impressions." I assumed, as there was nothing to the contrary, that a large proportion of these would present human beings. But it is not of much consequence whether they do so or not. Unless we adopt the telepathic theory at once, it is plain that this percipient is so excessively liable to hallucinations that a coincidence or two is no more than natural.

Mr. Gurney says that the percipient, having absolutely no ground for anxiety, was naturally not anxious. The decedent was a child of his, five years old, who had been removed from his parents, and from Paris to London, on account of an outburst of small-pox. Here I think is ground for such a degree of anxiety as would determine the hallucination to take the form it did.

I assume it to have been antecedently practically certain that any hallucination at that time would relate to the decedent. The antecedent probability of death, and therefore of coincidence, may be taken at 1 in 25,000. But, owing to the great liability to hallucinations, I multiply the probability of coincidence by 1,000, making it 1 in 25.

Case 195 (Vol. I, p. 528). See objections 5, 6, 8, and 14, and the reply of Mr. Gurney under the 8th.

Miss Rogers saw her mother and grandmother about the time of the death of the latter. This happened in 1878, and does not seem to have very profoundly impressed anybody at the time. It is only set down on paper in 1884, one of the family being then interested in telepathy. Consequently the memory of the witnesses is hardly adequate to giving correctly all the circumstances. The percipient "cannot fix exact times and hours; but, at the same time, she thinks her vision corresponded with the time of the death." Mr. Gurney, however, now adds a circumstance to the account (it is a pity he seldom cites any testimony for his numerous additions) which makes an error in the date less probable.

The percipient, I still think, was anxious. A witness whose house she was visiting, and who was therefore in a better condition to judge than we can be, says she "doubtless had gone to bed with an anxious mind."

The percipient herself is inclined to attribute the vision to the effect of a strong imagination. (This comes to us at second-hand. I should like to have her develop her views on this point.) Now, the imaginations of different persons differ enormously, and the percipient ought to know her own imagination better than Mr. Gurney can do,—expert if he be.

As two persons appeared in the vision, and the death of either of these would have been reckoned as a coincidence, the probability is doubled.

That the grandmother would be one of the two persons represented in any such coincident hallucination of the percipient at that time I take to be certain; for she says she was continually thinking of her grandmother. The antecedent probability of death, in view of the age of the decedent, her state of health, and the anxiety of her granddaughter, I take to have been 1 in 200, which is therefore the probability of the coincidence.

Case 197 (Vol. I, p. 531). The apparition of Mountain Jim. See objections 8 and 16, and Mr. Gurney's reply under the latter head. The following remarks were written before the discovery of the diary.

I carelessly represented the witness as saying that the time of death coincided with that of the apparition.[4] What she does say is, that the "date, allowing for difference of longitude, coincided." We are to conclude, then, that the dates would not have been the same without such allowance. The meridian of the death is seven and a half hours west of that of the apparition, and the apparition occurred at 7 A.M. Thus, what she probably means is, that the civil date of death was one day previous to that of the apparition. I consider the hypothesis that the witness applied the longitude the wrong way both gratuitous and improbable. It is true this would make the hour agree; but she seems to have no remembrance of the hour agreeing. Unfortunately

4. It was Mr. Gurney himself who first made this mistake and thus led me into it. For he says (p. 532), "The coincidence cannot have been as close as Mrs. Bishop imagines." But she says nothing of a closer coincidence than a day.

there is no record of the date of the apparition, and probably never was. The witness could not have heard of the death for some weeks, and hence there must be great doubt whether the apparition really came on the right day. On some Wednesday, she says it occurred, "a few days ago." Now, it should have occurred 1874, September 8. But that day was Tuesday. Eight days might conceivably have been called "a few days ago;" but, unless she had already forgotten the day, she would have been more likely to refer to that interval as "about a week ago." Is there no postmark on the letter? Does the hotel register show that she was there on Wednesday, September 16? What was the weather at Interlaken on September 8, at 7 A.M., since she speaks of the rose-flushed morning?

Mr. Gurney admits the coincidence of time is not proved to be within twelve hours, but still thinks the case should be allowed, because the limit of twelve hours is arbitrary, and might have been fixed at eighteen or twenty-four hours. But he is altogether wrong in this. The doctrine of chances supposes the instances to be drawn blindly; and the conditions of the drawings must not be modified so as to take in known cases. If a silver mine was to be sold, and Mr. Gurney, on the part of the sellers, and I, on the part of the buyers, were to be sent to the mine to collect a fair sample of the ore, and if, after we had done so honestly, Mr. Gurney were to propose to throw in a particular lump, because he could see, from its appearance, that it was rich in silver, and because it was lying close to another lump that had been taken, I should feel it my duty to say, "No, sir, that is just what you wished to do in Case 197!" But here, in point of fact, it is not a question of a few hours merely. It is quite likely that the time of the vision was several days from that of the death.

The testimony of the witness is not in every respect accurate. There was probably no record made, as she testifies that there was; and she was not writing a letter, but may have been dozing. These symptoms of inaccuracy make the coincidence still more uncertain.

The percipient was in bed, and the vision was very likely a dream.

She knew the decedent was ill; although she had heard he was getting well and going about. She had recently received news of him; and it is no wonder, after his impressive speech at parting with her to the effect that he should see her after death (meaning, I suppose, in another world), that any dream or vision she might have at that time should take that form.

I assume the antecedent probability that the hallucination would refer to the decedent to have been nine-tenths. The chance of death on a given day, since he was ill in Colorado, may have been one in a thousand. Owing to the uncertainty of the date, I multiply by 2, and thus find for the probability of the coincidence 1 in 550.

[The discovery of the diary, which, as I interpret it, makes the vision to have occurred September 5th (according to Mr. Gurney's view of the 6th), excludes the case altogether.]

Case 199 (Vol. I, pp. 534, lxxx). Mr. B. in bed with his wife sees a lady friend of his flit across the room. See objections 1, 6, 8, and 16.

Mr. Gurney states that the narrator says "nothing which independently marks the day of the week of the vision." I am at direct issue with him here, for I say the narrative reads as follows: "He was very disconcerted by seeing the form of a lady friend of his glide or flit across the room. He thereupon woke Mrs. B. and informed her of the fact. This was Saturday." The reader will please refer to the book, and decide whose statement is correct.

It may be that a real person was seen.

Mr. B. is a very careless witness. He vouches for an erroneous day and for an erroneous year.

The case is outside of the twelve-year limit; and it would be wholly unwarrantable to change that limit to thirteen years, as Mr. Gurney suggests doing, for the sake of including a known instance. However, he gives up the case, and it cannot be counted at all.

Case 201 (Vol. I, p. 542). A lady was lying down, when she seemed to see a man come in whom she afterwards identified with an old servant, the decedent. See objections 4, 6, 7, 8, and 9. I have twice mentioned Case 201 when I meant Case 249, as Mr. Gurney notes.

The percipient "had been in ill-health for some years." True she was better at that time than for long before, so that she says, "I felt a strength and enjoyment of life for its own sake, which was a delight to me." But these are the expressions of an invalid who is making a great improvement, and not those of a person in good health.

The percipient was lying down; and she herself suspected she might have been asleep. She applied a test, and so far deserves credit; but the test is not conclusive.

She totally failed to recognize the person. Mr. Gurney says I have misquoted the account. I have merely abridged the expression, by omitting some words that are altogether in favor of my view. She "knew the face quite well, but could not say whose it was," although "the suit of clothes impressed" her "strongly as being exactly like one which" her "husband had given to a servant named Ramsay the previous year." She thus appears to have recognized the clothes as Ramsay's, and also knew the face quite well; but notwithstanding this, could not say who it was! News of the man's death having arrived, she now adds, "I believe the face of the man I saw was that of Ramsay as I had known him at first, when I visited him as a dying man in the infirmary." She is thus not sure even now.

The date of the apparition is wholly uncertain. It occurred "about March."

Mr. Gurney gives up the case; and I am not inclined to give it any weight.

Case 202 (Vol. I, p. 544). A near-sighted lady sees a victoria, horse, driver, lady, and child. See objections 4, 8, and 9.

The percipient had "been ordered by [her] doctor to take absolute rest, not even to read at all, and to do no work whatever." At the same time, she was apparently allowed to drive about in an open landau. This suggests, at least, some nervous or mental derangement. At any rate, she was not in good health; so that the case is ruled out.

She is also near-sighted, so as to wear glasses,—a fact which is mentioned as if she was unable to recognize anybody without them. Had it been proved that the lady she thought she saw was, for example, travelling on the Continent at the time, she would doubtless herself have concluded the incident was due to her near-sightedness, and not have reported it in answer to the census-question say six years later, had she answered that question.

The agreement of the date is doubtful, especially as the sole witness may have been hysterical. Mr. Gurney's thinking the probability of the date being correct is "very high" should be noted in connection with objection 18.

The recognition was ambiguous. That is to say, two persons were seen (besides the driver), the death of either of whom would be counted as a coincidence.

I think it plainly a case of mistaken identity. I have often remarked furs worn in hot weather in July in London.

Case 214 (Vol. I, p. 563). An aunt, on receiving delayed news of the sudden death of her niece, falls down, and, after many days of delirium, unconsciousness, or oblivion, not having been out of bed for three months, at length declares that at the instant of the death she saw a startling apparition of the decedent. See objections 2, 4, 8, 13, and 15.

In the copy of my criticism sent to Mr. Gurney, owing to a confusion between this case and No. 236, I committed an oversight (though probably not a misstatement) in enumerating this case among those in which the percipients were not in good health.

Not having mentioned the apparition, as it would seem, on receiving news of the death a week after it occurred, "She fell off from the chair, remembering no more until days afterwards she found herself in bed, where she remained" for about three months. The doctor "said that she had received some great mental shock, and for some time he feared that she would not recover from it." She was in a delirious or oblivious condition for days; and her remaining in bed for three months in consequence of a mental shock suggests, to say the least, some nervous or mental affection.

In my opinion, it is altogether uncertain that she saw any vision before her illness, or, if she did, on what day she saw it. At any rate, it must be allowed that there is a chance amounting say to 1 in 100 that this is the case. The antecedent probability, then, of the event,— perhaps it was a coincidence and perhaps it was not, —is at least 1 in 100. I shall give the case this weight, although Mr. Gurney gives it up entirely.

Case 231 (Vol. II, p. 47). A volunteer officer in Zululand fancies he sees a dying comrade standing outside his tent. See objections 5 and 8.

The percipient's mind was not free from anxiety. It may not have been of a kind to produce hallucinations; but it would have prevented his truthfully answering the census-question in the affirmative. On account of this, I will multiply the probability of coincidence by 3.

There seems to have been an interval of two days between the apparition and the death. Mr. Gurney admits an even chance of this, but still argues that the case might be included. I do not think the chance as great as one-half; but still I will adopt this factor.

The case is most probably a mere instance of a dreadfully fatigued man looking at one person and fancying him another, and therefore not strictly a hallucination at all. In any such mistake that he might make at that time, he would be quite likely to think he saw the friend concerning whom his mind had been worried. We may take two-thirds as the antecedent probability of this.

As the decedent was known to be dreadfully ill, and to have suffered an utter collapse, and as the percipient had been told two days before that he was dying, we may assume as the antecedent probability of death on that day one-third. The probability of the coincidence was then, antecedently, two-ninths, or 1 in 4.5. In other words, there would, in the long run, be a coincidence as remarkable as this for every 4.5 hallucinations. But there is an even chance that there was no coincidence; so that this must be halved. Then, on account of anxiety, there is only a probability of one-third that the case should be counted, so that the number must again be divided by 3, which reduces it to less than unity, so that the case is, for the purposes of the present argument, of less value than the average hallucination. Mr. Gurney gives up the case altogether.

Case 236 (Vol. II, p. 52). A governess fancies she sees a dark figure just outside the [house?] door, in the evening, which reminded her of her brother. See objections 3 and 7, and Mr. Gurney's reply under the latter head.

The percipient had had for weeks a sound in her ears like the ticking of a watch, and shortly before, on several successive nights, had heard a tremendous crash like the smashing of a lot of china. Mr. Gurney admits that these were symptoms of a purely physical affection; and they certainly seem to indicate some disease of the brain. They render a hallucination at least ten times as probable as it would be under average circumstances.

The fright and weakness caused by the apparition, although it was only a dark figure, are most readily explained as physiological, and go to show that a genuine hallucination was experienced. The previous symptoms also render this probable.

The percipient does not say she saw her brother. "I saw what appeared to me to be a dark figure standing just outside the door, with outstretched arms." Later she says, "The apparition did remind me of my brother." This form of the indicative shows that she had either been shown some statement to that effect or had been asked some leading question equivalent to the exhibition of such testimony. (See objection 18.) In any case, the figure was not recognized as being her brother; it only reminded her of him.

In my opinion, the date of apparition is somewhat uncertain, as it was not recorded, and few persons remember days of the month accurately, especially against the influence of a mental suggestion tending to error. There is no circumstance, not even the day of the week, to corroborate the bare memory of the day of the month.

The second witness does not commend herself to my judgment so much as the percipient herself. This second witness, whose testimony is not in every respect consistent with that of the percipient, says the latter said she knew something must have happened to her brother. The percipient herself mentions no such effect; but there may have been a transitory fear for him, as he was at sea.

The antecedent probability that the hallucination would refer to the decedent may be taken as nineteen-twentieths. Assuming the brother to have been twenty-five years of age, his chance of dying on a given day would normally be 1 in 55,100. But his being a sailor would double this. Hence, there would be one coincidence as remarkable as this in 28,000 hallucinations. But this number should be divided by 2 on account of the defect of recognition, and again by 2 on account of the doubt about the date. Finally, it should be divided by 10 on account of the liability to hallucination. Thus, 1 hallucination out of 700 would be as extraordinary as this.

Case 237 (Vol. II, p. 54). A servant girl sitting with her mother in the evening and reading to herself distinctly saw a dear school-friend, the decedent. See objections 8 and 17.

We are obliged to trust to the apparently unaided memory of one witness as to the year. She says, nearly ten years after, that it happened in 1874. If it really occurred in 1873, of which there may perhaps be one chance in ten, it does not come within the twelve-year period.

We know little of the character of the witness, though the style of the narrative (if she wrote it unaided), as well as the impression she made on Mr. Gurney in a single interview, were very favorable.

We know nothing of the state of her health, which ought in every case to be closely inquired into.

The only person in the room at the time, her mother, thought she might have been dreaming. This is the more important, as the mother is not convinced by the occurrence, but continues to disbelieve in ghosts. Had there been no coincidence, the daughter would probably in time have fallen in with this view, and would consequently not have reported the vision in answer to the census-question.

After the lapse of ten years, it is impossible to be certain that the death and the vision occurred within twelve hours of one another, there being no record of either. Most persons' memory is very treacherous about coincidences. Mr. Gurney's thinking the probability that there was a 12-hour coincidence "very high" is remarkable.

Not so much as the name of the decedent is given.

We have no information about what kind of a room it was, nor have we any means of assuring ourselves that no real person could have been seen. I confess it seems more likely to have been a hallucination; but this is by no means established.

Mr. Gurney professes to consider this account as eminently satisfactory. But the story is too bald. From this point in the list on, the accounts are generally too meagre. With more details, some other explanation might offer itself.

There seems to have been no particular reason why the decedent should have been the object of the hallucination; so that we fall back on the general calculation that there is 1 chance in 17,000 of a coincidence. But owing to the doubt about the date, I multiply this by 3, making it 1 in 6,000. Since, if non-coincidental, it might have been set down as a dream, I multiply this again by 2, making 1 in 3,000. And on account of the baldness of the story, I multiply again by 2, making 1 in

1,500. I think this number, though I will adhere to it, is really much too favorable to the story.

Case 238 (Vol. II, p. 55). A laborer's wife sees her husband in the woods and speaks to him. See objection 2.

There was a strong hallucination, with faintness, causing the percipient to fall.

I assume that it was antecedently certain that the hallucination would refer to her husband, whom she seems to have loved. This is the assumption the most favorable to telepathy, since he was a well man. The probability that he would die on a given day might be 1 in 40,000; but, as he was exposed to accidents, I will take it at 1 in 30,000. But this probability is so microscopic that a very forced explanation is to be preferred to it, say, for instance, that the whole tale has been concocted. I cannot admit that the chance of there being some such explanation can be less than 1 in 20,000, which value I will therefore adopt.

Case 240 (Vol. II, p. 59). Mrs. Ellis three times during one day distinctly saw the face of an old friend. See objections 5 and 17.

The apparition occurred first at 10 A.M. and last at 6 P.M., so that the 24-hour period within which death would be considered as coincidental ought to be reckoned from 2 A.M. Only the date of the death being known, there is 1 chance in 12 that it did not fall within these 24 hours.

There is no record nor independent recollection of the date of the apparition.

Mr. Gurney says there was probably no anxiety, because the parties *"had not been"* on friendly terms. But the pluperfect, taken with the context, seems to signify that a reconciliation had recently taken place. The mother of the percipient, at the decedent's desire, went to see him just before his death. There was, thus, a redintegration of friendship.

As the decedent was an old friend and known to be near death (for the percipient says, "Nor did I know that he was *so* near death"), it may be taken as practically certain that one or more of the hallucinations would relate to him. The chance that he would die on that day may have been 1 in 5. Owing to various doubts, I will call it 1 in 4. Mr. Gurney abandons the case.

Case 249 (Vol. II, pp. 71, xxiii). This is the case depending on identification by means of a man's hat, the silver hair of the top part of his head, and the droop of his head, seen over a wall. See objections 7, 8, and 12.

No jury would hang a man on such an identification. Far less can such a theory as the telepathic be accepted on such evidence. For here we are dealing with explanations whose antecedent probability is microscopic.

My hypothesis of a slight degree of intoxication is needless and too gratuitous. It is, however, far more probable than the telepathic theory.

As the decedent was a neighbor of the percipient, and known to be ill, we will assume the antecedent probability that the hallucination would refer to him was one-half. As he was an aged man and ill, we will assume his chance of death was ten times the average. As he had silver hair and his head drooped, we will assume his age was eighty. Then, the probability that he would die on a given day was 1 in 256, and the antecedent probability of the coincidence was 1 in 500. But I do not believe there was any hallucination at all, and cannot admit anything more extraordinary than 1 in 100.

Case 298 (Vol. II, p. 143). A woman who is scrubbing a floor thinks she sees her old lover looking in at the window. See objections 3 and 17.

The percipient has "had an auditory hallucination on one other occasion, when she heard herself called by the voice of her husband, who, it turned out, had died at a distance two days before." Voices of absent loved ones are too common to be reported duly in a census.

There is little evidence that the percipient did not really see the person she thought she saw, except that a witness *says* that the decedent's employers in the city *said* that they had *received news*, the testimony of some witness in Madras, this testimony itself being very likely *second-hand*, that that person had died on that day. I am not convinced he ever went to India at all.

The coincidence of date is not certain. Mr. Hensleigh Wedgwood took a note of the apparition, May, 16, 1878. This note gives the time as "one Saturday evening, about six weeks ago." Six weeks before May

16 was April 4, and April 6 was Saturday; but the death was reported to have occurred on Saturday, March 30.

The whole circumstances are not sufficiently given.

The probability of coincidence would be 1 in 17,000; but, owing to the doubt about the date, this would have to be doubled. I prefer, however, the supposition that she saw the real person, since I do not think the probability of this hypothesis is less than 1 in 1,000. This measure of improbability I am willing to allow.

Case 300 (Vol. II, p. 146). A sailor sees his father on a voyage. See objections 11 and 17.

Women, children, sailors, and idiots are recognized by the law as classes peculiarly liable to imposition. If sailors' yarns are to be admitted, the reality of ghosts is put beyond doubt at once, and further discussion is superfluous.

The story is meagre. Mr. Gurney thinks it would be more credible if still more so. I disagree with him. I shall give it no weight whatever.

Case 350 (Vol. II, pp. 244, xxv). This is the ridiculous tale of the three maid-servants and the face in the window. See objection 10. My explanation given above is complete and satisfactory; and Mr. Gurney has not been able to pick any flaw in it of the least consequence. As tricksters invent strange things, and do not tell their secrets, I am at liberty to draw much upon my imagination in this kind of explanation. Nor is it at all necessary to suppose all the details of the testimony true. It is only necessary to invent an explanation which will strike a shrewd person as not utterly preposterous, and as sufficiently accounting for the stories told by the witnesses. Every amateur juggler will agree that it would be asking too much to require me to assume the witnesses saw precisely what they thought they saw. I acknowledge that the mistress says that it was not known that the person with whom the apparition was identified was near death. But that does not prove that the servants did not know all I have supposed they knew. I have said the decedent had a cancer. I may have confounded the case with 27; at any rate, there is no testimony that the disease was a cancer. Mr. Gurney endeavors to make much of this possible error; but it is quite insignificant; no part of my theory is based upon that. He also thinks that I have taken a great liberty with the evidence in changing the phrases "trying to look in" and having "come up [from the village] to make game" of the girls, into looking in and smiling at the girls, where I use no quotation marks. It seems to be the inferred smiling that offends him so. He splits hairs to find a weak point in my theory. He says the skull is inconsistent with some of the evidence, as if we were bound to admit that ghost-seers see all they think they see! I hope the reader will turn to the case and see which hypothesis he judges the more credible. I flatter myself common-sense will be upon my side.

Case 355 (Vol. II, p. 256). A nautical case occurring in 1853. Mr. Gurney withdraws it.

Case 695 (Vol. II, p. 693). A mother sees her son, who had died eight hours previously of enteric fever in the Soudan. See objections 2 and 17.

A meagre story, told at second-hand.

We know nothing of the state of health of the percipient.

Her husband says she was not anxious; but this is hard to believe. It is more likely she concealed her anxiety in order not to alarm her husband. The son had dictated a letter August 20, to say he had enteric fever, and had dictated another September 7, to say that he was better and expected soon to be home. There was nothing more till October 12, when he could not even dictate a letter; but a Sister Thomas wrote to say that he had been very ill, but "is getting on very nicely now." This last letter could not have been received long before October 24, the date of the apparition. How could a mother fail to be anxious? Is it not a calumny to say that she was not so? And if the hallucination had proved non-coincidental, would it not have been attributed to anxiety, and so not reported in answer to a census-question?

I assume that it was antecedently certain that the hallucination would relate to her son, and I estimate his chance of dying on a given day at 1 in 100, which is therefore the antecedent probability of the coincidence.

Case 697 (Vol. II, p. 695). The "practical" wife of a "practical business man," who informs us that "there can be no doubt whatever that there is some transmission for which no explanation has yet been given by the savants," sees, one night, an apparition which, the following evening, she recognizes as a clerk in her husband's counting-house, just as her husband is about to announce the death of this clerk. See objections 6 and 7, and Mr. Gurney's reply under the latter head.

The percipient's shivering fright lends color to the view that there was a genuine hallucination.

She may have heard of the death during the day, before she had made up her mind whom the apparition resembled. Mr. Gurney avers that this had not happened; but as he adduces no testimony but his own, the statement goes for nothing.

The practical business man gives us a hint when he says, "I should scarcely have believed [the story] if related to me of any one else." I am somewhat disposed to follow his example.

The lady had seen the unfortunate fellow; and the husband's expression, "I have some sad news to tell you," shows that her pity had been excited; so that we may assume that the antecedent probability that her hallucination would refer to the decedent was one-fourth. Considering what appears to have been the nature of the disease, and its history so far as we can make it out, the antecedent probability that he would die on a given day, though very uncertain, may be taken at 1 in 200. This would make the probability of the coincidence 1 in 800.

Case 702 (Vol. II, p. 703). The percipient, while laid up with Jamaica fever, had a dream, which, after sudden waking, was continued as a vision. It represented an old lady friend of his, who spoke. See objections 4, 5, 6, and 8.

The percipient, in his first account, says, I "believe the following was the result of illness." Although he has since been converted from that opinion by Mr. Gurney, it is clear that if the case had not been coincidental, it would not have been reported in answer to the census-question, with its good-health clause. Hence, it must positively be excluded from the argument.

The date is quite in doubt. In his original account the percipient has the year wrong. He now alters his recollected date by four days, in order to make it accord with that of the death. There is no independent evidence, and he was so ill that his memory was not to be trusted. My original statement conveys an entirely correct impression, except that I may have misunderstood the *altered* statement, that the vision took place "a few minutes past midnight, June 11." My professional habits led me to understand this in the sense in which an astronomer would use the expression. But, as the story has been cooked, I suppose the intention was to make it right.

An unnumbered case (Vol. I, p. 130, note). See objection 17. Mr. Gurney admits that the story is told in so meagre a form that it has no evidential value. Still he retains it. I cannot do so.

I will now collect and sum up the numbers of hallucinations that there would have to be in the long run, to have among them thirty-one coincidences as extraordinary as these. The following are the numbers already estimated:—

Case.	Number.	Case.	Number.	Case.	Number.
26	1,667	195	200	249	100
27	156	197	0	298	1,000
28	2,000	199	0	300	0
29	1,050	201	0	350	0
170	0	202	0	355	0
172	0	214	100	695	100
173	0	231	1	697	800
174	0	236	700	702	0
175	48	237	1,500	Unnumbered	0
182	400	238	20,000		
184	25	240	4	Total	29,851

Thus, 29,851 cases of hallucinations are called for, in order to produce as remarkable a series of coincidences as these. A believer in telepathy would, no doubt, reckon the number as larger; on the other hand, I have ascertained that many shrewd and experienced men would hold that I have not allowed sufficient weight to possibilities of fraud and concoction. I have, of course, been biassed; but I have endeavored to be on my guard against my bias. I am sure that hypotheses of small probability, say less than 1 in 500, have not been allowed their due weight. Especially, I have not sufficiently taken into account the possibilities of explanations that have not been thought of. On the other hand, it is easy to see that Mr. Gurney has not constructed the strongest possible argument of the same general nature. We can only conclude, then, that 30,000 coincidences *may be* the number called for. If we suppose that hallucinations are four times as common as the census shows, the 30,000 coincidences ought to have occurred in a population of two millions; but two-thirds of this number is wanted to account for Mrs. Duck's case alone, and no probable induction can, of course, be based on a single instance. This case, however, comes from the *Englishman* newspaper, which may recount the most remarkable experiences of more than a million of persons. It is likely that some of the other more valuable cases, such as 26, 237, etc., have been derived from the advertisements, which, for the reasons I have given, must have drawn the most remarkable experiences from a large population, going up perhaps into millions. A candid consideration of the whole matter will, I think, convince the reader that until the telepathic theory of ghost-stories has been rendered far more antecedently probable than it now is, it is useless to try to establish it as a scientific truth by any accumulation of unscientific observations.

19

Remarks on Mr. Peirce's Rejoinder

March 1889 ***Proceedings of the American Society for Psychical Research***

BY EDMUND GURNEY

I will endeavor to make the present reply as short as possible, my object being, not so much to make controversial points, as to ensure, as far as possible, that Mr. Peirce's treatment of the evidence and argument for telepathy shall not prevent his readers from studying them at length and at first-hand. Consequently I shall say little or nothing on matters where I believe that an impartial study of what has been said in *Phantasms of the Living*, or in my previous reply, obviates the necessity of further explanation and defence, nor shall I attempt to put what I have to say in connected literary form. It will be enough to state the points which need stating, one after another, with references to the pages in Mr. Peirce's last paper.

Mr. Peirce's treatment of the question of general probabilities (pp. 103–4) seems to me completely fallacious. My argument was, that a particular series of events, of the sort known as coincidences, could not, according to the doctrine of probabilities, be due to chance. My calculation made out the degree of probability against chance, as the cause of these coincidences, to be enormous; and Mr. Peirce objected to my figures, on the ground that in mundane affairs probabilities never really ran so high. I accordingly gave a simple practical instance where they ran higher,—an instance yielding a probability of almost incalculable magnitude that a particular series of events was not due to chance. The instance was that of a pair of dice turning up sixes a hundred times running, from which we should unhesitatingly conclude that the dice were loaded. Here was a case of an enormous *à posteriori* probability against a chance causation, exactly parallel to my case of the coincidences. Mr. Peirce, not being able to directly deny the legitimacy of the illustration, confuses the question by introducing a case of *à priori* probability, totally irrelevant to the matter in hand. He supposes the throw of a single die, which we should ordinarily regard as certain to turn up one or another of its faces, but in respect of which there is an appreciable possibility that it "may rest on its vertex, or fly up to heaven, or vanish altogether, or that, before it reaches the table, earth and heaven shall be annihilated." It would be easy, but it is unnecessary, to demur to this statement on its own account. The question is not of the appreciable possibility that *one* new and extraordinary event will occur at all; but of the appreciable possibility that a *series* of events, similar in character, but no one of them new or extraordinary, has occurred by chance. Mr. Peirce may hold, if he likes, that the probability, which plain men would describe as certainty, that his die will not accidentally fly up to heaven, rests on "assumptions," and "refers to an imaginary state of things"; it is enough for me that the probability which plain men would describe as certainty, that my dice did not accidentally turn up sixes a hundred times running, rests on no assumptions, and refers to the actually existing state of things. In what way, when estimating such a probability numerically in the analogous case of the coincidences, I can be held to "admit that the number has no real significance," I am at a loss to conceive.

As regards Mr. Peirce's remarks in the second paragraph on p. 104, it seems enough to refer to my former reply, p. 98. I do not "suppose that hallucinations are experiences particularly well remembered" (p. 105), in the sense which Mr. Peirce implies. I hold them to be neither better nor worse remembered than other equally rare and striking experiences.

Mr. Peirce cannot, I think, have given much time or care to the subject of hallucinations, or he could not have put forward (p. 106), as the one type of "genuine hallucination," "the product of an over-wrought brain, which is preceded by great depression, accompanied by faintness, and followed by an access of terror." Such hallucinations are very rare, and are no more "genuine" than numbers of others. (See *Phantasms of the Living*, Chap. XI, on "Transient Hallucinations of the Sane.")

So far from there being "no good reason for limiting the census-question to a period of twelve years" (p. 106), there were two very good reasons: (1) the imperfection of human memory, of which Mr. Peirce supplies an instance, since he describes a hallucination of his own, of thirty years ago, as having all but escaped his recollection; and (2) the fact that most of the best established coincidental cases, with which the non-coincidental cases had to be compared, fell within the assigned period.

The census inquiry was not limited, as Mr. Peirce represents, to hallucinations presenting persons really alive, but to hallucinations presenting persons who, as in the coincidental cases, were believed by the percipient to be alive; and so far from this involving a "fallacy," a fallacy would have been involved in reasoning conducted on any other basis.

The error in Mr. Peirce's argument at the top of p. 107 may be best shown by an illustration. Suppose I put an advertisement in the papers, asking persons who have had small-pox, though vaccinated in childhood, to communicate with me; and suppose my appeal to reach a circle of two hundred and fifty thousand people, strangers to me, of whom five take the trouble to write and tell me that they have had the experience in question. And suppose that I address inquiries on the same subject to the one thousand people most nearly connected with me and with my few intimate friends, and find that five out of the one thousand have been similarly affected. Mr. Peirce would apparently conclude that the one thousand form a class two hundred and fifty times as "fertile" in cases of small-pox as the general population. Most other people, I fancy, would conclude that only a very small proportion of the newspaper-readers who had had the experience had answered my appeal. As regards my alleged *petitio principii* (p. 107), I can but refer once more to the sentences from the opening of Chap. XIII of *Phantasms of the Living*, quoted in my last paper, p. 97.

P. 108. Mr. Peirce says: "Persons who, from the percipient's stand-point, appear particularly likely to die, are, we find, particularly apt to appear in hallucinations." I suppose that this statement is founded on those cases in *Phantasms of the Living*—an extremely small proportion of the whole number—where the so-called "agent" was known by the percipient to be seriously ill. But even if such hallucinations were numerous enough to justify Mr. Peirce's assertion, at least two strong objections may be urged to his conclusion, that they must have been due to the percipient's knowledge of the illness.

(1) By what right does he assume the correctness of the evidence for the fact and the circumstances of the hallucination, in these particular cases, while disputing it in the far more numerous cases where the "agent" was supposed by the percipient to be in normal health? The evidence must surely be judged, throughout, on its own account, and not be picked to suit a particular hypothesis. And of two rival hypotheses, that which covers all the facts, as telepathy does here, is naturally to be preferred to one which only covers a small, arbitrarily-selected group of the facts.

(2) How does he account for the close correspondence, in time, of the hallucination with the death, in the cases—of which the small class in question chiefly consist—where the more or less serious condition of the "agent's" health had been equally well known to the percipient for weeks, and even months, before?

Mr. Peirce's next sentence (p. 108) reproduces his gratuitous and erroneous view of "genuine hallucinations," already sufficiently noticed (p. 143). The "peculiar terror" is an extremely rare concomitant.

To the two pages 105–7 ("In the discussion of each story"—"destructive of sound judgment") I can give no better reply than is already given in the "General Criticism of the Evidence" (*Phantasms of the Living*, Vol. I, Chap. IV, pp. 161–72). I hope that Mr. Peirce's readers will consult that chapter before accepting his sweeping statement that telepathy is opposed to "some of the fundamental elements of the general conception of nature," and to "the main principles of science."[1] Even less defensible is the view, by which much of the remainder of his case is vitiated, that it is sufficient to suggest "an explanation for each story more probable than the telepathic explanation." This, of course, entirely ignores the quintessential point of the telepathic argument—the *cumulation* of similar instances. A single illustration—that of the dice—will again serve. If the dice turn up sixes once, by far the most probable explanation is, that they did so by chance, and no sane person will conclude that they are loaded; but if they turn up sixes a hundred times running, no sane person will conclude anything else.

1. As to the alleged *rarity* of telepathic effects "we must not be too positive that the telepathic action is confined to the well-marked or extensive instances on which the *proof* of it has to depend." (See *Phantasms of the Living*, Vol. I, p. 97.)

P. 111. I have never admitted that I had "the bias of an advocate;" what I admitted was some slight (very slight) justification for Mr. Peirce, if he chose to regard me as an advocate. I approached the subject quite as sceptically as he did; and to this day I agree with him in professing "a legitimate and well-founded prejudice against the supernatural."

P. 112, Mr. Peirce's bare assertion that one of his old objections is "logically sound" is less persuasive than would be some reply to the passage (p. 83) in which I have proved it, as I conceive, to be the reverse. But, as he withdraws the objection, I need say no more about it.

Mr. Peirce has certainly not added to the force of his third objection. The hallucinations in the coincidental cases of the class under debate were recognized as representing particular persons. It is of hallucinations of this class, and of no other, that account has to be taken in estimating the comparative frequency of non-coincidental cases. Whether a recorded hallucination was of the "recognized" class was one of the details as to which inquiry was made after the more general census question had been answered in the affirmative. (See *Phantasms of the Living*, Vol. II, p. 7, note.) Mr. Peirce's argument here is curiously suicidal; for, even if it were the case that persons who have had occasional impressions of a quite different kind were "abnormally subject" to this particular type of hallucination, they would be more, and not less, likely than other people to recall instances, which is just what not one of the percipients in the cases to which Mr. Peirce objects has been able to do.

P. 108. Objection 6. In his first comment Mr. Peirce seems to have missed my point. Once more let me repeat, what had to be done was to make a numerical comparison of certain coincidental hallucinations with non-coincidental cases similar in kind. For a non-coincidental case to be included in the statistics used it would be sufficient that the percipient *believed himself* to be awake at the time of his experience. I should not have been justified in rejecting a case merely because I had not conclusive proof that he *was* awake; and the coincidental cases had, of course, to be treated on the same principle. I may add that the belief in question is itself a very strong proof of its own truth, since it very rarely happens that after waking from a dream we continue to believe that it was a piece of real waking experience. To Mr. Peirce's second comment I can allow no weight. There is absolutely nothing in the fact of the coincidence to lead the percipient to conclude that he had been awake rather than asleep at the time of his experience. Rather is the tendency of percipients, shown in several cases, to persuade themselves, as time goes on, that what was clearly recognized at the moment as a rare thing, viz., a waking hallucination, had been no more than a common thing, viz., a vivid dream, likely to be increased by the fact of the coincidence; which is clearly easier to explain by the natural hypothesis of accident, if the percipient's experience belonged to a *common* class, than if it belonged to a *rare* class.

Objection 12. "The percipient may have been intoxicated," etc. So equally may the subjects of the non-coincidental cases have been. So equally, of course, were they not.

Objection 15. A. "He may be lying." The improbability of cumulative and concordant lying is ignored, like the whole of the cumulative argument. B. The hallucinations have in most cases been quite unlike "ordinary indistinct vision," or "dreams." They have been clear and definite. C. The memory of the hallucination has located it definitely in time and space, which entirely differentiates the cases from the common vague impression of having been in the same situation before.

Objection 16. I have nothing to add to the concluding sections of Chap. IV of *Phantasms,* already referred to. I will just repeat that "it is very important to avoid confounding the natural growths on the margin (so to speak) of a telepathic record with the vital point at its centre; or concluding that the latter is as likely to be unconsciously invented as the former."

Objection 17. I must maintain that the clearly-stated, unadorned, and corroborated piece of evidence which Mr. Peirce condemns as "meagre," differs completely from the narratives which one "may hear in an endless flood," by frequenting the company of marvel-mongers, or even in ordinary society, where unscientific credulity is often the prevailing temper. Whether or not such a piece of evidence "*must*" go for nothing, it certainly *will* not go for nothing, in the eyes of any impartial reader, in whose eyes I am not thoroughly incompetent for my work.

Case 26. I have nothing to add to my remarks on p. 88. I, of course, "use the case as a premise from which to draw a conclusion" of the high degree of probability which has so offended Mr. Peirce, just as I should use each of the hundred throws of sixes to support a similar highly probable conclusion that the dice were loaded.

Case 27. I dissent from Mr. Peirce's remarks, but am quite content to leave the question to the reader; merely protesting against the monstrous assumption "that the probability that this decedent would be represented in any hallucination that the percipient might have at this time was four-fifths." A little study of the subject of hallucinations would have taught Mr. Peirce that the hallucination was every bit as likely to represent the percipient's wife, or a servant in the house; and far more likely to represent one or another member of this daily-seen class.

Case 28. Again dissenting from Mr. Peirce's treatment, I am quite content to let the reader form his own opinion. It is amusing, by the way, to find Mr. Peirce driven by the momentum of his argument into eulogizing the judgment and observation of one witness, of whom all that appears is—that he believed in telepathic communications on insufficient evidence! Mr. Peirce concludes his comment with a similar monstrous assumption to that noticed in the last case.

Case 29. The percipient's testimony as to his health is this: "I never felt better in my life; there was nothing in the least amiss with me." In the original account he says that while peering forward, for a special purpose, he "slightly stumbled on a hassock of grass, and looked at my feet for a moment only." On the strength of this sentence Mr. Peirce describes the man as "stumbling about the churchyard,"—a very characteristic piece of misrepresentation, small in appearance, but eminently calculated to prejudice the reader. He proceeds to adduce as a suspicious circumstance that, "when the percipient got home, he half thought what he had seen must have been his fancy." I go further, for I have hardly a doubt that it was "his fancy,"—in other words, that what he saw was a hallucination. How does that affect the improbability that this fancy, and others of the same sort, would, by chance, closely coincide with the death of the person represented? A little further on, the "monstrous assumption"—as to the probability that this particular person would be the object of the hallucination—duly reappears; partly based in this instance on another—"as the news of the death reached the town the next morning, it is fair to assume that the gardener was aware of the illness of the decedent." This is a specimen of the assumptions which Mr. Peirce regards as "fair." The contrary of what he supposes seems sufficiently implied in the account; but the evidence is certainly improved by the following explicit statement: "I had no knowledge that Mrs. de F. was ill, and was not even aware that she was away from Hinxton. Alfred Bard."

Mr. Peirce says, "If we had a better acquaintance with the witness than is conveyed by the vicar's banal certificate to the man's character." The vicar's certificate may be "banal," but it is at any rate explicit and based on thorough knowledge. But "we" *have* "a better acquaintance," in so far as first-hand acquaintance is better than second-hand; for Mr. Myers and Mr. Hodgson[2] have seen and carefully examined the witness.

P. 120, top. Referring to a remark of mine on p. 92, line 28, I much regret the misprint, whereby a repetition of the last five letters of the word *through* has produced an interpolation of the adjective "rough" before "inadvertence." When I found, too late, that I had overlooked this word in the proof, I hoped that (apart from manners) its fatuity in point of style would suggest the nature of the error; but most authors have had occasion to mourn the baselessness of such hopes.[3]

Case 172. I dissent from Mr. Peirce's objections, and I, on my side, should be glad to know, (1) why he calls an apparition seen with the eyes open, and after the percipient had started up in bed and looked round, a dream; (2) how he would support his assertion that it was "practically certain that the dream would relate to the decedent," which implies, of course, that the witness could not dream of any human being except this particular friend during all the months of the friend's illness.

Case 173. Mr. Peirce's "explanation" involves, besides several assumptions, the conjunction of at least two improbabilities,—the production of a vivid dream by the mention of name outside the cabin, and the continuance, in waking hours, of the belief that the dream had been a piece of waking experience.

Case 174. Beyond noting once more the monstrous assumption of "an antecedent probability of nine-tenths" that the person who appeared would be the object of any hallucination which the percipient might have at the time, I need only refer to my former remarks, pp. 85, 96.

Case 175. I willingly leave to the reader the decision as to whether Mr. Peirce is justified in dismissing as a dream an experience of which the percipient uses such expressions as these: "I thought I saw him there after dreaming. I arose and rested on my right elbow, looking at him in the dusky light. I am sure that as the figure disap-

2. Mr. Bard was interviewed, I think in the summer of 1885, by Mr. Myers and myself, and we questioned him closely concerning his experience. R. H.

3. I may note here another misprint, which occurs on p. 97, line 8. The "case which happened a few months earlier" than case 199 is No. 500.

peared I was as wide awake as now." The percipient's former purely subjective dream-experiences, which he expressly distinguishes from the present case, were, as I rightly say, "not hallucinations at all in the sense in which I throughout employ the word." Mr. Peirce's assertion that they were "hallucinations, according to the definition of the census-question," is quite without foundation; for the census-question related expressly to waking experiences.

Case 182, with the corroboration of the percipient's cousin, given in my last paper, reduces Mr. Peirce to rather desperate straits; and as the "wonderful hypnotoid sensitiveness," leading up, weeks afterwards, to an accurately-timed hallucination, is in my view as groundless an assumption as the "important suppression or falsification of the testimony," I must continue to think the case a very strong one. Our old friend, the "monstrous assumption," reappears, in a particularly monstrous form, in the supposition that the antecedent probability that the hallucinations would relate to the decedent was one-half.

Case 184. In saying that the words "a vivid impression of seeing a human being" define what we have to understand by a hallucination, for the purposes of the present argument, Mr. Peirce has made a serious error. He does not seem to have observed—what is stated in *Phantasms of the Living*, Vol. II, p. 7—that the details of the hallucinations mentioned in answer to the original census-question were "a matter of subsequent inquiry." One of these details, as I have said, was whether the figure seen (or the voice heard) was recognized as that of a person known to the percipient. And I must, it seems, once more point out the obvious fact that the only hallucinations which could properly be included in my estimate are those of the same character as the coincidental group which I present as properly telepathic,—*i.e.*, they must be of the "recognized" class. It is worth noting that had I made the mistake which Mr. Peirce, it seems, would defend, of including *unrecognized* non-coincidental hallucinations in the reckoning, his own "monstrous assumption" of an immensely high probability, sometimes even of certainty, that any hallucination that befell the percipient in the coincidental cases would represent the person whom it did represent, would become more monstrous still, since it is only a minority of visual hallucinations that represent recognized figures at all.

Mr. Peirce's proof that the hallucination was determined by a state of anxiety on the part of the percipient is surely not one that he can reflect on with much satisfaction. He says: "The decedent was a child of his [the percipient's], five years old, who had been removed from his parents, and from Paris to London, on account of an outburst of small-pox." He omits to add that the removal took place in December, while the apparition did not take place till the 24th of January, and that in the course of the month's interval several letters had been received giving an excellent account of the little boy's health. More than this: the hallucination, which conveyed the impression of a happy laughing child, left the percipient saying to himself, "Thank God, little Isidore is happy as always"; and he describes the ensuing day as one of peculiar brightness and cheerfulness. The assumption that it was "antecedently practically certain that any hallucination at that time would relate to the decedent" is a robust specimen of its class.

Case 195. As to the supposed anxiety, I may simply refer to the remarks in my former paper, on p. 85–6. Mr. Peirce's point, that the percipient "ought to know her own imagination better than Mr. Gurney can do," has no force; for she has had no other hallucination, and therefore has no claim (such as some abnormally vivid visualizers might have) to speak with authority on the power of her imagination to conjure up fictitious sensory experiences. But of course the attribution of a sensory hallucination to "a strong imagination" would be a very natural and defensible hypothesis, even for a coincidental case, if the case stood alone; it is the ACCUMULATION of coincidental cases, of which the percipients themselves knew nothing, that justifies us in rejecting the hypothesis of a purely subjective origin for all of them. The matter is one of statistics, where the *collector* is an authority, and the *contributor*, as such, is none at all.

Case 197. I have here to admit a piece of inadvertence. When giving the additional evidence under head 16 (pp. 94–5), I did not recollect that it affected my remarks under head 8 (p. 88). The retention of those remarks is, however, of no importance, for in my summary (p. 97) I say, "As regards closeness of coincidence, the recent information as to case 197, though improving the quality of the evidence, removes it from this particular death-list."

Mr. Peirce's paragraph (p. 128), beginning "Mr. Gurney admits the coincidence of time is not proved to be within twelve hours," shows a curious misunderstanding of my meaning. I never dreamt of taking advantage of the fact that the twelve hours' limit was arbitrary, to include in a particular estimate, based on a twelve hours' limit, cases where that limit was known to have been exceeded, and I should not have thought that my remarks on page 88 could have been so interpreted. For the purpose of the estimate, the inclusion, with "due warning," of "two or three cases" where the chances are about even that the twelve hours' limit *was* or was *not* slightly exceeded, seems the more defensible in view of the large number of included cases where the coincidence was *much closer* than the said limit.

Mr. Peirce is so fond of assuming it as a certainty that the person actually represented would be the object of any hallucination that the percipient might have at the time, that we ought to be grateful for the probability of nine-tenths that he substitutes in this case, and which is, perhaps, not more than fifty times too large.

Lastly, unless Mr. Peirce could show how the words, "the coincidence cannot have been as close as Mrs. Bishop imagines," implied that Mrs. Bishop had imagined it to have been exact, he should not have labelled my perfectly true statement as a "mistake," in order to father his own upon it.

Case 199. I cannot conceive what Mr. Peirce finds *independent* of the vision to mark the day of the week on which the vision fell. The words which he quotes relate to the vision, and to nothing else.

His remark about changing the limit to thirteen years, "for the sake of including a known instance," is quite wide of the mark. Any limit of years that was selected would have included a certain number of "known instances"; and what is there "unwarrantable" in my true statement, that, had thirteen years been selected instead of twelve, "the numerical argument would not have suffered appreciably, if at all"?

Case 201. I willingly leave the case to the reader, merely drawing attention to the misleading brevity of Mr. Peirce's assertion that the percipient "suspected she might have been asleep." Her words, which he compels me to re-quote, are, "I tested myself as to whether I had been sleeping, seeing that it was ten minutes since I lay down. I said to myself what I thought I had read, began my chapter [of Kingsley's *Miscellanies*] again, and in ten minutes I had reached the same point."

Mr. Peirce says, "Mr. Gurney gives up the case, and I am not inclined to give it any weight." I concede its omission from this particular calculation, owing to the uncertainty as to the degree of closeness of the coincidence, but I continue to give it great weight.

On Case 202 I have nothing to add.

Case 214. I do not understand Mr. Peirce's probability of one in one hundred, but suppose that he means it as the probability that the story of the hallucination is untrue. I do not consider his suspicions well grounded, the account of the shock, and its sequel, having every appearance of truth. If the hallucination took place, its date, owing to the consequences, would be specially well marked, and the odds against the coincidence would be enormous.

My estimate of Case 231 differs considerably from that of Mr. Peirce, who, I think the reader will agree, overshoots his mark in making it count for *less than nothing*. But, owing to the uncertainty as to twelve hours' limit, I have conceded its omission from this particular list.

Case 236. I have nothing to add beyond noting that the assumption of the antecedent probability that the hallucination would refer to the decedent as *nineteen-twentieths* is perhaps Mr. Peirce's masterpiece in that line. Even if we neglect the facts of hallucination in general (as, for instance, their tendency to take the form of "after images," and to represent objects which the percipient is in the daily habit of seeing), the above exemption would at least imply—what there is not a syllable in the account to suggest—an utterly abnormal absorption of the percipient's mind by the thought of one particular relative.

Case 237. Mr. Peirce thinks it "important" that the mother of the percipient "thought she might have been dreaming." The mother does not say so in her own evidence, and all that her daughter says is, that she "was greatly amused at my scare, suggesting I had read too much or been dreaming." If Mr. Peirce ever has a waking hallucination while he is reading, and at once mentions it to some one in the room, I would wager a good deal that the same comment will be made; and if he is good enough to send me an account of the occurrence, I engage not to think the objection "important," even though the objector, like the mother in the case before us, should "continue to disbelieve in ghosts." If I were the "advocate" that Mr. Peirce considers me, I should certainly rely on his treatment of this case to do more for me with the jury than the best of my arguments.

Case 238. "I assume it as antecedently certain," we read, "that the hallucination would refer to her husband, whom she seems to have loved. This is the assumption the most favorable to telepathy, since he was a well man." Mr. Peirce omits to tell us how he has learned that she did not love any other "well" man, woman, or child; and by what statistics he has ascertained that a person must be loved, in order to become the object of a hallucination.

Case 240. The signification which Mr. Peirce quite unwarrantably squeezes out of a pluperfect is contrary to the fact. There had been no "reconciliation" between the percipient and the dying man; nor was she aware, at the time, of her mother's visiting him. I must continue to characterize Mr. Peirce's assumption of a practical certainty that the hallucination would relate to the decedent, as monstrous.

Case 249. In connection with this case, I would refer the reader to the remarks on mistakes of identity, and their relation to the cumulative argument in *Phantasms of the Living*, Vol. II, pp. 62–63. The percipient, it will be observed, had as little doubt as to who the person was whom he had seen as if the whole figure had been in view; in that sense the recognition was perfect, which is all that the argument requires. The "monstrous assumption" in this case (antecedent probability of one-half that the hallucination would represent the decedent, on the ground of his being a neighbor, not known to be seriously ill) is a veritable Mammoth.

Case 298. With our knowledge of the witness's character, we find it impossible to doubt that the news of the man's illness and death reached her in the way described.

Case 300. As to the case itself I have nothing to add. I wholly dissent, however, from Mr. Peirce's view that "the reality of ghosts is put beyond doubt at once," if sailors' yarns are believed; for the ghostly incidents in such yarns could almost always be explained on the hypothesis of purely subjective hallucination or illusion.

Case 350. I do not think that I endeavored to "make much" of Mr. Peirce's mistakes in relation to the facts of this case. Nor do I even complain of his hypothesis, except so far as the statement of it implies the erroneous view that a case has no legitimate place in a cumulative argument in favor of one explanation, merely because another explanation is conceivable. Personally, I think the hypothesis that the witnesses had a hallucination, decidedly more probable than Mr. Peirce's suggestion of the pendent skull; and I cannot help thinking that *had there been no coincident death*, and no telepathic theory to confute, he would have agreed with me. Yet it must be clear that, in estimating the relative probability of the two explanations (hallucination and skull), we have nothing whatever to do with the coincidence. We ought to forget it. And even if we remember it, it will, of course, tell for, and not against, the hypothesis of hallucination; since it brings in the chance (which Mr. Peirce would admit to exist, however infinitesimal he would consider it) that there was a hallucination of telepathic origin, in addition to the chance that there was a hallucination of purely subjective origin.

Case 695. As for the "meagreness" of the story, a clear statement of all the essential facts, given without a word suggestive of adornment or exaggeration, is not evidence which a disparaging epithet will much injure. The words "told at second-hand," though true, are misleading. I have explained (*Phantasms of the Living*, Vol. I, pp. 148–9) that "the evidence of a person who has been informed of the experience of the percipient, while the latter was still unaware of the corresponding event," is quite on a par with the percipient's own evidence; indeed, in some ways it is even preferable. And it is, of course, at its best when, as in this case, the information has led the witness at once to make a written note of the date, which leaves absolutely no doubt as to the coincidence. Mr. Peirce's hypothesis of anxiety, which Mrs. Teale "concealed in order not to alarm her husband," is quite gratuitous. Her husband says that she was not anxious, and not given to brooding, and the last news of her son had been reassuring. The "monstrous assumption"—of an antecedent certainty that the hallucination would relate to the son—reappears in due form.

Case 697. Mr. Peirce having surmised that the percipient had heard of the death during the day, I stated that the surmise was incorrect, as most readers of the account would perceive. He urbanely replies that *my* testimony "goes for nothing." I will not, however, do him the injustice of supposing that he really doubts my statement to have been made on authority,—that of our informant, Mr. B.

The assumption of a high antecedent probability (one-fourth) that the hallucination could relate to the decedent—a clerk in the office of the percipient's husband, whom she had only occasionally seen, and as to whom even her husband was "in no anxiety"—is in this case ludicrous as well as monstrous; for Mr. Peirce bases it on the fact that her husband, in telling her of the young man's death, used the hackneyed phrase "sad news," which, says Mr. Peirce, "shows that her pity had been excited"! He should really be a little more consistent in his view of the emotions which beget hallucinations. A little time ago it was *conjugal love.* A woman loved her husband, and this made it certain that any hallucination of hers could represent no one but him. But now the degree of *pity* which is implied in the fact that somebody who tells one of the death of an acquaintance calls the news "sad," is found to have immense power in the same direction. And hence a dilemma: for Mr. Peirce must assume either that the loving percipient had not this degree of pity for any human being, or that the pitying percipient did not love her husband.

Case 702. "In his original account the percipient has the year wrong." This is Mr. Peirce's version of the fact that, writing in May, 1886, without referring to documents, the witness describes an event which had really occurred three years and eleven months before as having occurred "some three years since." I have explained that the percipient's mistake as to the *date* of the coincidence has no importance, since it has no relation to his evidence as to the *fact* of the coincidence. When he handed me the longer account (giving the date of the death, which proved to have coincided with his vision on June 15) he said that he was trusting to memory for the date, but that he believed he could hunt up the letter which contained it. He did so the same evening, with the result which it pleases Mr. Peirce to describe as "cooking" the story. The date, June 15, actually occurs in the portion of the letter quoted, where it is given as the day of the *funeral,* the *death* being simply stated to have occurred "on St. Barnabas' day" (June 11). Thus the mistake was not only unimportant, but extremely natural.

As to the case in Vol. I, p. 130 [misprinted 230 in Mr. Peirce's rejoinder], note, though precluded from giving it in detail, I regard it as of great value. The difference between it and fully reported cases is merely that, in respect of it, the reader is more dependent on the judgment of those who present the evidence. I have said that the narrative was of the ordinary type and unsensational in character; and that the witness was not biased by a credulous love of marvels appears from her remark that, though "confident of having seen the vision" [of an old school-friend who died on that day at a distance], her common-sense makes her "wish to put it down to imagination."

Mr. Peirce's concluding remarks, where he repeats his heroic hypothesis as to the "millions" whom our appeal for evidence has tapped, call for no special reply. What I have to say on the important point of the value that may be attached to "unscientific observations" is said at length in *Phantasms of the Living,* Vol. I, Chap. IV.

POSTSCRIPT TO MR. GURNEY'S REPLY TO PROFESSOR PEIRCE.

By Frederic W. H. Myers.

Mr. Gurney did not live to give his final revision to the above paper; and in the course of correcting the proofs an inaccuracy in his earlier "Remarks on Prof. Peirce's Paper" has been observed by us, which, so far as it goes, tells in his own favor. I shall, therefore, correct it here, as my only addendum to this his latest word of controversy. I see, indeed, several arguments by which his chain of reasoning—strong as that seems to me already—might be reinforced. But I cannot say with certainty how far he would have pressed any of these arguments himself. And, on the other hand, I am absolutely sure that he would never knowingly have allowed a single sentence to stand which overstated his own case in the smallest particular.

In *Proceedings,* p. 85, fourth paragraph, Mr. Gurney states that, in his census of hallucinations, questions as to the person's bodily or mental state at the time of the experience were kept separate from the question as to the fact of the experience. This is entirely true of the *mental,* but only partially of the *bodily,* state. For the question on the census-paper was, "Have you ever, when in good health and completely awake, had a vivid impression of seeing, or being touched by, a human being, or of hearing a voice or sound which suggested a human presence, when no one was there?" Inquiries as to date, recognition, anxiety, as well as further inquiries as to health, were made subsequently. Thus, Mr. Gurney was the sole judge as to what degree of *anxiety* should exclude a case from the census; but the percipients themselves were, in the first instance, the judges as to what degree of *ill-health* should exclude a case from the census; and, consequently, Professor Peirce's objection to the inclusion in the group of evidential cases of certain cases where he thinks there was *anxiety* falls to the ground; his objection to the inclusion of cases where there was *ill-health* has logical validity. For, so far as the *anxiety* went, the same canon was applied by Mr. Gurney to both the groups which were compared together, the evidential group and the group of miscellaneous hallucinations; and the degree of anxiety which excluded a case from the one group excluded it also from the other. But, so far as the *ill-health* went, the respondents in the miscellaneous group might conceivably have answered "No" to the first question in the census-paper, if they had seen a hallucination when slightly unwell, and might then have judged themselves by a standard of health stricter than that used by Mr. Gurney in testing cases to be admitted into the evidential group. Cases 174 and 702 should, therefore, in strictness be dropped,—not, of course, from the evidence in general, but from this particular comparison between the two groups. And, in fact, Mr. Gurney admits this on pp. 96, 97. It is plain, therefore, that his erroneous statement on p. 85 was a mere slip of expression, due, no doubt, to the fact that, in actual practice, the appraisement of *ill-health* (as well as of anxiety), in the miscellaneous group, was mainly left by the respondents to Mr. Gurney himself. If the respondents had seen a hallucination at all they usually answered "Yes," whether they had been somewhat out of health at the time of seeing it or not. This we know partly from the testimony of those who collected the answers, and partly by the evidence on the face of the answers themselves. The error above pointed out, therefore, has probably had but very slight effect on the calculation; and, in any case, it is amply met by dropping cases 174 and 702 from the group used for comparison.

I may add that Mr. Gurney by no means considered that the information which he had obtained as to hallucinations, by his census and other methods, was enough. He always intended to take a further census before long. It is to be hoped that his example, in thus substituting the laborious but fruitful methods of statistics for the vague generalities current on this subject before him, may be followed in England and elsewhere; and, in any future census, it would probably be better to leave the percipient's state of *health,* as well as of *anxiety,* for subsequent inquiries, and to make the question first asked as short and simple as possible.

20

Number

c. 1887 *Houghton Library*

Definitions

$$\left\{\begin{array}{l} 1.\ \Pi_\alpha\Pi_i\Pi_j\Pi_k\ (\bar{t}_\alpha + \bar{r}_{\alpha ij} + \bar{r}_{\alpha jk} + r_{\alpha ik}) \\ 2.\ \Pi_\alpha\Sigma_i\Sigma_j\Sigma_k\ (r_{\alpha ij}r_{\alpha jk}\bar{r}_{\alpha ik} + t_\alpha) \end{array}\right.$$

$$\left\{\begin{array}{l} 3.\ \Pi_\alpha\Pi_i\Pi_j\ (\bar{e}_\alpha + \bar{q}_{\alpha i} + \bar{\mathrm{E}}_{ij} + q_{\alpha j}) \\ 4.\ \Pi_\alpha\Sigma_i\Sigma_j\ (q_{\alpha i}\mathrm{E}_{ij}\bar{q}_{\alpha j} + e_\alpha) \end{array}\right.$$

$$\left\{\begin{array}{l} 5.\ \Pi_i\Pi_j\Pi_\alpha\ (\bar{g}_{ij} + \bar{q}_{\alpha i} + \bar{e}_\alpha + q_{\alpha j}) \\ 6.\ \Pi_i\Pi_j\Sigma_\alpha\ (q_{\alpha i}e_\alpha\bar{q}_{\alpha j} + g_{ij}) \end{array}\right.$$

$$\left\{\begin{array}{l} 7.\ \Pi_i\Pi_j\ (\bar{\mathrm{U}}_i + g_{ij}) \\ 8.\ \Pi_i\Sigma_j\ (\bar{g}_{ij} + \mathrm{U}_i) \end{array}\right.$$

Properties of Number

A. $\Pi_i\Pi_j\Pi_k\ (\bar{\mathrm{E}}_{ij} + \bar{\mathrm{E}}_{ik} + 1_{jk})$ Axiom of Next.

B. $\Pi_i\Sigma_j\ \bar{\mathrm{E}}_{ij}$ Postulate of Next.

C. $\Pi_i\Pi_j\ (\bar{\mathrm{E}}_{ij} + \bar{g}_{ji})$ Axiom of As Great As.

D. $\Pi_i\Pi_j\ (\bar{\mathrm{U}}_i + \bar{\mathrm{U}}_j + 1_{ij})$ Axiom of One.

E. $\Sigma_i\ \mathrm{U}_i$ Postulate of One.

21

Logic of Number

c. 1887 **Houghton Library**

The fundamental premises concerning number may be stated as follows.

First Premise

There is a number such that whatever is true of it and also if of any number then of every next greater, is true of every number. If we write E_{jk} to signify that k is next greater than j, and $q_{\alpha i}$ to signify that i has the character α, this first proposition can be written

$$\Sigma_i \Pi_\alpha \Sigma_j \Sigma_k \Pi_l \, (\bar{q}_{\alpha i} + q_{\alpha j} E_{jk} \bar{q}_{\alpha k} + q_{\alpha l}).$$

It will be a useful abbreviation to call a character which if true of any number is true of the next greater (or of every next greater were there more than one) a *hereditary* character and to write

$$h_\alpha = \Pi_j \Pi_k \, (\bar{q}_{\alpha j} + \bar{E}_{jk} + q_{\alpha k}).$$

Thus, the first proposition is expressed by saying that there is a number all whose hereditary characters are possessed by all numbers, or

$$\Sigma_i \Pi_\alpha \Pi_l \, (\bar{q}_{\alpha i} + \bar{h}_\alpha + q_{\alpha l}).$$

It is usual and useful to say that a number which possesses all the hereditary characters of another is *at least as great as* that other. We may write g_{il} to signify that l is at least as great as i, so that

$$g_{il} = \Pi_\alpha \, (\bar{q}_{\alpha i} + \bar{h}_\alpha + q_{\alpha l}).$$

The first proposition is thus expressed by saying that there is a number that all numbers are at least as great as, or

$$\Sigma_i \Pi_l \; g_{il}.$$

A number that all numbers are at least as great as is called *one*. We may write U_i to signify that i is one, so that

$$U_i = \Pi_l \, g_{il} \,.$$

Then the first proposition is that there is a *one* or

$$\Sigma_i \, U_i .$$

Second Premise

This is the converse of the first, namely that there is but a single *one*, or I_{im} meaning that i and m are identical,

$$\Pi_i \Pi_m \, (\bar{U}_i + \bar{U}_m + I_{im}).$$

Other modes of expression will be

$$\Pi_i \Pi_m \Sigma_l \, (\bar{g}_{il} + \bar{g}_{ml} + I_{im})$$

$$\Pi_i \Pi_m \Sigma_\alpha \Sigma_l \, (q_{\alpha i} + q_{mi}) h_\alpha \bar{q}_{\alpha l} + I_{im}$$

$$\Sigma_l \Sigma_{l'} \Pi_i \Sigma_\alpha \Pi_{i'} \Sigma_{\alpha'} \Pi_j \Pi_{j'} \Pi_k \Pi_{k'}$$

$$q_{\alpha i}(\bar{q}_{\alpha j} + \bar{E}_{jk} + q_{\alpha k})\bar{q}_{\alpha l} + q_{\alpha' i'}(\bar{q}_{\alpha' j'} + \bar{E}_{j'k'} + q_{\alpha' k'})\bar{q}_{\alpha' l'} + I_{ii'}.$$

Third Premise

Every number has a next greater which it is not as great as; or

$$\Pi_i \Sigma_l \, (E_{il} \bar{g}_{li}).$$

At greater length

$$\Pi_i \Sigma_l \Sigma_\alpha \; q_{\alpha l} h_\alpha \bar{q}_{\alpha i} E_{il}$$

$$\Pi_i \Sigma_l \Sigma_\alpha \Pi_j \Pi_k \; (\bar{q}_{\alpha j} + \bar{E}_{jk} + q_{\alpha k}) q_{\alpha l} \bar{q}_{\alpha i} E_{il} .$$

Fourth Premise

No number has but one next greater than it.

$$\Pi_i \Pi_j \Pi_k \; (\bar{E}_{ij} + \bar{E}_{ik} + I_{jk}).$$

Theorems

I

The main procedure of inference consists in multiplying premises together or the same premise into itself, then identifying some of the indices (namely the index of a Π with any index to the left in the quantifier), then breaking down parentheses, and applying the principle of contradiction.

It is therefore natural to begin by multiplying g into itself. We have

$$g_{il}g_{mn} = \Pi_\alpha (\bar{q}_{\alpha i} + \bar{h}_\alpha + q_{\alpha l})\, \Pi_\beta (\bar{q}_{\beta m} + \bar{h}_\beta + q_{\beta n}).$$

We identify β with α, and we are led to take $m = l$. We thus have

$$\overline{g_{il}g_{ln}} \rceil\!\!\!\!+ \Pi_\alpha (\bar{q}_{\alpha i} + \bar{h}_\alpha + q_{\alpha l})(\bar{q}_{\alpha l} + \bar{h}_\alpha + q_{\alpha n}).$$

Breaking down the parenthesis the Boolian becomes

$$\bar{q}_{\alpha i} + \bar{h}_\alpha + q_{\alpha l}\bar{q}_{\alpha l} + \bar{h}_\alpha + q_{\alpha n},$$

and $q_{\alpha l}\bar{q}_{\alpha l}$ vanishes, by the principle of contradiction, while $\bar{h}_\alpha + \bar{h}_\alpha = \bar{h}_\alpha$ by the principle of excluded middle. We therefore have

$$\overline{g_{il}g_{ln}} \rceil\!\!\!\!+ \Pi_\alpha (\bar{q}_{\alpha i} + \bar{h}_\alpha + q_{\alpha n})$$

or

$$\overline{g_{il}g_{ln}} \rceil\!\!\!\!+ g_{in}.$$

Relations that have this property are called *transitive.* If we write $r_{\alpha xy}$ to signify that y is in the relation α to x, then if α is a transitive relation we have

$$\Pi_x \Pi_y \Pi_z (\bar{r}_{\alpha xy} + \bar{r}_{\alpha yz} + r_{\alpha xz}),$$

and if we write t_α to signify that α is transitive, t_α is equal to the proposition just written. The present theorem therefore is

$$\Sigma_\alpha \Pi_i \Pi_l (\bar{g}_{il} + t_\alpha r_{\alpha il}).$$

If this proposition were presented as a hypothesis whose truth had to be investigated we should endeavor to deduce something false either from the proposition or from the denial of it.

The denial of the proposition is

$$\Pi_\alpha \Sigma_i \Sigma_l\, g_{il}(\bar{t}_\alpha + \bar{r}_{\alpha il})$$

or, substituting for t_α its definition

$$\Pi_\alpha \Sigma_i \Sigma_l \Sigma_x \Sigma_y \Sigma_z\, g_{il}(r_{\alpha xy} r_{\alpha yz} \bar{r}_{\alpha xz} + \bar{r}_{\alpha il}).$$

Since α is distributed (i.e., its quantifier is Π), we may substitute any relative token for r_α. Substituting then g, we have

$$\Sigma_i \Sigma_l \Sigma_x \Sigma_y \Sigma_z \; g_{il}(g_{xy} g_{yz} \bar{g}_{xz} + \bar{g}_{il}).$$

Using the distributive principle, and observing that $g_{il}\bar{g}_{il} = 0$, we have

$$\Sigma_i \Sigma_l \Sigma_x \Sigma_y \Sigma_z \; g_{il} g_{xy} g_{yz} \bar{g}_{xz}.$$

We always have a right to drop a factor. Dropping g_{il}, we have

$$\Sigma_x \Sigma_y \Sigma_z \; g_{xy} g_{yz} \bar{g}_{xz}.$$

Now substituting for g its definition, we have

$$\Sigma_x \Sigma_y \Sigma_z \Sigma_\beta \Pi_\gamma \, (\bar{q}_{\gamma x} + \bar{h}_\gamma + q_{\gamma y})(\bar{q}_{\gamma y} + \bar{h}_\gamma + q_{\gamma z}) q_{\beta x} \bar{q}_{\beta z} h_\beta .$$

By dropping the parenthesis, and observing that $q_{\gamma y}\bar{q}_{\gamma y} = 0$, and that $\bar{h}_\gamma + \bar{h}_\gamma = \bar{h}_\gamma$, we get

$$\Sigma_x \Sigma_z \Sigma_\beta \Pi_\gamma \, (\bar{q}_{\gamma x} + \bar{h}_\gamma + q_{\gamma z}) q_{\beta x} \bar{q}_{\beta z} h_\beta .$$

We now identify γ with β, and apply this distributive principle. The first term disappears because it contains the factor $\bar{q}_{\beta x} q_{\beta x}$, the second because of $\bar{h}_\beta h_\beta$, and the third because of $q_{\beta z}\bar{q}_{\beta z}$; and thus the whole reduces to zero, or the denial of the theorem is reduced to absurdity.

II

The theorem which ought to be taken first, as being the simplest, is obtained by asking whether a number is as great as itself. In the definition of g

$$g_{il} = \Pi_\alpha \, (\bar{q}_{\alpha i} + \bar{h}_\alpha + q_{\alpha l})$$

substitute i for l and we have $\bar{q}_{\alpha i} + q_{\alpha i}$ which is necessarily true. Hence

$$\Pi_i \; g_{ii}$$

or everything is as great as itself.

These two theorems do not involve any of the properties of numbers, but only the definition of g.

III

Also quite independent of the properties of number, it can be shown that whatever is next greater than a number is at least as great as that number, or

$$\Pi_i \Pi_j \ (\bar{\mathrm{E}} + g)_{ij}.$$

For the denial of this is

$$\Sigma_i \Sigma_j \ \mathrm{E}_{ij} \bar{g}_{ij}.$$

Substitute for g its definition; then

$$\Sigma_i \Sigma_j \Sigma_\alpha \ \mathrm{E}_{ij} q_{\alpha i} h_\alpha \bar{q}_{\alpha j}.$$

Substitute for h its definition; then

$$\Sigma_i \Sigma_j \Sigma_\alpha \Pi_m \Pi_n \ \mathrm{E}_{ij} q_{\alpha i} (\bar{q}_{\alpha m} + \bar{\mathrm{E}}_{mn} + q_{\alpha n}) \bar{q}_{\alpha j}.$$

We identify m with i and n with j; then on applying the distributive principle all the terms vanish by the principle of contradiction.

IV

Of the same nature is the proposition that if j is as great as i, then whatever is next greater than j is as great as i; that is,

$$\Pi_i \Pi_j \Pi_k \ (\bar{g}_{ij} + \bar{\mathrm{E}}_{jk} + g_{ik}).$$

For the denial of this is

$$\Sigma_i \Sigma_j \Sigma_k \ g_{ij} \mathrm{E}_{jk} \bar{g}_{ik}.$$

The last theorem is

$$\Pi_j \Pi_k \ (\bar{\mathrm{E}}_{jk} + g_{jk}).$$

Multiplying this in, we get

$$\Sigma_i \Sigma_j \Sigma_k \ g_{ij} g_{jk} \bar{g}_{ik}.$$

This is the direct denial of the first theorem.

V

We now come to a genuine theorem concerning number, as distinguished from quantity in general. It is that if j is as great as i, it either is i or is as great as whatever is next greater than i; that is

$$\Pi_i \Pi_j \Pi_k \ (\bar{g}_{ij} + \bar{\mathrm{E}}_{ik} + g_{kj} + \mathrm{I}_{ij}).$$

Let us write

$$f_{ij} = \Pi_k (\bar{\mathrm{E}}_{ik} + g_{kj} + \mathrm{I}_{ij}).$$

Then f_i is a hereditary character; that is,

$$\Pi_p \Pi_q (\bar{f}_{ip} + \bar{\mathrm{E}}_{pq} + f_{iq}).$$

For the denial of this is

$$\Sigma_p \Sigma_q f_{ip} \mathrm{E}_{pq} \bar{f}_{iq},$$

or, substituting for the first f its definition

$$\Sigma_p \Sigma_q \Pi_k (\bar{\mathrm{E}}_{ik} + g_{kp} + \mathrm{I}_{ip}) \mathrm{E}_{pq} \bar{f}_{iq}$$

$$= \Sigma_p \Sigma_q \Pi_k \{(\bar{\mathrm{E}}_{ik} + g_{kp}) \mathrm{E}_{pq} + \mathrm{I}_{ip} \mathrm{E}_{pq}\} \bar{f}_{iq}.$$

Theorem III permits us to substitute g_{pq} for E_{pq} in the first term under the braces. This result, for instance, would be got by multiplying by theorem III in the form

$$\Pi_m \Pi_n (\bar{\mathrm{E}}_{mn} + g_{mn})$$

so as to get

$$\Sigma_p \Sigma_q \Pi_k \Pi_m \Pi_n \{(\bar{\mathrm{E}}_{mn} + g_{mn})(\bar{\mathrm{E}}_{ik} + g_{kp}) \mathrm{E}_{pq} + \mathrm{I}_{ip} \mathrm{E}_{pq}\} \bar{f}_{iq}$$

and then identifying m with p and n with q, so as to get

$$\Sigma_p \Sigma_q \Pi_k \{(\bar{\mathrm{E}}_{ik} + g_{kp}) g_{pq} + \mathrm{I}_{ip} \mathrm{E}_{pq}\} \bar{f}_{iq}.$$

Theorem II enables us to substitute in the second term under the braces $\Sigma_r \mathrm{E}_{pr} g_{rq}$ for E_{pq}. For first we multiply this term by itself, q being changed to r, and also by I_{rq}. This gives

$$\Sigma_r \Sigma_p \Sigma_q \Pi_k \{(\bar{\mathrm{E}}_{ik} + g_{kp}) g_{pq} + \mathrm{I}_{ip} \mathrm{E}_{pq} \mathrm{E}_{pr} \mathrm{I}_{rq}\} \bar{f}_{iq}.$$

We now multiply that term by theorem II in the form

$$\Pi_u \Pi_v (\bar{\mathrm{I}}_{uv} + g_{uv})$$

and then identifying u with r and v with q we get

$$\Sigma_r \Sigma_p \Sigma_q \Pi_k \{(\bar{\mathrm{E}}_{ik} + g_{kp}) g_{pq} + \mathrm{I}_{ip} \mathrm{E}_{pr} g_{rq}\} \bar{f}_{iq}.$$

We have now the right to substitute i for p in the multiplier of I_{ip} and thus get

$$\Sigma_p \Sigma_q \Sigma_r \Pi_k \{(\bar{\mathrm{E}}_{ik} + g_{kp}) g_{pq} + \mathrm{E}_{ir} g_{rq}\} \bar{f}_{iq}.$$

Breaking down the inner parenthesis, theorem I enables us to substitute g_{kq} for $g_{kp}g_{pq}$. Namely we multiply by that theorem in the form

$$\Pi_a\Pi_b\Pi_c\ (\bar{g}_{ab} + \bar{g}_{bc} + g_{ac})$$

and then identify a with k, b with p, and c with q.
We thus get

$$\Sigma_q\Sigma_r\Pi_k\ (\bar{\mathrm{E}}_{ik} + g_{kq} + \mathrm{E}_{ir}g_{rq})\bar{f}_{iq}\,.$$

The third property of number is

$$\Pi_a\Sigma_b\ \mathrm{E}_{ab}\bar{g}_{ba}$$

or dropping the last factor

$$\Pi_a\Sigma_b\ \mathrm{E}_{ab}.$$

Multiplying the last form of our proposition by this we have

$$\Pi_a\Sigma_b\Sigma_q\Sigma_r\Pi_k\ \mathrm{E}_{ab}(\bar{\mathrm{E}}_{ik} + g_{kq} + \mathrm{E}_{ir}g_{rq})\bar{f}_{iq}\,.$$

Identifying a with i and k with b we have

$$\Sigma_b\Sigma_q\Sigma_r\ (\mathrm{E}_{ib}g_{bq} + \mathrm{E}_{ir}g_{rq})\bar{f}_{iq}$$

$$= \Sigma_q\Sigma_r\ \mathrm{E}_{ir}g_{rq}\bar{f}_{iq}.$$

We now substitute for f its definition and so get

$$\Sigma_q\Sigma_r\Pi_k\ \mathrm{E}_{ir}g_{rq}\mathrm{E}_{ik}\bar{g}_{kq}\bar{\mathrm{I}}_{iq}.$$

On identifying k with r this vanishes, thus reducing the hypothesis that f_i is not an hereditary character to an absurdity.

Denoting this character by β, the proposition which we have proved is

$$h_\beta.$$

We multiply this by the first property of number, in the form

$$\Sigma_u\Pi_\alpha\Pi_v\ (\mathrm{U}_u\bar{q}_{\alpha u} + \bar{h}_\alpha + q_{\alpha v})$$

and then identifying α with β, we have

$$\Sigma_u\Pi_v\ (\mathrm{U}_u\bar{q}_{\beta u} + q_{\beta v}).$$

Now under the condition that unity is as great as i, β is true of unity; that is

$$\Pi_h\ (\bar{\mathrm{U}}_h + \bar{g}_{ih} + q_{\beta h}).$$

That is the same as to say that under the condition that the subject of β is as great as i, β is true of unity. But if β is true of a number it is true of the next greater. Hence, by the first property of number, under the condition that the subject of β is as great as i, β is true of every number. Q.E.D.

To put this algebraically, we multiply the last proposition by h_β which has just been proved and by the first property of number under the form

$$\Sigma_x \Pi_\alpha \Pi_y \; (\mathrm{U}_x \bar{q}_{\alpha x} + \bar{h}_\alpha + q_{\alpha y}).$$

This gives

$$\Sigma_x \Pi_\alpha \Pi_y \Pi_h \; (\mathrm{U}_x \bar{q}_{\alpha x} + \bar{h}_\alpha + q_{\alpha y}) h_\beta (\bar{\mathrm{U}}_h + \bar{g}_{ih} + q_{\beta h}).$$

We identify α with β, and h with x, when this reduces to

$$\Sigma_x \Pi_y \; h_\beta (\bar{g}_{ix} + q_{\beta y})$$

which is the theorem.

A Guess at the Riddle

22

[Contents]

Fall 1887–Winter 1888 ***Houghton Library***

Chapter 1. One, Two, Three. Already written.

Chapter 2. The triad in reasoning. Not touched. It is to be made as follows. 1. Three kinds of signs; as best shown in my last paper in the *American Journal of Mathematics.* 2. Term, proposition, and argument, mentioned in my paper on a new list of categories. 3. Three kinds of argument, deduction, induction, hypothesis, as shown in my paper in *Studies in Logic.* Also three figures of syllogism, as shown there and in my paper on the classification of arguments. 4. Three kinds of terms, absolute, relative, and conjugative, as shown in my first paper on the logic of relatives. There are various other triads which may be alluded to. The dual divisions of logic result from a false way of looking at things absolutely. Thus, besides affirmative and negative, there are really probable enunciations, which are intermediate. So besides universal and particular there are all sorts of propositions of numerical quantity. For example, the particular proposition Some A is B, means At least one A is B. But we can also say At least two A's are B's. Also, All the A's but one are B's, etc. etc. ad infinitum. We pass from dual quantity, or a system of quantity such as that of Boolian algebra, where there are only two values, to plural quantity.

Chapter 3. The triad in metaphysics. This chapter, one of the best, is to treat of the theory of cognition.

Chapter 4. The triad in psychology. The greater part is written.

Chapter 5. The triad in physiology. The greater part is written.

Chapter 6. The triad in biology. This is to show the true nature of the Darwinian hypothesis.

Chapter 7. The triad in physics. The germinal chapter. 1. The necessity of a natural history of the laws of nature, so that we may get some notion of what to expect. 2. The logical postulate for explanation forbids the assumption of any absolute. That is, it calls for the introduction of thirdness. 3. Metaphysics is an imitation of geometry; and mathematicians having declared against axioms, the metaphysical axioms are destined to fall too. 4. Absolute chance. 5. The universality of the principle of habit. 6. The whole theory stated. 7. Consequences.

Chapter 8. The triad in sociology or shall I say pneumatology. That the consciousness is a sort of public spirit among the nerve-cells. Man as a community of cells; compound animals and composite plants; society; nature. Feeling implied in firstness.

Chapter 9. The triad in theology. Faith requires us to be materialists without flinching.

23

Chapter I
Trichotomy

Fall 1887–Winter 1888 ***Houghton Library***

To erect a philosophical edifice that shall outlast the vicissitudes of time, my care must be, not so much to set each brick with nicest accuracy, as to lay the foundations deep and massive. Aristotle builded upon a few deliberately chosen concepts,—such as matter and form, act and power,—very broad, and in their outlines vague and rough, but solid, unshakable, and not easily undermined; and thence it has come to pass that Aristotelianism is babbled in every nursery; that "English Common Sense," for example, is thoroughly peripatetic; and that ordinary men live so completely within the house of the Stagyrite that whatever they see out of the windows appears to them incomprehensible and metaphysical. Long it has been only too manifest that, fondly habituated though we be to it, the old structure will not do for modern needs; and accordingly under Descartes, Hobbes, Kant, and others, repairs, alterations, and partial demolitions have been carried on for the last three centuries. One system, also, stands upon its own ground; I mean the new Schelling-Hegel mansion, lately run up in the German taste, but with such oversights in its construction that, although brand new, it is already pronounced uninhabitable. The undertaking which this volume inaugurates is to make a philosophy like that of Aristotle, that is to say, to outline a theory so comprehensive that, for a long time to come, the entire work of human reason, in philosophy of every school and kind, in mathematics, in psychology, in physical science, in history, in sociology, and in whatever other department there may be, shall appear as the filling up of its details. The first step toward this is to find simple concepts applicable to every subject.

But before all else, let me make the acquaintance of my reader, and express my sincere esteem for him and the deep pleasure it is to me to address one so wise and so patient. I know his character pretty well, for both the subject and the style of this book ensure his being one out of millions. He will comprehend that it has not been written for the purpose of confirming him in his preconceived opinions, and he would not take the trouble to read it if it had. He is prepared to meet with propositions that he is inclined at first to dissent from; and he looks to being convinced that some of them are true, after all. He will reflect, too, that the thinking and writing of this book has taken, I won't say how long, quite certainly more than a quarter of an hour; and consequently fundamental objections of so obvious a nature that they must strike everyone instantaneously will have occurred to the author, although the replies to them may not be of that kind whose full force can be instantly apprehended. For this wisdom let me show my serious and cordial gratitude by presenting only such matter as has been well-prepared, weighed, measured, and tested, expressed in language the best adapted I can find to the convenience of my reader, without caring whether the babes, the philistines, the hurried, and all the classes that will not read the book, at all, would, if they had read it, have gathered the right idea or a wrong one.

Accordingly, as my design is so ambitious, and as I happen to have a number of three-fold divisions to make, it will be advisable to examine, in the first place, the conceptions upon which all such divisions must rest. I mean no more than the ideas of First, Second, and Third,—ideas so broad that they may be looked upon rather as moods or tones of thought, than as definite notions, but which have great significance for all that. Of course, the popular prejudice against the doctrine that the numbers have any significance is nearly as great as was formerly the prejudice against that other Pythagorean idea of the earth moving round the sun; but equally of course, a book like this is not written merely for the purpose of confirming men in their preconceived ideas, and that is precisely why dull minds are unable to profit by such a book. If we merely wanted to make enumerations, it would, indeed, be out of place to ask for the significance of the numerals we should have to use; but then the distinctions of philosophy are supposed to attempt something far more than that; they are intended to go down to the very essence of things. If there are any three-fold distinctions that are more than verbal, their real nature will clearly be elucidated by an understanding of the meanings of the numbers one, two, three, provided that there are any such meanings. We shall presently find reason to admit that such meanings there are.

The question is what are the kinds of objects that are first, second, and third, not as being so counted, but in their own true characters. If there be any such kinds, the first will be that whose being is simply in itself, not referring to anything nor lying behind anything. The second will be that which is what it is by force of something to which it is second. The third will be that which is what it is owing to things between which it mediates and which it brings into relation to each other.

Now the reader already admits that there are things which are First, Second, and Third, not merely because they are so counted but because these numbers are appropriate to their nature. I say the reader already admits it; for I suppose he would not propose to expunge from the language such words as prior, prime, primitive, primeval, primary; secondary, second-class, consequent, object; tertium quid, medium, mediation; etc. All these words imply that things have the several ranks of first, second, and third, appropriate to them.

The idea of the absolutely First must be entirely separated from all conception of or reference to anything else; for what involves a second is itself a second to that second. The First must therefore be present and immediate, so as not to be second to a representation. It must be fresh and new, for if old it is second to its former state. It must be initiative, original, spontaneous, and free; otherwise it is second to a determining cause. It is also something vivid and conscious; so only it avoids being the object of some sensation. It precedes all synthesis and all differentiation: it has no unity and no parts. It cannot be articulately thought: assert it, and it has already lost its characteristic innocence; for assertion always implies a denial of something else. Stop to think of it, and it has flown! What the world was to Adam on the day he opened his eyes to it, before he had drawn any distinctions, or had become conscious of his own existence,—that is first, present, immediate, fresh, new, initiative, original, spontaneous, free, vivid, conscious, and evanescent. Only, remember that every description of it must be false to it.

Just as the first is not absolutely first if thought along with a second, so likewise to think the Second in its perfection we must banish every third. The Second is therefore the absolute last. But we need not, and must not, banish the idea of the first from the second; on the contrary, the Second is precisely that which cannot be without the first. It meets us in such facts as Another, Relation, Compulsion, Effect, Dependence, Independence, Negation, Occurrence, Reality, Result. A thing cannot be other, negative, or independent, without a first to or of which it shall be other, negative, or independent. Still, this is not a very deep kind of secondness; for the first might in these cases be destroyed yet leave the real character of the second absolutely unchanged. When the second suffers some change from the action of the first, and is dependent upon it, the secondness is more genuine. But the dependence must not go so far that the second is a mere accident or incident of the first; otherwise the secondness again degenerates. The genuine second suffers and yet resists, like dead matter, whose existence consists in its inertia. Note, too, that for the Second to have the Finality that we have seen belongs to it, it must be determined by the first immoveably, and thenceforth be fixed; so that unalterable fixity becomes one of its attributes. We find secondness in occurrence, because an occurrence is something whose existence consists in our knocking up against it. A hard fact is of the same sort; that is to say, it is something which is there, and which I cannot think away, but am forced to acknowledge as an object or second beside myself, the subject or number one, and which forms material for the exercise of my will.

The idea of second must be reckoned as an easy one to comprehend. That of first is so tender that you cannot touch it without spoiling it; but that of second is eminently hard and tangible. It is very familiar, too, it is forced upon us daily: it is the main lesson of life. In youth, the world is fresh and we seem free; but limitation, conflict, constraint, and secondness generally, make up the teaching of experience. With what firstness

The scarfed bark puts from her native bay;

with what secondness

doth she return,
With overweathered ribs and ragged sails.

But familiar as the notion is, and compelled as we are to acknowledge it at every turn, still we never can realize it; we never can be immediately conscious of finiteness, or of anything but a divine freedom that in its own original firstness knows no bounds.

First and Second, Agent and Patient, Yes and No, are categories which enable us roughly to describe the facts of experience, and they satisfy the mind for a very long time. But at last they are found inadequate, and the Third is the conception which is then called for. The Third is that which bridges over the chasm between the absolute first and last, and brings them into relationship. We are told that every science has its Qualitative and its Quantitative stage; now its qualitative stage is when dual distinctions,—whether a given subject has a given predicate or not,—suffice; the quantitative stage comes when, no longer content with such rough distinctions, we require to insert a possible half-way between every two possible conditions of the subject in regard to its possession of the quality indicated by the predicate. Ancient mechanics recognized forces as causes which produced motions as their immediate effects, looking no further than the essentially dual relation of cause and effect. That was why it could make no progress with dynamics. The work of Galileo and his successors lay in showing that forces are accelerations by which a state of velocity is gradually brought about. The words cause and effect still linger, but the old conceptions have been dropped from mechanical philosophy; for the fact now known is that in certain relative positions bodies undergo certain accelerations. Now an acceleration, instead of being like a velocity a relation between two successive positions, is a relation between three; so that the new doctrine has consisted in the suitable introduction of the conception of Threeness. On this idea, the whole of modern physics is built. The superiority of modern geometry, too, has certainly been due to nothing so much as to the bridging over of the innumerable distinct cases with which the ancient science was encumbered; and we may go so far as to say that all the great steps in the method of science in every department have consisted in bringing into relation cases previously discrete.

We can easily recognize the man whose thought is mainly in the dual stage by his unmeasured use of language. In former days, when he was natural, everything with him was unmitigated, absolute, ineffable, utter, matchless, supreme, unqualified, root and branch; but now that it is the fashion to be depreciatory, he is just as plainly marked by the ridiculous inadequacy of his expressions. The principle of contradiction is a shibboleth for such minds; to disprove a proposition they will always try to prove there lurks a contradiction in it, notwithstanding that it may be as clear and comprehensible as the day. Remark for your amusement the grand unconcern with which mathematics, since the invention of the calculus, has pursued its way, caring no more for the peppering of contradiction-mongers than an ironclad for an American fort.

We have seen that it is the immediate consciousness that is preeminently first, the external dead thing that is preeminently second. In like manner, it is evidently the representation mediating between these two that is preeminently third. Other examples, however, should not be neglected. The first is agent, the second patient, the third is the action by which the former influences the latter. Between the beginning as first, and the end as last, comes the process which leads from first to last.

According to the mathematicians, when we measure along a line, were our yardstick replaced by a yard marked off on an infinitely long rigid bar, then in all the shiftings of it which we make for the purpose of applying it to successive portions of the line to be measured, two points on that bar would remain fixed and unmoved. To that pair of points, the mathematicians accord the title of the absolute; they are the points that are at an infinite distance one way and the other as measured by that yard. These points are either really distinct, coincident, or imaginary (in which case there is but a finite distance completely round the line), according to the relation of the mode of measurement to the nature of the line upon which the measurement is made. These two points are the absolute first and the absolute last or second, while every measurable point on the line is of the nature of a third. We have seen that the conception of the absolute first eludes every attempt to grasp it; and so in another sense does that of the absolute second; but there is no absolute third, for the third is of its own nature relative, and this is what we are always thinking, even when we aim at the first or second. The starting-point of the universe, God the

Creator, is the Absolute First; the terminus of the universe, God completely revealed, is the Absolute Second; every state of the universe at a measurable point of time is the third. If you think the measurable is all there is, and deny it any definite tendency whence or whither, then you are considering the pair of points that makes the absolute to be imaginary and are an Epicurean. If you hold that there is a definite drift to the course of nature as a whole, but yet believe its absolute end is nothing but the nirvana from which it set out, you make the two points of the absolute to be coincident, and are a pessimist. But if your creed is that the whole universe is approaching in the infinitely distant future a state having a general character different from that toward which we look back in the infinitely distant past, you make the absolute to consist in two distinct real points and are an evolutionist.[1]

This is one of the matters concerning which a man can only learn from his own reflections, but I believe that if my suggestions are followed out, the reader will grant that One, Two, Three are more than mere count-words like "eeny, meeny, mony, mi," but carry vast, though vague ideas.

But it will be asked, why stop at three? Why not go on to find a distinct idea for Four, Five, and so on indefinitely? The reason is that while it is impossible to form a genuine three by any modification of the pair, without introducing something of a different nature from the unit and the pair, four, five, and every higher number can be formed by mere complications of threes. To make this clear, I will first show it in an example. The fact that A presents B with a gift C, is a triple relation, and as such cannot possibly be resolved into any combination of dual relations. Indeed, the very idea of a combination involves that of thirdness, for a combination is something which is what it is owing to the parts which it brings into mutual relationship. But we may waive that consideration, and still we cannot build up the fact that A presents C to B by any aggregate of dual relations between A and B, B and C, and C and A. A may enrich B, B may receive C, and A may part with C, and yet A need not necessarily give C to B. For

1. The last view is essentially that of Christian theology, too. The theologians hold the physical universe to be finite, but considering that universe which they will admit to have existed from all time, it would appear to be in a different condition in the end from what it was in the beginning, the whole spiritual creation having been accomplished, and abiding.

that, it would be necessary that these three dual relations should not only coexist, but be welded into one fact. Thus, we see that a triad cannot be analyzed into dyads. But now I will show by an example that a four can be analyzed into threes. Take the quadruple fact that A sells C to B for the price D. This is a compound of two facts: 1st, that A makes with B a certain transaction, which we may name E; and 2nd, that this transaction E is a sale of C for the price D. Each of these two facts is a triple fact, and their combination makes up as genuine a quadruple fact as can be found. The explanation of this striking difference is not far to seek. A dual relative term, such as "lover" or "servant," is a sort of blank form, where there are two places left blank. I mean that in building a sentence round lover, as the principal word of the predicate, we are at liberty to make anything we see fit the subject, and then, besides that, anything we please the object of the action of loving. But a triple relative term such as "giver" has two correlates, and is thus a blank form with three places left blank. Consequently, we can take two of these triple relatives and fill up one blank place in each with the same letter, X, which has only the force of a pronoun or identifying index, and then the two taken together will form a whole having four blank places; and from that we can go on in a similar way to any higher number. But when we attempt to imitate this proceeding with dual relatives, and combine two of them by means of an X, we find we only have two blank places in the combination, just as we had in either of the relatives taken by itself. A road with only three-way forkings may have any number of termini, but no number of straight roads put end on end will give more than two termini. Thus any number, however large, can be built out of triads; and consequently no idea can be involved in such a number, radically different from the idea of three. I do not mean to deny that the higher numbers may present interesting special configurations from which notions may be derived of more or less general applicability; but these cannot rise to the height of philosophical categories so fundamental as those that have been considered.

The argument of this book has been developed in the mind of the author, substantially as it is presented, as a following out of these three conceptions, in a sort of game of follow my leader from one field of thought into another. Their importance was originally brought home to me in the study of logic, where they play so remarkable a part that I was led to look for them in psychology. Finding them there again, I could not help asking myself whether they did not enter into the physiology of the nervous system. By drawing a little on hypothesis, I succeeded in detecting them there; and then the question naturally came how they would appear in the theory of protoplasm in general. Here I seemed to break into an interesting avenue of reflections giving instructive aperçus both into the nature of protoplasm and into the conceptions themselves; though it was not till later that I mapped out my thoughts on the subject as they are presented in Chapter V. I had no difficulty in following the lead into the domain of natural selection; and once arrived at that point, I was irresistibly carried on to speculations concerning physics. One bold saltus landed me in a garden of fruitful and beautiful suggestions, the exploration of which long prevented my looking further. As soon, however, as I was induced to look further, and to examine the application of the three ideas to the deepest problems of the soul, nature, and God, I saw at once that they must carry me far into the heart of those primeval mysteries. That is the way the book has grown in my mind: it is also the order in which I have written it; and only this first chapter is more or less an afterthought, since at an earlier stage of my studies I should have looked upon the matter here set down as too vague to have any value. I should have discerned in it too strong a resemblance to many a crack-brained book that I had laughed over. A deeper study has taught me that even out of the mouths of babes and sucklings strength may be brought forth, and that weak metaphysical trash has sometimes contained the germs of conceptions capable of growing up into important and positive doctrines.

Thus, the whole book being nothing but a continual exemplification of the triad of ideas, we need linger no longer upon this preliminary exposition of them. There is, however, one feature of them upon which it is quite indispensible to dwell. It is that there are two distinct grades of secondness and three grades of thirdness. There is a close analogy to this in geometry. Conic sections are either the curves usually so called, or they are pairs of straight lines. A pair of straight lines is called a degenerate conic. So plane cubic curves are either the genuine curves of the third order, or they are conics paired with straight lines, or they consist of three straight lines; so that there are two orders of degenerate cubics. Nearly in this same way, besides genuine secondness, there is a degenerate sort which does not exist as such, but is only so conceived. The medieval logicians (following a hint of Aristotle) distinguished between real relations and relations of reason. A real relation subsists in virtue of a fact which would be totally impossible were either of the related objects destroyed; while a relation of reason subsists in virtue of two facts, one of which only would disappear on the annihilation of either of the relates. Such are all resemblances: for any two objects in nature resemble each other, and indeed in themselves just as much as any other two; it is only with reference to our senses and needs that one resemblance counts for more than another. Rumford and Franklin resembled one another by virtue of being both Americans; but either would have been just as much an American if the other had never lived. On the other hand, the fact that Cain killed Abel cannot be stated as a mere aggregate of two facts, one concerning Cain and the other concerning Abel. Resemblances are not the only relations of reason, though they have that character in an eminent degree. Contrasts and comparisons are of the same sort. Resemblance is an identity of characters; and this is the same as to say that the mind gathers the resembling ideas together into one conception. Other relations of reason arise from ideas being connected by the mind in other ways; they consist in the relation between two parts of one complex concept, or, as we may say, in the relation of a complex concept to itself, in respect to two of its parts. This brings us to consider a sort of degenerate secondness that does not fulfill the definition of a relation of reason. Identity is the relation that everything bears to itself: Lucullus dines with Lucullus. Again, we speak of allurements and motives in the language of forces, as though a man suffered compulsion from within. So with the voice of conscience: and we observe our own feelings by a reflective sense. An echo is my own voice coming back to answer itself. So also, we speak of the abstract quality of a thing as if it were some second thing that the first thing possesses. But the relations of reason and these self-relations are alike in this, that they arise from the mind setting one part of a notion into relation to another. All degenerate seconds may be conveniently termed Internal, in contrast to External seconds, which are constituted by external fact, and are true actions of one thing upon another.

Among thirds, there are two degrees of degeneracy. The first is where there is in the fact itself no thirdness or mediation, but where there is true duality; the second degree is where there is not even true secondness in the fact itself.

Consider, first, the thirds degenerate in the first degree. A pin fastens two things together by sticking through one and also through the other: either might be annihilated, and the pin would continue to stick through the one which remained. A mixture brings its ingredients together by containing each. We may term these accidental thirds. "How did I slay thy son?" asked the merchant, and the genie replied, "When thou threwest away the date-stone, it smote my son who was passing at the time, on the breast, and he died forthright." Here there were two independent facts, first that the merchant threw away the date-stone, and second that the date-stone struck and killed the genie's son. Had it been aimed at him, the case would have been different; for then there would have been a relation of aiming which would have connected together the aimer, the thing aimed, and the object aimed at, in one fact. What monstrous injustice and inhumanity on the part of that genie to hold that poor merchant responsible for such an accident! I remember how I wept at it, as I lay in my father's arms and he first told me the story. It is certainly just that a man, even though he had no evil intention, should be held responsible for the immediate effects of his actions; but not for such as might result from them in a sporadic case here and there, but only for such as might have been guarded against by a reasonable rule of prudence. Nature herself often supplies the place of the intention of a rational agent in making a thirdness genuine and not merely accidental; as when a spark, as third, falling into a barrel of gunpowder, as first, causes an explosion, as second. But how does nature do this? By virtue of an intelligible law according to which she acts. If two forces are combined according to the parallelogram of forces, their resultant is a real third. Yet any force may, by the parallelogram of forces, be mathematically resolved into the sum of two others, in an infinity of different ways. Such components, however, are mere creations of the mind. What is the difference? As far as one isolated event goes, there is none; the real forces are no more present in the resultant than any components that the mathematician may imagine. But what makes the real forces really there is the general law of nature which calls for them, and not for any other components of the resultant. Thus, intelligibility, or reason objectified, is what makes thirdness genuine.

We now come to thirds degenerate in the second degree. The dramatist Marlowe had something of that character of diction in which Shakespeare and Bacon agree. This is a trivial example; but the mode of relation is important. In natural history, intermediate types serve to bring out the resemblance between forms whose similarity might otherwise escape attention, or not be duly appreciated. In portraiture, photographs mediate between the original and the likeness. In science, a diagram or analogue of the observed fact leads on to a further analogy. The relations of reason which go to the formation of such a triple relation need not be all resemblances. Washington was eminently free from the faults in which most great soldiers resemble one another. A centaur is a mixture of a man and a horse. Philadelphia lies between New York and Washington. Such thirds may be called Intermediate thirds or Thirds of comparison.

Nobody will suppose that I wish to claim any originality in reckoning the triad important in philosophy. Since Hegel, almost every fanciful thinker has done the same. Originality is the last of recommendations for fundamental conceptions. On the contrary, the fact that the minds of men have ever been inclined to threefold divisions is one of the considerations in favor of them. Other numbers have been objects of predilection to this philosopher and that, but three has been prominent at all times and with all schools. My whole method will be found to be in profound contrast with that of Hegel; I reject his philosophy in toto. Nevertheless, I have a certain sympathy with it, and fancy that if its author had only noticed a very few circumstances he would himself have been led to revolutionize his system. One of these is the double division or dichotomy of the second idea of the triad. He has usually overlooked external secondness, altogether. In other words, he has forgotten that there is a real world with real actions and reactions. Rather a serious oversight that. Then Hegel had the misfortune to be unusually deficient in mathematics. He shows this in the very elementary character of his reasoning. Worse still, while the whole burden of his song is that philosophers have neglected to take thirdness into account, which is true enough of the theological kind, with whom alone he was acquainted (for I do not call it acquaintance to look into a book without comprehending it), he unfortunately did not know, what it would have been of the utmost consequence for him to know, that the mathematical analysts had in great measure escaped this great fault, and that the thorough-going pursuit of the ideas and methods of the differential calculus would be sure to cure it altogether. Hegel's dialectical method is only a feeble and rudimentary application of the principles of the calculus to metaphysics. Finally, Hegel's plan of evolving everything out of the abstractest conception by a dialectical procedure, though far from being so absurd as the experientialists think, but on the contrary representing one of the indispensible parts of the course of science, overlooks the weakness of individual man, who wants the strength to wield such a weapon as that.

24

[Chapter III]
The Triad in Metaphysics

Fall 1887–Winter 1888 ***Houghton Library***

I will run over all the conceptions that played an important part in the pre-Socratic philosophy and see how far they can be expressed in terms of one, two, three.

1. The first of all the conceptions of philosophy is that of a primal matter out of which the world is made. Thales and the early Ionian philosophers busied themselves mainly with this. They called it the *arche,* the beginning; so that the conception of First was the quintessence of it. Nature was a wonder to them, and they asked its explanation; from what did it come? That was a good question, but it was rather stupid to suppose that they were going to learn much even if they could find out from what sort of matter it was made. But to ask how it had been formed, as they doubtless did, was not an exhaustive question, it would only carry them back a little way; they wished to go to the very beginning at once, and in the beginning there must have been a homogeneous something, for where there was variety they supposed there must be always an explanation to be sought. The first must be indeterminate, and the indeterminate first of anything is the material of which it is formed. Besides, their idea was that they could not tell how the world was formed unless they knew from what to begin their account. The inductive method of explaining phenomena by tracing them back step by step to their causes was foreign not only to them but to all ancient and medieval philosophy; that is the Baconian idea. Indeterminacy is really a character of the first. But not the indeterminacy of homogeneity. The first is full of life and variety. Yet that variety is only potential; it is not definitely there. Still, the notion of explaining the variety of the world, which was what they mainly wondered at, by non-variety was quite absurd. How is variety to come out of the womb of homogeneity; only by a principle of spontaneity, which is just that virtual variety that is the First.

25

Chapter IV
The Triad in Psychology

Fall 1887–Winter 1888 ***Houghton Library***

The line of reasoning which I propose to pursue is peculiar, and will need some careful study to estimate the strength of it. I shall review it critically in the last chapter, but meantime I desire to point out that the step I am about to take, which is analogous to others that will follow, is not so purely of the nature of a guess as might be supposed by persons expert in judging of scientific evidence. We have seen that the ideas of One, Two, Three, are forced upon us in logic, and really cannot be dispensed with. They meet us not once but at every turn. And we have found reason to think that they are equally important in metaphysics. How is the extraordinary prominence of these conceptions to be explained? Must it not be that they have their origin in the nature of the mind? This is the Kantian form of inference, which has been found so cogent in the hands of that hero of philosophy; and I do not know that modern studies have done anything to discredit it. It is true we no longer regard such a psychological explanation of a conception to be as final as Kant thought. It leaves further questions to be asked; but as far as it goes it seems to be satisfactory. We find the ideas of First, Second, Third, constant ingredients of our knowledge. It must then either be that they are continually given to us in the presentations of sense, or that it is the peculiar nature of the mind to mix them with our thoughts. Now we certainly cannot think that these ideas are given in sense. First, Second, and Third are not sensations. They can only be given in sense by things appearing labelled as first, second, and third, and such labels things do not usually bear. They ought therefore to have a psychological origin. A man must be a very uncompromising partisan of the theory of the *tabula rasa* to deny that the ideas of first, second, and third are due to congenital tendencies of the mind. So far there is nothing in my argument to distinguish it from that of many a Kantian. The noticeable thing is that I do not rest here, but seek to put the conclusion to the test by an independent examination of the facts of psychology, to see whether we can find any traces of the existence of three parts or faculties of the soul, or modes of consciousness, which might confirm the result just reached.

Now, three departments of the mind have been generally recognized since Kant; they are: Feeling, Knowing, and Willing. The unanimity with which this trisection of the mind has been accepted is, indeed, quite surprising. The division did not have its genesis in the peculiar ideas of Kant. On the contrary, it was borrowed by him from dogmatic philosophers, and his acceptance of it was, as has been well remarked, a concession to dogmatism. It has been allowed even by psychologists to whose general doctrines it seems positively hostile. This evidence that there is something true in it, is strengthened by the fact that it is impossible to make a critical examination of it, without coming to the conclusion that it is but a rough approximation to the truth, at best; and this has generally been conceded.

Where did this three-fold division of the functions of the mind come from? Kant took it ready-made from the Leibnitzian writer Tetens. He drew a suggestion from the rhetoricians of the sixteenth century and they found it, in an imperfect form, in their idolized Plato. In Plato, it appears under a poetical garb and distorted mien which we cannot believe to have been the original one; and it is easy to credit the statement of Diogenes Laertius that it came from the school of Pythagoras. Now in the doctrine of Pythagoras everything was connected with number, which was taken to be the foundation of the world. There is a hint in its history, then, that the three-fold division of the mind may be connected with the ideas of one, two, three.

By feelings, as constituting one of the great classes of mental activities, are meant according to Kant and most psychologists feelings of pleasure and pain. This is not, however, the original doctrine of Tetens, who includes under this head all that is immediately present, or at least the subjective element of it. Kant's modification suits his peculiar system better than the truth of nature. There is no good reason for giving such a peculiar place to pleasure and pain; as if they had no resemblance to anything else that we can feel. Pleasure and pain are nothing but secondary sensations, or feelings produced by feelings, whenever the latter reach a certain degree of subjective intensity, that is, produce a certain amount of commotion in the organism. If we could pay attention enough, we should probably recognize that every exertion and every cognition produces pleasure or pain. There is pleasure in the contemplation of a theorem of geometry. Pain is perhaps essential to the consciousness of exertion; what we do without pain we do without effort. But that peculiarity of feelings which makes them one of the great branches of mental phenomena is that they form the sum total of all of which we have in immediate and instantaneous consciousness; they are what is present. We cannot be immediately conscious of what is past and gone; we only remember it, though it be past by but the hundredth of a second. No more can we be immediately conscious of what is yet to come, however close at hand it may be. We can only infer it. Of nothing but the fleeting instant can we have absolutely immediate consciousness, or feeling, whether much or little; and this instant is no sooner present than it is gone. In it we can be conscious of no change; because we do that by making a little rehearsal of the process or imitation of it, and that occupies time. We can draw no inference in an instant, nor can we recognize any inferential conclusion. We can neither divide nor synthetize; we can only feel. When an instant has once passed, that immediate consciousness can never be recovered. It is totally and absolutely gone. We cannot compare any subsequent feeling with it, as immediate feeling, because we cannot have the second in our mind until the first has utterly gone from us. We remember it; that is to say, we have another cognition which professes to reproduce it; but we know that there is no resemblance between the memory and the sensation, because, in the first place, nothing can resemble an immediate feeling, for resemblance supposes a dismemberment and recomposition which is totally foreign to the immediate, and in the second place, memory is an articulated complex and worked-over product which differs infinitely and immeasurably from feeling. Look at a red surface, and try to feel what the sensation is, and then shut your eyes and remember it. No doubt different persons are different in this respect; to some the experiment will seem to yield an opposite result, but I have convinced myself that there is nothing in my memory that is in the least like the vision of the red. When red is not before my eyes, I do not see it at all. Some people tell me they see it faintly;—a most inconvenient kind of memory which would lead to remembering bright red as pale or dingy. I remember colors with unusual accuracy, because I have had much training in observing them; but my memory does not consist in any vision but in a habit by virtue of which I can recognize a newly presented color as like or unlike one I had seen before. But even if the memory of some persons is of the nature of an hallucination, enough arguments remain to show that immediate consciousness or feeling is absolutely unlike anything else.

There are grave objections to making a whole third of the mind of the will alone. One great psychologist has said that the will is nothing but the strongest desire. I cannot grant that; it seems to me to overlook that fact which of all that we observe is quite the most obtrusive, namely the difference between dreaming and doing. This is not a question of defining, but of noticing what we experience; and surely he who can confound desiring with willing must be a day-dreamer. The evidence, however, seems to be pretty strong that the consciousness of willing does not differ, at least not very much, from a sensation. The sense of hitting and of getting hit are nearly the same, and should be classed together. The common element is the sense of an actual occurrence, of actual action and reaction. There is an intense reality about this kind of experience, a sharp sundering of subject and object. While I am seated calmly in the dark, the lights are suddenly turned on, and at that instant I am conscious, not of a process of change, but yet of something more than can be contained in an instant. I have a sense of a saltus, of there being two sides to that instant. A consciousness of polarity would be a tolerably good phrase to describe what occurs. For will, then, as one of the great types of consciousness, we ought to substitute the polar sense.

But by far the most confused of the three members of the division, in its ordinary statement, is Cognition. In the first place every kind of consciousness enters into cognition. Feelings, in the sense in which alone they can be admitted as a great branch of mental phenomena, form the warp and woof of cognition, and even in the objectionable sense of pleasure and pain, they are constituents of cognition. The will, in the form of attention, constantly enters, and the sense of reality or objectivity, which is what we have found ought to take the place of will in the division of consciousness, is even more essential yet, if possible. But that element of cognition which is neither feeling nor polar sense, is the consciousness of a process, and this in the form of the sense of learning, of acquiring, of mental growth is eminently characteristic of cognition. This is a kind of consciousness which cannot be immediate, because it covers a time, and that not merely because it continues through every instant of that time, but because it cannot be contracted into an instant. It differs from immediate consciousness, as a melody does from one prolonged note. Neither can the consciousness of the two sides of an instant, of a sudden occurrence, in its individual reality, possibly embrace the consciousness of a process. This is the consciousness that binds our life together. It is the consciousness of synthesis.

Here then, we have indubitably three radically different elements of consciousness, these and no more. And they are evidently connected with the ideas of one–two–three. Immediate feeling is the consciousness of the first; the polar sense is the consciousness of the second; and synthetical consciousness is the consciousness of a Third or medium.

Note, too, that just as we have seen that there are two orders of secondness, so the polar sense splits into two, and that in two ways, for first, there is an active and a passive kind, or Will and Sense, and second, there are External Will and Sense, in opposition to Internal Will (self-control, inhibitory will) and Internal Sense (introspection). In like manner, just as there are three orders of thirdness, so there are three kinds of synthetical consciousness. The undegenerate and really typical form has not been made so familiar to us as the others, which have been more completely studied by psychologists; I shall therefore mention that last. Synthetical consciousness degenerate in the first degree, corresponding to accidental thirdness, is where there is an external compulsion upon us to think things together. Association by contiguity is an instance of this; but a still better instance is that in our first apprehension of our experiences, we cannot choose how we will arrange our ideas in reference to time and space, but are compelled to think certain things as nearer together than others. It would be putting the cart before the horse to say that we are compelled to think certain things together because they are together in time and space; the true way of stating it is that there is an exterior compulsion upon us to put them together in our construction of time and space, in our perspective. Synthetical consciousness degenerate in the second degree, corresponding to intermediate thirds, is where we think different feelings to be alike or different, which, since feelings in themselves cannot be compared and therefore cannot be alike, so that to say they are alike is merely to say that the synthetic consciousness regards them so, comes to this, that we are internally compelled to synthetize them or to sunder them. This kind of synthesis appears in a secondary form in association by resemblance. But the highest kind of synthesis is what the mind is compelled to make neither by the inward attractions of the feelings or representations themselves, nor by a transcendental force of haecceity, but in the interest of intelligibility, that is, in the interest of the synthetizing "I think" itself; and this it does by introducing an idea not contained in the data, which gives connections which they would not otherwise have had. This kind of synthesis has not been sufficiently studied, and especially the intimate relationship of its different varieties has not been duly considered. The work of the poet or novelist is not so utterly different from that of the scientific man. The artist introduces a fiction; but it is not an arbitrary one; it exhibits affinities to which the mind accords a certain approval in pronouncing them beautiful, which if it is not exactly the same as saying that the synthesis is true, is something of the same general kind. The geometer draws a diagram, which if not exactly a fiction, is at least a creation, and by means of observation of that diagram he is able to synthetize and show relations between elements which before seemed to have no necessary connection. The realities compel us to put some things into very close relation and others less so, in a highly complicated, and to the sense itself unintelligible, manner; but it is the genius of the mind, that takes up all these hints of sense, adds immensely to them, makes them precise, and shows them in intelligible form in the intuitions of space and time. Intuition is the regarding of the abstract in a concrete form, by the realistic hypostatization of relations; that is the one sole method of valuable thought. Very shallow is the prevalent notion that this is something to be avoided. You might as well say at once that reasoning is to be avoided because it has led to so much error; quite in the same philistine line of thought would that be and so well in accord with the spirit of nominalism that I wonder some one does not put it forward. The true precept is not to abstain from hypostatization, but to do it intelligently.

26

Chapter V
The Triad in Physiology

Fall 1887–Winter 1888 ***Houghton Library***

Granted that there are three fundamentally different kinds of consciousness, it follows as a matter of course that there must be something threefold in the physiology of the nervous system to account for them. No materialism is implied in this, further than that intimate dependence of the action of the mind upon the body, which every student of the subject must and does now acknowledge. Once more a prediction, as it were, is made by the theory; that is to say, certain consequences, not contemplated in the construction thereof, necessarily result from it; and these are of such a character that their truth or falsehood can be independently investigated. Were we to find them strikingly and certainly true, a remarkable confirmation of the theory would be afforded. So much as this, however, I cannot promise; I can only say that they are not certainly false; and we must be content to trace out these consequences, and see what they are, and leave them to the future judgment of physiologists.

Two of the three kinds of consciousness, indeed, the simple and dual, receive an instant physiological explanation. We know that the protoplasmic contents of every nerve-cell has its active and passive conditions, and argument is unnecessary to show that Feeling, or immediate consciousness, arises in an active state of nerve-cells. Experiments on the effects of cutting the nerves show that there is no feeling after communication with the central nerve-cells is severed, so that the phenomenon has certainly some connection with the nerve-cells; and feeling is excited by just such stimuli as would be likely to throw protoplasm into an active condition. Thus, though we cannot say that every nerve-cell in its active condition has feeling (which we cannot deny, however), there is scarce room to doubt that the activity of nerve-cells is the main physiological requisite for consciousness. On the other hand, the sense of action and reaction, or the polar sense, as we agreed to call it, is plainly connected with the discharge of nervous energy through the nerve-fibres. External volition, the most typical case of it, involves such a discharge into muscle cells. In external sensation, where the polar sense enters in a lower intensity, there is a discharge from the terminal nerve-cell through the afferent nerve upon a cell or cells in the brain. In internal volition, or self-control, there is some inhibitory action of the nerves, which is also known to involve the movement of nervous force; and in internal observation, or visceral sensation, there are doubtless transfers of energy from one central cell to another. Remembering that the polar sense is the sense of the difference between what was before and what is after a dividing instant, or the sense of an instant as having sides, we see clearly that the physiological concomitant of it must be some event which happens very quickly and leaves a more abiding effect, and this description suits the passage of a nervous discharge over a nerve-fibre so perfectly, that I do not think we need hesitate to set this phenomenon down as the condition of dual consciousness.

Synthetic consciousness offers a more difficult problem. Yet the explanation of the genuine form of that consciousness, the sense of learning, is easy enough; it is only the degenerate modes, the sense of similarity, and the sense of real connection, which oblige us to hesitate. With regard to these two degenerate forms, I am driven to make hypotheses.

When two ideas resemble one another, we say that they have something in common; a part of the one is said to be identical with a part of the other. In what does that identity consist? Having closed both eyes, I open first one and then shut it and open the other, and I say that the two sensations are alike. How can the impressions of two nerves be judged to be alike? It appears to me that in order that that should become possible, the two nerve-cells must probably discharge themselves into one common nerve-cell. In any case, it seems to me that the first supposition to make, for scientific observation to confirm or reject, is that two ideas are alike so far as the same nerve-cells have been concerned in the production of them. In short, the hypothesis is that resemblance consists in the identity of a common element, and that that identity lies in a part of the one idea and a part of the other idea being the feeling peculiar to the excitation of one or more nerve-cells.

When we find ourselves under a compulsion to think that two elements of experience which do not particularly resemble one another are, nevertheless, really connected, that connection must, I think, be due in some way to a discharge of nerve-energy; for the whole sense of reality is a determination of polar consciousness, which is itself due to such discharges. For example, I recognize that a certain surface on one side of a certain boundary is red, and on the other side is blue; or that any two qualities are immediately contiguous in space or time. If the contiguity is in time, it is by the polar sense directly that we are conscious of a dividing instant with its difference on the two sides. If the contiguity is in space, I think we have at first a completely confused feeling of the whole, as yet unanalyzed and unsynthetized, but afterward, when the analysis has been made, we find ourselves compelled, in recomposing the elements, to pass directly from what is on one side of the boundary to what is on the other. I suppose then that we are compelled to think the two feelings as contiguous because the nerve-cell whose excitation produces the feeling of one recalled sensation discharges itself into the nerve-cell whose excitation makes the feeling of the other recalled sensation.

The genuine synthetic consciousness, or the sense of the process of learning, which is the preeminent ingredient and quintessence of the reason, has its physiological basis quite evidently in the most characteristic property of the nervous system, the power of taking habits. This depends on five principles, as follows. 1st, when a stimulus or irritation is continued for some time, the excitation spreads from the cells directly affected to those that are associated with it, and from those to others, and so on, and at the same time increases in intensity. 2nd, after a time, fatigue begins to set in. Now besides the utter fatigue which consists in the cell's losing all excitability, and the nervous system refusing to react to the stimulus at all, there is a gentler fatigue, which plays a very important part in adapting the brain to serving as an organ of reason, this form of fatigue consisting in the reflex action or discharge of the nerve-cell ceasing on one path and either beginning on a path where there had been no discharge, or increasing the intensity of the discharge along a path on which there had been previously only a slight discharge. For example, a frog, whose cerebrum or brain has been removed, and whose hind leg has been irritated by putting a drop of acid upon it, after repeatedly rubbing the place with the other foot, as if to wipe off the acid, may at length be observed to give several hops, the first avenue of nervous discharge having become fatigued. 3rd, when from any cause the stimulus to a nerve-cell is removed, the excitation quickly subsides. That it does not do so instantly is well-known, and the phenomenon goes among physicists by the name of persistence of sensation. All noticeable feeling subsides in a fraction of a second, but a very small remnant continues for a much longer time. 4th, if the same cell which was once excited, and which by some chance had happened to discharge itself along a certain path or paths, comes to get excited a second time, it is more likely to discharge itself the second time along some or all of those paths along which it had previously discharged itself than it would have been had it not so discharged itself before. This is the central principle of habit; and the striking contrast of its modality to that of any mechanical law is most significant. The laws of physics know nothing of tendencies or probabilities; whatever they require at all they require absolutely and without fail, and they are never disobeyed. Were the tendency to take habits replaced by an absolute requirement that the cell should discharge itself always in the same way, or according to any rigidly fixed condition whatever, all possibility of habit developing into intelligence would be cut off at the outset; the virtue of thirdness would be absent. It is essential that there should be an element of chance in some sense as to how the cell shall discharge itself; and then that this chance or uncertainty shall not be entirely obliterated by the principle of habit, but only somewhat affected. 5th, when a considerable time has elapsed without a nerve having reacted in any particular way, there comes in a principle of forgetfulness or negative habit rendering it the less likely to react in that way. Now let us see what will be the result of these five principles taken in combination. When a nerve is stimulated, if the reflex activity is not at first of the right sort to remove the source of irritation, it will change its character again and again until the cause of irritation is removed, when the activity will quickly subside. When the nerve comes to be stimulated a second time in the same way, probably some of the other movements which had been made on the first occasion will be repeated; but, however this may be, one of them must ultimately be repeated, I mean that movement which removes the source of irritation, for the activity will continue until this does happen. On a third occasion, the process of forgetfulness will have been begun in regard to any tendency to repeat any of the actions of the first occasion which were not repeated on the second. Of those which were repeated, some will probably be repeated again, and some not; but always there remains that one which must be repeated before the activity comes to an end. The ultimate effect of this will inevitably be that a habit gets established of at once reacting in the way which removes the source of irritation; for this habit alone will be strengthened at each repetition of the experiment, while every other will tend to become weakened at an accelerated rate.

I have invented a little game or experiment with playing-cards to illustrate the working of these principles; and I can promise the reader that if he will try it half a dozen times he will be better able to estimate the value of the account of habit here proposed. The rules of this game are as follows. Take a good many cards of four suits, say a pack of 52, though fewer will do. The four suits are supposed to represent four modes in which a cell may react. Let one suit, say spades, represent that mode of reaction which removes the source of irritation and brings the activity to an end. In order readily to find a card of any suit as wanted, you had better lay all the cards down face up and distributed into four packets, each containing the cards of one suit only. Now take 2 spades, 2 diamonds, 2 clubs, and 2 hearts, to represent the original disposition of the nerve-cell, which is supposed to be equally likely to react in any of the four ways. You turn these 8 cards face down and shuffle them with extreme thoroughness.[1] Then turn up cards from the top of this pack, one by one until a spade is reached. This process

1. Cards are almost never shuffled enough to illustrate fairly the principles of probabilities; but if after being shuffled in any of the usual ways, they are dealt into three packs and taken up again, and then passed from one hand into the other one by one, every other one going to the top and every other to the bottom of the pack that thus accumulates in the second hand, and finally cut, the shuffling may be considered as sufficient for the purpose of this game. Whenever the direction is to shuffle, shuffling as thorough as this is meant.

represents the reaction of the cell. Take up the cards just dealt off, and add to the pack held in the hand one card of each of those suits that have just been turned up (for habit) and remove from the pack one card of each suit not turned up (for forgetfulness). Shuffle, and go through with this operation 13 times or until the spades are exhausted. It will then generally be found that you hold nothing but spades in your hand.

Thus we see how these principles not only lead to the establishment of habits, but to habits directed to definite ends, namely the removal of sources of irritation. Now it is precisely action according to final causes which distinguishes mental from mechanical action; and the general formula of all our desires may be taken as this: to remove a stimulus. Every man is busily working to bring to an end that state of things which now excites him to work.

But we are led yet deeper into physiology. The three fundamental functions of the nervous system, namely, 1st, the excitation of cells, 2nd, the transfer of excitation over fibres, 3rd, the fixing of definite tendencies under the influence of habit, are plainly due to three properties of the protoplasm or life-slime itself. Protoplasm has its active and its passive condition, its active state is transferred from one part of it to another, and it also exhibits the phenomena of habit. But these three facts do not seem to sum up the main properties of protoplasm, as our theory would lead us to expect them to do. Still, this may be because the nature of this strange substance is so little understood; and if we had the true secret of its constitution we might see that qualities that now appear unrelated really group themselves into one, so that it may be after all that it accords with our theory better than it seems to do. There have been at least two attempts to explain the properties of protoplasm by means of chemical suppositions; but inasmuch as chemical forces are as far as possible themselves from being understood, such hypotheses, even if they were known to be correct, would be of little avail. As for what a physicist would understand by a molecular explanation of protoplasm, such a thing seems hardly to have been thought of; yet I cannot see that it is any more difficult than the constitution of inorganic matter. The properties of protoplasm are enumerated as follows: contractility, irritability, automatism, nutrition, metabolism, respiration, and reproduction; but

5.

Thus we see how these principles not only lead to the establishment of habits, but to habits directed to definite ends, namely the removal of sources of irritation. Now it is precisely action according to final causes which distinguishes mental from mechanical action; and the general formula off all our desires may be taken as this: to remove a stimulus. Every man is busily working to bring to an end that state of things ~~make that thing~~ which now excites him to work.

But we are led ~~deeper yet~~ yet deeper into physiology. The three fundamental functions of the nervous system, namely, 1st, the excitation of cells, 2nd, the transfer of excitation over fibres, 3rd, the fixing of definite tendencies under the influence of habit, are plainly due to three properties of the protoplasm or life-slime itself. Protoplasm has its active and its passive condition; its active state is transfered from one part of it to another, and it also exhibits the phenomena of habit. But these three facts do not seem to sum up the main properties of protoplasm, as our theory would lead us to expect them to do. Still, this may ~~This may however~~ be because the nature of this strange substance ~~protoplasm~~ is so little understood; and if we had the true secret of its constitution we might see that qualities that now appear unrelated really group themselves into one, so that it may be ~~afte~~ after all that it accords with our theory better than it seems to do. There have been at least two attempts to explain the properties of protoplasm by means of chemical suppositions; ~~bu~~ but inasmuch as chemical forces are as far as possible themselves from being understood, such hypotheses, even if they were known to be correct, would be of little avail. . As for what a physicist would understand by a molecular explanation of protoplasm, such a thing seems hardly to have been thought of; yet I cannot see that it is any more difficult than the constitution of inorganic matter. The properties of protoplasm are enumerated as follows: contractility, irritability, automatism, nutrition, metabolism, respiration, and reproduction. ; but these can all be summed up ~~as a~~ under the heads of sensibility, motion, and growth. These three properties are respectively first, second, and third. Let us, however, draw up a brief statement of the facts which a molecular theory of protoplasm would have to account for. In the first place, then, protoplasm is a definite chemical substance, or class of substances, recognizable by ~~definitions~~ its characteristic reactions. "We do not at present," says Dr. Michael Foster (1879), "know anything definite about the molecular composition of active living protoplasm; but it is more than probable that its molecule is a large and complex one in which a proteid substance is peculiarly associated with a complex fat and with some representative of the carbohydrate group, i.e. that each molecule of protoplasm contains residues of each of these three great classes. The whole animal body is modified protoplasm." The chemical complexity of the protoplasm molecule must be amazing. A proteid is only one of its constituents, and doubtless very much simpler. Yet chemists do not attempt to infer from their analyses the ultimate atomic constitution of any of the proteids, the number of atoms

A typescript leaf from Chapter V of "A Guess of the Riddle" (R 909), showing Peirce's own revisions as well as subsequent retracings and annotations by the Collected Papers *editors. Editorial markings include the pagination (top right), the interlined text completing the transposition marked by Peirce in line 6, and complete or partial retracings of text above line 13 (substance) and in lines 22 (automatism) and 28 (active). (By permission of the Houghton Library, Harvard University.)*

these can all be summed up under the heads of sensibility, motion, and growth. These three properties are respectively first, second, and third. Let us, however, draw up a brief statement of the facts which a molecular theory of protoplasm would have to account for. In the first place, then, protoplasm is a definite chemical substance, or class of substances, recognizable by its characteristic reactions. "We do not at present," says Dr. Michael Foster (1879), "know anything definite about the molecular composition of active living protoplasm; but it is more than probable that its molecule is a large and complex one in which a proteid substance is peculiarly associated with a complex fat and with some representative of the carbohydrate group, i.e. that each molecule of protoplasm contains residues of each of these three great classes. The whole animal body is modified protoplasm." The chemical complexity of the protoplasm molecule must be amazing. A proteid is only one of its constituents, and doubtless very much simpler. Yet chemists do not attempt to infer from their analyses the ultimate atomic constitution of any of the proteids, the number of atoms entering into them being so great as almost to nullify the law of multiple proportions. I do find in the book just quoted the following formula for nuclein, a substance allied to the proteids. It is $C_{29}H_{49}N_9P_3O_{22}$. But as the sum of the numbers of atoms of hydrogen, nitrogen, and phosphorus ought to be even, this formula must be multiplied by some even number; so that the number of atoms in nuclein must be 224 at the very least. We can hardly imagine, then, that the number of atoms in protoplasm is much less than a thousand, and if one considers the very minute proportions of some necessary ingredients of animal and vegetable organisms, one is somewhat tempted to suspect that 50,000 might do better, or even come to be looked upon in the future as a ridiculously small guess. Protoplasm combines with water in all proportions, the mode of combination being apparently intermediate between solution and mechanical mixture. According to the amount of water it contains, it passes from being brittle, to being pliable, then gelatinous, then slimy, then liquid. Generally, it has the character of being elastico-viscous; that is to say, it springs back partially after a long strain, and wholly after a short one; but its viscosity is much more marked than its elasticity. It is generally full of granules, by which we can see slow streaming motions in it, continuing for some minutes in one way and then generally reversed.

The effect of this streaming is to cause protuberances in the mass, often very long and slender. They occasionally stick up against gravity; and their various forms are characteristic of the different kinds of protoplasm. When a mass of it is disturbed by a jar, a poke, an electric shock, heat, etc., the streams are arrested and the whole contracts into a ball; or if it were very much elongated it sometimes breaks up into separate spheres. When the external excitation is removed, the mass sinks down into something like its former condition. Protoplasm also grows; it absorbs material and converts it into the like of its own substance; and in all its growth and reproduction, it preserves its specific characters.

Such are the properties that have to be accounted for. What first arrests our attention as likely to afford the key to the problem, is the contraction of the mass of protoplasm on being disturbed. This is obviously due to a vast and sudden increase of what the physicists call "surface tension," or the pulling together of the outer parts, which phenomenon is always observed in liquids, and is the cause of their making drops. This surface tension is due to the cohesion, or attraction between neighboring molecules. The question is, then, how can a body, on having its equilibrium deranged, suddenly increase the attractions between its neighboring molecules? These attractions must increase rapidly as the distance is diminished; and thus the answer suggests itself that the distance between neighboring molecules is diminished. True, the average distance must remain nearly the same, but if the distances which had previously been nearly equal are rendered unequal, the attractions between the molecules that are brought nearer to one another will be much more increased than those between those that are removed from one another will be diminished. We are thus led to the supposition that in the ordinary state of the substance, its particles are moving for the most part in complicated orbital or quasi-orbital systems, instead of in the chemical molecules or more definite systems of atoms of less complex substances, these particles thus moving in orbits not being, however, atoms but chemical molecules. But we must suppose that the forces between these particles are just barely sufficient to hold them in their orbits, and that in fact, as long as the protoplasm is in an active condition, they are not all so held, but that one and another get occasionally thrown out of their orbits and wander about until they are drawn into some other system. We must suppose that these systems have some approximate composition, about so many of one kind of particles and so many of another kind, etc., entering into them. This is necessary to account for the nearly constant chemical composition of the whole. On the other hand, we cannot suppose that the number of the different kinds is rigidly exact; for in that case we should not know how to account for the power of assimilation. We must suppose then that there is considerable range in the numbers of particles that go to form an orbital system, and that the somewhat exact chemical composition of the whole is the exactitude of a statistical average; just as there is a close equality between the proportions of the two sexes in any nation or province, though there is considerable inequality in each of the different households. Owing to the very complexity of this arrangement, the moment that there is any molecular disturbance, producing perturbations, large numbers of the particles are thrown out of their orbits, the systems are more or less deranged in the immediate neighborhood of the disturbance, and the harmonic relations between the different revolutions are somewhat broken up. In consequence of this, the distances between neighboring particles, which had presented a systematic regularity, now become extremely unequal, and their average attractions, upon which the cohesion depends, is increased. At the same time, the particles thrown out of their systems shoot into other systems and derange these in their turn, and so the disturbance is propagated throughout the entire mass. The source of disturbance, however, being removed, interchanges of energy take place, in which there is a tendency to equalize the vis viva of the different particles, and they consequently tend to sink down into orbital motions again, and gradually something very like the original state of things is reestablished, the original orbital systems remaining, for the most part, and the wandering particles in large proportion finding places in these systems or forming new ones. Some of these particles will not find any places, and thus there will be a certain amount of wasting of the protoplasmic mass. If the same disturbance is repeated, so far as the orbital systems remain the same as they were before, there will be a repetition of almost exactly the same events. The same kinds of particles (the same I mean in mass, velocities, directions of movement, attractions, etc.) which were thrown out of the different systems before will generally get thrown out again, until, if the disturbance is repeated several times, there gets to be rather a deficiency of those kinds of particles in the different systems, when some new kinds will begin to be thrown out. These new kinds will differently perturb the systems into which they fly, tending to cause classes of particles like themselves to be thrown out, and, in that way, the direction of propagation of the disturbance, as well as its velocity and intensity, may be altered, and, in short, the phenomenon of fatigue will be manifested. Even when the protoplasmic mass is left to itself, there will be some wandering of particles, producing regions of slight disturbance, and so inequalities of tension; and thus, streams will be set up, movements of the mass will take place, and slender processes will be formed. If, however, the mass be left to itself for a very long time, all the particles that are readily thrown out, will, in all the changes that are rung on the combinations of situations and velocities in the orbital systems, get thrown out; while the others will constantly tend to settle down into more stable relations; and so the protoplasm will gradually take a passive state from which its orbital systems are not easily deranged. The food for those kinds of protoplasm that are capable of marked reaction has to be presented in chemically complex form. It must doubtless present particles just like those that revolve in the orbital systems of the protoplasm. In order to be drawn into an orbital system, a particle, whether of food matter or just thrown off from some other system, must have the right mass, must present itself at the right point, and move with the right velocity in the right direction and be subject to the right attractions. It will be right in all these respects, if it comes to take the place of a particle which has just been thrown off; and thus, particles taken in are particularly likely to be of the same material and masses and to take the same places in the orbits as those that have been shortly before thrown off. Now these particles, being the exact representatives of those thrown off, will be likely to be thrown off by the same disturbances, in the same directions, and with the same results, as those which were thrown off before; and this accounts for the principle of habit. All the higher kinds of protoplasm, those for example which have any marked power of contraction, are fed with matter chemically highly complex.

27

Chapter VI
The Triad in Biological Development

Fall 1887–Winter 1888 ***Houghton Library***

A very remarkable feature in the Darwinian theory is that it shows that merely fortuitous variations of individuals together with merely fortuitous mishaps to individuals (whether really fortuitous or not, they may be so for the purposes of the theory) should, under the action of heredity, result, not in mere irregularity, nor even in a mere statistical constancy, but in a continual and indefinite progress toward the adaptation of species to their environments. How can this be? What, abstractly stated, is the peculiar element in the conditions of the problem, which brings about this singular consequence?

Suppose a million persons, each provided with one dollar, to sit down to play a simple and fair game of chance, betting for example upon whether a die turns up an odd or even number. The players are supposed to make their bets independently of one another, and each to bet one dollar against a dollar on the part of the bank on the result of each throw. Of course, at the very first bet, one half of them would lose their only dollar and be out of the game, while the other half would win a dollar and so be worth \$2 each. After the second throw, 250,000 would have lost and so be worth \$1 each while the other 250,000 would have won and so be worth \$3 each. After the third throw, 125,000 more having been ruined, 250,000 would be worth \$2 (namely 125,000 of those that had had \$1 and 125,000 of those that had had \$3) and 125,000 would be worth \$4. It is a simple thing to calculate that after the sixteenth throw

21,821	players would have	\$ 1
52,369		\$ 3
55,542		\$ 5

38,879	\$ 7
19,226	\$ 9
6,714	\$11
1,587	\$13
229	\$15
15	\$17

More players would have \$5 than any smaller sum. At the end of the 36th throw more would have \$7 than any smaller sum; at the end of 64 throws \$9 would be the most frequent amount; at the end of 100 throws \$11. Here then would be a continual increase of wealth, which is a sort of "adaptation to one's environment" produced by the survival of the fittest, that is, by the going out of the game of all those who lose their last dollar. The reason of the phenomenon of increase is that wealth has an absolute minimum, but no absolute maximum. If the players could go on tick without ever stopping, no matter how much less than nothing they might be worth, the most frequent wealth would always remain \$1. On the other hand, if they were obliged to retire after they had won a certain fixed sum, the result would be that as the betting went on the most frequent amount of wealth would increase from \$1 up toward the half of the maximum sum, a point which it would indefinitely approach without ever reaching. The adaptation of a species to its environment consists in the capacity of one generation to bring forth another, for as long as another generation is brought forth the species will survive, and as soon as reproduction ceases it is doomed in one lifetime. This reproductive capacity, then, depending partly on direct fecundity, and partly on the animal's living through the age of procreation, is precisely what the theory of natural selection accounts for. It has an absolute minimum, for no animal can produce fewer offspring than none at all, and apparently no absolute maximum. It would therefore, under the influence of chance, be continually on the increase, like the wealth of our players.

The diagram shows curves of the distribution of wealth among the players at the end of the 100th, 400th, 900th, 1600th, and 2500th throws. What is called the moral wealth in probabilities is the logarithm of the wealth divided by the smallest amount on which a man can live. It is the earliest example of the recognition in a special case of the psychophysical law, which governs the relations of the outer and inner worlds. The moral wealth, then, measures the mental impression produced by physical wealth. I have reckoned the moral wealth along the horizontal axis of coordinates, and have taken the vertical coordinates of the different points of each curve so that the area included between two vertical lines, the curve, and the horizontal axis of coordinates should measure the number of players whose fortunes are intermediate between the two values corresponding to the two vertical lines.

But if the characters of animals have been developed under this influence, statistics will yield a sure indication of it, inasmuch as the frequency of the variation of a given magnitude would always be greater in the direction toward which the species is tending, than in the direction from which it has come. This is a most important principle, which if it does not absolutely disprove the theory, will always show what the progenitors of a given form must have been. I am not aware that such statistics have been collected even for man; in regard to all the characters that have been examined by Quetelet and others, it is found that plus and minus variations occur with equal frequency, which shows that these characters have not been formed under the direct action of natural selection; but it is hard to believe that men are born with brains only ½ the usual weight as often as men with brains 1½ times the average weight.

But it must be borne in mind that the rule just given supposes the magnitudes of the variations to be measured by equal probabilities of variation, that is to say, so that the offspring of a given individual are as likely to differ from their parents by a given amount in excess as in defect. If we estimate them by our feeling or judgment, the maxima may occur in some other place.

It is to be remarked that the phrase "survival of the fittest" in the formula of the principle does not mean the survival of the fittest individuals, but the survival of the fittest types; for the theory does not at all require that individuals ill-adapted to their environment should die at an earlier age than others, so long only as they do not reproduce so many offspring as others; and indeed it is not necessary that this should go so far as to extinguish the line of descent, provided there be some reason why the offspring of ill-adapted parents are less likely than others to inherit those parents' characteristics. It seems likely that the process, as a general rule, is something as follows. A given individual is in some respect ill-adapted to his environment, that is to say, he has characters which are generally unfavorable to the production of numerous offspring. These characters will be apt to weaken the reproductive system of that individual, for various reasons, so that its offspring are not up to the average strength of the species. This second generation will couple with other individuals, but owing to their weakness, their offspring will be more apt to resemble the other parent, and so the unfavorable character will gradually be eliminated, not merely by diminished numbers of offspring, but also by the offspring more resembling the stronger parent. There are other ways in which the unfavorable characters will disappear. When the procreative power is weakened, there are many examples to show that the principle of heredity becomes relaxed, and the race shows more tendency to sporting. This sporting will go on until in the course of it the unfavorable character has become obliterated. The general power of reproduction thereupon becomes strengthened, with it the direct procreative force is reinforced, the hereditary transmission of characters again becomes more strict, and the improved type is hardened.

But all these different cases are but so many different modes of one and the same principle, which is, the elimination of unfavorable characters. We see then that there are just three factors in the process of natural selection; to wit: 1st, the principle of individual variation or sporting; 2nd, the principle of hereditary transmission, which wars against the first principle; and 3rd, the principle of the elimination of unfavorable characters.

Let us see how far these principles correspond with the triads that we have already met with. The principle of sporting is the principle of irregularity, indeterminacy, chance. It corresponds with the irregular and manifold wandering of particles in the active state of the protoplasm. It is the bringing in of something fresh and first. The principle of heredity is the principle of the determination of something by what went before, the principle of compulsion, corresponding to the will and sense. The principle of the elimination of unfavorable characters is the principle of generalization by casting out of sporadic cases, corresponding particularly to the principle of forgetfulness in the action of the nervous system. We have, then, here, a somewhat imperfect reproduction of the same triad as before. Its imperfection may be the imperfection of the theory of development.

28

Chapter VII
The Triad in Physics

Fall 1887–Winter 1888 ***Houghton Library***

Metaphysical philosophy may almost be called the child of geometry. Of the three schools of early Greek philosophers, two, the Ionic and the Pythagorean, were all geometers, and the interest of the Eleatics in that science is often mentioned. Plato was a great figure in the history of both subjects; and Aristotle derived from the study of space some of his most potent conceptions. Metaphysics depends in great measure on the idea of rigid demonstration from first principles; and this idea, as well in regard to the process as the axioms from which it sets out, bears its paternity on its face. Moreover, the conviction that any metaphysical philosophy is possible has been upheld at all times, as Kant well says, by the example in geometry of a similar science.

The unconditional surrender, then, by the mathematicians of our time of the absolute exactitude of the axioms of geometry cannot prove an insignificant event for the history of philosophy. Gauss, the greatest of geometers, declares that "there is no reason to think that the sum of the three angles of a triangle is exactly equal to two right angles." It is true, experience shows that the deviation of that sum from that amount is so excessively small that language must be ingeniously used to express the degree of approximation: but experience never can show any truth to be exact, nor so much as give the least reason to think it to be so, unless it be supported by some other considerations. We can only say that the sum of the three angles of any given triangle cannot be much greater or less than two right angles; but that exact value is only one among an infinite number of others each of which is as possible as that. So say the mathematicians with unanimity.

The absolute exactitude of the geometrical axioms is exploded; and the corresponding belief in the metaphysical axioms, considering the dependence of metaphysics on geometry, must surely follow it to the tomb of extinct creeds. The first to go must be the proposition that every event in the universe is precisely determined by causes according to inviolable law. We have no reason to think that this is absolutely exact. Experience shows that it is so to a wonderful degree of approximation, and that is all. This degree of approximation will be a value for future scientific investigation to determine; but we have no more reason to think that the error of the ordinary statement is precisely zero, than any one of an infinity of values in that neighborhood. The odds are infinity to one that it is not zero; and we are bound to think of it as a quantity of which zero is only one possible value. Phoenix, in his "Lectures on Astronomy," referring to Joshua's commanding the sun to stand still, said that he could not help suspecting that it might have wiggled a very little when Joshua was not looking directly at it. We know that when we try to verify any law of nature by experiment, we always find discrepancies between the observations and the theory. These we rightly refer to errors of observation; but why may there not be similar aberrations due to the imperfect obedience of the facts to law?

Grant that this is conceivable and there can be nothing in experience to negative it. Strange to say, there are many people who will have a difficulty in conceiving of an element of absolute chance or lawlessness in the universe, and who may perhaps be tempted to reckon the doctrine of the perfect rule of causality as one of the original instinctive beliefs, like that of space having three dimensions. Far from that, it is historically altogether a modern notion, a loose inference from the discoveries of science. Aristotle often lays it down that some things are determined by causes while others happen by chance. Lucretius, following Democritus, supposes his primordial atoms to deviate from their rectilinear trajectories just fortuitously, and without any reason at all. To the ancients, there was nothing strange in such notions; they were matters of course; the strange thing would have been to have said that there was no chance. So we are under no inward necessity of believing in perfect causality when we do not find any facts to bear it out.

I am very far from holding that experience is our only light; Whewell's views of scientific method seem to me truer than Mill's; so much so that I should pronounce the known principles of physics to be but a development of original instinctive beliefs. Yet I cannot help acknowledging that the whole history of thought shows that our instinctive beliefs, in their original condition, are so mixed up with error that they can never be trusted till they have been corrected by experiment. Now the only thing that the inference from experience can ever teach us is the approximate value of a ratio. It all rests on the principle of sampling; we take a handful of coffee from a bag, and we judge that there is about the same proportion of sound beans in the whole bag that there is in that sample. At this rate, every proposition which we can be entitled to make about the real world must be an approximate one; we never can have the right to hold any truth to be exact. Approximation must be the fabric out of which our philosophy has to be built.

I come now to another point. Most systems of philosophy maintain certain facts or principles as ultimate. In truth, any fact is in one sense ultimate,—that is to say, in its isolated aggressive stubbornness and individual reality. What Scotus calls the haecceities of things, the hereness and nowness of them, are indeed ultimate. Why this which is here is such as it is, how, for instance, if it happens to be a grain of sand it came to be so small and so hard, we can ask; we can also ask how it got carried here, but the explanation in this case merely carries us back to the fact that it was once in some other place, where similar things might naturally be expected to be. Why IT, independently of its general characters, comes to have any definite place in the world, is not a question to be asked; it is simply an ultimate fact. There is also another class of facts of which it is not reasonable to expect an explanation, namely, facts of indeterminacy or variety. Why one definite kind of event is frequent and another rare, is a question to be asked, but a reason for the general fact that of events some kinds are common and some rare, it would be unfair to demand. If all births took place on a given day of the week, or if there were always more on Sundays than on Mondays, that would be a fact to be accounted for, but that they happen in about equal proportions on all the days requires no particular explanation. If we were to find that all the grains of sand on a certain beach separated themselves into two or more sharply discrete classes, as spherical and cubical ones, there would be something to be explained, but that they are of various sizes and shapes, of no definable character, can only be referred to the general manifoldness of nature. Indeterminacy, then, or pure firstness, and haecceity, or pure secondness, are facts not calling for and not capable of explanation. Indeterminacy affords us nothing to ask a question about; haecceity is the *ultima ratio,* the brutal fact that will not be questioned. But every fact of a general or orderly nature calls for an explanation; and logic forbids us to assume in regard to any given fact of that sort that it is of its own nature absolutely inexplicable. This is what Kant[1] calls a regulative principle, that is to say, an intellectual hope. The sole immediate purpose of thinking is to render things intelligible; and to think and yet in that very act to think a thing unintelligible is a self-stultification. It is as though a man furnished with a pistol to defend himself against an enemy were, on finding that enemy very redoubtable, to use his pistol to blow his own brains out to escape being killed by his enemy. Despair is insanity. True, there may be facts that will never get explained; but that any given fact is of the number, is what experience can never give us reason to think; far less can it show that any fact is of its own nature unintelligible. We must therefore be guided by the rule of hope, and consequently we must reject every philosophy or general conception of the universe which could ever lead to the conclusion that any given general fact is an ultimate one. We must look forward to the explanation, not of all things, but of any given thing whatever. There is no contradiction here, any more than there is in our holding each one of our opinions, while we are ready to admit that it is probable that not all are true; or any more than there is in saying that any future time will sometime be past, though there never will be a time when all time is past.

Of all the regular facts that have to be explained is Law or regularity itself. We enormously exaggerate the part that law plays in the universe. It is by means of regularities that we understand what little we do understand of the world, and thus there is a sort of mental perspective which brings regular phenomena to the foreground. We say that every event is determined by causes according to law. But apart from the fact that this must not be regarded as absolutely true, it does not mean so much as it seems to do. We do not mean, for example, that if a

1. After the scholastics. See Eckius in *Petrus Hispanus* 48b nota 1.

man and his antipode both sneeze at the same instant, that that event comes under any general law. That is merely what we call a coincidence. But what we mean is there was a cause for the first man's sneezing, and another cause for the second man's sneezing; and the aggregate of these two events makes up the first event about which we began by inquiring. The doctrine is that the events of the physical universe are merely motions of matter, and that these obey the laws of dynamics. But this only amounts to saying that among the countless systems of relationship existing among things we have found one that is universal and at the same time is subject to law. There is nothing except this singular character which makes this particular system of relationship any more important than the others. From this point of view, uniformity is seen to be really a highly exceptional phenomenon. But we pay no attention to irregular relationships, as having no interest for us.

We are brought, then, to this: conformity to law exists only within a limited range of events and even there is not perfect, for an element of pure spontaneity or lawless originality mingles, or at least must be supposed to mingle, with law everywhere. Moreover, conformity with law is a fact requiring to be explained; and since Law in general cannot be explained by any law in particular, the explanation must consist in showing how law is developed out of pure chance, irregularity, and indeterminacy.

To this problem we are bound to address ourselves; and it is particularly needful to do so in the present state of science. The theory of the molecular constitution of matter has now been carried as far as there are any clear indications to direct us, and we are now in the mists. To develope the mathematical consequences of any hypothesis as to the nature and laws of the minute parts of matter, and then to test it by physical experiment, will take fifty years; and out of the innumerable hypotheses that might be framed, there seems to be nothing to make one more antecedently probable than another. At this rate how long will it take to make any decided advance? We need some hint as to how molecules may be expected to behave; whether for instance, they would be likely to attract or repel one another inversely as the fifth power of the distance, so that we may be saved from many false suppositions, if we are not at once shown the way to the true one. Tell us how the laws of nature came about, and we may distinguish in some measure between laws that might and laws that could not have resulted from such a process of development.

To find that out is our task. I will begin the work with this guess. Uniformities in the modes of action of things have come about by their taking habits. At present, the course of events is approximately determined by law. In the past that approximation was less perfect; in the future it will be more perfect. The tendency to obey laws has always been and always will be growing. We look back toward a point in the infinitely distant past when there was no law but mere indeterminacy; we look forward to a point in the infinitely distant future when there will be no indeterminacy or chance but a complete reign of law. But at any assignable date in the past, however early, there was already some tendency toward uniformity; and at any assignable date in the future there will be some slight aberrancy from law. Moreover, all things have a tendency to take habits. For atoms and their parts, molecules and groups of molecules, and in short every conceivable real object, there is a greater probability of acting as on a former like occasion than otherwise. This tendency itself constitutes a regularity, and is continually on the increase. In looking back into the past we are looking towards periods when it was a less and less decided tendency. But its own essential nature is to grow. It is a generalizing tendency; it causes actions in the future to follow some generalization of past actions; and this tendency is itself something capable of similar generalization; and thus, it is self-generative. We have therefore only to suppose the smallest spur of it in the past, and that germ would have been bound to develope into a mighty and over-ruling principle, until it supersedes itself by strengthening habits into absolute laws regulating the action of all things in every respect in the indefinite future.

According to this, three elements are active in the world, first, chance; second, law; and third, habit-taking.

Such is our guess at the secret of the sphynx. To raise it from the rank of a philosophical speculation to that of a scientific hypothesis, we must show that consequences can be deduced from it with more or less probability which can be compared with observation. We must show that there is some method of deducing the characters of the laws which could result in this way by the action of habit-taking on purely fortuitous occurrences, and a method of ascertaining whether such characters belong to the actual laws of nature.

The existence of things consists in their regular behaviour. If an atom had no regular attractions and repulsions, if its mass was at one instant nothing, at another a ton, at another a negative quantity, if its motion instead of being continuous, consisted in a series of leaps from one place to another without passing through any intervening places, and if there were no definite relations between its different positions, velocities and directions of displacement, if it were at one time in one place and at another time in a dozen, such a disjointed plurality of phenomena would not make up any existing thing. Not only substances, but events, too, are constituted by regularities. The flow of time, for example, in itself is a regularity. The original chaos, therefore, where there was no regularity, was in effect a state of mere indeterminacy, in which nothing existed or really happened.

Our conceptions of the first stages of the development, before time yet existed, must be as vague and figurative as the expressions of the first chapter of Genesis. Out of the womb of indeterminacy we must say that there would have come something, by the principle of firstness, which we may call a flash. Then by the principle of habit there would have been a second flash. Though time would not yet have been, this second flash was in some sense after the first because resulting from it. Then there would have come other successions ever more and more closely connected, the habits and the tendency to take them ever strengthening themselves, until the events would have been bound together into something like a continuous flow. We have no reason to think that even now time is quite perfectly continuous and uniform in its flow. The quasi-flow which would result would, however, differ essentially from time in this respect, that it would not necessarily be in a single stream. Different flashes might start different streams, between which there should be no relations of contemporaneity or succession. So one stream might branch into two, or two might coalesce. But the further result of habit would inevitably be to separate utterly those that were long separated, and to make those which presented frequent common points coalesce into perfect union. Those that were completely separated would be so many different worlds which would know nothing of one another, so that the effect would be just what we actually observe.

But secondness is of two types. Consequently, besides flashes genuinely second to others, so as to come after them, there will be pairs of flashes, or, since time is now supposed to be developed, we had better say pairs of states, which are reciprocally second, each member of the pair to the other. This is the first germ of spatial extension. These states will undergo changes; and habits will be formed of passing from certain states to certain others, and of not passing from certain states to certain others. Those states to which a state will immediately pass, will be adjacent to it; and thus habits will be formed which will constitute a spatial continuum, but differing from our space by being very irregular in its connections, having, too, one number of dimensions in one place and another number in another place, and being different for one moving state from what it is for another.

Pairs of states will also begin to take habits, and thus each state, having different habits with reference to the different other states, will give rise to bundles of habits, which will be substances.[2] Some of these states will chance to take habits of persistency, and will get to be less and less liable to disappear; while those that fail to take such habits will fall out of existence. Thus, substances will get to be permanent.

In fact, habits, from the mode of their formation, necessarily consist in the permanence of some relation, and therefore, on this theory, each law of nature would consist in some permanence such as the permanence of mass, momentum, and energy. In this respect, the theory suits the facts admirably.

The substances, carrying their habits with them in their motions through space, will tend to render the different parts of space alike. Thus, the dimensionality of space will tend gradually to uniformity; and multiple connections, except at infinity, where substances never go, will be obliterated. At the outset, the connections of space were probably different for one substance and part of a substance from what they were for another; that is to say, points adjacent or near one another for the motions of one body would not be so for another; and this may possibly have contributed to break substances into little pieces or atoms. But the mutual actions of bodies would have tended to reduce their habits to uniformity in this respect; and besides there must have arisen conflicts between the habits of bodies and the habits of parts of space, which would never have ceased till they were brought into conformity.

2. I use substance, here, in the old sense of a thing, not in the modern chemical sense.

29
[Trichotomic]

Winter–Spring 1888 ***Houghton Library***

TRICHOTOMIC is the art of making three-fold divisions. Such division depends on the conceptions of 1st, 2nd, 3rd. First is the beginning, that which is fresh, original, spontaneous, free. Second is that which is determined, terminated, ended, correlative, object, necessitated, reacting. Third is the medium, becoming, developing, bringing about.

A thing considered in itself is a unit. A thing considered as a correlate or dependent, or as an effect, is second to something else. A thing which in any way brings one thing into relation with another is a third or medium between the two.

Firstness or freshness may have manifold varieties, or rather arbitrariness and variety is its essence, but it is absolute and unsusceptible of differences of degree. It may be present more or less, but it has no different orders of complication in itself. Secondness, on the other hand, may be genuine or degenerate. Degenerate secondness has two varieties, for a single object considered as second to itself is a degenerate second, and an object considered as second to another with which it has no real connection, so that were that other taken away it would still have those same characters which are implied in the relation, is also a degenerate second. Genuine secondness is dynamical connection; degenerate secondness is a relation of reason, as a mere resemblance. Thirdness has two different orders of degeneracy. Genuine thirdness is where of the three terms *A*, *B*, *C*, each is related to each of the others, but by a relation which only subsists by virtue of the third term, and each has a character which belongs to it only so long as the others really influence it. It would not be enough to say that the connection between the terms is dynamical, for forces only subsist between pairs of objects; we had better use the word "vital" to express the mode of connection, for wherever there is life, generation, growth, development, there and there alone is such genuine thirdness. Thirdness of the first order of degeneracy is where two of the three terms are identical, so that the other only mediates between two aspects of the same object, or where in some other way there is no vital connection between *A*, *B*, and *C*, but only a dynamical connection between *A* and *B*, and another between *B* and *C*, thus bringing about a dynamical connection between *A* and *C*. The second order of degeneracy is where there is not even any dynamical connection between the terms, or at least where the thirdness does not consist in that (although it may be necessary for the establishment of the thirdness), but where all three terms are virtually identical or are connected by mere relations of reason.

Expression is a kind of representation or signification. A sign is a third mediating between the mind addressed and the object represented. If the thirdness is undegenerate, the relation of the sign to the thing signified is one which only subsists by virtue of the relation of the sign to the mind addressed; that is to say, the sign is related to its object by virtue of a mental association. Conventional modes of expression, and other modes dependent on the force of association, enter largely into every art. They make up the bulk of language. If the thirdness is degenerate in the first degree, the sign mediates between the object and the mind by virtue of dynamical connections with the object on the one hand and with the mind on the other. This is the only kind of sign which can demonstrate the reality of things, or distinguish between things exactly alike. As I am walking alone on a dark night, a man suddenly jumps out of a corner with a "Boh!" and thus brings his presence home to me in a particularly forcible manner. It would be impossible to follow a geometrical proof without the letters which are attached to the different parts of the figure and thus forcibly direct the attention to the right object. So a desired frame of mind on the part of the audience is often brought about by the dramatist in a forcible way by directly affecting the nervous system, without appealing to association; or the attention of the audience may be awakened, as a clergyman shouts out the commencement of a new head to his sermon, or may be directed to a particular part of the stage, as the jugglers do. If the thirdness is degenerate in the second degree, the idea in the mind addressed, the object represented, and the representation of it, are only connected by a mutual resemblance. The sign is a likeness; and this is the main mode of representation in all art. Here there is no sharp discrimination between the sign and the thing signified, the mind floats in an ideal world and does not ask or care whether it be real or not. This character makes a striking point of difference between this kind of representation and the second; and that is why the use of the second mode of representation is so unartistic. Again, the third mode of representation is unanalytic, it presents the total object as it exists in the concrete, and not merely abstract relations and points in that object; and this constitutes a marked contrast from the first mode of representation; and this is what makes the first mode of representation unartistic. Mr. MacKaye divides dramatic expression into pantomime, voice, and language. A person would at first glance make the division into speech and gesture, and this would doubtless answer some purposes better. But with reference to the value of the different instruments at our command it is important to make a division which shall correspond as nearly as may be with the different kinds of representation. Now language is in the main representation by the force of association; it involves the analysis of whatever is to be conveyed (on the part of the hearer as well as on the part of the author) and the separate expression of abstract points. Voice, on the other hand, awakes attention, directs it to particular channels, calls up feelings, and modifies consciousness generally, in a physiological way in the main; and is therefore a mode of expression of the second kind. Pantomime alone is mainly representation of the purely artistic kind, to be contemplated without analysis and without discrimination of the sign from the thing signified. Pantomime may itself be divided, on the same principle, into three varieties: artistic pantomime which merely exhibits the man, his general disposition and what there is uppermost in him at the moment, and is to be contemplated without analysis; dynamical pantomime, as where one points with finger or shakes or holds up the finger to impress what one is saying, or when one shakes the fist, or knocks the interlocutor down; and sign-language, mostly (owing to the peculiar nature of pantomime) of an imitative kind but yet involving analysis and being really rather language than pantomime proper.

CONSCIOUSNESS has three elements, Single, Dual, and Plural consciousness. Single or simple consciousness is consciousness as it can exist in a single instant, the consciousness of all that is immediately present, for which all that is not immediately present is an absolute blank. This is the pure Feeling which forms the warp and woof of consciousness, or in Kant's phrase its matter. In this kind of consciousness subject and object are nowise discriminated, in fact there is no discrimination, no parts, no analysis, there is no considering a thing for anything else, no relation, no representation, but just a pure indescribable quale which is gone in the twinkling of an eye and which bears no resemblance to any memory of it. It is just the quality of the immediately present, which is continually pouring through us, always here but never stopping to be examined. It is always fresh, always new, sporting in unbounded manifoldness. Dual consciousness is a sense of another, not present, a sense of hitting and of getting hit, of action and reciprocal reaction, of energy. This is the most wide-awake kind of consciousness; it strenuously sets object over against subject, in place of the dreamy failure to recognize the situation which belongs to Feeling. Dual consciousness includes Will, but the consciousness of hitting and that of being hit have been shown by conclusive experiments not to differ, and Sense in its direct reference to an object is likewise consciousness of action and reaction. It is the energetic and real character of the dual consciousness that principally distinguishes it. It consists of a sense of "can" which is at the same time a sense of "cannot." Force implies resistance, and power limitation. There is always an opposite, always a but, always a second, in the dual consciousness. It has nothing to do with may-be's; it is always right there. Plural or synthetic consciousness is not the mere feeling of what is immediately present, nor yet the mere sense of something without, but is the being aware of the bridge which unites the present and the absent, of a Process as such. Zeno showed how motion is impossible if you refuse to open the eyes of the synthetic consciousness. It is the perception of motion and change. I am soundly asleep and my bed-clothes take fire. At first, the warmth merely tinges my consciousness, so to speak; that is pure Feeling; then I become energetically conscious of something and start up without knowing what it is; that is Dual consciousness, Sense with Will; last I begin to collect myself, I am aware of a process of learning, I put things together; that is Perception and Synthetic consciousness, which collects present and absent into a whole.

Dual consciousness, because it is consciousness of a second, has two degrees, the dynamical and the statical or degenerate form. Dynamical dual consciousness consists of outward action and reaction, External Sense and Volition; statical dual consciousness consists of inward action and reaction, Self-consciousness and Self-control. Plural consciousness, because it is consciousness of a third, has two degrees of degeneracy. The genuine synthetic consciousness, the consciousness of that which has its being in its thirdness, is Reason. The dynamical variety is a consciousness of a coordination between acts of sense and will, it is the looking upon the phenomena of sense and will as rational, which we may call Desire, though that does not precisely define it. The statical variety is the comparison of feelings, and may be called esthetic understanding.

Mr. MacKaye's division of the principles of being has considerable resemblance with this. What he calls the vital or passional principle, which sustains life, seems to be nearly what I call the simple consciousness of Feeling; what he calls the affectional or impulsive principle is my dual consciousness plus Desire and minus Sense; what he calls Reflection is probably Reason with the esthetic understanding.

The functions of the Nervous System are three, corresponding to the three kinds of consciousness. They are, first, Irritability, for the capacity of a nerve-cell to be thrown into an excited condition is undoubtedly the physiological ground of feeling; second, the power of conveying nervous disturbance over the nerve-fibres, for it is by this property of the nerves that we are placed in relation with the outward world; and third, the power of acquiring habits, which is the ground of our faculty of learning.

The properties of protoplasm in general are three, first, its capacity of being thrown into a state in which it is more liquid and at the same time has a stronger cohesion and surface-tension; second, the tendency of this condition to spread throughout the entire mass; and third, its power, when passing into or out of this condition, of assimilating new material, provided this is presented so as to be subject to the same forces as that which is deranged,—in other words the power of growth with all that that implies.

30

Pendulum Observations at Fort Conger

Fall 1888 ***Report on the Proceedings of the U.S. Expedition to Lady Franklin Bay***

In 1881 the Chief Signal Officer applied to the Superintendent of the Coast and Geodetic Survey for pendulum apparatus, instructions, etc., to enable Lieutenant Greely to determine the acceleration of gravity at Lady Franklin Bay. Mr. Carlile P. Patterson, then Superintendent of the Survey, was a man of high intelligence, and though he did not class himself among scientific men, yet had for so many years conducted investigations in association with them that he understood most of the conditions of success in scientific work. He at once put me into personal communication with Lieutenant Greely, and instructed me to do what was necessary to further the end in view, without hampering the business by requiring the observance of intricate forms. We were just then commencing the construction of the series of Peirce pendulums. These instruments will be elsewhere described, and it is only necessary to say here that they are invariable reversible pendulums of nearly cylindrical contour, so that the effects of viscosity can be theoretically ascertained.

It was agreed that Lieutenant Greely should take with him No. 1 of this series of pendulums, and that he should send me one of his companions, Mr. E. Israel, to be instructed in the use of the instrument. Very little time remained, however, after the completion of the pendulum before it was necessary to pack it up for transportation. The preliminary operations in Washington were therefore somewhat hurried. Eight swingings of the pendulum were made in room No. 6, in the basement of the Coast Survey building. This station had never been used before, and I unhappily found out, too late, that the sandstone piers had the peculiarity of bending back and forth by a considerable amount under the oscillating pendulum, without elastic restoration. Accordingly, it became of the very highest moment for the success of the whole work that these piers, or rather the entire dolmen, should be preserved intact, so that the pendulum could be again swung on the same support after its return. Unfortunately, while I was afterwards in the field, a naval officer was permitted to remove the stone capping the piers, to carry with him to South America, in order, apparently, to save the trouble of cutting a hole in a plank. The result is that these preliminary swingings must be regarded as of no value. The position of the center of mass of the pendulum was determined by me before it was sent out; and the distance between the knife-edges was carefully compared with the German Normal Meter, No. 49, to which I have referred the lengths of all the reversible pendulums used by me.

The pendulum was finally placed in a wooden box having holes bored in it in such a way as to permit air to be blown through it and through the hollow stem of the pendulum; and a current of air, thoroughly dried with chloride of calcium, was passed for a long time through the box, which was then stoppered, placed in a tin case, and soldered up. The object of this proceeding was to prevent the pendulum being found covered with frost when wanted for use in its arctic destination. Then the pendulum was carried to Fort Conger, by far the most northerly station which ever has been or is ever likely to be occupied for exact scientific observations, and it was there swung on sixteen days by Lieutenant Greely, aided by Mr. Israel, with a remarkable degree of skill and energy.

The directions accompanying the instrument were that the pendulum should be swung on eight days, once each day with heavy end down and twice with heavy end up, the one swinging in the former position being intermediate in time between the two in the latter. After these eight days' swingings the knives were to be removed and interchanged, and eight days' more work was to be done in the same manner in the new position of the knives. This programme was faithfully carried out; but after the interchange of knives the periods of oscillation show a large change, and this is of such a character as not to be eliminated by the formula for the reversible pendulum. This seems to have been due to a difference in the cylindricity of the edges, combined with the effect of some accident to the pendulum. The result is that only the observations made after the interchange of knives can be used.

On the abandonment of Fort Conger the head upon which the pendulum had been supported in its oscillations (the bearings of the knife-edges forming a part of it) was left behind; but the pendulum itself was courageously brought away and carried down to the camp, from which the survivors of the party, of whom the lamented Israel was not one, were rescued. It seems almost inconceivable that any instrument could have gone through that terrible journey over ice hummocks, etc., intact. The chronometer brought back at the same time arrived almost smashed to pieces. Nevertheless, a remeasurement of the pendulum after its return to Washington shows that it had only undergone an increase of 1/30000, a change which might almost be expected without any special accident: namely, in June, 1881, the pendulum was found 397.2 microns longer than Meter 49, and in December, 1884, it was found 429.3 microns longer, both at 20° C. The pendulum was oscillated at the Smithsonian Institution, and, using the formula for the reversible pendulum, these experiments give a value for gravity at that station agreeing closely with that given by our best pendulum, Peirce No. 2, and in accordance with other results: namely, the period of oscillation of a metre pendulum (subject to some small corrections) was, according to No. 1, 1.0063191^{s}; while according to No. 2 it was 1.0063186^{s}. This shows that the knives of Pendulum No. 1 never underwent any permanent damage.

But, though there was so little change in the length of the pendulum, there is evidence that it lost a large part of its mass. In 1881 illness prevented my weighing the pendulum myself, and it was not weighed at all in its finished state. But my assistant reported that while still symmetrical, and after having been polished, its mass was 6477 grammes, that the added load was 3985 grammes, and that in the adjustment 4.6 grammes were deducted, so that its total mass must have been 10457 grammes. My experience in the construction of other pendulums shows that the mass so calculated was probably in excess by 5 or 10 grammes, owing to the operation of polishing. But the pendulum now weighs only 10436 grammes, so that it would seem to have lost from 10 to 15 grammes, probably on the journey from Fort Conger to Camp

Peirce's pendulum case marks the stone cairn on Stalknecht Island where the Greely Arctic expedition stored records and instruments from October 1883 until the survivors were rescued in June 1884. (Greely, Three Years of Arctic Service *(NY: Scribner's, 1886), Vol. II, p. 179.)*

Clay. The centre of mass, too, was apparently moved 0.32 millimetre toward the centre of figure. Namely, I found in 1881 that the distance from the centre of mass to the nearest knife-edge was 25.105 centimetres, while Mr. Farquhar now finds that with the same arrangement of the knives the same distance is 25.137 centimetres; yet as economical considerations have always prevented our expending the sum of $50 required for a suitable instrument to measure this quantity, I should not think these measures by themselves conclusively proved a change. This, however, is not all. The excess of the period of oscillation with the heavy end down over that with the heavy end up, corrected for flexure and brought to the standard pressure and temperature (one absolute atmosphere and 15° C.), was +0.0006514^{s}; while the corresponding difference at Washington, after the return, was found to be +0.0007009^{s}. The difference between these corrected for difference of gravity is +0.0000494^{s}. This result, not depending upon the coefficient of expansion, is probably nearly correct. But there is an equation to be satisfied between the loss of weight, the shifting of the centre of mass, and the change of period. Moreover, any two of these quantities determine the point (supposed on the axis of the pendulum) where the loss took place; and the question arises whether this was a point at which such a loss could take place. Now, there are but three points where the loss was possible. One of these is 3 centimetres outside of the knife-edge at the heavy end. If 12 grammes were lost at that point the centre of mass would be shifted by 0.32 millimetre, the amount observed; and the excess of the period with heavy end down over that with heavy end up would be increased by +0.0000472^{s}; or very nearly the amount observed. The agreement of these numbers tends to show that the alteration which the pendulum underwent during its homeward journey did not involve any difference in the distance between the knife-edges, so that the pendulum may still be treated as invariably reversible, though not as two invariable pendulums.

Having thus narrated the history of the instrument, I proceed to consider the difficulties of deducing any result from the observations. The atmospheric pressure at Fort Conger exhibits no great range, and does not differ much from that at Washington, so that the small corrections can be satisfactorily calculated from theory. The case is far otherwise with the temperature corrections. The difference of temperature between the two stations was about 50° C. This would make so much difference in the effect of the atmosphere as to involve it in some doubt. Still, as long as the pendulum is treated as reversible, but not as invariable, except as to the distance between the knife-edges (a treatment necessitated by the circumstances just narrated), this is a matter of little consequence.

The coefficient of expansion of this pendulum, and of another, Peirce No. 4, constructed of brass purchased at the same time as the material of No. 1, was determined by comparisons of those pendulums with a metre marked U. S. C. S.—C. S. P.—1878—B., at different temperatures. This bar was made at the same time as and is in every respect a match with the Metre A, whose coefficient of expansion was carefully determined by me and published in my "Measurements of Gravity at Initial Stations."[1] This Metre B has a series of different lines at one end. The mean of ten skillful comparisons by Mr. D. C. Chapman, on five days of December, 1884, between Pendulum No. 1 and Metre B, taken at its outer line, makes the pendulum longer by $+251.6^{\mu}$ $\pm 0.3^{\mu}$ at 18.46°; and the mean of five comparisons on two days by the same observer during the same month makes the same excess $242.7^{\mu} \pm$ 0.1^{μ} at 30.99° C. The expansion of the pendulum was, according to these measures, 0.71^{μ} less than that of the metre per degree. Six comparisons of Peirce No. 4 with the same metre at the third line from the end, made in the previous October, on three days, make the excess of the pendulum $-0.9^{\mu} \pm 0.3^{\mu}$ at 16.83°, and six comparisons on four days in the same month, all by the same excellent observer, make the excess $-6.5^{\mu} \pm 0.4^{\mu}$ at 25.42°. This gives for the excess of the expansion per degree centigrade of the pendulum over Metre B, -0.65^{μ}; but I prefer to use the comparisons of Pendulum No. 1; and since the coefficient of Metre A was found to be 18.95^{μ} we assume 18.24^{μ} for the pendulum. At an extremely low temperature this coefficient would, of course, be smaller. The coefficient 18.24^{μ} is for the temperature of 24.6° C. Now, Fizeau (*Comptes rendus*, LXVIII, p. 1125) examined a specimen of brass whose coefficient of expansion at 24.6° C. was 18.28 millionths; and this coefficient was found to increase 1.96 millionths per 100° C. of elevation of temperature. As the first coefficient was so nearly the same as that of Pendulum No. 1, we may assume that the

1. *U. S. Coast Survey Report* for 1876, Appendix 15.

second would be so, too. The observations at Fort Conger after the interchange of the knives were at a mean temperature of –30.4° C. To reduce them to +15° C. we must use the coefficient for –7.7° C., and since this is 32.3° below the temperature for which the coefficient was observed, we calculate the coefficient to be used as follows:

Coefficient of expansion at 24.6°	= 18.24 microns per degree C.
Correction to –7.7° C. = 1.96 × .323	= .63
∴ Coefficient of expansion at –7.7° C.	= 17.61

Experiments at different stations, especially in Washington and in Ithaca, show, however, conclusively, that while the effects of temperature calculated from the expansion and the atmospheric theory answer well enough for heavy end up (in which position the atmospheric effects, being three times as great as with heavy end down, greatly reduce the effect of expansion), yet with heavy end down the effect of temperature on the period is much larger in fact than the theory indicates. Similar phenomena have presented themselves to many experimenters; and the later Repsold pendulums may be said to be almost exceptional in not showing anything of the sort to any marked extent. The cause of the phenomenon can only be surmised. In order to determine the proper value of the expansion to be used in reducing the periods it would be necessary to leave a pendulum support undisturbed for six months and re-occupy the same station at the end of that time; and in order to understand the effect sufficiently to allow for it with certainty it should be studied through a large range of temperature. For this purpose a station like Minneapolis should be chosen. But in the present state of our knowledge, and in a case like this, the expansion deduced from linear measures must be used.

Elaborate observations upon the descent of the arc were made by Mr. Israel, and these have been reduced by Mr. H. Farquhar, of the Coast and Geodetic Survey, according to the method given in my "Measurements of Gravity at Initial Stations," with some improvements in detail. In the following tables these observations with the reductions are first given, and are followed by the observations of periods, and then by the measure of flexure. In these Mr. Israel says he used "the weight of 2.5 pounds"; but I think that this must have been the weight which in the *Coast Survey Report* for 1881, p. 377, is said to weigh 1.0818^k = 2.38 lb., and I have so treated it in the reductions.

Decrement of arc.—Observed $D_{\varphi}t$ in swings with heavy end up.

φ	1		3		4		6		7		9		10		13		16		18		19	
	m.	*m.*	*m.*	*m.*	*m.*	*m.*	*m.*	*m.*	*m.*	*m.*	*m.*	*m.*	*m.*	*m.*	*m.*	*m.*	*m.*	*m.*	*m.*	*m.*	*m.*	*m.*
.030	---	---	---	---	---	---	1.0	1.1	---	---	---	1.5	---	---	---	---	---	---	---	---	---	---
.029	---	---	---	---	---	---	1.0	1.0	---	---	---	---	---	---	---	---	---	---	---	---	---	---
.028	---	---	---	---	---	---	---	1.3	1.3	1.1	---	---	---	---	---	---	---	---	---	---	.9	1.0
.027	---	---	---	---	---	---	---	---	1.1	1.0	---	---	---	---	---	---	---	---	---	---	---	---
.026	---	---	---	---	1.0	---	---	---	.9	.9	---	---	---	---	---	---	---	---	.9	---	---	---
.025	---	---	---	---	---	---	---	---	---	---	---	---	---	---	---	---	---	---	---	---	---	---
.024	---	---	---	---	---	---	---	---	---	---	---	---	---	---	---	---	---	---	---	---	---	---
.023	---	---	---	---	---	---	---	---	---	---	---	---	---	---	---	---	---	---	---	---	---	---
.022	---	---	---	---	---	---	---	---	---	---	---	---	---	---	---	---	---	---	---	---	---	---
.021	---	---	---	---	---	---	---	---	---	---	---	---	---	---	---	---	---	---	1.5	---	---	---
.020	---	---	---	1.9	---	---	1.1	1.0	1.5	1.5	1.7	---	---	---	---	---	---	---	1.3	1.3	---	---
.019	---	---	1.2	1.3	---	---	1.6	1.6	1.6	1.6	2.1	2.2	1.3	---	---	---	---	2.0	2.0	1.7	1.7	1.8
.018	---	---	1.7	1.7	1.5	---	1.5	1.9	1.8	1.7	2.5	1.8	2.1	1.9	---	1.9	1.8	2.0	2.0	1.8	1.8	1.8
.017	---	---	1.7	1.9	1.7	---	2.3	1.5	1.7	1.7	2.0	2.2	1.8	1.8	---	2.2	1.9	1.9	1.8	1.9	1.7	2.0
.016	---	---	2.0	2.2	1.8	1.3	2.1	2.2	2.0	2.1	2.1	2.0	2.1	2.1	---	2.5	2.1	2.1	2.0	2.1	1.9	2.0
.015	---	---	2.4	2.6	2.5	2.2	2.0	1.9	2.1	2.0	1.9	2.0	2.1	2.0	2.0	2.3	2.1	2.1	2.5	2.1	2.3	2.5
.014	---	---	2.4	2.2	2.1	2.0	2.5	2.2	2.3	2.6	2.3	1.9	2.2	2.1	2.3	2.7	2.4	2.5	2.4	2.2	2.6	2.5
.013	---	---	2.1	2.2	2.7	2.0	2.7	2.7	2.6	2.7	2.5	2.3	2.8	2.7	2.2	2.7	2.3	2.4	2.8	2.8	2.6	3.1
.012	---	3.3	2.5	3.0	2.8	2.2	3.2	2.9	2.8	2.9	3.2	2.6	3.1	3.0	2.3	3.2	3.1	3.1	3.5	3.2	2.9	3.2
.011	2.7	2.8	3.7	3.2	3.3	3.4	3.9	3.9	2.9	2.8	3.5	3.4	3.1	3.0	2.5	4.0	3.2	3.4	3.6	3.2	3.0	3.1
.010	2.7	3.0	3.7	3.9	3.4	3.2	3.5	3.4	3.6	3.9	4.1	3.5	3.7	3.3	2.8	4.9	3.9	3.8	3.6	3.8	3.2	3.7
.009	3.7	3.8	3.6	4.1	4.4	3.9	4.4	4.0	4.1	4.2	4.9	3.9	3.9	3.6	3.6	5.3	4.7	4.0	4.1	4.1	4.1	5.2
.008	4.2	4.8	4.5	4.9	5.1	4.2	4.9	4.2	4.5	5.0	4.9	5.0	4.5	4.1	4.5	5.6	5.1	4.9	5.0	4.2	4.8	4.7
.007	5.0	4.8	5.3	4.7	5.2	4.2	5.2	5.4	5.2	5.6	5.7	5.1	5.5	5.4	4.7	7.0	5.0	5.7	5.9	5.5	4.9	6.4
.006	4.9	5.8	[5.3]	---	5.8	5.7	6.6	5.6	[6.4]	---	5.8	5.6	---	[7.1]	[5.2]	---	[5.9]	---	---	[6.3]	6.3	7.1
.005	[7.8]	[7.8]	[7.7]	---	---	---	[6.9]	---	[6.3]	---	---	---	---	---	---	---	[6.5]	---	---	[7.0]	---	---
.004																						

Decrement of arc.—Observed $D_\varphi t$ in swings with heavy end up (continued).

φ	21		22		23		28		31		33		36		39		43		46	
	m.	*m.*	*m.*	*m.*	*m.*	*m.*	*m.*	*m.*	*m.*	*m.*	*m.*	*m.*	*m.*	*m.*	*m.*	*m.*	*m.*	*m.*	*m.*	*m.*
.030	---	---	---	---	---	---	.9	.9	---	---	---	---	.9	---	---	---	---	---	---	---
.029	---	---	---	---	---	---	---	---	---	---	---	---	---	---	---	---	---	---	---	---
.028	---	---	---	---	---	---	---	---	---	---	---	.8	---	---	---	---	---	---	---	---
.027	---	---	---	---	---	---	1.2	1.0	---	---	---	---	---	---	---	---	---	---	---	---
.026	---	---	---	---	---	---	---	.8	---	1.0	---	---	---	---	---	---	---	---	---	---
.025	---	---	---	---	---	---	---	---	---	---	---	---	---	---	---	---	---	---	---	---
.024	---	---	---	---	---	---	---	---	---	---	---	---	---	---	---	---	---	---	---	---
.023	---	---	---	---	---	---	---	---	---	---	---	---	---	---	---	---	---	---	---	---
.022	---	---	---	---	---	---	---	---	---	---	---	---	---	---	---	---	---	---	---	---
.021	---	---	---	---	---	---	---	---	---	---	---	---	---	---	---	---	---	---	---	---
.020	1.6	1.5	2.0	---	---	1.7	---	---	---	---	1.8	---	---	---	---	1.5	---	---	---	---
.019	1.4	1.6	---	2.0	1.5	1.6	1.5	1.9	---	---	1.7	---	---	---	1.6	2.1	---	---	1.7	---
.018	1.6	1.7	---	---	1.6	1.8	1.9	1.7	---	---	1.9	1.7	---	---	2.1	1.8	---	1.6	---	1.9
.017	1.9	1.8	---	---	1.7	1.9	1.6	1.8	---	---	2.0	1.9	---	---	1.8	2.2	1.9	1.9	---	---
.016	2.0	2.0	---	---	2.0	2.1	1.8	2.1	---	---	2.3	2.0	---	---	2.0	2.2	1.9	2.2	---	---
.015	2.0	2.3	2.0	2.5	2.3	2.2	2.1	2.1	---	---	2.3	2.1	---	---	2.1	2.6	2.0	2.2	---	---
.014	2.2	2.6	2.2	2.1	2.4	2.5	2.1	2.4	---	---	2.6	2.3	---	---	2.5	2.3	2.4	2.4	2.4	---
.013	2.7	2.5	2.8	2.4	2.9	2.8	2.5	2.9	2.7	2.7	2.8	2.6	---	---	2.3	2.8	2.5	2.8	3.1	3.1
.012	2.9	2.6	3.6	2.9	3.1	3.1	2.9	3.0	2.8	3.0	3.6	2.9	---	---	2.5	3.2	3.0	2.9	3.2	2.7
.011	3.1	3.1	3.4	3.4	3.0	3.8	2.9	3.2	3.1	3.5	3.7	3.1	---	3.8	3.3	4.0	2.9	3.3	3.2	3.2
.010	3.7	3.5	4.4	3.5	3.6	4.0	2.3	3.9	3.4	3.7	4.3	3.6	---	4.7	3.8	4.3	3.3	3.5	3.9	3.8
.009	3.5	4.2	4.5	4.5	3.9	4.2	3.8	4.1	3.7	4.2	4.5	3.4	---	5.2	4.0	4.9	3.6	4.5	4.5	4.6
.008	3.9	5.3	5.3	4.6	4.2	4.8	4.5	5.1	4.3	5.1	5.4	4.3	3.5	---	4.5	4.8	4.6	4.5	4.5	4.3
.007	5.1	5.3	5.5	5.1	5.0	5.8	4.8	5.8	5.1	5.8	---	5.4	4.1	---	4.8	6.3	5.0	5.2	6.1	5.5
.006	[5.7]	---	6.4	5.7	6.2	6.7	5.9	6.8	6.4	6.9	---	[5.8]	[5.1]	---	[5.6]	---	5.3	7.0	---	[5.9]
.005	[6.2]	---	---	---	---	---	---	---	---	---	---	[6.1]	[5.2]	---	[7.4]	---	---	---	---	[8.4]
.004																				

NOTE.—The notation is that of "Measurements of Gravity at Initial Stations."

Observed $D_{\varphi} t$ in swings with heavy end down.

φ	2		5		8		11		17		23		38		41		44	
	m.	*m.*	*m.*	*m.*	*m.*	*m.*	*m.*	*m.*	*m.*	*m.*	*m.*	*m.*	*m.*	*m.*	*m.*	*m.*	*m.*	*m.*
.030	3.0	----	----	----	----	1.6	----	2.5	2.3	2.3	----	2.4	----	2.0	----	----	----	----
.029	3.0	----	2.8	----	----	2.3	2.1	2.7	2.4	2.3	2.6	2.5	2.2	2.5	----	----	----	----
.028	3.1	----	2.2	1.9	2.1	3.0	2.7	2.5	2.5	2.7	2.2	2.6	2.7	2.7	----	----	1.8	----
.027	3.1	3.0	3.2	3.5	3.0	3.3	3.0	2.7	2.7	3.1	2.8	2.6	2.9	3.3	----	----	3.1	2.3
.026	----	2.9	3.5	3.4	3.5	----	2.5	2.8	2.7	----	3.0	3.1	3.3	2.9	----	----	2.4	3.0
.025	----	3.2	----	----	----	----	----	----	----	----	----	----	----	----	----	----	----	----
.024	----	----	----	----	----	3.3	----	----	----	----	----	----	----	----	----	----	----	----
.023	4.0	----	3.7	3.3	2.9	2.8	2.5	2.4	3.9	3.6	3.3	3.3	----	3.6	----	----	----	----
.022	4.4	3.8	3.2	3.4	3.3	4.5	2.9	3.4	3.8	3.8	3.5	3.9	3.8	3.6	----	----	4.3	3.8
.021	3.7	4.1	4.0	3.8	4.1	4.7	4.4	4.5	3.9	4.6	4.1	4.1	3.8	4.4	4.1	----	3.9	4.0
.020	4.4	3.7	4.0	3.9	5.0	5.0	4.3	5.3	4.5	4.6	4.2	4.0	4.3	5.6	3.9	3.5	3.9	4.2
.019	4.5	4.3	5.0	5.1	4.9	5.3	5.8	4.6	4.4	5.2	4.2	4.4	5.5	5.1	4.8	3.9	4.1	4.1
.018	4.7	4.7	4.9	4.7	5.1	5.1	4.0	4.1	5.5	6.2	4.6	4.8	5.3	5.9	5.2	5.4	4.1	4.9
.017	5.5	4.7	5.1	4.7	5.1	5.1	4.9	6.1	6.1	5.1	5.0	5.1	6.0	6.2	4.9	4.9	5.1	6.0
.016	4.6	5.5	5.4	5.0	5.2	6.5	5.1	6.1	5.1	6.0	5.4	5.7	6.3	6.1	5.1	5.8	6.2	6.3
.015	5.9	4.5	5.5	6.2	6.5	6.1	6.0	5.7	5.8	7.3	5.9	6.1	6.1	6.1	5.7	5.6	6.4	6.8
.014	8.2	6.2	8.7	6.5	6.3	8.1	6.9	7.0	7.6	7.0	6.3	6.6	6.6	7.3	6.0	5.9	7.0	7.7
.013	6.9	8.0	7.8	8.3	7.9	7.8	6.3	7.7	6.7	7.9	8.6	8.5	7.0	7.5	6.1	6.0	7.5	7.8
.012	8.1	7.0	8.5	9.1	7.7	9.0	9.0	9.1	7.8	9.3	8.7	8.6	9.0	9.1	7.5	7.1	7.7	8.4
.011	9.6	9.1	8.2	9.3	9.1	9.8	8.9	10.0	9.9	10.3	9.5	9.4	9.1	10.6	8.3	7.9	8.4	8.8
.010	11.0	10.1	10.9	10.1	9.9	11.7	10.3	11.1	9.8	11.1	10.5	12.5	9.5	12.0	9.4	8.7	9.0	10.6
.009	11.9	11.4	10.6	11.1	11.5	12.1	11.4	11.8	11.2	13.1	11.7	12.6	12.5	11.8	10.4	10.0	11.1	11.6
.008	12.5	11.7	11.8	11.3	12.4	14.4	12.2	13.8	13.9	13.8	11.6	12.4	11.7	14.7	12.5	12.5	12.6	13.9
.007	15.9	13.8	14.7	13.7	14.4	15.0	14.8	15.1	12.9	14.2	13.4	16.5	14.8	15.9	13.7	12.7	14.1	15.3
.006	23.4	16.3	18.8	16.3	15.0	17.7	17.4	21.2	14.1	17.0	17.3	21.4	16.7	20.3	16.7	15.6	15.1	17.6
.005																		

Calculation of time of infinite arc from approximate $\frac{1}{b}$.

φ	(1)	10^h	(2)	11^h	(3)	4^h	(4)	9^h	(5)	10^h	(6)	3^h
	m.	*m.*	*m.*	*m.*	*m.*	*m.*	*m.*	*m.*	*m.*	*m.*	*m.*	*m.*
.030	----	53.7	60.5	----	----	42.0	----	----	----	19.2	26.1	25.4
.029	----	----	61.1	----	42.1	----	----	----	19.1	----	26.3	25.7
.028	----	----	61.5	----	----	42.2	----	----	19.3	18.4	26.4	25.8
.027	53.1	----	61.8	55.2	42.1	----	----	----	18.7	17.5	----	26.1
.026	----	53.5	62.1	55.4	----	42.1	39.7	38.5	19.1	18.2	26.0	----
.025	53.0	----	----	55.2	41.9	----	39.7	----	19.5	18.5	----	26.2
.024	----	----	----	55.3	----	----	----	----	----	----	----	----
.023	----	----	59.3	----	----	----	----	----	19.3	18.5	----	----
.022	----	----	59.7	56.6	----	----	----	----	19.4	18.2	----	----
.021	----	----	60.4	56.7	----	----	----	----	18.9	17.9	----	----
.020	----	52.8	60.1	56.8	----	41.9	39.1	----	18.9	17.7	25.9	25.3
.019	52.5	----	60.2	56.2	41.7	42.4	----	----	18.6	17.3	25.6	24.9
.018	----	52.8	60.2	56.0	41.3	42.1	39.6	37.4	19.1	17.9	25.6	24.9
.017	52.3	----	60.0	55.8	41.3	42.1	39.4	----	19.1	17.7	25.4	25.1
.016	----	52.7	60.2	55.2	41.1	42.1	39.2	36.8	18.9	17.1	25.8	24.7
.015	52.1	----	59.2	55.1	41.2	42.4	39.1	36.2	18.7	16.5	26.0	25.0
.014	----	52.6	58.9	53.4	41.4	42.8	39.4	36.2	18.0	16.5	25.8	24.7
.013	51.7	----	60.5	53.0	41.5	42.7	39.2	35.9	20.1	16.4	26.0	24.6
.012	----	52.6	60.0	53.6	41.1	42.4	39.4	35.4	20.5	17.3	26.2	24.8
.011	52.5	53.0	60.0	52.5	40.7	42.5	39.3	34.7	20.9	18.3	26.5	24.8
.010	52.1	52.7	60.6	52.6	41.3	42.6	39.5	35.0	20.1	18.6	27.3	25.6
.009	51.3	52.2	61.6	52.7	41.5	43.0	39.4	34.7	21.0	18.7	27.3	25.5
.008	51.0	52.0	62.0	52.6	41.1	43.1	39.8	34.6	20.1	18.3	27.7	25.5
.007	50.6	52.2	61.3	51.1	41.0	43.4	40.3	34.2	18.7	16.4	28.0	25.1
.006	50.2	51.6	61.7	49.4	40.9	42.7	40.1	33.0	17.9	14.6	27.8	25.1
.005	48.6	50.9	66.5	47.1	39.7	----	39.4	32.2	18.1	12.3	27.9	24.2
.004	48.4	50.7	----	----	39.4	----	----	----	----	----	26.8	----
.003	----	----	----	----	----	----	----	----	----	----	----	----
Summary. .0280	53.1	53.6	61.2	55.2	42.0	42.1	39.7	38.5	19.1	18.4	26.2	25.8
.0148	52.2	52.7	59.9	54.7	41.3	42.4	39.3	36.4	19.2	17.2	25.9	24.9
.0084	51.2	52.2	61.2	52.4	41.1	43.0	39.7	34.6	20.0	18.0	27.4	25.3
.0050	49.0	51.0	64.9	47.1	39.9	42.9	39.5	32.2	18.0	12.3	27.6	24.4

Calculation of time of infinite arc, etc.—Continued.

	φ	(7)	9h	(8)	9h	(9)	2h	(10)	9h	(11)	9h	(12)	1h
		m.	*m.*	*m.*	*m.*	*m.*	*m.*	*m.*	*m.*	*m.*	*m.*	*m.*	*m.*
	.030	----	20.2	44.1	46.8	9.7	8.8	----	28.4	----	49.8	----	----
	.029	----	----	----	46.0	----	9.5	28.6	----	48.8	49.9	----	----
	.028	19.2	20.0	44.1	45.7	----	----	----	----	48.3	50.0	----	----
	.027	19.5	20.1	43.4	45.9	10.1	----	----	28.0	48.2	49.7	----	----
	.026	19.6	20.1	43.6	46.4	----	----	28.5	----	48.4	49.6	----	----
	.025	19.5	20.0	44.0	----	----	9.1	----	27.7	47.8	49.3	----	----
	.024	----	----	----	46.1	----	----	----	----	----	----	----	----
	.023	----	----	43.4	46.0	----	----	----	----	47.6	48.8	----	----
	.022	----	----	42.7	45.2	----	----	----	----	46.5	47.6	----	----
	.021	----	----	42.3	46.0	----	----	----	----	45.7	47.3	----	----
	.020	18.6	19.6	42.4	46.7	9.4	----	----	----	46.1	47.8	----	----
	.019	18.7	19.7	43.1	47.4	9.7	8.8	28.0	----	46.1	48.8	----	----
	.018	18.7	19.7	43.5	48.2	10.2	9.4	27.7	27.0	47.4	48.9	----	----
	.017	18.8	19.7	43.7	48.4	11.0	9.5	28.1	27.2	46.5	48.1	----	----
	.016	18.6	19.5	43.5	48.2	11.1	9.8	28.0	27.1	46.1	48.9	----	----
	.015	18.7	19.7	43.1	49.1	11.3	9.9	28.2	27.3	45.6	49.4	----	----
	.014	18.6	19.5	43.4	49.0	11.0	9.7	28.1	27.1	45.4	48.9	68.8	----
	.013	18.6	19.8	43.1	50.5	11.0	9.3	28.0	26.9	45.7	49.3	----	67.7
	.012	18.7	20.0	44.6	50.9	11.0	9.1	28.3	27.1	44.6	49.6	66.5	----
	.011	18.6	20.0	43.2	51.8	11.3	8.8	28.5	27.2	45.5	50.6	----	65.2
	.010	18.4	19.7	43.3	52.6	11.7	9.1	28.5	27.1	45.4	51.6	64.5	----
	.009	18.5	20.1	43.2	54.3	12.3	9.1	28.7	26.9	45.7	52.7	----	62.0
	.008	18.6	20.3	43.2	54.9	12.2	9.0	28.6	26.5	45.6	53.0	60.5	----
	.007	18.5	20.7	42.4	56.1	13.5	9.4	28.5	26.0	44.6	53.6	----	58.0
	.006	18.3	20.9	41.3	55.6	13.8	9.1	28.6	26.0	43.9	53.2	55.8	57.1
	.005	18.2	----	37.7	54.7	13.1	8.2	----	26.6	42.7	55.8	53.6	----
	.004	16.5	----	----	----	----	----	----	----	----	----	51.6	----
	.003	----	----	----	----	----	----	----	23.7	----	----	----	----
Summary.	.0280	19.5	20.1	43.8	46.1	9.8	9.1	28.5	28.0	48.3	49.7	----	----
	.0148	18.7	19.7	43.3	49.0	10.8	9.4	28.1	27.1	45.9	49.0	69.6	69.6
	.0084	18.5	20.2	43.1	54.3	12.2	9.1	28.6	26.7	45.4	52.6	61.5	60.9
	.0050	17.9	21.1	38.5	54.8	13.4	8.4	28.6	26.0	42.9	55.0	53.8	54.1

Calculation of time of infinite arc, etc.—Continued.

φ	(13)	11^h	(14)	10^h	(15)	3^h	(16)	10^h	(17)	10^h	(18)	3^h
	m.	*m.*	*m.*	*m.*	*m.*	*m.*	*m.*	*m.*	*m.*	*m.*	*m.*	*m.*
.030	----	34.6	104.7	107.7	----	55.2	35.1	----	50.2	51.7	24.7	----
.029	----	----	103.3	106.6	55.2	----	----	35.2	50.1	51.6	----	----
.028	----	34.5	101.8	105.4	----	----	35.2	----	49.9	51.3	24.9	24.0
.027	----	----	100.3	104.0	----	54.2	----	35.0	49.6	51.2	----	----
.026	31.9	34.0	99.2	102.4	53.9	----	35.0	----	49.5	51.5	25.0	23.9
.025	----	----	97.3	----	----	53.4	----	35.1	49.1	----	24.9	----
.024	31.0	----	95.6	----	----	----	----	----	----	----	----	----
.023	----	----	----	----	----	----	----	----	48.5	51.7	----	----
.022	----	----	----	----	----	---	----	----	48.8	51.7	----	----
.021	----	----	----	----	----	----	----	----	48.9	51.8	25.1	----
.020	----	----	87.5	92.0	----	----	34.8	----	48.8	52.4	25.2	24.1
.019	----	----	85.0	90.0	----	----	----	35.0	49.0	52.7	25.1	24.0
.018	----	33.6	82.5	88.2	----	49.4	34.9	35.4	48.9	53.4	25.5	24.1
.017	----	33.8	79.7	86.2	48.9	----	35.0	35.7	49.5	54.7	25.8	24.2
.016	----	34.1	77.3	83.7	----	47.8	35.0	35.7	50.3	54.5	25.8	24.1
.015	29.1	34.7	74.4	81.1	47.0	----	35.2	35.9	49.8	54.9	25.9	24.3
.014	28.9	34.8	71.1	78.3	----	45.6	35.1	35.8	49.4	56.0	26.2	24.2
.013	28.9	35.2	67.5	76.4	44.3	----	35.2	36.0	50.4	56.4	26.3	24.1
.012	28.6	35.4	63.4	72.6	----	42.6	35.0	35.9	49.7	56.9	26.6	24.4
.011	28.0	35.7	59.7	70.1	41.2	----	35.2	36.1	49.4	58.1	27.2	24.7
.010	27.4	36.6	54.1	67.0	39.5	39.1	35.3	36.4	50.3	59.4	27.7	24.8
.009	26.7	38.0	48.4	64.5	37.4	37.1	35.7	36.7	50.1	60.5	27.8	25.1
.008	26.3	39.3	42.0	63.4	34.8	34.5	35.4	36.7	49.8	62.1	27.9	25.2
.007	26.2	40.3	35.7	62.2	31.5	31.1	35.9	37.0	50.5	62.7	28.3	24.8
.006	25.5	41.9	29.1	63.3	27.6	27.3	35.5	37.3	47.9	61.4	28.8	24.9
.005	24.2	----	21.5	----	22.8	22.4	34.9	----	43.4	59.8	----	24.7
.004	----	----	12.7	----	----	----	33.4	----	----	----	----	23.7
.003	----	----	59.1	----	9.0	----	----	----	----	----	----	----
Summary. .0280	32.6	34.4	101.9	105.3	54.8	54.5	35.1	35.1	49.7	51.5	24.9	24.0
.0148	29.2	34.6	73.7	80.4	46.6	46.3	35.1	35.8	49.5	55.0	26.0	24.2
.0084	26.7	38.4	44.7	64.2	35.9	35.5	35.5	36.6	50.0	61.1	27.8	24.9
.0050	24.4	43.5	21.7	61.9	22.9	22.4	34.7	37.6	43.8	59.9	29.1	24.5

Calculation of time of infinite arc, etc.—Continued.

φ	(19)	11^h	(20)	11^h	(21)	4^h	(22)	11^h	(23)	0^h	(24)	4^h
	m.	*m.*	*m.*	*m.*	*m.*	*m.*	*m.*	*m.*	*m.*	*m.*	*m.*	*m.*
.030	----	38.2	54.3	----	40.4	----	----	----	----	4.9	----	34.1
.029	----	----	----	53.9	----	40.5	----	----	3.6	4.9	----	----
.028	37.6	38.2	53.6	----	40.3	----	----	----	3.6	4.8	----	34.1
.027	37.5	38.2	----	53.0	----	40.5	----	----	3.0	4.6	----	----
.026	----	----	52.9	----	40.0	----	----	----	3.0	4.4	32.9	34.0
.025	37.3	----	----	52.4	----	40.5	52.2	----	2.9	4.4	----	34.2
.024	----	----	----	----	----	----	----	----	----	----	----	----
.023	----	----	----	52.6	----	----	----	----	3.5	5.3	----	----
.022	----	----	52.4	----	----	----	----	----	3.2	5.0	----	----
.021	----	----	----	52.8	----	----	----	----	3.0	5.2	----	----
.020	----	----	52.3	----	39.6	40.5	51.9	----	3.1	5.3	----	----
.019	37.0	38.1	----	52.7	39.8	40.6	52.5	51.4	3.0	5.0	32.9	34.6
.018	37.1	38.3	52.5	----	39.6	40.6	----	51.8	2.7	4.9	----	----
.017	37.2	38.4	----	52.7	39.5	40.6	53.5	----	2.4	4.8	32.8	35.6
.016	37.0	38.5	52.5	----	39.5	40.5	----	----	2.1	4.6	----	----
.015	37.0	38.6	----	52.4	39.6	40.6	53.7	51.4	1.9	4.7	33.2	35.7
.014	37.1	38.9	51.9	----	39.4	40.7	53.5	51.7	1.6	4.6	----	----
.013	37.4	39.1	----	53.4	39.3	41.0	53.4	51.5	1.3	4.6	33.5	35.9
.012	37.5	39.7	54.7	----	39.5	41.0	53.7	51.4	2.5	5.7	----	----
.011	37.5	40.0	----	55.5	39.5	40.7	54.4	51.4	3.1	6.2	33.3	36.2
.010	37.4	40.0	55.7	----	39.5	40.7	54.7	51.7	3.6	6.6	----	----
.009	37.1	40.2	----	55.8	39.7	40.7	55.6	51.7	4.1	9.1	34.0	37.2
.008	37.2	41.4	54.6	----	39.2	40.9	56.1	52.2	4.3	10.2	----	----
.007	37.4	41.5	----	56.9	38.5	41.6	56.8	52.2	2.7	9.4	33.7	38.8
.006	36.9	42.5	54.0	----	38.2	41.5	56.9	51.9	0.6	10.4	----	----
.005	36.5	43.1	----	55.8	37.4	----	56.8	51.1	59.3	13.2	33.2	39.7
.004	----	----	50.4	----	35.6	----	----	----	----	----	----	----
.003	----	----	----	----	----	----	----	----	----	----	----	----
Summary.												
.0280	37.5	38.2	53.6	53.1	40.2	40.5	----	----	3.2	4.7	32.9	34.1
.0148	37.2	38.7	53.0	52.9	39.5	40.7	53.4	51.5	2.4	5.0	33.1	35.7
.0084	37.3	40.7	54.6	55.9	39.3	40.9	55.8	51.9	3.7	8.8	33.7	37.7
.0050	36.5	43.2	52.4	56.2	37.2	41.5	56.9	51.3	59.0	12.8	33.2	39.7

Calculation of time of infinite arc, etc.—Continued.

φ	(25)	0^h	(26)	0^h	(27)	5^h	(28)	11^h	(29)	0^h	(30)	5^h
	m.	*m.*	*m.*	*m.*	*m.*	*m.*	*m.*	*m.*	*m.*	*m.*	*m.*	*m.*
.030	21.7	----	34.3	----	28.2	29.1	55.4	55.8	6.5	----	9.4	----
.029	----	22.3	----	----	----	----	55.5	55.9	----	6.6	----	9.7
.028	----	----	33.7	31.6	28.4	29.2	----	----	6.6	----	9.4	----
.027	21.7	22.7	----	----	----	----	55.1	55.8	----	6.1	----	9.4
.026	----	----	32.9	30.5	28.4	29.4	55.3	55.8	6.1	----	9.2	----
.025	21.8	----	32.4	----	----	29.4	----	55.6	----	5.3	----	9.4
.024	----	----	----	----	----	----	----	----	----	----	----	----
.023	----	----	----	----	----	----	----	----	4.8	----	----	----
.022	----	----	----	----	----	----	----	----	----	5.4	----	----
.021	----	----	31.6	27.5	----	----	----	54.4	6.5	----	----	----
.020	----	22.4	----	----	28.3	29.7	----	----	----	6.5	8.9	----
.019	21.7	22.7	31.4	27.5	----	----	54.1	55.2	6.5	----	----	9.5
.018	21.6	22.7	----	----	28.3	29.9	54.0	55.5	----	6.4	9.4	----
.017	21.5	22.8	31.7	27.2	----	----	54.2	55.5	6.0	----	----	9.8
.016	21.3	22.8	----	----	28.1	30.4	53.9	55.4	----	5.8	9.7	----
.015	21.4	23.0	31.6	26.8	----	----	53.8	55.6	4.9	----	----	10.1
.014	21.5	23.0	----	----	28.3	30.8	53.7	55.5	----	6.1	9.7	----
.013	21.6	23.2	32.8	26.2	----	----	53.5	55.6	5.6	----	----	10.1
.012	22.0	23.5	----	----	28.5	31.5	53.5	56.0	----	7.2	9.6	----
.011	22.2	23.7	33.6	27.4	----	----	53.5	56.1	7.7	----	----	10.5
.010	22.1	24.4	----	----	28.5	31.9	53.3	56.2	----	7.9	9.9	----
.009	22.2	24.9	36.7	26.5	----	----	53.1	56.6	8.8	----	----	10.6
.008	22.1	25.1	----	----	28.9	33.2	52.9	56.7	----	7.1	10.1	----
.007	21.7	25.3	37.4	25.4	----	----	52.8	57.2	7.8	----	----	10.3
.006	21.3	25.7	40.5	23.7	29.0	----	52.2	57.6	----	9.1	9.8	----
.005	21.0	25.9	43.0	23.8	28.5	34.9	51.6	57.9	8.7	----	----	9.9
.004	----	----	----	----	----	----	----	----	----	7.3	8.1	----
.003	----	----	----	----	----	----	----	----	----	----	----	----
Summary. .0280	21.7	22.5	33.5	31.5	28.3	29.3	55.3	55.8	6.3	5.9	9.3	9.5
Summary. .0148	21.6	23.0	32.2	27.0	28.3	30.7	53.8	55.6	6.1	6.3	9.6	10.0
Summary. .0084	22.0	24.9	36.3	26.2	28.7	32.9	53.0	56.7	8.1	7.4	10.0	10.5
Summary. .0050	21.0	25.9	43.3	23.3	28.6	34.9	51.6	58.0	8.7	8.3	9.0	9.9

Calculation of time of infinite arc, etc.—Continued.

φ	(31)	11h	(32)	11h	(33)	4h	(34)	11h	(35)	0h	(36)	4h
	m.	*m.*	*m.*	*m.*	*m.*	*m.*	*m.*	*m.*	*m.*	*m.*	*m.*	*m.*
.030	53.5	54.4	64.5	67.6	45.1	----	51.4	----	16.5	----	----	39.7
.029	----	----	----	----	----	----	----	51.4	----	17.9	----	39.8
.028	53.7	54.4	64.3	67.4	----	43.9	51.4	----	16.4	----	----	----
.027	----	----	----	----	45.2	43.7	----	51.4	----	17.2	----	----
.026	53.3	54.2	64.3	----	----	----	51.2	----	16.0	----	----	40.1
.025	----	54.2	63.8	----	----	43.7	----	51.2	----	17.1	38.4	----
.024	----	----	----	----	----	----	----	----	----	----	----	----
.023	----	----	----	----	----	----	----	----	----	----	----	----
.022	----	----	62.8	67.7	----	----	----	----	----	17.5	----	----
.021	----	----	----	----	----	----	----	----	15.8	----	----	40.7
.020	----	----	62.6	68.2	45.8	43.6	50.8	----	----	18.0	----	----
.019	53.0	54.4	----	----	46.2	----	----	50.9	15.7	----	----	40.9
.018	----	----	61.6	68.7	46.3	43.6	50.7	----	----	17.7	35.4	----
.017	52.7	54.5	----	----	46.5	43.6	----	51.0	14.9	----	----	41.7
.016	----	----	61.3	69.6	46.6	43.6	51.0	----	----	19.0	34.8	----
.015	52.6	54.7	----	----	47.0	43.7	----	51.2	15.9	----	----	42.6
.014	----	----	60.7	70.9	47.1	43.6	50.8	----	----	19.3	34.7	----
.013	52.6	55.0	----	----	47.4	43.6	----	51.2	15.4	----	----	43.1
.012	52.8	55.2	60.3	72.3	47.7	43.7	50.7	----	----	19.7	34.4	----
.011	52.7	55.3	----	----	48.4	43.7	----	50.8	14.5	----	----	44.0
.010	52.7	55.7	58.5	72.0	49.0	43.7	51.1	----	----	20.5	33.7	44.7
.009	52.6	55.9	----	----	49.8	43.8	----	51.5	14.7	----	----	45.9
.008	52.3	56.1	55.1	77.1	50.3	43.2	50.9	----	----	23.6	31.9	47.1
.007	52.0	56.6	----	----	51.1	42.9	----	51.0	15.4	----	30.8	----
.006	51.7	57.0	53.5	81.4	----	42.9	50.8	----	----	24.3	29.5	48.6
.005	51.6	57.4	51.9	83.3	----	42.2	----	50.5	10.9	20.5	28.1	----
.004	----	----	----	----	----	40.3	49.6	----	----	----	25.3	----
.003	----	----	----	----	----	----	----	----	----	----	----	----
Summary. .0280	53.5	54.3	64.2	67.6	45.2	43.8	51.3	51.4	16.3	17.4	38.4	39.9
Summary. .0148	52.7	54.8	60.9	70.3	47.0	43.6	50.8	51.0	15.3	19.0	34.8	42.5
Summary. .0084	52.4	56.1	56.0	75.8	50.1	43.4	50.9	51.3	14.9	22.8	32.3	46.4
Summary. .0050	51.5	57.4	51.9	83.3	52.9	42.0	50.3	50.5	10.9	21.5	27.9	49.6

Calculation of time of infinite arc, etc.—Continued.

φ	(37)	1^h	(38)	2^h	(39)	7^h	(40)	0^h	(41)	0^h	(42)	5^h
	m.	*m.*	*m.*	*m.*	*m.*	*m.*	*m.*	*m.*	*m.*	*m.*	*m.*	*m.*
.030	46.7	47.7	----	10.6	----	14.9	----	----	----	60.4	9.5	----
.029	----	----	9.0	10.2	----	----	50.2	----	60.4	----	----	9.5
.028	46.7	----	8.6	10.1	----	15.2	----	50.0	----	60.2	9.4	----
.027	46.5	47.9	8.5	10.0	13.5	----	50.0	----	60.9	----	----	9.4
.026	----	----	8.6	10.5	----	----	----	49.8	----	59.8	9.4	----
.025	46.4	----	8.8	10.3	13.5	15.1	49.9	----	60.9	----	----	9.4
.024	----	----	----	----	----	----	----	----	----	----	----	----
.023	----	----	----	11.2	----	----	----	----	----	----	----	----
.022	----	----	8.5	11.2	----	----	----	----	----	58.9	----	----
.021	----	----	8.6	11.1	----	----	----	----	60.5	----	----	----
.020	46.4	48.1	8.4	11.5	----	15.8	----	49.3	60.6	59.3	9.3	----
.019	----	----	8.4	12.8	13.6	15.9	49.3	----	60.2	58.5	----	9.4
.018	46.3	48.7	9.4	13.4	13.6	16.4	----	49.0	60.5	57.9	9.5	----
.017	----	----	9.8	14.4	14.0	16.5	48.7	----	60.8	58.4	----	9.6
.016	46.5	49.4	10.5	15.3	13.9	16.8	----	49.1	60.4	58.0	9.5	----
.015	----	----	11.2	15.8	14.0	17.1	48.9	----	59.9	58.2	----	10.2
.014	46.5	49.6	11.1	15.7	13.9	17.5	----	49.2	59.4	57.6	10.1	----
.013	----	----	11.1	16.4	14.1	17.5	49.0	----	58.8	56.9	----	10.4
.012	46.3	50.4	10.7	16.5	13.9	17.8	----	49.2	57.5	55.5	10.5	----
.011	----	----	11.6	17.5	13.5	18.1	49.2	----	55.9	54.5	----	10.6
.010	46.1	51.5	11.7	19.1	13.7	19.0	----	49.1	56.2	53.4	10.6	----
.009	----	----	11.2	21.1	14.0	19.8	49.3	----	55.6	52.1	----	11.1
.008	46.2	52.9	12.2	21.4	14.0	20.7	----	49.5	54.5	50.6	10.5	----
.007	----	54.0	10.7	22.9	13.9	20.9	49.3	----	53.8	49.9	----	11.8
.006	44.6	----	10.0	23.3	13.3	21.8	----	49.2	52.0	47.1	10.2	----
.005	45.6	55.2	8.1	25.0	12.4	----	48.4	----	50.1	44.1	----	11.2
.004	----	----	----	----	11.8	----	----	----	----	----	----	----
.003	----	----	----	----	----	----	----	----	----	----	----	----
Summary. .0280	46.6	47.8	8.7	10.3	13.5	15.1	50.1	49.9	60.9	60.1	9.4	9.4
Summary. .0148	46.4	49.6	10.8	15.5	13.8	17.1	49.0	49.1	59.6	57.7	9.9	10.0
Summary. .0084	46.1	52.6	11.4	21.1	13.9	20.1	49.3	49.4	55.0	51.5	10.5	11.3
Summary. .0050	45.3	55.2	8.2	24.7	12.5	22.9	48.4	49.0	50.0	44.0	10.0	11.5

Calculation of time of infinite arc, etc.—Continued.

	φ	(43)	0^h	(44)	0^h	(45)	4^h	(46)	0^h	(47)	0^h	(48)	5^h
		m.	*m.*	*m.*	*m.*	*m.*	*m.*	*m.*	*m.*	*m.*	*m.*	*m.*	*m.*
	.030	23.7	----	37.1	----	59.2	----	----	40.3	57.7	----	5.2	----
	.029	----	24.2	----	39.1	----	59.9	40.6	----	----	57.1	----	5.3
	.028	23.7	----	37.0	----	----	59.9	----	----	56.4	----	5.3	----
	.027	----	23.9	36.0	38.7	----	----	----	40.2	----	55.2	----	5.3
	.026	22.3	----	36.3	38.2	58.9	59.8	40.4	----	55.0	----	5.3	----
	.025	----	23.6	35.6	38.1	----	60.0	----	40.2	----	53.7	----	5.4
	.024	----	----	----	----	----	----	----	----	----	----	----	----
	.023	----	----	----	----	----	----	----	----	----	----	----	----
	.022	----	----	35.2	38.9	----	----	----	----	----	----	----	----
	.021	----	----	35.8	39.0	----	----	----	----	----	----	----	5.7
	.020	----	24.0	35.7	39.0	----	----	----	----	50.5	----	5.6	----
	.019	23.0	----	35.3	38.9	58.6	60.2	41.1	----	----	49.7	----	5.6
	.018	----	24.1	34.9	38.5	----	----	41.2	40.6	49.6	----	5.8	----
	.017	22.7	24.0	34.1	38.5	58.5	60.5	----	40.8	----	49.5	----	6.2
	.016	22.7	24.0	33.9	39.2	----	----	41.3	----	48.9	----	5.9	----
	.015	22.7	24.3	34.5	39.9	58.4	60.4	----	41.0	----	49.4	----	6.5
	.014	22.5	24.3	34.7	40.5	----	----	41.6	----	49.2	----	6.2	----
	.013	22.6	24.4	35.1	41.6	58.2	60.5	41.7	41.1	----	48.5	----	6.9
	.012	22.6	24.7	35.2	42.0	----	----	42.3	41.7	47.2	----	7.0	----
	.011	22.7	24.7	34.8	42.3	58.3	61.1	42.6	41.5	----	47.8	----	7.0
	.010	22.5	24.9	34.2	42.1	----	----	42.7	41.6	47.9	----	7.2	----
	.009	22.3	24.9	33.2	42.7	57.9	61.5	43.1	41.9	----	48.7	----	7.6
	.008	21.9	25.4	32.8	42.8	----	----	43.6	42.5	47.2	----	7.6	----
	.007	21.9	25.3	32.2	43.5	57.6	62.1	43.5	42.2	----	46.1	----	7.8
	.006	21.5	25.1	30.8	43.3	----	----	44.2	42.3	47.6	----	7.3	----
	.005	20.3	25.6	27.3	42.3	55.9	63.6	----	41.7	49.6	45.6	----	7.9
	.004	----	----	----	----	----	----	----	42.1	----	----	6.4	----
	.003	----	----	----	----	----	----	----	----	----	----	----	----
Summary.	.0280	23.4	23.9	36.6	38.6	59.1	59.9	40.5	40.2	56.4	55.8	5.3	5.3
	.0148	22.7	24.3	34.7	40.2	58.4	60.5	41.7	41.0	48.9	49.0	6.2	6.5
	.0084	22.2	25.1	33.1	42.8	57.8	61.7	43.2	42.0	47.4	47.4	7.4	7.5
	.0050	20.6	25.4	27.8	42.6	55.9	63.6	44.5	42.0	49.2	45.6	6.9	7.9

Values of $\frac{1}{b}$ *and of the ratio heavy end down to heavy end up.*

No. of swings.	$\frac{1}{b}$			Ratio, down : up.
	Heavy end down.	Heavy end up.		
	m.	*m.*	*m.*	
1, 2, 3	110.3	37.0	38.7	2.91
4, 5, 6	111.1	36.6	38.6	.95
7, 8, 9	114.9	38.3	40.3	.92
10, 11, 12	110.7	38.1	[21.5]	.91
13, 14, 15	[59.3]	37.3	[19.3]	----
16, 17, 18	115.7	39.9	40.7	.87
19, 20, 21	112.6	39.9	38.5	.87
22, 23, 24	113.1	41.5	41.1	.74
25, 26, 27	109.1	39.9	40.9	.70
28, 29, 30	113.1	37.9	39.7	.91
31, 32, 33	112.0	39.1	41.1	.79
34, 35, 36	113.0	38.4	38.6	.94
37, 38, 39	119.0	41.0	41.6	.88
40, 41, 42	105.4	37.7	40.3	.70
43, 44, 45	111.7	38.8	39.1	.87
46, 47, 48	100.9	41.2	41.1	.45

Fort Conger. Pendulum, Peirce No. 1.

HEAVY END DOWN.

No. of swing and face.	Temperature (F).	Pressure.	Mean instant, first transits.	Mean instant, last transits.	Arc correction.	Interval.	No. of oscillations.	Uncorrected period.	Rate.
	°	*in.*	*h. m. s.*	*h. m. s.*	*s.*	*s.*		*s.*	
2 B	–9.5	29.892	8 01 50.956	10 18 58.229	0.085	8227.187	8190	1.0045405	+293
5 F	–10.1	29.936	6 21 54.677	8 43 25.124	0.087	8490.360	8452	1.0045337	+293
8 F	–10.8	29.825	5 45 40.006	8 07 51.636	0.096	8531.535	8493	1.0045372	+293
11 F	–14.6	29.919	5 51 16.941	8 12 45.177	0.088	8488.148	8450	1.0045145	+293
14 B	–18.3	30.041	7 41 37.613	9 16 14.876	0.044	5677.219	5652	1.0044619	+293
17 B	–16.1	29.841	6 51 10.445	9 14 29.119	0.096	8598.578	8560	1.0045068	+293
20 B	–16.0	29.286	7 53 56.610	10 25 41.479	0.093	9104.776	9064	1.0044986	+293
23 F	–15.4	29.789	8 05 37.325	10 28 47.998	0.090	8590.584	8552	1.0045117	+293
26 F	–18.9	29.717	8 35 09.007	10 53 36.815	0.083	8307.725	8271	1.0044402	+294
29 F	–20.8	29.975	8 06 30.184	10 37 34.324	0.093	9064.047	9024	1.0044378	+294
32 B	–21.3	29.776	8 05 19.742	10 32 42.974	0.094	8843.138	8804	1.0044455	+294
35 F	–21.5	29.999	8 18 25.331	10 41 07.292	0.090	8561.871	8524	1.0044429	+294
38 B	–21.6	29.446	10 11 28.548	12 37 41.455	0.095	8772.812	8734	1.0044438	+340
41 F	–25.0	29.872	9 01 36.205	11 13 17.033	0.084	7900.744	7866	1.0044170	+340
44 F	–26.6	29.821	8 38 44.315	10 56 14.706	0.089	8250.302	8214	1.0044195	+340
47 B	–25.9	29.287	9 01 45.782	11 08 54.270	0.068	7628.420	7595	1.0044003	+340

FORT CONGER. PENDULUM, PEIRCE NO.1—CONTINUED.

HEAVY END UP.

No. of swing and face.	Temperature (F).	Pressure.	Mean instant, first transits.			Mean instant, last transits.			Arc correction.	Interval.	No. of oscillations.	Uncorrected period.	Rate.
	°	*in.*	*h.*	*m.*	*s.*	*h.*	*m.*	*s.*	*s.*	*s.*		*s.*	
1 B	−9.9	29.873	5	29	15.364	6	18	43.118	0.027	2967.727	2956	1.0039671	+293
3 F	−10.1	29.908	11	18	41.202	12	08	01.892	0.027	2960.663	2949	1.0039550	+293
4 F	−10.0	29.942	4	15	55.413	5	02	06.354	0.024	2770.917	2760	1.0039553	+293
6 B	−9.2	29.928	10	02	43.028	10	55	39.548	0.027	3176.493	3164	1.0039485	+293
7 B	−11.5	29.829	3	55	39.382	4	46	01.286	0.028	3021.876	3010	1.0039455	+293
9 B	−10.8	29.830	8	46	03.706	9	35	21.373	0.028	2957.639	2946	1.0039509	+293
10 B	−15.5	29.900	4	06	24.949	5	00	13.573	0.024	3228.600	3216	1.0039179	+293
12 F	−13.8	29.948	8	56	31.588	9	21	12.127	0.008	1480.531	1476	1.0030699	+293
13 F	−16.8	30.043	6	13	57.083	6	56	51.168	0.019	2574.067	2564	1.0039261	+293
15 F	−15.0	30.036	10	29	25.625	10	50	40.955	0.011	1275.218	1271	1.0033190	+293
16 F	−16.5	29.892	5	11	23.928	6	10	35.691	0.029	3551.735	3538	1.0038821	+293
18 B	−15.6	29.780	10	00	37.269	10	52	11.182	0.029	3093.884	3082	1.0038559	+293
19 B	−16.6	29.338	6	13	05.985	7	04	07.873	0.029	3061.859	3050	1.0038881	+293
21 B	−16.0	29.267	11	15	58.320	12	05	21.808	0.028	2963.460	2952	1.0038822	+293
22 B	−15.8	29.796	6	28	32.893	7	18	06.475	0.027	2973.555	2962	1.0039010	+293
24 F	−16.0	29.786	11	09	37.201	12	00	37.098	0.029	3059.868	3048	1.0038938	+293
25 B	−18.5	29.665	6	57	23.116	7	47	58.915	0.029	3035.770	3024	1.0038921	+293
27 F	−18.2	29.755	12	04	34.987	12	55	40.873	0.029	3065.857	3054	1.0038825	+293
28 F	−20.3	29.969	6	30	42.121	7	18	43.286	0.027	2881.138	2870	1.0038807	+293
30 B	−20.2	29.958	11	44	29.864	12	37	02.015	0.029	3152.122	3140	1.0038605	+293
31 B	−21.5	29.766	6	29	20.535	7	19	48.195	0.028	3027.633	3016	1.0038571	+293
33 B	−21.1	29.793	11	18	57.889	12	09	35.592	0.031	3037.672	3026	1.0038572	+293
34 B	−22.4	29.997	6	26	13.701	7	17	17.528	0.028	3063.799	3052	1.0038661	+293
36 B	−22.2	29.996	11	14	31.568	12	00	54.307	0.027	2782.713	2772	1.0038647	+293
37 B	−21.0	29.485	8	22	01.236	9	12	33.904	0.030	3032.638	3021	1.0038523	+340
39 B	−21.4	29.393	13	50	29.471	14	41	55.326	0.028	3085.826	3074	1.0038471	+340
40 B	−25.4	29.842	7	24	44.646	8	09	22.960	0.026	2678.287	2668	1.0038558	+340
42 F	−25.0	29.899	11	44	32.245	12	30	30.926	0.028	2758.653	2748	1.0038767	+340
43 F	−26.1	29.834	6	58	38.207	7	46	15.284	0.028	2857.050	2846	1.0038825	+340
45 F	−25.9	29.830	11	34	56.301	12	22	43.212	0.025	2866.886	2796	1.0038933	+340
46 F	−26.4	29.373	7	14	59.632	8	08	09.968	0.031	3190.275	3178	1.0038625	+340
48	−26.4	29.218	11	40	04.803	12	35	03.470	0.030	3298.636	3286	1.0038455	+340

PENDULUM, PEIRCE NO. 1.

HEAVY END DOWN.

Before interchange of knives.

No. of swing.	Temperature, +13.2° F.	Pressure, –29.736 in.	Period corrected for rate.	Temperature correction.	Pressure correction.	Period corrected to mean pressure and temperature.
	°	*In.*	*s*			*s*
2	+3.7	+0.108	1.0045698	–174	–15	1.0045509
5	+3.1	+0.152	5630	–146	–22	5462
8	+2.4	+0.041	5665	–113	–6	5546
11	–1.4	+0.135	5438	+66	–19	5485
14*	. . .	. . .	. . .	. . .	. . .	. . .
17	–2.9	+0.057	5361	+136	–8	5489
20	–2.8	–0.498	5279	+132	+71	5482
23	–2.2	+0.005	5410	+103	–1	5512
Mean						1.0045498

* Necessarily rejected on account of irregular descent of the arc.

After interchange of knives.

No. of swing.	Temperature, +22.7° F.	Pressure, –29.737 in.	Period corrected for rate.	Temperature correction.	Pressure correction.	Period corrected to mean pressure and temperature.
	°	*In.*	*s*			*s*
26	+3.8	–0.020	1.0044696	–179	+3	1.0044520
29	+1.9	+0.238	4672	–89	–34	4549
32	+1.4	+0.039	4749	–66	–6	4677
35	+1.2	+0.262	4723	–56	–37	4630
38	+1.1	–0.291	4778	–52	+41	4767
41	–2.3	+0.135	4510	+108	–19	4599
44	–3.9	+0.084	4535	+183	–12	4706
47	–3.2	–0.450	4343	+150	+64	4557
Time of oscillation at –22.7° F. and 29.737in pressure.						1.0044626
Correction to standard atmosphere						–681
Expansion to 15° C.						+4014
Flexure						–655
Elevation, 23 feet.						–11
Corrected period.						1.0047293

HEAVY END UP.

Before interchange of knives.

No. of swing.	Temperature, +13.6° F.	Pressure, –29.736 in.	Period corrected for rate.	Temperature correction.	Pressure correction.	Period corrected to mean pressure and temperature.
	°	*In.*	*s*			*s*
1	+3.7	+.079	1.0039964	–106	–33	1.0039825
3	+3.5	+.114	9843	–100	–48	9695
4	+3.6	+.148	9846	–103	–63	9680
6	+4.4	+.134	9778	–126	–57	9595
7	+2.1	+.035	9748	–60	–15	9673
9	+2.8	+.036	9802	–80	–15	9707
10	–1.9	+.106	9472	+55	–45	9482
12*	. . .	. . .	. . .	. . .	. . .	. . .
13	–3.2	+.249	9554	+92	–106	9540
15*	. . .	. . .	. . .	. . .	. . .	. . .
16	–2.9	+.098	9114	+83	–42	9155
18	–2.0	–.014	8852	+57	+6	8915
19	–3.0	–.456	9174	+86	+193	9453
21	–2.4	–.527	9115	+69	+223	9407
22	–2.2	+.002	9303	+63	–1	9365
24	–2.4	–.008	9231	+69	+3	9303
Mean						1.0039485

*Necessarily rejected on account of irregular descent of the arc.

After interchange of knives.

No. of swing.	Temperature, +22.6° F.	Pressure, –29.736 in.	Period corrected for rate.	Temperature correction.	Pressure correction.	Period corrected to mean pressure and temperature.
	°	*In.*	*s*			*s*
25	+4.1	–.071	1.0039214	–118	+30	1.0039126
27	+4.4	+.019	9118	–126	–8	8984
28	+2.3	+.233	9100	–63	–99	8938
30	+2.4	+.222	8898	–69	–94	8735
31	+1.1	+.030	8864	–32	–13	8819
33	+1.5	+.057	8865	–43	–24	8798
34	+0.2	+.261	8954	–6	–111	8837
36	+0.4	+.260	8940	–11	–110	8819
37	+1.6	–.251	8863	–46	+106	8923
39	+1.2	–.343	8811	–34	+145	8922
40	–2.8	+.106	8898	+80	–45	8933
42	–2.4	+.163	9107	+69	–69	9107
43	–3.5	+.098	9165	+100	–42	9223
45	–3.3	+.094	9273	+95	–40	9328
46	–3.8	–.363	8965	+109	+154	9228
48	–3.8	–.518	8795	+109	+220	9124

Time of oscillation at–22.6° F. and 29.736^{in} pressure	1.0038990
Correction to standard atmosphere	–2026
Expansion to 15° C.	+4006
Flexure	–220
Elevation, 23 feet.	–11
Corrected period.	1.0040739

Flexure of Pendulum Piers.
Observer, E. Israel,1882.
Deflecting force, the weight of 2.5 pounds. [Treated as 2.38 lb.]

1 rev. micr. at –12° F.	= 0.001704^{in}
	Flexure.
	r.
Scale 7.843^{in} forward	0.299
Scale 15.858 back	0.656
At centre knife-edge	0.414
	= 0.000710^{in}
Wt. pend. 23.0 lb. ∴ *MS*	= 0.00686^{in} = 174.2$^{\mu}$

Pendulum, Peirce No. 1.
1881, June 11–14.
Comparison with Metre No. 49, middle plugs.

Temperature F.		Length observed excess pendulum.	Correction for mean to 70°.	Correction for difference.	Excess, corrected.
Mean pendulum and metre.	Excess pendulum over metre.				
°	°	μ	μ	μ	μ
70.3	+0.2	399.5	+0.1	–2.1	397.5
69.3	–0.1	397.5	–0.2	+1.0	398.3
69.5	0.0	398.0	–0.2	0.0	397.8
69.6	–0.2	400.0	–0.1	+2.1	402.0
69.8	0.0	397.5	–0.1	0.0	397.4
70.0	–0.2	393.5	0.0	+2.1	395.6
70.2	–0.1	396.5	+0.1	+1.0	397.6
69.9	–0.4	390.0	0.0	+4.1	394.1
69.9	–0.2	391.5	0.0	+2.1	393.6
70.0	–0.2	393.0	0.0	+2.1	395.1
70.1	–0.2	396.5	0.0	+2.1	398.6
70.2	–0.2	393.0	+0.1	+2.1	395.2
70.3	–0.2	394.0	+0.1	+2.1	396.2
69.5	–0.1	400.0	–0.2	+1.0	400.8
69.6	–0.1	393.0	–0.1	+1.0	392.9
69.8	–0.2	395.5	–0.1	+2.1	397.5
					396.9
Corr. error of thermometers					396.6
At 68°					397.2

PENDULUM, PEIRCE NO. 1.
1884, December 1–10.
Comparison with outer line of Metre B.

Temperature C.	Pendulum–Metre.	Reduced to 20° C.
°	μ	μ
17.24	+252.4	+251.1
18.11	+252.8	251.6
17.98	+253.2	250.1
18.19	+252.7	253.9
18.38	+252.3	252.5
18.82	+251.4	251.7
19.00	+249.0	250.3
19.74	+249.8	250.9
19.32	+249.6	251.1
19.83	+248.0	250.9
30.30	+242.5	250.7
30.57	+241.9	250.9
30.92	+242.1	250.7
31.45	+241.9	250.4
31.71	+242.2	250.9
Mean pendulum – *B* 1st line		+251.2
1st line – 3rd line		+199.4
B 3rd line – No. 49		−12.0
Correction to thermometers		+0.7
		+429.3

I now give a summary of the observations made with this pendulum in Washington in 1884–85 by me, with the assistance of Mr. W. B. Fairfield.

PENDULUM NO. 1.

1884–85.

At Smithsonian Institution, Washington, D. C.

Heavy end down.				Heavy end up.			
No. of swing.	Tempera-ture.	Pressure.	*nT.*	No. of swing.	Tempera-ture.	Pressure.	*nT.*
	°	*In.*	*s.*		°	*In.*	*s.*
1	20.15	29.711	15095.265	1	20.75	30.256	5028.101
2	20.58	29.643	.230	2	21.02	30.266	.043
3	20.63	29.753	.212	3	21.23	30.282	.106
4	20.53	30.044	.229	4	21.21	30.300	.093
5	20.20	29.624	.274	5	20.96	30.348	.028
6	20.69	29.618	.232	6	20.98	30.336	.061
7	21.04	29.866	.216	7	21.00	30.344	.048
8	21.18	30.078	.202	8	20.99	30.402	.084
9	20.33	30.681	.251	Means	21.02	30.317	5028.070
10	20.54	30.640	.276				
11	20.48	30.608	.282	Corr. to stand. atmos.			−.033
12	20.10	30.462	.246	Expansion to 15° C.			−.273
Means	20.54	30.061	15095.243	Flexure			−.116
				Corrected time			5027.648
Corr. to stand. atmos.			+.005				
Expansion to 15° C.			−.752				
Flexure			−1.037				
Corrected time			15093.459				
10,000 osc. simple pendulum 10065.819^s							

In comparing the observations made at Fort Conger with those at Washington I shall make use of a figure of the earth which I have deduced from the totality of the experiments with Kater invariable pendulums down to and including the expedition of Mr. Edwin Smith. In this discussion I have ascertained by least squares that the correction for elevation is 0.00406^s.[2] The coefficient of $\sin^2\varphi$ is 225.94^s, and I have also introduced a term in $\sin^3\varphi - 3/5 \sin\varphi$, the coefficient of which is 1.22^s, this operating to increase the last effect at

2. Here, as elsewhere, by 1 second in such a connection I mean one unit in the fifth place of the common logarithm of gravity.

the north pole. According to this discussion gravity is in excess at Washington by + 0.76^s.

Inasmuch as it is certain that the pendulum underwent some alteration between its last swinging at Fort Conger and its swinging at Washington, but of such a nature that the distance between the knife-edges was not altered, we have to compare the periods of the pendulum at the two stations, reduced according to the principle of the reversible pendulum. This period for this pendulum is obtained by adding 8 in the seventh place of decimals to 3/2 the period of heavy end down, minus 1/2 the period of heavy end up. This gives, at Fort Conger, 1.0050578^s as the period of oscillation of the simple pendulum of the same length between the knife-edges. We now proceed as follows:

2 log. of period at Fort Conger	+ 0.0043821
Correction to equator	+ 0.0022174
Correction from equator and sea-level to Washington	– 0.0008904
– station error at Washington	– 76
– 2 log. period at Washington	– 0.0056982
– station error at Fort Conger	+ 0.0000033

It appears from this that gravity is slightly in deficiency at Fort Conger, by only –0.33^s; and since a careful scrutiny of these observations has fully convinced me that they are by far the best that ever have been made within the arctic circle, it is gratifying to find that they satisfy so well the figure already deduced by me, and that they go to confirm the reality of some small harmonic function of the third order, such as that which I have introduced.

MEMORANDUM BY THE OFFICER COMMANDING THE EXPEDITION

It only appears proper, in a matter of such importance to the scientific world as the pendulum observations of the Lady Franklin Bay Expedition, that its commanding officer should make some brief statements bearing on the opinions of Professor C. S. Peirce, which are believed to be erroneous. An opinion is expressed on pages 217–18, as follows: "This seems to have been due to a difference of cylindricity of the edges, combined with the effect of some accident to the pendulum." No accident in any way, shape, or manner, occurred to this pendulum. It was never handled by any one in reversion or suspension excepting by myself; so that I can speak with a personal and positive knowledge that the pendulum was never harmed while at Fort Conger. As soon as the series of observations was completed, the pendulum was carefully removed, wiped dry, and again soldered up in the original tin box.

The statement is also made, that "on abandonment of Fort Conger, the head upon which the pendulum had been supported in its oscillations (the bearings of the knife-edge forming part of it) was left behind." The metal piece referred to never was, in any way, shape, or manner, alluded to by either the Superintendent of the Coast Survey, the late Carlile P. Patterson, or Professor Peirce, as being of the slightest utility, and the instructions given me were to the effect that the only important part to be brought back was the pendulum, then soldered in a tin box. If the omission to bring back the plate has any bearing on these observations, as does not plainly appear from Professor Peirce's remarks, it is simply the fault of either the late Mr. Patterson or Professor Peirce himself.

Later the statement is made, "But, though there was little change in the length of the pendulum, it is evident it lost a large part of its mass." In the very next line it is admitted by Professor Peirce that the pendulum was not weighed at all in its finished state, and that the loss in adjustment, 4.6 grams, was calculated. Consequently the statement that "It (the pendulum) would seem to have lost from ten to fifteen grams, probably on the journey from Fort Conger to Camp Clay," rests on a surmise and an estimate. The pendulum was brought back to Camp Clay soldered in the original metal box, in which it was so carefully packed that no vibratory motion could occur in such manner as to cause loss of weight. The pendulum, although handled hundreds of times, was always treated with special consideration, as was also a box containing photographic negatives; and as an instance of the care exercised with these packages, may be mentioned the fact, that out of forty-eight glass negatives only four were fractured, although necessarily handled scores of times, under circumstances when a moment's delay apparently entailed a loss of boats and life.

It is possible, as suggested in the following Supplementary Report, that during the observations the screws holding one of the pendulum edges in place might have been loosened or tightened, and this seems very probable, as the wrong screw might easily have been touched under the extremely disadvantageous circumstances in connection with the swinging of the pendulum, which was done in an ice-house, where one's breath congealed the moment it left the mouth, and the darkness was broken simply by the light from a single candle so that the temperature of the pendulum might not be affected. On one occasion something of this kind undoubtedly occurred, for the pendulum was stopped after swinging a few minutes, as its arc of oscillation decreased so rapidly as to show conclusively that its vibrations would cease in about one-quarter of the usual time.

It seems but justice to the late Mr. Israel, the astronomer of the expedition, who had charge of the pendulum, both during our stay at Fort Conger and our retreat later, that these statements should be made. Besides, they may have a bearing in other scientific discussions of these observations and so be of a certain importance. It would not be just to those who consult these results to deprive them of the fullest and most complete information on this point. The commanding officer of the expedition has had too much experience with physical observations not to realize the importance of a full and free statement of all the facts in any case. He realizes clearly that accidents and mishaps may occur in any set of observations. While a full statement of such accidents and mishaps enables those discussing the observations to apply suitable corrections, on the other hand any misstatements or denials might result in misleading the zealous student of such observations.

It is admitted that the preliminary observations with this pendulum in Washington, under conditions left entirely to Professor Peirce, were practically failures, through whose fault I know not. To the embarrassments, discomforts, and privations which Mr. Israel and myself (the former very indifferently instructed in pendulum work, and myself without any definite verbal and no written instructions) experienced in making these observations should not be added the charge of having injured the pendulum (which was *never weighed in its finished state until after its return*) and caused a considerable loss of mass without adducing the clearest proof that such mass had been lost while in our possession. These statements of Professor Peirce have been maturely made after being assured by me that no injury came to the pendulum and that no such loss of mass was possible. I leave it to the scientific world to pass on this matter.

A. W. GREELY,
Late Commanding Lady Franklin Bay Expedition.

WASHINGTON, D. C., *July*, 1888.

Explanatory Note

Mr. Peirce, upon seeing the memorandum by General Greely on pages 243–244, desires to say that he is shocked to find that any words of his are construed as imputing blame—or, indeed, anything less than the highest honor—to General Greely or to Mr. Israel in regard to the treatment of the pendulum apparatus. He therefore asks leave to make the following corrections to his report:

Page 218, line 6, before the words "left behind" insert "very properly."

Page 220, at the end of the first paragraph, insert: It will be seen that I merely set forth the circumstantial evidence in favor of a loss of mass for what it is worth, while limiting myself to the conclusion stated in the first four lines of the second paragraph on page 242. Moreover, whatever may have been the nature of the alteration of the pendulum, I hold, as implied in the sentence on page 218, beginning "It seems almost inconceivable," etc., that it was absolutely unavoidable. Pendulums frequently undergo such changes under the most careful handling.

Mr. Peirce desires further to say that his report contains no kind of reflection upon the management of the Coast and Geodetic Survey, except that it does make a quite unavoidable protest against a certain derangement of apparatus under a former administration of the Survey. Mr. Peirce wishes to say as little as possible about a matter now past and gone; but he must not be understood to admit that the various surmises offered in defense of the act complained of are in accordance with the facts, nor that they would constitute a sufficient vindication even if they were so.

In regard to the many criticisms in this Appendix upon himself, Mr. Peirce will reply to them in another place. He has here only space to remark that the determination of gravity has been signally successful, and that the only doubt which affects the result, namely, that which relates to the temperature-correction, is destined to be resolved in due time by the means indicated toward the end of the middle paragraph on page 222.

31

Reflections on the Logic of Science

1–17 January 1889 ***Houghton Library***

Chapter I

Those who view the results of science from the outside, who judge from the telephone, the Brush and incandescent lights, instantaneous photography, the phonograph, etc., imagine that science is now making rapid strides; but those who are within the circle of research know better.

The truth is that the description of the properties of matter, so far as they can be directly observed, has been for some years, approximately speaking, and barring details and niceties, complete. Whoever will look through the *Beiblätter* to the *Annalen der Physik und Chemie,* which forms a compendious record of all that has been done in physics since 1875, will be impressed at once with the immense activity and skill of physicists during that period, and at the same time with the very little that they have accomplished. The truth is their task, so far as the description of what can be directly observed goes, is drawing, I will not say towards a close,—for with no limit to the number of substances to be examined and no limit to the accuracy demanded, the time required has obviously no limit,—but towards completion in this sense, that the importance of all that remains to be discovered is small as compared with what is known already.

But to ascertain, not merely empirical formulae connecting the quantities observed with the quantities fixed by the conditions of the experiments, but the real laws of their connection, to find the real coördinations between the properties of one body and those of another, to answer *why* a body which has certain properties should have certain others having no apparent relation to the former,—why, for example, the only element whose atomic weight is intermediate between that of the platinum metals and thallium should have all the properties of mercury,—and to apply all this undiscovered theory to the production of new practical results, and it may be of quite new phenomena, that is a further affair devolving upon the physicists and chemists, which has as yet been scarcely broached.

Let it not be said that these things are beyond the province of human science. It is a good maxim for a young man that in advance of a careful consideration of his situation, of having learned how far the limits of his forces and resources extend, and of having surveyed the obstacles in his path, he should no more fear to attempt anything as too ambitious than he should hope for any success however easy it may appear. Now what is a good rule for a young man is a good rule for science, for the human race is young yet, and has plenty of time before it. No predictions have turned out more unfortunate than predictions that this, that, and the other could never be discovered. Auguste Comte in one of his lectures had occasion to give an instance of a fact which should beyond all doubt lie beyond the possibility of discovery. In order to be quite sure, he gave the rein to his imagination, and pronounced that nobody could be so extravagant as to dream that man should ever learn the chemical constitution of the fixed stars. Yet the ink was scarcely dry upon the printed page, before the supposed impossibility was a fact. Legendre in his *Théorie des nombres,* after penetrating more deeply into the higher arithmetic, and after having studied the nature of mathematical proof more accurately than any man before him had ever done, gave it as his opinion that the demonstration of a certain proposition,—though the proposition itself seemed to be true,—was probably beyond the powers of the human mind. Yet the very next important book upon the subject published a few years later gave six proofs of this theorem, resting upon as many different principles.

It is, however, hardly worth while to discuss this somewhat metaphysical question; because powerful minds are now actively engaged upon these problems, and their solution might perhaps come before so large a discussion was closed. Let us rather limit ourselves to the more practical question of how far the existing equipment of physicists, in ideas, in methods of reasoning, and in means of observation are likely to serve them in the task before them.

That all matter such as we can see and touch is composed of molecules of some sort, of very minute parts more or less separated from one another and acting upon one another in ways very different from those in which large masses act, is fully acknowledged by all students of physics. Sir William Thomson himself, than whom no physicist is less wedded to existing theories, admits that all ordinary matter has a "grain" or "grained structure," as a proposition fully proved. Some chemists, accustomed to think that the arguments for the atomic theory are mainly drawn from their science, have called it in question; and I myself was one of them, before I had examined the evidences from general physics. But the arguments shall be examined in another chapter: here I provisionally assume the conclusion to be out of doubt.

If this be true, then it is plain that none of those further advances in physics which the world now awaits are possible until we more definitely ascertain what the nature of molecules is; and to that problem the higher work of physicists has long been directed.

Now the only method for studying the nature of molecules which is in the possession of physicists today is this. Gathering such hints as they may from striking phenomena, and resting upon analogies drawn from the behaviour of large masses, especially the heavenly bodies, they set up provisional hypotheses as to the attractions, motions, etc. of molecules; they then undertake to deduce mathematically from these hypotheses consequences other than those which led to their provisional adoption and yet capable of experimental verification or falsification; and finally they would propose to accept any theory which might resist the test of every imaginable experiment. Were such a theory only once met with, and being so treated were its consequences all found agreeable to observed fact, there could be no resisting the evidence of its truth. But how long will it probably take to determine the true theory in that way? This is the method by which Kepler discovered his three laws of planetary motion. In that case, the truth happened to depend on extremely simple laws, and consequently he only had to try about 20 different hypotheses before he lit on the right one. But it is impossible to doubt that the constitution of matter is far more complicated than that of the solar system; the thousands of different varieties of matter sufficiently show that, not to speak of other arguments. It is therefore not extravagant to guess that a million hypotheses may be drawn out of the grab-bag of possibility, before the single prize is had; nor is it extravagant to allow on the average a century for the mathematicians of the world to work out the consequences of each. There is, therefore, no particular reason to hope that the human race may live long enough to solve the problem in that way. But this consideration is not the worst. These hypotheses, according to the present haphazard way of framing them, all rest upon a supposed analogy between these molecules, so small that a powerful microscope can scarce make spaces equal to their mutual distances visible, and the vast bodies of the solar system, for they all make the molecules obey the three laws of mechanics whose exactitude is hardly beyond doubt even for ordinary terrestrial masses. For instance, one of the physical hypotheses which is now lying on the table of the mathematician awaiting his study when the mathematics may have made such progress as to encourage him to attack it, is the vortex-theory of molecules. This is quite as promising a supposition as any of those that are current concerning the constitution of matter, and has recommended itself above others to several of the most enlightened of the higher physicists of our day. The peculiarity of the hypothesis is that it explains molecules by analogies drawn not from ordinary rigid or elastic bodies but from fluids. Since fluids are less complex and organic than solids, the hypothesis is so much the simpler; it certainly would seem unnecessary to suppose the parts to have more complicated properties than the wholes they compose. One of the curious consequences which mathematicians have succeeded in deducing from the definition of a perfect fluid is that if any part of such a fluid has a rotational motion,—like an eddy in a stream or a smoke-ring in the air,—the particles which partake of this whirling motion will never cease to move in this way, unless the fluid be supposed viscous; and only by virtue of viscosity can such a motion ever be set up. The following propositions are also proved. 1. Every such vortex, or whirl, must have an axis, which is a line, generally curved, all along which the particles are rotating round it. 2. Every such axis must extend to the boundary of the fluid (like an eddy) or to infinity, or else return into itself, like the axis of a smoke ring. 3. As the motion goes on, such a vortex-axis may be elongated or contracted and distorted in almost any way; but it can never, in any of these movements, cut through itself, nor can two such vortices cut one another. The vortex-ring may have been knotted in any manner, from the first, or several of them may be interlaced; but none can *become* knotted nor unknotted, nor can two of them enlace nor unlace themselves. 4. Two vortex-rings attract or repel one another according to their positions. 5. In these actions, the reactions depend upon the ratio of the velocity or strengths of the two whirls, and these are indestructible. 6. A vortex-ring free from the attraction or repulsion of another moves forward along a straight line with a uniform velocity.

Now, the vortex-theory of matter is that each atom, or molecule, is a vortex-ring in a primordial ether, free from viscosity; so that the different chemical elements would correspond to the different kinds of knots and enlacements. That which specially merits attention just now is that according to this theory the three laws of mechanics,—that a particle moves uniformly in a straight line if left to itself; that the instantaneous effects of forces are accelerations; and that reactions depend on the ratio of the masses of the two bodies, these *masses* being unchangeable quantities,—these laws are explained as results of the hypothesis. Thus, the primordial ether being supposed homogeneous and incompressible, no such idea as mass or density would be introduced into the hydrodynamical discussion of its motions; but this idea, or an analogous one, would be evolved from the discussion. But if there be a primordial ether which is not itself what we call matter, but is only a something whose vortices are matter,—a supposition perfectly open to us,—what reason have we to ascribe to it any of the properties of matter, such, for example, as the three laws of mechanics describe? We may, no doubt, suppose that it has these or any other properties from which the phenomena observed can be deduced; but we are not at all limited to such suppositions. We may ascribe to it any other imaginable modes of action which may serve the purpose. In short, we are swimming in a boundless ocean of possibilities, and of this ocean only one individual drop contains the truth we seek. The whole existing method of framing mechanical theories of the constitution of matter is based on the assumption that the elementary particles which the theory supposes are strictly subject to the three laws of mechanics; and yet the vortex-theory is an illustration of how perfectly arbitrary such an assumption may be. The primordial ether, if there be any, may be subject to any laws. It is assumed that the instantaneous effect of a force upon one of its particles is to change the second fluxion of the position; but there is an infinite series of successive fluxions, and no antecedent reason whatever for preferring the second to any other for this purpose; so that the chance of our choosing the right one is as one to infinity, or as near the impossible as chance can come.

But not merely the laws of mechanics, even those of arithmetic itself fall away from under our feet in such a method of inquiry. The German mathematician G. Cantor has shown that the number of all whole numbers, multiplied into itself as many times as this number itself represents, and this operation performed the same number of times, and then all of this again repeated the same number of times, etc. will never amount to the number of points upon any line however short. Now he supposes that while the number of molecules of ordinary matter is infinite, in the former sense, that of molecules of luminiferous ether is infinite in the second sense. This is a perfectly open hypothesis; there is no reason why it should not be admitted to citizenship and equal rights in the great democracy of may-bes. Only, Cantor has limited far too much the varieties of infinity. He admits the proposition of Euclid that if there be two infinite series of rational numbers A_1, A_2, A_3, etc. and B_1, B_2, B_3 etc., the former continually increasing, the latter continually decreasing, and yet every one of the former smaller than every one of the latter, but so that, given any quantity, an A and a B can be found which differ by less than that quantity, then there can at most be but one quantity larger than all the A's and smaller than all the B's. But the so-called proof of this amounts to nothing, for it assumes that no quantity can be too small to be a "given" quantity, and without the word "given" or some equivalent the proposition cannot be stated. We must therefore admit along with Cantor's a limitless series of other similar hypotheses.

In short, suppose there to be one single grain in a whole elevator of wheat which it is desirable to find, and that the only way of finding it is to take grains at random and devote 50 or 100 years to the examination of each in order to ascertain whether it is the one sought, and the illustration is miserably inadequate to expressing the hopelessness of the existing method of physical speculation. Instead of wasting your time in that way, it would be better to spend your days in wandering about Wall Street in the hope of picking up gold pieces.

In lieu of the unsystematic speculation which has hitherto been practised, it will be necessary to resort to a method analogous to that Rule of False by which so many mathematical calculations are performed. When a computer has a complicated arithmetical problem,—say to solve a hundred equations between a hundred unknown quantities,—he begins by making such a guess at the solution as he can, finds how nearly this will satisfy all the conditions and tries successive corrections to the values assumed for the unknowns with a view to satisfying the equations better. But it is found that, even in arithmetic, the success of this proceeding depends greatly on the skill of the computer. In applying the same principle to the correction of molecular hypotheses, it will be necessary to make an elaborate study of the kind of effect which every possible element introduced into a hypothesis can produce.

This process of successive corrections to our hypotheses in general physics will be at best arduous and costly,—I mean as compared with other great works of the human race extending over centuries,—and its success must depend in great measure upon the original hypothesis selected for correction. The question arises, then, whether any of those which are now current are suitable for the purpose. I believe not. The difficulty with all of these hypotheses is that they assume some property of matter to be original, underived, and inexplicable. Thus, Mr. Herbert Spencer assumes this to be the case with the conservation of energy. Now, there cannot, from the nature of things, be a scintilla of evidence, not the faintest indication in phenomena, that either the conservation of energy or any other property of matter, is absolute, unchangeable, and underived. For inductive evidence is all there could be; but it will be shown in the next chapter, that inductive inference is incompetent to establish any proposition as absolute. This is, in fact, what Leibniz said: a necessary property cannot be known as such from experience. The assumption, then, that certain given properties of matter are ultimate and absolute, must be a purely arbitrary assumption, disproof of which may come to us at any time, but which there never can be now or in the future the slightest reason for believing true. Why should we base our whole theory of matter on such an idle surmise? The history of science shows that arbitrary suppositions have uniformly come to grief, as they might naturally be expected to do.

Indeed, I do not believe that anybody ever would have proposed an explanation of matter which began by assuming certain of its properties to be inexplicable, except that they could not conceive that an explanation could help being based on some fundamental law. From the hypothesis, A, they said, whatever that hypothesis may be, we are to show that the phenomena, C, necessarily result. This can be done if we grant a law of nature, according to which one thing necessarily results from another; but if we are allowed to assume nothing of the kind, how we are ever to explain anything, we cannot imagine.

Such has been the state of mind of the fabricator of suppositions. His inability to imagine how else to proceed, has blinded him to the grave and fatal objection to proceeding as he has done. He ought to have kept steadily before the eye of reason both the inability and the objection; and then he would have seen that his first business was to overcome that inability, and that till that was done it was idle to make hypotheses.

He did not, however, use the phrase "I cannot imagine that another kind of explanation should be possible," but "it is evident that no other kind of explanation is possible." Has it not been remarked, that that alone is *evident* which is plainly *seen* to be true; so that, impossibilities, not belonging to the category of things seen, cannot be *evident.* Calling propositions *evident* is only a way of accepting them without evidence. To this we shall return in another chapter.

The purpose of this book is

1. To inquire by what sort of hypothesis we can imagine the phenomena of matter to be explained without the assumption of any absolute and inexplicable law.
2. To inquire in what manner we ought to proceed to frame an initial hypothesis of that kind for subsequent correction.
3. To inquire what will be the general cast of philosophy in its other branches which will harmonize with this philosophy of physics.

Now, how shall we commence the first inquiry, the inquiry which is to teach us to imagine something which we cannot imagine at the outset. We will use the way of experience. We will examine other cases in which we have learned to imagine what we could not at first imagine, in which the "evident" has become inevident; and we will see how we learned in those cases, and try whether we cannot learn in the same way in this case.

Chapter II *[First Version]*. The Doctrine of Chances

I am tempted to recognize for the calculus of probability the title of the logic of modern science. Taking its rise with Galileo and Pascal, it has constantly grown in scientific importance until now in the exacter branches of physics the statement of a value generally carries with it an estimate of the probable error of the evaluation.

Thus, taking the first book at hand of Geodesy I read that __________ determined the difference of longitude between __________ & __________ to be __________ ± __________. This ± __________ signifies that they consider it as likely as not that their number departs by __________ from the truth in excess or in defect. If a physicist has to estimate the strength of any argument, he resorts to the calculus of probability as the only method whose validity he will acknowledge.

Thus it would seem that all that the old rules of syllogistic were supposed to do, the calculation of chances really does.

Nevertheless, we must not forget that there is a great part of reasoning which has nothing to do with probability,—I mean necessary reasoning. For this kind of inference, the logic of modern science is mathematics. The doctrine of chances is no more a *branch* of mathematics than is mechanics or thermodynamics. It is treated by an application of mathematics; but all the mathematician's reasoning in probabilities is as strictly necessary as in geometry itself. It is true, too, that a mathematician in his researches may make use of probable reasonings, provisionally; but that will be a mere scaffolding, useful in erecting his doctrine, but intended to be knocked away when all is complete; while in the positive sciences probabilities remain probabilities forever, and mathematical demonstration is unattainable.

Mathematics, on the one hand, then, and probabilities, on the other, are two distinct branches of the logic of science. It is important to apprehend clearly the gulf which separates these two arts. The reasonings and conclusions of the mathematician do not in the least depend upon there being in the real world any such objects as those which he supposes. The devoted mathematician cares little for the real world. He lives in a world of ideas; and his heart vibrates to the saying of his brother Plato that actuality is the roof of a dark and sordid cave which shuts out from our direct view the splendors and beauties of the vast and more truly real world,—the world of forms beyond. A great mathematician of our day said with gustful emphasis: "A great satisfaction in the study of the theory of numbers is that it never has been, and never can be, prostituted to any practical application whatever."

In such a noumenal world, there is no room for probability. For what is probability? It is primarily an attribute of an argument or inference belonging to a class of inferences which from true premises sometimes lead to true and sometimes to false conclusions. The probability of the inference is the ratio of true conclusions to all the conclusions which would be drawn in the long run from true premises by inferences of the same kind. Probability is therefore essentially based on the existence of a *statistical average,* by which I mean a ratio between the number of objects of one class and the number of connected objects of another class, according to their actual occurrence in the long run; and the doctrine of chances may advantageously be extended so as to embrace the entire theory of *statistical averages*. Such *averages* have nothing to do with the essences or forms of things, but merely with frequencies of different kinds of actual occurrences in nature. Thus, probability has as little concern with the ideal world as mathematics has with the actual world.

There is no need of enlarging upon the great importance of statistics and statistical averages; for it is universally felt and acknowledged. To this unanimity the works of Quetelet have contributed the most. When one rises from their perusal, he is impressed that between any two classes of connected objects there must subsist a statistical ratio. Quetelet and his followers seem to think it a mere mathematical truism to say, for example, that every species of animal, at least under given conditions, must have an average length of life, that the stars must have an average direction and distance of proper motion, and that at any kind of game there must be an average loss or gain. But the existence of an average is not in truth a matter of mathematical necessity but of observed fact; and the general prevalence of such averages in nature, which renders the application of probable reasoning possible, may fairly be reckoned as the first in importance of the Laws of Nature.

To show this, let us begin with the case of a game. Two men, A and B, toss up a coin until heads turns up, when the game ends. Thereupon, if n is the number of times the coin was tossed up, one player pays the other 2^n dollars; only, if n is odd, it is A who pays B, while if n is even, it is B who pays A. What will be the average loss of A? Let g be the number of games played, which must be assumed infinite. Then, the following table gives the items of the calculation.

Value of n	Number of games when it has this value	Loss of A per game	Total loss of A from games where n has this value
1	½ g	\$2	g × \$1
2	¼ g	–\$4	– g × \$1
3	⅛ g	+\$8	+ g × \$1
4	1/16 g	–\$16	– g × \$1
5	1/32 g	+\$32	+ g × \$1
etc.	etc.	etc.	etc.

Then the total loss of A will be represented by the infinite series

$$\$g - \$g + \$g - \$g + \$g - \text{etc.}$$

and the average loss per game will be this divided by g, or

$$\$1 - \$1 + \$1 - \$1 + \$1 - \text{etc.}$$

But this series carried to infinity has no definite value. It is what the mathematicians call a divergent series. No matter how far the play might be carried, there would never be any approximation to an average gain or loss, but simply continual fluctuations. If instead of the gain or loss being 2^n dollars, they had been by the rules of the game

3^n dollars, these fluctuations would have a tendency to become greater and greater without limit as the number of games played was increased.

In like manner, *[ ]*

Chapter II *[Second Version]*. Mathematics
Arithmetic

We have, then, to make a survey of all the resources of the Natural Philosopher. The first of these is mathematics, by which alone the consequences of a physical hypothesis can be deduced.

What is mathematics? It is the ideal construction of "ensembles" (that is, wholes or systems) and the discovery in them of relations other than those which served for the rule of construction. "Mathematics is the science which draws necessary conclusions" (Benjamin Peirce, *Linear Associative Algebra*, §1). The reader exclaims: I thought logic was the art of reasoning, and mathematics the science of quantity. That mathematics is not the science of quantity has long been agreed. Indeed, that definition is an example of the numerous class of consecrated phrases, which having gained credence in one sense, have lost their original meaning without losing popular acknowledgment. What was originally meant was that mathematics was the science of *quanta*,—or those things which Aristotle placed under the predicament of How much? After Aristotle's predicaments had been exploded, the phrase remained, no longer meaning the science of things that are so much, but the science of the muchness of things. An ancient Greek geometer would have rejected this last definition, because he was familiar with the fact that a large part of geometry, though dealing with points, lines, and surfaces, which were called *quanta*, yet had nothing to do with the measures of those elements. The fact is still more clear now. Through any point draw three unlimited straight lines, a, b, c. Take any point on each of these lines, and through pairs of these points, draw three more unlimited straight lines, l, m, n. Take another point on each of the three lines, a, b, c, and through pairs of them draw three more unlimited straight lines, l', m', n'. Then the intersections of l and l', of m and m', and of n and n', will all lie on one straight line. As Sylvester says:— "It seems to me absurd to suppose that there exists in the science of pure logic anything which bears a resemblance to the infinitely developable and interminable heuristic processes of mathematical science." Logic ought, I agree, to be or to include, the art of reasoning; but those who have written about it have been, almost all, mere children in that art; while all the really difficult and accurate reasonings *of the necessary kind* have been performed by mathematicians at their proper work.

How far this reasoning includes the whole business of the mathematician the reader will judge after I have described what that business is as the mathematician himself understands it.

The mathematician lives in another world from the rest of us, in a world of pure forms. Here he is domiciled and spends part of his time; but he is a mere sojourner; this is not the world that he knows or that he cares for. If you tell him that something in the world of mathematical forms corresponds to something in the real world, be cautious not to speak as if such a correspondence could impart any value to the mathematical object, or he may consider you impertinent. Of what consequence is reality to him? That passage of the mathematician, Plato, strikes a sympathetic chord in every mathematician's breast where he says that these heavens and earth we gaze upon are but the walls and floor of a dismal cavern which shut out from our direct view the glories of the world of forms beyond. Gauss, the acknowledged chief of the mathematicians of our century, said of the Theory of Numbers, his favorite study, that it was a great satisfaction to think that it never had been, and never *could* be prostituted to any practical application whatever. Yet what would steam-engines, electric cables, turbine wheels, life-insurance, and a thousand things be but for the hints which mathematicians have vouchsafed?

The mathematician begins his work by making a diagram or scheme. Sometimes, it is something which can be drawn on paper; sometimes it cannot be adequately drawn. Sometimes it can be held steadily before the mind's eye, and sometimes it cannot be adequately represented even to the imagination. But in every case the different parts are matters that can be schematically seen and drawn. Some reader will immediately dispute this and say that a geometrical line, since it has no breadth, cannot be drawn. But this is a misunderstanding. It cannot be exactly drawn, but it can be schematically drawn. A diagram or scheme is a figure whose parts are connected according to a prescription or rule; and any figure whose parts are so connected is as good as any other, except that that one is preferable which makes the prescribed connections most prominent, and features not prescribed the least prominent. Allow me to call the mathematician's diagram or scheme an *icon*. Then, an *icon* is a mere figure of connected units; and just as the number 3 is equally well shown by ∴ or ≡, so a triangle is as well shown by as by the finest drawing. Perhaps it is still better shown by

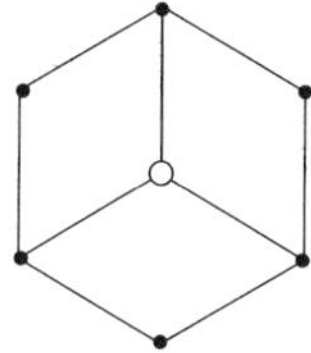

Here the dots connected with the little circle represent points, the other dots lines. Again, the triangle may be represented as in trigonometry by A, B, C, a, b, c, where the capitals are points, the small letters lines, and where each large letter is connected with every small one except that which corresponds to it and *vice versa*.

32

Note on the Analytical Representation of Space as a Section of a Higher Dimensional Space

17–25 January 1889 ***Houghton Library***

With the three coordinates, x, y, z, of a point in space, let a fourth meaningless variable, u, be associated. Then, any pair of equations linear in x, y, z, u, will, after the elimination of u, determine a plane. Any 3 such equations, taken in pairs, will determine 3 coaxal planes, the axis being determined by all three equations. Any 4 such equations, taken in pairs, will determine 6 planes passing in threes through 4 lines meeting in one point, determined by all four equations together. Any 5 such equations, taken in pairs, will determine 10 planes, passing in threes through 10 lines, and in fours through 5 points. So far, we have nothing recognizable as a proposition. But if none of the equations contain u, from any pair of them z may be eliminated. Thus, any 2 equations will determine a line in a plane, and any 3 a point in the plane. Any 5 equations, then, will determine 10 lines passing in threes through 10 points. Thus, $A = 0$ $B = 0$ $C = 0$, may be so taken as to represent in pairs any three concurrent lines. The two independent constants of a fourth equation, $D = 0$, may be so determined that

$$A = 0 \quad B = 0 \quad D = 0,$$
$$A = 0 \quad C = 0 \quad D = 0,$$
$$B = 0 \quad C = 0 \quad D = 0,$$

may represent any three points on the three lines $A = 0$ $B = 0$, $A = 0$ $C = 0$, and $B = 0$ $C = 0$. The same will be the case with a fifth equation E = 0. But the lines A = 0 D = 0 and A = 0 E = 0 will meet in the point A = 0 D = 0 E = 0; the lines B = 0 D = 0 and B = 0 E = 0 will meet in the point B = 0 D = 0 E = 0, and the lines C = 0 D = 0 and C = 0 E = 0 will meet in the point C = 0 D = 0 E = 0. These three points

A = 0 D = 0 E = 0,
B = 0 D = 0 E = 0,
C = 0 D = 0 E = 0,

lie all on the line D = 0 E = 0. Thus, we demonstrate an elementary proposition in projective geometry, substantially after von Staudt.

Returning to space of three dimensions, any 6 equations, taken in pairs, represent 15 planes passing in threes through 20 lines and in fours through 15 points. Hence, if 4 lines be drawn through a point, and 2 tetrahedra be formed having each a vertex on each of those 4 lines, corresponding faces of the two tetrahedra will intersect in 4 coplanar lines. The planes will be

Through the first point	6
Faces of the tetrahedra	8
New plane	1
	15

The lines will be

Through the first point	4
Edges of the tetrahedra	12
In the new plane	4
	20

The points will be

The first point	1
Vertices of the tetrahedra	8
In the new plane	6
	15

In two dimensions, the same 6 equations give the proposition that if through any point, 3 lines *a, b, c,* be drawn, and upon each of these 3 points be assumed,

on *a*, the points	A, A′, A″,
on *b*,	B, B′, B″,
on *c*,	C, C′, C″,

then the three lines through the intersections of AB and A′B′ and of AC and A′C′, through the intersections of AB and A″B″ and of AC and A″C″, and through the intersections of A′B′ and A″B″ and of A′C′ and A″C″, will all meet in 1 point. *[. . .]*

Returning to space of three dimensions, any 7 equations, taken in pairs, determine 21 planes passing in threes through 35 lines and in fours through 35 points. This gives the proposition that if 4 lines be drawn through a point and 3 tetrahedra have their vertices severally on these lines, the 3 planes in which lie intersections of pairs of corresponding faces of the tetrahedra are coaxal.

The same 7 equations in two dimensions represent 21 lines passing in threes through 35 points. This gives the proposition that if 4 triangles have their vertices on 3 concurrent lines, then the 6 lines on which corresponding sides of the triangles intersect meet by threes in 4 points.

Returning to three dimensions, suppose we associate a fifth variable v with x, y, z, u. Then 3 equations linear in x, y, z, u, v will, by the elimination of u and v, determine a plane. 7 equations will then represent 35 planes passing by fours through 35 lines and by fives through 21 points. This will only give the reciprocal of the last proposition in three dimensions.

In two dimensions, if z does not occur in the equations, any 3 equations will represent a line in the plane. Thus 7 equations will represent 35 lines passing by fours through 35 points.

33
Ordinal Geometry

19 January 1889 ***Houghton Library***

By ordinal geometry, I mean the theory of the arrangements of segments.

I make use of the notation of the algebra of logic. If a denotes a part of the line, plane, or solid considered, $\bar{a}$ denotes the complementary part. "Qualification" is the respect in which a and $\bar{a}$ differ. To change the qualification of a letter is to "requalify" it. The expression $a \prec b$ means a is included in b. The product of two segments is their common part. The sum includes all that is included in either. A fraction, as $\frac{a}{\bar{b}}$, is equal at once to a and to $a\bar{b}$, implying that $a \prec \bar{b}$.

In ordinal geometry, it is best to use no fiction in respect to passing through infinity, whether that of projective geometry or that of the theory of functions.

Ordinal geometry on a line

A point, A, put upon a line separates it into two segments a and $\bar{a}$. A second point, B, put upon the line separates it, irrespective of A, into two segments b and $\bar{b}$. As it is a mere matter of designation which is considered as the positive and which the negative side of a point, it will be best to assume that towards infinity in one direction is the positive side of all points. The following rules are self-evident for all dimensions:

Rule 1. In passing from one segment to a bounding segment, one letter only is requalified.

Rule 2. In passing along a line through segments made by flat secants each letter is requalified once and once only.

Hence, in the case of two points on the line, the succession of segments is either

$$ab, \quad \bar{a}b, \quad \bar{a}\bar{b},$$

or

$$ab, \quad a\bar{b}, \quad \bar{a}\bar{b};$$

and these arrangements are essentially the same since the symbols for one are converted into those for the other by a mere change of lettering.

For any higher number of points, beginning with the segment $abcd$ etc., the others in succession are obtained by successively requalifying the different letters, until $\bar{a}\bar{b}\bar{c}\bar{d}$ etc. is reached. Thus, the number of segments is one more than that of the letters.

Plane ordinal geometry

A line drawn in the plane separates it into two regions. A second line cuts the first and thus penetrates both regions and adds two regions; and so on successively, the nth line adding n to the number of regions. Hence, the total number of regions is $\frac{1}{2}(n^2 + n) + 1$, of which $2n$ are infinite, leaving $\frac{1}{2}(n^2 - 3n) + 1$ limited. The total number of segments of lines is n^2, of which $2n$ are infinite, leaving $n^2 - 2n$ finite; and that of points of intersection is $\frac{1}{2}(n^2 - n)$. Of course, coincidences are not now considered.

The following rule is self-evident:

Rule 3. In passing along infinity in a plane which is separated by unlimited curves, we pass from the region $\alpha\beta\gamma\delta$ etc. by successive requalifications of single letters, just as in a line separated by points, until we reach $\bar{\alpha}\bar{\beta}\bar{\gamma}\bar{\delta}$ etc. when we pass by new requalifications of the letters in the same order as before back to $\alpha\beta\gamma\delta$ etc.

The secant lines may be assumed to be so lettered that these requalifications take place in alphabetical order.

A single line, a, divides the plane into two regions α and $\bar{\alpha}$, which are unilateral. A second line, b, gives as the succession of regions round infinity $\alpha\beta$, $\alpha\bar{\beta}$, $\bar{\alpha}\bar{\beta}$, $\bar{\alpha}\beta$; these are all the regions and are bilateral. A third line gives for the succession of regions round infinity $\alpha\beta\gamma$, $\alpha\beta\bar{\gamma}$, $\alpha\bar{\beta}\bar{\gamma}$, $\bar{\alpha}\bar{\beta}\bar{\gamma}$, $\bar{\alpha}\bar{\beta}\gamma$, $\bar{\alpha}\beta\gamma$. But let us consider the succession in which the regions $\alpha\beta$, $\alpha\bar{\beta}$, $\bar{\alpha}\bar{\beta}$, $\bar{\alpha}\beta$ are penetrated by the third line. We see that it appears in the region $\alpha\beta$; for we have both regions $\alpha\beta\gamma$ and $\alpha\beta\bar{\gamma}$. The succession of regions which it penetrates may, therefore, be

$$\alpha\beta, \quad \alpha\bar{\beta}, \quad \bar{\alpha}\bar{\beta}$$

or

$$\alpha\beta, \quad \bar{\alpha}\beta, \quad \bar{\alpha}\bar{\beta}\,.$$

These two cases are converted into one another by a mere change of lettering; we may therefore assume the latter to be the case. Then $\alpha\bar{\beta}$ is not penetrated by γ and we have the region $\alpha\bar{\beta}\bar{\gamma} = \dfrac{\alpha\bar{\beta}}{\bar{\gamma}}$, or $\alpha\bar{\beta} \prec \bar{\gamma}$. It follows by the rule of contraposition in logic that $\gamma\alpha \prec \beta$ or $\gamma\alpha\beta = \dfrac{\gamma\alpha}{\beta}$ and $\beta\bar{\gamma} \prec \bar{\alpha}$ or $\bar{\beta}\gamma\bar{\alpha} = \dfrac{\bar{\beta}\gamma}{\bar{\alpha}}$. Thus, the succession of regions round infinity is

$$\frac{\gamma\alpha}{\beta}, \;\; \beta\bar{\gamma}\alpha, \;\; \frac{\alpha\bar{\beta}}{\bar{\gamma}}, \;\; \bar{\gamma}\bar{\alpha}\bar{\beta}, \;\; \frac{\bar{\beta}\gamma}{\bar{\alpha}}, \;\; \bar{\alpha}\beta\gamma.$$

A fraction may be said to be reduced to the utmost when it is put into the form which contains the smallest number of letters in the numerator. Then, since every fraction equals its numerator, we have the following rule:—

Rule 4. When a fraction denoting a region by means of letters referring to the sides of single secants is reduced to the utmost, the number of letters in the numerator equals the number of secants bounding the region it denotes.

We, thus, see that in the case of 3 lines, the regions round infinity are alternately bilateral and trilateral. Since the third line penetrates the region $\bar{\alpha}\beta$, we have the regions $\bar{\alpha}\beta\gamma$ and $\bar{\alpha}\beta\bar{\gamma}$. The former extends to infinity, as we have seen. But the latter $\bar{\alpha}\beta\bar{\gamma}$ is a finite trilateral or triangle. If we desire by the succession of the letters in each symbol for a region extending to infinity to show the order of the bounding lines, we have only to observe that the letters which are requalified in passing from this region to the next on the two sides along infinity are necessarily the boundaries extending to infinity. We thus finally write

$$\frac{\alpha\gamma}{\beta}, \;\; \bar{\gamma}\alpha\beta, \;\; \frac{\bar{\beta}\alpha}{\bar{\gamma}}, \;\; \bar{\alpha}\bar{\beta}\bar{\gamma}, \;\; \frac{\gamma\bar{\beta}}{\bar{\alpha}}, \;\; \beta\gamma\bar{\alpha}.$$

In the case of four lines, the fourth (according to our convention) first appears in the region $\frac{\alpha\gamma}{\beta}$. From that, it may pass to either of the trilateral regions $\bar{\gamma}\alpha\beta$ or $\beta\gamma\bar{\alpha}$. As these are precisely alike, suppose the former. From $\bar{\gamma}\alpha\beta$, it may pass to $\bar{\gamma}\bar{\alpha}\beta$, which is the triangle, or to $\frac{\bar{\beta}\alpha}{\bar{\gamma}}$. In the former case, the succession of regions penetrated is

$$\frac{\alpha\gamma}{\beta}, \quad \bar{\gamma}\alpha\beta, \quad \bar{\gamma}\bar{\alpha}\beta, \quad \bar{\alpha}\bar{\beta}\bar{\gamma}.$$

The unpenetrated regions are $\frac{\bar{\beta}\alpha}{\bar{\gamma}}$, $\frac{\gamma\bar{\beta}}{\bar{\alpha}}$, and $\beta\gamma\bar{\alpha}$. Two of these are adjacent; for from $\frac{\gamma\bar{\beta}}{\bar{\alpha}}$ we pass to $\beta\gamma\bar{\alpha}$ by a single requalification. But from $\frac{\bar{\beta}\alpha}{\bar{\gamma}}$ we pass only to $\bar{\gamma}\alpha\beta$ and to $\bar{\alpha}\bar{\beta}\bar{\gamma}$; so that this is on the other side of the fourth line. The regions round infinity are

$$\frac{\alpha\gamma}{\beta}\delta, \quad \frac{\alpha\gamma}{\beta}\bar{\delta}, \quad \bar{\gamma}\alpha\beta\bar{\delta}, \quad \frac{\bar{\beta}\alpha}{\bar{\gamma}}\bar{\delta}, \quad \bar{\alpha}\bar{\beta}\bar{\gamma}\bar{\delta}, \quad \bar{\alpha}\bar{\beta}\bar{\gamma}\delta, \quad \frac{\gamma\bar{\beta}}{\bar{\alpha}}\delta, \quad \beta\gamma\bar{\alpha}\delta.$$

Comparing these with the unpenetrated regions we see that all the regions are

$$\frac{\alpha\gamma}{\beta}\delta, \quad \frac{\alpha\gamma}{\beta}\bar{\delta}, \quad \bar{\gamma}\alpha\beta\delta, \quad \bar{\gamma}\alpha\beta\bar{\delta}, \quad \bar{\gamma}\bar{\alpha}\beta\delta, \quad \bar{\gamma}\bar{\alpha}\beta\bar{\delta}, \quad \bar{\alpha}\bar{\beta}\bar{\gamma}\delta,$$

$$\bar{\alpha}\bar{\beta}\bar{\gamma}\bar{\delta}, \quad \frac{\bar{\beta}\alpha}{\bar{\gamma}\bar{\delta}}, \quad \frac{\gamma\bar{\beta}}{\bar{\alpha}\delta}, \quad \frac{\beta\gamma\bar{\alpha}}{\delta}.$$

The last three symbols show us that

$$\bar{\beta}\alpha \prec \bar{\delta} \quad \gamma\bar{\beta} \prec \delta \quad \beta\gamma\bar{\alpha} \prec \delta,$$

which give by contraposition

$$\alpha\delta \prec \beta \quad \bar{\beta}\delta \prec \bar{\alpha}$$

$$\gamma\bar{\delta} \prec \beta \quad \bar{\beta}\bar{\delta} \prec \bar{\gamma}$$

$$\gamma\bar{\delta} \prec \alpha \quad \bar{\alpha}\bar{\delta} \prec \bar{\gamma}.$$

These propositions reduce the symbols to

$\frac{\alpha\gamma\delta}{\beta}$, $\frac{\gamma\bar{\delta}}{\alpha\beta}$, $\frac{\bar{\gamma}\alpha\delta}{\beta}$, $\bar{\gamma}\alpha\beta\bar{\delta}$, $\bar{\gamma}\bar{\alpha}\beta\delta$, $\frac{\bar{\alpha}\beta\bar{\delta}}{\bar{\gamma}}$, $\frac{\bar{\beta}\bar{\gamma}\delta}{\bar{\alpha}}$, $\frac{\bar{\alpha}\bar{\beta}\bar{\delta}}{\bar{\gamma}}$, $\frac{\bar{\beta}\alpha}{\bar{\gamma}\bar{\bar{\delta}}}$, $\frac{\gamma\bar{\beta}}{\bar{\alpha}\delta}$, $\frac{\beta\gamma\bar{\alpha}}{\delta}$.
We see that there are 3 bilateral, 6 trilateral, and 2 quadrilateral regions.

In the second case, the succession of regions penetrated is $\frac{\alpha\gamma}{\beta}$, $\bar{\gamma}\alpha\beta$, $\frac{\bar{\beta}\alpha}{\bar{\gamma}}$, $\bar{\alpha}\bar{\beta}\bar{\gamma}$. The unpenetrated regions are $\bar{\gamma}\bar{\alpha}\beta$, $\frac{\gamma\bar{\beta}}{\bar{\alpha}}$, and $\beta\gamma\bar{\alpha}$. These regions lie together, for we can pass from $\beta\gamma\bar{\alpha}$ to either of the others by a single requalification. But if we interchange β and δ, α and $\bar{\alpha}$, we get the last case.

Of the two quadrilaterals, $\bar{\gamma}\bar{\alpha}\beta\bar{\delta}$ is finite, and of the 6 trilaterals, $\frac{\bar{\alpha}\beta\bar{\delta}}{\bar{\gamma}}$ and $\frac{\bar{\gamma}\alpha\delta}{\beta}$ are finite, as the symbols immediately show.

As to the order of the letters, the fourth line separates $\frac{\alpha\gamma}{\beta}$ into $\frac{\bar{\delta}\gamma}{\alpha\beta}$ and $\frac{\alpha\gamma\delta}{\beta}$; it separates $\bar{\gamma}\alpha\beta$ into $\bar{\gamma}\bar{\delta}\alpha\beta$ and $\frac{\bar{\gamma}\alpha\delta}{\beta}$; it separates $\bar{\alpha}\beta\bar{\gamma}$ into $\frac{\bar{\alpha}\beta\bar{\delta}}{\bar{\gamma}}$ and $\bar{\alpha}\delta\beta\bar{\gamma}$; and it separates $\bar{\alpha}\bar{\beta}\bar{\gamma}$ into $\frac{\bar{\alpha}\bar{\beta}\bar{\delta}}{\bar{\gamma}}$ and $\frac{\delta\bar{\beta}\bar{\gamma}}{\bar{\alpha}}$.

34

[Mathematical Monads]

23 January 1889 ***Houghton Library***

As the mathematics are now understood, each branch,—or, if you please, each problem,—is but the study of the relations of a collection of connected objects, without parts, without any distinctive characters, except their names or designating letters. These objects are commonly called *points;* but to remove all notion of space relations, it may be better to name them *monads.* The relations between these points are mere complications of two different kinds of elementary relations, which may be termed immediate connection and immediate non-connection. All the monads except such as serve as intermediaries for the connections have distinctive designations.

As an example of such a collection of monads, I will describe one of the simplest, that of the Boolian algebra of logic. Here, the single letters signify statements; but what they signify is nothing to the mathematician. For him, they are so many points or monads denoted by different letters. Statements have in logic to be compared, and consequently taken in pairs. Every such pair is for the mathematician a new monad. Thus, every two monads denoted by letters are connected with a third monad which is connected with no other lettered monads than them. These new monads may be termed the monads of the second order. A pair of statements may be taken conjunctively or disjunctively; for example, "It lightens *and* it thunders," is conjunctive, "It lightens *or* it thunders" is disjunctive. Each such individual act of connecting a pair of statements is a new monad for the mathematician. That is, he conceives each monad of the second order to be connected with two new monads, which we may call monads of the third order. Each monad of the third order is connected with one monad of the second order and with only one. But the mathematician has to recognize the distinction in kind between conjunction and disjunction. For this purpose he takes two new monads, which he names severally "conjunction" and "disjunction" and collectively the *modes of operation;* and of the two monads of the third order which are connected with a monad of the second order, one he connects with the monad "conjunction," while the other he connects with the monad "disjunction." But each conjunction and disjunction of statements is itself a statement; so that every monad of the third order is, as it were, a lettered or letterable monad. To take account of this, the mathematician devotes an algebraical sign, ×, to conjunction, and another, +, to disjunction. He then takes a new monad for every such expression as $a+b$, $c \times d$, and these monads he conceives to be comprehended under the class of lettered monads, but each of these is connected with a monad of the third order. Thus, every monad of the third order is immediately connected with just one lettered monad, and no lettered monad is immediately connected with more than one of the third order. But the lettered monads with which we set out are not connected with monads of the third order. Those which are so connected make a second batch of lettered monads, infinite in number.

Now, every statement is either true or false, and none is both true and false. To take account of this, the mathematician takes two new monads, which he respectively names Truth and Falsehood, and collectively, the *values.* He connects Truth with disjunction and Falsehood with conjunction. Every lettered monad is connected with one of these and not with the other. Every lettered monad of the second batch which is connected through a monad of the third order, and then one of the second order, with two lettered monads which are connected with one and the same value, is itself connected with that same value. But when these two lettered monads are of different values, the first monad (of the second batch) is connected with that value which is connected with that monad "mode of operation" which is connected with that monad of the third order with which this first monad is connected.

The scheme of the mathematician is now complete. Here, for example, is a bit of it in graphical form.

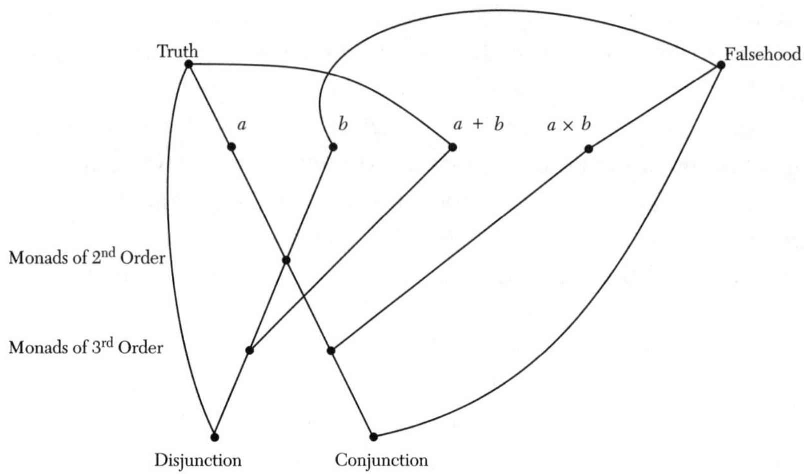

But now suppose that the following problem is proposed: To enumerate all the ways in which one statement implies the truth of another. The mathematician at once sees that his scheme has to be modified to meet this question. Instead of truth and falsehood, he has now to deal with the known and unknown, and with assertion and denial, and questions. He doubles the lettered monads by placing beside each another, its denial. He takes two new monads which he names assertion and denial, and joins all the old lettered monads to assertion, all the new to denial. Each pair consisting of an assertion or denial is also to be joined to a new monad, which is a question. He also takes a new monad, the known, and this is joined to all statements which are known to be true.

35

Review of Stock's *Deductive Logic*

15 August 1889 ***The Nation***

Deductive Logic. By St. George Stock, M.A. Longmans, Green & Co., 1889. Pp. 356.

One of the author's friends who looked over this book in manuscript advised him not to publish it because it was too like all other Logics; another advised him to cut out a considerable amount of new matter. We cannot help being of the opinion that both of these friends were persons of a great deal of wisdom. In spite of the fact that the latter advice was followed, a good part of the new matter which is retained is, as we shall presently show, erroneous, and the old matter is, to say the least, not better set forth than in several other text-books which we could name.

This is not saying that it is not, at many points, fresh and admirably expressed and fully mastered by good sense. It would be impossible for a man who has been studying and teaching logic at Oxford for seventeen years to write a thoroughly bad book on the subject. It is merely saying that the teacher who should decide to adopt this book in his class-room instead of Bain, for instance, would be doing his pupils an injury. The trouble which the student usually has with his book on Logic is that it seems to him too much like a mixture of dry bones and sawdust. The best exposition of the subject is one which forces him, at every step, to see that there is an intimate connection between its formal rules and the trains of thought which actually go on in his own mind. Mill is still the only book for "the gentleman and the scholar" to read; but, for the young person who must be put quickly through the drill established by the schoolmen, and who must at the same time see that it has a close bearing upon the present perplexities of the scientific man and the practical thinker, hardly anything is so good as Bain. Bain, it is true, is open to plenty of objections of another kind; and there is no subject in which there is more urgent need of a new book which shall embody the recent improvements in the science, and which shall at the same time exhibit a kindly consideration for the weaknesses of immature minds.

Mr. Stock, as far as appears from his book, is wholly unacquainted with Symbolic Logic. That is a subject which throws so much light on logical theory that a brief treatment of it ought to be introduced into every text-book; but even if that is not done, no one who writes a book should be content to be ignorant of it. The conventions which Symbolic Logic finds absolutely essential are a source of very great simplicity and consistency in ordinary Logic. Mr. Stock does not mention Venn among the writers who have helped him, and he can hardly have read his persuasive plea for the thoroughgoing introduction of De Morgan's idea of a limited universe, and of the convention that particular propositions must imply the existence of terms, and universal must not. With this convention, it is true that we must "accept the awkward corollary" of the collapse of the time-honored jingle about opposition; but worse things than that have been lived through. If it has been shown that black swans are not found in Africa, and that they are not found anywhere else, what follows in real life is that there are no black swans; but what the old-fashioned logician wishes us to believe is that one or other of the two statements must be false. It is evident that the former is the more reasonable conclusion.

Mr. Stock calls the statement "If *a* is *b*, *c* is *d*" a complex proposition. It should be called a compound proposition, that is, a proposition about propositions, or, better still, a sequence. The term complex proposition is needed for such as have subjects or predicates that are to be broken up in the course of the reasoning, as when we infer from the statement, "Citizen-students are always revolutionists," the other statement, "All students are revolutionists, or else they are not citizens." The three things which logic considers would then be the concept, the judgment and the sequence, the last being defined to be the statement that one proposition *follows* from another or from several others, either logically (that is, as inference), or materially (that is, as matter of fact).[1]

Mr. Stock's introduction, on the whole, is good, though a more psychological account of the concept might have been given; and good, also, is his treatment of extension and intension. But he has a curious idea of what constitutes induction. The concluding from "All the metals which we have examined are fusible" to "All metals are fusible," he gives as an example of what induction is not, and then he argues that it is a mistake to talk of inductive reasoning as though it were a species distinct from deductive. The above kind of reasoning he stigmatizes as a "vague instinct," but he forgets that before the days of Aristotle the strictest syllogistic reasoning was vague instinct in everybody's mind, that it is so now in the minds of all but a very few, and that it is so even in their minds in all but a very few hours of their existence. Another "curiosity of literature" Mr. Stock furnishes when he argues, under fallacies, that it is wrong to ask your opponent to grant the point under dispute, because it is violating "the first of the general rules of syllogism, inasmuch as a conclusion is derived from a single premise, to wit, itself."

But the most original part of the book is the treatment of immediate inference as applied to compound propositions, and this, unfortunately, is almost wholly erroneous. In the first place, the treatment is totally inadequate on account of the fact that it applies only to singular propositions. The denial of "No kings are tyrants" is "Some kings are tyrants," not "All kings are tyrants." "If all men are gentle, all women are brave" is the same thing as "If any women are not brave, some men are not gentle," but it is far from being the same thing as "If no women are brave, no men are gentle." But even for singular propositions, in which "The sun shines" and "The sun does not shine," for instance, contradict each other, Mr. Stock is still chock-full of error. His mistakes are due to two causes—to his ignorance of the fact that particular propositions necessarily imply the existence, real or logical, of their terms, and to his ignorance of the fact, admirably

1. The distinction between the logical and the material sequence is very much the same as that between the verbal and the real proposition.

set forth by the late Prof. O. H. Mitchell, in the *Studies in Logic,* that propositions in two dimensions are necessarily six and not four in number. The reason for this latter fact is, that "All rivers are sometimes dry" may mean either that there are times when every river is dry, or that every river is dry at one time or another; and that reasoning cannot proceed with safety until it is known which of these two things is meant. We shall not take time to set forth the effects of these two fundamental errors. It is sufficient to point out that no one but a hardened logician would suppose the statement, "Either operators must be careful, or telegrams will sometimes not be correct," to be the same thing as "Either telegrams are correct, or operators are sometimes not careful"; nor would he suppose that in order to deny the statement, "Either men fight, or tyrants reign," we say "Either men fight, or tyrants do sometimes not reign." It gives one a distinct feeling of dizziness, if not of nausea, to be told that these two statements are the denials of each other. To refute him who says, "Either corruption ceased, or the country went to the dogs," it would be necessary to establish *both* that corruption did not cease *and* that the country did not go to the dogs. It happens that statements in *either or* and in *if* are abbreviated forms for *universal* sequences, and that it is impossible to express with those words the particular sequences which are necessary for denying them. All this is as plain as daylight to any one who has been trained in Symbolic Logic, as well as to any one who has not studied Logic at all.

If this author showed greater strength than he does in plain questions of Logic, more interest would attach to the fact, which appears from an advertisement in the end of the book, that he attributes "importance to spiritualism, and gives a degree of credit to its phenomena." There is an admirable collection of examples.

36

Report on Gravity at the Smithsonian, Ann Arbor, Madison, and Cornell

22 November 1889 ***Washington National Record Center***

THESE DETERMINATIONS WERE MADE AT THE FOLLOWING STATIONS:

Smithsonian. This station is in the North East corner of the cellar of the building of the Smithsonian Institution in Washington D.C. The station was selected by Colonel Herschel and me, and was first occupied by him. Since that time considerable changes have been made in the building, and the station was at the time of the observations herein described some 6 feet higher than when Col. Herschel occupied it. My station is about 15 feet further south than Herschel's. It is about 0′.3 south of the Washington Observatory, so that its latitude is 38°53′.3. It is about 1.3 statute mile east of the observatory. Its height above sea-level is about 28 feet. The pendulum room was never entered during the swingings, the observations being made through a small hole in the door. Professor Baird, the late Secretary of the Smithsonian, kindly devoted the two connected rooms to our purposes.

Cornell. Two stations were simultaneously occupied there. They are distinguished by the names of the pendulum supports placed in them, being distinguished as "Old Stand" and "New Stand." The Old Stand was in a large dark inner closet ordinarily used for keeping acid and dangerous chemicals, in the cellar of the Physical Laboratory of Cornell University, in Ithaca, New York. The supports rested upon three stones which had been placed there some months before, under the obliging superintendence of my friend Professor E. A. Fuertes. The closet was never entered during the swingings, the pendulum being observed through a small hole in the door. The room in which the closet was, was exclusively devoted to my work. The New Stand was in a small wooden observatory attached to the Engineering School of the University. This observatory has four rooms, first, an office into which the outer door opens, next a transit-room, in which was the transit instrument with which time was observed, then, a round room with a dome-room for a small equatorial above it. The whole observatory having been placed entirely at my disposition, I determined to use the room under the dome-room as a pendulum room. I had its one window doubled with glass, and all its walls tightly ceiled with wood. The floor was cut away just sufficiently not to touch two stone piers which were sunk to rest the pendulum on. The stairway into the dome-room was allowed to remain open in order to allow the heated air from the observer's body to quickly escape. But the pendulum-room was never entered during the swingings, the pendulum being observed through a small hole in the door; nor was the building entered during the swingings except for the initial and final observations of each set. The station was a bad one, owing to its exposure to sudden changes of temperature and to wind. It was selected as being suitable for the determination of the temperature-coefficients of the pendulums. The latitude of the observatory is stated to be 42°27.′0. The Old Stand was a few hundred feet north-west of it. The elevation of the Old Stand was 802.3 foot and of the New Stand 815.2 foot above the sea-level. It would be impossible for me to acknowledge my obligations to Presidents White and Adams of the Cornell University, and to Professors Fuertes, Anthony, and others, for their many generous acts in furtherance of my operations there. Professor Fuertes allowed me the observatory, an office, and the exclusive use of a chronograph, and put himself to a great deal of serious inconvenience on my account. Professor Anthony gave up several large rooms to me, allowed me the use of a Villarceau régulateur, needed thermometers, a very fine barometer, and many other instruments. Professor Newberry gave me the two rooms in which the pendulum work was done. In short, so much was done to contribute to my success, that I should weary the reader were I to recount it all.

Ann Arbor. The station was situated near the western extremity of the library of the University of Michigan, at Ann Arbor, in that state. The Old Stand was toward the south, and the outer wall; the New Stand was toward the north and inner wall, and was better placed. The geographical position according to Professor Schaeberle is: latitude, 42°16′28″ N; longitude, $5^h 34^m 56\overset{s}{.}7$ from Greenwich. I found the station to be 105 foot above the Michigan Central Railway at the station, which is said to be 193 foot above the Detroit River in 1869, and 771 foot above sea-level. The pendulums were protected by paper screens. I am indebted to President Angell, and to Professors Schaeberle, Langley, and others, for every possible aid in making my observations here.

Madison. The station was at the north end of the cellar of the library of the State University of Wisconsin at Madison, in that state. The Old Stand was toward the west, the New Stand toward the east. The middle point between them was 10 feet south and 30 feet east of the north-west corner of the building. That corner bears 214 feet, 42°7′ East of South from the astronomical station of the Coast and Geodetic Survey, the latitude of which is 43°04′33″. I found the station to be 26.6 foot below the Madison station of the Chicago, Milwaukee, and St. Paul Railway, which I am informed is 278 foot above Lake Michigan, itself 578 foot above the level of the sea. The floor of the cellar was a concrete laid down on gravel, not very hard nor good. The Old Stand rested on three heavy pieces of iron about one foot square each. The New Stand had two pieces of iron under one end. The half of the cellar used was partitioned off with scantling and asphalt paper, which made an absolutely dark room. The pendulums were further protected by screens. Asphalt paper was put upon the pendulum stands to keep off rats. My thanks are due to the Trustees of the University for the facilities extended to me, and especially to my friend Professor Holden. Time was admirably determined for me at the Washburn Observatory by Mr. M. Updegraff. At this station, my chronograph having broken down, Professor Fuertes of Ithaca most generously sent me his own, the instant he heard of my mishap.

Positions of the Several Stations

	Latitude	Longitude	Height in feet
Smithsonian	38°53′.3	$5^h\ 8^m\ 6^s$	28
Cornell	42 27 .0		815.2
Ann Arbor	42 16 .5	5 34 57	876
Madison	43 4 .5		829

GENERAL DESCRIPTION OF THE INSTRUMENTS

The pendulums with which these determinations were made are marked Peirce, having been constructed in the office of the Survey under my immediate direction, and after my design. They are intended to be used at once as invariable and as reversible pendulums. The advantages of this plan are as follows. First, relative determinations of gravity by means of invariable pendulums are less affected by accidental errors than relative determinations derived from the comparison of absolute determinations. By accidental errors, I mean those which in the different swingings at each station would be in the long run as often in excess as in defect by any given amount. This is evident, since in an absolute determination part of the observations have to be made with the centre of mass at a smaller distance from the support than one would like; and also since two series of observations have to be combined with weights not inversely proportional to the squares of their probable errors. Indeed, the weight given to one set must be negative. Thus, if we use a reversible pendulum, having its centre of mass at the distances h_d and h_u from the two edges, and T_d and T_u are the observed periods of oscillations, then T the period of oscillation of the corresponding simple pendulum is calculated by the formula $T^2 = \frac{T_d^2 h_d - T_u^2 h_u}{h_d - h_u}$, where T_u^2 is seen to have a negative weight. But this advantage of the invariable pendulum disappears if the swingings are sufficiently numerous to make the accidental error of the mean small in comparison with constant errors; and such a multiplication of the swingings will commonly add little to the expense of the determination. In regard to the far more serious constant errors, the advantage is on the side of the reversible pendulum. Erroneous constants for corrections for pressure and temperature will generally give rise to constant errors in the determinations of gravity of different magnitudes at the different stations. The corrections for the pressure and temperature of the air have no effect upon the determinations by the reversible pendulum, except owing to the small and accidental difference for the two positions of the instrument. The same error in the coefficient of expansion will produce the same error in the result with the two forms of apparatus; but the difficulty of determining this coefficient is much greater for the invariable pendulum, where its effect is masked by atmospheric effects of various kinds. Some eminent geodesists consider the slower descent of arc of the invariable pendulum an important advantage, because if the pendulum swings from one star-observation to another, we do not depend upon the clock, which presumably does not move as uniformly as the pendulum, nor upon the chronometer, which must move much less uniformly. But it seems to be forgotten how very small is the error against which this consideration is directed. Many clocks go so accurately that it would be better to depend upon their rates for 24 hours, as calculated from star-observations at longer intervals, than to use the star-observations at the limits of the 24 hour interval. A chronometer doubtless moves much less uniformly than a gravity pendulum, because it is subject to sudden changes of rate. But when these have been detected by comparisons of several chronometers, and duly allowed for, the error of rate for any portion of the day will not amount to a quarter of a second per diem. Supposing, then, that the pendulum swings only 1/3 of the day, the error of rate due to the cause supposed will be less than a tenth of a second, which is almost insignificant. But if the intervals during which the pendulum is swinging are distributed somewhat uniformly through the 24 hours, the error will be very much less. I assume that the chronometer is a good one, and that the oil in it is in a good state; for otherwise the instrument should be rejected. But I think by far the most economical course is to have a good clock. An exceedingly fine clock by Krille was to have been used in the work herein described; but it reached me in bad order, and I preferred a chronometer. A less unimportant reason for letting the pendulum swing nearly all day is that under these circumstances its mean temperature must be nearly that of the surrounding air, so that the indications of the thermometers can be relied upon in the mean. The pendulums here described swing from night till morning with heavy end down, and in that position are practically kept in oscillation for 24 hours. In the other position, the observations extend with intervals over some 12 hours. I see no reason to think that the results would be sensibly better if in the latter position the observations were spread more uniformly over the 24 hours, which could, of course, be easily done. The only really serious objection to the plan of making an absolute determination at each station is that the pendulum would have to be measured at each station. Now a station very well adapted to swingings may be very ill-adapted to accurate measurements. For example, I never knew a better place to oscillate a pendulum than the Allegheny Observatory. But I found it impossible to measure the pendulum in the room where it was swung there; for the effect upon the temperature of the illumination, the observer's person, etc. would have been too great; and I never had so much trouble in measuring the pendulum as at that station. The idea of the reversible pendulum supposes the knives to be interchanged. But, as a matter of observed fact, if the knives are in good condition (without which the whole method is futile), their interchange produces no effect on the period, except by altering the distances from the centre of mass, or possibly also the moment of inertia about that centre, effects calculable beforehand. Even if this were not so, it would be quite unnecessary to interchange the knives at each station. But if the knives are not so interchanged, there is no necessity of measuring the pendulum at each station. Indeed, we may suppose the knives to be different and that they are never interchanged, and the pendulum never measured, and still, assuming (what has to be assumed in the case of the invariable pendulum) namely, that the pendulum is transported uninjured from station to station, we can still determine the relative values of gravity, and preserve the substantial advantages of the reversible pendulum in regard to the elimination of the atmospheric effects, and consequent better determinations of the temperature coefficients. One of the most serious objections to the invariable pendulum is that it is assumed that a bar will be transported unchanged, when experience shows that there is considerable risk of its alteration. If several pendulums are carried, the change can be detected. But then some of the observations have to be rejected, either arbitrarily or by the application of the Criterion. There is no means by which the effect of the alteration can be allowed for. Moved by these considerations, I designed these pendulums to be used as invariable, reversible pendulums. That is to say, they are so constructed that the atmospheric effect can be ascertained, at least approximately, and the plan was not to meddle with the knives, and only to measure them once a year at Washington. They are thus supposed to reunite the one substantial merit of invariable pendulums, namely that the length need not be frequently measured, with the several advantages of reversible pendulums, 1st, that the atmospheric effect, if its amount is in doubt, can be eliminated, 2nd, that the temperature coefficient is less doubtful, and 3rd, that an injury to the pendulum destroys none of the work. For the remeasurement of the pendulum on its return to Washington shows whether any alteration has taken place; and the change in the difference of the periods in the two positions, after correction for atmospheric effect,[1] shows at what epoch the alteration took place; and thus the work is all utilized as if nothing had happened. Colonel Herschel has pronounced a sweeping condemnation of my system. His objections are two; first, inasmuch as I secure the knives by thumb-screws, the pendulums are not invariable, since it is possible for human beings to alter them; and second, since the knives are not interchanged, they are not reversible in the full sense of the word. The first objection is directed against an inessential detail. My method itself is perfectly consistent with any attainable approach to invariability. Colonel Herschel's objection has proved well-founded as far as it goes; since, regardless of my earnest protest, the knives have been taken out. Still, I do not feel sure the thumb-screws made any difference. As for the knives not being reversed, the worst effect this can have is to make a small constant error in the absolute determinations. It leaves the relative determinations, which are the most important, intact. Let it be clearly understood that the object of making the pendulums reversible is not to make absolute determinations for their own sake (though this is an incidental advantage), but to make more accurate relative determinations. At first sight, this seems an absurd plan, because the accidental errors must be greater than with invariable pendulums. But the accidental errors can easily be brought down to reasonable limits. The constant errors are the important ones; and these largely spring from erroneous pressure-and-temperature-coefficients, and from alterations of the pendulums in transportation. The pendulums are so constructed that if we were to disregard the observations with heavy end up, they would be very good invariable pendulums. True, they have thumb-screws; but no successful gravity determinations can be made in any way if the instruments are

1. Were this correction not effected, the advantage would be lost.

tampered with. Regard the pendulum with heavy end up as another inferior invariable pendulum. Now, suppose the differential results between two stations with heavy end up agree with those with heavy end down. Our confidence in the conclusion is certainly increased. Suppose, however, they differ markedly. Then, surely it is an advantage to know the precise relation between the effects of all possible sources of error upon the two invariable pendulums used. In order to treat the pendulums as invariable, we must know the coefficients of the atmospheric effects. These are two, the first depending upon the density of the air, and the second upon its viscosity. It would be very desirable to know these coefficients with certainty and accuracy. This knowledge may be attained when the pendulums can be transported to high lands, and there swung under greatly diminished pressures and at widely differing temperatures. But in the mean time, approximate values of the coefficients will answer the purpose of ascertaining when the pendulums suffer any alteration. These simply involve the disadvantages of possibly forcing us to combine heavy end up with heavy end down according to the formula of the reversible pendulum, to get the best attainable result. These approximate values can be calculated a priori if the pendulums are nearly cylindrical in form. For this reason, I have modified the large Repsold pattern for reversible pendulums in the following particulars. First, the entire loads of the pendulums are placed in the interior of the tubes which form the stems; second, these tubes are made larger, so that the frames which hold the knives project less; and third, the tubes are terminated at both ends by hemispheres. It seemed best to use two pendulums at each station; for it is generally nearly as easy to swing two simultaneously as one, and thus observations are multiplied at little cost. But these pendulums must have incommensurable periods; so that there shall be no danger of their influencing one another. Now the only lengths readily measured with great accuracy are a metre and a yard. Thus, it was directly suggested that one of the two pendulums to be used together should measure a metre between the knife-edges and the other a yard. Besides, it was conceived that the ratio between the lengths of the yard and the metre might be determined in this way. The success of this did not quite meet my anticipations, but there were other advantages in the plan which will appear in the

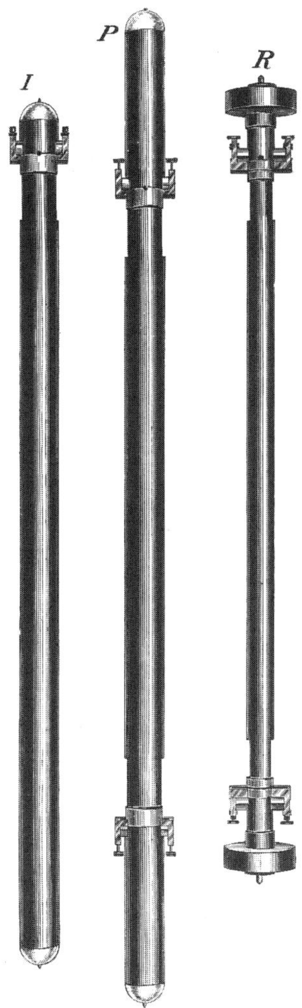

"I have modified the large Repsold pattern for reversible pendulums. . ." A Peirce reversible pendulum (P) is flanked by examples of the Peirce invariable (I) and the Repsold (R). Four Peirce reversibles were built during 1881–82. No. 1 (a meter length) was swung by the Greely Arctic expedition in 1882. Between 1882 and 1885, Peirce swung No. 2 (a meter) and No. 3 (a yard) at various North American field stations. (Coast and Geodetic Survey Report, *Appendix 12, 1890*)

sequel. The centre of mass was made to divide the distance between the knife-edges in the ratio of three to one. This was judged to be a choice which would not make the formula for the reversible pendulum too disadvantageous (making $T^2 = 3/2 T_d^2 - 1/2 T_u^2$), while, on the other hand, it would leave a considerable independent value to the observations with heavy end up. The ratio was made as exact as possible to facilitate the computations. The tubes are in length 3/2 the distance between the edges. The load is in two parts, one being a thick brass tube fitting closely into the stem of the pendulum and placed centrally, and the other a solid brass-piece fitting into the tube between the extremity and one of the knives. The other features of the pendulum were copied from the large Repsold pattern. The knives are exactly like those, and can be used in that pendulum. In order to eliminate the correction for the flexure of the support, in the determination of the ratio between the yard and metre, the masses of Nos. 1 and 3 were made proportional to their lengths. The weakest part of these pendulums is just inside the knife-edges, where the tube composing the stem is cut away to receive the supporting bracket. At the heavy end, there is plainly great danger of alteration of this part in transportation. But if any portion of the pendulum was so situated that its centre of mass was distant from the functioning knife-edge by half the length of the synchronous simple pendulum, a variation of the distance of this part from the knife-edge would not alter the period. Now, when the pendulum has its heavy end up, the centre of mass of the part below the knife is not far from this point; and hence the alteration most likely to occur will change the period with heavy end up but very little. The pendulums rest on "heads" so called, because copied from the heads of the Repsold tripod, though they are a little larger. The mode of raising and lowering the pendulum is simplified. The workmanship is very inferior to that of the Repsolds, and I never was satisfied that the steel planes bearing the knives were at all temperatures quite rigidly fixed to the brass. I regard the general plan of resting a pendulum on a projecting bracket or tongue as highly objectionable; but at the time the pendulums were made, this seemed the only construction which I could get executed. In order not to recur to the subject, I may mention that four of these heads were made, numbered 0, 1, 2, 3. No. 1 was abandoned at Lady Franklin Bay by Lieutenant Greely's party. No. 2 has also been lost. There remain only Nos. 0 and 3. They are denoted by H_0 and H_3 respectively. These heads are intended to be bolted to heavy wooden stands; and these will be described below. The first step toward the construction of the pendulums was to purchase in April 1881 sufficient drawn brass tubing to make four pendulums. This tube has an external diameter of 6¼ centimetres. Its thickness is about 1 millimetre. I then endeavored to obtain drawn brass wire to fit this tube. Finding this impossible, I contented myself with some remarkably perfect castings. The density of this brass was found to be 8.43. Four rectangular holes to admit the supporting bracket or tongue were cut in this tube, and rings carrying frames to hold the knives were fixed upon it. Cast brass hemispherical cups formed the ends. A piece of the brass rod 20 centimetres in length was then cut off, and a core of ⅔ of its diameter was centrally bored out. This was then fixed exactly in the centre of the tube. In this state, pendulum No. 1 (a metre) weighed 6477 grammes, No. 2 (a metre) 6613 grammes, No. 3 (the yard) 6230 grammes, and No. 4 (a metre) 6447 grammes. These weights included the knives which weigh about 154 grammes each. In this state, the period of oscillation of No. 4 was $0\overset{s}{.}8934$ and $0\overset{s}{.}8938$ sidereal time. The pendulum was then polished and lacquered with one gram of shellac. This reduced the mass of No. 4 by 35 grammes. After this the load was put into the end, so that its centre should be about 15.4 centimetres from the knife-edge. This load for No. 1 weighed 3985 grammes, for No. 2 about 4055 grammes, for No. 3, 3767 grammes, and for No. 4, 4163 grammes. Nos. 1 and 3 were finally adjusted by adding brass screws to the end loads, Nos. 2 and 4 by melting solder into the hemispherical cups. The resulting masses were found to be:

	M
Pendulum No. 1	10127
No. 2	10324
No. 3	9676
No. 4	10348

Constants of the Different Pendulums, 1884				
	Length at 15°	h_d/h_u	Mass with knives in grammes	$\log(T_d/T_u)^2$
No. 4	$1^{m}.0002410$	2.988	10657	$+6^{s}.$
No. 1	1.0006915	2.982	10439	+60.58
No. 2	0.9998666	3.001	10633	− 6.18
No. 3	$Yd - 98^{\mu}.8$	2.981	9972	+15.55

DESCRIPTION OF THE STANDS

Two wooden stands were used for the support of the pendulums. They are distinguished as Old Stand [O. S.] and New Stand [N. S.]. The Old Stand, constructed in 1884, is shown in Plate 1. The material of it is yellow pine. A is a plank 2 inches thick, 6 feet long, and 18½ inches wide. B is a similar plank 5 feet long, with a hole in the middle through which the pendulum hangs. These two planks are kept apart by the two X braces, C, 3 by 3 inches in section which set in sockets below, and abut against the cleats D, D above. The two planks are drawn together by four upright iron bolts an inch in diameter. This structure is screwed down to an equilateral triangular base, E, the extreme length of sides being 6 feet, and the beams 4½ inches square. This base is tied together by three bolts F, F, F. The three bolts G, G, G at the joints have conical heads below which form the feet of the whole stand. Finally, two light bars H, H are intended to hold the structure steady in a fore and aft direction. The New Stand, constructed in 1885, is shown in Plate 2. The material of it is red oak. The frame consists of two upright and parallel equilateral triangles. The sides of this are composed of beams 3 inches square. The sides of these triangles measured along the axes of the beams are 6 feet long.

ASSISTANTS EMPLOYED IN THIS WORK

At the Smithsonian, the larger part of the transits and observations of arc were made by Mr. W. B. Fairfield, a very faithful and accurate observer. At Ithaca, a few of the transits and the leveling were the work of Mr. W. B. Curtis, and were quite satisfactory. The measurements of Pendulum No. 3 were made by Mr. E. D. Preston, whose own gravity determinations are known. The measurements of the other pendulums were made with consummate skill and patience by Mr. D. C. Chapman.

Plate 1. Front and side views of Peirce's old pendulum stand (constructed 1884). Peirce had Survey personnel photograph the stand for eventual use in preparing drawings for the North American gravity report. His labels for support members and fastening bolts, along with his stand dimensions, appear in black ink on the photographs. They may have been drawn to aid the artist, but no drawings of this stand have been located. The handwritten annotations match Peirce's narrative descriptions in the text. (By permission of the Houghton Library, Harvard University.)

Plate 2. Front and side views of Peirce's new pendulum stand (constructed 1885). Coast Survey photographs of this stand were to be used in preparing drawings for the North American gravity report. None have been located, but a drawing from the side view appeared in the Coast Survey Report of 1890. Peirce's handwritten dimensions appear on the photographs in black ink. Those dimensions not included in the report narrative are: overall height from pendulum support board to bottom of base (5 ft. 3 in.); the total width (from end to end) of the base support beams (6 ft. 5 1/2 in.); the interior space between the front and back triangular support structures (14 in.); and dimensions of the pendulum support board (19 1/2 in. wide by 20 in. deep). (By permission of the Houghton Library, Harvard University.)

Form of the Geoid According to the Observations

Though the data are as yet too scanty to enable us to calculate the form of the geoid, yet we can from the observations assign values which its departure from the mean spheroid cannot probably exceed.

Table I

Provisional Maximum Values of the Height of the Geoid above the Mean Spheroid

Smithsonian	+ 275 feet
Ann Arbor	+ 199 feet
Madison	+ 23 feet
Cornell	− 86 feet

These quantities are the products of 1000 feet into the quotients of the excesses of the "reduced station-numbers" over 86400 "logarithmic seconds," divided by 0.69 "logarithmic seconds." I proceed to explain the meanings of these phrases.

The Mode Used in This Paper for Expressing the Relative Gravity at the Several Stations

It happens that a pendulum which at the equator beats seconds, or makes 86400 oscillations a day, at any other station makes very nearly as many more oscillations a day as there are units in the fifth place of decimals in the Briggsian logarithm of the ratio of gravity at the two stations. For instance, at the pole such a pendulum would make about 86626 oscillations a day, and the following figures verify the statement.

Numbers	Double logs
86400	9.87303
86626	9.87530
226	227

The reason of this is that the modulus of Briggsian logarithms multiplied by 200000 gives 86859, which is nearly the number of seconds in a day.

Taking advantage of this circumstance, I find it convenient to express the relative gravity logarithmically. Namely, if g be the acceleration of gravity, the number I use is

$$N = A + 100000 \log g,$$

where A is such a constant that, after reduction to the equator and sea-level, the mean value of N for all stations shall be 86400. I call N the "station number"; and it is "reduced" if the reductions for the latitude and elevation above the sea have been applied. The unit of N may be termed a "logarithmic second"; for a variation of a unit in N corresponds very closely to a variation of an oscillation per day in the rate of a pendulum beating seconds at the equator. I denote the logarithmic second by σ.

Whether the value assumed for A is precisely right or not is a matter of small moment. I determine it so that the reduced station number for Washington shall be 86401.90. I also term this the logarithmically expressed oscillations per diem at the station of the equatorial seconds pendulum, whether reduced or not.

FORMULA FOR CALCULATING THE RADIUS VECTOR FROM THE REDUCED STATION-NUMBERS

Stokes ("On the Variation of Gravity," 1849) has shown that if the distribution of gravity be represented by the formula

$$g = G\left[1 - \frac{5}{2}m\left(\frac{1}{3} - \sin^2\phi\right) + u_2 + u_3 + u_4 + \text{etc.}\right],$$

where m is the ratio of equatorial centrifugal force to gravity, ϕ is the latitude, and u_2, u_3, u_4, etc. are spherical harmonics of the same orders as their subjacent indices, then the radius vector is

$$r = R\left[1 + \varepsilon\left(\frac{1}{3} - \sin^2\phi\right) + u_2 + \frac{1}{2}u_3 + \frac{1}{3}u_4 + \text{etc.}\right].$$

There cannot be any considerable spherical harmonic of either the second or third order in the distribution of gravity, except what is already taken account of. Since the coefficients of all the other higher terms are as small as ⅓ in the development of r, we may probably conclude that $\Delta r/R \leq \frac{1}{3}\Delta g/G$.

Since $$\Delta g/g = (1/86859)\Delta N,$$

we have, neglecting the difference between g and G,

$$\Delta r \leq (1/260577)\mathrm{R}\Delta\mathrm{N}.$$

But R = 20,900,000 feet. Hence,

$$\Delta r\ (in\ feet) \leq (1/0\overset{\sigma}{.}00069)\Delta\mathrm{N}.$$

This is the formula by which the provisional maximum elevations of the geoid above the mean spheroid have been calculated.

Reduced Station Numbers

The logarithmic station numbers defined above, reduced to the equator and sea-level, are found to be

Table II

Smithsonian	$86401\overset{\sigma}{.}90$
Ann Arbor	86401.37
Madison	86400.16
Cornell	86399.41

The first of these numbers is assumed, from the result of an unpublished investigation. The differences from this of the others result from the observations herein described. The reductions to the equator and sea-level which have been applied are as follows:

Table III

Station	*Latitude*		*Height*	*Red. for lat.*	*Red. for height*
	°	′		σ	σ
Smithsonian	38	53.3	28 feet	−189.56	+0.12
Ann Arbor	42	16.5	876 "	−102.81	+3.64
Madison	43	4.5	829 "	−105.97	+3.45
Cornell	42	27.0	815 " [N. S.]	−103.50	+3.39
			802 " [O. S.]		+3.34

The reduction for latitude has been calculated from the formula

$$g = g_0[1 + 0.0052375\ \sin^2\phi]$$

and the logarithm of the coefficient is 7.71912. This is the value obtained by me in a discussion published in the *Coast Survey Report for 1881,* Appendix 15; but it now rests on a new investigation, which I do not intend to publish, as some of the data, those of Colonel Herschel, were confidentially communicated. In this unpublished work, I have concluded *a posteriori* that the mean correction for elevation is 0.004156 logarithmic seconds per foot; and this value has been used in the present work.

COMPARISON OF RESULTS WITH DIFFERENT APPARATUS

The station numbers were obtained by least squares, along with two empirical temperature corrections and with 8 constants, one for each of 8 forms of pendulum apparatus, which were employed independently at each station.[2] The Smithsonian was, indeed, twice occupied; and on the first occasion only 4 of these forms of apparatus were used. The residuals for the different stations are shown in the following table.

TABLE IV

Smithsonian		*Ann Arbor*	*Madison*	*Cornell*
σ		σ	σ	σ
[0.00]	−0.11	+0.05	+0.06	+0.55
+0.15		+0.12	−0.26	+0.66
−0.17	0.28	+0.19	+0.09	−2.22
[0.00]		−0.10	+0.09	−0.55
−0.09	+0.28	+0.14	−0.43	+1.82
[0.00]		−0.27	+0.27	+0.88
−0.48	+0.22	−0.39	+0.18	−0.15
−0.25		−0.12	+0.38	−0.97

The same calculation gave the following "logarithmic pendulum numbers." It will be noticed that those for the New Stand are about $0^{\sigma}.84$ less than those for the Old Stand. This difference is owing, no doubt, to the fact that in the flexure of a stand under an oscillating pendulum it does not move in one rigid piece; for it is easy to show mathematically that under those circumstances a part of the effect of flexure

2. But the numbers given were obtained by a common sense calculation, and not by an exact application of the method of least squares. The values given by the least squares calculation where the observations at Cornell are allowed ¼ weight, and no difference of weight is allowed for the different pendulums, their positions or the stands, are as follows:

Additional temperature correction of No. 2 per Degree C. + $0^{\sigma}.1212$
" " " No. 3 " " " + 0.9933

[Logarithmic] Oscillations [reduced to Equator and Sea-level] per diem at the different stations of the equatorial seconds pendulum.

Smithsonian	86401.90
Ann Arbor	86401.37
Madison	86400.25
Cornell	86399.48

would be independent of $h:l$, the ratio of the centre of mass from the axis of rotation to the length of the synchronous simple pendulum.

TABLE V

Logarithmic excess of oscillations per diem of each pendulum over Equatorial Seconds Pendulum		
	Old Stand	*New Stand*
No. 2, H.e.d.	– 390.15[3]	–389.53
H.e.u.	– 397.0	–397.18[4]
No. 3, H.e.d.	+3510.0	+3512.66[5]
H.e.u.	+3524.70	+3525.43

3. But for Smithsonian 1885, –391.46
4. But for Smithsonian 1886, –395.77
5. But for Smithsonian 1886, and Cornell, +3509.06

THE EMPIRICAL TEMPERATURE CORRECTION

The empirical temperature corrections determined along with the above numbers are additional to the corrections already applied for

---

Excess of [logarithmic] oscillations per diem of each pendulum, for each position and on each stand over seconds pendulum.

	Old Stand	*New Stand*
No. 2, H.e.d.	– $390^{\sigma}.15$	– $389^{\sigma}.52$
H.e.u.	– 397.16	– 397.29
No. 3, H.e.d.	+3510.12	+3512.60[6]
H.e.u.	+3524.53	+3525.31

6. This is for Ann Arbor and Madison. For Cornell and Smithsonian, 3509.21.

RESIDUALS

	Smithsonian '85.	*Smithsonian* '86.	*Ann Arbor*	*Madison*	*Cornell*
No. 2, H.e.d., O.S.	—	–0.12	+0.04	–0.04	+0.48
N.S.		+0.12	+0.10	–0.39	+0.66
H.e.u., O.S.	+0.28	–0.16	+0.31	+0.12	–0.21
N.S.		—	0.00	+0.10	–0.41
No. 3, H.e.d., O.S.	+0.01	+0.19	+0.04	–0.61	+1.62
N.S.		–0.18	–0.24	+0.21	+0.73
H.e.u., O.S.	–0.32	+0.36	–0.44	+0.22	–0.06
N.S.		–0.16	–0.02	+0.39	+0.85

expansion from the standard temperature of 15°, and for atmospheric effects. For pendulum No. 2, it is equivalent to an addition to the coefficient of 2$^{\mu}$.895 per metre per degree centigrade; and is in logarithmic seconds 1/8 of excess of the temperature Centigrade over the standard temperature. (For the product of 2.895 by the modulus of Briggsian logarithms is 1.25.) For pendulum No. 3, it is 0.10 per degree. In neither case is its effect, therefore, very serious except for extreme temperatures. The mean temperatures will be given below under the head of Expansion Correction; but meantime, the following table shows the means at the several stations and on the two supports.

TABLE VI
Mean Temperatures

	Old Stand	*New Stand*
	°	
Smithsonian 1885	18.90	°
Smithsonian 1886	18.93	19.67
Ann Arbor	18.26	18.16
Madison	18.68	18.68
Cornell	16.73	− 5.27

It will be seen that this correction depends almost entirely on the observations at Cornell; and the extreme temperatures of the New Stand at that station will suggest a reason for the large residuals at that station.

A *PRIORI* CORRECTIONS

The observed periods of an invariable pendulum require to receive corrections,

1. For the rate of the time-keeper,
2. For the amplitude of oscillation,
3. For the atmospheric effects,
4. For the expansion of the pendulum by heat,
5. For the unequal expansion of its upper and lower parts,
6. For the inclination of the knife-edge to the horizon,
7. For the flexure of the support,
8. For the state of the tide.

I do not mention any correction (9) for the wear of the knives, because I do not believe in such wear; and I omit the corrections (10) for the slip of the knife, (11) for the figure of the knife-edge, and (12) for the flexure of the pendulum itself, because I assume that these will not vary from station to station. I have also assumed that the correction for tide will not affect the inland stations to which this memoir relates. The remaining seven corrections have been applied in two different ways, a part of them to each swinging (or uninterrupted series of oscillations), and a part to the mean results of each form of apparatus at each station. The correction for flexure is, however, the only one which has been entirely applied in the second way; while the corrections for rate, arc, unequal expansion, and inclination have been wholly applied in the first way. The atmospheric corrections and that for expansion have been applied, first differentially, to bring the different swingings of each pendulum in each position and on each support, at each station, to their mean pressures and temperatures; and afterwards new corrections have been applied to reduce to the standard temperature and pressure.

Correction for Flexure

The station-numbers given above have not been corrected for the flexure of the pendulum itself, though this correction is known to be considerable. They have, however, been corrected for the flexure of the support. The corrections which have been applied on this account are as follows:—

Table VII

Corrections of the Station Numbers for Flexure						
		Ann Arbor	*Madison*	*Cornell*	*Smithsonian*	
					'84–5	*1886*
		σ	σ	σ	σ	σ
No. 2, H.e.d.	O. S.	4.58	4.16	6.14	4.91	3.83
	N. S.	5.17	4.48	5.07		3.00
H.e.u.	O. S.	1.52	1.39	2.04	1.64	1.28
	N. S.	1.72	1.49	1.69		1.00
No. 3, H.e.d.	O. S.	4.69	4.26	6.28	5.03	3.92
	N. S.	5.29	4.58	5.18		3.07
H.e.u.	O. S.	1.57	1.43	2.11	1.69	1.31
	N. S.	1.77	1.54	1.74		1.03

These corrections are the products each of two factors, one the horizontal flexure of the support of the middle point of the knife-edge under a horizontal force perpendicular to the knife-edge equal to the weight of one kilogram, while the other factor is the effect upon the vibration-number of the particular pendulum in its position of a flexibility, measured by a unit of the first factor. The formula (*C. S. Report*, 1881, p. 430) is

$$\Delta T^2 = \frac{\partial^2}{g} MS\frac{h}{l}.$$

But since

$$T^2 = \partial^2\frac{l}{g},$$

$$\Delta T^2 = -\partial^2\frac{l}{g^2}\Delta g$$

and

$$\Delta N = 43429\frac{\Delta g}{g}.$$

Hence

$$\Delta N = 0.43429\ M\frac{h}{l^2}\ S,$$

where M is the mass of the pendulum in kilograms, h is the distance of the centre of mass from the functioning knife-edge, l is the equivalent length in metres, and S is the flexure in microns under a force of a kilogram-weight. The value of the factor peculiar to the pendulum and its position, or 0.0434 $M\frac{h}{l^2}$ is shown in the following table, in which I include the values for two other pendulums; and also corrections to nT.

TABLE VIII

Pendulum-Factor of Flexure Correction to the Station Numbers; and to nT (in Sidereal Time)

	M	h/l	l	$0.0434M\ h/l^2$	$n\Delta T/S$
No. 1. H.e.d.	10.439	.7489	1.0007	0.114	0.0589
H.e.u.		.2511		0.339	0.00659
No. 2. H.e.d.	10.633	.7501	0.9999	0.115	0.0602
H.e.u.		.2499		0.347	0.00669
No. 3. H.e.d.	9.972	.7488	0.9139	0.119	0.0589
H.e.u.		.2512		0.355	0.00659
No. 4. H.e.d.	10.657	.7492	1.0002	0.116	0.0602
H.e.u.		.2508		0.347	0.00672

The value found for S, or the horizontal flexure in microns of the knife-edge under a horizontal force perpendicular to the knife-edge of one kilogram weight, is shown in the following table:

TABLE IX

Value of S

	Old Stand	*New Stand*
Smithsonian 1884–5	14.16	
Ann Arbor	13.2	14.9
Madison	12.0	12.9
Cornell	17.7	14.6
Smithsonian 1886	11.05	8.64

The discrepancies between these values are serious, and have engaged my careful study. If the measure of the flexure is wrong for one stand and not for the other, the residuals for the two stands should be different; and these differences should be three times as great for heavy end down as for heavy end up.

TABLE X

Residuals Old Stand Minus New Stand

	Ann Arbor	*Madison*	*Smithsonian 1886*
		Heavy end down	
No. 2	$-0^{\sigma}.07$	$+0^{\sigma}.32$	$-0^{\sigma}.26$
No. 3	+0.41	−0.70	
		Heavy end up	
No. 2	+0.29	+0.00	
No. 3	−0.27	−0.20	+0.47

These numbers do not support any suspicion of erroneous flexure. Thus, the values of the error due to erroneous flexure with probable errors would be

TABLE XI

	Heavy end down		*Heavy end up*	
Ann Arbor	$-0^{\sigma}.52$	$\pm 0^{\sigma}.86$	$+0^{\sigma}.49$	$\pm 0^{\sigma}.67$
Madison	−1.34	± 1.18	+0.12	± 0.74
Smithsonian 1886	−0.44	± 0.62	−0.20	± 0.74

Measures of flexure were made at the Smithsonian, 1885 Feb. 16, 17, and 18. The deflections were produced by a weight of 52675 grains attached to a cord passing over a pulley and thence horizontally to the knife-edge plane. The measures were made by an eye-piece micrometer looking at a stage micrometer. The value of the divisions of the latter were not known at the time; for the record reads "the divisions are supposed to be tenths of millimetres." From experiments with the same eye-piece micrometer, I am satisfied they were really 200ths of an inch. Measures were made at 9.5 cm above and 3 cm below the middle of the knife-edge (in both cases at 14 cm to the left) In the former position, the deflection was 34 eye-piece divisions, of which 87.1 made a division of the stage micrometer. In the other position, I found

Flexure in eye-piece divisions	*Eye-piece divisions in div. stage micr.*		*Flexure in div. stage micrometer*
23.0	61.5		37.4
28.0	75.0		37.3
28.5	75.5		37.7
		Mean	37.5

The agreement of these results proves nothing, as such measures will agree almost perfectly if made at the same time, although, owing to neglect of proper precautions, they may really be far in error. The result is confirmed by experiments with the noddy.

At Ann Arbor, 1885 Sept. 15 and 16, the deflections were produced by the method of Colonel Herschel. Namely, for the sake of using a heavier weight, the pulley was discarded, and the weight was attached directly to the cord in such a manner that the latter was inclined 45° to the horizon from its fixed attachment to the point from which the weight was suspended, while it was horizontal from that point to the knife-edge support. A stage-micrometer was used which is positively stated to have divisions of 10 microns; and this statement I accept, although it disagrees with a statement made from memory a month later and inserted in the record for another station. But I do not think this sufficient to shake the statement recorded at the time. The measures were made with a filar micrometer. But I did not succeed in mounting this solidly enough to be able to use it in the ordinary way. In fact, I could only estimate the tenths of the divisions of the stage micrometer. A number of experiments were made but as they appeared to agree exactly they were set down as one. The angle of the cords was traced upon paper, and subsequently measured.

At Madison, Oct. 10 and 11, very careful measures were made. The weight was one half of that employed at Ann Arbor, the micrometer had divisions of 10 microns (without any possible doubt), and the microscope was used in the same way.

At Cornell, 1885 Dec. 21, the flexure of the New Stand was measured as at Madison, only with weight used at Ann Arbor; and 1886 Jan. 22, the flexure of the New Stand was measured in the same way.

At the Smithsonian, 1886 March 6, and April 9, measures were made with a filar micrometer compared with a stage micrometer. The same weight was employed as in 1885. The measures are probably unusually accurate.

Correction for Expansion

All the station numbers have been corrected for the expansion of the pendulum from 15°. The corrections applied are shown in the following table, which includes corrections to swingings of pendulums Nos. 1 and 4 at the Smithsonian in 1884–5.

Table XII

	Old Stand		*New Stand*	
	Smithsonian 1884–5			
	H.e.d.	H.e.u.	H.e.d.	H.e.u.
	σ	σ		
No. 1	+4.39	+4.77		
2nd set.	−0.24			
No. 2	+3.70	+3.87		
No. 3	+2.65	+2.17		
No. 4	+2.89	+2.73		
2nd set.	+1.47	+1.62		
	Ann Arbor			
			σ	σ
No. 2	+2.42	+2.43	+2.91	+2.53
No. 3	+2.90	+2.59	+2.31	+2.30
	Madison			
No. 2	+3.22	+2.96	+2.65	+2.77
No. 3	+2.67	+2.69	+3.18	+3.10
	Cornell			
No. 2	+1.17	+0.86	−17.09	−19.56
No. 3	+1.39	+2.08	−14.21	−13.48
	Smithsonian 1886			
No. 2	+2.66	+2.98	+3.51	+3.35
No. 3	+3.37	+3.47	+3.79	+4.16

These are the products of the excesses of the mean temperature over 15°C by 0.795 for pendulums Nos. 2 and 4, and by 0.792 for pendulums Nos. 1 and 3. These coefficients are the coefficients of expansion, k, multiplied by the modulus of common logarithms. For N, the station number having been calculated from the period of oscillation, depends, like the periods, upon the length, l, of the pendulum, so that we may write

$$N = B + \log l$$

Introducing $\Delta\tau$ the excess of the temperature over the standard temperature, we have

$$N = N_0 + \Delta N = B + \log l_0 + \log(1 + k\Delta\tau) = B + \log l_0 + Mk\Delta\tau$$

or

$$\Delta N = Mk\Delta\tau.$$

For the coefficients of expansion I have found

k. [No. 4] = 18.30 microns per meter per degree C.
k. [No. 1] = 18.24 " " " " " "

Owing to the circumstances of the manufacture, pendulum No. 2 is supposed to have the same coefficient as No. 4, and No. 3 the same as No. 1. The coefficients of expansion were derived from comparisons of the lengths of the pendulum between the knife-edges with a certain Metre B, which was made at the same time and is assumed to have the same coefficient as Metre A. The coefficient of expansion of this is shown ("Measurements of Gravity at Initial Stations," p. 74) to be 18.95 microns per meter per degree C. The means of the comparisons are as follows:

TABLE XIII
Comparisons of the Pendulums with Metre B
at Different Temperatures

Pendulum No. 1

	Temp.	*Length Pend.* – *B*
	°	μ
	18.46	–251.6
	30.99	–242.7
Diffs	12.53	– 8.9
Relative expan per degree		– 0.71
Absolute " " "		18.24

Pendulum No. 4

	Temp.	*Length Pend.* – *B*
	°	μ
	16.83	0.9
	25.42	6.5
Diffs	8.59	5.6
Relative expan per degree		0.65
Absolute " " "		18.30

For the further details of these comparisons, see the closing discussion on the lengths of the pendulums.

The mean temperatures used in calculating the corrections for expansion are shown in the following table.

TABLE XIV

Mean Temperatures of the Pendulums				
	Old Stand		*New Stand*	
	H.e.d.	H.e.u.	H.e.d.	H.e.u.
	Smithsonian 1884–5			
	°	°		
No. 1	20.54	21.02		
2nd set	14.70			
No. 2	19.65	19.87		
No. 3	18.34	17.74		
No. 4	18.65	18.44		
2nd set	16.85	17.02		
	Ann Arbor			
			°	°
No. 2	18.05	18.06	18.66	18.18
No. 3	18.66	18.27	17.92	17.90
	Madison			
No. 2	19.05	18.72	18.33	18.48
No. 3	18.37	18.40	19.02	18.91
	Cornell			
No. 2	16.47	16.08	–6.50	–9.61
No. 3	16.74	17.63	–2.94	–2.02
	Smithsonian 1886			
No. 2	18.35	18.75	19.43	19.22
No. 3	19.25	19.38	19.79	20.25

Atmospheric Effects

The station-numbers given above have also received two corrections to bring the periods of oscillation to their values in a standard atmosphere of one million C.G.S. units of pressure and at a temperature of 15°C. The absolute zero has been assumed to be –273°.1 C, and departures from the laws of Boyle and Charles have been neglected. The absolute atmosphere, or one million C.G.S. units of pressure, has been taken at the following values in inches of mercury at the freezing point.

TABLE XV

One Absolute Atmosphere in Inches of the Reduced Barometer	
	in
Smithsonian	29.546
Ann Arbor	29.540
Madison	29.539
Cornell	29.540

These numbers have been calculated from the following data:

Density of Mercury at 0°C	13.5959
Centimeters in an inch	2.5400
Gravity at the Smithsonian	980.14
" " Ann Arbor	980.34
" " Madison	980.39
" " Cornell	980.34

The density of mercury is not that found at Breteuil, but Regnault's as corrected by Wüllner, as it is supposed that this represents the mercury actually used.

The first atmospheric correction is proportional to the density of the air, and corrects for the effects of buoyancy, enclosed air, and a hydrodynamic effect equivalent to carrying a volume of air equal to the cylindrical parts and half the hemispherical ends of the pendulum. The calculation of it is purely *a priori*.

The second atmospheric correction is for the effect of viscosity. It is calculated from the rate of descent of the amplitude of oscillation as in my "Measurements of Gravity at Initial Stations." The *a priori* calculation from Stokes's theory has been made, also.

The amounts of these corrections are as follows:

TABLE XVI

First Atmospheric Effect					
Smithsonian 1884–5		*Ann Arbor*	*Madison*	*Cornell*	*Smithsonian 1886*
	σ	σ	σ	σ	σ
No. 2. H.e.d. O. S.	+0.30	−0.79	−1.01	−0.17	−0.06
N. S.		−0.89	−0.65	+1.76	−0.03
H.e.u. O. S.	+1.40	−2.24	−2.49	−1.16	+0.46
N. S.		−2.41	−2.15	+5.83	+0.56
No. 3. H.e.d. O. S.	+0.08	−0.56	−0.65	−0.57	−0.20
N. S.		−0.77	−0.99	+1.82	−0.11
H.e.u. O. S.	+0.20	−2.38	−2.07	−3.16	−0.66
N. S.		−2.15	−2.46	+4.51	−0.70

TABLE XVI *(continued)*

Second Atmospheric Effect						
Smithsonian 1884–5		*Ann Arbor*	*Madison*	*Cornell*	*Smithsonian 1886*
	σ	σ	σ	σ	σ
No. 2. H.e.d. O. S.	+0.04	–0.04	–0.04	–0.00	+0.01
N. S.	–	–0.04	–0.03	–0.00	+0.02
H.e.u. O. S.	+0.15	–0.10	–0.10	–0.06	+0.08
N. S.		–0.10	–0.08	–0.01	+0.09
No. 3. H.e.d. O. S.	+0.01	–0.04	–0.02	–0.03	+0.01
N. S.		–0.03	–0.04	+0.02	+0.01
H.e.u. O. S.	+0.05	–0.10	–0.08	–0.16	+0.02
N. S.		–0.09	–0.10	+0.03	+0.03

These are calculated from the temperatures given under Expansion and the following pressures:

TABLE XVII

Mean Pressures in inches of mercury at the freezing point				
	Old Stand		*New Stand*	
	H.e.d.	H.e.u.	H.e.d.	H.e.u.
Smithsonian 1884–5				
No. 1	30.061	30.317		
2d set	30.324			
No. 2	30.335	30.533		
No. 3	29.967	29.899		
No. 4	30.108	29.988		
Ann Arbor				
No. 2	29.022	29.077	28.990	29.030
No. 3	28.990	29.030	29.022	29.077
Madison				
No. 2	28.904	29.053	29.190	29.150
No. 3	29.190	29.150	28.894	29.066
Cornell				
No. 2	29.521	29.250	29.009	28.817
No. 3	29.108	28.694	29.485	29.285
Smithsonian 1886				
No. 2	29.830	30.092	29.977	30.170
No. 3	29.765	29.760	29.907	29.833

The following table exhibits the detailed calculation of the coefficients of the atmospheric effects. The algebraical notation is as follows:

Letters.

r, the radius of a cylinder or sphere;
l, the length of a cylinder;
V, a volume;
M, a mass;
D, a density;
γ, a radius of gyration;
J, a moment of inertia of a volume of unit density;
h, the distance of a centre of mass from an axis of rotation;
I, a moment of inertia;
T, a period of oscillation;
μ, the dynamical coefficient of viscosity;
ν, the kinetical coefficient of viscosity;
k, a coefficient of air carried by the pendulum;
℧ = 3.14159.

In the dimensions, G is a gramme, C a centimetre, S a solar second, S′ a sidereal second.

Accents Applied to the Letters above the Line.

These indicate the things whose density, mass, volume, etc. are denoted by the letters, as follows:

One dot, indicates the brass part of the pendulum;
Two dots, one steel knife;
One accent, air displaced by the metal of the pendulum;
Two accents, air enclosed in the hollow parts;
Three accents, air displaced plus that enclosed;
iv, the air displaced *plus* enclosed by the cylindrical part of the pendulum considered as solid;
v, the air displaced *plus* enclosed by one hemispherical terminal;
vi, the air displaced *plus* enclosed by parts of the knives and the attachments projecting beyond the cylindrical surface of the pendulum.

Subjacent Indices.

These distinguish different axes of rotation (all parallel to the knife-edge) as follows:

No index, the axis through the centre of mass;
Index 0, the axis through the centre of volume;
Index *d*, the functioning knife-edge with heavy end down;
Index *u*, the functioning knife-edge with heavy end up.

TABLE XVIII

Calculation of Atmospheric Coefficients

Quantity	*Dimensions*	*Pend. No. 2*		*Pend. No. 3*	
		Number	*Log*	*Number*	*Log*
r^{iv}, by measure	C	3.13	0.4955	3.13	0.4955
$(r^{iv})^2$	C^2		0.9910		0.9910
l^{iv}, by measure	C	150	2.1761	137.16	2.1372
∂			0.4971		0.4971
$V^{iv} = \partial(r^{iv})^2 l^{iv}$	C^3	4615	3.6642	4220	3.6253
$(r^{v})^3 = (r^{iv})^3$	C^3		1.4865		1.4865
4/3			0.1249		0.1249
$2V^{v} = \frac{4}{3}\partial(r^{v})^3$	C^3	128	2.1085	128	2.1085
$2V^{vi}$ by estimation	C^3	88	1.9445	88	1.9445
$V''' = V^{iv} + 2V^{v} + 2V^{vi}$	C^3	4831	3.6840	4436	3.6470
$M^{\cdot}$, by weighing	G	10324	4.0139	9663	3.9851
$D^{\cdot}$, by weighings	GC^{-3}	8.43	0.9258	8.43	0.9258
$V^{\cdot} = M^{\cdot}/D^{\cdot}$	C^3	1225	3.0881	1146	3.0593
$2M^{\cdot\cdot}$	G	309	2.4900	309	2.4900
$D^{\cdot\cdot}$, assumed	GC^3	7.85	0.8950	7.85	0.8950
$2V^{\cdot\cdot} = 2M^{\cdot\cdot}/D^{\cdot\cdot}$	C^3	1.5950	39	.5950	
$V = V^{\cdot} + 2V^{\cdot\cdot}$	C^3	1264	3.1017	1185	3.0737
$V'' = V''' - V$	C^3	3567	3.5523	3251	3.5120
$\frac{1}{4}(r^{iv})^2$	C^2	2		2	
$\frac{1}{12}(l^{iv})^2$	C^2	1878	1567		
$(\gamma^{iv})^2 = \frac{1}{4}(r^{iv})^2 + \frac{1}{12}(l^{iv})^2$	C	1880	3.2742	1569	3.1956

TABLE XVIII *(continued)*

Calculation of Atmospheric Coefficients					
		Pend. No. 2		*Pend. No. 3*	
Quantity	*Dimensions*	*Number*	*Log*	*Number*	*Log*
$J_0^{iv} = V^{iv}(\gamma^{iv})^2$	C^5	8678×10^3	6.9384	6621×10^3	6.8209
$\frac{2}{5}(r^{v})^2$	C^5	4		4	
h^{v}, estimated	C	1		1	
$(\gamma^{v})^2 = \frac{2}{5}(r^{v})^2 - (h^{v})^2$	C^2	3		3	
$h_0^{v} = \frac{1}{2}l^{iv} + h^{v}$	C	76		70	
$(h_0^{v})^2$	C^2	5776	4900		
$(\gamma_0^{v})^2 = (\gamma^{v})^2 + (h_0^{v})^2$	C^2	5779	3.7618	4627	3.6653
$2J_0^{v} = 2V^{v}(\gamma_0^{v})^2$	C^5	742×10^3	5.8703	594×10^3	5.7738
h^{vi}, by estimation	C	51.5	1.7120	47.2	1.6739
$(h_0^{vi})^2$	C^2		3.4240		3.3478
$2J_0^{vi} = 2V^{vi}(h_0^{vi})^2$	C^5	234×10^3	5.3685	196×10^3	5.2923
$J_0''' = J_0^{iv} + 2J_0^{v} + 2J_0^{vi}$	C^5	9654×10^3	6.9847	7411×10^3	6.8699
$(h_d + h_u)$, by measure	C	100.00		91.4	
$(h_d - h_u)$, by measure	C	50.04		45.5	
$h_d = \frac{1}{2}(h_d + h_u) + \frac{1}{2}(h_d - h_u)$	C	75.02	1.8751	68.45	1.8354
$h_u = \frac{1}{2}(h_d + h_u) - \frac{1}{2}(h_d - h_u)$	C	24.98	1.3976	2.95	21.3608
$h_d h_u$	C^2		3.2727		3.1962
T_d, *in vacuo*, by approx.	S′	1.0060	0.0026	0.9618	9.9830
T_u, *in vacuo*, by approx.	S′	1.0054	0.0024	0.9605	9.9825
T_u/T_d			9.9998		9.9995
$(T_u/T_d)^2$		0.9990	9.9996	0.9979	9.9990
$T_u^2/T_d^2 - 1$			–0.0010		–0.0021
$1 + (T_u^2/T_d^2 - 1)(h_d + h_u)/(h_d - h_u)$		0.9980	9.9991	0.9958	9.9982

TABLE XVIII *(continued)*

Calculation of Atmospheric Coefficients					
Quantity	*Dimensions*	*Pend. No. 2*		*Pend. No. 3*	
		Number	*Log*	*Number*	*Log*
$\gamma^2 = h_d h_u[1 + (T_u^2/T_d^2 - 1) \times (h_d + h_u)/(h_d - h_u)]$		1870	3.2718	1565	3.1944
$h_0 = \frac{1}{2}(h_d - h_u)$	C	25.02	1.3982	22.75	1.3570
h_0^2	C^2	626		518	
$\gamma_0^2 = \gamma^2 + h_0^2$	C^2	2496	3.3972	2083	3.3390
$J_0' = V(\gamma_0)^2$	C^5	3152×10^3	6.4989	2586×10^3	6.4127
$J_0'' = J_0''' - J_0'$	C^5	6502×10^3	6.8130	4825×10^3	6.6834
$h_0'' = h_0(V/V'')$	C	8.86	0.9476	8.29	0.9187
$(h_0'')^2$	C^2	79	1.8952	69	1.8374
$(\gamma_0'')^2 = J_0''/V''$	C^2	1823	3.2607	1484	3.1714
$(\gamma'')^2 = (\gamma_0'')^2 - (h_0'')^2$	C^2	1744		1415	
$h_d'' = \frac{1}{2}(h_d + h_u) - h_0''$	C	41.14		37.41	
$(h_d'')^2$	C^2	1692		1400	
$(\gamma_d'')^2 = (\gamma'')^2 + (h_d'')^2$	C^2	3436	3.5361	2815	3.4494
$h_u'' = \frac{1}{2}(h_d + h_u) + h_0''$	C	58.86		53.99	
$(h_u'')^2$	C^2	3464		2915	
$(\gamma_u'')^2 = (\gamma'')^2 + (h_u'')^2$	C^2	5208	3.7166	4330	3.6365
$(\gamma''')^2 = J_0'''/V'''$	C^2	1998	3.3007	1671	3.2229
$(\gamma_d''')^2 = (\gamma_u''')^2 = (\gamma''')^2 + \frac{1}{4}(h_d + h_u)^2$	C^2	4498	3.6530	3761	3.5753
$J_d'' = V''(\gamma_d'')^2$	C^5	12258×10^3	7.0884	9150×10^3	6.9614
$J_u'' = V''(\gamma_u'')^2$	C^5	18575×10^3	7.2689	14077×10^3	7.1485
$J_d''' = J_u''' = V'''(\gamma_d''')^2$	C^5	21725×10^3	7.3370	16683×10^3	7.2223
$\gamma_d^2 = \gamma^2 + h_d^2$	C^2	7498	3.8750	6250	3.7959
$\gamma_d^2 = \gamma^2 + h_u^2$	C^2	2494	3.3969	2092	3.3206

TABLE XVIII *(continued)*

Calculation of Atmospheric Coefficients					
Quantity	*Dimensions*	*Pend. No. 2*		*Pend. No. 3*	
		Number	*Log*	*Number*	*Log*
$M = M^{\cdot} + 2M^{\cdot\cdot}$	G	10633	4.0266	9972	3.9988
$D = M/V$	GC^{-3}		0.9249		0.9251
$D^{\cdot} - D^{\cdot\cdot}$	GC^{-3}	0.58		0.58	
$(D^{\cdot} - D^{\cdot\cdot})/D^{\cdot}$		0.0688		0.0668	
$2M^{\cdot\cdot}/M$		0.0291		0.0310	
$2M^{\cdot\cdot}(D^{\cdot} - D^{\cdot\cdot})/MD^{\cdot}$		0.00200		0.00214	
$(h_d - h_u)M^{\cdot\cdot}(D^{\cdot} - D^{\cdot\cdot})/MD^{\cdot}$	C	0.0500		0.0487	
$h'_d = h_d + (h_d - h_u)M^{\cdot\cdot} \times (D^{\cdot} - D^{\cdot\cdot})/MD^{\cdot}$	C	74.97	1.8749	68.40	1.8351
$h'_u = h_u + (h_d - h_u)M^{\cdot\cdot} \times (D^{\cdot} - D^{\cdot\cdot})/MD^{\cdot}$	C	25.03	1.3984	23.00	1.3617
h'_d/h_d			9.9998		9.9997
h'_u/h_u			0.0008		0.0009
D'	GC^{-3}		97.0827		97.0827
D'/D			96.1578		96.1576
$(D'/D)(h'_d/h_d)$		.0001437	96.1576	.0001436	96.1573
$(D'/D)(h'_u/h_u)$		.0001441	96.1586	.0001440	96.1585
$I_d = M\gamma_d^2$			7.9016		7.7947
$I_u = M\gamma_u^2$			7.4235		7.3194
$I''_d/I_d = J''_d D'/I_d$		.0001860	96.2695	.0001776	96.2494
$I''_u/I_u = J''_u D'/I_u$		.0008474	96.9281	.0008162	96.9118
$I'''_d/I_d = J'''_d D'/I_d$		.0003297	96.5181	.0003241	96.5103
$I'''_u/I_u = J'''_u D'/I_u$		.0009912	96.9962	.0009674	96.9856
$A_d = (D'/D)(h'_d/h_d) + (I''_d + I'''_d)/I_d$		.0006594		.0006453	
$A_u = (D'/D)(h'_u/h_u) + (I''_u + I'''_u)/I_u$		.0019827		.0019276	
$\log(1 + A_d) = A_d \log 6$		28″.63		28″.03	
$\log(1 + A_u)$		86.02		83.63	

A Priori Calculation of the Second Effect					
v			9.1937		9.1937
T_d	S	1.0035	0.0015		9.9820
∂^{-1}			9.5029		9.5029
$vT_d\partial^{-1}$			8.6982		9.6787
$\sqrt{vT_d\partial^{-1}}$			9.3491		9.3394
$2\sqrt{2}$			0.4515		0.4515
$k-1 = 2\sqrt{2}\sqrt{vT_d\partial^{-1}}/r^{v}$			9.3051		9.2954
$(I_d'''/I_d)(k-1) = B_d$			95.8232		95.8057
$(I_u'''/I_u)(k-1) = B_u$			96.3013		96.2810
		σ		σ	
$\log(1+B_d)$		2.89		2.78	
$\log(1+B_u)$		8.69		8.29	
Calc b'		.0000477	95.6782		

A Posteriori Calculation of the Second Effect				
b_d' at 20°C and 30 in	.0000579	95.7628	.0000575	95.7597
$\log$ б		99.6378		99.6378
$b_d = b_d'/\log$ б		96.1250		96.1219
∂		0.4971		0.4971
b_d/∂		95.6279		95.6248
$1-b_d/\partial$		0.0000		0.0000
$2(b_d/\partial)(I_d/I_d''')$		99.4108		99.4155
$1+2(b_d/\partial)(I_d/I_d''')(1-b_d/\partial)^{-2}$		0.0995		0.1005
$\sqrt{1+2(b_d/\partial)(I_d/I_d''')(1-b_d/\partial)^{-2}}$		0.0498		0.0502
$(1-b_d/\partial)^2 \times \sqrt{1+2(b_d/\partial)(I_d/I_d''')(1-b_d/\partial)^{-2}}$	2.2427	0.0497	2.2452	0.0501
$(k-1)$ at 20°C and 30 in	0.2429	99.3854	0.2454	99.3899
$(k-1)$ at 15°C and 29.56 in		99.3821		99.3866
$(I_d'''/I_d)(k-1) = B_d$		95.9002		95.8969
$(I_u'''/I_u)(k-1) = B_u$		96.3783		96.3721
	σ		σ	
$\log(1+B_d)$	3.45		3.43	
$\log(1+B_u)$	10.38		10.23	

DESCENT OF THE ARC

The theory of the effect of the air on the pendulum must be admitted to be in a very unsatisfactory condition. Newton showed vaguely that there would be a resistance proportional to the square of the velocity; but nobody has determined how large this ought to be. It is evident that a "resistance" proportional to any power of the velocity can only affect the period by a quantity of the second order, since the velocities for the ascending pendulum are nearly the same as in the descent. Green first considered the problem as one of hydrodynamics, and showed what would be the effect on an ellipsoid making infinitesimal oscillations in a perfect fluid; namely, the period of oscillation would be affected by a certain amount, while the amplitude would not suffer any diminution at all. Stokes undertook to determine the effect of the viscosity of the air, and has produced solutions of the problem for a sphere making infinitesimal oscillations in a concentric spherical envelope, and for a cylinder oscillating in infinite space. Oscar Emil Meyer finds a different value from Stokes for the effect on the decrement of the arc; and this accords somewhat better with the observations.

In order to express the observations of the descent of the arc, we may make use of the old resistential formula

$$\mathrm{D}_n \Phi = -a - b\Phi - 2c\Phi^2.$$

The signification of this equation is that Φ is the simplest function of n fulfilling the following conditions:

1st, that $\mathrm{D}_n \Phi = 0$ when

$$a + b\Phi + c\Phi^2 = 0,$$

that is, when Φ has either of the values

$$\Phi = -\frac{1}{2}\frac{b}{c}\left(1 \pm \sqrt{1 - 4\frac{ac}{b^2}}\right)$$

2nd, that when Φ has one other value, $\mathrm{D}_n \Phi$ has the value determined by the differential equation;

3rd, that for one value of n, Φ takes an arbitrary value.

Now, if $b^2 > 4ac$, the two values of Φ for which $\mathrm{D}_n \Phi = 0$ are real, though both are negative. Consider, then, any value of n for which $\mathrm{D}_n \Phi = 0$. By the differential equation

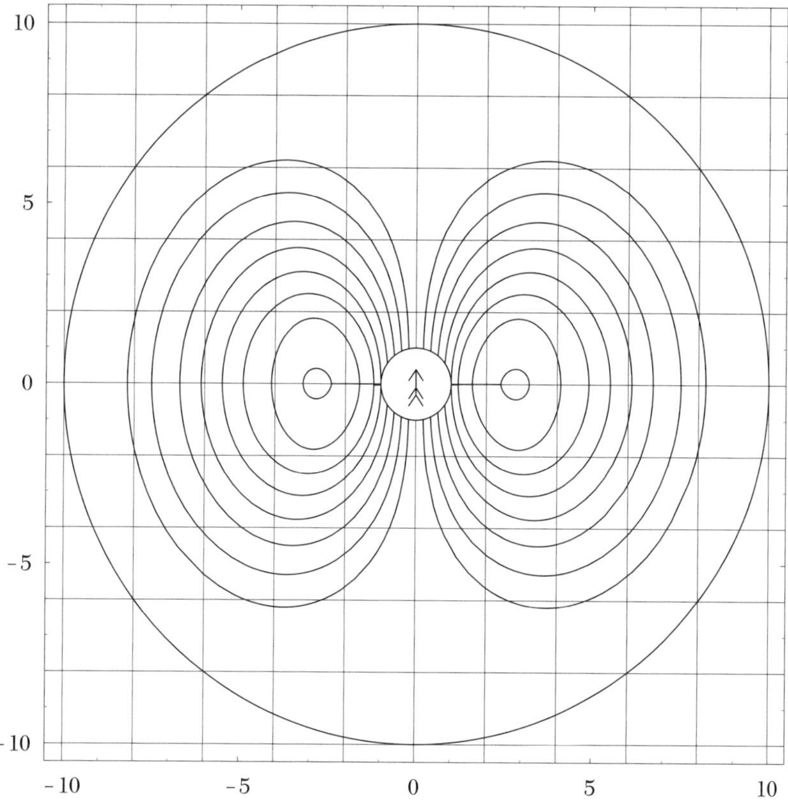

On 3 September 1887, Peirce sent the Coast Survey a partial diagram of stream lines surrounding an overhead cross-sectional view of a cylindrical Peirce pendulum, along with a provisional caption and coordinates to assist in completing the diagram. His cover letter identified this drawing as "the first of a series of diagrams intended to illustrate my report now in preparation." Peirce never completed the diagram, nor did he provide any others with his November 1889 submission of the North American gravity report. The diagram above represents a conception of the finished illustration, completed using the coordinates Peirce supplied in 1887. Peirce's provisional caption reads, "Streamlines of air about a cylindrical pendulum enclosed in a cylindrical vessel of ten times its diameter. The air viscous but of infinitesimal density."

$$\mathrm{D}_n^2\,\Phi \;=\; (-b - c\,\Phi)\mathrm{D}_n\,\Phi,$$

and evidently all the differential coefficients of Φ relative to n will vanish, so that n must change by an infinite amount to produce any finite change of Φ; and consequently, n is infinite. Thus, Φ has two different values for $n = \infty$, although by the third condition above, it generally has but one value for a given value of n. Hence, it must be represented by a function having an essential singularity at $n = -\infty$, and the simplest such function is б^n. The simplest one involving two constants is $\mathrm{H}\text{б}^{kn}$. When $n = +\infty$, this equals ∞, but when $n = \infty$ it vanishes. Then, the simplest way of giving to Φ its required values for these values of $\mathrm{H}\text{б}^{kn}$ is to write

$$\Phi = -\frac{1}{2}\frac{b}{c}\left[1 - \left(1 - \frac{2}{1+\mathrm{H}\text{б}^{kn}}\right)\sqrt{1 - 4\frac{ac}{b^2}}\right].$$

The differential coefficient of this is

$$\mathrm{D}_n\Phi = \frac{\mathrm{H}\text{б}^{kn}}{(1+\mathrm{H}\text{б}^{kn})^2}k\frac{b}{c}\sqrt{1-4\frac{ac}{b^2}}$$

$$= \left(\frac{1}{1+\mathrm{H}\text{б}^{kn}} - \frac{1}{(1+\mathrm{H}\text{б}^{kn})^2}\right)k\frac{b}{c}\sqrt{1-4\frac{ac}{b^2}}.$$

On the other hand,

$$c\,\Phi + b = \frac{1}{2}b\left[1 + \left(1 - \frac{2}{1+\mathrm{H}\text{б}^{kn}}\right)\sqrt{1-4\frac{ac}{b^2}}\right]$$

$$c\,\Phi^2 + b\,\Phi = -\frac{1}{4}\frac{b^2}{c}\left[1 - \left(1 - \frac{2}{1+\mathrm{H}\text{б}^{kn}}\right)^2\left(1 - 4\frac{ac}{b^2}\right)\right]$$

$$= -a - \frac{1}{4}\frac{b^2}{c}\left(-\frac{4}{1+\mathrm{H}\text{б}^{kn}} + \frac{4}{(1+\mathrm{H}\text{б}^{kn})^2}\right)\left(1 - 4\frac{ac}{b^2}\right)$$

$$-a - b\,\Phi - c\,\Phi^2 = \frac{b^2}{c}\left(-\frac{1}{1+\mathrm{H}\text{б}^{kn}} + \frac{1}{(1+\mathrm{H}\text{б}^{kn})^2}\right)\left(1 - 4\frac{ac}{b^2}\right).$$

The comparison of the two values shows that

$$k = \sqrt{b^2 - 4ac}.$$

If the square root vanishes, $\Phi = -\dfrac{b}{2c}$ for $n = \infty$, so that we have most simply

$$\Phi = -\frac{1}{2}\frac{b}{c} + \mathrm{F}n,$$

where $\mathrm{F}n = 0$ for $n = \infty$. The simplest function having this property, and involving two constants, is $\mathrm{P}/(\mathrm{Q}+n)$, so that

$$\Phi = -\frac{1}{2}\frac{b}{c} + \frac{\mathrm{P}}{\mathrm{Q}+n}.$$

If Φ and n are plotted as rectangular coordinates, the curve will be an equilateral hyperbola. The differential coefficient of this equation is

$$\mathrm{D}_n\Phi = -\frac{\mathrm{P}}{(\mathrm{Q}+n)^2} = -\frac{1}{\mathrm{P}}\left(\Phi + \frac{1}{2}\frac{b}{c}\right)^2.$$

Consequently, $\mathrm{P} = 1/c$.

When the square root is imaginary, the exponential becomes a circular function, and it will be convenient to introduce a tangent, since Φ evidently passes through infinity in this case. Now, we have the formula

$$\tan(\mathrm{B}i) = \left(1 - \frac{2}{1+\mathfrak{e}^{2\mathrm{B}}}\right)i.$$

This gives

$$\Phi = -\frac{1}{2}\frac{b}{c}\left[1 + \tan(kn+n_0)\sqrt{4\frac{ac}{b^2} - 1}\right]$$

where k has the value

$$k = \sqrt{4ac - b^2}.$$

It is a matter of no small labour to determine the values of these constants for a given series of observations of the descending amplitude; so that I should not think it worth while to do so unless the series were well observed. The observations of arc herein detailed were made as follows. Upon a brass plane perpendicular to the knife-edge making a part of the pendulum, namely, of the frame holding the knife, was stuck a horizontal scale of fortieths of an inch, so that the edge of the scale observed was exactly at the level of the lower knife-edge. Then, a wire in the focus of the reading-telescope being brought into a vertical position, its positions on the scale, estimated to the nearest tenth of a division, were read at the two extremities of the excursion. The difference of the two readings was the measure of the double amplitude. Such readings were made at every hundredth oscillation of the pendulum, for about 2000 oscillations, and afterward at every 500th or 1000th oscillation. The probable error of a reading did not, I am sure, exceed 1:400 inch. It was found convenient to carry the calculations to the nearest half of a tenth of a division of the scale; but the practice in the observations and calculations was to place the decimal point so as to make the unit a quarter of an inch. The first step toward calculating the curve of decrement of the arc was to compare the series of observations with an approximate curve for the purpose of smoothing off the variations of individual observations. The observations, as thus smoothed off, were evidently in most cases correct to the nearest 800th of an inch. Four observations, thus corrected, were then selected to be absolutely satisfied by the curve to be calculated. The first step was to use the three of largest amplitudes to compare with the formula for which k vanishes, in order to determine, by means of the fourth observation, whether the exponential or the tangential formula was to be used. In the case of the Repsold pendulum, the coefficient of friction, a, was decidedly in excess of the value for which k vanishes; but for the pendulums now considered the reverse was the case. Consequently, after having compared the observations with the intermediate formula, it was next proper to compare them with the formula with friction equal to zero, in order to see whether it was positive or negative. I then proceeded by the rule of false position to determine the constants so as to satisfy exactly the four selected values taken from the smoothed curve. As the computation is decidedly troublesome if not rightly conducted, computers will not be sorry to be furnished with an example. The 7th swinging of pendulum No. 4, with heavy end down, furnished the following observations of the descent of the arc, which I compare with a curve provisionally adapted to the purpose, and not of the form prescribed.

TABLE XIX

Descent of Arc				
Pendulum No. 4. Heavy end down. 7th Swinging				
No. of oscillations	*Observed amplitude*	*Provisional curve*	*Excess*	*Smoothed values*
300	5.58	5.57½	+0½	
400	5.46	5.47½	−1½	
500	5.38	5.37½	+0½	5.37½
600	5.28	5.28	0	
700	5.20	5.18½	+1½	
800	5.09	5.09½	−0½	
900	5.00	5.00½	−0½	
1000	4.94	4.91½	+2½	
1100	4.82	4.83	−1	
1200	4.76	4.75	+1	
1300	4.66	4.66½	−0½	
1400	4.60	4.58½	+1½	
1500	4.53	4.50½	+2½	4.51½
1600	4.44	4.43	+1	
1700	4.38	4.35½	+2½	
1800	4.29	4.28	+1	
1900	4.20	4.21	−1	
2000	4.14	4.14	0	4.14½
2500	3.81	3.81	0	
3000	3.52	3.51	+1	
3500	3.23	3.24	−1	
4000	3.00	2.99½	+0½	
4500	2.78	2.77	+1	
5000	2.58	2.56½	+1½	
5500	2.38	2.37½	+0½	2.38
6000	2.20	2.20	0	
6500	2.04	2.04	0	
7000	1.89	1.89½	−0½	
7500	1.77	1.76	+1	
8000	1.63	1.63½	−0½	
9000	1.41	1.41	0	
10000		1.22		
11000		1.05		
12000	0.90	0.88½	+1½	
13000	0.78	0.78	0	0.78½
14000	0.68	0.67	+1	

From the smoothed values in the last column, I select the following three.

n	Φ
500	5.37½
2000	4.14½
5500	2.38

By means of these, I proceed to calculate the values of Q′, b, and c, in the formula

$$\left(c\Phi + \frac{1}{2}b\right)(Q' + n) = 1.$$

I find $Q' = 7486.43$, $b = 0.0000386944$, $c = 0.0000160963$. These constants thus known, I proceed to calculate values of Φ for the following values of n. Their comparison with the smoothed values are here given.

n	Calc.	Smoothed	S – C
300	5.57½	5.57½	0
500	5.37½	5.37½	0
1000	4.91½	4.92	½
1500	4.51	4.51½	½
2000	4.14½	4.14½	0
3000	3.52	3.51½	½
4000	3.00½	3.00	½
5500	2.38	2.38	0
8000	1.60½	1.63½	3
13000	0.63	0.78½	15 ½
14000	0.49	0.68	19

Every one of the differences serves to show that the friction is here taken too great. I now begin again with the same three smoothed observations, and calculate the constants for the theory of no friction, where $\frac{c}{b}\Phi(10^{qn+Q} - 1) = 1$. To do this, I reflect that the friction being supposed to vanish, the value of c must now be cut down to balance the loss of a. Since, therefore, we previously got $c/b = .416$, I will begin by trying the value $c/b = 0.1$. Here is my calculation.

Φ	$10\,\Phi^{-1}$	$qn + Q$	*Diff.*
5.375	1.860465	.4564366	
			766418
4.145	2.412545	.5330784	
			1830653
2.380	4.201681	.7161437	

Since the numbers in the last column are not proportional to 1500:4000, the differences of n, it follows that the assumed value of $c{:}b$ will not do. I next assume $c{:}b = .07$, and now prefer to make the calculation with a table of addition-logarithms, in place of a table of reciprocals.

$\log \Phi$	$\log \frac{b}{c\,\Phi}$	$qn + Q$	*Diffs.*
0.7303785	0.4245235	0.5632209	
			847968
0.6175245	0.5373775	0.6480177	
			1972493
0.3765770	0.7783250	0.8452670	

The ratio of the numbers in the last column is now out in the opposite direction; and after two more assumptions, with the results of which I will not trouble the reader, I am led to $c{:}b = 0.0733$. This gives me $b = 0.00012865$, $c = 0.00000943$, $Q = 0.5208392$. I now calculate the values of Φ for different values of n, and find

n	*Calc.* Φ	*Obs.* Φ
500	5.375	$5.37\frac{1}{2}$
2000	4.145	$4.14\frac{1}{2}$
5500	2.380	2.38
13000	0.818	$0.78\frac{1}{2}$

These numbers suffice to show that there is a small amount of friction. I now assume $q = 0.00005$, $500q + Q = 0.5$, and give to p and P such values as exactly to satisfy the second and third smoothed observations of the four just compared with the no friction formula. The calculation is as follows.

$n' = n - 300$	$qn' + Q$	$1/(10^{qn'+Q} - 1)$	$\log(\Phi + P)$	$\Phi + P$	Calc. Φ
0	.500	9.6650886	0.7467611	5.5816	5.3512
1500	.575	9.5593469	0.6410194	4.3754	4.1450
5000	.750	9.3350373	0.4167098	2.6104	2.3800
12500	1.125	8.9088533	9.9905258	.9784	0.7480
	2nd–3rd	0.2243096			
	Subtr. log	9.8300349			
	Last + 3rd	9.1650722			
	log Ratio Φ	0.2467447			
$\log \frac{c}{b}$ = Diff. two last		1.0816725			

We next try $q = 0.00005$ $Q = 0.47 - 500q$

n'	$qn' + Q$	$1/(10^{qn'+Q} - 1)$	$\log(\Phi + P)$	$\Phi + P$	Calc. Φ
0	.470	9.7096962	0.7431890	5.5359	5.3732
1500	.545	.6007558	0.6342486	4.3077	4.1450
5000	.720	.3718077	0.4053005	2.5427	2.3800
12500	1.095	.9413787	9.9748715	0.9438	0.7811
	2nd – 3rd	0.2289481			
	Tech. Subtr. log.	0.3875039			
	2nd – log	9.2132519			
	log Ratio Φ	0.2467447			
$\log \frac{c}{b}$ = Diff. last 2		1.0334928			

We next try $q = 0.000051$ $Q = 0.5 - 500q$

n'	$qn' + Q$	$1/(10^{qn'+Q} - 1)$	$\log(\Phi + P)$	$\Phi + P$	Calc. Φ
0	.5000	9.6650886	0.7429092	5.5323	5.3609
1500	.5765	9.5573043	0.6351249	4.3164	4.1450
5000	.7550	9.3289634	0.4067840	2.5514	2.3800
12500	1.1375	9.8953555	9.9731761	0.9391	0.7677
	2nd – 3rd	0.2283409			
	Tech. Subtr. log	0.3883802			
	2nd – log	9.1689241			
	log Ratio Φ	0.2467447			
	$\log \frac{c}{b}$	1.0778206			

Proceeding in this way we find $Q + 500q = 0.4975$, $q = 0.00005$, and from this the following table has been calculated.

TABLE XX

Descent of Arc				
Pend. No 4. Heavy End Down. 7th Swinging				
No. Oscill.	*Calc. Arc.*	*Obs. Arc.*	*O.–C.*	*Smoothed*
300	5.57½	5.58	+0½	5.57½
400	5.47½	5.46	–1½	
500	5.37½	5.38	+0½	5.37½
600	5.28	5.28	0	
700	5.18	5.20	+1½	
800	5.09½	5.09	–0½	
900	5.00½	5.00	–0½	
1000	4.92	4.94	+2	4.92
1100	4.83½	4.82	–1½	
1200	4.75	4.76	+1	
1300	4.67	4.66	–1	
1400	4.59	4.60	+1	
1500	4.51	4.53	+2	4.51½
1600	4.43½	4.44	+0½	
1700	4.36	4.38	+2	
1800	4.28½	4.29	+0½	
1900	4.21½	4.20	–1½	
2000	4.14½	4.14	–0½	4.14½
2500	3.81½	3.81	–0½	
3000	3.51½	3.52	+0½	3.51½
3500	3.24½	3.23	–1½	
4000	3.00	3.00	0	3.00
4500	2.77½	2.78	+0½	
5000	2.57	2.58	+1	
5500	2.38	2.38	0	2.38
6000	2.20½	2.20	–0½	
6500	2.05	2.04	–1	
7000	1.90	1.89	–1	
7500	1.76½	1.77	+0½	
8000	1.64	1.63	–1	1.63½
9000	1.41½	1.41	–0½	
10000	1.22			
11000	1.06			
12000	.91	.90	–1	
13000	.78½	.78	–0½	0.78½
14000	.67½	.68	+0½	0.68

But although this formula thus satisfied the observations, there cannot really have been as much friction as this represents; for, according to this, the pendulum would come to rest when $n = 27954$, whereas in fact, observations of transits were often made at $n = 30000$, and were entirely satisfactory, the value of Φ being

0.060. I therefore construct a new formula to satisfy the following values

$n - 500$	Φ
0	5.375
5000	2.38
12500	0.785
29500	0.060

This time, for the sake of the illustration, I do not use the rule of false, but work algebraically. We have, then, the four equations

$$(1) \qquad \frac{1}{\mathrm{K}-1} = 5.375p + \mathrm{P}$$

$$(2) \qquad \frac{1}{\mathrm{K}k^{10}-1} = 2.380p + \mathrm{P}$$

$$(3) \qquad \frac{1}{\mathrm{K}k^{25}-1} = 0.785p + \mathrm{P}$$

$$(4) \qquad \frac{1}{\mathrm{K}k^{58}-1} = 0.060p + \mathrm{P}$$

$$(5) = (1)-(2) \qquad \frac{1}{\mathrm{K}-1} - \frac{1}{\mathrm{K}k^{10}-1} = 2.995p$$

$$(6) = (1)-(3) \qquad \frac{1}{\mathrm{K}-1} - \frac{1}{\mathrm{K}k^{25}-1} = 4.590p$$

$$(7) = (1)-(4) \qquad \frac{1}{\mathrm{K}-1} - \frac{1}{\mathrm{K}k^{58}-1} = 5.315p$$

$$(8) = (6)/(5) \qquad \frac{\dfrac{1}{\mathrm{K}-1} - \dfrac{1}{\mathrm{K}k^{25}-1}}{\dfrac{1}{\mathrm{K}-1} - \dfrac{1}{\mathrm{K}k^{10}-1}} = 1.53255$$

$$(9) = (7)/(5) \qquad \frac{\dfrac{1}{\mathrm{K}-1} - \dfrac{1}{\mathrm{K}k^{58}-1}}{\dfrac{1}{\mathrm{K}-1} - \dfrac{1}{\mathrm{K}k^{10}-1}} = 1.77462$$

Write

$$a = 0.53255 \qquad b = 0.77462$$

Clearing (8) and (9) from fractions and dividing by K (for the four equations have the trivial solution $K = 0,\ p = 0,\ P = -1$) we get

$$(10)\quad K[-ak^{35} + (1+a)k^{25} - k^{10}] = k^{25} - (1+a)k^{10} + a$$

$$(11)\quad K[-bk^{68} + (1+b)k^{58} - k^{10}] = k^{58} - (1+b)k^{10} + b$$

$$(12) = (11)/(10)\quad \frac{bk^{68} - (1+b)k^{58} + k^{10}}{ak^{35} - (1+a)k^{25} + k^{10}} = \frac{k^{58} - (1+b)k^{10} + b}{k^{25} - (1+a)k^{10} + a}$$

clearing from fractions and dividing by k^{10}, we get

$$(13)\quad (b-a)(k^{83}-1) - (b-a)k^{10}(k^{63}-1) - (1+a)bk^{15}(k^{53}-1) + (a+b+2ab)k^{25}(k^{33}-1) - a(1+b)k^{35}(k^{13}-1) = 0.$$

This is divisible by $k^9 + k^8 + k^7 + k^6 + k^5 + k^4 + k^3 + k^2 + k + 1$ and the remaining factor is

$$(b-a)(k^{73}+1) - (1+a)bk^{15}(k^{43}+1) + a(1+b)k^{25}(k^{23}+1) = 0.$$

This is again divisible by $(k^5-1)(k+1)$, but there is no need of dividing out this factor at present; but we may at once find the numerical solution. We soon find $\log k = 0.0291$, $p = .056434$, $P = .001424$. With these values, we calculate the following table:

TABLE XXI

Descent of Arc			
Pend. No 4. Heavy end Down. 7th Swinging			
No. of Oscillation	*Calc. Arc.*	*Smoothed Obs. Arc.*	*O.– C.*
–200	5.57	5.57½	+0½
0	5.37½	5.37½	0
500	4.92½	4.92	–0½
1000	4.52½	4.51½	–1
1500	4.16	4.14½	–1½
2500	3.53	3.51½	–1½
3500	3.00½	3.00	–0½
5000	2.38	2.38	0
7500	1.63	1.63½	+0½
12500	0.78½	0.78½	0
13500	0.68	0.68	0
29500	0.05½	0.05½	0

This shows that no formula of the kind assumed can perfectly agree with the facts.

For different pendulums having the same figure and dimensions, it is plain that b' will be inversely as the moment of inertia; that is, $b'\mathrm{M}hl$ will be constant, where M is the mass, h the distance of the functioning edge from the centre of mass, and l the length of the synchronal simple pendulum. Writing λ' for the length of the sidereal seconds pendulum at Washington, and expressing M in grammes, h in centimetres, I find for the metre pendulums $\frac{\mathrm{M}hl}{\lambda'}b' = 46.8$ at 30 inches pressure and 20°C. The value of P is independent of the moment of inertia, and I find for the same pressure and temperature, $\log \mathrm{P} = -1.2225$. These values are the means of the numbers shown in the following table (rejecting No. 2, Heavy end down, on account of the inferiority of the observations, and giving the observations with heavy end up one third weight).

TABLE XXII. Constants for the Descent of the Arc.

Pend.	Position	$\log {}^1/_{\mathrm{P}}$	$1000b'$	$\frac{\mathrm{M}hl}{1000\lambda'}$	$\frac{\mathrm{M}hl}{\lambda'}b'$
No. 4	Heavy end down	1.2232	0.0581	809	47.0
No. 1		1.2240	0.0597	784	46.8
No. 2		1.2215	0.0613	808	49.5
No. 4	Heavy end up	1.2172	0.1775	270.7	48.1
No. 1		1.2213	0.1727	262.6	45.3
No. 2		1.2227	0.1728	268.9	46.5

The values in this table are means of the observed swingings reduced to the above pressure and temperature. The constant b' ought to consist of two terms (see "Measurements of Gravity at Initial Stations," p. 66) the larger proportional to the square root of the pressure and inversely as the 8th root of the absolute temperature, and the other, theoretically only of 1/20 the magnitude of the first, independent of the pressure and directly as the ¾th power of the absolute temperature. The theory of the effect of viscosity upon the pendulum is not sufficiently perfect for us to rely on magnitudes of these terms; yet one may safely assume that b' is pretty nearly proportional to $\sqrt{p}$. It is impossible at present to say how the temperature will affect, further than it cannot have a large effect. Pendulum No. 1 was swung at Lady Franklin Bay by General Greely at –27°C, and the value of b there was larger than at the Smithsonian at +20°C in ratio of the square roots of the absolute temperatures. But we cannot believe the coefficient is really so large. In view of all the facts, I have not attempted to correct b' for temperature, but have assumed it proportional to $\sqrt{p}$. The constant $c' = b'\mathrm{P}$ seems clearly proportional to the air, so that P is proportional to the absolute temperature and inversely as the square root of the pressure. That is, taking 30 inches as the mean pressure and 20°C as the mean temperature, every additional inch of pressure subtracts .0072 from log 1/P and every additional degree centigrade adds .0015 to it. The constant Q is altered by ¾ of these amounts.

I add the comparison of some of the curves with the observations, and the records of the descent of the arc in those swingings in which it was the most carefully observed.

[*Table XXIII omitted.*]

TABLE XXIV

Calculation of Constants of Formula of Descent of Arc				
Smithsonian. Pendulum. No. 2. Heavy end down.				
No. of Oscil.	*Calc.*	*Obs.*	*O. – C.*	*Smoothed*
0	5.87½	5.85	–2½	5.85
500	5.31	5.31	0	5.31
1000	4.82	4.83	+1	4.83
1500	4.41½	4.41	–0½	4.40½
2000	4.00	4.02	+2	4.02
2500	3.65½	3.68	+2½	3.67
3000	3.35	3.36	+1	3.35½
3500	3.07½	3.08	+0½	3.07½
4000	2.82½	2.83	+0½	2.82½
4500	2.60	2.60	0	2.60
5000	2.40	2.44	+4	2.39½
5500	2.21½	2.21	–0½	2.21
6000	2.04	2.03½	–0½	2.04
6500	1.89	1.88½	–0½	1.88½
7000	1.74½	1.75	+0½	1.74½
7500	1.62	1.61½	–0½	1.61½
8000	1.49½	1.49½	0	1.49½
8500	1.39	1.39	0	1.39
9000	1.29	1.30	+1	1.29½
9500	1.19½	1.20	+0½	1.21
10000	1.11			1.13

TABLE XXIV *(continued)*

No. of Oscil.	*Calc.*	*Obs.*	*O. – C.*	*Smoothed.*
10500	1.03½	1.04	+0½	1.06
11000	0.96	0.98½	+2½	0.99½
11500	0.89½	0.91	+1½	0.94
12000	0.83	0.84½	+1½	0.89
12500	0.77½	0.79	+1½	0.85
13000	0.72	0.74	+2	0.82
13500	0.67	0.67½	+0½	0.80
14000	0.62½	0.63	+0½	
14500	0.58½	0.59	+0½	
15000	0.54½	0.55	+0½	

[Tables XXV–XXX omitted.]

TABLE XXXI

Smithsonian 1884–85. Decrement of Arc. Pendulum No. 2. Heavy End Down											
Oscillations are counted from the first transit.											
No. of oscill.	180	200	300	400	500	600	700	800	900	1000	1100
1	5.50									4.95	
2	5.55								4.97		
3			5.55						4.97		
4			5.55						4.95		
5			5.50						4.96		
6	5.64		5.54						4.94		
7		5.58	5.48	5.37	5.26	5.18	5.07	4.98	4.88		
8		5.64									4.92
9		5.66	5.56						4.95		
10	5.64		5.57	5.41	5.34	5.21	5.16	5.03	4.97	4.84	4.78
11	5.64		5.52	5.41	5.32	5.20	5.11	5.04	4.93	4.83	
12	5.60		5.51	5.40	5.27	5.20	5.09	5.00	4.89	4.81	4.72
13	5.64		5.55	5.41	5.31						
Means	5.64	5.65	5.54	5.41	5.31	5.20	5.12	5.01	4.94	4.83	4.75

TABLE XXXI *(continued)*

Smithsonian 1884–85. Decrement of Arc. Pendulum No. 2. Heavy End Down. Oscillations are counted from the first transit.											
No. of oscill.	1200	1300	1400	1500	1600	1700	1800	1900	2000	2100	2200
1				4.45					4.07		
2				4.45			4.21	4.14	4.07	3.99	3.92
3											
4					4.36	4.26	4.20	4.11	4.06	3.98	3.89
5				4.42	4.35	4.28	4.20	4.12	4.05	3.98	3.88
6											
7											
8											
9											
10	4.66	4.60	4.50	4.42	4.37	4.26	4.19	4.11	4.02	3.98	3.89
11				4.40					4.02		
12	4.62	4.57	4.45	4.40	4.31	4.22	4.18	4.08	4.01	3.96	3.85
13											
								4.11	4.04	3.98	3.89
Means	4.64	4.59	4.48	4.42	4.35	1700	1800	1900	2000	2100	2200
No. of oscill.	2300	2400	2500	3000	3500	4000	4500	5000	5500	6000	6500
1			3.43					2.49			
2	3.86	3.76	3.74								
3											
4	3.84	3.76	3.70					2.44			
5	3.82	3.77	3.69					2.38			
6				3.36	3.06	2.81	2.59			2.01	1.86
7											
8											
9											
10	3.80	3.76	3.68								
11			3.68	3.34	3.08	2.84	2.60				
12	3.80	3.74	3.66	3.38	3.09	2.83	2.61	2.38	2.21	2.06	1.91
Means	3.82	3.76	3.69	3.36	3.08	2.83	2.60	2.44	2.21	2.04	1.89

TABLE XXXI *(continued)*

Smithsonian 1884–85. Decrement of Arc. Pendulum No. 2. Heavy End Down.								
No. of oscill.	7000	7500	8000	8500	9000	9500	10000	10500
1								
2								
3								
4								
5								
6								1.12
7	1.73	1.60	1.47	1.38	1.28	1.19		1.08
8		1.64	1.52	1.41	1.31	1.21		
9								
10								
11								1.05
12								
13	1.77	1.63	1.52	1.40	1.32	1.21		1.03
Means	1.75	1.62	1.50	1.40	1.30	1.20		1.04
No. of oscill.	11000	11500	12000	12500	13000	13500	14000	14500
1								
2								
3			0.87					
4								
5								
6								
7								
8								
9								
10	0.98	0.91	0.86	0.79	0.73	0.67	0.63	0.59
11								
12	0.99	0.91	0.83	0.79	0.75	0.68	0.63	0.59
Means	0.99	0.91	0.85	0.79	0.74	0.67½	0.63	0.59

[Tables XXXII – XXXIX omitted.]

RESULTS OF SINGLE SWINGINGS

The station-numbers given above are calculated from the periods of oscillation of the different pendulums in their two positions and in the two stands, which periods are commonly the means each of the results obtained from eight swingings. The first tables following show, first, the synopsis of each such series reduced to its mean pressure and temperature, and corrected for rate of time keeper, arc, inclination, and difference of temperature above and below. Following these tables will be found another set showing these corrections to each swinging, the clock-time of the beginning and ending of each, and the number of oscillations it comprises.

TABLE XL. Smithsonian 1884–85. Pendulum No. 1.

Heavy end down					Heavy end up				
No. of swinging	Temp.	Pressure	*n*T	Excess over mean	No. of swinging	Temp.	Pressure	*n*T	Excess over mean
	°	*in*	*s*			°	*in*	*s*	
1	20.15	29.711	15095.265	+.022	1	20.75	30.256	5028.101	+.031
2	20.58	29.643	.230	−.013	2	21.02	30.266	.043	−.027
3	20.63	29.753	.212	−.031	3	21.23	30.282	.106	+.036
4	20.53	30.044	.229	−.014	4	21.21	30.300	.093	+.023
5	20.20	29.624	.274	+.031	5	20.96	30.348	.028	−.042
6	20.69	29.618	.232	−.011	6	20.98	30.336	.061	−.009
7	21.04	29.866	.216	−.027	7	21.00	30.344	.048	−.022
8	21.18	30.078	.202	−.041	8	20.99	30.402	.084	+.014
9	20.33	30.681	.251	+.008					
10	20.54	30.640	.276	+.033					
11	20.48	30.608	.282	+.039					
12	20.10	30.462	.246	+.003					
Means	20.54	30.061.	15095.243	±.006	Means	21.02	30.317	5028.070	±.008
Corr. to standard atmos.			+ .005		Corr. to standard atmos.			−.033	
Expansion			− .766		Expansion			−.277	
Flexure			− 1.037		Flexure			−.116	
Corrected time			15093.445		Corrected time			5027.644	
	°	*in*	*s*		10000 osc. simple pend.			10065.809	±.0⅛1
13	13.64	30.453	15094.637	+.012					
14	13.98	30.390	.569	−.056					
15	15.43	30.295	.636	+.011					
16	15.75	30.160	.656	+.030					
Means	14.70	30.324	15094.625						
Corr. to standard atmos.			−.149						
Expansion			+.041						
Flexure			−1.037						
Corrected time			15093.489						

TABLE XLI. Smithsonian 1884–85. Pendulum No. 2.

Heavy end down					Heavy end up				
No. of swinging	Temp.	Pressure	nT	Excess over mean	No. of swinging	Temp.	Pressure	nT	Excess over mean
	°	*in*	*s*			°	*in*	*s*	
1	19.60	30.356	15094.798	+.015	1	19.04	30.539	5031.817	+.017
2	19.31	30.297	.779	−.004	2	19.25	30.538	.831	+.031
3	19.35	30.174	.826	+.043	3	19.50	30.564	.828	+.028
4	19.41	30.116	.772	−.011	4	19.45	30.596	.843	+.043
5	19.30	30.167	.784	+.001	5	20.26	30.540	.763	−.037
6	18.72	30.608	.765	−.018	6	20.44	30.516	.771	−.029
7	19.01	30.590	.807	+.024	7	20.52	30.490	.767	−.033
8	19.06	30.585	.798	+.015	8	20.50	30.482	.787	−.013
9	19.20	30.494	.772	−.011					
10	20.43	30.354	.738	−.045					
11	20.68	30.270	.760	−.023					
12	20.54	30.211	.771	−.012					
13	20.84	30.131	.803	+.020					
Means	19.65	30.335	15094.783	±.002	Means	19.87	30.533	5031.800	±.009
logT^2			547.13		logT^2			550.67	
same in mean time			309.65		same in mean time			313.19	
(log) oscill. per diem			86090.35		(log) oscill. per diem			86086.81	
Emp. Temp. Cor.			+0.58		Emp. Temp. Cor.			+0.61	
Flexure			+4.91		Flexure			+1.64	
Expansion			+3.70		Expansion			+3.87	
1st Atm. Effect			+0.30		1st Atm. Effect			+1.40	
2nd Atm. Effect			+0.04		2nd Atm. Effect			+0.15	
Cor. oscill. per diem			86099.88		Cor. oscill. per diem			86094.48	

TABLE XLII. Smithsonian 1884–85. Pendulum No. 3.

Heavy end down					Heavy end up				
No. of swinging	Temp.	Pressure	nT	Excess over mean	No. of swinging	Temp.	Pressure	nT	Excess over mean
	°	*in*	*s*	*s*		°	*in*	*s*	*s*
1	20.50	29.871	14431.557	+0.045	1	17.96	29.807	4809.523	+0.006
2	20.91	29.734	.533	+0.021	2	18.17	29.776	.526	+0.009
3	20.72	29.556	.567	+0.055	3	18.34	29.771	.501	−0.016
4	20.54	29.905	.601	+0.089	4	18.40	29.782	.516	−0.001
5	18.09	29.720	.463	−0.049	5	16.89	30.080	.525	+0.008
6	17.26	29.716	.518	+0.006	6	17.22	30.046	.527	+0.010
7	17.15	29.921	.529	+0.017	7	17.52	29.994	.502	−0.015
8	16.79	30.101	.458	−0.054	8	17.44	29.935	.519	+0.002
9	16.99	30.461	.451	−0.061					
10	17.13	30.446	.529	+0.017					
11	16.74	30.242	.446	−0.066					
12	17.20	29.933	.486	−0.026					
Means	18.34	29.967	14431.512	±0.011	Means	17.74	29.899	4809.517	±0.003
$\log T^2$			−3355.90		$\log T^2$			3373.70	
same in mean time			−3593.38		same in mean time			3611.18	
(log) oscill. per diem			89993.38		(log) oscill. per diem			90011.18	
Emp. Temp.			+0.42		Emp. Temp.			+0.34	
Flexure			+5.03		Flexure			+1.69	
Expansion			+2.65		Expansion			+2.17	
1st Atm. Effect			+0.08		1st Atm. Effect			+0.20	
2nd Atm. Effect			+0.01		2nd Atm. Effect			+0.05	
Cor. oscill. per diem			90001.57		Cor. oscill. per diem			90015.63	

TABLE XLIII. Smithsonian 1885. Pendulum No. 4.

Before wrenching					*After wrenching*				
Heavy end down									
No. of swing-ing	Temp.	Pres-sure	nT	Excess over mean	No. of swing-ing	Temp.	Pres-sure	nT	Excess over mean
	°	*in*	*s*			°	*in*	*s*	
1	18.81	30.430	15097.126	+.002	17	16.76	30.225	15097.776	−.003
2	19.26	30.526	.150	+.026	18	16.96	30.156	.817	+.038
3	19.11	30.704	.139	+.015	19	16.83	30.136	.745	−.034
4	18.77	30.804	.111	−.013					
5	18.96	30.212	.054	−.070					
6	19.02	30.138	.090	−.034					
7	18.86	30.041	.137	+.013					
8	18.66	29.843	.116	−.008					
9	19.98	29.648	.090	−.034					
10	20.10	29.782	.130	+.006					
11	20.08	29.886	.090	−.034					
12	19.89	29.989	.122	−.002					
13	17.40	29.492	.195	+.071					
14	17.49	29.656	.204	+.080					
15	16.05	30.277	.161	+.037					
16	15.94	30.306	.078	−.046					
Means	18.65	30.108	15097.124		Means	16.85	30.172	15097.779	
Corr. to standard atmos.									
Heavy end up									
	°	*in*	*s*			°	*in*	*s*	
1	18.96	30.823	5031.987		13	16.74	30.084	5031.841	
2	19.30	30.734	.960		14	17.03	30.052	.827	
3	19.40	30.714	.927		15	17.22	30.036	.816	
4	19.34	30.700	.979		16	16.83	29.954	.824	
5	18.87	29.624	.884		17	17.14	29.902	.829	
6	19.30	29.518	.891		18	17.27	29.898	.854	
7	19.52	29.503	.828						
8	19.56	29.494	.826						
9	17.14	29.886	.775						
10	16.94	29.950	.793						
11	16.46	30.185	.746						
12	16.47	30.176	.793						
Means	18.44	30.109	5031.866		Means	17.04	29.988	5031.832	

TABLE XLIV. Smithsonian 1886. Pendulum No. 2.

Old Stand					New Stand				
Heavy end down									
No. of swinging	Temp.	Pressure	*n*T	Excess over mean	No. of swinging	Temp.	Pressure	*n*T	Excess over mean
	°	*in*	*s*			°	*in*	*s*	
1	18.39	29.425	15094.073	−.038	1	19.39	29.883	15094.006	+.015
2	18.35	.492	.161	+.050	2	19.41	.849	.050	+.059
3	18.24	.644	.115	+.004	3	19.22	.893	.028	+.037
4	18.00	.849	.084	−.027	4	19.13	.937	.025	+.032
5	18.53	.931	.093	−.018	5	19.56	30.037	15093.942	−.048
6	18.78	.990	.109	−.002	6	19.81	.002	15094.005	+.014
7	18.34	30.099	.160	+.049	7	19.58	.045	15093.947	−.050
8	18.23	.210	.093	−.018	8	19.38	.167	.928	−.063
Means	18.35	29.830	15094.111	±.008	Means	19.43	29.977	15093.991	±.013
logT^2			543.26		logT^2			542.57	
same in mean time			305.78		same in mean time			305.09	
(log) oscill. per diem			86094.22		(log) oscill. per diem			86094.91	
Emp. Temp. Cor.			+0.42		Emp. Temp. Cor.			+0.55	
Flexure			+3.83		Flexure			+3.00	
Expansion			+2.66		Expansion			+3.51	
1st Atm. Effect			−0.06		1st Atm. Effect			0.03	
2nd Atm. Effect			+0.01		2nd Atm. Effect			+0.02	
Cor. oscill. per diem			86101.08		Cor. oscill. per diem			86101.96	
Heavy end up									
	°	*in*	*s*			°	*in*	*s*	
1	17.93	30.011	5031.714	+.027	1	19.33	30.109	5031.614	+.001
2	18.40	29.976	.731	+.044	2	19.57	.090	.574	−.039
3	18.77	.942	.709	+.022	3	19.74	.073	.584	−.029
4	18.85	.928	.687	−.000	4	19.70	.067	.592	−.021
5	18.74	30.249	.673	−.014	5	18.48	.327	.641	+.028
6	19.04	.225	.672	−.015	6	18.77	.312	.652	+.039
7	19.20	.205	.672	−.015	7	19.02	.221	.652	+.039
8	19.07	.199	.640	−.047	8	19.17	.160	.596	−.017
Means	18.75	30.092	5031.687	±.007	Means	19.22	30.170	5031.613	±.008
logT^2			548.72		logT^2			547.44	
same in mean time			311.24		same in mean time			309.96	
(log) oscill. per diem			86088.76		(log) oscill. per diem			86090.04	
Emp. Temp. Cor.			+0.47		Emp. Temp. Cor.			+0.53	
Flexure			+1.28		Flexure			+1.00	
Expansion			+2.98		Expansion			+3.35	
1st Atm. Effect			+0.46		1st Atm. Effect			+0.56	
2nd Atm. Effect			+0.08		2nd Atm. Effect			+0.09	
Cor. oscill. per diem			86094.03		Cor. oscill. per diem			86095.57	

TABLE XLV. Smithsonian 1886. Pendulum No. 3.

Old Stand					New Stand				
Heavy end down									
No. of swinging	Temp.	Pressure	*n*T	Excess over mean	No. of swinging	Temp.	Pressure	*n*T	Excess over mean
	°	*in*	*s*			°	*in*	*s*	
1	19.20	30.070	14431.463	+.077	1	19.16	30.061	14431.185	−.065
2	19.26	.006	.471	+.085	2	19.52	29.934	.525	−.024
3	18.98	.003	.456	+.070	3	19.19	.873	.553	+.004
4	18.88	29.989	.405	+.019	4	19.27	.783	.503	−.046
5	19.39	.693	.346	−.040	5	20.30	.855	.553	+.004
6	19.48	.566	.316	−.070	6	20.26	.873	.559	+.010
7	19.46	.419	.355	−.031	7	20.25	.906	.617	+.068
8	19.38	.376	.277	−.109	8	20.39	.972	.597	+.048
Means	19.25	29.765	14431.386	±.020		19.79	29.907	14431.549	±.011
$\log T^2$			−3356.66		$\log T^2$			−3355.68	
same in mean time			−3594.14		same in mean time			−3593.16	
(log) oscill. per diem			89994.14		(log) oscill. per diem			89993.16	
Emp. Temp. Cor.			+0.53		Emp. Temp. Cor.			+0.60	
Flexure			+3.92		Flexure			+3.07	
Expansion			+3.37		Expansion			+3.79	
1st Atm. Effect			−0.20		1st Atm. Effect			−0.11	
2nd Atm. Effect			+0.01		2nd Atm. Effect			+0.01	
Cor. oscill. per diem			90001.77		Cor. oscill. per diem			90000.52	
Heavy end up									
	°	*in*	*s*			°	*in*	*s*	
1	19.21	29.967	4809.480	−.009	1	19.87	29.720	4809.487	−.014
2	19.49	.945	.485	−.004	2	19.86	.685	.493	−.008
3	19.66	.916	.453	−.036	3	19.89	.631	.472	−.029
4	19.62	.881	.479	−.010	4	19.97	.544	.472	−.029
5	18.94	.574	.514	+.025	5	20.57	30.036	.529	+.028
6	19.11	.586	.516	+.027	6	20.59	.036	.533	+.032
7	19.43	.594	.495	+.006	7	20.63	.023	.504	+.003
8	19.60	.615	.492	+.003	8	20.62	29.992	.521	+.020
Means	19.38	29.760	4809.489	±.003	Means	20.25	29.833	4809.501	±.007
$\log T^2$			3374.20		$\log T^2$			−3373.99	
same in mean time			3611.68		same in mean time			−3611.47	
(log) oscill. per diem			90011.68		(log) oscill. per diem			90011.47	
Emp. Temp. Cor.			+0.55		Emp. Temp. Cor.			+0.66	
Flexure			+1.31		Flexure			+1.03	
Expansion			+3.47		Expansion			+4.16	
1st Atm. Effect			−0.66		1st Atm. Effect			−0.70	
2nd Atm. Effect			+0.02		2nd Atm. Effect			+0.03	
Cor. oscill. per diem			90016.37		Cor. oscill. per diem			90016.65	

TABLE XLVI. Ann Arbor. Pendulum No. 2.

Old Stand					New Stand				
Heavy end down									
No. of swinging	Temp	Pressure	nT	Excess over Mean	No. of swingings	Temp	Pressure	nT	Excess over Mean
	°	*in*	*s*			°	*in*	*s*	
1	17.70	29.100	15092.438	+.007	1	18.61	29.183	15092.548	+.053
2	17.24	29.144	.471	+.040	2	18.65	28.984	.512	+.017
3	17.24	29.182	.467	+.036	3	18.71	28.969	.538	+.043
4	17.09	29.204	.470	+.039	4	19.13	28.821	.485	−.010
5	18.99	28.699	.405	−.026	5	18.31	29.118	.532	+.037
6	18.88	28.791	.377	−.054	6	18.23	29.040	.445	−.050
7	18.95	28.897	.442	+.011	7	19.08	28.946	.476	−.019
8	18.31	29.162	.376	−.055	8	18.56	28.858	.423	−.072
Means	18.05	29.022	15092.431	±.011	Means	18.66	28.990	15092.495	±.012
log T^2			533.59		log T^2			533.96	
same in mean time			296.11		same in mean time			296.48	
(log) oscill. per diem			86103.89		(log) oscill. per diem			86103.52	
Emp. Temp. Cor.			+0.38		Emp. Temp. Cor.			+0.46	
Flexure			+4.58		Flexure			+5.17	
Expansion			+2.42		Expansion			+2.91	
1st Atm. Effect			−0.79		1st Atm. Effect			−0.89	
2nd Atm. Effect			−0.04		2nd Atm. Effect			−0.04	
Cor. oscill. per diem			86110.44		Cor. oscill. per diem			86111.13	
Heavy end up									
	°	*in*	*s*			°	*in*	*s*	
1	16.93	29.214	5030.931	−.010	1	17.70	29.079	5030.971	.000
2	18.25	29.164	.960	+.028	2	18.07	29.165	.974	+.003
3	17.98	28.808	.904	−.037	3	17.15	29.066	.974	+.013
4	18.65	28.608	.946	+.005	4	17.14	29.021	.992	+.021
5	17.79	29.280	.928	.000	5	18.53	29.118	.949	−.022
6	17.84	29.197	.937	+.012	6	18.76	28.987	.949	−.022
7	18.01	29.176	.915	−.026	7	18.91	28.948	.971	.000
8	18.03	29.172	.971	+.030	8	19.20	28.858	.981	+.010
Means	18.06	29.077	5030.937	±.006	Means	18.18	29.030	5030.971	±.004
log T^2			535.77		log T^2			536.36	
same in mean time			298.29		same in mean time			298.88	
(log) oscill. per diem			86101.71		(log) oscill. per diem			86101.12	
Emp. Temp. Cor.			+0.38		Emp. Temp. Cor.			+0.40	
Flexure			+1.52		Flexure			+1.72	
Expansion			+2.43		Expansion			+2.53	
1st Atm. Effect			−2.24		1st Atm. Effect			−2.41	
2nd Atm. Effect			−0.10		2nd Atm. Effect			−0.10	
Cor. oscill. per diem			86103.70		Cor. oscill. per diem			86103.26	

TABLE XLVII. Ann Arbor. Pendulum No. 3.

Old Stand					New Stand				
Heavy end down									
No. of swinging	Temp	Pressure	nT	Excess over Mean	No. of swingings	Temp	Pressure	nT	Excess over Mean
	o	*in*	*s*			*o*	*in*	*s*	
1	18.63	29.183	14429.809	+.006	1	17.63	29.100	14429.415	–.027
2	18.69	28.984	.811	+.008	2	17.23	29.144	.496	+.054
3	18.69	28.969	.836	+.033	3	17.21	29.182	.491	+.049
4	19.20	28.821	.798	–.005	4	17.05	29.204	.476	+.034
5	18.33	29.118	.747	–.056	5	18.79	28.699	.441	–.001
6	17.89	29.040	.854	+.051	6	18.61	28.791	.368	–.074
7	19.27	28.946	.811	‘+.008	7	18.69	28.897	.427	–.015
8	18.59	28.858	.761	–.042	8	18.19	29.162	.420	–.022
Means	18.66	28.990	14429.803	±.008	Means	17.92	29.022	14429.442	±.011
log T^2			–3366.19		log T^2			–3368.36	
same in mean time			–3603.67		same in mean time			–3605.84	
(log) oscill. per diem			90003.67		(log) oscill. per diem			90005.84	
Emp. Temp. Cor.			+0.46		Emp. Temp. Cor.			+0.36	
Flexure			+4.69		Flexure			+5.29	
Expansion			+2.90		Expansion			+2.31	
1st Atm. Effect			–0.86		1st Atm. Effect			–0.77	
2nd Atm. Effect			–0.04		2nd Atm. Effec			–0.03	
Cor. oscill. per diem			90010.82		Cor. oscill. per diem			90013.00	
Heavy end up									
	o	*in*	*s*			*o*	*in*	*s*	
1	17.73	29.079	4808.871	+.000	1	16.93	29.214	4808.843	+.021
2	18.33	29.165	.775	–.096	2	18.04	29.164	.837	+.015
3	17.14	29.066	.892	+.021	3	17.91	28.808	.789	–.033
4	17.17	29.021	.979	+.108	4	18.55	28.608	.833	+.011
5	18.49	29.118	.856	–.015	5	17.81	29.280	.816	–.006
6	18.87	28.987	.849	–.022	6	17.89	29.197	.833	+.011
7	19.03	28.946	.873	+.002	7	18.03	29.176	.815	–.007
8	19.41	28.858	.876	+.005	8	18.03	29.172	.812	–.010
Means	18.27	29.030	4808.871	±.011	Means	17.90	29.077	4808.822	±.005
log T^2			–3385.36		log T^2			–3386.25	
same in mean time			–3622.84		same in mean time			–3623.73	
(log) oscill. per diem			90022.84		(log) oscill. per diem			90023.73	
Emp. Temp. Cor.			+0.41		Emp. Temp. Cor.			+0.36	
Flexure			+1.57		Flexure			+1.77	
Expansion			+2.59		Expansion			+2.30	
1st Atm. Effect					1st Atm. Effect				
2nd Atm. Effect					2nd Atm. Effect				
Cor. oscill. per diem			90024.93		Cor. oscill. per diem			90025.92	

TABLE XLVIII. Madison. Pendulum No. 2.

Old Stand					New Stand				
Heavy End Down									
No. of swinging	Temp	Pressure	*n*T	Excess over Mean	No. of swinging	Temp	Pressure	*n*T	Excess over Mean
	o	*in*	*s*			*o*	*in*	*s*	
1	19.30	28.794	15092.155	+.047	1	18.36	29.148	15092.088	+.009
3	19.56	28.783	.108	+.001	2	18.28	29.159	.072	−.007
4	19.71	28.803	.109	+.001	3	18.61	29.090	.049	−.030
5	18.92	28.772	.082	−.026	4	18.25	29.216	.081	+.002
6	19.05	28.812	.104	−.004	5	18.20	29.302	.078	−.001
7	18.67	29.075	.069	−.039	6	18.28	29.260	.095	+.016
8	18.76	29.072	.123	+.015	7	18.32	29.155	.090	+.011
9	18.71	29.028	.108	.000					
10	18.75	28.972	.109	+.001					
Means	19.05	28.901	15092.108	±.004	Means	18.33	29.190	15092.079	±.004
$\log T^2$			531.73		$\log T^2$			531.56	
same in mean time			294.25		same in mean time			294.8	
(log) oscill. per diem			86105.75		(log) oscill. per diem			86105.92	
Emp. Temp. Cor.			+0.51		Emp. Temp. Cor.			+0.42	
Flexure			+4.16		Flexure			+4.48	
Expansion			+3.22		Expansion			+2.65	
1st Atm. Effect			−1.01		1st Atm. Effect			−0.65	
2nd Atm. Effect			−0.04		2nd Atm. Effect			−0.03	
Cor. oscill. per diem			86112.59		Cor. oscill. per diem			86112.79	
Heavy end up									
	o	*in*	*s*			*o*	*in*	*s*	
1	17.62	28.990	5030.879	+.045	1	18.58	29.058	5030.845	−.010
2	18.11	29.010	.828	+.004	2	18.54	29.135	.878	+.023
3	18.21	29.039	.882	+.048	3	18.55	29.174	.875	+.020
4	18.82	29.087	.853	+.019	4	18.44	29.215	.828	−.027
5	18.94	29.034	.783	−.051	5	18.41	29.218	.860	+.005
5½	19.06	29.038	.862	+.028	6	18.39	29.119	.864	+.009
6	19.37	29.120	.792	−.042	7	18.45	29.129	.838	−.017
7	19.66	29.106	.780	−.054					
Means	18.72	29.053	5030.832	±.012	Means	18.48	29.150	5030.855	±.005
$\log T^2$			533.96		$\log T^2$			534.36	
same in mean time			296.48		same in mean time			296.88	
(log) oscill. per diem			86103.52		(log) oscill. per diem			86103.12	
Emp. Temp. Cor.			+0.46		Emp. Temp. Cor.			+0.44	
Flexure			+1.39		Flexure			+2.77	
Expansion			+2.96		Expansion				
1st Atm. Effect			−2.49		1st Atm. Effect			−2.15	
2nd Atm. Effect			−0.10		2nd Atm. Effect			−0.08	
Cor. oscill. per diem			86105.74		Cor. oscill. per diem			86105.59	

TABLE XLIX. Madison. Pendulum No. 3.

Old Stand					New Stand				
Heavy end down									
No. of swinging	Temp	Pressure	nT	Excess over Mean	No. of swingings	Temp	Pressure	nT	Excess over Mean
	o	in	s			o	in	s	
1	18.24	29.148	14429.469	+.004	1	19.26	28.794	14429.113	+.110
2	18.18	29.159	.450	−.015	2	19.20	28.824	.064	+.061
3	18.59	29.090	.446	−.019	3	19.55	28.783	.004	+.001
4	18.31	29.216	.491	+.026	4	19.55	28.803	.030	+.027
5	18.41	29.302	.436	−.029	5	19.00	28.772	14428.942	−.061
6	18.47	29.260	.481	+.016	6	18.80	28.812	14429.004	+.001
7	18.42	29.155	.485	+.020	7	18.63	29.075	14428.962	−.041
					8	18.82	29.072	.940	−.063
					9	18.73	29.028	14429.040	+.037
					10	18.71	28.972	14428.932	−.071
Means	18.37	29.190	14429.465	±.006	Means	19.02	28.894	14429.003	±.013
logT^2			−3368.22		logT^2			−3371.00	
same in mean time			−3605.70		same in mean time			−3608.48	
(log) oscill. per diem			90005.70		(log) oscill. per diem			90008.48	
Emp. Temp. Cor.			+0.42		Emp. Temp. Cor.			+0.50	
Flexure			+4.26		Flexure			+4.50	
Expansion			+2.67		Expansion			+3.18	
1st Atm. Effect			−0.65		1st Atm. Effect			−0.99	
2nd Atm. Effect			−0.02		2nd Atm. Effect			−0.04	
Cor. oscill. per diem			90012.38		Cor. oscill. per diem			90015.63	
Heavy end up									
	o	in	s			o	in	s	
1	18.48	29.058	4808.770	+.027					
2	18.40	29.135	.728	−.015	2	18.22	29.010	4808.705	+.010
3	18.46	29.174	.752	+.009	3	18.50	29.039	.698	+.003
4	18.38	29.215	.694	−.049	4	18.54	29.087	.699	+.004
5	18.39	29.218	.766	+.023	5	19.02	29.036	.704	+.009
6	18.34	29.119	.720	−.023	6	19.46	29.120	.697	+.002
7	18.38	29.129	.768	+.025	7	19.74	29.106	.667	−.028
Means	18.40	29.150	4808.743	±.008	Means	18.91	29.066	4808.695	±.004
logT^2			−3387.67		logT^2			−3388.54	
same in mean time			3625.15		same in mean time			−3626.02	
(log) oscill. per diem					(log) oscill. per diem			90026.02	
Emp. Temp. Cor.			−0.42		Emp. Temp. Cor.			0.49	
Flexure			+1.43		Flexure			+1.54	
Expansion			+2.69		Expansion			+3.10	
1st Atm. Effect			−2.07		1st Atm. Effect			−2.46	
2nd Atm. Effect			−0.08		2nd Atm. Effect			−0.10	
Cor. oscill. per diem			90027.64		Cor. oscill. per diem			90028.59	

TABLE L. Cornell. Pendulum No. 2.

Old Stand

No. of swinging	Temp	Pressure	nT	Excess over Mean
Heavy end down				
	o	in	s	
5	14.58	29.310	15092.583	−.064
6	14.86	29.329	.612	−.035
7	15.05	29.298	.589	−.058
8	15.35	29.298	.568	−.079
9	17.04	29.737	.736	+.089
10	17.88	29.818	.679	+.032
11	18.00	29.792	.691	+.044
12	17.35	29.700	.719	+.072
13	18.15	29.405	.649	+.002
Means	16.47	29.521	15092.647	−.016
logT²			534.83	
same in mean time			297.35	
(log) oscill. per diem			86102.65	
Emp. Temp. Cor.			+0.18	
Flexure			+6.14	
Expansion			+1.17	
1st Atm. Effect			−0.17	
2nd Atm. Effect			−0.00	
Cor. oscill. per diem			86109.97	
Heavy end up				
	o	in	s	
1	13.60	29.596	5031.134	+.012
2	13.76	29.177	.105	−.017
3	14.02	29.182	.115	−.007
4	14.18	29.198	.082	−.040
5	14.62	29.145	.126	+.004
6	17.67	29.476	.154	+.032
7	18.76	29.076	.132	+.010
8	18.10	29.112	.121	−.001
9	18.00	29.176	.116	−.006
10	18.16	29.366	.134	+.012
Means	16.08	29.250	5031.122	±004
logT²			538.97	
same in mean time			301.49	
(log) oscill. per diem			86098.51	
Emp. Temp. Cor.			+0.14	
Flexure			+2.04	
Expansion			+0.86	
1st Atm. Effect			−1.16	
2nd Atm. Effect			−0.06	
Cor. oscill. per diem			86100.33	

New Stand

No. of swingings	Temp	Pressure	nT	Excess over Mean
Heavy end down				
	o	in	s	
2	+3.15	28.701	15089.188	+.125
4	−7.50	29.141	15088.908	−.155
5	−6.23	28.979	15089.120	+.057
6	−7.72	28.743	15089.086	+.023
7	−8.18	29.113	15089.109	+.046
10	−12.55	29.371	15088.968	−.095
Means	− 6.50	29.009	15089.063	±.027
logT²			514.20	
same in mean time			276.72	
(log) oscill. per diem			86123.28	
Emp. Temp. Cor.			−2.67	
Flexure			+5.07	
Expansion			−17.09	
1st Atm. Effect			+1.76	
2nd Atm. Effect			−0.00	
Cor. oscill. per diem			86110.33	
Heavy end up				
	o	in	s	
1	−9.27	28.123	5030.141	+.091
2	−8.85	28.157	.119	+.069
5	−8.17	29.487	5029.992	−.058
6	−12.14	29.501	.946	−.104
Means	−9.61	28.817	5030.050	±.040
logT²			520.46	
same in mean time			282.98	
(log) oscill. per diem			86117.02	
Emp. Temp. Cor.			−3.08	
Flexure			+1.69	
Expansion			−19.56	
1st Atm. Effect			+5.73	
2nd Atm. Effect			−0.01	
Cor. oscill. per diem			86101.79	

TABLE LI. Cornell. Pendulum No. 3.

Old Stand					New Stand				
Heavy end down									
No. of swing-ing	Temp	Pres-sure	*n*T	Excess over Mean	No. of swing-ings	Temp	Pres-sure	*n*T	Excess over Mean
	°	*in*	*s*			°	*in*	*s*	
1	17.02	29.365	14429.664	−.058	5	+1.28	29.295	14427.432	+.080
2	17.55	28.731	.797	+.075	6	+0.88	29.313	.475	+.122
3	17.66	29.130	.744	+.022	7	+2.08	29.359	.469	+.116
4	17.38	29.145	.717	−.005	8	+3.54	29.513	.419	+.066
5	17.38	29.022	.740	+.018	9	−15.00	29.796	.115	−.238
6	17.51	28.772	.749	+.027	12	−9.96	29.713	.348	−.005
7	15.76	29.096	.730	+.008	13	−3.43	29.407	.212	−.141
8	15.66	29.164	.691	−.031					
9	15.68	29.257	.696	−.026					
10	15.78	29.399	.695	−.027					
Means	16.74	29.108	4429.722	±.008	Means	− 2.94	29.485	14427.353	±.040
$\log T^2$			−3366.67		$\log T^2$			−3380.91	
same in mean time			−3604.15		same in mean time			−3618.39	
(log) oscill. per diem			90004.15		(log) oscill. per diem			90018.39	
Emp. Temp. Cor.			+0.22		Emp. Temp. Cor.			−2.24	
Flexure			+6.28		Flexure			+5.18	
Expansion			+1.39		Expansion			−14.21	
1st Atm. Effect			−0.57		1st Atm. Effect			+1.82	
2nd Atm. Effect			−0.03		2nd Atm. Effect			+0.02	
Cor. oscill. per diem			90011.44		Cor. oscill. per diem			90008.96	
Heavy end up									
	°	*in*	*s*			°	*in*	*s*	
1	19.24	28.139	4808.852	−.011	4	+0.75	29.195	4808.345	+.027
2	18.24	28.151	.847	−.016	5	−3.06	29.223	.359	+.041
3	18.29	28.184	.850	−.013	6	+0.08	29.469	.327	+.009
4	16.16	29.486	.888	+.025	9	−1.80	29.141	.271	−.047
6	16.20	29.508	.879	+.016	10	−6.05	29.397	.287	−.031
Means	17.63	28.694	4808.863		Means	−2.02	29.285	4808.318	−.014
$\log T^2$			−3385.52		$\log T^2$			−3395.35	
same in mean time			−3623.00		same in mean time			−3632.83	
(log) oscill. per diem			90023.00		(log) oscill. per diem			90032.83	
Emp. Temp. Cor.			+0.33		Emp. Temp. Cor.			−2.13	
Flexure			+2.11		Flexure			+1.74	
Expansion			+2.08		Expansion			−13.48	
1st Atm. Effect			−3.16		1st Atm. Effect			+4.51	
2nd Atm. Effect			−0.16		2nd Atm. Effect			+0.03	
Cor. oscill. per diem			90024.20		Cor. oscill. per diem			90023.50	

Corrected Times for Temperature, Pressure, and Inclination

[Tables LII–LX omitted.]

Table LXI

Smithsonian 1886. Pend. No. 2. Heavy end down. Old Stand				
No. of swing	1	2	3	4
Date	March 13	March 13	March 13	March 14
Time 1st Transit	$10^h\ 6^m\ 17^s.238$	$3^h\ 17^m 51^s.53$	$7^h\ 47^m\ 38^s.043$	$12^h\ 17^m 22^s.177$
" last "	2 17 51.378	7 29 26.088	11 59 12.250	8 40 32.499
Duration	4 11 34.140	4 11 34.235	4 11 34.207	8 23 10.322
Cor. for arc	−.063	−.063	−.062	−.063
No. of oscill.	15000	15000	15000	30002
Time 15000	4 11 34.077	4 11 34.172	4 11 34.145	4 11 34.123
Cor. for rate	−.078	−.078	−.083	−.085
" " pres.	+.072	+.060	+.033	−.004
" " temp.	−.005	−.000	+.013	+.042
" " diff. temp.	+.008	+.008	+.008	+.008
" " inclin.	−.001	−.001	−.001	−.001
Cor. time	4 11 34.073	4 11 34.161	4 11 34.115	4 11 34.083
Old Stand *(continued)*				
No. of swing	5	6	7	8
Date	March 16	March 16	Mar 16	Mar 16
Time 1st Transit	$9^h 42^m\ 32^s.348$	$2^h\ 8^m\ 3^s.651$	$6^h\ 34^m\ 19^s.114$	$0^h\ 39^m 57^s.624$
" last "	1 54 6.605	6 19 37.922	10 45 53.409	9 3 8.006
Duration	4 11 34.257	4 11 34.271	4 11 34.295	8 23 10.382
Cor. for arc	−.062	−.062	−.062	−.063
No. of oscill.	15000	15000	15000	30002
Time 15000	4 11 34.195	4 11 34.209	4 11 34.232	4 11 34.153
Cor. for rate	−.036	−.036	−.079	−.012
" " pres.	−.018	−.028	−.048	−.067
" " temp.	−.022	−.040	+.001	+.015
" " diff. temp.	+.005	+.005	+.005	+.005
" " inclin.	−.001	−.001	−.001	−.001
Cor. time	4 11 34.123	4 11 34.109	4 11 34.110	4 11 34.093

[Tables LXII–XCII omitted.]

CORRECTION FOR INCLINATION

This is the correction for the inclination of the knife-edge, or axis of rotation, to the horizon. Denoting the angle of inclination by i, gravity as observed has to be multiplied by sec i, or the time of oscillation by $\sqrt{\cos i} = 1 - \frac{1}{4}\sin^2 i$; so that the correction is $\frac{1}{4}n\mathrm{T}\sin^2 i$. For $i = 4'$, this is 1/4000000, so that it is a very trifling correction, and only needs a rough observation of the pitch of the knife–edge plane. A small spirit level whose divisions were about 50″ was from time to time put upon the knife-edge plane to test its horizontality. I have not thought it worth while to give all these observations in detail; but the following tables will serve as specimens of the proceeding.

TABLE XCIII

Smithsonian 1886. Inclination. Old Stand.					
	Forward	*Back*	*Value*	*Means*	*Corr.*
March 13	2.6	1.7			
	3.5	0.8			
			1′.3		
Pendulum No. 2. Heavy end down					
March 14	2.6	1.8		1.4	0ˢ.001
	4.0	0.4			
			1′.6		
Heavy end up					
March 15	2.5	1.8		1.6	0.000
	4.0	0.3			
			1′.6½		
Heavy end down					
March 16	2.6 A	1.7		1.6	0.001
	4.0	0.3 A			
			1′.5		
Heavy end up					
March 17	2.6 A	1.7		1.5	0.000
	4.0	0.3 A			
			1′.5		

Table XCIII *(continued)*

No. 3. Heavy end down					
March 18	2.7 A 4.0	1.6 0.3 A	 1′.6	1.6	0.001
Heavy end up					
March 19	2.7 A 4.0	1.6 0.3 A	 1′.6	1.6	0.000
Heavy end down					
March 21	2.7 A 4.0	1.6 0.3 A	 1′.6	1.6	0.001
Heavy end up					
March 22	2.8 A 4.1	1.5 0.2	 1′.8	1.7	0.000

[Tables XCIV–XCVIII omitted.]

Correction for Difference of Temperature

This is the correction for the fact that the upper part of the pendulum is warmer and consequently more expanded than the lower. We can only infer the rate of increase of temperature with the height from the readings of thermometers hung near the pendulum so as to have their bulbs nearly at the level of the upper and lower knife-edges. Fortunately, however, the correction is not great, so that there is not room for large error in estimating it. The coefficient of the correction to nT (which is always additive for heavy end down and subtractive for heavy end up) per degree centigrade, for $n = 15000$ H.e.d. and $n = 5000$ H.e.u., is

	s	
Metre pendulums	0.00856	solar time
Yard pendulum	0.00863	" "

Correction for Rate

It is unnecessary to say that this is one of the most important corrections to the results. If the time-piece is of the first excellence and the star observations precise, there is no room to suspect that any error can be imported into the determinations by faulty rates. On the other hand, when these conditions are not fulfilled, it may easily happen that the errors of rates exceed the uncorrected irregularities of movement of the invariable reversible pendulums.

The corrections of rate at the Smithsonian were, as far as I was concerned, very simple. Twice each day, time signals were telegraphed from the National Observatory by the courtesy of the Director. A correction to each set of signals was afterward communicated, which I had simply to apply, without knowing anything further about the observations. The rates are evidently sufficiently accurate.

At Ann Arbor, a mean time chronometer was employed, which had just been repaired, and which proved to go very badly. A circuit was arranged so that this chronometer could be compared with the Tiede clock of the observatory as often as I liked, but this arrangement was partly improvised, electricity not being habitually used there, and did not work with perfect uniformity. The clock was rated by means of eye and ear observations by Professor Schaeberle. The rates, however, are, I believe, unquestionable. They certainly cannot be otherwise, in the mean.

In Madison, a circuit was arranged so that I used the very fine clock of the Washburn Observatory directly upon my chronograph. The time was observed for me with great skill by Mr. Updegraff, with the magnificent meridian instrument of the observatory. The result of these arrangements was a better agreement than usual in the pendulum work.

At Cornell University, I used upon the chronograph, a complicated mean time clock with a gravity escapement, belonging to the physical department of the University. As might be expected of such a clock, its going was somewhat irregular. Time was observed by me with a good chronometer and a transit instrument belonging to the engineering department of the University. This transit was rather an inferior instrument in several respects, and the time is not so good as if observed with one of the larger instruments belonging to the Survey. The weather was also stormy; so that the irregularities of the clock were of the more importance. Still, no large errors can have been introduced in this way.

The following tables give all the necessary information concerning the correction for rate. But the star observations, not coming within my cognizance, except at a single station, are not exhibited.

TABLE XCIX

Smithsonian. 1884–85. Chronometer Times of Signals from the Observatory.						
Corrected date and time			Chron. time	Chron. gains on clock in 12h	Gain of clock	Gain of Chron.
1884	Dec 23 A.M.	h m	4h04m11^s.247			
	......					
	Dec 24 P.M.	9 30	4 08 9.273	+0.735	+0.065	+0.800
	Dec 25 A.M.	9 30	4 10 8.286	+0.735	+0.071	+0.806
	P.M.	9 30	4 12 7.294	+0.730	−0.071	+0.659
	......					
	Dec 26 P.M.	9 30	4 15 45.136	+0.671	−0.075	+0.596
	Dec 27 A.M.		4 18 4.177	+0.708	−0.040	+0.668
	P.M.		4 20 3.083	+0.628	−0.020	+0.608
	Dec 28 A.M.	9 30	4 22 2.036	+0.680	−0.040	+0.640
	P.M.	9 30	4 24 0.962	+0.648	−0.030	+0.618
	Dec 29 A.M.	9 30	4 25 59.932	+0.692	−0.030	+0.662
	P.M.	9 30	4 27 58.875	+0.665	−0.040	+0.625
	Dec 30 A.M.	9 30	4 29 57.862	+0.709	−0.080	+0.629
	P.M.	9 30	4 31 56.811	+0.671	−0.050	+0.621
	Dec 31 A.M.	9 30	4 33 55.809	+0.720	−0.050	+0.670
	......					

[Balance of Table XCIX omitted; Tables C–CVII omitted.]

NUMBERS OF OSCILLATIONS

The number of oscillations was, of course, never counted, but is in no case open to the smallest doubt. In the first place, during the observations of the times of beginning and ending, every third transit up to 60 was observed and recorded on the chronograph; and in this way we have at each station many hundred observations of counted intervals of 120 oscillations. These observations have been used to determine approximate periods which are found to be slightly too great in most cases, owing to the effect of fatigue in retarding the signals at the latter part of a set of 60 observations in 3 minutes. At every station, transits of each pendulum were observed at the beginning and end of a series of about 1000 oscillations, the precise number being determined by the approximate period determined as just described; and this observation served to give a second approximate period, sufficient to determine the number of oscillations, when this reached the neighborhood of 15000. Every set of transits began with one from right to left; so that the numbers of oscillations must in most cases be even and cannot be in error, if at all, by less than 2 oscillations. The approximate period need, therefore, only have been determined to the 7500th part. In no case was the hypothesis of an odd number of oscillations admitted, unless there was something in the record to compel such an hypothesis, or at least, something to destroy the presumption of an even number.

It would have been sufficient to determine this at a single station, for with heavy end up, the period is only needed accurate to the 2500th part; and station errors as large as this were out of the question; and, in point of fact, the method here indicated was employed as a check upon the direct determination.

CORRECTION FOR ARC

The amplitude of oscillation was rather small, being at the beginning ¾ of an inch upon a radius of 39.37 or 36 inches as the case might be, so that the correction for arc is small. Moreover, great care was taken to have the amplitude at the beginning of the swingings always the same. The tables of the descent of arc given above show that the pendulum behaved with great uniformity in this respect in different swingings. It is therefore only necessary to calculate the correction of arc once for all, for each pendulum in each position. The formula obtained by integrating that for the descent for the arc and given in my "Determinations of Gravity at Initial Stations" is

$$\frac{1}{16}\int \varphi^2 dt = \frac{b}{16c^2}\{bt - \text{Nat. log. } (\mathfrak{S}^{bt} - 1) - (\mathfrak{S}^{bt} - 1)^{-1}\} + \text{C.}$$

$$= \frac{b}{16c^2}\left\{\text{Nat. log. } \left(1 + \frac{c}{b}\varphi\right) - \frac{c}{b}\varphi\right\} + \text{C.}$$

On the Times of Beginning and Ending of the Swingings

Each time of beginning and ending is the mean of 60 transits, being every third one of 180 oscillations, always beginning with a transit from apparent left to apparent right. These were registered, as observed, upon a Fauth chronometer. After being read, each set was treated as in the example shown in Table CVIII.

Table CVIII

Old Stand. Yard Pendulum. Heavy End Down, Seventh Swing.								
9h.58m *Transits.*	*Red. to mean*	*Residuals*	*Transits.*	*Red. to mean*	*Residuals.*	*Transits.*	*Red. to mean*	*Residuals.*
s			s			s		
52.14	05	0	49.70	04	−1	47.28	06	+1
55.05	08	+6	52.58	04	+2	50.13	03	+1
57.90	05	0	55.47	06	+1	53.01	99	−6
			58.30	01	−1	55.89	04	+2
3.65	04	−1	1.18	01	−4	58.78	05	0
6.47	98	−4	3.96	91	−11	1.64	03	+1
9.42	06	+1	6.94	01	−4	4.58	09	+4
12.25	01	−1	9.80	00	−2	7.42	05	+3
15.20	08	+3	12.72	04	−1	10.29	04	−1
18.03	03	+1	15.58	02	0	13.14	02	0
20.99	11	+6	18.47	03	−2	16.05	05	0
23.78	03	+1	21.33	01	−1	18.87	99	−3
26.70	07	+2	24.24	04	−1	21.80	04	−1
29.55	04	+2	27.07	00	−2	24.67	03	+1
32.44	05	0	30.00	05	0	27.56	05	0
35.30	03	+1	32.87	04	+2	30.40	01	−1
38.17	02	−3	35.79	08	+3	33.30	03	−2
41.00	98	−4	38.61	02	0	36.14	99	−3
43.92	02	−3	41.51	05	0	39.06	03	−2
46.81	03	+1	44.36	02	0	41.92	01	−1
Mean.	R to L	$10^{h}\ 00^{m}17^{s}.046$		±.002				
	L to R	17.027		±.002				
	Mean	10 00 17.031		±.002				

A much higher magnifying power was always employed at the end than at the beginning of a swinging, and when the swinging was of double length a still higher third power was employed. Nevertheless, as a personal equation dependent upon the amplitude might be feared, at Cornell two scales having been fixed to a pendulum, one near the centre of rotation and the other below, the pendulum was then arranged to register automatically upon a régulateur Villarceau, while my observations were also registered. The results of five sets on each scale were,

With large amplitude, Observations $0^{s}.003$ before event.
With excessively small amplitude, Observations $0^{s}.022$ after event.

No correction has been applied on this account. It could only affect the absolute determinations, and that by a very small amount.

The minute was carefully marked upon the chronograph sheet just after starting and again just before stopping the instrument.

At the Smithsonian, there is no room for doubt or hesitation in regard to the time on any occasion.

In Ann Arbor, where a foreman was employed to note these times, there are one or two cases of a discrepancy between the first and second time noted on the sheet, but still there is no possibility of a real doubt.

At Madison, the chronograph was nearly half a mile from the clock, and made no indication of the beginning of the minute, and as I happened to have only a very bad watch, the only way of getting the seconds right was to send the foreman to the observatory where he would carry the beats of the clock from the clock room into the transit-room, and there make a rattle indicating the beginning of the minute. There was, of course, much room for error in this proceeding, and the results had to be submitted to an elaborate study. As a check upon these results, I noted the chronometer time of the first transit, at the beginning and ending of each swinging, and I trust that I have in that way avoided all error.

A table is given below showing the details of this comparison.

At Cornell, the clock of the physical department of the University was used on the chronograph. This clock made a special signal every 15 minutes, but as its error was about 9 minutes, it was possible to wrongly mark the 15 minute signal on the sheet.

As explained above, two stations were simultaneously occupied at the Cornell University, and two different chronographs were habitually used in one circuit, so that all signals were recorded upon both and the times were generally marked independently upon the two sheets. I do not think, therefore, that there can be any error in regard to these times, especially as they are checked by frequent comparisons between the mean time clock and a sidereal time chronometer.

TABLE CIX

Madison. Notes on Times of Transits.

The time piece used on the chronometer was the sidereal clock of the observatory, which gave no indication of the commencement of the minute. To show this, the sidereal chronometer, Negus 1589, was switched on from time to time. The minute of this chronometer was marked directly on the sheet at the time from the reading of its face. This was done by the foreman. An independent record was made by C. S. P. of the times at which he intended to commence each set of transits. This record marked P is here compared with the adopted times, marked A. The time of the mean of each set of transits is later than that of the first of the set by $1^{m}29^{s}0$ for No. 2 and $1^{m}25^{s}1$ for No. 3.

Date	Chron. sheet	Heavy end	No. of swing	Begin. or end	Old Stand	New Stand	Pend. on N. S.
Oct. 12	1	D	1	b P	5 25^{m} 12^{s}	5 11^{m} 25^{s}	Y
				A	13 43 18.9	13 29 31.6	
				diff.	8 18 6.9	8 18 6.6	
				e P	1 48 17.6	1 28 27	
				A	10 6 23.7	9 46 34.1	
				diff.	8 18 6.1	8 18 7.1	

The chronometer was not on at all; so that the times can only be determined by C. S. P.'s record.

It is unnecessary to explain how the absolute times have been fixed. The swinging lasted from the night of Oct. 12 to the following morning. C. S. P.'s record presents a slight inconsistency of one second, that is, as this is the record of an intention only, one of the pendulums was not in the expected phase of oscillation at the intended instant. The second has been so taken as best to satisfy C. S. P.'s record. A change would introduce extravagant residuals, since the numbers of oscillations were divisible by 2.

[Table entries from Oct. 13 through Oct. 27 omitted.]

ON THE ABSOLUTE VALUE OF GRAVITY

The length of the equatorial seconds pendulum according to my observations in Hoboken and Kew, combined with the station errors found in my unpublished investigation on the figure of the earth (these two station errors depending mainly on the observations of Herschel), is 990.^{mm}95. The value obtained by me in Paris using station error mainly depending on Sabine's work is somewhat different. I cannot admit the view of Helmert expressed in his *Höhere Geodäsie* that the discrepancy is owing to the unusual rigidity of the support used by me in Paris, although this opinion is based upon a suggestion in my own Memoir; but further study in the matter of the flexure of pendulum supports, together with the comparison of my result at Paris with those of previous and of subsequent observers, inclined me rather to the belief of an error in the relative course of gravity as determined by Sabine. In any case, however, it is indisputable that the value of the length of the equatorial seconds pendulum, as deduced from my work in Paris, although probably really nearer the truth than other careful determinations, is nevertheless not comparable with them, the large correction due to the flexure of the pendulum staff itself during the swingings never having been allowed for.

The swingings for the Smithsonian in the year 1885 with pendulums 1 and 2 differ but little from those deduced from the previous work at Hoboken and Kew. One of the knives of pendulum No. 4 having been found to be loose it is not surprising that the value obtained with this pendulum differs considerably. It seems, however, that it is difficult to account for the difference of about 1/7 of a millimetre in the value given by the yard pendulum No. 3.

When the deductions were first made this seemed to fall in very well with the others, but this appearance of agreement seems demonstrably due to the combined effect of several errors; and the discrepancy remains one for which I am unable to account. The following tables give the results, calculations, and comparisons of length.

TABLE CX

Mean Equatorial Seconds Pendulum	
Peirce Pendulum	*mm*
No. 1.	990.9540
No. 2.	990.9553
No. 3.	991.1058
No. 4.	990.8730
Mean Equatorial Seconds Pendulum from Determinations with the Repsold Pendulum	
	mm
Hoboken	990.9531
Kew	990.9442
Paris	990.9931

TABLE CXI

Repsold Pendulum				
		Hoboken	*Paris*	*Kew*
Seconds Pendulum per *C. S. Rep. 1875*		993.2052	993.9337	994.1776
Correction *C. S. Rep. 1881*		−162	−162	−162
Corrected		993.1890	993.9175	994.1614
Logarithm		2.9970319	2.9973503	2.9974569
To equator and sea level		−9761	−12891	−14007
Neg. of station error		−27	+94	−70
Logarithm of Equatorial sec. pend.		2.9960531	2.9960706	2.9960492
Equatorial seconds pendulum		990.9531	990.9931	990.9442
Peirce Pendulums				
	No. 1	*No. 2*	*No. 3*	*No. 4*
Log. oscill. per diem H.e.d.	86097.53	86099.88	90001.48	86085.36
H.e.u.	86158.74	86094.48	90015.56	86090.75
H.e.d. – H.e.u.	−61.21	+5.40	−14.08	−5.39
$1/(h_d/h_u - 1)$	.5045	.4998	.5048	.5030
Product two last	−30.88	+2.70	−7.11	−2.71
H.e.d. + last	86066.65	86102.58	89994.37	86082.65
Length standard	$1000000^{\mu}.0$	$1000000^{\mu}.0$	$914400^{\mu}.0$	$1000000^{\mu}.0$
Excess length pend. over stand	$+692^{\mu}.1$	$-134^{\mu}.0$	$-97^{\mu}.9$	$+241^{\mu}.6$
Length pendulum	$1000^{mm}.6921$	$999^{mm}.8660$	$914^{mm}.3021$	$1000^{mm}.2416$
Log. length	+30.05	−5.82	−3891.03	+10.49
Log. excess over sec. pend.	−333.35	−297.42	+3594.37	−317.35
Log. sec. pend.	−303.30	−303.24	−296.66	−306.86
To equator	−89.56	−89.56	−89.56	−89.56
To sea level	±.12	+.12	+.12	+.12
Neg. station error	−1.90	−1.90	−1.90	−1.90
Log. Equatorial sec. pend.	−394.64	−394.58	−388.00	−398.20
Equatorial sec. pend.	990.9540	990.9553	991.1058	990.8730

Two sets of quantities used in this calculation depend upon special observations. One of these is the difference of the distance of the centre of mass from the two ends of the pendulum. This was observed in a rather unsatisfactory way, but is, I hope, not more than a millimetre in error.

The other is the series of lengths of the pendulums.

The pendulums were compared with their standards by means of a vertical comparator constructed on the principle of that belonging to the Repsold pendulum apparatus. In fact, the new comparator was made by simply replacing the standard carrying the microscopes in the Repsold apparatus by a tube of the same size and material as the pendulums herein described. This tube was pierced with holes about 1/10 inches in diameter in a helicoidal line from top to bottom, in order to facilitate the circulation of air. There is also a suitable tripod to support the apparatus. The yard pendulum No. 3 was compared with the yard of Yard and Metre Bar No. 1, which yard I denote by Y_1. This bar has been determined by Mr. Blair to be standard at 63°.53 F, but I assume 63°.45 owing to a recalculation of Mr. Blair's results. The other pendulums were compared with a metre bar marked "U.S.C.S. C.S.P. 1878B." This metre has three lines engraved on a plug at one end at distances of 100^{μ} and at the other end has 7 such lines. The original intention was to set always on three lines at each end and to define the length of the bar as the distance between the mean of three at the other. But in measuring the pendulums, it was deemed best to set only on one line at each end. At the end having three lines, the middle one was always used; but at the other end different lines were used with different pendulums. I designate the length from the middle line of the three at one end to the 1st, 3rd, and 7th at the other end as B_1, B_3, B_7. The distances of these 7 lines were carefully measured both with the upper and the lower microscopes of the vertical comparator, in order to determine the values of the screw-revolutions. The length of Metre B has been determined by comparing it with German Normal Metre 49, as shown below. For the length of Metre 49, see my papers in the *Coast Survey Report for 1875,* and *1881.* There are also other data, as shown below. The distances of the 7 lines at the end of Metre B were determined by Dr. Clarke, who compared them with the screw-revolutions of the Blair comparator, as shown below.

TABLE CXII

Lengths of the Pendulums	
Pendulum No. 1	
No. 1 at 15° – B_1 at 15°	= +254$^{\mu}$.3
$B_1 - B_3$	= +98.6
B_3 at 15° – No. 49 at 15°	= −21.8
No. 49 at 15° – No. 49 at 0°	= +282.4
No. 49 at 0° – Metre	= −21.4
∴No. 1 at 15° – Metre	= +692.1
Pendulum No. 2	
No. 2 at 15° – B_7 at 15°	= +25.1
$B_7 - B_3$	= −397.1
B_3 at 15° – No. 49 at 15°	= −21.8
No. 49 at 15° – No. 49 at 0°	= +282.4
No. 49 at 0° – Metre	= −21.4
∴No. 2 at 15° – Metre	= −134.0
Pendulum No. 4	
No. 4 at 15° – B_3 at 15°	= +2.2
B_3 at 15° – No. 49 at 15°	= −21.8
No. 49 at 15° – No. 49 at 0°	= +282.4
No. 49 at 0° – Metre	= −21.4
∴No. 4 at 15° – Metre	= +241.6
Pendulum No. 3	
No. 3 at 15° – Y_1 at 15°	= −57.4
Y_1 at 15° – Yard	= −40.5
∴No. 3 at 15° – Yard	= −97.9

TABLE CXIII

1	2	3	4	5	6	7	8	9	10	11	12	13	14	15	16
Date	Upper micr. reading of pendulum	Upper micr. reading of standard	Lower micr. reading of pendulum	Lower micr. reading of standard	Mean temp.	Excess temp.	(2) – (3)	(4)–(5)	(8) in microns.	(9) in microns.	(10)–(11)	(12) Corr. for (7).	Corr. for mean temp.	Corr. for mean temp.	Excess over temp.
Measures of Pendulum No. 1															
1884															
Dec. 1	2.774	0.258	0.205	0.213	17.°24	+ 0.°03	+ 2.516	−0.008	+251μ.4	−00μ.8	+252μ.2	+252.8	+1μ.6	+254μ.4	+0μ.1
Dec. 1	2.812	0.391	0.353	0.455	16.12	+0.03	+2.421	−0.102	+241.9	−10.3	+252.2	+252.8	+0.8	+253.6	−0.1
[Dec. 2–10 measurements omitted.]															
Measures of Pendulum No. 2															
1884															
Nov. 14	0.699	0.391	3.448	3.345	20.°40	+ 0.°01	+0.308	+0.103	+30μ.7	+10.4	+20μ.3	+20.5	+3μ.8	+24μ.3	
Nov. 14	0.695	0.394	3.434	3.330	21.89	−0.03	+0.301	0.104	+30.0	+10.5	+19.5	+20.1	+4.9	+25.0	
[Nov. 15–19 measurements omitted.]															
Measurements of Pendulum No. 4															
1884															
Oct. 15	2.528	2.435	2.159	2.041	17.°48	+0.°03	+ 0.093	+0.118	+09μ.2	+11μ.9	−02μ.7	−02.1	+1μ.8	− 0μ.3	
Oct. 15	2.526	2.423	2.169	2.035	17.08	+0.05	+0.103	+0.134	+10.2	+13.5	−03.3	−02.4	+1.5	−0.9	
[Oct. 16–24 measurements omitted.]															
Measures of Pendulum No. 3															
1883															
Dec. 17	2.681	3.535	3.702	4.063	21.°59	−0.28	− 0.854	−0.361	−85.2	−36.4	−48.4	−54.2			
Dec. 17	2.715	3.540	3.735	4.061	23.38	−0.19	−0.825	−0.326	−82.3	−32.9	−49.4	−52.8			
Dec. 17	2.724	3.565	3.728	4.052	24.58	−0.13	−0 84	−0.326	−83.9	−32.9	−51.0	−53.3			
[Dec. 18–22 measurements omitted.]															

TABLE CXIV

Pendulum No 3. Compared with the Yard of Yard and Metre Standard No. 1												
Date 1885	*Time*	*Pend.*	*Above Stand.*	$P-S$		*Pend.*	*Below Stand.*	$P-S$		*Diff. length*	*Mean temp.*	*at 15°*
		r	*r*	*r*		*r*	*r*					
Nov. 9	11 AM	6.243	13.687	−7.444	−744.8 μ	13.432	5.754	7.678	+768.8 μ	−58.8 μ	24.29	−60.7
	1 PM	6.200	13.641	−7.441	−744.4	13.377	5.684	7.693	+770.3	−60.1	25.10	−62.1
	3 PM	6.216	13.386	−7.440	−744.3	13.386	5.682	7.705	+771.5	−61.2	25.69	−63.3

[November 10–11 measurements omitted.]

TABLE CXV

Calculation of the number of millimetres in an inch	
Capt. Kater	25.39954
Col. Clarke	25.39977
Mr. Rogers	25.39988
C.S. Peirce	25.39994
Heaviside and Peirce	25.40005
Gen. Comstock	25.40015

37

[Reasoning]

c. 1889 ***Houghton Library***

The first thing to remark about reasoning is that it is a passage from one belief to another. The propositions embodying the earlier and later beliefs are called respectively the *premises* and *conclusion:* the latter is said to be *inferred* or *concluded* from the former by the process of *inference* or *reasoning.*

But that one belief is subsequent to another signifies nothing, unless it also results from that other. When this is the case we have something like inference: it may be called by that name in a broad sense. Only if we are not conscious that the resulting belief is caused by one already adopted, we cannot watch the process nor control it; so that there can be no art of reasoning applicable to inference in that sense. Therefore, the name of reasoning is best confined to those processes in which we are directly aware that the concluded belief is an effect of another.

But when we say that one belief is determined by another, what do we mean, precisely what positive and sensible facts do we refer to?

In answering this, it will be useful to have a bit of reasoning before us as an example. What is the sum of the angles of a plane polygon? Let the polygon be cut in two by means of a diagonal between two vertices, the two parts similarly cut in two, and so on until the pieces are reduced to triangles. Each such cut leaves the total sum of all the angles the same, increases the number of polygons by one, and increases the number of sides by two. Thus, the number of cuts increased by one gives the number of polygons, and if these are all triangles, three times this or thrice the number of cuts *plus* three is the number of their sides; but this is also equal to twice the number of cuts *plus* the number of sides of the original polygon; so that the number of cuts *plus* three is the original number of sides. Then, the number of triangles is the original number of sides less two; and as each triangle has two right angles, the sum of the angles of a polygon is twice as many right angles as it has sides less four right angles.

We are thus led to believe that the sum of the angles of the N-gon is 2N – 4 right angles, *because* they are equal to the angles of N – 2 triangles having each the sum of its angles equal to two right angles. The question is what we are conscious of which induces us to use this word "because." As the etymology of the word shows, it implies that we feel a compulsion upon us to believe the conclusion, which compulsion we refer to the premises as its subject. There is a sense of compulsion in all belief; we are compelled to see what we see. But the compulsion of reason produces a different sensation. It seems to derive its force from our most intimate self. But all this is of little interest to the logician as such, who need not care how men feel, nor even too much how they think, but rather how they ought to think and will think when they reflect. What is far more essential to the significance of the "because," in that it is more important to the fulfilling of the function expressed by that word, is the implication that the conclusion is derived from the contemplation of an ideal construction. This ideal construction is not a mere product of casual experience; but is regarded as something that will hold good everywhere and always. In whatever world we may find ourselves, we are confident that the truth of premises such as those of the inference before us would be accompanied by the truth of such a conclusion, according to a rule which commends itself to our intelligence. We have in the above example the idea of the measurement of angles by superposition; and we see clearly that measuring them in this way the sum of the angles of the polygon will be equal to that of the triangles into which it is dissected, in every case whatever. In regard to the number of triangles, the reasoning has intentionally been left rather loose, so as to resemble our ordinary inferences. But except in certain vaguely conceived cases, this part of the reasoning also is seen to hold in every possible world.

The next character of reasoning to be noticed is that it is capable of being right and wrong. It is unnecessary at this time to open the difficult question of what the truth of a proposition consists in. Suffice it that some propositions are what we wish them to be; they are *true.* Others are not; they are *false.* An inference is good or bad according to the character of the habit which governs it. A habit of inference such that we can assure ourselves that from true premises it will in every possible case lead to a true conclusion is good reasoning. But if it is within the bounds of possibility (that is, of what we do not know to be false) that an inference governed by the habit in question should have true premises and a false conclusion, then it is not demonstrative, and if it pretends to be *[. . .]*

38

On a Geometrical Notation

c. 1889 ***Houghton Library***

Let A, B, C, D, etc., be multiple quantities determining points in space. Let (ABCD) be such a function of the quantities A, B, C, D, that (ABCD) = 0 shall signify that the points A, B, C, D, are coplanar. We may write (ABC.) = 0 to mean that (ABCX) = 0 holds no matter what point X may be, so that A, B, C, are collinear. In like manner, (AB..) = 0 will mean that A = B.

Any three points, A, B, C, lie in one plane; for A = A, or (AA..) = 0. Hence, (AABC) = 0.

For the purposes of this notation, a plane is defined as the locus of X when (ABCX) = 0. Consequently, a plane is completely determined by three points, or through three points only one plane can be drawn. This shows that if we have given the two equations (PQRS) = 0 and (PQRT) = 0, we can infer (PQST)(PQR.) = 0; that is, either (PQST) = 0 or (PQR.) = 0.

Through any two points, A and B, one straight line only can be drawn. Since (AA..) = 0, we have (AAB.) = 0; so that any two points are collinear. But for the purposes of this notation, a line is defined as the locus of a point X subject to an equation of the form (ABX.) = 0; so that two points suffice to determine a line. Stating this symbolically, if (ABX.) = 0 and (ABY.) = 0, then (AXY.)(AB..) = 0; so that in the transformation of the last paragraph a dot may be treated precisely like a letter.

A line and a plane have one point and one only in common, unless every point of the line is in the plane. The first part of this proposition involves the continuity and tridimensionality of space,—characters not yet taken account of. It furnishes the rule that any two equations of the forms (ABCX) = 0 and (DEX.) = 0 can be satisfied simultaneously. That a line and a plane cannot have more than one point in common, may be proved as follows. For suppose (ABCX) = 0 and (ABCY) = 0 and (XYU.) = 0. Then, we have only to prove that (XY..)(ABCU) = 0. Now from the first two premises we have (ABC.)(ABXY) = 0. But if (ABC.) = 0, the desired conclusion follows at once; so that we need not notice that alternative, and may say, for short, that (ABXY) = 0 follows from the first two premises. Combining this with (XYUA) = 0, which is an immediate corollary from the third premise, we find (AXY.) (ABXU) = 0. And in like manner, as symmetry shows, (AXY.) (ACXU) = 0. Thus, either (AXY.) = 0 or both (ABXU) = 0 and (ACXU) = 0. And by symmetry, either (BXY.) = 0 or both (ABXU) = 0 and (BCXU) = 0. Also, either (CXY.) = 0 or both (ACXU) = 0 and (BCXU) = 0. But if of the three equations, (AXY.) = 0, (BXY.) = 0, (CXY.) = 0, any two hold good, I shall show that we can draw the desired conclusion; while if only one of them holds, two of the alternatives must hold, and from them we can again draw the desired conclusion. To show this, suppose (AXY.) = 0; then, since (XYU.) = 0, we have (XY..) (AXU.) = 0. If then we further suppose (BXY.) = 0, we have (XY..)(BXU.) = 0. But from (AXU.) = 0 and (BXU.) = 0, we could conclude (XU..) (ABU.) = 0. If the first factor held good, we should have X = U and by the first premise (ABCU) = 0, and if the second factor held good, the same thing would follow immediately. So that from (AXY.) = 0 and (BXY.) = 0, we could infer (XY..)(ABCU) = 0, which would be the desired conclusion. Let us now suppose a pair of the other set of alternatives to hold good. Whichever these may be, we shall have (ABXU) = 0, (BCXU) = 0, (CAXU) = 0. The first two of these give (ABCU) (BXU.) = 0, and the last two give (ABCU)(CXU.) = 0. The first factor of each equation is the desired conclusion, which therefore follows unless both (BXU.) = 0 and (CXU.) = 0. But from these follows (XU..)(BCU.) = 0. We have already seen how the conclusion follows from the first factor, and from the second it evidently does so. Thus, the proposition is proved.

Two planes have a line, and only one, in common. The first part of this proposition is as much as to say that any two equations of the forms (ABCX) = 0 and (DEFX) = 0 can be satisfied simultaneously in two different ways. Now these two equations are satisfied by any point that satisfies (ABCX) = 0 and also either (DEX.) = 0, (EFX.) = 0, or (FDX.) = 0. Each of these three pairs of equations has a solution, but the three solutions may coincide. In that case, however, I shall show that the first pair of equations is satisfied by any point that satisfies the first. Namely, the two equations (DEX.) = 0 and (EFX.) = 0 are satisfied by E and not by any other point, because two straight lines have but one point in common. So that X = E, and the second equation becomes (DEFE) = 0 which is true identically, because there is a plane through any three points.

That any two lines in a plane have a point in common follows obviously in a similar manner.

SECTION II. We are now prepared to consider qualitative geometry of the first order.

Suppose 6 points, A, B, C, D, E, F, subject to the condition that there shall be a solution to the simultaneous equations (ADX.) = 0, (BEX.) = 0, (CFX.) = 0. I follow the usual practice of not stopping to show that this is possible: I simply assume it. Then we know that the following pairs of equations have solutions: (ABU.) = 0 and (DEU.) = 0, (BCV.) = 0 and (EFV.) = 0, (CAW.) = 0 and (FDW.) = 0. I shall show that these solutions are related by the equation (UVW.) = 0.

39

On the Numbers of Forms of Sets

c. 1889 **Houghton Library**

The number of objects (say, letters) in a set may be called the *plurality* of the set. If the places for single objects in a set are all distinguished from one another (say, as *first, second,* etc.), the set may be called a perfectly ordered set, or *ad;* or, according to its plurality, a *monad, dyad, triad, tetrad,* etc. Some of the objects of a set may be alike, so that the same kind may go in several places, although one place can contain but one kind. Two sets of the same plurality and diversity are said to have the same *form,* if one can be changed into the other by simply changing the characters of its objects; but an interchange of two places is regarded as a change of form. Thus, AAB and BBA are of the same form; but ABA is of a different form. The number of different forms may be called the *formality*.

The forms of $(x+1)$-ads of diversity $y+1$ consist of all the forms obtained by affixing to each x-ad of diversity y a new kind of object in a new place, together with all the forms obtained by affixing to each x-ad of diversity $y+1$ an object of any one of its $y+1$ kinds in a new place, and the forms so derived from different forms are all different. Hence, putting $[x, y]$ for the formality of x-ads of diversity y, we have (E being the symbol of enlargement, or $\Delta + 1$)

$$\mathrm{E}_x\mathrm{E}_y[x, y] = (y+1)\mathrm{E}_y[x, y] + [x, y].$$

We also have

$$[x, 0] = 0 \quad [1, 1] = 1.$$

The solution of these equations is

$$[x, y] = \sum_{1\;i}^{y} \frac{(-)^{i} i^{x-1}}{(i-1)!(y-i-2)!},$$

whence

$$\Delta_x^n\ [1, y] = [n, y-1]\ .$$

Also $\Sigma_y [x, y]$ has the value given by me, *American Journal of Mathematics,* Vol. III, p. 48. I will set down a few forms.

Monads	*Dyads*	*Triads*	*Tetrads*
A	AA	AAA	AAAA
	AB	AAB	AAAB
		ABA	AABA
		ABB	AABB
			ABAA
			ABAB
			ABBA
			ABBB
		ABC	AABC
			ABAC
			ABBC
			ABCA
			ABCB
			ABCC
			ABCD

Table of Formalities.

No. of places	1	2	3	4	5	6	7	8	9
No. of letters 0	0	0	0	0	0	0	0	0	0
1	1	1	1	1	1	1	1	1	1
2	0	1	3	7	15	31	63	127	255
3	0	0	1	6	25	90	301	966	3025
4	0	0	0	1	10	65	350	1701	7770
5	0	0	0	0	1	15	140	1050	6951
6	0	0	0	0	0	1	21	266	2646
7	0	0	0	0	0	0	1	28	462
8	0	0	0	0	0	0	0	1	36
9	0	0	0	0	0	0	0	0	1

Taking the differences of the 6th line we have:

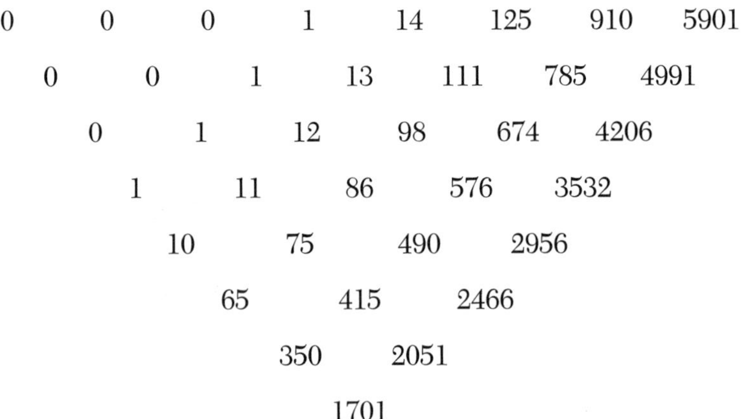

0 0 0 1 14 125 910 5901
0 0 1 13 111 785 4991
0 1 12 98 674 4206
1 11 86 576 3532
10 75 490 2956
65 415 2466
350 2051
1701

This illustrates the last equation.

40

The Formal Classification of Relations

c. 1889 **Houghton Library**

1. Relations may be classified without regard to the form of their elements.
    11. As to what they contain.
        111. Whether an element or not. The latter class embraces only the relation 0.
        112. Whether a pair of elements or not. A relation embracing one element but not a pair is *individual.*
        113, etc. This system of classification may be extended to sets of any number of elements.
        $11\infty^0$. Whether an infinity of elements or not. The names *infinite* and *finite* may be applied to these classes.
        11∞. Whether a continuum of elements or not. The names *continuous* and *discrete* may be applied to these classes. *Continuous relations* may be classified according to the manifoldness of the continuum.
    12. As to what they exclude, the classifications being parallel to those under 11.
2. Relatives may be classified in regard to the form of the elements; especially, as to whether they subsist between two or more individuals. These are *dual* and *plural* relations; and the plural are distinguished as to the number of their plurality. I assume that all relations have a definite plurality.

Dual Relations

1. Dual relations may be classified as containing *all, part,* or *none* of the pairs in the universe of the forms A:A, a selfcouple, and A:B, an aliocouple, respectively.

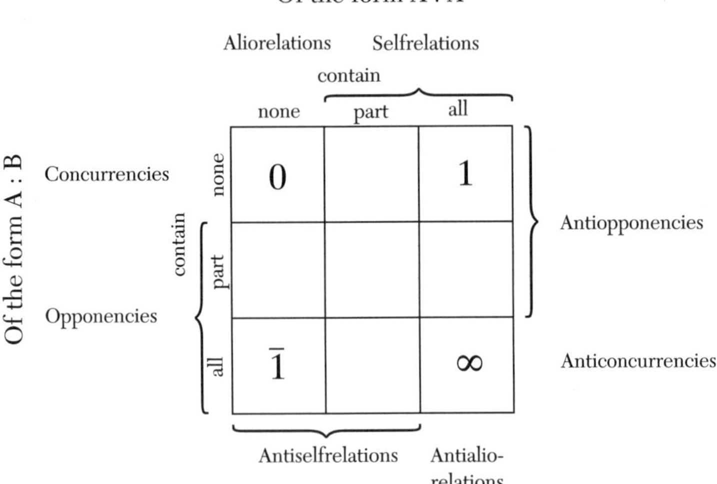

The prefix *anti-* means negative of. Thus, an anticoncurrency is the negative of a concurrency.

There is but one alioconcurrency, the relation of *incompossibility.* There is but one antialioconcurrency, the relation of *identity.* There is but one alioanticoncurrency, the relation of *otherness.* There is but one antialioanticoncurrency, the relation of *coexistence.* Classing these together as *logical relations,* we have on the other hand *real relations* of five kinds, as follows. 1st, *alioopponencies,* and these are antiopponencies as well; 2nd, *selfconcurrencies,* and these are antiselfrelations as well; 3rd, *antialioopponencies,* and these are antiopponencies as well; 4th, *selfanticoncurrencies,* and these are antiselfrelations as well; and 5th, *variform* relations, or those which are at once opponencies and antiopponencies, selfrelations and antiselfrelations.

2. Dual relatives may be classified in reference to their including or excluding one or both of every or some *pair* of couples of one of the nine forms following.

A:A B:B	A:A A:B	A:A B:A	A:A B:C	
A:B B:A	A:B C:A	A:B A:C	B:A C:A	A:B C:D

21. A dual relative may contain just one couple of the form A:A (selfindividual), or it may only exclude just one such couple (selfsimple), or it may belong to neither of these classes (selfgeneral).

22. With reference to the second pair of couples.

221. Either it excludes some selfpair A:A and also some other pair A:B having the same relate, or it includes all the alio pairs whose selfrelate pairs it excludes (if not so related to itself it is to everything else; *omni-vel-sibi*).

222. Either it includes an alio pair with its selfrelate pair, or it excludes all the alio pairs whose selfrelate pairs it includes *(nullo-si-sibi)*.

223. Either it includes an alio pair while excluding its selfrelate pair, or it excludes every alio pair whose selfrelate pair it excludes *(nullo-vel-sibi)*.

224. Either it excludes an alio pair while including its selfrelate pair, or it includes every alio pair whose selfrelate pair it includes *(omni-si-sibi)*.

The only relatives which belong at once to the second class of 221 and the second of 224 are identity and otherness. The only relatives which belong at once to the second classes of 222 and 223 are coexistence and incompossibility.

The only relatives which belong at once to the second classes
of 223 and 224 are aliorelatives,
of 221 and 222 are antialiorelatives,
of 222 and 224 are concurrencies,
of 221 and 223 are anticoncurrencies.

The first class of 222 is a species of selfopponency, that of 221 is an antiselfantiopponency, that of 223 is an antiselfopponency and that of 224 is a selfantiopponency.

23. With reference to the third pair of couples the division is parallel.

24. With reference to pairs of couples A:A and B:C.

241. Either it excludes a selfpair and also an alteroalio pair or it includes every alteroalio pair of every excluded selfpair *(sibi-vel-altero-alio).*

242. Either it includes a selfpair and also an alteroalio pair or it excludes every alteroalio pair of every included selfpair *(si-sibi-non-altero-alio).*

243. Either it excludes a selfpair and includes an alteroalio pair or it excludes every alteroalio pair of every excluded selfpair *(sibi-si-altero-alio).*

244. Either it includes a selfpair and excludes an alteroalio pair or it includes every alteroalio pair of every included selfpair *(altero-alio-si-sibi).*

25. With reference to pairs of couples A:B and B:A.

251. It either includes an alio pair and its converse or excludes one in every case. Admits or excludes reciprocity.

252. It either excludes an alio pair and its converse or includes one or other in every case. Linear. Exists one way between any two.

253. It either includes an alio pair while excluding its converse or in every case includes one or other. Requires reciprocity.

26. With reference to pairs of couples A:B and C:A.

261. It either includes an alio pair and a prior pair or it admits no prior nor posterior. Excludes sequence.

262. It either excludes an alio pair and a prior pair or it includes every pair prior and posterior to an excluded pair.

263. It either includes an alio pair while excluding its prior or it includes every prior of an included pair. Necessitates priority.

264. It either excludes an alio pair while including its prior or it includes every posterior of an included pair. Necessitates posteriority.

27. With reference to pairs of couples A:B and A:C.

271. It is either pluricorrelative or not.
272. It is either plurinoncorrelative or not.
273. It either admits A:B while excluding A:C or in every case includes all or excludes all. Whatever is in that relation to anything else is not related to everything else.

28. With reference to the pairs of couples B:A and C:A. Parallel classification.

29. With reference to the pair of couples A:B and C:D.
291. Either it admits two (altioplural) or of any two excludes at least one.
292. Either it excludes two (antialioplural)
293. Either it excludes one and admits another, or it excludes both or admits both.

41

Dual Relatives

c. 1889 **Houghton Library**

1. These may be classified, first, with regard to the forms of their single couples. These forms are two, A:A and A:B.

11. A relation may contain *(a)* none, *(b)* a part, or *(c)* all the couples of the form A:A in the universe.

12. A relation may contain *(a)* none, *(b)* a part, or *(c)* all the couples of the form A:B.

The only relation which contains none of either form is that of incompossibility. The only relation which contains all of both forms is that of coexistence. The only relation which contains all of the form A:A and none of the form A:B is that of identity. The only relation which contains all of the form A:B and none of the form A:A is otherness. These are logical relations. The real relations are of five classes:

(a) relations such as nothing has to itself;
(b) relations such as everything has to itself;
(c) relations such as nothing has to anything else;
(d) relations such as everything has to everything else;
(e) relations such as some things have and some have not to themselves and which exist between some pairs of different things and not others.

2. Dual relatives may also be classified in regard to the forms of pairs of couples. These are nine as follows:

(a) A:A and B:B
(b) A:A and A:B
(c) A:A and B:A
(d) A:A and B:C
(e) A:B and B:A
(f) A:B and C:A

(*g*) A:B and A:C
(*h*) A:B and C:B
(*i*) A:B and C:D

21. A relation may be (*a*) such that only one thing is so related to itself, or (*b*) so that only one thing is not so related to itself, or (*c*) so that either all, no, or a plurality of things are so related to themselves.

22. With reference to the pair of couples A:A and A:B.

221. A relation may be (*a*) such that there is something not so related to itself nor to // everything / anything // else, or (*b*) so that everything is either so related to itself or to //everything / something // else.

222. A relation may be (*a*) such that there is something so related to itself and to // something / everything // else, or (*b*) so that nothing so related to itself is so related to // anything / everything // else.

223. A relation may be (*a*) such that there is something so related to itself but not to // everything else / anything else //, or (*b*) so that whatever is so related to itself is so related to // everything / something // else.

224. A relation may be (*a*) such that there is something not so related to itself but so related to // something / everything // else, or (*b*) such that whatever is so related to // anything / everything // else is so related to itself.

The combination of these four dichotomies only gives fifteen classes because 221 (*b*), 222 (*b*), 223 (*b*), 224 (*b*) are incompossible.

23. There is a parallel classification in regard to A:A and B:A.

24. With reference to the pair of couples, A:A and B:C.

241. A relation may be (*a*) such that there is something not so related to another and a third thing not so related to itself, or (*b*) such that taking any two objects whatever either each is so related to the other or // everything / something // else is so related to itself. That is, the relation is such that everything is so related to itself or everything to everything else, or except two things everything to itself and to everything else.

242. A relation may be *(a)* such that something is so related to a second and a third thing so to itself, or *(b)* such that either nothing is so related to itself or nothing to anything else or there are only two things between which or to themselves the relation subsists.

243. A relation may be *(a)* such that something is so related to a second and a third thing not so to itself, or *(b)* such that if anything is so related to anything else every third thing is so related to itself.

244. A relation may be *(a)* such that something is not so related to a certain second while a third thing is so related to itself, or *(b)* such that if anything is so related to itself every second and third things are so related to one another.

25. With reference to the pair of couples A:B and B:A.

251. A relation may be *(a)* such that two things are so related to one another, or *(b)* such that there is no such reciprocity.

252. A relation may be *(a)* such that neither of two things is so related to the other, or *(b)* such that of any two things one is so related to the other.

253. A relation may be *(a)* such that one thing is so related to the other without that other being so related to it, or *(b)* such that if anything is so related to another that other is so related to it.

26. With reference to the pair of couples A:B and C:A.

261. A relation may be *(a)* such that the same thing can be relate and correlate of the relation to two different things, or *(b)* such that nothing to which a second is in that relation can be in the same relation to a third.

262. A relation may be *(a)* such that there may be a thing to which a second is not in that relation, while it is itself not in that relation to a third, or *(b)* such that if anything be not in that relation to a second that second is in that relation to every third.

263. A relation may be *(a)* such that there is something so related to a second, that second not being so related to every third, or *(b)* such that if anything is so related to a second that second is so related to every third.

264. A relation may be *(a)* such that a thing is not in that relation to a second which is so related to a third, or *(b)* such that everything is either so related to a second or that second not so related to any third.

27. With reference to the pair of couples A:B and A:C.

271. A relation may be *(a)* such that the same thing is so related to two things, or *(b)* such that nothing is so related to more than one thing.

272. A relation may be *(a)* such that the same thing is not so related to two things, or *(b)* such that nothing fails to be so related to more than one thing.

273. A relation may be *(a)* such that the same thing is so related to a second but not to a third, or *(b)* such that everything is in that relation to everything else or to nothing else.

28. Parallel classifications relative to A:B and C:B.

29. With reference to the pair of couples A:B and C:D.

291. A relative may be *(a)* such that it exists between two entirely different pairs, or *(b)* such that it does not.

292. A relative may be *(a)* such that there are two entirely different pairs between which it subsists, or *(b)* such that taking any two such pairs it subsists between one or the other.

293. A relative may be *(a)* such that of two entirely different pairs it subsists between one and not the other, or *(b)* such that if it subsists between any couple it does so between every entirely different couple.

42

Notes on Geometry of Plane Curves *without Imaginaries*

c. 1889 ***Houghton Library***

I. *Point.* From every point in plane one tangent.
No line intersects it.

II. *Line.* No tangent to it.
Every line intersects it.

III. Oval without singularities divides plane into two regions.

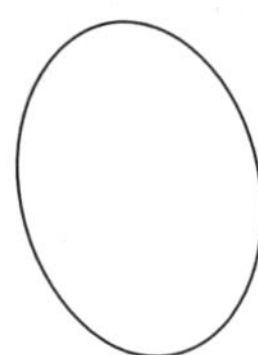

Inner lines 2 intersections
Outer lines 0 "
From Inner points 0 tangents
From Outer points 2 "

Two ovals either	(1) have	0 common tang.	0 com. pt.	
	(2)	4 " "	0 " "	
	(3)	0 " "	4 " "	
	(4)	$2n$ " "	$2n$ " "	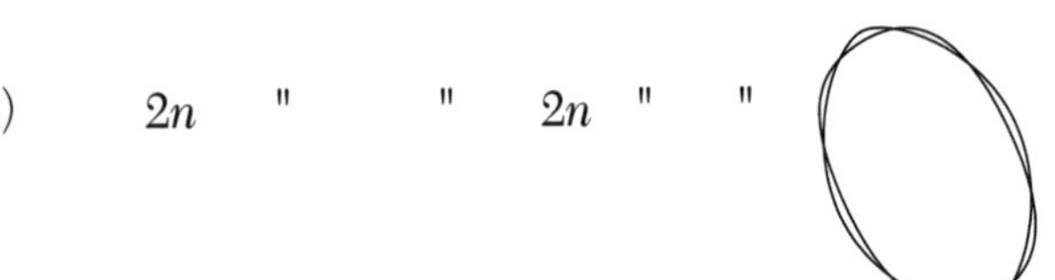

IV. Ovals with 1 node and 1 bitangent.
No cusp nor inflexion.

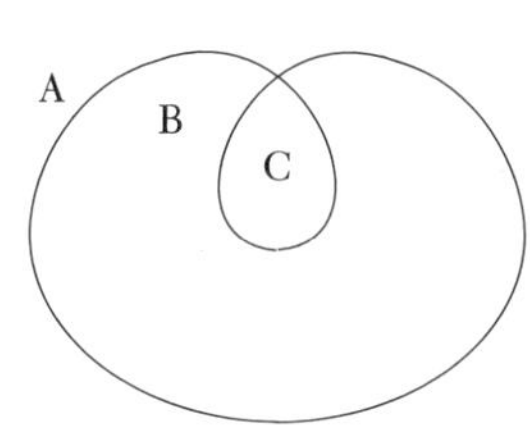

Three regions.		
From points in	A	4 tangents
" " "	B	2 "
" " "	C	0 "
Lines through	C	4 intersections
" "	B not C	2 "
" "	A not B	0 "

V. Ovals with 1 node and 1 inflexion.
No cusp nor bitangent.

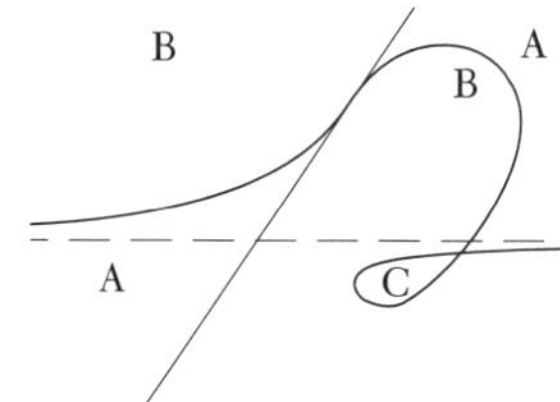

Three regions.		
From points in	A	4 tangents
" " "	B	2 "
" " "	C	0 "
Line cutting curve		3 intersections
		1 "

VI. Ovals with 1 bitangent and 1 cusp.

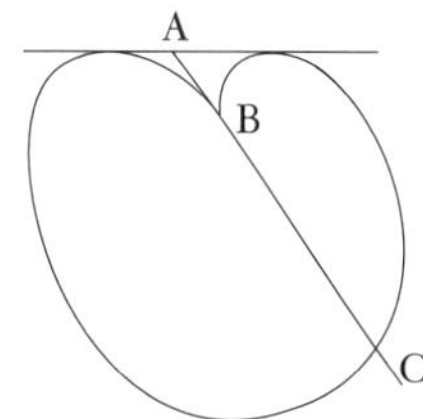

Line cutting tangent at cusp between AB	4 intersections
	2 "
outside	0 "
	3 tangents
	1 tangent

VII. Ovals with 1 cusp and 1 inflexion.
No node nor bitangent.
2 Kinds

First Kind

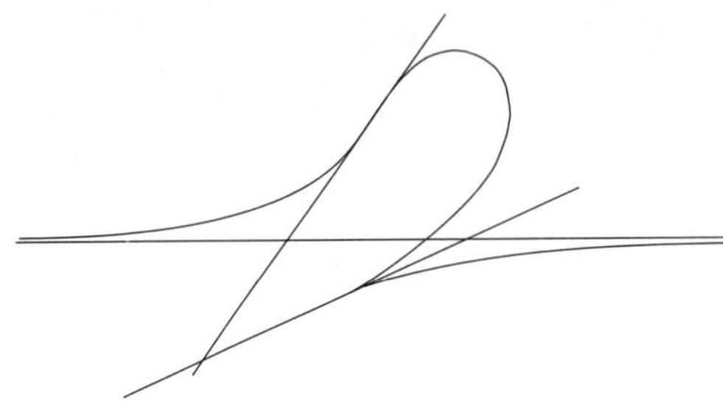

Tangents 3 or 1
Intersections 3 or 1

Second Kind

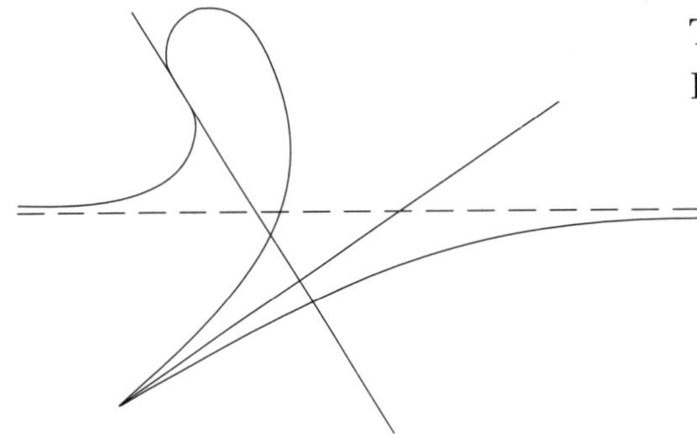

Tangents 5, 3, or 1
Intersections 5, 3, or 1

Curves with 3 *singularities.*

VIII. Three cusps.

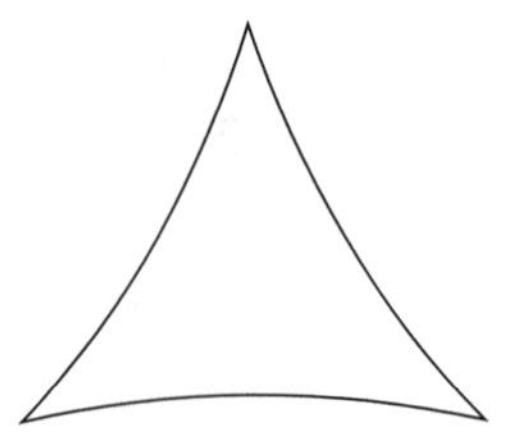

Intersections 4, 2, or 0
Tangents 3 or 1

IX. Three inflexions.

Intersections 3 or 1
Tangents 4, 2, or 0

[These two curves seem to falsify Klein's Formula, *Mathematische Annalen* x, 199.]

X. A cusp and two inflexions.

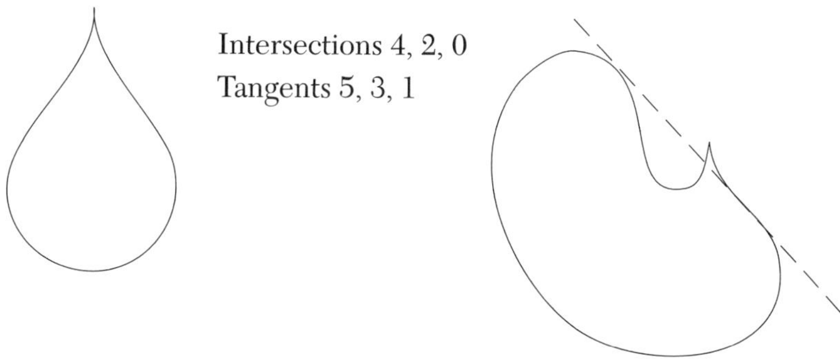

XI. Two cusps and an inflexion.

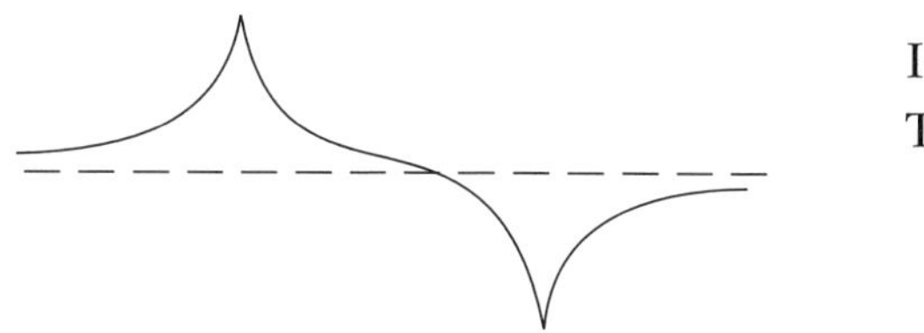

Intersections 5, 3, 1
Tangents 4, 2, 0

XII. Two cusps and a node.

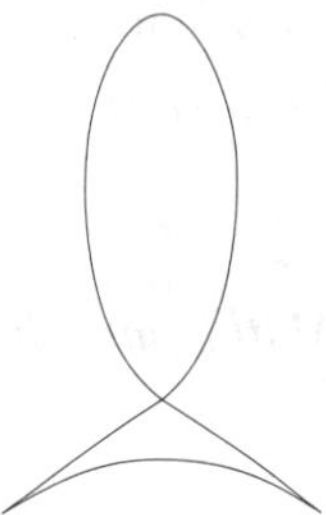

Intersections 4, 2, 0
Tangents 4, 2, 0

XIII. Two inflexions and a bitangent.

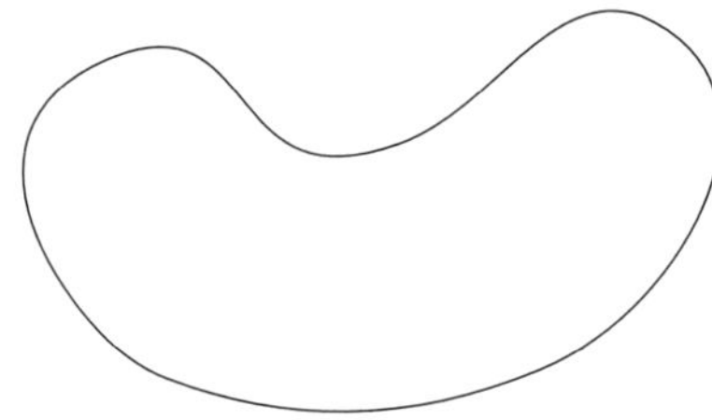

Intersections 4, 2, 0
Tangents 4, 2, 0

Most of above satisfy the formula
$3M + 2\delta + \iota = 3N + 2\tau + \kappa$

43

Review of Noel's *The Science of Metrology*

27 February 1890 **The Nation**

The Science of Metrology; or, Natural Weights and Measures. A Challenge to the Metric System. By the Hon. E. Noel, Captain Rifle Brigade. London: Edward Stanford. 1889.

The metric system is now supposed to be taught in the arithmetic course in every school. If it were well taught—say, if a quarter of an hour twice a week for half a school year were intelligently devoted to it—the pupils would forever after be more familiar with millimetres, centimetres, metres, and kilometres, with grammes and kilogrammes, with ares and hectares, and with litres, than they are ever likely to be with the English units. Who, except an occasional grocer, can guess at a pound within two ounces; or how many, besides engineers and carpenters, can distinguish seven-eighths of an inch from an inch at sight? Yet these are things easily taught. But schools will gradually get better conducted, and foreign intercourse seems destined before very long to receive an almost sudden augmentation; so that the metric system will pretty certainly become more and more familiar, and there may be expected to be some practical movement towards its use in trade. It is quite within the bounds of possibility that, even in a country with as little governmental initiative as ours, fashion may lead to the partial superseding of the old weights and measures, just as the avoirdupois pound superseded the Troy and merchants' pounds, as ells and nails have given place to yards and inches, as lasts and stones, firlots, kilderkins, long tons, great hundreds, and innumerable other units have disappeared within this century. If the litre, the half-kilo, and the metre were only not all severally greater than the quart, the pound, and the yard, there might be shops today where the keepers would affect to be unacquainted with English weights and measures.

There is little real difficulty in changing units of weight and bulk, were there any positive motive for it, for the things they weigh and measure are mostly used up within a twelvemonth. But with linear and square measure it is otherwise. The whole country having been measured and parcelled in quarter sections, acres, and house-lots, it would be most inconvenient to change the numerical measures of the pieces. Then we have to consider the immense treasures of machinery with which the country is filled, every piece of which is liable to break or wear out, and must be replaced by another of the same gauge almost to a thousandth of an inch. Every measure in all this apparatus, every diameter of a roll or wheel, every bearing, every screw-thread, is some multiple or aliquot part of an English inch, and this must hold that inch with us, at least until the Socialists, in the course of another century or two, shall, perhaps, have given us a strong-handed government.

We can thus make a reasonable prognosis of our metrological destinies. The metric system must make considerable advances, but it cannot entirely supplant the old units. These things being so, to "challenge" the metric system is like challenging the rising tide. Nothing more futile can well be proposed, unless it be a change in the length of the inch. Nevertheless, there is a goodly company of writers to keep the Hon. Capt. Noel in countenance in conjoining these two sapient projects. None of these gentlemen supports the constructive parts of the other's propositions; but they are unanimous against the metric system and the existing inch.

Mr. Noel's system is nearly as complicated and hard to learn as our present one, with which it would be fearfully confused, owing to its retaining the old names of measures while altering their ratios. Thus we should have to learn that 2½ feet would make a yard, 4 miles a league, 5 feet a fathom, 625 acres a square mile, 1.953125 cubic ells a cubic yard, 216 cubic inches a gallon, 24 ounces a pound, etc. But it is not intended that this complication shall last forever, for this lesson, once digested, is to be followed by a clean sweeping away of the decimal numeration and the substitution of duodecimals. Mr. Noel enumerates sixty-eight advantages of his proposal, among them the following: "Mile, one-quarter hour's walk, better than kilometre"; "cubic foot worthier base than cubic decimetre"; "old London mile restored." The scheme is not without merit, and might have been useful to Edward I. Even at this day it must at least have afforded some agreeable occupation to its ingenious and noble author, not to speak of the arithmetical practice.

44

[Logic and Spiritualism]

March–April 1890 ***Houghton Library***

Facts, new or newly published, rappings, table-turnings, with different predispositions opining differently, started controversy concerning Spiritualism. In course of time, other facts, as planchette, public exhibitions, mind-reading, trances, apparitions, physical manifestations in great variety, many hundred well-attested strange experiences, attempts at scientific experimentation,—contrariwise, important mediums and mind-readers detected rogues, new psychological laws explanatory of various illusions,—all these facts doubtless had influence, one or other way, upon men's opinions. Meantime, a mighty flood, literature and talk, deluged the subject,—observations highly judicious, delicious satire, ingenious speculations, a large part sadly rash, a very little too timorous. But doubted whether all this comment has changed one individual's mind.

In this impotence of argumentation, sole hope of contributing anything useful to the discussion lies in breathing a spirit so candid, unsophisticated, direct, yielding, that the impartial mind, he who alone can get good from such reading, he who looks upon speculative opinions as so many objects of natural history, calculated to excite lively interest by curious relationships and affinities, more so perhaps by being false than being true, but who lays them upon his dissection-table as things not calling for sympathy, as vivisection-subjects whose vehement logic-squirmings need excite no concern whatever,—that this man may be aided in picking to pieces, disentangling, studying the intellectual component impulses urgent to the opinion in hand, in appreciating them, in considering their just limits of action, not so much himself to form definitive judgment *pro* or *con* (which mostly is not safe while controversy rages), as to assign it its schematic place in the natural history of opinion.

First, I state plainly what I dispute. Hypnotism I question not, nor double and triple personality. That these things yet remain imperfectly classified, is admitted, too; and not alone these phenomena, but much in everyday life, communication of ideas in ordinary conversation. Only vague, doubtful explanations are deliverable for phenomena resembling clairvoyance. Not altogether improbably, unrecognized avenues of sense may exist. Possibly *so* the blind avoid trees and walls. Phenomena in abundance await explanation from future science about every stock and stone; how much more about mind? But here, with parting salutation, I diverge from spiritualistic paths, for I think no mind with which man can communicate can act or feel otherwise than through its residential nerve-matter, which in turn can act and react upon external bodies only according to recognized laws of mechanics. Not that telepathy is absurd or in its nature impossible, but in the coarse form it has been imagined, impracticable as voyage to planet Mars. Belief in telepathy ought to be ranked as variation of spiritualism.

I run up my colors and confess myself scientific specialist. Spiritualists do not take kindly to scientific men, and never forego opportunities of instancing scientific follies. Though eminent scientists be their allies, they would not have spiritualism judged by the scientific kind of intelligence, surely anticipating disfavor from such judgment. For scientific men, we may as well acknowledge it, are, as such, mere specialists. That stigma! We are blind to our own blindness; but the world seems to declare us simply incapable of rising from narrowness and specialism to take broad view of any facts whatsoever.

"Myopy" and "presbyopy": inability to focus objects too far away; corresponding inability for objects too near. I suppose we scientific specialists, technical sharps, connoisseurs, travellers, scholars, are myopic minds, seeing microscopically, but only things under our several noses. Presbyopic minds, with defective accommodation, would be able to see only what stands open to all men's apprehension: these are fogies, average board-members, men whom one believes to be very wise, but whom one perceives to be very ignorant.

First, I state plainly what I dispute. I do not call hypnotism in question, nor double and triple personality. That these things yet remain imperfectly classified is admitted, too; and not alone these phenomena, but others of everyday life, communication of ideas in ordinary conversation. Only vague doubtful explanations are available of much resembling clairvoyance. Not very improbably, unrecognized avenues of sense may exist. Possibly so the blind avoid trees and walls. Phenomena galore about every stock and stone await explanation from future science; and ignorance of mind exceeds that of matter. But there, I diverge from the Spiritualists path with a parting salutation, for I think that no mind with which we can communicate can act or feel otherwise than through its residential nervematter, which in its turn can act upon external matter only according to the regular laws of mechanics.

A holograph leaf from Peirce's initial draft of "Logic and Spiritualism" (R 879). Hand revisions include the diagonal slashes Peirce would use to cut the word count throughout his negotiations with Forum *editor Lorettus Sutton Metcalf; Peirce's word count annotations are visible beneath each counted line. (By permission of the Houghton Library, Harvard University.)*

Is there a corresponding contrast between objects themselves? Some paintings are not easily made out because done in miniature, requiring narrow examination. Others, large and executed broadly, when looked at closely show only brush marks, the design quite invisible. So, some experiences are inapprehensible because minute and recondite. They are *(a)* scientific observations, only feasible with special instrumental aids, under special precautions, by virtue of special skill; they are *(b)* strange adventures, happenings dependent on rare chances fallen to few people, unrepeatable at pleasure. In contrast with these phenomena, remote from everyday life, others (let us hasten to acknowledge) are as hard or harder to see, simply because they surround us on every hand; we are immersed in them and have no background against which to view them. A person's heart stops beating, he perceives it; but let it keep on its regular course, and he knows not he has a heart. People do not hear how their own voices sound, nor feel their own manners. Writers are unaware of the peculiar impressions produced by their own styles. What is the most obvious characteristic of the universe we live in, puzzles one to answer otherwise than by rote.

Curious, how little impression experience too familiar makes upon men's minds, how little attention is paid to it. With an oversecure, not to say ridiculous, contempt, I bethink me, we are despising everyday experience, we specialists and half the world besides,—except where its lessons are followed irreflectively. Recondite experiences, whether scientific or autobiographic, are cherished as very precious. They are rare; the means for acquiring them have been costly; they distinguish their possessor over other men; they are all that many a man has to show for life's labor. Have we professional men often been found *underrating* the importance of special orders of facts we have spent our lives in acquiring and in learning how to acquire? Has it happened to any of us, I wonder, to detect smiles on circumspicient faces at our contrary tendency? Or has it been generally remarked that persons who have gazed upon the midnight sun, or attended the Nijni Novgorod fair, or seen the effigies in Westminster Abbey, have set *less* store by these experiences than their untravelled interlocutors would seem inclined to do?

Let us ask ourselves whether not only scientific specialists, not only professional men, not only all educated men, but whether the bulk of mankind do not place too much stress on particulars, and regard too little the universal. Two persons, casually meeting with wish to develop mild sympathy, call one another's attention to the fair weather or the foul weather,—insignificant details. The deeper ground of common feeling, that it is day-time, nobody is ever asked to remark; still less the good cheer that earth contains fellow creatures, heaven a Father. Commonplaces these? Granted. But what are commonplaces but universal experiences?

Ask a thoughtful company the general question, where lies the intellectual superiority of one set of experiences over another, and reply will be made with some concord: facts are important only, first, as they are massed and concentrated upon one or more positions, and, secondly, as these positions are themselves important.

Go on, however, to inquire of relative values of experiences familiar and recondite, and differences will emerge. Respectability will remark that worth of anything is equivalent of trouble requisite to supply it, familiar experiences, like air and water, commanding no price;—answer veritably redolent of the frankincense and the myrrh of the temple of Solomon. Science will hold scientific experiences more capable of systematic marshalling to great ends than civilian facts. Young America will call familiar phenomena squeezed lemons, whatever they had to teach already learned, things to be left behind in pressing on to things new; and it will recall dazzling inventions sprung from recondite experiences, gunpowder, mariner's compass, steam-engine, electric telegraph, india-rubber, anæsthetics, sewing-machine, telephone, electric light.

But all these voices will not drown those that decry and revile specialism, extolling and magnifying perfections of the all-pervading. These will be heard to say that those things are not most intellectually helpful which most dazzle imagination; that great facts of nature which familiar experiences embody are not of the number of those things which can have their juices sucked out of them and be cast aside; that (returning to the principle upon which alone the question can be properly answered) the very circumstance which renders facts familiar is their being grouped into uniformed hordes, in consequence of which no collection of scientific observations can well be vast enough to withstand their concurrent testimony.

These protestants against worship of scientific specialties, deeper-thinking of the spiritualists included, will be averse from admitting that the discovery of phenomena of electricity, establishment of its laws, determination of its constants, and application to the uses of life, rank as the greatest triumph of modern knowledge. That distinction they will rather reserve for the evolution of the principle of conservation of energy, *résumé* of all that man has ever learned about force, great governing principle of all physics, whose history reaches from Archimedes to our day. That history shows that this great investigation has, from first to last, rested almost exclusively upon familiar experiences.

Its completion was involved in the discovery that heat, instead of being something ingenerable, indestructible, is but mechanical work transformed. Humanity wanted time to master that subtilty, energy being yet only a letter in an algebraic formula, and even *vis viva* no commanding feature of ordinary conceptions of mechanics. Accordingly, the doctrine having been accepted, a vestige of mental confusion remained in disagreements as to the nature of the evidence that had demonstrated it. Tyndall and Clausius, sound logicians, uphold Mayer's proof drawn from facts to be reckoned as familiar; but Tait, patriotic Scot, finds adherents for attribution to more special considerations adduced by countrymen. Others, however, had found it out long before, Rumford, Sadi Carnot, and if I am rightly informed, Uriah Boyden.

Be those doubts what they may, there can be none that previous steps used familiar experiences as almost their sole premises. Archimedes proves the property of the lever, Stevinus that of the inclined plane, Huygens that of moments of inertia, by mathematical reasoning from propositions assumed as self-evident,—dictates of common sense. Galileo, demonstrating the mechanical parallelogram, merely asks imagination how a body would move upon a vessel itself moving, no outward experiment demanded. Newton, establishing the law of action and reaction, treats his facts as matters of course. Even Galileo arguing the first, substantially too the second, law of motion in the teeth of supposed established facts, though keen observer, though experimenter, rests almost exclusively on familiar experience, and *il lume naturale,* adducing but few simple experiments, after all not needed.

Dr. Thomas Young, name to conjure with among physicists, thought, in the first quarter of this century, scientific experimentation had gone far enough and should stop till facts already collected were digested. Every scientist will jeer. My individual notion, doubtless warped with specialism, is this. Reasoning is strictly experimentation. Euclid having constructed a diagram according to prescription, draws an extra line, whereupon his mind's eye observes new relations not among those prescribed, quite as surprising as new metals or new stars. Experimentation is strictly appeal to reason. Chemist sets up retort, introduces ingredients, lights fire, awaits result. Why so confident? Because he trusts that what happens once happens always; nature follows general laws, in other words, has a reason. Successful research,—say Faraday's,—is conversation with nature; the macrocosmic reason, and the equally occult microcosmic law, must act together or alternately, till the mind is in tune with nature. This, the distinctively scientific procedure, linked experimentation and reasoning (suppose we say *indagation*), essentially involves special, new experiences. A scientific man is simply one who has been trained to conduct observations of some special kind, with which his distinctive business begins and ends. Nevertheless, reasoning from familiar experience plays a great role in science: it lays the indispensable foundation, is needful in frequent later conjunctures. The part so built is the strongest of the structure, upholding the rest.

Such reasoning is sometimes elaborate, self-critical; but at its best it is simple, sleepy. The doctrine of Descartes, that the mind consists solely of that which directly asserts itself in unitary consciousness, modern scientific psychologists altogether reject. Swarming facts positively leave no doubt that vivid consciousness, subject to attention and control, embraces at any one moment a mere scrap of our psychical activity. Without attempting accuracy of statement demanding long explanations, and irrelevant to present purposes, three propositions may be laid down. 1. The obscure part of the mind is the principal part. 2. It acts with far more unerring accuracy than the rest. 3. It is almost infinitely more delicate in its sensibilities. Man's fully-conscious inferences have no quantitative delicacy, except where they repose on arithmetic and measurement, which are mechanical processes; and they are almost as likely as not to be downright blunders. But unconscious or semi-conscious irreflective judgments of mother-wit, like instinctive inferences of brutes, answer questions of "how much" with curious accuracy; and are seldom totally mistaken.

Conclusions men reach they know not how, are better than those fortified by unscientific logic. By logic, *Aquinas*,[1] if not *Calvin*, persuaded himself that one of the chief joys of the blest will be to peer over heaven's parapet and watch the damned writhing in torments and rage below: by instinct, or half-conscious inference, a poor peasant girl will inwardly reject the doctrine, for all revered pastor may say. No moral sentiment more universally violent than reprobation of intermarriage of near relatives. Assassin will shudder at thought of incest. But had a man to depend upon conscious reasoning to instruct conscience in this matter, while he might be led to condemn the act, he would be unlikely to regard it with the extreme horror in which actually all share. Generation after generation has, in almost unconscious mode, taken measure of ordinary experiences about family relationships, has transmitted its impression to the next, partly by tradition, partly one guesses by congenital bequest, this next has made its observations and discussions, has modified in some insensible degree the sentiment it derived from its fathers, and so at last our strong feeling has been developed. That races tolerating occasional incest have died out and that *so* horror of it has been bred, there is scant room to believe.

This transmission from father to son of dictates of good judgment, makes the growth of common sense. Based on large, ordinary experience, far more valuable reservoir of truth than the aggregate of man's special experiences (scientific and extraordinary), worked up in that part of the mind that functions the most delicately and unerringly, reconsidered and revised by countless generations, such conclusion, if

1. Thus in the *Scriptum in quartum librum sententiarum Magistri Petri Lombardi,* (Distinctio 50, quæstio 2, articulus 4), he says: "Dicendum . . . quod . . . ut beatitudo sanctorum eis magis complaceat et de ea uberiores gratias Deo agant, dantur eis ut poenam impiorum perfecte intueantur." In his 8th Quodlibet, question 7, article 1, he says: "Dicendum quod videre miseriam damnatorum omnino erit sanctis ad gloriam, gaudebunt enim de justicia Dei et de sua visione." And in another place: "lætantur de justa punitione." "A horrible doctrine, I confess," says Calvin of election to damnation; but logic forced him to it.

unequivocal and pertaining to matter plainly within the competency of good sense, who shall dare to dispute?

Let not conscious reason look down upon it as inadequate to problems high, intellectual, intricate. From data of sensations proper to hundreds of nerve-terminals in the optic retina, combined with certain muscular sensations,—premises more tangled and confused than tongue can tell or brain can think,— common sense has extricated the marvellously clear and beautiful conception, Space. What a simple theory, reducing to order what infinitely complicated facts! Can the whole history of science show any discovery whatever half so practically important, half so intrinsically difficult, half so intellectually interesting? It is conceivable that future science should find some principles of geometry to be measurably erroneous. Such discovery would be the most remarkable ever made by science. Yet what insignificant detail compared with that which common sense has taught us of space!

Common sense corrects itself, improves its conclusions. The history of the science of dynamics is that of gradual correction by inference from familiar experience (essentially an operation of good sense), of the primitive conceptions of "force" and "matter." There, however, the reasoning was of the self-conscious kind. But we see social, political, religious common sense modifying itself insensibly in the course of generations, ideas of rights of man acquiring new meaning, thaumaturgic elements of Christianity sinking, spiritual rising in religious consciousness.

Common sense improves; it does not, then, attain infallibility. Then, its decisions are subject to review. But in case there be evidence that such a conclusion is definitive, not a mere stage in a changing estimate; if it appears to have been formed under guidance of general experience and to be of the kind such experience can warrant; finally, if its substance is in harmony with individual good judgment from general experience, then the authority of common sense as to the practical truth of the conclusion (subject to minute modification) is so weighty, that special experience can hardly attain sufficient strength to overthrow it.

How will this rule work in practice? Dr. Zöllner, eminent astronomer and mathematical physicist, man of true genius, keen and subtle, has Mr. Slade, the celebrated medium, visitor in his house. One night he ties the ends of a string together, putting seal upon the knot. Next day, he hands this string to Slade, who thereupon before his eyes makes (or seems to make) a knot in the single string (in contradistinction, I mean, to the doubled string), and hands it back for examination. The ends of the string not being free, this was impossible according to common sense. But had space a fourth dimension, additional to its three of length, breadth, and thickness, there would be no such impossibility. Hence Dr. Zöllner concludes that space really has four dimensions. Now, it must be admitted that no experiences, familiar or otherwise, are absolutely inconsistent with space having four dimensions. For example, this refutation might be proposed: steam can be subjected to great pressure in a boiler; now if space were open in a fourth dimension, there would be a way round from the inside to the outside of the boiler, and why should not the steam escape? It might, however, be replied that the molecules having no component velocities in that direction, and there being no component pressure in that direction, there would be no tendency to motion in that direction; indeed various other loopholes in the argument are discoverable. Only suppose, then, that space really has a fourth dimension, and suppose that one single muscle-cell of Mr. Slade's had somehow got displaced so as to project in that direction, and a force is thus supplied in that direction which, in the total absence of resistance in that direction, would suffice to carry Mr. Slade's fingers and with them the string round by that path so as to tie the knot; and here we have explanation, simple and beautiful, of the phenomenon;—a gentlemanly explanation, too, not unnecessarily offensive to Mr. Slade's honor. Should it be urged that all experience is against space having a fourth dimension, because on that hypothesis phenomena similar to that tying of the knot ought to be more common, ready reply comes: if space has a fourth dimension there is no determining *a priori* how often it would happen that something would project into it; experience seems to show it happens so rarely that Mr. Slade furnishes the first conclusive instance of it. Now, it is certainly true that no experience whatever can furnish the slightest reason for thinking that an event of any conceivable kind will *absolutely never* happen. Take a thousand people at random among the inhabitants of the United States, and upon inquiry it may probably be found that not one of them will ever have read a line of Martin Farquhar Tupper. It will be fair to conclude that not one in a thousand of all the people in the country ever read a line of this poet; but not to conclude he has *no* readers in the country, since it might be not one in a thousand were readers of his works, while still those poems were devoured by sixty thousand people. Upon the same principle, all accumulable experience will never furnish any smallest reason for thinking that no one, or no million for that matter, of all the bodies in the universe juts out into a fourth dimension. Nay, presumption rather holds that this does somewhere occur, since every rule has exceptions; for how could an absolutely universal law ever come about? But the whole of our personal experience, itself an amazing flood, together with the experience of all history as embodied in common sense, compels us to hold such jutting to be so excessively infrequent that the probability of its occurrence in any particular case, as in the person of Mr. Slade, is beyond all compare smaller than the probability of trick, even were we at a loss to conceive how trick could be.

Of course, popular belief has often fallen into gross errors. Primitive man peopled woods, streams, earth, air, clouds, stars, with spirits. If intercourse with these beings could be shown to have been believed customary, happening every day, it would be an inference of a kind legitimately to be drawn from familiar experience, and we should have to inquire seriously into its truth. But I fancy intercourse with spirits was never considered matter of course. Belief in it was not formed under guidance of experience, but was hot, extravagant fancy, classable with those superstitions that have inspired or terrified mankind,—fountain of perpetual youth, philosopher's stone, fairies, ogres, ghosts, magic, personal devil, jinns sealed up by Solomon, archei, oracles of Apollo, Eleusinian mysteries, metempsychosis, and all other romances about substantial spirits.

Faith in these things is fading out; where people are enlightened mere traces of it remain. The essence of these rapidly-decadent beliefs is the doctrine that soul (such as we can know) is able to feel and act independently of its animal body. State the proposition in the abstract, and most men will subscribe to it. Find a practical case, and willingness to risk great interests upon the truth of the principle will commonly be deemed symptomatic of aberration of mind.

Common sense is coming to reject the doctrine, good sense does reject it. All the ordinary phenomena of life, which crowd upon us every minute, together with such familiar matters as sleep, faintings, bodily illness, insanity, death, show as plainly, as conclusively, dependence of mind upon body, as familiar facts of lifeless things show the first law of motion. That law which Galileo substantially first told the world, is that a moving body left to itself, will move on with no diminution, no increase of speed, in one straight line forever. They say the first thing that made him think so was seeing a lamp hung by a chain from the roof of the beautiful cathedral at Pisa, just before the choir, swinging backward and forward, through a small arc, once in about four seconds, and continuing so to move all through high mass, without any perceptible decrement of the amplitude of its oscillations. I can well believe this true. Performance of good judgment is a sluggish movement, a mental peristalsis that is favored by beautiful and peaceful surroundings, even by a certain luxurious tedium, which, in that most satisfying of cathedrals, ceremonies, performed with an elegance in manner, a refinement in spirit, caught it might seem from the architecture, would well produce in mind of boy attending them too often. I remember myself giving that same lamp, as no doubt it was, a small impulse shortly before a function more than ordinarily prolonged,—obsequies of a prince of the church,—and to have watched its grave, impressive, though soft assertion of the first law of motion, all through the service, wondering whether the obvious lesson of mortality which that corpse, that whole scene, was bearing in upon me, could be less true, less infallible than that.

Completely satisfactory discussion of the question of Spiritualism would involve satisfactory theory of connection of soul and body, which is not perhaps forthcoming.

The obsolete Cartesian dualism, that soul and body are two substances, distinct, independent, untenable as positing a double absolute, rendering connection of soul and body absolutely inexplicable either on mechanical or on psychological principles, had a single element of philosophical strength, its recognition of real reaction between *ego* and *non-ego*. Development of this naturally leads to thinking that minds can communicate only through bodies,—doctrine unfavorable to Spiritualism.

Philosophy tries to understand. In so doing, it is committed to the assumption that things are intelligible, that the process of nature and the process of reason are one. Its explanation must be derivation. Explanation, derivation, involve suggestion of starting-point,—starting-point in its own nature not requiring explanation nor admitting of derivation. Also, there is suggestion of goal or stopping-point, where the process of reason and nature is perfected. A principle of movement must be assumed to be universal. It cannot be supposed that things ever actually reach the stopping-point, for there movement would stop and the principle of movement would not be universal; and similarly with the starting-point. Starting-point and stopping-point can only be ideal, like the two points where the hyperbola leaves one asymptote and where it joins the other. In regard to the principle of movement, three philosophies are possible.

1. Elliptic philosophy. Starting-point and stopping-point are not even ideal. Movement of nature recedes from no point, advances toward no point, has no definite tendency, but only flits from position to position.

2. Parabolic philosophy. Reason or nature develops itself according to one universal formula; but the point toward which that development tends is the very same nothingness from which it advances.

3. Hyperbolic philosophy. Reason marches from premises to conclusion; nature has ideal end different from its origin.

The choice of elliptic philosophy, which refuses to acknowledge the ideal, supposes more interest in nature than in reason. The philosophy which sees nothing in nature but the washing of waves on a beach, cannot consistently regard mind as primordial, must rather take mind to be a specialization of matter. Bent on outward studies, it will find the statement that nerve-matter feels, just as carmine is red, a convenient disposition of a troublesome question. Elliptic philosophy is irreconcileable with Spiritualism.

He who feels himself and his neighbors under the constraints of overwhelming power, from which they long to take refuge in annihilation,—situation less common in this country and age than in other places and times,—viewing this little life as rounded with a sleep, readily accepts the idea that the world, too, sprang out of the womb of nothingness to evolve its destiny, and into nothingness back to return. Such life as this philosophy recognizes,—a fatal struggle, a mere death-throe,—it should extend throughout nature. Soul should be a mere aspect of the body, not tied to it, therefore, but identical with it. Nothing can be more hostile to Spiritualism than this parabolic philosophy.

Hyperbolic philosophy has to assume for starting-point something *free,* as neither requiring explanation nor admitting derivation. The free is living; the immediately living is *feeling.* Feeling, then, is assumed as starting-point; but feeling uncoördinated, having its manifoldness implicit. For principle of progress or growth, something must be taken not in the starting-point, but which from infinitesimal beginning will strengthen itself continually. This can only be a principle of growth of principles, a tendency to generalization. Assume, then, that feeling tends to be associated with and assimilated to feeling, action under general formula or habit tending to replace the living freedom and inward intensity of feeling. This tendency to take habits will itself increase by habit. Habit tends to coördinate feelings, which are thus brought into the order of Time, into the order of Space. Feelings coördinated in a certain way, to a certain degree, constitute a person; on their being dissociated (as habits do sometimes get broken up), the personality disappears. Feelings over whose relations to their neighbors habit has acquired such an empire that we detect no trace of spontaneity in their actions, are known as dead matter. The hypothesis here sketched, whose consequences, traceable with precision to considerable detail in various directions, appear to accord with observation, to an extent of which I can here give no idea, affords a rational account of the connection of body and soul. This theory, so far as I have been able as yet to trace its consequences, gives little or no countenance to Spiritualism, because, according to it, personality belongs only to feelings coördinated through matter. Still, it is evidently less unfavorable than any other reasonable philosophy.

The myriad strange stories prove nothing. Tell me a marvel; I cannot explain it. Does that teach you or me anything? True, you offer explanation, the spiritualistic one; but that is in conflict with good sense, while we know so little of the mind, at present, that it is not surprising that many things are yet inexplicable. Taking these stories in the gross, the only profitable way, we can roughly compare the phenomena with the general facts at our command for their explanation. These facts are four. First, the fact that all men are liars. Secondly, the fact of deranged imagination, hypnotism, hysteria. Thirdly, the fact that we may receive and act upon indications of which we are quite unconscious, and which, owing to the low sensibility of the conscious part of the mind, seem impossible. Fourthly, the fact that a certain number of coincidences will occur by chance. The result of such rough comparison is that, notwithstanding these four considerations, there are some stories truly surprising. If you have already admitted the general proposition of Spiritualism, you will naturally be inclined to use it to explain some of these stories. If, on the other hand, your judgment is that general experience is emphatically opposed to that proposition, these stories will assuredly not shake that judgment.

Meantime, those who are engaged in psychical research should receive every encouragement. They may have reached little or no result, so far; perhaps will not till they dismiss the phantom of telepathy from their minds. But scientific men, working in something like scientific ways, must ultimately reach scientific results. Psychology is destined to be the most important experimental research of the twentieth century; fifty years hence its wonders may be expected to occupy popular imagination as wonders of electricity do now.

45

Herbert Spencer's Philosophy

March 1890 ***Houghton Library***

Is It Unscientific and Unsound?—Its Pretensions Attacked and a Demonstration Called For

Herbert Spencer's philosophy has been before the public now for some thirty years; it seems time that some one should tell the truth about it, and inform the public what value has been accorded to it by men competent to judge it. We know well enough that Hegelians and such like scorn it, and also that the "general reader" reveres it. But what we would like to have told is whether the pretensions of Mr. Spencer are acknowledged to be well founded; whether, for example, since his doctrine partly rests upon mathematical considerations, he ranks high as a mathematician among mathematicians; whether biologists have awarded him those tokens of respect (such as medals and foreign memberships of academies) which usually mark their recognition of a leader; whether the modern school of psychology reckons him as one of its chiefs, and whether anthropologists hold that his sociological tables have been drawn up in a truly scientific and critical method; or whether, on the other hand, each of these specialists is accustomed to think of Mr. Spencer as eminent in every branch but his own.

Are his methods of reasoning in each of the sciences in which he professes to instruct the world such as its adepts will pronounce the most powerful and unexceptionable at their command? An outsider is often tempted to doubt this. For example, in laying down his first principles, he makes the following statement:

> This method is to compare all opinions of the same genus; to set aside, as more or less discrediting one another, those various special and concrete

elements in which such opinions disagree, to observe what remains after the discordant constituents have been eliminated, and to find for this remaining constituent that abstract expression which holds true throughout its divergent modifications.

Is it possible, then, to deduce truth from a mere opinion, or from any number of opinions, these having sprung, it may be, from temperamental hopes or superstitious fears acting in a field of utter ignorance? Would not the result of this method, had it, for instance, been applied before the rise of modern science to the different systems of astrology, have been that the stars in some way influence the destinies of men; and would this have been a conclusion to "rank next in certainty to the postulates of exact science"? Are thinkers ever really obliged to give all opinions equal votes without educational qualification, and shall not the doubts which must instantly spring up when any proposition is found to rest on no better ground than that be allowed their vote, too?

It is one of Mr. Spencer's first principles which he is content to establish in this fashion, and particularly important is it that a thinker of the mold in which he is cast should set out with premises true beyond all manner of doubt. For he is not one of those philosophers who launch upon a voyage of discovery, supported by the pressure of a fluid experience renewed at every step, subject to incessant change, a thing to be vigilantly watched, through which (advancing most when almost overwhelmed) they are propelled toward their goal by skillful adaptations of the force of elemental and cosmical thought, the breath of the universe; but he is one of those who build Babel systems to scale the heights of knowledge; structures standing upon hard, unchangeable foundations of "first principles," so that no stage of their erection can be more secure than their cornerstones—cornerstones too often resting on quaggy ground which gives way beneath them more and more with time.

Next, readers would like to be informed whether Mr. Spencer's system is logically put together. Does he fully understand his own theory; does he accurately distinguish all the different elements of it; does he recognize precisely what part each has to play; does he justly assign them their relative ranks, and does he use this knowledge of his own theory to form with it a consistent and thoroughgoing philosophy? These are the respects in which English thinkers have generally been at fault. The oft-signalized inconsistency of Berkeley in admitting the substantial soul while denying corporeal matter is only a specimen of the common patchwork of English philosophers, who would one and all dread to carry even the all-salutary multiplication table too far. It is true that the English have gone to great extremes in philosophy, witness Ockham, Hobbes, Mandeville, Hume, Jonathan Edwards, James Mill, Bentham. They are extreme without being thoroughgoing; it is a part of their inconsistency. Indeed, the extreme character of their thought is itself due to their omission to reflect upon the precise sorts of effect which the different general elements of their hypotheses are fitted to account for. John Mill, for example, pronounces the mind to be a succession of feelings. This proposition is the garland that crowns him a philosopher. But if he had ever sat down to consider as a general question what continuity was, and how the occurrence of the conception of it could be accounted for, perhaps he might not have taken up that extreme position. Such being the deformity to which English thought is liable, we naturally inquire whether or not Mr. Spencer has been able to escape it. Since his is a philosophy of evolution, has he sought to apply this principle to the explanation of everything capable of being explained and presenting those characters which belong to phenomena such as may be developed by evolution?

There are philosophies of evolution which undertake to explain everything, or rather to render everything explicable. Hegel's, for example, accepts nothing as primordial but blank immediacy itself. But Mr. Spencer's is not one of these. There are certain things which his somewhat clumsy conception of evolution has left him no room to explain in any evolutionary sense. It is not, perhaps, a fault that he leaves Matter one of these; for blank indeterminate matter, the mere germ of existence, presents no order, no relationship, no characters at all that call for explanation; and it is posited as primordial by the great father of metaphysical evolutionism, Aristotle himself. Nor would it be fair to complain that Time remains behind the starting point of Spencer's evolution, although time is a system of relationship in most intimate analogy with the consecution of thought; for great analytic power would undoubtedly be required to detach the idea of evolution from that of time. But Space, does not space call for some explanation? Is not that a half-way philosophy which in these our days does not explain, or at least hold out some promise of explaining, why space is continuous, why it has such a wonderful uniformity in all its parts, why there are neither more nor less than three dimensions everywhere, why every closed curve can, by a continuous change of position, size, and form, be brought into coincidence with every other, and why the three angles of a triangle make exactly one hundred and eighty degrees, or at least so very closely so that we cannot tell whether they make more or less? The study of philosophy seems to exist only by virtue of a presumption that all the regularities of the universe are to be explained upon some one principle; and we might expect that, were this principle once grasped, these regularities of space, so intelligible as they are, so universal, so fundamental, would, among the first and easiest of things, get explained with mathematical precision and clearness. The general laws of mechanics are of much the same character. There, however, we have to thank Mr. Spencer for an easy but important generalization, namely, that each of these laws is a statement that in every motion a certain quantity definitely related to that motion, remains unchanged. It follows from this, according to Spencer, that these laws are themselves immutable, and consequently not to be explained by evolution. But one cannot help asking whether, if so, it is not so much the worse for evolution, and whether, in fact, this would not show at once that evolution is not that El Dorado of which philosophy is in quest. But then Mr. Spencer says that these inexplicables spring directly from the Unknowable, and this seems to be at any rate a somewhat imposing *substitute* for an explanation. But is it not something like the doctrine of Special Creations; is this resort to the Unknowable thoroughgoing evolutionism? One would like to hear, too, about this Unknowable, or is it not merely this Unknown of Mr. Spencer's; is it the good, authentic, practical, working God of religion, or is it a poor, decayed divinity, exercising no functions in this evolutionary world, but retained on half pay for the sake of auld lang syne?

The most remarkable feature of Spencer's evolutionism would seem to some readers to be that for him evolution is only a secondary result of another principle, namely, that of the conservation of energy, which he holds to be primordial. He belongs, in short, to that generation who, after they have opened such eyes as they have been blessed with, and have looked upon the world, teeming and bursting with life all over, having asked themselves whether the principle of growth would seem to be something primary and *sui generis* or something secondary and a special variety of something else, have been able to reply, "It is undoubtedly an incidental result of mechanical principles." Of course, it would require quite an intricate combination of lifeless elements to make a living, growing thing; and consequently the definition of life is decidedly complicated, and as life is a special kind of mechanism, so consciousness is an aspect of a special kind of life. Now, do those who know all about it really tell us to believe that feeling is merely an aspect of a special mechanical contrivance? It must be a remarkably clever trick. Do mathematicians consider the demonstrations of that chapter to be perfectly rigid and perspicuous in which Spencer professes to show, from mathematical considerations, that evolution is a necessary result of the principle of living forces? We have heard that this last was equivalent to saying, that if the directions of motion of all the bodies in the world were at one instant all to be reversed while the velocities remained the same, the universe would pass back through all the configurations by which its parts had arrived where they were when their velocities were reversed, and, in short, it would go through all its motions backward; the man that had been knocked down would fly up to meet the fist, at contact of which his pain would disappear, he would walk home backward, and would grow to be a boy and a baby again, and back we should go to the primeval nebula. This, at least, is the dictum of the conservation of energy. But this would not be evolution, but counter-evolution—not growth, but ungrowth, one would think. That which prevents anything like this from generally happening would seem to be something different from the conservation of energy, and yet something that has to do with the law of development.

Enough of these questions. Herbert Spencer claims to have produced, not a philosophy comparable with former systems, but a great scientific theory, a philosophy worthy to form the crown of modern science; and, indeed, a less pretension would be simply a confession of nility. Now, the recognized touchstone of a scientific theory is successful prediction. A theory which brings forth bad fruit is rejected, and one that brings forth none at all is brushed aside. Spencer's theory, therefore, having been before the world now these thirty years, no doubt can point to considerable discoveries directly resulting from its predictions—not, be it understood, from the general doctrine of evolution, or from the Darwinian theory, but from the seventeen articles of the Spencerian confession. No doubt other even greater additions to our knowledge have been brought about by it indirectly. For the doctrine of Spencer, if worth anything at all, is a far greater thing than that of Sir Isaac Newton. Now, we know what Newtonianism accomplished for the world. It began by staking its entire credit without reservation upon a formal prediction that the earth would be found flattened at the poles. Geodesists set themselves to work to ascertain whether this was so in fact. The early results were doubtful; then for a time it seemed to have been shown that the globe was *prolate,* or elongated. But the Newtonians never flinched, hedged, straddled the question, or shifted their ground, but simply awaited the final issue.

That final decision about the flattening of the earth made the Newtonian philosophy king and master of speculation. So much for its direct predictions; as for its indirect achievements, we may reckon among them the molecular philosophy, modern physics, and a great part of modern mathematics. We wish some competent persons would give a condensed résumé, in not over fifty pages, of all the similar discoveries which the synthetic philosophy of Spencer, as drawn up by him in those seventeen propositions, has thus far given to the world.

OUTSIDER

46

Review of Collins's *Epitome of the Synthetic Philosophy*

27 March 1890 ***The Nation***

Epitome of the Synthetic Philosophy. By F. Howard Collins. With a preface by Herbert Spencer. D. Appleton & Co. 1889.

A more admirably executed second-hand synopsis of a system of philosophy never was. Considered simply as an index to Spencer's systematic works, this *Epitome* is invaluable; and to persons who read and reread those thick volumes, not because they believe in them, but only because they want to know what it is that so many others believe, and to whom the writings of the dreariest scholastic doctor are less heartbreakingly tedious, this one volume of 500 pages in place of a library of 5,000 pages is like balm of Gilead. Would it only embraced an introduction boiling the whole thing down to 50 pages! It is printed uniformly with Spencer's works, upon agreeable paper with clear type, and published by the same eminent firm which, by the dissemination of those writings, has contributed so much to the culture and thought of our people.

47

"Outsider" Wants More Light

13 April 1890 ***The New York Times***

He Cometh After His Critics and Searcheth Them—Spencer's Standing in Science—His Theory of Evolution—"Outsider" Is an Inquirer, Not an Assailant.

To the Editor of the New York Times:

I am an individual who three weeks ago gave utterance in your columns to questions weighing on me respecting Herbert Spencer's philosophy. I wanted a lesson. I did not argue, except so far as was necessary to setting forth my doubts. I simply begged to be informed what the special students of the different branches of science upon which Spencer has written books and papers really think of his work in its relation to their several studies. It is now time I should express grateful thanks to the gentlemen who have kindly responded to my appeal.

Above all they are due to the eminent biologist, Prof. Osborn, for his truly admirable paper last Sunday. Though many of your readers have, I am sure, perused it more than once, they will not blame my calling to their minds a few of his pregnant sentences in altered coloration. Prof. Osborn fully comprehends the essence of Spencerianism. It is not that nature and man are the result of evolution; for that had been said before by biologists, and, let me add, by wide-swaying philosophers as well. But what characterizes Spencerianism is the doctrine that *evolution is purely mechanical.* As Prof. Osborn well says, Spencer holds that "an organism is a machine, self-lubricating, constantly repairing all effects of wear and tear, with its internal relations constantly adjusted to its external relations." In Spencer's biology "all the processes which living matter has in common with non-living matter are magnified, all the processes peculiar to living matter are minimized."

We learn that there is "perhaps a large class of original investigators who have little respect for the hypothetical anatomy of Spencer," who "has never claimed to be a practical investigator." But, says the Professor, "every great leader in biology has gone directly to nature as the source of his inspiration," and "all permanent advances in the solution of the marvelous phenomena of life come from original thinkers in the laboratory and the field." Accordingly, Prof. Osborn has not implicit confidence in the permanent value of Spencer's work. "The sum of several works of transient value does not foot up to one work of permanent value." "It appears now as if Weismann's discoveries would mark an epoch in the history of the evolution theory." Weismann contends that acquired characters are not transmitted, and "it is perfectly evident that if they demonstrate this proposition one great section of Spencer's philosophy falls to the ground." Spencer has mainly been merely a follower of Lamarck in biology, though a follower with independent thought. Nevertheless, "many of his purely hypothetical deductions have been confirmed by the very latest discoveries," and Sedgwick writes from a laboratory where non-specialist generalizers are not objects of admiration that "Herbert Spencer's view of the origin of the nervous system may perhaps not be so far from the mark as at first sight appeared." All these judgments carry conviction to an outsider of fair-minded justice and truth. Some of my doubts they dissolve, but the more ponderous they greatly strengthen.

Another gentleman, Mr. H. J. Messenger, Jr., of the Department of Mathematics in New York University, comes forward to inform me regarding Spencer's competency from the mathematical standpoint. To this gentleman also thanks are due. He gives as a reason why Mr. Spencer has not been elected foreign associate of scientific academies that his religious views are not sufficiently orthodox. I am surprised to hear that the academies of Paris, Berlin, and St. Petersburg insist so strongly on orthodoxy. Chancing today upon a volume of the *Transactions of the Royal Society of Edinburgh*—a city where, if anywhere, theology should weigh—among the nineteen names selected, from all the philosophers of England and Ireland to receive the distinguished honor of membership in the Edinburgh Society, I found, to my surprise after the information accorded by Mr. Messenger, that of Huxley, although Huxley is, if anything, more heterodox than Spencer (whose name, of course, was not there). In the list of thirty-six foreign associates, a list formed with the utmost care, whom should I find but Haeckel, a notorious infidel! Of course Mr. Messenger, who comes forward as an expert, is intimately acquainted with the great academies, in their personnel and spirit, but without his positive testimony I should have hardly believed that they would proscribe great scientific men because they were agnostics. What bigots the European scientists must be! In this country the clergy contains the most numerous class of readers of Spencer.

Mr. Messenger is so good as to report what "the professor of chemistry in one of our leading medical colleges" thinks of Herbert Spencer. I suppose the first rank of theoretical chemists is connected with the larger universities, with governmental institutions, and with great manufactories, so that "the professor of chemistry in one of our leading medical colleges" might chance not to be the kind of man whose testimony would be the most valuable. Nevertheless, we may listen to it. It is that the first volume of Spencer's *Biology* contains a "very large number" of predictions in chemistry which recent laboratory investigations bear out. I should not have estimated at a "very large number" all the chemical remarks in the volume; of those, the greater part seems to express known truths, and of the rest many are glittering and slippery generalities, hard to transfix.

Mr. Messenger declares, as a mathematician, that "he has read Mr. Spencer's writings with considerable care and completeness," and "has not been able to find any" mathematical errors in them. He says he shall be glad to have any such pointed out. I thought I had already pointed out something that looked like a mathematical error, though it seems to have escaped Mr. Messenger's scrutiny. Namely, suppose all the molecules in the universe to have the positions which they actually have at any moment, but suppose them to have all precisely the reverse velocities. There is nothing in those positions or in those velocities contrary to the principle of the persistence of force. But it would follow from the same principle that, going on from that instant, history would be the precise reverse of what it actually had been up to the instant when all the particles actually had those positions. Such a backward motion of all history would then be perfectly consistent with the principle of the persistence of force. But Mr. Spencer, after defining evolution, etc., says: "All these phenomena, from their great features down to their minutest details, are necessary results of the persistence of force." One phenomenon of evolution actually observed is that eggs grow to birds, not birds back to eggs. Yet this cannot be a mathematical consequence of the persistence of force, since, on the contrary, the reverse proceeding would be perfectly consistent with that law. Is there no mathematical error here? If there be, is it not a fundamental one? Does not its correction show at once that evolution has not that mechanical nature which it is the great distinguishing characteristic of Spencer's philosophy to assign to it?

No other scientific adept seems to have favored me with answers to my questions, unless such be Mr. Edgar R. Dawson, who vouchsafes me little instruction, but subjects me to severe catechizing. He first asks: "Is it necessary for us to change our method of reasoning when we drop mathematics, for example, to take up chemistry?" How can I answer that, indeed! What a pity the authors of those great treatises on methods of reasoning which have distinguished our age had not bethought them of this sockdologer of a question before indicting their un-Dawsonian books! He next challenges me to "state any way in which one is more likely to arrive at truth which cannot be reached by exact science" than in adopting from all beliefs "that portion which all men admit, the most learned as well as the most ignorant." I reply: If we all hold to any given position without shadow of doubt—all from Edgar R. Dawson down to lowly "Outsider"—I do not think there is any possible way of arriving at that position where we appear already to be. At the same time, I must tell you, Mr. Editor, that, for my humble part, when I find a belief has no better warrant than a general tendency to believe in it, I am very apt indeed to turn it over in what I call my mind, and to commence doubting it, very strongly, and my doubt, once set in, does not yield to certification that others believe it if I know they have no other reason for believing it than the Spencerian one that they do believe it. If Mr. Dawson, however, insists on inquiring for a likelier way of arriving at truth, I can only say that a better way, as it seems to me, would be to keep one's eyes and ears open, and if that way does not teach me about the Absolutely Unknowable, I fear I shall have to go disgracefully ignorant of that branch of learning.

Another question is whether "astrology can properly be said to have had an existence since the rise of exact science." Exact science took its rise with Hipparchus and Archimedes; astrology was practiced by all astronomers from Ptolemy to Kepler, inclusive, themselves two of the greatest scientists that ever lived. Again, "Does 'Outsider' expect Mr. Spencer to start with nothing and explain everything? Does he admit no necessary truths?" Following the greatest students of the theory of cognition, I am disinclined to admit any proposition as absolutely necessary. I would not absolutely require philosophy to start with nothing, though some systems do this, but I should think it very hazardous to commence with a hard and fast set of "first principles." I should certainly demand some prospect of an explanation of so definite and regular a fact as the law of energy. I need not remind Mr. Dawson that philosophies which are far from "starting with nothing," and in this halting imbecility are not remote from Spencer's, do, nevertheless, give explanations of Matter perfectly rational and intelligible from their standpoint. I will touch on the question of explaining Space below.

One more question Mr. Dawson puts, more drastic, perhaps, than all the rest. I had said that, if all particles had their motions reversed, all the previous history would be run over backward, which I take to be a commonplace of dynamics, and he thereupon asks whether this would not suppose "that thereafter motion would follow the line of greatest resistance?" Our mathematician, Mr. Messenger, will answer this authoritatively. Meanwhile, my impression would be that, if an electric current finds a certain wire to contain the line of lowest resistance in going from New York to Philadelphia, that same wire would not necessarily be the line of greatest resistance for a current going from Philadelphia to New York.

Having thus noticed those correspondents who have signed their names (except Mr. "Carl Opperg," whose communication concerns "Kappa," not me), I proceed to those who have given their initials.

"W. H. B." wishes to place Matter on the throne of the intellectual heavens, a desire I cannot share, though it is entirely opposed to Spencer. "R. G. E." entertains the very lowest opinion of my intelligence. He answers my prayer for light by reviling me for a barking cur; and he even questions my sincerity, probably suspecting me of a clandestine worship of Spencer. Had I the honor of his personal acquaintance, such controversial atavisms would naturally have their zest. In actual circumstances they must be sacrificed. I think I agree in the main with what "R. G. E." says. He lifts his voice in favor of evolution, and I am altogether with him. I suspect he does not perceive that my dissatisfaction with Spencer is not that he is evolutionist, but that he is not evolutionist enough. He subordinates life to force; as to that, I venture to entertain my doubts.

"Kappa," delightful writer and good thinker, conveys his wisdom amiably, without cruel allusions to mental deficiency. He has a pleasant way of almost persuading me I know some of these things already. He says: "'Outsider' doubtless knows that there are two kinds of scientists—the specialist and the generalizer, or philosopher." Between you and me, Mr. Editor, I really had not known this at all. I thought, on the contrary, that scientific men attached such supreme importance to making inference and observation go hand in hand, the deduction of one hour checked by the observation of the next, and that serving as suggestion for the meditations of the following, that no class of non-specialists were recognized as scientific men. I know there was Herbert Spencer, but I cannot yet make out that he is a recognized scientist. Who are our generalizers in this country? I have heard of Prof. Cope, whose book is famous, but I am assured he is one of the foremost of paleontologists, a specialist of the specialists. There is Prof. J. P. Cooke, one of whose ideas, I believe, is destined to form one of the world elements of future philosophy; but he is, I am told, devoted to a special branch of inorganic chemistry. There are generalizing geologists of eminence. It is very creditable to our country to have produced so few, and those few so strong. But where are the non-specialist generalizers?

"Kappa" gives up Mr. Spencer's *vox populi* method of attaining truth, thus admitting his idol has feet of clay. But when I ask whether Spencer's system is logically put together or not, "Kappa" declares this "purely a new method of criticism. Readers who have to be told whether a system of philosophy is logical or not—" oh, well, they are in a truly pitiable condition! As nearly as can be estimated, down to the date of Mr. Spencer's first principles, 282 systems of philosophy had been given to the world, and each of these had, for certain, at least one reader, namely, the man who originated it. It is equally certain that in at least 282 out of these 283 instances, the one and only guaranteed reader proved unequal to the task of determining whether that system was logically put together or no. But it is easy to see that "Kappa" is a born critic himself, and that he consequently knows well enough—better than any of us—what a piece of work the logical critic of a philosophic system has in hand. It is not merely to ascertain the validity and estimate the probability of the different argumentations, though even this, in the field of philosophy, is matter, I fancy, for a serious student of methods of reasoning. But that is the least of the critic's task. He has, first, to seize the central idea and gist of the system, omitting nothing essential, inserting nothing accidental; second, completely to analyze this essence of the doctrine and take account of every element of thought belonging to it; third, to study each of these principles, to appreciate it, to find exactly what logical application can be made of it; fourth, to go through every part of the system and see whether every one of these principles has been applied in a completely thoroughgoing manner wherever it was applicable, and nowhere else; fifth, to examine whether every philosophical question has been included which ought to have been included; sixth, to consider what the system would become if its logical defects were to be corrected—whether it would be disrupted or only reformed, and, seventh, to compare it with other philosophies, existent and possible, so as to learn what its logical advantages and disadvantages may be. If "Kappa" finds all this so easy, please let him lend his aid to me.

"Kappa" and others seem genuinely confounded at my asking whether philosophy should not in our day be required to explain the properties of space. I am informed that all geometers now profess to understand that those properties might have been different from what they appear to be. Mathematicians no longer say that the sum of the three angles of a triangle are equal to two right angles, but only that it is so nearly so that we cannot tell whether it be more or less. Though this view has not reached the text books as yet, I am told it is adopted with unanimity by mathematicians. Then why is it not reasonable to ask philosophy how the angles of a triangle come to sum up to two right angles as nearly as they do? There is nothing really incomprehensible or confounding in the question; it only seems so to Spencerians because in the firmament of their beautiful and wondrous system there happens to be a coal-sack just here. If my question about space seems to give every man of them symptoms of blind staggers, that seems to indicate a malady in their philosophy. The cognition-theory explanation of space given by Spencer, to which "Kappa" refers me, is no explanation in the sense intended. But really, in this day, I know not what polite epithet to apply to a theory of space which does not undertake to show why the propositions of geometry should be such as they are.

Finally, "Kappa" reads me a lecture about the logical function of explanation. His method of weighing the logical import of a question before undertaking to answer it certainly commends itself to every thoughtful mind. But he concludes that "that which has never changed in our experience or in the experience of our long line of ancestors, beginning, say, with the jelly-fish, cannot be explained." I can see no good ground for this. Explanation is a rational account of things. It simply discovers and points out a reason or general principle, operative in nature to a given result. Does nature only behave regularly and reasonably while we have our eye upon her? The motions of the double stars are explicable by gravitation. Some of them may be so far distant that the light which reaches us left them before our revered jelly-fish existed. Does that vitiate the explanation? "Kappa's" principle makes a curious variety of nominalism repugnant to all science. It is also in downright conflict with Spencer, who undertakes to explain the evolution of the solar system from the primitive nebula, and, what is much more, makes life nothing but a cunning mechanism. Let it not be supposed I am attacking Spencerianism. An attack would be very different. At present I am only seeking light.

OUTSIDER

Editorial Backmatter

Editorial Symbols

Within the Text

Peirce's writings are presented (as nearly as possible) in a clear-text format. Omitted passages in abridged selections are identified (by page or table reference) within italic brackets at the point of abridgement. All other insertions are the result of authorial rather than editorial circumstances. Situations caused by various kinds of interruptions or incompleteness in Peirce's surviving texts are indicated as follows:

Italic brackets enclose titles and other text supplied by the editors (including parts of words in damaged documents that have been reconstructed).

Italic brackets enclosing three ellipsis points indicate one or more lost manuscript pages.

Italic brackets enclosing a blank indicate that an incomplete discussion occurs before the end of the manuscript page.

Sets of double slashes mark the beginning and end of Peirce's undecided alternate readings; the single slash divides the original from the alternative inscription.

Selections by writers other than Peirce are reduced in size and, for ease of reference, are identified by vertical rules running down both margins.

Within the Apparatus and Annotations

PAGE AND LINE REFERENCES

All page, column, and line numbers refer to the present edition (each selection's opening page title block, running heads, diagrams, drawings, and illustrations do not count as lines). In most cases, text or titles within a diagram or drawing will not need a line reference; if necessary for clarity, line numbers are counted independently within each figure.

Unbordered data tables are included in the page line count, but lines in complicated data tables are enclosed in lined borders and counted independently from the surrounding text lines. Since some columns often span two or more subordinate columns in Peirce's scientific tables, the boundary lines around column blocks (counted left to right, top to bottom) are used to locate a point of variation. In such bordered table references, the page number is followed by a column block number (in parenthesis) and a row number within the block. If a page includes more than one table, a table number (t1, t2, etc.) will be included with the parenthetical block number. Footnote lines are also counted separately from the text and are indicated by "n" following the page number.

A line may include more than one occurrence of a word. If such a word is the subject of an apparatus entry, a parenthetical number following the line number indicates the specific occurrence of the keyed reading in that line. When the keyed reading refers to more than one occurrence, all are identified parenthetically.

General Editorial Symbols

Bibliographical references used throughout the editorial portions of the volume are identifed in the "Bibliographical Abbreviations" summary that immediately precedes the Introduction. Editorial symbols found in the editorial back-matter are defined as follows:

An asterisk (*) preceding page and line numbers indicates that the reading is discussed in a textual note.

A roman closing bracket (]) follows the initial reading of an apparatus entry. In most cases this initial reading, or lemma, represents the reading of the present (critically edited) edition. Rejected readings (either from the copy-text or subsequent forms of the text) appear to the right of the bracket.

A caret (‸) in the rejected reading to the right of the bracket signals the absence of punctuation, operational signs (e.g., +, –, or the mid-line multiplication dot), or mathematical and scientific symbols (e.g., degrees, minutes, seconds). Absence of punctuation in the accepted reading (lemma) will be represented as clear text, without the caret.

A wavy dash (~) in the rejected reading to the right of the bracket stands for the same word in the accepted reading to the left of the bracket. It is used as a place holder for words in an entry where the only variant is a symbol such as a mark of punctuation or an operational sign.

The word *[formula]* or *[equation]*, used (as shown here) in italic brackets, stands for a lengthy or intricate mathematical reading. It is used in the lemma as a place holder representing the accepted reading in the present (critically edited) edition when the rejected reading to the right involves only a few simple changes (such as a mark of punctuation or an operational sign).

A vertical stroke (|) indicates a line-end break and is used to clarify an emendation or an alteration description; when, in the Alterations, it indicates a page break, it is noted as such.

An arrow (→) within the pagination descriptions of Peirce's manuscripts indicates that a page has been renumbered within the sequence. Thus, 1→2 indicates that Peirce renumbered manuscript page 1 as page 2.

A pilcrow (¶) represents a paragraph indention.

IN EMENDATIONS AND REJECTED SUBSTANTIVES ONLY:

The abbreviation *et seq.* after a page and line number indicates a "class-emendation": all readings subsequent to the cited reading are identically emended (and exceptions are listed after the word *Except*). If the same emendation occurs more than once, but in scattered places in a given item, the additional instances are listed after the word *Also*.

The abbreviations *ital.* and *rom.* indicate that the reading in the lemma was originally printed either in italic type (underlined in manuscripts) or in roman type (not underlined in manuscripts or in italic typescripts).

The abbreviation *om.* (for omitted) signifies the lack of corresponding text in the copy-text or other collated source texts.

An imploded diamond (✧) preceding an emendation indicates that the reading has a significant history of authorial alteration within the copy-text, and invites the reader to examine the corresponding entry in the Alterations list.

IN ALTERATIONS ONLY:

In a few cases, when Peirce's own alteration to a passage has to be emended, an imploded diamond (✧) preceding page and line numbers indicates that all or part of the lemma in the Alterations list represents the superseded reading to the right of the lemma at the same point in the Emendations list. The imploded diamond makes this connection across the two lists, and invites the reader to examine the corresponding lemma in the Emendations list for the exact reading in the edition text.

The following non-punctuated italicized abbreviations are adopted to sometimes describe the nature of the alteration: *ab* for *above*, *add* for *added* (i.e., inscribed either on the line without being squeezed in, or very close to the line without interlining, or in the margin), *aft* for *after*, *bef* for *before*, *bel* for *below*, *del* for *deleted by hand*, *del-t* for *deleted by typing over*, *ins* for *inserted* (i.e., squeezed in on the line), *intl* for *interlined* (i.e., set between two lines, or above or below a line), and *intl-c* for *interlined with caret or a careted line.*

A small black diamond (♦) within an alteration description indicates that the immediately following words are affected by the description enclosed within the next set of square brackets. When there is no ambiguity as to the words affected by the description within brackets, no black diamond is used.

Identical alterations are listed after the word *Also* at the end of their first keyed description, but only if they immediately follow each other. Otherwise, their description is repeated.

Annotations

The annotations given below are keyed to page and line number. For details see Editorial Symbols. Some annotations identify persons whose names may not be widely known, or who are insufficiently identified in the text, and the sources of quotations and paraphrases. For the identification of sources every effort has been made to cite the editions Peirce is known to have owned or had available to him. When this is unknown, or when the edition he used was unavailable to us, the edition referred to is one that was accessible to him. See the Bibliography of Peirce's References for more details. Where Peirce's quotations differ from their sources, either the original is provided or the differences are noted.

Other annotations clarify passages, provide historical background, identify and explain philosophical, mathematical, and scientific terms (often using Peirce's own entries for the *Century Dictionary*), or refer to relevant passages elsewhere in Peirce's work. Several annotations contain transcriptions of relevant correspondence, passages from earlier drafts, annotations by Peirce in offprints, etc., that are not incorporated in the text. Sometimes comments and evaluations made by Peirce himself, or by others, are also included. The transcriptions contain occasional corrections in italic brackets, and spelling and punctuation improvements. Mistakes made in tables and calculations that may affect other values given by Peirce or the conclusions he draws, and which for that reason remain uncorrected in Peirce's text, are also identified and explained.

Works quoted by Peirce are cited in shortened form. Complete bibliographic information for them can be found in the Bibliography of Peirce's References. Works referred to by the editors are fully cited in the annotations. For abbreviations used see Bibliographical Abbreviations in Editorial Matter.

1. *Boolian Algebra—Elementary Explanations*

3.16 the first is $,] For Peirce's use of 0 and $, see also W5:382–83, 1886.

5.13 Mr. Hugh McColl.] The Scottish logician Hugh MacColl (or McColl, 1837–1909) introduced the colon as a symbol for implication, here adopted by Peirce for want of a more suitable key on his typewriter, in "The Calculus of Equivalent Statements (Second Paper)" (1878), p. 177, Def. 12. Peirce's first reference to MacColl is in his 1880 paper "On the Algebra of Logic" (W4:173).

7.11 Laurentius Valla.] Laurentius (or Lorenzo) Valla (1407–1457), Italian humanist. Peirce probably refers to Valla's *Dialecticae disputationes*, ch. 13, "De dilemmate et antistrephonte," published posthumously in 1509.

7.20–23 The old . . . *Logic,*1599).] Thomas Blundeville (fl. 1561), bk. 5, ch. 27, 154:

Dilemma is an argument made of two members repugnant to one another, whereof whichsoever thou grantest, thou art by and by taken, as thus, it is not good to marrie a wife, for if she be fayre she wil be common, if fowle then loathesome.

In "Qualitative Logic" (W5:355, 1886), Peirce attributes this standard example to Aulus Gellius (c. 123–c. 165). In his *Noctium Atticarum,* bk. 5, ch. 11, Gellius attributes it to Bias of Priene (6th century B.C.), although Diogenes Laertius in his *Lives of Eminent Philosophers,* bk. 4, ch. 7, 48, attributes it to Bion of Borysthenes (3rd century B.C.). It is worth noting that the Greek plays on the words: "common" is κοινήν, and "loathesome" is ποινήν.

2. *Circular for Course on the Art of Reasoning*

10.7–14 The education . . . science of thought itself.] Peirce became convinced early on that logic formed the core of a liberal education. Already in 1861, in the "Treatise on Metaphysics," he wrote that "to learn how to analyze ideas . . . and to analyze them will be *par excellence* education" (W1:65). In an 1872 review of educational books, he stressed that logic well taught will strengthen and enlighten a young man, but added the caveat that deductive logic was almost utterly worthless in education, "except as an introduction to the logic of science" (W3:3). It was in his "Introductory Lecture on the Study of Logic," given in 1882 at the Johns Hopkins University, that he made his point most dramatically: "when new paths have to be struck out, a spinal cord is not enough; a brain is needed, and that brain an organ of mind, and that mind perfected by a liberal education. And a liberal education—so far as its relation to the understanding goes—means logic. That is indispensible to it, and no other one thing is" (W4:380). He repeated this conviction in 1903 while addressing a Harvard audience: "I cannot but think it deeply lamentable that true, modern, exact, non-psychological logic, which ought to form the background of a liberal education, does not receive sufficient attention here to be at all in evidence. As time goes on the consequence of this neglect will be deeply graven" (EP2:527n.1).

10.19–20 "dialectic . . . all methods."] This phrase, often quoted by Peirce, is the opening sentence of the first treatise in Petrus Hispanus's *Summulae logicales,* also known as the *Tractatus,* which was composed sometime before 1245 (Peirce thought it had been written around 1270: see W3:3, 1872) and was the standard logic text for three hundred years.

12.31–32 A complete course . . . three years.] There is no evidence that any student achieved the complete course, or even a complete quarter. If the state of the extant correspondence can serve as an indication, most students seem to have abandoned the course after a few lessons, either because the lessons were too difficult for them, or because Peirce could not keep up with the correspondence to their satisfaction—despite Peirce's demonstrably extensive epistolary activity. A number of students dropped the course for personal reasons, such as illness or the demands of their profession.

3. *Follow-up Letter to Circular*

16.6–7 Prof. Allan Marquand] Allan Marquand (1853–1924) was a fellow in ethics and logic at Johns Hopkins University from 1878 to 1880, where he studied under Peirce. It was to Marquand that Peirce addressed his famous 30

December 1886 letter, in which he suggested an electrical circuit as the basis for the construction of a logical machine (W5:421–23). Marquand published a short paper, "A Machine for Producing Syllogistic Variations," in Peirce's 1883 *Studies in Logic,* pp. 12–15. See also Marquand's paper "A New Logical Machine," in *Proceedings of the American Academy of Arts and Sciences* 21 (1886): 303–307.

16.11–12 forthcoming number . . . *Psychology).*] See sel. 14.

17.12–32 A young king . . . drawn?] Peirce discusses the "young king" example at the end of "An Elementary Account of the Logic of Relatives" (W5:386–87, 1886). The original source of the exercise, assuming Peirce did not invent it, has not been identified. It returns in sel. 4 in this volume. A later algebraic analysis of this example is published in NEM 2:634–35 (c. 1893).

18.8 "Political Economy,"] Peirce's few contributions to political economy include his 1873 letter to Abraham Conger in W3:109–10, his 1874 discussion of it in W3:173–76, and his 1884 discussion of the Spanish Treaty in W5:144–48.

18.10 doctrine of chances] Peirce's writings on this subject up to this time include his "Illustrations of the Logic of Science" papers from 1878, especially "The Doctrine of Chances," "The Probability of Induction," and "The Order of Nature" (W3:276–322), and "A Theory of Probable Inference" in *Studies in Logic* (W4:408–49, 1883).

18.12–13 method . . . errors of observation.] For Peirce's theory of errors of observation, besides a short note in W3:111–13, see especially his long 1873 article in W3:114–60.

4. *A Few Specimens of Exercises in the Art of Reasoning*

19.1 CONFIDENTIALLY COMMUNICATED.] See sel. 5, 25.19–24.

19.13 A young king,] See ann. 17.12–32. As far as known, no student was ever assigned this exercise, which seems to have caused difficulty for Peirce himself.

20.26 Every Corsican kills a Corsican;] This syllogism is a recurrent example of Peirce to illustrate that the "syllogism of transposed quantity" holds only for finite collections. See W5:188–89 (1885) for Peirce's first discussion of this kind of syllogism (attributed to De Morgan), and other examples in "The Law of Mind" (EP1:316–17, 1892).

20.32–33 proximate . . . effects.] Francis Bacon, *The Elements of the Common Lawes of England* (1630), part 1, regula 1. At the time of Peirce's writing the distinction had become a standard one in American tort law. See also Peirce's definition of "proximate" in Baldwin's *Dictionary,* reproduced in CP 6.391 (1902).

20.35 Criticise . . . pronoun,] The phrasing of this exercise appears to be the earliest indication (not fully spelled out since the answer is not provided) of Peirce's having come to theorize, as a result of his reflection on the role of indices in the logic of relatives, that pronouns do not serve to replace nouns, as the common definition holds, but that on the contrary nouns serve to replace pronouns. As he put it in 1895: "There is no reason for saying that *I, thou, that, this,* stand in place of nouns; they *indicate* things in the directest possible way. . . . A pronoun is an index. A noun, on the other hand, does not indicate the object it denotes. . . . Thus, a noun is an imperfect substitute for a pronoun" (EP2:15n).

20.37 the ordinary definition of a circle] In the *Imperial Dictionary,* which provided the basis for the *Century Dictionary,* the circle is defined as follows: "a plane figure, comprehended by a single curve, called its circumference, every part of which is equally distant from a point within it called the centre." In the *Century Dictionary*, Peirce defined the circle as "a plane figure whose periphery is everywhere equally distant from a point within it, the center" (p. 1006). Peirce thus omitted the phrase "comprehended by a single curve line," suggesting that this was the part he found superfluous in the ordinary definition. In a later, undated document, Peirce stated that his definition was "perhaps superior to the definition that a circle (circumference) is a plane curve of the second order having double contact with the absolute" (RS 25:173).

5. *Directions to Agents*

22.16 one ticket,] This is the ticket agents were asked to sell to recruited students. For reproductions see p. 31. Students were required to pay the agent $2 (which presumably the agent could keep), and Peirce $28. The tickets seems to have been rarely used. The only evidence of their use is found in Peirce's notebook "Pupils. List of letters etc," which shows that on 2 March 1887, Miss S. M. Hawes paid $2 to a certain Francfort and sent Peirce a $28 check. The notebook shows that many students followed the instructions printed in the circular, first paying $5 upon registration, and the balance of $25 upon admission. Others paid the $30 in full, and at least one other student paid only $10, on a trial basis. In the surviving draft of the first leaf of this text, Peirce advised his agents to get their prospect:

> in a state of excessively strained and tired attention, when he will do whatever you tell him. Tell him to do any little thing, and if he does it make him pay down completely for one quarter, if not for a whole course of six, and have him take a half dozen tickets at $2 besides. With some experience and natural turn for this sort of thing, you will find it of frequent use. In almost every case, what you want to do is not to convince a person but to persuade him, win him, seduce him.

25.15–19 The third part . . . a few months.] In the next subsection "Facts about the instruction," Peirce presents the actual content of the three parts of his course. In the third part he intended a course of exercises designed to strengthen "judgments about matters of fact" but there is no evidence that Peirce actually wrote up such a course of exercises. The exercises he sent his students were confined to the first two parts, especially the second one, since some students were only sent Boolean algebra exercises.

25.20–21 a secret . . . pupils,] See sel. 4, 19.1.

25.22 upon which Mr. Peirce is now engaged.] If Peirce was engaged upon such a book it could have been "A Guess at the Riddle" or an outgrowth of "Qualitative Logic" (W5:323–71, 1886), a manuscript which Peirce had an assistant turn into a typescript (WMS 593) at some time during this period. "Boolian Algebra," published in NEM 3/2:1126–31, and "Boolian Algebra. First Lection," published in NEM 3/1:269–283, both written c. 1890, appear to be part of another attempt to write a logic textbook based on Boolian algebra. A further indication that Peirce may have been working on such a book is found in a letter of 26 March 1888 to Marcus Benjamin, in which he stated, with likely exaggeration: "I also wish to say that I have a book in press called the Art of Reasoning." The writings that survive, however, concentrate only on an introduction to matters of formal logic, not on the matters described in the third part of the course.

26.19–21 three degrees . . . appended,] Peirce's three degrees were an A.B. (1859), A.M. (1862) and Sc.B. (1863, *summa cum laude*).

26.31–27.35 In 1875 . . . by a unanimous vote.] See Peirce's report "On the Flexure of Pendulum Supports" in W4:515–28, especially 516–20. For a later account by Peirce of this episode, see R 641:39–42, 1909. See also Max H. Fisch's introduction in W3:xxiv–xxvi.

26.31–32 to attend the meetings] These are the meetings of the European Geodetic Association. For Peirce's involvement, see Victor F. Lenzen's "Charles S. Peirce and Die Europäische Gradmessung" in *Proceedings of the Tenth International Congress of the History of Science* (Paris: Hermann, 1964), 781–83.

27.8–9 Brussels meeting . . . reports were received] This is the meeting of the Permanent Commission of the European Geodetic Association, held in Brussels from 5 to 10 October 1876.

27.19 Mr. Randall] Samuel Jackson Randall (1828–1890), U.S. congressman who served for nearly thirty years and who, as Speaker of the House of Representatives (1876–81), codified the rules of the House and strengthened the role of speaker. He was also chairman of the House Appropriations Committee. The episode Peirce relates occurred in 1877, when Randall was Speaker of the House.

27.20 European Surveys] For the discussion of Peirce's work at the Brussels meeting, see *Verhandlungen der vom 5 bis 10 Oktober 1876 in Brüssel vereinigten Permanenten Commission der Europäischen Gradmessung* (Berlin: Georg Reimer, 1877), pp. 2, 3, 12, 16–21, 41–42, 45–49.

27.22 New York newspapers . . . protested against this view,] Editorials discussing the importance of a U.S. representation at the meeting of the International Geodetic Association appeared in the *New York Tribune* on 21 August 1877, and in the *New York Times* on 25 August 1877. Peirce does not make here the claim made later that he orchestrated this protest himself. In 1909 he wrote (R 641:41):

> I should not have been able to appear at the meeting if I had not resorted to a ruse, by which I got a paragraph inserted in the editorial page of that New York Daily that was most influential in Washington, strongly urging that some Coast Survey officer be dispatched to the meeting.

27.24–25 entered . . . a heated discussion] On his arrival he wrote in a letter to his mother of 2 November 1877 (RL 341):

> They had already had one days sitting but that was only a formal one. As for the views which I wished to enforce, they had a complete triumph and the extreme importance of the matter was acknowledged by everybody, so that I was quite the hero of the moment. I addressed the meeting 4 times and also made an after dinner speech.

27.25–26 General Baeyer] Lieutenant General Johann Jakob Baeyer (1794–1885), founder and president of the Royal Prussian Geodetic Institute, and of the European Geodetic Association. For an earlier account of Peirce's first meeting with Baeyer, see W3:217, 1877. For the views of Baeyer and Peirce on the pendulum stands, see also Victor F. Lenzen's "Charles S. Peirce and Die Europäische Gradmessung" cited in ann. 26.31–32.

27.37 king . . . dinner.] It is unlikely that Peirce refers to the German Kaiser Wilhelm I, who had become emperor of a united Germany in 1871. Since the conference met in Stuttgart, capital of the kingdom of Württemberg within the empire, it is probable that Peirce met King Karl (reigned 1864–1891) of Württemberg. Since there is no mention of a king in his otherwise very detailed letter about this meeting to his mother (2 November 1877; RL 341), what Peirce here presents as a personal invitation from the king was probably a reception for the conference attendees.

28.2–4 He has lectured . . . etc.] These are the Lowell Lectures of 1866 (W1:358–504), and the Harvard Lectures of 1865 (W1:162–302) and of 1869–70 (W2:310–46). Peirce taught at Johns Hopkins from 1879 to 1884.

28.14 Professor Schroeder,] Friedrich Wilhelm Karl Ernst Schröder (1841–1902), German mathematician who did important work in algebra, set theory, and logic. Peirce first took notice of Schröder's work in 1879, when he read his 1877 *Der Operationskreis des Logikkalkuls.* Peirce and Schröder corresponded when Peirce was at Johns Hopkins and they resumed their correspondence in 1890.

28.16–20 "It has been . . . pupils."] Peirce's source for this is an announcement (*Anzeige*) for Schröder's *Vorlesungen über die Algebra der Logik* that appeared in the *Mitteilungen der Verlagsbuchhandlung B. G. Teubner in Leipzig* (vol. 3, 44–45) in 1886. The quotation is a rather loose translation of the following (45): "Seit der Erscheinen von des Verfassers 'Operationskreis des Logikkalkuls' [1877] hat diese Behandlung noch höchst bedeutende Fortschritte gemacht: vor allem durch die Arbeiten des Amerikaners Charles S. Peirce und seiner Schule." Schröder incorporated the text of the *Anzeige,* including this quotation, on p. iii of the foreword of the *Vorlesungen,* whose first volume appeared in 1890.

30.11–12 But the Colleges . . . teaching.] In a draft fragment Peirce typed the following (RL 100):

> A wise old college professor asked a student in the class what he came to College for. Some answer was given, and he put the question to the next; and so it went round the class. Now said the professor, at last, it is strange none of you will say the real object which you one and all have in coming here: it is to learn to think. Unfortunately, the weak point about American Colleges is, that while the students learn a number of things, a few of them useful and the rest not so, they generally come out hardly more able to think than when they entered; and for the most part less able to think than those who have spent the same time in the practical business of life. Why is this? It is for the same reason that college students after seven years spent in learning latin cannot write it elegantly; cannot even speak it fluently; can hardly read it at sight. It is simply because it is not taught in the only way in which anything can be taught. All teaching worthy of the name is teaching to do something. And the only way to teach anybody to do anything is to have them do it. It is the way in which people learn to swim. Practical exercises in the doing of that thing which they have to learn to do well. Mr. Peirce's instruction has this advantage over the Colleges, that it actually does teach that thing which it is the main business of a college to teach, but which in point of fact, is generally not taught at all. Logic, which is the method of finding a method of doing anything, is not taught at all or hardly taught in some of the greatest universities in the land.

32.7–8 Cornelius Vanderbilt and his grandfather.] Cornelius Vanderbilt (1843–1899) was regarded as the head of the Vanderbilt family from 1885 on. His father, William Henry Vanderbilt, died in 1886. The grandfather was Cornelius Vanderbilt (1794–1877).

6. *Letter to New Students*

33.12 Cyrus Field] Cyrus West Field (1819–1892), American financier and businessman (paper and railroad). He was the driving force behind the first submarine telegraph line from the United States to Europe (1857–66). Peirce seems to have found Field a source of personal inspiration. In a draft of a letter to Field he wrote (RL 142a):

> You are in some sort the father of the scheme set forth in the circular which I take the liberty of sending you herewith, concerning practical exercises in the Art of Reasoning. For years I had been carrying in my pocket-book a newspaper clipping which reported you as saying, "My fortune was made by working a gold-mine, and that gold-mine is the power of right reason." I had long admired the truth of the observation, until it suggested to me that the new Logic of Science which has been developed during the first half-century ought in some way to be made useful to the youth of our land, who are still commonly taught the logic of the Middle Ages by some broken down Minister.

Peirce considered using Field's remark in a short advertisement for his course, but did not do so.

34.26–27 at the end . . . same subject,] It is doubtful whether any student reached the end of the first quarter and submitted a new letter; no supporting documentation has been found.

7. *Orientation Letter to Marie Noble*

35.18 *vis a tergo*] A force operating from behind, a propulsive force (mostly used as a medical phrase, in contradistinction to *vis a fronte,* a force operating from in front, as in attraction or suction).

36.16–17 Law of the Medes and Persians.] Allusion to Dan. 6:15.

8. *Letter to Noble on the Nature of Reasoning*

37.6 All reasoning involves observation.] Compare with W5:163–64 (1885).

38.7 this simple proposition] This proposition is known as the theorem of Desargues and as the ten-ray theorem. Karl von Staudt gave a proof of it in his *Geometrie der Lage* (Nürnberg: Korn, 1847), theorem 90, p. 41. The theorem is also mentioned in sels. 9 (see ann. 45.1), 15, 31, and 32 in this volume.

39.24–40.18 As another illustration . . . product of products)] This example is known as Fermat's Little Theorem and was first presented by the French mathematician Pierre de Fermat (1601–1665) in 1640. Peirce's non-symbolic argument might be continued thus:

> Consequently, the product of products will be divisible by the prime number with a remainder equal to the product of numbers less than the prime number. Note that the product of products, however, consists of two factors: one is the base with exponent one less than the prime number and the other is the product of numbers less than the prime number. Thus dividing the first factor by the prime number must give a remainder equal to 1 since the second factor is equal to the remainder for the product of products.

9. *Reasoning Exercises*

41.2 Fermat's series:] Two series named after Pierre de Fermat. Each term in the first series is found by adding 1 to twice the term immediately preceding it. In the second series, each term is found by subtracting 1 from twice the term immediately preceding it.

41.7–13 Fibonacci's series,] Leonardo of Pisa (c. 1170–after 1240) studied mathematics in North Africa, introduced the Arabic numeral system in Europe, and discovered the Fibonacci sequence of numbers. Each term in the series (except the first two) is found by adding the two terms immediately preceding (this relation was not recognized until about 1600). The Fibonacci numbers are also exemplified by the botanical phenomenon known as phyllotaxis: the arrangement of whorls on a pinecone, of petals on a sunflower, etc.

41.14–16 Pell's series:] John Pell (1611–1685), an English mathematician who wrote *Idea of Mathematics* (1638) and *Controversiae de vera circuli mensura* (1647), the latter related to a controversy over the value of π. The first series is called the Pell Number series, and the second the Pell-Lucas series. Both follow the same rule: each term in the series (except the first two) is found by adding twice the immediately preceding term to the term preceding the latter.

44.1 Fig. 3] This figure yields a plane representation consisting of thirteen straight lines and thirteen points, nine of which intersect four lines, and four of which intersect three lines.

45.1 Fig. 7] Peirce's figures are clearly inspired by Kempe's "A Memoir on the Theory of Mathematical Form" in *Philosophical Transactions of the Royal Society of London* 177 (1886): 1–70, in which Kempe made much use of dots and lines (called "links" when straight, "wavy" when wavy, "barbed" or "arrowed" when arrowed). Peirce's fig. 7 matches exactly (apart from being upside down) Kempe's fig. 13 (Kempe 1886: 11). Kempe explicitly connected his fig. 13 to the ten-ray theorem that von Staudt demonstrated (Kempe 1886: 63), the same theorem Peirce alludes to in commenting on his fig. 7 (see EP2:174, fig. 3, for the figure Peirce is asking the students to draw). Kempe commented (Kempe 1886: 10–11):

> The single system shown in fig. 13 is one of considerable interest; it is that dealt with in the case of the theorem that if two coplanar triangles are coaxial they are also copolar. The graphical units [i.e., the dots] may be taken to represent either the ten straight lines of the theorem, or the ten points of intersection; the form is the same in either case. Taking the former case, the pairs of graphical units which are joined by links correspond to pairs of lines whose points of intersection are points other than the ten considered in the theorem.

In his copy of Kempe's paper Peirce wrote that Kempe's figure "hardly" dealt with the theorem, "for that theorem depends on remarking the collinearity of 3 points which is not represented at all in the diagram he gives." Peirce also drew three alternate figures in the margin, with the comment "the same in more obvious shape." The third of his drawings is equivalent to that reproduced in the third Harvard Lecture of 1903 (see EP2:174, fig. 4). The second sentence in the above quotation from Kempe contains the answer to the question Peirce asked his students.

10. *Boolian Algebra. Three Lessons*

50.12–13 every possible state of things] From 1880 on, Peirce was interested in what is currently referred to as possible-worlds semantics for modal logic (see W4:170, 1880, and CP 2.349, c. 1896). The crux lies in the distinction between the *de inesse* conditional, which only states that "here and now either the antecedent is false or the consequent is true," and the ordinary hypothetical, which asserts that "in a certain possible state of things throughout a certain well understood range of possibility either the antecedent is false or the consequent true" (NEM 4:169, 1898). The latter needs a worked-out theory of quantification, so that possible states of things can be quantified over. See also W5:169f., 1885; W5:330–335, 372, 1886; as well as CP 4.514, 1903, where Peirce attempts to describe the relation between possibilities and actual fact. Peirce's later developments in logic, especially his Existential Graphs, are in large part aimed at sophisticating the expression of this "possible worlds" approach. For a further discussion see Jay Zeman, "Peirce and Philo," in Nathan Houser, Don Roberts, and James Van Evra (eds.), *Studies in the Logic of Charles Sanders Peirce* (Bloomington: Indiana University Press, 1997), 402–17. See also sel. 37 below.

50.18–19 the possible is that which is not known to be non-existent,] This view, later called the nominalistic conception of possibility (CP 6.367, 1902), Peirce came to reject in 1897 (CP 3.527):

> I formerly defined the possible as that which in a given state of information (real or feigned) we do not know not to be true. But this definition today seems to me only a twisted phrase which, by means of two negatives, conceals an anacoluthon.

For a discussion of this change in Peirce's thought, and its bearing on the nominalist-realist issue, see Max Fisch's *Peirce, Semeiotic, and Pragmatism* (Bloomington: Indiana University Press, 1986), 194. See also sel. 37 below.

53.14–17 Let the sign of dollars . . . be false.] See ann. 3.16.

11. *Two Letters from Loring on Algebra Lessons*

54.27 J. B. Loring] J. B. Loring sent his introductory letter to Peirce (enclosing $5) on 12 September 1887. He was born in 1837, left school when he was 14, and took a job in 1860 with the Equitable Life Assurance Society, where he spent most of his life. He promised Peirce: "Am very desirous of coming under your instruction & if I break down & fail to get through part 1, all right, you may keep the $30." In his next letter of 22 October 1887, he added: "For years past my work has consisted principally in criticising, analyzing, comparing and looking after other people. Both tongue & pen have been very silent. You will have to put me way down to the foot of your class & begin with A–B–C."

12. *Reply to Loring*

56.5–7 You will please . . . when the quarter ends;] In his short reply of 3 January 1888, Loring indicated that, up to the Dec. 27 letter, he had spent at least fourteen hours working over the first two lessons on Boolian algebra.

57.24–25 I will not send you . . . at least.] Loring apparently progressed no further in the course. His letter of 19 March 1888 indicates that he would attempt to return to the lessons by autumn but no further correspondence survives.

13. *Additional Exercises in Boolian Algebra*

59.18 The members of a board] This exercise was conceived by John Venn (*Mind,* October 1876) and was reproduced by Christine Ladd-Franklin in "On the Algebra of Logic," published in Peirce's 1883 *Studies in Logic,* 51–52. Peirce used it as his "Example 2" in "An Elementary Account of the Logic of Relatives" (W5:385–86, 1886).

59.27 The members of a scientific society] This exercise was conceived by W. B. Grove, who published it in *Educational Times,* 1 Feb. 1881, p. 6616. Peirce's version follows the original wording closely. This exercise is reproduced by Christine

Ladd-Franklin in her paper (p. 54) cited in ann. 59.18. Her answer to the question of what is the least addition to the rules is that "No one who has not paid his subscription can be a member of all three sections and deliver a lecture, or of *a* and *c* and perform an experiment without lecturing" (p. 55).

60.9 In a certain lot of calicos,] This exercise is based on one originally conceived by George Boole in his 1854 *An Investigation of the Laws of Thought,* ch. 15, pp. 237–38. It was proposed by W. B. Grove for a simpler solution in *Educational Times,* 1 April 1881, and reproduced by Christine Ladd-Franklin in her paper (pp. 55–56) cited in ann 59.18. Peirce's version is closer to the latter, with some differences in word choice.

14. *Science and Immortality*

61.15–16 English Psychical Research Society] The English Psychical Research Society, which later became the English Society for Psychical Research, was founded in 1882 for the purpose of examining allegedly paranormal phenomena in a scientific manner. Former past presidents include Henry Sidgwick, F. W. H. Myers, C. D. Broad, Henri Bergson, H. H. Price, and William James.

61.17–18 *Phantasms of the Living.*] A short account of the history behind *Phantasms of the Living* can be found in Janet Oppenheim, *The Other World: Spiritualism and Psychical Research in England, 1850–1914* (Cambridge: Cambridge University Press, 1985), 141–49. Apart from Peirce, informed attacks on the book came from: W. Preyer, "Telepathie und Geisterseherei in England," *Deutsche Rundschau* (Berlin, January 1886): 30–51; and A. Taylor Innes, "Where are the Letters? A Cross-Examination of Certain Phantasms," *The Nineteenth Century* (London, August 1887): 174–94. Innes's attack proved the most devastating. In many of his cases Gurney had referred to corroborating evidence from contemporary documents, such as postmarked letters. Innes notes that there was no indication in the book that such letters were received and examined by Gurney and his assistants. In his reply to Innes (op. cit., October 1887, 522–33), Gurney could only point at three cases that met Innes's requirements, one of which later turned out to be a fraud.

61.23 Gurney,] Edmund Gurney (1847–1888), English philosopher and psychologist, and co-founder of the English Society for Psychical Research (1882). He was the main author of *Phantasms,* which was based on research done by his assistants Frank Podmore and George Albert Smith. For a biography with a detailed account of the *Phantasms* episode, see Trevor H. Hall, *The Strange Case of Edmund Gurney* (London: Duckworth, 1980). Hall defends the claim that Gurney committed suicide upon discovering he had been consistently deceived by his assistants and that this deception nullified the entire enterprise. For a different perspective on Gurney, see Gordon Epperson's *The Mind of Edmund Gurney* (Madison: Fairleigh Dickinson Press, 1997).

61.23 Myers,] Frederick William Henry Myers (1843–1901), English essayist and lecturer at Cambridge. He took the lead among the founders of the English Society for Psychical Research and edited their *Proceedings*. Myers wrote the introduction and the "Note on a Suggested Mode of Psychical Interaction" in *Phantasms of the Living.*

61.23 Podmore] Frank Podmore (1855–1910), a spiritualist and a socialist writer who argued for psychological causality. He is believed to have coined the name of the Fabian Society of which he was one of the founders (1884). Podmore assisted Gurney in the collection, examination, and appraisal of the material presented in *Phantasms of the Living*.

63.1 "The flower that once has bloomed forever dies."] This is a rendition of the last verse of stanza 26 from the *Rubáiyát of Omar Khayyám* translated by Edward FitzGerald in 1859.

63.11–12 the world is not governed altogether by mechanism,] In his *First Principles* Herbert Spencer (1820–1903) defended the view that the world evolved through a redistribution of matter and motion from a more diffused, uniform, and indeterminate arrangement, to a more concentrated, multiform, and determinate arrangement.

63.19 Then there is the great fact of growth,] In the draft-typescript, just after the sentence corresponding to this one, Peirce added the following sentence (R 537:10): "Now, law does not produce growth."

63.20–21 a consequence of the mechanical principle of the conservation of energy.] Spencer defended such a view in ch. 18 of *First Principles*, "The Interpretation of Evolution," where he characterized the persistence of force (his expression for the law of the conservation of energy) as the basic mechanism of evolution.

63.21–22 his chapter on the subject] *First Principles*, bk. II, ch. 18.

64.9 the proposition of Kant,] This is a major theme in Kant's *Critique,* for instance in B xix: "For we are brought to the conclusion that we can never transcend the limits of possible experience."

64.15–16 Comte said . . . fixed stars,] Auguste Comte (1798–1857), French philosopher and founder of positivism, made this claim in his *Cours de philosophie positive*, vol. 2, part 1. Comte argued that since we cannot directly observe the stars, we cannot know their chemical composition (p. 2, 5). By 1859, however, Gustav Kirchhoff, of Heidelberg University, had developed spectroscopic methods which enabled the chemical composition of stars to be investigated (*Sonnenspectrum,* Berlin: Ferd. Dümmler, 1862). Compare sel. 31, 247.17–24.

64.18 Legendre] Adrien-Marie Legendre (1752–1833), French mathematician known for his work in number theory and his theory of elliptic functions.

64.18–21 Legendre said . . . to prove it;] Peirce probably refers to the law of quadratic reciprocity, which first appears in Legendre's paper "Recherches d'analyse indéterminée," *Mem. Acad. Roy. des Sciences* 1785 (publ. 1787), 465–559. There Legendre wrote, much less radically than Peirce made it sound, that the "proposition is quite difficult to prove" (*The History of Mathematics: A Reader,* John Fauvel and Jeremy Gray, eds., New York: Macmillan Press , 1988, p. 500). Later, in the preface to his *Essai sur la théorie des nombres* (Paris, 1798), Legendre stated that his 1785 paper contained "the proof of a general law existing between any two prime numbers, which one might call the law of reciprocity" (p. viii). In Book II of the *Essai*, Legendre provided again a demonstration of the law of quadratic reciprocity, writing that it caused "almost insurmountable difficulties" (p. 393 in the second edition). Peirce's exaggerated claim about Legendre is repeated in sel. 31, 247.24–32.

64.21–22 the next writer . . . theorem] Carl Friedrich Gauss (1777–1855), German mathematician and astronomer, was director and professor of astronomy of the Göttingen observatory and author of *Disquisitiones arithmeticae* (1801), a work that had a profound impact on Peirce and his father. In this work Gauss called the law of quadratic reciprocity the "gem of arithmetic" and offered six rigorous proofs of it (sect. IV, arts. 130–152).

64.33 sanction of good sense.] The typescript in which Peirce first drafted this article adds at this point a new paragraph containing the following afterthought (R 537:11):

> I will take the liberty of adding one word not directly connected with the subject. Modern materialistic and skeptical views are not of that nature that they can be suppressed. Now if the dogmas of religion are true, these modern views must be erroneous and will necessarily be brought to naught. If then they are to be refuted, but cannot be suppressed, there is but one [way] in which their refutation can come about; it is by the thought of the age going through them, fully developing all their consequences, in the completest manner, and finding some difficulties connected with them, which do not at present fully appear. If therefore there be anybody now whose belief in the truth of religion is perfect, he ought to wish to see these materialistic views develop themselves as rapidly as possible, because the quicker they grow the quicker they will run their course, and to that development he should lend all his aid and countenance.

15. *Logical Machines*

65.1 "Voyage to Laputa"] Part III of Jonathan Swift's *Gulliver's Travels*, "A Voyage to Laputa, Balnibarbi, Glubbdubdrib, Luggnagg, and Japan," describes Gulliver's visit to the floating island of Laputa whose inhabitants are so engulfed in abstract speculation that they have mostly lost their common sense and show very poor practical skills.

65.2–5 "By this contrivance, . . . or study."] From ch. 5 of "A Voyage to Laputa," where Swift describes the machine of a professor from a division of the grand academy of Lagado that is reserved for the "advancers of speculative learning."

65.6 *Organon* of Bacon,] Francis Bacon (1561–1626) described in his *Novum Organum* (1620) a method of scientific investigation designed to force natural philosophy out of its scholastic slumber.

65.8–9 logical machines of Jevons and Marquand] Influenced by Boole's logic, W. Stanley Jevons constructed in 1869 a logical machine that could draw conclusions from premises in a mechanical manner. The following year he gave a demonstration of the machine, which resembled a portable piano, to the Royal Society. It is described in his "On the Mechanical Performance of Logical Inference," *Philosophical Transactions of the Royal Society of London* 160 (1870): 497–518. For Allan Marquand, see sel. 3, ann. 16.6–7. See also the entry "Logical Machine" by J. M. Baldwin in his *Dictionary of Philosophy and Psychology*, vol. 2 (1902), 28–30, for a description of the machines of Jevons, Venn and Marquand.

65.11–12 Webb's adder] Charles Henry Webb (1834–1905), American inventor, poet, and satirist, who invented several adding machines. Advertisements for different models of a "Webb's adder" began to appear in the late 1860s. Webb invented the "ribbon adder" in 1886, but it was not a commercial success. In this device, slide bars and notches found in slide adders were replaced by continuous bands and holes. In 1889 he patented a circular adding machine with two tangential circles, the first for the units (from 1 to 99), the other for the hundreds.

65.12 Babbage's] Charles Babbage (1791–1871), English mathematician and inventor who is generally credited with having conceived the first automatic digital computer. Peirce was much impressed by the different machines of Babbage and wrote an obituary of him for the *Nation* (W2:457–59, 1871). In 1822 Babbage completed a mechanical calculator that could calculate tables of logarithmic and trigonometric functions up to six decimal places. This calculator formed the basis of his work on the "Difference Engine," which, if the first few numbers of a table were supplied to it, would calculate the others successively according to the same principle. In 1834, Babbage began work on the "Analytical Engine," which consisted of a punched-card-fed processor combined with a memory unit and a printer. It was never built but could theoretically perform complicated algebraical processes and make decisions based on the calculations it had performed.

66.12 Mr. Mitchell] Oscar Howard Mitchell (1851–1889) held the chair of Mathematics and Astronomy at Marietta College, Ohio, and was a student of Peirce at Johns Hopkins. The paper referred to is Mitchell's "On a New Algebra of Logic" in *Studies in Logic*, pp. 72–106.

67n.1 Mrs. Franklin's system.] Christine Ladd-Franklin (1847–1930), American psychologist, logician, and mathematician, was a student of Peirce at Johns Hopkins. She described this system in "On the Algebra of Logic" in *Studies in Logic*, pp. 17–71.

68.1–2 *solvet ambulando*] The *OED* has *solvitur ambulando, solvitur* being in the third person of the indicative present (passive) of the verb *solvo*, while Peirce's *solvet* is in the third person of the indicative future (active). Literally meaning "it is solved by walking around," the phrase calls for the solution of a problem or for the proof of a statement through an appeal to practical experience. Originally the phrase alluded to Diogenes the Cynic's method of disproving the inexistence of motion by getting up and walking around (Diogenes Laertius VI. 39). In a similar context Peirce uses the phrase *probatio ambulandi* (CP 5.539, c. 1902).

68.5–11 One peculiarity . . . complicated.] See also W5:173n and W4:572n184.3.

70.13–16 Every reasoning machine . . . procedures.] Compare with what Peirce wrote some twenty years later, in January 1906 (EP2:387):

> [A]ll the operations of reason can receive perfect logical explanation by principles which apply as much to real signs as to the imaginary signs called concepts, although it is quite true that we cannot make a machine that will reason as the human mind reasons until we can make a logical machine (logical machines, of course, exist) which shall not only be automatic, which is comparatively a small matter, but which shall be endowed with a genuine power of self-control; and we have as little hopes of doing that as we have of endowing a machine made of inorganic materials with life.

70.18 simplest proposition of projective geometry,] On the ten-ray theorem, see anns. 38.7 and 45.1.

70.19 von Staudt] Karl Georg Christian von Staudt (1798–1867), author of *Geometrie der Lage* (Nürnberg, 1847), and *Beiträge zur Geometrie der Lage* (Nürnberg, 1856–60), developed the theory of imaginary lines and points in projective geometry.

72.12 a Jacquard loom,] An attachment to a weaving loom which made automated pattern weaving possible. The attachment, invented by Joseph-Marie Jacquard (1752–1834) in 1801, was fed with cards punched with rectangular holes that directed the feeding of various threads into the loom. Jacquard's system of punched cards, which created a rudimentary sequence control mechanism that allowed for primitive programmability, greatly influenced Charles Babbage in the development of his analytical engine.

16. *Criticism on* Phantasms of the Living

74.title An Examination of an Argument] William James, who was one of the founders of the American Society for Psychical Research, published a far more positive review of *Phantasms* than Peirce's in *Science* 9 (7 January 1887) 18–20, now reprinted in his *Works, Essays in Psychical Research* (Cambridge, Harvard University Press, 1986), 24–28.

74.1–2 Messrs. Gurney, Myers, and Podmore,] Sel. 14, ann. 61.23.

74.2 spontaneous telepathy,] The authors define telepathy in the following terms: "the ability of one mind to impress or to be impressed by another mind otherwise than through the recognized channels of sense" (*Phantasms* 1:6). Most of the cases were of spontaneous occurrence.

74.3 *of the Living*] On the rationale for designating phantasms projected by agents at or near death as "of the living" see *Phantasms* 1:lxiii–lxv.

74.3–4 Only one person . . . hallucination.] To obtain this ratio, Peirce took Gurney's statement (*Phantasms* 2:16) that, out of 5705 persons taken at random, only twenty-three recalled having had a visual hallucination over a period of twelve years, yielding a ratio of 1/248 over twelve years, and thus a ratio of approximately 1/3000 over one year.

74.5 annual death-rate] This annual death-rate amounts to 22/1000, according to the "official returns" quoted by Gurney in *Phantasms* 2:13. The proportion of anyone's relatives and acquaintances who die within twelve years is taken as 264/1000 (2:13–14).

74.6 fifty millions] To obtain this figure, Peirce multiplied Gurney's 4,114,545 by twelve to reach a ratio applicable to one year instead of twelve years.

74.10 thirty-one indubitable cases] In ch. 13 on "The Theory of Chance-Coincidence" (*Phantasms* 2:17), these cases are listed in a footnote to Gurney's assertion that "our collection includes 31 first-hand and well-attested coincidental cases of this type, which have occurred in this country within the specified time." The cases are of people who have experienced a visual hallucination representing a living person, known to them, who died within twelve hours before or after the hallucination.

74.11–12 some very enormous odds] Gurney calculated these odds to be about 10^{48} to 1 (*Phantasms* 2:17). If only cases are reckoned where the visual phantasm was recorded before the news of the death arrived, the odds are reduced to about 10^{23} to 1 (ibid., 2:iii).

75.6–8 According to their calculations . . . fortuitously.] Peirce is inferring this from the odds calculated by Gurney in ch. 13 of *Phantasms*.

75.17–18 *"while in good health . . . and wide awake."*] *Phantasms* 2:7:

> Since January 1, 1874, have you—when in good health, free from anxiety, and completely awake—had a vivid impression of seeing or being touched by a human being, or of hearing a voice or sound which suggested a human presence, when no one was there? Yes or no?

75.21 in Cases 28, 174, 201, 202, 236, and 702.] In the uncorrected galleys which were sent to Gurney, Peirce had written 29 for 28 and 214 for 236. Gurney objects to the inclusion of 214 on the ground that the percipient became ill *after* she had the vision, namely when receiving the note informing her of the death of her niece. Interestingly, case 236 with which Peirce replaces this case shows no indication that the percipient, a young woman, is not in good health.

75.29–30 "I cannot yet . . . asleep."] *Phantasms* 1:433:

> I reflected, 'Am I awake, or is this a dream?' I cannot yet answer this question to my own satisfaction; I cannot tell when my dream merged in my waking thoughts.

75.30–31 "vivid dream."] *Phantasms* 1:530.
76.4 "could not say who it was."] *Phantasms* 1:542; "I knew the face quite well, but could not say whose it was."
76.5 "a dark figure"] *Phantasms* 2:53.
76.7 "resembled her [the percipient's] brother,"] *Phantasms* 2:53; Peirce is mistaken in saying that the percipient, Miss Bale, was shown, and assented to, the statement made by a second witness, Mrs. Hart. Bale wrote "The apparition did remind me of my brother" and, in a letter Bale did not get to see, Hart confirmed: "She said it reminded her of her brother."
76.9–11 the percipient . . . reached her.] Peirce's rendition is not entirely accurate. *Phantasms* 2:696:

> When I got home in the evening, my wife met me as usual at the door, and I said to her, "I have some sad news to tell you." Before I could say more she replied, "I know what it is; poor Z. is dead. It was his face which I saw looking at you last night."

76.26–28 "The next day, . . . that day, Saturday."] *Phantasms* 1:207.
76.29–32 he says the vision occurred . . . the night of Friday at 2 A.M.] The percipient said quite clearly, however, that his experience occurred at "about 2 o'clock on the morning of October 21st, 1881," which was a Friday (*Phantasms* 1:207).
76.38–77.1 "Time passed, and all was forgotten."] *Phantasms* 1:428; "Time passed on, and all seemed forgotten."
77.11–13 "had been ordered . . . no work whatever,"] *Phantasms* 1:544.
77.21–24 He turned round . . . anything at all.] Peirce's account is incorrect: the percipient, Mr. Carr, did not turn round to remark upon it to other people in the room, and did not wait for a knock at the door. Instead, alone in his room, Carr waited near the window to watch unseen his friend pass close to the terrace, but the friend vanished out of view (*Phantasms* 2:71).
77.37–38 They could see all around it,] From Helen Robinson's testimony reproduced in "Additions and Corrections," *Phantasms* 2:xxv–xxvi.
78.15 "face of a skeleton"] *Phantasms* 2:246.
78.31–32 This applies to Nos. 29 and 249;] There is no indication in the descriptions for either of the two cases that the percipient had been drinking, or was intoxicated in any other way.
79.20 She . . . past ten;] The percipient doesn't state the exact time of the vision, surmised by Gurney to have taken place soon after midnight. The 10:30 P.M. time corresponds to the actual time of death of the agent (*Phantasms* 1:441–43).
79.30–33 Now, since taking this testimony . . . May 4th.] Peirce correctly notes that the percipient could have received her father's notification from England before writing the June 5 letter, but he mistakes this letter for the missing first letter from the Cape she allegedly wrote to her father upon arriving at Capetown on May 10. Her father wrote: "The letter I most wanted I cannot find, but have one dated June 5th, in which my daughter again refers to Miss B.'s death, and adds, 'On the 2nd of May, . . ." (*Phantasms* 1:442–43). The correct date is thus given in this second letter, contrary to Peirce's reading of it. In spite of these confusions, Peirce's general point is sound—with no surviving letter dated earlier than June

5, there is no corroborating evidence that she wrote about the incident prior to receiving word of her friend's death. In his "Remarks" (sel. 17, 93.5–19), Gurney does, however, corroborate that she told others of the vision before docking at Capetown, by quoting from a letter he received later from one of her fellow travelers (unnamed). Gurney agrees nonetheless that it is best to assume that she did not send any letter to her father prior to June 5.

80.1 the percipient is a lady.] As Gurney notes, this lady was the well-known traveler and authoress, Isabella L. Bird (1831–1904).

80.15–18 We . . . to the minute.] In his "Remarks," Gurney is right in pointing out that Miss Bird did not state that the coincidence was exact "to the minute." In an earlier draft, Peirce closed his discussion of Case 197 with this observation: "It appears to me strange that these gentlemen should think that this coincidence is established beyond a reasonable doubt, unless to the mind of a person who has already admitted the existence of ghosts on telepathic phantasms."

80.28 an unnumbered case,] *Phantasms* 1:130n. The percipient requested that details not be published. Gurney identifies it as one of his 31 well-attested visual cases in his chapter on chance-coincidence, 2:17n.

81.15–17 I also strongly dissent . . . 300,000.] Gurney justifies his estimate in *Phantasms* 2:14–15, and replies to Peirce in his "Remarks," sel. 17, 99.5–36.

17. *Remarks on Professor Peirce's Paper*

82.30–83.10 Referring . . . Mr. Peirce.] Sel. 16, 74.3–15 with corresponding annotations. In the fourth Cambridge Conferences lecture of 1898, Peirce wrote:

> Strictly speaking, it is not certain that twice two is four. If on an average in every thousand figures obtained by addition by the average man there be one error, and if a thousand million men have each added 2 to 2 ten thousand times, there is still a possibility that they have all committed the same error of addition every time. If everything were fairly taken into account, I do not suppose that twice two is four is more certain than Edmund Gurney held the existence of veridical phantasms of the dying or dead to be. (EP 2:44)

83.18 the list in Chap. XIII,] *Phantasms* 2:17n.2.

83.41–42 (see Vol. I, p. 148)] In *Phantasms* 1:148, Gurney wrote:

> There is one, and only one, sort of second-hand evidence which can on the whole be placed on a par with first-hand; namely, the evidence of a person who has been informed of the experience of the percipient while the latter was still unaware of the corresponding event; and who has had equal opportunities with the percipient for learning the truth of that event, and confirming the coincidence.

84.3 237, is, I suppose, a mistake for 238).] Here and at 84.37, 85.15, 85.24–26, 90.4, 91.3–8, and 92.24–25, Gurney is noting errors found in his copy of the uncorrected proof of Peirce's "Criticism." Peirce's erroneous case references were corrected before the paper was printed (along with Gurney's "Response" and Peirce's "Rejoinder") in the *Proceedings*, and thus do not appear in the text itself. Peirce published an errata note at the beginning of his "Rejoinder" (sel. 18) to explain why Gurney, in sel. 17, is pointing out incorrect references that are absent in sel. 16. See ann. 75.21.

85.16 I have explained (p. 7) . . . in separate parts] In *Phantasms* 2:7n.1, Gurney wrote that the "comprehensive question [cited in ann. 75.17–18] has been actually asked in several parts." The original question did not state the *terminus a quo*

(1 January 1874), so that the time of the recorded experience had to be ascertained in subsequent correspondence, as were the factual details of the experience itself.

86.18–24 "to cases . . . phenomenon."] *Phantasms* 2:48–49.

86.26 "did not know he was so near death."] *Phantasms* 2:59.

87.1–4 "several cases . . . evidence."] *Phantasms* 2:16n.1.

87.19 Kingsley's *Miscellanies,*] Charles Kingsley (English clergyman and novelist, 1819–1875), *Miscellanies* (London: John W. Parker and Son, 1859).

87.27 Vol. II, p. 12, second note.)] This note contains the following relevant passage:

> The question as to hallucinations specially included the condition *of being awake;* but naturally some of the experiences recorded had taken place when the hallucinated person was *in bed* (Vol. i, p. 393). I reckon these cases among the *yeses;* and I include similar experiences in the group of *coincidental hallucinations* which appears later in the calculation.

87.35–37 "I knew . . . previous year."] *Phantasms* 1:542.

87.38 a very reasonable explanation] *Phantasms* 1:543: "I will only add that I believe the face of the man I saw was that of Ramsay as I had known him at first, when I visited him as a dying man in the infirmary. But seeing him every day as my servant, and in health, it had passed from my mind, or rather I did not connect itself with this man in my memory." Prior to entering service with the percipient, Archibald Ramsay was a discharged soldier recovering from a near-fatal illness in the Inverness infirmary.

87.40–88.2 Case 236 . . . occurred.] See ann. 76.7. In sel. 18, 133.5–12, Peirce subsequently shows that Gurney's own interrogation may have established in the percipient's mind the connection between the apparition and her brother.

88.29 I have myself pointed out] *Phantasms* 1:532.

92.24 Case 180.] This is not one of the 31 cases under review—Peirce had misprinted 180 for 170 in his typescript, and this error was transmitted to the uncorrected proofs upon which Gurney based his response.

92.25 through rough inadvertence.] See ann. 120.28.

92.28–29 'Borderland' hallucination] Gurney discusses "borderland" hallucinations in *Phantasms* 1:389–456. Borderland telepathic phenomena occur in the transition states between sleeping and waking, when the percipient is neither dreaming nor fully awake.

93.6–8 one of the persons told . . . ascertained.] This person was the percipient's cousin, Mr. Jenour, as can be inferred from *Phantasms* 1:442.

97.8 No. 500),] This is not one of Gurney's 31 cases, but he considers it as well-attested as any of these; it only fails to make the list because it seems "as likely as not that the 12 hours' limit was somewhat exceeded" (*Phantasms* 2:17n.2).

97.32–39 "It is very necessary . . . recorded."] *Phantasms* 2:1.

98.12 Vol. II, pp. 10, 11.] Gurney rightly points out that Peirce misread what was written in *Phantasms* 2:10–11, where the objection was addressed and answered with this rhetorical question:

> Now, can it be a common thing for an experience as unusual and surprising as this to be, within a dozen years or any shorter period, so utterly obliterated from a person's mind that his memory remains a blank, even when he is pointedly asked to try and recall whether he has had such an experience or not?

99.6–7 Of the 64 coincidental experiences] Gurney's revised approximation of the population size appears in a footnote in *Phantasms* 2:15n.1.

100.17–20 More cases . . . will come.] In 1889 the English Society for Psychical Research undertook a much larger census of 17,000 persons (Gurney had only surveyed 5705 persons), called the Census of Hallucinations. The American Society for Psychical Research assisted in the effort by circulating its own questionnaire. The English report was published in the Society's *Proceedings* 10 (August 1894): 25–422, and the results of the American survey were published in the report's Appendix B. William James played a significant role in this matter; see his contributions published in his *Works, Essays in Psychical Research* (Cambridge: Harvard University Press, 1986), 56–78. More information about this Census can be found in Alan Gauld's *The Founders of Psychical Research*, (New York: Schoken Books, 1968), ch. 8, "Edmund Gurney and Phantasms of the Living," 153–85. Regarding that Census, Peirce wrote the following in a 1903 manuscript on telepathy (R 881; CP 7.603):

> I was . . . moved to write an elaborate criticism of [*Phantasms of the Living*] to show that hallucinations were so very common, while hallucinations coincident with truth beyond the ken of sense were so very rare, after the suspicious cases had been weeded out, that these coincidences might very well be supposed to be fortuitous. At the same time, I essayed to determine by logical analysis what were the conditions to which a census of hallucinations must conform in order to afford sound support to the contention of the telepathists that the veridical hallucinations were too numerous to be accounted chance coincidences. The Society at once set about making a new census. I wish I could pay them the compliment of averring that, in doing so, they were influenced by my reasons or by any better considered reasons. But I am obliged to say that they so far failed to conform to the conditions which I had shown to be requisite,—and in the direction of favoring their doctrine of telepathy,—that now the question stands as it did before, a question which each man will answer according to his predilections, whether these owe their birth to his general experience of the ways of nature or to some episode of his private life.

In his work just cited, Alan Gauld, however, believes that the Census of Hallucinations gave a final answer to Peirce's objections.

18. *Mr. Peirce's Rejoinder*

101.1 In the copy of the above criticism,] Gurney based his "Remarks" on a set of uncorrected galleys of Peirce's "Criticism." Peirce's errata indicate what corrections were made in the final proofs. In a later footnote (119n.1–2) Peirce indicates that he himself was sent both first and second galleys of Gurney's "Remarks" on which to base his rejoinder. See ann. 84.3.

101.18–19 I found myself in the possession of a good many notes] See *[*Notes for a review of *Phantasms of the Living]* (1887.13). These are notes Peirce typed while going through the 31 relevant cases in Gurney's book.

101.22–23 American Psychical Research Society] The American Society for Psychical Research (A.S.P.R.) was organized in the fall of 1884 in Boston with Simon Newcomb as its first president. Its first officers included William James, Henry P. Bowditch, James Mills Peirce, and G. Stanley Hall. The research work of the A.S.P.R. was conducted by Richard Hodgson from 1887 until his death in 1905. In 1890, the American Society became officially the American Branch of the

Society for Psychical Research (see ann 61.15–16). This Branch was dissolved in May 1906 but soon reorganized as the American Society for Psychical Research.

103.8–10 Gurney has, for the first time . . . question to rest;] Probability analysis had been used earlier to study telepathy. In 1884, Charles Richet published his "La suggestion mentale et le calcul des probabilités" (*Revue Philosophique de la France et de l'Etranger* 18 [1884]: 609–74). This paper, which was reviewed by Gurney in "M. Richet's Recent Researches in Thought-Transference" (*Proceedings of the Society for Psychical Research* 2 [1884]: 239–57), inspired Gurney to work on *Phantasms*. Interestingly, Peirce's brother Jem also preceded Gurney. See James M. Peirce and E. C. Pickering, "Report of Thought-Transference Committee: Appendix B," *Proceedings of the American Society for Psychical Research* 1 (1885): 19–34. Both the Richet study and the Peirce-Pickering study led to negative results. Gurney discusses the two researches in *Phantasms* 1:31–35. For a discussion of the early use of probability theory in the study of telepathy, see Ian Hacking, "Telepathy: Origins of Randomization in Experimental Design," *Isis* 79 (1988): 427–51.

103.13 "as far as the evidence goes."] The phrase as quoted is slightly modified; it appears in the last but one sentence of "Criticism" (sel. 16).

103.14–15 "in view of the uncertainty . . . at all."] From the last but two line in "Criticism" (sel. 16), which has "utter uncertainty."

103.17-18 though I decidedly . . . ghost-stories.)] In a letter to William Benjamin Smith of 25 July 1908 (RL 408:17), Peirce wrote that "there is *something* in the spiritist theory," holding that "there is *some* life after death, at least for some people, though it may be a brief butterfly life." He immediately cautioned, however, "But what I have ever seen of manifestations was odious beyond words."

103.20–24 "It may be calculated that . . . trillions to one."] *Phantasms* 1:17.

104.21–24 I have pointed out . . . coincidence!] Sel. 16, 81.7–9.

104.27–28 Mr. Gurney sharply censures me] Sel. 17, 98.8–23.

104.28–29 for saying . . . a few months.] Sel. 16, 81.6–13.

104.33–34 "totally forgotten" is "thoroughly misleading,"] Sel. 17, 98.16–17.

104.35–36 "and was . . . death."] Sel. 17, 98.14–15

104.36–37 Mr. Gurney doubts . . . in the book.] Sel. 17, 98.15–16.

105.7–8 "happened to remember"] *Phantasms* 2:87. Peirce here is mistaken; it was not the percipient who "happened to remember," but her husband.

105.8–9 "recurred to it from time to time,"] *Phantasms* 2:159. The husband's account, however, suggests that his wife did refer to the "apparition" regularly in conversation; it was the husband, who wrote the letter, who was much more likely to have forgotten the event had it not been for the coincidence.

105.12–14 Mr. Gurney . . . an error.] This error is already noted by Gurney in *Phantasms* 2:511n.2 and 2:xxvii (in "Additions and Corrections").

106.27–30 "Had the cases . . . blunder."] Sel. 17, 98.31–32.

106.31–32 "Only five cases . . . in this way."] Sel. 17, 98.37–99.1.

107.6–10 "Would any one . . . might be sent?"] *Phantasms* 2:15.

107.17–19 5 of his 64 . . . at random.] *Phantasms* 2:15n.1 and sel. 17, 99.6–21.

107.19–22 The other . . . half-a-dozen persons.] Sel. 17, 99.26–35.

107.28 31 visual and 33 auditory cases] The auditory cases are identified, but not listed, in *Phantasms* 2:13; the visual cases are identified and listed by case number in 2:17 and 17n.

107.31 the case of Mrs. Duck,] *Phantasms* 2:55–57.

110.37–111.1 On the contrary . . . at all times.] Stephen E. Braude formulates a number of objections against this statement in "Peirce on the Paranormal," *Transactions of the Charles S. Peirce Society* 34 (1998): 207–9.

111.31–32 Mr. Gurney, in his reply . . . have so too.] Sel. 17, 100.6–9.

112.25–27 Mr. Gurney . . . awake.] Sel. 17, 87.29–31.

114.10 There is a doubt about the date;] Peirce is right in pointing out this problem; Gurney believed that by "the next day" the percipient meant " the day following the night of the experience," thus some time during Friday, Oct. 21 (*Phantasms*, 1:207n.2), while Peirce thought, on good textual ground, that the percipient meant Saturday.

114.18–19 "about two o'clock . . . October 21st;"] See ann. 76.29–32.

115.34–35 "I can scarcely . . . due to anxiety."] Sel. 17, 86.8–9.

117.11–13 Mr. Gurney, . . . an attack of indigestion.] Sel. 17, 85.35.

119.1 See objections 4 and 12,] In the original "Criticism," Peirce does not cite objection 4 for this case. Other variations in objections cited in the "Rejoinder" include the addition of objection 3 to case 182, objection 9 to case 201, objection 4 to case 214, objection 8 to case 249, and objection 5 to case 702. Conversely, the "Rejoinder" omits other objections cited in the original "Criticism," including the omission of objection 17 from case 231, objection 4 from case 236, objection 9 from case 249, and objection 5 from case 695.

119.1–4 Mr. Gurney's replies . . . in perfect health.] Sel. 17, 84.35 and 90.35–41.

119.8 Ingoldsby legend.] Under the pseudonym Thomas Ingoldsby, Richard Harris Barham (1788–1845) wrote *The Ingoldsby Legends, or, Mirth and Marvels.* The book was published by his son, Richard Harris Dalton Barham, in 1846.

120.28 "rough inadvertency."] Sel. 17, 92.25. In sel. 19, 147.16–18 Gurney explains that the word "rough" was a misprint repeating unintentionally the last five letters of the preceding word, "through."

121.1 Mr. Gurney gracefully surrenders this case,] Sel. 17, 87.32–33 and 88.24–25.

121.19–20 Mr. Gurney replies . . . the word.] Sel. 17, 86.12–14.

122.14–16 Mr. Gurney says . . . of no consequence.] Sel. 17, 85.10–13.

122.16–17 But he himself . . . summing up.] Sel. 17, 96.22–32.

122.22 He says he cannot tell] Sel. 17, 85.10.

122n.1–3 The passage . . . constructed.] Sel. 17, 85.16–21.

123.7–8 in a critical condition."] *Phantasms* 1:433: "known to be fatally ill."

123.23–25 "There . . . the word."] Sel. 17, 84.25–26.

124.17–28. I will put . . . 48.] Peirce's calculations in this passage are roughly done. Since the antecedent probability, 1 in 2500, is estimated at two-thirds, the probability of coincidence is 1 in 3750, and not 1 in 3700 or 1 in 3800 as Peirce has it inconsistently in the text. Dividing 3750 by 4 gives 187.5. Rounded up to 188 and divided by 4, we reach the number 47, instead of Peirce's 48.

124.33 furnishes new testimony,] Sel. 17, 93.5–25. See also ann. 93.6–8.

125.27–29 "He has had . . . figure."] Sel. 17, 84.13.

125.29 The census–question] *Phantasms* 2:7.

126.14–15 Mr. Gurney says . . . not anxious.] Sel. 17, 85.31–32.

126.25–26 reply of Mr. Gurney under the 8th.] Sel. 17, 88.40–44.

126.32–34 cannot fix ... of the death.] *Phantasms* 1:529; original has "at the time" where Peirce has "at the same time."
126.35 now adds a circumstance to the account] Sel. 17, 88.40–44.
127.24-25 I carelessly represented . . . the apparition.] Sel. 16, 80.9–10.
128.4–5 On some Wednesday . . . "a few days ago."] Sel. 17, 95.20.
128.13–16 Mr. Gurney admits . . . twenty-four hours.] *Phantasms* 1:532.
129.8 The discovery of the diary,] Sel. 17, 95.4 and 95n.5–6.
129.13–14 "nothing which . . . the vision."] Sel. 17, 94.3.
129.15–18 He was very disconcerted . . . Saturday."] *Phantasms* 1:534.
129.24–25 as Mr. Gurney suggests doing,] Sel. 17, 83.20–22.
129.29–30 I have twice mentioned . . . notes.] Sel. 17, 90.3 and 91.6–7. Peirce made the errors in sel. 16, 77.18 and 78.32 (they have been corrected in this edition).
130.4 Mr. Gurney says] Sel. 17, 87.34; the "misquotation" occurs in sel. 16, 76.4.
130.21 Mr. Gurney gives up the case;] Sel. 17, 96.35–36.
130.35–36 Mr. Gurney's thinking . . . is "very high"] Sel. 17, 89.1–3.
131.12–13 a confusion . . . 236,] Sel. 16, 75.21 (in this edition 214 is corrected to 236).
131.30–31 Mr. Gurney gives it up entirely.] Sel. 17, 84.6–11 and 96.22–23.
132.4 Mr. Gurney admits an even chance of this,] *Phantasms* 2:48.
132.24–25 Mr. Gurney gives up the case altogether.] Sel. 17, 96.33–36.
132.28 Mr. Gurney's reply] Sel. 17, 88.5–8.
132.32–33 Mr. Gurney admits] *Phantasms* 2:54.
134.20–21 Mr. Gurney's thinking . . . is remarkable.] Sel. 17, 89.4–6.
134.27–28 Mr. Gurney professes . . . satisfactory.] Sel. 17, 96.4–8.
135.27 *"had not been"*] *Phantasms* 2:59, italics added. Sel. 17, 86.26–27.
135.36–37 Mr. Gurney abandons the case.] Sel. 17, 86.29–30.
137.15–16 Mr. Gurney thinks . . . if still more so.] Sel. 17, 96.10–12.
137.19–20 Mr. Gurney has not . . . any flaw in it] Sel. 17, 90.12–17.
137.34 Mr. Gurney endeavors . . . this possible error;] Ibid.
138.9–10 Mr. Gurney withdraws it.] Sel. 17, 9.18.
139.2–3 Mr. Gurney's reply under the latter head.] Sel. 17, 88.5–8.
139.7–8 Mr. Gurney avers . . . not happened;] Ibid.
140.4–6 Mr. Gurney admits . . . value.] See ann. 80.28.
141.4–5 no probable induction . . . on a single instance.] See also W3:281 (1878), where Peirce argues that in such a case "probability can have no meaning." For a recent discussion see Hilary Putnam, *The Many Faces of Realism* (La Salle: Open Court, 1987), pp. 80–86, "The Importance of Peirce's Puzzle."

19. *Remarks on Mr. Peirce's Rejoinder*

147.16–18 I much regret . . . "inadvertence."] See sel. 17, 92.25, and ann. 120.28.
147n.3–4 I may note . . . No. 500.] The misprint here reported by Gurney was corrected in sel. 17, 97.8 (see corresponding emendation).

20. *Number*

155.2–3 1. *[formula]* . . . 2. *[formula]*] The letter *t* stands for "transitive," *a* for some unspecified character or relation, and *r* for "is a relation between" (a dyadic relative: see W5:187 [1885] lines 16–19). The first two formulas define transitivity. Compare with sel. 21, 158.15–20, and Peirce's 1881 paper "On the Logic of Number," W4:299, lines 20–22.

155.4–5 3. *[formula]* . . . 4. *[formula]*] The lowercase letter *e* may stand for "being a number"; in the next selection Peirce turns it into *h*, standing for "a hereditary character." The capital roman letter E stands for "next greater than," and *q* (as explained in sel. 21, 156.6–7 and in Peirce's 1885 "On the Algebra of Logic," W5:185 lines 16–17 and 25–26) for "has the character of" (a monadic predicate). Formulas 3 and 4 state the third axiom found in Peirce's 1880–81 "The Axiom of Number," W4:222: "Whatever is greater than a number is a number."

155.6–7 5. *[formula]* . . . 6. *[formula]*] The letter g stands for "at least as great as." For *j* to be as great as *i*, they must belong *(e)* to the same number system (i.e., possess the same hereditary characters: compare with sel. 21, 156.16–19.

155.8–9 7. *[formula]* . . . 8. *[formula]*] The letter U stands for "unity." The formula implies the "Postulate of One" or the sixth axiom found in Peirce's 1880–81 "The Axiom of Number," W4:222: "Unity is the minimum number." For a number to be as great as another, that other must be at least 1; see sel. 21, 157.1–3.

155.11–12 A. *[formula]* . . . B. *[formula]*] Both the axiom and the postulate of next are also stated in Peirce's 1885 manuscript "Studies in Logical Algebra," W5:220, lines 9 and 6, respectively. The axiom becomes the "fourth premise" in sel. 21 while the postulate is the "third premise" with the g factor dropped.

155.14–15 D. *[formula]* . . . E. *[formula]*] The axiom of one becomes the "second premise" in sel. 21, and the postulate is the "first premise."

21. *Logic of Number*

156.11 *hereditary* character] The notion of heredity plays a central role in the logic of relations. Gottlob Frege is generally credited as being the first to precisely define heredity, or ancestral relation, in his *Begriffschrift* (Halle, 1879); see e.g. I. M. Bochenski, *A History of Formal Logic* (Univ. of Notre Dame Press, 1961), 384. Peirce's use of the phrase "hereditary character" in this context is independent of Frege and appears to be his own device.

156.12 $\Pi_j\Pi_k(\bar{q}_{\alpha j} + \bar{E}_{jk} + q_{\alpha k})$] This formula follows the same format as Frege's definition of heredity. On Frege's account (as rendered in Michael D. Resnik, *Frege and the Philosophy of Mathematics*, Ithaca: Cornell University Press, 1980, p. 203), for any relation R (like Peirce's "next greater than"):

$$\text{F is R-hereditary} \equiv (x)(y)((\text{F}x \cdot x\text{R}y) \supset \text{F}y)$$

which may be taken as equivalent to: $(x)(y)(-\text{F}x \vee -x\text{R}y \vee \text{F}y)$.

157.26 The main procedure of inference] Peirce explains this procedure in detail in his 1885 paper "On the Algebra of Logic," W5:182–85.

22. A *Guess at the Riddle: Contents*

165.title A Guess at the Riddle] It is commonly assumed that Peirce chose the title on account of Emerson's famous poem "The Sphinx," some verses of which he frequently quoted. But there is no convincing evidence that Peirce wanted to make a specific allusion to Emerson or anyone else. That the title might refer to F. C. S. Schiller's *Riddles of the Sphinx: A Study in the Philosophy of Humanism* must be ruled out since that book was only published in May 1891. Other candidates are Francis E. Abbot and Peirce's father Benjamin (see W5:xli–xlii). It is clear that Peirce did not need any special source of inspiration to come up with his title, as the metaphor was culturally well established. What is the riddle? A clue is suggested by the fact that Peirce had engrossed himself in the study of presocratic thinkers for one or two years, as manifested in R 1574: 217–19 (see ann. 181.4–5) and in "One, Two, Three" (W5:294–98, 1886), where Peirce compares his own research with that of the first Greek philosophers on "primal matter." The riddle Peirce tries to guess at is substantially the same: "What is the world made of?" (W5:295). The last chapter, "The Triad in Physics," gives the answer (sel. 28, 208.29–31). On how much of a guess it is, see sel. 25, 182.3–6.

166.title *[Contents]*] This table of contents is remarkably close to the outline given in "One, Two Three," W5:294–98 (1886), with which it ought to be compared.

166.1 One, Two, Three. Already written.] This refers, not to the actual first chapter printed in this volume (it was written later than the table of contents), but to sel. 35 or (a more developed form of) one of the chapters in sels. 47–50 in W5, which were all intended for the projected book "One, Two, Three."

166.2 Chapter 2. . . . Not touched.] Although Peirce probably never wrote this chapter, its substance can be deduced from the five papers referred to (and identified in the next five annotations). For this chapter, the *Collected Papers* editors used part of R 901 (CP 1.369–72; published in W5:242–47, 1885).

166.3 my last paper] "On the Algebra of Logic: A Contribution to the Philosophy of Notation" (1885), W5:162–90, especially 162–65.

166.5 my paper on a new list of categories] "On a New List of Categories" (1867), W2:49–59, especially 56–59.

166.6–7 my paper in *Studies in Logic.*] "A Theory of Probable Inference" (1883), W4:408–50, especially 408–23.

166.8 my paper on the classification of arguments.] "On the Natural Classification of Arguments" (1867), W2:23–48, especially 29–42.

166.9–10 my first paper on the logic of relatives.] "Description of a Notation for the Logic of Relatives" (1870), W2:359–429, especially 364–66.

166.11–15 The dual . . . numerical quantity.] See "Segment 4" of "Notes on the Categories" (W5:240–41, 1885), which expresses the same idea more fully.

166.18–19 dual quantity . . . Boolian algebra,] See for instance W5:382.

167.7 pneumatology.] CD 4574: "2. The branch of philosophy which treats of the nature and operations of mind or spirit, or a treatise on it." This is followed by a quotation from William Hamilton: "The terms Psychology and Pneumatology, or Pneumatic, are not equivalent. The latter word was used for the doctrine of spirit in general, which was subdivided into three branches, as it treated of the three orders of spiritual substances—God, Angels and Devils, and Man." Under pneumatic philosophy, Peirce gives the following definition: "the science of metaphysics or psychology; pneumatology."

167.8 consciousness is a sort of public spirit] Compare with R 954:12–13 (c. 1892):

> Such is a slight outline of some of the features of the philosophy which I am persuaded will soon be recognized as that which is the most in harmony with the methods and discoveries of physical science. I have not developed its psychological side, because that part of it is difficult of apprehension. I must however mention that according to this everything is of the nature of the mind,—even material phenomena. But mind is not necessarily person. A person is mind whose parts are coordinated in a particular way. Something of the general nature of personality there is in all general ideas. These conceptions are in a certain sense creations of the human intelligence; but in another aspect the human mind is the creation of these conceptions working together. These general conceptions are no figments, they are

real things,—more than that, they are living beings with something like life and something like personality. Mind acts upon mind by virtue of its continuity; and this continuity involves generality. In regard to the concerns of the soul, religion, immortality, morality, the synechistic philosophy, as I call it, that is the philosophy of continuity, leaves all such questions to the jury to be decided according to the evidence.

167.11 Chapter 9. The triad in theology.] See Peirce's 1885 review of Royce's *The Religious Aspect of Philosophy,* W5:221–34, especially 229.

167.11–12 Faith . . . without flinching.] In his "Peirce's Arisbe" paper (*Peirce, Semeiotic, and Pragmatism,* p. 234), Max Fisch wrote by way of explanation:

> The clue is in the address on "Design and Chance," where [Peirce] chides even Epicurus for flinching, by exempting his gods from the absolute chance that gives rise to his infinite worlds. For he places his gods in the spaces between the worlds and rests their divinity on the fineness of the atoms that compose them. "Thus, divineness comes from a special cause & does not originate by chance from elements not containing it. Darwin's view is nearer to mine. Indeed my opinion is only Darwinism analyzed, generalized, and brought into the realm of Ontology" (W4:552).

23. *A Guess at the Riddle: Chapter I*

168.1–3 To erect . . . massive.] Thinking that this text was written c. 1890, Max Fisch connected this architectonic metaphor to Peirce's "making the architect's drawings and supervising construction to body forth Juliette's dream-house" Arisbe (*Peirce, Semeiotic, and Pragmatism,* 238), but evidence indicates that it was written during the year in Milford that preceded the purchase of the house.

168.3–6 Aristotle . . . undermined;] Aristotle distinguishes the "few chosen concepts" in *De anima,* bk. 2, ch. 1. Peirce is intimating that Aristotle's real "categories" were not those of substance and the nine accidents, but rather these "broader, unshakable" concepts.

168.16 the new Schelling-Hegel mansion,] For the connection between Peirce and Schelling, see Gerhard Schönrich's "Schellings Metaphysik in der Naturphilosophie von Peirce," *Allgemeine Zeitschrift für Philosophie* 16.1 (1991): 1–22.

169.3–5 But before all else . . . patient.] This passage is reminiscent of, and in fact contemporary to "Private Thought" no. LXXV, 17 March 1888: "The best maxim in writing, perhaps, is really to love your reader for his own sake" (W1:9).

169.24–27 Accordingly . . . rest.] To this part corresponds the following passage with which Peirce initially started the first chapter in R 909:5 (R 909:38, draft):

> Perhaps I might begin by noticing how different numbers have found their champions. Two was extolled by Peter Ramus, Four by Pythagoras, Five by Sir Thomas Browne, and so on. For my part, I am a determined foe of no innocent number; I respect and esteem them all their several ways; but I am forced to confess to a leaning to the number three in philosophy. In fact, I make so much use of three-fold divisions in my speculations, that it seems best to commence by making a slight preliminary study of the conceptions upon which all such divisions must rest.

Petrus Ramus sought to organize discourse by dividing his subject into a tree-like chain of dichotomies. Pythagoreans believed that the number four, or the tetrad, contained the fount and root of eternal nature. Sir Thomas Browne (1605–1682) wrote *The Garden of Cyrus,* or *Quincuncial Lozenge* (1658), a mystical text in which the number five (quincunx) plays an important role.

169.27–30 I mean no more . . . for all that.] Douglas Greenlee discussed this passage in his "Peirce's Hypostatic and Factorial Categories," *Transactions of the Charles S. Peirce Society* 4 (1968): 49–58, especially 50.

170.9–10 The question is . . . third,] For comparable accounts of the three categories see W5:238–40, 446 (1885), 293, 294–95, 298–308, and 455–57 (1886).

170.11–16 the first . . . each other.] These three propositions are Peirce's standard, short, formulaic definitions of the categories; compare with their first occurrences in W5:299 and 304.

171.3–4 Only, . . . false to it.] That firsts are indescribable is an essential character of firstness. See e.g. Thomas A. Goudge, "The View of Charles Peirce on the Given in Experience," *Journal of Philosophy* 32 (1935): 533–44, and his "Further Reflections on Peirce's Doctrine of the Given," ibid. 33 (1936): 289–95.

171.34–36 limitation, conflict . . . experience.] This seems to be the first time Peirce formulates this explicit, definitional, connection between experience and secondness, a constant of his later philosophy.

172.1–4 The scarfed bark . . . ragged sails.] Shakespeare, *The Merchant of Venice,* act 2, sc. 6, 15–18 (also quoted in W5:300 and 304).

172.14–21 We are told that . . . by the predicate.] Charles Hartshorne inserted an editorial footnote after this sentence in the typescript, not printed in CP: "This sentence is exceedingly important. It shows that the principle of exact science is applicable to *any* subject matter which involves relative distinctions." Hartshorne presumably meant that for Peirce, wherever differences of degree are observable, they are quantifiable in principle, and that qualitative sciences are not equipped to analyze such differences. Compare with W5:306.

172.36–38 all the great steps . . . cases previously discrete.] For a more detailed discussion of the point made here, see Peirce's "Introductory Lecture on the Study of Logic" in W4:378–82 or EP1:210–14 (1882).

173.22–29 According . . . that yard.] See W5:250–51 (1885) for an earlier parallel discussion of the "absolute," and W5:450, ann. 248.6.

174.3–17 If you think . . . an evolutionist.] Compare with W5:251 (1885) and EP1:294–95 (1891).

174.14–18 This is one . . . vague ideas.] This one-sentence paragraph replaces the following paragraph in the draft (R 909:47): "Things, as well as processes are thirds. The subject of a sentence is first, the direct object is second, and the instrument or other circumstance is third."

174.19–24 But it will be asked . . . complications of threes.] Peirce is here presenting what is known as his "reduction thesis," first stated in his "Description of a Notation for the Logic of Relatives" of 1870 (W2:365), and then subsequently in W4:211 (1880), W5:243 (1885), 306–7, 455–56 (1886), and later—for instance in EP2:169–70, 174–76, 240 (1903), 364–65 (1905).

174.19–175.29 But it will be asked . . . idea of three.] Compare for instance with W4:332 (1882), CP 7.537 (c. 1899), and EP2:364–66 (1905).

174.27–29 the very idea . . . relationship.] In his 1973 dissertation "The Concept of Continuity in Charles Peirce's Synechism" (SUNY, Buffalo), 20–34, George A. Benedict establishes a distinction between *combination* and *connection* based on the fact that parts that are *combined* are of a different nature than parts that are *connected,* to the effect that degenerate thirds involve combinations, while genuine thirds involve connections. Benedict thus suggests that the word "combination" in this sentence be replaced with the word "connection."

175.25–27 A road . . . two termini.] The same analogy is found in W5:244 (1885) and W5:300, 306 (1886). In a draft of this page this sentence is followed by the following passage here omitted (R 909:40):

> So chemical monads will only yield binary combinations alone; but let dyads be admitted into the compound and it may have any number of atoms. In like manner, a radicle formed of dyads alone can have but two free bonds; but if triads are admitted it may have any number. These are all examples of one and the same mathematical principle, that any number N of objects, each capable of being directly joined to but one object, can be indirectly connected by means of N – 2 objects each capable of being directly joined to the three objects.

175.34–37 The argument . . . into another.] For the beginning of this development, see for example W4:544–54 (1883–84) and W5:242–47 (1885).

175.34–176.28 The argument . . . positive doctrines.] Compare this account with what Peirce told Paul Carus in "Reply to the Necessitarians" (CP 6.604, 1893).

176.13–14 One bold saltus . . . suggestions,] Max H. Fisch identified the "garden" as that of Epicurus. See his "Peirce's Arisbe" in *Peirce, Semeiotic, and Pragmatism,* 229–32, 236–37. See also H. William Davenport's 1977 dissertation "Peirce's Evolutionary Explanation of Laws of Nature: 1880–1893" (University of Illinois at Urbana-Champaign), ch. 2.

176.20–21 this first chapter . . . afterthought,] Although Peirce composed this first chapter after the others, it is clear, from the "One, Two, Three" texts in W5, that its substance was not exactly an "afterthought."

176.32–33 It is that . . . grades of thirdness.] The notion of degeneracy is evoked for the first time in Peirce's 1885 "On the Algebra of Logic," W5:162–63, and then surfaces in three of the 1886 "One, Two, Three" texts (W5:300–1, 306–8, 455–56). Felicia Kruse offers a pointed discussion in her paper "Genuineness and Degeneracy in Peirce's Categories," *Transactions of the Charles S. Peirce Society* 27 (1991): 267–98. See also Ulrich Baltzer's *Erkenntnis als Relationengeflecht: Kategorien bei Charles S. Peirce* (Paderborn: Ferdinand Schöningh, 1994), part 2, ch. 5.

176.34–177.2 Conic sections . . . degenerate cubics.] See Peirce's CD definition of "conic section" reproduced in EP2:544–45n.24. Peirce uses the example of a degenerate conic every time he discusses categorial degeneracy.

177.2–4 Nearly in the same way . . . only so conceived.] In the draft this sentence is followed by the following passage subsequently omitted (R 909:40):

> Degenerate seconds are of two families; for either there are two independent objects, not coupled together in existence, but only in the mind, or there is but one object which is second to itself, or to which an abstraction is taken as second.

177.34–36 But the relations . . . to another.] The earlier draft (R 909:41) has:

> In all these cases, the secondness lies not in the fact, but in the mind. In the case of the relations of reason, the mind makes the synthesis of the two objects; in the relations of identity, the mind sets the thing over against itself.

177.36–178.2 All degenerate seconds . . . another.] On degenerate secondness, see especially W5:306–7, 455 top, and sel. 29 in this volume.

178.11–12 We may term . . . accidental thirds.] Peirce also distinguished two other sorts of thirds degenerate in the first degree: the associating third and the reflective third. He first did so in WMS 577, quoted in W5:456n.301.26–27. In a draft of the present chapter, Peirce provided the following examples (R 909:41, 48):

> An example of another family of thirds degenerate in the first degree is that of a man looking at himself in a looking-glass. Here, if we regard the light as a third object besides the man and the mirror, no doubt there is genuine thirdness. But leaving that out of account, the only fact is that the man and the glass are in somewhat complicated dual relation to one another. Namely the glass imparts to the man the temporary power of self-vision. We may call this a case of a reflective third. Any dual relation may be so regarded as involving a third. If A loves B, then by the medium of B, A is co-lover with himself. The difference is that in some cases, this way of regarding the matter leads to some convenient classification of facts, and in other cases not.
>
> Very much of the same sort are cases where a resemblance or other relation of reason between first and second are constituted by their real relations to a third. Thus, Mercury and Venus are alike in that both revolve around the sun. Such a third may be called an associating third.

178.12–27 "How did I slay thy son?" . . . rule of prudence.] Peirce owned Edward W. Lane's 1840 translation of the collection of Arabic tales entitled *Thousand and One Nights*. In the first chapter, Scheherazade tells of a negligent merchant who, while resting in a garden, ate a date and threw away its stone (seed). The stone struck and killed the nearby but invisible son of a genie. In retribution, the genie decided to kill the merchant but allowed him one year so that he could go home and settle his affairs before returning for his punishment. According to Lane, the genie was not unjust by the standards of the tale, for custom required that the merchant cry out in warning to invisible genies before casting the stone away.

178.17–20 Had it been aimed at him . . . in one fact.] See W5:456n.301.27–29. Peirce put it this way in the typed draft (R 909:48):

> If we compare these thirds degenerate in the first degree with genuine thirds, we are struck with their mechanical character. Genuine thirdness is rational. Thus, the difference between the genie's son being accidentally hit and being aimed at lies in the intention of the action.

178.20–32 What monstrous injustice . . . which she acts.] This passage replaces the following lines from an earlier draft (R 909:41):

> Even without evil intention, a man may be responsible for the immediate effects of his actions; but these are those in which the effect follows the cause not in a sporadic case here and there, but in the regular course of nature. The three things are then brought together by the law of nature, and not merely because there is something that suggests putting them together. But even where there is no responsibility, there is a real connection of cause and effect.

178.37 What is the difference?] Peirce adds this explanation in the typed draft (R 909:48):

> But when two real forces are combined the difference is that these have a real existence in the laws of nature. The real thirdness lies then in nature's having a rational or intelligible constitution. The degenerate secondness is that which lies merely in the mind but not in the thing; that is very different from the real intelligibility which constitutes the genuine thirdness. Diamond and corundum both scratch glass; they are thus made alike by a fact

which presents itself as if it were ultimate and unintelligible. But let this be explained, and brought under any law of nature, and the statement that one scratches glass will virtually involve the other's doing so, and in so far the thirdness will be made genuine. Mercury and Venus are alike in revolving around the sun. As far as this depends on the two individual facts that both are small bodies near the sun, it is accidental; but that once granted, the motion is the result of a universal law, which would not have the character it has if only some bodies were under its influence. The observation does not however appear to be true with regard to the reflective thirds; and I must leave that as a point requiring further elucidation.

179.6 thirds degenerate in the second degree.] See "Types of Third Degenerate in the Second Degree" in W5:252–53 (dated 1885 in W5, but more likely to be from 1886), and sel. 29 below.

179.28–29 of Hegel; I reject his philosophy in toto.] For a preliminary discussion of whether Peirce is here exaggerating, see Max H. Fisch's "Hegel and Peirce," *Peirce, Semeiotic, and Pragmatism*, 261–82.

24. *A Guess at the Riddle: Chapter III*

181.1–3 I will . . . one, two, three.] This third chapter is closely connected to the third chapter (numbered IIa) of "One, Two, Three" (W5:295–98, 1886), which also describes the appearance of the three conceptions "in metaphysics" and starts with the Presocratics. The table of contents (sel. 22) reveals that Peirce intended to devote this chapter to the theory of cognition. Its Presocratic underpinning and the connection with W5:295–98 suggests that the central part of this chapter would have discussed the cognitive passage from the many to the one (the reduction of the manifold to unity).

181.4–5 The first of all . . . made.] The following is an incomplete list of citations, paraphrases and notes on presocratic philosophers compiled by Peirce possibly for this chapter. The original document consisted of three large typed sheets, but only the last two are extant (R 1574:217–19). The missing first sheet probably contained entries starting with Thales, Anaximander, and Anaximenes. The text begins in the middle of entry 19 and ends with entry 56. Entries 20, 22, 26, 29, 36, 38, 42, 43, 48, and 50–53 are marked with an x in the margin, and entry 31 is marked with a vertical line. The remarks following entry 25 link it to Peirce's reflection on the categories in chapter 1 (see also W5:295–98, 304):

[. . .] things. Identical with the world. The all, as being thought. [Xenophanes.]
20. That all things are one and that one unchangeable, the absolute. [Xenophanes.]
21. That unity and eternity are necessary characters of reality. [Parmenides.] This seems to be an exaggeration of consistency. That is, the truth is one, error only manifold.
22. Plurality and variability are appearances only. [Parmenides.]
23. The existent as the "full." Only being is and nothing is altogether not and cannot be thought. That is to say, you cannot even imagine to yourself a thing in a state of non-existence. [Parmenides.]
24. There is no becoming. What is neither was nor will be, but just is. [Parmenides.] This is the same as 21.
25. Now is at once all one indivisible. [Parmenides.] This seems to be the very apotheosis of the First, its intrinsic manifoldness being however overlooked. Remember that that manifoldness is only potential. But after all, there is a sort of synthetical idea here. The freshness, newness and life of the First is overlooked.
26. Logos, or reason, as the knowledge of the one and therefore true and better than the

senses which show us the variable. [Parmenides.]
27. The ethereal fire of light is being, and the night, the dark, the heavy, the cold, the earth, is non-being placed beside it. [Parmenides.]
28. Being is active, non-being is passive. [Parmenides.]
29. Besides being and non-being is the mythic form of the goddess who guides all things. [Parmenides, according to Theophrastus; but it seems hard to believe that he admitted a third, after his "Being only is."]
30. He devised Love the very first of all the gods. [Parmenides as quoted verbatim by Plato.] But this doctrine was of course infinitely more ancient. Hesiod, quoted by Plato in the same place in the *Symposium,* puts Chaos first, earth second, and love third.
31. I remark that the view of Parmenides is that if we were to find the ultimate explanation of things, that would be absolute unity, for if not, it would require further explanation.
32. The like knows its like, the corpse feels cold, and the man with more of the heavenly fire in his composition knows more of the truth. [Parmenides.]
33. What thinks is extended in space. [Parmenides.]
34. Continuity impossible. [Zeno.]
35. That there is no void. Implies the conception of a vacuum, which I suspect is not a very ancient idea, for I have often seen persons who had a difficulty with it. [Melissus of Samos.]
36. All things in constant flux. Cannot descend twice into the same stream. [Heraclitus.]
37. All comes from one, and one from all. [Heraclitus.] This shows clearly enough the synthetic idea in the One of the ancients. Heraclitus also calls it the One for all.
38. Strife, opposites contemporaneous in change. [Heraclitus.] *Polemos* is the Greek word.
39. The idea of action and reaction. That which strives against another supports itself. [Heraclitus.]
40. Fate is Heraclitus but of course infinitely earlier.
41. Chresmosyne, divided being. [Heraclitus.]
42. The same stream and not the same. [Heraclitus.]
43. Elements, or roots of things roots of all, that is different kinds of simple matter. Idea due entirely to Empedocles.
44. Attraction and repulsion, observed by Thales in the case of the magnet, for which reason he said the magnet has life; were regarded by Empedocles as general phenomena of nature, though he calls them by psychical terms Love and Hate, or Affection and inveterate Hate, *philotes* or *storge* and *neikos* or *kotos*. But they do not act on any mechanical or fixed laws.
45. Attractions are the result of development.
46. Non-being is the vacuum. [Leucippus.]
47. Effluences. [Empedocles.]
48. Impact the only form of force. [Democritus.]
49. As Leucippus insisted on there being a non-being because he was convinced by the arguments of Parmenides that that was the only way in which genesis was possible, and he could not give that up, it would follow I should think that he must have believed that matter did have a genesis. Therefore that doctrine of the imperishability and eternity of atoms could not have been his but must have belonged to Democritus. No, this is not so.
50. All the properties of things depend on the form, magnitude, arrangement, and position of their atoms. [Democritus.]
51. Matter is inert. [Anaxagoras.]
52. There is no fate. [Anaxagoras.]
53. There is no chance. [Anaxagoras.] This is a highly original doctrine.
54. Like is not perceived by like, but by unlike. [Anaxagoras.] Action & reaction.
55. Mind as something utterly unlike matter belongs apparently to Anaxagoras. Mind is simple.
56. Of all matters the measure is man; of those that are how they are and of those that are

not how they are not. [Protagoras.] This is of course the principle of relativity, and very near if not quite the principle of idealism.

181.5–7 Thales . . . the beginning;] The first of the Ionians to search for a natural explanation of the origin and constitution of the universe, Thales of Miletus (6th century B.C.) thought that the *arche* was water, maybe in a physical sense as Aristotle suggests, but more probably in a metaphysical sense. Anaximander believed it to be the *apeiron,* an infinite reservoir of swirling possibilities according to one plausible reading, endowed with a power of determination (for which reason he could have been one of Peirce's favorite Presocratics). His follower Anaximenes theorized that the basic principle was air, more determinate than the somewhat ad-hoc *apeiron,* but less so than water.

181.22–23 Baconian idea.] Francis Bacon (1561–1626), English philosopher. Peirce gives a similar account of the "Baconian idea" in 1886, and calls it "Baconian induction" (W5:296). In "The Fixation of Belief" Baconian induction marks the step from the a priori method to the scientific method (W3:253, 1877). Bacon's own account is given in his *Novum Organum* (1620), where he sought to replace Aristotle's deductive logic with an inductive method of interpreting nature.

181.23–24 not the indeterminacy of homogeneity.] This is most likely a reference to Herbert Spencer, who holds in his *First Principles* (1862) that the initial state of the world is an unstable homogeneity that develops through a necessary and uniform process of evolution into a coherent heterogeneity. See especially chapter 13 "The Instability of the Homogeneous." Peirce refers to this idea for the first time in "Design and Chance," W4:548 (1883–84).

25. *A Guess at the Riddle: Chapter IV*

182.6–7 We have seen . . . logic,] This refers to the unwritten chapter 2 mentioned in sel. 22, 166.2–19.

182.15–16 a psychological explanation . . . as Kant thought.] Although the *Critique* does not purport to be a psychological tract, since it instead offers a transcendental argument, psychology certainly influenced Kant's critical philosophy, as the categories are "psychological" in the broader sense of explaining the limits of knowledge for the human mind.

183.8–9 three departments . . . Willing.] Kant may be seen as examining three faculties of the mind: knowing in his *Critique of Pure Reason,* willing in his *Critique of Practical Reason,* and feeling in his *Critique of Judgment.*

183.12–13 dogmatic philosophers,] Kant distinguishes three viewpoints within philosophy: the dogmatic, the skeptical, and the critical. Of these, the dogmatist assumes that human reason can comprehend ultimate reality, without inquiring whether this is possible, and proceeds on that assumption. Kant sees Descartes and Leibniz as typical examples of this.

183.14–15 even by psychologists . . . hostile.] These are probably references to Christian Wolff (1679–1754), Alexander Gottlieb Baumgarten (1714–1762), Moses Mendelssohn (1729–1786), and Johannes Tetens (1736–1807), psychologists and philosophers who all held some kind of faculty theory of the mind.

183.21–22 Kant took it . . . Tetens.] Johannes Nickolaus Tetens (1736–1807), German mathematician and philosopher, and author of *Über die allgemeine spekulativische Philosophie* (1775) and *Philosophische Versuche über die men-*

schliche Natur und ihre Entwickelung (1777). For Tetens, the three fundamental faculties, or powers, are knowing, feeling, and willing (*Versuche*, pp. 618 and 625). Peirce may have known the claim made by Johann Georg Hammann in a 17 May 1779 letter to Herder, that "Kant is at work on his Ethics of Pure Reason and always has Tetens lying before him."

183.22–23 rhetoricians . . . idolized Plato.] Peirce may be referring to the Ramist tradition, but it is not clear to whom exactly he is referring. Aristotle's *De anima* and other works remained at the epicenter of the vast majority of philosophical/psychological discussions among Renaissance thinkers in the sixteenth century, starting with the influential *Margarita philosophica* of Gregor Reisch (of which Peirce owned three copies), which contains an elaborate classification of the faculties based on the tripartite division of the souls (vegetative, sensitive, and intellectual). Marsilio Ficino's Latin 1484 edition of Plato's works and his own commentaries inaugurated the "countercultural" movement of Renaissance Platonism in Florence and contributed to its propagation throughout the sixteenth century, as did the Stephanus edition of 1578. A similar discussion of Tetens is found in CP 7.541 (c. 1896), where Peirce refers to the ancient writers upon rhetoric instead.

183.24 In Plato, it appears under a poetical garb] This refers probably to *Phaedrus* 246–56, where Plato's tripartite division of the soul into reason, spirit and appetite is captured in the narrative of the bad horse of appetite, the charioteer of reason, and the good horse of spirit.

183.26–27 Diogenes Laertius . . . of Pythagoras.] In Book VIII of *Lives of Eminent Philosophers*, "Pythagoras," line 30, Diogenes writes that for Pythagoras the soul of man is divided into three parts: intelligence, reason, and passion.

183.31–33 By feelings . . . and pain.] *Critique of Judgment*, introduction, § 3.

183.33–35 This is not . . . element of it.] In his 1777 *Philosophische Versuche* (vol. 1, ch. 10, § 5) Tetens distinguished, as Kant did after him, between sensation *(Empfindung)* and feeling *(Gefühl)*, but as regards feelings he made a further distinction between, first, the rather crude receptivity to pleasant and unpleasant experiences *(Empfindnisse)* and emotions *(Rührungen)*, and, second, the refined inner sense of one's bodily and mental states, for which he reserved such terms as "impressions" *(Eindrucke)* and "representations" *(Vorstellungen)*—what Peirce calls the subjective element. Thus for Tetens feeling is both a complex cognitive faculty, and "sentiment" or sensibility *(Empfindsamkeit)*—the susceptibility to pleasure and displeasure.

185.3–5 I remember colors . . . observing them;] Peirce's interest in color studies originated in 1869 in his work in spectrum analysis (W2:285–93), which constituted a significant part of his astronomical research, as shown especially in his *Photometric Researches* of 1878 (W3:382–92). A number of notebooks have survived that show his continual interest in the measurement of wavelengths of light and colorimetry, and his work with Ogden N. Rood's colored disks: see for instance WMSS 245, 246, 257, 258, 289, 311, and 571. In the period of this volume, Peirce read a paper "On Sensations of Color" at the April 1889 meeting of the National Academy of Sciences in Washington, D.C. (no related document has been identified), wrote extensive color definitions for the *Century Dictionary* (see R 1155), did night observations with Rood's disks in November 1886 and June 1887, and made color experiments in April 1889 (R 1017).

185.12–13 One great psychologist . . . desire.] This psychologist has not been identified and may be a straw man.

187.30–31 Intuition is the . . . relations;] As defined here, intuition is not the immediate, asemiotic, cognition Peirce attacked in his 1868 articles, but the active contemplation of a diagram, i.e., of a concrete representation of abstract relations, likely to display new connections that had gone unnoticed until then.

26. *A Guess at the Riddle: Chapter V*

188.1 Granted that. . . .] The following alternative beginning for this chapter (R 909:54, 19) contains a number of statements not found elsewhere. The last seven sentences (starting with "But Kant") were published in CP 1.384. The theory of local signs Peirce refers to was introduced by Rudolf H. Lotze in 1852, and taken up by Wundt and others; William James commented on it in his *Principles of Psychology*.

These three fundamentally different kinds of consciousness must be accounted for by something in the physiology of the nervous system. This inference, in the present state of psychology, is a matter of course. There are practically no psychologists now who wish to be classed as materialists; still, the dependence of psychical phenomena, at least in the present life, is so far admitted that it would hardly be necessary to argue at length that three kinds or elements of consciousness imply three kinds or elements of nervous activity. Our theory, then, may be taken as predicting that three such functions of the nerves will be found. Let us see if we can make out what they are.

We know that there is an active and a passive state of a nerve-cell, and there can be no doubt that Feeling, or immediate consciousness, is a feeling of an active state of nerve-cells. We are not in a condition to say, with positiveness, whether or not every excitation of a nerve-cell is accompanied with consciousness; the existing evidence seems to be rather against such a supposition. But probably nobody will dispute that immediate Feeling implies active nerve-cells as its chief physiological condition. The sense of action and reaction, or the polar sense, as we agreed to call it, is evidently connected with the discharge of nerve-cells through the nerve-fibres. In the exercise of external volition, the discharge is upon the muscle-cells; and the large quantities of nervous *[energy]* involved explains why Volition should have been taken as the type of the polar sense. In external sensation, the discharge is from the peripheral nerve-cell; and the quantity of energy involved is slight. In internal volition, or self-control, there is an inhibitory nervous action, the precise nature of which it is not necessary to specify.

I think that everybody must admit that the condition of excitation of nerve-cells is, broadly speaking, the physiological basis of Feeling, and that the discharge of nerve-cells, or the movement of nervous energy, is the physiological basis of the sense of action and reaction. But almost everybody will say that these two phenomena exhaust the functions of the nerves, and leave nothing to explain mediate consciousness; for we are so restricted to the plane of dual thought in regard to physiology, that the most remarkable property of the nerves, and of living tissue generally, is commonly left out of sight. This most characteristic power is that of taking habits.* [*See the instructive work J. J. Murphy, *Habit and Intelligence*.] It seems clear that this is the physiological basis of the consciousness of learning. In order to test this, let us see whether it will account for the three modes of mental synthesis, namely, synthesis due to relations of reason, synthesis due to external compulsion, and genuine learning, or synthesis by the construction of a synthetizing concept. Now synthesis by internal compulsion is plainly due to the fact that like feelings affect the same, or intimately associated, nerve-cells; this is the physiological cause of our judging those feelings to be alike. This view generalizes the conception of a local sign, and makes all similarity of that same nature. There is a certain current theory of "local signs" which is commonly admitted for the purposes of the psychological explanation of vision. The theory is simply that there is something in the feeling to distinguish the excitation of one peripheral nerve-cell from that of another, however similar the feelings may be. I would go a step further and say that all resemblances and differences of feelings are of the nature of local signs. How can the feelings of the excitations of different nerve-cells have any relation whatever? Must it not be by virtue of their being associated with one and the same cell? I suppose we distinguish the excitation of one part of the retina from that of another in consequence of different nerve-cells being concerned, and that we feel them to be similar in color in consequence of both leading to the excitation of one cell nearer the centre. According to this, ideas would be more or less similar according to the greater or less number of common nerve-cells involved in their production. At any rate, here is something to serve as a "working hypothesis" or doctrine in the course of refuting which knowledge is advanced. The physiological explanation of synthesis by external compulsion is less transcendental; it is simply that ideas are thought as externally connected in consequence of their having resulted from the same general nervous disturbance, or in other words, they are more or less nearly related according as one and the same discharge over one and the same nerve-fibre, has been more or less concerned in the production of them. Ideas are thought as directly connected, when one is discharged into the other, that is to say, when one is present just before a movement of nervous energy and the other just after it. But Kant gives the erroneous view that ideas are presented separated and then thought together by the mind. This is his doctrine that a mental synthesis precedes every analysis. What really happens is that something is presented which in itself has no parts, but which nevertheless is analyzed by the mind, that is to say, its having parts consists in this that the mind afterward recognizes those parts in it. Those partial ideas are really not in the first idea, in itself, though they are separated out from it. It is a case of destructive distillation. When having thus separated them, we think over them, we are carried in spite of ourselves from one thought to another, and therein lies the first real synthesis. An earlier synthesis than that is a fiction. The whole conception of time belongs to genuine synthesis, and is not to be considered under this head.

188.3 physiology of the nervous system] Previous texts related to this topic include "Logic. Chapter I. Of Thinking as Cerebration," W4:38–44 (1879), W4:45–46 (1880); "On the Algebra of Logic," W4:163–65 (1880); "An American Plato," W5:225 (1885); "One, Two, Three: Fundamental Categories of Thought and of Nature," W5:242–47, especially pp. 246–47 (1885). The issue continues to occupy Peirce and plays an important role in the *Monist* series, especially in "Man's Glassy Essence," EP1:334–351 (1892).

190.28–192.16 depends on five principles . . . accelerated rate.] Compare this passage with an earlier version, which discusses only three principles, found in the last paragraph of R 909:55. Note especially the last sentence.

The essentials of the power of taking habits are these. First, over whatever path a nerve-cell has discharged itself, it is somewhat more likely to discharge itself a second time. If this rule had the absolute inviolability of a physical law, if it were that over the path along which a nerve-cell had once discharged itself, it must forever discharge itself, there would be no room for the gradual development of habit, and mediation or thirdness, which is the essence of mind, would have no place in the universe. But while mechanical laws have nothing to do with probabilities or tendencies, it is the slight tendency to act in a given way that is peculiarly characteristic of a physiological principle. I do not now stop to ask how this peculiarity is to be explained; but I wish to draw attention to its all-important consequences. The second essential part of the power of taking habits, is forgetfulness or the tendency of old habits, old tendencies to discharge energy over particular paths, to become obliterated. The third essential ingredient of the same power is the tendency to fatigue, which, as it seems to me, physiologists have sometimes failed correctly to define. There is, no doubt, a total exhaustion of a nerve-cell, when it refuses to respond to any stimulus whatever; but the primary and more important effect of fatigue is that a cell ceases to discharge itself in one channel, and begins to discharge itself with a certain energy in another. It necessarily results from the action of these three principles, that the actions of the nervous system are directed toward ends, which is the essential property of mind.

191.19 This is the central principle of habit;] In a draft page (R 909:54; cited above), Peirce refers to the Irish writer Joseph John Murphy's *Habit and Intelligence* (London: Macmillan & Co., 1869)—see also W4:39, 1879 (Peirce corresponded with Murphy in 1880–81, and sought unsuccessfully to invite him to give a course of lectures at Johns Hopkins in 1881). In vol. 1, p. 169, Murphy wrote:

All vital actions whatever come under the laws of habit: and none but vital actions do so. By vital actions I mean all those actions which organisms perform in virtue of being alive: and when I speak of actions, I include all functions, even those in which the organism is usually said to be passive, as in sensation.

The definitions of habit, and its primary law, is that all vital actions tend to repeat themselves; or, if they are not such as can repeat themselves, they tend to become easier on repetition.

195.7 Dr. Michael Foster (1879),] Sir Michael Foster (1836–1907), first professor of physiology at the University of Cambridge (1883–1903) and founding editor of the *Journal of Physiology* (1878–94). His *Textbook of Physiology* (1877) became a standard reference work; much of Peirce's information in this chapter derived from it. Peirce owned a copy of the third edition of 1879.

195.6–13 "We do not at present . . . modified protoplasm."] *A Textbook of Physiology*, p. 647 (4th. ed., 1883), which is the first page of the appendix entitled "On the Chemical Basis of the Animal Body."

195.19–20 I do find in the book . . . proteids.] Ibid., p. 727.

197.25 vis viva] CD 6768:

Vis viva, in older writers, the mass into the square of the velocity, or the measure of the mass multiplied by the square of that of the velocity: but recent writers frequently use the phrase to denote one half of the above quantity. The term was invented by Leibnitz. Also called *active* or *living force*.

27. *A Guess at the Riddle: Chapter VI*

199.1 A very remarkable feature in the Darwinian theory] Five distinct openings for this chapter survive. In the first two (R 909:43 and 39), which are incomplete fragments, Peirce belittles the biologists of his day for paying too much attention to inessential details while disregarding the method from which all modern sciences have sprung, the method of analysis, also called the "Newtonian philosophy." The following is a transcription of the second fragment (909:39):

The theory of natural selection strongly resembles the kinetical theory of gases, and both were no doubt suggested by statistical science. The general idea is that in many cases where it is perfectly hopeless to think of tracing out the behavior of individuals,—living beings in the one case, molecules in the other,—we find it easy to make out statistical regularities about them. The striking conception in the Darwinian idea is that chance, the mere action of chance, may lead to a determinate end, the adaptation of living forms to their environments. Unfortunately, the whole tendency of biological studies is to load down the mind with a mass of details, exceptions, and modifications, under which it staggers. But let it not be forgotten that after all modern science is but a following out of the Newtonian philosophy. Its great achievements are the triumphs of analysis; which consists in the diagrammatic representation of the main features of a problem, and the complete mastery of the ideas of such an outline view before undertaking to account for the modifications of it. Consider, for example, how the true explanation of the motions of the planets was reached. The first great step was taken by Hipparchus, or some earlier astronomer, who showed that the motion of every planet has two inequalities, the first or *inaequalitas soluta* being brought to light when we consider only the times and places at which the planet comes to opposition with the sun, or crosses the meridian at midnight, which facts show that the planet moves faster on one side and slower on the other side of its orbit, the second inequality or *inaequalitas alligata* appearing when we compare the place of the planet when it is not in opposition with what would be its place if it had moved without any other than the first inequality. The popular notion is that the ancient astronomy was simply false; the real truth was that it pursued so profoundly scientific a method of logic that the best modern studies of little understood periodical phenomena proceed by an exact imitation of the ancient system of epicycles, translated only from the language of geometry to that of algebra.

The third draft (909:56, 58, 51) puts a similar emphasis on the benefits of analysis, though more briefly as it shifts the main topic to biological evolution. Here is how it begins:

It will be interesting to trace out the connection between the theory of protoplasm proposed in the last chapter with the Darwinian theory on the origin of species. For this purpose it will be necessary to state the latter theory in its most abstract form. I remark that the biologists themselves have little sympathy for such an attempt to put their doctrine in an abstract undress. The whole tendency of their mental organization is toward detail; and they seem to think that there is error in analysis. But this must not deter us; we have to remember that the Newtonian philosophy, upon which all modern science is founded, consists in substituting for the infinitely complicated problems of nature, simpler ones resembling those as near as may be, which are within the grasp of the mind. As we are accustomed, in analytical mechanics, to leave out of account various considerations without which it would be utterly impossible to gain any conception of the reasons of the phenomena presented to our observation, so I propose to state what appears to be the most essential elements of the theory of natural selection in as diagrammatic a form as possible, neglecting altogether a multitude of circumstances which, however important they may be as modifying the application of the principle of natural selection, do not seem to form any part of that principle.

199.10 Suppose a million persons,] Peirce refers to the "million players" example on several other occasions, such as in "The Architecture of Theories" (EP1:289, 1891). For an early occurrence, see "Design and Chance" (W4:549–50 or EP1:220–21, 1883–84). A later version is found in the first Harvard Lecture of 1903, EP2:135–36, 138–39.

199.22–23 It is a . . . sixteenth throw] An earlier version of this chapter shows a fuller calculation table, with numbers for the first ten and the sixteenth throws. It has been reproduced with corrections in EP1:271. In the later version of the chapter here published, Peirce took the numbers from the last column of that earlier table, corresponding to the sixteenth throw. The first two and the fourth numbers have been corrected (Peirce's error occurred earlier in the table and was then propagated through to the last column).

200.11-12 survival of the fittest] This phrase was first coined by Herbert Spencer in his *Principles of Biology* ([1864], vol. 1, p. 444). In the 6th edition of *The Origin of Species* (1870), Darwin wrote that "the expression often used by Mr. Herbert

Spencer, of the Survival of the Fittest, is more accurate, and is sometimes more convenient" and he added the phrase to the title of his fourth chapter.

200.15 could go on tick] The phrase "to go on tick" means to buy on credit.

200.32–201.9 The diagram shows curves . . . two vertical lines.] No diagram has been found. The diagram below is a reconstruction made by Stephen Pollard, who bases it on the following reasoning. The probability p that a player will have m dollars after n rounds of the game (or throws) is:

$$p(n, m) = \frac{n!m}{2^n\left(\frac{n+m+1}{2}\right)!\left(\frac{n-m+1}{2}\right)!}.$$

If we graph the probability $p(n,m)$ against the dollar amount m for some fixed number of throws n, we obtain the distribution of non-zero wealth after n throws. But dollar amounts are not the best way to measure the utility of money, as Peirce recognized (1 dollar has more utility for a poor man than for a rich man), and it is thus better to represent the utility (x coordinate) by the logarithm of the dollar amount. Peirce's "moral wealth" differs from this utility only by a change of scale, through multiplication by the "smallest amount on which a man can live." Having transformed the x coordinates in this way ($\ln m$), we need to modify the y coordinates so that the area under a curve between two x coordinates measures "the number of players whose fortunes are intermediate between" the values of those coordinates. We thus need a function P such that, for any fixed n, the area under P between $\ln(a)$ and $\ln(b)$ is the same as the area under the probability function p between a and b. It is a theorem of calculus that

$$\int_{\ln(a)}^{\ln(b)} e^x f(e^x)dx = \int_a^b f(x)dx.$$

The value that needs to be associated with $\ln(m)$, for a given n, is therefore not $p(n,m)$, but $e^{\ln(m)}p(n,e^{\ln(m)})$, that is, $m{\cdot}p(n,m)$. This yields five successive curves (from highest to lowest) indicating the distribution of utility after 100, 400, 900, 1600, and 2500 throws. As the number of rounds increases, the curves widen and flatten, while their maxima move further and further to the right. The widening represents an increasing disparity between the richest and poorest players. This does not mean that the wealth is distributed ever more unequally. The game can be shown to produce an increasing degree of equality among richer and richer survivors as long as losers are somehow made to disappear.

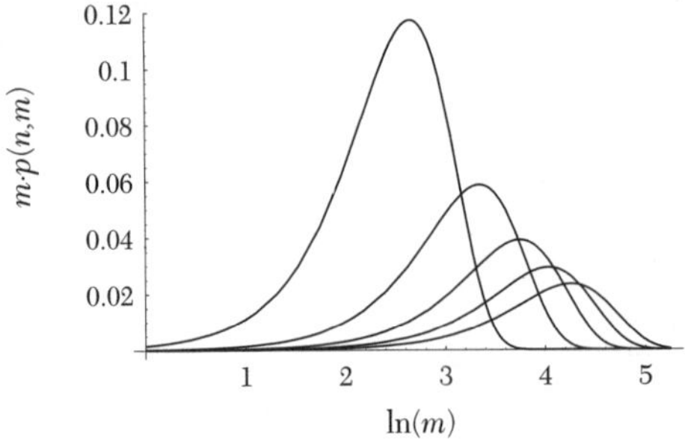

201.18 Quetelet] The Belgian statistician and astronomer Lambert Adolphe Jacques Quetelet (1796–1874), pioneered the application of statistics to human psychology and physiology, and he developed a theory of "the average man" in *Sur l'homme* (1835). Peirce may be referring to Quetelet's *Letters on the Application of Probabilities to the Moral and Political Sciences,* translated into English by O. G. Downes in 1849.

202.21–25 We see then . . . unfavorable characters.] Compare with what Peirce wrote in an earlier version (R 909:58, 51).

> The following elements are the essentials then of the action of natural selection. First, there is an element of chance or sporting,—individual variation is the phrase of Darwin,—connected with the occurrence of very high numbers which are sure to bring about every possible variety. Second, each individual inherits nearly the procreative power of its parents. (I will not say the mean procreative power of its two parents, because that would be wandering into considerations foreign to the present abstract and diagrammatic view of the subject. We are leaving out of account all that results from the circumstance that an individual has two parents, rather than one,—a circumstance as important for biology as you please but not belonging to that minimum of circumstances which are necessary to give the principle of natural selection standing room.) If this were not so, there would be nothing to develop any hereditary characters at all, any more than there would be any tendency in our surviving players to develop greater average wealth, if the money were all going to be given back after each bet to be distributed by chance, or if every player at each bet risked his whole pile against $1, or any other possible gain independent of what he has already. In other words, the players would not get rich if the wealth after a bet had no connection with the wealth before the bet. Third, there is the tendency of these individual variations themselves to become hereditary; only in order to become strongly so, there must be something or other to concentrate them. This concentrating agent in the case of natural selection and in that of our players, is the cutting off of all who fail to accommodate themselves to circumstances. In the case of a habit, it is somewhat different, being the fact that the irritation will always go on until the action removing it is performed. Such a cause may very likely have been that in the early stages of the development of the animal and vegetable kingdoms forms had very much more tendency to sport than they have now. So much so that no permanent species were formed until the course of variations accidentally led to those having stronger hereditary tendencies. This would be a cause going back of natural selection inasmuch as it would account for the development of the principle of heredity itself, which natural selection has to take for granted.

202.36–38 We have then . . . of development.] Peirce realizes that the three principles of evolution as stated do not match the one-two-three scheme satisfactorily, and he attributes this to the imperfect development of biology rather than to the imperfect development of his categorial theory. He insists on the promising heuristic power of his three categories: if biologists would pay attention to the categories, they could formulate better working hypotheses.

28. *A Guess at the Riddle: Chapter VII*

203.1–2 Metaphysical philosophy . . . the child of geometry.] See also W5:292–93 (1886), where Peirce showed how "metaphysics is an imitation of geometry."

203.2 Ionic] Thales of Miletus is said to have been the first to introduce geometry to Greece, and that he used it to determine the distance of ships at sea. Anaximander, in turn, is said to have introduced the gnomon and made known an outline of geometry. See also Peirce's extensive discussion of Thales's geometry in his 1892–93 "History of Science Lectures" (R 1277:17–34).

203.3–4 Eleatics] Early school of thought originating with Parmenides of Elea and including Zeno of Elea and Melissus of Samos. Of special interest for Peirce was Zeno, who wrote a treatise consisting of forty arguments, including the famous ones about motion, which rely on geometric concepts and were advanced to defend Parmenides's views.

203.5–6 Aristotle . . . potent conceptions.] Geometry, as the study of space, plays a central part in Aristotle's work. In *Posterior Analytics,* geometry provides a model for predication in the sciences; in *Physics,* the distinction of physics and mathematics leads Aristotle to further distinguish matter from form and to describe the four causes; in *Metaphysics,* geometry and mathematics provide the models for investigating being, distinguishing potentiality and actuality, etc.

203.9–11 the conviction . . . a similar science.] This is one of the convictions that Kant criticized in his *Critique:* see the preface to the second edition, especially Bx–xxii, and also A712/B740–A738/B766.

203.12–13 The unconditional surrender . . . of geometry] See also W4:544–46 (December 1883–January 1884), and W5:292–93 (1886).

203.14 Gauss,] Carl Friedrich Gauss (1777–1855), see ann. 64.21–22.

203.15–16 "there is no reason . . . two right angles."] An exact match for this quotation has not been found. Peirce implies that this was Gauss's stand on the issue of the Euclidean or non-Euclidean nature of physical space. However, Gauss is not known to have taken such a definite position on this question. Gauss was, nevertheless, well acquainted with mathematical instances of non-Euclidean triangles. An example is in his 8 November 1824 letter to F. A. Taurinus (*Werke*, vol. 8, 186–87), where he wrote that "the assumption that the sum of the three angles is smaller than 180 degrees leads to a peculiar geometry, quite distinct from the Euclidean, and which is quite consistent."

203.19–21 but experience . . . considerations.] In an earlier version Peirce added at this point: "Induction is utterly incompetent to establish any proposition at all as absolutely exact; and therefore if we are to rest on induction we cannot think that any general proposition is absolutely exact" (R 1600:10).

204.2–4 The first to go . . . inviolable law.] The criticism of determinism, or as it is also called necessitarianism, plays a prominent role in Peirce's 1892–93 *Monist* papers. See especially "The Doctrine of Necessity Examined" (EP1:298–311, April 1892) and "Reply to the Necessitarians: Rejoinder to Dr. Carus" (CP 6.588–618, July 1893). Although the argument does not return in the printed version of either, it does appear in one of the drafts of the rejoinder to Dr. Carus, where Peirce connects it with the doctrine of infallibilism (R 958:61, 1893).

204.11–12 Phoenix, . . . on Astronomy,"] John Phoenix was the pseudonym of George Horatio Derby (1823–1862), American humorist. The story is given in the first chapter of his humorous "Lectures on Astronomy" (1854), reprinted in his *Phoenixiana; or, Sketches and Burlesques* (New York: Appleton & Co., 1856), 57. The story of Joshua alludes to Jos. 10:12–13. See also CP 1.156 (1892).

204.27–28 Aristotle often lays . . . by chance.] *Physics,* 195b31–198a13.

204.28–31 Lucretius . . . reason at all.] Titus Lucretius Carus (c. 99–55 B.C.), Roman philosophical poet, disciple of Epicurus (and thereby of Democritus of Abdera), author of *De rerum natura,* in which he sought to abolish in an Epicurean vein the fear of gods and of death by demonstrating that the soul is mortal and the world not governed by gods but by mechanical laws. Lucretius expounded the doctrine of the "swerve" of atoms *(clinamen)*, with which Epicurus sought to undermine the determinism of the earlier atomists, in *De rerum natura* II, 216–93. Compare with what Peirce wrote in 1898:

> But there is *another* class of objectors for whom I have more respect. They are shocked at the atheism of Lucretius and his great master. They do not perceive that that which offends them is not the Firstness in the swerving atoms, because they themselves are just as much advocates of Firstness as the ancient Atomists were. But what they cannot accept is the attribution of this firstness to things perfectly dead and material. Now I am quite with them there. I think too that whatever is First is *ipso facto* sentient. If I make atoms swerve,—as I do,—I make them swerve but very very little, because I conceive they are not absolutely dead (CP 6.201, RLT 260–61).

204.37 Whewell's views . . . truer than Mill's;] William Whewell (1794–1866), English philosopher and mathematician. John Stuart Mill (1806–1873), English philosopher and economist. For Peirce's earlier views, see his 1865 "Lecture on the Theories of Whewell, Mill, and Comte" (W1:205–23), where he draws on Whewell's *Novum Organon Renovatum* (1858) and Mill's *A System of Logic.* See also Peirce's 1869 lecture on Whewell's logic of science (W2:337–45).

205.17 haecceities] In CD 2677 Peirce gives the following definition: "That element of existence which confers individuality upon a nature . . . so that it is in a particular place at a particular time; hereness and nowness." The term is introduced by Scotus in *Ordinatio*, bk. II, dist. 3, part 1, qu. 6 (*Opera omnia studio et cura Commissionis Scotisticae ad fidem codicum edita,* Vatican City: Typis Polyglottis Vaticanis, 1950–). English transl.: P. V. Spade, *Five Texts on the Medieval Problem of Universals* (Indianapolis: Hackett, 1994), 96–113.

206.5–8 But every fact . . . inexplicable.] Peirce began an earlier version of this chapter with a call for a natural history of the laws of nature (R 909:60):

> We need a Natural History of the laws of nature. For physical speculation is now in this condition; the mathematical development and physical testing of any hypothesis as to the ultimate or molecular constitution of matter, beyond what is now substantially demonstrated, will take at least fifty years, and the antecedent probability of any given hypothesis being correct, since the possible false hypotheses are indefinitely numerous, while there is but one true one, is practically infinitesimal. How long, at that rate, will it take to make any valuable advance in our knowledge. We made a great leap in dynamics, as soon as it began to be studied scientifically, because we were guided by our inborn instincts concerning force, which only needed to be corrected in the light of experiment, to yield the truth. In other words, we had sufficient innate tendency to believe that which was true, that if not the first, then the second or third idea which came into our heads, was the right one. So with astronomy, it so happened that the conic sections, nearly the easiest of curves for us to think about, were those in which the heavenly bodies really moved. But this guide of natural instinct seems to fail us in regard to the molecular constitution of matter; and we are embarrassed to know what sort of behaviour to expect from a molecule. Let us then treat the laws of nature as objects of natural history, and study them as we do animals and plants, comparing them, classing them, arranging them, in regard to their different characteristics. In this way, we may perhaps get, not to hope for a positive criterion, yet a hint or clue, to aid our guesses about the nature of atoms. The hypothesis which I am about to propose in this chapter is designed to form a nucleus for such a natural //history/study// of physical laws.

206.8–9 This is what Kant calls a regulative principle,] See for instance *Critique of the Pure Reason*, A179–80/B222–23, A509/B537.

206.9–10 The sole immediate purpose . . . things intelligible;] Compare with what Peirce wrote in the following incomplete fragment (R 1600:8–9).

> The chief philosophies of the universe that are now current trace things back to certain laws which are supported to be ultimate and inexplicable, such as the conservation of force. But I maintain that every philosophy is illogical that posits an ultimate and inexplicable fact. This is a variety of the absolutely incognizeable; and we can have no right to suppose that any thing whatever is absolutely unknowable. The only function of thought is to make things intelligible and it is a stultification of thought to think things to be unintelligible; and whatever is inexplicable and ultimate is unintelligible. It is true, that it may be that some things are unintelligible; perhaps it is not unlikely. But to lay your finger on any one and say I believe this to be an ultimate and inexplicable fact, is as unwarrantable as it would be,—because we hold no doubt to many erroneous opinions,—to pick out one and say this is my opinion but I think it is erroneous. A given problem may be insoluble, but if we are to think about it at all, since the only use of reason is to solve problems, the only consistent course is to hope it will be found soluble, and to proceed upon that hope; and not to think about it, which thinking really consists in an attempt to understand it, and yet think that the right mode of understanding it is to be to understand it as not understandable. Abstain by all means from inquiring how it happens that energy is always conserved, if you do not find any interest in the problem; but do not ask the question and seek to put yourself off with the ridiculous answer that the question is irresolvable. Your mind was given you to resolve questions; and in point of fact you cannot use it otherwise. To say that a fact is ultimate and inexplicable is an attempt to give an account of it, but it is an absurd and self-stultifying attempt. It is as though a man having arms in his hand to resist an enemy, should become frightened and use his arms to commit suicide to prevent being killed by the enemy.
>
> If the reader goes with me so far, and will allow that we are to admit that any given question, whose answer can make any conceivable practical or sensible difference, must always be assumed to be answerable if we had sufficient time to investigate it, then I think that he must also go a step further.

Peirce repeats this in nearly the same words in a second draft (R 909:60, R 1600:11, 10), where he added:

> Does the reader admit the truth of this principle of hope? If not, I fear we must part company here; but if he does, then he will allow that we must seek for a philosophy of the universe according to which it shall always be possible to find an explanation for every phenomenon for which an explanation can be asked. Every regular phenomenon is of this kind; and we are entitled to ask for an explanation for Law itself.

206.28–29 Law or regularity itself.] In CD 3375 Peirce defines law in terms of regularity, catering to both his own view and the one he here opposes:

> A proposition which expresses the constant or regular order of certain phenomena, or the constant mode of action of a force; a general formula or rule to which all things, or all things or phenomena within the limits of a certain class or group, conform, precisely and without exception; a rule to which events really tend to conform.

206n.1 Eckius] Johann Eck, original name Johann Maier (1486–1543), German theologian and Martin Luther's principal Roman Catholic opponent. The work referred to is his *In summulas Petri Hispani extemporaria et succincta explanatio; sed succosa explanatio* (1516).

207.13–14 But we pay . . . us.] In an earlier version (R 1600:11) Peirce wrote:

> The only kind of phenomenon which does not required to be explained is mere irregularity. For example, when in the kinetical theory of gases we are told that the reason why gases press their enveloping vessels equally in all directions is that the molecules move irregularly, it is unreasonable to ask why they should move irregularly. In like manner, our explanations of the universe cannot stop or pause, until we get some notion of how regularity can emerge from irregularity.

Later, in 1898, he wrote: "fortuitous distribution, that is, utter irregularity, is the only thing which it is legitimate to explain by the absence of any reason to the contrary" (CP 7.521, RLT 211).

209.14 Our conceptions of the first stages of the development,] Compare with Peirce's later cosmological accounts, such as CP 6.215–19 (Dec. 1897) and CP 6.200 (RLT 260), 1898.

29. *Trichotomic*

211.1 three-fold divisions.] See "One, Two, Three," W5:294 (1886).

211.2 the conceptions of 1st, 2nd, 3rd.] See sel. 23 and related annotations for a corresponding treatment of the categories and their degeneracies.

211.22 Thirdness has . . . of degeneracy.] The surviving typed sheet (R 1600:7) containing a shorter variant of this document includes the following:

> Thirdness may also be of a degenerate type, and that in two different degrees, and in more than one mode in each degree. The first degree of degeneracy is where though there is no real thirdness, there is real secondness; the second degree is where there is not even any real secondness.

212.19 a mental association.] In R 1600:7 this paragraph continues thus:

> Such is every conventional sign, and every mode of expression so far as it depends on the force of association. If the thirdness is degenerated [*sic*] in the first degree, the sign has a real dynamical relation with the object on the one hand and a real dynamical connection with the mind on the other hand, and thus enables the object to act on the mind. As I am walking quietly on a dark night, a man suddenly jumps out of a corner with an exclamation of "Bo!" and thus brings his presence home to me in a particularly forcible way; so agitating music at a thrilling crisis of a melodrama acts upon the audience in a sort of psycho-physical way quite independent of any association. If the thirdness is degenerate in the second degree, the sign has no real dynamical connection with its object, but only has a resemblance, or relation of reason, with it. In this case, the mind forgets the distinction between the sign and the thing represented, and loses sight of reality altogether. Theatrical representation is in the main of this kind.

212.36–37 If the thirdness is degenerate in the second degree,] The original typescript mistakenly has "third" for "second." Compare the distinction between the first and the second order of degeneracy of thirdness with the discussion of thirdness degenerate in the second degree in sel. 23, 179.6–19, and "Types of Third Degenerate in the Second Degree" in W5:252–53 (1885).

213.7–12 the second mode of representation . . . first mode of representation unartistic.] Peirce's use of ordinals may be somewhat confusing: as used here in the "first," "second," and "third" modes of representation, they are not categorial. The first mode is related to genuine thirdness, the second to thirdness degenerate in the first degree (with admixture of secondness), and the third to thirdness degenerate in the second degree (with admixture of firstness).

213.12–13 Mr. MacKaye . . . language.] James Morrison Steele MacKaye (1842–1894), New York playwright, actor, inventor in theatrical scene design, boyhood friend of William James, and (with his wife Mary) a friend of the Peirces. Juliette Peirce started taking acting lessons with him in late 1886. Apparently "Trichotomic" was inspired by MacKaye's theory of dramatic expression. MacKaye was the only American pupil of the French acting, singing, and aesthetics teacher, François Delsarte, and was the principal person responsible for bringing the Delsarte System of Aesthetics (Delsartism) to the U.S. MacKaye opened the Madison Square Theatre in 1879, where his most successful melodrama, "Hazel Kirke," was presented in 1880. He then took over the Lyceum where he established the first school of acting in New York (later known as the American Academy of Dramatic Art). This is probably where Juliette took her lessons.

213.36 CONSCIOUSNESS . . .] In R 1600:6 this paragraph runs as follows:

> Consciousness has three elements, the Singular, Dual, and Plural consciousness. Singular consciousness is that to which whatever is present for a minute is so only by being present for every second of that minute, and whatever is present for a second is so only by being present for every fraction of that second. This is the consciousness of the present, or immediate consciousness, or the element of pure feeling in the flow of life. It is present only while it is present, and when it is past it is utterly gone as such. Dual consciousness, or consciousness of Other, is the vivid lively sense of action and reaction, as when something hits me or I get hit; this embraces not only Will, but also an important element of Sense. Plural or true synthetic consciousness is the consciousness of a passage from one state to another; it is experience, or the sense of learning. This is the characteristic element in cognition.

214.4 or in Kant's phrase its matter.] *Critique of Pure Reason*, A20/B34.

215.1 Dual consciousness . . .] In R 1600:6 this paragraph runs thus:

> Dual consciousness is either undegenerate or degenerate. Undegenerate dual consciousness is the sense of a real other; degenerate dual consciousness is the consciousness of self regarded as an other or object; thus we have External volition and sense and Internal volition and sense, or self-control and self-consciousness. Synthetic consciousness is either undegenerate, or degenerate in the 1st or the 2nd degree.

30. *Pendulum Observations at Fort Conger*

216.1 the Chief Signal Officer] General William Babcock Hazen (1830–1887) was in charge of organizing the Greely expedition. In a letter of 30 November 1888, however, Greely wrote to Peirce (RL 174:7):

> The statement in the opening line of your report is incorrect. The Chief Signal Officer did not apply to the Superintendent, but the Superintendent applied to me, asking if I would make the observations, and, as I then understood, this application was made owing to your interest and zeal in the matter.

216.1–2 Superintendent of . . . Survey] Carlile P. Patterson (see ann. 216.4).

216.3 Lieutenant Greely] Adolphus Washington Greely (1844–1935), commander of the twenty-five men expedition that was sent by the U.S. Army to establish a metereological station at Lady Franklin Bay. For Greely's account of the expedition see his *Three Years of Arctic Service: An Account of the Lady Franklin Bay Expedition of 1881–84, and the Attainment of the Farthest North* (New York: C. Scribner's Sons, 1886), and his *Report on the Proceedings of the United States*

Expedition to Lady Franklin Bay, Grinnell Land (2 vols., New York: Government Printing Office, 1888), of which the current selection is appendix 141.

216.4 Lady Franklin Bay] At Lady Franklin Bay, which is on the eastern shore of Ellesmere Island, Greely established his base camp, Fort Conger.

216.4 Carlile P. Patterson] Carlile Pollock Patterson (1816–1881), superintendent of the U.S. Coast and Geodetic Survey from 1874 until his death in 1881.

216.7–8 that he understood . . . scientific work] With this comment, and the comment in the next sentence on hampering scientific inquiry by excessive bureaucratic regulations, Peirce shows discontent with the changes that have been taking place in the Coast Survey under Superintendent F. M. Thorn, who was a politician, not a scientist.

216.12–13 series of Peirce Pendulums] During 1881–82 four invariable, reversible pendulums, called Peirce Nos. 1, 2, 3, 4, were constructed at the Office of the Coast and Geodetic Survey after an original design of Peirce. Nos. 1, 2, and 4, were meter pendulums; No 3 was a yard pendulum. For a description of the Peirce pendulum, see Victor F. Lenzen and Robert P. Multhauf, "Development of Gravity Pendulums in the 19th Century," *United States National Museum Bulletin* 240 (Washington: Smithsonian Institution, 1965), 301–48; esp. 327–31. See also W4, introduction, pp. xxx–xxxi.

216.13 will be elsewhere described] A full description of the Peirce pendulums and the theory behind their development is given in the opening narrative of sel. 36.

216.14–15 invariable reversible pendulums] In a 24 February 1886 letter to Thorn (NARG 23/22), Peirce explained:

> We have been using for several years, a kind of pendulum designed by me and known as the "Peirce" pendulums. There has been much controversy as to whether determinations of gravity ought to be made with *invariable* or with *reversible* pendulums. Our method consists in using pendulums which are at once *reversible and invariable.*

216.19 Mr. E. Israel] Sergeant Edward Israel (d. 1884), graduate in astronomy from the University of Michigan at Ann Arbor, was assigned to the Greely expedition along with other members of the U.S. Army Signal Corps. See also ann. 218.8.

216.19 to be instructed . . . the instrument] In a 8 Sept. 1881 letter to Superintendent Hilgard, Peirce explained: "The enclosed paper is a copy of the written instructions given by me to Mr. Israel and Lieut. Greely. They were of course supplemented by careful training of Mr. Israel in all the details of the operations." The paper referred to was probably the document transcribed below, of which two different amanuensis copies exist among the Greely expedition papers (NARG 27 entry 138 NC 3). Both amanuenses were found only after publication of Volume 4, and thus were not included in its Chronological List. Neither is in Peirce's hand, and one is a transcription of the other. For Greely's comments on Peirce's instruction see 244.18–19 with ann.

> General Instructions for Observing Oscillating Pendulums.
>
> The point requiring the greatest attention of all is the temperature. The temperature of the pendulum is to be ascertained to a fraction of a Fahrenheit degree throughout the observations. As no thermometer can be attached to the pendulum, it follows that the temperature of the room in which the observations are made must be extremely constant. Should this not be the case, the temperature of two thermometers—one at the top, and the other at the bottom of the pendulum—would not indicate the temperature of the pen-

dulum itself, which requires a long time to take the temperature. It will probably be necessary therefore to seize those opportunities on which during the winter the temperature happens to remain constant for a long time. Should the temperature be erroneously determined, it will be impossible to detect the error, and on this account especially great pains must be taken.

Great solidity of the pendulum-support is absolutely essential. When a horizontal force of one kilogram applied to the middle of the point of support of the knife-edge produces a deflection of 1/30 mm, it is ascertained that with the Repsold's Reversible Pendulum, an error of no less than 1/4 mm in the deduced length of the Seconds Pendulum was due to this cause alone. For the pendulum transmitted, this correction would be considerably larger. The support ought to be so stiff that the deflection produced as above should not exceed 1/200 mm. The piers have to be solidly built of brick, laid with Portland cement, and connected at the top by a 2^{in} plank. These piers should be constructed in the Summer, and the observations should be made in Winter, when the piers will be very solid, and when time can be obtained. The distance between the piers on the inside should be half a metre. The flexure of the piers should be measured under the circumstances under which the experiments have been made. This is done by passing a cord carrying the end of it to the middle point of the tongue upon which the pendulum rests, in such a way as to give a horizontal strain parallel to the motion of the pendulum. A long wooden tongue is then to be attached to the tongue upon which the pendulum rests—its general direction being perpendicular to the plane of the motion of the pendulum, that is, parallel to the knife-edges. At the end of this wooden tongue, which may be of any convenient but accurately measured length, is to be attached a micrometer scale, the plane of which is in the plane of motion of the pendulum, and the direction of measurement of which is parallel to the direction of measurement of the pendulum. A microscope carrying a filar micrometer is then set up so as to observe on this scale, and the kilogram weight is to be alternately taken off and put on, so that its effect in producing flexure can be measured. The micrometer scale is to be mounted in two separate positions—one preferably forward, and the other back of the pendulum-support. By means of an arithmetical proportion we shall then obtain from the flexure at the end of the tongue in the two positions the flexure at the middle of the knife-edge.

In setting up the pendulum, the brass head upon which the pendulum rests will first be attached to the 2^{in} plank, either by plaster of Paris or by some other cement, or preferably, by bolts with leaden washers. The leaden washers have the convenience of enabling us to level the plane upon which the pendulum rests by tightening up the bolts, so as more or less to compress the washers. The pendulum can be lifted off of its support so as to rest in the brass Ys. When the pendulum is first put on, these Ys must of course be raised, so that the knife comes down into them, and care must be taken to see that there is no rubbing, either forward or back. It is needless to say, that the greatest pains must be used in handling the pendulum, as the smallest accident might be serious.

The method of observing the pendulum has been fully studied by Mr. Israel. The arc of oscillation had best be neither greater than $25{:}1000^{ths}$ nor less than $5{:}1000^{ths}$ of the radius. Extreme accuracy in the observations of amplitude of oscillation is not essential. The difficulty lies much more in the observation of the transits of the pendulum. It is recommended that Mr. Israel should practice further in making this sort of observations. An equal number of transits have to be observed from left to right, and right to left. The point from which they are observed is the zero of the scale, and this is done by placing a wire of the telescope in coincidence with the zero line of the scale. The pendulum is to be experimented with on each day, both with heavy end up, and heavy end down. The oscillation with heavy end down should occupy at least an hour and a half, and that with heavy end up about half an hour. It is recommended that two experiments be made each day with heavy end up. If the whole operation is doubled, so as to give four experiments with heavy end up, and two with heavy end down, with good time observations at the beginning and end of the whole series, so much the better. All the chronometers should be compared about the time of making time observations, and also at the beginning and end of the pendulum experiments. The time should be so observed that the probable error of determination does not exceed one-tenth of a second. After eight different days observations have been obtained resting upon different sets of time observations the knife-edges should be taken out and interchanged. The thumbscrews should then be loosened while the pendulum is in horizontal position, and the knives slipped out carefully and immediately interchanged. The thumbscrews should then be tightened up—as tight as the fingers can readily tighten them. In performing this operation the greatest care must be used that no snow, or any other substance gets between the steel and the brass upon which it bears. After this operation is concluded eight more nights oscillations should be obtained. The pendulum should then be put in its box, soldered up, and returned to Washington at the first opportunity. Great care has been used here to have the pendulum quite dry, and the air in the pendulum-box also quite dry at the moment of packing. It is expected that the box will be opened at a low temperature, when there will be little or no moisture in the air; and should the observations terminate the first winter, no particular precautions need be used in packing it up, since the air will have been dry all the time. On the other hand, should it be necessary to make observations on two winters, the box had better be sealed up during the summer to keep it dry. The pendulum sent is intended to be an invariable one, and the observations when received will be reduced upon that principle. But should the principle of invariability fail owing to any injury which the pendulum may receive, it is expected that the observation will still be valuable, on account of its being a reversible pendulum.

In transmitting the records to the office, they should be accompanied by the record of barometric pressure. It is highly desirable that the chronograph sheets should be read off as soon after the observations are made as possible. Should this not be done, however, they can be sent to the office in a tin box, and all the necessary computations will be made here.

If, as we hope, these important pendulum observations should be successful, the gentlemen concerned in making them will deserve great credit, on account of the unusual difficulties which must attend them, and also on account of the great need that there is of the results to be obtained.

216.21–22 preliminary operations in Washington] In a 27 October 1886 letter to Thorn (NARG 23/22), Peirce explained:

The pendulum was oscillated under my direction in June 1881, by Messrs. Farquhar and Israel . . . This work was done in the C. S. Office, Room No. 6, and Professor Hilgard in an oblivious moment, in my absence, allowed Lieutenant Very to take down the pier. It was ascertained that the pier had a peculiar kind of flexure, owing partly to the bad foundation, and partly to the singular sandstone of which it was built; and all things considered, I doubt whether the work done in June 1881 is of any value.

See also ann. 217.9–10 for Farquhar's discussion of this.

217.6–9 Unfortunately . . . plank.] As is clear from his 27 October 1886 letter to Thorn (see ann. 216.21–22), Peirce is referring to Lieutenant S. W. Very, who used a Peirce pendulum to measure gravity in Patagonia in 1882 (*Coast Survey Report for 1890*, 652), and who may have taken the stone cap to use as a support for the pendulum head at the South American station.

217.9–10 The result . . . no value.] Peirce hoped initially that the preliminary swingings of the pendulum at the Smithsonian might have some long-range value. His April 1887 submission of the report added, "although some result may possibly be deduced from them hereafter." In "On the Pendulum Observations at Fort Conger" which is included in the same appendix, Henry Farquhar (identified at ann. 220.4), commented (716):

The failure, probably complete, of the observations in room 6 of this building is correctly ascribed to the absence of a reliable determination of the flexure of the support. That the deficiency has been irremediable since the removal of the cap-stone is not denied, though, as the flexure must be largely due to the unfortunate situation of the piers over a brick archway, even this is doubtful. But when it is remembered that in such researches large corrections are usually, especially where their exact determination is difficult, variable corrections, that in this case the yielding is described as having been of such a character as would naturally be produced by a cause like imperfectly-hardened mortar under the recently erected piers, and that it might have become essentially changed by a settling of the archway beneath, an accurate measurement of the flexure at the time of the observations is seen to have been the chief desideratum, and the maintenance of this confessedly unreliable stand to have been of far less importance. Results from a later swinging on the same support would not improbably have been misleading. That observations of flexure were not prevented by lack of time, notwithstanding Professor Peirce's illness at the most unfortunate point, is clear, for the stone was removed in August or September, 1882, the pendulum having been swung from it in June, 1881. And as if to fix the responsibility beyond possible question, Mr. Peirce in this report calls especial attention to the liberal discretion allowed him by Mr. Patterson, who was Superintendent until August, 1881. It is certain that Superintendent Hilgard would not have permitted the removal of the stone had not Mr. Peirce failed to impress upon him the importance of retaining it, or had it been given him to understand that observations essential to the availability of work done months before were yet unmade. The simple truth I believe to be, that because of the want of time for proper preparations, the unsuitability of the place, and the newness of the observer, Mr. Peirce expected no valuable results at the time from the swingings in room 6, and attached no such importance to them as he now appears to attach.

217.13 German Normal Meter] For the precise measuments of length required for absolute determinations of gravity, Peirce acquired a line meter from the German Imperial Standards Office in Berlin. For a description of Standard No. 49, see Victor F. Lenzen, "The Contributions of Charles S. Peirce to Metrology," *Proceedings of the American Philosophical Society* 109 (1965): 29–46.

217.22 Fort Conger] See ann 216.4.

217.27 The directions accompanying the instrument] See ann. 216.19.

217.33–34 This programme was faithfully carried out] In *Three Years of Arctic Service*, Greely gave the following account (vol. I, p. 180):

the severe cold made the work of the most trying character to our astronomer, Sergeant Israel. He made the observations on the 14th, in temperatures varying from –54° (–47.8° C.) to –56° (–48.8° C.). A few days later, being exposed for a long time to a temperature of –48° (–44.4° C.) in the open observatory, he froze superficially one of his feet. Apart from this the pendulum experiments, though tedious, and involving exposure and suffering, were most fortunately and successfully conducted.

217.34–218.3 but after . . . can be used] Peirce worked for over a year to account for a significant change in the period of oscillation for swingings conducted after the interchange of knives: on average, the pendulum beat slightly longer seconds with the heavy end down than it did with the heavy end up (see also ann. 217.36–218.1). At the time of his April 1887 submission of the report, Peirce was in the midst of an intense and sometimes heated correspondence with Coast Survey colleagues (and with General Greely himself) over his own contention that the anomalous readings were due to some kind of damage to the pendulum. Peirce's eventual decision was to use only swingings made after the interchange of knives, as these could be corroborated with future experiments with the pendulum (see ann. 222.25–27). Farquhar's supplementary report concurs with Peirce's decision but explains how the change in the pendulum may have been due to an accidental loosening of the heavy-end knife edge (718):

One explanation remains: That there was a real difference in the length of the pendulum, as swung before and after the interchange. The mean periods in the two positions were for temperature –20° F. and pressure 29.75^{in} (using the coefficient .00000489):

	s.	s.
First days	T_d = 1.0045145±10	T_u = 1.0039287±47
Last days	T_d = 1.0044656±20	T_u = 1.0039009±29
Differences	.0000489±22	.0000278±55
Differences, calculated . . .	.0000560	.0001672

The distance of edge 9 from its bearing-plane, as measured by Dr. J. J. Clark in January, 1887, is 504.0$^{\mu}$, and that of edge 10 is 670.6$^{\mu}$; difference, 166.6$^{\mu}$. Hence is calculated the theoretical decrease in period, entered above; nearly the observed amount for heavy end down and very different for heavy end up. It seems highly probable, therefore, that the edge at the heavy end was farther from the center of mass at the earlier observations than at the later. This edge, that is to say, was loose, so as to have a play of an eighth of a millimeter on the average until the transposition was made, and was properly tightened after it. Inspection of the earlier heavy-end-up corrected periods plainly suggests (when the lower expansion-coefficient is used more plainly yet) that the play of this edge may have increased progressively, as they show a pretty steady diminution. . . .

A loosening of the heavy-end edge, after the measures made in 1881, might have taken place in one of several conceivable ways. The observer, whose zeal and industry surpassed his experience, could have turned one of the screws holding this edge in place, about the beginning of the experiments, mistaking it for a similar screw by which the pendulum is raised or lowered. An artisan, in packing the instrument, could accidentally have touched the screw. Dirt of some kind could have remained on one of the brass slides holding the edge in place (a recent examination shows that the slide at the name end of the heavy edge-holder is considerably stained with rust, verdigris, etc., over its inner surface, which may be a trace of it) and this dirt not have been squeezed out till after the measures of length (June 11 to 14, 1881, before the pendulum had been swung even in Washington), but become so, gradually perhaps, before the edges were transposed. Without committing ourselves to any one of these possible explanations, we must admit that the hypothesis of a slight loosening of one edge during the first swings is the only one yet suggested that seems to meet the facts.

217.36–218.1 This seems to . . . the pendulum.] For Greely's reply see 243.6–12. See also sel. 36, 280.25–28. At the conclusion of a typescript (1887.28) prepared for the report Peirce gave the following account (R 1076:11–12):

On the first eight days of the swingings at Fort Conger, before the interchange of the knives, the temperature being –13° F., the period of oscillation of an equivalent simple pendulum, uncorrected for flexure, but corrected to bring the pendulum to the length it had after the interchange of knives (on the supposition that the change of length observed in Washington to have taken place during the journey happened at the time of the interchange of knives), was, according to the observations, $1\overset{\text{s}}{.}0048432$. After the interchange, on the following eight days, the temperature being –23° F., the same quantity appears as only $1\overset{\text{s}}{.}0047795$. The discrepancy cannot be attributed to a change of the distance between the knife-edges, for according to the observations at Washington, there was no material change of length during the whole journey. It cannot be attributed to a permanent damage of a knife, because the pendulum after its return gave an excellent value for the gravity at Washington. It might possibly be attributed to a large improvement in the rigidity of the supporting piers, but General Greely does not think that possible. It seems to me most probably due to some frost having been deposited on one or both knives at the time of their interchange. Whatever the cause may be, however, we shall probably ascertain which value to prefer, when we shall have determined by experiment the effect of an interchange of knives upon the periods in the two positions. These experiments should be conducted at extremely low temperatures, so as to reproduce the same conditions, as nearly as possible.

218.4–6 the head . . . was left behind] See 243.13–15 and 244.37.

218.6–7 The pendulum itself was courageously brought away] In his report in the first volume of the *Proceedings*, Greely elaborated (61):

The pendulum being a heavy and cumbersome instrument, I informed the men that while the saving of it was much to be desired, from the value of subsequent comparative observations, yet it could not weigh against the chances of any man's life, and that whenever any one thought his life endangered by hauling it or anyone insisted on its abandonment I would do so. To the credit of the party no man ever hinted at the abandonment, and most of them were outspoken for its retention to the last.

218.8 the survivors . . . Israel was not one] As supply and relief ships failed to reach the base camp in 1882 and in 1883, Greely and his men decided in August of 1883 to try to make their way south by boat. They reached Cape Sabine, where they were stranded. With dwindling provisions they wintered there. When relief finally arrived on 23 June 1884, only Greely and six of his twenty-four man party were still alive. Sergeant Israel had died of starvation on May 27.

218.9–11 It seems almost inconceivable . . . intact.] See 243.29–36 and 245.4–6.

218.11–12 The chronometer . . . to pieces.] In *Three Years of Arctic Service*, Greely wrote (vol. I, p. 130):

In default of a break-circuit chronometer, for use with the chronograph in time observations, Professor Pierce [*sic*] kindly loaned his own chronometer, which was used in the pendulum work. As a recognition of this action, I felt it incumbent on me to see that the instrument was returned, and so, in all the dark days of our retreat, that chronometer was carefully looked after, and has since been delivered to Professor Pierce.

In a letter of 10 April 1888, to Superintendent F. M. Thorn, Peirce described the damage to the chronometer as follows (NARG 23–22):

A day or two before Lieut. (now Genl.) Greely sailed for Lady Franklin Bay, he found himself in sudden straits for want of a breakcircuit chronometer. By direction of the Acting Superintendent, I let him take Frodsham 2490. When he came back he surrendered it in a terrible state. It was then put in running order and regulated to mean time. I used it at Ann Arbor; but it was found to go very irregularly, and it is probable that some of the spindles or other parts have been slightly bent in a way impossible to detect or remedy and to cause irregular going.

218.14 $^{1}/_{30000}$] Peirce appears to have used the fractional ratio as an approximation of the increase in the length of the pendulum. The actual increase is closer to a value of $^{1}/_{31100}$, according to the measurements summarized at 218.15–17.

218.17 429.3 microns] This value represents the number of microns by which the pendulum exceeded the length of the meter standard (after corrections) as expressed at 240(c7).5. The actual value should be 439.3 microns, unless there is an error in one or more of the correction factors in the table. If the actual value is 439.3, then the fractional variation in pre- and post-expedition length measurements expressed at 218.14 should read $^{1}/_{23700}$. Since the calculations underlying the correction factors have not been recovered, the pendulum length value as expressed in the copy-text is retained.

218.17–18 The pendulum was oscillated at the Smithsonian] To remedy the removal of the piers in Room No. 6, the pendulum was compared with the other Peirce pendulums, as Peirce explained in a 27 October 1886 letter to Thorn:

> I bestowed much care on the comparison of the pendulum with the other Peirce pendulums. These operations, which were conducted at the Smithsonian by Mr. W. B. Fairfield and myself, lasted almost continuously from 1884 December 19 to 1885 February 18, all the Peirce pendulums being oscillated.

218.36–37 lost from 10 to 15 grammes] For Greely's comments, see 243.23–36. In an earlier hectograph of the report (1887.18), Peirce presented the issue as follows:

> Now, on the return of the pendulum it was weighed and found near 10436 grams, so that it must certainly have lost at least fifteen grams upon the journey from Fort Conger to Camp *[Clay]*, unless we are to suppose some great error had been committed in the weighing. Moreover, we find that at Fort Conger, during the last eight days swingings, the difference in time of the oscillation of the pendulum in its two positions was $0^{s}.0005689$, this was at about –30° C. On the return of the pendulum to Washington, the same difference was found to be $0^{s}.0007514$ at + 20° C. The difference of temperature would account for about two thirds of this discrepancy; the rest must have been due to a change in the pendulum, unless it can be accounted for by the difference of the flexure of the supports. On the whole, then, we seem to have positive evidence that some piece of metal of considerable size came away from the pendulum. I was extremely desirous of making further experiments upon the pendulum before the knives were removed, but contrary to my earnest representations, and without my knowledge, they were taken out of the pendulum in January 1887; and doubtless sustained some injuries at that time. At any rate, the invariability of the pendulum has been destroyed; and it will be fortunate if the whole value of the magnificent work done by Greely and his party, in the determination of gravity and the figure of the earth, does not turn out to have been brought to naught in a single day, by an act which might well be called criminal, were officials considered bound to exercise intelligence.

218.37–220.1 Camp Clay] The encampment at Cape Sabine, named after Henri Clay who wrote an article for the *Louisville Courier* predicting the disaster awaiting the expedition, and urging that Cape Sabine be provisioned. A copy of this article was included among the provisions brought to Cape Sabine which allowed the expedition to survive the winter (see ann. 218.8).

220.1–8 The centre . . . a change] In his supplementary report Farquhar commented (716):

> The loss to the service from the necessity of using for the Peirce pendulums a center-of-mass apparatus adapted to a smaller stem Professor Peirce slightly overrates. In conse-

quence of the forced removal of parts of the apparatus the measure is rendered more difficult with the new pendulums; but as two independent determinations of the distance h_u, made last January, gave (when reduced to edge 9 at heavy end) 25.140^{cm} and 25.135^{cm}, it is improbable that the uncertainty of the result can be so great as to admit the earlier value, 25.105^{cm}, as an equally exact observation of the same quantity. I have not examined the 1881 observations with care, but I believe them to have been less complete than those of 1887.

220.4 Mr. Farquhar] Henry Farquhar, Coast Survey employee who assisted Peirce in his *Photometric Researches* and in pendulum research; see W4:116 (1879) and W5:8 (1884). Farquhar wrote a report discussing the charges made by Peirce, which was added to the appendix in which Peirce's report appeared.

221.3–6 Still . . . consequences] The greatest obstacle Peirce encountered in reducing the Arctic gravity data involved the 47° C difference in temperature between the calibration station in the Smithsonian and the Arctic field station at Fort Conger. The initial submission (1887.21) identifies the first- and second-order atmospheric effects on such pendulum operations, and also speculates about "other atmospheric effects, not yet taken into account in reducing pendulum operations." In rewriting the report, Peirce came to the conclusion that these factors were, in effect, cancelled out "as long as the pendulum is treated as reversible." This conclusion allowed him to remove the lengthy tables of atmospheric effects, which appeared in the initial submission (1887.21), the subsequent typescript (1887.28), and the uncorrected first galleys (1887.3) between pages 236 and 237. In 1889, Peirce prepared a more fully developed form of the atmospheric notations and tables for the 1889 Gravity Report (sel. 36).

221.10 U.S.C.S.—C.S.P.—1878—B] As measurements are made at different temperatures, the coefficients of expansion of the pendulum and of the meter scales need to be determined. To establish this the pendulum meter, which is assumed to have the same coefficient as the pendulum, was compared at different temperatures with meter No. 49. To determine the coefficient of expansion of No. 49 itself, Peirce compared it with one of two meters he had made for the purpose, which are marked U.S.C.S.—C.S.P.—1878—A and U.S.C.S.—C.S.P.—1878—B respectively (also called Meter A and Meter B). See also ann. 350.19–20, and W4:120ff. (1879). For a description of the comparison of meter bars and the use of a comparator, see Victor F. Lenzen, "The Contributions of Charles S. Peirce to Metrology" (cited at ann. 217.13), pp. 34ff.

221.13–14 "Measurements . . . at Initial Stations."] W4:79–145 (1879).

221.15–16 D. C. Chapman] Coast Survey mechanician; see also ann. 286.28–29.

221.31–222.8 The coefficient 18.24^{μ} . . . 17.61] In his supplementary report Farquhar provided the following comment, reemphasizing his rival hypothesis of a loose knife-edge (719):

> The probability of a loose knife-edge is the real justification of the course properly followed by Mr. Peirce in depending on the latter half of the observations alone for a value of gravity. One correction to his final result appears, however, to be needed: An increase of the expansion allowance by 0.0000074^{s}. He states that his expansion "coefficient 18.24^{μ} is for the temperature of 24.6° C.," apparently because the comparisons between Pendulum No. 1 and Meter B were made about that temperature. But the observations of Meter A, on which the adopted coefficient for B depends, were made (1876 Report, page 274) about 8° C.; taking

this as the temperature at which the coefficient 18.24^{μ} holds good, we have as the value for −7.7° C. 17.93^{μ}.

221.32 Fizeau] Armand Hippolyte Louis Fizeau (1819–1896), French physicist. On page 1129 of the paper referred to, Fizeau gives an expansion coefficient for yellow brass of 18.59 millionths at 40° C with a variation of 1.96 millionth per 100° C. This gives an expansion coefficient at 24.6° C of 18.29 millionths (rounded up).

222.17 Repsold pendulums] For a detailed description of this type of pendulum and Peirce's involvement with it, see Lenzen and Multhauf, "Development of Gravity Pendulums in the 19th Century" (op. cit.), 320–27.

222.25 Minneapolis] Peirce suggested this location to examine the influence of low temperatures on the pendulum, so as to better evaluate the results obtained on the Arctic expedition. Reacting to the Survey's refusal to honor his requests for further cold-weather observations, Peirce ended the first draft of his report with the following attack on the Coast Survey (1887.18):

> Consequently, it would be utterly impossible, in the present state of our knowledge, to make the slightest use of Greely's observations to determine the force of gravity at Fort Conger. For the error due to erroneous expansion through 40° C might easily, and indeed probably would surpass the error of the general formula from the form of the earth as known. Meantime, until the Coast Survey does the part which it agreed to do, the observations remain monument to the strict scientific care, industry, and skill of Greely and his companions; and if they are not rendered nugatory by the various blunders of the Survey may at some future time (when scientific questions shall again be treated as matters of legitimate inquiry by those in whose hands the power of government resides), completed according to the original plan, furnish an important contribution to human knowledge.

222.25–27 But . . . be used] In galley revision, this brief passage replaced a long section in the April 1887 initial submission describing how expansion (due to temperature) and the apparent change of length of the pendulum during the Arctic journey prevented Peirce from calculating a value for gravity at the Arctic station. In the original submission, Peirce provided a version of the linear interpolation for temperature expansion, but cautioned against using it for the extreme range of temperatures involved in the Arctic work (R 1076:11):

> At present, I can only say that for moderate differences of temperature the expansion should be taken at about 22 microns per degree centigrade. But over a range of 47 degrees, this might involve an error of over a third of a millimeter.

Peirce continued the original discussion by revisiting the issue of damage to the pendulum, which he felt occurred at the time of interchange of the knives. Without further observations at low temperatures, Peirce felt that "the reductions can proceed no further." Peirce's subsequent decision to use "only the observations made after the interchange of knives" (218.1–3) apparently cleared the way for him to use linear calculations to determine expansion per degree centigrade and to complete the gravity determinations.

222.28–32 Elaborate . . . detail.] This statement appears in the initial submission after the table at 241, which concludes the data run on the descent of the pendulum arc during oscillations. In the original, Peirce commented further on Farquhar's corrections for arc (1887.21, 10): "His reductions have a value in showing the general uniformity of the descent of arc. An improved method of reduction will, however, be given in my description of the Peirce Pendulums." Neither this reference, nor Peirce's description of the pendulums appeared in the final report; he eventually completed a draft of the description for the 1889 Gravity Report (sel. 36).

235(c19).3 1.0045337] Calculation from previous data shows that this uncorrected period should read 1.0045386 .

236(c17).11 1275.218] Calculation from previous data shows that this interval should read 1275.319.

236(c17).32 3190.275] Calculation from previous data gives an interval of 3190.305.

237(t1,c15).1 1.0045498] In his offprint copy, Peirce has made additional working calculations around the mean value for the period of swings made with the heavy end down and before interchange of the knives. The result is a correction of +0.0000428 seconds, correcting the mean period of oscillation for these swings to 1.0045926 seconds. The calculations for this correction cannot be verified, nor can it be known if this correction alters subsequent stages in the determination of gravity for the Arctic station. Given this degree of uncertainty, the original copy-text reading is retained.

238(t1,c11).10 1.0039554] Given the previous data, this corrected period value ought to read 1.0039464. The error affects the subsequent corrected period.

238(t1,c11).13 1.0038852] Based on previous data, this corrected period value ought to read 1.0039174. The error affects the subsequent corrected period.

238(t1,c15).1 1.0039485] In addition to the correction of mean period of oscillation for heavy end down swingings of the pendulum prior to exchange of knives, Peirce also made further calculations in his offprint for the mean period of heavy end up swings prior to exchange of knives. The result is a correction of +0.0000261 seconds, correcting the mean period for these swings to 1.0039746 seconds. The basis for these calculations is unknown, as is the effect on subsequent stages in the gravity determinations; with no certain basis for emendation, the original copy-text reading is retained.

239(c13).16 392.9] Based on previous data, this corrected excess ought to read 393.9.

240(c7).5 +429.3] The final addition should give 439.3. See ann. 218.17.

240.2–3 Mr. W. B. Fairfield] See ann. 286.23.

241.1-242.1 In comparing . . . north pole] Farquhar continued his discussion of the increase of the expansion allowance by describing the effect on the station error in Peirce's final results (719):

> Increasing T_d, T_u, and the "reversible pendulum" period by 0.0000074^s, we must increase the double logarithm by 0.0000064, when the "station error" becomes –0.0000097, and the conclusion in favor of a term in odd powers of the sine of the latitude is correspondingly weakened. It should be remembered that this result is subject to three uncertainties: Whether the latter observations were alone made with a pendulum of the length found in 1884; whether, in correcting periods of the simple pendulum for temperature, allowance for the expansion of the metal is sufficient, and whether the unusually rapid decrement of arc at this station was due to a cause that left the period unaffected. Another point, which does not appreciably affect this result, is nevertheless worth noting. If the reversible-pendulum period equals $(74.914T_d - 25.160T_u)$:49.754, $\frac{3}{2}T_d - \frac{1}{2}T_u$ must be increased by $0.0057(T_d - T_u) = 0.0000040^s$ at the Smithsonian, 0.0000037^s at Fort Conger. This might be

diminished by 2 in the seventh place to allow for the factor under the radical in the first formula above. Professor Peirce, at the end of his report, uses a quite different correction.

241.2–3 a figure of the earth which I have deduced] Peirce is probably referring to his "On the Mean Figure of the Earth from Determinations of Gravity. Second Paper. The formula for the Earth's ellipticity in terms of the variation of gravity with the latitude" (1888.4).

241.3–4 Kater invariable pendulums] Henry Kater (1777–1835), English geodesist who introduced in 1819 an invariable compound pendulum with a single knife-edge of which thirteen were constructed and swung throughout the world. See also W4:148 (1880); W4:529 (1883).

241.4–5 the expedition of Mr. Edwin Smith] Assistant at the U.S. Coast Survey. This is probably the expedition for the determination of gravity at various points in the Pacific Ocean under Smith's charge. This expedition used a Kater pendulum that was on loan from the Royal Society. See Peirce's 24 February 1886 letter to Thorn (NARG 23/22).

243.7–8 No accident . . . to this pendulum] In his report in the first volume of the *Proceedings*, Greely also stressed that no damage came to the pendulum (15):

> The instructions of Assistant Charles Peirce, of that service, were followed as closely as practicable, and fortunately no accident or mishap occurred in the course of the observations. The pendulum itself was brought back in good condition, so that further comparable observations may be made with that instrument.

In reply to a letter Peirce wrote after seeing Greely's memorandum, Greely again explained (RL 174:6, 30 November 1888):

> I have never considered this question otherwise than impersonally and I should in no way have considered the question as involving any imputation upon Mr. Israel or myself. It would have been a grave reflection upon both of us if the scientific world believed that an accident having occurred, the commanding officer failed to fully and clearly set forth the nature of such accident. The whole question for the scientific world to pass upon is whether your hypothesis is correct or not.

243.12 again soldered up in the original tin box] See ann. 216.19.

243.13–15 The statement . . . left behind] See 218.4–7, and 244.37–38.

243.23–36 Later the statement . . . and life.] See 218.26–220.1, and 244.39–245.1.

243.37 as suggested in the following Supplementary Report] Henry Farquhar's "On the Pendulum Observations at Fort Conger" which he was requested to write by Superintendent Thorn (716): "to clear up the question of responsibility with regard to certain charges explicitly or implicitly made by Assistant C. S. Peirce against the management of this office in his report on the Pendulum Observations at Fort Conger." See also 245.7–11.

243.44–244.2 On one occasion . . . one-quarter of the usual time] In a 30 November 1888 letter to Peirce, Greely explained (RL 174:6):

> On one occasion, when the decrease of arc of oscillation was so rapid as to show conclusively that the vibration would not continue more than one-fourth the usual time, Mr. Israel suggested that one of the screws might be loose, and on that occasion he entered the pendulum house alone and stopped the pendulum, readjusted the screws, and set the pendulum again in motion.

244.18–19 the former . . . written instructions] See ann 216.19. Also, in *Three Years of Arctic Service*, Greely wrote (vol. I, 130): "My astronomer, Sergeant Edward Israel, had received from Professor Pierce [*sic*] careful and detailed instructions concerning the pendulum work."

244.33 imputing blame] See the Peirce-Greely correspondence in RL 174:3–10.

245.4–5 was absolutely unavoidable] After seeing Greely's memorandum, Peirce wrote to Greely on 27 November 1888 (RL 174:4; draft):

> Looking at the question from a purely impersonal point of view myself, and advancing my hypothesis as a means of strengthening, and not of weakening, the determination, I did not realize that you would consider an accident, which in my opinion was absolutely unavoidable, as involving any imputation upon you or Mr. Israel.

245.9–10 a certain derangement of apparatus] See 217.6–9 and corresponding ann.

31. *Reflections on the Logic of Science*

246.3 the Brush . . . lights] The Brush light is an electric arc lamp so called after its inventor, Charles Francis Brush (1849–1929).

246.10–11 *Beiblätter* . . . *Chemie*] The *Beiblätter zu den Annalen der Physik und Chemie,* published by Johann Ambrosius Barth, appeared from 1877 to 1899 as a supplement to the *Annalen der Physik und Chemie,* which later became the *Annalen der Physik.*

247.17–22 Auguste Comte . . . the fixed stars.] See ann. 64.15–16.

247.24–32 Legendre . . . different principles.] See anns. 64.18–21 and 64.21–22.

248.7–9 Sir William Thomson . . . fully proved.] William Thomson, first Baron Kelvin of Largs, also known as Lord Kelvin (1824–1907), British physicist and mathematician. Thomson supposed that all matter, including the luminiferous ether, had "molecular structure." In this he differed from chemists like Ostwald, who denied the existence of atoms, and from instrumentalist physicists like Mach, who denied the reality of unobservable particles. For Thomson's view on matter, see his lecture "The Size of Atoms" (*Popular Lectures*, pp. 154–224), first delivered in 1883.

248.29–30 Were such . . . met with] With this awkward use of the phrase "only once," Peirce does not mean "If such a theory was met just one time" but rather "As soon as such a theory is met with," etc.

248.34 Kepler] Johannes Kepler (1571–1630), German astronomer and mathematician who discovered the laws of planetary motion and founded modern optics.

249.19 vortex-theory of molecules] The discovery in 1858 by Hermann von Helmholtz of the permanence of vortex motions in perfectly inviscid fluids encouraged the invention, throughout the latter half of the 19th century and especially in Great Britain, of models in which vortices in a structureless ether played the part otherwise assigned to atoms. In 1866 William Thomson proposed that these vortices could act exactly like primeval atoms of solid matter.

251.13 G. Cantor] Georg Ferdinand Ludwig Philipp Cantor (1845–1918), pioneer in set theory and theory of transfinite numbers.

251.13–18 has shown . . . however short] Cantor shows this in a number of papers; an offprint of one (found in R 1599, now in WMS 530) has been annotated by Peirce: "Une contribution à la théorie des ensembles" *Acta Mathematica,* 2

(1883): 311–328, see esp. 314. This paper, originally published in 1877, was one of seven papers by Cantor that were translated into French and that were published in *Acta Mathematica* 2 (1883): 305–414.

251.18–20 Now he supposes . . . second sense] The discussion of the potential application of Cantor's theory of transfinite numbers to physical science occurs on pp. 123–24 in Cantor's "Über Verschiedene Theoreme aus der Theorie der Punktmengen in einem n-fach ausgedehnten stetigen Raume G_n" (1885), reprinted in Cantor's *Gesammelte Abhandlungen mathematischen und philosophischen Inhalts,* ed. Ernst Zermelo (Berlin: J. Springer, 1932), 261–76. Following Leibniz, Cantor calls the ultimate particles of matter "monads," and he makes the hypothesis Peirce attributes to him about the monads of ordinary matter and of ether. See also Peirce's response to Royce's "Supplementary Essay" in *The World and the Individual* (CP 3.570; 16 March 1900) where he makes the same point.

251.22–23 Only, Cantor . . . of infinity.] On a working sheet Peirce formulates this idea a little more explicitly (R 1574:656):

> Cantor's theory. Describe it. It is a perfectly reasonable supposition. But why limit ourselves so to two *classes* of *infinity*? This limitation springs from no more being needed in mathematics*[,]* nothing else. Rational & irrational numbers.

251.24–30 the proposition of Euclid . . . all the B's.] This type of limit argument is used most prominently in Book XII of Euclid's Elements and relies on Proposition 1 in Book X.

251.31–32 it assumes . . . "given" quantity] Peirce's point seems to be that this proof relies on a definition of real numbers that does not allow for infinitesimals and that there is no good reason for this restriction.

252.8 Rule of False] Of this rule, Peirce's father Benjamin wrote: "this admirable rule, the principle of which is obviously at the foundation of all higher mathematics, and pervades all practical science in some form or other, is sufficient for obtaining, with ease and accuracy, the most important numerical results" (*Elementary Treatise on Curves, Functions, and Forces,* vol. 2, Boston: James Munroe and Co., 1846, p. 38). Peirce gives a good illustration of it at the beginning of his 1898 lecture on "The First Rule of Logic," EP2:42–43. See also Peirce's *Century Dictionary* definition of "position" (4635):

> In *arith.,* the act of assuming an approximate value for an unknown quantity, and thence determining that quantity by means of the data of a given question. A value of the unknown quantity is posited or assumed, and then by means of the given connection between the unknown and a known quantity, from the assumed value of the unknown a value of the known is calculated. A new value of the unknown is then assumed, so as to make the error less. In the rule of *simple position,* only one assumption is made at the outset, and this is corrected by the rule of three. In the far superior rule of *double position,* two values are assumed, and the corrected value of the unknown is ascertained by the solution of a linear equation. Also called the *rule of supposition, rule of false,* and *rule of trial and error.*

252.26–29 The difficulty . . . of energy.] See chapter 6 of Spencer's *First Principles,* which discusses "the persistence of force," Spencer's expression for the conservation of energy: "By the Persistence of Force we really mean the persistence of some Cause which transcends our knowledge and conception" (p. 192d, 2nd ed.).

252.35–36 Leibniz said . . . experience.] The reference is likely to the *New Essays on Human Understanding* (1704). In bk. I, ch. i ("Are There Innate Principles?"), Leibniz argues that necessary truths are not learned from experience. Between 1885 and 1888, the first English translation of parts of the *New Essays* (bk. I, chs. i–iii, and bk. II, chs. i–xi) appeared in four installments in the *Journal of Speculative Philosophy* under the title "Leibnitz's Critique of Locke." The book was thus the subject of renewed interest at the time of Peirce's writing.

255.8–10 Plato . . . real world] *Republic,* bk. VII, 514–519d. See also 258.17–21.

255.12–14 A great . . . whatever] Gauss; see 258.21–25 and corresponding ann.

255.16 what is probability?] Compare with "The Doctrine of Chances," W3:281 (1878), and "A Theory of Probable Inference," W4:408–50 (1883).

256.9–257.3 To show this . . . was increased.] A similar version of this game is discussed in the first Harvard Lecture of 1903; see EP2:138.

257.21–22 *quanta,*—or . . . How much?] Aristotle's word *πόσον* for the predicament of quantity (*Categories,* chs. 4 and 6) is both an interrogative and an indefinite adjective, not an abstract noun. Instead of listing quantitative properties (like that of being a cubit long) or corresponding quantitative predicates (like "a cubit long"), Aristotle lists all the owners of quantitative properties, whether discrete (number, speech) or continuous (lines, surfaces, solids, time, place).

257.29–35 Through any point . . . straight line.] See ann. 38.7.

257.35 Sylvester] James Joseph Sylvester (1814–1897). English mathematician who also wrote poetry, was mathematics professor at Johns Hopkins when Peirce taught there. On the quotation see textual note.

258.21–25 Gauss . . . application whatever.] An exact source for this statement has not been found, although it is consistent with other statements by Gauss, who said that mathematics was the queen of the sciences and the theory of number the queen of mathematics. See also 255.12–14; and on Gauss ann. 64.21–22.

32. *On the Analytical Representation of Space*

261.10–11 von Staudt.] On von Staudt's ten-ray theorem, see ann. 38.7.

262.10 will all meet in 1 point.] An incomplete diagrammatic construction (R 278:58) suggests how Peirce may have completed this example on the missing page. The diagram as described so far consists of 12 lines and 17 points. Let us call the intersection of A′B′ and A″B″, α; of AB and A″B″, α'; of AB and A′B′, α''; of A′C′ and A″C″, β; of AC and A″C″, β'; and of AC and A′C′, β''. Thus, what Peirce has told us so far is that the lines through α and β, α' and β', and α'' and β'' meet in one point, say 0. In the missing page Peirce probably instructed to draw 3 more lines, BC, B′C′, and B″C″ (for a total of 15 lines) and to consider 3 more points: the intersection of B′C′ and B″C″, γ; of BC and B″C″, γ'; and of BC and B′C′, γ''. He would then have remarked that γ was collinear with α and β, γ' with α' and β', and γ'' with α'' and β'', the three lines all meeting in the same point 0, and the total number of points being 20.

33. *Ordinal Geometry*

263.title Ordinal Geometry] Moritz Pasch (1843–1930) has been credited with presenting the first axioms for ordering points and line segments in his *Vorlesungen über neuere Geometrie* (Leipzig: Teubner, 1882), but Peirce's combinatorial scheme for describing the ordering appears to be his own invention.

263.1–2 theory of the arrangements of segments.] It appears that in previous drafts Peirce started out by defining ordinal geometry as "the theory of the arrangement of segments, regions and spaces" (R 249:5), then he restricted it to only "regions and segments" (R 249:2), before realizing that the three notions all denoted kinds of segments in each of the three dimensions. Accordingly, he generalized the definition to segments only, as a term valid in all three dimensions. The paper begins with a short consideration of ordinal geometry upon a line, then moves on to regions, but does not extend to spaces (or solids).

263.5 "Qualification" . . . differ.] In the previous draft (R 249:9), Peirce put it thus: "The being or not being overscored may be called the qualification of the letter."

263.8–9 A fraction] In the previous draft (R 249:9), Peirce explained: "A fraction denotes the space denoted by its numerator with the implication that this is wholly included in the space denoted by the denominator."

34. *Mathematical Monads*

268.6 *monads.*] The word has to be understood in the context of Peirce's recent rereading of Kempe's 1886 "Memoir on the Theory of Mathematical Form," the first "fundamental principle" of which was that "whatever may be the true nature of things and of the conceptions which we have of them . . . in the operations of reasoning they are dealt with as a number of separate entities or *units*" (2). At this point in the margin Peirce commented:

> "unit" should be restricted to the quantitative sense. "Monad" is a good word here, or individual or term.

Peirce added that such monads or individuals were not definite, but indefinite.

268.9–10 except such . . . connections] Such are the monads of the second and third order described in the next paragraph, which have no distinctive designations.

35. *Stock's* Deductive Logic

271.1 St. George Stock] Saint George William Joseph Stock (1850–1911), Oxford philosopher, grammarian, Latinist, logician, and chemist. In addition to *Deductive Logic,* he wrote *Attempts at Truth* (London, 1882), *Logic* (1900; 1903), and *Outlines of Logic* (1902).

271.3–6 One of the author's friends . . . matter.] *Deductive Logic,* Preface, p. v.

271.17 Bain] Alexander Bain (1818–1903), Scottish philosopher and psychologist and founder of the periodical *Mind.* The reference is to Bain's *Logic* (2 vols., London: Longmans, Green & Co., 1870). In 1870 Peirce published a not so positive review of Bain's *Logic* in the *Nation* (W2:441–44), which ended with the conclusion that "[a]s a school-book the work has some advantages."

271.23–24 Mill is . . . the scholar"] John Stuart Mill, *A System of Logic* (London: J. W. Parker, 1843).

272.3–4 Bain . . . another kind] A number of these objections can be found in Peirce's 1870 review mentioned in ann 271.17.

272.16 Venn] John Venn (1834–1923), English logician who developed Boole's mathematical logic; author of *Symbolic Logic* (London: MacMillan and Co., 1881).

272.17–19 his persuasive plea . . . limited universe,] See Venn's *Symbolic Logic* (1881), ch. 6, especially pp. 131–53, and his *The Principles of Empirical or Inductive Logic* (London: Macmillan, 1889), 257–58 (cf. 181–82). De Morgan's "universe of discourse" was introduced in 1846 in "On the Syllogism, I: On the Structure of the Syllogism" (*Transactions of the Cambridge Philosophical Society* 8 [1846]: 379–408), where the universe was restricted to the names that are to be applied to a proposition, and hence called the "universe of a proposition." In "On the Syllogism, II: On the Symbols of Logic, the Theory of the Syllogism, and in Particular of the Copula" (ibid., 9 [1850]: 79–127), the universe became "the whole universe of thought, or a conceivably separate portion of it."

272.19–20 particular . . . of terms,] The requirement of the existential import of particular propositions was introduced by Peirce in "Grounds of Validity of the Laws of Logic" (W2:242–72, 1868).

272.21–22 "accept the . . . opposition.] *Deductive Logic,* 140: "accepting the awkward corollary of the collapse of the doctrine of contradiction."

272.29 Mr. Stock calls . . . proposition.] *Deductive Logic,* 61, in the subsection "Simple and Complex Propositions."

273.7–9 The concluding . . . are fusible,"] Abbreviated from *Deductive Logic,* 127.

273.10–11 it is a mistake . . . deductive.] *Deductive Logic,* 128.

273.12 "vague instinct,"] *Deductive Logic,* 127: "We are led to this conclusion, not by reason, but by an instinct which teaches us to expect like results, under like circumstances." Also 128: "The fact is that inductive inferences are either wholly instinctive, and so unsusceptible of logical vindication, or else they may be exhibited under the form of deductive inferences."

273.17–18 it is wrong to . . . dispute] *Deductive Logic,* 314, where Stock says "the very proposition originally propounded for discussion." See also 315. Stock lists asking to grant such a proposition as one of five ways of begging the question.

273.18–20 "the first . . . to wit, itself."] *Deductive Logic,* 315–16.

273.21–22 the treatment . . . compound propositions,] *Deductive Logic,* 134–46.

273.25–29 The denial . . . are gentle."] These examples are not found in the book, but are of a kind Stock ought to have considered had he treated non-singular (quantified) propositions.

274.1–3 O. H. Mitchell . . . in number.] Oscar Howard Mitchell, see ann. 66.12. The reference is to his article "On a New Algebra of Logic," in *Studies in Logic* (edited and published by Peirce in 1883), 87–96. The second dimension being time, Mitchell can be seen as presenting a temporal logic. Stock gives only four forms of conjunctive propositions in *Deductive Logic,* 234: If A is B, (A) C is always D; (E) C is never D; (I) C is sometimes D; (O) C is sometimes not D.

274.9–12 "Either operators . . . not careful"] *Deductive Logic,* 243: (O) Either care must be taken or telegrams will sometimes not be correct. / Either telegrams are correct or carelessness is sometimes shown (I).

274.27–29 an advertisement . . . its phenomena."] Stock's book contains a series of advertisements at the end. This quotation appears on p. 4 of it, from an ad that appeared originally in the *Cosmopolitan.*

36. *Report on Gravity*

275.4 Colonel Herschel] John Herschel (1837–1921), English astronomer who came to the U.S. to connect the English gravity survey with that going on in the U.S. Herschel oscillated Kater pendulums of the Royal Society, first at the

Stevens Institute in Hoboken, N.J., and later at the Smithsonian. Herschel participated in the Conference on Gravity Determinations which was held in Washington D.C. in May 1882. The report of this conference, of which Peirce was the editor, includes work by Herschel (see W4:349–77).

275.9 Washington Observatory] The U.S. Naval Observatory in Washington, D. C., which was then located on the hill north of where the Lincoln Memorial now stands (i.e. Foggy Bottom). The observatory was established in 1830 as the Depot of Charts and Instruments. In 1844 its mission was expanded, and the observatory became an important center for scientific research.

275.13 Professor Baird] Spencer Fullerton Baird (1823–1887), American zoologist.

275.16 Cornell.] On the day Peirce completed his work at Cornell, the *Cornell Daily Sun* (5 February 1886) described his work as follows (p. 1):

> Professor Peirce employed himself in observing the vibration of two pendulums which were kept swinging, one a cold pendulum, in the equatorial room of the Engineering building and the other, a warm one, in a closely walled room in the basement of the Physical laboratory, allowing only a small aperture through which to observe the vibrations by means of a telescope.

275.23–24 Professor E. A. Fuertes] Estevan Antonio Fuertes (1838–1903), American engineer, Dean of the Department of Civil Engineering, Cornell University, 1873–90. On 8 January 1886, Peirce wrote to Edward S. Holden a glowing letter of recommendation expressing his hope that Fuertes could become the next Coast Survey Superintendent.

276.25 White] Andrew Dickson White (1832–1918), founder and first president of Cornell University.

276.25 Adams] Charles Kendall Adams (1835–1902), president of Cornell University 1885–92.

276.26 Anthony] William Arnold Anthony (1835–1908), professor of physics at Cornell University 1872–87.

276.31 Villarceau régulateur] Instrument made by Antoine Joseph Francois Yvon Villarceau (1813–1883), French engineer who constructed an equatorial meridian-instrument and an isochronometric regulator for the Paris Observatory.

276.33 Professor Newberry] John Strong Newberry (1822–1892), American paleontologist and geologist.

277.2 Professor Schaeberle] John Martin Schaeberle (1853–1924), American astronomer.

277.7 President Angell] James Burrill Angell (1829–1916), President of the University of Michigan, Ann Arbor, 1871–1909.

277.8 Langley] Samuel Pierpont Langley (1834–1906), director of the Allegheny Observatory (1867–1887). He supervised the construction of the observatory's first telescope and clock. From 1887 until his death he was secretary of the Smithsonian Institution.

277.28 Professor Holden] Edward Singleton Holden (1846–1914), director of the Washburn observatory from 1881 until 1885.

277.29 Washburn Observatory] The observatory at the University of Wisconsin, named after Wisconsin governor Cadwallader C. Washburn and completed in 1881.

277.29 Mr. M. Updegraff] Milton Updegraff, an assistant at the Observatory from 15 August 1884 to about 1888, who worked primarily on observations and reductions of the positions of stars using a meridian circle. Circa 1890, after spending two years at the national observatory in Argentina, he became director of the observatory at the University of Missouri in Columbia, Missouri.

279.26 Krille] Peirce seems to have had first hand experience with the Krille clock, whose maker could not be further identified. On 25 August 1885 he sent B. A. Colonna an inventory of Coast Survey property in his possession at Ann Arbor, which listed a Krille clock with accessories.

280.4 Allegheny Observatory] The Allegheny Observatory is located ten miles north of Pittsburgh, Pennsylvania, in Allegheny City. It was constructed in the 1860s and affiliated with the Western University of Pennsylvania in Pittsburgh.

280.30 the Criterion] See Benjamin Peirce, "Criterion for the Rejection of Doubtful Observations," *Astronomical Journal* 2 (1852): 161–63. Though cumbersome to apply, Peirce's Criterion received some renown. There is no sign that Charles Peirce used it in the present report. For a discussion and statement of the Criterion see W3:132 and the corresponding annotation in W3. In CD Charles Peirce wrote simply that it was a "certain rule for preventing observations from being rejected without sufficient reason." The criticism of R. M. Stewart is now regarded as having revealed a fatal flaw in the procedure ("Peirce's Criterion," *Popular Astronomy* 28 [1920]: 2–3). Further references are given in Raymond Clare Archibald, *Benjamin Peirce, 1809–1880: Biographical Sketch and Bibliography* (Oberlin, Ohio: The Mathematical Association of America, 1925).

284.37 No. 1 was abandoned] Greely brought back Pendulum No. 1 with the expedition records at the time of their 1884 rescue (see 218.6–7 with ann.). Commander Robert E. Peary retrieved Pendulum Head No. 1 several years later.

286.3 New Stand] Peirce described the development of the second pendulum stand in a letter of 1 Sept. 1885 from Ann Arbor:

> I have had an expensive oaken pendulum support constructed, costing about $80. This was necessary for two reasons; because the old stand was not sufficiently stiff, so that the pendulum made 4 oscillations too few *per diem* upon it, and also because I desired to economize by oscillating two pendulums at once and so abridging the time consumed at each station. The new support is a great success, and has been much admired by scientific men.

286.20 6 feet long.] R 1096 (1889.8) contains two large typed sheets. One lists the instruments that are needed for fieldwork (R 1096:4), and the other describes how to work with the pendulum (R 1096:5).

> § 26. Rules for the use of these pendulums.
>
> 1st. The following instruments will be needed in the field:
>
> 2 Peirce pendulums,
> 2 heads,
> Bolts and leaden washers,
> 2 wooden pendulum stands,
> 1 mercurial barometer,
> 7 thermometers graduated to tenths of a Centrigrade degree,
> 1 microscope with eye-piece micrometer and ⅔ inch objective
> 1 paper double pointed tacks,
> 2 vulcanite observing-keys with cords,
> 2 fine glass scales for reading chronograph sheets,
> 1 five-inch lens mounted on castors,
> 1 reading lens (convenient with handle),
> 1 large Steinheil reading telescope,
> 2 condensing lenses,
> 3 Rochester lamps,

1 stage microscope with fine lines, divided into tenths and hundredths of a millimetre,
1 holder for the micrometre,
1 Atwood machine pulley, strongly made,
3 salmon lines,
1 weight of 10 kilograms and 2 of 5 kilograms,
1 spring balance,
1 small spirit level for leveling knife-edge plane, the divisions about 1′ each,
1 box of tools, including monkey wrenches, wood clamps, etc.
1 high support for microscope,
1 astronomical clock (if possible),
1 box-chronometer,
1 accurate pocket time-piece with second hand,
1 Fauth chronometer,
Chronometer sheets,
Tin boxes for chronograph sheets,
8 large cells gravity battery with blue and white vitriol,
1 reel paraffin-coated wire,
1 spool silk covered wire,
2 shunts,
1 oil can with pump,
1 engine divided scale, 40 lines to the inch,
1 army prescription scales, with weights down to a centigramme,
2 pendulum rests for laying pendulum down,
1 rest for end of pendulum,
1 large transit instrument,
1 current *American Ephemeris,*
1 Crelle's *Rechentafeln,*
1 four place table of natural trigonometric functions,
1 *Barlow's tables,*
Stationary, record books, etc.
1 step ladder,
1 chronograph table,
1 computing table,
1 observing table,
4 chairs,
1 cot bed and blankets,
2 foot rugs,
1 petroleum stove,
1 levelling instrument and staves.

The pendulum should first be compared in Washington, by means of the vertical comparator, a metre pendulum with Metre B, and the Yard pendulum with Yard and Metre Bar No. 1.

The knife-edges should first be carefully scrutinized; but they should not be removed unnecessarily. The thumb screws should be made very tight, and scratches made on their heads to detect any subsequent loosening. The positions of these should be noted in the record.

The values of the screw-revolutions of both microscopes of the vertical comparator should first be ascertained by measuring spaces on Metre B. State whether the screw head reading increases or decreases as the wire descends. The sum of the distances of the lines on the abutting pieces should be measured. A perfect illumination should be arranged with special precautions against the shifting of the lines. The comparator should be adjusted. 1st, its length should be intermediate between that of the pendulum, and the most nearly equal length on the standard. 2nd, it must be adjusted so that when its axis of rotation is vertical a plumb-line falls on the vertical lines of both microscopes at once, and is in focus of both microscopes at once. 3rd, the microscopes must be level, when the axis is vertical. 4th, the whole staff carrying the microscopes must be put in such a position, that with its axis of rotation vertical the defining line of the piece on which the pendulum rests is in focus. The lower piece should then also be in focus. 5th, the standard is brought into the vertical, and into focus. Thermometers should have been bound with tin-foil to the middles of the pendulum and standard. Sufficient time should be allowed for the temperature to settle. Two persons should not enter the comparing room at once; but the recorder should stand just without the door. The observer should work as quickly as possible, in the following order. 1st, lamps lighted to illuminate thermometers. 2nd, readings of thermometers by telescope, first on standard, second, on pendulum. Lights turned down. 3rd, one reading of micrometer on standard below, one on standard above. Comparator carefully turned on pendulum. One reading on pendulum above, two on pendulum below, one on pendulum above. Comparator turned back onto standard. One reading on standard above, one on standard below. 4th, lights turned up on thermometers. Thermometer-readings, first on the pendulum, second on the standard. The observer now goes out and reduces his observations. Two comparisons should be made in a day, at intervals of two hours. At least one complete readjustment of the comparator should be made before concluding the measurements of each pendulum.

After the measures are completed, the two thermometers should be immersed in water at the same temperature as the comparing-room, together with a third; and the three should be compared. The zero of the third should then be determined by immersing it for about three minutes in a pail of melting pounded ice, from which the water is not allowed to drain off.

3rd. The pendulums should be swung at the station in the Smithsonian building. The error of the barometer should be ascertained. In setting up the stand, pains should be taken to have the bearings of the parts, as well as the floor under the feet of the stand as clean as possible.

The stand having been set up, and wrenched up which such force as almost to endanger the perfect coherency of the wood, one of the brass heads is put on. The top of the stand should be already nearly level, and the head should be bolted on with the use of the leaden washers. By compressing these it should be leveled pretty accurately.

The next step is to measure the flexure. A weight of 10 kilograms should be hung from the middle of the knife-edge plane, during these measures. A flexible and inelastic cord must be bound to the middle of the knife-edge plane, and, passing off horizontally and at right angles to the direction of the knife-edge, pass over the Atwood machine pulley and carry a weight of 5 or 10 kilograms. No soft or yielding substances should be interposed between the cord and the steel. The centre of the cord must be exactly on the level of the plane. The stage micrometer must have its plane vertically and the line of readings coincident with the line of the cord produced on the other side of the knife-edge plane. The microscope should be supported in the finest possible way independently of the pendulum stand.

The observer should record his own observations while his assistant gently lets the weight bear and relieves it alternately. This may be done by a spring balance. Both should be sitting and neither must stir. The one who raises and lowers the weight may very well be seated on a shelf below the pulley. The observer must cautiously assure himself that there is no mistake about his measure of the flexure. The inclination of the knife-edge must now be measured. These measures having been concluded, the thermometers should be attached. One of these should have the centre of its bulk on the level of the lower knife-edge, or if the Yard and Metre pendulums are both used, half way between the levels of the two lower knife-edges. It must be in front of the stand and a little to one side. Another thermometer should be on the level of the upper knife-edge, towards the back of the stand and as far to one side as the lower thermometer is to the other.

The observer, wearing lined leather gloves, should then hang the pendulum upon the raised Y's, an operation requiring a certain dexterity. A weighed piece of engine-divided scale [divisions 40 to the inch] 1 11/20 inch long and 1/2 inch wide should already have been fixed to the pendulum with two weighed bits of wax. The observing telescope and illuminating lamp, mirror and lens should be a*[*djusted.*]*

286.23 W. B. Fairfield] Walter B. Fairfield, who was employed by the Coast Survey as "extra observer," assisted Peirce in his pendulum observations at Key West, on which occasion Peirce spoke very highly of him. Fairfield also assisted Peirce for the Greely Report (sel. 30).

286.25 W. B. Curtis] Unidentified.

286.26 E. D. Preston] Erasmus Darwin Preston (1851–1906), subassistant at the Coast Survey; after 1900, editor of publications of the Coast and Geodetic Survey.

286.28–29 D. C. Chapman] Coast Survey mechanician; see also sel. 30, 221.15–16.

289.8–11 + 275 . . . – 86 feet] These values are obtained by multiplying by 100, not 1,000 feet as Peirce has it. This implies that the denominator in the formula at 291.4 should be 0.0069 rather than 0.00069 logarithmic seconds.

289.13–14 "logarithmic seconds,"] The "logarithmic second" is Peirce's own invention. On 19 July 1890, Superintendent T. C. Mendenhall objected to Peirce's system for expressing gravity; Peirce's eight-page written response defended the use of the concept as a way of simplifying calculations involving values of relative gravity (Peirce to Mendenhall, 22 July 1890, NARG 23):

> I apprehend that what you mean by saying my system is *unnecessarily* obscure, is that the C.G.S. system affords an unexceptionable mode of expressing gravity. In this, I am entirely with you. I have no idea of using any other system for expressing any quantity which the C.G.S. system expresses. But you will agree that there are innumerable cases in which we have to record physical determinations which have not yet been carried to the point at which we can compare them with the centimetre, the gramme, and the second. There is no more marked instance of this than determinations of the relative acceleration of gravity. These are much more accurate than absolute determinations. Their principal use, that of ascertaining the figure of the geoid, would be in no degree subserved by knowing the absolute value. The measurement of the absolute value and its calculation from observations is most advantageously separated from the relative determinations. Thus, we are often in the situation of having to express gravity *relatively*, with high precision, when we are quite unable to assign its *absolute* value with anything like that precision. In such a case, we plainly cannot make use of absolute units. . . . Values of *relative* gravity to be of any use must be carried to six significant figures. The only way they can be reduced, or used after they are reduced, is by multiplying and dividing them. If, therefore, they are expressed in a logarithmic form, that generally saves going twice or more to the table of seven place logarithms every time you have to do with one. . . . [Logarithmic seconds] have the effect of making all the operations of reduction and comparison additions & subtractions in place of multiplications and divisions.

The basic relation between two values of gravity, g_1 and g_2, and the corresponding oscillations n_1 and n_2, is $g_1/g_2 = (n_1/n_2)^2$. Consequently, $100{,}000\log(g_1/g_2) = 200{,}000\log(n_1/n_2) = 200{,}000\log(e)\ln(n_1/n_2)$ which Peirce takes as approximately equal to $86859 \times 2 \times (n_1 - n_2) / 2n_1$ or, equivalently, $(n_1 - n_2)$ (see Victor Lenzen, "An Unpublished Scientific Monograph by C. S. Peirce," *Transactions of the Charles S. Peirce Society* 5 [1969]: 5–24, esp. 13–14, 21–22).

290.22 $g = \ldots$] See ann. 291.22–23.

291.15–16 unpublished investigation] This investigation has not been found.

291.22–23 *Coast Survey Report* for 1881, Appendix 15] "On the Deduction of the Ellipticity of the Earth from Pendulum Experiments," *Report of the Superintendent of the United States Coast an Geodetic Survey . . . 1881* (Washington: Government Printing Office, 1883), 442–56 (W4:529–34). On p. 445 (W4:534) Peirce gives a value for the ellipticity of the earth "taking $\eta = .0052375$." There is no explicit explanation of the calculation, of what η represents, or of the formula used in this conclusion to his 1881 writing. The formula used in the present report for reduction for latitude is based on Clairaut's Theorem, and the coefficient, to which Peirce has assigned the value of 0.0052375, is equal to $5m/2 - e$ where m is the ratio of the centrifugal force at the equator to the force of gravity at the equator and e is the ellipticity of the earth. A standard theoretical derivation of this formula is given in A. R. Clarke, *Geodesy* (Oxford: Clarendon Press, 1880), 66–82.

292.7 8 forms of pendulum apparatus] The eight forms of apparatus which Peirce usually used were the following:

(1) Pendulum 2, heavy end down, Old Stand
(2) Pendulum 2, heavy end down, New Stand
(3) Pendulum 2, heavy end up, Old Stand
(4) Pendulum 2, heavy end up, New Stand
(5) Pendulum 3, heavy end down, Old Stand
(6) Pendulum 3, heavy end down, New Stand
(7) Pendulum 3, heavy end up, Old Stand
(8) Pendulum 3, heavy end up, New Stand

At the Smithsonian in 1884–85 the four forms were (1), (3), (5), and (7). The reduced station numbers are calculated on the basis of the data contained in the first set of "Results of Single Swingings" charts (R 1096a:49 and following). Richard Tursman determined that the corrected oscillations per diem for each of the eight forms of apparatus (when reduced to sea level and to the equator) are:

Form	Smithsonian 1884–85	Smithsonian 1886	Ann Arbor	Madison	Cornell
(1)	86010.44	86011.64	86011.27	86010.07	86009.81
(2)	—	86012.52	86011.96	86010.37	86010.22
(3)	86005.04	86004.59	86004.53	86003.22	86000.17
(4)	—	86006.13	86004.09	86003.07	86001.68
(5)	89912.13	89912.33	89911.65	89909.86	89911.28
(6)	—	89911.06	89913.83	89913.19	89908.85
(7)	89926.19	89926.93	89925.76	89925.12	89924.04
(8)	—	89927.21	89926.75	89926.07	89923.39

It is not clear in these concluding steps of his work how Peirce obtained precisely the values he gives for either of the two sets of station numbers he provides in Table II and in the footnote. It is possible to arrive at numbers close to Peirce's by the following procedure. Starting with the data in the above table, for each of the eight forms of apparatus (but excluding the incomplete Smithsonian 1884–85 for purposes of this example), subtract 86401.9 from the value given for Smithsonian 86 (in form (1) for example: 86011.64 – 86401.9 = –390.26) and add the difference to each value in the form (obtaining in (1): 86401.9, 86401.53,

86400.33, 86400.07). After completing these calculations for each of the eight forms, apply some best-fit scheme for each station; simply averaging the results across the forms would give 86401.9, 86401.58, 86400.53, and 86399.03 for Smithsonian, Ann Arbor, Madison, and Cornell respectively. Dropping some of the more anomalous values of forms and using a least-squares approximation it is possible to get values closer to those of Peirce. However, for the second set at least, Peirce apparently applied temperature corrections in addition to those already applied in the tables under "Results of Single Swingings" (324), and gave a reduced weight to the results at Cornell (290n.1–6).

296.4 The formula] In his "On the Flexure of Pendulum Supports," *Report of the Superintendent . . . 1881*, 359–441 (W4:515–28); see p. 430 (not printed in W4).

296.4–5 *C. S. Report* . . . 430] "On the Flexure of Pendulum Supports," partially printed in W4:515–28 (1883). The page here referred to is not included in W4.

296.9 43429] This is half the coefficient used at 290.32 in what appears to be the same relationship. In the following line a conversion of units probably explains the appearance of the decimal point in 0.43429. Another value of this coefficient, 0.0434, is given a few lines later and is used in Table VIII.

296 TABLE VIII] The heading of the penultimate column was left blank by Peirce. The column gives the values of the coefficient of S in the formula preceding the table. In the heading of the last column Peirce or his typist appears to have failed to put in the delta and the solidus by hand (items which were normally added by hand) and these have been supplied.

300.20 "Measurements . . . p. 74] "Measurements of Gravity at Initial Stations in America and Europe," *Coast Survey Report* for 1876, 202–337, 410–16 (W4:79–144). Peirce's page comes from a separate, later printing and corresponds to p. 273 of the published report (or W4:122).

302.8 Breteuil] The Pavillon de Breteuil, located in the Parc de Saint-Cloud, at Sèvres, in the suburbs south-west of Paris, is since 1875 the site of the International Bureau of Weights and Measures.

302.8 Regnault's] Henri Victor Regnault (1810–1878), French chemist.

302.9 Wüllner] Adolph Wüllner (1839–1908).

302.18 "Measurements . . . stations"] See ann. 300.20. Peirce's reference is probably to his discussion of the effect of viscosity in W4:104–5.

302.18–19 The *a priori* . . . made, also.] This sentence was added in ink by Peirce to the typescript. Despite Peirce's explanation, it is not made clear in the following pages just what formulas he is using in Table XVIII. In his 1890 review of the typescript, Professor Ferrel stated his belief that Peirce's method might be "a better way" of determining the atmospheric effects but that Peirce had not yet published on this and that he, Ferrel, could make little sense of how the calculations presented in "Atmospheric Effects" and in "Descent of the Arc" were made or how they fitted together. He gave considerable attention, however, to Peirce's key expression in the "Descent of the Arc" (310), for the rate of change of the amplitude of oscillation. He wrote that "it at once seemed to me that there must be something wrong, and after mature consideration, and fruitless efforts to understand some parts of the methods, I am constrained to come to the conclusion that the whole matter is not only unnecessarily complicated, but the first part even erroneous." "I know of no such expression as that of $D_n \Phi$" he asserted. Peirce had published the same expression in "Measurements of Gravity" (264;

W4:93), but Ferrel did not have access to any literature while composing his report. In any case, Peirce is not much more helpful in justifying this expression in his earlier report. Peirce once stated that to find out what the matter was with Stokes's theory was "one of the most difficult mathematical problems conceivable" (Peirce to Thorn, 29 Aug. 1887, NARG 23/22). Ferrel pointed out the failure of Peirce's efforts to make the formula fit the data and proceded to derive an expression that differed only in the constant term, $-a$, from Peirce's. In the course of doing this he showed how the second term, $-b\Phi$, came from Stokes's theory, which takes atmospheric viscosity only into account, and that Peirce's contribution was essentially the addition of the second-order term, $-c\Phi^2$, which attempts to account for additional atmospheric effects. The motivation for this term could come, as Ferrel described it, by first obtaining the decrement of arc through an application of Stokes's theory for the oscillations given in Table XIX for Pendulum No. 4, and then comparing those values with the decrement of arc calculated from the observed amplitudes given in the table. Ferrel found that the former were on the whole one-fifth less than the latter. After completing his report Ferrel added a postscript stating that he had overlooked Peirce's tables for the "A Priori Calculation of the Second Effect" and "A Posteriori Calculation of the Second Effect" where the final values of the former are one-fifth those of the latter. He stated that as he was "not acquainted with the formulae and notation I am not quite certain as to what the final results refer to," but the one-fifth difference was evidently sufficient cause for Ferrel to conclude that "Peirce's method is therefore the better, as I at first surmised, since it takes into account other resistances than those from viscosity, if there happen to be such." (Ferrel to Mendenhall, 19 Oct. 1890, NARG 23, Vol. 657, p. 20.)

302.19 Stokes's] Sir George Gabriel Stokes (1819–1903), British physicist and mathematician, and a pioneer in geodesy.

305(c8).11 9663] The mass of Pendulum No. 3 is given earlier as 9676 (see 285.32).

307(c8).5 3.3390] Instead of log 2083, this value is that of log 2183. It is used to calculate the logarithm in the next row but does not affect subsequent calculations.

309(t2,c2).10 2.2427] This and the corresponding value for Pendulum No. 3, 2.2452, appear to be twice the correct values. The corresponding logarithms are computed using the correct values.

310.9–11 Green . . . perfect fluid;] George Green (1793–1841), British mathematician. Peirce is probably referring to Green's "Researches on the Vibrations of Pendulums in Fluid Media," *Transactions of the Royal Society of Edinburgh* 13 (1836): 54–62.

310.13–17 Stokes . . . space.] See George Gabriel Stokes, "On the Effect of the Internal Friction of Fluids on the Motion of Pendulums," *Transactions of the Cambridge Philosophical Society* 9 (1856): 8–106, esp. 23.

310.17 Meyer] Oskar Emil Meyer (1834–1909), physicist and professor and director of the Department of Physics and the Mathematical Institute at the University of Breslau.

310.21 the old resistential formula] Peirce's equation was inspired by Coulomb's formula for the electrostatic force between two charged particles. In his "Gravity at Initial Stations" (W4:93), Peirce cites Benjamin Peirce's *Analytic Mechanics* where it occurs on p. 46. Peirce seems not to have succeeded here in determining appropriate values of a, b, and c. See ann. 302.18–19.

316.10–11 Their comparison . . . given.] The calculated values in the second column of the table are 1.2 less than those the formula gives. This indicates that one or both of the two values given for *b* and *c* is wrong, probably through mistyping.

317.9–10 I now calculate . . . and find] It is not clear what formula is being used; the first three values are identical to those before, as expected.

317.14–15 The calculation is as follows.] In the second table: instead of the stated value of Q as $0.47 - 500q$, Q is taken as 0.47.

319 TABLE XX] How the values in the second column are obtained is not clear. In the fourth column, the fifth data value should be +2 based on the corresponding values in the previous two columns.

320.3–4 rule of false,] See ann. 252.8.

322.3–4 For different . . . will be] Since the present edition only includes the descent of the arc data for one of the meter pendulums, the constants for the descent of the arc for the yard pendulum, No. 3, are given below (from R 1096a:36):

log $^1/$P =	1.201	
b' =	0.0000575	[H. e. down]
	0.000169	[H. e. up]
Q =	0.5782	[H. e. down]
	0.5792	[H. e. up]

322.18–9 "Measurements . . . p. 66] See ann. 300.20. The page number corresponds to p. 265 of the published report (or W4:105–6).

322.27–323.1 Pendulum No. 1 . . . Greely] See sel. 30.

323.16 *[Table XXIII omitted.]*] Peirce next includes Tables XXIII–XXIX, which give "smoothed out" mean values for curves showing the descent of the arc—that is, the descending amplitude of the swinging arc—for each pendulum as it was oscillated at the Smithsonian station. Tables XXX–XXXIX, which give the descent of the arc for individual swingings, provide the observed mean values used to calculate the curves. Only representative samples are needed to illustrate Peirce's calculation of the decrement of the arc; the present edition abridges these sections by including only Table XXIV, which gives the smoothed curve for Pendulum 2 (swung heavy end down), and Table XXXI, which provides the observed decrement for each of the 13 heavy-end-down swingings of Pendulum 2 as well as the uncorrected mean values.

323 TABLE XXIV] A formula similar to that used in Table XXI appears to have been used here but what the corresponding constants are is not clear.

326.5–327.6 The first tables . . . comprises.] The first set of the two sets of tables to which Peirce refers is here presented in its entirety (Tables XL–LI). Each table in this set summarizes all swingings for a given pendulum at a given site *after* initial corrections for arc, rate, pressure, temperature, and inclination of the axis of rotation. Peirce uses the data to determine a mean value which is then further corrected for atmosphere, flexure, and expansion; at the end of each chart in this series, he projects the number of oscillations per diem for a given pendulum at a given site. These calculations will reduce to the logarithmic station number for each site as shown in Table II (see 291.10).

The second set (Tables LII–XCII) shows the individual swingings in detail, and provides the initial corrections summarized in the first set. The second set records the results of individual swingings for the eight forms of the gravity apparatus. This adds up to thirty-two tables for the four locations (Smithsonian 1886, Ann Arbor, Madison, Cornell). In addition Peirce swung nine forms of apparatus (all on the Old Stand and five involving Pendulums 1 and 4) at the Smithsonian in 1884–85 (see ann. 292.7). This gives a total of forty-one forms of apparatus, which corresponds to the data recorded in Tables LII–XCII. Each of these forty-one tables gives the same kind of information; only one (Table LXI) has been included in the present edition to illustrate the way that Peirce determined the number of oscillations and corrected them for use in Tables XL–LI.

Table LXI gives the results of eight swingings of Pendulum 2 heavy end down on the Old Stand at the Smithsonian in 1886. Each swinging in this case lasted a little over four hours (Peirce usually swung the invariables with heavy end down for 4 hours 11 minutes and with heavy end up for 1 hour 23 minutes). The exact time for the first swinging recorded in Table LXI, after initial corrections, is 4 hours 11 minutes and 34.073 seconds, or 15,094.073 seconds. Peirce repeats such results of the times for the individual swingings in the third column of each table in the first set (Tables XL–LI); for example, the exact time for the first swinging of Table LXI is repeated in Table XLIV, first entry, where it then receives final corrections before the number of oscillations per day is projected. See also ann. 331.

327 TABLE XL] The summary tables for Pendulums 2 and 3 (XLI–XLII, XLIV–LI) are fully reduced to the number of oscillations per diem. But Pendulums 1 and 4 (Tables XL and XLIII), which were only oscillated at the base station, are not reduced beyond the corrected time of swing (Table XLIII contains no reductions at all). Although the reductions are missing, the number of oscillations per diem for Pendulums 1 and 4 appear in Peirce's calculations for the absolute value of gravity at the close of the report. See 349(t2,c8–11).2–3.

331 TABLE XLIV] In this, as in all the tables of this type, the values in the fourth column of each sub-table give the corrected time for a fixed number of oscillations, usually 15000. It is implied that these are taken from the subsequent tables of the report of which one, Table LXI for the eight values for heavy end down, Old Stand, is printed here on p. 339. Comparison of the two shows that most of the eight values match (where, for example, 4 hours, 11 minutes, and 34.073 seconds corresponds to 15094.073 seconds). However, three of the values do not match exactly and this lack of a complete correspondence is typical for all of the tables for all of the pendulums.

332 TABLE XLV] For heavy end down, New Stand, only if the first value of nT is taken as 14431.484 instead of 14431.185 are the given values for error and mean correct. The source, Table LXVI (not printed here), gives this value as 14431.485, but in transferring these values to the present table all but the eighth value from Table XLVI have, without explanation, been similarly changed by 0.001.

333 TABLE XLVI] For heavy end up, New Stand, three values of nT have been altered by hand: .960 from .968, .928 from .941, .937 from .953. These changes result from changes made to Table LXXI (not printed here); Peirce has not, however, changed the corresponding differences from the mean.

334 TABLE XLVII] For heavy end down: $\log T^2$ should be –3366.17 for Old Stand and –3368.34 for New Stand based on the previous data values. Subsequent calculations, however, use the given values.

334 TABLE XLIX] For heavy end up, Old Stand, the final value should be 90027.70 based on previous values, some of which have been altered by hand.

336 Table L] Problems with the Ithaca oscillations led Peirce to reject or even cancel a number of swingings at this site. He describes these circumstances on the tables for individual swingings at Ithaca (Tables LXXXV–XCII), which are not included in the critical edition. Swingings missing from the final corrections at Ithaca (Tables L–LI) of the present edition were omitted by Peirce for various reasons, including random vibrations, rapid changes in temperature, and disturbance of the air around the pendulum.

337 TABLE L] For heavy end down, New Stand, the last two digits of the oscillations per diem, 86110.33, have been written by hand over typed numerals; the value should be 86110.35 based on the previous entries.

339 TABLE LXI] In the seventh swinging the time for 15000 oscillations should be 4 11 34.233 based on the previous data; this would change the final corrected time to 4 11 34.111. In any case, as noted above (ann. 331), Peirce uses a different corrected time in tables that draw on this table.

340.1 CORRECTION FOR INCLINATION] This correction appears not to have been made by Peirce in his previous gravity work nor by others in the field before or since.

340.10–11 but . . . proceeding.] Peirce provides six sample tables (XCIII–XCVIII) of the correction for inclination: Smithsonian (1886) Old and New Stands; Madison Old and New Stands; and Ithaca Old and New Stands (no corrections for Ann Arbor are given). The initial table in this sequence (XCIII) is included as an example of this work.

341.2 CORRECTION . . . TEMPERATURE] The values are those derived by Peirce in "On the Effect of Unequal Temperature upon a Reversible Pendulum" (W5:319–22).

342.15 Tiede clock] Sidereal clock made by M. Tiede of Berlin and housed in the Detroit Observatory since 1854.

343.1–3 The following . . . exhibited.] Peirce included nine tables (XCIX–CVII) of time signals and clock corrections covering the periods of time that he swung pendulums at the various stations in 1884, 1885, and 1886. These are abridged in the present edition; only the initial entries of Table XCIX, listing Peirce's first clock signals from the Naval Observatory (23–31 December 1884) and the recorded loss/gain of his own instruments, are included as samples of this calculation.

344.14 station errors] Peirce previously referred to these as the excesses of the reduced station-numbers over 86400 logarithmic seconds.

344.27–29 "Determinations . . . [Formula]] See W4:96.

345.5 Fauth chronometer] Most likely a chronometer produced by Fauth & Co., Washington D.C. (1874–1900). The company was founded by George N. Saegmuller (1847–1934), then a Coast Survey employee, and his two brother-in-laws Henry Lockwood (1834–1897) and Camill Fauth (1847–1925), the latter having started a business making surveying and astronomical instruments.

345(c2).1 9h.58m] Peirce does not state which station is represented in this example, but the time of last transit given here is that of the seventh swing of the yard pendulum (No. 3) on the Old Stand (heavy end down) at Ann Arbor.

346.5 a régulateur Villarceau] See ann. 276.31.

347.12 Negus 1589] Chronometer made by T. S. & J. D. Negus, New York (1850–).

348.4 unpublished investigation . . . earth] Probably 1888.4; see also ann. 241.2–3.

348.7 Sabine's] Sir Edward Sabine (1788–1883), British soldier and astronomer who participated in expeditions to find the Northwest Passage (1818, 1819–20), and conducted pendulum experiments at many locations world-wide.

348.8–11 I cannot admit . . . my own Memoir.] Friedrich Robert Helmert (1843–1917) discussed Peirce's work in *Die mathematischen und physikalischen Theorien der Höheren Geodäsie* (1884), vol. II, 209–212. The memoir Helmert was referring to is Peirce's "De l'influence de la flexibilité du trépied sur l'oscillation du pendule à réversion" (*Verhandlungen der allgemeinen Konferenz der europäischen Gradmessung zu Stuttgart 1877*, Berlin: Georg Reimer, 1878, 171–87). Helmert referred in particular to page 173 of Peirce's introduction. Note that this introduction differs slighty from that in the English version that appeared in the *Coast Survey Report* of 1881 (W3:217–34). Helmert objected to Peirce's finding (210): "Nur beachtete Peirce nach E. Plantamour und Cellerier noch nicht genügend die Verschiedenheit des Fundaments." Helmert thus believed that Peirce's failure to take into account differences in the foundation was why Peirce's Paris measurement departed so radically from the measurements of others ("mit den älteren Bestimmungen ganz und gar nicht stimmt"), and he discarded Peirce's result on this ground (212). The Paris measurements listed by Helmert are 3860, 3860, 3860, 3859, 3899, and 3950 respectively, of which the last measurement is Peirce's (211). The value 3950 does not stem directly from Peirce, but from Förster's article in the *American Journal of Science* 20 (1880): 327. Helmert seems to have been unaware of Peirce's discussion of Förster's paper in a later addition to his "On the Value of Gravity at Paris" (published in 1881), where Peirce gave a new measure of 3917.5 (W4:150–51).

348.31 unable to account] Peirce's inability to account for the discrepancy was a major issue in Simon Newcomb's analysis of the report. In a 28 April 1890 letter to Superintendent Mendenhall, Newcomb referred to the difference as an "extraordinary discrepancy," stating that more investigation was needed than Peirce had given it.

349(t2,c8,9).18 990.9540 . . . 9553] The final values for the equatorial seconds pendulum for No. 1 and No. 2 should be 990.9542 and 990.9556 respectively based on the given data. Since these values differ considerably from those given by Peirce, and since it is not clear how Peirce arrived at his figures, Peirce's original values are retained.

350.17 Mr. Blair] Henry Wayne Blair (1851–1884), Coast Survey assistant.

350.19–20 U.S.C.S. C.S.P. 1878B] See ann. 221.10.

350.36 Clarke] Alexander Ross Clarke (1828–1914), English geodesist and author of *Geodesy*. See also ann. 291.22–23.

351.1 Blair comparator] Comparator designed by Henry Blair. See ann. 350.17.

351 TABLE CXII] The value for No. 2 at 15° – Metre should be –132.8, instead of –134, based on the previous values. The value for No 4 at 15° – Metre should be 241.4, instead of 241.6, based on the previous values. The original values are

retained because the above values differ considerably from Peirce's, and since it is not entirely clear how Peirce arrived at them.

353 TABLE CXV] See also R 1095a:68 (1892) "Length of Metre in Inches," and R 1095a:60 (1892) "Inch in Millimetres," where in the latter Peirce gives a figure of 25.4001, based upon Clarke's value for the number of inches per meter as corrected by Benoît. In his 1892 *Nation* review of Hussey's *Logarithmic Tables,* Peirce gives a more precise figure of 25.40003 millimeters in an inch. Today the relationship between the inch and millimeters is not a matter of measurement but of definition: one inch = 25.4 mm exactly. See *American National Standard "Metric Practice," ANSI/IEEE Standard 268–1982,* American National Standards Institute, New York.

353(t2,c2).1 Kater] See ann. 241.3–4.

353(t2,c2).2 Clarke] See ann. 350.36. Peirce is most likely referring to Clarke's 1867 paper in *Philosophical Transactions.*

353(t2,c2).3 Rogers] Fairman Rogers (1833–1900), American engineer and a founding member of the National Academy of Sciences.

353(t2,c2).5 Heaviside] William James Heaviside (1840–1915), British geodesist.

353(t2,c2).6 Comstock] General Cyrus Ballou Comstock (1831–1910), U.S. Army Corps of Engineers.

37. *Reasoning*

354.1–14 The first thing . . . of another.] Compare this passage with W4:245 (1881), W5:327, 328 (1886), and W5:372 (1886), for instance.

354.8–9 it may be . . . broad sense.] In the draft Peirce explained (R 839:16–17):

> In all this I am aiming at a verbal definition of reasoning; I do not care whether the word does involve these implications (though I think it does), the point is that this is what the word *should* mean to fulfill its uses.

355.9 As the etymology of the word shows] The word "because" derives from the Middle English "bi cause" or "by cause." The word "cause" comes from the Latin *causa,* whose own etymology is somewhat uncertain. Some speculate that it comes from the Latin verb *cavere,* to take care, in its primitive legal sense of ordering or decreeing, which was the role of jurisconsults (who also took care of their *causae* and were called *causidici*). Thus the compulsion Peirce refers to would be a legal binding. Others link the word "because," via *caud-ta* (a striking), to *cudere,* to strike, beat or knock, thus connoting a compulsion marked by greater secondness. It is unclear which etymology Peirce had in mind, as neither CD nor Murray's Dictionary (which became the *OED*) provide it.

355.33–34 to hold in every possible world] See ann. 50.12–13

356.6–7 of what we do not know to be false] See ann. 50.18–19.

38. *On a Geometrical Notation*

357.1 Let A, B, C, D, etc.] An earlier experiment with this notation appears on three pages in a portion of a notebook called "Formulae" (R 124:10–12), and is reproduced below with punctuation corrections.

> Let (A, B, C, D) = 0 signify that the four points A, B, C, D are coplanar. Then, if (A, B, C, D) = 0 then (A, B, D, C) = 0 etc., and if (A, B, C, D) = 0, and (A, B, C, E) = 0, any one of the

letters common to the equations, as A, may be eliminated, giving (B, C, D, E) = 0, or else (A, B, C, 1) = 0. We may write (A, B, C, 1) = 0 to signify that (A, B, C, X) = 0 whatever point X may be, so that (A, B, C, 1) = 0 will mean that A, B, C are collinear. In every case (A, B, C, A) = 0. If (A, B, C, D) = 0, (A, E, F, G) = 0, (A, H, I, J) = 0, (A, K, L, M) = 0, the four planes are confocal, and A may be eliminated. If (A, B, C, D) = 0, (A, B, E, F) = 0, (A, B, G, H) = 0, the three planes are coaxial, and either A or B may be eliminated.

Let the result of the last elimination but one be written [(1, B, C, D)(1, E, F, G)(1, H, I, J)(1, K, L, M)] = 0. Then, [1(1, B, C, D)(1, B, E, F)(1, B, G, H)] = 0 will be the result of the last elimination.

There is just one point X which will satisfy the two equations (X, A, B, C) = 0 and (1, X, D, E) = 0, unless (A, B, C, D) = 0 and (A, B, C, E) = 0 when every point that satisfies (1, X, D, E) = 0 satisfies (X, A, B, C) = 0. From (A, B, C, D) = 0 and (A, B, C, E) = 0, we have (A, B, D, E) = 0. From this and (A, X, D, E) = 0 [at once from (1, X, D, E) = 0] we have (X, A, B, D) = 0. From this and (A, B, C, D) = 0 we have (X, A, B, C) = 0.

That is, if (X, A, B, C) = 0, (1, X, D, E) = 0, (Y, A, B, C) = 0, (1, Y, D, E) = 0 we can eliminate A, B, C, D, E and get (X, Y, 1, 1)(A, B, C, D) = 0.

39. *On the Numbers of Forms of Sets*

360.7–8 diversity] Peirce considers the maximum number of distinct elements (letters in this case) included in the set, arranged vertically in the first column of his table of formalities on 362.

361.4–5 *American* . . . p. 48.] "On the Algebra of Logic," W4:163–209 (1880). The reference is to W4:199–200.

362.1 Taking the . . . 6th line] The sixth line is the row facing "5" in the "No. of letters" column; to get the first line of his triangle of figures, Peirce subtracts each number from the next one in that row, thus: 1 – 0 = 1, 15 – 1 = 14, 140 – 15 = 125, 1050 – 140 = 910, and 6951 – 1050 = 5901. The same procedure of taking the differences of each row newly produced is used to generate successive rows in the triangle.

40. *The Formal Classification of Relations*

364.1–18 1. Dual relations . . . antiselfrelations.] Compare with Peirce's earlier accounts, such as in "Description of a Notation for the Logic of Relatives" (W2:417–20, 1870); "On the Algebra of Logic" (W4:198–200, 1880); "On Relative Terms" (W4:342–44, 1882); "Note B" (W4:457, 1883); "Lecture XII. General formulae of the logic of relatives" (W4:481, 1883). A slightly later account is in R 555:9–12 (Fall 1892), which is a draft of the never published "Critic of Arguments III" written for the *Open Court*. See also the third entry for "relation" (CD 5057), and Peirce's letter to Francis C. Russell of 27 September 1892 (RL 387:80–82). Peirce's ultimate classification is found in his 1903 "Nomenclature and Divisions of Dyadic Relations" (R 539, CP 3.571–608).

364.2 selfcouple] This term, and the next one, aliocouple, were later inserted in the text by Peirce. Throughout the rest of the text, however, Peirce retained the word "selfpair" and "aliopair" without correction. Unqualified, the word "pair" is only used to designate a pair of couples. Elsewhere, Peirce refers to selfcouples as identitive couples, selfpairs, selfrelatives, and selfdyads; they must be distinguished from selfrelations.

364.3 aliocouple,] Also called aliotive couples, aliopairs, aliorelatives, aliodyads; to be distinguished from aliorelations.

364.fig. *[figure]*] The figure drawn by Peirce is incomplete so far as it contains only the four logical relations and not the five real relations. Peirce gives a similar figure in a letter to Francis Russell of 27 September 1892 (RL 387:81). Based on that figure, and the description given below the current figure, the diagram could be reconstructed and completed as follows. First row, from left to right: incompossibility, selfconcurrencies, identity; second row: alioopponencies, variform relations, antialioopponencies; third row: otherness, selfanticoncurrencies, coexistence. Peirce uses this figure several times, often in a reverse order. For an early version, see W4:481 (1883); for a later version, see CP 3.581 (1903).

364.fig. aliorelations] CD 5058: "A relation of such a nature that a thing cannot be in that relation to itself; as, being previous to."

364.fig. concurrencies] CD 5057: "relations which nothing can bear to anything else, as self-consciousness." Note that this definition differs from the one Peirce gives at W4:198 (1880). Peirce also calls these relations sibi-relations, and, in a draft for this dictionary entry, selfrelations (R 536:15)

364.fig. opponencies] In R 555:10 (1892) Peirce gives the following definition: "By an opponency, may be meant a relation applicable to all aliodyads *[*= aliocouples*]*; such is that expressed by '—— is conscious of something besides ——.'"

364.6 negative] In his 27 September 1892 letter to Francis Russell, Peirce explains (RL 387:81): "The negative of a dual relative is a dual relative which includes every individual dual relative the former does not include and includes none the former does include."

364.10 relation of *coexistence*.] An earlier draft continues here as follows (R 534:4):

> Excepting these four relations, all other concurrencies and anticoncurrencies are selfantiself relations, and all other aliorelations and antialiorelations are both opponencies and antiopponencies. Finally we have a ninth class which are at once opponencies and antiopponencies, self and antiself relations. These may be called *variform* relations.

364.11 *logical relations*] In CD 5057 Peirce explained: "*Logical relations* are those which are known from logical reflection: opposed to *real relations*, which are known by generalization and abstraction from ordinary observations."

364.11–12 *real relations* of five kinds] In a draft of the CD entry "relation" Peirce presents these five kinds as follows (R 536:15–16):

> Real dual relations are of five classes, as follows: (1) relations which nothing can bear to itself, or *aliorelations*, as being greater than; (2) relations which nothing can bear to anything else, or *selfrelations*, as selfconsciousness; (3) relations which everything bears to itself, or *assimilations*, as similarity; (4) relations which everything bears to everything else, or *opponencies*, as distances; (5) relations which some things only bear to themselves and which subsist between some pairs only of different things, or *variform* relations.

365.2 *pair* of couples] A "pair of couples" is given the form "x:y and u:v" where ":" is not commutative (x:y in general differs from y:x); the "and" connecting the couples as a pair is, however, commutative; thus each couple is an ordered pair but the pair of couples is not ordered.

365.2–3 of the nine forms following] The following table lays out the possibilities; either, or both, of the members of the non-A:A couple may be A, B, or C, for a total of 3^2 possibilities. Instructions are given for converting pairs to the equivalent member of the nine. With the base couple A:B we get sixteen possibilities.

"Base" Couple	Other Couple	Makes it pair
A:A	A:A	same as simple A:A (idempotency of "and")
A:A	A:B	pair 2
A:A	A:C	same as pair 2; B for C
A:A	B:A	pair 3
A:A	B:B	pair 1
A:A	B:C	pair 4
A:A	C:A	same as pair 2; B for C
A:A	C:B	same as pair 4; B for C and C for B
A:A	C:C	same as pair 1; B for C
A:B	A:A	same as pair 2; commute couples
A:B	A:B	same as simple A:B (idempotency of "and")
A:B	A:C	pair 7
A:B	A:D	same as pair 7; C for D
A:B	B:A	pair 5
A:B	B:B	same as pair 3; commute couples, A for B, B for A
A:B	B:C	same as pair 6; commute couples, A for B, B for C, C for A
A:B	B:D	same as pair 6; commute couples, A for B, B for D, C for A
A:B	C:A	pair 6
A:B	C:B	pair 8; the equivalent of B:A and C:A (see below)
A:B	C:C	same as pair 4; commute couples, A for C, B for A, C for B
A:B	C:D	pair 9
A:B	D:A	same as pair 6; C for D
A:B	D:B	same as pair 8; C for D
A:B	D:C	same as pair 9; C for D, D for C
A:B	D:D	same as pair 4; commute couples, A for D, B for A, C for B

In a different draft Peirce gives the same account (note the identical anomaly for class eight) of these nine classes, using a different vocabulary. (R 533:12):

A:A and B:B, other sibicouples.
A:A and A:B, the latter is *obalien* of the former, the former *subidentical* of the latter.
A:A and B:A, the latter is *subalien* of the former, the former *obidentical* of the latter.
A:A and B:C, the latter is *ambialien* of the former, the former *aliosibicouple* of the latter.
A:B and B:A, each is *converse* or *anticouple* of the other.
A:B and C:A, the latter *prior* of the former, the former *posterior* of the latter.
A:B and A:C, each is *divergent* of the other.
B:A and C:A, each is *convergent* of the other.
A:B and C:D, each is *remote* from the other.

365.6–7 B:A . . . C:A] This anomaly in Peirce's list returns also in the manuscript of "Dual Relatives" (sel. 41), and in R 533:12, cited above. In sel. 41, however, Peirce does give the equivalent "A:B and C:B" under division 2.8, which is more consistent with the lettering scheme of the list, and which was therefore emended in its corresponding list location there. See also textual note.

365.8–24 A dual relative . . . *(omni-si-sibi).*] In a different draft Peirce gives the following account (R 534:7; see also ann. 365.2–3):

> 21. *Sibi-individual,* containing just one sibicouple. *Sibisimple,* containing every sibicouple but one. *Sibigeneral,* containing and excluding several sibicouples, unless containing none or excluding none.
> 22. With reference to obaliens and subidenticals.
> 221. Including an aliocouple and its subidentical. *Sibietalio.*
> Excluding the subidentical of every included aliocouple. *Nulloaliosisibi.*
> 222. Excluding an aliocouple and its subidentical. *Nonsibinecalio.*
> Including the subidentical of every excluded aliocouple. *Omnivelsibi.*
> 223. Including an aliocouple while excluding its subidentical. *Aliosednonsibi.*
> Including the subidentical of every included aliocouple. *Sibisialio.*
> 224. Excluding an aliocouple while including its subidentical. *Sibisinealio.*
> Excluding the subidentical of every excluded aliocouple. *Omnisisibi.*
>
> A *sibisialio* relation which is *omnisisibi* may be called *obtotal* since it has everything for correlate to every relate it has.
> A *nulloaliosisibi omnivelsibi* has for each relate either the identical correlate and no other or all other correlates except that.

41. *Dual Relatives*

368.9 coexistence.] Peirce means that any two possible objects are compatible, compossible, or possibly co-exist, not that all such objects actually do so.

368.22 These are nine as follows:] See ann. 365.6–7.

42. *Geometry of Plane Curves* without Imaginaries

372.title *without Imaginaries*] In general, a line in the plane intersects an oval (to take Peirce's first example) in either two distinct or coincident real points, or two imaginary points. In these pages Peirce enumerates only real intersection points.

372.1 tangent] Peirce's definition for tangent (CD 6179) includes the statement that "a curve has only one tangent at an ordinary point, or a mere line singularity, or a cusp, but has two or more tangents at a node."

372.5 oval] Peirce's definition of oval (CD 4192) is threefold:

> (a) A closed curve everywhere convex, without nodes, and more pointed at one end than at the other. (b) A curve or part of a curve returning into itself without a node or cusp. (c) A part of a curve returning into itself without inflections or double tangents.

372.5 singularities] Peirce defines singularity in geometry as (CD 5648):

> a projective character of a locus consisting in certain points, lines, or planes being exceptional in their relations to it. . . . An ordinary singularity is one of a set of singularities of which all others are modifications or compounds. Thus, an actual node upon a skew curve is a modification of an apparent node, and ought not to be reckoned as an ordinary singularity. But cusps and inflections, as stationary points and tangents, are ordinary singularities. A higher singularity is one which differs indefinitely little from an aggregation of ordinary singularities.

372.13 (4)] The fourth case applies to situations where at least one of the two ovals is a carpenter's oval, defined in CD 4192 as: "an irregular closed curve, formed of four arcs of circles having their centers at the vertices of a rhombus and joining one another so as not to make angles." Carpenter's ovals may conceivably be formed of more than four arcs of circles.

373.1 Ovals . . . 1 bitangent] Here, as in V, VI, and VII, Peirce is not speaking of ovals proper, since by definition these cannot have nodes, bitangents or cusps (see ann. 372.5), but rather of ovaloids depicting specific deviations of the oval.

373.1 node] A node is defined by Peirce as (CD 4006):

> (a) A point upon a curve such that any line passing through it cuts the curve at fewer distinct points than lines in general do. . . . (b) A double point of a surface; a point where there are more than one tangent-plane . . . (c) A point of a surface: so called because it is a node of the curve of intersection of the surface with the tangent-plane at that point.

373.2 cusp] A cusp is defined by Peirce as (CD 1412): "a stationary point on a curve where a point describing the curve has its motion precisely reversed" (p. 1412).

373.2 inflexion] An inflexion is defined by Peirce as (CD 3086): "the place on a curve where a tangent moving along the curve by a rolling motion changes the direction of its turning, and begins to turn back; a stationary tangent."

374.10 *Curves*] Note that Peirce changes the wording here from "oval" to "curve."

375.4 These two curves] In addition to the last two curves, VIII and IX, curves V and VI do not fit Klein's formula either, where Peirce's highest number for line intersections is taken as the order and his highest number for tangents is taken as the class. Klein proved his formula using general algebraical geometrical arguments which take into account tangents and inflexions with multiplicities, for example, whereas Peirce seems to rely exclusively on the geometrical diagrams he has drawn here.

375.4–5 seem to falsify . . . 199.] Felix Klein (1849–1925) offered, in "Eine neue Relation zwischen den Singularitäten einer algebraischen Curve" (*Mathematische Annalen* 10 [1876]: 199–209), a proof of the following Plückerian formula for plane curves (200): $n + w' + 2t'' = k + r' + 2d''$ where n is the order of the plane curve, k its rank, w' the number of real inflexions (inflexion points), t'' the number of real isolated bitangents, r' the number of real cusps, and d'' the number of real, isolated nodes (double points). Peirce may have copied his incomplete reference from the endnote (no. 6, p. 335) attached to the reproduction of Klein's formula in ch. 1, p. 17, of Hermann Schubert's *Kalkül der Abzählenden Geometrie* (Leipzig: B. G. Teubner, 1879).

376.8 $3M + 2\delta + \iota = 3N + 2\tau + \kappa$] Taking M as the order, N as the class, δ as the number of nodes, ι the number of inflexions, τ the number of bitangents, κ the number of cusps, and using Peirce's enumerations, the formula, which appears to be Peirce's own, is satisfied by all but X and XI.

43. *Noel's* The Science of Metrology

377.2 Hon. E. Noel,] Edward Noel (1852–1917), English soldier and author of *International Time* (1892) and *Gustaf Adolf: The Father of Modern War* (1908).

377.4–5 The metric system . . . in every school.] The use of the metric system was made legal (but not mandatory) in the United States by the Metric Act of 1866.

Within the scientific community the system quickly took over, but in other areas it lagged behind. In 1975 Congress passed the Metric Conversion Act to accelerate the conversion, but failed to set firm deadlines.

377.21 avoirdupois pound] A standard system of weights introduced in England c. 1300 A.D., in which the pound equals 453.6 grams in the metric system. Peirce wrote the avoirdupois entry in CD 397, and he did extensive research on pounds; see also WMS 592, CP 1.106 and CP 1.209.

378.32–34 2½ feet . . . etc.] *Science of Metrology,* 24, 24, 25, 29, 72 table VI, 34, and 42.

378.37–379.4 Mr. Noel . . . restored."] These advantages, including the three quoted are listed in *Science of Metrology,* 58–61, with an additional one on 59. They are assessed in relation both to the metric and to the English system.

379.5 Edward I.] Peirce may be thinking of Edward I (king of England, 1272–1307) because his reign was particularly noted for increased administrative efficiency and a vast reform of English common law.

44. *Logic and Spiritualism*

380.3 Spiritualism.] In a draft, Peirce wrote on his own position (R 880:2–3):

> I know nothing in particular about spiritualism. I mean I have never attended a successful spiritualistic séance, nor even had enough interest in the subject to participate at all earnestly even in unsuccessful ones. I am what might be called a hide-bound sceptic. . . . The editor of this review asks me to state what I conceive to be the direct argument against spiritualism, and I shall take the liberty to put telepathy, or the influence of mind upon mind at a distance, without ordinary physical communication, in one category with spiritualism. The task is delightfully easy. Strictly speaking, there is no direct argument against spiritualism and telepathy. All the direct reasons are just the other way.

380.4 planchette,] Invented in 1853 by a French spiritualist, a planchette is a triangular polished board on rollers, resting on a pencil in the socket at the apex. The medium places his hand on the board. If it moves the front leg, the pencil leaves markings on the paper placed beneath. These markings may assume the form of letters and spell out connected messages.

383.34 Nijni Novgorod fair,] The Russian city Nijni Novgorod (Gorki between 1932 and 1990) played an important role in the barter trade with the Orient through Siberia and Turkistan. The fair Peirce refers to was established in 1817, and became the largest in Russia, attracting traders and goods from across Europe and Asia. The Russian Revolution of 1917 ended it until its revival in 1991.

383.34–35 Westminster Abbey,] The London church where English monarchs are crowned. Effigies of such monarchs as Charles II and Henry III can be found in the Abbey.

385.17 *vis viva*] See ann. 197.25.

385.21 Tyndall] John Tyndall (1820–1893), Irish physicist who studied the transmission, radiation, and absorption of heat by vapors and gases; author of *Radiant Heat in its Relation to Gases and Vapors* (1859–71), and *Heat Considered as a Mode of Motion* (1863).

385.21 Clausius] Rudolf Julius Emmanuel Clausius (1822–1888), German mathematician and physicist. His work on heat and molecular motion appeared in

English translation in 1867: *The Mechanical Theory of Heat*, ed. T. A. Hirst (London).

385.21–22 Mayer's proof] Julius Robert von Mayer (1814–1878), German chemist. Tyndall and Tait (see below) debated von Mayer's contribution to the establishment of the principle of energy conservation. Tyndall thought von Mayer's 1842 paper "Bemerkungen über die Kräfte der unbelebten Nature" (*Annalen der Chemie und Pharmacie* 42 [1842]: 233–40) had established this claim, for von Mayer had there calculated "the mechanical equivalent of heat from the heat involved in the compression of a gas." Tait disputed this claim, and criticized von Mayer's work. For Tyndall's defense, see his "On Force" (*Philosophical Magazine* 24 [1862]: 57–66), and his "Remarks on the Dynamical Theory of Heat" (ibid. 25 [1863]: 380). For Tait's criticisms, see "On the History of Thermodynamics" (ibid. 28 [1864]: 292), and "On the Conservation of Energy" (ibid. 25/26 [1863]).

385.22 Tait] Peter Guthrie Tait (1831–1901), Scottish physicist who specialized in thermodynamics, theory of dissipation of energy, and kinetic theory of gases.

385.23–24 finds . . . countrymen.] See Tait's *Sketch of Thermodynamics*, §§ 30–39.

385.25 Rumford] Count Rumford, or Benjamin Thompson (1753–1814), American physicist who conducted cannon experiments that showed heat to be a mode of motion, thereby disproving the prevalent notion that heat was a fluid. See Peirce's remark on Rumford in W4:152–53 (1880).

385.25 Sadi Carnot,] Nicolas Léonard Sadi Carnot (1796–1832), French physicist and founder of modern thermodynamics whose principles were developed into the second law of thermodynamics. Carnot's cycle showed the relationship between heat and mechanical energy, and his work contains the germinal ideas of entropy. See especially his *Réflexions sur la puissance motrice du feu et sur les machines propres à développer cette puissance* (Paris: Bachelier, 1824).

385.25 Uriah Boyden.] Uriah Atherton Boyden (1804–1879), described as "Boston's reproach" by Peirce in a draft (R 879:30), was an American engineer and inventor who occasionally visited the Peirce house during Peirce's youth. Of Boyden's role in this matter, Peirce wrote later (R 778:4, c. 1909):

> The mechanical theory of heat, when put forward at the American Academy by Uriah Boyden, so frightened the fogies that they would not print his paper any more than Poggendorff would print Mayer's great paper, and the poor fellow went mad with his pent up truth.

385.28 Archimedes . . . the lever.] *On the Equilibrium of Planes*, bk. 1, props. 6–7. Peirce discusses Archimedes's principle of the lever extensively in his 1892–93 Lowell Lectures (R 1275:80–87, 89). In the draft of the present text (R 879:30), he describes Archimedes's common-sense premisses as being:

> 1st, that equal weights in the pans of a balance having equal arms will be in equilibrium, and 2nd, that the balance with the weights in the pans will weigh the same as the balance with the weights lying beside it.

385.28–29 Stevinus . . . plane.] Simon Stevin (1548–1620), Dutch mathematician and engineer. Stevin's "clootcrans" proof for the principle of the inclined plane can be found in *De Beghinselen der Weeghconst (The Principles of the Art of Weighing)* (Antwerp: Christoffel Plantijn, 1586). In his 1892–93 Lowell Lectures, Peirce discusses Stevin's clootcrans proof also immediately after a discussion of Archimedes's principle of the lever (R 1275:88, 90–91). In R 879:30, the simple premise assumed by Stevinus's proof is described as that "the weight of a chain having its first and last links joined to make a ring and hung over any support will not cause it to move round and round unceasingly."

385.29 Huygens . . . inertia,] Christiaan Huygens (1629–1695), Dutch mathematician and physicist, discussed the moments of inertia as part of the center of oscillation problem in *The Pendulum Clock, or Geometrical Demonstrations Concerning the Motion of Pendula as Applied to Clocks,* pt. IV, "The Center of Oscillation," especially props. 3–5. In R 879:21, Huygens's proof is said to assume only "that if a pendulum is drawn to one side and allowed to fall, its centre of gravity will never rise higher than it was at the instant the pendulum was set free."

385.31–33 Galileo . . . moving,] Peirce refers to Galileo's use of thought experiments instead of empirical data in the *Dialogue Concerning the Two Chief World Systems* (transl. by Stillman Drake; University of California Press, 1953, pp. 126–55) where the character of Salviati asks Simplicius to imagine an object being dropped from the mast of a moving ship. This object would fall directly under the mast, not behind the moving ship. For Galileo this thought experiment was the key to explaining why, if the earth moved, falling objects still landed directly under the point from which they were dropped. Peirce argues that Galileo was the first to discover the law of "inertia" (Newton's first law of motion).

385.33–34 Newton . . . reaction,] This is the third of three axioms Newton introduced in the opening section of *Philosophiae naturalis principia mathematica* (1687).

386.3–6 Thomas Young . . . digested.] English physician, physicist, and Egyptologist (1773–1829), commented in his 1802 *A Course of Lectures on Natural Philosophy and the Mechanical Arts,* vol. 1, lect. 20 on "The History of Mechanics":

> There is the greatest reason to apprehend, that from the continual multiplication of new essays, which are merely repetitious of others that have been forgotten, the sciences will shortly be overwhelmed by their unwieldy bulk, that the pile will begin to totter under its own weight, and that all the additional matter that we heap on it, will only tend to add to the extent of the basis, without increasing the elevation and dignity of the fabric.

386.15 say Faraday's,] Michael Faraday (1791–1867), English chemist and physicist; author of *Experimental Researches in Electricity* (1839–1855), and *Experimental Researches in Chemistry and Physics* (1859).

386.19 *indagation*),] This obsolete word is derived from the Latin *indagare* and means the action of searching or tracking out; investigation.

386.22 begins and ends.] Peirce crossed out the following paragraph after the corresponding sentence in the draft (R 879:33–34):

> I may here slip in, as a little corollary from this view, that when people talk of its being a "scandal to science" that spiritualistic stories are not explained, and say that scientific men ought to "investigate" them, they betray a complete misconception of the scientific business. Investigation? It is not a scientific man's trade to take testimony: get a lawyer for that. Until the scientific man can find opportunity *[for]* the special kind of observations which he has been trained to make, he is quite out of his element. However, that scientific men who do not believe in spiritualism are altogether scandalous, is a proposition which cannot be seriously disputed.

386.25 upholding the rest.] Peirce makes this additional remark about reasoning from familiar experience in the draft (R 879:34):

> This it must do in every branch, for science can have no other starting point than the common ground of familiar knowledge. Not merely at the outset either, but throughout the whole progress of science, good sense must often be called in.

386.27–28 The doctrine of Descartes . . . unitary consciousness,] See the second of Descartes's *Metaphysical Meditations Concerning First Philosophy.*

386.32 psychical activity.] In a draft Peirce adds at this point the following comment about vivid consciousness (R 879:37–38):

> The alert and agile part of us, it pays for its superior activity by an according absence not only of accuracy, but also of sensitiveness. Our ordinary inferences from familiar phenomena are performed unconsciously, or at least irreflectively; and thus escape being controlled by our too often worse than valueless theory of what a good argument should be. But then, were our logical views never so unexceptionable, the shadowed side of the mind is so much more delicate in its sensibilities (like a shaded eye) and so much more unerring in its operation (as mechanism ought to be) that whatever it produces must be far superior to the handiwork of conscious reason. The "monarch Thought," seated upon the throne of attention, is all very fine and gorgeous, and with the aid of his grand vizier, Language, and his lord high executioner, the obflexible thumb, has given the genus *homo* ascendency and immeasurable superiority.

387n.1–4 Thus in the . . . intueantur."] "I answer that . . . in order for the blessedness of the saints to be more pleasing to them, and that they give more abundant thanks to God for this, it is given to them that they see perfectly the punishment of the damned." This citation appears close to the end of the fourth book of Aquinas's commentary on Petrus Lombardus's *Sentences* (In IV sent. dist. 50, art. 4 co), as Aquinas replies to the question whether the blessed in heaven will see the punishment of the damned. At issue is the last verse in Isaiah 66:24, which raises the problem whether the perception of such horror is compatible with a state of complete happiness in the perceiver. Aquinas thinks it is, arguing that the perception of such horror heightens the happiness of the blessed on the ground that placing two contraries side by side heightens their respective distinctiveness. References to Aquinas are to the Piana Edition (1570): *Opera Omnia gratiis privilegiisque Pii V Pont. Max.* Typis Excusa. Ant. Bladus & J. Osm. Lil soc. Roma.

387n.4–6 In his 8th Quodlibet . . . sua visione."] "[To the first objection] I reply that seeing the misery of the damned is for the saints fully to their glory; for they will take pleasure in the justice of God and in seeing it." This citation is from the *Quaestiones Quodlibetales* (Quodl. 8, qu. 7, art. 16, ad 1), where Aquinas replies to the opposite question, whether the damned will see the happiness of the saints after judgment day. The first objection here addressed by Aquinas is that, if seeing the suffering of the damned heightens the happiness of the blessed, then seeing the happiness of the blessed would similarly heighten the sufferings of the damned. Aquinas denies this because seeing the happiness of the saints requires an element of perfection, of which the damned are deprived, so that they cannot see the happiness of the saints. Aquinas also denies that the blessed will pity the damned. See also *Summa Theologica,* Supplementum, qu. 94, art. 1, "Whether the Blessed in Heaven Will See the Sufferings of the Damned?"

387n.6 "lætantur de justa punitione."] The reference is probably to Aquinas's commentary on Lombardus's *Sentences* (In II sent. dist. 11, qu. 1, art. 5 co): "laetantur de justa permissione et punitione."

387n.6–7 "A horrible doctrine, I confess,"] This remark is found in John Calvin's *Institutes of the Christian Religion,* bk. 3, ch. 23, § 7. Calvin, however, was not talking about the saints' undistressed witnessing of the hellish suffering of the damned, but about God's chasing Adam out of Eden and decreeing that all humanity was henceforth, for the crime of one, liable to eternal death. For Peirce's views on the Calvinistic notion of salvation, see also R 865:7–8 (c. 1893).

388.12–13 It is conceivable . . . erroneous.] Peirce gives the following example in the draft (R 879:42–43):

> It may perhaps be found, for instance, in the far distant future, that space is measurable, that setting out from any given point and going north in a beeline for a certain number of vigintillions of miles, we should return to our starting-point from the south, something like a ship sailing round the world. This would be a result directly counter to the dictum of common sense. Yet mathematicians are now agreed that there is no reason in the world why this may not be the true state of the case. For nice as the judgment of common sense may be, it would be against common sense to hold it for infinitely nice. And even were it so, the sensations on which that judgment is based cannot posibly be so infinitely fine as to exclude this supposition. Here, then, we reach a limit to the trustworthiness of common sense. And yet even the discovery of the finitude of space, than which none more marvellous can be imagined, would be but a small detail regarding space compared with our present knowledge of it. No mathematician in his most refined calculations, no astronomer in his nicest measurements would think it worth while to take account of such a trifle. Practically speaking, the conclusion of common sense would remain unshaken.

388.21–25 But we see social . . . religious consciousness.] This is more fully developed in the draft (R 879:44):

> But in the department of religion, of politics, of social ideas, instances are not far to seek where the first opinion has been insensibly modified from generation to generation. The discussion of last winter *[Peirce is referring to discussions about doctrinal revision in the Presbyterian church that took place in the winter of 1890]* revealed the fact that a certain element of religious conviction has become strengthened at the expense of another among the Presbyterians, since the date of the Westminster confession. Christianity has two elements, the thaumaturgic and the spiritual: the latter has been gradually gaining over the former in the minds of believers from the very earliest times until now, and that, notwithstanding the swaddling clothes that reflective theology has bound about the faith to prevent its development. In the future history of protestant churches, I believe we can descry a still more rapid growth, almost a hypertrophy, of some elements of religious belief.

388.36–389.1 Dr. Zöllner . . . his house.] Johann Karl Friedrich Zöllner (1834–1882), German astrophysicist and inventor of the astrophotometer and reversion spectroscope. Seeking an empirical foundation for his theory of a fourth dimension of space, he investigated the American medium Henry Slade (d. 1905), the best-known slate writer over whose performances sceptics and believers remained bitterly divided. Zöllner's investigation and his subsequent account in his *Transcendental Physics: An Account of Experimental Investigations* (English translation appeared in 1880) made him famous in the annals of psychical research and subjected him to the contempt of the scientific community. His experiments began in December 1877, with the assistance of other physicists. Knots tied in an endless cord was the first phenomenon Zöllner witnessed. He made a loop of strong cord by tying the ends together. The ends projected beyond the knot and were sealed down to a piece of paper. In the seance room he put the sealed knots on a table, placed his thumbs on each side of the knot and dropped the loop over the edge of the table on his knees. Slade kept his hands in sight and touched Zöllner's hands above the table. A few minutes later four symmetrical single knots were found on the cord. Slade was caught in fraud several times, as in 1885 by the Seybert Commission, appointed to investigate spiritualism by the University of Pennsylvania. Their report was published in 1887.

390.2 Tupper.] English writer (1810–1889) and author of *Proverbial Philosophy* (1838–76), containing didactic and moralizing commonplaces in free verse.

390.18 how trick could be.] At this point Peirce added in the draft the following paragraph (R 879:49–50):

I am informed that Professor S. P. Langley in his superb volume entitled *The New Astronomy* (which is far beyond the purse of a poor student) objects to this kind of reasoning, that the first well attested aerolite was found about the beginning of this century, that the falling of a stone out of the sky was as counter to all familiar experience as anything could be, and yet that there neither was nor ought to have been any great difficulty in accepting the testimony to its first occurrence. As I have not seen the passage, I may be misstating Professor Langley's position, but I think it is something like that. It is, at any rate, an example worth considering. In my opinion, common experience was not against such an occurrence. That the other bodies of the solar system were composed of materials essentially similar to those found on this globe had been unquestionable for centuries. In particular, this was the accepted opinion about the shooting stars, which were generally supposed (though erroneously) to be stones thrown out by the volcanoes on the moon. There were plenty of stories of stones falling from the sky, and if they were not generally believed, it was merely because the common sense of mankind attaches very little credit to extraordinary stories (and surely if common belief is entitled to be regarded about anything, it should be about the average veracity of men). The common experience, therefore, so far as it went, was quite in favor of such occurrences, not as exceedingly common, but as happening now and then. The only remaining question is whether the absence of conclusive evidence was such as to have rendered any given story extremely improbable. There had previously been very few men likely to go to the bottom of such a report, there were beginning to be a great many; the roads over which the report and the investigator would have to be trained had mostly been execrable and were beginning to be admirable; the area of the earth's surface under civilization had increased. Finally, as a matter of fact, the story was not felt at the time by the bulk of judicious persons to be in conflict with common sense.

390.19 Of course, . . . errors.] The draft has the following paragraph in lieu of this sentence (R 879:50–51):

But am I then proposing to maintain, I hear the disgusted scientist exclaim, that popular belief falls into no gross errors? Oh no, only "so long as it remains under the guidance of general experience, and confines itself to conclusions of the kind to which such experience is plainly competent to testify." But how are we to decide whether these conditions are satisfied or not? Well, the question has to be submitted to good judgment. If it appears on a review of experience that similar conclusions are inferrable, the testimony of common sense is to be taken to determine more precisely what those conclusions shall be. Then these conclusions will again be submitted to individual good judgment to see whether a further revision may be needed or not.

391.3–4 Common sense . . . reject it.] Peirce adds the following comment in the draft (R 879:55):

> If it be urged that neither common sense nor good sense can be made to favor the doctrine *[that]* consciousness is an accident or "ultimate property" of nervematter, I willingly grant that. Sooner than make mind a modification of matter, I would make matter a modification of mind. But no speculations about the connection of body and soul can shake the proposition of the dependence of feeling and action upon the nervematter in which it resides; for this stands solidly upon universal experience.

391.8–10 law which Galileo . . . no diminution,] See ann. 385.31–33.

391.10–12 the first thing . . . at Pisa,] This was reported by Vincenzo Viviani (1622–1703), Galileo's student and assistant, and early biographer of Galileo. However, Stillman Drake, in *Galileo at Work: His Scientific Biography* (Chicago: University of Chicago Press, 1978, pp. 20–21), casts serious doubt on this. For background, see Galileo's discussion of the pendulum principles in his *Discourses and Mathematical Demonstrations Concerning Two New Sciences* (1638). For an extensive discussion of Galileo's dynamics, and the role of the swinging lamp, see Peirce's 1892–93 Lowell lectures, R 1282, 1283.

392.15–25 In regard to . . . from its origin.] The three possible philosophies listed here, elliptic, parabolic, and hyperbolic, which are also mentioned in "Sketch of a New Philosophy" (R 928, 1890), correspond respectively to the Epicurean, pessimist, and evolutionist views depicted in the first chapter of "A Guess at the Riddle" (sel. 23) and first distinguished in W5:251 (1885). See also R 150, which is reprinted as NEM 2:474–75.

393.35 The myriad strange stories prove nothing.] Of these stories Peirce says in his draft (R 879:55–56):

> If I am asked whether I will not allow that they prove there are phenomena of the human mind that we cannot explain, I reply that I suppose no rational man, certainly no physicist, thinks that he can satisfactorily explain all the ordinary phenomena of stocks and stones, far less that he knows all about the action of the mind. So that the strange stories cannot be said to prove what was as evident as could be before. Mr. Gurney, in *Phantasms of the Living*, undertook to make something out of some of these stories by the aid of the mathematical theory of probabilities. After a full examination of his method, I came to the conclusion that it could yield no valuable results; and I set forth my views at length. . . . If these stories were examined in large numbers,—say if twenty men of first rate ability were *[to]* devote a year exclusive of all other occupation to the investigation of a thousand of them, something might be learned, but probably nothing at all adequate to the expenditure.

45. *Herbert Spencer's Philosophy*

395.6–7 Hegelians and such like scorn it,] Peirce may have in mind British Hegelians such as Thomas Hill Green (1836–1882) and Edward Caird (1835–1908). Green, who agreed with Hegel's view of history, but not his dialectical method, was especially critical of Spencer.

395.22–23 An outsider . . . to doubt this.] Note that Peirce wrote this piece under the pseudonym "Outsider" (see also sel. 47). The *New York Times* editor wrote, in his introduction to the debate, that:

the writer of the article signs himself 'Outsider,' too modestly, we think, for while for the purposes of his inquiry he may desire to stand apart from the adepts whom he calls upon to speak their minds about Herbert Spencer, he is himself eminent for his attainments in science and might speak with some authority upon the questions he raises.

395.25–396.4 This method . . . divergent modifications.] Strangely enough, Peirce's quotation appears to conflate Spencer's original statement and the abbreviated version found in F. Howard Collins's 1889 *An Epitome of The Synthetic Philosophy* which he read and noticed for the *Nation* during the same weeks (sel. 46). Spencer wrote: "This way is to compare all opinions of the same genus; to set aside as more or less discrediting one another those special and concrete elements in which such opinions disagree; to observe what remains after these have been eliminated; and to find for the remaining constituent that expression which holds true throughout its various disguises" (*First Principles,* pt. I, ch. 1, § 2). Collins summarized: "Our method to find this postulate is:—To compare all opinions of one genus; to set aside the special and concrete elements in which they disagree; and to find for the remainder that abstract expression which holds true throughout its divergent modifications" (*An Epitome,* ch. 1, § 2, p. 4).

396.11–12 "rank next in certainty . . . exact science"?] F. Howard Collins, *An Epitome of The Synthetic Philosophy,* ch. 1, § 2, p. 4.

397.2–3 inconsistency of Berkeley . . . corporeal matter] In his 1871 Berkeley review, Peirce called the fact that Berkeley did not treat mind and matter in the same way "the great inconsistency of the Berkeleyan theory" (W2:483). For a discussion of Berkeley's different treatment of mind and matter, and Peirce's criticism thereof, see Cornelis de Waal, "The Quest for Reality: Charles S. Peirce and the Empiricists" (dissertation, University of Miami, 1997), ch. 4.

397.6–8 the English . . . Bentham.] Jonathan Edwards (1703–1758), American philosopher who was strongly influenced by the Cambridge Platonists and John Locke. Bernard de Mandeville (1670–1733), Dutch physician who moved to London after receiving his medical degree from the University of Leiden.

397.12–13 John Mill . . . of feelings.] See *Logic* (1886), bk. I, ch. 3, § 8, "Mind."

397.24–26 There are philosophies . . . immediacy itself.] Hegel's philosophy is a paradigmatic example of a philosophy that is both evolutionary and complete, as it is based on the idea that the categories of thought correspond precisely with the determining characteristics of things. The phrase "blank immediacy" refers to Hegel's basic or "primordial" category of Pure Being. See his *Science of Logic* (London: George Allen & Unwin, 1929, 81–82).

397.27–33 There are certain things . . . evolutionary sense.] In the first part of his *First Principles,* entitled "The Unknowable," Spencer explains that Matter, Motion, Force, Space, and Time are all notions fully incomprehensible and inexplicable, given the antinomies to which reflection upon them inevitably leads.

397.30–34 blank indeterminate matter . . . Aristotle himself.] Compare with what Aristotle says in *Metaphysics* VII, *Physics* II, and *Generation of Animals* I.

398.18–20 an easy but important . . . remains unchanged.] *First Principles,* pt. II, ch. 5, "Continuity of Motion." Also Collins's *An Epitome,* ch. 2, para. 59, p. 24.

398.20–22 It follows . . . evolution.] *First Principles,* pt. 2, ch. 11, "Recapitulation, Criticism, and Recommencement." In his evolutionary cosmology, Peirce himself goes a major step further as he seeks to explain the very origin of the general laws of mechanics. See sel. 28 above, and also the 1891–93 *Monist* series.

398.25–26 Mr. Spencer . . . Unknowable,] *First Principles*, pt. II, ch. 2, § 43.

398.35–399.1 The most remarkable . . . to be primordial.] Spencer defends this view in pt. II, ch. 6, "The Persistence of Force," which is the name he gives to the law of conservation of energy. Also, in pt. II, ch. 18, "The Interpretation of Evolution," the persistence of force is the basic mechanism of evolution.

399.7–8 "It is undoubtedly . . . principles."] Compare with Spencer's statement in *First Principles*, pt. II, ch. 16, § 138, that "all Evolution is from the homogeneous to the heterogeneous" and that "this advance in definiteness is not a primary but a secondary phenomenon—is a result incidental on other changes. . . . That is to say, the increasing definiteness is a concomitant of the increasing consolidation, general and local. While the secondary re-distributions are ever adding to the heterogeneity, the primary redistribution, while augmenting the integration, is incidentally giving distinctness to the increasingly unlike parts as well as to the aggregate of them. . . . The more specific idea of Evolution now reached is—a change from an indefinite, incoherent homogeneity, to a definite coherent heterogeneity, accompanying the dissipation of motion and integration of matter." See also pt. II, ch. 24, § 187.

399.15–18 that chapter . . . forces?] Which chapter of *First Principles* Peirce is referring to is unclear. A hint on 404.30–36 suggests ch. 18 as the most likely.

400.6–7 the seventeen articles of the Spencerian confession] These "seventeen" articles are really sixteen, and are listed by Herbert Spencer in his preface to F. Howard Collins's *An Epitome*, pp. viii–xi. It is a summary list Spencer first wrote around 1871 for an American friend who had asked him to furnish a succinct statement of the cardinal principles developed in his successive works.

400.10–19 Now, we know . . . of speculation.] Based on pendulum experiments Newton (1642–1727) posited in the first edition of the *Principia* (1687), and again in the the third edition (1726), that the earth was not a perfect sphere, but was flattened at the poles, and that this was due to the centrifugal force of the earth's rotation. In Paris the dominant view at that time, based on measures of arcs of longitude, was that the earth was slightly elongated at the poles. The subsequent debate has commonly been depicted as pitting the older French Cartesian and the new British Newtonian schools against one another.

400.22–23 We wish . . . in not over fifty pages,] See also 401.10–11.

46. *Collins's* Epitome of the Synthetic Philosophy

401.1 F. Howard Collins] Frederick Howard Collins (1857–1910).

401.4–5 Spencer's systematic works,] This is Spencer's *The Synthetic Philosophy*, a comprehensive work which he began in 1860 and completed in 1896. It contains volumes on the principles of biology, psychology, morality, and sociology. See sels. 45 and 47 for Peirce's discussion of Spencer's system.

47. *"Outsider" Wants More Light*

402.14 Prof. Osborn,] Henry Fairfield Osborn (1857–1935), American paleontologist. Osborn's letter to the *New York Times* appeared on Sunday, 6 April 1890, on p. 13, cols. 1 and 2, under the title "The Spencerian Biology, the Philosopher's Standing as a Biologist—The Soundness of His Views Tested by Time."

402.22–25 As Prof. Osborn . . . its external relations."] H. F. Osborn, ibid., col. 2.
403.1–3 "all the processes . . . minimized."] Ibid.
403.4–5 "perhaps a large class . . . of Spencer, "] Ibid.
403.6 "has never claimed to be a practical investigator."] Ibid., col. 1.
403.7–8 "every great leader . . . inspiration,"] Ibid., col. 2.
403.8–10 "all permanent advances . . . the field."] Ibid.
403.11–13 "The sum of several works . . . value."] Ibid., col. 1.
403.13–14 "It appears now . . . evolution theory."] Ibid., col. 2.
403.13 Weismann's] August Friedrich Leopold Weismann (1834–1914), German biologist who developed a "germ plasm" theory of heredity, according to which hereditary elements are carried by sex cells. Cf. EP1:359–60 (1893).
403.14–15 Weismann contends . . . transmitted] The relevant work of Weismann prior to 1890 consists of his *Studien zur Descendenz-Theorie* (1875), and of articles of which some appeared in English translation in *Essays on Heredity* (1889), just one year prior to the present controversy over Spencer.
403.15–17 "it is perfectly evident . . . the ground."] H. F. Osborn, ibid., col. 2:

> What the issue will be is the present bone of contention between the Lamarckians, Darwinians, and Neo-Darwinians, the latter school holding that there is absolutely no transmission of acquired characters, and it is perfectly evident that if they demonstrate this proposition one great section of Spencer's system falls to the ground!

The 'they' in Peirce's quotation thus refers to Osborn's Neo-Darwinians. Osborn distinguishes Darwinians who allow that the transmission of acquired characteristics may be one factor among many in evolution, from Neo-Darwinians who do not admit this mechanism, and make natural selection the sole mechanism of evolution. Osborn uses the term "Neo-Darwinian" because in *The Origin of Species* Darwin took a hard line against Lamarckian evolution, a view which he later softened, in light of possible evidence for the heritability of acquired characteristics.

403.18 Lamarck] Jean Baptiste Pierre Antoine de Monet de Lamarck (1744–1829), French naturalist who proposed an evolutionary theory according to which acquired characteristics are heritable.
403.19–21 "many of . . . discoveries,"] H. F. Osborn, ibid., col. 2. After "confirmed" Osborn had added "or are apparently in accordance with," which Peirce omits.
403.21–24 Sedgwick writes . . . appeared."] Quoted by H. F. Osborn, ibid., col. 2. As Osborn intimates in his letter to the *New York Times*, the English zoologist Adam Sedgwick (1854–1913) was the favorite pupil of the British embryologist Francis Maitland Balfour, who died unexpectedly in 1883. Sedgwick continued Balfour's work in the same laboratory. In 1880, Balfour had published a paper in which he refuted Spencer's view of the formation of the nervous system. Balfour's own explanation of this process was shown to be incorrect by Sedgwick five years later (and not eight as Osborn contends), in a paper entitled "On the Fertilised Ovum and Formation of the Layers of the South African Peripatus" (*Proceedings of the Royal Society of London* 39/240 [1885]: 239–44). The quoted concession to Spencer is found on its last page.
403.28 H. J. Messenger] Hiram John Messenger (1855–1913), mathematics professor and social statistician. Messenger's letter to the *New York Times* appeared Sunday, 30 March 1890, p. 13, col. 4, under the title "Two Points Fairly Met, Mr.

Spencer Relies on Acknowledged Specialists—The Soundness of His Conclusions Attested."

403.31–33 He gives as a reason . . . orthodox.] H. J. Messenger, ibid., col. 4:

> Another point should be borne in mind when considering the reason why Mr. Spencer has not been covered with the honors which the learned societies generally shower upon many other men who have not done one-tenth as much for the progress of science. Every one knows that Mr. Spencer is one of the boldest and most original of thinkers. As a natural result, he has arrived at, and given expression to, conclusions which have brought upon him the hostility of the orthodox element, and nearly every learned society has an orthodox element large enough and hostile enough to prevent it from giving the great philosopher a single honor, and so he, like all great reformers, will have to be content with being called infidel, atheist, materialist, godless, in his own lifetime, and will have to wait for the next generation to sing his praises.

403.35–404.7 Chancing today . . . infidel!] *Transactions of the Royal Society* 35 (1890): 1118–19. Huxley and Haeckel do appear in the respective lists. Peirce cites the number of foreign fellows as thirty-six, but this was the limit on the number of foreign fellows allowed. In 1890 there were only thirty-four elected foreign fellows.

404.4 Huxley,] Thomas Henry Huxley (1825–1895), English biologist and advocate of Darwinian evolutionary theory.

404.7 Haeckel,] Ernst Heinrich Philipp August Haeckel (1834–1919), German biologist who was greatly influenced by Darwin's *Origin of Species,* a book he used both to attack entrenched religious dogma and to build his own cosmology.

404.14–23 Mr. Messenger is so good . . . bear out.] H. J. Messenger, *New York Times*, 30 March 1890, p. 13, col. 4:

> The first volume of Mr. Spencer's biology, written some twenty-five years ago, deals very largely in the introductory chapters with the subject of organic chemistry. The professor of chemistry in one of our leading medical colleges, who was reading the volume last year, recently said to me that the one thing in the book which particularly impressed him was the very large number of correct conclusions drawn, and the very large number of possibilities and probabilities hinted at in the chapters referred to, which were not known when the book was written, but which recent work in the chemical laboratory has shown to be true.

404.27–30 Mr. Messenger declares . . . pointed out.] Ibid., col. 4

404.30–31 I thought I had already pointed out] Sel. 45, 399.14–32.

405.5–7 "All these phenomena, . . . of force."] This is the beginning of cardinal principle no. 15 given by Spencer in his preface to Collins's *An Epitome,* p. xi. Spencer's sentence, after "force," finished with the words "under its forms of matter and motion." Compare with *First Principles*, pt. II, ch. 18, "The Interpretation of Evolution," § 147: "In other words, the phenomena of Evolution have to be deduced from the Persistence of Force." The conception of "evolution" is developed in chapters 12 to 17 and is eventually defined as "an integration of matter and concomitant dissipation of motion; during which the matter passes from a relatively indefinite, incoherent homogeneity to a relatively definite, coherent heterogeneity and during which the retained motion undergoes a parallel transformation" (pt. II, ch. 17, § 145).

405.17 Edgar R. Dawson,] Dawson's first letter to the editor of the *New York Times* appeared on Sunday, 6 April 1890, p. 13, cols. 2 and 3, under the title "Asking Too

Much, 'Outsider' Should Accept as True Those Things about Which Everybody Is Agreed—Space and Time." After Peirce's reply of 13 April, another letter from Dawson appeared on April 20 under the title "As to 'Reversed Velocities.' Some Illustrations of 'Outsider's' Hypothesis of a Universe Moving Backward."

405.19–20 "Is it necessary . . . chemistry?"] Dawson, *New York Times*, 6 April 1890, p. 13, col. 2.

405.24–27 "state any . . . ignorant."] Ibid., col. 2. Peirce's "than in adopting from all beliefs" replaces Dawsons's "than in deducing from all experiences."

406.6–7 "astrology . . . exact science."] Ibid., col. 2: "For it must be remembered that Mr. Spencer proposes only to apply this to cases that exact science does not reach, and can astrology be said to have had an existence since the rise of exact science?" Dawson's "this" refers to Spencer's method of obtaining first principles in areas where we lack scientific knowledge by finding the core of common opinion on a given topic. In his first article Peirce had pointed out that the Spencerian consensus method would not so long ago have led to the inclusion of general astrological opinions among the first principles. Dawson replies that this would not have been the case because the method is only applied to subjects that "exact science does not reach," while the subject-matter of astrology is properly scientific—and hence, Peirce did not understand the purpose of the consensus method. Peirce, however, said in his first article that Spencer's method was meant to arrive at principles that "rank next in certainty" to the results of exact science, which indicates that Peirce understood that the consensus method did not apply to scientific topics.

406.8 Hipparchus] Hipparchus (fl. 146–127 B.C.), Greek astronomer and mathematician, believed to be the author of the first catalogue of stars, on which Ptolemy's based his catalogue in the *Almagest*.

406.10–12 "Does 'Outsider' . . . necessary truths?"] Dawson, ibid., col. 3.

406.25–27 I had said that . . . dynamics,] See sel. 45, 399.14–32, and ann. 404.30–31.

406.28–29 "that thereafter . . . resistance?"] Dawson, ibid., col. 3. On the idea that motion must follow the "line of least resistance," see Spencer's *First Principles*, pt. II, ch. 9.

406.36 "Carl Opperg,"] This letter appeared in the *New York Times*, Sunday, 6 April 1890, p. 13, cols. 3–4, under the title "Experience and Intuition. A Dissenter from Spencer's Theory of the Source of Knowledge as Explained by 'Kappa'."

407.1–2 "W. H. B." . . . heavens,] W. H. B.'s letter appeared in the *New York Times* on Sunday 6 April 1890, p. 13, col. 4, under the title "A Philosophical Critic. He Goes Pretty Deeply into the Subject of Matter, Space, and the Unknowable." Peirce alludes to the following sentence: "Instead of making matter revolve around force the need of the times is for some Copernicus to recentre Mr. Spencer's system and call matter the sun and place him on the throne of the intellectual heavens." W. H. B. wrote a second letter which appeared in the 20 April 1890 issue of the newspaper, p. 13, col. 3.

407.3–6 "R. G. E." . . . of Spencer.] R. G. E.'s letter appeared in the *New York Times* on Sunday, 30 March 1890, p. 13, cols. 2–4 as "A Call for Specifications. Opponents of Spencer's Philosophy Must Point Out its Imperfections—Countless Prophecies Have Been Based on It." Peirce is alluding to a sentence in col. 2: "Had 'Outsider' waited until his last paper appeared before writing that Mr. Spencer 'is one of those who build Babel systems to scale the heights of knowledge' we might have looked upon him as a candid disbeliever. But when he makes such a statement at the outset, without giving a single reason for the assertion, the analogy of a noisy barker that does no biting forces itself upon us." R. G. E. wrote a second letter which appeared in the 20 April 1890 issue of the newspaper, cols. 1–2, under the title "Force and Life. A Mechanical Theory of Evolution and of Life the Only Possible—Spencer and the Learned Societies."

407.14 "Kappa,"] Kappa's letter to the editor was the first reply printed in the *New York Times* on Sunday, 30 March 1890, p. 13, cols. 1–2, under the title "Flaws in 'Outsider's' Reasoning. His Attention Called to the Fixed Line between the Knowable and the Unknowable—Experience and Intuition."

407.17–18 "'Outsider' doubtless . . . philosopher."] Ibid., col. 1.

407.27 Prof. Cope, whose book is famous,] Edward Drinker Cope (1840–1897), American paleontologist and advocate of Lamarckian evolution. The book is probably Cope's *The Origin of the Fittest, Essays on Evolution* (New York: Macmillan, 1887).

407.29 Prof. J. P. Cooke,] Josiah Parsons Cooke (1827–1894), American chemist, and professor at Harvard University (1850–94). He was Charles Peirce's chemistry teacher at the Lawrence Scientific School.

408.1–2 "purely . . . logical or not—"] Kappa, ibid., col. 1; 'purely' for 'surely.'

408.4–5 282 systems . . . to the world,] It is unclear where this estimate comes from, if it is not purely fanciful. In a two-page unfinished fragment entitled "How many Philosophies have there been?" (R 1573:10–11), Peirce distinguishes seventy-two philosophies from that of Thales to that of Victor Cousin (1792–1867).

409.10–12 The cognition-theory . . . intended.] In his letter (col. 1), Kappa refers Outsider to the second volume of Spencer's *Principles of Psychology* for the best account of space available (vol. II, pt. 6, ch. 14, "The Perception of Space").

409.16–21 Finally, "Kappa" . . . cannot be explained."] Kappa, *New York Times*, 30 March 1890, p. 13, col. 2. Kappa takes a sort of Kantian view of scientific explanation as the explanation of events that occur within phenomenal experience. Space is a condition of possibility of experience; as such we do not experience it as something that "changes in our experience," and thus we cannot have a scientific explanation of space. Kappa writes:

> Since knowledge is limited by experience, and the reason for the existence of a thing involves the predication of a change in its state or condition within experience, it follows that that which has never changed in our experience or in the experience of our long line of ancestors beginning, say, with the jelly fish, cannot be explained by our mental organization. As our organism has never experienced an environment containing a different number of dimensions, antecedent to the space in which we live, we are therefore, and shall ever be, unable to explain the whyness of this thusness; we might as well attempt to lift ourselves by our boot straps, or explain why two and two make four.

409.30–32 Spencer, . . . nebula,] This refers to Spencer's "The Nebular Hypothesis," reprinted in vol. 1 of his *Essays, Scientific, Political and Speculative* (1858).

Bibliography of Peirce's References

For Peirce's references preference is given to the edition he is most likely to have used, based on a variety of evidence like library charging records, book lists made by him, and clues from his correspondence. It should be noted, however, that a reconstruction of Peirce's library is still in its infancy and that the list is provisional. Much work in this area has been done by José Vericat, who also assisted with the bibliography given below.

The bibliographical entries are divided into three categories. First, items for which there is no evidence that Peirce owned them, but which he had in his physical possession at some point in time as evidenced by library charging records or correspondence. Items in this category are labeled "Consulted."

Second, items that Peirce owned or considered part of his personal library. The main evidence for this category is the several lists Peirce composed of the books he owned (e.g., R 1556, 1557, 1559) and library cards of his personal library (R 1596). Although these lists include books of which Peirce was not strictly the owner, that they are listed suggests that they have been in his physical possession for a prolonged period of time. Entries falling in this second category are labeled "Library." When there is evidence pointing to the actual copy owned by Peirce, like an autograph, marginalia in Peirce's hand, or testimony by third parties, an asterisk is added. Third party evidence includes the books reported as "Gift of Mrs. Peirce" in Widener Library Old Cards and Widener Library Shelf Lists, the books listed by Johns Hopkins University as sold to them by Peirce, and the books listed by Mrs. James Bryce of Milford.

Books that are not listed by Peirce, and for which there is no evidence that Peirce owned them, remain unlabeled. For this last group preference is given to the edition that seems to have been most currently available at the time.

Aristotle. *Opera*. Edidit Academia regia Borussica. 5 vols. Berlin: Georg Reimer, 1831[–70]. (Library; also owned the 1489 *Omnia opera*.)

———. *Organon*. Translated by O. F. Owen. 2 vols. London: Henry G. Bohn, 1853. (Library.)

Bacon, Francis. *Novum Organum; or, True Suggestions for the Interpretation of Nature*. Translated by Andrew Johnson. London: Bell & Daldy, 1859. (Library; also owned the 1665 *Opera omnia*.)

Berkeley, George. *The Works of George Berkeley*. 4 vols. Edited by Alexander Campbell Fraser. Oxford: Clarendon, 1871. (Library.)

Blundeville, Thomas. *The Arte of Logicke. Plainly Taught in the English Tongue, by M. Blundeuil of Newton Flotman in Norfolke, aswell According to the Doctrine of Aristotle, as of all Other Moderne and Best Accounted Authors thereof*. London: printed by William Stansby, and are to be sold by M. Lownes, 1619. (Library*.)

Boole, George. *The Mathematical Analysis of Logic, being an Essay towards a Calculus of Deductive Reasoning*. Cambridge: Macmillan, Barclay and McMillan, 1847.

———. *An Investigation of the Laws of Thought, on which are Founded the Mathematical Theories of Logic and Probabilities*. London: Walton and Maberly, 1854. (Consulted.)

Butler, Joseph. *The Analogy of Religion, Natural and Revealed to the Constitution and Course of Nature, to which are Added two Brief Sermons: I. On Personal Identity. II. On the Nature of Virtue*. With a preface by Samuel Halifax. New edition. London: G. Bohn, 1852. (Library.)

Calvin, John. *Institutes of the Christian Religion*. Translation by Henry Beveridge. 3 vols. Edinburgh: Calvin Translation Society, 1845–1846.

Cantor, Georg. "Über Verschiedene Theoreme aus der Theorie der Punktmengen in einem *n*—fach ausgedehnten stetigen Raume G*n*." *Acta Mathematica* 7 (1885): 105–124.

Clarke, Alexander Ross. *Geodesy*. Oxford: Clarendon Press, 1880.

Collins, F. Howard. *Epitome of the Synthetic Philosophy*. New York: D. Appleton & Co., 1889. (Library.)

Comte, Auguste. *Cours de philosophie positive*. 6 vols. Paris/New York: Bachelier, 1864. (Consulted.)

Descartes, René. *Oeuvres choisies*. New ed. Paris: Garnier Frères, libraires-éditeurs, 1865. (Library*; also owned the 1650 *Opera philosophica*.)

Diogenes Laertius. *The Lives and Opinions of Eminent Philosophers*. Translated by C. D. Yonge. London: Henry G. Bohn, 1853. (Library; also owned a 1692 Greek-Latin edition.)

Duns Scotus, John. *Quæstiones quodlibetales ex quatuor voluminibus scripti Oxoniensis*. Edited by Salvator Bartholutius. 8 vols. in 4. Venetiis: apud Hæredes Melchioris Sessæ, 1580. (Library*; also owned a 1477, 1481, 1609, and a 1639 edition.)

Eck, Johann. *In summulas Petri Hispani extemporaria et succincta explanatio; sed succosa explanatio*. Augusta Vindelicorum: Ex officina Millerane, 1516. (Library*.)

Euclid. *Elementa. (Opera omnia Vols. I–IV. Libri I–XIII.)* Greek, with Latin translation. Edited by I. L. Heiberg. Lipsiae: B. G. Teubner, 1883–85. (Library; also owned 1570, 1651, and 1752 edition of the *Elements*.)

Faraday, Michael. *Experimental Researches in Electricity*. 3 vols. London: R. and J. E. Taylor, 1849–1855. (Consulted volume one.)

Fizeau, Armand. "Tableau des dilatations par la chaleur de divers corps simples métalliques ou non métalliques, et de quelques composés hydrogénés du carbone." *Comte Rendu des Séances de L'Academie des Sciences* 68 (1869): 1125–31.

Foster, Michael. *A Textbook of Physiology*. 3rd. revised ed. London: Macmillan and Co., 1879. (Library.)

Galilei, Galileo. *Le opere de Galileo Galilei. Prima edizione completa, condotta sugli autentici manoscritti palatini*. 15 vols. in 16. Firenze: Societa Editrice Fiorentina, 1842–56. (Library*.)

Gauss, Carl Friedrich. *Disquisitiones arithmeticae*. Leipzig: G. Fleischer, 1801. (Library.)

———. *Werke*. Leipzig: B. G. Teubner, 1900.

George, Henry. *Progress and Poverty. An Inquiry into the Causes of Industrial Depression and of Increase of Want with Increase of Wealth. The Remedy by Henry George*. London: William Reeves, 1882.

Green, George. "Researches on the Vibrations of Pendulums in Fluid Media." *Transactions of the Royal Society of Edinburgh* 13 (1836): 54–62.

Gurney, Edmund, Frederic W. H. Myers, and Frank Podmore. *Phantasms of the Living*. London: Trubner and Co., 1886. (Library.)

Hegel, Georg Wilhelm Friedrich. *Encyklopaedie der philosophischen Wissenschaften im Grundrisse*. 2nd ed. Heidelberg: August Osswald, 1827. (Library*.)

Helmert, Friedrich Robert. *Die mathematischen und physikalischen Theorien der höheren Geodäsie*. 2 vols. Leipzig: B. G. Teubner, 1880. (Library.)

Huygens, Christiaan. *Horologium oscillatorium, sive, De motu pendulorum ad horologia aptato demonstrationes geometricae*. Parisiis: Apud F. Muguet, 1673. (Library.)

Jevons, William Stanley. "On the Mechanical Performance of Logical Inference." *Philosophical Transactions of the Royal Society of London* 160 (1870): 497–518.

Kant, Immanuel. *Critique of Pure Reason*. Edited by M. D. Meiklejohn. London: Henry G. Bohn, 1855. (Library*.)

Khayyám, Omar. *Rubáiyát of Omar Khayyám in English Verse*. Translator Edward FitzGerald. New York and Boston: Houghton, Mifflin and Company, 1888. (Library*.)

Klein, Felix. "Eine neue Relation zwischen den Singularitäten einer algebraischen Curve." *Mathematische Annalen* 10 (1876): 199–209. (Library.)

Langley, Alfred G., "Leibnitz's Critique of Locke." *The Journal of Speculative Philosophy* 19 (1885): 275–299.

Legendre, Adrien Marie. *Essai sur la Théorie des Nombres*. Paris: 1794.

Marquand, Allan. "A Machine for Producing Syllogistic Variations." In *Studies in Logic. By Members of the Johns Hopkins University*, 12–15. Boston: Little, Brown, & Co., 1883. [Edited by Peirce.] (Library*.)

McColl, Hugh."The Calculus of Equivalent Statements (Second Paper)." *Proceedings of the London Mathematical Society* 9 (1878): 177–86.

———. "Symbolical Reasoning." *Mind* 5 (1880): pp. 45–60. (Library*.)

Mill, John Stuart. *A System of Logic, Ratiocinative and Inductive. Being a Connected View of the Principles of Evidence, and the Methods of Scientific Investigation*. London: Longmans, Green, and Co., 1886. (Library*.)

Mitchell, Oscar Howard. "On a New Algebra of Logic." *Studies in Logic. By Members of the Johns Hopkins University*, 72–106. Boston: Little Brown & Co., 1883. [Edited by Peirce.] (Library*.)

Newton, Isaac. *Philosophiae naturalis principia mathematica*. New edition by Thomas Le Seur, and Franciscus Jacquier. 2 vols. in 1. Glasuaem: T. T. and J. Tegg, 1833. (Library*.)

Noel, E. *The Science of Metrology; or, Natural Weights and Measures. A Challenge to the Metric System*. London: Edward Stanford, 1889. (Library*.)

Peirce, Benjamin. *Linear Associative Algebra*. Read before the National Academy of Sciences. New Edition, with Addenda and Notes by C. S. Peirce, Son of the Author. New York: D. Van Nostrand, 1882. (Library.)

Petrus Hispanus. *Compendiarius parvorum logicalium liber continens perutiles Petri Hispani tractatus priores sex & clarissimi philosophi Marsilij dialectices documenta: cum utilissimis commentarijs: per virum preclarum Chunradum Pschlacher*. Vienne: 1512. (Library*.)

Phoenix, John [pseud.] (George Horatio Derby). *Phoenixiana; or, Sketches and Burlesques*. 8th ed. New York: D. Appleton & Co., 1856. (Library.)

Plato. *The Works of Plato. A New Literal Version, Chiefly from the Text of Stallbaum*. Translated by Cary, Davis, and Burges. 6 vols. London: Henry G. Bohn, 1851–55. (Library*.)

Quetelet, Lambert Adolphe. *Théorie des Probabilités*. Bruxelles: A. Jamar, 1853. (Consulted.)

Shakespeare, William. *The Works of William Shakespeare*. Edited by Richard Grant White. 12 vols. Boston: Little, Brown & Co., 1857–65. (Library*.)

Spencer, Herbert. *Essays, Scientific, Political and Speculative*. London: Longman, Brown, Green, Longmans, and Roberts, 1858.

———. *First Principles*. 1st ed. London: Williams and Norgate, 1862. (Library.)

———. *The Principles of Biology*. 2 vols. New York: D. Appleton and Co., 1864–67.

Stock, St. George. *Deductive Logic*. London: Longmans, Green & Co., 1889. (Library*.)

Stokes, George Gabriel. "On the Variation of Gravity at the Surface of the Earth." *Transactions of the Cambridge Philosophical Society* 8 (1849): 672–95.

Studies in Logic. By Members of the Johns Hopkins University. Edited by Charles S. Peirce. Boston: Little, Brown, & Co., 1883. (Library*.)

Swift, Jonathan. *Travels into Several Remote Nations of the World, by Lemuel Gulliver*. Philadelphia: Porter & Coates, [n.d.]. (Consulted.)

Tait, Peter Guthrie. *Sketch of Thermodynamics*. 2nd ed. Edinburgh: David Douglas, 1877.

Tetens, Johan Nicolai. *Philosophische Versuche über die menschliche Natur und ihre Entwickelung*. Leipzig: M. G. Weidmanns Erben und Reich, 1777.

The Thousand and One Nights, Commonly Called, in England, The Arabian Nights' Entertainments. A new translation from the Arabic with notes, by Edward William Lane. Illustrated by W. Harvey. 3 vols. London: Charles Knight & Co., 1840–41. (Consulted.)

Thomas Aquinas. *Divi Thomae Aquinatis ordinis praedicatorum, doctoris angelici, secundum scriptum appellatum, Super quatuor libros Sententiarium, ad Hannibaldum Hannibaldensem. Nunc primum in lucem æditum cum duobus indicibus copiosissimis, & quibusdam scholijs in margine additis*. Romae: Vincentius Luchinus excudebat, 1560. (Library*.)

———. *Quaestiones de duodecim quodlibet*. Nurmberg: Johann Sensenschmidt and Andreas Frisner, 1474. (Library*.)

Thomson, Sir William. *Popular Lectures and Addresses*. 3 vols. London: MacMillian & Co., 1889.

Transactions of the Royal Society of Edinburgh 10 (April 1890). Edinburgh: Robert Grant and Son.

Tupper, Martin Farquhar. *Proverbial Philosophy, in Four Series: Now First Complete Including the Fiftieth Edition of the Two First Series*. London: E. Moxon & Son, [1880?].

"Vorlesungen über die Algebra der Logik." *Mitteilungen der Verlagsbuchhandlung B. G. Teubner in Leipzig* 3 (June 1886), pp. 44–45.

Weismann, August. *Essays upon Heredity and Kindred Biological Problems*. Oxford: Clarendon Press, 1889.

Whewell, William. *Novum organon renovatum.* 3rd ed. London: John W. Parker and Son, 1858.

Wüllner, Adolph. *Lehrbuch der Experimentalphysik.* 4 vols. B. G. Leipzig: Teubner, 1875.

Young, Thomas. *A Course of Lectures on Natural Philosophy and the Mechanical Arts.* London: Printed for J. Johnson by W. Savage, 1807.

Zöllner, Johann. *Transcendental Physics: An Account of Experimental Investigations. From the Scientific Treatises of Johann Karl Friedrich Zöllner.* Translated from the German, with a preface and appendices, by Charles Carlton Massey. 2nd. edition. London: W. H. Harrison, 1882.

Chronological Catalog
January 1887–April 1890

Beginning with this volume, what in previous volumes was called the "Chronological List" is taking on a new appearance. This is partly due to a change of policy that took place in the fall of 1996. At that time the Project and its advisors came to understand that the greatest impediment to the Project's pace of production was the commitment to reorganize all the manuscripts, including every page of every fragment, and to arrange all the writings in strict compositional order, whether they were going to be published or not. This was necessary for the preparation of a new catalog numbering system reflecting the Project's rearrangement of the manuscripts. This requirement has now been dropped, for it is not central to the Project's principal mission of producing a selected chronological edition. Consequently, the editors no longer spend as much time trying to identify, resequence, repaginate, and date, every Peirce document. This intensive work is performed only on documents deemed publishable—or closely connected to publishable documents (such as drafts)—after preliminary, but thorough, inspection, with the help of specialized contributing editors. Documents clearly not candidates for a chronological edition are simply entered into the Project's manuscript database, stored in a folder, and given a catalog entry. All other documents undergo the usual reorganization process, until their publishability is finally assessed. Since exact compositional sequencing and dating of Peirce's writings cannot be fully established, the numbering system used in previous volumes, which tended to convey the misrepresentation that the definitive reordering had been achieved, is abandoned. Also abandoned is the mere chronological list format which provided little useful information about the documents not selected for publication. The editors now provide a "chronological catalog" with an internal organization inspired both from Arthur Burks's bibliography of Peirce's works published in CP 8, pp. 251–330, and from Richard S. Robin's *Annotated Catalogue of the Papers of Charles S. Peirce.*

The catalog lists and provides information about the following kinds of documents.

(1) All of Peirce's known publications, identified by P followed by a number whenever the publication is listed in Kenneth L. Ketner's *A Comprehensive Bibliography of the Published Works of Charles Sanders Peirce*.

(2) All of Peirce's manuscripts (holograph or amanuensis), typescripts, offprints, notebooks, galleys, proof pages, prospectuses, which are archived in the Houghton Library of Harvard University or in any other known collection.

(3) The very few letters, generic or personal, and letter drafts that are included in the edition, identified by RL and a number as found in Robin's *Catalogue* when they are in the Harvard Peirce Papers.

(4) Titles of papers read by Peirce at professional meetings (such as the National Academy of Sciences), or known to have been written by him, even though no corresponding manuscripts have as yet been identified.

Not included here are those items in the *Comprehensive Bibliography* that merely mention Peirce's Coast Survey duties and observations in the annual *Report of the Superintendent of the United States Coast Survey.*

Information for each item includes: (a) the title provided by Peirce, or, if not available, a title provided by the editors, enclosed in italic square brackets; (b) the document type (holograph, typescript, etc.); (c) the number of sheets it contains, i.e., the number of inscribed rectos and versos; (d) the archival source (Houghton, Peirce Papers, most of the time); (e) the archival call number if any, or, in most cases, the Robin *Catalogue* number preceded by R and followed by the ISP pagination as resequenced; (f) the date, followed in parenthesis by an abbreviated rationale (see below); (g) supplementary information such as cross-references to other documents, content clues, and previous places of publication, such as NEM or CP.

All documents have been arranged chronologically according to the following principles.

(1) Documents whose composition is known to have taken place or begun in a given year are all listed under that year, which serves as a subtitle in the catalog. Within each year, the documents are arranged chronologically month by month in a decreasing order of date exactitude: first the documents dated to a precise day or range of days within a given month, then those dated simply within that month, then those dated within a month range beginning in that month, then those of the following month if that month falls in the same trimester, then those within a trimester indicated by a season (thus, "winter" documents follow the March documents, "spring" documents follow the June documents, "summer" documents follow the September documents, and "fall" documents follow the December documents), then those dated within a season range (spring–summer, for instance), then those of the next trimester, and so on until the end of the year, and finally those dated within the year or a year range beginning in that year.

(2) Documents whose composition is not assuredly known, but only vaguely suspected, to have taken place or begun within a given year are

listed separately after those mentioned above, under a new subtitle representing the *circa* year.

(3) Documents that bear an identical date are grouped thematically as far as feasible, so that papers on Non Euclidean geometry are not scattered among papers on metaphysics for instance, and are arranged alphabetically within those themes (the order of which is arbitrary).

(4) All documents are numbered in the final catalog order, restarting at 1 each time a new year or circa year is reached (following Burks's practice in CP 8). In this way it will be easier to add later discovered documents to the catalog, without disrupting the numbering system. One advantage is that readers will be more aware of the provisional and fallible state of the arrangement here offered. It also yields a convenient reference and filing system that allows users to refer to any document by its year and catalog number: 1887.2 or c. 1889.4, for example.

Whenever the date is not provided by Peirce himself with sufficient exactitude, it is followed, usually between parentheses, by a short rationale that summarizes the grounds on which the editors based their dating. These rationales are normally self-explanatory: "paper" means that the document was written on a kind of paper stock mostly used within the period; "watermark" means that the paper's watermark contained a manufacturing year, before which Peirce could not have written the document; "handwriting" means that comparison of Peirce's handwriting in many documents of the period and later indicate a pattern that is characteristic of the volume's period; "context" means that the document touches matters also dealt with in other documents of the period, or reflects a research interest Peirce is known to have had at the time. Rationales for circa years may also indicate that they were a mean in a range of possible years: some c. 1889 paper might have been written anywhere between 1887 and 1891, for instance.

Documents that have been selected for publication in this volume have their title introduced by the boldfaced word **Selection** followed by the number they were assigned in the table of contents. Selection 1 does not appear in the catalog below, but does so in the "Supplement to W5 Chronological List, 1884–1886" which follows the catalog. This supplement lists a number of writings, mostly related to pendulum work, which could not have been identified as belonging to the W5 period before work was completed on the W6 papers. This supplement is arranged in the same fashion as the catalog, but each item is preceded by a decimaled WMS number that indicates the position that item would occupy in the W5 Chronological List. Wherever in the W6 Catalog the letters WMS plus a number are used, they refer to some document listed in one of the previous chronological lists. It is partly to avoid confusion that the letters MS that were customarily used to refer to a document listed in Robin's *Catalogue* have been replaced by the less ambiguous letter R.

1887

1. **Selection 2.** [Circular for Course on The Art of Reasoning]

Holograph, 10 sheets, proofs, and offprints, Houghton, Peirce Papers, from folder RL 100. The manuscript was composed in December 1886 and printed during the first week of January 1887. Peirce used this brochure to advertise his correspondence course. The offprint serves as copy-text.

2. [Circular Letter to Bishops, accompanying the Correspondence Course Circular]

Four amanuensis, 3 pages each, letters to Bishops of Louisiana (J. N. Gallaher), of Northern New Jersey (I. A. Starkey), of Michigan (Samuel Smith Harris), and of Pittsburgh (Cortlandt Whitehead). First and fourth dated 11 January 1887; second and third dated 13 January 1887. Houghton, Peirce Papers, folder RL 100.

3. Pupils. List of letters etc.

Notebook, 19 sheets, Houghton, Peirce Papers, RL 100; 22 January–14 April 1887. Record of correspondence between Peirce and his students prior to Peirce's move to Milford.

4. **Selection 6.** [Letter to New Students]

Holograph, 5 sheets, plus 1 typed sheet (illegible carbon), Houghton, Peirce Papers, RL 100; January 1887.

5. [Correspondence Course. Letters from Students and Applicants]

Houghton, Peirce Papers, part of folder RL 100. This portion of the folder contains many letters between Peirce and his pupils concerning the correspondence course: letters of inquiry, typed exercises, students' answers to exercises, and Peirce's letters of correction/explanation. Portions of selections 2 to 9 and 11 to 12 in W6 come from folder RL 100 (some of these items are listed separately). The dates of the materials range from January 1887 to April 1889 (plus one 1890 and two 1893 letters of inquiry), the majority being from 1887 and early 1888. Names of students who actually began the course and of whom a few letters are still extant include: Walter Scott Andrews, George William Armstrong, A. M. Backus, Henry P. Goodenow, J. W. Grace, S. M. Hawes, Rev. Edgard L. Heermance, M. P. Janney, H. B. Kinghorn, Walter S. Langley, J. B. Loring, William Noyes, Louis C. Smith, Anna C. Vincent, and W. L. Winchester. There were a number of other students, some listed in the notebook "Pupils. List of letters, etc" (1887.3), whose correspondence did not survive.

6. **Selection 3.** [Follow-up Letter to Circular]

Typescript, 2 sheets plus carbon copy of first sheet, Houghton, Peirce Papers, folder RL 100. Dated 13 March 1887 after the date found on a 2-sheet typed draft of the document. This is a generic letter explaining the machinery of the correspondence course in greater detail than the circular.

7. [On Science and Immortality]

Typescript, 7 sheets. Houghton, Peirce Papers, R 884 (1st series): 3, R 884 (2nd series): 6–10; R 537: 10–11; March–April 1887. Partial early draft of P 347 and P 348 (selection 14, 1887.17 and 1887.51). Text from R 884 (2nd series): 6 (line 14) to 10 (line 39) were later extracted by Peirce to be reshaped into typescript R 884 (2nd series): 2–5, 1, the copy-text for P 352 (selection 16; 1887.27 and 1887.48).

8. *[*Receipt ticket for the Correspondence Course on the Art of Reasoning*]*

Printed ticket, Houghton, Peirce Papers, RL 100; winter 1887. Used as illustration in this volume.

9. *[*Syllogism Lesson and Exercises*]*

Typescript, 2 sheets (not continuous), Houghton, Peirce Papers, R 699: 15, 11; winter 1887.

10. *[*Fragment of letter to Correspondence Course student with three exercises*]*

Italic typescript, 2 sheets including carbon copy, Houghton, Peirce Papers, RL 100; winter 1887. Ending portion of a letter introducing the student to three kinds of consciousness, and assigning three exercises.

11. **Selection 9.** *[*Reasoning Exercises: Number Series, Relational Graphs, and Card Games*]*

Holograph, amanuensis, and typescript, 22 sheets including a number of duplicates, Houghton, Peirce Papers, R 699: 2–10 and 16–20, RS 25: 27, RS 62: 2, RL 100: 1 sheet, RL 173 (exercise questions extracted from J. W. Grace's 14 April 1887 letter); winter 1887 (as evidenced from correspondence and Peirce's study of Kempe).

12. **Selection 10.** Boolian Algebra. *[*Three Lessons*]*

Holograph, 2 sheets, Houghton, Peirce Papers, RS 39: 3, 2; winter 1887. These two sheets were first sent out by Peirce to students on 25 March 1887. Selection 13 (1887.31) seems to be a continuation. Published in NEM 3/1: 294–297.

13. *[*Notes for a review of *Phantasms of the Living]*

Typescript, 5 sheets. Houghton, Peirce papers. R 884 (1st series): 5, 4, 6–13; winter 1887. Precedes the draft of *[*On Science and Immortality*]* (P 347, P 348, selection 14, 1887.17 and 1887.51). Notes Peirce typed while examining the 31 relevant cases in Gurney's book (see selection 16, 1887.27 and 1887.48). Peirce used those notes first in the draft of *[*On Science and Immortality*]*, five pages of which were pulled out and reshaped into the Gurney review itself.

14. *[*Greely Report: Draft Pages for Opening Narrative*]*

Holograph, 1 sheet in Peirce's hand and 3 amanuensis sheets, Houghton, Peirce Papers, R 1095: 312, R 1087: 5–7; winter 1887 (internal evidence, context).

15. Calculation of Atmospheric Effects *[*(Greely report)*]*

Holograph, 16 sheets including two drafts with missing pages, and scratch sheets. Houghton, Peirce Papers, R 1095: 401, 392, 393, 378, 377; R 1095: 384–91; R 1095: 20, 19, 399; winter–spring 1887 (context). Most of these sheets describe Peirce's notational conventions for his calculation of atmospheric effects on the pendulum. R 1095: 20 is titled "Calculation of the effects of the atmosphere on the movement of the pendulums of Peirce pattern and metre length." All these sheets are draft material for pages 14 to 24 of the April 1887 report (NARG 23, pre-copy-text of selection 30, 1888.5).

16. **Selection 5.** Directions to Agents

Typescript, 5 sheets, Houghton, Peirce Papers, RL 100; winter–spring 1887, from internal evidence and connection to other correspondence course materials. Folder also includes two typed sheets belonging to an earlier draft.

17. **Selection 14.** [Science and Immortality]

P 347. *The Christian Register*, Boston, vol. 66, p. 214, cols. 2–4, 7 April 1887. Reprinted in P 348 (1887.51). Published in CP 6.548–556.

18. The United States Coast and Geodetic Survey

Typescript, 2 sets of 3 sheets, one with Peirce's corrections, Max H. Fisch Papers, Peirce Edition Project; 11 April 1887 (context). Draft of opening narrative of the April 1887 report (NARG 23 below, pre-copy-text of selection 30, 1888.5).

19. [Greely Report: Hectograph Fragments from Opening Narrative]

Typescript, 2 hectograph sheets, corresponding to pp. 3 and 11 of narrative portion of Greely report (NARG 23 below), with Peirce's corrections; Max H. Fisch Papers, Peirce Edition Project; 11 April 1887 (context).

20. Report upon the Pendulum Observations at Fort Conger British America

Typescript, 3 hectograph sheets, bound at the Coast and Geodetic Survey, and filed in National Archives, Record group 23, Entry 22, as 11 P 1881–84 Greely & others, 40909 (received stamp 12 Feb 1892); 11 April 1887 (context). Narrative portion of the April 1887 report (NARG 23 below, pre-copy-text of selection 30, 1888.5).

21. On the Pendulum Observations at Fort Conger

Holograph and typescript, 28 sheets, National Archives, Record Group 23, Entry 22, Item 36, Vol. 657, (6) Gravity; 11 April 1887 (date of cover letter sent to Coast Survey superintendent F. M. Thorn). This is the initial version of the Greely report on the Artic expedition (selection 30, 1888.5).

22. **Selection 4.** A Few Specimens of Exercises in the Art of Reasoning

Typescript (carbon copy), 1 sheet, Houghton, Peirce Papers, RL 100; April–May 1887 (typewriter clue). Folder includes another carbon copy, RS 64: 62, reproducing four of the exercises.

23. **Selection 7.** [Orientation Letter to Marie Noble]

Italic typescript (carbon), 1 sheet, Houghton, Peirce Papers, RL 100; 11 May 1887.

24. **Selection 8.** [Letter to Noble on the Nature of Reasoning]

Italic typescript (carbon, incomplete), 2 sheets, Houghton, Peirce Papers, RL 100; 28 May 1887.

25. [Advertisement in the *Century Magazine* for the Correspondence Course]

Offprint, Houghton, Peirce Papers, RL 100; full-page ad published in the schools section of the advertisement section of the *Century Monthly Illustrated Magazine* (cut out in bound copies) in May 1887, p. 10; possibly in other issues as well. Published as illustration on page 14, above.

26. [Translation of part of the first act of Ernest Legouvé's *Medea*]

Holograph, 19 sheets, Houghton, Peirce Papers, R 1562: 16–34; spring–summer 1887. Verse translation of an excerpt of the first act of Ernest Legouvé's tragedy *Médée* (1856), which Juliette Peirce rehearsed under Steele MacKaye's guidance.

27. **Selection 16.** An Examination of an Argument of Messrs. Gurney, Myers, and Podmore

Typescript, 5 sheets, Houghton, Peirce Papers, R 884 (2nd series): 2–5, 1; spring–summer 1887. This is the typescript of P 352, "Criticism on *Phantasms of the Living*" (1887.48), and is used as copy-text for that selection.

28. On the Pendulum Observations at Fort Conger

Typescript, 16 sheets, and one holograph amanuensis sheet at the end; the document was retitled "Pendulum Observations" by Middleton Smith. The typescript served as the printer's copy (called "folio") by Government Printing Office. This copy is in Houghton, Peirce Papers, R 1076: 2–18. The National Archives folder has a carbon-copy version in place. The folio pagination is 2899–2936. Missing pages are 2899, 2911–24, 2930–33, 2935–36. This printer's copy was made after NARG 23, Entry 22 (6), sometime between late spring and early fall 1887.

29. [Calculations of Atmospheric Effects on Pendulum Swings]

Holograph, 12 sheets, discontinuous fragments, Houghton, Peirce Papers, R 1095: 265–66, 314–16, 318, 321–22, 381, 400, 403, 418; August–September 1887. Related to 1889 Report (1889.18), §14, Table 18. Various titles: §13. Of the Atmospheric Effects/Atmospheric Effects. Pendulum No 2/Calculation Atmospheric Effects.

30. Stream-lines of air about a cylindrical pendulum enclosed in a cylindrical vessel of ten times its diameter

Diagram on gridded graph paper enclosed with letter, Peirce to F. M. Thorn, 3 September 1887, National Archives, Record Group 23, Entry 22. Also enclosed is a ledger sheet titled "Coordinates of points on Stream Lines." Diagram intended to illustrate the 1889 Report and reproduced in this volume, p. 311.

31. **Selection 13.** [Additional Exercises in Boolian Algebra]

Holograph, 3 sheets, Houghton, Peirce Papers, R 699: 13–14, 12; summer 1887. The R 699 sheets were sent out in early July 1887 (letters from student Anna Vincent to Peirce), as a continuation of the RS 39 lessons (selection 10, 1887.12).

32. [Atmospheric Effects—Differential Equations]

Holograph, 3 sheets, Houghton, Peirce Papers, R 1095: 291–93; summer 1887.

33. *[*Atmospheric Effects: Isolated Fragments*]*

Holograph, 22 sheets, Houghton, Peirce Papers, R 1095: 106, 167, 171–74, 209, 212, 283, 297, 317, 462–63, 470–71, 484, 497; R 1574: 33–37; summer 1887.

34. *[*Atmospheric Effects. Pendulum Hydrodynamics: theoretical equations*]*

Holograph, 46 sheets, Houghton, Peirce Papers, R 278: 423–27, 429, 431, 434–37; R 1095: 402, 421–24, 427, 429, 431–35, 440, 442, 445, 447, 469, 476–79, 482–83, 488–89, 492–95, 498–500, 519, 521, 524; summer 1887.

35. Cylindrical pendulum in viscous air of no inertia, but incompressible

Holograph, 6 sheets, Houghton, Peirce Papers, R 1095: 464, 473, 485–87, 490; summer 1887. Related to Peirce's research on atmospheric effects on the pendulum.

36. *[*Effects of Viscosity on motion and velocity: theoretical equations*]*

Holograph, 17 sheets, Houghton, Peirce Papers, R 1095: 60, 281–82, 284–88, 289–90, 296, 298–302; summer 1887.

37. *[*Equation of continuity for an ellipsoidal solid*]*

Holograph, 3 sheets, Houghton, Peirce Papers, R 1095: 185–87; summer 1887.

38. *[*Fragments: Determination of b′ as a constant for the descent of the arc*]*

Holograph, 2 sheets, Houghton, Peirce Papers, R 1095: 379–80; summer 1887. Related to R 1096a: 31 (1889.18).

39. Motion of air about cylinder with $\mu = 0$ *[*Theoretical equations*]*

Holograph, 6 sheets, Houghton, Peirce Papers, R 1095: 161–65, 472; summer 1887.

40. Motion of the Air caused by the pendulum on the supposition of No Viscosity

Diagram on gridded graph paper, 2 sheets, plus 2 sheets titled "Calc. Stream & velocity lines"; Houghton, Peirce Papers, R 1095: 458–61; summer 1887. Related to letter, Peirce to F. M. Thorn, 3 Sept. 1887 (NARG 23/22).

41. *[*Pendulum Hydrodynamics: Theoretical Equations*]*

Holograph, 5 sheets, Houghton, Peirce Papers, R 1095: 126–30 and R 194: 17; summer 1887. Related to diagram of stream-lines of air about a cylindrical pendulum (1887.30); see letter Peirce to F. M. Thorn, 3 Sept. 1887.

42. *[*Pendulum Hydrodynamics: Theoretical Study of Equation Solutions*]*

Holograph, 27 sheets, Houghton, Peirce Papers, R 278: 428, 430, 432–33, 438–39, 441–43; R 1095: 419–20, 425–26, 428, 430, 436–39, 441, 443–44, 446, 520, 522–23, 525; summer 1887.

43. *[*Pendulum Hydrodynamics: Viscosity and Velocity (theoretical equations)*]*

Holograph, 10 sheets, Houghton, Peirce Papers, R 1095: 465–68, 474–75, 480–81, 491, 496; summer 1887.

44. Transformations of the 4 Systems of Coordinates

Holograph, 20 sheets, Houghton, Peirce Papers, R 1095: 448–57, 509–18 (set of duplicates); summer 1887. Part of Peirce's study of atmospheric effects for the 1889 Report.

45. **Selection 15.** Logical Machines

P 344. *The American Journal of Psychology,* vol. 1, pp. 165–70, November 1887. Published in NEM 3/1: 625–32.

46. Determinations of the Lengths of Decimetre Scales Nos. 3, 4, and 5

Amanuensis with inscriptions in Peirce's hand, 8 sheets. National Archives, Record Group no. 167. Records of the National Bureau of Standards—Records of the Office of Weights and Measures—Computations of "Comparisons" of Weights and Measures—Volume 5, Length Nos. 1131–1189 — (1882–1887). According to the cover sheet, the length determinations were made in July 1879, January and February 1880, October, November and December 1884. The document itself was made in November 1887, as evidenced from Coast Survey correspondence. Connection with R 1089: 11–12 (WMS 564).

47. **Selection 12.** *[*Reply to Loring*]*

Typescript, 1 sheet, Houghton, Peirce Papers, RL 100; 30 December 1887. Answer to J. B. Loring's letters (selection 11).

48. Criticism on *Phantasms of the Living.* An Examination of an Argument of Messrs. Gurney, Myers, and Podmore

P 352. *Proceedings of the American Society for Psychical Research,* old series vol. 1, 150–57, December 1887 (Peirce signed the article on 14 May 1887, however). Emendation source for selection 16, whose copy-text is typescript R 884 (2nd series): 2–5, 1 (1887.27).

49. **Selection 18.** Mr. Peirce's Rejoinder

P 354. *Proceedings of the American Society for Psychical Research,* old series vol. 1, 180–215, December 1887.

50. *[*Survey of Scientific Opinions about the Belief in Immortality*]*

Holograph, USCGS letterhead, 3 sheets, Houghton, Peirce Papers, RS 74: 2–4; fall 1887 (direct connection with P 348, 1887.51).

51. **Selection 14.** *[*Contribution to the *Christian Register* Symposium on Science and Immortality*]*

P 348. *Science and Immortality; the Christian Register Symposium,* Revised and Enlarged, edited and reviewed by Samuel J. Barrows, Boston: Geo. H. Ellis, 1887, pp. 69–76; fall 1887. Comments on Peirce's contribution are pp. 109–11, and a brief biographical statement on Peirce is at p. 135. CP 6.548–56. Reprint of 1887.17.

52. **Selections 22–28.** A Guess at the Riddle *[*1887–1888*]*

Typescript, 67 sheets, Houghton, Peirce Papers, R 909, R 1600, RS 104; fall 1887–winter 1888. Published in CP 1.1–2, 1.354–416, and in EP1:245–279.
*[*Contents*]*, R 909: 4

Chapter I. Trichotomy. (a) First draft: R 909: 62, 42, 46, 47, 40, 41, 48; (b) final version: R 909: 5–13, including rejected draft pages: R 909: 38, 64–67; (c) three alternative openings: R 909: 3, 68; R 909: 2; and CP 1.1–2.
Chapter III. The Triad in Metaphysics. R 909: 14.
Chapter IV. The Triad in Psychology. R 909: 15, 45, 16–18.
Chapter V. The Triad in Physiology. (a) First start: 909: 54, 19; (b) second start: R 909: 53, 55; (c) final version: R 909: 20–27.
Chapter VI. The Triad in Biological Development (other title, used in (c) only: The Triad in Biology). (a) First opening: R 909: 43–44; (b) second opening: R 909: 39; (c) first fuller version: R 909: 56, 58, 51; (d) second version: R 909: 28–30; (e) third version: R 909: 59, 57, 50.
Chapter VII. The Triad in Physics. (a) First start: R 1600: 9, 8; (b) second start: R 909: 60 and R 1600: 11, 10; (c) a residual sheet RS 104: 127; (d) final version: R 909: 31–37.

53. *[*Comparisons of Values between Stations, 1887–1888*]*

Holograph, 10 sheets, Houghton, Peirce Papers, R 1095: 351, 368–73, 397, 404–405; 1887–1888. Preliminary to 1889 Report, §9, Tables 3–5. Various titles are: Reduction for Lat. & Elevation/Madison compared with Smithsonian 1886/Madison compared with Ann Arbor/Ann Arbor–Smithsonian 1886.

54. *[*Number of Swingings per Station, 1887–1888*]*

Holograph, 2 sheets, Houghton, Peirce Papers, R 1095: 501–502; 1887–1888. Data from Smithsonian, Ithaca, Ann Arbor, and Madison.

55. *[*Mathematical Fragments, 1887–1890*]*

Holograph, 11 sheets, Houghton, Peirce Papers, R 105: 9; R 112: 8–11, 13–14; R 194: 20; R 1095: 195–96; R 1574: 343; 1887–1890. This folder contains all unidentified mathematical fragments for the period of W6.

56. *[*Miscellaneous Fragments, 1887–1890*]*

Holograph, 3 fragment sheets, Houghton, Peirce Papers, R 1095: 363; R 1572: 37; 1887–1890 (any time during W6 period).

c. 1887

1. **Selection 20.** Number

Holograph, 1 sheet, Houghton, Peirce Papers, R 278: 867; c. 1887 (paper, handwriting, connection with R 39, c. 1887.2).

2. **Selection 21.** Logic of Number

Holograph, 16 sheets, Houghton, Peirce Papers, R 39: 2–5, 8, 17, 6–7, 9–10, 12, 18, 11, 14, 16, 15; c. 1887 (handwriting; mean within a range of possible years). Folder also contains 2 draft sheets (R 39: 19, 13) and a related fragment titled “Theorems of Numbers” (R 227: 2–3).

3. *[*Calculations related to Pendulum no. 2 at the Smithsonian*]*

Holograph, 1 sheet, Houghton, Peirce Papers, R 1095: 112; c. 1887 (context).

4. Correction to J for Regular Hoboken Set

Holograph, 1 sheet, Houghton, Peirce Papers, R 1095: 18; c. 1887 (context). Perhaps related to viscosity calculations or seconds pendulum calculations. J = moment of inertia of a volume of unit density.

5. Correction to the Standard Atmosphere

Holograph, 1 sheet, crossed out fragment, Houghton, Peirce Papers, R 1095: 122; c. 1887 (context). Related to 1889 Report, §14, narrative and Tables 15–17; draft for R 1096a: 17, 18 (1889.18).

6. *[*Drafts of Tables for 1889 Report*]*

Holograph, 3 sheets, Houghton, Peirce Papers, R 1095: 304, 326, 303; c. 1887 (context). Related to tables in 1889 Report, R 1096a: 138–140 (1889.18).

7. Kew–London

Holograph, 1 sheet, Houghton, Peirce Papers, R 1095: 17; c. 1887 (context). Comparison of values at international stations.

8. On the Absolute Value of Gravity

Amanuensis, 3 sheets, Houghton, Peirce Papers, R 1087: 2–4; c. 1887 (context). Draft of 1889 Report (1889.18), top of R 1096a: 138.

9. On the times of the beginning and ending of the swingings

Amanuensis, 3 sheets, Houghton, Peirce Papers, R 1095: 24–26; c. 1887 (context). Draft of 1889 Report (1889.18), §22 (R 1096a: 127–128).

10. *[*Fragment on three-dimensional geometry and spherical projection*]*

Holograph, 3 sheets, Houghton, Peirce Papers, R 278: 44–45, and R 839: 56 (draft of 278: 44); c. 1887 (handwriting). The two pages are numbered 7 and 8 by Peirce. The rest of the document is missing.

11. *[*Presocratic Fragments with Some Comments*]*

Typescript, 2 sheets, Houghton, Peirce Papers, R 1574: 217–19, c. 1887. First TS sheet missing. Probably related to third chapter of "A Guess at the Riddle" (selection 24, 1887.52); printed in W6 Annotations.

1888

1. Annual Assay. 1888

P 368. Offprint of "Annual Assay. 1888" in *Proceedings of the Assay Commission of 1888,* Treasury Department, Document No. 1089, from the Director of the Mint, pp. 1–17. Peirce's offprint is in R 1600. Appointed by President Grover Cleveland on 9 January 1888, the Commission met at the Philadelphia mint from February 8 to 10, 1888. One of the fifteen commissioners, Peirce was a member of two subcommittees, on counting and on weighing, of which he helped write the reports included in the larger report.

2. **Selection 29.** *[*Trichotomic*]*

Typescript, 4 sheets, Houghton, Peirce Papers, R 1600: 1–7; winter–spring 1888 (composed shortly after "A Guess at the Riddle"; reference to MacKaye). The fourth sheet (R 1600: 7) is a condensed version of the ideas presented in the other three sheets. Published in EP1:280–84.

3. Pendulum Observations

Nine galley sheets numbered 49EEE, 50EEE/1FFF, 2FFF–8FFF, in National Archives, Record Group 27, Records of Polar Expeditions, 1881–1923, NC-3, Entry 138, Box 5 of 25; May–June 1888 (context). These are the first proofs of the Greely report (selection 30, 1888.5), revised by H. Farquhar on 19 June 1888, who proofread it against NARG 23 (6) to match the typescript R 1076 Peirce had not sent back in time, so as to replace it as printer's copy "folio" in printer's files. These galleys correspond to folios 2899 to 2936 (partially found in R 1076), according to an inscription by Middleton Smith. Peirce's text comes under the main title "Pendulum Observations. Appendix 141." The folder also includes seven sheets of various sizes, which are notes from the editor M. Smith, the printer Wm. Barnum, and cover sheets.

4. On the mean figure of the Earth from determinations of gravity. Second Paper. The formula for the Earth's ellipticity in terms of the variation of gravity with the latitude

Document of at least 37 pages, missing from the National Archives, received and acknowledged on 10 August 1888 by Coast Survey Superintendent F. M. Thorn, commented upon by C. A. Schott, and alluded to both at the end of the Greely Expedition report (selection 30, 1888.5) and in the "Lost Report" (selection 36, 1889.18). Part of the "first paper" (1883) is published in W5:529–34.

5. **Selection 30.** Pendulum Observations at Fort Conger

P 369. Appendix no. 141 in *International Polar Expedition. Report on the Proceedings of the United States Expedition to Lady Franklin Bay, Grinnell Land,* by Adolphus W. Greely, House Misc. Doc. 393, Part 2, 49th Congress, 1st Session, Washington: Government Printing Office, pp. 701–714; fall 1888. The report, titled "Pendulum Operations," is followed by Greely's objections stated in his "Memorandum by the Officer Commanding the Expedition" at p. 715; Peirce's half-page response, titled "Explanatory Note" (which he sent to Greely on 28 November 1888, and which was inserted in the report at the last minute in December 1888, between pp. 714–15); and comments (challenging Peirce's hypotheses about the pendulum having lost some mass) and tables by Henry Farquhar at pp. 716–29. Apart from R 1076, there were two sets of galley proofs which Peirce corrected prior to the final printing of this report, one on 7 July 1888, and one between 21 and 24 July 1888. These two sets of proofs have not been located.

6. *[*Three Annotated Pages from Offprint of "Pendulum Observations"*]*

Offprint, 3 sheets, pp. 710, 711, and 718, surviving from Peirce's offprint of the Greely report on pendulum observations (selection 30, 1888.5); Houghton, Peirce Papers, R 1600; fall 1888. Each of the three sheets contain handwritten calculations in Peirce's hand.

c. 1888

1. Effect on Peirce Metre Pendulum of Upper part being warmer than lower

Holograph, 3 sheets, Houghton, Peirce Papers, R 1095: 178, 294, 295; c. 1888. Connected to 1889 Report (1889.18), §18 (R 1096a: 112). Corrections for difference of temperature.

2. Geodesic Arc from northernmost point to equator

Holograph, 1 sheet, Houghton, Peirce Papers, R 194: 7; c. 1888 (context, paper, handwriting).

3. *[Instrumental Constants and Related Calculations]*

Holograph, 6 sheets, Houghton, Peirce Papers, R 1095: 307–308, 333, 374–76; c. 1888. Various sheets calculating pendulum-related constants. There are two titles: Table IX. Constants of the Different Pendulums, 1884 / To calculate γ^2 for the different pendulums. Connection to 1889 Report (1889.18), §2, Table 9 (R 1096a: 7).

4. *[Conic and Jacobian]*

Holograph, 2 sheets, first page missing, Houghton, Peirce Papers, R 278: 1392–1393; c. 1888 (handwriting, paper, topic).

5. *[The sum of an odd and an even square]*

Holograph, 2 sheets, fragmentary, Houghton, Peirce Papers, R 278: 869–70; c. 1888 (handwriting, paper, mean in W6 period).

1889

1. **Selection 31.** Reflections on the Logic of Science

Holograph, 38 sheets, Houghton, Peirce Papers, R 246, 247, 248, 278, 1573, 1574; 1–3, 7–9, and 17 January 1889.
[Chapter I]: R 1573: 270 (same as R 278: 214) and R 246: 2–22; also a working sheet, R 1574: 656 and a false start, R 1574: 657.
Chapter II. The Doctrine of Chances: R 247: 2–6, 8–9, 7.
Chapter II. Mathematics: R 248: 2–8.

2. Excelsior Diary for 1889

Holograph, 25 sheets, diary book, pages after 15 February are missing, Houghton, Peirce Papers, R 1616: 2–26. First entry on January 1, last entry on January 27, 1889.

3. Newton's Enumeration of Cubic Curves

Holograph, 8 sheets, Houghton, Peirce Papers, R 115: 2–9; 6 January 1889 (dated from diary entry in 1889.2). Classification of Newton's 72 species of cubic curves.

4. Height of road in front of house

Holograph, 1 sheet, Houghton, Peirce Papers, R 1095: 197; possibly 14 January 1889 (diary entry in 1889.2).

5. Notes on Kempe's Paper on Mathematical Forms

Holograph, 7 sheets, Houghton, Peirce Papers, R 714: 2, 4–6, 12–13, 3; 15 January 1889.

6. **Selection 32.** Note on the analytical representation of space as a section of a higher dimensional space

Holograph, 6 sheets, Houghton, Peirce Papers, R 259: 2, R 278: 140, R 260: 3–4, (missing page), RL 339: 156, R 278: 1005; 17–25 January 1889 (letter to Simon Newcomb, 17 Jan. 1889, and letter to James Mills Peirce, 25 Jan. 1889). Folder contains many draft pages, variants, and scratch notes: R 260: 2, RL 314: 7; R 839: 170; R 278: 57, 159, 58, 141, 156; R 278: 157–58, 67, 62–63, 146, 150–51, 147, 143, 149, 154–55, 152–53; R 278: 59, 145; R 278: 148.

7. **Selection 33.** Ordinal Geometry

Holograph, 35 sheets, Houghton, Peirce Papers, R 249: 2–36; 18–19 January 1889. Selection 33 consists of 10 sheets in R 249: 15, 6–7, 31, 8, 32–36, all dated 19 January 1889. The folder contains two other opening pages, three incomplete drafts, and a number of rejected sheets.

8. **Selection 34.** *[*Mathematical Monads*]*

Holograph, 6 sheets, Houghton, Peirce Papers, R 536: 2–6, R 278: 144; 23 January 1889.

9. *[*Fragments of Coast Survey Report of 1889*]*

Typescript, 18 sheets, Houghton, Peirce Papers, R 1096: 7–10, 3, 13, 11–12, 16, 6, 14–15, 17–20, 4–5; January 1889. These sheets were originally part of a full draft of the report, which Peirce subsequently dismembered, cutting and pasting vast portions of it into the final typescript version (R 1096a, selection 36, 1889.18).

10. *[*Notes on Plane Geometry*]*

Holograph, 7 pages in a ledger, Houghton, Peirce Papers, R 966: 2–8; January 1889 (based on strong connection with selection 32, R 260, 1889.6).

11. The graph of Boolian Algebra

Holograph, 2 sheets, Houghton, Peirce Papers, RS 40: 2, R 714: 7; January 1889 (from allusion in R 714: 2–3; watermark).

12. *[*Hue Studies*]*

Small notebook labeled "HUE," 15 pages with holograph notes, dozens of sheets missing, Houghton, Peirce Papers, R 1017: 2–13; 4 April 1889 (date on first page). Notes on colorimetry, work with color disks.

13. *[*Catalog of Plants for Cultivation at the Farm*]*

Holograph notebook, 98 pages, Houghton, Peirce Papers, RS 2: 2–99; 15 April 1889 (internal date). Peirce used this notebook for two different purposes fifteen years apart. In April 1889 he used it to make an alphabetical list of plants he and Juliette might want to plant on their farm. But in October 1904, since most of the leaves were blank except for plant names, he used it for mathematical work (notes on topology, census theorem).

14. On Sensations of Color

P 379. Paper read by Peirce during the first session of the National Academy of Sciences, which took place at the regular annual meeting of the Academy in Washington, D.C., April 16 to 19, 1889, in the National Museum. No related document has been identified in the Peirce Papers.

15. On Determinations of Gravity

P 380. Paper read by Peirce during the first session of the National Academy of Sciences, which took place at the regular annual meeting of the Academy in Washington, D.C., April 16 to 19, 1889, in the National Museum. No related document has been identified in the Peirce Papers.

16. The *Century Dictionary*

P 376. Peirce's reply to Simon Newcomb's letter to the editor published by the *Nation* on 13 June 1889; in the *Nation*, vol. 48, 504–505; 20 June 1889. Published in CN 1: 75–77. Will be published in W7.

17. **Selection 35.** Review of Stock's *Deductive Logic*

P 378. *The Nation,* vol. 49, no. 1259, 136–37; 15 August 1889. Published in CN 1: 78–80.

18. **Selection 36.** Report on Gravity at the Smithsonian, Ann Arbor, Madison, and Cornell

P 385. Typescript and holograph, 145 sheets, Washington National Record Center, Suitland Compound, Maryland, Accession no. WNRC 370-73-002, Box 23. R 1096a: 1–146. It is supplemented with one sheet from the Peirce Papers at Houghton: R 1095: 398. The report was sent by Peirce on 20 November 1889 to the US Coast and Geodetic Survey, where it was received two days later, but mislaid and not found for about two weeks.

19. *[*Photographs of Old and New Pendulum Stands*]*

Blue prints, 4 photographs with ink marks by Peirce, Houghton, Peirce Papers, R 1096: 2 and R 1574: 201–202; 1889 (context). These photographs were made for the 1889 pendulum report. They show the two pendulum stands Peirce used in his gravity work, each from two different angles. Both the "Old Stand" and the "New Stand" are described in the report (selection 36, 1889.18), on page 6 of the original typescript, where the photographs are referred to as Plates 1 and 2. Used as illustrations in W6.

20. *[*Question on what proportion of non-Poles speak Polish*]*

Holograph, 2 sheets, Houghton, Peirce Papers, RL 483: 3–4; 1889 (context, description of household matching diary R 1616: 3 in 1889.2).

21. *[*Peirce's Definitions for the *Century Dictionary and Cyclopedia,* 1889–1891*]*

P 373. William D. Whitney, Editor-in-Chief, 10 volumes, New York: The Century Company, 1889–1891. Peirce was responsible for definitions in the fields of Logic, Metaphysics, Mathematics, Mechanics, Astronomy, Weights and Measures, Color Terms, and many common words of philosophical import. By his own reckoning,

Peirce worked on 16,000 entries, half of them in mathematics, and a third in logic. More than 6,000 entries have been identified in the actual publication of the *Century Dictionary* as having been contributed to by Peirce, thanks to the latter's own marked interleaved copy. A selection of Peirce's significant definitions, philosophic and scientific, as published in the *Century Dictionary*, will appear in W7.

c. 1889

1. **Selection 37.** *[*Reasoning*]*

Holograph, 6 sheets, Houghton, Peirce Papers, R 830: 2, R 278: 240, 243, 269, 268, 267, 266 (= R 1573: 250); c. 1889 (mean between 1886 and 1891). Folder also contains variant pages R 839: 16–17; R 830: 5, 3–4; R 278: 241, 242.

2. Kempe translated into English

Holograph, 1 sheet, Houghton, Peirce Papers, R 715: 2; c. 1889 (watermark, connection to R 714 (c. 1889.3), handwriting). Terminological remarks on Kempe's 1886 paper.

3. Notes to Kempe

Holograph, 5 sheets, Houghton, Peirce Papers, R 714: 8–11 and R 249: 37; c. 1889 (handwriting, connection with rest of R 714). Remarks of terminology on §§ 3–7, 16, 19, 27, and 37 of Kempe's 1886 paper.

4. The Logic of Relatives

Holograph, 3 sheets. Houghton, Peirce papers, R 534: 2, R 747: 6. Also R 547: 3, an incomplete definition probably for the *Century Dictionary;* c. 1889 (mean between 1887 and 1890; handwriting; ref. to Kempe).

5. Logical Papers, by C. S. Peirce

Holograph, 3 sheets, Houghton, Peirce Papers, R 1577: 2–4; c. 1889 (watermark, handwriting). List of 33 papers in logic published by Peirce.

6. The Theory of Force

Holograph, 9 sheets, Houghton, Peirce Papers, R 1568: 2–3; R 1314: 4; R 1568: 8. Unfinished document with draft in R 1568: 5–7; 1314: 2–3; c. 1889 (paper and handwriting same as in selection 31, 1889.1).

7. **Selection 38.** On a Geometrical Notation

Typescript (carbon), 3 sheets, Houghton, Peirce Papers, R 275: 5, 6, 4; c. 1889 (mean between 1887 and 1891). Folder contains another carbon copy from R 1600, completed by RS 5: 2. R 275: 2 reproduces part of R 275: 5–6, and R 275: 3 is same as R 275: 4. Document connected to R 124: 9–12 (c. 1889.9).

8. **Selection 39.** On the Number of Forms of Sets

Holograph, 3 sheets, Houghton, Peirce Papers, R 37: 2–4; c. 1889 (watermark, handwriting, connected to Peirce's reading of Kempe).

9. Formulae

Holograph, first 13 pages of a notebook, Houghton, Peirce Papers, R 124: 2–14; c. 1889 (handwriting, mean between 1887 and 1891, connection with selection 38, c. 1889.7). Topics covered: solution of quadratic equation and of the general cubic, trigonometrical formulae, plane and spherical triangles, analytic geometry, and density. Second portion of notebook (R 124: 15–44) separated and dated much later, c. 1909.

10. Method of Solving a Numerical Equation

Holograph, 2 sheets, Houghton, Peirce Papers, R 1150: 19–20; c. 1889 (paper, handwriting, connection to R 246: 7, 1889.1). Published in NEM 2: 559–60.

11. Solutions of Spherical Triangles without logarithms

Holograph, 4 sheets, Houghton, Peirce papers, R 194: 19, 43–44, 130; c. 1889 (handwriting, possible connection to R 124, c. 1889.9). Internal titles: spherical triangles; quadrantal triangles.

12. *[Rectangular to polar transformation]*

Holograph, 5 sheets, Houghton, Peirce Papers, R 194: 52–56; c. 1889 (very uncertain; handwriting).

13. In the Game of Go as You Please

Holograph, 1 sheet, Houghton, Peirce Papers, R 1537: 8; c. 1889 (watermark, handwriting). Exercise in probability.

14. *[Fragments on the Four-Color Problem]*

Holograph, 7 sheets, Houghton, Peirce Papers, R 112: 12, R 113: 16–17, and R 249: 38–41; c. 1889 or 1890 (paper, connections to other documents).

15. *[Arithmetical and Mathematical Books with Appraisal]*

Holograph, 3 ledger sheets, Houghton, Peirce Papers, R 1542: 2–4; c. 1889 (internal evidence may defend an earlier date, but it may also be later). Internal subtitles: Old Arithmetics, historically valuable; History of Mathematics; Ancient Mathematical Works.

16. Dual Relations

Holograph, 2 sheets, Houghton, Peirce Papers, R 533: 3–4; c. 1889. Connected to selections 40 and 41.

17. **Selection 40.** The Formal Classification of Relations

Holograph, 16 sheets, Houghton, Peirce Papers, R 533: 2, 5–14, R 534: 4–7, and RS 64: 111; c. 1889 (paper, handwriting, connection to *Century Dictionary* work, and mean within a range of possible years). Copy-text pages are R 533: 6, 5, 14, 9; R 534: 6; R 533: 10–11; and RS 64: 111. Folder includes false starts, draft pages, and working sheets.

18. **Selection 41.** Dual Relatives

Holograph, 8 sheets, Houghton, Peirce Papers, R 536: 7–14; c. 1889. Variant of selection 40.

19. **Selection 42.** Notes on Geometry of Plane Curves *without Imaginaries*

Holograph, 5 sheets, Houghton, Peirce Papers, R 261: 2–6; c. 1889 (paper, handwriting, connection to other curve documents). Folder also includes 8 draft sheets: R 261: 7–12 and RS 12: 44–45.

20. On the Real Qualitative Characters of Plane Curves

Typescript (all italic), 12 sheets, Houghton, Peirce Papers, R 262: 2–13; c. 1889 (mean within range of possible years, TS quality, topic). Folder consists of five aborted attempts to write the paper; it includes several false starts and draft pages. Best run consists of R 262: 2, 3, 9, 4. Connected to RS 12 (c. 1889.22).

21. On the Real Singularities of Plane Curves

Holograph, 9 sheets, Houghton, Peirce Papers, R 264: 2–10; c. 1889 (mean within range of possible years, paper, handwriting, topic). Document very fragmentary. Related to R 261 and 262 (c. 1889.19 and 20).

22. *[*Rakers and Rakees*]*

Holograph, 76 sheets, Houghton, Peirce Papers, RS 12: 2–43, R 1574: 573–580, 584–608, RS 25: 126; c. 1889 (mean within range of possible years, topic, handwriting). Includes an attempt to classify curves according to rakers and rakees. Connected to R 262 (c. 1889.20).

23. Analysis of the *Almagest*

Holograph, 23 sheets, Houghton, Peirce Papers, R 1304: 2–24; c. 1889 (handwriting, watermark). Reading notes on Ptolemy's *Almagest.*

1890

1. **Selection 43.** Review of Noel's *The Science of Metrology*

P 389. *The Nation,* vol. 50, no. 1287, 184; 27 February 1890. Published in CN 1: 81–82.

2. Is This the Truth About Herbert Spencer?

Galleys, first set, cut-and-paste copy, Max H. Fisch Papers, folder G-1890-2. Set of galleys for selection 45 (P 402); March 1890.

3. **Selection 45.** Is This the Truth About Herbert Spencer?

Galleys, second set, Houghton, Peirce Papers, R 1600; March 1890. These galleys contain Peirce's handwritten word and line count, and serve as copy-text, emended from P 402 (1890.4).

4. Herbert Spencer's Philosophy. Is It Unscientific and Unsound—Its Pretensions Attacked and a Demonstration Called For

P 402. *The New York Times,* vol. 39, p. 4, cols. 6–7; Sunday, 23 March 1890. Signed "Outsider." Galleys serve as copy-text.

5. **Selection 46.** Review of Collins's *Epitome of the Synthetic Philosophy*

P 389. *The Nation,* vol. 50, 265; 27 March 1890. Published in CN 1: 82.

6. *[*Logic and Spiritualism*]*

Holograph, 11 sheets, Houghton, Peirce Papers, R 880: 2–12; winter 1890. Peirce's first attempt at writing this paper, at the invitation of L. M. Metcalf, editor of *The Forum,* some time in early 1890. In Robin's *Catalogue,* this document is titled *[*On Spiritualism, Telepathy, and Miracles*]*.

7. *[*Logic and Spiritualism*]*

Holograph, 42 sheets, Houghton, Peirce papers, R 879: 17–58; winter–spring 1890. Second attempt (after R 880) to write the *Forum* article (R 878, selection 44, 1890.9). At least two sheets are missing.

8. *[*Logic and Spiritualism*]*

Holograph, 15 sheets, Houghton, Peirce Papers, R 879: 2–16; winter–spring 1890. Third attempt to write the *Forum* article (R 878, selection 44, 1890.9). Many sheets missing.

9. **Selection 44.** *[*Logic and Spiritualism*]*

Galleys, 5 sheets heavily corrected by Peirce, Houghton, Peirce Papers, R 878: 2–6; 7 April 1890 (galleys' typesetting date). Galleys returned by *The Forum* to Peirce, who corrected them but did not send them back. The galleys were made after a manuscript that is no longer extant (March–April 1890). The uncorrected underlayer of the galleys serves as copy-text. Earlier manuscripts are in R 879 and 880. R 882 is a later, though related, document (c. 1894).

10. **Selection 47.** "Outsider" Wants More Light. He Cometh After his Critics and Searcheth Them—Spencer's Standing in Science—His Theory of Evolution—"Outsider" is an Inquirer, Not an Assailant

P 416. *The New York Times,* vol. 39, p. 13, cols. 1–2; Sunday, 13 April 1890. Signed "Outsider."

11. *[*Logic and Spiritualism*]*

Typescript, 20 sheets, Houghton, Peirce Papers, R 878: 26–45 (with duplicate in R 878: 7–25); April–May 1890. Typescript made from the corrected galleys (selection 44, 1890.9), with additional corrections in Peirce's hand, and markup by the editors of the *Collected Papers.* Published in CP 6.557–87. Peirce sent the TS to Samuel P. Langley, who commented on it in an 8 May 1890 letter.

Supplement to W5 Chronological List 1884–1886

1884

WMS 522.1 Temperatures in Room 99

Amanuensis, 1 sheet, Houghton, Peirce Papers, R 1098: 16; 17–21 December 1884. Readings preparatory to the swings of Meter Pendulum 2, begun 23 Dec. 1884.

1885

WMS 537.1 Clock Signals Sheets

Holograph, 6 sheets, Houghton, Peirce Papers, R 1095: 254–57, 327–28; 18–20 January 1885. Smithsonian Time Signals, related to 1889 Report (1889.18), §19, Table 100.

WMS 537.2 [Pendulum Swing Sheets, Smithsonian 1885]

Holograph, 7 sheets, Houghton, Peirce Papers, R 1095: 367, 365, 364, 366, 113–15; January 1885. Related to 1889 Report (1889.18), §16, Tables 52–60.

WMS 549.1 [Pendulum Swing Sheet, Ann Arbor 1885]

Holograph, 1 sheet, Houghton, Peirce Papers, R 1095: 180; September 1885. Related to 1889 Report (1889.18), §16, Table 75. Yard pendulum no. 3.

WMS 557.1 [Pendulum Swing Sheets, Ithaca 1885–1886]

Holograph and amanuensis, 14 sheets, Houghton, Peirce Papers, R 1095: 406–13, 503–508; December 1885–January 1886. Related to R 1096 (1889.9), §14, Tables 62–69, and to 1889 Report (1889.18), §19, Tables 85–92.

c. 1885

WMS 561.1 End of Swing. Beginning of Swing. [Instructions for operating the pendulum]

Amanuensis, 1 sheet, Houghton, Peirce Papers, R 1095: 15; c. 1885 (composed while Peirce was doing fieldwork in 1885 or 1886).

WMS 561.2 [Ithaca, Individual Swingings, §16] or [Smithsonian, Pendulum Calculations]

Holograph, 11 sheets, Houghton, Peirce Papers, R 1095: 352–62, winter 1885 *or* winter 1886. All these sheets are indexed by Peirce under Ithaca in his letter to

Thorn (2/1/1889), in which case they could be dated December 1885–January 1886, but they correlate better with Smithsonian tables than with Ithaca tables in the 1889 Report, in which case they could be dated January–February 1885. Numbers do not match up exactly, however. Related to 1889 Report (1889.18), §16, Tables 85–92. Possibly temperature corrections of swing values.

1886

WMS 567.1 *[Calculations related to Sidereal Time Observations in Ithaca]*
Amanuensis, 1 sheet, Houghton, Peirce Papers, R 1095: 350; 12–14 and 24 January 1886 (or later in the year: Aug./ Sep., or Dec., when Ithaca results were reworked).

WMS 568.1 *[Pendulum Swing Sheets, Smithsonian 1886]*
Holograph, 16 sheets, Houghton, Peirce Papers, R 1095: 349, 337–48, 336, 334–35; March 1886 (work done in February/March at the Smithsonian). Related to 1889 Report (1889.18), §16, Tables 61–62, 65–66.

WMS 570.1 Swingings of the Kater Pendulum at Hoboken, 1886
Amanuensis, 1 sheet, Houghton, Peirce Papers, R 1095: 16; spring 1886 (Peirce worked at Hoboken from April to June 1886).

WMS 582.1 *[Notes for letter, Peirce to F. M. Thorn]*
Holograph, 1 sheet, Houghton, Peirce Papers, R 1095: 123; 6 December 1886.

WMS 582.2 *[Partial draft of letter, Peirce to F. M. Thorn]*
Holograph, 3 sheets, Houghton, Peirce Papers, R 1095: 394–96; 15 December 1886. Partial draft of letter, concerning Ithaca work, including temperature coefficient tables related to R 1096 (1889.9), §10, Tables 14, 16, or 1889 Report (1889.18), §13, Table 12.

WMS 583.1 *[Flexure and Gravity Calculations for Fort Conger (Greely Report)]*
Holograph, 2 fragment sheets, Houghton, Peirce Papers, R 1095: 23, 221; fall 1886. First sheet not in Peirce's hand. Related to work on Greely report (selection 30, 1888.5).

WMS 583.2 **Selection 1.** Boolian Algebra—Elementary Explanations
Typescript, 4 sheets, Houghton, Peirce Papers, RS 38: 2–4, R 1573: 185. Folder also contains a false start of the first page, with identical title, from RL 100. Fall 1886: the document was written after selection 56 in W5 (MS 585, R 537) and before the Correspondence Course Peirce started in early 1887. Published in NEM 3/1: 284–89.

c. 1886

WMS 594 Effect on Amplitudes
Holograph, 2 sheets, Houghton, Peirce Papers, R 1095: 382–83; late 1886, or 1887. Determination of constant for Repsold pendulum experiments.

WMS 595 Residuals

Holograph, 1 sheet, Houghton, Peirce Papers, R 1095: 305; c. 1886 or 1887. Draft of 1889 Report, §9, Table 4 (draft for final section, R 1096a: 10, 1889.18); residuals at four different stations.

WMS 596 *[An Improvement on Boole's Treatment of the Function]*

Holograph, 4 sheets, Houghton, Peirce Papers, R 563: 2–5; c. 1886 (some time in the mid-1880s).

1886–1891

[Drafts of Peirce's Definitions for the *Century Dictionary and Cyclopedia*]

Very little of Peirce's handwritten or typewritten notes for the *Century Dictionary* are extant, since the Century Company's archives for the most part have disappeared, and all that is left in the Peirce Papers consists of about 600 sheets, scattered among many folders, which have been arranged alphabetically, some of which will be published in W7. These are drafts of definitions composed between 1886 and 1891, the year the last fascicle of the *Dictionary*'s first edition appeared. The Chronological List in W7 will provide a detailed listing of all the draft sheets. Here is a list of the Robin folders that contain *Century Dictionary*-related sheets (from 1886 to 1890): R 228, 258, 272, 278, 534, 536, 884, 967, 1059c, 1095, 1150, 1151, 1155, 1157, 1165, 1166, 1168, 1170, 1173, 1177, 1253, 1261, 1284, 1306, 1324, 1573, 1574, R S96, R S98, and R S104.

[Notecards with quotations, bibliographical references, tentative definitions for *Century Dictionary* entries]

Listed as item R 1596 in Robin's *Catalogue,* these notecards are found in four large boxes filled with 3 × 5 size cards and one box filled with 2 × 5 cards. There are several thousands of them. They still need to be identified and reorganized. The Chronological List in W7 will give a more detailed account of the content of those boxes. Their contents are in large part related to *Century Dictionary* work, and thus dated 1886–1891.

Essay on Editorial Theory and Method

In 1890, Peirce joined with Alexander Campbell Fraser, John Locke's then-most recent biographer, in a public plea for a new edition of Locke's works. Peirce firmly maintained that Locke, "whose utterances still have their lessons for the world . . . should be studied in a complete, correct, and critical edition." He wished no less for his own work, and fought a well-documented battle with editors throughout his publishing career. But it was his misfortune to write for editors who often were not qualified to edit (or even to understand) his work; those few who understood and believed in Peirce had to contend with authorial chaos at every turn, for the eccentricities of his personal life and his unusual methods of composition led Peirce himself to despair at the chances of ordering his papers in his own lifetime. This formidable task is now in the hands of modern-day critical editors whose basic focus—the recovery and annotations of texts—is very much in line with Peirce's own critical vision as an editor and translator of scientific and philosophical writers.

But the domain of scholarly editing—both critical and documentary editing—is far more of a forensic domain than had yet developed in Peirce's day. The *Writings of Charles S. Peirce* consists of chronological volumes prepared in the critical editing tradition as it has evolved in the twentieth century. Our central goal is to provide critically edited and reliable texts of Peirce's work across the wide range of disciplines to which he contributed. Where the documentary editor focuses on preserving the text, the critical editor focuses on recovering the author's discernible *intention* for the text. Rather than simply reproducing a single surviving form of a document, we (as critical editors) identify the most mature coherent form closest to Peirce's composing hand, and, by incorporating identifiable authorial revisions and corrections from subsequent forms, produce an eclectic text which aims to represent his most fully developed intention. Variants from subsequent published forms of the text judged to be editorial sophistications and compositorial errors are rejected; Peirce's own errors of content are corrected. This new text, when combined with an apparatus documenting the evolution of the various forms of the work, listing the historical variants, and identifying all of our editorial emendations (and their sources), constitutes the "critical edition" of Peirce's work.

Critical editors normally work within a narrow and well-studied range of surviving forms of a text—published documents, galleys, printer's copy, or, at the worst, fair-copy manuscripts. Peirce's complex habits of composition, and the unfinished state of many of his manuscripts, create a number of problematic editing situations for the unpublished materials which constitute—by far—the greater portion of his surviving canon. Peirce often composed parallel versions of a document without indicating which was the preferred form, and we must deal with variant passages and entire variant documents, any one of which might be worthy of publication. Even when only one finished form of a work exists, the editing problems will almost always go beyond simple cases of missing punctuation or incomplete revision. Often Peirce's "finished" work falls far short of fair-copy form in terms of textual development, and may also contain unfinished revisions to mathematical formulae, diagrams, and illustrations.

These complications make it all the more important to describe in the clearest terms how editors establish critical texts of Peirce's writings. Our specific editing policies for Peirce's published and unpublished work follow an overview of the general principles of critical editing as we have applied them to our own edition. The essay closes with a brief textual survey of the W6 selections and an overview of special editing challenges encountered in establishing the texts for this volume.

I. General Editing Guidelines

We apply the editorial standards and guidelines of the Modern Language Association's Committee on Scholarly Editions, and have received the CSE's emblem, "An Approved Edition," for all our volumes. The CSE does not dictate a step-by-step procedure for critical editing, but rather identifies the essential elements (a textual essay, a textual apparatus, and a proofreading plan) and recommends the inclusion of a general introduction providing either an interpretive or historical frame for each volume. Beyond these elements, CSE stipulates that the editing theory and procedures be appropriate for the particular author. Implicit in the statement of standards put forward in "Aims and Services of the Committee on Scholarly Editions" (January 1992 printing) is a system of evaluation based on three expected outcomes: accuracy, consistency, and clarity of editorial discussion. Accordingly, our editorial procedures are based on the following general goals:

1. We are committed to producing a critical, unmodernized edition of Peirce's published and unpublished work.[1] This edition is critical because our central goal is to produce a text that recovers Peirce's intentions as an author.

1. Occasionally, we include direct rejoinders or commentaries by other writers (identified by vertical rules running down both margins). These are edited with a minimum of editorial intrusion.

It is unmodernized because, rather than update its accidentals for the benefit of the modern reader, our goal is to present a text that retains the author's general preferences in punctuation, spelling, and capitalization while eliminating (by emendation) careless errors or confusing inconsistencies.

2. Although we work from master sets of microfilm, microfiche, and photographic copies of Peirce's papers, we are committed to proofreading our transcriptions against the original documents to verify the accuracy of the transcribed readings, to ascertain the physical characteristics of paper and ink, and to resolve any problematic marks or revisions on the document.

3. We are committed to determining, as clearly as possible, the transmission of each text and its relationship to other writings in the corpus. We use standard collation schedules for horizontal comparisons of Peirce's printed articles with his own corrected and annotated offprints, with errata sheets, and with other copies of the original printing to discover variant readings. Texts transmitted vertically through two or more manuscript, typescript, or copy-set forms are also collated to identify variations. We also compare parallel but distant versions of a text to recover the full family tree for a given document.

4. When more than one form of a text exists, we are committed to a consistent procedure for copy-text selection and emendation based on Sir Walter W. Greg's "The Rationale of Copy-Text" (*Studies in Bibliography* 3 [1950–51]: 19–36) and modified for nineteenth- and twentieth-century editing situations by Fredson Bowers and G. Thomas Tanselle.[2] As Greg pointed out, the copy-text concept is not an abstract principle but rather a pragmatic rationale for editing when there exists no compelling evidence for making choices among variant readings from surviving texts. Peirce's tendency to continuously develop a document in many forms over many years has led us to modify copy-text selection in certain cases where "text" cannot be traditionally defined.

5. In terms of presentation, we are committed to a chronological edition published in a clear reading text. The chronological order of presentation allows us to fit the transmission of individual texts into the larger perspective sought by scholars since Murray Murphey's *The Development of Peirce's Philosophy* appeared in 1961; our volumes show the evolving nature of Peirce's work in each of his many disciplines, the breadth of materials that Peirce worked on (often simultaneously) in particular historical periods, and the emerging patterns of Peirce's intellectual development throughout his entire lifetime. The clear reading text is made possible by our construction of a textual apparatus keyed to the pages and lines of the clear text.

2. The Center for Scholarly Edition's "An Introductory Statement" (NY: Modern Language Association, 1977), includes a bibliographical essay by G. Thomas Tanselle. His "A Fourth Interim Supplement" (1993) supersedes supplements of 1990, 1991, and 1992, and is available from the chair of MLA's Committee on Scholarly Editions—the body which has evolved from the original CEAA and CSE structures. Beth Luey's *Editing Documents and Texts: An Annotated Bibliography* (Madison, WI: Madison House, 1990) contains annotated citations for essays published across all the fields of scholarly editing.

The multiple text situations described in the third goal require further general comment. If there are two or more texts of a work, the text which represents the most mature form that is closest to the author's hand will usually become the copy-text. A mature manuscript—representing the final draft if more than one manuscript form survives—provides the ideal basis for a critical edition. Such a manuscript (or a typescript prepared by Peirce or under his supervision) is preferable to subsequent printed forms where compositorial error and editorial styling may have corrupted the text. The copy-text is the most authoritative source for accidentals, especially when it is a holograph manuscript; when no holograph forms survive, the typed or printed document that is closest to Peirce's unmediated hand (that is, the form in which the fewest intermediaries have had a chance to interfere) will become copy-text. If there is only one version of a document, it automatically becomes copy-text.

Because of Peirce's complex habit of constantly rethinking and revising his work, a number of texts survive in distinct versions which are collatable sentence-by-sentence or paragraph-by-paragraph rather than word-for-word. In many of these cases, he diverges radically from the direction of a previous draft and produces an entirely different work. As a consequence, each such version has its own textual authority and each would serve as its own copy-text for publication. When collation provides a chronological order to the divergent forms, we generally publish the final or most mature version, and designate the others as pre-copy-text forms. There will be times when more than one form is mature and significant, but Peirce shows no clear preference; in such a case, we will consider publication of multiple forms of the single basic work. In general practice, however, earlier divergent forms will be consigned to non-critical facsimile representation in an expanded electronic edition of our volumes.

Earlier manuscript drafts, whether divergent or not, are certainly important in documenting the evolution of the work, but these drafts are pre-copy-text forms representing superseded authorial intention. The variant readings in these earlier forms are carefully studied, for these forms may provide clues to the content of missing, damaged, or erroneous text in the more mature copy-text document; but such preliminary drafts have no real authority in the process of establishing the new edition's text. Even the copy-text itself may contain pre-copy-text forms, especially when copy-text is a manuscript or a typescript prepared by Peirce and containing multiple layers of revision. In the vast majority of cases, the text as represented in the final layer of revision is accepted as copy-text—the words and punctuation of this layer stand as the basis for emendation from subsequent authoritative forms. In very rare cases, severe editorial pressure on Peirce's revising hand (such as *The Forum's* editorial pressure on Peirce's revision of "Logic and Spiritualism") will make Peirce's final layer of revision suspect; in such a case, the unrevised layer may provide the best choice for copy-text, a choice which allows the editors to evaluate the "revised" variant forms on a case-by-case basis.

II. Specific Editing Guidelines

Copy-text rationale is not meant to stand as an ironclad principle or an inflexible rule; it simply provides an authoritative textual basis whenever variants in the subsequent texts aren't supported by convincing evidence. Under copy-text rationale, all variants are suspect; whether accidentals or substantives, they must be rejected unless there is supportable evidence that they represent Peirce's intended revisions. What is supportable evidence? It will range from conclusive to suggestive—in each case, the editor must exercise critical judgment in accepting or rejecting the variant.

As critical editors we do not "style" Peirce's texts in the traditional sense; in fact, one of the principal purposes of critical editing is to recover the author's intentions from compositorial corruptions and house styling imposed in the past. But we do edit Peirce's texts with an eye for (1) extending his consistent habits in scientific notation, spelling and punctuation throughout the working period covered by the volume, (2) for correcting unacceptable errors (those errors in spelling, grammar, or formulae which confuse or mislead the reader), and (3) for completing Peirce's sometimes incomplete revisions. Editing within these categories will be more extensive than that of most critical editions, which normally deal with authors more successful in bringing work to press or at least to fair-copy forms of manuscript. In Peirce's case, more extensive intervention is dictated by the high proportion of manuscript material which never reached a fair-copy draft stage, let alone publication. Many emendations to the unpublished selections simply bring these texts to a publishable level of presentation in ways which follow (as closely as possible) Peirce's own expectations and usages.

But Peirce's more fully developed copy-texts often approached or achieved publication in his lifetime, generating typescripts, galleys, or page proofs containing both authorial revisions and non-authorial corruptions. Besides a record of emendation, such selections may require a record of substantive variations occurring after the accepted reading, which has already been established either by the source copy-text or by emendation from an intervening form (for example, a point in a manuscript may be revised by the author in first galleys, then mis-set by the compositor in revised galleys). A variant of this type will appear in a Rejected Substantives list rather than an Emendations list—it falls outside the process of establishing the critical text, but within the period in which the author was actively engaged in work on the text. Accidentals in this category are documented in collation, but do not appear in the volume; editorial corruptions introduced by the CP editors decades after Peirce's death are not relevant and are not recorded here.

The material we are committed to edit consists of article-length compositions published in newspapers, periodicals, scholarly journals, proceedings, dictionaries, and encyclopedias, and a far larger body of significant manuscripts from Peirce's many fields of study that remained unpublished during his lifetime.[3] This volume contains 47 individual items, diverse in content, and ranging in form from outlines, notes and preliminary drafts of articles intended for eventual publication to published reviews, published articles, and fair-copy drafts of manuscripts which, for various reasons, never went to press. This broad range in form, typical of the volumes in this edition, requires different editing techniques for the two major categories of materials—papers published by Peirce and his unpublished manuscripts.

1. Previously published writings

Peirce's publications sometimes have no known pre-publication forms, but many others can be traced to surviving manuscript drafts, printer's galleys, and page proofs. In those cases that require a choice among possible copy-texts, a historical collation is used to identify all variants among the relevant forms and to determine the transmission of the text. Generally, a manuscript form (or the last draft if a sequence of manuscripts survive) is selected as copy-text because it represents Peirce's preference in accidentals (spelling and punctuation) and is the best authority for his word choice. This text will be emended by revisions to the publication layers judged to be Peirce's, and by corrections imposed by Peirce's editors (or by the present editors) required to correct errors of content and eliminate confusion. These interventions are recorded in the Emendations list appended to each selection's headnote.

Variants (in the copy-text and in later forms) judged to be the result of non-authorial intervention, such as compositorial errors, compositorial misreadings, or editorial changes in grammar or style, are rejected and noted in the historical collation; a non-authorial variant introduced prior to the accepted reading is part of the emendation record and will appear in the Emendations list. A few non-authorial variants will occur in a form of the text subsequent to that containing the accepted reading; substantive readings of this kind will appear in the list of Rejected Substantives. Finally, any revisions by Peirce in the copy-text itself supersede his earlier pre-copy-text layers; a full record of authorial alterations within the copy-text is made, and substantive alterations within this category appear in each selection's Alterations list. The complete list of alterations will be included in the electronic version of the *Writings*.

3. Longer works do survive; at various times, Peirce began writing books he intended as major contributions to philosophy, logic, mathematics, and other disciplines. Some of these went well beyond the planning stage—such as the lengthy manuscripts entitled "How to Reason" and "Minute Logic"—and will fill individual volumes.

An important source of emendation to the published papers lies in Peirce's own offprints, which he habitually corrected and annotated partly because of constant feuding with publishers (including the Government Printing Office) over his technical charts and often complex scientific notational signs. His offprint corrections are emended into the text, unless they involve calculations which cannot be verified or which cause untraceable cascading changes through an entire series of subsequent calculations. Such problematic authorial corrections are not emended into the copy-text, but are fully described in Annotations. Peirce's marginal comments in his offprints are quoted in textual notes. Further documentary sources for emendation include published errata lists as well as errors that Peirce mentions in letters or reports. Even when there is no documentary evidence, we emend other typographical errors and erroneous readings, all of which are reported in the list of emendations.

We verify all of Peirce's quotations against source books he is known to have owned or had available. But unless there is a nonsensical reading, we do not emend substantive variations (changes in wording) between the original quotation and Peirce's rendering; instead, the original quotation is cited in the volume's Annotations, while the variations are pointed out and discussed in the textual notes. When Peirce refers to any of his other publications, and that work also appears in this volume, we replace his reference numbers with the present page numbers; we do not emend Peirce's references to his own work published in other volumes of this edition.

Peirce's publications appeared in many different journals and periodicals, each with its own house style. We emend all title references to conform to our own edition style (*Chicago Manual of Style*, 14th ed.); thus we italicize book titles, place chapter titles in quotation marks, and so on. Lengthy quotations set in the text of Peirce's original publications are offset and reduced in size to conform with our own style for printing extracts.

All emendations to the texts are listed, and the sources for each cited, in the selection's Emendations list. Any changes not listed there are described generically in the Essay on Editorial Theory and Method or in the selection's headnote in the Apparatus. These include purely visual characteristics, such as the uppercase styling of opening words in a publication, or the Attic font Peirce tended to use in his own typescripts. Other physical characteristics involve footnote numbers and variation in ellipsis points. The symbols or page-by-page numbering systems Peirce's publishers used for footnotes are replaced by a single series of arabic numerals; though this is not Peirce's usual method for indicating footnotes in manuscript (he preferred page-by-page repeating symbols), changes in pagination between original printings and our edition also necessitate changes in numbers or symbols. In place of varying numbers of ellipsis points to mark omissions in quoted material (a device used by some compositors to help justify right-hand margins), we follow modern standard form.

When no manuscript survives and the proof or published form must serve as copy-text, we emend printer's styling to conform to Peirce's own style of punctuation and spelling only if Peirce has demonstrated a clear preference in established practice during the period of his life covered by the volume. For instance, Peirce's preference for the spelling 'premiss' (after 1900) and the compound form 'seconds-pendulum' is well established in both his usage and his commentaries on style. Peirce's preference for acceptable nineteenth-century spelling forms, as well as acceptable variant spellings of proper names, are allowed to stand as they appear. For the most part, Peirce shows no clear preferences in such matters as routine punctuation; he occasionally corrected or revised punctuation in his typescripts, but collations of publications against surviving typescripts or manuscripts reveal that he typically retained house styling of commas and dashes in otherwise heavily corrected proofs. The ampersand (&) and related combinations (such as &c.), which Peirce often used for convenience in draft documents, rarely carried over into his publications and is emended to "and" and "etc." when encountered in copy-text. Peirce preferred to superscript the ordinal number suffixes "st," "nd," "rd," and "th," as well as "Mr" and similar titles of address. We emend published pieces to conform to Peirce's usage, including his preference for "2nd" and "3rd" over "2d" and "3d." However, we do not reproduce Peirce's nineteenth-century calligraphic convention of double-underlining the superscript portions, or his inconsistent use of a period after ordinals.

2. *Unpublished writings*

A. *Selection*

The general editing guidelines described earlier in this essay are applied in editing all selections, but specific copy-text selection is often more complex for Peirce's unpublished manuscripts than it is for his publications. With published items, especially those where no prepublication forms of the text survive to serve as copy-text, we focus our effort on locating and eliminating editorial or printing corruptions. With unpublished holograph and typescript items, the focus is on identifying the sequence of Peirce's revisions—both across drafts and within single drafts—that show evidence of one or more layers of revision. In general, the search for copy-text follows the same rationale used for published items: a mature manuscript form in Peirce's hand represents the best authority. Where more than one manuscript draft survives, collation will generally reveal the order of composition and lead to a fairly simple editing decision. Sometimes, a mature manuscript is followed by a typescript (or an amanuensis draft) prepared under Peirce's supervision, which contains his holograph corrections and revisions, but varies significantly in both substantives and accidentals from the manuscript. If the two mature versions are collatable word-for-word, we accept the authority of the manuscript (copy-text) and emend it with those substantive revisions (and corrections to accidentals) in the typescript that can be attributed to Peirce with a fair degree of confidence. If the typescript is so thoroughly rewritten (which usually indicates a missing intervening draft) that word-by-word collation is not possible, we conclude that Peirce rewrote the document, and use the typescript as copy-text. The surviving earlier stage will be designated a pre-copy-text form and important variant readings will be reproduced or described in editors' annotations.

In fact, situations involving widely diverging forms (that derive from single original drafts) represent the most common copy-text dilemma found in the unpublished materials. Successive manuscript versions may repeat the title or have the same or a similar opening sentence, but will often diverge into a related but new line of inquiry or method of argument. Paragraph or outline collation will usually yield a chronological order, but we are left with two or more discrete documents, generally parallel in content but distinct in presentation and development. When parallel versions are equally significant in terms of documenting Peirce's evolving ideas or scientific findings, we may publish them as discrete items. Each serves as its own copy-text, and will not be emended from subsequent parallel forms; we may refer to other parallel versions for Annotations, but not for textual authority.

B. Recording Peirce's alterations to the manuscript

We archive the full record of Peirce's pre-copy-text alterations, but only those alterations that manifest a "critically significant" change of intention in the process of composition will appear in each volume's apparatus. To decide whether a correction is critically significant, the following maxim, inspired by Peirce's own pragmatic maxim, is applied: "consider whether the change of intention possibly manifested in the alteration produces an effect which might conceivably modify a reader's perception or understanding of the altered passage; if there is any such conceivable effect, then the alteration is critically significant."[4] Given this selective process, there are some manuscripts for which we do not publish an alterations list, even though they do contain alterations recorded in our master files.

After examining different linear methods based on special symbols for insertions, deletions, transpositions, and the like, we settled on a modified version of the method created by Fredson Bowers (*Studies in Bibliography* 29 [1976]: 212–264). A physical description of the method of insertion or deletion is archived for each reading, but in most cases only the text of each superseded reading appears in the volume's Alterations lists, presented in the sequence that evolved as Peirce revised toward the final copy-text form.

4. André De Tienne, "Selecting Alterations for the Apparatus of a Critical Edition," *Text* 9 (1996): 37.

C. Editing unpublished selections

In emending Peirce's manuscripts, the range of our interventions is based in large part on the distinctions between public and private writings defined by G. Thomas Tanselle in his statement of textual policy for the Northwestern-Newberry critical edition of Melville's *Journals* (Evanston, IL: Northwestern Univ. Press and the Newberry Library, 1989, 236–42). This policy is also the editing basis for Melville's *Correspondence* (Evanston, IL: Northwestern Univ. Press and the Newberry Library, 1993), and is summarized in Tanselle's *A Rationale of Textual Criticism* (Philadelphia: Univ. of Pennsylvania Press, 1989).

Public documents include those that conform to genres normally intended for publication, whether they are personal working copies, early drafts, worksheets, or outlines; lectures written, in outline or fair-copy form, for presentation in lecture courses or at public conferences. All manuscripts or typescripts devoted to topics and ideas that are related to those Peirce published and that he would have been willing to submit for public comment and criticism are so regarded. These might be thought of as works Peirce composed with the general reader in mind. Although we go farther in extending the definition of public documents than Tanselle does, our definition is due to Peirce's lifelong habit of leaving unfinished much of the work he intended for presentation or publication, and of submitting premature stages of work to his various publishers. By far the larger part of the unpublished manuscripts are considered public documents, and we edit this category in the following specific ways.

Spelling and grammatical errors are corrected, missing punctuation is inserted, and lowercase variables (sometimes left in roman style through haste or carelessness on Peirce's part) are emended to italics. A dash, parenthesis, or quotation mark is added when it is the missing half of a pair. Numbers, expressed in either arabic or numeral form, are left as he wrote them unless his usage is confusing. Spelling presents the greatest difficulty, for Peirce was inconsistent even when a general preference can be identified. Fortunately, his long-standing association with the development of the *Century Dictionary* provides a late nineteenth-century standard when emendation is necessary. Simple spelling errors are resolved by the *Century* standard. Where two different spellings are acceptable by that standard, we allow him to vary unless he has a clear and generally consistent preference for one form over another, or unless the occurrences might lead to confusion. Texts where variant spellings appear in close proximity, or where the variations involve a technical term, fall into the latter category.

Because of Peirce's own patterns of revision, manuscripts intended for publication occasionally require deeper editorial intervention. While revising, he sometimes created grammatical errors; at other times he failed to complete his intended revision by crossing out a needed word or phrase but not going back to replace it. If there is no convincing evidence identifying Peirce's intentions, we return to his original word or phrase, citing each occurrence in a textual note. When he added introductory clauses to already inscribed sentences, but failed to lowercase the first word of the original sentence, we emend his misplaced capitalization. Occasionally, Peirce will misspeak himself or produce a confusing or vague passage. We emend when we are confident of his intent. If such confidence is lacking, his eccentricities and anomalies are left as written. Here, as in Peirce's published pieces, we change his footnote symbols to sequential numbers, and reproduce quotations as he gives them. Abbreviated or erroneous titles cited in Peirce's texts or in his footnotes are corrected. All of the interventions described above are recorded in the volume's emendations lists.

Private documents include letters, drafts of letters, journals and notebooks. Some were never intended for publication, and their content was for personal use only. But most of the journals, however cryptic and abbreviated their contents may be, were preparatory for eventual presentation in a public forum. Even certain letters fall into this category—Peirce's long letters to William James were often formally developed, and written with the knowledge that James might use them in his Harvard classroom (and with the expectation that they would be preserved with James's papers for future scholars). Peirce's letters to the Coast Survey contain technical material designed to amplify his formal reports and even to appear in them; in fact, his monthly letters to the Survey *were* formal reports required by law. Given these circumstances, we modify the notion of private document in the following way.

For private documents that we identify as clearly personal in nature, composed with a particular reader (perhaps only himself) in mind, we will generally not interfere with the private character of the presentation—we will not substantially interfere with Peirce's private usages, including his page formatting, his idiosyncratic syntax and grammar, and unconventional (but nevertheless intended) spellings. These personalized characteristics of presentation would not be allowed to stand by a publisher in Peirce's day, but these materials—especially the journals—are really "idea books" used by Peirce to work out problems before going on to future development for presentation. When no further development of the text survives, we edit and publish them as private documents, emending only those idiosyncrasies which do not reflect authorial intention (such as transposed letters and other slips of the pen). All interventions appear in the volume's emendations lists.

Even for "private documents" we identify as probably intended for eventual presentation, we will still retain the character of Peirce's work wherever possible; but while we make every effort to preserve the surface features of these documents, we correct mistakes in content—the evolving technical and analytical nature of Peirce's ideas calls for clarity of presentation. For this reason, we intervene to represent clearly Peirce's intentions, especially in his use of logic signs, mathematical formulae, and scientific notation. But in terms of accidentals, private documents which Peirce intended for eventual presentation are generally emended only in the following four instances: Peirce's unintended spellings (transpositions and slips of the pen) are corrected, periods are added at the ends of sentences except before the beginning of a new paragraph, apostrophes are inserted in the plural forms of variables (but not in the possessive forms of proper names or other substantive words), and Peirce's incomplete revisions are completed when necessary for clarity. These editorial interventions are all recorded in the volume's emendations lists.

D. Scientific notation

It remains to define the policies used to edit Peirce's scientific usages and preferences. As a mathematician and logician, Peirce knew that lowercase variables are represented as italics; he expected that in publications, but did not always carry through in manuscript composition. Wherever Peirce is inconsistent in his underlining of variables, or where he simply leaves it to editors to properly set long sequences of variables, we will generally emend to italics and record the emendation so that the original state of each variable can be reconstructed as it was in the copy-text reading. Greek variables (uppercase and lowercase) follow the same pattern of usage and are handled in the same way, but the quantifiers Π and Σ remain roman. Uppercase letters are italicized in the relatively few cases where they clearly stand for variables; otherwise they remain roman, as when they are used to designate relatives in logical algebra or to label geometric lines. These practices represent the styles that Peirce generally used in manuscript, or at least accepted in his scientific publications; any exceptions that are allowed to stand unemended, as when Peirce explicitly modifies these conventions, will be annotated.

In his charts and related texts, several physical characteristics will be regularized, but not noted as emendations: decimal points are lowered from mid-line to on-line; multiplication dots are raised to mid-line from the on-line position; place-holding zeros in long columns are supplied as Peirce intended; and ambiguous dashes for omitted words, phrases, or numeric values are placed mid-line and given the appropriate em-length required by *Chicago* style. Long equations broken across lines of text in the present edition may require insertion of a multiplication sign if the break point falls between expressions where multiplication is implied but not expressed by a sign. Since the sign operates, like a hyphen, to indicate continuation across lines, it is not entered as an emendation. These regularizations will be noted in the item's apparatus headnote.

E. Editing Peirce's typescripts

Many of Peirce's scientific documents, and indeed a significant portion of his work in many fields, survive in one or more typewritten drafts. Between

1880 and 1893, Peirce used a number of different machines to create these documents, and became a fairly accomplished typist. Analysis of known typescripts indicates that Peirce used a Remington and a Caligraph during the early 1880s; from 1885 on, however, he showed a clear preference for the Hammond Model 1, a highly sophisticated machine with interchangeable type shuttles and a double-shift mechanism that was ahead of its time.

Surviving correspondence indicates that Peirce used two and possibly three Hammonds during the W6 time period, and acquired at least a half dozen interchangeable font shuttles for these machines. Peirce would often use multiple fonts in a single document to set italic variables within a roman typescript, to style headings, or simply to expand his range of characters. However, there were limitations; some of the type shuttles included parentheses, but some did not, and Peirce or his typists often used square brackets to offset parenthetical text. The present edition emends brackets to parentheses unless the brackets offset an interpolation by Peirce, or serve a mathematical or logic function.

Peirce would sometimes employ typists, but many of the documents contain typed revisions and corrections in progress that indicate authorial composition. A line in progress was not visible on the Model 1, and he often typed his corrections and revisions above the original reading without returning to cancel the superseded text. The Hammond allowed Peirce to overstrike the superseded reading, and he sometimes did so; but this took time, and a quick interlinear revision is often all we find. The lack of a true platen made hand cancellation difficult, and he rarely took the time to make the cancellation after the completed page left the machine. His preference for the interlined text is clearly evident in many typed interlineations, and these revisions will be transcribed as the author's intended form. In such cases, the original reading will be recorded as an implicit alteration. Where there is any doubt, the interlined typing is transcribed as a parallel reading.

Peirce's implicit alterations within the layered fabric of a typescript copy-text will usually be significant, and will appear in the volume's listing of significant pre-copy-text alterations. The Emendations list will include any post-copy-text revisions by Peirce, as well as our own emendations to the textual elements; however, purely physical characteristics or mechanical faults found in the typescripts are visual elements of the copy-text, and will not be recorded in the textual apparatus. Significant visual characteristics will be discussed in headnotes, but in general the visual elements will be handled during editing in the following ways.

Marginal errors caused by the typing medium will be transcribed, but will be silently removed or regularized during the editing process. These include missing terminal letters or hyphenation due to right margin overrun, as well as false starts of words or entire phrases due to right margin and even bottom margin overrun. Peirce also ran together words and associated punctuation by missing the space bar. At times Peirce would switch type shuttles to italicize a mathematical expression or to italicize for emphasis, then fail to switch back to one of his roman shuttles without discovering the error until several characters, words or lines later. All of these anomalies are transcribed as typed by Peirce; however, since they are purely physical characteristics of the typescript, they are regularized during the editing phase and do not appear in the Emendations list.

Other physical characteristics will not appear in transcription at all. Paragraph indentation is normalized in transcription, unless Peirce has indicated subordinating or sequential variations in successive paragraphs or formulae. Extra spacing before and after punctuation is also normalized in transcription. In the same way, defects in the typography are neither annotated in transcription nor considered in the establishment of the text. For example, occasional off-center strikes (especially the lowercase n, s, u, w, and y letterfaces) on the Hammond result in the partial image of two letters in a single space, or a vacant space where no strike is evident at all. In such cases, with no evidence to the contrary, we assume the proper key was struck. Characters completely superimposed (that is, typewritten in the same space) are considered consecutive and are transcribed in the proper sequence.

III. Survey of Texts in the Volume

The years 1886–1890 were years of movement from city to country for Peirce, and marked as well a time of great professional turmoil as long-term stress in his working relationship with the Coast Survey boiled over into open conflict. The documents of this period are largely undated, unpublished, and greatly disordered. The table of contents for Volume 6 represents the first focused effort to recover the record of Peirce's work for those years, and pieces together texts that, in their entirety, are somewhat unfamiliar even to Peirce scholars. The present volume contains 44 selections composed by Peirce between the fall of 1886 and the spring of 1890. Three more selections are by other writers: two direct responses to Peirce's "Criticism of *Phantasms of the Living*" by *Phantasms* principal author Edmund Gurney are grouped with Peirce's original review and his own rejoinder to Gurney's first response; and a two-part student response to Peirce's correspondence course in "The Art of Reasoning" precedes Peirce's written reply. Of the 44 Peirce texts, only 10 were published in his lifetime. Three are reviews published in the *Nation*, and two others are *New York Times* editorial letters. For four of these popular press items, no pre-publication forms have been located. Pre-publication forms do survive for three of the five remaining texts that Peirce saw through to publication; although all contain valuable clues to the evolution of Peirce's texts (and some have allowed us to detect and eliminate errors in the original publications), none is developed enough to stand as a copy-text document. Of the 34 texts in this volume that Peirce never brought to press, 22 are here first published. All or parts of nine selections appeared in a topical arrangement in the *Collected Papers*; three other complete selections appeared (again in topical order) in the *New Elements of Mathematics*. These are published here in Peirce's original order of composition.

Five major texts or text sequences from this period of Peirce's life have complicated textual histories requiring special critical editing applications: Peirce's correspondence course in "The Art of Reasoning"; his milestone manuscript for "A Guess at the Riddle," representing the culmination and consolidation of earlier cosmological studies from the Volume 5 period; his controversial Arctic gravity determinations for the Greely expedition; Peirce's long-lost gravity report of 1889, a book-length magnum opus of unpublished geodetic theory and application; and the unpublished "Logic and Spiritualism," a victim of an editing war between Peirce and *Forum* editor Lorettus Sutton Metcalf during the spring of 1890. The editing problems and the solutions developed to establish these critical texts are overviewed below; a more specific discussion is found in the headnotes prefacing the apparatus lists for each selection.

1. "THE ART OF REASONING" (SELS. 2–13)

Peirce's periodic desire to leave the Coast & Geodetic Survey flared up again early in 1887—he was under extreme pressure to produce a significant report from the complex Arctic gravity observations brought back by the survivors of the Greely Expedition in 1884. His refusal to work in Washington, and the Survey's budget austerity during this period, made it extremely difficult for Peirce to receive the computational support he desperately needed for the gravity work. By May 1887 he had turned in a preliminary version of the report and left his New York flat for the country in order to save money and plan a new future. From the countryside around Milford, Pennsylvania he would continue to work for the Survey while writing and proofing thousands of entries for the *Century Dictionary*. But he would simultaneously work for nearly two years on a correspondence course in "The Art of Reasoning" which he had developed and implemented in the months just prior to his departure from New York.

The surviving texts of this project are similar in content and voice to the textbooks he was beginning to develop in logic, arithmetic, geometry, and higher mathematics. But the epistolary nature of the course materials, and the supporting body of advertising that also survives, represent a different notion of text than we find elsewhere in his work. The exploration of yet another kind of Peircean text is complicated by the incomplete and chaotic state of the course materials that do survive.

Much of the course advertising, and a fragmentary record of the student correspondence itself, is located in two badly overcrowded and unsorted folders designated RL 100 and assigned to the "correspondence" category within the Harvard Peirce Papers. The folders include a notebook with abbreviated entries on student progress which, when decoded, provide vital clues for dating and for understanding just how the course developed—off and on—through the winter and spring of 1887. But most of the course lessons and exercises are spread through a number of widely scattered manuscripts; reassembly of each document (and its related drafts) is only the beginning of the recovery process. None of the surviving texts are titled within the hierarchy of the course itself, and many are prototypes, drafts, or damaged hectograph copies of the lessons that actually went out to students. Until very recently, it was unclear whether or not enough materials could be identified to complete a meaningful (and publishable) skeleton of "The Art of Reasoning."

Much advertising and marketing material for the course survives in RL 100, and these documents provide the blueprint for the course as Peirce intended it. The following synopsis correlates the organization of the course as expressed in selections 2, 3 and 5 of the present volume and in a full-page advertisement which ran in the May issue of the *Century Magazine:*

Circular	Follow-up Letter to Circular	Letter to Agents	*Century* Advertisement
Part 1 Traditional logic 1–2 quarters (30–60 lessons, 120–240 hours)	Part 1 Non-quantifiable reasoning	Part 1 Logical language and thought	Part 1 The old logic
Part 2 Mathematical reasoning 2–3 quarters (60–90 lessons, 240–360 hours)	Part 2 Quantifiable reasoning	Part 2 Mathematical reasoning	Part 2 Mathematical precision in reasoning
Part 3 Scientific reasoning 2 quarters (60 lessons, 240 hours)	Part 3 How to deal with real facts	Part 3 Judgments about matters of fact	Part 3 The art of investigation

With the help of the detailed descriptions contained in these documents, a number of surviving exercises and lessons from the first part of the course can be pieced together; but it is the epistolary structure of the course that reveals just how these bricolage-like materials worked together in the context of the larger whole. Peirce cast a wide net (100,000 copies of the circular were planned) to secure what he felt would be a large enough "school" of corespondents to make a living at the business. A query brought in by the brochure was answered by a generic follow-up letter from Peirce (sel. 3); a commitment to try the course (secured by all or part of the "tuition") was answered by Peirce's generic letter to new students (sel. 6), which included a request for a writing sample so that he could properly "place" each student at the right point in the curriculum; alternatively, Peirce would send a personalized orientation letter requesting the writing sample (sel. 7). Actual lessons (sel. 8), sometimes with exercises (sel. 10), would follow. Other stand-alone exercise sheets also survive (sels. 9 and 13). Successful responses to the exercises brought the next set of exercises; unsuccessful responses (and there were many) would trigger remedial instruction letters from Peirce (sels. 11 and 12).

Production of the course materials was, for the times, fairly high-tech. The circular itself was jobbed out to a printer. The generic letters (and some of the lessons and exercises) were typed on a hectograph master and run off in purple copies for mass distribution. The individual letters of remedial instruction, the section overviews, and occasional letters on student progress were typed individually, as revealed by a few surviving discarded sheets and carbon record copies. All of the typed hectograph masters and the personal letters were composed on one of the Hammond Model 1 typewriters that Peirce owned or used during this period. The type-shuttles were interchangeable between machines, and could be used on a single machine to compose exercises in a number of different fonts. Peirce took full advantage of this capability—nearly all of the surviving typescripts were composed in multiple fonts by Peirce or under his direct supervision.

Other exercise sheets and some of the lessons were hand-written on hectograph masters for mass distribution. Often the hand is Peirce's, but an amanuensis was also employed. Holograph drafts also survive for the marketing letters as well. But recognizable portions of Parts 2 and 3 have not been located; these materials may never have been composed, for Peirce lost interest in the work and let the program die out when he was unable to realize a viable income from it.[5] Although the surviving materials cannot be reconstructed into the formal three-part program that Peirce envisioned, his marketing materials and the surviving lessons and problem sets provide a meaningful picture of the course at work. Dating rationale for individual components of the course is explained in the individual selection headnotes. Copy-text decisions and sources of emendation are also described in selection headnotes, but some general comments on editorial decisions here follow.

Peirce's advertising and marketing materials (sels. 2–5) are entrepreneurial texts, designed to persuade the general public (1) that the ability to reason

5. An advertisement in the 1 September 1892 issue of the *Monist* announced the resumption of the course, but there is no evidence that any students enrolled.

is essential in all activities and (2) that traditional logic lessons derived from medieval curricula were only a point of departure for a new form of mathematical reasoning that could be applied to any problem of everyday life. The circular and its follow-up letter mapped out a road to success through correspondence learning that was not at all new to America of the Gilded Age. Peirce's strategy of reiterating his academic credentials on almost every page of these documents is reminiscent of the "confidence man"; indeed, his private correspondence on the subject shows an intriguing mixture of idealism and materialism in his attitude toward the course—a course designed to raise money for Peirce while it also raised the quality of life for the nation.[6]

The wide audience intended for these marketing materials argues for viewing even those formatted as letters in the context of public documents. The circular is clearly a public document,[7] intended for nationwide distribution; his follow-up letter was intended for those relatively few he might hook from recipients of the brochure, but it too is essentially a public document in every sense of the word. The "Directions to Agents," however, seems more private, and, in content, much darker than the rest of the surviving marketing texts. It reveals an obsession with gaining the confidence of prospective students in the small towns and rural communities of America, and describes many techniques that his "agents" might use in drumming up interest. It must be distinguished from selections 3 and 4, which were meant for his students and were open to review by the general public. But Peirce's private correspondence reveals his intention for a nationwide network of agents; therefore, "Directions to Agents" is edited as a public document intended for finished form and distribution to a multiple-reader audience.

The letter to new students (sel. 6) was Peirce's way of initiating a tutorial relationship with a student, and it was the last generic letter that a student would receive. In fact, Peirce may have abandoned the generic form for more personalized orientation letters (sel. 7) fairly early in the evolution of the course. From this point on, the letters (even those topical introductions containing boiler-plate information) would have personalized headers and saluta-

6. Letters to his brother James Mills Peirce (dated by context to January 1887) and to his cousin Henry Cabot Lodge (4 January 1887) outline in great detail Peirce's strategies for advertising the course. The letter to his brother is reliable in its candor: "If I could send 10000 *[circulars]* to 5000 whom I should easily select from my lists, I believe I should within a month get as returns 5 pupils and within 3 months 10 more perhaps, because my first lessons are especially arranged to make the common people *think* it is gaining a great deal, so as to give encouragement." Later in the month, he outlined for his brother a fall-back scheme to advertise gratuitous lessons, clearly banking on the indisputable quality of his material: "I know that whoever will take my lessons will think highly of them, whether he be uneducated or educated. The test of the improvement is too positive to be contested."

7. Beyond the text of the document itself, which describes a nationwide strategy for selling the course, Peirce alludes to the agents in a calculating way to his brother James: "I am thinking of sending agents out to get me scholars paying $10 for each *new* scholar—This would cost me nothing to speak of even if the agents starved" (c. 20 January 1887).

tions. The few surviving carbons and discards indicate that all letters were typed individually, perhaps not always by Peirce but always on one of his Hammond machines. The exercises and the Boolean Algebra lessons were not personalized and went out in hectograph form as attachments or perhaps as separate mailings.

The result of this reconstructed presentation reveals the course dynamic as Peirce implemented it during 1887 and 1888; yet the central question remains how to edit these correspondence materials. The format is epistolary, personal, and on the surface appears by the usual definition of "correspondence" to be private in nature. But these texts are also documents of public education, intended for mass distribution to many students. Even the personalized overview letters and letters of remediation were developed for assembly-line production and dissemination. Peirce outlined the process for his cousin Henry Cabot Lodge on 4 January 1887: "Now I have planned a system which I won't trouble you with, with passages written out answering every conceivable difficulty in the whole course, type-writers, and assistants (upon whom I can lay my hands when I need them) by which I can write say 500 letters a day, or take charge of 1500 students." A 4 April 1887 letter to his mother shows this process little changed, and although letters to his mother (and presumably to Lodge, of whom he asked a loan of up to a thousand dollars to support the scheme) might not be entirely revelatory, they show nonetheless an unmistakable intention to make the course a public venture in mass marketing. Therefore, the reconstructed texts of "The Art of Reasoning," although epistolary in form, are treated as public documents in the present edition and edited according to the policies outlined in the opening pages of this essay.

Two completely rewritten and greatly expanded versions of the first Boolean algebra lesson (opening sel. 10) have been recovered from a score of Harvard manuscripts. Yet neither of these items were prepared for the first version of this course; student responses trail off after April 1889, and the major overhaul to the Boolean lessons probably dates from late 1890. Both of these distinct variants are significant, but they are also beyond both the scope and the time frame of the "Art of Reasoning" materials, and will appear in the next chronological volume.

2. "A GUESS AT THE RIDDLE" (SELS. 22–28)

Peirce's draft for a book on his evolving cosmology is most directly rooted in his "Notes on the Categories" and related items from the summer or fall of 1885 (W5, Items 34–37), and more detailed descriptions of the categories from the summer and fall of 1886 which the present edition has gathered under Peirce's general title of "One, Two, Three" (W5, Items 47–50). "A Guess at the Riddle," Peirce's first bold testing of his grand hypothesis that three elements (or categories) fundamentally underlie the active structuring of thought and nature, dates from the 1887–88 period; it survives short of fair-copy in the form of a 67-leaf typescript of Chapters 1, 3 (in outline), and 4 through 7; Chapters 2, 3, 8, and 9 were not yet written at this stage of the work, but are described in some detail in the surviving outline/table of contents for the book. The textual history of "A Guess at the Riddle" is further complicated by the fact that R 909 was removed from Harvard during the early 1940s when faculty and friends of the Philosophy Department were allowed to take certain manuscripts as mementos of the *Collected Papers* project. R 909 was returned years later, but the most mature version of the opening two paragraphs, which served as printer's copy for *CP,* are no longer part of the holding.

What survives is clearly a work in progress, and the typescript chapters of R 909 reveal just how Peirce was working his way through examples of triadic structure in the major fields of knowledge. There is a cascading series of starts for nearly every chapter, some more or less finished, others broken off early on. The Harvard page order is not sequential, but shows a rough chapter-by-chapter progression that may be the result of heavy editing by Hartshorne and Weiss for the *Collected Papers*—their pagination, annotations, correction, and styling appear throughout the typescript. Beneath these layers are corrections (both typed and holograph) by Peirce himself. The task of editing is further complicated by the fact that Peirce broke off this work just as he was preparing his finished drafts; for several chapters, the mature form breaks off early and without autograph revision by Peirce, leaving an intermediate form to serve as copy-text for the rest of the chapter. Choice of copy-text becomes a chapter-by-chapter affair, and is described thus in the respective apparatus headnotes.

3. "PENDULUM OBSERVATIONS" (SEL. 30)

The raw data for Peirce's report was recorded by members of a U.S. Arctic team, the northernmost expedition involved in a worldwide effort to gather scientific data during the first International Polar Year (1882–83). The expedition, under the command of Army Lieutenant Adolphus W. Greely, was equipped with Peirce Pendulum Number 1, a prototype reversible and invariable gravity pendulum. On 11 April 1887, Peirce submitted his 28-page report on the Arctic gravity work, which included his assertion (based on circumstantial evidence) that the pendulum had been damaged during the expedition. In the opening narrative portion Peirce also concluded that reckless experimental procedures at the Coast Survey headquarters had ruined the calibration data, and therefore no actual gravity values could be calculated. The three-page narrative, prepared on a new Hammond Model 1 typewriter, was followed by 25 holograph pages of swing summaries and partial reduction of the raw data. But correspondence from the expedition leader and from Coast Survey technicians disputed this conclusion and persuaded Peirce to explore the possibility that anomalies in the pendulum's period (it beat slightly longer seconds with the heavy end down than it did with heavy end up) involved some complex and as yet unidentified atmospheric correction involving the extremely cold Arctic January temperatures.

The ensuing year between submission (April 1887) and the correction of galleys (July 1888) allowed Peirce to calculate a reliable value of gravity for the final page of the report. Peirce heavily re-wrote the first galleys, and within a month had made final corrections to a second set. Neither set has been located, but Peirce's letters of transmission survive and reveal that he completely re-wrote the report. Since the surviving initial submission proved to be preliminary, the publication itself (in the absence of the re-written galleys) serves as copy-text for the present edition.

But collation reveals numerous variants between the data tables of the initial submission and those of the final publication. Patterns of variation indicate that some of the tables were clearly and sequentially revised by Peirce; but many of the tables recording the decrement of the pendulum's arc show seemingly random and isolated variation. In his 7 July 1888 letter returning the first corrected proofs to Greely, Peirce noted that "I have not been able to compare all the numbers in the printed proofs, but have verified them to some extent. Should it afterwards turn out that there is time for me to read another proof I will thank you to send with it my original copy, as I may then be able to verify some numbers which I have not been able to do, as it is." We know from Peirce's cover letter of 24 July that he did revise second proofs as well, but he makes no mention of checking the unrevised figures. In the absence of any compelling evidence that Peirce checked the data tables, we have retraced (as far as possible) Peirce's calculations to determine which of the isolated table variations in the published version reflect calculated correction, and which simply introduce new errors, and emend or reject these accidentals on a case-by-case basis.

4. "Report on Gravity at the Smithsonian, Ann Arbor, Madison, and Cornell" (sel. 36)

The same challenge of correcting for atmospheric effects also plagued his work on systematic gravity determinations at stations across the United States; as he worked on the Greely Report, he was also working on a much larger report for stations across the 43rd parallel and down a vast meridional arc from Montreal to Key West. Peirce finally submitted results for the 43rd parallel stations in November 1889, but it went unpublished and was lost in the Survey archives for decades. The details surrounding the Survey's refusal to publish the report as submitted, its rediscovery in the 1960s, and the physical characteristics of the document are contained in the selection's headnote and the volume Introduction.

The 43rd parallel station data was recorded during 1885, but it would take Peirce several years of painstaking work to reduce the data to a meaningful form and compensate for the complex effects of air pressure and temperature on the gravity pendulums. On two occasions, Survey Superintendent Thorn forced Peirce to submit preliminary versions for inspection. The initial submission, a massive set of data sheets accompanied by a handwritten draft report, was turned in during January 1888. The following January, Peirce submitted more than 2000 pages consisting of the data sheets, the handwritten draft, and a new typewritten draft. Thorn was not satisfied with the preliminary nature of the second submission, but the change in administrations resulting from the March 1889 inauguration of Benjamin Harrison allowed Peirce to delay final submission for nearly another year.

The copy-text document itself—a 140-page conflation of new and old typescript pages—was submitted under pressure in November 1889, less than two years prior to his forced resignation from the Coast Survey. Peirce's haste in preparation for final submission is especially evident in the physical form of the document. Most of the report consists of sequences of highly complex tables with only the most preliminary headings. Column and row titles are inconsistently displayed, and in the case of iterative tables, these headings are abbreviated or missing. While Peirce's narrative passages and table data are treated as text (and emended accordingly), the table headings and layout are treated as presentation characteristics of the document. Headings are silently regularized, and layout adjusted to the standards which Peirce accepted for his published survey reports of earlier years.

All emendations to the text itself are recorded in the selection's emendations list, but Peirce's data tables and his complex mathematical corrections for the effects of atmosphere and peripheral station equipment (such as pendulum stands, pivot heads and timepieces) are not easy to verify. Many of the data points are reduced from pendulum worksheets which, even when they survive, can no longer be attributed to discrete calculations in the submitted report. Those data points which derive from identifiable calculations elsewhere in the report have been checked for accuracy and emended if error is detected. Textual notes describing these situations are keyed to the emendations list for this selection.

5. "Logic and Spiritualism" (sel. 44)

The apparatus headnote for this selection describes why, in the absence of any surviving printer's copy, the unrevised underlayer of the *Forum's* galleys represent the text closest to Peirce's intentions. This choice of copy-text represents a departure from the norm, where the final layer of authorial revision is usually regarded as the copy-text "layer." But even before the galleys were pulled, there is evidence (in surviving manuscript drafts and printer's-copy discards) that Peirce was deeply engaged in an editing war with *Forum* editor Lorettus Sutton Metcalf and his inflexible 5000-word limit. As Peirce added words to clarify his points, he would cut articles, pronouns, and even verbs to stay within Metcalf's limit. Peirce's unusual but calculated strategy appears in successive layers of the galleys and continues through a typescript prepared from the galleys. This process is almost entirely in Peirce's hand, and no doubt represents his frustration with Metcalf's editorial dictatorship; but it also destabilizes the only documents that can serve as copy-text. In this case, the most stable form is the unrevised *underlayer* of the galley sheets, which includes compositorial corruptions but which is free of the five most destructive layers of editing warfare between Metcalf and Peirce, a war which, in terms of surviving texts, Metcalf apparently won. Peirce's true revisions within these successive layers—that is, those alterations which develop or clarify the galleys—have been accepted as emendations; but his destabilizing attempts to cut the word count are rejected.

* * * * *

The remaining selections in this volume received the same care in editing as the problem texts described above, but the apparatus sections for these less complex pieces require no further amplification in this essay. Individual apparatus sections for each of the volume's 47 selections follow with detailed discussions of (and documentation for) the editing decisions applied in establishing the texts of the 1886–1890 period.

Textual Apparatus

The Textual Apparatus provides (together with the Essay on Editorial Theory and Method) a nearly complete record of what has been done in the editing process, and it presents the necessary evidence for the editorial decisions that have been made in this critical edition. It consists of forty-seven sections, corresponding to the number of selections published in the present volume, and each section contains up to five separate subdivisions. Each of the forty-seven sections begins with its identifying number in the volume and its (running-head) short title. It is followed by an untitled headnote, Textual Notes, and lists of Emendations, Rejected Substantives, Line-End Hyphenation, and, if the selection is a manuscript, Alterations. Textual Notes and all apparatus lists are printed in reduced type; apparatus lists are set in double columns. The rationale involved in establishing each type of apparatus list is discussed in detail in the Essay on Editorial Theory and Method; symbols and editorial abbreviations used throughout the apparatus are described in the brief survey of Symbols found at the beginning of the editorial back matter.

The headnote describes the genesis of the text and the occasion for which it was written. It designates the copy-text and identifies (by sigla) all collated variant documents composed before and after the copy-text. It provides information on copy-text dating, and gives a physical description of the manuscript (including number of leaves, paper size, watermarks, medium of inscription, and so on); it also describes fragmentary pages and other portions of the manuscript not included in the edition, and presents source information for all manuscript items not deposited in the Harvard Peirce Papers.

The Textual Notes discuss and explain in detail readings adopted in the edition that represent complex or interesting textual cruxes. They represent either an emendation or a retention of the copy-text reading and specify why, in certain problematical or anomalous instances, the copy-text has or has not been emended. They explain problematic emendations of missing or incomplete revisions by Peirce that have been incorporated into the text or, when Peirce's final intention in those revisions is unclear, they record those revisions and annotations that cannot be incorporated. They also provide fuller verbal description of certain complex alterations that could not be represented adequately in the Alterations.

Emendations provide a record of all changes, in both substantives and accidentals, made in the copy-text to produce the critical text. They record the addition or deletion of passages and the change or correction of words, of mathematical and scientific formulas, and of such accidentals as spelling and punctuation. With the exception of selection 36, where an abbreviated record of accidentals is presented for Peirce's italic variables and data table headings, the emendation lists record all changes introduced into the copy-text. For each entry, the accepted emendation from the present (critically edited) edition appears in the lemma to the left of the bracket; an abbreviation (or siglum) identifying the authority for that reading, followed by a semicolon, the original reading of the copy-text, and variant readings of texts after the copy-text but before the reading accepted in the present text appear to the right of the bracket. Sigla identifying the source for all readings, other than the editors (E), is given in the headnote for each item. Readings of texts which fall between the copy-text and the accepted reading which agree with the original (copy-text) reading will not be duplicated in an entry; instead, the superseded copy-text reading will include the siglum of both. Any substantive variations in texts subsequent to the accepted reading will appear in a Rejected Substantives list immediately following the Emendations list.

The Rejected Substantives list records all substantive variants subsequent to the accepted reading which have been rejected as nonauthorial. For each rejected substantive entry, the reading of the present edition is cited to the left of the bracket; an abbreviation (or siglum) identifying the source of the accepted reading, followed by a semicolon and any subsequent variant readings and their sigla appear to the right of the bracket. If the authority for the accepted reading is not the copy-text, the copy-text reading can be found in the Emendations list. Other relevant readings not listed here agree with the accepted reading unless recorded as emendations.

Line-End Hyphenation is a list of those compounds or possible compounds that are hyphenated at the ends of lines in the copy-text. They are resolved according to known Peirce usage and, consequently, are printed in this edition either as hyphenated words or as single unhyphenated words. (This list of compounds hyphenated at the ends of lines in the present volume appears as a separate section before the Index.)

Alterations provide a selected list of changes made by the author in the course of writing the manuscript or upon reviewing it. Such changes include deletions, simple and complex insertions, simple and complex transpositions, superimpositions of letters or words, typeface and character-style alterations, and cancellations. Only those alterations that are critically significant and either dispensable or informative are recorded in this list.

Beginning with this volume, the technical description of alterations has been simplified on the pragmatic assumption that what really needs to be represented is the sequence of intermediary readings as they evolved through the alteration process rather than the alteration process itself which involves different kinds of insertions and deletions. Consequently, wherever possible the alteration descriptions simply consist of a sequence of readings, each separated by a closing square bracket. The first reading (the lemma) reproduces the exact reading in the edition text, except when it is preceded by an imploded diamond (explained in Editorial Symbols), and thus represents the final stage of the alteration. Each subsequent reading reproduces the result of the immediately preceding stage of the alteration, so that the last reading in the sequence actually reproduces the initial text, prior to alteration. For example, the sequence "mien] shape] form" tells the reader that Peirce initially wrote the word "form," then changed it to "shape," and finally to "mien." That he did so by deleting or inserting this or that is left out of this simplified description. Full technical descriptions of each alteration will be made available on the Peirce Project's website.

In some cases, a technical description is provided whenever the nature of the alteration makes it more practical (this concerns mostly simple deletions and simple interlineations). For example, the entry "garb] *intl-c*" indicates economically that the word was interlined with a caret at the place it now occupies in the sentence.

Two further lists are prepared in the editing process—a full Historical Collations list and a complete List of Alterations in the Manuscripts, which yields the published selected Alterations lists—but neither is published in the edition. (They are available to interested persons for the cost of photocopying.)

1. *Boolian Algebra—Elementary Explanations, 1886*

Copy-text has been recovered from two Harvard manuscripts. It consists of three hectographed sheets in R S38 and a final sheet in R 1573(x), all run off from a now-lost set of masters. The first three leaves are 9½" × 15" sheets of white wove paper bearing a "Montauk Mills" watermark. The hectograph run is in purple, reproducing the typed single-spaced text of the missing masters. The text is typed in an italic font struck from an interchangeable type-shuttle mounted on one of Peirce's Hammond Model 1 machines. Peirce's handwritten corrections were apparently made to the master and were transferred down in the same blue ink at the time of printing. Peirce went over most of these corrections in black on the sheets themselves, and added at least one additional point of revision. The only surviving legible run of the fourth leaf appears to have been an early test run—there are no mastered corrections or any other marks by Peirce. This sheet is a cut half-sheet of the Montauk Mills paper (9½" × 7½") bearing a lightly inked or faded run of the final master page. All four leaves of the copy-text are missing corners but are otherwise intact. Leaf four is soiled across the top and creased across both bottom corners.

A full-page test run of leaf four is located in R S64, but this leaf was also used as a test run for selection 4 and is illegible. A false start of the first leaf survives in the RL 100 grouping of correspondence course materials. It appears to be run off from a preliminary draft of the first fifteen lines of text. The complete 4-page text bridges the material in W5.54 and W5.56 (Fall 1886) into the actual correspondence course materials sent to students beginning early in 1887, but this elementary lesson does not appear to have been used. A fuller discussion of the genealogical connections to other teaching documents appears in the Essay on Editorial Theory and Method.

The typescript is poorly typed and contains many errors; the many run-on sentences suggest that Peirce dictated the piece. The combination of carelessness and spoken patterns (especially in punctuation) resulted in a very confusing and sometimes incoherent text that required deeper emendation than usual.

Textual Notes

1.11 $a = b$] The entire document was typed with an italic type-shuttle on the Hammond typewriter. All lowercase variables thus appear italicized, as does the rest of the text. The present edition retains the italic form of the variables but converts the rest of the document to roman type, without listing the change in the emendations.

1.25–26 false. With] Peirce's run-on sentences here and at such points as 2.29 through 2.33, 3.16, 4.21–22, 8.3 reflect the spoken pace and rhythms of dictation rather than carelessness. However, the clarity of the written text requires emendation of these commas to fuller stops.

4.13 $\bar{a}$] Apparent underlining of the negatived variables here and throughout the remainder of the typescript is the result of a misalignment in shifting the Hammond to strike the negative bar across the top of the variable.

Emendations

Title Explanations] E; ~.
1.11 etc.,] E; &c‸, *Also* 1.21
1.12 sense that,] E; ~, ~‸
1.14 and *b*,] E; ~ b‸
1.20 words "or both"] E; ~, ‸~ ~,‸
1.25 and false] E; and are false
*1.25–26 is false. With] E; are false, with
2.3 parenthesis. Thus,] E; ~, thus,
2.6 $(a+b)c$,] E; $(a+b)$,
2.11–12 reasoning. Thus,] E; ~, thus,
2.13 $a+a$,] E; $a+a$‸
2.26 $(a+c)$,] E; $(a+c)$‸
2.27 *a* is true,] E; *a*,
2.27 are true,] E; ~ ~‸
2.29 true. As] E; ~, as
2.30–31 *bc*. Now] E; *bc*, now
2.32 letters. We] E; ~, we
2.33 *bx*. Now] E; *bx*, now
2.33 whatever. Let] E; ~, let
2.35 conclusion;] E; ~,
2.36 principle] E; principal *Also* 3.8
2.37 *ac*,] E; *ac*‸
3.5 false,] E; ~‸
3.5 is,] E; ~‸
3.5 two,] E; ~‸
3.11 principles] E; principals
3.11 $ac+bc$] E; $ab+ac$

3.16 true. All] E; ~, all
3.25 for] E; fot
3.27 Second,] E; ~:
3.31 Third, since] E; third: Since
3.36 proving] E; providing
3.37 instance] E; intsance
3.37(2) formula] E; formulae *Also* 4.4, 4.7
4.4 \$ = \$\$] E; \$ = \$\$5
4.11 But] E; but
4.11 yet no] E; yet, not
4.15 time;] E; ~,
4.16 Second,] ~‸
4.21–22 rule. Thus,] E; ~, thus,
4.32(1) therefore] E; ~,
4.33 asserts *b*] E; ~ B
4.34 course] E; ~,
5.1 example that] E; example
5.6 $a(b + c)$] E; $a(b + c$‸
5.10 $\prec$,] E; $\prec$‸
5.12 typewriter,] E; type-writer
5.26 $(b{:}c)$.] E; $(b{:}c)$‸
5.27 have] E; hawe
6.3 $[(a{:}c){:}d]$]E; $[(a{:}c)\,d]$
6.12 equivalent] E; equevalent
6.18(2) $0\bar{c}$] E; $0c$
6.27 \$;] E; \$.;
6.28 premise,] E; ~‸
6.33 *d*,] E; ~‸
6.33 $c\bar{c}$] E; $\bar{c}$
6.34 *d*,] E; ~‸
6.37 All] E; all
6.38 a man] E; man
6.39 mortal,] E; ~‸
7.10 on] E; op
7.15 signs,] E; ~‸
7.15 about] E; aboutt
7.22 then] E; ~,
7.22 loathesome"] E; ~",
7.22 Blundeville] E; Blunderviles
7.22–23 *Art of Logic*] E; *rom.*
7.34 $b(\bar{b} + \bar{d})$] E; $b(\bar{b} + \bar{d}$ ‸
7.38 eligible] E; elegible
8.2 is all] E; are all
8.3 ways. First,] ~, first
8.6 Secondly, the] E; ~: The
8.7 things,] E; ~;
8.8 aid.] E; ~‸

Alterations

2.19 addition and] addition is
5.15 and I] I
°6.18(2) $0c$] $0 + c$
6.37 Take the premises, Translated persons are not mortal] Take the premise not translated persons are mortal
7.12 middle ages] middle age
7.17–18 either non-*a* or *b*.] either *a* or *b*.
7.19 the case of the dilemma. Syllogistic reasoning is] the cases of the dilemma and of syllogistic reasoning,

2. *Circular for Course on the Art of Reasoning, 1887*

The hand-corrected first state of Peirce's privately published circular for his "Art of Reasoning" correspondence course serves as copy-text. The circular, which is printed on all four surfaces of an unwatermarked folio sheet folded into a pair of 8½" × 11" conjugate leaves, survives in two states; a copy of the first state, with a correction in Peirce's hand, appears to be the source for the corrected second state. Examples of both of these states survive in the RL 100 letter folders at Harvard, but only one example of the first state has been hand-corrected by Peirce.

Nine unnumbered manuscript leaves located within the RL 100 correspondence course manuscript nest comprise a draft for the circular. The ninth leaf contains an isolated paragraph of text subsequently inserted in the published form; a tenth sheet contains an incomplete first draft of the insertion. The large number of substantive revisions contained in the printed brochure-style circular suggests that Peirce worked through at least one unlocated intermediate stage of revision (presumably printer's copy) as he designed and printed the document. Extra leading appears between some words and phrases of the printed form; collation reveals that these spaces coincide with points of variation, suggesting that some of Peirce's final revisions were made in at least one set of unlocated page proofs. Only two variants can be ascribed to compositorial error. Since Peirce was his own editor for the printed brochure, the few remaining variations in punctuation, along with all the substantives, can be attributed to Peirce with a high degree of certainty. The first surviving printed state thus represents the most mature form over which Peirce exercised complete control. Given the unusual degree of authority attributable to the published form, the draft manuscript (already separated from Peirce's final intention by the more mature but missing stages of printer's copy and page proofs) is relegated to pre-copy-text status.

Although the circular is undated, external sources clearly identify the period of composition. A 4 January 1887 letter from Peirce to his cousin Henry Cabot Lodge appealing for start-up money briefly describes two circulars, the shorter of which was "now printing." File or discard copies of generic letters from Peirce to various clergy (RL 100) dated 11 and 13 January 1887 apparently covered mailings of the brochure. An undated letter to his brother Jem can be dated by Jem's 17 January reply and indicates that 1400 copies of the brochure had already gone out by mid-month, thus confirming the rationale for a January date.

There is no further evidence to identify the longer circular, but it may be that the unpublished follow-up letter to the circular (selection 3) may have been intended for this purpose. The pressing deadlines for his gravity reports, along with his more profitable moonlighting for the *Century Dictionary*, led to abandonment of the correspondence course during 1888. A resumption of the course was briefly announced in successive issues of *The Open Court* (December 1891 to 1 September 1892), but there is no evidence that Peirce's advertising brochure was ever used after the 1887–88 period.

Peirce's printed brochure contains large and small capitals and bolded phrases that are not marked for such treatment in the pre-copy-text manuscript. Without evidence of authorial intent in the surviving pre-publication form, such physical characteristics would normally be considered editorial styling. However, Peirce exercised more control than normal over his privately printed advertisements, and in this case Peirce's authorial intentions clearly extend to the physical layout of the brochure itself—that is, Peirce used both words and physical layout to communicate the quality of his program to his prospective students. The importance of image in selling his course to the public is further clarified in his correspondence with his brother, with Henry Cabot Lodge, and in his detailed "Directions to Agents" (selection 5). Therefore the present edition retains these font characteristics. Other layout elements, such as the positioning of titles and text blocks, are silently regularized.

Textual Notes

11.1–2 The theory of reasoning is not neglected] The circular's first state erroneously reads "is neglected", except for one copy which Peirce corrected by hand in black ink. The second state incorporates the revision.

12.24 Under this system, the student] Five pencil revisions and a marginal comment, all in another hand, appear at various points in the pre-copy-text manuscript. The context of the non-authorial marginal comment that refers to the course fee at 12.33 ("$45 is better; a leisurely class is in question") indicates that the pencil revisions were made by an advisor (probably Peirce's brother Jem) shortly after composition. Peirce actually incorporated one of these revisions at the beginning of the present paragraph, to replace his initial words "The student", thus providing a better textual bridge between paragraphs.

12.29 MR. PEIRCE] Peirce deliberately and clearly wrote "Mrs. Peirce" in the pre-copy-text manuscript. The subsequent change to Mr. Peirce in the final circular may be compositorial error. Juliette Peirce managed the personal accounts throughout their married lives, but Peirce may have decided that direct correspondence was more practical (the address direction given at the end of the letter is to "C. S. Peirce").

Emendations

11.24 college] E; College

11.29 instruction] E; instrucfion

Line-End Hyphenation

11.33 common–sense

Alteration

*11.1 is not] is

3. *Follow-up Letter to Circular, 1887*

Copy-text consists of two typewritten leaves from RL 100, a chaotic nest of two folders in the Harvard Papers consisting of letters and materials for Peirce's correspondence course in "The Art of Reasoning." The leaves are 15" × 9½" first-layer carbon sheets of lightweight unwatermarked manifold paper. A nearly illegible second-layer carbon of leaf 1 also survives. The bottom half-inch of leaf 1 has been cut off to dispose of a line of text slanting down off the page; this text, which begins a sample student exercise, is restarted on leaf 2. Both leaves are discolored by exposure to light around the left, top, and right margins. Oil staining obscures but does not obliterate the text at the top of leaf 2. Text is single-spaced in a roman serif typeface from a Hammond type-shuttle mounted on Peirce's Hammond Model 1 typewriter. The carbon strike is in black with good alignment—only one line (leaf 1 midpage) and several characters throughout the typescript are misaligned. These purely physical characteristics do not require emendation. Peirce's corrections during composition are made by overstrike; his subsequent handwritten corrections and revisions are in black ink. An ink smear near the right margin of leaf 2 partially obscures two lines of still-readable text.

A draft typescript dated 13 March 1887 is the direct source for the copy-text; this draft, along with the surviving record of correspondence between Peirce and his students, provides the rationale for dating the letter. Variations of the "Young Prince" exercise appear in selections 4 and 13. A long but incomplete draft of the exercise and the associated algebraic calculations dates from a later period (1894) and is spread through R S59 and R S64. The original source of the exercise is unknown.

Emendations

15.21 etc.,] E; &c.,
16.1 quarter.] E; ~,
16.6 Allan] E; Allen
16.7 Marquand] E; ~,
16.6–7 (there . . . pupils)] E; [~ . . . ~],
16.8–9 conclusions] E; conlusions
16.10 books] E; ~,
16.10–12 (I . . . *Psychology*)] E; [~ . . . ~]
16.11–12 *American . . . Psychology*] E; *rom.*
16.13 mind's] E; mind‸s
17.1 learning] E; the learning
17.4 take up] E; take it up
17.14 great] E; gret
17.20 people] E; peopIe
18.1 *Progress and Poverty*] E; *rom.*
18.1 *Analogy*]E; *rom.*
18.3 course,] E; ~,
18.8 Economy," etc.] E; ~", &c.

Alterations

15.6 see only] see
16.9 are turned out,] turn out,
16.20 test,] test
16.28 experience of the realities] reality of the experiences
16.34 without always] without

4. *A Few Specimens of Exercises in the Art of Reasoning*, 1887

A single typed manifold sheet of 15" × 9½" lightweight unwatermarked carbon paper recovered from the RL 100 folders of materials for "The Art of Reasoning" correspondence course serves as copy-text. The black carbon strike is barely legible; the sheet itself is chipped all around with missing top and bottom right corners and heavy damage and staining to the lower left edge from midpoint down. Carbon smudging slightly obscures the entire sheet. The text is single-spaced in three typefaces—roman serif, roman small/large capitals sans serif, and ecclesiastical small/large capitals—from three different Hammond type-shuttles interchanged while typing. The carbon is uncorrected, and only a few overstrikes can be detected. The typescript was prepared on one of Peirce's Model 1 Hammond machines; the ecclesiastical type-shuttle was probably one of two purchased for Peirce by the Coast Survey office in early April 1887. The font evidence, other surviving advertisement documents for "The Art of Reasoning," and the peak period of student enrollment in Peirce's correspondence course (spring/summer 1887) provide the rationale for dating. Peirce's case selection, including the use of large and small capitals, reflects his own intention for the form of presentation for "The Art of Reasoning" samples, and is retained in the present edition text.

The sample exercises represent problems used in the portions of the course devoted to definitions, syllogistic, and logical algebra; a version of the pronoun definition exercise appears in a discarded sheet of a student exercise; versions of the "powder mill" and "young king" exercises are among the Boolian word exercises of selection 13.

Emendations

19.2 NUMBER] E; NUMBERS
20.12–13 (But. . . recitations.)]E; [~. . . ~.]
20.20–21 accuses] E; excuses
20.21 other to] E; otherto
20.31 true"?] E; ~‸?

Alterations

20.2 If I do not conquer in the first campaign] If I am positively popular with the army
20.20 one of whom] the first of whom
20.21 that] the

5. *Directions to Agents, 1887*

Copy-text consists of five typewritten leaves from Harvard's RL 100 folders of materials for Peirce's correspondence course in "The Art of Reasoning." The leaves are 14 15/16" × 9 7/16" sheets of lightweight unwatermarked paper; the first four leaves are numbered in the upper right hand corner in ink, possibly by Peirce. All leaves are slightly darkened by exposure to light. Leaves 1 through 4 have been double-folded horizontally; leaf 5 has been folded once across the page. Text is single-spaced in a roman partial serif typeface from a Hammond type-shuttle mounted on Peirce's Hammond Model 1 typewriter. The strike is in black with good alignment, but the last lines of leaves 1 and 3 slant down toward the lower margins. Two draft leaves, prepared with the same typeface and on the same paper, also survive.

Peirce's corrections during composition are made by overstrike; his subsequent revisions are typed interlinearly between the lines without insertion marks. The few handwritten notations are found only on the third leaf and are not authorial. These notes include the year "1886" penciled in the upper margin and blue-penciled check marks at two points (one with underlining) that mark passages containing clues to the date of the document. The left margin of this leaf bears a red pencil line (parallel to the mid-page text) which is a characteristic mark of the CP editors.

Peirce's internal allusions to his "resignation" from regular duty at the Survey, and to the near break-up of the Survey as a government agency, place the document after the Cleveland administration's 1885 investigation of the Survey and Peirce's highly publicized (and unaccepted) offer of resignation; his statement of age places the work between September 1886 and September 1887. Schröder's advertisement as quoted by Peirce appeared in Europe in 1886, even though the work it refers to was not published until 1890. Three more pieces of evidence place the document firmly in 1887. Peirce notes in a January 1887 exchange of letters with his brother Jem that "I am thinking of sending agents out to get me scholars paying $10 for each new scholar—This would cost me nothing to speak of even if the agents starved." Peirce's own "Art of Reasoning" course notebook indicates payment of $2.00 to one of the recruiting "agents" in early March 1887; this was the (apparently reduced) finder's fee set out on the face of Peirce's enrollment "tickets" and in one of the draft leaves of "Directions to Agents." Finally, the font from this particular Hammond type-shuttle does not appear in Peirce's typescripts before his early April 1887 acquisition of a new Hammond machine and two new shuttles.

Textual Notes

23.24 advantageous.] Although lacking a period, both context and physical positioning suggest that this word concludes the paragraph as well as the first page of text. The copy-text and through the middle of the second leaf represents a major and continuous reworking of the material found on the preliminary first draft leaf.

28.26 a page like this] Peirce is referring to the oversize (14 15/16" × 9 7/16") leaves he used in typing the "Directions to Agents," which could hold 63 lines of up to 98 characters.

32.30 Mr. Peirce] These final words may represent a typed signature, or the beginning of a continuation of text that was never completed.

Emendations

21.2–3 (having] E; [~
21.4 teachers).] E; ~.]‸
21.5 Teachers] E; Teachrs
21.6 divinity] E; divinty
21.9 interest] E; interist
21.24 (resident) E; [~]
22.3 almost] E; aomost
22.7 of] E; odf
22.15–16 gentleman] E; geutleman
22.19 able] E; abla
23.7 attentively] E; attentiwely
23.12 showing] E; showeng

23.19–20 (unless . . . away)] E; [~ . . . ~]
*23.24 advantageous.] E; ~‸
23.25 will] E; will will
23.30 better] E; ~,
23.33 for some] E; from ~
24.3 few] E; feu
24.4 have] E; hawe
24.35 useful, showing] E; usefulshowing
25.4 recognition] E; reognition
25.15 matters] E; matter
25.35 go] E; gon
26.5 résumé] E; resume
26.19 successively] E; sucessively
26.19 last, Doctor] E; lastDoctor
26.20 Science,] E; ~‸
26.20 *summa cum laude,*] E; *rom.*
26.24 etc.,] E; ~.‸
26.28 fellow countrymen] E; fellow-countrymen
26.30 Survey] E; survey
26.32 Surveys] E; surveys *Also* 27.10, 27.12, 27.16, 27.20, 27.28
27.5–6 lengthened] E; lenthened
27.7 surprised] E; surprized
27.9 (at . . . present)] E; [~ . . . ~]
27.17 Stuttgart] E; Stuttgard
27.26 Baeyer of Berlin,] E; Bayer ~ ~‸
27.28 the experiments] E; tthe ~
27.29 bring] E; pring
27.32 led] E; lead
27.33 views] E; wiews
27.34 themselves] E; himself
28.15 today,] E; to-day,
28.16 says:] E; ~ :.
28.18 very] E; verny
28.18 *(hoechst bedeutende)*] E; [*rom.*]
28.20 pupils."] E; ~.‸
28.20–21 yourself] E; nourself
28.24 *Harper's Magazine*] E; *rom.*
28.25 *Harper's*] E; Harper
28.29 habit.] E; ~..
28.35 deceived] E; deceiwed
29.2 juggles as are] E; juggles are
29.2 served] E; serwed
29.18–19 logic formed by] E; logic. according to formed by
29.19 algebra of logic] E; Algebra of Logic
29.23 have] E; hawe
29.28–29 up and] E; ~. And
29.33 reasoning] E; ~,
30.10 It is] E; It
30.16 years,] E; ~‸
30.20–21 instruction.] E; ~‸
30.23 (grammar, . . rhetoric)] E; [~, . . . ~]
30.26–27 subtleties,] E; subtilties
30.29–30 worthless] E; wothless
32.5 successful] E; sucessful
32.25 learn,] E; ~‸
32.26 learning?] E; ~.

Alterations

24.16 cause him] give hi[m]
25.11 habituating] teaching
25.17 inventing] finding
27.13 investigations] *bef del-t* to determine
*27.26 Berlin] *bef del-t* fell u[pon]
28.12 and philosophical] *intl*
28.29 habit.] thing.
30.1–2 Quasi-periodic phenomena.] *intl*
32.28 not too old] *intl*

Line-End Hyphenation

25.7 clear-headed
25.18 lifetime

6. *Letter to New Students, 1887*

Copy-text consists of five 7 15/16" × 9 7/8" unnumbered leaves recovered from the RL 100 nest of correspondence course materials for "The Art of

Reasoning." The leaves are laid paper with vertical chain lines and a "Massasoit" watermark. They are blue-ruled at single-space intervals; each rule is indented 3/4" from the left margin. All the leaves are faded yellow to brown, with leaf 2 most heavily soiled. The top right corner of the first leaf is black-stained and partially torn away, and the entire leaf is stained blue with bleed-off from the hecto of "Boolian Algebra—Elementary Explanations" (selection 1), which has rested upon it for years in the RL 100 folder. The leaves are inscribed by Peirce in black ink, with many holograph revisions by Peirce also in black ink. The manuscript is in letter form, signed but undated.

This copy-text is emended from another RL 100 leaf, a typed hectograph which represents the only known revision to the student letter. The paper is a partial leaf of a heavyweight laid but unwatermarked folio sheet (10" × 16") initially folded into a quarto-size conjugate pair of leaves with printed blue guidelines at single-spaced intervals and bordered by blue external and internal gutter margins to form four 8" × 10" writing sides. This leaf was opened out, re-folded, and torn along the new fold to create a rough 10" × 10 1/2" leaf. The letter text is double-spaced in blue ink with an italic font running across the printed guidelines and down the surviving portion of the opened-out leaf. The lack of any typing key impressions, the faded and blotted letters, and the doubled lines of text in the final portion indicate that this copy was probably a trial hectograph run. The text can no longer be read without backlighting, and was not identified within the RL 100 manuscript leaves until late 1993; subsequent comparisons reveal that the microfilm print still retains some resolution. The page is waterstained and yellowed along the left margin, rendering the text illegible at several points. Black ink on the verso suggests that this leaf was used as blotting paper. No hand revisions appear, but the hectograph contains significant substantive variations from the manuscript text.

The hectograph master was prepared on one of Peirce's Hammond Model 1 machines with an italic type-shuttle, but corruptions suggest it was prepared by one of the typists Peirce occasionally employed for this work. The reliability of the hecto is further eroded by a number of end-line overruns, false line starts, several illegible words, and nearly invisible punctuation throughout the document caused by a lightly inked print run. The hecto version appears to be an intermediate draft of an introductory form letter for distribution to new students; however, given the unpolished state of much of the "Art of Reasoning" materials, it may be as close as Peirce ever came to a fair-copy version of the student letter. The many substantive revisions represent the most mature known form of the letter, but the condition of the hecto, and the possibility that it may have been typed by another, render it unreliable as a copy-text. Peirce's earlier holograph version provides the most reliable basis for the new edition, and serves as copy-text; the typed hectograph serves as the source of emendation for Peirce's substantive revisions and for accidentals that correct errors or confusing readings in the holograph. Further points of error of confusion left unresolved (or unreadable) in the hectograph are emended on the authority of the present edition.

Dating is circumstantial; Peirce's "Art of Reasoning" circular (selection 2) was in circulation by the first week of January 1887; his student logbook (also in RL 100) indicates that a letter to new students was sent to each of his first two pupils (Walter Andrews and Helen Pearson) on 28 and 29 January, respectively. The single surviving typed hectograph includes a header with Peirce's 36 West 15th Street address in New York, a flat which he occupied from mid-1886 until his departure for Milford, Pennsylvania, in May 1887. Discarded leaves from new student letters of this period contain a much more personalized text, and indicate that he may have moved away from the form letter soon after January and well before he moved to Milford; in fact, there is no proof that this prototype letter went out at all. A full discussion of the correspondence course texts appears in the Essay on Editorial Theory and Method.

Textual Notes

33.12 be today] Substantive revisions here (for "today be") and at two points along 33.16 ("that" for "which" and "the" for "an") are editorial stylings; but since Peirce was the editor and printer (and possibly the typist) of the "Art of Reasoning" hectographs, these variants are accepted as authorial revisions, and emended into the copy-text.

33.25 men's] The apostrophe added in the hectograph TS represents completion of the possessive; at 33.26, the addition of a comma in the TS completes a substantive revision started in the manuscript. These variants may be Peirce's, but they may have been introduced by a typist; nevertheless, both are required for clarity and are emended from the hectograph text.

34.7–8 Then . . . am.] The reading "better man" in this passage is a best guess based on the number of characters discernible in this illegible two-word passage of the TS. The use of a gender-specific term is consistent with usage at 33.13 and 33.24, as well as with masculine pronouns appearing throughout the text; however, given the illegibility of the hectograph, the reading is emended on the authority of the present edition.

34.15–16 personal, local, or technical,] A revision in the manuscript changed a pair of adjectives ("personal or local") into a series. The three commas in the hecto TS complete the manuscript revision.

Emendations

33.1 36 W 15th St, New York City] TS; *om.*

33.7 for the purchaser] TS; *om.*

33.9 the carpenter] TS; a carpenter's

*33.12 be today] E; today be AMS; be to-day TS

33.15 declare] TS; say

33.15–16 proclaim to the general public] TS; say in my published circulars

33.16 do not wish to make] TS; am not fond of making

33.16 that] TS; which

33.16 have the] TS; have an

33.17 declare] TS; will say
33.17 intend] TS; am going
33.23–24 level. ¶Few] TS; level. Now very few
33.24 excel in all] E; raise all AMS; excell in all TS
33.24 mind.] TS; mind much above the general level.
*33.25 men's] TS; men‸s
33.25 various] TS; different
33.26 multitudes,] TS; ~‸
34.3 remarkable] TS; extraordinary
34.5 amount . . . could] TS; amount distributed among the different branches of the art of reasoning in any other way could
34.6 prescribe . . . . patient's] TS; give a patient I must accurately note his
*34.7–8 Then . . . am] E; *om.* AMS; Then, I may be able to make him a *[two illegible words]* than I myself am TS
34.8 make] TS; form
34.10 begin by] TS; begin, then, by
*34.15–16 personal, local, or technical,] TS; ~‸ ~‸ ~‸
34.16 could not possibly] TS; cannot
34.19 a subject] TS; something
34.20 ask] TS; wish
34.21–22 directions.] TS; directions about this.
34.22 Do the thing] TS; Do it
34.23–25 It . . . directed.] TS; It will supply me with necessary information.
34.28–29 these . . . strength.] TS; these letters will serve as evidence, to you and to me, of successive increments of your mental vigour.

Alterations

33.5 my] this
33.8 every day-laborer knew how to work with wood] every laborer could work wood and build a house
33.9 trade] business
33.11 foreseen] seen
✧33.16 am] do
33.16 may not] am not going to
33.19 It is] That would be
33.22 is extended to] profits one child as
33.23 level.] *bef del* Now class-instruction can only be really well done when done on a large scale.
✧33.24 all their powers of mind much above] themselves above
✧33.24 much above the general level.] . *ins bef del* in respect to all human powers. B Every man Men's minds are as infinitely diverse as their faces. ◆A [*intl aft del* One] man o Each will be
33.24 experience has] observations have
33.25–26 Having minutely studied multitudes] I have minutely studied ◆a multitude [thousands] and
34.2 pupil] man
34.3 have to] *bef del* put in my work where it will be most effective, and carefully consider
34.3–4 arrange his] adjust the
34.4–5 the same amount] a like all] *bef del* differently
✧34.5 art] *aft del* subjects
34.14 think] *aft del* have
34.14–15 No matter what subject you select. Perhaps it had] The subject selected had
✧34.15 personal local or technical] personal or local
34.17 matters are not] subjects should not be
34.17–18 not to think] to take
34.21 will] wish to
34.21–22 directions] instructions
34.26 our] my
✧34.28–29 successive increments] the development

7. *Orientation Letter to Marie Noble, 1887*

A single typewritten leaf from RL 100 serves as copy-text. The leaf is a 15" × 9 ½" sheet of wove paper watermarked "Montauk Mills," and appears by the strike to have been a carbon record copy. This orientation letter, which answers an unlocated application letter from student Marie Noble, provides a good illustration of Peirce's pedagogical experiment with his correspondence program. The date and postscript indicate that the letter was one of the first written after Peirce's move to Milford, Pennsylvania; by this time, nearly five months into the course, Peirce may have discontinued the standard letter to new students (selection 6) and replaced it with a personalized reply that included the request for a writing sample found in the standard letter. One reason for doing so may have been the realization that the male gender-specific language of the standard letter was not appropriate for the growing number of female students enrolled in his course. Another reason may have been a need to condense the program's protracted preliminary correspondence.

The leaf is yellowed around the right and top edges; there are orange spots on the lower half of the page. Text is single-spaced in an italic serif typeface from a Hammond type-shuttle mounted on one of Peirce's Hammond Model 1 typewriters. The carbon strike is in black with good alignment; the imprint is legible but has faded over time. The letter was almost certainly typed from a now-lost draft—there is only one overstrike correction and one typed interlined correction in the entire text. Peirce may have further corrected the outgoing original, but there is no evidence of such correction on the surviving carbon.

Emendations

35.2 B.] E; B,
35.4 City.] E; ~,
35.7 being able] E; be able
35.18 *vis a tergo*] E; *rom.*
35.18 reasons.] E; ~. .

8. *Letter to Noble on the Nature of Reasoning, 1887*

Copy-text survives on two typewritten leaves from the Harvard RL 100 nest of correspondence course materials for "The Art of Reasoning." The leaves are 15" × 9 ½" sheets of cream-colored wove paper watermarked "Montauk Mills;" both sheets appear by the strike to have been carbon record copies. These leaves remain folded horizontally in the RL 100 folders, and are yellowed along the left and top margins from past exposure to sunlight; leaf 2 has fold lines at the top right corner as well. These leaves contain only the first two pages of text for a longer letter; the closing leaf or leaves remain unlocated.

The text is double-spaced in a roman serif typeface from a Hammond type-shuttle mounted on Peirce's Hammond Model 1 typewriter. Italics added for emphasis were struck from a second type-shuttle interchanged with the first. The carbon strike is in black with good alignment, but the imprint has faded over time. The letter was almost certainly typed from a now-lost draft—there are few typographical errors and no typed interlineations in the surviving leaves. Peirce may have further corrected the outgoing original, but there is no evidence of such correction on the surviving carbon.

This letter fragment contains an introduction to reasoning in general for Peirce's student Marie Noble. Two examples of mathematical reasoning occupy much of the extant letter text and serve to illustrate Peirce's point that "all reasoning involves observation." The surviving fragment, along with his earlier orientation letter to Noble (selection 7), provide a valuable look at the way Peirce introduced students to the "Art of Reasoning" coursework as the program continued to develop through the spring and summer of 1887. Although Noble's correspondence is not recorded in the student record book, the record of mailings to other students indicates that the missing final portion of this letter fragment probably included an initial set of mathematical exercises.

Textual Note

39.14 planes 1 and 2.] The reference to "planes 2 and 3" in the previous sentence probably led to a doubling error by Peirce's typist. The mathematical context requires "1 and 2" which has thus been emended in.

Emendations

37.3 City.] E; ~,
37.5 some] E; ssme
37.9 procedure] E; proceedure
37.16 so] E; ro
38.18 Z] E; ~,
38.21 (produced if necessary)] E; [~ ~ ~] *Also brackets to parens at* 38.31–33 *and* 40.18
38.29 plane.] E; ~‸
38.33 Consequently,] E; Consequentl,
*39.14 1 and 2.] E; 2 and 3.
39.28 4th] E; 4th
39.28 2401,] E; 3401,
39.29 etc.,] E; &c.,

Alterations

38.22 imagine] draw
39.5 points] lines
39.37 between them] *intl*

9. *Reasoning Exercises, 1887*

With the exception of three exercises recovered from a student letter (RL 173), copy-text is assembled from purple hectograph sheets of exercises preserved in Harvard manuscript R 699. All of these exercises can be traced (through either format or student records) to Peirce's "Art of Reasoning" correspondence course, and seem to represent a rough grouping of exercises used by Peirce at an early stage of the coursework.

The two pages of number series exercises survive as two single-sided hectos run from an unlocated master. Each leaf is a medium weight 15" x 9 ½" wove sheet bearing the watermark "Montauk Mills" and run off in purple ink. These two pages are clearly continuous, and were probably intended for two-sided printing; the surviving rectos may be Peirce's file copies. The number diagram exercises concluding this sequence survive on an overinked single-sided hectograph run on the "Montauk Mills" paper; a second hecto run is underinked, and lacks the top of circles A and B; both sheets appear to be discarded runs. The unlocated masters for all of the number exercise sheets were handwritten by Peirce and transferred to the hecto runs in blue ink.

The first three exercises on relational graphs are preserved in RL 173, a student response from Mr. J. W. Grace which includes a restatement (in Grace's hand) of Peirce's exercises, Grace's initial colored graph solutions, and Grace's corrected solutions with notations of the time required to reaccomplish the graphs. Peirce's original exercise set and his letter of remediation have not survived. The nine-figure set of relational graphs (following the Grace materials in the present edition) survives in R 699 on a single hectograph sheet printed head-to-head on the "Montauk Mills" paper. The text and graphs of the master were inscribed by Peirce; the text accompanying Figure 3 is squeezed into the right margin of the recto, and was clearly a last-minute addition to the master copy. A duplicate run also survives; both are poorly inked on the bottom verso, obscuring the notations appended to Figure 9.

The card exercises survive on three single-sided hectos or carbons run (or typed) on the "Montauk Mills" paper. The first two leaves are continuous and include two distinct exercises. The second leaf includes the first sentence of a third exercise, but the text breaks off at mid-page; these two leaves may be a discarded draft question bank for card exercises. The third sheet, which includes a longer two-stage variation of the second card exercise, differs in format and may be part of a different bank of card exercises. The masters for all these sheets were typed with Peirce's italic type-shuttle mounted on one of his Hammond Model 1 machines; the sheets themselves are black carbon or hecto impressions.

The three R 699 leaves serve as copy-text for the two card exercises and the two-stage variant of the second exercise. The second stage of the variant also appears as exercise 23 on a single sheet of the same "Montauk Mills" paper in RL 100, but it is a leaf from a discarded (or file) copy of a multiple-page letter sent to another of Peirce's students (Miss. S. M. Hawes). The fragment is not a suitable copy-text, but its variations from the copy-text form of the two-stage exercise are worth further comment. The first stage is referred to in the letter as exercise 22, but the letter page including this portion has not been located. The RL 100 fragment was composed on one of

Peirce's Hammond machines (this time using one of the roman type-shuttles), but probably by one of his hired typists. Variations in the RL 100 version suggest that Peirce dictated the entire letter, reading in the appropriate exercises from a copy of the R 699 exercise bank version. Periods are replaced with conjunctions to give the exercise in the letter text more of a spoken quality consistent with the body of the letter; other variations, such as omitted words and commas and close misreadings, also make the case for dictation. Although it lacks the accuracy and completeness of the exercise bank copy, the RL 100 fragment provides important insight into the way that Peirce constructed and "packaged" individualized versions of correspondence course exercises.

There is evidence among the student responses in the RL 100 folders that the number exercises and the card exercises were sent out to correspondence course students during the winter and spring of 1887. Peirce's notebook of student progress, which also indicates the numbers assigned to many of these exercises in the student mailings, runs through the spring and confirms the rationale for dating. This is also true for the color graphs, for which April 1887 solutions survive in letters from two students (Grace and Heermance).

Although the hectograph format of the nine relational graph figures strongly indicates association with the correspondence course, no student letters make any reference to them. But there is no doubt that they were prepared for use in the course—three of the nine figures (numbers 3, 7, and 8) come with exercise instructions, and Peirce used a discussion of Figure 7 as an example of reasoning in a letter to his student Marie Noble (selection 8). Finally, Peirce's deep interest in these graphs coincides exactly with the early correspondence course period. The figures are clearly inspired by Peirce's reading of A. B. Kempe's 1886 "Memoir on the Theory of Mathematical Form," which Peirce received from Kempe in December 1886 and read with great care in January 1887. The color graph exercises, for which dating evidence survives as noted above, were also inspired by Peirce's reading of Kempe.

A discussion of the general history of the correspondence course texts appears in the Essay on Editorial Theory and Method.

Textual Notes

43.4 and A] These words were double-transferred from the master during the hectograph run. The doubling, which includes the preceding comma as well as the words, appears interlinearly and is not considered text.

44.5 *straight*] Peirce surrounded this interlineal insertion with parenthesis-like insertion marks for clarity; these non-textual marks have been silently removed.

48.12 relation.] Peirce began a third exercise designed as a variation to the final portion of the "kingless" first exercise, but broke it off at mid-page after this single opening sentence: "Having gone through with the operations of the spades and hearts of problem [1], all except spreading the cards out on the table, you put the king of spades at the top or bottom of the pack of spades."

Emendations

41.2 series:] E; ~‸ *Also* 41.14
41.3 etc.] E; ~‸ *Also* 41.4, 41.15, 41.16, 41.18, 42.11
42.9 it?] E; ~.
43.7 another.] E ~‸
43.8 grandmother.] E; ~‸
43.9 sisters.] E; ~‸
43.11 mother-in-law.] E; motherin-law‸
43.12 B,] E; B.,
43.14 of E] E; ~ ~,
43.15 of B,] E; ~ ~.
43.16 mentioned.] E; ~‸
43.17 spot] E; spots
43.19 you] E; *om. Also* 43.24
43.26(1,2) Fig.] E; ~‸ *Also* 44.1, 44.6, 44.7(2,3), 45(c2).1
44.2 Let] E; Lett
44.5 *Problem:*] E; ~‸
44.7 Fig. 4] E; Fi 4
44.8 Figs.] E; ~‸
44.8 Fig.] E; ig‸
45(c1).5 necessary,] E; ~‸
45.9 Fig. 9] E; Fig. 9.
46.7 bill.] E; bills‸
46.9 ┼┼┼┼┼┼┼┼┼.] E; ~‸
46.15 — — — —.] E; ~‸
46.17 +———.] E; ~‸
46.26 Disappearance] E; disappearance
46.26–27 line. ¶ [F] Quarrel between parties joined by plain lines.] E; line. ‸ [F] Quarrel between parties joined by *[illegible]*
46.31 Knave] E; knave
46.31 Queen,—the] E; queen, king,—the
46.32 front.] E; fronta‸
46.32 pile,] E; ~,.
47.31 the two.] E; themtwo.
48.9 44 45 46 47 48 49 50 51 52] E; 45 46 47 48 49 50 59 52 53
48.10(2) a] E; *om.*
48.11(2) their] E; theirs
48.12 Try] E; try
48.19 2, 3, 5, 6, 10,] E; 2. 3. 5. 6. 10.
48.19 The cards] E; THe cards
48.31 their] E; there

Alterations

43.2 relation] arran*[gement]*
*44.5 *straight*] *intl-c*
46.1–2 a later] following

10. *Boolian Algebra. Three Lessons, 1887*

Copy-text is a single hectograph sheet printed on both sides (head to head) from a two-page master. The master has not been located, but the surviving hecto run is in the nest of correspondence course materials for "The Art of Reasoning" in two Harvard folders designated RL 100. The hecto is a medium weight 15" × 9 ½" wove sheet bearing the watermark "Montauk Mills" and run off in purple ink. The master was hand-inscribed by Peirce; both recto and verso include corrections and careted additions to the master in Peirce's hand as well. The surviving hecto is a defective run that was not sent out to students; it is barely legible toward the corners on both sides, and the closing line of the verso is not legible at all. Student copies may have been defective as well—the final line has been recovered from a draft response by Peirce to a student's request for the text of the final exercise (see selections 11–12).

The "Boolian Algebra" lesson evolved from "Boolian Algebra—Elementary Explanations" (selection 1). It was sent out to students on 25 March 1887 for the first time. Among students known to have worked on these lessons were W. L. Winchester, Anna C. Vincent, J. B. Loring, and Walter S. Langley.

Emendations

50.1–2 abbreviated] E; abbrieviated
50.4–5 abbreviated] E; abbrievated
50.5 statement.] E; ~,
50.8 $x = y$] E; x = y *Also all subsequent lowercase variables are italicized*
51.11 $x + x = x$,] E; $x + x = x$ ‸
51.17 Algebra] E; algebra
51.25 *(xy)z*] E; *(xy)z*.
51.32–52.10 N.B. The . . . further. ¶*Boolian Algebra—Second Lesson*] E; Boolian Algebra-Second Lesson ¶N.B. The . . . further.
51.32 exercises] E; exercises on the other side
51.34 example:] E; ~.
52.1 2nd] E; second
52.8 these] E; those
52.14–15 Principle of Addition and Multiplication] E; principle of addition and multiplication
52.29 $(b+d)$] E; (b + d).
52.32 *ca*] E; ca.
52.35 *cd*] E; ~. *Also* 52.37
53.4 *bcd*] E; ~.
53.7 *efgh*] E; ~.
53.8 *Lesson*] E; ~.
53.14 dollars] E; Dollars
53.19 *Exercises.*] E; ~:
53.19 Show] E; show
53.24 contradiction.] E; ~‸
53.25 excluded middle] E; Excluded Middle.

Line-End Hyphenation

50.19 non-existent

Alterations

50.13–14 is or would be a state] is a state
50.14 is or would be true] is true
51.4 denotes] means
52.19 with $x + x = x$ and $xx = x$] *intl-c*
53.1 $(a+e)(b+f)(c+d)$] *aft del* (a + c)(b + d) =
53.4 *acd* + *bcd*] bce + caf
53.7 + *efgh*] *intl-c*

11. *Two Letters from Loring on Algebra Lessons, 1887*

A composite document comprised of two handwritten letters from Peirce's "Art of Reasoning" correspondent student J. B. Loring, serves as copy-text. Loring's two-page letter of 22 December 1887, and the supplemental single-page letter of the 27th, respond to Lesson 1 of "Boolian Algebra" (selection 10). The letters are located in the Harvard RL 100 nest of correspondence course materials. Context indicates that the 22 December letter originally included penciled solutions to the first algebra lesson, but only the cover letter (with a detailed solution to the final problem) has been located, and Peirce's reply of the 30th makes no reference to the penciled solutions. It consists of a single leaf of 10 ¾" × 16" cream-colored wove paper, bi-folded to form two 8" × 10 ¾" writing leaves. The first verso thus formed is embossed top left with a "Congress Carew Co" emblem. Light blue ruled lines run across the four writing surfaces of the conjugate pair; the text covers the two rectos. The 27 December supplemental letter is written on a single sheet of 8 ½" × 11" cream letterhead from the Finance Department of The Equitable Life Assurance Society of New York. The letterhead leaf is wove, very yellowed, and has been folded horizontally in half. Left, top, and bottom margins are darkened by exposure to light. Both letters are composed and lightly corrected by Loring in black ink.

Peirce's outgoing lessons and letters to students were designed for public distribution and, as noted in the Essay on Editorial Theory and Method, are edited as public documents. Student responses, on the other hand, were designed for private evaluation, and Loring's letters are therefore edited as private documents. His consistent holograph formation of uncrossed t's and ligatured double-s's are regularized as purely physical appurtenances of the copy-text; Loring's punctuation irregularities, including his preference for the English style of placing final punctuation after quotation marks, are retained.

Loring's solution to the final algebra problem, as well as his requests for clarification on several points of the lesson, refer to specific passages in selection 10; Peirce's critique of Loring's work, and his clarifications of the lesson, follows as selection 12. Both Peirce's and Loring's references to the selection 10 algebra lesson are identified in the Annotations. Surviving responses from other students confirm that Peirce sent the three brief "Boolian Algebra" lessons of selection 10 to a number of students enrolled in the "Mathematical Reasoning" quarter of the course. Peirce's exchange with Loring is the most complete and clear example of how this portion of the course worked.

Textual Notes

54.8 other] Loring initially wrote "other solution" and then tried (unsuccessfully) to erase the final word. The word "solution" also appears in the previous sentence, and there it serves as a clear antecedent for "other." Loring appears to have attempted to remove the unnecessary repetition. Although the ink image remains transcribable, the original reading is clearly superseded by Loring's erasure; no emendation is necessary.

54.25 oblige] Loring's final sentence closes with an unpunctuated courtesy used as a transition into the letter's closing salutation. This form is clearly Loring's intention, and no punctuation is required.

Emendations

54.9 *et seq.* $(x+y)$] E; *rom. All lower-case variables rom. to ital.*
54.15 parenthesis] E; parenthisis
55.15 $(a+b)d$—is] E; (a + b)d‸~

12. *Reply to Loring, 1887*

Copy-text is a carbon record copy of a single-leaf letter to Peirce's "Art of Reasoning" correspondent student J. B. Loring. Peirce's response to Loring's letters of 22 and 27 December 1887 (selection 11) offers a detailed critique of Loring's solution to the final problem of the "Boolian Algebra" Lesson 1 (selection 10), and answers Loring's questions on two points of the lesson text itself. The letter carbon is located in the second of two RL 100 correspondence course folders at Harvard. It consists of a single leaf of 9½" by 15" wove paper bearing the "Montauk Mills" watermark. The leaf is folded in half horizontally; when opened, it reveals darkened areas along the left and lower margins from exposure to light in earlier times. The top margin is badly chipped all the way across, nearly obliterating the date. A penciled mark "VA2" in the top right corner dates from the manuscript reorganization initiative of the 1960s. The carbon impression is light but readable; the double-spaced italic serif font was struck from a type-shuttle mounted on one of several Hammond Model 1 typewriters used by Peirce during this period. The date and heading were struck on the same machine from a roman serif type-shuttle of the same font family. Two overstrikes during composition represent Peirce's only corrections to the carbon; other errors may have been corrected by Peirce in the unlocated original, which Loring acknowledged in a letter of 3 January 1888.

Both Peirce's and Loring's references to the algebra lesson are identified in the annotations. Fragment drafts or carbons of critique letters to two other students survive in RL 100, but only the Peirce–Loring exchange is complete enough to merit publication. The italic face has not been reproduced, but all variables have been emended to italic form.

Emendations

56.2 York.] E; ~,
56.5 please] E; plese
56.7 determined] E; deteemined
56.10 *[equation]*] E; *rom. All lower-case variables rom. to ital.*
56.17 principle] E; *om.*
57.21 contradiction.] E; ~‸
57.21 $x+\bar{x} = \$$] E; x + x = $
57.24 exercise] E; excercise

Alteration

56.6 four] *aft del-t* 30

13. *Additional Exercises in Boolian Algebra, 1887*

Copy-text consists of a single purple hectograph sheet printed on both sides (head to head) from an unlocated two-page master. The hecto run survives at Harvard in the R 699 folder of exercises used in Peirce's "Art of Reasoning" correspondence course. The hecto is a medium weight 15" × 9 1/2" wove sheet bearing the watermark "Montauk Mills" and run off in purple ink. Both surfaces are in good condition but slightly worn at the corners (one lower corner is torn away at the margins). The leaf has been folded once horizontally at mid-page. The master was hand-inscribed by Peirce; both recto and verso include corrections and careted additions to the master in Peirce's hand as well. In spite of these light corrections, each side was clearly composed in a carefully aligned single-spaced body of text designed for use in the correspondence course. Both surfaces are lightly inked and barely legible in spots at the bottom of the leaf. The text of the short exercises has been verified from an over-inked and damaged single-sided discarded hecto sheet which also survives in the R 699 folder.

The hecto is similar to the handwritten Boolean Algebra lessons of selection 10. There is evidence among the student responses in the RL 100 folders that these exercises were sent out with or just after the Algebra lessons; these responses, along with Peirce's notebook of student progress, provide the rationale for a summer 1887 dating. A full discussion of the history of the correspondence course texts appears in the Essay on Editorial Theory and Method.

The untitled recto appears to be a sample exercise with solution provided (as evidenced in Anna C. Vincent's letter of 8 July 1887 to Peirce). The sequence of the verso exercises (numbered 6, 4, 5, 2, 3, 1) has been silently regularized to place each one in its numbered order. The physical alignment of the exercise numbers (which angle slightly outward down the left margin of the hecto) suggests that they may have been added later by Peirce to transform an unnumbered "text bank" master page of exercises into a specific sequence students were required to follow (A. C. Vincent tackled exercises 1 to 4, in that order, in her letter of 20 July 1887); number six is certainly the most difficult, and reordering seems to fulfill Peirce's settled intention for the sheet as it survives. Each problem is an exercise in algebraic translation, and Peirce's specialized syntax, which is designed to help the student form algebraic representations of the data, has not been disrupted by emendation.

Textual Notes

58.1 I saw] This full-page sample exercise is numbered "1" on the original hectograph run. The recto page of exercises was then numbered 1–6 in a non-sequential order designed to create a sequence of increasing difficulty. Since there is only one sample exercise, its exercise number has been emended out to avoid confusion with the numbers of the six student exercises that follow.

58.2–3 near-sighted] Peirce's frequent use of hyphenated compounds in this exercise is inconsistent. His preference for the compound forms "absent-minded," "horse-car," "bob-tailed," and "near-sighted" is clear until he comes to the mathematical expression of the premises in the final portion of the exercise. Six of Peirce's eight uses of unhyphenated forms (single-word or two-word) occur in these equations, suggesting that he was concentrating on logical rather than grammatical consistency as he completed the exercise text. On that basis, these exceptions are emended to Peirce's preferred compound form. The longer forms "absentmindedness" and "nearsightedness" are consistently treated as single words by Peirce, and this usage is retained in the present edition.

59.13 He] The final line of the long sample exercise is severely obscured by the lightly-inked hectograph run. The first word is not visible, but the progression toward the product of the premises suggests the emended reading.

59.19 shareholder] Peirce's usage of the single-word form is established in an earlier statement of this exercise (W5:385).

Emendations

*58.1 ¶I saw] E; *[no ¶]* 1. I saw
*58.2–3 near-sighted] E; nearsighted *Also* 58.7, 59.3, 59.5
58.8 sat] E; sats
58.23 absent-minded] E; absent‸minded *Also* 59.1
59.2 bob-tailed] E; bobtailed *Also* 59.4
59.2 horse-car] E; car *Also* 59.4, 59.6, 59.13
59.3 he thought] E; the thought *Also* 59.5–6
59.11 $\bar{f}\bar{n}$] E; $\bar{f}\bar{a}$
*59.13 He] E; *om.*
59.18–19 shareholders,] E; share‸holders, *Also* 56.19 (share‸holder;), 56.21 (share‸holders.)
60.1 whoever] E; Whoever
60.22 state] E; State

Line-End Hyphenation

58.16 near-sighted
59.20 bondholders

Alterations

58.5 slit] hole
58.13 bob-tailed] *intl-c*
60.9 lilac spots and] lilac and
60.10 black spots and] black and
60.11 red spots and] red and
60.14 freemen] men
60.20(1) men] those

14. *Science and Immortality, 1887*

Copy-text is P 347, Peirce's contribution to the *Christian Register* survey article "Science and Immortality" compiled by *Register* editor Samuel J. Barrows and published in the April 7, 1887 issue, pp. 210–215 (with Peirce's article on p. 214). It is emended by P 348, Chapter XX of *Science and Im-*

mortality, subtitled *The Christian Register Symposium, Revised and Enlarged.* (Boston: Geo. H. Ellis, 1887), pp. 69–76. P 347 descends from a draft typescript recently recovered from two distinct manuscript groupings at Harvard. Five leaves from R 884 (ISP 6–10, second series) and two leaves recovered in 1993 from R 537 (ISP 10–11) represent a complete typescript that is much longer than the published text, for it includes at its center the earliest surviving version of his "Criticism on *Phantasms of the Living*" (P 352), Peirce's review of a casebook by members of the English Psychical Research Society. The central review section was prepared from a series of detailed notes also located in R 884 (ISP 5, 4, 6–13, first series); at some point after completing the long dual-purpose draft of "Science and Immortality," Peirce altered his intention and prepared an independent fair-copy typescript (R 884: ISP 2–5, 1, second series) of the book review portion for separate publication in the Psychical Research Society's *Proceedings* (selection 16, December 1887).

The unlocated printer's copy of "Science and Immortality" apparently went forward without the review section, for neither P 347 nor the subsequent book version (P 348) include any of the review material. The opening and closing pages of the restored typescript (R 884/537) were probably used to prepare printer's copy—collation against the published forms reveals a close textual correspondence. Two passages (59.19–26 and 60.19–28 in this volume) were expanded in the publication form. The final paragraph of the typescript, where Peirce digresses to speculate on the clash of religion and materialism in the modern world, is omitted in both published versions.

The R 884 leaves are legible first carbons, but the punctuation is obscured throughout by smudging and light impressions; the R 537 leaves are barely legible second or third carbons, which may explain how they migrated to a mathematics MS at Harvard. Punctuation and even words are not legible at a number of points; the poor state of the typescript, and the fact that two-thirds of the material was removed for separate publication, militate against the selection of R 884/537 as copy-text. In the absence of printer's copy, P 347 stands as copy-text, and the significant closing passage of the typescript appears in the Annotations.

The surviving history of publication is preserved in the editor's prefatory material for both P 347 and P 348. Sometime before the spring of 1887, *Christian Register* editor Samuel J. Barrows submitted to prominent men of science these three survey questions on "the relation of science to the question of immortality":

1. Are there any facts in the possession of modern science which make it difficult to believe in the immortality of the personal consciousness?
2. Is there anything in such discoveries to support or strengthen a belief in immortality?
3. Or do you consider the question out of the pale of science altogether?

In the April 7th issue, Barrows published responses from Peirce and twenty-two other lay and professional scientists, including Simon Newcomb, James D. Dana, Asa Gray, Josiah Parsons Cook, William James, Benjamin A. Gould, Asaph Hall, Herbert Spencer, and T. H. Huxley. Peirce's closely related work reviewing *Phantasms of the Living* led him to address the broader issue in detail—his response to the survey questions is longer and more fully developed than any of the others. In the original *Christian Register* publication, Peirce's response appears between entries from Herbert Spencer and Daniel Coit Gilman (it was Gilman, as President of the Johns Hopkins University, who had removed Peirce from the Philosophy department in 1884). The positioning of Peirce's contribution before Gilman's is undoubtedly coincidental, but Barrows may have placed Peirce directly after Spencer because of the direct attack on Spencer's view of mechanistic evolution contained in Peirce's portion of the article. By the spring of 1890, Peirce's position on Spencer would lead to an open debate in the pages of the *New York Times* (selections 45 and 47).

Reader interest in the article led Barrows to publish the responses as a "symposium" in book form under the same short title as the original (P 348). Prior to publication, he returned the contributions to the authors for revision and expanded the symposium with entries from five new participants, including Joseph Le Conte, Alexander Graham Bell and Gen. Adolphus W. Greely, the commander of the Arctic expedition for which Peirce was just then completing a controversial interpretation of gravity readings (selection 30).

Peirce's P 347 by-line (CHARLES S. PEIRCE, MEMBER OF THE U.S. NATIONAL ACADEMY) has been silently removed. Collation of the published forms indicates that Peirce made several substantive revisions for the book publication. Both P 347 and P 348 include a brief biographical note on Peirce; P 348 also contains editorial comments on Peirce's contribution.

Textual Notes

61.2–3 life? ¶By] There is a significant loss of emphasis in the paragraphing introduced in P 348 at this point. The deleted paragraph break in P 348 cannot be considered authorial or contextually necessary; it is more likely the result of a copy-editor's desire for uniform paragraphing. Therefore, the original P 347 opening paragraph break is retained. Such a loss of emphasis must be considered substantive, and the P 348 version is thus recorded as a rejected substantive reading.

62.3–4 But, . . . prove?] The P 348 revisions from "manifestations" to "manifestation" and from "it" to "they" appear to be editorial regularizations intended to eliminate Peirce's use of the collective singular in the first case, and in the second case to force number agreement between the pronoun and "stories" (62.3). The singular pronoun of the original reading actually refers to the gerundial act of "granting"

(62.3) rather than to "stories"; consequently, both of the P 348 revisions are rejected and recorded as rejected substantives.

64.33 has] The P 348 revision may or may not be Peirce's, but it brings the passage into agreement with the singular form of "deduction" found at 64.30 and is consequently accepted for emendation.

Emendations

61.6–11 The question . . . it?] 348; *om.*
61.15 Catholic] E; catholic
63.1 "The] 348; '~
64.4 As well . . . times] 348; In my opinion
64.22 I really cannot] 348; For my part, I do not
*64.32–33 deduction has] 348; deductions have

Rejected Substantives

*61.2–3 life? ¶By] 347; ~ ? ~ 348
*62.4 manifestations] 347; manifestation 348
*62.4 it] 347; they 348

15. *Logical Machines, 1887*

Copy-text is a six-page publication appearing under Peirce's by-line in the November 1887 issue of *The American Journal of Psychology*, pp. 165–170 (P 344). There are no known pre-copy-text materials, but Peirce's 30 December 1886 letter to his former student Allan Marquand critiques Marquand's initial attempt at developing a logical machine (W5:421–23). In selection 3, Peirce makes use of Marquand's invention as a high-end example of general logic, which Peirce considered less interesting than the "living process" of reasoning (16.15). Context indicates that Peirce may have expected "Logical Machines" to appear in an earlier issue of *AJP*, but there is no known correspondence to document the publication.

AJP was published in Baltimore under the editorship of G. Stanley Hall, a professor of Psychology and Pedagogics at the Johns Hopkins. Peirce had been his colleague during the early 1880s, and continued to correspond with him after Hall took a position with the fledgling Clark University faculty. Peirce's Hopkins students included Marquand and the subsequently eminent psychologists Joseph Jastrow and Christine Ladd. Although Peirce would continue to work in psychological studies for many years, he never again placed an article with *AJP.*

The original page-by-page numbering system used by *AJP* for footnotes is a purely visual characteristic of the copy-text, and has been silently replaced by a single series of numbers in the present edition. The by-line C. S. Peirce, which follows the text in the published form, has been silently removed.

Textual Note

66.7 A=B] In the original, none of the capital or lowercase letters representing propositions, machine handles, or letters on machine dials, were italicized. With the exception of the sentence at 71.10, which contains lowercase variables here italicized, all other letters in this selection have been kept roman, since in most cases Peirce is concerned more with describing the appearance of logical operations on the face of the machine than with propositional logic per se. This exceptional retention of roman characters also avoids the risk of confusion or ambiguity a partial italicization would introduce.

Emendations

Title Logical Machines] E; ~ ~.
65.6(1,2) *Organon*] E; *rom.*
66n.1 *Philosophical Transactions*] E; Phil. Trans.
68.1–2 *solvet ambulando*] E; *rom.*
68.7 (A+B)C] E; (A+BC)
71.5 today] E; to-day
71.5 tomorrow] E; to-morrow
71.10–11 $(a+b)c=d$, . . . The letter *t*] E; *all lowercase variables rom.*
71.27–28 (The . . . negative.)] E; [~ . . . ~.]

16. *Criticism on* Phantasms of the Living, *1887*

Copy-text (designated TS2) consists of five leaves from R 884, a complete carbon typescript fair-copy form of his essay-review of *Phantasms of the Living* (1886), a collaborative two-volume set of paranormal case studies compiled by Gurney, Myers, and Podmore of the English Society for Psychical Research. It is emended by P 352, the published form of the review in the *Proceedings of the American Society for Psychical Research,* 1:3 (December 1887), which also included "Remarks on Professor Peirce's Paper" by Edmund Gurney (O 353) and "Mr. Peirce's Rejoinder" to Gurney's remarks (P 354). The copy-text is corrected at several points by Peirce's own errata note opening the P 354 "Rejoinder," but these errata were corrected in P 352's galleys prior to publication. The headnote to Peirce's errata listing in his "Rejoinder" indicates that Gurney was sent uncorrected galleys of the "Criticism" prior to publication so that Gurney's first "Remarks" could appear in the same issue of the *Proceedings;* no galleys, corrected or otherwise, have been located.

The five TS2 copy-text leaves (R 884:2–5, 1, 2nd series) are first carbons with no typed corrections other than a few strikeovers and an interlined revision in type. The pages are typed on a Hammond Model 1 using several different steel font shuttles. Recent research teams have marked the first leaf "Ms. 884" in black ink at the top right of the recto; other ink marks (such as the opening and closing quotation marks at 75.17–18) appear to be Peirce's. A brief headnote, "For the American Society for Psychical Research," appears in brackets at the top of R 884:2, along with Peirce's working title (in Attic) and by-line (in roman), AN EXAMINATION OF AN ARGUMENT OF MESSRS. GURNEY, MYERS, AND PODMORE. BY C. S. PEIRCE.; subsequent pages bear (with variations in punctuation) the running head, EXAMINATION OF GURNEY, MYER [*sic*], AND PODMORE. Leaf R 884:2 is unnumbered; R 884:3–5 and 1 are numbered in type ("2" through "5") in the top right corner of the recto. Dimensions are 9 ½" × 15", lightweight and watermarked "Montauk Mills." All are faded at bottom and right margins by exposure to light; leaves 3 and 5 (R 884:4, 1) are yellowed and moderately chipped. Leaves 1–3 (R 884:2–4) are damp stained, including a dark stain at the right margin of leaf one; feline pawprints darken the stain across the lower half of leaf 2.

Two pre-copy-text forms of the review survive. R 884:5, 4, 6–13 (1st series) consists of a sequence of detailed notes and analysis on *Phantasms;* these pages probably date from late 1886 or early 1887. R 884:6–10, 2nd series, and R 537:10, 11 together represent a complete typescript carbon draft of Peirce's speculative essay on science and immortality (selection 14), solicited by the *Christian Register*'s editor as one of a series of essays on the subject by great men of science; this draft (designated TS1) contains the first fully developed version of the *Phantasms* review, embedded between R 884:6.14 and R 537:10.6 and taking up by far the largest part of the essay. Sometime before publication of the science and immortality essay in the *Christian Register* (7 April 1887), Peirce removed the *Phantasms* review portion and prepared the TS2 independent fair-copy draft of this material which stands as copy-text for the present edition. The earlier combined TS1 draft is clearly the direct source, but collation indicates a complete reworking of the review for independent publication that relegates TS1 to pre-copy-text status.

Peirce's punctuation and spelling are only emended if required for clarity or correction of obvious errors. His typed running heads and pagination are regularized, as are his margin overruns and run-together words. Words superseded by typed interlineal or in-line passages, often left undeleted by Peirce in his typescripts, are recorded as implicit deletions in the list of significant alterations. Peirce's single-line headnote, by-line, and running heads described above are silently removed.

Peirce's essay-review is published here in its entirety, followed by Gurney's "Remarks" (selection 17), Peirce's "Rejoinder" (selection 18), and Gurney's posthumous "Remarks on Mr. Peirce's Rejoinder" (selection 19). A synoptic outline of the cases Peirce criticizes will appear in the Electronic Companion for Volume 6 (www.iupui.edu/~peirce). A few points of error by both Peirce and Gurney surface as the exchange evolves through the four papers. These points have been emended and annotated to clarify the context of discussions of error by both men at subsequent points in the debate.

Textual Notes

74.3 this. Only] P 352 replaces Peirce's period with a colon, a styling which incorrectly limits the "most imposing argument" to the following sentence only, when it actually encompasses the following four. The period is thus retained.

74.6 fifty millions] E; Peirce's inconsistent use of Arabic numerals would not normally require emendation, but in this article numbers indicating quantity and duration should be clearly distinguished from the case numbers used with great frequency throughout the text. The present edition emends to the P 352 style for such numbers; the only exception concerns round hundreds and hundreds of thousands, where Peirce's consistent use of numerals is not confusing for the reader.

75.12 Cases 173 and 298] Collation of both surviving typescripts reveals that in the TS2 copy-text form, Peirce was developing a standard of capitalization for the word "Case" when used with specific case studies identified by number. Peirce's remaining lowercase usage was capitalized in P 352; since this was clearly Peirce's intention, the present text is emended to "Case" at these points as listed in Emendations.

77.5 all,] Here and at 78.20, the end-line punctuation was probably struck on the original, but lies beyond the manifold margin for the carbon strike. Both are emended from P 352.

77.12–13 rest, and not read at all, and do no work whatever,"] The correct internal punctuation of the quotation is emended from P 352, but that publication did not correct Peirce's errors in wording; the original reads, "rest, not even to read at all, and to do no work whatever." The second internal comma (all,) and the closing comma appear in the pre-copy-text TS1; these pre-copy-text readings are not authoritative, but have supplied circumstantial evidence of haste rather than intent for commas dropped from the copy-text typescript. The commas are restored here, at 77.18 (man,), and at 80.27 (355,).

Emendations

Title Criticism . . . *Living:*] E; *om.* TS2; CRITICISM ON "PHANTASMS OF THE LIVING." P352
Title Podmore] E; ~. TS 2, P 352
74.1 Myers] P 352; Myer *Also* 80.6, 80.32, and 81.23
74.3 *Phantasms of the Living*] E; *rom.* TS 2; "~ ~ ~ ~" P 352 *Also* 81.37–38
*74.6 fifty] P 352; 50
74.7 twelve] P 352; 12 *Also* 70.11, 72.13
74.10 thirty-one] P 352; 31 *Also* 74.16, 76.18, 80.36
74.14 reaches] P 352; can be measured by
74.14–15 trillions, or even billions to one.] P 352; trillions.
74.17 eighteen] E; sixteen
75.5 238] P 352, P 354; 237
75.6 3rd.] P 352; ~,
75.11 frequently] P 352; frequetly
*75.12 Cases] P 352; cases *Also* 77.4, 79.15
75.21 28] P 352, P 354; 29
75.21 236] P 352, P 354; 214
75.25 695] P 352, P 354; 702
75.26 6th.] P 352; *om.*
75.31 Case] E; case *Also* 76.3, 76.8, 76.9, 76.37, 77.5, 77.11, 77.13, 77.36, 79.2, 79.16
76.20 twelve-hour] P 352; ~‸|~
*77.5 all,] P 352; ~‸
*77.12 rest,] P 352; ~‸
*77.12 all,] P 352; ~‸

*77.13 whatever,"] P 352; ~‸"
77.15–16 (although . . . away)] E; [~ . . . ~]
77.18 249] P 352, P 354; 201 *Also* 74.32
77.18 man,] P 352; ~‸
77.19 saw,] P 352; ~‸
77.22 first] P 352; forst
77.22 came] P 352; ~,
77.23 (we . . . minute).] E; [~ . . . ~].
78.20 entitled.] P 352; ~‸
78.34 In] P 354; I
78.35 or] P 352, P 354; and
79.3 vision] P 352; ~,
79.9 on] P 352; at on
79.15 170] P 352, P 354; 180
79.33 three] P 352; 3
80.7 avers,] P 352; avars,
80.27 355,] P 352; ~‸
80.29 worthless.] P 352; ~‸
80.35 logicians.] P 352; logicianss.
81.17 300,000] E; 300‸000

Alterations

77.10 is] was
78.28 or skipper] *intl-t*
79.18 or acquaintance] *intl-t*

17. *Remarks on Professor Peirce's Paper, 1887*

Copy-text is O 353, Edmund Gurney's response to Peirce's "Criticism on *Phantasms of the Living*" (selection 16). Gurney was principal author of *Phantasms* (1886), a collaborative two-volume set of paranormal case studies compiled by three members of the English Society for Psychical Research. Peirce's follow-on "Rejoinder" (selection 18) indicates that Peirce was supplied with uncorrected and corrected galleys of Gurney's "Remarks," but no galleys have been located. All three articles—Peirce's "Criticism," Gurney's "Remarks," and Peirce's "Rejoinder" to Gurney—appeared in the *Proceedings of the American Society for Psychical Research,* 1:3 (December 1887).

Gurney based his "Remarks" on uncorrected galleys of Peirce's "Criticism." Peirce did correct galleys prior to publication, but his "Rejoinder" to Gurney's "Remarks" opens with a list of the galley corrections to explain why Gurney refers to errors in the "Criticism" which, by the time of publication, no longer existed.

Gurney's by-line is retained (and his text is set between black line borders in smaller type) to remind readers that the "Remarks" are not Peirce's. Quotation marks enclosing offset letter excerpts have been removed to eliminate inconsistency of presentation. Gurney's closing address (19 BUCKINGHAM STREET, ADELPHI, LONDON, W.C.) is removed. None of these changes appear in the Emendations list.

Textual Notes

83.41 first-hand] Here and at two subsequent points, the single-word form in O 353 is emended to the compound form found throughout Gurney's *Phantasms* text (1:148 and elsewhere). Emendation is based on the assumption that Gurney had more control of the text in his own book than in the *Proceedings.*

86.18 a war, where] The source of emendation is Gurney's own *Phantasms* text (2:48), from which he is quoting. Style impositions by the *Proceedings* editors are emended out of subsequent direct quotations from *Phantasms* at 87.19–22, 87.23, and 97.32–39.

97.8 199 (and . . . No. 500),] This passage has been emended to conform to Gurney's correction in the third footnote of his final "Remarks" (selection 19).

98n.5 not calculated] The context of the passage which the footnote annotates requires the negative construction as emended. The clear compositorial error emended earlier in the same line of the note suggests that this follow-on passage may have been misread as well.

Emendations

Title Paper] E; ~.
82.1 Gurney] E; ~.
82.30 *Phantasms of the Living,*] E; "Phantasms of the Living," *Also* 100.15
82.30 XIII,] E; XIII., *Also* 83.23, 99.8
83.26 2nd] E; 2d
*83.41 first-hand] E; firsthand *Also* 84.5, 84.10
83.42 Vol. I, p. 148))] E; ~.~., ~. ~)‸
84.12 3rd] E; 3d
*86.18 a war, where] E; war, when
86n.7 idea] E; dea
87.19 *Miscellanies,*] E; "Miscellanies,"
87.20 10] E; ten *Also* 87.22
87.26 Vol. II,] E; Vol. II., *Also* 98.12
89.26 5:20] E; 5.20
93n.4–5 essentials.] E; ~‸
94.2 2nd] E; 2d *Also* 94.13
95n.3 7:30] E; 7.30
97.6 at all in] E; in at all
*97.8 199 (and . . . No. 500),] E; 199, ‸and . . . Nos. 500‸,
97.32–33 questions—whether] E; questions: Whether
97.33 trusted; and] E; ~, ~,
98n.5 XIII] E; ~.
98n.5 Vol. II,] E; V. of II.,
*98n.5 not calculated] E; calculated
99.8 VIII] E; ~.
99.8 five,] E; 5,

Line-End Hyphenation

86.15 non-coincidental
87.29 census-cases
89.38 near-sighted
96.34 death-list

18. *Mr. Peirce's Rejoinder, 1887*

Copy-text is P 354, the third article in a series of exchanges between Peirce and Edmund Gurney, principal author of *Phantasms of the Living.* Peirce's "Rejoinder" was written in response to Gurney's "Remarks on Professor Peirce's Paper" (selection 17); "Remarks" was a response to Peirce's "Criticisms on *Phantasms of the Living.*" All three articles appeared in the *Proceedings of the American Society for Psychical Research,* 1:3 (December 1887).

Internal evidence indicates that Peirce worked both from uncorrected and corrected galleys of Gurney's "Remarks." There is no reference to galleys for Peirce's "Rejoinder" here or in Gurney's posthumous "Remarks on Mr. Peirce's Rejoinder" (selection 19); none have been located.

Textual Notes

101.1–2 In the copy of the above criticism, which was sent to Mr. Gurney] Peirce keys his corrections to line numbers within the published text of his "Criticism on *Phantasms of the Living*," indicating that Gurney was sent a set of uncorrected galleys on which to base his "Remarks"; It is possible, but far less likely, that Gurney was sent Peirce's typescript setting copy or a carbon (Peirce's own record copy of the typescript is a carbon).

101.5 Peirce's line count (second column in the table) starts at the first line of each objection, not at the first line of the corresponding page. Only the first line number needed to be emended (from 6 to 5) so as to correspond to the text of selection 16; the other seven line numbers happen to match those in the present edition.

102.17–18 never such] Peirce's readers would have understood this older usage of "never such" as a more emphatic equivalent of "ever such." The reading is retained on this basis.

103.24 to one."] Here and at 107.6–10, the variations in Peirce's quotation from Gurney's published "Remarks" (selection 17) suggest that Peirce's source was the first set of galleys, which appear to be uncorrected and unstyled. Other comments at 118n.1–3 and 139.36 indicate that Peirce also studied a second set of "Remarks" galleys prior to publication of the "Rejoinder."

127.21 Jim] The case narrative reads "Mountain Jim" at all points but in his discussion Peirce spells it "Jem," perhaps inadvertently substituting the nickname used for his own brother James Mills Peirce.

132.27 [house?]] The narrative context suggests that the apparition appears in the doorway of the dining room, but, as Peirce's parenthetical implies, Gurney's summary is not entirely clear.

140.4 130] Peirce had "230" as the page number, an error Gurney pointed out in his final "Remarks" (selection 19), and it is thus here corrected.

Emendations

Title Rejoinder] E; ~.
*101.5 5] E; 6
101.14 *Phantasms of the Living*] E; "Phantasms of the Living" *Also* 106.25
105.2 170] E; 165
105.5 "but] E; "But
105.26–27 remembered.] E; ~‸
106n.1 II,] E; II., *Also* 131.32, 132.26, 133.34, 135.3, 135.17, 136.1, 136.21, 137.9, 137.17, 138.9, 138.11, 138.33, 139.21
107.33 *Englishman*] E; "Englishman" *Also* 141.6
112.4 2nd] E; 2^{d}
112.11 3rd] E; 3^{d}
113.31 truth,—] E; ~‸—
113.31 one,—] E; ~‸—
114.1 company,—] E; ~‸—
114.2 too,—] E; ~‸—
114.7 I,] E; I., *Also* 114.35, 116.23, 119.1, 120.24, 121.3, 121.29, 122.4, 123.12, 124.29, 125.23, 125.33, 126.25, 127.21, 129.11, 129.27, 130.20, 131.6, 140.4
119.29 one-third.] E; ~-~‸
121.18 Moreover] E; Morever
124.23(1,2) 3,800] E; 3700
124.28 48] E; forty-eight
*127.21 Jim] E; Jem
129.30(1,2) Case] E; case
130.9 Ramsay] *Phantasms* 1:542; Ramsey *Also* 130.10–11, 130.13
135.32–33 (for . . . death")] E; [~ . . . ~"]
137.9 p.] E; p-

*140.4 130] E; 230
140.13 0] E; 50
141.7 persons.] E; persons‸
141.12 the reader] E; thereader

Line-End Hyphenation

112.5–6 newspapers
122.19 census-question
127.6 second-hand

19. *Remarks on Mr. Peirce's Rejoinder, 1889*

Copy-text is O 381, Edmund Gurney's second and final response to Peirce's "Criticism on *Phantasms of the Living*" (selection 16). Gurney's initial "Remarks" (selection 17) responded directly to Peirce's "Criticism"; these final remarks focus on Peirce's "Rejoinder" (selection 18) to Gurney's initial remarks, and appeared in the *Proceedings of the American Society for Psychical Research*, 1:4 (March 1889).

Gurney's untimely death occurred before he could revise the text for publication. It was revised by Frederic W. H. Myers, a fellow-member of the English Society for Psychical Research and co-author of *Phantasms of the Living*. Myers's "Postscript to Mr. Gurney's Reply to Professor Peirce" concludes this selection in the original *Proceedings* publication, and is included in the present edition.

Emendations

142.2 will] E; WILL
142.7 *Phantasms of the Living*] E; "Phantasms of the Living" *Also* 143.23, 144.4, 144.7, 144.29, 144n.3, 145.16, 146.6 ("Phantasms,"), 148.18, 151.9–10, 151.40, 153.7
142.11 (pp. 103–4)] E; (p. 182)
143.7 things";] E; ~;"
143.13 in the second paragraph on p. 104,] E; p. 182, bottom, and p. 183, top
143.14 p. 98] E; p. 176, bottom, and 177
143.15 105] E; 183
143.19 106] E; 184 *Also* 143.25
143.23 Chap.] E; ~‸
143.23 XI] E; XI. *Also stops after volume and chapter roman numerals at* 144.4, 144.29, 144n.3, 145.16, 146.5, 148.18, 151.10, 151.40, 152.40, 153.7
143.35 107] E; 185 *Also* 144.3
144.4 97] E; 176
144.5 108] E; 186 *Also* 144.24
144.13 (1)] E; (1.)
144.20 (2)] E; (2.)
144.25 143] E; 288
144.27 105–7] E; 187–9
145.1 111] E; 189
145.6 P. 112] E; A little lower
145.7 (p. 83)] E; (pp. 158–9)
145.22 108] E; 190
146.17 p. 88] E; pp. 164–5
147.16 120] E; 197
147.16 p. 92, line 28] E; p. 170, line 8
147.35 85, 96] E; 160–1, 174–5
147n.3 97, line 8] E; 175, ~ 27
148.41 always";] E; ~;"
149.2 pp. 85–6] E; p. 161
149.14 94–5] E; 172–3
149.15 88] E; 165 *Also* 149.24
149.16 97] E; 175
149.19 128] E; 203
149.42 instances";] E; ~;"
150.11 Case 202] E; case 202

153.2 vision"] E; ~‸
153.10 Mr. Gurney] E; MR. GURNEY
153.12 Paper] E; paper
153.19 *Proceedings,*] E; *rom.*
153.19 85, fourth] E; 161, first
154.1 96, 97] E; 174, 175
154.1 85] E; 161

Line-End Hyphenation

143.20 over-wrought
143.24 census-question; *Also* 148.5
146.13 marvel-mongers

20. *Number, c. 1887*

Copy-text is a single self-contained page of definitions recovered from the Harvard R 278 fragment folder (ISP 867). The definitions are inscribed by Peirce in faded blue ink on the first recto of a conjugate pair of white medium-weight laid pages with vertical chain lines but no watermark. Each leaf measures 7 7/16" × 10" and contains horizontal rules starting from a vertical line 5/8" in from the left edge and running to the right margins. The two leaves are joined at the left edge to form a four-page folio, but only the first recto bears text.

This document has been dated c. 1887 on account of its handwriting and its connection to selection 21, which must have been composed not long after it. Although the leaf is unnumbered, it probably used to be part of a larger set of pages which have not been located.

Emendations

155.2 *et seq.* Π_α] E; $\Pi_{\mathrm{\alpha}}$ *Also all subsequent lowercase letters used in formulas*
155.2 $r_{\alpha ik}$] E; $\bar{r}_{\mathrm{\alpha ik}}$
155.10 Number] E; ~.
155.11 Next.] E; ~‸ *Also* 151.12
155.12 B.] E; ~‸
155.13 C.] E; ~‸
155.13 As Great As.] E; as great as.
155.14 D.] E; ~‸
155.15 E.] E; ~‸

Alterations

155.2 $\bar{r}_{\alpha ij}$] $\bar{\mathrm{q}}_{\mathrm{\alpha ij}}$
155.5 Σ_j] Π_{j}
155.7 $q_{\alpha i}$] $\bar{\mathrm{q}}_{\mathrm{\alpha i}}$
155.11 A.] *bef del* $\Sigma_{\mathrm{i}}\mathrm{U}_{\mathrm{i}}$
✧155.12 B] *bef del* $\Pi_{\mathrm{i}}\ \Pi$

21. *Logic of Number, c. 1887*

Copy-text is Harvard R 39, eighteen sheets of 8" × 9 15/16" medium-weight laid paper bearing vertical chain lines. The leaves are white, unwatermarked, and horizontally ruled beginning 13/16" in from the left margin and running to the right edge. All are in good condition but slightly darkened from age; several leaves have chipped corners. The document was composed by Peirce in black ink; his few ink cancellations and revisions generally involve an interlined terminology change from "Proposition" to "Premise" in his headings. The neatness of the composition and the very few revisions to running text suggest that Peirce was working from an unlocated earlier draft. The leaves have been reordered from the Harvard sequence (as recorded in ISP numbers) to recover Peirce's compositional sequence (2–5, 8, 17, 6–7, 9–10, 12, 18, 11, 14, 16, 15).

The manuscript is undated, but the handwriting and paper suggest a date around 1887. The content evolves from earlier work on the axiomatization of natural numbers and the broader logical origins of these propositions, including "Axioms of Number" (W4, winter 1880–81), "On the Logic of Number" (W4, 1881), and "Fundamental Properties of Number" (W5, 5 January 1886). Peirce's use of the "streamer" (which combines the negation bar over a variable and the disjunction sign "+" to create a new sign of implication) first appears in "Qualitative Logic" (W5, fall–winter 1886).

For the most part, Peirce punctuated his offset axiomatic expressions as if they were part of the running text. Occasionally Peirce failed to point a sentence ending in an expression; in these cases, periods are supplied by emendation. Peirce's lowercase variables and relationals are emended to italic form where Peirce has forgotten to do so; roman form is retained for uppercase variables, relationals, quantifiers and numbers. Peirce's by-line ("C. S. Peirce") has been silently removed.

Textual Notes

157.8 *m*] Here and at 160.11, 160.17, 163.9, and 163.13, Peirce has failed to complete a revision to the subscript variables, or simply placed the wrong subscript variable in a theorem or proposition. These errors are corrected by emendation.

159.11 $\Sigma_x\Sigma_z\Sigma_\beta\Sigma_\gamma$] In passing to this proposition, Peirce forgot to drop Σ_y from the quantifiers; it has been emended out to conform to the seventh procedural step described in W5:184.

Emendations

Title Number] E; ~.

156.3 *Premise*] E; ~. *Also* 157.6 *and* 157.21

156.6 E_{jk}] E; E_{jk} *Also all lowercase letters within algebraic expressions, all lowercase Greek letters within the text, and the isolated variables at* 156.6, 158.6, 159.7, 159.20, 159.27, 160.8, 161.7, 161.20, 162.4, 162.16, 163.12

156.9 abbreviation] E; abbrieviation

156.15 $+q_{\alpha l}$).] E; $+q_{\alpha l}$)$_\wedge$ *Further periods after propositions at* 157.9, 157.14, 158.5, 158.7, 159.1, 159.8, 160.5, 160.9, 160.11, 160.19, 160.21, 160.29, 161.9, 161.17, 161.21, 161.25, 161.28, 162.6, 162.10, 162.15, 162.17, 162.22, 162.26, 163.9, 163.11

*157.8 *m*] E; *j*

157.20 Π_i] E; Π_α

157.25 I] E; ~. *Also subheading numbers at* 159.17, 160.1, 160.14, *and* 160.25
157.26 procedure] E; proceedure
158.2 the principle] E; principle
158.6(2) We] E; we
158.30 i.e.,] E; i.e.‸
*159.11 $\Sigma_x\Sigma_z\Sigma_\beta\Pi_\gamma$] E; $\Sigma_x\Sigma_y\Sigma_z\Sigma_\beta\Pi_\gamma$
159.14 $q_{\beta z}\bar{q}_{\beta z}$;]E; $q_{\beta x}\bar{q}_{\beta x}$;
159.18 simplest,] E; ~‸
160.11 Σ_α] E; Σ_k
160.13 contradiction.] E; ~‸
160.17 g_{ik}] E; g_{jk}
163.2(2) true] E; as true
163.4–5 number.] E; ~‸
163.9 q_{ay}] E; $\bar{q}_{al}$
163.10 gives] E; ~.
163.13 $\bar{g}_{ix}$] E; $\bar{g}_{iy}$

Alterations

156.1 premises] propositions
156.3 *Premise*] *proposition*
156.5(1) every] the
156.5(2) every] any
157.6 *Premise*] *Proposition Also* 157.15, 157.21
157.12 $(q_{\alpha i}+q_{mi})h_\alpha\bar{q}_{\alpha l}+\mathrm{I}_{im}$] $(\bar{q}_{\alpha i}+\bar{q}_{\alpha m}$
157.27 some] certai*[*n*]*
158.5 $(\bar{q}_{\beta m}+\bar{h}_\beta+q_{\beta n})$] $(\bar{q}_{\alpha m}+\bar{h}_\alpha+q_{\alpha n})$
158.6 β with α] α with β
159.1 $\Sigma_x\Sigma_y\Sigma_z$] $\Sigma_a\Sigma_b\Sigma_c$ (
159.9–10 and that] we get
✧159.14 $q_{\beta x}$] $q_{\gamma x}$
160.11 $q_{\alpha i}$] *intl-c*
160.12 We identify] *bel del* On applying the dis*[*tributive principle*]*
160.16 whatever] the
160.19 $\bar{g}_{ik}$] $\bar{g}_{jk}$
160.24 is the] multi
161.20 and] will
162.12 E_{ab}] (E_{ab}
162.17 E_{ik}] $\bar{\mathrm{E}}_{ik}$
163.2 unity.] every number.
163.2 a] any
163.3 under] *aft del* if β
163.4 as great as *i*] true
163.13 h_β] *aft del* $q_{\alpha y}$
✧163.13 $\bar{g}_{iy}$] $\bar{g}_{ih}$

22–28. *A Guess at the Riddle, 1887–88 (General Headnote)*

The copy-text has been assembled from R 909, a 67-page typescript representing work-in-progress for the projected book-length study, "A Guess at the Riddle." The leaves are 9 3/8" × 12 7/16" sheets of laid lightweight unwatermarked paper typed on one of Peirce's Hammond Model 1 typewriters using a roman sans serif type shuttle. Leaf 68 is a heavier sheet of laid 8 1/2" × 11" paper watermarked "SYSTEMS BOND"; the last lines of 909:3 have been cut away and glued to the top of this leaf. The typescript is a series of working drafts or outlines for chapters 1 and 3–7 of a planned 9-chapter book, with typed and black-ink handwritten corrections by Peirce in some of the drafts. Some of the chapter headings are typed with a roman small capital shuttle. The volume title found at the head of two versions of the opening chapter is in an ecclesiastic-styled font marketed by Hammond as "Attic". Peirce obtained an Attic type-shuttle for his machines in

April 1887; it is likely that the sans serif roman font used in the body text was obtained at the same time.

Peirce did not write these chapters sequentially, nor did he bring them all to the same stage of revision. Overstrike and typed interlinear revisions are characteristic of the entire typescript, but Peirce's handwritten corrections only appear in the leaves of Chapters IV and V, which the contents outline (selection 22) reveals to be the first chapters that Peirce completed. Seventeen pages are struck in black, and the remainder in blue ink; the blues (and most of the black pages) appear to be carbon manifold impressions. Peirce indicates in Chapter I ("Trichotomy") that this first chapter was written last of those that survive; in fact, the seventeen black manifolds represent the final two drafts of Chapter I, two further expansions of the Chapter I opening, and the sole surviving fragmentary start of Chapter III. The blue carbon drafts of Chapters IV–VII appear to predate these leaves, as does the working outline (R 909:4), which lists a version of Chapter I ("One, Two, Three") written more than a year earlier (W5:291–308).

Many leaves throughout the typescript were heavily corrected by the CP editors in black ink, and actually served as marked-up printer's copy for that edition. Instructions to the printer, footnote instructions, and editorial corrections appear throughout the typescript, often retracing (but sometimes overruling) Peirce's own less obvious revisions. Draft chapters selected for CP publication have non-cumulative page numbers in red grease pencil at top right; other drafts rejected by CP editors simply have a red grease pencil "x" at top left. In general, the cumulative ISP numbering sequence imposed in the Texas Tech electroprint copies is based on the page sequence of chapter drafts as published in CP, followed by those earlier (and in some cases more mature) leaves discarded by CP editors. Peirce left these pages unnumbered; since the CP numbering is both incomplete and in error at several points, the ISP system is used to identify pages in the headnote descriptions that follow.

Partial or full drafts exist for Chapters I, IV, V, VI, and VII, and the selection of copy-text follows the most mature form. Split-copy-text decisions, where an earlier chapter draft carries on where more mature draft fragments leave off, have been used in establishing the texts of Chapters I and VI; the full explanation of copy-text rationale, and a discussion of how the selection and arrangement of text differs from CP, appears in the individual selection headnotes.

Purely physical characteristics of Peirce's typescripts, such as misstruck or double-struck letters and his font selections, are not recorded as textual variants of any kind. Editorial marks by the CP editors are ignored throughout the typescript. Although "A Guess at the Riddle" is clearly work-in-progress, it is edited as a document intended for publication. Missing words and punctuation are emended into the copy-text at all points in the narrative chapters. Peirce's working outline of contents, written as an abbreviated text rather than a full narrative, has been left largely unemended to retain the synoptic form that Peirce intended.

Peirce also showed a preference for capitalizing the chapter number prefix for each title, but varied widely in his capitalization of the descriptive subtitles that follow each prefix. As Peirce shows no preference in form, these descriptive subtitles have been emended to title case for substantive words. The volume title appears in various fonts at the top of Peirce's successive drafts of Chapter I. This title, along with his accompanying instructions to insert a vignette of a sphinx, have been silently removed.

In the 1930s the CP editors dated "A Guess at the Riddle" c. 1890, probably speculating that the document was closely connected to Peirce's first *Monist* articles. But more direct evidence indicates that Peirce began conceiving the idea of writing such a book as "A Guess at the Riddle" toward the end of 1885. On October 25 of that year, he wrote to his brother Jem that the one goal of his life was to set forth the true nature of logic and of scientific methods of thought and discovery:

> "I have a great and momentous thing to say on this subject. Without it, molecular science must remain at a stand-still. It must continue what it is, idle guess-work. The true theory of the constitution of matter, which can only be based on sound scientific logic, must have the most important consequences in every direction. On psychology too, which is to be the great science of the coming hundred years, logic must exert weighty influences. About logic, I have something to say which other men have not thought of, and probably may not soon think of."

Three days later, Peirce repeated this statement to William James, adding: "I have something very vast now. I shall write it for *Mind.* They will say it is too vast for them. It is, or within it has as a part of it, an attempt to explain the laws of nature, to show their general characteristics and to trace them to their origin & predict new laws by the laws of the laws of nature." This program announces chapter VII of Peirce's "Guess," where he remarks that the only way further progress can be achieved in molecular science is to answer the question of the origin of the laws of nature, an origin that may be explained in terms of the three elements of chance, law, and habit-taking. On 20 August 1886, Peirce wrote to his friend Edward S. Holden about an "evolutionist speculation" of his (see selection 49 in W5) that had grown much in two directions, those of natural science and philosophy:

> "In the first place, I have found how to make mathematical deductions from it respecting nature, and have quite a list of these, which agree remarkably with some of the most striking characters of the laws of physics; so that it is no longer a mere speculation but a great working hypothesis of science. . . . In the second place, the skeleton of my ideas has filled itself out on the philosophical side, so that my book will be a real manual of philosophy, leaving no question untouched. . . . [T]he duty immediately before me is to write that book."

There is little doubt that the projected book was "A Guess at the Riddle," since nothing else in the corpus fits this description of Peirce's intention so well. During 1886 Peirce wrote several short papers (W5:291–308) on the categories, the wording of much of which is shared by the first chapter on "Trichotomy."

It is not entirely clear when Peirce began to write "A Guess at the Riddle," but there are grounds for believing that he worked on it from late fall 1887 to the end of the winter 1888,—after he had settled in his rented house in Milford, and prior to his purchase of a nearby farm. A new Hammond and Model 1 typewriter, and at least one of the type shuttles used in the surviving typescript, were provided for Peirce by the Coast Survey in April 1887. From June to September 1887, Peirce was exceedingly busy with Coast Survey work and became ill several times from overwork. It also appears that for much of the summer Peirce had lent his new typewriter to a friend, Titus Munson Coan, who returned it at the end of September. Peirce's mother died on 10 October, and he spent a good part of that month in Cambridge. Upon his return to Milford, he resumed work for the Coast Survey, but with diminished enthusiasm, as he did not feel the Coast Survey was treating him fairly. His gravity report was progressing very slowly, and in early November he had to hire a clerk, paying him from his own pocket, to help him do the work. Indeed, internal evidence indicates that at least part of "A Guess" was typed by a clerk from a now-lost manuscript.

At the end of November, Peirce was asked by the Coast Survey to return the Hammond typewriter, but he refused to comply, claiming that he still needed it. On January 8th, 1888, he wrote to Francis Russell, an admirer who was to become one of his staunchest supporters, a letter in which he must have mentioned something about his philosophical research, for Russell replied one week later with enthusiasm: "I am delighted to hear that your Scientific Organon is soon to appear. . . . It seems to me that this epoch calls loudly, almost vociferously, for the organic principles capable of stating the Universe mental and physical with thorough convenience. I look for this to be done on the lines laid down by you, outside of which I can discern no mental salvation." That the "Scientific Organon" was "A Guess at the Riddle" is probable, since the description provided by Russell fits Peirce's program better than any other known document of the period.

Peirce is thus likely to have worked intermittently on the book from November 1887 on, and he may have been forced to stop sometime in March 1888. Internal evidence suggests that the first chapter was composed after the other chapters were completed, and that the opening statement ("To erect a philosophical edifice . . .") was itself composed last, after the first chapter. This statement contains, among other things, a most appreciative address to the reader (this volume, p. 169), an address which matches perfectly the spirit of the last remark Peirce recorded in his notebook, "Private thoughts principally on the conduct of life," on 17 March 1888: "The best maxim in writing, perhaps, is really to love your reader for his own sake" (W1:9). By the end of March, too, Peirce's interests started to shift, as he was thinking of writing another book, related to his correspondence course in logic, to be called "The Art of Reasoning." At about the same time, he got a letter from Superintendent Thorn complaining about the backwardness of his Coast Survey work. One may reasonably speculate that Peirce was forced to lay aside his "Guess at the Riddle" by the demands of his other duties and undertakings. Lastly, "A Guess" appears to have been written before the text titled "Trichotomic," as appears from a comparison of the two documents, and there is good reason to believe that "Trichotomic" was itself composed in late winter/early spring 1888 (see the headnote to selection 29).

22. *[Contents], 1887–88*

Copy-text is Peirce's single-leaf outline of contents from the typescript of "A Guess at the Riddle" (R 909:4). It is a purple-ink carbon with dark black ink corrections and editorial comments by the CP editors. The type and paper characteristics are described in the general headnote above.

Peirce's working outline serves as a table of contents here in the absence of a true table; the blue carbon strike probably predates the black carbons from Peirce's final stage of work (the revised and expanded drafts of Chapter I and the Chapter III fragment); in fact, it is very similar to one developed in 1886 for "One, Two, Three" (W5:294). This text has been lightly emended to preserve its intended synoptic form as an outline-in-progress. It remains the only evidence for the content of the unlocated Chapter 2. This chapter may never have been written, but it is carefully outlined here. Peirce planned to use the material from five previously written sources, then bridge and revise to form a new work. These source writings have appeared in earlier volumes of the present edition and are recorded in the Annotations for this chapter in the present volume. Peirce's title, A GUESS AT THE RIDDLE, and by-line, "By C. S. Peirce" have been silently removed.

Emendations

166.4 *American Journal of Mathematics*] E; Am. Jour. Math.
166.7 *Studies in Logic*] E; *rom.*
166.9 absolute,] E; $\sim_\wedge$
166.10 the logic of relatives] E; Logic of Relatives
166.12 affirmative] E; affirmatiue
166.14 sorts] E; sort
166.16 two] E; 2
166.18 Boolian] E; Booliau
166.20 chapter,] E; $\sim_\wedge$
166.22 Chapter] E; Fhapter
166.22 psychology] E; Psychology
166.26 germinal] E; germiual
167.11 requires] E; reouires
167.11 us] E; *om.*

23. *A Guess at the Riddle:* Chapter I, 1887–1888

There are three drafts of Chapter I within R 909, but only the third version represents a complete chapter. These drafts document Peirce's initial intention to overview and then define the trichotomy that is the subject of Chapter I. The earliest surviving form (R 909:62, 42, 46, 47, 40, 41, 48) is nearly complete, lacking (based on collation against the complete version three) only a final continuation page. The second version is fragmentary, representing an opening page and four subsequent pages (in sequential pairs of two) from the middle of the chapter (R 909:38, 64–67). Collation places these fragments between the first and third versions in the order of composition, and indicates as well that there may have been a further layer of revision for all or part of the chapter at some time. Version three (R 909:5–13) is the only complete form of the chapter that survives, and those nine leaves represent the best choice of copy-text for the vast majority of the chapter content; but version three also includes a headnote that Peirce would expand into at least three further versions of the chapter opening. These three fragment forms reveal a developing intention to open the first chapter with a more general and grandiloquent overview of his purpose for the book and a description of his intended readership.

The first new opening (R 909:3, 68) is pivotal to understanding Peirce's evolving intention for the first chapter. Its opening sentence draws its tone and even one key phrase from Peirce's grand headnote to version three ("births of time" in the headnote becomes "storms of time" and eventually "vicissitudes of time" in the final two openings). Peirce also introduces references to historical philosophical systems and to his intended readership. But this first expanded opening still retains a shortened version of the "Trichotomy" overview found in the opening of the third draft, and actually continues in close approximation of the complete draft until it breaks off at mid-page 68.

A significant evolution occurs in the second new opening (R 909:2). It consists of two tightly focused paragraphs—the first describing the need for a new philosophical system, and the second defining his intended readership for the volume. The specific overview of Chapter I's concepts has been squeezed out completely. Yet this version still retains the subtitle "Chapter I. Trichotomy" and ends at the bottom of the first page, with no indication that a fuller digression from earlier versions of Chapter I was planned. The revising process documented in the first and second expanded openings suggests that the new material, which had initially been woven into the opening of the third full draft, ended up as a self-contained expansion of the third draft headnote from which it had originated.

Interlinear typed revisions by Peirce run throughout the second opening, and finally take over as a continuous layer of revision between the lines of the second paragraph. Peirce apparently retyped this somewhat confusing page, but that final form is preserved only in the published text of the *Collected Papers.* The editors used this now-lost third opening to introduce Volume I of the *Collected Papers* (CP 1.1–2), and thus isolated it from the chapters of "A Guess at the Riddle." The text was probably lost while serving as printer's copy for CP, but one can infer that the title remained the same as the earlier versions of the expanded opening—an editorial note in CP 1.355 indicates that this lost opening was "called" Chapter I. The complete Chapter I (R 909:5–13) supplies further supporting evidence; in that draft, Peirce developed a long paragraph toward the end of the chapter which overviews how the book took shape in his mind, and how he wrote the chapters. Thus Peirce's final discernible intention for Chapter I was to nest the specific "trichotomy" concept (upon which the book is based) within the context of a general overview of the book and its purpose. The present edition uses this evidence to reintegrate the expanded introduction and the Chapter I draft as a single textual unit.

The second expanded opening (R 909:2), which represents his most fully developed opening to the chapter, will serve as copy-text for the first two paragraphs; substantive variant readings from CP 1.1–2 (the missing third opening) are emended into the copy-text if they are more likely authorial than editorial. The entire complete text of version three (R 909:5–13) will serve as copy-text for the remainder of the chapter; it will be emended from the first expanded opening (R 909:3,68), which includes minor revisions to the first few sentences of the copy-text draft. Physical descriptions of these leaves are included in the general headnote to selections 22–28.

Textual Notes

169.17–23 For this wisdom . . . wrong one.] This last sentence of the paragraph concludes the second revised opening (R 909:2), the most mature opening that survives. The CP editors used a now-lost third revise to serve as preface to the CP volumes (CP 1.2), but did not include the final sentence, with which Peirce apparently intended to bridge the expanded revision back into Chapter I.

169.24–170.24 Accordingly . . . them.] These three paragraphs come from the first expanded opening (R 909:3, 68), thus continuing the most mature form, where Peirce's second revised opening (R 909:2) breaks off. Peirce had used the first sentence of 909:3 to anchor his second and (now lost) third expansions of the opening. Resuming the copy-text at this point requires that its second sentence (beginning with "Accordingly,") be offset by paragraph indentation.

170.25 The idea] The expanded opening fragments (909:2 and 909:3, 68) have superseded the first two paragraphs of the chapter as originally drafted. The copy-text continues with the third paragraph of version three (909:5–13), the only complete form of the chapter. Peirce's occasional holograph alterations appear throughout this draft and the incomplete pre-copy-text forms (versions one and two).

175.6 with B] In the example showing that all higher numbers can be formed by combinations of threes, Peirce had in his first surviving version of the chapter used the example "A presents C with a gift B," but in the present version he changed the example to "A presents B with a gift C" (168.25). Peirce failed to revise the subsequent B and C references at 169.6 and 169.7; the letters at these points have been emended to complete his intended revision.

179.34 forgotten] Peirce typed the interlinear revision "forgotten" with the intention of superseding the original "committed the trifling oversight of forgetting", and not uncharacteristically failed to line out the earlier form when the page left his machine. This compositional evidence, as well as the sense of the subsequent lines of text, confirms that the original passage is an implied deletion; it is recorded in the Alterations list, and Peirce's intended reading (cancelled in the R 909 typescript by the CP editors) appears in the present edition.

Emendations

Title Chapter I] E; ~ ~.
Title Trichotomy] E; ~.
168.7 that] CP; *om.*
168.8 Sense,"] CP; ~‸"
168.8 for example,] CP; *om.*
168.9 that ordinary] CP; *om.*
168.10 whatever] CP; whatevar
168.10 appears] CP; seems
168.11 Long . . . only] CP; But it has long been quite
168.12 fondly . . . the] CP; fond though we be of it, and habituated to it, this
168.13–14 Hobbes, Kant] CP; Hobbes, Locke, Kant
168.15 system, also,] CP; system‸ only‸
168.16 upon its own] CP; on new
168.16 Schelling] CP; Shelling
168.17 but] E; and
168.17 oversights] CP; overSights
168.18 that] CP; in that
168.18–169.5 uninhabitable. . . . know] CP; uninhabitable. ¶But the bottommost and most constantly useful of all conceptions, the life-blood of philosophy and wise conduct, better yet conducive to the satisfaction of our physical needs, the attainment of power, the lining of our pockets, and the prolongation of life, as the sequel shall abundantly show, are those to which I am now about to introduce the reader. Very happy am I to be able to offer him something so worthy of his attention; happier still to have a reader so exceptionally worthy of all that I have to offer him. How do I know
169.5–6 character pretty well,] CP; character? Simply by having chosen him,—
169.6 for . . . ensure] CP; for I have so written my book as to insure
169.7 comprehend] CP; ~ well
169.7 written] CP; published
169.8–9 opinions, . . . had.] CP; opinions; if it were he would not take the trouble to read it.
169.9–11 He . . . all.] CP; *om.*
169.12 reflect, too,] CP; also‸ reflect‸
169.12 book has] CP; book including the thinking of it out has
169.13 quite] CP; but quite
169.14 consequently] CP; therefore
169.15 strike . . . instantaneously] CP; instantly occur to everybody,
169.15–16 will . . . although the] CP; will not altogether have escaped the writer's attention, and
169.16–17 may . . . apprehended.] CP; may be expected to develope themselves in the course of the work.
169.30 course] E; cousse
170.1 indeed] E; indde
170.2 philosophy] E; philossphy
170.8 such] E; suuch
170.17 things] E; thiogs

172.9 Patient,] E; ~, ,
172.25 a state] E; state
173.10 which] E; which the
173.30–31 (in . . . line)] E; [~ . . . ~]
174.8 nirvana] E; nirwana
174.16 Three] E; ~,
174n.3 time] E; tima
*175.6 B] E; C
175.7 C] E; B
175.8–9 as genuine a] E; a genuine
175.10 difference] E; differnce
175.11 "servant,"] E; Tservaut",
175.15 term] E; terg
176.8 aperçus] E; apercus
176.11 V] E; IV
177.4–5 (following . . . Aristotle)] E; [~ . . . ~]
177.17 facts,] E; ~‸
177.25 parts.] E; ~ . .
179.23 for] E; for for
179.26 but three] E; but three, but three
180.3–4 (for . . . it)] E; [~ . . . ~]
180.7 thorough-going] E; thorough-ooing
180.11 Finally,] E; ~‸

Alterations

168.2 care] main care
168.2 nicest] the nicest
168.5 and in their outlines vague and rough] rough] vague and so rough in their outlines
168.6–7 and thence it has come to pass] the result is
†168.11 long] *intl*
168.15 stands] has been run up
†168.18–169.5 better yet] and highly
†168.18–169.5 satisfaction of our physical needs] enjoyment of passtimes] enjoyment of life
†168.18–169.5(1) him] the reader
†168.18–169.5 all that] what
†169.6 for I have] by having
169.7 millions] *aft del-t* fifty
169.7 will comprehend] knows
†169.7 it has not been published] my book is not written
†169.12 will also reflect] also considers
169.12 thinking and] *intl*
†169.12 thinking of] *aft del-t* work
169.13 quite] *intl*
169.17–19 For this wisdom . . . measured,] And for this kind patience I am most cordially grateful to my wise reader. Let me on my side endeavour to merit this his esteem measured, [me *in* measured *typed over* em *in* esteem]
169.20 my reader] *aft del-t* allll
169.22 that] who
169.24 happen to have] have
169.28 be looked upon rather] rather be considered
169.35 why] the reason
170.5 three-fold] *intl*
170.5 verbal,] *bef del-t* or at least if there are any that convey any ideas of the nature of th things, and there be any positive notions connected with the numbers one, two, three, which we propose to apply to these distinctions, then it will be necessary to
170.5 their real nature] the real nature of such
170.6 meanings] ideas
170.33 all differentiation] all *add by hand*
171.35 make up] that is
172.19 every] any
172.20 indicated by] o*[f]*
172.22 motions] for*[ces]*
172.38 discrete.] distinct.
173.1 mainly] *intl*
173.19 by which the former influences the latter.] mediating between these two.
173.33–34 last or second,] second or last
174.19–20 distinct idea for] new conception in

174.31 C] B
175.28 no idea can be] there can be no idea
176.29–30 exemplification] exposition
177.1 two] thr*[ee]*
177.11 just] *intl-c*
177.13 one another] one *aft impl del* each
177.21 gathers] embraces
177.22 arise from] consist in t
177.25 a complex concept] an idea
177.33 a thing] an object
177.34 first thing] object
178.7–8 fastens] sti*[cks]*
178.30 as first] the first
178.31 as second] the second
178.32 acts.] *bef del-t* Thus, intelligibility or reason objectified, is neces sary to making thirdness genuine.
179.5 genuine.] *bef del-t* ¶It may be remarked that a degenerate third cannot from as o a thing bringing two others into a relation of reason or bringing an object into relation with itself; for a degenerate second can be created only by the mind.
179.34 forgotten] commi[t]*ted the trifling oversight of forgetting
180.16 that.] *bef del-t* Nor could Hegel himself, as he must surely sometimes have felt, succeed in bending the bow of Ulysses.

24. *A Guess at the Riddle: Chapter III*, 1887–88

Copy-text is the sole surviving single-page fragment of this chapter (R 909:14). The chapter number supplied for the present edition is based on a match with the contents outline (sel. 22), which was prepared very early in the process and before Chapter III had been attempted. The chapter is titled but unnumbered; CP editors supplied the chapter number as well as a number of retracings, corrections and the insertion of two missing words in Peirce's typescript. All of their marks are in black and blue ink; there are no typed corrections or revisions of any kind by Peirce. The general headnote for selections 22–28 contains a description of paper and type characteristics.

The typescript breaks off below mid-page, just as Peirce is concluding his summary of the first of three important pre-Socratic philosophical conceptions. There is no evidence that this chapter was ever continued; as the general headnote indicates, the carbon characteristics suggest that Peirce prepared the first and third chapters last, and this single incomplete sheet may mark the point at which the project was dropped forever.

Textual Notes

181.1 part] The emended readings here and at 181.20 (method) are interpolations which supply what may have been Peirce's choice for missing nouns in this very preliminary partial draft of Chapter III.

Emendations

Title Chapter III. The . . . Metaphysics] E; The . . . Metaphysics.
*181.1 part] E; *om.*
181.7 *arche*] E; *om.*
181.20 method] E; *om.*
181.22 philosophy] E; philossphy

25. *A Guess at the Riddle: Chapter IV, 1887–88*

Copy-text is the sole surviving form, a continuous five-page run of leaves (15, 45, 16–18) from the R 909 typescript. It contains a few interlined typing revisions, but most of Peirce's revisions are by hand in light (thin) black ink; years later the CP editors made further retracings and alterations in dark (thick) black ink and light pencil. Their editorial notations, pagination, and printing directions appear throughout in red pencil or red ink. Editorial cancellations of passages by the CP editors appear at the top of pages 16 and 17. The general headnote to selections 22–28 contains a physical description of Peirce's paper and type characteristics.

In his annotated content outline (selection 22) Peirce stated that Chapters IV and V were the first chapters written in the development of the R 909 drafts for "A Guess at the Riddle." Only these chapters contain handwritten authorial revisions and corrections to typing errors beneath the editorial impositions of the CP editors.

Textual Notes

183.15–184.26 This evidence . . . from us.] This passage does not appear in CP 1; at that time, R 909:45 had not been identified as the connective between leaves 15 and 16. In its place, the CP editors published a portion of the earlier R 901 related work, "One, Two, Three: Fundamental Categories of Thought and of Nature" (W5:245.40–247.4).

185.17 desiring with willing] CP 1.380 inserts "doing" for "willing" in the published text; in the TS, Peirce initially typed "desiring and doing" but typed "willing" interlined above "doing" as an implicit alteration. He later revisited the text and in black ink cancelled "doing" while making other revisions to the sentence. The CP editors have made further interlines to introduce what may be intended as a parallel reading ("willing, doing"), but settled on reinstating "doing" over Peirce's intended "willing" in the published text. The present edition retains Peirce's revised reading.

187.26–27 in a highly complicated, and to the sense itself unintelligible, manner;] Instead of "to the sense" Peirce typed "in the sense"; this created an infelicitous reading which the CP editors attempted to improve, first by altering it to "in a sense", then to "to sense", and finally (in CP 1.383) to "in the [to?] sense". Since the preposition "to" in conjunction with the word "unintelligible" offers a better construction, the editors replaced "in" with "to" and added a comma after "unintelligible" to clarify Peirce's intended distinction between "mind" and "sense".

187.37–38 intelligently.] The CP editors believed there were missing pages following R 909:18, even though it closes conclusively well before the lower margin. They added a portion of R 909:19 here (CP 1.384), which is actually a portion of the first draft for Chapter V (reproduced in the Annotations).

Emendations

Title IV] E; ~.

Title Triad in Psychology] E; triad in psychology.

182.4 follow,] E; ~‸

182.11 they] E; ~ they
182.22 Third] E; Third,
182.26 *tabula rasa*] E; *rom.*
183.6 soul,] E; ~‸
183.17 without] E; with
183.21 ready-made] E; ~‸~
183.22 suggestion from] E; ~ of ~
183.23 form,] E; ~‸
183.24 mien] E; mein
183.32 most psychologists] E; ~ of ~
183.35–36 system] E; sytem
184.12 though] E; thoogh
184.15 we have] E; have
184.19 rehearsal] E; rehersal
184.21 neither] E; naither
184.21 synthetize] E; synthetise *Also* 187.6
184.21 we] E; We
184.22 passed] E; past
184.25 our] E; oor
184.34 is,] E; ~, :
184.36 result,] E; ~‸
185.4 colors] E; colours
185.6 color as] E; colour ar
185.8 hallucination,] E; ~;
185.29 to] E; ~ to
185.34 phenomena,] E; ~‸
185.36 of cognition] E; cognition
186.1 will] E; ~,
186.5 growth] E; ~ .
186.6 cognition.] E; ~‸
186.14 radically] E; raically
186.23 (self-control . . . will)] E; [~ . . . ~]
186.23 (introspection)] E; [~]
186.33 reference] E; rference
187.10 nor] E; not
187.10 force] E; foree
187.11–12 synthetizing] E; synthetising
187.13 gives] E; give
*187.26 to] E; in
*187.27 unintelligible,] E; ~‸
187.30 Intuition] E; Intuiteon
187.31 hypostatization] E; hypostatisation *Also* 182.4

Alterations

182.3 critically] carefully from this point of
182.14 studies] speculation
182.16 asked] answere
182.21 sense.] *bef del-t* Things do promenade like sandwich men with
182.22 Second, and Third] second, and third
182.23 appearing] being so
182.23 and such labels] labels which
183.5 traces] *bef del* there
183.8 Now,] Now
183.9 since Kant; they are: Feeling,] since Kant, Feeling,
183.20 three-fold] *intl-c*
183.22 drew] found
183.22 from] in
183.24 garb] *intl-c*
◇183.24 mein] shape] form,
183.25–26 it is easy to credit the statement of Diogenes Laertius that] we easily give credit to Diogenes Laertius, who says that
183.28–29 a hint in its history] a hint, here
183.33 This is not, however, the original doctrine] This is not the doctrine
183.35–36 Kant's modification suits his peculiar system better than the truth of nature. There] But Kant made the modification to suit his system. It is not an improvement; there
184.8 But that peculiarity of feelings which] What there is about feelings that
184.13 hundredth] thirtieth
184.15 Of nothing but the fleeting instant can] We can
184.16–17 whether much or little;] neither much nor little,

184.17 and this instant] of anything but the fleeting instant, which
184.17 In it] In this instant,
184.18 of no change; because we do that by] of no change. We can cognise no process, because we only cognise a process by
184.19 the process] it
184.19 that occupies time.] this we cannot do in an instant.
°184.21 synthetise;] synthetise.
184.29 feeling] cognition
184.29–30 resemblance] that
184.34 No doubt] Perhaps
184.35–36 to some the experiment will seem to yield an opposite result but I have convinced myself that] but I am sure, for my part, that
185.2 memory which] memory I should think, which
185.9 or feeling] *intl*
185.11 are] are also
185.13 the strongest desire.] that desire which prevails as being the strongest.
185.14 quite] altogether
185.15–16 This is not a question of] It is not an affair of
°185.16–17 experience; and surely he who can confound desiring with willing must be a day-dreamer.] experience. It seems to me that he who does not see the difference between desiring and doing is dreaming.
185.26 I have a sense] I am conscious
185.28 occurs.] is meant
185.31 the most confused] the worst
185.32 Cognition.] Cognition, as a branch of the mind.
185.34 alone they can] they c
185.34 great] *intl-c*
185.35 form the warp and woof of cognition] *intl-c*
185.36 they are constituents of cognition.] enter into cognitions as a part of them.
185.36 will,] *bef del* as a
186.3 But that element of cognition which is neither feeling nor polar sense,] But what there is in cognition which is ◆at once [*intl-c*] other than feeling, and other than the sense of a saltus,
186.4 consciousness] sense
186.4–6 and this in the form of the sense of learning, of acquiring, of mental growth is eminently characteristic of cognition.] and more especially the sense of learning, of acquiring, of mental growth.
186.7 covers] cannot
186.7–8 and that not merely because it continues through every instant] not merely because it is every instant
186.8 but because] for
186.13 life] ego
186.27–28 by psychologists; I shall therefore mention] by psychologists and therefore I shall mention
186.29–30 where there is an external compulsion] where an external force compels us
186.32 cannot choose] are compelled
186.38 in our] of our
187.4 alike] compared
187.8–9 what the mind is compelled to make neither by] where the mind is neither compelled to make by
187.17 The artist] He
187.35 and] ;

26. *A Guess at the Riddle: Chapter V, 1887–88*

An incomplete but comprehensive run of eight pages from the R 909 typescript serves as copy-text for Chapter V. Interlinear typed revisions appear occasionally throughout this draft, but many substantive revisions in

Peirce's hand appear in narrow-point black ink. The CP editors have retraced lightly struck or mis-struck characters as well as some of Peirce's hand revisions; other corrections and editorial annotations appear throughout the draft. The general headnote to selections 22–28 includes a description of Peirce's paper and type characteristics.

There are three discrete versions of this chapter: two two-leaf fragments (R 909: 54, 19; R 909: 53, 55), both just under 1000 words in length; and the eight-leaf, 4000-word copy-text version (R 909: 20–27) that, though not apparently complete, carries on a far fuller discussion than the two earlier versions. In the fragments, Peirce defines the physiological triad and describes parallels with the correspondent psychological triad of Chapter IV. The third version, which contains a fuller treatment of these definitions and parallels, goes on to speculate on the nature of protoplasm as it might be analyzed within Peirce's framework of categories. Peirce's handwritten revisions, along with his notes in the contents outline for the projected volume (selection 22), reveal that Chapters IV and V were written and apparently revised during the initial stages of composition; no other developed chapters show evidence of revision.

Textual Notes

188.18 contents] Peirce uses the usually plural form "protoplasmic contents of every nerve-cell" with the singular "has its active and passive conditions." Context indicates that he intended the singular form expressed in the verb and possessive adjective; these forms, as well as Peirce's unusual (but not unacceptable) usage of "contents" as singular, are retained.

192.5–6 irritation,] This emendation restores the comma originally joining the two clauses of the compound sentence, and completes Peirce's transposition of a nonrestrictive clause and the second clause of the original compound. CP 1.390 ignores Peirce's transposition entirely.

198.21 particle,] the emended comma offsets the nonrestrictive phrase and completes the revision begun by Peirce's interlinear insertion of "a particle" following the original offsetting punctuation.

198.34 complex.] The typescript of Chapter V ends here, four-fifths down the eighth page. Peirce added in black ink the cryptic "Here the chemical idea.", apparently a notational reminder to pick up the chapter with this subtopic. The "chemical idea" has not been identified.

Emendations

Title V] E; ~.
Title Triad in Physiology] E; triad in physiology.
188.6 acknowledge.] E; ~ . .
188.13 say] E; san
188.13 content] E; contant
189.1–2 (which . . . however),] E; [~ . . . ~]‸
189.10 self-control] E; self control
189.29 common] E; commoo
190.8 way] E; ~,
190.10 surface] E; ~,
190.14 of a] E; of
190.16 unanalyzed] E; unanalysed
190.16 unsynthetized] E; unsynthetised

191.8 when] E; ~,
191.32 any] E; aoy
*192.5–6 irritation,] E; ~‸
192.6 until] E; untill
192.15 repetition] E; repitition
192.28 spades,] E; ~‸
193.3 (for habit)] E; [~ ~]
193.4 (for forgetfulness)] E; [~ ~]
193.12 of] E; off
193.20 transferred] E; transfered
193.32 avail.] E; ~..
195.7 (1879)] E; [~]
195.28 to be] E; to
195.36 elasticity.] E; ~..
196.4 protoplasm.] E; ~..
196.5 etc.,] E; ~.‸
196.6 it sometimes] E; sometimes
196.8 condition.] E; ~..
196.13 likely to] E; likely to likely to
196.27(1) those] E; thsse
197.2 entering] E; enteriog
197.4 number of] E; numbers of of
197.25 equalize] E; equalise
197.31 wasting] E; wastiog
197.33 will be] E; will
197.35–36 (the . . . etc.)] E; [~ . . . ~.]
198.14 thrown] E; thrown thrown
*198.21 particle,] E; ~‸
198.29 particles,] E; ~‸

Alterations

188.6 Once more] Again
188.8 not] *bef del* th
188.8 thereof] of the theory
188.9–10 or falsehood] *intl-c*
188.21 feeling] *bef del* wh
189.1–2 which we cannot deny,] [nor can we deny this
189.2 however] however, neither
189.25 which oblige] which afford some
190.2–3 that identity] that *intl-c*
190.8 to a discharge] to that
190.8 nerve-energy;] nerve-energy:
190.21 produces] constitutes
190.25 and] or
190.26 reason] understanding] mind
190.26 quite evidently] most plainly
190.28 five] four] three
190.36 serving] bei*[ng]*
190.37 ceasing] *bef del* to oo
191.2 increasing] *bef del* in
191.3 a frog,] one ◆may [will] sometimes see a frog,
191.6–7 may at length be observed to give] at length give
191.20–21 The laws of physics] *aft del-t* In the realm of physics, all
191.27 virtue] element
191.35 activity] action
192.1 activity] action
192.4 repeated; but,] repeated, but
192.5 I mean that movement] for the action will continue until ◆this does happen [it is repeated], I mean that action
◇192.5–6 irritation for the activity will continue untill this does happen.] irritation for the action will continue untill this does *bef illegible word*]. irritation.
192.12 activity] action
192.12–13 be that] be, that] be that
192.13 gets] is
192.24–25 brings the activity to an end.] stops the action.
192.25 readily] *intl-c*
192.25 as] *intl-c*
192.26 you had better lay all the cards down face up and distributed] you lay them all down face up separated
192.27 Now] You now
192n.3 going] being
193.2–3 each of those suits that have just been turned up] each suit just turned up
193.13 bring to an end that state of things] make that thing
193.15 yet deeper] deeper yet

193.23–24 Still, this may] This may however
193.24 this strange substance] protoplasm
193.37 reproduction;] reproduction.
195.1 under] *aft del* as s
195.5–6 or class of substances,] *intl-c and , add*
195.6 by] *bef del-t* definite on
195.6 characteristic] *intl-c*
195.25–26 and if] and it is quite as likely to be fifty times that number. Indeed, if
195.26 minute] small
195.28 might do better, or even] may
195.29 a ridiculously small guess.] an estimate absurdly small.
196.4 When a] When any
196.4 it] protoplasm
196.4–5 is disturbed by a jar, a poke, an electric shock, heat, etc.] receives a disturbance
196.6 ball;] ball,
196.6 it were] it
196.16–17 which phenomenon is] which is phenomenon
196.17 and is] and
196.20 suddenly increase] have
196.21 molecules?] molecules vastly increased?
196.31 instead of] which replace
196.33 But we] *aft del* Then, when
197.9 the exactitude of] *intl-c*
197.9 average;] average.
197.11–12 inequality in each of the different households.] inequality in the different households.] range in each household.
197.12 Owing] *aft del* We must also suppose that these orbital systems are not separated from one another, but that they are rather interlaced.
°197.35–36 [the same I mean in mass, velocities, directions of movement, attractions, etc.]] *intl*
198.8–9 particles,] particles
198.14 out;] out,
198.15 relations;] relations
198.16 from which] in whi
198.21 matter] matter not
198.24 and be subject to the right attractions] *intl-c*
198.28 as] and
198.29 being] being taken

27. *A Guess at the Riddle: Chapter VI*, 1887–88

Copy-text is split between Peirce's incomplete third draft (R 909:59, 57, 50) and, for the remainder of the chapter, the final two leaves of his second draft (R 909:29-30). Typed cancellations and interlined revisions appear occasionally on all the leaves related to this chapter, but there are no handwritten revisions by Peirce in any of the three developed drafts of Chapter VI. The CP editors have made many corrections in black ink, and used red grease pencil in the corners to record page numbers (top right) or rejection X's (top left) as indicators of their intent to publish or not to publish individual pages. A physical description of Peirce's "A Guess at the Riddle" typescript and its sequences of chapters may be found in the general headnote to selections 22–28. In terms of content, the complex textual history of this chapter is not readily apparent from earlier publications of the work. Both the *Collected Papers* Vol. I (1931) and *The Essential Peirce* (1992) published what collation shows to be the second draft, the most complete but not (by itself) the most fully developed form of Chapter VI.

Peirce's initial concept of the chapter survives in two preliminary openings (R 909:43, 44; R 909:39). In these fragments, Peirce belittles the biologists of his day for paying too much attention to inessential details while disregarding the method from which all modern sciences have sprung: the method of analysis, also called the "Newtonian philosophy." Both fragments present an example taken from the history of astronomy to show how analysis led to the eventual explanation of planetary motion, but neither brings the discussion of this example to a conclusion.

The first complete draft (R 909:56, 58, 51) puts a similar emphasis on the benefits of analysis, though more briefly as it shifts the main topic to biological evolution. The astronomy example disappears, and Peirce goes instead into an "abstract" and "diagrammatic" discussion of the role of chance in the theory of natural selection. He again resorts to an example, that of a statistical game of chance (repeated in drafts 2 and 3), no longer to substantiate the power of analysis, but to draw an analogy between the wealth of the players and a species' power of procreation. This example is then followed with the identification of the three elements at work in natural selection: chance or sporting (individual variations), inheritance of procreative power, and hereditary fixation of beneficial variations. Part of the latter discussion does not reappear in versions 2 and 3, but because it illuminates the way Peirce's thoughts developed, it is recorded in the Annotations.

In draft 2 (R 909:28–30), Peirce omits the preliminary considerations about analysis and tackles directly the theory of natural selection and survival of the fittest by questioning how fortuitous variations can reinforce the adaptation of a species to its environment. The "game of chance" statistical example appears in revised form, but augmented with a chart carrying the game of chance through sixteen iterations. Draft 2 concludes with a significant section describing how adaptation is based on a process of elimination of unfavorable characters and how the three principles (now called sporting, hereditary transmission, and elimination of characters) are connected to the triad consisting of chance, compulsion, and generalization.

The third and final surviving draft (R 909:59, 57, 50) begins as a revision of the second draft. The gaming chart is reduced to a summary of the sixteenth throw, but is followed with a much more expanded explanation of the analogy between the increasing wealth of some players and the procreative power of species. Included in this explanation is the description of a statistical chart (now lost) from which Peirce formulates a "most important principle"—that the frequency of a given variation is greater in the direction of the future than of the origin of a species. Peirce maintains that this opens a new line of statistical research not explored by Quetelet or others. Here draft 3 ends abruptly, without going into the triadic considerations present in draft 2.

These forms of the text indicate that once Peirce had settled on his approach, the three major drafts evolve without radical departure in organization or content. Draft 2 is the most complete in terms of structure, since it dwells also at some length on the connection with the three fundamental elements, but draft 3 promised to be more fully developed, as shown by the extended considerations on statistics and probabilities. It is impossible to tell why Peirce broke off this most comprehensive version in mid-page and in mid-chapter. But Peirce does not indicate a preference for either of the earlier drafts; since all three were typed by or for Peirce in sequence, the third draft remains the final form over which Peirce exercised complete compositional control of both accidentals and substantives. As far as it goes, the third draft presents the fullest development of the material and serves as copy-text for the first half of chapter VI. The second draft represents the most mature surviving form of the remaining portion of the chapter, and serves as copy-text beginning where the third draft breaks off. Significant passages from the first draft and from the earlier fragment openings appear in the Annotations.

Textual Notes

199.24–200.4 The numbers of players holding $1, $3, and $7 after sixteen throws are emended to reflect the correct computation. The number of players holding $7 has been correctly rounded (down rather than up) to reflect Peirce's intent throughout the chart to round to the nearest whole number. The much larger errors for players holding $1 and $3 are the result of progressive errors in the fourth through tenth throw computations charted on R 909:28 (published in EP 1:271 with corrections, it is the immediate source of the table summarized here in the final draft fragment). Throws eleven through fifteen do not appear in the earlier chart; Peirce apparently tired of the longhand process and recalculated using an algorithm. Such a change in approach would explain why only two of the nine final values contain significant error.

200.32–201.9 This diagram has not survived, but Peirce's narrative analysis provides enough information for the reconstruction found in the Annotations.

201.19–20 frequency, which] Peirce's interlined revision of "which" for "This" indicates an intention to run these two sentences together. The present reading completes the revision by emending the full stop to a comma.

201.20 these characters have not] The word "characters" is followed in the typescript by the incomplete word "variat" breaking off at the very end of the line, the next line beginning with "have not been formed". The word "variat" was crossed out by the CP editors, not by Peirce, which leaves open the possibility that he could have meant the word "variations" to replace the word "characters" or to be appended to it to form the compound "character variations." Analysis suggests, however, that Peirce meant to reject the word "variations": natural selection forms and develops characters, while variations, which do contribute to this development, are fortuitous and thus due to chance.

201.29 place.] Peirce's final uncorrected draft of Chapter VI ends here, breaking off abruptly near the top of the third leaf (R 909:50). The remainder of the chapter carries on the penultimate draft, beginning in mid-paragraph at R 909:29.13.

Emendations

Title VI] E; ~.
199.1 is that] E; is that that
199.3–4 (whether . . . theory)] E; [~ . . . ~]
199.4 so for] E; so a for
199.4 should,] E; ~‸
199.10 Suppose] E; Soppose
199.21–22 (namely . . . $3)] E; [~ . . . ~]
*199.24 21,821] E; 31744
199.25 52,369] E; 52292
199.26 55,542] E; 55‸542
200.1 38,879] E; 38880
200.2 19,226] E; 19‸226
200.3 6,714] E; 6‸714
200.4 1,587] E; 1‸587
200.7 sum.] E; ~. .
200.11 "adaptation] E; ‸~
200.14 has] E; is has
200.15 tick] E; ~ tick
200.15–16 much less] E; much they less
200.18 after they] E; afterhe
200.20 sum,] E; som,
200.21 The] E; TTe
200.25 lifetime] E; life-time
200.27 theory] E; Thheory
201.7 curve,] E; corve,
201.15 which] E; wtich
201.18 Quetelet] E; Quetelt
*201.19 frequency,] E; ~.
201.30 ¶It] E; It
201.37 offspring] E; off-spring
202.4 reproductive] E; reproductiwe
202.16 the direct] E; the pro direct
202.17 reinforced, the] E; reinforced, and the
202.30 is the] E; the
202.33 unfavorable] E; onfavorable

Alterations

199.17 each.] *bef del-t* At the end
199.18 throw,] bet,
200.14 has] is
◇200.21 TTe] By the
200.24 reproduction] produ
201.4 physical] *intl*
201.12 would] will
201.17 such statistics] there
201.19 occur with equal frequency] are equally
*201.20 which] This
*201.20 characters have] characters variat have
201.35 and indeed] *aft del* indeed, they may even do that, so long as these offspring as not so closely like their ◆ill-adapted parents [parents] as usual. In fact, it seems likely that as a general ◆rule [thing], when the circumstances under which a race is are not favorable to reproduction for any reason, the fecundity or procreative power of the race becomes weakened. Now there are many examples to show that when the procreative power is weakened the principle of heredity becomes relaxed, and the race shows more tendency to sporting, iu which the type is in danger of obliteration. And so, on the other hand, as soon as a race begins to be adapted to its environment, the procreative power is strengthened, the hereditary transmission of characters becomes more strict, and so the type is hardened.
202.5 its] his
202.11 disappear] be obliterated
202.22–23 individual variation or sporting] sporting or individual variation
202.27 already met with] pre
202.34 casting] n

28. *A Guess at the Riddle: Chapter VII*, 1887–88

Copy-text is a run of seven pages (31–37) from the R 909 typescript. There are in-line cancellations and interlineal revisions, all in type, but there are no authorial hand revisions of any kind. Peirce's superseded passages beneath the interline typing are cancelled by the CP editors in black ink; further editorial corrections and revisions appear in black ink throughout the draft. A sequence of CP page numbers has been imposed at the top-right corner in red grease pencil. Paper and type characteristics are recorded in the general headnote to selections 22–28.

Three attempts at this chapter survive in different Harvard manuscript locations: a 600-word fragment on an oversize leaf recovered from the R 1600 miscellaneous boxes (R 1600:8/9); a two-leaf, 1000-word fragment recovered from R 909 (leaf 60) and R 1600 (leaf 10/11); and the seven-leaf, 3000-word apparently complete version (R 909:31–37) which serves as copy-text. The R 1600 first draft is typed in an italic font, the second draft in the roman font used in R 909. The 3000-word version is a full development of the ideas expressed in the earlier fragments, and extends beyond into new material that rounds out a chapter-length portion of the book. Illustrative examples Peirce used in the fragments but deleted from the final surviving version appear in the Annotations.

Textual Notes

204.22–23 absolute chance or lawlessness] Peirce failed to type the word "chance," as a result of which the CP editors crossed out the words "absolute or" so as to provide the reading "an element of lawlessness." Previous texts, however, make it clear that Peirce meant to write "absolute chance" (see W4:549, W5:293, and selection 22 in this volume), and the word has thus been emended in while the crossed out words have been restored.

208.31–38 This paragraph is preceded in the typescript by directions in brackets to "Insert the following before the last paragraph." Context indicates that "the following" refers only to this single-paragraph passage, which has been transposed here (as in CP) according to Peirce's directions.

209.20 been,] The comma here is required for clarity, and may have been lost to margin overrun. But as one cannot assume that Peirce provided the punctuation, it is added by emendation rather than silently regularized.

210.8 having, too,] Peirce awkwardly uses the term "too" to mean "also" or "as well as" in the second of three characteristics for the spatial continuum of paired secondness. CP eliminated the reading as a typographical error; the present text emends in offsetting commas to clarify Peirce's usage.

210.13 substances.[2]] A full paragraph intervenes between the parenthetical note (after 210.13) and the passage to which it applies (210.22–27). The term defined by the note ("substances") appears twice in the referent passage, but Peirce failed to tag either spot with the asterisk used for notation in the R 909 typescript. The note tag appears in the present edition at the point where Peirce first identifies this usage of the term.

Emendations

Title VII] E; ~.
Title The Triad in Physics] E; The triad in physics.
203.14 event] E; ewent
204.11–12 "Lectures on Astronomy,"] E; ‸~ ~ ~‸‸
*204.22 chance or] E; or
205.4 condition,] E; ~‸
205.4 error] E; ~,
206.5 *ultima ratio*] E; *rom.*
206.18 hope,] E; ~.
206.20 universe] E; ~,
206.23 than] E; thhan
206.26 past,] E; passed,
206n.1 *Petrus Hispanus*] E; Petr. Hisp.
207.5 makes] E; make
207.17 least] E; ~;
207.28 nature] E; ~,
207.28 of the] E; of of the
207.30 nothing] E; ~,
208.15 atoms] E; Atoms
208.16 in] E; io
208.31 at] E; ot
209.16 Genesis] E; genesis
209.17–18 firstness,] E; ~‸
*209.20 been,] E; ~‸
209.21 more] E; mor
209.37 Consequently,] E; ~‸
*210.8 having, too,] E; ~‸ ~‸
210.11 state,] E; ~‸
210.15 disappear] E; dissappear
210.17 formation,] E; ~‸
210.22 substances,] E; ~‸
210.29 another] E; aonther

Alterations

203.4 that science] geometry
203.5–6 Aristotle derived from the study of space some of his most potent conceptions.] some of the most important of the metaphysical conceptions of Aristotle, as Form, and the Abstract, are borrowed from geometry.
203.9 bears its paternity on its face.] came without doubt directly from geometry.
203.9–11 the conviction that any metaphysical philosophy is possible has been upheld at all times, as Kant] metaphysics has been sustained, a*[s]* Kant
204.8 the error of the ordinary statement is precisely] its value is precisely
204.23–24 reckon the doctrine of] *[t]*hink that
204.28 are determined] happen
204.28 while] a
204.28 happen] ar*[e]*
204.34 when] if
205.3(1) that] *bef del-t* our instinctive beliefs
205.17 reality.] *bef del-t* But that any fact, so far as it has general characters is ultimate and inexplicable, is an assumption which logic can never warrant. It violates a fu*[n]*damental regulative principle of reason.
206.5 every] a
206.28 all the] the
207.16 for] but
207.18 mingle] do so
207.30–31 make one] direct us
208.5 the course] *aft impl del* there is
208.15 For] *intl*
208.16–17 there is] has
*208.31–38 Such is our guess . . . laws of nature.] *paragraph ins per Peirce's instruction*
208.35–37 there is some method . . . fortuitous occurrences] the laws which could ◆result [be] from the action of chance, and habit-taking would have certain characters, and

there is a method by which others could be deduced, and then we
209.7–8 in one place] in one ◆time [place]
209.8 such] ju[st]
209.17–18 by the principle of firstness] *intl*
209.26 uniform] regular
209.32 separate utterly] utterly separate
209.37 But] *aft 3 paragraphs del per Peirce's instruction* ¶But secondness is of two types; so that besides flashes coming second to others, so as to be genuinely second or after them, there would be pairs of flashes of which each one would be second to the other, reciprocally. Habit-taking will here also give rise to a continuum; only here there will be nothing to restrict the number of dimensions to one or indeed to any other particular number. The connections of this continuum will also be excessively complicated. This would be Space in an early form of its development. ¶Habit groups would be formed; and these would be substances. There would be nothing to form the material of these habits but the relations of the habit-groups to one another, which would be the relations of space and time. ¶Having thus reached substances moving in a sort of space; we find somewhat more tangible ideas, which we can reason about without any extraordinary difficulty.
210.3 habits] *aft impl del* a
210.14–15 less and less liable] more and more permanent or

29. *Trichotomic, 1888*

Copy-text is recovered from the first box of the large nest of papers and offprints known as R 1600. It consists of three medium-weight leaves of 12" × 9½" hectograph or carbon sheets (no watermark). All three leaves are heavily worn at the edges, chipped all around, and missing corners. The missing top left corners on leaves 2 and 3 have taken away text; however, the missing text is intact on electroprint copies, allowing complete transcriptions of the document for the present edition. The leaves are typed on one of Peirce's Hammond Model 1 machines using a roman serif font shuttle. Occasional misstrikes for lowercase o, u, y, and s are discernible and here transcribed as the intended letters. The strike is in purple throughout the typescript, which is likely the result of either a carbon manifold impression or a hectograph run from a master. Peirce's interlinear corrections-in-progress appear in purple type; his further revisions (along with carets for some of the interlines) appear in black ink. A surviving variant leaf (of similar strike and paper) appears to be an abstracted version and parts of it are recorded in the Annotations.

A comparison of this text with the first and fourth chapters of "A Guess at the Riddle" (selections 23 and 25) shows that "Trichotomic" must have been composed a short time later in 1888. The three-page typescript offers a summary of some of the main arguments in the those chapters, while at the same time going a step further in providing a trichotomic analysis of "expression" or representation, and of consciousness in general. There are also datable references to the work of the New York playwright and theater manager Steele MacKaye. Juliette Peirce began acting lessons with MacKaye late in 1886, prompting a close social relationship between the two families that peaked in early 1888. A connection also exists between "Trichotomic" and the earlier document "One, Two, Three" (W5.48), which similarly defines trichotomic as "the art of making threefold divisions." In fact, the term "Trichotomic" was one of the alternative titles Peirce used for the earlier work (see textual note 294.3, W5:578).

Textual Notes

215.6 consciousness,] Punctuation missing at Peirce's typescript endlines is normally assumed lost in margin overrun, and silently restored. But the required comma cannot be assumed here, where the text falls more than a full space short of the carbon margin as established by adjacent lines of type; it is therefore supplied by emendation.

Emendations

211.1 ¶TRICHOTOMIC] E; ‸~
211.5 reacting.] E; ~. .
211.23 *et seq.* *A, B, C,*] E; A, B, C, *All capital variables rom.*
211.24 relation] E; relations
212.5 object,] E; ~‸
212.11–12 (although . . . thirdness),] E; [~ . . . ~]‸
212.37 second] E; third
213.10 constitutes] E; constituter
213.12 MacKaye] E; Mackaye
213.19–20 (on . . . author)] E; [~ . . . ~]
213.28 varieties:] E; ~;
214.5 in] E; iu
214.5–6 discrimination, no parts,] E; ~‸ ~ ~‸
214.17(1) consciousness] E; consciousnass
214.18 that of] E; of
214.20 energetic] E; ~,
214.22 "cannot."] E; "~".
214.25–26 consciousness] E; ~,
214.33 conscious] E; consciouss
*215.6(1) consciousness,] E; ~‸
215.14 MacKaye's] E; Mackaye's
215.17 Feeling;] E; ~,
215.26 the power] E; power
215.33 presented] E; preseuted

Alterations

211.25 term] *intl-c*
212.15 addressed] *intl-c*
212.23 connections] relations
212.29 follow] understand
213.17 shall] may
✧214.20 energetic,] lively] vivid,
214.28 a Process] the Process
215.17 of Feeling] or Feeling
215.32 passing into or out of this condition,] in this condition

30. *Pendulum Observations at Fort Conger, 1888*

The initial publication of Peirce's report on the Greely Arctic expedition's gravity measurements serves as copy-text. Although not a member of the

1881–84 expedition, Peirce instructed General (then First Lieutenant) Greely and his astronomer, Sergeant Edward Israel, in the use of gravity pendulums; in January 1882, they used Peirce's pendulum apparatus and his written instructions to swing the pendulum and record the raw data for subsequent reduction and interpretation by Peirce. Peirce's determination of gravity from the Greely expedition data was eventually published as "Pendulum Observations. |Report by C.S. Peirce" in the official *Report on the Proceedings of the United States Expedition to Lady Franklin Bay, Grinnell Land* (Washington: GPO, 1888), Volume II, as Appendix 141 (pp. 701–714). General Greely's brief prefatory comments appear in the Annotations; the report designation "Appendix 141," as well as Peirce's by-line, have been silently removed.

Two partial and two complete pre-copy-text versions of this report survive; together they document the monumental difficulties Peirce encountered in publishing what would be his last report on gravity determinations to reach print. The relevant forms of the text are described below; abbreviations used for each form is followed by the corresponding chronological catalog number in parenthesis.

TS(1887.18) A three-page preliminary draft of the opening narrative, titled "The United States Coast and Geodetic Survey," survives in the Max Fisch Papers at the Peirce Edition Project. It breaks off with an emotional discussion of the factors which made a conclusive report impossible. This fragment, typed on one of Peirce's Hammond machines using both italic and roman type-shuttles, probably dates from early 1887. Carbons of the first and third leaves also survive, as does an earlier typed version of the second leaf bearing black ink corrections by Peirce. Both versions are carefully typed, suggesting that Peirce only discarded this form of the opening narrative when he decided that an interim report was possible, showing the results of the Arctic experiments but not the Washington base station data or the final deductions for gravity at the Arctic station.

ATS(1887.21) A 28-page combination of typed hectograph and handwritten leaves representing the initial submission of Peirce's reductions of the Greely Arctic expedition's gravity determinations of January 1882. The manuscript, titled "On the Pendulum Observations at Fort Conger," was submitted to the Coast Survey with a cover letter in Peirce's hand dated 11 April 1887, and survives today as National Archives Record Group 23, Entry 22, Item 36, Volume 657 (NARG 23/22). Extra copies of the typed hecto sheets have also survived. The document contains three unnumbered runs of page 11 below the revised (in type and in Peirce's hand) numbered page 11 which Peirce sent in on 13 April as a replacement. In the same way, a revised (in Peirce's hand) page 12 is bound in above an original unnumbered and unrevised run. A poor run

(1887.20) of the narrative (pages 1–3) and the typed tables (pages 11–12) is separately bound in papered boards at the National Archive under the old Coast Survey file system as 11P 1881–4, 40909.

1076(1887.28) Harvard R 1076, a portion of the printer's copy prepared by Coast Survey or Government Printing Office (GPO) typists from the ATS sometime after April 1887. The fragment includes only the opening narrative and a heavily damaged version of the calculations of atmospheric effects. Its title, originally the same as that of the ATS, was deleted and replaced with "Pendulum Observations."

G1(1888.3) A record set of the GPO's first galleys survives in National Archives Record Group 27, regressively corrected to match the copy-text by Survey Assistant Farquhar but untouched by Peirce. Compositorial errors abound, but the G1 text includes a companion chart to Peirce's first chart (decrement of the pendulum arc). This chart was not included in the ATS, and was presumably supplied later under separate cover for setting. Peirce's corrected set of the G1 galleys has not been located, nor has any set of the G2 revised galleys; however, letters of transmittal from Peirce to General Greely for both the first and second galleys survive in NARG 27, indicating that Peirce corrected both sets of galleys during July 1888.

P 369(1888.5) Peirce's Arctic gravity determinations were published under the title "Pendulum Observations" in *Report on the Proceedings of the United States Expedition to Lady Franklin Bay, Grinnell Land* (Washington: GPO, 1888), Volume II, Appendix 141: 701–714. For the published report, Peirce omitted the final data correction category (atmospheric effects on the oscillating pendulum) and substituted a new closing section that included the actual gravity determinations for Greely's Arctic pendulum station. The opening narrative was revised to reflect these modifications in the published version. General Greely's brief opening overview, as well as his closing rejoinder and Peirce's tipped-in comment to the rejoinder, appear only in the published form of the *Report*. Peirce's hand-corrected offprint survives in the Harvard Peirce Papers.

ATS, 1076, and G1 all represent a preliminary form of the report which, although set in galleys, would prove to be unpublishable as written. Peirce submitted his study of Greely's pendulum oscillations under extreme pressure from government officials intent on satisfying Congressional requirements for an official Arctic expedition report. The pressure was magnified by the complex mathematical corrections required to neutralize the effects of extreme weather conditions encountered by Greely's men in the Arctic. On 22 March 1887, Peirce wrote to Survey Superintendent Thorn:

> You are aware that my judgment is averse to the publication of the Greely matter; but as you were plainly determined upon it, I thought it my duty to do all I possibly could

to try to render that publication useful, and especially, to that end, to try to make out a more secure value for the temperature coefficient from the Ithaca work. (ATS)

His most complex calculations, those involving corrections for atmospheric effects, are clearly provisional—portions of four drafts for this material survive in Harvard R 1095 and R 1076, and Peirce ultimately pulled this section prior to publication. Peirce's 11 April 1887 cover letter to the original submission offers "the whole ready for the press," but internally he made no effort to conceal the fact that it was only an interim document, and deliberately refrained from offering a value for gravity at the Arctic station; the original narrative simply concludes that "the final deductions will be published hereafter" (ATS, p. 3).

Peirce completely rewrote the report and provided a conclusion based on his decision to treat the pendulum as reversible but not invariable, and to use only the readings after interchange of knives in the reductions. By these modifications to the data reductions, he was able to provide an actual value for gravity at the Arctic station. Although the basic organization of the report remained intact, a major portion—the notations and corrections for atmospheric effects—was removed entirely, and the tables on the period of oscillation for each swinging were heavily revised. The rewritten report also had a conclusion, which completed the post-expedition instrument measurements and added the crucial calculation of the value of gravity for the Arctic station.

The transformation of the report from an interim submission to a comprehensive determination of gravity took place in galley revisions during the early summer of 1888. Although his own copies of the first and second galleys have not been located, the surviving cover letters for each set summarize extensive revisions by Peirce in his own copy of G1. In returning the first proofs to General Greely, he offered the following assessment of the process:

> The printer will be dismayed at the state in which I return the proofs. You will remember that I earnestly protested against writing the report at the time I did, because I was not then prepared to do your observations justice. Had my report been delayed as I judged that it ought to be, it would have been finished long before this, perhaps more satisfactorily than I have now been able to complete it. I have now done my best within the time allowed and if the proofs afford trouble you have to thank those who overruled my judgment. Had I another day I would send with the proofs a complete copy of the text so that the reading should be made clear. (NARG 27)

Peirce asked for and received final data on elevation at the Arctic station, and in late July he made further recalculations in a revised set of galleys. In his monthly Coast Survey report for July 1888, Peirce took a final shot at those who forced the premature submission of the report:

Gen[l] Greely, having sent me the proofs of my report on his pendulum experiments, which report, you will remember, I made contrary to my own judgment at a time when I was not yet ready to undertake it, I was obliged to do most of the work over again, and rewrite the report. This time I brought it to a final result. This was sent on to Gen[l] Greely and another set of proofs sent me, corrected, and returned. (NARG 23)

The ideal copy-text would be the first set of heavily revised galleys, emended from the second galleys. But in the absence of these forms, the published version of the report stands as copy-text. Peirce received offprints from General Greely in late November 1888, and Peirce's handwritten corrections to calculated values at two points have survived in an offprint at Harvard. Since these corrections cannot be evaluated for accuracy, and may distort other unaltered stages of the gravity determinations in unknown ways, they are noted in the annotations but are not emended into the copy-text.

General Greely's rebuttal of Peirce's contention that the Pendulum had been damaged in transit was appended to Peirce's report; Peirce's brief half-sheet rejoinder was subsequently inserted into the 750 copies of the published volume distributed by the War Department; it is not known if the rejoinder went into the copies distributed by the GPO. These postscripts follow the report text; relevant excerpts from Henry Farquhar's supplemental report on the gravity determinations appear as annotations. The Annotations also identify corrected values at a number of points in Peirce's tables which cannot be emended due to the resulting effects which such impositions would have on subsequent calculations.

Congressional report styling, which varies from Peirce's usage in his Coast Survey publications, involves spelling of metric units, capitalization of metric standards, and the expression of temperature values. Such variations are emended to restore Peirce's preferred style.

Textual Notes

216 title] Peirce's report was published under the short title "Pendulum Observations" which was sufficient in the context of the larger report of which it was an appendix, but is no longer so when deprived of that context. The title has thus been emended to make it more explicit on the basis of Peirce's pre-copy-text title. The following short note by A. W. Greely prefaced Peirce's report (p. 701 in the original publication):

> A pendulum furnished by the U.S. Coast and Geodetic Survey was swung forty-eight times under favorable conditions, as regards equable temperature, and corresponding sets of time observations were made.
>
> Detailed information on this point has been given the Coast Survey, to which office these observations were sent September 24, 1886.

The date provided by Greely appears to be erroneous: the pendulum records were actually received by the Coast Survey two years earlier, on 15 September 1884.

221.22 of Peirce No. 4] The copy-text reading ("pendulum Peirce No. 4") first appeared in Peirce's initial submission (ATS) and probably represents an incomplete revision to "Peirce No. 4" from an original intent to type "Pendulum No. 4". The printer's copy (R 1076) capitalizes "Pendulum", but that reading is not authoritative and probably represents a typists' attempt to solve the dilemma. The reading is resolved by emendation as Peirce most likely intended.

221.31–222.8 The coefficient . . . 17.61.] During the early summer of 1888, Peirce substantively rewrote the (unlocated) first and second galleys, adding this narrative passage describing the process of calculating the coefficient of expansion for the pendulum at Arctic temperatures.

223(c23).15 1.8 1.9] This reading in the copy-text appears to be a composing error. The pre-copy-text typescript (ATS) contains the original and presumably correct reading. Similar readings in adjacent columns and rows may have led to the transposition error, which has been emended out in the present edition.

225.1 *Observed . . . down.*] This chart was not part of the initial submission in April 1887. It first appeared in the uncorrected first galleys; in final publication, the compositor added a signature notation (H. Mis. 393, pt 2—45) to mark the final leaf of the 45th gathering in Volume II of the Arctic report. This notation has been emended out of the present edition.

227(c10).13–27 43.1 . . . 54.7] The tables of the initial submission are all typed or are in the hand of an amanuensis, with only a few handwritten corrections by Peirce. At this point, the amanuensis appears to have repeated the values in rows 18 and 19 of this column, causing a downward shift of two rows for the remainder of the column. The extra rows were omitted in galley and publication forms, and the published form is retained at these points.

228(c10).29 59.1] This value appears with an overbar in the ATS and was printed in smaller type in P 369, presumably to indicate a rejected value. In 229(c14).27 and 229(c21).4 the two values 59.3 and 59.0 also appear with an overbar in the ATS, but were printed in normal type in P 369 perhaps because, though anomalous, they were not rejected.

229(c12).12 51.9] Here and at a number of subsequent points in the tables, variations appear between the copy-text publication of 1888 (P 369) and the pre-copy-text initial submission of April 1887 (ATS). In the initial submission, the tables in question were inscribed by an amanuensis [228(c6, 7, 13, 14, 20, 21)–235] or typed [236–237(t1)]. Peirce made very few handwritten revisions to these leaves, and his heavily revised first and second galleys have not been located, although surviving correspondence indicates his intention to check all the table values as he rewrote the report. The calculations for these tables cannot be reproduced from the fragmentary worksheets that survive at Harvard and the National Archives. Taken together, all these factors militate against any effort to determine if the copy-text readings (which in all cases agree with the single surviving set of uncorrected first galleys) are corruptions. All of the copy-text variants conform as well as (or better than) the pre-copy-text variants to the general pattern of change in the pendulum arc; since Peirce made many large-scale columnar revisions to these charts in the first and second galleys, and since none of the isolated copy-text variations are anomalous, the copy-text readings are retained at all points. Points of variation are as follows:

	pre-copy-text		copy text	
228(c10).29	57.9	----	51.9	----
230(c11).22	38.5	31.9	28.5	31.9
230(c11).24	28.9	32.2	28.9	33.2
230(c11).27	28.5	24.9	28.5	34.9
232(c13).3	60.9	----	60.4	----
234(c9).2		.96		.95
234(c9).10		.92		.91
236(c16).31		0.030		0.025

230(c11).27 28.5 34.9] These values appear a row below this position in the pre-copy-text initial report submission, but were transposed in the uncorrected first galleys. This may be a compositorial error carried forward to publication, but the lack of raw data sheets prevents verification for either form, and thus the copy-text readings stand.

236(c17).31 2866.886] The compositor misread the data point as typed on p. 12 of the initial submission. The first decimal figure was obscured by an overstrike correction.

242(t1).4 – 76] In the tabular presentation of station error, the copy-text displays spaces to the fifth decimal (rather than zeros) as placeholders; these spaces are retained without emendation to preserve Peirce's notational form.

244.30 Explanatory Note] Peirce wrote his reply after Greely sent him, on 22 November 1888, advance copies of the Appendix (RL 174:2). He wrote back to Greely on 27 November (RL 174:3–5; Greely's 30 November reply is in RL 174:6–8), and again on the next day. Greely's assistant, Lieutenant Craig, acknowledged receipt of Peirce's 28 November letter together with "two notes for insertion in volume 2, Report of the Lady Franklin Bay Expedition" (RL 174:9). This exchange, and the frequent use of the phrase "Mr. Peirce," suggest that the Note in its final form was edited by Greely on the basis of material sent by Peirce.

Emendations

Title Pendulum . . . Conger] E; Pendulum Observations.

216.4 Carlile] E; Carlisle *Also* 243.17

217.13 Normal Meter,] E; normal meter,

217.32 days'] E; ~‸

218.14 1/30000] E; 1:30,000 NARG 23; 1/30‸000 P 369

218.22 *et seq.* metre] E; meter

218.30 grammes] E; grams *Also* 218.31, 218.32, 218.33, 218.35, 218.36, 218.37, 220.23

220.1 centre] E; center *Also* 220.2, 220.3, 220.17, 239.9
220.1 millimetre] E; millimeter *Also* 220.24
220.3–4 centimetres] E; centimeter *Also* 220.5, 220.22
221.12 *et. seq.* Metre]E; meter
221.13–14 "Measurements . . . Stations."] E; ‸~ . . . ~‸
221.16 Pendulum] E; pendulum
*221.22 Peirce No.] E; pendulum Peirce no.
221n.1 *U.S. Coast Survey Report*] E; *rom. Also* 222.36 (*Coast Survey Report*)
222.35 pounds";] E; ~;"
*223(c23).15 1.8 1.9] E; 1.9 1.8
225 *[Table]*] E; *[Table]* H. Mis. 393, pt 2——45
*236(c17).31 2866.886] E; 2806.886
239.14 *Metre No.* 49,] E; *Meter No.* 49,
240.5 1884–85.] E; 1884-'85. *Also* 241.2
243.1 EXPEDITION] E; ~.
243.6 217–218] E; 702
244.30 Note] E; ~.
244.32 pages 243–244,] E; page 715,
244.37 Page 218, line 6,] E; Page 702, third paragraph from the bottom, line 2,
244.37–28 properly."] E; ~".
244.39 Page 220,] E; same page,
244.39 first] E; last
244.39 paragraph,] E; paragraph but one,
245.1 four] E; two
245.1 second] E; third
245.1 242.] E; 714.
245.3 on page 218,] E; above,
245.4 inconceivable,"] E; ~",
245.21–22 middle] E; second
245.22 222.] E; 703.

31. *Reflections on the Logic of Science, 1889*

Copy-text is recovered from R 1573x (a single-page preface), R 246 (an unnumbered introductory chapter), R 247 (an incomplete initial version of Chapter II, titled "The Doctrine of Chances"), and R 248 (an incomplete second version of Chapter II, titled "Mathematics"). It is apparent from content that "The Doctrine of Chances" is a distinct variant superseded by the entirely different "Mathematics" version of Chapter II. "Chances" is broader in outline than "Mathematics" and indicates that Peirce may have originally intended to continue with a discussion of the role of probability in the physical sciences, including mathematical probability. But Peirce's page-by-page dating record reveals that he suddenly began the new "Mathematics" Chapter II—completely different in content and bearing the identical pagination of the earlier version—before going any further in his "Reflections." In fact, no further text has survived; Peirce failed to complete the new Chapter II, and apparently abandoned the project without revealing how he intended to use the displaced (but clearly not discarded) material of the original Chapter II. No transition to a discussion of chance is part of the "Mathematics" version of Chapter II as it stands, and the displaced "Chances" version could not have followed the new Chapter II without substantial rewriting.

The initial "chances" version clearly links best with the introductory Chapter I, which includes explicit references to the chances topic. But the subsequent "Mathematics" version is also significant, for it offers a glimpse of a more settled intention that, if continued, would no doubt have led to a rewriting of the opening chapter as well. The "Mathematics" version also documents Peirce's shift of interest from his reflections to the more narrowly focused mathematical writings that followed in quick succession. Given Peirce's unsettled intentions and the early stage at which he broke off work on the project, both versions of Chapter II are published here in the original order of composition.

The pages of all three manuscripts are 8 3/16" × 10 1/2" sheets of white laid paper with horizontal chain lines bearing the watermark "A. PIRIE & SONS | 1888." The leaves of the "Chances" chapter (MS 247) are marked in red grease pencil with an "X" across every page by the CP editors to indicate the decision not to publish. The first leaf of each chapter is inscribed with the Robin manuscript number (top left, in pencil) as part of the initial manuscript reorganization initiative of the early 1960s; the single-page preface leaf from R 1573x is marked "MS 1572" in pencil at top right. This preface leaf has a somewhat confusing history of movement through the Harvard Papers. It was microfilmed as part of R 278, and then microfilmed again after its removal to R 1573x. A false start of Chapter I's second leaf was recovered from R 1574. All of the leaves are in good condition, but those of Chapter I show some chipping and fading due to exposure to light. A tear in the lower edge of leaf 21 has been repaired by tape.

Peirce's text is inscribed by hand in black ink with numerous authorial corrections and revisions. The inserted preface is undated, but every other leaf in R 246, R 247, and R 248 is dated in sequence from 1 to 17 January 1889. Peirce wrote Chapter I from 1 to 8 January, the "Chances" version of Chapter II on 8–9 January, and the "Mathematics" version of Chapter II from 9 to 17 January. Pagination is continuous from 1 to 22 (the introductory Chapter I), 23 to 27→[29] ("Chances" Chapter II), and 23 to 29 ("Mathematics" Chapter II). Page numbers appear in the upper right corners, and dates of composition appear in the upper left, all in Peirce's hand.

Successive revisions in the pagination of leaves 1–7 reveal details of composition. Peirce composed and numbered the first 5 leaves (as well as a discarded false start for leaf 2). He next moved the original leaf 1 ("That . . . doubt") to the end of the sequence, transferred the volume title line to the second leaf, and renumbered these leaves (originally 2–5, 1) as 1–5. He made revisions to improve the flow of this new page sequence (including a bridge passage at the foot of leaf 5), and began a continuation leaf 6. The same day (1 January) he cancelled his new leaf 1 title line, and added a preface page bearing the volume title. He numbered this sequence, beginning with the preface, 1–7; all subsequent leaves are numbered without revision from 8–22 and dated from 1 to 8 January 1889. The pagination of the manuscript is as follows: 1, 2→1→2, 3→2→3, 4→3→4, 5→4→5, 1→5→6, 6→7,

8–22 (Ch. I); 23–28, 27→[29] (Ch. II, "Chances"); 23–29 (Ch. II, "Mathematics"). An abortive re-write for the last three pages of "Chances" survives as leaf R 247:7 (numbered 27 by Peirce; see Textual Note 255.31).

The content of Chapter I, along with Peirce's January diary and an 8 January 1889 letter to Francis Russell, provides ample evidence that these "Reflections" were to become a book-length project. Content suggests that Chapter 7 of "A Guess at the Riddle" (selection 28) may have served as the catalyst for the opening chapters. But other dated manuscripts show that Peirce quickly turned to more specialized mathematical projects such as his notes on Kempe's paper (15 January) and his "Ordinal Geometry" paper (19 January). His January household move from temporary lodgings to Arisbe may also have prevented Peirce from returning to the "Reflections" project, but no direct connection is known. A major outside interruption came on 28 January from the Superintendent of the Coast Survey, who demanded a full accounting of progress on Peirce's gravity determinations of the early and mid-1880s; by month's end, Peirce had assembled more than 2,000 pages of text and data, and would be embroiled in a battle over these documents for the rest of 1889.

Peirce's habitual use of a comma/dash combination to offset digressive or explanatory passages within a sentence, and his similar use of colon/dash to offset a quotation, are retained at all points. His lowercase variables are emended to italics in the cases where Peirce failed to do so.

Textual Notes

246.1 Chapter I] Peirce begins chapter designations in Chapter II, and refers to the introductory chapter as the first chapter in the text of Chapter II. The chapter designation has been emended in on the basis of this internal evidence.

249.19 This] Here and at 252.5, Peirce inserted an interlineal date of ("Jan 2" and "1889 Jan 3" respectively) to indicate where he resumed work on the second and third days of composition.

252.6–16 In lieu . . . computer.] These lines are a rewrite of the immediately preceding paragraph in the manuscript. The original, dated 3 January, concludes the run of pages Peirce dated 2 January; the rewrite begins the next sequence of pages, dated 7 January. Although Peirce failed to cancel the original, it has been treated as an implicit deletion and recorded in the Alterations.

253.16 the fabricator] The definite article is supplied to complete the revision Peirce began by deleting the final "s" of "fabricators." The singular form continues throughout the paragraph.

253.19 reason] Peirce had originally intended to construct a phrase offset by his habitual comma and dash combination, but he failed to delete the comma when he modified the sentence and deleted the dash.

253.31–37 To . . . physics.] Peirce originally wrote only two objectives for his projected volume of Reflections; the third appears in a dated appendix to the final manuscript page (R 246:22) along with instructions to "Add to the two objects above". The note is dated "1889 Jan 8," the day after Peirce completed the chapter proper.

254.15–18 The six underlines in this passage stand for blank spaces Peirce left in the manuscript with the unfulfilled intention of filling them in at a later time.

255.31 A brief second attempt to rewrite the chapter from this point begins on a discarded leaf (R 247:7). It opens a similar discussion of probability defined as a statistical average, but Peirce planned to use the work of Laplace instead of Quetelet. Peirce had broken off the original Chapter II in mid-sentence on 8 January after completing the discussion of Quetelet's work. His brief attempt to rework the chapter on leaf R 247:7 (numbered 27 by Peirce to replace the original leaves 27, 28 and [*sic*] 27) is dated 9 January. The "Mathematics" version of Chapter II is also dated 9 January, indicating that Peirce had broken off the partial revise to restart the chapter in an entirely new direction.

257.35–258.2 "It seems . . . science."] Peirce did not provide this quotation in the manuscript but left a blank space he intended to fill in at a later time. The quotation is one found in Peirce's 1881 review of Jevons's *Studies in Deductive Logic* (W4:238), which seems to fit the context quite well. Jevons himself quoted this statement in his book (London: Macmillan & Co., 1880, p. xi). The original is in Sylvester's *The Laws of Verse, or Principles of Verification* (London: Longmans Green & Co., 1870, p. 19). Where Sylvester and Jevons have "euristic" Peirce wrote "heuristic" instead.

259.8 better shown by] Peirce drew four successive versions of his schematic triangle across the page at this point. The first and third are crossed out, but context at 259.10 indicates that the second schema was superseded as well. Only the third and fourth diagrams include the "little circle," leaving the uncanceled fourth diagram as the intended "reading" and relegating the second diagram to the status of an implicit deletion.

Emendations

246.1 Chapter I] E; *om.*
246.3 Brush] E; brush
246.4 photography,] E; ~ ‸
246.4 etc.,] E; ~.‸
246.8 years,] E; ~‸
246.10–11 *Chemie,*] E; *der Chimie,*
247.1 former,—] E; ~,‸
247.3 platinum] E; Platinum
247.3 thallium] E; Thallium
247.10 situation] E; situating
248.10 accustomed] E; accostomed
248.12 one] E; ~ one
248.25 molecules;] E; ~:
248.28 falsification;] E; ~:
249.2 show] E; shows
250.28 we] E; *om.*
251.22 Only,] E; ~‸
251.25 A3, etc.] E; A3,.etc
251.25 B3 etc.,] E; B3 ~.‸
251.30 A's] E; As
251.30 B's] E; Bs
*253.16 of the] E; of
*253.19 reason] E; ~,
253.36 cast] E; caste
254.8 Chances] E; Chances.
254.9 for the] E; ~ The
254.29 mathematician's] E; mathematicians
254.30 probabilities] E; probabities
255.3 clearly] E; ~,
255.19 ratio of] E; ratio
255.23 class and] E; class to
255.26 *statistical*] E; *rom.*
255.27 *averages.*] E; ~‸
256.15 calculation.] E; ~‸
256(c2).3 value] E; ~.

256(c5).(1,2) g] E; *rom. All instances. Also* 256.17(1–5)
256(c5).6 etc.] E; etc‸ *All instances. Also* 256.17, 256.19
257.5 *[Second Version].*] E; *om.*‸
257.11 is,] E; ~‸
257.13 conclusions"] E; ~."
257.14 *Linear Associative Algebra,*] E; *rom.*
257.14 1).] E; ~.)
257.23 remained,] E; ~‸
257.32 *m*] E; *rom.*
257.34(2) *m*ʹ]E; *rom.*
257.34 *n* and *n*ʹ] E; n′ and n′
*257.35–258.2 "It . . . science."] E; *om.*
258.15 to speak] E; speak
259.10 lines.] E; ~‸
259.10–11 trigonometry] E; Trigonometry
259.11 points,] E; ~‸
259.12 lines,] E; ~‸

Alterations

246.2–3 instantaneous photography] *intl-c*
246.7 The truth is that] *intl-c bel del centered underlined title* Reflections on the logic of Science
246.7 the description] The description
246.8 has been for some years] is now, in a general way,
246.9 Whoever] Any physicist who
246.11 compendious] complete
246.12 at once] *intl-c*
246.13 at the same time] *intl-c*
246.14–15 so far] *bef del* as it can be done
246.15 directly] *intl-c*
246.15–16 drawing,] *bef del* towards
247.1 having no apparent relations] apparently unrelated
247.1 why,] why the body
247.4 to apply] from
247.4 undiscovered theory] theory
247.5 quite new] ne*[w]*
247.6 that is a further affair] that is a further business] all that is a further aim of the physicists and chemists,] that is another task
247.7 scarcely] ha*[rdly]*
247.9 of] *bef del* having
247.10 how] what
247.11 having] *bef del* accurately
247.12 to attempt anything] any attempt
247.17 discovered.] foun*[d]*
247.19 beyond] *bef del* all
247.25 penetrating more deeply into the higher arithmetic,] the most profound study of arithmetic than ever any man had yet gone,
247.26 proof] demonstration
247.26 accurately] nicely
247.27–28 the demonstration of] *intl-c*
247.28 the proposition itself] it
247.31 proofs] independent proofs
247.33 It is, however, hardly worth while to discuss] It is not, however, worth while to pause to discuss
247.33–34 somewhat metaphysical question;] general question;] point;
247.34 powerful minds] physicists
247.35 perhaps] not improbably
247.36 so large a] our] so large a] our
247.36 Let us] *aft del intl-c* But
247.36–248.2 Let us rather . . . before them] *add*
247.36 limit ourselves to] consider
248.2 the] their new
248.3 That] *bel del centered underlined title* Reflections of the Logic of Science
248.9 "grain" or] *intl-c*
248.13 But the] The
248.14 provisionally assume] content myself with stating
248.14–15 to be out of doubt.] as indubitable.
248.16 plain] true

248.17 are] is
248.20 Now] But
248.22 may] may,
248.23 masses] bodies
°248.25 molecules:] molecules;
248.27 yet] *intl-c*
248.29 the] this
248.30 once met with, and being so treated] found and treated in that
248.30 were its] were it to satis*[fy]*
248.31 could be] can be no do*[ubt]* is
248.33 determine] make out
248.35 extremely simple laws] an extremely simple law
249.1–2 the thousands of different] the different] its
249.4 may] must
249.5 had] drawn of
249.5 allow] give
249.7 There is] It is
249.9 consideration] *intl-c*
249.9 hypotheses,] *bef del* as they the
249.10–11 rest upon] suppose
249.12 spaces] lines] dis*[tances]*
249.12 mutual] *intl-c*
249.13 the vast bodies of the solar system,] the planets of our system, which are so large
249.13 system,] *comma ov period ov comma*
249.14–15 whose exactitude is] which are only
249.16 physical] *intl-c*
249.16 now] *intl-c*
249.17 the mathematics] the *intl-c*
249.19 supposition] hypot*[hesis]*
249.22 the higher] the *intl-c*
249.23 explains molecules by] refers to
249.24 or elastic] *intl-c*
249.24 Since fluids] As a fluid
249.26 would seem] seems
249.26–27 the parts to have more complicated properties] parts more complex
249.31 whirling] *intl-c*
249.32 unless] until
249.34–35 The following propositions are also proved. 1. Every such vortex] Wherever there is such a vortex
249.35 must have] there must be
249.37 (like an eddy)] *intl-c*
250.2 elongated] distorted
250.5–6 several] two
250.6 nor] or
250.9 In these actions, the reactions depend] Their reactions are
250.9 ratio of the velocity] velocities] velocity
250.10 strengths] strength
250.11 from the] from any
250.13 atom] molecule
250.14 ether] fluid
250.14 that the] *bef del* supposition
250.14–15 different] *bef del* kinds of
250.19 forces] the forces
250.21 are explained as] appear as mere secondary
250.22 hypothesis] hypotheses
250.27–28 —a supposition perfectly open to us,—] *intl-c bel del intl*—a perfectly reason*[able]*
250.29 matter,] matter?
250.33 imaginable] *intl-c*
250.35 and of this ocean only one individual drop] only one of which is the truth we seek
251.2–3 illustration] example
251.7 antecedent] *intl-c*
251.9 choosing] lighting
251.14–15 this number itself] itself
251.17 etc.] *intl-c*
251.17 any line] *aft del* the shortest
251.19 in the former sense,] in the first sense,] that of
251.21 open hypothesis] admissible supposition
°251.22–23 Only Cantor] He a*[dmits]*
251.27 any] any given] any finite
251.35 suppose there to be] if there were
251.36 is] was

251.37 devote] ex*[amine]*

*252.6–16 In lieu of . . . computer.] *aft impl del* ¶In reply to all that has been urged, it may be said that after all we have only to apply the great rule of false, the method by which almost all mathematical calculations are made. Make any hypothesis you please, and compare its results with observed fact, and you have some indication of how the hypothesis ought to be modified. Then, if the modified hypothesis is nearer [nearl*[y]*] the truth than the first, a repetition of the process may be expected to bring it still closer. Every mathematician knows that this rule [process] works admirably if you only have a sufficiently close approximation at the outset

252.6 the] this

252.9 a computer has] mathematicians have

252.10 equations] ques*[tions]*

252.12 satisfy all the] solve the

252.13 to the values assumed for the unknowns] *intl-c*

252.14 the equations] them

252.20–21 hypotheses in general physics] physical hypotheses] hypotheses of

252.25–26 purpose.] purpose?

252.27 original, underived,] ultimate and underived

252.28 Mr.] *intl-c*

252.30 a scintilla] *aft del* the

252.30–31 phenomena,] nature

252.32 absolute,] absolute and

252.37 that certain given properties] of certain pr*[operties]*

253.2 now or in the future] *intl-c*

253.4 matter] physics

253.5 suppositions] hypo*[theses]*] a

253.8 an explanation] a theory

253.8 of its] *intl-c*

253.9 could] would

253.10 law.] assum*[p]*tion.

253.12 This can] We cannot

253.13 grant] are in

253.13 law of nature,] necessary law

253.16 fabricator] fabricators

253.23 He did not, however,] But he did not

253.26 true;] true.

253.26 so that,] while] But

253.27 not belonging to] not being of] be

253.31 by what sort of hypothesis we can imagine] in what manner a hypothesis

253.32 matter] q

253.32 the assumption] any assumption

*253.36–37 To inquire . . . physics] *add*

253.36 what will be the] what general] how other branches of

253.37 this] the

254.1 Now, how] How

254.6 how] *bef del* those

254.9 I am tempted to recognize for] *intl-c*

254.9–10 the title of] may be named] may be called

254.12 value] quantity

254.13 an] the

254.13 evaluation.] evaluation, and physicists hardly recognize [know] any way of estimating the strength of an argument than by its probability.

254.18 departs] is

254.19 has] wishes

254.22–23 were supposed to do] did

254.24 part] province

254.28 mechanics] dynamics

254.28–29 an application] means

254.34 complete;] complete:

254.34 the positive] other

255.3 arts.] methods.

255.4–5 do not in the least depend] are not in the least affected

255.7–8 his heart vibrates to the saying of his brother Plato that] for him, as for a Platonist,

255.8 his brother] *intl-c*
255.8–9 actuality is the roof of a dark and sordid cave] actuality is a mere cave
255.9 shuts] tends to shut] shuts
255.9 direct] *intl-c*
255.10 —the world] *intl-c*
255.11 of our day] *intl-c*
255.11 with gustful emphasis.] *intl-c*
255.16–17 argument or inference belonging to a class of inferences] *argument*
255.17 inferences] arguments
255.17 premises] *bef del* may
255.18 to true] to a true
255.18 to false conclusions] to a false conclusion
255.19 inference] argument
255.19 all] *aft del* false
255.20–21 from true premises by inferences] for arguments
255.21–22 essentially] s
255.22 the] a
255.22 *average*] *proportion*
255.23 a ratio] the ratio
255.25 chances] probabilities
255.27 *averages*] proportions.
255.27 Such *averages*] Such an *average*
255.28–29 frequencies of different kinds of actual] order of
255.29 concern] to do
255.30 actual] real
255.36 followers] readers
255.37 that] than in
256.1 least] least,
256.1 length of life] adult weight
256.2 stars] stars, if we could weight them,
256.2–3 direction and distance of proper motion,] weight,
256.4 in truth,] *intl-c*
256.7 reasoning] logic
256.9–10 A and B,] *intl-c*
256.11 the coin was tossed up,] tails was turned up,
256.12 *n*] A
256.13 loss] losing] winning
256.13 Let g] *aft del* ¶In $\frac{1}{2}$ the number of games, $n = 0$, and he wins $1 making
256.14 infinite.] infinite:
256.15 items] elements
256(c3).1 Loss of] Gain per
256(c4).1 loss] gain
256.16 the infinite series] *ins*
256.21 the play] you play
257.10–11 It is the ideal construction of "ensembles" (that is wholes or systems)] It is the ideal constructions of wholes, ensembles, or systems] It is the ◆framing of [discovery of [tracing out of]] relations involved in ◆ideal constructions [an ideal construction,]
257.11–12 and the discovery in them of relations other] of relations other] other
257.12 served for the rule of construction.] were explicitly contained in the conditions of the construction.
257.17–18 the numerous class of consecrated phrases] a consecrated phrase
257.18 having gained] have gained] first gained
257.18–19 have lost their] and then lost its
257.19 popular acknowledgment] the general respect
257.26 a large] many pro–
257.27 lines] curves] lines
257.28 elements] po*[ints]*
257.29 Through any point] *aft del* Take a point in a plane
257.29–30 unlimited straight lines,] lines (in a plane or otherwise)
257.30 Take any] Assume any
257.31 pairs of these] these
257.33 unlimited] *intl-c*
258.4 that art] every kind of art
258.5–6 *of the necessary kind*] *intl-c*
258.6 proper] *intl-c*
258.6 work.] *bef del* (Outside their province, mathematicians have rea-

soned scarcely better than others.) This reasoning also includes the whole business of mathematicians, excepting the invention [ideal construction] of their ensembles. [systems]

258.12 but he is a mere sojourner] but his] but these are his

258.13 If you tell] Be cautious about telling

258.14 world,] *bef del* as if it were a matter for him to be glad of

258.16–17 Of what consequence is reality to him?] What is it to him

258.17 reality] it

258.17 to him?] *bef del* what is real? and Gauss Plato

258.19 these] this

258.22 chief] head

258.26 life-insurance] insurance

258.30 be held] be fully held

258.33 parts] elements

258.33 schematically] *intl-c*

258.35 since it has] having

258.35 breadth] thickness

258.37 is a] is] shows a

258.37 figure] *bef del* which simply represents the connections of parts

259.1 prescription or rule] prescribed rule

259.3 prescribed] *intl-c*

259.4 prescribed] required

259.4 prominent.] *bef del* Thus, a

259.9 the dots] every point

32. *On the Analytical Representation of Space, 1889*

The copy-text has been recovered from five widely scattered manuscript and letter files in the Harvard Peirce Papers. All of the six reassembled leaves are heavy pages of 8 ¼" × 10 ½" laid white paper with horizontal chain lines and the watermark "A. Pirie & Sons | 1888." Leaf 6 also bears light blue horizontal writing guidelines at single-spaced intervals from edge to edge. All leaves show wear and staining toward the margins. Leaf 5 is severely chewed across the top margin by a small rodent; what remains of the top left margin is dark-stained. Except for one reconstructed word (262.20, "[mee]t"), the entire text of this leaf is recoverable. The manuscript is unnumbered and undated; it is inscribed and lightly revised by Peirce in black ink. His by-line, which is silently removed in the present text, appears below the title as "By C. S. Peirce." In addition to the reassembled documents, false starts of leaves 2 and 3 also survive.

The reconstructed manuscript yields an exercise in incidence geometry that describes how spatial elements (that is, the points, lines and planes of three-dimensional space and of its one-and two-dimensional subspaces) can be represented as intersections of higher-dimensional planes. There is a lacuna between leaves 4 and 5—probably a single leaf describing the geometric pattern formed by pairings of six linear equations in two-dimensional space. The two concluding leaves that survive (leaves 5 and 6) analyze three-dimensional and two-dimensional space as represented by seven linear equations.

The manuscript is closely related to letters on this subject written to Peirce's brother James Mills Peirce (RL 339, 25 January 1889) and to Simon Newcomb (RL 314, 17 January 1889); in fact, leaves 2 (RL 314) and 5 (RL 339) were filed with surviving drafts of these letters in the Peirce Papers for many years. The date of these drafts, the common paper source between the letters and the manuscript, and the watermark provide the rationale for dating the document 17–25 January 1889. Many working pages of diagrams and calculations are contained in R 260. Another document, R 966 (1889.9), is related to this work on projective geometry; it is a small notebook with 12 pages of calculations and equations that appear to date from the same period. But neither the letter drafts nor the related manuscripts contain a discussion of the equations applied to two-dimensional space, and shed no light on the content of the missing page.

Textual Notes

262.7 A′B′] Peirce adopted a shorthand form in designating this line (AB′) and the three subsequent lines (AC′, AB″, AC″). This form has been emended at all four points for clarity.

262.10 point.] The final word of the sentence has been deduced from context and emended in, but the rest of the missing page can only be recovered in general terms (see Annotations).

Emendations

Title Space] E; ~.
260.5 three] E; 3 *Also* 262.7, 262.22, 262.27,
261.11–12 von Staudt] E; VON STAUDT
261.15 4] E; four
261.16 2] E; two
261.16–17 coplanar] E; complanar
261.31 15] E; 15.
262.1 6] E; six
262.2 3] E; three *Also* 262.3, 262.15, 262.19, 262.28
*262.7 A′B′] E; AB′ *Also* 262.9
262.8 A′C′] E; AC′ *Also* 262.10
262.8 A″B″] E; AB″ *Also* 262.9
262.9 A″C″] E; AC″ *Also* 262.10
262.10 1] E; one
*262.10 point.] E; *om.*
262.12 pairs,] E; ~‸
262.20 meet] E; t

Alterations

260.1 With] To
260.4 Any 3 such equations,] *aft del* Any three such equations will determine a right line, and the three pairs which can be selected from these 3 equations will determine 3
260.4 coaxal planes] planes
260.6–7 passing in threes through] thr*[ough]*
260.7 determined] represented
260.9 and] which pass
260.15 in pairs] *intl-c*
261.1 a] any
261.9 lie] ha
261.9 line D] line E
262.2 through] from
◊262.7 the 3 lines] the lines
262.8 and of] , of
262.13 4 lines] 4 poi*[nts]*
262.15 these lines] these points
262.15 planes in] planes of
◊262.19 on three] severall*[y]*
262.28 z] v

33. *Ordinal Geometry, 1889*

Copy-text consists of 10 leaves recovered from a nest of 40 pages in R 249. The copy-text leaves are all 8 ¼" × 10 ½" medium weight sheets of laid paper with horizontal chain lines and watermarked "A. Pirie & Sons | 1888." The leaves are in good condition, although the top right corner (including the page number but excluding any text) has been torn off of the final sheet. The text is inscribed by Peirce in black ink; his date of composition, "1889 Jan 19," is also inscribed top left on all but the first leaf (most of the draft leaves are dated a day earlier, January 18). The pages are numbered top right by Peirce [1], 2–5, 6 over 5, 7–9, [10].

The disorder of the R 249 manuscript nest was only recently put right, yielding no less than four substantial drafts and three other single-page starts. The order of composition leads to a nine-page final draft lacking only an opening page. The surviving page 2 begins a new paragraph; context suggests that one of the single-page starts, a complete half-page opening, is Peirce's replacement page for the unlocated first leaf. Indeed, this half-page contains, besides the title, all the information that is necessary to understand the special vocabulary and conventions Peirce uses in page 2 and thereafter; he defines ordinal geometry, explains his notation ($a, \bar{a}, a/b$, etc.), and defines the term "qualification." It is likely that the half-page was written after the main part of the document was composed, and then attached in place of the original. Two draft leaves, numbered 4 and 5 (early forms of pages 4 and 5→6 respectively) also survive. Peirce's numbering of the draft leaf 5 and his final leaf 5→6, along with a close reading of the final leaf 5 text, indicates that the final leaves 4 and 5 represent an expanded opening of his subsection on "Plane Ordinal Geometry."

Emendations

263.3 denotes] E; denote
263.6–7 expression] E; express
263.9 $a \prec \bar{b}$] E; *rom. Also all subsequent lowercase and Greek variables*
263.13 *line*] E; ~.
264.14 *geometry*] E; ~.
264.19 2*n*] E; *rom. Also all following* n-*terms*
264.20 infinite,] E; ~‸
266.1 fourth] E; fourth first
266.5 $\frac{\bar{\beta}\alpha}{\bar{\gamma}}$.] E; ~‸
267.1 $\frac{\bar{\beta}\bar{\gamma}\delta}{\bar{\alpha}}$,] E; ~‸
267.13 it] E; its

Alterations

263.3 algebra of logic] logic*[*al algebra*]*
°263.6–7 The expression $a \prec b$ means a is included in b.] *intl-c*
263.9 at once to] t*[*o*]*
263.14 separates] di*[*vides*]*
263.15 put] pla*[*ced*]*
263.19 rules] R*[*ules*]*
263.21 a] another
264.7–8 the symbols for one] one is] once
264.16 line] line b

264.16–17 regions; and] regions. And
264.17–18 to the number of regions] new re[gions]
264.18–19 + 1, of . . . limited.] + 1.
264.20–21 of which . . . finite;] *intl*
264.29 these] the
265.1 in which the regions $\alpha\beta$, $\alpha\bar{\beta}$, $\bar{\alpha}\bar{\beta}$, $\bar{\alpha}\beta$ are] of the regions $\alpha\beta$, $\alpha\bar{\beta}$, $\bar{\alpha}\bar{\beta}$, $\bar{\alpha}\beta$ wh[ich]
265.2 it appears] it first appears
265.3 The succession] *aft del* From $\alpha\beta$, it pen[etrates]
265.8 latter] last
265.10 the rule of contraposition in logic] a rule of logic
265.10 $\gamma\alpha$] $\alpha\gamma$
265.16 every] the
265.20–21 secants bounding] bounding secants to
265.24–25 extends] is adjacent
265.25 finite] bounded
265.28 bounding lines] boundaries] boundary
265.29 next on the two] next tw[o]
265.32 $\frac{\alpha\gamma}{\beta}$ . . . $\beta\gamma\bar{\alpha}$.] $\alpha\beta{\equiv}\gamma$, $\bar{\gamma}\alpha\beta$, $\bar{\beta}\bar{\gamma}{\equiv}\alpha$, $\bar{\alpha}\bar{\beta}\bar{\gamma}$, $\gamma\bar{\alpha}{\equiv}\bar{\beta}$,
266.1 lines,] *bef del* the succession of regions round in
266.1–2 the fourth (according to our convention) first appears] the fourth first penetr[ates]
266.4 which is the triangle,] the triangle,
266.5 In the former case,] *aft del* In the first case, the 11 regions are ¶ $\frac{\alpha\gamma}{\beta}\delta$, $\frac{\alpha\gamma}{\beta}\bar{\delta}$, $\bar{\gamma}\alpha\beta\delta$, $\bar{\gamma}\alpha\beta\bar{\delta}$,
266.8 by] with
266.15 $\frac{\beta\gamma\bar{\alpha}}{\delta}$.] *bef del* ¶In the second case, the succession of regions penetrated is ¶ $\frac{\alpha\gamma}{\beta}$, $\bar{\gamma}\alpha\beta$ [*bef del* $\bar{\gamma}\bar{\alpha}\beta$] $\frac{\bar{\beta}\alpha}{\bar{\gamma}}$, $\bar{\alpha}\bar{\beta}\bar{\gamma}$.¶The unpenetrated regions are $\bar{\gamma}\bar{\alpha}\beta$, $\frac{\gamma\bar{\beta}}{\bar{\alpha}}$, and $\beta\gamma\bar{\alpha}$. These regions lie together, for we can pass from $\beta\gamma\bar{\alpha}$ to either of the others by a single requalification.
266.18 which give] and those
266.21 $\gamma\bar{\delta} \prec \alpha$] α *ov* β
267.2 3] two
267.5 $\bar{\alpha}\bar{\beta}\bar{\gamma}$] $\bar{\beta}$ *ov* γ

34. *Mathematical Monads, 1889*

Copy-text is reconstructed from part of R 536 (5 leaves) and R 278A (1 final leaf), and consists of white 8 1/4" × 10 7/16 " heavy laid paper with horizontal chain lines and the watermark "A. Pirie & Sons | 1888." The pages are glossy or coated, and bear faint blue horizontal guidelines (recto only) at single-spaced intervals. The final leaf bears the same watermark and physical characteristics as the others, but lacks the blue guidelines. Leaves are lightly worn except for the opening page, which is chipped at the lower left margin and faded from light exposure around all edges. Leaves 2–5 are also faded, but only along the bottom and lower right margins of each sheet (the final leaf does not share the same storage history and is not faded). The manuscript is unnumbered, but the opening leaf begins at upper left with the date "1889 Jan 23" in Peirce's hand; the entire document is inscribed and moderately revised by Peirce in black ink. The penciled notation "from 'The Dual Relatives'" and editorial references to early Harvard filing systems appear in black ink at the top right of the opening leaf; these markings probably date from the CP editing period. The cataloging efforts of the 1960s retained the "Dual Relatives" material within the R 536 folder, but the relationship between these items goes no further than the common paper type. Peirce's short-lived habit of dating documents written during January 1889 reveals that "Mathematical Monads" was one of a series of mathematical and scientific pieces begun at that time. Of these, it is most closely related to notes on Kempe's paper on mathematical forms, that Peirce wrote during the first two weeks of January 1889 (R 714).

Textual Notes

269.5 *operation.*] Peirce's interlined insertion doubles the punctuation of the running text at this point, and is emended to complete the author's revision.

270.12 to be true.] Copy-text for this selection ends here, which corresponds to the fourth line of the last leaf (R 278:144) of the manuscript. That leaf, however, contains ten additional lines of working notes in which Peirce tries to give algebraic expression to conditional propositions whose values are the known or the unknown. These lines are so preliminary and incomplete that they were clearly not meant to be part of the text, and they have thus been here omitted.

Emendations

268.20 order.] E; ~‸
*269.5 *operation;*] E; ~; ;
269.11 +,] E; ~‸
269.15–16 immediately] E; immediate
269.19 Those] E; ~,
269.25 conjunction.] E; ~‸
270.1 proposed:] E; ~.

Alterations

268.1 the mathematics are] mathematics is
268.3 without parts, without any] without parts & without anything
268.11 collection] con/nection/
268.14 mathematician] mathematicians
268.14 denoted] indicated] designated] dis
268.15 in logic] *intl-c*
268.17 denoted] con/nected/
268.19–20 These new monads may be termed the monads of the second order] *intl-c*
268.24–25 of the second order to be connected with two new monads] connected with two lettered monads to be connected again with two monads neither
269.1 with only one.] with none of the lettered monads.] one of the
269.2 has to] must
269.3 takes] has
269.3–4 names severally] calls
269.4–5 and collectively the *modes of operation;*] *intl-c*
269.9 statement;] statement. In order to let
269.15–16 immediately] *intl-c*
269.16 monad,] monad.
^269.16–18 and no lettered monad is immediate connected with more than one of the third order.] which is neither of the lettered monads with which is connected that monad of the second order with which the monad of the third order is connected. In this way, the class of ◆let-

tered [*intl-c*] monads [*bef del* of the] becomes ◆infinite in number. [*intl ab del* innumerable, or rather, not completely numerable, for we shall see presently that there is a distinction to be drawn here.]

269.20–21 number. ¶Now,] number. Now

269.23–24 Falsehood, and collectively] Falsehood.

269.27 through] w*[ith]*

269.32 monad] *intl-c*

270.1 ¶But] *aft del flush left* We see, at once

270.1–2 enumerate] state

270.2 one statement] statements] the truth or falsity of certain propositions] the truth of certain propositions

270.2–3 one statement implies the truth of another] statements imply the truth of othe*[r]*

270.5–6 unknown, and with assertion and denial, and questions.] unknown.

270.7 its denial.] having the same letter with a line over it to signify denial.

270.9 Each] He

270.11–12 statements which are known to be true.] questions the answer to which is known

35. *Stock's* Deductive Logic, *1889*

Copy-text is P 378, an untitled and unsigned review published on 15 August 1889 in the *Nation* and reprinted from the same standing type in the *New York Evening Post* the following day. There is no by-line in the index of either paper, or in Haskell's *Index to* The Nation, and no manuscript evidence for attribution survives; Max H. Fisch attributed the review to Peirce on the basis of an internal reference to O. H. Mitchell's paper in *Studies in Logic,* which Peirce edited (Fisch, "First Supplement to Burks," p. 483). The tone and style of the review as well as the points it addresses are also so typical of Peirce that his authorship is not in doubt. The standard UMI microfilm was collated against a letterpress copy (Indiana Univ.) with no internal variation noted.

Emendations

272.18 thoroughgoing] E; thorough-going

274.1 *Studies in Logic,*] E; 'Studies in Logic,'

Line-End Hyphenation

271.25 schoolmen

272.34 Citizen-students

274.22 daylight

36. *Report on Gravity, 1889*

Copy-text is R1096a (NARG 23/22), a complete composite typescript of 140 leaves of heavy, laid and unlined white paper (watermarked "Montauk Mills") measuring 9½" × 14¹⁵⁄₁₆" and numbered [1]–8, 8½, 9–75, [75½], 76–120, [120½], 121–137. Three leaves (35, [75½], [120½]) are cut short in length; all leaves are foxed and brittle, and numbered with paste-down arabic numerals; exceptions are 8 ½, which is paginated in ink, and the unnumbered leaves following 75 and 120. Peirce composed the report on his Hammond Model 1, using a variety of roman and italic type shuttles. Eighty pages are blue manifold carbons, 48 are black manifold carbons inserted (along with 12 sheets of blue and black carbon fragments cut and pasted together) in the process of revising and expanding the report for possible publication by the Coast and Geodetic Survey. Peirce's further revisions appear throughout in pencil, black ink, or blue carbon pressed through from the original typed page hand corrections. Six leaves have false typing starts on the versos; most of the blue carbon leaves are numbered by Peirce in red and blue on the versos, indicating that they were once part of a large body of working papers on the gravity report numbered inversely from 1 to 2038 in each color (red 1 is blue 2038). Although the report was never published, this composite typescript remains in Record Group 23 in the National Archives. It has been given a Robin catalog number (R 1096a) to indicate its close relationship to R 1096, discarded sheets of the original typescript which remain in the Harvard collection.

The "Report on Gravity" represents the only portion of Peirce's North American gravity report to approach a state of completion. The larger project originally included the 43rd parallel determinations through Ann Arbor, Madison and Cornell (Ithaca) as well as Peirce's earlier gravity determinations along a vast meridional arc from Montreal to Key West.[1] As he worked to complete determinations for the 43rd parallel stations and the base or calibration station in the Smithsonian Institution, Peirce developed a "results first" format that ran against the accepted scientific reporting practices of his day. Peirce finally submitted this portion of his magnum opus in November 1889, but it went unpublished and was lost in the Survey archives for decades.[2]

The document that Peirce turned over to Mendenhall in November 1889 was a 140-page conflation of new and old typescript carbons. It evolved from three earlier bodies of work: reductions of the raw data from the gravity measurement sites; a handwritten draft of the report narrative and tables; and a typescript prepared directly from the draft. In January 1888, Peirce was pressured into turning over his report materials to the Coast Survey for review, which at that time included the reductions and at least part of the handwritten draft. In January 1889, lame-duck Superintendent Thorn demanded another submission for review before he himself departed with the

1. Peirce's original 18-section report outline survives in a 29 September 1887 letter to Survey Superintendent Thorn. Discarded fragments of Peirce's first typescript (R 1096) show that the report grew to 26 numbered sections; the final submitted typescript (R 1096a) consists of 23 unnumbered sections. Correspondence indicates that Peirce twice attempted the complete North American Report before submitting the partial report in November 1889.

2. A full discussion of the circumstances surrounding the survey's refusal to publish the report as submitted is found in the volume Introduction.

rest of the Cleveland administration's appointees. Peirce sent in the data reductions, the handwritten draft, and a blue carbon of the first typescript draft. The package was massive and, perhaps intentionally, difficult to break down into its component parts. Each leaf was coded on the verso with a series of blue (ascending) and red (descending) numbers running from 1 to 2038. Peirce eventually supplied a Rosetta Stone of sorts—a document which identified each leaf by subject and sequence in the blue series.[1]

During 1889, corrections to the atmospheric data led Peirce to rework much of the report; his final submission of November 1889 consisted of 48 newly-typed sheets interleaved with 80 of the old blue carbon sheets and 12 cut-and-paste sheets combining pieces of both the old and new typescripts (R 1096a). The handwritten draft, which a 5 February 1889 Coast Survey memo identifies as leaves 1776 through 1911 of the second submission, has not survived. Most of the first typescript (leaves 1912 to 2038 of the second submission) was used to construct the final conflated text, or was destroyed. A total of 18 unincorporated leaves from the first typescript survive in the Harvard Peirce Papers as R 1096.

Copy-text for the "Lost Report" is the final submitted conflation of the first and second typescripts, which includes Peirce's handwritten corrections and revisions throughout. The unincorporated leaves of the first typescript include a version of the opening narrative that is very close to the final form, but Peirce's decision not to incorporate these leaves into the conflated final report relegates the unincorporated leaves of the first typescript to pre-copy-text status.

R 1095, a massive pocket of disordered calculations, includes many of the early reduction sheets from the field sites; several hundreds are from the early layers of the 2038-page initial submission. A few lines of draft narrative text survive on some of these manuscript pages, but all are isolated fragments. R 1087 contains an early manuscript version of the first three paragraphs of the report's final section, "On the Absolute Value of Gravity." This fragment appears to be the direct source of the typescript text, but it is an amanuensis draft; punctuation and spelling suggest that the fragment may have been taken from dictation. Since Peirce exercised an equal or greater degree of authorial control over his own typescript, the R 1095 and R 1087 narrative fragments are relegated to pre-copy-text status.

The great difficulties Peirce encountered in reducing his data were magnified by constant pressure to publish from successive Survey superintendents. The submitted report was by no means a finished document, and this is especially evident in the state of the data tables which form the

1. National Archives Record Group 23, Entry 22 includes Peirce's 1 February 1889 cover letter for 20 loose quarto books of working papers for the gravity report, his 2 February index of the blue verso number sequence arranged by gravity station and by the stages of calculations, and a 5 February internal memo identifying the two report drafts within the blue sequence.

greater part of R 1096a. Most of these tables were pulled forward from the earlier typescript (R 1096) which Peirce had submitted as working papers nearly a year earlier. The table numbers were revised two, three, and even four times as Peirce cut up the original tables to construct more comprehensive layouts. Not surprisingly, the row and column headings are abbreviated and, judging by the great inconsistency in abbreviations and punctuation, clearly provisional. These draft titles and headings are only partially carried through for tables in a series, indicating that Peirce expected editors at the Survey or the GPO to lay out his technical data in the usual way, as prelude to his own galley corrections.

But, unlike the Greely Report (selection 30), the "Lost Report" was never typeset. Given this situation, Peirce's tentative templates for table titles and headings have been emended to conform with Peirce's layout and compositional intentions as they can best be determined from the typescript and from his published gravity reports. Emendations to these templates, which include hundreds of spelling and punctuation regularizations, are not recorded in the volume; however, the entire record of editorial intervention in these templates are documented in the transcription prepared for this edition and are on file in the project archives.

Besides the unfinished table headings, the typescript copy-text also contains hundreds of font inconsistencies involving mathematical variables. In many cases, Peirce left the italicization of variables unresolved as he moved between typed passages and handwritten insertions of formulae too complex for his Hammond machines to reproduce. In other cases, he used an italic type shuttle to express variables, but then failed to switch back to one of his roman font shuttles until several more equation characters or words of text had been typed in italics. The present edition emends to correct these slips of the typist, and consistently emends to italics for lowercase variables; capitalized constants are emended to roman where Peirce has occasionally italicized them. But this class of emendation runs into the hundreds, and since the cause of variation is mechanical rather than a matter of authorial intention, these occurences are silently emended. The physical positioning of table text is likewise silently modified to eliminate the inconsistent and confusing layout patterns found in the typescript forms.

The present text omits long runs of data that do not contribute to an understanding of Peirce's methodology. The important numbers reduced from these data runs are repeated in the tables which remain. These omissions are identified at the point of omission in the text, and are described in the Textual Notes. Multiplication signs inserted within long equations at 308.xx, xx indicate continuity across line breaks introduced in the present edition. Since they serve the same extra-textual function as a hyphen, these signs are not recorded as emendations.

Textual Notes

275.1–18 Title . . . and] The first page of the report has doubled as the inner wrapper for more than a century, and the type is barely readable. A typed transcription has been pasted to the first page, but it contains errors and is not authorial. The opening passage in the present edition is based on the original.

276.23 foot] Here and throughout the report, Peirce changed "feet" to "foot" in ink for measurements of elevation. The usage is unusual, but may be an attempt to distinguish distances (which Peirce keys in "feet") from elevations (all but two of which are in "foot").

277.3 $5^{h}34^{m}56^{s}.7$] The correct longitude reading is recovered from the pre-copy-text 1096 fragment.

277.32 POSITIONS] Here and at 286(c1).1, old table numbers were carried over from the R 1096 typescript to the opening pages of the final submitted typescript (R 1096a). A revised run of tables numbered I to CXII begins in R 1096a at 289(c1).1. The sequence numbers carried over in the two earlier tables (numbered VIII and IX respectively) represent a superseded intention, and are therefore omitted from the present edition. These emendations are in line with Peirce's intention for the final numbering sequence, and also reflect Peirce's occasional practice of not numbering short runs of tabular information.

279.3–4 descent of arc of the] The pre-copy-text reading was likely misread in typing the copy-text; it is restored by emendation.

279.23 oil in it is in] The copy-text reading is probably a corruption of the pre-copy-text source; the original reading is restored by emendation.

281.26 incidental] Peirce's ink revision ("incidental" over "accidental") in the pre-copy-text was misread by the typist as [*sic*] "acidental."

285.17 6613 grammes,] The opening portion of the pre-copy-text fragment ends at this point close to the bottom of R 1096:10 (Peirce's page 9), but the text does not run to the end of the line. Other non-sequential leaves remain among the R 1096 discards; other portions of the first typescript are tipped or pasted into the R 1096a typescript of the complete report. A full discussion of the textual history appears in the selection headnote.

285.29 M] Peirce inserted a capital "M" just above and between the second and third digit of 10127, as though it was a unit of measurement. Since the actual unit is the gram and Peirce never gives the letter "g" such a position, "M" is interpreted as expressing the Mass (as in 1096a:18) and is moved to the column's header position.

286.4 Plate 1] Plates 1 and 2 (286.16–17) are not included in the composite report at the National Archives (R 1096a), but the pre-copy-text Harvard fragment (R 1096) includes photographic prints of both stands. These prints are inserted as Plates 1 and 2 in the present edition, and are annotated according to Peirce's description.

292n.1–2 by an exact . . . squares.] What follows this sentence in this footnote was written by Peirce on a sheet he tipped into the typescript between p. 8 and p. 9 and numbered 8½. He wrote "See p 8½" after the end of the first sentence at the bottom of p. 8, and the editors have taken this as an indication to incorporate p. 8½ into the footnote. Peirce's "See p 8½" has been emended out once this was done.

296(c6).1 0.0434M h/l^2] This untitled column of Table VIII gives the values for "the factor peculiar to the pendulum and its position" expressed at 296.15 as 0.0434M h/l^2. It is possible that Peirce has the pairs of values for each pendulum (that is, heavy end down and heavy end up) reversed in this column; if so, the values should be stacked to read 0.339, 0.114, 0.347, 0.115, 0.355, 0.119, 0.347, 0.116. Such a transposition would explain the serious discrepancies which Peirce speaks of at 297.4–8.

310.22 *[formula]*] Peirce wrote $-c$ in the formula, but the mathematical context requires $-2c$ instead; the missing factor has thus been emended in.

313.17 *[formula]*] Peirce wrote +1 under the square root at the end of the formula, but the mathematical context requires –1; the minus sign has thus been emended in.

316.9 of Φ for] Peirce failed to insert a variable by hand at this point in the typescript. Context indicates that the variable should be Φ.

322(c7).2 No. 1] Peirce has typed "No. 2" in the row heading, but the progression of constants reveals this to be a typographical error.

339(c2).5 Duration] Tables for the earlier Smithsonian swingings of 1884 use the term "Interval" instead of "Duration" as the heading for rows that list the total time of oscillation for each swinging.

346.5 régulateur Villarceau] Peirce uses the French equivalent of "Villarceau regulator,"

347.8 Table CIX] Table CIX is a long, annotated record of the times of each set of transits at the Madison station. The times for the initial swinging of Pendulum 2 at Madison (12 October 1885) and Peirce's annotations for that date are included as a sample of these readings.

348.26 1/7] The fraction of a millimeter difference between the yard pendulum's value and the value of the equatorial seconds pendulum as determined by Peirce at Hoboken and Kew was left as a blank in the report typescript. But the decimal difference is 0.1558 mm, or the difference between the Kew and Hoboken average (990.95 mm) and the value yielded by Pendulum 3 (991.1058 mm). A pre-copy-text narrative fragment (R 1087) gives the fraction as 1/7, which is the closest unit fraction to 0.1556; this value has been emended into the present edition as the fraction Peirce would most likely have penned into the typescript had he remembered to do so.

348.28 deductions] The pre-copy-text amanuensis fragment in R 1087 reads "reduction"; context confirms that the R 1096a typescript's "deductions" is a corruption.

349 Table CXI] "On the Absolute Value of Gravity" may have been intended as the closing section of the never completed North American gravity report. Most of it was apparently pulled forward from the earlier R 1096 typescript to become the conclusion of the partial report as submitted in 1889 (R 1096a) without integrating the section's table numbers with the report proper. The first two tables were cut out of their original pages, and any table numbers which they may have been given in 1096 were not included in the cuts. The remaining tables are either unnumbered or carry superseded numbers. The present edition has provided table numbers (CX–CXIV) that continue the numbering system of the main body of the submitted report, and recorded these impositions in the Emendations list.

352.1 Table CXIII] Peirce concludes the report with an unnumbered table of pendulum lengths as measured each day for the meter pendulums (1, 2, and 4) and the yard pendulum (3). This table is a conflation of smaller tables extracted from the earlier R 1096 typescript; two of these tables still carry the original table numbers (CXXIII and CXXXIII). These superseded internal numbers have been emended out. The present edition prints only the first day's measurements for each pendulum, and gives this abridged table what would be the next number in the report sequence (CXIII). Peirce sequences the pendulums by type in this table, with the meter pendulums (1, 2, and 4) preceding the yard pendulum (3). This sequence is consistent with Peirce's general practice of presentation, and is retained here.

352(c38).3 Oct. 15 2.526 . . . –0.9] The final surviving page of the report is a badly torn leaf pulled forward from the R 1096 typescript fragment. It is a continuation of the daily length measurements of Pendulum 4 found in Table CXIII, but follows an unnumbered table of length calibrations for Pendulum 3. The Pendulum 4 measurements from this page are transposed ahead of the calibration table and into Table CXIII, but since this table has been abridged in the present edition to show only the first day's measurement for each pendulum, the continuation entries for Pendulum 4 are omitted.

353 Table CXIV] Table CXIII is followed by an unnumbered table comparing the yard pendulum (number 3) with one of Yard Standards at different hours on each of three days. The editors have included only the initial comparison, and have given this abridged table what would be the next number in the report sequence (CXIV).

353 Table CXV] One small 3" × 5" card buried in the unsorted R 1095 folders appears to contain the missing final table of the report. The verso bears blue (1080) and red (959) pagination that places it in the midst of Peirce's 2038-page run of working papers. It is emended into the copy-text under Peirce's final line of text, an uncancelled title line for "Calculation of the Number of Millimeters in an Inch." Since it is a short run of data, no table number is imposed.

353 Table CXV] The pre-copy-text typescript fragment (R 1096) includes references to three sections originally following "On the Absolute Value of Gravity," which closes the final report typescript (R 1096a). Only one of these sections ("§25 Assistants Employed in This Work") was carried forward to the final conflated typescript. The uncancelled heading for a missing chart, "§24 Calculation of the Number of mm/inch," was pulled forward on a sheet of R 1096 that became the last page of the submitted report; the data for this chart has been restored from a worksheet in the mass of gravity papers known as R 1095. But a final section of the earlier draft report, "§26 Rules for the Use of These Pendulums," remains in the R 1096 fragment. Peirce held this out of the report as submitted, but may have intended to include this section as an appendix to the complete version of the North American Gravity Report. The Rules (missing an unlocated final leaf) appear in the Annotations to the present volume; see also the note for the instructions for swinging Pendulum 1 transmitted to the astronomer of the Greely Arctic expedition of 1881–84 (selection 30).

Emendations

275.1 THESE . . . STATIONS:] E; THESE DETERMINATIONS WERE MADE AT THE FOLLOWING STATIONS:

275.10 statute] E; statue

275.18 Old Stand] E; old stand *Also* 276.22, 276.23, 276.38, 277.12, 277.21, 286.4

275.18 Stand."] E; ~".

275.21 University] E; Universtiy

276.22 42°27.′0.] E; 42°27.′0‸

276.23 New Stand] E; new stand *Also* 276.38, 277.12, 277.22, 286.16. 294.13–14, 299.3, 299.5

276.31 régulateur] E; regulateur *Also* 346.5

276.34 done.] ~‸

277.2 Schaeberle] Schaebele *Also* 277.7–8, 342.18
*277.3 $5^h34^m56^s.7$] E; $5^h34^{mm}6^s.7$
277.4 foot] E; feet *Also* 277.5
277.17–18 Milwaukee] E; Milwaukie
277.24 absolutely] E; absolutly
277.29 Updegraff] E; Updegraf *Also* 342.23
277.28 Professor] E; Professos
278.1 GENERAL DESCRIPTIONS OF THE INSTRUMENTS] E; *ital., ending with a period. Also section heading at* 286.1
278.20 pendulum] E; *om.*
278.21 formula] E; ~.
278.21 *[formula]*] E;

$$T^2 = \frac{T^2 h_d - T^2 h_u}{h_d - h_u}$$

278.25 will] E; well
*279.4 arc of] E; *om.*
279.13 interval.] E; ~,
*279.23 in it] E; *om.*
280.4 Allegheny] E; Alleghany
280.8 measuring] E; measureing
280.14 beforehand] E; before-hand
280.29 detected.] E; ~,
280.35 approximately,] E; ~‸
281.2 1st,] E; ~.
281.4 2nd,] E; ~.
281.4 3rd,] E; 3rd. .
281.5–6 remeasurement] E; remeasurements
281.7 place;] E; ~:
281.19 been] E; *om.*
*281.26 incidental] E; acidental
281.32 alterations] E; alter.-|tions
282.1 up] E; ~,
284.4 making] E; *ital.*
284.37 abandoned] E; abondoned
285.1 Lieutenant] E; Lieut.
285.2–3 respectively] E; respectfully
285.8 endeavored] E; endeavered
285.26 grammes.] E; ~. .
285.27 loads,] E; ~.
285.28 be:] E; ~.
286.4 Plate 1.] E; Plate I.
286.6 feet long,] E; feet,
286.9 cleats] E; cleets
286.9 D, D] E; DD
286.9 are drawn] E; drawn
286.13 F.] E; F,
286.15 H, H] E; H H
286.17 The] E; the
286.21 ASSISTANTS EMPLOYED IN THIS WORK] E; *rom., with ending period. Also section heading at* 345.1
286.28 consummate] E; consumate
289.1 ACCORDING TO THE OBSERVATIONS] E; ACCORDING TO THE OBSERVATIONS.
289.14 seconds."] E; ~,"
289.16–17 THE MODE USED IN THE PAPER FOR EXPRESSING THE RELATIVE GRAVITY AT THE SEVERAL STATIONS] E; *all small caps with the first word uppercased, ending with a period. Also section headings at* 290.18–19, 291.7, 295.18, 341.3
289.23 day,] E; ~.
289.30 86859,] E; ~‸
290.5–6 sea-level] E; sealevel *Also* 291.9, 291.18
290.7 number";] E; ~;"
290.11 equator.] E; ~‸
290.20 "On the Variation of Gravity, 1849"] E; [On the variation of gravity, 1849.]
290.22 *[formula]*,] E; ~‸
290.23 where] E; Where
290.26 *[formula]*.] E; ~‸
290.29 Since] E; ~,
290.30 development] E; developement
291.2 RΔN.] E; R.ΔN.
291.3 20,900,000] E; 20900000
291.4 ΔN.] E; ΔN‸
291.23–24 *Coast . . . 1881*,] E; *rom.*
291.24 15;] E; ~.;
291.25 data, those] E; ~‸ ~
291.25 Colonel Herschel,] E; Col Herschel‸
292.1 *a posteriori*] E; *rom.*
292.4 DIFFERENT APPARATUS] E; DIFFERENT APPARATUS.

292.5 least] E; ~.
292(c7).9 +0.38] E; +0 = 38
292.14 numbers."] ~,"
292n.2 squares.] E; ~‸ See p. 8 ½.
292n.5 No. 2] E; No‸ 2 *Also* 294.2, 300.14
292n.6 No. 3] E; No‸ *Also* 294.6, 300.15, 348.27, 350.15
292n.7 Sea-level] E; Sea‸level
293.4 THE . . . CORRECTION] E; ~ . . . ~. *Also ending periods in section headings at* 301.6, 310.1, 326.2, 343.6, 348.1
294.2 pendulum] E; Pendulum
294.2–3 coefficient] E; coefficieut
294.5–6 (For . . . 1.25.)] E; [~ . . . ~‸] *Brackets replaced by parentheses also at* 295.1, 295.2, 295.3(1,2), 295.8, 296.4–5, 298.6, 299.1, 300.9, 300.20, 304.33–34, 322.19–20, 341.11–12
294.7 very] E; not very
294.7 except] E; ~ in
294.9 meantime] E; mean time
294.24 *A Priori* CORRECTIONS] E; A PRIORI CORRECTIONS.
295.26–296.1 knife-edge] E; ~‸~
296.4–5 *C. S. Report,*] E; *rom.*
*296(c6).1 0.0434M h/l^2] E; *om.*
296(c7).1 $n\,\Delta$T/S] E; n T S
297.2 perpendicular] E; perpeudicular
297.3 weight,] E; ~‸
297.30 $-0^{\sigma}\!.52$] E; –0. .052
298.2 record] E; recosd
298.7 34] 34."
298.21 pulley] E; pully
298.36 1885 Oct.] E; Oct. 1885 Oct.
299.3 Dec.] E; ~‸
299.5 Jan.] E; ~‸
299.12 Nos.] E; ~‸
300.2 For] E; ~,
300.9 $(1 + k\Delta\tau)$] E; ~.
300.12 No. 4] E; No‸ 4 *Also* 300.15, 348.23
300.13 No. 1] E; No‸ 1 *Also* 350.16
300.14 pendulum] E; Pend.
300.16 No.] E; NO‸
300.18 Metre] E; Meter *Also* 300.19
300.20 "Measurements . . . Stations,"] E; ‸Mearurements . . . ~,‸
300.28 μ] E; *om.*
301.1–2 see the closing discussion on . . . pendulums.] E; see On . . . pendulums.
301.4 table.] E; ~‸
302.9 mercury] E; Mercury
302.12 ¶The first] E; ‸~ ~
302.16 *a priori*] E; *apriori*
302.17 ¶The second] E; ‸~ ~
302.19 "Measurements of Gravity at Initial Stations."] E; ‸*Determinations of Gravity at Initial Stations.*‸
302.19 *a priori*] E; *à priori*
303.2–3 Expansion] E; *Expansion.*
303.3 pressures:] E; ~: -
303.5 exhibits] E; exibits
303.6–7 follows:] E; ~‸
304.14 pendulum;] E; ~.
304.15 3.14159.] E; ~‸
304.17 sidereal] E; siderial *Also* 347.10
304.19 etc.] E; ~‸
305.1 index,] E; ~;
305.2 0,] E; ~;
305.3 d,] E; ~;
305.4 u,] E; ~;
305(c6).11 3.9851] E; 3.9951
305(c6).13 3.0881] E; 3.0891
305(c6).13 1146] E; 1225
306(c6).6 4900] E; 5776
306(c6).11 196×10^3] E; 196 × 10 *Third power also inserted at* 307(c6).5(2), 6(2), 21(2), 22(2), 23(2)
306(c6).12 $2\mathrm{J}_0^{\mathrm{vi}}$] E; $2\mathrm{J}_0^6$
306(c6).12 7411×10^3] E; 7411 10
306(c6).22 $\mathrm{T}_u^2/\mathrm{T}_d^2$]E; $\mathrm{T}_u^2/\mathrm{T}_d$
306(c6).23 $(\mathrm{T}_u^2/\mathrm{T}_d^2 - 1)$] E; $(\mathrm{T}_u/\mathrm{T}_d - 1)$
307(c6).1 $\mathrm{T}_u^2/\mathrm{T}_d^2$] E; $\mathrm{T}_u/\mathrm{T}_d$

307(c6).10 J_0''] E; J''
307(c6).13 $(h_d'')^2$] E; h_d''
307(c6).14 $(\gamma'')^2 + (h_d'')^2$] E; $(\gamma'') + (h_d$
307(c6).16 $(h_u'')^2$E; $h\,{}^{2}_{u}$
307(c6).17 $(\gamma_u'')^2 = (\gamma'')^2 + (h_u'')^2$] E; $(\gamma_u^2) = (\gamma'')^2 + h$
307(c6).23 J_u''']E; J'''
308(c6).1 $2\ddot{M}$] E; ${}^2\ddot{M}$
308(c6).4(1,2) 0.0688] E; 0.688
308(c6).19 $M\gamma_u^2$]E; $M\gamma^2$
308(c6).23 =] E; –
308(c6).21 .0008162] E; .000[162
308(c6).11 1.3617] E; 1.3717
309(t1,c2).4 $\nu T_d \partial^{-1}$] E; $\nu T_d 6^{-1}$ *Also* 309(t1,c2).5, 309(t1,c2).7
309(t1,c2).6 $2\sqrt{2}$] E; 2v2 *Also* 309(t1,c2).7
309(t2,c2).3 96.1250] E; 95.1250
*310.22 $-2c\Phi^2$.] E; $-c\Phi^2$‸
310.26 0,] E; ~‸
310.29 D_n]E; Dn
312.9 equals] E; equalls
312.20 *[formula]*.] E; ~‸
312.21 *[formula]*.] E; ~‸
313.9 *[formula]*.] E; ~‸
*313.17 $\sqrt{4\frac{ac}{b^2} - 1}$] E; $\sqrt{4\frac{ac}{b^2} + 1}$
313.19 *[formula]*.] E; ~‸
314.4 double amplitude] E; ~-~
314.19 observation,] E; ~‸
316.6 in] E; iu
316.7 *[formula]*.] E; ~‸
*316.9 of Φ for] E; of for
316.10 smoothed] E; smootheed
316(c1).3 500] E; 300
316(c1).11 13000] E; 3000
316(c1).12 14000] E; 4000
316.13 great] E; mreat
317.9 0.00000943,] E; ~.
317.12 0.00005,] E; ~‸
318(t1,c4).1 $\log(\Phi + P)$] E; $\log\Phi + P$ *Also* 318(t3,c4).1
318(t2,c4).1 $\log(\Phi + P)$] E; $\log\Phi - P$
318(t2,c12).1 5.3732] E; 5.53732
318.2 $q = 0.000051$] E; $q - 0.000051$
318(t3,c9).4 9.8953555] E; 9.9853555
318.3 0.4975,] E; ~‸
318.4 0.00005,] E; ~‸
318.4 following] E; fsdlowing
319.2 for,] E; ~‸
319.3 this,] E; ~‸
320.4 work] E; word
320.13 (9)=] E; (9)–
321.10 divisible] E; divisable
321.16 table:] E; tables:
321(c3).3 –200] E; 200
321(c6).1 *O.–C.*] E; *O. C.*
322.3 ¶For] E; ‸~
322.4 is,] E; ~‸
322.8 seconds] E; second's
322.12 log] E; ~.
322.13 down,] E; ~‸
322.15 weight).] E; ~‸.
322(c3).1 log 1/P] E; log A
322.19–20 "Measurements . . . Stations,"] E; ‸Measures . . . ~.‸
322.27 $\sqrt{p}$] E; *vp* *Also* 323.6
322.27 than] E; that
323.6 clearly] E; ~,
323.8 That is,] E; ~ ~‸
323.8 inches] E; in
324(t1,c3,4).9 0.63 $+0\frac{1}{2}$] E; 0.63 $+0\frac{1}{2}+0$.
324(t2,c11).4 5.04] E; 5.004
327.3 temperature] E; tepperature
327.4 corrections] E; correction
329(c4).16 –3355.90] E; 3355.90
329(c4).18 89993.38] E; 87993.37
331(c11).10 30.092] E; 30.92
331(c11).12 $\log T^2$] E; $\log T$
331(c12).16 +2.98] E; +.98
332(c12).17 –0.66] E; –0.06
333(c11).3 17.98] E; 17‸98
333(c12).18 86103.70] E; *om.*
333(c15).16 –2.41] E; +2.41

333(c15).17 –0.10] E; +0.10
334(c15).11 –3386.25] E; –3388.25
335(c7).11 531.56] E; 531.66
335(c7).12 294.08] E; 294.8
335(c7).19 86112.79] E; 86112.89
335(c14).17 86105.59] E; *om.*
335(c15).3 +.020] E; +‸020
335(c15).4 –.027] E; –‸027
335(c15).5 +.005] E; +‸005
335(c15).6 +.009] E; +‸009
335(c15).7 –.017] E; –‸017
335(c15).8 ±.005] E; ±‸005
336(c8).15 –3608.48] E; –3608.15
336(c8).22 90015.63] E; 90015.71
336(c15).13 +1.54] E; –1.54
336(c15).14 +3.10] E; –3.10
337(c6).7 –.079] E; –‸079
337(c6).8 +.089] E; +‸089
337(c6).9 +.032] E; +‸032
337(c6).10 +.044] E; +‸044
337(c6).11 +.072] E; +‸072
337(c6).12 +.002] E; +‸002
337(c6).13 –.016] E; –‸016
337(c7).7 –6.23] E; ~ , ,
337(c8).5 15089.120] E; .120
337(c8).6 15089.086] E; .086
337(c8).7 15089.109] E; .109
337(c8–9).2 514.20] E; 514.20 -.
338(c5).14 –3366.67] E; 3366.67
338(c5).15 –3604.15] E; 3604.15
338(c6).5 +.075] E; +075
338(c8).11 –3380.91] E; 3380.91
338(c8).12 –3618.39] E; 3618.39
338(c9).4 +.080] E; +‸080
338(c9).6 +.116] E; +‸116
338(c9).7 +.066] E; +‸066
338(c9).8 –.238] E; –‸238
338(c9).9 –.005] E; –‸005
338(c13).1 –.011] E; –‸011
338(c13).2 –.016] E; –‸016
338(c13).3 –.013] E; –‸013
338(c13).4 +.025] E; +‸025
338(c13).5 +.016] E; +‸016
339.1 CORRECTED TIMES FOR TEMPERATURE, PRESSURE, AND INCLINATION] E; *om.*
339(c12).14 4 11 34.093] E; 4 11 34.93
340.1 INCLINATION] E; INCLINATION.
340.3 horizon] E; horizen
340.7(2) of the] E; of tae
340(c9).1 14] E; 15
340(c16).1 15] E; 16
340(c23).1 16] E; 17
341(c2).1 18] E; 19
341(c9).1 19] E; 20
341(c23).1 22] E; 23
341.16 pendulum] E; pendulums
341.17 CORRECTION FOR RATE] E; COHRECTION ~ ~.
342.10 anything] E; any thing
342.15 Tiede] E; Thiede
342.17 work] E; wirk
342.17 uniformity] uniformitn
342.24 observatory] E; obsrvatory
342.29 physical] E; Physical *Also* 346.32
342.29 University] E; university *Also* 346.32
342.37 introduced] E; intrhoduced
343.3 station] E; statiin
343.3 exhibited] E; exhibitad
343.7 counted,] E; ~;
344.8 case] E; ~,
344.10 compel] E; ~,
344.17 CORRECTION FOR ARC] E; ~ ~ ARC.
344.19 case] E; casa
344.20 Moreover,] E; ~‸
344.22 above] E; ~,
344.26 integrating] E; integrading
344.27 "Measurements of Gravity at Initial Stations"] E; determinations of gravity at initial stations
345.2 ¶Each] E; ‸~
345(c3).22 R to L] E; RLL
345.8 ¶A much] E; ‸~ ~
*346.5 Villarceau] E; Villarcean
346.10 affect] E; effect
347.5 think,] E; ~‸
347.12 1589,] E; ~‸
347.13 of its] E; of i'ts

347.15 transits.] E; ~‸
347.15 P] E; P.
347.18 P.'s] E; P's *Also* 347.21, 24
347.19 record.] E; ~‸
347.20 unnecessary] E; unnecesary
347.21 Oct. 12] E; Oct. 121
347.22 intention] E; ~,
347.24 change would] E; change one is would
348.2 of] E; op
348.4 earth] E; ~;
348.5 (these] E; ‸tetese
348.5 errors] E; errohs
348.6 Herschel),] E; ~‸‸
348.8–9 *Höhere Geodäsie*] E; Hohere Geodasie
348.9 owing] E; ouing
348.10 Paris,] E; ~.
348.11 Memoir;] E; ~:
348.13 Paris] E; ~;
348.15 case,] E; ~‸
348.17 as] E; ar
348.17 although] E; alttough
348.17 really] E; rally
348.18 than] E; thah
348.18 nevertheless] E; never-the-less
348.19 them,] E; ~.
348.19(1) the] E; The
348.21 1885] E; 1885.
348.22 2] E; 2,
348.24 surprising] E; suprizing
348.25 however] E; howewer
*348.26 1/7] E; *om.*
348.29 appearance] E; apaearance
348.29–30 demonstrably] E; deponstrably
348.31 one] E; over
348.32 calculations] E; cacculations
348.32 and] E; ~,
349.1 Table CX] E; *om.*
349.2 Table CXI] E; *om.*
349(t2,c8).6 –30.88] E; 30.88
349(t2,c9).2 86099.88] E; 86099 88
350.4 way,] E; ~;
350.11 apparatus] E; ~.
350.16 No. 1] E; No‸ 1.
350.33 Normal Metre] E; normal metre
350.34 *Coast . . . 1875*] E; *rom.*
350.35 *1881*] E; *rom.*
350.35 distances] E; distance
351(c3).1 +254″.3] E; +254.3
352(c10).1 9] E; *om.*
352(c11).1 10] E; *om.*
352(c12).1 11] E; *om.*
352(c13).1 12] E; *om.*
352(c14).1 13] E; *om.*
352(c25).1 (2)–(3)] E; 2–3
352(c40).2 –0.361] E; –0:361
353 *[Table CXV]*] E; §24. Calculation of the Number of Millimeters in an inch.

Alterations

276.23 foot] feet
276.36 in that state.] Michigan.
277.6 foot] feet
277.17 foot] feet
277.18 foot] feet
277.19 foot] feet
278.1 General] *aft del* §7.
278.1 Instruments] Pendulums
278.2 with which these determinations were made] to which this report relates
278.28 corrections for pressure and temperature] correction for pressure, and temperature,
278.31 of the air] *intl-c*
279.17 per diem] a day
279.27–28 unimportant] important
281.18 well-founded] well-\founded
282.14 in the mean time,] mean time
282.36–37 anticipations, but] anticipation though the numerical result is very close to that of other recent determinations. But
284.30 Repsolds,] Repsold,
286.1 Description] *aft del* § 8
286.21 Assistants] *aft del* §25.
289.9 199] 239
289.10 23] 020

289.11 86] 90
290.15 86401.90] 86400.76
290.15–17 I also term...or not.] *add by hand*
291.24 now] *intl-c*
291.25 those of Col Herschel] *intl-c*
292.5 numbers] *bef del* given above
292.6 two empirical temperature corrections] an empirical temperature correction,
292(c6).7 –0.27] –0.33
292(c7).7 +0.27] +0.33
292n.1–2 But the numbers. . . squares.] *footnote added by hand*
292n.1 were] are
292.13 The same calculation] *aft del* ¶In the calculation by least squares, the results with heavy end up were allowed ⅔ the weight of those with heavy end down; but since the ratios of periods in the two positions are in pretty good agreement, the precise value of the relative weight is a matter of little moment.
293.5–6 corrections determined along with the above numbers are] correction which was determined by least squares is
294.2 For Pendulum No 2, it] It
294.6–7 For pendulum No 3, it is 0.10 per degree. In neither case is its effect, therefore,] Its effect is, therefore,
*294.7 for] in the case of
295.20 flexure of the] *intl-c*
296.16 include] conclude
297 *[Table X]] all numbers in Table X corrected by hand:* –0.07] +0.35; +0.32] 0.16; –0.26] +0.17; +0.41] 1.38; –0.70] –2.51; *blank space under* –0.26] –1.06; +0.29] –1.16; +0.00] –0.87; *blank space above* +0.47] –0.95; –0.27] –0.18; –0.20] –0.62; +0.47] –0.54
297.31 –1.34] –0.87
299(c19).2 +2.69] +2.82
301(c19).2 18.40] 18.56
302.19–20 The à priori...also.] *add by hand*
302(t2,c4).9 –2.07] –2.12
312.19 $\left(-\frac{4}{1+\mathrm{H}\sigma^{\mathrm{kn}}}\right)$] $\left(1-\frac{4}{1+\mathrm{H}\sigma^{kn}}\right)$
312.22 $\sqrt{b^2-4ac}$] $\sqrt{1-\frac{4ac}{b^2}}$
313.26 stuck] pasted
316.7 $(c\Phi$] aft del $\Phi+\frac{1}{2}\frac{b}{c}=$
316.14–15 friction, where. . . = 1] friction, where $\Phi=\frac{b}{c}(10^{qn+\mathrm{Q}}-1)^{-1}$] friction. I thus find
317.3 c:b] b:c
317.3 c:b] b:c
317.12 $500q+\mathrm{Q}$] Q
321.10 This is] *bef erased again*
327.7 XL] XVII
328.1 XLI] XVIII
329.1 XLII] XIX
330.1 XLIII] XX
333.1 Table XLVI] Table XXI] §10Table XXI
333(c12).2 .960] .968
333(c12).5 .928] .941
333(c12).6 .937] .953
333(c12).9 5030.937] 5030.941
334.1 Table XLVII] Table XXII] §10 Table XXII
336(c11).9 18.40] 18.56
336(c12).14 2.69] 2.82
336(c12).15 2.07] 2.12
337.1 L] XXV
337(c8).9 15089.063] 15089.080
337(c8).10 514.20] 514.31
337(c8).11 276.72] 276.83
337(c8).12 86123.28] 86123.1
337(c8).18 86110.33] 86110.22
337(c9).4 .125] .108
337(c9).5 .155] .172
337(c9).6 .057] .040
337(c9).7 .023] .006

337(c9).8 .046] .029
337(c9).9 .095] .112
338.1 Table LI] Table XXVI] §10. Table XXVI
338.1 Cornell] ITHACA
338(c5).12 .695] .747
338(c5).13 4429.722] 4429.728
338(c6).4 058] 064
338(c6).5 075] 068
338(c6).6 022] 016
338(c6).7 005] 011
338(c6).8 018] 012
338(c6).9 .027] 021
338(c6).10 008] 002
338(c6).11 031] 037
338(c6).12 026] 032
338(c6).13 –.027] +.039
338(c8).10 14427.353] 14427.329] 14427.324
338(c8).11 3380.91] 3381.08
338(c8).12 3618.39] 3618.56
338(c8).13 90018.39] 90018.56
338(c8).19 90008.96] 90009.13
338(c9).4 +.080] +.103] +.108
338(c9).5 +.122] +.146] +.151
338(c9).6 +.116] +.140] +.145
338(c9).7 +.066] +.072] +.037
338(c9).8 –.238] –.214] –.209
338(c9).9 –.005] +.019] –.014
338(c9).10 –.141] –.117] –.112
338(c11).4 18.29] 18.24
338(c12).2 4808.852] 4808.827
338(c12).3 .847] .822
338(c12).4 .850] .825
338(c12).5 .888] .576
338(c12).6 .879] .854
338(c12).7 4808.863] 4808.872
338(c12).8 –3385.52] –3386.0
338(c12).9 3623.00] 3623.55
338(c12).10 90023.00] 90023.55
338(c12).16 90024.20] 90024.75
338(c13).1 011] 005
338(c13).2 016] 010
338(c13).3 013] 007
338(c13).5 016] 022
343.9–10 up to 60] *intl-c*
344.15 the method here indicated] this method
345.1 On the times] *aft del* §21.
345.6 CVIII] CXXVIII
345.7 CVIII] CXXVIII
346.3 at Cornell two scales having been] two scales were
346.11 amount.] *bef del* The simple results are shown in Table CXXIX.
346.32 Cornell] Ithaca
347.8 Table CIX] §21
348.34 9] 8
349(t1,c3).2 990.9540] 990.9569
349(t1,c3).3 990.9553] 990.9558
349(t1,c3).4 991.1058] 991.1081
349(t2,c5).4 1614] 1414
350.18 results.] results shown below.

Line-End Hyphenation

276.22 north-west
281.18 well-founded

37. *Reasoning, c. 1889*

Copy-text consists of an opening leaf from R 830 and five leaves recently recovered from the 1400-page manuscript fragment nest designated R 278. A seventh (apparently continuous) leaf appears in the microfilm in both R 278 and in the R 1573 miscellaneous fragment nest, but the leaf can no longer be located; copy-text for this page was prepared from the surviving electroprint record. All leaves are 7 7/8" × 9 13/16" sheets of unwatermarked medium-weight white wove paper inscribed in black ink. Peirce's occasional revisions appear as cancellations in the running text and twice as interlineations, all in the same black ink. Thick red pencil underlining (characteristic of the CP editors) appears on the first page, as does a lightly pencilled "Ms 830" (top left) dating from the 1960s.

The reassembled manuscript describes the first character of reasoning, ending with a paragraph break above mid-page on the sixth leaf. The seventh leaf picks up with a second character of reasoning, but subsequent pages remain unlocated. The c. 1889 date reflects the fact that Peirce could have written this document any time between 1886 and 1891. It could have been intended as a lesson in his correspondence course of 1887 just as much as it could have been written to become part of the 1892 "Critic of Arguments" series of articles Peirce published in the *Open Court*.

Emendation

356.1 *true.*] E; ~:

Alterations

354.8 broad] generalized
354.9 caused] a result
354.21–22 the total sum of all the angles] the sum of the angles
354.23 two] three
354.25 *plus*] less
354.26 twice] *aft del* the
355.1 original] *intl-c*
355.8 induces] makes
355.11–12 a sense of compulsion] a compulsion
355.26 intelligence] reason
355.28–29 the sum of the angles] the angles
355.29 that] those
355.35 character] f*[eature]*
355.36 unnecessary] not necessary
356.2 is] is made
356.3 inference] *bef del* which from true premises
356.4 it will] it can lead
356.7 inference] *bef del* of

38. *On a Geometrical Notation, c. 1889*

The two pages of "On a Geometrical Notation" survive only in hectograph form; two sets are known, both run off from a single unlocated typewritten master. Harvard R 275 (imaged as ISP 2, 5, 6 and 3, 4) was printed on two 9 ½" × 15" leaves of medium weight white paper bearing a "Montauk Mills" watermark. It represents an inferior hecto run, with additional damage from water spots and punctures. Two leaves—R 1600 (unpaginated) and R S5:2—represent the better hecto run, and are used as copy-text for most of the piece. Both sheets were printed in black ink on a fragile unwatermarked 9 ½" × 15" carbon stock. Portions of paragraphs 4 and 5, which have been eaten away from the right-hand margin of the R 1600 leaf by a small rodent, are recovered from R 275:2, 5, 6.

The black lightly-run type impression (recto only) is identical on both hecto sets, and includes specimens of three distinct type-shuttles from the Model 1 Hammond typewriters Peirce used almost exclusively after 1885.

The body font is struck from an italic serif type-shuttle, the title line from a small capital ecclesiastic-style (Hammond's "Attic") shuttle, and the second page running head from a small capital roman sans serif shuttle. Typed deletions (all deriving from the master) were made by striking out the superseded text with a dollar sign. There is one typed interlinear revision on the first page of both sets; however, a single black ink correction on line 36 of the copy-text hecto (U over X in ABU) does not appear in the R 275 run.

"On a Geometrical Notation" includes five basic geometric proofs constructed in an abbreviated notation of Peirce's own design. It breaks off after a brief introduction to a second section on qualitative geometry of the first order. A roughly parallel piece, "A Few Formulae of Analytical Geometry," survives in a notebook (R 124:9–12) which Peirce seems to have started around 1889 and continued to write in for nearly twenty years. These notebook pages are likely to have been composed shortly before the R 275 typescript, and the last three have been reproduced in Annotations.

Dating of "On a Geometric Notation" is based on both physical and content aspects of the document. The scholastic font begins to appear in Peirce's typescripts shortly after he received a new Hammond and several new shuttles in April 1887. The general formulae and notational conventions developed in "On a Geometric Notation" are either preliminary to or an alternative for Peirce's datable geometry work of January 1889; this concentration of activity makes it likely that the selection was composed toward the middle of the 1887–91 year range.

The physical characteristics of the italic body font are not reproduced in the present edition; the letter designations, which designate geometric points rather than mathematical variables, are likewise expressed in roman type.

Emendations

Title Notation] E; ~.
357.3–4 coplanar] E; complanar
357.10 (ABCX)] E; (ABCK)
357.10–11 determined] E; defermined
357.17 But] E; but
357.17 line] E; lina
357.18 subject to] E; subjectto
357.19 Stating] E; Shating
357.20 symbolically] E; symbollically
357.25 characters] E; charcaters
357.27 satisfied] E; satiisfied
358.2 follows] E; follws
358.5 the desired] E; and the desired
358.13 (BCXU) = 0.] E; (PCXU) = 0.
358.15 hold] E; old
358.28 good.] E; ~,
358.28–29 (ABXU) = 0, (BCXU) = 0,] E; ~$_\wedge$ ~$_\wedge$
358.30 (CXU.)] E; (CXU$_\wedge$)
359.1–2 simultaneously] E; ~.
359.3 satisfies] E; satisfie

Alterations

357.6 (AB ..)] (ABC
*358.5 and] *aft del-t* (ABCY) = 0
358.16 I shall show that] *intl*
358.28 Whichever] *aft del-t* say
359.18 there] *aft del-t* they shall satisfy

39. *On the Numbers of Forms of Sets, c. 1889*

The brief but intact Harvard R 37 serves as copy-text. The three leaves are 8 3⁄16" × 10 1⁄2" sheets of medium-weight white laid paper with horizontal chain lines and the watermark "A Pirie & Sons | 1888." The pages are coated to form a glossy surface; the darker shade of the first leaf may be due to exposure of the coating to light. Each page is ruled horizontally from edge to edge. Peirce's text is composed in black ink on the rectos, with very few revisions to the text of the first two pages and moderate revisions through the "Table of Formalities" and illustration which comprise the third page. His ink pagination appears at the top right of each page above a curved line.

The Robin manuscript number (R 37) assigned during the 1960s has been pencilled into the top left corner of the first leaf; but in earlier times, the far more intrusive format designations of the CP editors were superimposed on Peirce's text. The first page is most heavily modified, with a tentative CP section number (§1.) prefixed to the title and CP paragraph numbers (435 and 436) pencilled into the paragraph indentation spaces. Other pencilled CP editorial marks on this page include the cancellation of Peirce's by-line (silently removed in the present text), the addition of a tentative date (c. 1880) in brackets below the last line of text, two sets of editor's markings to the right of the title line, and a manuscript location note and short title written above Peirce's title line. Peirce's page numbers have been superseded (p. 1) or incorporated (pp. 2–3) into a larger page run as pages 471, 472, and 473. Taken together, these markings indicate careful preparation of R 37 as printer's copy for insertion into a volume of CP, but the piece does not appear in any of the CP volumes. In spite of the detailed nature of the editorial mark-up, the piece's intended place in the CP arrangement (or the reason for its deletion) cannot be established.

The document has been dated c. 1889 because it can be connected to Peirce's rereading of A. B. Kempe's paper on mathematical forms in January 1889; it is written on the same paper as selection 41, "Dual Relatives," and its handwriting is typical of the period. The watermarked year of 1888 precludes an earlier dating.

Textual Notes

360.20 *[formula]*] Peirce probably intended to write the formula expressing the enlargement of a formality as emended here; the emendation of $(y + 1)$ for y better matches the description he has just given and allows the reader to find the next values in the Table of Formalities, where x = "number of places" and y = "number of letters."

361.1 *[formula]*] This formula produces the results in the Table of Formalities if "$i!$" in the denominator is emended to read "$(i - 1)!$".

361.table Peirce's four-column progression of forms was misaligned in the manuscript due to a lack of space on the page. Rather than going to another, Peirce compressed the final entry in the Triads column and carried the Tetrads column over to a fifth column. The present text vertically aligns the Tetrads entries into a single column, horizontally aligns the final entry in the Triads column (ABC) with the corresponding row of the Tetrads column (AABC). This silent alignment establishes the layout that Peirce intended.

362(c19).5 1701] Peirce's application of the formula to the sixth row reveals an error at position [8, 4] in the fifth row of the Table of Formalities. Peirce may have designed the exercise to expose the error, since it is the only value in the table which is incorrect, and Peirce did not alter the value. However, since there is no explanatory text, it is at least as likely that Peirce merely forgot to correct an error exposed by an apparently random exercise check. Therefore, Peirce's correct value (as calculated in the sample exercise) is emended into the Table.

Emendations

Title Sets] E; ~.
360.3 etc.),] E; ~‸),
360.16 any one] E; anyone
*360.20 $y+1$] E; y
*361.1 $(i-1)!$] E; $i!$
361.4–5 *American Journal of Mathematics*, Vol. III,] E; A. *Jour. Math.* Vol‸ III‸
362(c11).1 No.] E; ~‸
*362(c19).5 1701] E; 1704
362.2 have:] E; ~.

40. *The Formal Classification of Relations, c. 1889*

Copy-text consists of 8 leaves (6 from R 533, 1 from R 534, and 1 from R S64) of 7 13/16" × 9 13/16" white heavy laid paper with vertical chain lines and the watermark "Massasoit Company." The pages bear blue horizontal guidelines at single-spaced intervals which are indented from the left edge but run to the right edge of each recto. The leaves are in good condition, although some have torn or folded lower corners. The reassembled manuscript is unnumbered and undated; it is inscribed and lightly revised by Peirce on the rectos in black ink. Dual readings appear within some of the classification descriptions, but the manuscript also contains a number of notations by Peirce in the margins and within the document itself. These notations are described and recorded in textual notes. The R 533 and R 534 manuscript nest also includes two false starts for the opening page, fuller drafts for each of the first four pages of the final draft, and two worksheets for the classifications (the penciled notation of Robin MS numbers appears at the top left of several of these leaves).

The close relationship of this piece with "Dual Relatives" (selection 41) provides the basis for dating. The discussion of dating rationale, along with an account of genealogical connections with earlier and later documents, appears in the headnote for selection 41 and in the Annotations. Although the two manuscripts are closely connected, the priority of composition between these two selections cannot be established with full certainty. "Dual Relatives" is clear and simple in terminology, while "Formal Classification" is more complex—it begins with a few important distinctions not made in

"Dual Relatives" and includes a specialized systematic vocabulary of both Greek and Latin derivatives.

A case for priority can be made in both directions. Peirce may have written the heavily annotated and altered "Formal Classification" first, and then rewritten it in more straightforward terms as "Dual Relatives," a more carefully prepared manuscript containing very few alterations. But content suggests that the reverse may be true—Peirce may have worked from "Dual Relatives" while composing "Formal Classification," since the special vocabulary in the latter text condenses somewhat the lengthier descriptions in the former. But Peirce could easily have composed the rough "Formal Classification" without "Dual Relatives" having been written yet. Peirce's *Century Dictionary* definition of "relation" clearly antecedes both writings; all they have in common is the distinction between the four logical relations and the five classes of real relations. The *Century* definition doesn't provide the detailed classification found in either document, but instead reproduces the divisions already produced in Peirce's 1870 "Description of a Notation for the Logic of Relatives" (W2:418–20). Peirce's work on the dictionary definition may have given him the incentive to explore the classification of dual relations more systematically through the neologisms developed in these two documents.

Even though the two selections follow the same pattern of classes, the analysis and attendant vocabulary is sufficiently distinct to warrant their conjoined publication in the present edition.

Textual Notes

364 *table of dual relations*] An anonymous hand, by no means Peirce's, scribbled four words on the top and left sides of the grid which have not been reproduced here. These words are: contrasuilation (above "Aliorelations"), juxtambilation (next to "Selfrelations"), contrambilation (above "Concurrencies"), and juxtambilation (under "Opponencies"). They reflect the vocabulary Peirce devised in his 1903 "Nomenclature and Divisions of Dyadic Relations" (R 539; CP 3.571–608).

365.17 alio pairs] Peirce's general preference is to avoid compound or single word forms when combining a classification term with the word "pair" or "pairs." "Selfpair," which Peirce prefers as a single word, is the only exception. Inconsistencies in his use of "pair" here and in subsequent cases are emended to Peirce's preferred form.

367.11 (antialioplural)] Peirce did not complete this sentence.

Emendations

Title Relations] E; ~.

363.1–2 elements.] E; ~‸

363.11 classes.] E; ~‸

364.1 1.] E; ~‸ *Also classification numbers at* 365.19, 365.22, 366.7, 366.10, 366.13, 366.16, 366.20, 366.22, 366.25, 366.34, 367.3, 367.8, 367.11, 367.12

364.2 A:A, a selfcouple,] E; A:A ‸~ ~‸

364.2–3 A:B, an aliocouple,] E; A:B ‸~ ~‸

364.10 alioconcurrency,] E; alio-concurrency,
364.17 *alioopponencies*] E; *alio opponencies*
364.18–19 antiselfrelations] E; anti-self relations
364.19 *antialioopponencies*] E; *anti-alio opponencies*
364.20 4th,] E; ~‸
364.21 antiselfrelations] E; anti self-relations *Also* 364.22–23
ᐩ365.8–9 A:A (selfindividual),] E; A:A, ‸~‸‸
ᐩ365.9–10 couple (selfsimple),] E; ~, ‸~‸‸
ᐩ365.10 (selfgeneral).] E; ‸~‸‸
365.11 couples.] E; pairs‸
ᐩ365.14–15 (if . . . else; *omni-vel-sibi*).] E; ‸~ . . . ~‸ omni-vel-sibi‸‸
*365.17 alio pairs] E; aliopairs
365.17 selfrelate pairs] E; selfrelates
365.18–19 includes *(nullo-si-sibi)*.] E; ~. ‸nullo-si-sibi‸‸
365.20–21 excludes *(nullo-vel-sibi)*.] E; ~. ‸nullo-vel-sibi‸‸
365.23–24 includes *(omni-si-sibi)*.] E; ~. ‸omni-si-sibi‸‸
366.2 223 is] E; 223
366.6 B:C.] E; B:C‸*Also all subsequent periods following text except* 366.21 (case.) 366.29 (posterior.)
366.7 selfpair] E; self pair *Also* 366.13, 366.17
366.7 alteroalio] E; alter-alio
366.8–9 selfpair *(sibi-vel-altero-alio)*.] E; ~; ‸sibi-vel-altero-alio‸‸
366.11 alteroalio] E; altero alio *Also* 366.13, 366.16, 366.17
366.11–12 *(si-sibi-non-altero-alio)*.] E; ‸si-sibi-non-altero-alio‸‸
366.15 *(sibi-si-altero-alio)*.] E; ‸sibi-si-altero-alio‸‸
366.16 it] E; in
366.18 *(altero-alio-si-sibi)*.] E; ‸altero-alio-si-sibi‸‸
¶$(s + a)(\bar{s} + \bar{a})$
366.20 excludes] E; Excludes
366.31 and] E; &
366.33 priority] E; priorit
367.5 not] E; no
367.6 B:A and C:A.] B:A C:A‸
367.6 Parallel] E; parallel
367.9 (alioplural)] E; ‸alio plural‸
*367.11 (antialioplural)] E; ‸anti alio plura‸
367.12 293.] E; 239‸
367.12 another,] E; ~‸
367.13 both or] both & or

Alterations

363.6 Whether] *bef del* they
364.2 a selfcouple] *intl-c*
364.2–3 an aliocouple] *intl-c*
364.17 antiselfrelations] anticoncurrences
365.2 couples] pairs
365.8 couple] pair
365.9 selfindividual] *add intl*
365.9 one such couple] one pair
365.9–10 selfsimple] *add intl*
365.10 selfgeneral] *add intl*
365.12 selfpair] selfpair while] pair of the fo*[rm]*
365.13–14 it includes all the alio pairs] if it excludes any selfpair
365.14 excludes] includes
365.14–15 if . . . else] *add*
ᐩ365.15 omni-vel-sibi] *add*
365.17 includes] excludes
ᐩ365.18 nullo-si-sibi] *add;* nullo-vel-non-sibi
ᐩ365.21 nullo-vel-sibi] *add*
ᐩ365.24 omni-si-sibi] *add*
365.32 224] 223
366.1 selfopponency] selfconcurrency
366.4 couples] pairs
366.4–5 parallel] the same
ᐩ366.7 altero-alio pair] alio pair

°366.8–9 *sibi-vel-altero-alio*] *add*
°366.11–12 *si-sibi-non-altero-alio*] *add;* si-sibi-altero
°366.15 *sibi-si-altero-alio*] *add*
°366.18 altero-alio-si-sibi] *add*
366.21 Admits or Excludes reciprocity] *add;* Excludes reciprocity
366.23–24 Linear . . . two] *add and* Linear *intl ab* Exists one
366.26 Requires reciprocity] *add*
366.28(2) pair] aliop[air]
366.29 nor] and
366.29 Excludes sequence] *add*
366.31 posterior] alio
366.33 Necessitates priority] *add*
366.35–36 Necessitates posteriority] *add*
367.2 plurinoncorrelative] plurianticorrelative
367.3 It] *bef del* is
°367.4–5 Whatever is in that relation to anything else is no related to everything else] *add*
367.5 else] *bef del* but itself
°367.9 alio plural] *add intl*
367.9 of any two excludes] *intl ab del* if it adm[its]
°367.11 anti alio plura] *add intl*

Line-End Hyphenation

364.8 anticoncurrency
364.11 antialioconcurrency
364.20 antiopponencies

41. *Dual Relatives, c. 1889*

Copy-text is R 536, 7 leaves of white 8 1/4" × 10 7/16" heavy laid paper with horizontal chain lines and the watermark "A. Pirie & Sons | 1888." The pages are glossy or coated, and bear faint blue horizontal guidelines (recto only) at single-spaced intervals. Leaves are lightly worn except for the opening page, which is chipped, edgeworn and faded at all margins. A faded and edgeworn false start of the fourth leaf also survives. The manuscript is unnumbered and undated; it is inscribed and lightly revised by Peirce in black ink. Parallel readings stand for a few of the dual-relative descriptions. The penciled notation "Ms. 536" appears at the top left of the opening leaf.

Robin's 1889 dating of this piece is primarily based on evidence from the first five pages of the 536 manuscript nest. These pages, bearing the date 23 January 1889, have subsequently been separated out as the distinct item "Mathematical Monads" (selection 34). The two pieces share little in the way of subject matter, but were written on the same source paper with a watermark of 1888. The *Writings* editors retain the 1889 date of "Dual Relatives" for additional reasons. "Dual Relatives" appears to be a direct expansion of Peirce's *Century Dictionary* definition of "relation." Three surviving pages of drafts for the *CD* definition are written on the same paper, indicating a working date for the *CD* drafts no earlier than 1888. By the end of that year, Peirce was already marking proofs for *CD* publication. The volumes were in press from 1889 to 1891; presumably, Peirce's definitions would have been in the revision stage by the time the *CD* started into press. Composition of "Dual Relatives," which most likely runs parallel to the revision and publication of the "relation" definition, may then be dated circa 1889 as the midpoint in the range of possible dates.

Peirce would also return to the *CD* definition in the first of his *Open Court* essays entitled "The Critic of Arguments" (1892), and in a 23 September 1892 letter to fellow *Open Court* contributor Francis C. Russell.

It appears likely that "Dual Relatives" was written a short time after selection 40, "The Formal Classification of Relations," but see the headnote of that item for a full discussion of issues of priority. Like the earlier piece, the "Dual Relatives" manuscript is in an exceptionally rough and unfinished form. Peirce appears to have concentrated on the classification system itself, rather than aspects of formal presentation; he initiated patterns of punctuation as well as patterns of syntax for parallel layers of subordination, but quickly abandoned any consistency of form as the draft progressed. Sometimes he omitted words necessary to make his meaning clear, and on occasion he left unresolved dual readings. These readings are preserved as Peirce left them, but the general inconsistencies within this clearly preliminary form have been emended for fair copy presentation.

Textual Notes

369.2 A:B and C:B] Peirce wrote originally B:A and C:A (as he did in selection 40), which as far as the pairs of couples go is correct, but it does disrupt the continuity of the list. But when this pair resurfaces in subsection 28 later in the text, it is under the equivalent form A:B and C:B. Peirce's reformulation at that point thus allows the editors to substitute it here by emendation, a move which could not be carried out in selection 40 where Peirce made no correction.

369.6 all, no, or] The editors regard the earlier punctuation of this line as a template of how Peirce wanted the relatives punctuated; he promptly abandoned this as he "gained momentum," perhaps intending to emend in the necessary clarifying punctuation later. At any rate, the present edition has been emended on the basis of that pattern.

371.3 everything] Peirce's interlined substitution of "every" for "either a" is closed up to complete the revision and to conform with his normal usage.

Emendations

368.2 two,] E; ~$_{\wedge}$
368.2 A:B.] E; AB.
368.3 *et seq.* (*a*)] E; (*a*) *All parentheses around lowercase letters rom.*
368.4 universe.] E; ~$_{\wedge}$
368.13 classes:] E; ~$_{\wedge}$
368.18 some things] E; somethings
368.22 follows:] E; ~$_{\wedge}$
368.23 (*a*)] E; *rom. Also parentheses and inclusive letters from* 368.23 *to* 369.3
368.23 B:B] E; ~.
368.24 A:B] E; ~.
*369.2 A:B and C:B] E; B:A and C:A
369.3 C:D] E; ~.
369.4 (*a*) such] E; such (*a*) *Also* 369.9, 370.15, 370.17
*369.6 all, no,] E; ~$_{\wedge}$ ~$_{\wedge}$
369.8 A:B.] A:B$_{\wedge}$
369.13 (*a*) such that] E; such that (*a*) *Also* 369.17, 369.21, 370.20
369.23 else,] E; ~$_{\wedge}$

369.25 four] E; 4
369.25 fifteen] E; 15
369.26 221*(b)*, 222*(b)*, 223*(b)*, 224*(b)*] E; 221*b*, 222*b*, 223*b*, 224*b*
369.31 itself,] E; ~‸ *Also* 370.11
369.32 such] E; may be such
369.36 else.] ~‸
370.1 242.] ~‸ *Also classification numbers at* 370.6, 370.10, 370.20, 370.34, 371.1, 371.9, 371.12, 371.19, 371.22
370.2 to itself] E; to a third
370.5 subsists.] E; ~‸
370.9 itself.] E; ~‸
370.12 anything] E; any thing
370.18 other,] E; ~‸
370.19 other.] E; ~‸
370.24 C:A.] E; C:A‸
370.26 things,] E; ~‸ *Also* 371.7
370.31 third,] E; ~‸ *Also* 370.35, 371.13
370.37 third.] E; ~‸
371.1 may be] E; maybe *Also* 371.22
371.1 such] E; *om.*
*371.3 everything] E; every thing
371.5 A:C.] A:C‸
371.8 thing.] E; ~‸ *Also* 371.11
371.16 C:D.] E; C:D,
371.18 pairs,] E; ~‸
371.19 *(a)*] E; *om.*
371.20 subsists,] E; ~‸
371.23 other,] E; ~‸

Alterations

368.8 all of both] both
*°369.2 B:A] B *ov* A
369.22 but so] but
370.1 *(a)* such] *(a)* that
370.9 the pair] pairs
370.16 no such reciprocity] no reci
371.1 a thing] the s*[econd]*] a s*[econd]*
*°371.3 every thing is either] either a thing is
371.7 nothing] anything
371.15 Parallel] A parallel
371.17 that it exists between] that two different

42. *Geometry of Plane Curves* without Imaginaries, *c. 1889*

Copy-text consists of five sequential leaves from Harvard R 261, 7 15/16" × 9 15/16" sheets of medium-weight white laid paper with vertical chain lines and the watermark "Whiting Paper Co." The leaves are wide-ruled, beginning 3/4" in from the left margin and running to the right edge. The pages are slightly darkened by exposure to light, but otherwise well preserved. Peirce's text is inscribed in blue ink on the rectos; his page numbers appear in the top right corners. The Robin manuscript number has been pencilled in the top left corner by latter-day researchers.

As early as 1887 Peirce developed an interest in identifying properties that are common to curves of given kinds (see letter, Alan Risteen to Peirce, 4 August 1887). Peirce's work on mathematical definitions for the *Century Dictionary* led him to study curves in some detail, and we find him, for instance, reading Newton's 1704 treatise on cubic curves in January 1889 (R 115). There are a number of manuscripts in this period that show various attempts by Peirce to work out plane curve properties: R 262 "On the Real Qualitative Characters of Plane Curves," R 264 "On the Real Singularities of

Plane Curves," R S12 *[Rakers and Rakees]* (all dated c. 1889), and "On Real Curves. First Paper" (1890). None of these documents are publishable, given their fragmentariness. The present selection is relatively complete and self-contained. It has been dated c. 1889 on the basis of its handwriting, the kind of paper used, and its connection to the other documents just mentioned.

Emendations

Title *Imaginaries*] E; ~.
372.3 *et seq.* II.] II‸ *Also no periods after all subsequent roman numeral headings.*
372.3 *Line.*] E; ~‸
372.3 it.] E; ~‸
372.13(1,2) 2*n*] E; 2n
373.1 bitangent.] E; ~‸ *Also subsequent periods in text except* 373.18
373.3 Three regions.] E; 3 Regions‸ *Also* 373.12
373.13 points] E; point
374.5 1] E; ~. *Also* 375.8
374.12 4,] E; ~‸ *Also* 375.3
375.3 0] E; ~.
375.4–5 Formula, *Mathematische Annalen* x, 199.] E; ~‸ Ann Math x. 199‸
376.8 $3M + 2\delta + \iota = 3N + 2\tau + \kappa$] E; *All Greek letters rom.*

Alterations

373.17 1] 0
373.20 2] *aft del* BC
374.12 2] or 2 *Also* 375.3
376.7 Most] *bel del* XIV

43. *Noel's* The Science of Metrology, *1890*

Copy-text is P 389, an untitled review published on 27 February 1890 in *The Nation.* It is unsigned, and unattributed in both the volume index and Haskell's *Index to* The Nation (1951), but Peirce's own listing of his contributions to Volumes 50 through 56 of *The Nation* (R 1365) begins with this piece. The standard UMI microfilm was collated against a letterpress copy (Indiana University) with no internal variation noted.

Emendations

377.1–2 *or . . . System.*] E; *rom.*
377.7 forever] E; for ever *Also* 378.35
377.20 superseding] E; super|seding
378.2 today] E; to-day
378.36–37 decimal] E; deci|mal

Line-End Hyphenation

378.37 duodecimals

44. *Logic and Spiritualism, 1890*

Copy-text is one of the two documents comprising Harvard R 878—the untitled revised galleys for an unpublished article on psychic phenomena solicited from Peirce by Lorettus Sutton Metcalf, founding editor of *The Forum.* The five pages are each 20" × 4 7/8" sheets of wove galley-length paper with multiple horizontal folds; all corners are bent or torn, and wear along the fold lines has resulted in tears and chips along the left and right margins. The provisional running head identifies the compositor (Josie), the journal, the sheet sequence (8–12), and includes a date (April 7). The sheets are hand-numbered (1–5) in the top right corners and heavily revised in black ink by Peirce, but several editorial hands have also left annotations. Editorial queries (probably by Metcalf) and circled words run throughout the text. Another editorial hand has annotated the running head on each sheet to indicate the revised state of the galleys ("Rev. 2d F[olio]") as well as the range of page numbers from Peirce's (now lost) manuscript to which each galley sheet corresponds. Still another hand has penciled and underscored "11" in the top left corner of each sheet.

A struggle between Peirce and Metcalf over article length makes all of Peirce's revisions to the galleys a priori suspect; thus the uncorrected underlayer of the galleys provides copy-text, and those galley revisions by Peirce which are not simply concessions to Metcalf's constraints are emended into the text. The copy-text is further emended by a typescript prepared from the revised second galleys, but this document also bears the scars of Peirce's editorial battle with Metcalf. The following discussion identifies the way that Peirce's true revisions have been identified in establishing the critical text for this volume.

Peirce's earliest attempt survives as R 880, eleven handwritten pages that directly respond to Metcalf's request for "the direct argument against spiritualism." Peirce went on to explain that no direct argument can be made against spiritualism, but he discarded this fragmentary preamble before taking the subject fully in hand with an entirely different approach.

In addition to this fragment, four more or less complete forms of the text also survive in Peirce's Harvard Papers—a draft manuscript (R 879:17–58), discards from a revised manuscript (R 879:2–16), the second galleys selected as copy-text for the present edition, and a typescript revised by Peirce that postdates the *Forum*'s galley sheets (together forming R 878). Each document includes multiple layers of revision by Peirce, but the revisions reveal an unusual mixture of intentions—sometimes expanding, but more often abridging—caused by Peirce's stylistic solution to his tough back-and-forth struggle with his editor.

Late in 1889 Metcalf orchestrated a debate on spiritualism in the pages of his journal, a publishing strategy he often followed with controversial issues throughout his tenure as editor (1886–1891). Mary J. Savage opened the debate through "Experiences with Spiritualism" in the December 1889 issue: "I am to ask a question; others are to answer it. I am to present a problem; others are to solve it—if they can. Such is the task assigned me by the editor of the *Forum* . . ." (*Forum* 8: 449). Richard Hodgson, Secretary and Assistant Treasurer of the American Society for Psychical Research, followed with "Truth and Fraud in Spiritualism" in the April 1890 issue. Peirce was invited to write the next response, and by April he had already completed a long (6700-word) untitled version of his own essay in manuscript. Fragments from a completely rewritten version, shortened to near Metcalf's ironclad limit of 5000 words, survive in the Harvard Papers; these appear to be discarded draft sheets from the unlocated printer's copy. The surviving second galleys (also untitled) are dated 7 April in the running head, but without a year indicated. The typescript, prepared from the galleys as revised by Peirce, is undated; however, it continues the battle over word count evident in the galley revisions and represents the final stage of that struggle.

Peirce sent a revised form of the text, probably a carbon of the subsequent typescript, to Samuel Pierpont Langley for review. Langley, by this time governing Secretary of the Smithsonian Institution, wrote back on 8 May 1890 with interest and some suggested modifications to Peirce's discussion of probability and human perception.[1] The previous year, Langley began a term as President of the American Society for Psychical Research, and was just one of a number of Peirce's colleagues in the scientific community who were involved in investigating the cresting wave of reported psychic phenomena in America. But Langley's suggestions would bear no fruit; by late June, the battle over the essay was decided. A letter from Metcalf to Peirce, dated 21 June (with no year indicated), reveals Metcalf's final offer:

> If you are endeavoring to carry out the idea that you proposed to me, of writing a new article, will you please let me know what you will be able to do as to date. My hope was that the papers on Spiritism might follow one another quite closely, and already several months have passed since Mr. Hodgson's appeared. And the length—please remember not to exceed 5000 words.[2]

The letter implies that the editing impasse was tentatively resolved by an agreement to start over with a new article, but no such text is known today. The surviving forms of the first article bear the scars of the battle as it raged through the spring of 1890, and these scars must be separated from Peirce's true revisions with the greatest care before the critical text can be established.

Metcalf was notorious for bending authors to his unyielding length requirement, but he nearly met his match in Peirce. Peirce's efforts to "buy" space for the full expression of his thoughts had taken the form of cutting ar-

1. The letter is not year-dated, but internal references in this letter and in a subsequent Langley-to-Peirce correspondence dated 12 May 1890 confirm the year. Both letters are located in RL 409. Langley's quotations from "Logic and Spiritualism" in the 8 May letter verify that he was reading a revised form of the text.

2. RL 282.

ticles, pronouns, and even verbs. The original 6700-word draft, and surviving discarded fragments of the rewrite, show his consistent diagonal marks through many of the words in these manuscripts; his word counts, marked off in hundreds, run through many of these pages as well. In the surviving second galleys, Peirce's cutting continued to develop into a telegraphic style reflecting an alternative to Metcalf's more conventional desire that Peirce cut blocks of text. But instead of cutting blocks, Peirce retained all his observations and presented them condensedly without the full complement of words. The resulting text reads like an outline in places, but Peirce's consistent adoption of this one-time style through the galley stage is readable and reflects the full scope of the original content.

Much of what happened in the missing printer's copy and first galley stages can be deduced from the surviving second galley sheets. These galleys came in at 5045 words, only one percent over the limit and clearly workable in revision. But collation against the surviving preliminary manuscripts reveals that the second galleys also include new punctuation variations and the restoration of many articles Peirce had cut in manuscript; presumably Metcalf had imposed these changes in the missing first galleys in an effort to house-style the piece while restoring the full complement of words (and thereby forcing Peirce to cut actual sections of text in revision). Instead, Peirce set out to remove these impositions by hand wherever they worked against either the original meaning or against his now fully-developed telegraphic style. In this process, Peirce also added several handwritten passages for clarity, and counterbalanced the new material with still more cuts to articles and pronouns. As revised by Peirce, the galleys came in at 4999 words.

But handwritten changes to the "post-galley" typescript, which was prepared from Peirce's revised second galleys, reveals that the battle was not nearly over. In the first layer of typescript revision, he apparently added 43 words for clarity, and two new sentences with 59 words, for a total of 102. To compensate, he went through with his now-familiar diagonal slashes and cut 100 more words, again mostly articles and pronouns but some phrases were shortened as well. However, the steady process of cutting articles had now gone beyond styling, and this final layer of cuts resulted in a number of confusing and ambiguous readings. At great price, the typescript was finally "restored" to the 5000-word limit.

Presumably the entire project was abandoned at this point—Metcalf's 21 June letter suggests that Peirce was to start all over again with a new article, but Peirce had already shown great reluctance to cutting text in the traditional way, and there is no evidence that he ever worked on this piece again. Long after Peirce's death, the CP editors restored 77 of the articles and pronouns that Peirce had deleted in his final unsuccessful layer of cuts. But these editorial restorations were subsequently cancelled, and the article appeared in CP with a new title and annotations but with a text essentially as Peirce left it in 1890.

For the present edition, all four surviving documents (as well as their respective layers of revision) were considered in establishing copy-text. The original (and only complete) manuscript contains the least evidence of editorial pressure to cut words, but it is a rough version that clearly represents a superseded authorial intention, and is essentially a completely different document. Interesting variants and significant passages not carried through in Peirce's synoptic revisions are reproduced in the present edition's Annotations.

Peirce's work toward a "fair copy" form created an entirely new document which retained all his ideas within the protective shell of his new elliptic style—a style which Peirce hoped would protect the full development of his points from Metcalf's editing hand. The only manuscript of the revised version consists of rejected pages for a little more than half of the now-lost printer's copy manuscript, and collation against the galley sheets reveals many further authorial changes in the missing printer's copy—presumably the last stage of work in which Peirce exercised any significant degree of control. The surviving text closest to Peirce's intentions, then, is represented by the galleys, but a further distinction is necessary.

The two layers of revision in the galleys—one eliminating Metcalf's impositions in the lost first galleys, the other making new revisions to the evolving synoptic form of the text—must be considered in the copy-text decision. In this case, the most stable form is the unrevised underlayer of the galley sheets—the closest surviving form to the lost printer's copy. Peirce's revisions, made in response to (and under the continuing pressure of) Metcalf's editorial control, can then be evaluated on a case-by-case basis. Those authorial revisions in the galleys which undo compositorial corruptions and editorial impositions are emended into the copy-text. Peirce's handwritten expansions of the galley text, as well as his further refinements to the elliptic style, are also emended into the copy-text. Only those relatively few ill-advised galley revisions, where context indicates that Peirce has deleted galley readings purely to save space, are rejected and recorded in the list of rejected substantives.

The post-galley typescript is yet another generation away from the lost printer's copy. It was prepared from Peirce's revised second galleys, probably in an effort to continue revisions on the now-overworked galleys, but collation indicates that Peirce was not the typist. It is unreliable in its accidentals, but the typescript does contain two handwritten layers of authorial revision that can (with effort) be distinguished from the heavy markings of Peirce's posthumous Harvard editors. His handwritten expansions and corrections of text in the typescript are emended into the copy-text, but his final layer of cuts (marked with the distinctive diagonal slashes he had used from the very first version of the essay) go beyond any sense of refinement to his abbreviated style of presentation. There were simply no expendable words left to cut, and this final layer of 100 deletions degrades the outline style he had more or less perfected in earlier layers of revision. These final destructive revisions served only to accommodate Metcalf's word limit in a way that Metcalf had already indicated he would never accept, and are relegated to the list of rejected substantives in the present edition. The net result is a text that remains very close to the final typescript form, but which will once again have the full complement of words intended by Peirce for one of his major statements on paranormal psychology and the exploration of the unknown.

Key to copy-text and sources of emendation:

G unmarked underlayer of second galleys (copy-text)
Gr Revised layer of second galleys
TS unmarked underlayer of typescript
TSr Revised typescript, disregarding all revisions not in Peirce's hand

Textual Notes

380.3–4 as planchette,] Peirce's holograph elimination of "as" in the galley revision was dictated more by word-count considerations than syntactical ones, and works against clarity to no good effect. This regressive revision is thus relegated to the list of rejected substantives.

380.21–22 dissection-table] Here as well as 380.22, 380.23, 384.7 and 388.5, Peirce restored hyphens to G which were in his pre-copy-text manuscripts (879), but were apparently removed by Metcalf from the now-missing printer's copy. His restorations in these places suggest that other hyphenations at 392.6–7, 392.8, 392.11, 392.13, 392.17, and 392.31 were also restorations rather than new changes.

380.24 man may] The reading in G, "reader may," makes a poor grammatical fit with the antecedent "mind" which Peirce emended in after "impartial" in TSr. In the surviving preliminary manuscripts of 879, Peirce had the word "impartial" standing alone and wrote "man may" where G subsequently has "reader may." In Gr Peirce deleted the word "reader" after "impartial," thus restoring the reading in 879, which suggests that it was Metcalf who added "reader" after "impartial" in G (a poor choice of word, given the broader context) and substituted it for "man" in the subsequent phrase. Peirce failed to notice the latter substitution, with the consequence that his TSr addition of "mind" in the first phrase makes "reader" untenable in the second. Peirce's original (and at any rate more accurate) "man" has thus been emended in.

381.1 its schematic place] The dropping of "its" in G and TS is suspect; this possessive adjective is present in both pre-copy-texts (879), and its elimination works against the precision of the text. Its indirect antecedent is the phrase "the opinion in hand," thirty-four words earlier in the sentence. Since the dropping of "its" may not have been Peirce's choice but an overlooked typesetter's mistake, the editors have restored the adjective to the benefit of the sentence.

381.6 everyday] Peirce's preference for the unhyphenated form of this word is documented from other usage and is the way he spelled it in 879. Though the printer's copy does not survive, evidence of heavy editorial intrusion by Metcalf elsewhere leads editors to infer that Peirce's spelling was altered. The word has been emended accordingly here and at 383.10 and 383.23.

381.31 travellers] Peirce's preference for the double "l" where allowable is documented from other usage and is the way he spelled in 879. Assuming Metcalf's editorial intrusion, the editors have emended to Peirce's preferred spelling here and have restored a missing "l" in "untravelled" (383.35), "marshalling" (384.22), and "marvellously" (388.8).

383.22 we are] The G reading "are we" is an infelicitous inversion of the wording found in 879, and may be the result of an incomplete revision of the entire sentence; it is here rejected.

383.23 besides,—] In 879 Peirce follows his almost invariable custom of preceding dashes with a comma. These commas, all of which were eliminated by the house-styling of the *Forum,* have all been restored.

383.31–32 circumspicient] Here and at 380.17, 381.10, 384.22, 385.4, 386.10, 387.7, 393.4, the *Forum's* compositor or editor has queried Peirce for word choice. In this one case the editor's mark is an underline rather than a circle, but the meaning is clearly to query rather than to italicize. The subsequent typescript does not italicize, nor do we. Peirce rejected the query by writing "stet" in the margin.

383.34 the Nijni Novgorod fair] Peirce deleted the article "the" in Gr, but as he did not delete the other articles in the sentence, the result is a distracting stylistic imbalance. His deletion is therefore rejected. See textual note 391.11–12 for a similar case.

384.13 concord:] The punctuation in this sentence has been emended to restore its appearance in the pre-copy-text. It was clearly altered by Metcalf in the first galleys, in a way that obscures the original syntactical clarity of the sentence.

384.27 india-rubber] The spelling 'India rubber' in G is probably Metcalf's alteration of Peirce's spelling, here restored as found in 879 and as recommended in the *Century Dictionary.*

385.21 Clausius] Spelled "Claussius" in G and subsequent versions, Peirce had correctly spelled the name in 879.

385.35 first, substantially too the second, law] In Gr, Peirce emended to "substantially the first two laws," sacrificing an important nuance to obtain brevity. In order to preserve this nuance the editors have retained the original reading.

386.7 warped with specialism] In the TS, "with" is deleted by hand and the word "by" is interlined above it. The word "warped," which had been mistyped, is rewritten above itself in Hartshorne's hand. The word "by" may also be in Hartshorne's hand but its attribution remains doubtful; it is quite dissimilar from another occurrence of the same word, clearly in Peirce's hand, five pages later in the TS. This uncertainty leads the editors to make no emendation.

389.5 doubled string] TS alters to "double." Here and elsewhere TS alters a word which Peirce allowed to stand in the three subsequent layers of revision. Since these changes are "unforced" by length constraints, it might be argued that the TS reading should be adopted. But Peirce did not type the TS himself and he failed to correct a number of obvious typographical mistakes. His failure to "catch" such changes does not provide compelling evidence to emend copy-text.

389.14–15 a way round from the inside to the outside] Peirce altered these words in TS to read: ways round from inside to outside. Since this holograph alteration was dictated solely by length constraints, as indicated by Peirce's telltale oblique cross-out pattern through the original reading, it has not been emended in.

391.11–12 a chain from the roof] Peirce in Gr revised to "chain from roof" by deleting the two articles. His alteration creates a stylistic imbalance within the sentence, since other articles in the immediate vicinity (before "lamp" and before "beautiful cathedral") were left undeleted. The alteration is rejected to preserve the integrity of the larger passage.

391.16–17 sluggish movement, a mental peristalsis] In G, Metcalf circled the word "peristalsis" to query this word choice. Peirce as a result deleted the five words and replaced them with "plant-movement in the mind, slow, obscure,". In the TS, however, the typist misunderstood Peirce's alteration and typed "sluggish movement, a mental plant-movement in the mind, slow, obscure,". Peirce then made only a partial correction by replacing "plant-movement in the mind," with "peristalsis,". His restoration of "peristalsis" and the fact that he did not delete "sluggish movement" in the TS indicate that he wanted to return to the original wording in G. Although he did not delete the words "slow, obscure," in the TS, preserving both "sluggish movement" and "peristalsis" makes those two adjectives redundant, and the editors have decided not to emend them in.

391.18 a certain luxurious] This Gr emendation by Peirce does not appear in TS. Since the phrase "a certain" is written in the margin at a distance from the word "luxurious," the editors have assumed the typist simply missed it, and have retained the Gr reading.

392.11 actually reach] Whoever prepared the TS altered this present-tense "reach" to a past-tense "reached." Peirce himself did not correct the word in the three subsequent layers of revisions, and it might be argued that this is an "intended" authorial change. However, the context and sense of the passage requires the use of the simple present. Lacking any compelling evidence that Peirce "accepted" the TS change, the copy-text reading is allowed to stand.

392.13 similarly] In the TS the typist wrongly typed "simply" instead. The error was crossed out and the word "similarly" written above it by later editors.

393.4 it should extend] In G, Metcalf questioned the use of "it" by circling the word and suggesting deletion. Peirce rejected the suggestion by deleting Metcalf's marginal query. Peirce, however, inserted "be" before "extend" in Gr, without altering "extend" to "extended". In the TS, the typist typed "it should be extended," but Peirce undid the correction by deleting both "be" and the ending "ed," thereby restoring the original G reading, here preserved.

393.31–32 because . . . matter] Peirce deleted this explanation in Gr. This is the only deletion of an extended integral passage in the post-copy-text forms, and thus runs against Peirce's established practice of preserving at least a component form of every idea. Since Peirce's deletion of this significant passage only reflects a desire to comply with length constraints, the original copy-text reading is retained.

Emendations

380.3 other facts] TS; otherf acts
380.6 experimentation,—] Gr; ~;
380.7 detected] Gr; ~ and proved to be
380.8 illusions,—] Gr; ~;
380.10–11 subject,—] E; ~‸—
380.12 But] Gr; ~ it is
380.13 all this] Gr; this

380.13 comment has] Gr; ~, any or all, ~
380.15 sole hope] Gr; hope
380.16 in breathing] Gr; only in bringing into it
380.17 mind] TSr; reader
380.21(2) being] Gr; by being
*380.21–22 dissection-table] Gr; ~‸~
380.22 vivisection-subjects] Gr; ~‸~
380.23 logic-squirmings] Gr; ~‸~
380.23 whatever,—] Gr; ~;
*380.24 man] E; reader
380.25 urgent] Gr; favoring
380.27 *con*] E; ~.
*381.1 it its] E; it
*381.6 everyday] E; every-day; *Also* 383.10, 383.23
381.6 life,] Gr; ~, in the
381.9 *so*] Gr; because of these
381.10 in abundance] Gr; galore
381.12 mind?] Gr; ~.
381.14 nerve-matter] E; ~‸~ *Also* 392.31
381.16–19 Not . . . spiritualism.] TSr; *om.*
381.28 take] Gr; ~ a
*381.31 travellers] E; travelers
381.35 board-members] Gr; ~‸~
383.13–14 beating,] E; ~;
383.16 feel] Gr; know
383.18 puzzles one] TSr; is a puzzling question
*383.22 we are] E; are we
*383.23 besides,—] E; ~‸—
383.31 smiles on] Gr; ~ or
383.35 *less*] Gr; *rom.*
383.35 untravelled] E; untraveled
384.6 weather,—] E; ~‸—
384.7 day-time] Gr; ~‸~
384.11 question,] E; ~‸
*384.13 concord:] E; ~;
384.16 relative] Gr; the ~
384.18 equivalent] Gr; an ~
384.18 trouble] Gr; the ~
384.20 price;—] E; ~‸—
384.20 answer] Gr; an ~
384.22 marshalling] E; marshaling
*384.27 india-rubber] E; India‸rubber
384.30 perfections] Gr; the ~
384.34 them] E; ~,
385.4–5 deeper-thinking] Gr; the ~-~
385.5 establishment] Gr; the ~
385.6 determination] Gr; the ~
385.6 application] Gr; its ~
385.9 *résumé*] E; *resumé*
385.12 almost exclusively upon] Gr; upon
385.13 experiences.] TS; experiences, almost exclusively. G; experiences,. Gr
385.17 formula,] E; ~‸
385.17–18 *vis viva* no commanding feature of] Gr; *vis viva* cutting no particular figure in
385.19 having been accepted] Gr; accepted
385.21 Tyndall] E; Tindall
*385.21 Clausius] E; Claussius
385.21 Mayer's] E; Meyer's
385.22 facts] Gr; facts that are
385.24 by] Gr; ~ certain of his
385.28 the property] E; the principle G; property TSr
385.28 Stevinus] Gr; Cavaglieri
385.30 self-evident,—] E; ~-~‸—
386.1 and *il lume naturale,*] E; *om.* G; and "il lume naturale," Gr
386.10 quite as] TSr; as
386.10 metals] Gr; plants
386.11 Chemist] Gr; The chemist
386.12 retort] Gr; his ~
386.12 fire,] Gr; the ~,
386.12 result.] Gr; the ~.
386.15 research,—] E; ~‸—
386.15 Faraday's,—] E; ~‸—
386.24 part] Gr; ~ of science
387.7–8 *Aquinas,*[1] if not *Calvin,* persuaded himself] TS; Aquinas‸‸ and Calvin‸ persuaded themselves G; *Aquinas**, if not *Calvin,* persuaded himself Gr;
387.8 peer] Gr; lean

387.9 torments] Gr; the ~
387.10 below] Gr; of hell
387.11 all] Gr; ~ that a
387.13 Assassin] Gr; An assassin
387.13 thought] Gr; the ~
387.20 partly one guesses] TSr; partly
387.23–25 That . . . believe.] TSr; *om.*
387n.1–7 1. Thus . . . it.] E; *om.* G; *Thus . . . it. Gr, TS
387n.1 *Scriptum . . . Lombardi,*] E; *rom.* Gr, TS
387n.2 quaestio 2] E; ~ 5 Gr; questio 3 TSr
387n.2 "Dicendum] E; ‸~ *Also* 6n.4
387n.3 eis ut] E; eis
387n.4 intueantur."] E; ~.‸
387n.4 article 1] E; ~ 16 Gr, TS
387n.6 visione."] E; evasione.‸ Gr, TS
387n.6 "laetantur . . . punitione."] E; ‸~ . . . ~.‸
388.5 nerve-terminals] Gr; ~‸~
388.6 sensations,—] E; ~‸—
388.7 think,—] E; ~‸—
388.8 marvellously] E; marvelously
388.12 find] TSr; show
388.29 changing] Gr; charging
388.31 its substance] Gr; the substance of it
388.35–36 it. ¶How] Gr; ~. ‸~
388.36 practice? Dr. Zöllner] Gr; ~? ¶~ ~
389.1 visitor] Gr; as a ~
389.2 seal] Gr; a ~
389.4–5 in contradistinction, I mean, to] Gr; not in
389.12 refutation] TSr; argument
389.12 proposed] TSr; advanced
389.16 It might, however,] TSr; But it might
389.19 indeed] TSr; and
389.19 loopholes] E; loop-holes
389.20 are discoverable] TSr; might be found
389.21 one single muscle-cell of Mr. Slade's] TSr; a single one of Mr. Slade's muscle-cells
389.22 somehow] TSr; in some way
389.23 which,] Gr; ~‸
389.24 direction,] Gr ~‸
389.25 by that path] TSr; in that way
389.26 an explanation, simple and beautiful,] TSr; a simple and beautiful explanation
389.26–27 phenomenon;— a] TSr; ~, and a
389.30 that tying] TSr; the tying
389.31 ready reply comes: if] Gr; the ready reply is that if
389.31–32 there is no determining] TSr; it is impossible to determine
389.32 *a priori*] E; *à priori*
389.32 something] TSr; a thing
389.33 it; experience] TSr; it, and that experience G; it, and experience Gr
389.33 happens] TSr; to happen
390.4 to conclude he] TSr; that he
390.5 it might be] TSr; *om.*
390.5 were] TSr; might be
390.6 while] TSr; and
390.6 those poems were devoured] TSr; they might be read
390.7–8 accumulable experience] TSr; the experience we can ever accumulate
390.8 smallest] TSr; *om.*
390.10 Nay, presumption rather holds] TSr; There is rather a presumption
390.11 occur, since] TSr; take place, on the ground that
390.11 exceptions;] TSr; an exception;
390.15 such] Gr; that ~
390.15 to be] Gr; is
390.24 I fancy] TSr; probably
390.26 guidance] Gr; the ~
390.26 hot] Gr; a ~
390.27 classable] TSr; to be classed
390.27 those] Gr; the
390.28 mankind,— fountain] Gr; ~ with‸‸ the ~
390.28 philosopher's] Gr; the ~

390.33 rapidly-decadent] Gr; ~‸~
390.34 soul] Gr; the ~
391.2 commonly be] Gr; be commonly
391.5 together with] Gr; all
391.8 substantially] Gr; *om.*
391.14 high] Gr; the ~
*391.18 a certain] Gr; that
391.19–20 an elegance] Gr; elegance
391.20 a refinement] Gr; refinement
391.20 might] TSr; would
391.21 would] TSr; might
391.21 attending] TSr; who had attended
391.22 no] TSr; I have no
391.24 prolonged,] E; ~‸—
391.24 church,—] E; ~‸—
391.27 scene,] Gr; ~‸
391.31 perhaps] TSr; *om.*
391.33–34 absolute,] Gr; ~‸
391.35 a single] TSr; but one
392.1 bodies,—] E; ~‸—
392.1–2 doctrine] Gr; a doctrine
392.6–7 starting-point,—starting-point] E; a starting‸point,—a starting‸point G; a starting-point,—starting-point Gr
392.8 stopping-point] Gr; ~‸~ *Also* 392.11, 392.13, 392.17
392.13(1) starting-point] Gr; ~‸~ *Also* 393.8, 393.11, 393.13
392.13(2) Starting-point] Gr; ~‸~ *Also* 392.17
392.25 origin.] Gr; starting point.
392.32–33 Elliptic . . . Spiritualism] TSr; *om.* G; Elliptic . . . spiritualism. Gr
392.35–36 annihilation,—] E; ~‸—
392.36 situation] Gr; a ~
392.37 times,—] E; ~‸—
393.1 world, too,] Gr; world‸
393.3 recognizes,—] E; ~‸—
393.4 death-throe,—] E; ~-~‸—
393.6–7 Spiritualism . . . philosophy.] Gr; Spiritualism.
393.16 associated with and] Gr; *om.*
393.19 itself] Gr; *om.*
394.8 which,] E; ~‸ seem impossible
394.9 mind, seem impossible.] Gr; mind.

Rejected Substantives

*380.3–4 as planchette,] G; planchette, Gr
380.12 a large] G; large TSr
380.16 a spirit] G; spirit TSr
383.16 the peculiar] G; peculiar TSr
383.29 the importance] G; importance TSr;
*383.34 the Nijni] G; Nijni Gr
385.3–4 deeper-thinking] G; deep-thinking TS; deeper-thinking TSr
385.17 a letter] G; letter TSr
385.17 an algebraic] G; algebraic TSr
385.20 the nature] G; nature TSr;
385.28 the lever] G; lever TSr
385.28–29 the inclined] G; inclined TSr
385.31 the mechanical] G; mechanical TSr
385.34 the law] G; law TSr
*385.35 the first, substantially too, the second, law] G; substantially the first two laws Gr; substantially first two laws TSr
385.36 the teeth] G; teeth TSr
388.8–9 a simple] G; simple TSr
388.10 the whole] G; whole TSr
388.20 the primitive] G; primitive TSr
388.23 the course] G; course TSr
*389.5 doubled] G; double TS
*389.14–15 a way round from the inside to the outside] G; ways round from inside to outside TSr
389.20 a fourth] G; fourth TSr
389.22–23 a force] G; force TSr
389.23 the total] G; total TSr
389.24 Mr. Slade's] G; Slade's TSr
389.29 a fourth] G; fourth TSr

389.30 the knot] G; knot TSr
389.31 a fourth] G; fourth TSr
390.2 a line] G; line TSr
390.7 the same] G; same TSr
390.10 a fourth] G; fourth TSr
391.4 the ordinary] G; ordinary TSr
391.7–8 the first] G; first TSr
*391.11–12 a chain from the roof] G; chain from roof Gr
*391.16–17 a sluggish . . . peristalsis that] G; a plant-movement in the mind, slow, obscure, that Gr; a sluggish movement, a mental plant-movement in the mind, slow, obscure, that TS; a sluggish movement, a mental peristalsis, slow, obscure, that TSr
391.18 a certain luxurious] G; luxurious TS
391.19 that most] G; most TSr
391.24 a prince] G; prince TSr
391.26 the service] G; service TSr
*392.11 reach] G; reached TS
*392.13 similarly] G; simply TS
*393.31–32 Spiritualism . . . matter.] G; Spiritualism. Gr

45. *Herbert Spencer's Philosophy, 1890*

Copy-text is Peirce's annotated but unrevised galley proof of P 402, a *New York Times* editorial by Peirce writing as "Outsider" and questioning the tenets of Spencer's philosophy; the proof (located in the R 1600 maze of offprints and proofs by Peirce and others) is emended by the actual newspaper publication. Attribution was initially made by Fisch in his "First Supplement to Burks" (1964), p. 480.

Composed some time in March 1890, the letter was published on 23 March 1890 as the catalyst for a six-week debate on Spencer in the pages of the Sunday *Times.* The unnamed "editor" provided a summary of Peirce's "Outsider" text framed within a call for responses in the same issue (O 401). Both articles appeared on page 4; on 30 March, the editor ran a summary of the published responses for that issue, again on page 4 (O 403), and established page 13 as the battleground with a brief headline note (O 404) introducing responses by a lawyer, a physician and a New York University mathematician (O 405–407). The same editorial pattern was followed in the next four issues of the Sunday *Times,* although no editor's summary or headliner preceded the responses of 20 April. A total of eighteen responses to "Outsider" appeared on page 13 of these successive Sunday issues. Half were anonymous, and all but four offered a strong defense of Spencer. Peirce re-entered the fray on 13 April (P 416, selection 47) with a response to the seven letters published on 30 March and 6 April. The headnote for selection 47 provides complementary information.

No manuscript for selection 45 survives, but Peirce probably corrected and returned galleys; R 1600 contains what is apparently Peirce's file copy of these galleys, numbered 35 and 36 and stamped WAITS FOR ORDERS. The galleys are annotated by Peirce in black ink to indicate the word count and number of words per line for the first 500 words. Photocopies of a second set survive in the Max Fisch Papers, but the original (apparently a paste-up used by earlier researchers) cannot be located. There is no variation between these galleys, and they show only two variations in accidentals from the published piece (caused by dropped type along the left margin in P 402); however, the galleys do vary in three substantive instances outside the article text itself: the galley title, *"Is This the Truth about Herbert Spencer?"*; the lack of a by-line anywhere in the galley; and a closing citation in the galley for Collins's *Epitome of the Synthetic Philosophy*, a book which Peirce reviewed in the same week's issue of *The Nation* (selection 46). The citation is not keyed by footnote to the text, but it was meant to provide documentation for the passage Peirce quotes from Spencer's preface to this volume.

Peirce's annotation in the R 1600 galley suggests that he carefully reviewed the text prior to publication; he may have supplied the final title and deleted the endnote citation, but these changes may also have been the result of editorial intervention to bring the piece in line (both in terms of tone and format) with a standard editorial page. Nevertheless, Peirce's continuing complicity as the "Outsider" in selection 47 suggests that he endorsed both the by-line and the titles of the published versions. These substantive changes, and the deletion of the Collins citation, are therefore accepted as emendations. The *Times*'s house-styled titles have been silently regularized.

Although Peirce apparently approved the editorial subheading, it was designed to initiate controversy and does not reflect Peirce's more neutral stance both in this essay and in the rejoinder (selection 47). However, since the subheading reflects the journalistic tone established for the exchange by the editors (and apparently with Peirce's implied consent), it is retained.

Emendations

Title Herbert . . . Philosophy] E; Herbert . . . Philosophy. P402; *Is This the Truth about Herbert Spencer?*
395.1–2 Is It . . . For] P 402; *om.*
395.2 For] E; ~.
395.25–396.4 "This . . . modifications."] E; "~ . . . ~"
397.9 thoroughgoing] E; thorough-going
400.27 OUTSIDER] E; OUTSIDER. P402; Epitome of the Synthetic Philosophy. By F. Howard Collins. With a preface by Herbert Spencer. New York: 1889.

46. *Collins's* Epitome of the Synthetic Philosophy, *1890*

Copy-text is P 390, a very brief and untitled review/note published in *The Nation* on 27 March 1890. It is unsigned, and unattributed in both the volume index and Haskell's *Index to* The Nation, but it is included in Peirce's own listing of his contributions to Volumes 50 through 56 of *The Nation* (R 1365). The standard UMI microfilm copy was collated against a letterpress copy (Indiana University) with no internal variation noted.

Emendation

401.5 *Epitome*] E; 'Epitome'

47. "Outsider" Wants More Light, 1890

Copy-text is P 416, a letter to the editor of the *New York Times* in which Peirce, signing as "Outsider," responds to criticism of his "Outsider" critique of Herbert Spencer's philosophy that appeared in the 23 March issue of the *Times.* Attribution was initially made by Fisch in his "First Supplement to Burks" (1964), p. 480.

The letter was published on 13 April 1890 to extend a three-week debate on Spencer masterminded by an unnamed "editor" in the pages of the Sunday *Times.* Peirce's first "Outsider" piece (selection 45) elicited a number of responses, seven of which had appeared in the 30 March and 6 April issues. "'Outsider' Wants More Light" responds to six of these authors and dismisses the seventh (who had focused his argument on one of the other respondents to Peirce). Three of the six published rejoinders the following week. The original passages by these authors addressed by Peirce on the 13th, as well as passages that rejoin the argument with Peirce on the 20th, are identified and recorded in Annotations. The debate continued in the 27 April Sunday *Times,* but the three responses focused on Outsider's first letter and on a retrospective celebration of Spencer's 70th birthday, the event for which the Outsider debate seems to have served as preamble.

No galleys have been recovered for selection 47; with only a week to prepare his response, and no external evidence that he might have been in New York rather than Milford that week, Peirce may not have seen galleys at all.

Textual Notes

404.27 "he has] The opening quotation mark would appear to belong after "has", but Peirce's placement is in fact correct—at the point quoted in Messenger's response, the passage is written in the third person.

405.22 on] Given the similarity in letter form between "n" and "r", and the fact that both "on" and "or" are grammatically correct, the P 416 printing "or" is probably a compositorial misreading uncorrected in the proof stage. Peirce is not referring to "authors" of methods, but rather to authors of treatises on methods.

Emendations

402.4 *New York*] E; ~~~
402.17–18 coloration] E; colloration
402.21 philosophers] E; philosopers
402.22 doctrine] E; gocterine
403.17 philosophy] E; philosopy
403.29 New York] ~~~ *Also* 406.32, 406.34
403.35 today] E; to-day
403.36 *Transactions . . . Edinburgh*] E; "Transactions . . . Edinburgh" *(rom.)*
404.5 Spencer] E; ~,
404.5 there).] E; ~.)
404.21 *Biology*] E; *rom.*
405.5 etc.,] E; &c.,
405.18 He] E; The; *Also* 4.13
*405.22 on] E; or
405.24 books] E; hooks
406.36–37 names (except . . . me),] E; ~, (~ . . . ~,)
407.35 Spencer's] E; Spencer‸s
409.11 cognition-theory] E; ~‸~
409.12 me,] E; ~‸

Line-End Hyphenation in the Edition Text

The following lists those compound words hyphenated at the ends of lines in the critical text of the present edition that, in being quoted or transcribed from the text, must retain their hyphens. All other possible compounds hyphenated at the ends of lines should be transcribed as single words.

20.8 well-drawn
33.5 custom-made
34.1 two-fold
35.8 ill-health
58.2 near-sighted
77.36 maid-servants
90.6 conscience-stricken
91.9 Christmas-day
102.4 proof-sheets
109.11 ghost-story
120.9 coal-scuttle
132.11 two-thirds
138.27 census-question *Also* 139.28
138.37 counting-house
140.8 thirty-one
144.1 newspaper-readers
153.37 census-paper
154.2 *ill-health*
189.2 nerve-cells *Also* 190.20
201.1 psycho-physical
218.5 knife-edges *Also* 242.5, 282.33, 341.8
268.8 non-connection
276.12 stair-way
280.2 ill-adapted
281.12 thumb-screws
290.5 sea-level
295.26–296.1 knife-edge, *Also* 313.27
350.31 screw-revolutions
360.15 *x*-ad
366.8 *sibi-vel-altero-alio*
366.11 *si-sibi-non-altero-alio*
378.14 screw-thread
378.17 strong-handed
380.21 dissection-table
384.27 sewing-machine
385.3 deeper-thinking
386.36 fully-conscious
387.3 mother-wit
392.6 starting-point
392.13 stopping-point
399.28 counter-evolution
403.1 non-living
403.21 non-specialist
404.5 thirty-six

Index

Peirce's "Arisbe"

Milford, Pennsylvania

1888

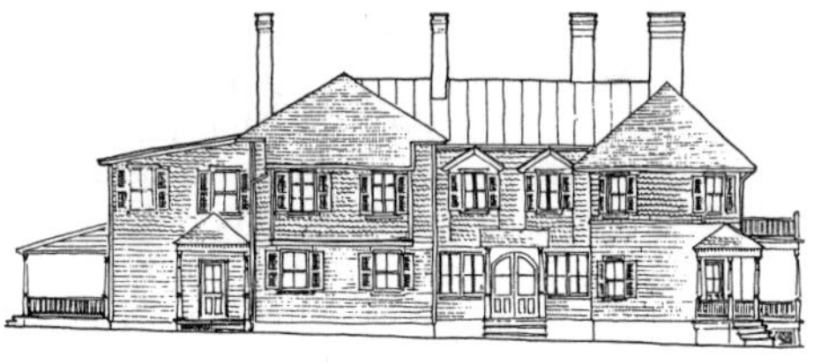

1892

1909

1914

South elevation through successive periods of renovation and expansion. (Drawings by Penelope Hartshorne Batcheler, from "Charles S. Peirce House," a 1983 National Park Service Historic Structure Report.)